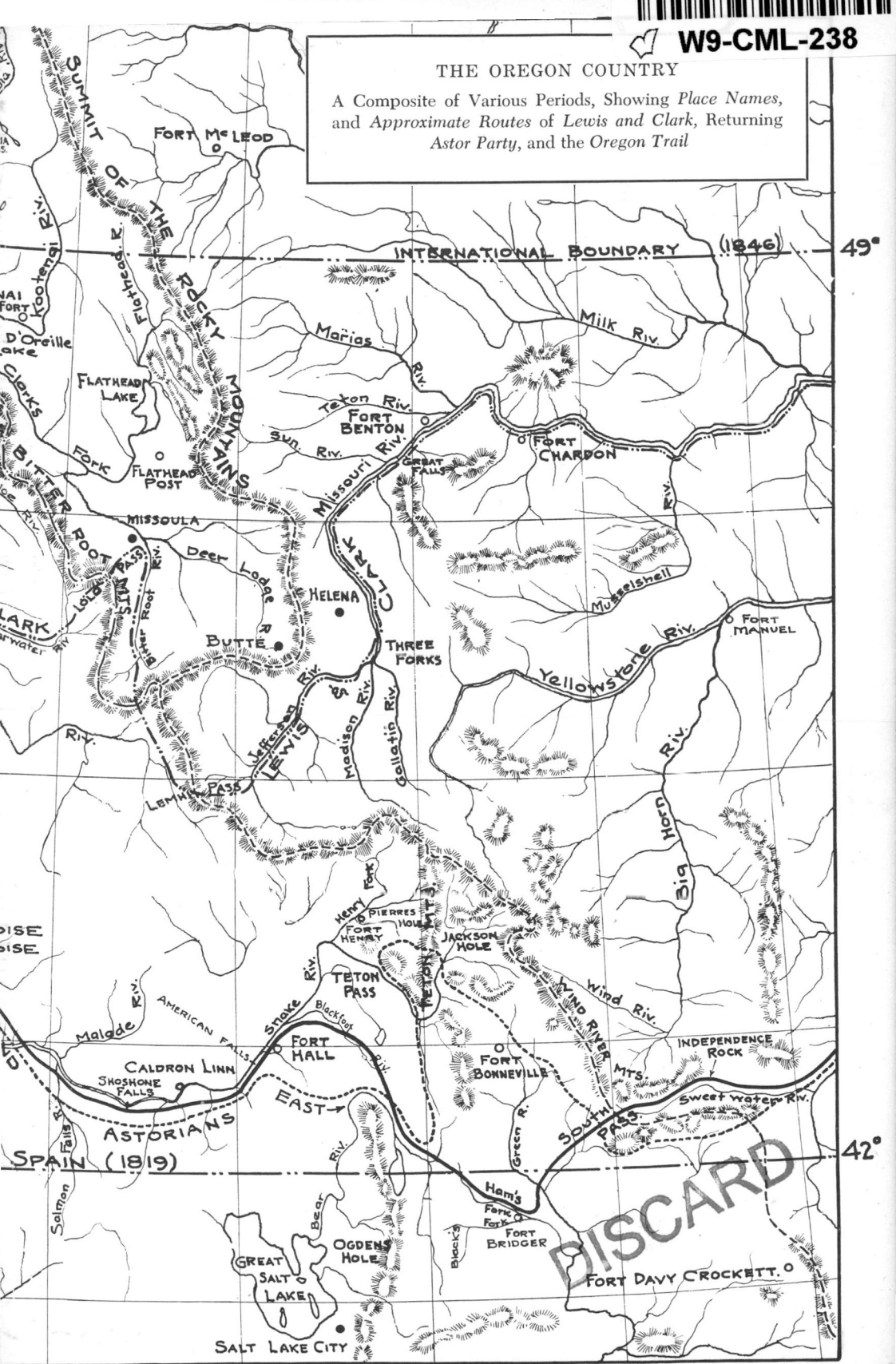

THE OREGON COUNTRY

A Composite of Various Periods, Showing *Place Names*,
and *Approximate Routes* of *Lewis and Clark*, Returning
Astor Party, and the *Oregon Trail*

C   979.5 Care
Carey
General history of Oregon through
early statehood
1971

General History of Oregon

Through Early Statehood

By CHARLES H. CAREY, LLD.

Published by

BINFORDS & MORT, *Publishers*
for the
PETER BINFORD FOUNDATION

Portland   •   Oregon   •   97242

General History of Oregon

LIBRARY OF CONGRESS CATALOG CARD No. 70-140122
ISBN: 0-8323-0221-X

Printed in the United States of America

THIRD EDITION 1971

To Peter Binford

who founded Binfords & Mort, Publishers, and established the Peter Binford Foundation because of his deep and abiding interest in the history of the Pacific Northwest and his dedication to the preservation and distribution of books about this region.

PUBLISHERS' PREFACE

For some eighty years we have been concerned with the publishing of excellent books for reading and reference in Pacific Northwest history. Of the many volumes we have brought out during these years, the present reprint of the timeless work of Charles Henry Carey, "General History of Oregon," is monumental among them. By scholars everywhere it is recognized as the standard reference authority on the history of the Oregon Country from the time outsiders first examined this remarkable region—through shrouded sun by sailors and with cautious steps on soil by more permanent invaders—up through the years of early statehood.

For half a century, with comprehensiveness and accuracy, Carey compiled and wrote Northwest history. He wrote substantial portions of Elwood Evans' "History of the Pacific Northwest," published in 1889; and of Harvey W. Scott's "History of Portland," published in 1890. For a young lawyer just starting out and faced with the necessity of earning a living, these were considerable contributions; also an augury of what was to come.

Until his death some fifty years later, Carey was an inveterate reader of regional history and keeper of copious notes—the latter always benefiting from his disciplined scholarship. Many writers, overwhelmed at the immensity of the task of researching every point from original sources in order to be safe, have found that there is the necessary reliability in Carey's writings; saying an item is "according to Carey" is in no small way comparable to the time-worn "according to Webster." Carey's name is to be found in most of the biographical dictionaries and the Who's Who lists published in the United States. His achievements were of such size and excellence that he belonged in such publications.

The exhaustive research, the clarity and organization, and the over-all scholarship have made this book irreplaceable among histories of the region since its original publication by the Pioneer Historical Publishing Company in 1922. This edition was in three volumes titled "History of Oregon," with the first volume containing the history, and the others, biographies. Carey disclaimed any responsibility for the biographical volumes. In 1935-36, a revised two-volume edition of the history — re-titled "General History of Oregon"—was brought out by Metropolitan Press, now Binfords & Mort, Publishers. This edition incorporated discoveries of new materials, along with minor corrections and adjustments traditionally necessary following a first edition. It is this revised edition that is here reprinted.

The first edition was not produced entirely as planned. Carey had seen himself as editor and contributor to a manuscript compiled by other competent writers—much as in the case of Evans' and Scott's books. The submitted manuscript, however, did not satisfy him—and by that time the word had got around that he was the sole author of the forthcoming history, and advance orders were arriving; his reputation was selling the book even before publication. For a man of Carey's integrity, there was no alternative: he had to assume full responsibility for both writing and accuracy. This decision enriched for all time the written history of the Pacific Northwest.

"General History of Oregon" begins with a graphic description of the region itself, next presents a sympathetic account of the original inhabitants, then takes up the exciting narrative of discovery and settlement. Carey writes:

"Discovery, exploration, fur trading, missionary evangelism, settlement by home seekers, the pageant of history flashes its scenes and then pauses to show how pioneers created a simple but effective local government, without instruction or command from recognized political authority. Thereafter, boundary dispute is compromised, a territory is created, the Old Oregon domain is subdivided and new territories are organized. Indian wars are courageously faced and homes are defended with comparatively little help from the distant federal government. A state is then created, and the responsibilities of statehood are assumed on the eve of the war that divides the nation."

On February 14, 1859, Oregon was admitted to the Union as the thirty-third state . . . and to the pioneers of those early years, Carey pays tribute:

"Oregon's early history is picturesque, and is unique in many of its features, but, if it had no pages excepting those of the pioneers, it would still have a brilliant story to tell. The early pioneer period, before the discovery of gold in California, by an Oregonian, has been called idyllic. Settlers had come as homeseekers, hoping to aid in building an American government and

to strengthen the claim of the United States. Conditions of home life were simple, even primitive, but there was a total lack of pretense and artificiality. Wealth there was none, and there were no grades of social classes. Agriculture was the leading, and almost the sole industry. The production of sufficient food for the necessities of a growing population was generally recognized as the prime need of the hour. . . ."

The death of Charles Henry Carey, August 26, 1941, when he was just two months short of his eighty-fourth birthday, closed the career of one of the Northwest's most remarkable and productive citizens. Though he successfully practiced law for half a century he is best known as Oregon's leading historian. He was born in Cincinnati, Ohio, October 27, 1857, just two years before Oregon achieved statehood. He was educated in the public schools of Cincinnati, graduating from Denison University in 1881, with a bachelor's degree in philosophy; and from Cincinnati College of Law in 1883.

At the age of twenty-six, heeding Horace Greeley's advice, "Go west, young man, go west," he moved west to Portland, Oregon, which became his home for the rest of his life. The story goes that on his arrival in Portland his worldly wealth consisted of a single twenty-dollar gold piece. Otherwise he was well equipped; he carried a law degree and was an experienced newspaper reporter.

Following a brief newspaper career here, he joined the law office of Thayer & Williams. Two years later he formed a partnership with A. H. Tanner, and in 1894 founded the law firm of Carey and Mays. Three years later he became associated with James B. Kerr, with whom he practiced till the death of the latter in 1930. In another three years he himself resigned from active practice.

Occasionally there is a question regarding his use of the title Judge; he was generally addressed as Judge Carey. Surely he would have been an excellent judge, but it seemed to be a position to which he never aspired—except for serving as municipal judge in Portland from 1892-1895. He was nominated by all the political parties and on election day received the highest vote cast for any office for any candidate.

Despite his large practice, he constantly gave time and energy to matters other than law—which could not absorb his total interests. His practice was of a civil nature rather than criminal, involving considerable amounts of counseling beyond litigation. In later years he became known more or less as a corporation lawyer, but actually he represented and advised clients whether they were individuals or corporations and regardless of whether they were rich or poor.

During the decade of the nineties he was active in Republican politics. Son of a Union soldier, a staunch Republican, Carey was following his earlier bent. For him the key to political success was strong party organization, and during those years his activities resulted in his law offices being literally overrun at times with office seekers and party workers.

He found time to serve as vice-president of the Oregon Electric Railway Company and the Oregon Trunk Railway. He was on the board of the Oregon Law Review and in 1904 was a delegate to the International Congress of Lawyers and Jurists. He was a member of the American Society of International Law and was chairman of the Oregon State Commission to revise judicial organization and procedure. He was president of the Oregon Historical Society from 1927-1937, and director from 1916-1941. He frequently contributed historical articles to the Society's "Quarterly" as well as other periodicals. In 1927 he received an honorary degree for public service from the University of Oregon, and in 1931, an honorary law degree from Denison University.

Almost as soon as he had taken up residence in the Northwest, he became interested in the historic roots of the region. His avid interest led him to purchase ever more books, in time building up a formidable collection of Northwest Americana, including hundreds of maps and other historical material in addition to books; and most of it was on the Oregon Country.

Judge Carey was vice-president of the American Bar Association and president of the Oregon Bar Association; president of the Lang Syne Society and of the Portland Art Association. But whether his work involved history or art, law or community service, the old hallmarks of the Carey mind were in evidence—precision, authority, clarity, and a remarkable ability for realistic judgment and action.

CONTENTS

PART ONE —

TO THE TERRITORIAL GOVERNMENT

CHAPTER I

First Conceptions of Oregon

1

THREE CENTURIES after Columbus first sighted land in the western hemisphere, Capt. Robert Gray sailed into, and named, the Columbia river. During the three centuries, rich as they were with the achievements of a modern world, and remarkable as they were for geographic research, practically all the coast lines of all the continents of the entire globe had been examined and charted, saving the Oregon coast line, and saving those of the polar regions.

The definite discovery of the strait of Juan de Fuca was by the Englishman, Barkley, 1787, and that of the Columbia river was by the American, Gray, 1792; but for years prior to these important discoveries, Spanish, British and American vessels in considerable numbers had passed along the Oregon coast without finding either strait or river, notwithstanding some of them had been sent for the very purpose of exploring and reporting upon such geographical features. Morcover, the coasts of Alaska had been fairly well explored, chiefly by the Russians and the British, long before any thorough examination of the Oregon coast was made.

As for the strait, its location had been approximately indicated on maps of North America ever since Michael Lok, an English merchant, about 1596, began to circulate the story that a Greek, called Juan de Fuca, in 1592, had discovered and entered such a waterway. It was accordingly shown upon the maps, but more than one able explorer afterward looked for it in vain, and reported that there was no strait in that location.

The Spanish pilot, d'Aguilar, as early as 1603, and again, the navigator, Heceta, of the same nation, 1775, had reported an opening, or entrance, having the appearance of a great river, near where the Columbia river actually is. Maps, based upon these reports, had indicated the location of this entrance, and had even given the river the name of one or the other of these explorers, but no one had pursued the inquiry further. Numerous maps nevertheless continued through three centuries to outline a coast, sometimes shown as though bulging out far to the west, but sometimes indicated by lines expressing doubt and uncertainty. Imaginary kingdoms were named on many of these early maps, although other maps more cautiously marked the country as un-known.

However, on the eastern side of the continent, there had been rumors of the existence of a great River of the West. French Cana-dians, from very early times, had favored an expedition to go overland in search of the western sea by the route of this river. This culminated, about 1728, in express commands for such an ex-pedition. Authorized by the French government at Paris, and di-rected by the colonial government at Montreal, Pierre Gaultier de Varennes, known better by his title, Sieur de la Verendrye, fur trader and explorer, was commissioned to undertake the task. A native chief, Ochagach or Auchagah, told him of a river, and traced a map, showing its course. Another map made by three chiefs of the Cree or Christinaux tribe confirmed this report, and it appeared that this river flowed westward, through a series of lakes, passing mountains of Bright Stones, finally reaching waters unsuitable for drinking, where tides ebbed and flowed. From this information a map was made up and sent to Paris where it is still preserved.

Verendrye and his sons spent years thereafter in the interior and remote parts of North America, and endeavored to reach the western sea and to locate this great river. Two of the sons, Fran-cois and Pierre, 1742, reached a place in Montana or Wyoming, not now easy of exact identification, from which they saw the Rocky mountain range, the mountains of Bright Stones, but they did not reach the fabled River of the West. The work was after-ward taken up and pursued by others under government orders, as long as the French controlled Canada. Many maps issued by French geographers in the 18th century, therefore, show the sup-posed location of this undiscovered River of the West, more or less founded upon the crude Indian map of Ochagach.

It is evident that in the various stories of a great river, there is at times a confusion of the River of the West with the Colorado river, or even with the Mississippi river, since the direction in which the river of Indian tradition was supposed to be located was not always clearly expressed or understood.

An account of Baron La Hontan in the latter part of the 17th century, of the discoveries made by him in the region of the Great lakes and the Mississippi, passed through several editions, and the later editions added a fictitious account of the discovery of the

"Long river" which he described with much detail, and which was perhaps the Missouri. After travelling up the Mississippi, and then up this imaginary stream six weeks, as he reported, he learned of a lake of salt water, 300 leagues in circumference, located far toward the west. He gave many fictitious details as to cities and inhabitants in the vicinity of the distant lake and said that he had obtained from the natives a map, which he reproduced in his book. Although there are many inconsistencies, this lake is located on the map about in the region of Great Salt lake. In 1710, an English map maker of good repute, John Senex, F. R. S., reproduced the La Hontan map as a part of his own map of North America, and thus the actual discovery of Great Salt lake was anticipated by a century or more.

In something of the same manner, Puget sound, or rather, a large inland sea in the location of Puget sound, was also shown on 18th century maps, long before it was actually discovered and named. There was a detailed description of the early visit to this inland sea, by a romancer, Admiral Pedro Bartolome de Fonte, 1640, whose story was taken with a degree of seriousness, so that learned geographers wrote books about it, and published these maps, which still may be studied by those who are curious to see how myths and rumors have anticipated and antedated geographical certainty. A great archipelago in the vicinity was called archipelago of St. Lazarus, and owed its fancied existence to the description of de Fonte. The story is attributed to James Petiver, editor of a London magazine, in which it was printed, 1708.

The general region in which the modern state of Oregon lies, was variously known, before discovery, by the now forgotten names, kingdom of Anian, kingdom of Quivira, and New Albion; and those countries, with cities and towns, lakes, rivers and capes, all bearing fictitious names, were shown on numerous maps published in various European countries, to the close of the American Revolution, although, as already indicated, a few map makers, less confident, marked the Oregon region simply as Terra Incognita.

The name Quivira, applied to both the kingdom of that name and to one of several mythical cities therein located, was obtained by Francisco Vasquez Coronado, a Spanish explorer, 1540, from a story he had from the natives of the New Mexico region. A futile search for this wonderful kingdom, by Coronado, and by others from Mexico, led through the eastern part of the present New Mexico, rather than toward the coast, although the early maps placed Quivira in the Oregon region, above New Albion, or California. The original story supplied a detail about ships from the orient on this coast, bearing pelicans of silver and gold upon their prows, and told how the vessels had sailed 30 days to reach these shores, bearing cargoes of merchandise.

It was Sir Francis Drake who originated the name New Albion, 1579, when he landed just above the present San Francisco bay, and took possession of the country for the British crown, but many of the old maps extended the kingdom of New Albion far enough northward to include the modern state of Oregon.

Another error of map makers was in showing imaginary straits of Anian, separating North America from Asia. The idea that the two continents were separated by a strait or a sea may be traced to a time shortly after the discovery of the Pacific ocean, and took many forms upon the maps of two or three centuries before actual discovery and exploration. It was not until after Bering had discovered and explored the strait that bears his name, 1728, that the world knew definitely that the continents were not joined.

As early as the middle of the 16th century stories of voyages that included passage through, or north of America began to gain circulation. Sir Humphrey Gilbert mentions some of them in his famous "Discourse of a Discovery for a New Passage to Cataia," published in London, 1576. It was largely for the finding of such a passage that the voyages of Frobisher, Davis, Hudson and Baffin to the northeast coast were undertaken.

The name Anian, as applied to the strait and the kingdom of that name, and as appearing on early maps of North America, is of Asiatic origin. The romantic story of Marco Polo, the great traveller, was responsible for new and strange oriental names on world maps made after his return to Europe from his famous visit to Cathay and eastern Asia. Therefore, after Columbus made his great discovery, which he believed to be in the neighborhood of India, the first maps followed the Columbus theory, and the kingdom of Anian (the same as the Indo-Chinese kingdom of Annan or Anam), was very properly located in the vicinity of India and Cathay, but, of course, near the newly discovered Columbus islands. Soon, however, the Italian geographer Gastaldi conceived a new idea, nothing less than that Asia and North America were separate continents. Not because of any explorer's report of new discoveries, he split the new world from the old by inserting the imaginary strait of Anian between the two. The kingdom of Anian thus lost its footing on the continent of Asia, but remained for some two centuries or so in North America, about where Oregon later appeared on the maps. Nonetheless, numerous other stories were told about the origin of the Anian name, ascribing it to various voyagers, of diverse nationalities, who were supposed to have passed through the northwest passage, some of whom told romantic stories of their experiences.

The first actual British search for the mythical northwest passage was that of Martin Frobisher, 1576. He did not find it, but his voyage began the long series of Arctic expeditions by his nation, including those of Sir Humphrey Gilbert, and other English navigators, already mentioned. In preparation for his own voyage, Sir Humphrey, 1579, had a map drawn based largely upon the theory of the Italian, Giovanni da Verrazana, who had commanded an early French expedition to North America, of a great inland sea stretching across North America, sometimes called the sea of Verrazana. Gilbert's map extended this sea westward through the Canada region, reaching, indeed, to what would now be called the gulf of California, then designated by geographers as the Mare Vermelio. It was so located on the map that there was no room for an Oregon.

Sir Francis Drake heard in a roundabout way that one Urdenada, or Urdaneta, a Spanish friar, had passed successfully through from sea to sea, and this led, later, to Drake's attempt to find the passage, as a possible route for his return to England from his voyage, 1579, into the north Pacific waters, as will be related in the following pages.

Mention has been made of the Iberian romancer, Admiral Pedro Bartolome de Fonte, who published, with a wealth of circumstantial detail, an account of his discovery in latitude 53, on the Pacific coast of North America, of the mouth of a great river, which he claimed to have ascended until he found himself sailing upon the bosom of a great lake. Thence another river took him into still another lake, whose waters were connected with those of the Atlantic. As further embellishments to his tale, he described great cities occupied by friendly natives, and he told of meeting with

a ship from Boston, the "Maltechusetts," commanded by one
Nicholas Shapley.

Another history fakir, and the best known of them all because
his name has been given to the great strait connecting Puget
sound with the Pacific ocean, is Juan de Fuca, as already mentioned. This romancer was not a Spaniard, as his name might indicate, but was a Greek, whose real name was Apostolos Valerianos,
a ship pilot by profession. Whether he, or Michael Lok, a reput-
able English merchant, who gave credence to the story, should be
blamed for this distortion of history, is a matter of some uncertainty; but Lok, apparently a sincere believer, is responsible for
the publicity. He published, 1596, "A Note made by me, Michael
Lok, the elder, touching the Strate of Sea, commonly called Fretum Anian, in the South Sea, through the Northwest Passage of
Meta Incognita." He says he was told by Juan de Fuca that, in
1592, he was sent out by the viceroy of Mexico to discover the
strait of Anian and the passage into the North sea. That he
sailed along the California coast until he came to latitude 47 north,
where he found the land trended north and northeast, with a
broad inlet of sea, between 47 and 48 degrees. That he entered the
strait, sailing more than 20 days, finding land, sometimes veering
northwest, then northeast, and then north, as well as eastward
and southeastward, and that he passed by divers islands. He saw
some people wearing beast's skins, and the land was very fruitful
and rich in gold and silver, pearls and other things, like New
Spain. The strait, he said, was 30 or 40 miles wide at the mouth.

It will be seen that the details do not fit. But because of de
Fuca's guess as to the location of the entrance of the strait, it has
been sometimes believed that he was the discoverer. The real discoverer, as already stated, was an Englishman, Capt. Charles William Barkley, and the strait ought rather to be named after him.

Two centuries later, or, to be exact, in the year 1768, Thomas
Jeffreys, Geographer to the King, published at London his book,
entitled, "The Probability of a Northwest Passage, deduced from
Observations on the Letter of Admiral De Fonte, who sailed from
the Callao, of Lima, on the Discovery of a Communication between the South Sea and the Atlantic Ocean" etc., with maps.
Jeffreys was of different type from the fakirs, and he most earnestly believed in the existence of the passage, and sought to revive interest in the subject. The principal map of his book con-

nects the "Straits passed by Juan de Fuca" with the "Lake de Fonte," the "Straits of Ronquilla," and the sea opening into Baffin bay. Incidentally, the map follows a then recent French map and shows the River of the West by dotted lines, in the two locations "according to the Russian Maps," and "according to ye French," respectively, both reaching the South sea at the "Entrance of Martin d'Aguilar" at 45 degrees north.

War broke out between Spain and England, 1779, and when Spain again turned her attention to the northwest coast, Capt. James Cook, the great British navigator, and the many American and British fur traders who followed him, had done much to make known the coast line, and to dispel the myths about the northwest passage. A Spanish voyage under Perez had reached Nootka sound four years before Cook's visit to the harbor, but the account of the Perez voyage was not published by Spain until several years after the account of the Cook voyage had been published. The official exploring expedition of Captain Cook prepared the way for that of Captain Vancouver, under whom the coast geography was most elaborately determined, and Puget sound and the Columbia river were made known to the world. Oregon was no longer a mere fabulous river, it acquired a place on the maps and both Americans and British sought possession of the country drained by it.

In spite of the discovery by Bering of the strait that bears his name, 1728, and the many voyages of Cook and others along the coast in the following half century, there was a curious recrudescence of the old theory of a northwest passage, beginning in the latter part of the 18th century, and gaining adherents in the early years of the 19th century. This was due to publicity given to a fictitious tale written in 1609, but brought to modern notice about 1788. It purported to have been written by a Portuguese, Lorenzo Ferrer Maldonado, as early as 1588, asking leave to lead an expedition by sea, and reciting the details of a purely imaginary voyage through an inland sea and waterways leading across the continent. The story was believed by some, and, as late as 1790, the Spanish government sent ships to investigate and, if possible, to find the strait and the passage. But it soon became manifest by the reports of Vancouver, and others, that the whole story was a fiction, and that Captain Cook had reached an unimpeachable conclusion in deciding that there was no passage.

The voyages of these romancers were by no means the only ones supposed to have reached a northwest passage; and, while some of these reports were generally accepted when first promulgated, it is a curious fact that it was after the discovery of Bering strait, 1728, that the Fuca, Fonte and Maldonado tales gained credence. A part of the story of Fuca's voyage may have a basis of truth; but either his telling, or that of Michael Lok embellished it with fiction, so that little of truth can now be segregated and identified. There was little real corroboration of the Fonte narrative, but, in 1744, it was given a new impetus by Arthur Dobbs of London, an active advocate and promoter of voyages to find the northwest passage, who published an abstract of the Fonte letter in a book in which he gave an account of an Indian expedition across the continent to the western sea.

These old stories and old maps relate to periods before actual discovery and exploration, but they have a real bearing upon the history of Oregon, for many of the fictions anticipated fact. Perhaps in no other part of the world has early myth so often foreshadowed actuality.

2

So far as known, the name Oregon did not appear in any book or upon any map until after Major Robert Rogers made use of it, 1765, in some writings bearing his name. He submitted to King George the Third and his ministers an offer, or Proposal, as he called it, to take 200 men under proper officers and to make an overland search for the northwest passage. It seems probable that he had obtained some information regarding the explorations of the Verendryes, since his proposal largely follows and makes use of what had been reported by them a few years before to the French authorities, before the British acquired the Canada country at the end of the French and Indian war. Rogers shrewdly turned to his own account the then active interest of the British nation in the elusive northwest passage.

In his Proposal he told of his qualifications for such an undertaking, and called attention to the fact that he had spent eight years in the least known part of North America, and that he had "been very attentive to, and prosecuted with the utmost assiduity every inquiry in his power in reference to the real Existance of a Northwest passage, in consequence of which he has obtained a

Moral certainty that such a passage there really is!" He proposed to take Indian guides, and, having water a great part of the way, he intended to carry bark canoes from one river to another, or perhaps, to resort to felling trees on the banks and making fresh canoes where it would be found necessary.

In this interesting document, which is in the Public Records Office of the British government, in London, occurs this now important passage, containing the first form and use of the name Oregon: "The Rout Major Rogers proposes to take, is from the Great Lakes towards the Head of the Mississippi, and from thence to the River called by the Indians Ouragon, which flows into a Bay that projects North-Eastwardly into the [country] from the Pacific Ocean, and there to Explore the said Bay and its Outletts, and also the Western Margin of the Continent to such a Northern Latitude as shall be thought necessary."

His application brought him an appointment as governor-commandant at Fort Mackinac, at the head of Lake Michigan. Here he served from August, 1766, to December, 1767, and the first thing he did after arriving and taking up his duties was to outfit an expedition to do through others what he had sought the opportunity to do himself.

In the records and files of the court of King's Bench, at London, signed by Rogers in his official capacity, are his instructions to Capt. James Tute, who was to set out from Mackinac and to conduct an overland expedition to the Pacific ocean, and in these instructions Major Rogers gives careful and minute orders as to the route to be followed, which is much like the route he had described in his first petition.

Tute was instructed to proceed with his detachment to the falls of St. Anthony on the Mississippi, where he was to find one Jonathan Carver, who had gone on to this point under previous orders, and who was to act as draftsman for the expedition. The second officer, Goddard, was named, and an interpreter also, and all of these were to constitute a council or governing body. The first winter was to be spent at St. Anthony falls, or in that vicinity, but an early start was to be made from there in the spring with Indian guides, from the Sioux nation. The course was to follow the Ouragon to its mouth, making careful record of the journey, and the approximate location of the bay or estuary into which the great river was supposed to empty was given at 48, 49, or 50 degrees, north latitude. The object of finding the northwest passage was to be kept clearly in view.

This expedition got under way and reached St. Anthony falls, where Carver was found, but the council decided, perhaps for lack of promised supplies for the proposed western journey, to return by way of Chippewa river. This was done in the following spring, and the project was abandoned. But the definiteness with which the Ouragon was described, and the fact that a part of the description fits very well the Columbia river as it really is, leaves it to be supposed that Rogers had some information that he at least deemed reliable, and upon which he was acting. There is a noticeable trace of Verendrye in the Rogers itinerary.

Rogers soon returned to London, as did Carver also, and both of them became petitioners asking recognition from the government. In the new petition filed by Rogers, February 11, 1772, the object of which, like that of his previous application, was to get leave to "Atempt by Land the Discovery of a navigable Passage by the North-West from the atlantic into the great Pacific Ocean," he gives with great detail the overland route to be followed. The part of the proposed plan, after reaching St. Anthony falls, where it was proposed to spend the first winter, was as follows:

"From the Falls of Saint Antoine, it is proposed to depart in the month of April of the second Year; to enter the River Saint Pierre, and to stem that to the Source in about the fourty-fourth Degree of Latitude; to cross the twenty Mile Portage into a Branch of the Missouri, and to stem that northwesterly to the source: To cross thence a Portage of about thirty Miles, into the great River Ourigan: to follow this great River, through a vast, and most populos Tract of Indian Country to the Straits of Anian, and the Gulf or Bay projecting thence north-easterly into the Continent and there to pass the second Winter. Here an Intercourse of Traffic will be opened with the Indians, to procure every necessary Article of Subsistence. A Store of Codfish and other Victualling, will be cured, & a Purchase of Boats or craft, peculiar to these Parts will be completed. Early in the Spring the Adventurers will proceed to explore every Inlet, Nook, or Bay, from the Straits of Anian to Hudson's Bay, between which it is expected to find the navigable Passage, or Communication in Question." This is much like the plan covered by his instructions to Tute,

1766, and is substantially the main part of the route of Lewis and Clark three decades later.

Jonathan Carver had been a captain of a company of provincial troops of Massachusetts bay in the French and Indian war, and claimed some knowledge of Indian languages and customs, and some acquaintance with the interior and unfrequented parts of America. He had done some creditable engineering and map making at Quebec. It was doubtless for these reasons that he had been selected for the overland expedition, and sent by Rogers to the region already mentioned, near the sources of the Mississippi. There he spent some part of 1766 and 1767 among the Indians. On his return he went to London, as stated. Some years afterward, 1778, there was published in that city his book of Travels, in which for the first time, so far as known, the word Oregon appeared in print and upon a map.

Carver himself had filed a petition, 1769, and another, 1773, praying pecuniary relief and employment from the British government, based upon his military service and knowledge of the west, and in both of these petitions he mentions his plans, or maps, and also refers to his journals, which he says were "acquired by Hardships and Dangers of every Kind and that only with the utmost Resolution and Perserverance."

His popular book, which was entitled "Travels through the Interior Parts of North America in the Years 1766, 1767 and 1768," contained two maps, both made in London, dated 1778, one of which used the name "Origan," and the other of which showed the "River of the West."

The word Oregon is also found in the following passages in his book: "From the intelligence I gained from the Naudowessie Indians, among whom I arrived on the 7th of December, and whose language I perfectly acquired during a residence of seven months; and also from the accounts I afterward obtained from the Assinipoils, who speak the same tongue, being a revolted band of the Naudowessies; and from the Killistinoes, neighbors of the Assinipoils, who speak the Chipeway language, and inhabit the heads of the River Bourbon;—I say, from these nations, together with my own observations, I have learned that the four most capital rivers on the Continent of North America, viz, the St. Lawrence, the Mississippi, the River Bourbon, and the Oregon or River of the West (as I hinted in my introduction), have their sources in the same neighborhood. The waters of the three former are within thirty miles of each other; the latter however, is rather farther west." This quoted statement about having received from Indians the information as to the sources of the four great rivers, may, of course, be literally true, but the information itself is almost identical with that reported by Sieur Verendrye, in his report to the French Canadian government 40 years earlier.

At another place in his book, Carver speaks of the "River Oregon, or the River of the West, that falls into the Pacific Ocean at the Straits of Annian," and again, he says that Robert Whitworth, 1774, planned a journey upon nearly the same route as that followed by himself, with the intention of extending it westward, "till having discovered the source of the Oregon, or River of the West, on the other side of the summit of the lands that divide the waters which run into the Gulph of Mexico from those that fall into the Pacific Ocean, he would have sailed down that river to the place where it is said to empty itself near the Straits of Annian." This project, he adds, was interfered with by the Revolution in America, before the preparations were completed. He makes no allusion to the earlier project of the same kind, of Verendrye, or of the latter's successors, under orders of the French Canadian government. He does not mention the earlier project of Major Rogers. On the contrary, he boldly asserts that he had "the honor of first planning and attempting" an expedition of the same kind.

Speaking of the Rocky mountains, called by him the Shining Mountains (as also by Verendrye, from whose reports the picturesque name was probably derived), he says: "Among these mountains, those that lie to the west of the river St. Pierre [now known as the Minnesota] are called the Shining Mountains, from an infinite number of crystal stones, of an amazing size, with which they are covered, and which, when the sun shines full upon them, sparkle so as to be seen at a very great distance."

Where Rogers and Carver got this name, Oregon, will always be a matter of interest. A book advocating a search for the northwest passage by Arthur Dobbs, London, 1744, gives a story from an Indian who claimed to have been with a party that had reached the ocean, and had seen a whale, and met Indians called Flatheads. Rogers, who had spent years on the frontier before 1765, when he made the first use of the name Oregon in his Proposal, may have learned of the explorations and map of the Verendryes.

ing pages; and am fatisfied that the
greateft part of them have never been
publifhed by any perfon that has hitherto
treated of the interior Nations of the
Indians; particularly, the account I give
of the Naudowefies, and the fituation of
the Heads of the four great rivers that
take their rife within a few leagues of
each other, nearly about the center of this
great continent; viz. The River Bourbon,
which empties itfelf into Hudfon's Bay;
the Waters of Saint Lawrence; the Mif-
fiffippi, and the River Oregon, or the
River of the Weft, that falls into the
Pacific Ocean at the ftraits of Annian.

The impediments that occafioned my
returning, before I had accomplifhed my
purpofes, were thefe. On my arrival at
Michillimackinac, the remoteft Englifh
poft, in September 1766, I applied to
Mr. Rogers, who was then governor of
it, to furnifh me with a proper affortment
of goods, as prefents for the Indians who
in-

First Printed Use of the Name Oregon
Page from Carver's "Travels," 1778.

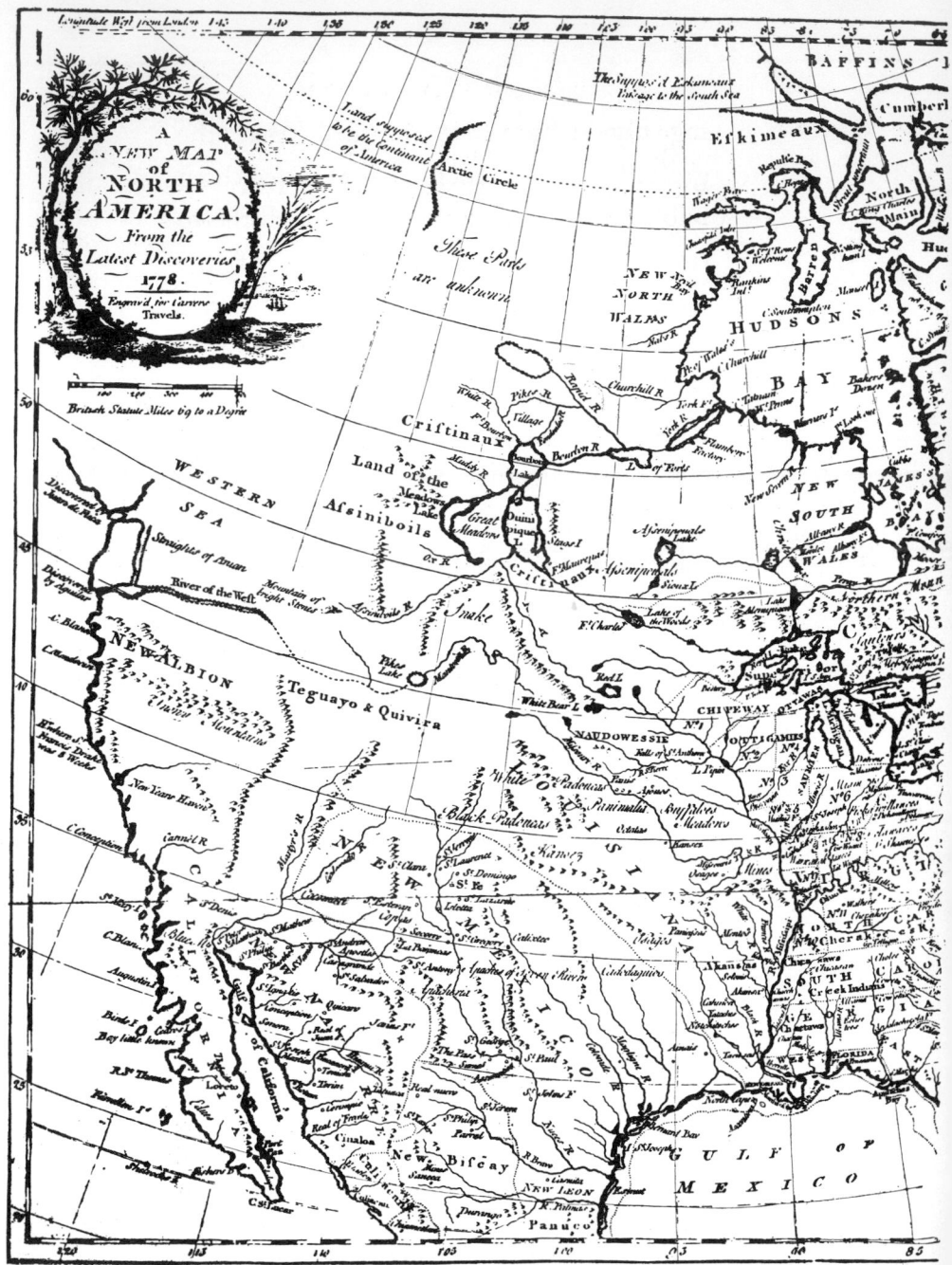

One of Jonathan Carver's Maps, 1778

From the first edition of Carver's "Travels." This map indicates the Columbia as the River of the West, near the Mountains of Bright Stones.

They do not appear to have reported the name Oregon, as applied to the river, but they did use the name of the mountains of Bright Stones, which Carver repeats as though he got it from the Indians. The Jesuit priests had reported in their "Relations" Indian information as to the country in the interior and in these reports of their mission work they often indicated a belief in a great River of the West.

A list of names of tribes and of places, as found in Algonquin Indian dialects, was reprinted from the newspaper, Courrier du Canada, in the Quebec Annual Mission Report, 1857. The Algonquin native family, among the most wide spread, once occupied much of the eastern United States and Canada, and in the time of Carver and Rogers were neighbors of the Chippewas, or Sautees. According to this vocabulary, which was issued under the authority of Seminaire de Nicolet, the name Oragan, or Oregon, is traced to the native Sautee language, meaning a casket or plate of bark; a situation, seat, or site of bark. While the application to the River of the West is not apparent, the suggestion has some interest, because the Sautee tribe, a Chippewa branch of the great Sioux (or otherwise the Naudowessie family), occupied Minnesota and the Canadian region west of Lake Superior. Carver seems to have spent months near them, and in his book he frequently refers to these natives by the name Naudowessies, and speaks of the Assinipoils, who used the same language.

As both Carver and Rogers assert its Indian origin, there is no basis for the arguments, sometimes advanced, that the word Oregon may have come from some French or Spanish word, for which there is no historic support whatever. Rogers, as already shown, had used it in one of his petitions, before Carver had made his visit to the west, and therefore Carver did not originate it. The word was repeated in the written instructions, prepared by Rogers, and given by him to each of the three principal men of his proposed expedition, including Carver. The second Rogers petition shows by an endorsement thereon that Rogers lent both of his petitions, and his plans as he called them, to Carver, as early as February 15, 1775, which was before Carver printed the word in his book.

However, it was from Carver's map showing "Heads of Origan," that the "first official map of the United States" was prepared and published, 1784, by William McMurray, an ex-soldier who had served during the Revolution as captain of the American forces, and who signed the map as "Assistant Geographer to the United States." The limit of that map, on the west, was at the Mississippi river. Inscriptions thereon show that the northwestern part was "taken from Carver, compared with later travels," and the drawing of the lakes and rivers in the upper Mississippi region is similar to that of Carver, though not identical in outline. The words "Head br. Origan," no doubt were intended to indicate the head branch of that supposed river.

Another American map was published, 1785, by John Fitch, entitled the "Northwest Parts of America." He follows McMurray, and marks the "Head of Origan" in similar position, although altering the drawing. Fitch, who may be characterized as a surveyor or engineer, was a native of Connecticut, but had lived in Kentucky, and he claimed to have been the first to invent and apply steam as a motive power to vessels upon water. He had never visited the headwaters of the Mississippi, or seen the district in which he located the waters of the Oregon.

It was probably from Carver's book, though perhaps more directly from the Hudson's Bay Company office, that Captain Meares, an English mariner, obtained the name Oregon, which he marked as a river upon a map in his book published in London, 1790. He was there discussing the probability of a passage or strait from Hudson bay to the Pacific, and incidentally he mentioned the fact that the Hudson's Bay Company had many curious maps, some by Indians, of the interior part of the country towards the northwest and the Pacific. He said: "On the face of these charts, particularly the one described by two Indians, appear several rivers or inlets, unknown to Europeans, which communicate with the Arathapescow lake, and from this lake the river Kiscachewan [Saskatchewan] runs northwest into the Pacific Ocean, communicating perhaps with Cook's River, the Northern Archipelago, or what we shall call the Straits of John de Fuca. These charts have great resemblance to those made by the Canadian traders, which renders them exceedingly interesting."

A search has failed to locate these Indian maps in the archives of the company in London. The description suggests resemblance to the map inspired by the Indian Ochagach. The Meares map indicates a doubt whether the river Oregan empties into the strait just mentioned, or into an inland sea. The map was made two

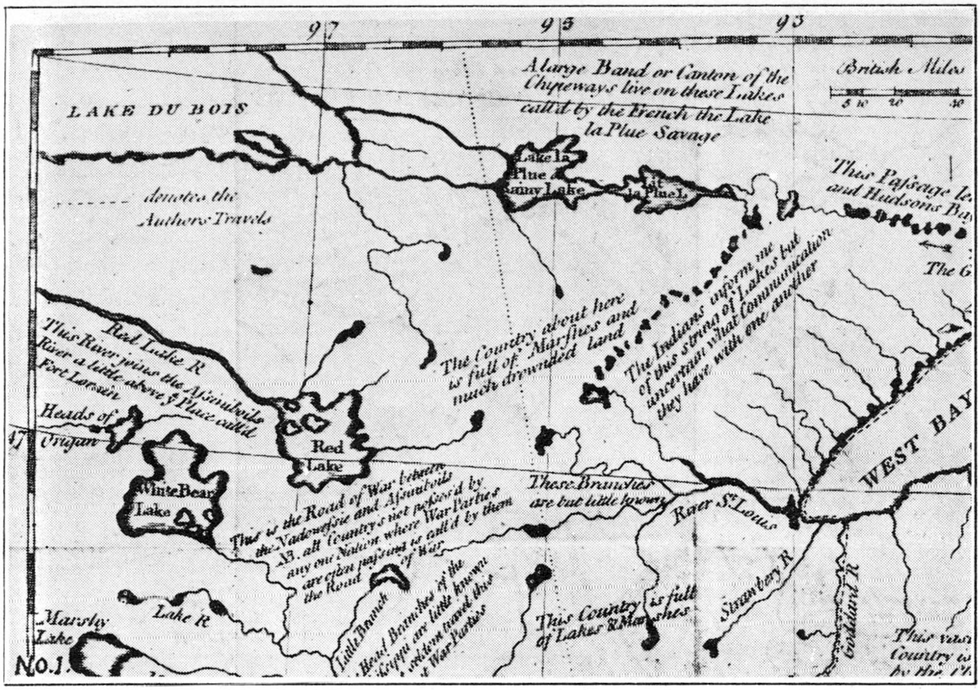

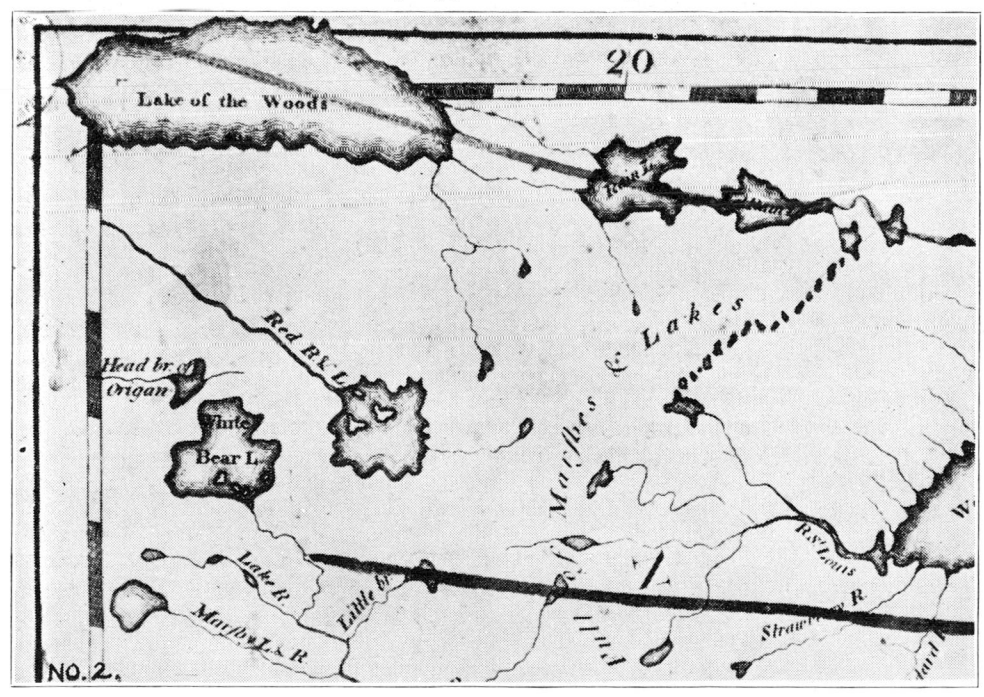

From Carver's "Travels," 1778

The district shown is west of Lake Superior. "Heads of Origan" represent the source of supposed River Oregon.

From William McMurray's (First Official) Map of the United States, 1784

Head branch of the Origan is evidently copied from Carver's map showing the name Oregon.

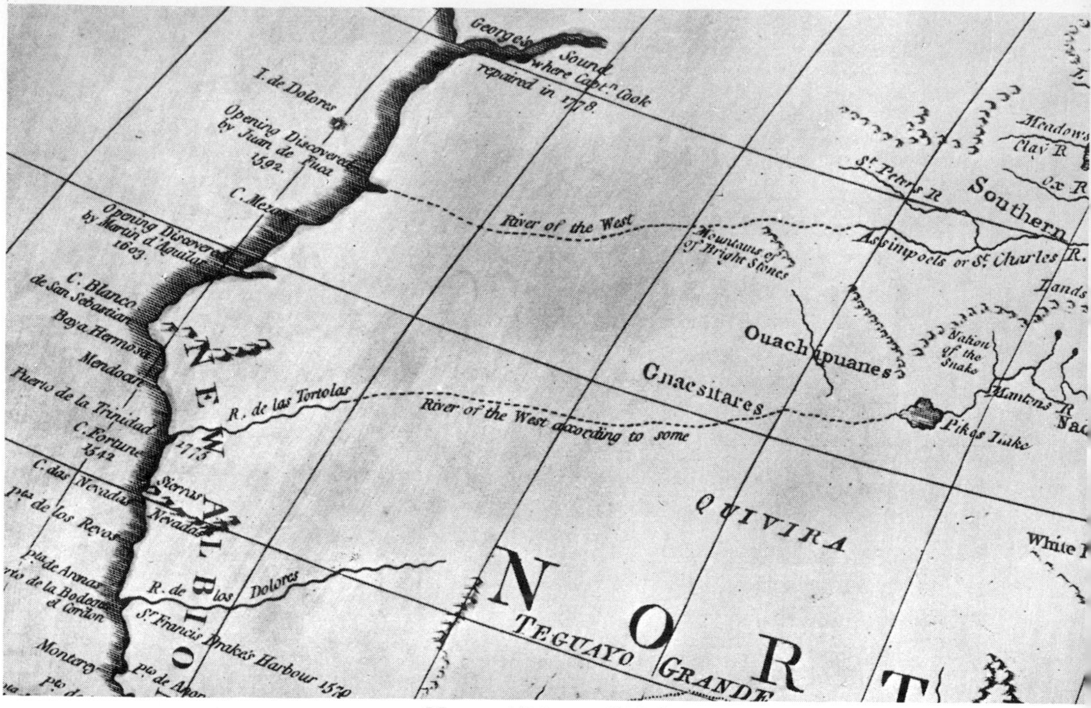

New Albion, 1786

Part of a Map of North and South America showing New Albion, published for Robert Sayer, No. 53 Fleet Street, August 15, 1786. This section shows two Rivers of the West with the "Mountains of Bright Stones."

New Albion, 1787

This is a part of a Map of North America, engraved for John Harrison, No. 115 Newgate Street, September 29, 1787. T. Kitchen drew the map and the engraver was G. Terry. Note the River of the West; also the "Mountains of Bright Stones."

years before Gray discovered and named the Columbia river, and four years after Meares himself had examined the neighborhood of the mouth of that river and had decided that "there is no such river."

On the whole, the evidence is clear that Oregon is a word of Indian origin; that it was first used in writing by Rogers, first printed by Carver, and perhaps originated with the Sautee or Chippewa branch of the Sioux. Thus, there was added to modern civilized language the new name, Oregon, of liquid sound and romantic significance. Thomas Jefferson knew of it and as shown by his correspondence, he called the river by that name, 1793, and again in 1803. Its acceptance by him, and by others, was due to the wide circulation of the printed reference to Oregon in the many editions of the Carver book, as also to the distribution of the various maps, on which the name was used.

The young poet, William Cullen Bryant, used the word Oregon in the year 1811, although his poem did not get into print until 1817, when it appeared in a revised and improved form. He was apparently impressed with Carver's book of travel and adventure, and found the sonorous word well adapted to the meter of his Thanatopsis. It could not fail to attract attention when immortalized in that masterpiece and embedded in the much quoted verse:

"Where rolls the Oregon and hears no sound
Save his own dashings—yet the dead are there!"

When the poem was published the river had already been christened the Columbia, upon its discovery, 1792, and it was usually, although not always, so designated upon maps after that date.

The attempts to reach the western sea by following a western river culminated in the great feat of Alexander Mackenzie, who first found the Pacific by an overland route, 1793, although not by following one stream. Afterward, Lewis and Clark, 1804-06, went up the Missouri and down the Columbia to the ocean; and, 1807, Simon Fraser went down Fraser river, although not to its mouth. These great expeditions were followed by the explorations of David Thompson, which led him to follow the entire length of the Columbia river, from source to mouth, 1811, although not by a single continuous passage.

December 19, 1820, there was brought up in Congress, by Representative John Floyd, of Virginia, a motion for appointment of a committee for inquiry into the situation of the settlements upon the Pacific ocean, and "the expediency of occupying the Columbia river." A month later, as chairman of a committee, he brought in an elaborate report upon the subject. It is probable that he had had some information about Oregon from the Astor partners, whose expedition to the Columbia river, 1811-14, was then a matter of keen public interest, but at any rate his proposal for use of the name in a bill that was brought in by him, January 18, 1822, for the creation of an "Origon Territory," for all time fixed the name as a designation of the region, rather than as the name of the river itself. That the name still continued to be used for the river, in the departments at Washington, as well as in popular parlance, is illustrated by the fact that the secretary of state, as late as 1836, in giving written instructions to Lieut. William A. Slacum, directed him to go to the Oregon river, and the maps in the navy department at that time still continued to so designate that stream.

It was here that the Oregon Question made its appearance as a matter of debate and public interest, later becoming an international question long unsettled, as will be shown in these pages. It may be added that the name Oregon, as applied to the country, soon gained further publicity through the many pamphlets and publications of Hall J. Kelley, a new England school teacher, who became zealous in promoting interest in the regions of the northwest, and in urging congressional legislation and early settlement.

Thus, the Oregon Country became a familiar name. There is still a pleasant aroma of mystery about the name taken from an impossible river, of no existence, arising in the interior basin and finding an unknown and devious way through lakes and across mountains and valleys as yet unseen by any white man, until in its wanderings it should reach the imaginary strait of Anian, somewhere in the remote regions of the Pacific. The great river, Columbia, named by its discoverer, Robert Gray, almost, though not quite, discovered by many before him, had been marked upon old maps with such names as the River of the West, River d'Aguilar, River de los Estrechos, River Thegayo, Esenada de Heceta, River of San Roc, and other names given by those who had never been upon its mighty waters, or penetrated its fertile valley, or seen its mountain stronghold.

CHAPTER II

WORLD DISCOVERY AND SPANISH ACTIVITIES

1

THE 15TH CENTURY that witnessed the great geographical discoveries by Portugal and Spain, forms, as it were, a bridge between the mediaeval and the modern in history. It was in 1486 that the Portuguese rounded the cape of Good Hope. They reached the famous Malabar coast of India, 1498. Spanish ships under Columbus had found the western hemisphere, 1492. Prior to these epoch making events Europe knew little at first hand of the other continents, even the nearer parts of Asia and Africa. But now the long dormant period was over and European nations entered upon that marvelous era of awakening that has given meaning to those expressions, the Revival of Learning, the Renaissance and the Reformation. Europe, that had itself been subject for centuries past to successive inundations of the restless populations of the east, now began to be the source of world migration, and her people poured out to explore, conquer and settle far countries.

Europe had been, in great measure, dependent upon the overland eastern caravan trade for her rarities and luxuries. The capture of Constantinople by the Turks, 1453, had interrupted this traffic. The discovery, therefore, of the ocean route around Africa, and the return of rich cargoes brought home by the bold Portuguese navigators, stimulated the imagination and excited a new interest in exploration, not less than did Spanish discoveries in the west. In the years to follow, the vast quantities of gold brought to Europe increased the volume of money in circulation and made commerce in a more modern sense possible between nations; and greater comforts, conveniences and luxuries soon had their effect upon social conditions. It was an age of growing curiosity as to nature and her manifestations. Science, the arts, learning, philosophy and religion felt the impetus; and the isolation of towns and provinces that was so characteristic of the dark ages, when travel was difficult and dangerous, began to give way, while local governments grouped themselves together with a new sense of national interest, and the map of Europe took form much like that of more recent times.

In order to understand the history of Oregon, particularly the beginnings of that history, there is some advantage to be gained by bringing to mind the conditions under which the first visits of white men to this region were made. The earliest voyages to the western coasts of the continent were under the Spanish flag, and these, while not less hazardous than the more famous voyages of Columbus and De Gama, are scarcely less important in final results. On the tomb of the discoverer of America was inscribed the words, "To Castile and to Leon, Columbus gave a New World." But a new world was also given to civilization by those who penetrated the mysteries of the unknown ocean beyond the western continents, and who explored the Pacific coast. The ocean itself was then vaguely designated as the South sea, a name which persisted long after the name Pacific was established by Spanish discovery.

Meantime, there were practical inventions and improvements in aid of navigation that made these long voyages possible. The compass no longer floated in its bowl of water, but was made more useful by being mounted upon a pivot. The astrolabe was perfected, and cartographers abandoned the Ptolemy map of the second century that had been used as the foundation for the various maps of the middle ages, and began to draw maps that reflected the actual observation and experience of sea-faring men, and aimed to conform to the latest theories of the shape of the world, its land masses, and its oceans. Great improvement was made in the architecture of the ship, for until this time naval construction had showed the influence of the ancient use of oars as a propelling force. The emporiums of commerce shifted from Genoa, Venice and Alexandria to Lisbon and Barcelona, and the Mediterranean no longer limited the scope of commercial ventures by ships.

By force of circumstances Spain was led to the golden shores of America before she found the western route to Asia. A growing belief that an ocean lay between Asia and the country discovered by Columbus was confirmed by Vasco Nunez de Balboa, who, from the heights of Darien, 1513, looked out upon the limitless water and asserted the rights of his sovereign, not only to the land on which he stood, but to the peaceful sea he beheld, and to all the territory washed by it.

From native chiefs, Balboa learned of lands, rich in gold, lying to the southward. Before they were attained, however, adventurers had begun exploitation of the coast to the northward. Cordova plundered Yucatan, the home of the Maya civilization, and Cortes despoiled Mexico, the seat of Aztec culture. It is surprising how soon thereafter Spanish explorers and Jesuit missionaries found their way overland to Lower California and beyond.

While the land of Montezuma was being conquered by Cortes, there occurred an event which opened a new era in the Pacific. It was the voyage of Fernando Magelhaes, or as the name is anglicised, Ferdinand Magellan. Immediately after the first voyage of Columbus, the world had been divided by papal decree between Spain and Portugal. The division line extended from pole to pole, and as subsequently modified, contemplated a free field for Spain to the westward and for Portugal to the eastward. If their paths should cross, ownership was to be determined by priority of discovery. The Portuguese had reached India, 1498, but did not actually attain the Spice islands until 1512, when they won the race for the control of the trade in cloves, pepper and nutmegs. In the absence of knowledge of the true dimensions of the earth, information that the islands of Spice lay far to the east of India revived the hopes of Magellan and the original project of Columbus to seek them by the western route.

2

Magellan submitted his plan to the king of Portugal, but being in disfavor, was not encouraged. He then renounced his Portuguese citizenship and took service with the king of Spain, whom he approached with the argument that, as the Moluccas lay so far east of India, they were probably in the Spanish half of the world, and if approached from the west might be won by Spain. The argument appealed to the Spanish monarch. In accordance with the custom that had grown up, the king and Magellan entered into a sharing contract, and by its terms Magellan was to receive a sum of money with which to equip his fleet and was to be allowed one-twentieth of the profits of the expedition for himself and friends, as well as the government of any land discovered.

September 20, 1519, Magellan's fleet, consisting of the flagship Trinidad and four other vessels with a well armed crew of 280 men, (of whom only 35 finally returned to Spain,) dropped down the Guadalquivir river in San Lucar, from whence it sailed under conditions strongly contrasting with those under which Columbus had set out on his first voyage. Steering southwest, Magellan sighted the coast of South America at Cape St. Augustine, near

Pernambuco, November 29, 1519; thence he followed the coast to
La Plata estuary, where he hoped to find the southern passage.
March 13, of the following year, he arrived at Port St. Julien,
where he spent the winter in overhauling his ships. Here he held
a trial, in summary fashion, and crushed a mutiny instigated by
one of his captains. He cultivated the acquaintance of the natives,
whom he named Patagonians on account of their big feet. Leaving
Port St. Julien, August 24, 1520, Magellan discovered, October
21, the cape of Eleven Thousand Virgins, the eastern entrance of
the hoped for passage. Through the narrow strait, 360 miles
long, its tortuous course fringed by snow clad mountains, he guided for 38 days his armada, then weakened by the desertion of one
vessel, the Antonio. November 21, a council of pilots was held to
determine whether to continue the voyage. It was decided to go
on. November 28, Cape Deseado, the Desired, the western terminus of the strait, was rounded. It has been variously called
"Victoria strait," "strait of the Patagonians," "All Saints," "The
Eleven Thousand Virgins." It is known to the modern world as
strait of Magellan.

To the south Magellan observed a forbidding land "stark with
eternal cold" which, from the many fires, he called Tierra del
Fuego. The expedition now entered the great ocean which had
been first sighted by Balboa, but which was now christened "Pacific," by Magellan. Its steady and gentle winds drove the expedition onward during 98 days of hope and doubt, in which period
fresh provisions became exhausted, and there was left but little
of fresh water, and that not good. Ox hides, sawdust and rats became coveted food. At last, March 6, 1521, the Ladrones came in
sight. The first port of call was Guam. Here the fleet rested, repaired and revictualed.

The route across the Pacific has generally been assumed as having been direct from the strait to Guam; but a recent writer in
the American Geographical Magazine has developed the theory
that the expedition did not turn westward from the South American continent until it had followed the coast as far north as latitude 20 degrees, south. In any case, it is certain that Magellan did
not see the Oregon coast, although he led the van of explorers in
opening the Pacific to world knowledge.

The journey westward was resumed, and March 16, 1521, Magellan sighted the south point of Samar island in the archipelago

of the Philippines. April 7, he arrived at the island, Cebu. He there established an alliance with the local sovereign, who, the better to utilize his new found friends, professed Christianity. Magellan was persuaded by his ally to accompany an expedition to conquer the inhabitants of a neighboring island. In a fight with these natives, September 27, 1521, the great navigator received a mortal wound. Like Captain Cook in later times, his death in the islands of the Pacific cut him off from a triumphal return home. Like Moses, he had but caught a glimpse of the promised land.

The king of Cebu murdered several of Magellan's companions, and the survivors, after burning one of the three remaining vessels, made their way to Molucca in the other two. One of these, the Trinidad, was seized by the Portuguese. The other, the Vittoria, under Juan Sebastian del Cano, proceeded to Europe by way of the cape of Good Hope, suffering from scurvy and short rations, but, September 6, 1522, del Cano dropped anchor at San Lucar, in Spain. The first vessel that ever made the tour around the earth had reached a home port.

No greater feat of persistence under discouraging circumstances has ever been recorded. It is one of the tragedies of history that Magellan should lose his life when in sight of his goal, but before he died he had carried the flag of Spain into the Portuguese monopoly from the rear, and he had given Spain a foothold on Asiatic soil.

The great era of maritime discovery had reached a climax in the circumnavigation of the globe. The theory of Columbus that the world was not flat but round had been worked out successfully. Portugal and Spain, the one departing toward the orient, the other toward the occident, had met and encompassed a newly discovered world. Under authority of the pope of Rome one had a monopoly on trade with Asia by the south and east, the other by the west.

The king of Portugal, jealous of his monopoly of Africa and of the right of eastern exploration, and the sovereigns of Castile, desiring to build their colonial empire on solid and unquestioned foundations, both appealed to the fountain of their religious faith for a definition of their rights. As early as 1454, Pope Nicholas had given the Portuguese the exclusive right to exploration and conquest on the road to India. His decree contemplated the use of the route by way of Africa, to the south and east. But after the return of Columbus, and his supposed demonstration that the Indies could be reached from the west, ground was opened for a bitter dispute. The Catholic sovereigns again appealed to Rome. Alexander VI was the pope at this time. To compromise the differences he drew a line from north to south through the Atlantic ocean, 100 leagues west of the Azores and Cape Verde islands. To Spain he gave all the firm lands and islands found or to be found, discovered or to be discovered toward the west and south of the line of demarcation. This decree was dated May 4, 1493. The king of Portugal, however, was not satisfied, and entered a protest. A conference was held between the two powers, 1494, and an agreement, known as the Treaty of Tordescillas, was reached, by which the line of demarcation was shifted to 37 degrees west of the Cape Verde islands. This line corresponded to what is now the 50th degree of longitude west of Greenwich. It touched the mainland of South America about the mouth of the Amazon, thus enabling Portugal to claim rights in Brazil. Upon this settlement, and her early voyages, Spain's claim of exclusive right to the Pacific coast of North America was founded and maintained.

The voyage of Magellan disclosed a continent divided by a vast stretch of ocean from Asia, and mostly lying within the sphere of Spanish influence. But it was inevitable in the great political and religious upheaval of the Reformation, and with the consequent weakening of papal authority, that the bulls of the popes would be violated and defied, especially by Protestant nations.

The maps of the Spanish navigators contained valuable and much coveted secrets of the sea lanes that competitors could not secure, but England was already asserting the right to trade with all Spanish possessions in or out of Europe, claiming, indeed, a free sea. The lack of accurate maps did not stay her enterprise, and English sea rovers, Huguenot corsairs and Dutch buccaneers, between their fights among themselves, raided the Spanish main and captured the Spanish galleons, laden with the looted wealth of America. It was this prize and the love of adventure that first led the great English freebooter, Sir Francis Drake, into the Pacific, as will be related in the following pages, after a brief review of Spanish activities upon the coast. This review will involve to some extent an examination of voyages to the northward, sometimes beyond the north limits of the old Oregon Country.

Delay in making a systematic survey of the northwest coast of

North America was due to a combination of circumstances. In the 16th and 17th centuries, when Spain was the nation most vitally concerned, and best able to make the exploration, her attention was fully engaged elsewhere. Gold was eagerly sought, and was chiefly found in Mexico, Ecuador and Peru. Discovery and exploitation of those countries brought wealth to Spain, and indirectly all Europe felt the impetus that was due to raising the standard of living through the increase of gold, and introduction of new comforts and luxuries. But, while Spain found it profitable to develop trade with the Philippines and other distant possessions, it soon became convinced that there was little gold to be gained from the aborigines of the more northern parts of North America. The nearer coast of California was visited, but the regular trade route for ships returning from the islands of spice and sugar did not pass the Oregon shores, and required no examination of coast lines north of California.

As for other nations, the 16th and 17th centuries developed no such maritime ambition as would warrant mercantile ventures around Cape Horn, or into ports of the west coast of the Americas, monopolized by Spain. In the 18th century there came a change in this respect. That century developed a new interest, in Russia, first, then Great Britain, and finally the United States. France was not seriously interested. Holland was absorbed in her island possessions in the Indian ocean. It was due to threatened competition and danger of conflict of interests, that Spain finally awoke to the need of exploring and mapping the northwest coast, and strengthening its hold in western North America.

3

Balboa's discovery was in 1513; and by 1517, that enterprising captain of industry had built and launched ships at Panama, and actually had begun navigation upon the ocean waters. While he accomplished little in the way of exploration, others did begin short voyages. By 1525, the coast of Nicaragua was known, and a route through the lake of that name was even at this early period suggested as practicable for a passage way for ships between the two oceans. Other voyages followed the west coast of Mexico and into the gulf of California.

Toward the distant Oregon the quest was gradually approaching. Juan Rodriguez Cabrillo. 1542, skirted the California coast to a point just north of San Francisco bay. It is possible that his pilot, Bartolome Ferrelo, who succeeded to the command upon Cabrillo's death on the voyage, reached the present south boundary of Oregon at 42 degrees, or even sailed as far north as 44 degrees; but no critical examination of the coast was made, and so far as known there was no attempt to make a landing.

It was at this juncture, however, that the energies of the Spaniards turned more particularly to conquest of the trade of the Indies, by a direct route across the Pacific, so that these new interests, together with the growing harvest of wealth from Mexico itself, so absorbed their attention that they had no urgent motive for further exploration of the Pacific coast to the northward, save perhaps that of safeguarding the possessions already acquired. Gradual decay of Spanish maritime supremacy followed the destruction of the Armada, 1588; and, indeed, the interest of the British nation in far countries and far voyages was greatly stimulated by this disaster to Spanish prestige.

Near the close of the 16th century, Monterey, the viceroy of Mexico, received orders from Philip II of Spain, to equip an expedition at his own charge, and to explore the coast of California. Monterey sent Sebastian Viscaino, a distinguished officer, who made a futile attempt to plant a colony in Lower California. After the death of Philip, his successor ordered the survey renewed, and as a consequence, a well equipped expedition consisting of two large ships and one of smaller dimensions sailed northward, 1602, entered the bay of Monterey, and gave it the name of the viceroy. On leaving this beautiful harbor, however, a storm arose that separated the ships of the small flotilla. Viscaino, in command of one of the larger vessels, took refuge in a bay, near present San Francisco bay, after which he explored the coast as far north as the 42d degree of latitude and discovered the white bluffs of a promontory, which may have been the present Cape Blanco, or Cape Orford, on the Oregon coast.

The small frigate of the expedition was commanded by d'Aguilar, who, assuming that Viscaino had preceded him, sailed still further northward. He was favored with a close view of the Oregon coast, in latitude 43, or above, and his log, the first written description of the Oregon coast, is worthy of being quoted. He says: "The Fragata parted from the Capitana, and, supposing that she had gone onward, sailed in pursuit of her. Being in the latitude of 41 the wind began to blow from the southwest, and the Fragata, being unable to withstand the waves on her beam, ran before the wind until she found shelter under the land, and anchored near Cape Mendocino [on the California coast,] behind a great rock, where she remained until the gale had passed over. When the wind became less violent they continued their voyage close along the shore, and, on the 19th of January, the pilot, Antonio Flores, found that they were in a latitude of 43 degrees, where they found a cape, or point, which they named Cape Blanco. From that point the coast begins to turn northwest; and near it was discovered a rapid and abundant river, with ash trees, willows, and brambles, and other trees of Castile on its banks, which they endeavored to enter, but could not from the force of the current."

This entry in the vessel's log presents questions that are still unsettled. Cape Blanco is usually identified with a prominent cape not far north of the south boundary of the state of Oregon, which was renamed, 1792, by the British explorer, Lieutenant Vancouver, as Cape Orford. There is no river at that location, and the coast line trends rather to the eastward, instead of westerly. It is sometimes assumed that the river may have been the Columbia, although the location given is not near the mouth of that stream, and the features described do not apply.

The narrator proceeds to say that as the vessel had already sailed farther north than instructions commanded, and as there was much sickness on board, it was decided to return to Mexico. He also gives it as his opinion that the river, which they had not been able to enter, was in reality the famous strait of Anian, connecting the Pacific with the Atlantic; in other words, the much sought northwest passage. However, as has already been stated, it is a fact that the name of d'Aguilar was thereafter put on numerous maps, opposite a supposed river, somewhere near the actual location of Columbia river.

The Spanish viceroys went no further toward ascertaining the nature of the country, or in making settlements. They had, using Mexico as a base, examined the Lower California peninsula, and had explored the gulf, and had even established missions in southern California. They also had explored the country that is now covered by Arizona and New Mexico, then comprising parts of New Spain and New Galicia. But they had little or no interest in following up the inquiry as to whether the strait of Anian had at last been found by d'Aguilar. During the 17th century a belief prevailed that California was an island, and many maps were issued, based upon this theory, and showing Cape Mendocino and Cape Blanco at the northern extremity of this great island.

A century and a half passed away. The home bound ships sailing from the Philippines to Spain with heavy cargoes found that they could take advantage of the trade winds and come direct in quick time to California, or Mexico, and thence turn southward and away to Spain. This discovery made it desirable to have safe ports on the California coast, and, in furtherance of this, the Spanish Council of the Indies gave orders, 1768, to fortify San Diego and Monterey. Expeditions for the purpose were organized. Galvez had charge of the expeditions by sea, and two overland parties were placed in charge of Portola and Rivera. A religious character was given the expeditions by inclusion of a number of Franciscans, headed by their president, Junipero Serra, and attended by a number of Indian neophytes. Occupation of the new land was to be spiritual, as well as practical and military. From the missions was gathered up all the livestock that could be spared for the new colonization.

After a long march of four months an overland expedition arrived at San Diego, July, 1769, where it was met by the party that came by water. Remaining four days at San Diego, Portola started out again for Monterey, with 64 men, including Fathers Crespi and Gomez. The party followed along the coast, but passed Monterey, not recognizing the place from the description the sailors had given of it. Before retracing their steps, they went as far north as San Francisco bay, of which they were the discoverers. Finally however, they wandered back to San Diego, reaching there, January, 1770.

April 17, Portola again started for Monterey, this time with more definite description, and succeeded in finding it. Here a mission was founded, as had already been done at San Diego. In a few years, the Franciscan fathers had their missions at San Gabriel, San Buenaventura, San Luis Obispo, San Antonio de Padua, Santa Clara and San Francisco. Spanish authority spread westward, across upper Mexico, to New Spain and New Galicia. Occupation of California was now complete. Cortes, Guzman and Mendoza, listening to fanciful tales of rich countries to the north-

ward and westward, sent out expeditions to find the mythical city
of Quivira, and the fabled "seven cities." As has been stated in
our first chapter, numerous maps of this period showed this kingdom and these cities in the region now called Oregon. Moreover,
the vicinity of the Colorado river was minutely explored, as well
as the gulf of California. Colonies were set up by the Jesuits on
the east coast of Lower, or Baya, California. But it was found
that Quivira and its fabled wealth was a myth.

Expulsion of the Jesuits from all Spain was decreed by Charles
III, (1767). Their missions in Mexico and California were taken
over by the Franciscan fathers. To this may be attributed, in great
part, the new impetus to extend Spanish development in upper
California. About this time it became evident to the Spaniards,
that, unless they bestirred themselves, their claim to mastery of
the Pacific would be contested. The English were becoming more
and more active in western waters, and the Russians, who had
long before established themselves on the north Pacific coast,
seemed about to push their activities farther southward. The
Spanish were no longer the powerful maritime nation of former
days, and realized that the most discreet method of securing their
hold over the unoccupied northern coast, and to prevent rivals
from finding and controlling the northwest passage, was to locate
and seize the entrance of the elusive strait of Anian. With this
object in view, three expeditions were sent out between the years
1774 and 1779.

4

The first of these important expeditions sailed in the corvette
Santiago, under the command of Juan Perez, who left Mexico,
January, 1774, touching at San Diego and Monterey, and sailing,
according to orders, as far north as the 54th degree of latitude,
which he reached on the 18th of July. At this point, because of
the ever prevalent scurvy on board, he turned about. He then
began a leisurely exploration of the coast to the southward.

Some further details may be of interest. Perez had been instructed to sail as far as 60 degrees north, and to explore the
whole coast and take possession of it. With him went Estevan
Martinez, as navigator, who was later to acquire prominence, because of his part in the Spanish activities that now followed. There were also two Franciscan friars, Crespi and Pena,

who embarked at Monterey under instructions of Father Junipero Serra. Land sighted, July 15, was the western seaboard of Queen Charlotte islands, as afterward named by the British, but Perez made no landing. On the following day, the main coast was plainly seen, seven or eight leagues distant, and in the afternoon the vessel advanced within three leagues of land, but, owing to the lateness of the hour, no landing was attempted. Next day, a canoe load of Haida Indians approached, singing a native song and scattering feathers on the water, apparently to propitiate the strangers. The Indians, however, stood off at first, but were later induced to approach, by display of beads, biscuits and handkerchiefs. They took what was thrown to them, but did not go aboard the Santiago. Perez named the cliff first sighted as Santa Margarita, since this happened to be the day of the saint so named. He also bestowed the same name on a group of three islands. Some 40 or 50 miles north of this point was a promontory covered with trees, which Perez called Santa Maria Magdalena. An island near by was christened Santa Christina, and the snow capped mountains in the interior were called San Cristobal.

In seeking land so far below the latitude of his instructions, Perez was influenced by the fact that his fresh water barrels needed refilling. But on leaving Santa Margarita, he went no farther north, and turned south, sighting land again, August 18, about latitude 49 degrees. Here, he anchored, about one league from shore, but a storm came up suddenly and it was necessary to cut the cable and sail to the southwest. The vessel again lay to, while the long boat which had started to land with sailors could be picked up.

This place was called by Perez, San Lorenzo. Its exact location is questioned, and priorities between Spanish and British claims have been much debated. By some it is said that Perez was the first discoverer of Nootka sound, on the west shore of Vancouver island. Others, who are supported by statements in the diary of Robert Haswell, the American, affirm that Nootka sound was really discovered by the British explorer, Capt. James Cook, four years later, who called it King George's sound. Father Crespi, however, in his journal of the Perez voyage, describes San Lorenzo as lying between two points, of which that on the southwest was called San Estevan, and the one to the northwest, Santa

Clara. It is probable that the place of anchorage was in the small harbor not far from Nootka, Vancouver island.

However this may be, the results of the Perez expedition were considered by the Spanish government as meagre and unsatisfactory, and a second was sent out soon afterwards, consisting of the ship Santiago, commanded by Bruno Heceta, and the schooner Sonora, under the command of Lieutenant Juan Francisco de Bodega y Quadra. Their first landing was March, 1775, just north of Cape Mendocino, perhaps on the coast of the present state of Oregon. Repairs were made, and some trading was done with the Indians, who were found to be using small articles of copper and iron, evidence of former contact with white men. The vessels were then driven far out to sea and did not make land again until the coast of Washington was sighted, in latitude 47 or 48 degrees, not far south of strait of Juan de Fuca. A boat was sent ashore, but the boat crew was ambushed and immediately murdered by the natives.

Shortly after this tragedy the two vessels were separated by a storm, whereupon Heceta, because of scurvy and the loss of men, decided to turn about. Anchor was cast near Point Grenville, in 47 degrees, 20 minutes. On this point, Heceta and some of his officers went ashore. They erected a cross, and with due ceremony took formal possession of the country in the name of the king of Spain. It was while the officers of the Santiago were thus engaged that Quadra, in the Sonora, became involved in serious difficulty.

A few men had been sent ashore in the only small boat, for water. They had scarcely landed when a large number of Indians rushed out of the woods and overwhelmed them. The tragedy was observed from the Sonora, but no aid could be sent, and the shore was out of range from the schooner. All those on shore were murdered, reducing the Sonora's crew to five men and one boy, in health, and four men, ill. The Indians next attacked the schooner in canoes, but were repulsed with loss of six men. Maurelle, the schooner's pilot, is quoted as saying that there were only three men on board the Sonora able to handle a musket, and that these were the captain, his servant and himself. By this time, the Santiago arrived on the scene and rescued her consort, and in commemoration of the tragedy the point was called Punta de Martires, or Martyr's point. The island lying a little to the northward was named Isla de Dolores, Isle of Sorrows. It may be here mentioned that the coast of Washington, south of the strait, was inhabited by fierce tribes. Twelve years later, the location came to be the scene of another tragedy and to be christened Destruction bay, by the Englishman, Barkley, because some of his crew were killed in a similar manner, on the mainland opposite.

Between the officers of the Heceta expedition a difference of opinion arose. The question of returning was discussed, for Heceta had grown weary of fighting head winds, and was anxious to return, while Quadra and Maurelle favored going ahead. The result was that all again resumed the voyage northward for a time, but it was not long afterward that a storm came up and separated the vessels, whereupon Heceta seized his opportunity and slipped away. He first made land on the west coast of Vancouver island, near the 50th parallel, and then sailed south. Meanwhile, the schooner, under Quadra, continued northward and explored the Alaska coast, as far as Mount Edgecumbe.

It is the southward voyage of Heceta, however, that is of the greatest interest to us, because of a near discovery of the Columbia river, and his belief that he had found the fictitious strait of Juan de Fuca. Let Heceta tell his story in his own words:

"In the evening of this day, [August 17, 1775,] I discovered a large bay, to which I gave the name of Assumption bay, and of which a plan will be found in this journal. Its latitude and longitude are determined according to the most exact means afforded by theory and practice. The latitude of the two most prominent capes of this bay are calculated from the observations of this day.

"Having arrived opposite this bay at six in the evening, and placed the ship nearly midway between the two capes, I sounded and found bottom in four brazas [about four fathoms]. The current and eddies were so strong that, notwithstanding a press of sail, it was difficult to get clear of the northern cape, towards which the current ran, though its direction was eastward in consequence of the tide being at flood. These currents and eddies caused me to believe that the place is the mouth of some great river, or of some passage to another sea. Had I not been certain of the latitude of this bay, from my observations of the same day, I might easily have believed it to have been the passage discovered by Juan de Fuca, in 1592, which is placed on the charts between the 47th and the 48th degrees, where I am certain no such strait exists; because, I anchored on July 14 midway between these latitudes, and carefully examined everything around. Notwithstanding the great difference between this bay and the passage mentioned by de Fuca, I have little difficulty in conceiving that they may be the same, having observed equal or greater difference in the latitude of other capes and ports on this coast, as I will show at the proper time; and in all cases latitudes thus assigned are higher than the real ones.

"I did not enter and anchor in this port, which in my plan I supposed to be formed by an island, notwithstanding my strong desire to do so; because, having consulted with the second captain, Don Juan Perez, and the pilot, Don Christoval Revilla, they insisted I ought not attempt it, as, if we let go the anchor, we should not have men enough to get it up and to attend to the other operations which would be thereby necessary. Considering this, and also that in order to reach the anchorage, I should be obliged to lower my long boat (the only boat that I had) and to man it with at least 14 of the crew, as I could not manage it with fewer, and also as it was then late in the day, I resolved to put out; and at the distance of three leagues I lay to. In the course of that night I experienced heavy currents to the southwest, which made it impossible to enter the bay on the following morning, as I had planned, as I was far to the leeward. These currents, however, convinced me that a great quantity of water rushed from this bay on the ebb of the tide.

"The two capes which I name in my plan, Cape San Roque [Cape Disappointment] and Cape Frondoso [Point Adams], lie in the angle of ten degrees of the third quadrant. They are both faced with red earth and are of little elevation.

"On the 18th, I observed Cape Frondoso, with another cape, to which I gave the name of Cape Falcon [Cape Lookout], situated in the latitude of 45 degrees, 43 minutes, and they lay at an angle of 22 degrees to the third quadrant; and from the last named cape I traced the coast running in the angle of five degrees of the second quadrant. This land is mountainous, but not very high, nor so well wooded as that lying between the latitudes of 48 degrees, 30 minutes, and 46 degrees. * * * * In some places that coast presents a beach, in others it is rocky.

"A flat topped mountain, which I named The Table, will enable any navigator to know the position of Cape Falcon without observing it; as it is in the latitude of 45 degrees, 28 minutes, and may be seen at a great distance, being somewhat elevated."

This description is of interest as being the first recognizable description to be written of the mouth of the Columbia river and of the coast to the south. The water outside of the bar can hardly be recognized as a "large bay," but reference to Heceta's plan, or map, alluded to in his journal, shows that his Assumption bay embraces the waters visible from his position at sea, and includes the lower reaches of Columbia river as far inland as Tongue point and Cathlamet bay. Any one familiar with this coast will easily recognize the salient features of beach and cliff, and the rugged mass of Mount Neahkahnie so accurately described by Heceta. But the navigator did not enter the river, and no attempt was made, afterward, to follow up the investigation. Spanish maps for nearly two centuries had marked the entrance of Martin d'Aguilar, but now showed Heceta's name in near the same location. His name of Assumption bay did not gain recognition but many maps after that time indicate the near discovery of Columbia river, by the name Esenada de Heceta.

In the meantime, Quadra and Maurelle, in their small vessel, only 27 feet in length, were making an effort to reach 65 degrees north. They sailed northwest without sighting land, until a snow capped mountain appeared above the horizon. It was called San Jacinto, or St. Hyacinth. A little farther on, ports Remedios and Guadelupe were visited. San Jacinto is believed to be Mount Edgecumbe. Port Remedios probably was what Cook later called the bay of Islands, while Guadelupe is now known as Norfolk sound. At Norfolk sound, Quadra sent a boat ashore for wood and water without offering payment, and here again the natives resisted, and here also a cross was erected; but it was torn down by the natives after the Spanish returned to their vessel. While in the neighborhood of the 50th parallel Quadra decided to return to Mexico, consoling himself with the thought that if he did not follow out instructions, he had at least gone farther north than any other navigator. On the way homeward, he discovered Bucareli sound, on the west side of the largest of the Prince Edward islands. It still retains the name he gave it. Here he landed and took possession of the country with due formality. From Bucareli, Quadra sailed south across Dixon entrance, to which he gave the name Entrada de Perez, and sighted Cape North. He arrived at

San Blas, Mexico, November 20, 1775, after eight months' absence.

The next explorer to leave San Blas was Ignacio Arteaga, who was accompanied by Quadra and Maurelle. They sailed, February 17, 1779, in the Princesa and Favorita, along a course very similar to that of Cook in the year following. After voyaging four months they reached Bucareli sound, where they remained several weeks surveying and trading with the Indians. Leaving this port they made the highest point reached by Spanish explorers on the northwest coast, and sighted Mount Saint Elias, as it had been named by Vitus Bering, 1741. While searching for a passage which might lead into the Arctic they entered a large bay containing many islands, which they called Isla de Magdalena. Port Santiago was also discovered and named.

This ends the tale of early Spanish attempts at exploration along the Oregon coast, meagre enough, it is true, and purely negative in result, so far as Oregon itself is concerned.

CHAPTER III

SIR FRANCIS DRAKE

1

FOR MORE THAN a century following the discovery of America, Spain pressed its advantage to the utmost. West Indies, South American coasts, Central America, and especially Mexico and Peru, were seized and occupied. Portugal, meanwhile, took possession of Brazil and pushed explorations in the East Indies, far away in the eastern hemisphere. South Africa, India, the islands of the Indian ocean, and even parts of the Chinese coast, fell more or less under Portuguese sway. While these nations were revelling in the conquest of the west and the east, it seemed that the British were to have no part. Too weak at this period to dispute with the Spaniards their claim to the supremacy of the seas, England's mariners, as already explained, at first devoted their energies to the north Atlantic, and the Arctic, toward the discovery of either a northeast or a northwest passage which would enable them to reach the coveted South sea without running the gauntlet of the armed ships of their rivals.

These efforts led, after discovery of Labrador, by Cabot, to exploration of the bleak coast of Baffin bay, the object being to reach India and the orient. But it was not decreed by fate that the British were to have a subordinate role in the drama of world exploitation. Elizabeth and her knights errant of the sea refused to recognize the validity of the papal line of demarcation. It was the virgin queen who first asserted the doctrine of the freedom of the seas and the policy of the "open door." To the complaint of the Spanish ambassador that the English were infringing upon the commercial prerogatives of his sovereign, she replied "that she did not understand why either her subjects, or those of any other European prince, should be debarred from traffic in the Indies; that as she did not acknowledge the Spaniards to have any title by donation of the bishop of Rome, so she knew no right they had to other places than those they were in actual possession of; for that, their having touched only here and there upon a coast, and given names to a few rivers and capes, were such insignificant things as could in no way entitle them to a proprietary right, further than in the parts where they actually settled and continued to inhabit."

This bold challenge was taken up by the Spanish, and there began a warfare that was none the less brilliant in its exploits from being at times carried on during periods when the nations were apparently and theoretically at peace with each other. Let it be remembered that in the days of Elizabeth, privateering and letters of marque were not contrary to international law and usage, and that this was true even until 1856, when it was for the first time agreed among nations: "Privateering is and remains abolished."

The famous English naval heroes, Hawkins, Oxenham, Drake, and others, were buccaneers and sea rovers, pirates if you will, but they had, secretly or openly, the countenance of their government, with the public blessing of their church, and so long as they robbed and looted on the Spanish main there was no one at home to call them to account.

One of the picturesque characters of history is Sir Francis Drake, whose name is linked with the early history of Oregon as the first of his nation to sail the north Pacific and to land upon the western coast. It was he who gave the name New Albion to the lands he discovered, a name which was carried upon maps, especially English maps, until long after the American Revolution, two centuries later.

To tell the story of his spectacular and interesting career will not be practicable here, excepting in so far as it bears upon the story of Oregon. But, at the close of his eventful life, he had passed through all of the stages from poor clergyman's son to ship captain and naval hero. He had become one of the richest men of England, had been knighted by his queen, and was worshipped by his countrymen. He was a great national figure, one who had accomplished marvelous feats of courage and seamanship, and he had had a great part in the defeat of the Spanish Armada itself. In his time, the English nation had advanced to front rank as ruler of the seas, and the prestige of the powerful Spanish maritime forces had been seriously impaired.

It was in 1573, when he was still in his twenties, that he first saw the Pacific. With Oxenham, a daring freebooter like himself, he had pounced upon a Spanish settlement on the isthmus, and then had invaded the country for the purpose of waylaying and seizing a treasure train upon the forest hidden trail, over which the gold of Peru and Ecquador would be carried to the Atlantic seaboard. It was an audacious scheme, an adventure of a mere handful of bold men, a project full of danger and of incredible escapes, but a raid that was successful in accomplishing its primary objects. On this errand, it is related, he came to a hill where there was a great tree that had been provided by the natives with stepping places to some sort of bower, or look-out at the top. It was from this vantage point that he looked out over the vast expanse of the Pacific, or South sea, its blue rim melting into the western sky. Then and there, he determined that he would set sail upon that sea, and as the old chronicler puts it, he "resolved to be the pioneer of England in the Pacific; and on this resolution he solemnly besought the blessing of God."

A few years after this, Drake left England in command of his own fleet of five vessels, three of them so small that it now seems incredible that they would be provided for his contemplated voyage to the Pacific. But, for that matter the same remark may be made about all of the early expeditions and the puny ships that ventured the far seas. At that time England was nominally at peace with Spain, but there can be no doubt that Drake's purpose was known to his government and that he was secretly aided in the enterprise. It is believed that Elizabeth had a share in the profits. He sailed from Plymouth, December 13, 1577, with a crew of 164 men, "Gentlemen and Saylors," ostensibly bound for Egypt, but he directed his course on a very different route.

He touched at the coast of Patagonia, where Magellan had punished mutineers when on the famous voyage around South America and across the Pacific, and here Drake proceeded to make use of the very gibbet that had been constructed and used by Magellan, left standing in this forsaken spot. Drake's lieutenant, Doughty, who was charged with insubordination, was tried, convicted and executed. The crew was there told of the real object of the voyage, which was to invade the Spanish preserves and to prey upon the treasure ships on the Pacific shores. Of the five ships that had left England, the flagship alone, the Golden Hind, with a crew of but 60 men, and of a burden of but 100 tons, succeeded in threading the dangerous straits and reaching the Pacific ocean.

But the intrepid commander sailed on without his consorts, and lost no time in proceeding to accomplish his piratical design. One after the other, the surprised and unprepared Spanish ports were entered, and were stripped of gold and silver, and ship after ship fell into his hands almost without resistance. The Golden Hind became so heavy with loot that a part of the cargo, including precious oriental silks and spices, had to be thrown overboard. One of the last Spanish ships to be taken was the great treasure ship whose name was Nuestra Senora de la Concepcion, but called by the Spanish sailors the Cacafuego. Vast treasure was secured by the sea rovers. On one of the smaller vessels it is reported that he obtained valuable emeralds, half a finger long, probably the same that he afterward gave to Queen Elizabeth.

Drake knew that to return by the same route would be dangerous in the extreme, for aroused Spanish authorities would be lying in wait, with all the ships they could muster, to overhaul him. Besides, he knew that the prevailing winds would not favor him on that route. His little vessel is said to have had on board not less than 26 tons of silver, 80 pounds of pure gold, 13 chests of gold plate, besides emeralds and pearls and other precious stones. A recent author estimates that there were 10 or 15 tons of cannon and arms, and she had bales of valuable products of the orient to weight her down.

2

The raid, so far, had been successful beyond all hopes. Whether he then made up his mind to try another course, and, instead of turning south, to continue northward along the Mexican coast, and determined to try for the strait of Anian, and to find the northwest passage, or, whether he merely pretended that such was his purpose and had already decided to return home by way of the Indian ocean, is a matter of debate. At this time Englishmen knew nothing of the existence of Oregon. The popular belief, as shown by the maps of the period, was that California was an island, and many supposed that an archipelago of islands lay west of the Labrador coast. Drake is said to have captured some Spanish maps showing the route to the Philippines, but if so, they could have shed little light upon the perilous journey through unknown northern seas that were supposed to afford a sailing route to England.

Reports of his experiences in the north Pacific leave much doubt as to just how far he ventured before he finally gave up this plan, if it really was his plan. One narrative fixed his northernmost latitude at 43 degrees, another at 48 degrees. The south boundary of Oregon is 42 degrees, and so in any case he was the first Englishman to sail along the Oregon coast, as he was the first to sail the Pacific ocean.

In a book published in London, 1630, entitled "Relations of the Most Famous Kingdoms and Commonwealths throwout the World," is a quaint and curious description of "America, commonly called West India," which serves to show the state of knowledge at that time concerning the new world. This was over 50 years after Drake's famous voyage was made, and reading it makes plain the stupendous undertaking that confronted that navigator, if he actually made a decision to try for a way across North America. The colonies in Virginia and in Massachusetts had but recently been planted, when the book was published, and, according to it, America was "bounded on the east with the Atlanticke or North Sea; upon the south with the Magellan Straights; upon the west with Mare Pacificum, or Mar del Zur; and on the north with Terra Incognita." Concerning the north, the book tells us that "authors affirme that under the very Pole lyeth a black and high Rocke and three and thirty leagues in compasse, and there these ilands. Among which the Ocean disgorging itself by 19 channels maketh foure whirllpooles or currents, by which the waters are finally carried towards the North, and there swallowed into the bowels of the earth. That Euripus or whirle-poole, which Sythicke [Pacific] ocean maketh, have five inlets; and by reason of his streight passage and violent course is never frozen. The other Euripus on the backside of Groneland [Greenland] hath three inlets, and remaines frozen three moneths yearely; its length is thirty seven leagues. Betweene these two raging Euripi lyeth an Iland (about Lappia and Biarmia) the habitation (they say) of the Pigmies. A certaine schollar of Oxford reporteth that these foure Euripi are ingulphed with such furious violence into some inward receptacle that no ship is able, with never so strong or opposite a gale, to stem the current. And that at no time there bloweth so much wind as will move a windmill." The author concludes that this is merely a "folly and a fable which some mens boldnesse made other mens ignorance to believe." But from this, it will be understood that Drake's courage was never greater than when he decided to take the chances and to sail his ship homeward by the uncharted northern route.

The ship entered a belt of cold and fog by the time it reached the latitude of the present Oregon south boundary line, and the early chronicler does not fail to make us understand how disagreeable was this voyage. It was June 3, 1578, and the crew, just from the tropics, "did grievously complain thereof, some of them feeling their health much impaired thereby, neither was it that this chanced in the night alone, but the day following carried with it not only the markes, but the stings and force of the night." We are told that "the very ropes of our ship were stiffe, and the rain which fell was an unnatural congealed and frozen substance, so that we seemed to be rather in the frozen Zone than any where so neere unto the sun, or these hotter climates."

At two degrees farther north, these conditions were still worse, "yet would not our general be discouraged, but (answered) as well, by comfortable speeches, of the divine providence, and of God's loving care over his children, out of the scriptures." They noted that the land in that part of America "beares farther out into the West than we had before imagined, we were nearer on it than we were aware; yet the neerer still we came to it, the more extremity of cold did sease upon us."

Then they made shore, but the description is so indefinite that it is a matter of uncertainty just where this was. The narrative says: "The fifth of June we were forced by contrary windes to runne in with the shoare, which we then first descried, and to cast anchor in a bad bay, the best roade we could for the present meete with, where we were not without some danger by reason of the many extreme gusts and flawes that beate upon us, which if they ceased, and were still at any time * * * there followed most vile, thicke and stinking fogges, against which the sea prevailed nothing." The cold and wind forced them as soon as they were clear of land to turn southward, and they ran from 48 to 38 degrees by June 17, and found a "convenient and fit harborough and sunshine." This harbor has been identified, and is now called Drakes bay, opposite the Farralones on the California coast. It is the same bay known to the Spaniards, 1595, as Port Francisco, not far north of the present bay of San Francisco.

According to this account, the fourteen days of this northward venture were so overcast that no observation of sun or stars could be secured, and for this reason, as well as because of the discrepancy in the accounts, the assertion that the Golden Hind reached 48 degrees, north, is open to some question; but if the weather was as bad as stated another question arises as to the accuracy of the narrator's description of the Oregon coast, for the chronicle says, in telling of the "generall squalidnesse and barrennesse of the countrie," that they saw "trees without leaves and the ground without greenes in these months of June and July." This is ascribed to the fact that the "high and snow covered mountains make the north and northwest winds to send abroad their frozen nimphes [winds], to the infecting of the whole air with incredible sharpnesse. Snow hardly departs in the midst of summer." The shrewd opinion was ventured that Asia and America come near together "if not fully joyned," and also that there is either no passage at all through these northern coasts, which is most likely, or if there be, that yet it is unnavigable. A recent and very thorough author, after careful consideration, expresses the view that Drake's voyage to the north was not to find the northwest passage, but to evade capture.

It is hard to reconcile the description given with the verdant shores of the Oregon Country, as it is now known, or even to apply the description to the Alaskan coasts, and surely "nimphes" of the kind experienced by Drake and his bold fellows are not often found in these latitudes in the summer months. But it is evident from all the narratives that the ship needed overhauling, before undertaking the long homeward voyage, and that the return to the California coast afforded the opportunity.

It would be interesting to quote in full the old descriptions of the visit of these mariners during the period from June 17 to July 23 in Drakes bay, where the ship was overhauled. The country was formally taken possession of by the navigator for his sovereign, but this was in California and not in limits of present Oregon. One account says: "Our Generall called this Countrey Nova Albion, and that for two causes: the one in respect to the White Bankes and Cliffes, which lie toward the Sea; and the other, because it might have some affinity with our country in name, which sometimes was so called. There is no part of Earth here to be taken up, wherein there is not some probable show of Gold or

Silver." The name New Albion was afterward shown on maps until recent times, and was usually applied not only to modern California, but to Oregon and beyond, on the north.

Drake and his crew spent the weeks pleasantly in the California harbor, living on amicable terms with the natives, whose manners and customs interested them. With great ceremony Drake was adopted into the tribe, or, as he thought, was made king. The old account says: "On our departure hence our Generall set up a monument of our being there, and also of her Majesties Right and Title to the same, namely a Plate, nayled upon a faire great Poste, whereupon was engraven her Majesties name, the day and yeere of our arrivall there, with the free giving up of the Province and the People into her Majesties hands, together with her Highnesse Picture and Armes, in a piece of six pence of current English Money, under the Plate, whereunder was also written the name of our Generall."

Drake found the Spanish maps that he had captured to come into practical use now, and he used them to cross the Pacific and the Indian oceans, stopping at various points. At Sierra Leona, in Guinea, on the African coast, he found, according to the veracious report, "necessarie provisions, great store of Elephants, Oisters upon trees of one kinde, spawning and increasing infinitely, the Oister suffering no bud to grow." The reader may believe it, or not. The expedition arrived in England in the autumn of 1580, three years after departure.

The Golden Hind was the first English ship to circumnavigate the globe. The queen received valuable gifts from the treasures, and graciously dined on board, and then conferred knighthood upon the bold commander. The ship was afterward preserved in the Thames, as a public relic. It was casually mentioned by Ben Johnson in the play Every Man in his Humor, published, 1596, in the phrase: "Drake's old ship at Deptford may sooner circle the world again," showing that at that date it was still in existence.

Drake was 32 years old when he sailed away on this voyage. His subsequent career was full of interest. He died at 51 years of age, when on an expedition against the Spanish under his old commander, Admiral Hawkins. He did not succeed in finding a northwest passage, but it was primarily upon his visit to Oregon and to California that England based its claim in after years to the Oregon Country and the north Pacific coast of North America.

After Drake's example, Cavendish, 1586, undertook a voyage to the South sea, and followed Drake's course up the coast of America as far as Cape San Lucas, California, when he struck across the Pacific and returned to England, 1588. Sir Richard Hawkins, 1593, reached the Pacific, but was fought by the Spanish and forced to surrender before he had passed far beyond the equator. Two other British voyages, 1670 and 1685, reached the Pacific, but did not attempt to follow the coast line of North America.

3

During the 200 years that followed Drake's discovery the British nation did nothing to secure dominion over the western part of that continent. No doubt the wars and revolutions of Europe made it difficult for England or for any other European power to embark upon any great overseas undertaking. Nevertheless, it will afford a subject for speculation and for debate that, during this period of intense maritime activity in other directions, covering the span of two centuries, Britain gave no attention to the country on the west coast of North America reported upon by Drake. It sent no other expeditions there for discovery or barter, although it promptly followed up his report of what he had seen of the coast of India, going thither by way of the cape of Good Hope.

It was as early as 1600 that the "Governor and Company of Merchants of London trading to the East Indies," generally known as the East India Company, was founded, under Queen Elizabeth. India was the famed storehouse of all that wealth and luxury most coveted at the time, and competition between the British and the Dutch for that trade was particularly keen during the 17th century. But, even the fact that Spain had for years past been able to bring great sums of gold from Peru, Mexico, **Ecuador**, and elsewhere in the western Americas, seems not to have tempted the great maritime nations, the British or the Dutch, to follow Drake's path around to the Pacific northwest in search of information concerning the regions claimed by the Spanish monopoly. And, as already shown, Spain itself did little, so far as the world knows, during this period further to explore and occupy the northerly coasts.

The South Sea Company was formed, 1711, in London, and was given a monopoly of British trade with the Pacific islands and South America, which monopoly existed until 1807. Ships flying the British flag were required to have a special permit to sail thither. Its actual operations upon the Pacific were unimportant, but out of it grew the South Sea Bubble, and the era of wild speculation in England, culminating in 1720. The British merchant ships that engaged in the fur trade on the north Pacific coast in the late years of the 18th century were hampered by this monopoly.

There was one event of this early period that had a profound influence, albeit indirectly, upon the history of the Pacific northwest. King Charles II, of England, May 2, 1670, issued a charter to the Hudson's Bay Company, officially known at that time as "The Company of Adventurers of England Trading into Hudson Bay." Although it was provided in the charter that the company should pursue active exploration of all the region draining into Hudson bay, little was done in furtherance of this object, until a century later the British victory in the Seven Years' war took Canada from France (1763), and removed the obstacle of French opposition. It was a few years after this, 1783-84, that another British fur company, the North West Company, was organized at Montreal. It soon proved to be a formidable competitor of the Hudson's Bay Company, and, between the two, western exploration advanced rapidly. Not only was all of Canada opened, but the valleys of the St. Lawrence, and of the Mississippi as well.

By acquisition of the French colonies in Canada, the English gained a new interest in searching for the northwest passage, and perchance even for a route by land to the Pacific coast, especially in view of their final conquest and domination over India, that had been secured, 1751. The effort made by Verendrye, and his successors, to reach the western sea overland, during the period of French domination, were now to be renewed by the British fur trading companies, and under their enterprising management a number of adventurous explorers penetrated the unknown parts of the continent.

CHAPTER IV

CAPTAIN COOK AND COAST FUR TRADE

1

SOON AFTER the conclusion of the Seven Years' War, 1763, by which France lost its Canadian colonies, we find the British taking advantage of the opportunity thus presented to them to explore the western sea. Parliament had offered, 1745, a reward of £20,000 sterling to a ship privately owned discovering a passage opening into Hudson Bay. A new act, 1776, extended the operation of the law to ships of the royal navy, and provided that the passage might be sought in any direction above 52 degrees north, for interest in finding a route eastward, to the north of Europe, was as keen as in the long sought northwest passage. An additional reward of £5000 was offered any ship reaching within one degree of the north pole.

Capt. James Cook has the honor of being the first Englishman, after the long period of inactivity, to carry the flag of his country into the antipodes. He had spent his boyhood upon a small English farm, but at an early age he entered the service of the East India Company, and thus secured nautical training. Rising rapidly in rank, he was entrusted with numerous important missions, the successful execution of which brought to him, 1768, the command of a scientific expedition sent into the south seas for the purpose of observing the transit of Venus. Upon his return to England, he was entrusted with the task, 1773, of searching in the Antarctic ocean for a habitable continent, supposed to be in that quarter of the globe. The first of these expeditions added greatly to the geographical knowledge of the world by the discovery of New Zealand and the Sandwich islands, while the second showed conclusively that the supposed Antarctic continent was a myth.

His third and last voyage into the Pacific was primarily in search of the long sought northwest passage, the control of which, if it really did exist, was a matter of great importance, because of its strategic value. It is a coincidence that when, July 6, 1776, two days after the date of American Declaration of Independence, Cook's vessels were at anchor in Plymouth sound and ready for sea, three British war vessels and a fleet of transports, bound to America with the last division of Hessian troops and some cavalry, were driven into Plymouth sound by adverse winds. Commenting on this, Cook observed that it seemed a singular circumstance that at the very instant of his departure upon a voyage, the object of which was to benefit Europe by making fresh discoveries in North America, there should be the unhappy necessity of employing others of his Majesty's ships and of conveying numerous bodies of forces to secure the obedience of those parts of that land which had been discovered and settled by his countrymen.

July 12, 1776, Captain Cook set sail, in command of two ships, the Resolution and the Discovery. The Resolution was the warship in which he had made his second voyage. The Discovery was a small vessel of 300 tons, under the command of Captain Clerke. Cook's orders were to proceed by way of the cape of Good Hope, thence, after arriving in the Pacific, to sail by New Zealand to Tahiti, or Society islands, from which islands he was to steer directly for New Albion, seeking its coast line at about the latitude of 45 degrees, north. Retention of the name, New Albion, for the coast of the North American continent above California, shows that the British had never given up their claim of proprietary rights in that region, first established by Drake.

The American coast was first reached at latitude 43 degrees, and Cook was the first Englishman to view the Oregon littoral, unless that distinction belongs to Drake. No sooner had Cook reached that coast than a storm arose which drove his ships southward, probably as far as the California line; but favorable weather then succeeding, the northward voyage was resumed. March 7, 1778, the Oregon coast was again sighted. The expedition was now near Yaquina bay. The land appeared to be moderately high and diversified with hill and valley. Almost everywhere it was covered with trees but there were no distinguishing promontories or capes to mark its shore line except a flat topped hill to which Cook gave the name of Cape Foulweather, a name it still bears.

Slowly up the coast he sailed through blustery March weather, keeping the land in sight almost continuously. The coast appeared almost straight, without an inlet or opening. At 43 degrees, 30 minutes, arose a point, which was called Cape Gregory. At 44 degrees, 6 minutes, came another to which he gave the name Cape Perpetua. It is noted that in his narrative Cook remarks that almost in this place geographers had placed the cape called Blanco, supposed to have been discovered by d'Aguilar, 1603, and the large entrance or strait, the discovery of which was also attributed to d'Aguilar. A careful search failed to verify the statements. March 22, a small round hill to the northward had the appearance of an island and "between this island, or rock, and the northern extreme of the land, there appeared to be a small opening which flattered us with hopes of finding an harbor." But the hopes were not realized, for as the vessels drew near it appeared that the wished for opening was closed by low land. "On this account," says Cook, "I called the point of land to the north of it Cape Flattery." Thus did one of the great landmarks of the northwest coast get its name. Cook describes the land to the southward as of moderate height, covered with forests, and pleasant and fertile in appearance.

He utterly missed the mouth of the Columbia river, as well as the entrance to the strait of Juan de Fuca. He landed upon the western shore of Vancouver island, in Nootka bay. Regarding his failure to find the entrance to the strait, Cook wrote: "It is in this very latitude where we now were that geographers have placed the pretended strait of Juan de Fuca. But we saw nothing like it; nor is there the least probability that ever any such thing existed." It seems strange that Cook could have spent a full month at Nootka without learning from the natives of the existence of the great strait that was so near; but neither did Drake, who spent five weeks at Drake's bay, learn of San Francisco bay.

2

During his month's sojourn on Vancouver island, Cook cultivated and won the friendship of the natives, and he carried on with them a lively trade in skins, chiefly those of the wolf, fox, bear, deer, marten and sea otter, for which were given pieces and implements of brass and iron. Cook was surprised, as the Spaniards had been before, at their possession of fish hooks and other implements of brass and iron. He found two silver spoons of Spanish make there, and his mention of this fact in his report figured later in the controversy between the British and the Spanish over the sovereignty of Nootka.

Spanish officials believed San Lorenzo, named by Perez, 1774, to be identical with Nootka, and Martinez, who was with Perez and who afterward represented the Spanish interests at Nootka, produced proofs that he had been at this very place before Cook's visit, not the least of which proofs was Cook's statement that he

Captain James Cook
From an original picture by Dance in the Gallery of
Greenwich Hospital (engraving by E. Scriven).

A Man from Nootka Sound

A Woman from Nootka Sound

Various Articles Used by the Nootkans
Reproductions from plates in Captain James Cook's "Voyage to the Pacific Ocean, 1776-1780." Drawings were made by R. Webber during the voyage.

found Spanish spoons in the possession of the natives. The statement of the Spanish claim to priority is shown by the official correspondence in the Nootka sound controversy papers, but the British view was that the finding of the articles by Cook, did not conclusively show that the Spanish had left these articles at the exact place where they were found.

It is possible that in early times ships had been wrecked on the northwest coast, and that thus the natives first came into possession of these articles. This is indicated by the fact that there are several legendary accounts of prehistoric visits of white men to the Oregon coast, such as the "treasure ship" which landed near Neahkahnie mountain, the "beeswax" ship wrecked near Nehalem, in the same vicinity. There was a story of a Yazoo Indian seen in his old age in the lower Mississippi region by a French scholar and writer. This Indian claimed to have visited the Pacific coast in 1745, or about that time, and to have learned there of the regular visits of a ship to that coast, and to have seen bearded visitors ambushed and slain by the natives on landing. Konapee, a young man, having dark red hair, and much freckled, is mentioned by several of the very early visitors to Oregon. He lived south of the Columbia river among the Tillamook tribe. There was also an old man named Soto, who claimed to be a son of a Spaniard, one of the four that are said to have survived a wreck at the mouth of the Columbia river, about 1725. Lewis and Clark, on reaching the Rocky Mountains, 1805, were told by Flathead Indians of an old man, living alone by the sea, who had given handkerchiefs to men of that tribe, who had visited the coast in the previous autumn. Within the range of actual history, 1833, a Japanese vessel, laden with crockery, was wrecked near Cape Flattery, and three of the crew of seventeen were held as slaves by the natives until rescued by Capt. William McNeill, of the Hudson's Bay Company vessel, Llama. They were sent to England by Dr. John McLoughlin, and thence taken to China.

With Cook on his expedition were two Americans, Gore and Ledyard, the first Americans to visit the Pacific northwest. Cook found the Indians very eager to obtain possession of pieces of metal of any kind, and several times he caught them stealing. He seems, however, to have been the first voyager to understand the Indian code of ethics in this particular. Indian tribes, according

to their own theory, had a communal proprietary right in everything pertaining to their tribal locality. Earth, air, water, everything, in fact, about them, whether subject to ownership according to the white man's idea or not, was the exclusive property of
the tribe. They thought that when the white strangers needed
water or wood for their ships, they should ask permission before
taking it, and that they should make some payment to the tribe.
The white men did not do this, and therefore the natives considered that they had an equal right to help themselves to some
of the white men's property.

Leaving Nootka, Cook sailed northward along the Alaska coast,
where he sighted Mount Edgecumbe and Mount Saint Elias. He
passed through Cook inlet, named after himself, penetrated the
Aleutian islands, touched the Asiatic continent and came at last
to Bering strait, through which he sailed into the Arctic ocean,
until he found his way blocked with ice. Thus was the myth of the
northwest passage forever discredited. For, although it is stated
in the Introduction to Cook's Voyages, written afterwards for the
Lords Commissioners of the Admiralty, it was already "pretty certain that no such passage existed through Hudson Bay," it was
Cook's expedition that made this certain. Attainment of this
geographical knowledge was epochal, inasmuch as it established
the fact of the closed polar sea. The long voyage around Cape Horn
required to reach these coasts, and the comparative isolation of
the Oregon Country, made certain that whoever in the future
should secure control over this region must perforce establish communication therewith by land rather than by sea.

Turning his back then upon the inhospitable Arctic sea, Cook
afterward explored Norton sound, north of the Yukon, and touched
again at the Aleutian islands where he met some Russian fur
traders. He then directed his course toward the Sandwich islands,
where he intended to winter before extending his explorations
farther. There, however, February 14, 1779, while at Kealakekua
bay, Hawaii, Captain Cook was killed in an unfortunate conflict
with the natives. Command of the expedition now devolved upon
Clerke, who sailed from the islands the next season once more
into the Arctic, where he found the ice worse than before. He was
in frail health, and, upon the return voyage, he died upon the Si-

berian coast, August 22, 1779, and the command was assumed by Gore.

Proceeding to Canton, it was found that furs which had been acquired for mere scraps of iron, old knives and the like, were in great demand among the Chinese, and, in spite of their poor condition, brought what to Cook's men seemed fabulous prices. The members of the crews desired to return immediately to the American coast, in order to procure more furs, and it was only by the exercise of the severest authority that Gore prevailed upon them to continue on their homeward way. Arriving in England, 1780, the report about the fur trade was at first suppressed by the government, but before the official account of the voyage was published the news leaked. After the end of the Spanish war, accounts of the voyages were given out, and news was soon spread abroad of the profits to be made. Thus was laid the foundation for a new era in the history of the Pacific northwest, the Era of the Fur Trader.

CHAPTER V
ERA OF FUR TRADING VESSELS
1

IT IS NOT THE purpose to detail the history of exploration on the northwest coast, but some circumstances may be given as having a bearing upon the history of Oregon itself.

Until the beginning of the 18th century Russia was Asiatic, rather than European, and was little affected by the European wars, or political entanglements. But with the rise of the power of Peter the Great a new era began. Russian interest in Siberia had already been shown, the eastern coast had been reached, 1711, when the extension of the fur trade to that vast district brought it to the particular attention of the emperor. In 1724, just before his death, he commissioned a Danish naval officer, Vitus Bering, to explore Kamschatka. The language of the commission is interesting: "At Kamschatka, or somewhere else, two decked boats are to be built. With these you are to sail northward along the coast, and, as the end of the coast is not known, this land is undoubtedly America. For this reason you are to inquire where the American coast begins, and go to some European colony; and when European ships are seen you are to ask what the coast is called, note it down, make a landing, obtain reliable information, and then, having charted the coast, return."

Bering and his men suffered great hardships in making their way to the Siberian coast; and, in building the required sea going vessels they were mostly dependent upon their own ingenuity and resourcefulness. They succeeded in constructing a small ship, which was named the Gabriel, the timber for which was hauled from the forest by dogs. Tar was manufactured by the sailors themselves. Cables, rigging and anchors had been dragged 2000 miles through Siberian wilderness. Food was scarce. Fish oil was the sailor's butter, and dried fish his beef. The sea gave up its salt, and spirits were distilled from straw.

After great hardships the vessel was made ready and Bering started out on a voyage of discovery along an unknown coast. July 13, 1728, the Gabriel headed north, keeping in sight of land, and proceeded to a point near 67 degrees, 18 minutes, north latitude, and 195 degrees, seven minutes, east, by Greenwich longitude. Thus was established the fact that the two continents were separated by the strait or sea, which is now known as Bering strait, although owing to cloudy weather Bering was unable to see the American shore.

From St. Petersburg, it was announced that "Bering has ascertained that there really does exist a northwest passage, and that from the Lena river it is possible, provided one is not prevented by polar ice, to sail to Kamschatka and thence to Japan and China and the East Indies." In 1729, Bering made another voyage charting the Kamschatka peninsula and northern Kurile islands. After these achievements, he went into retirement, and it was not until 1741 that he returned and then sailed upon his last ill fated voyage of discovery. In that year he sailed from Avatcha, on the Siberian coast, with two inadequately equipped vessels, the St. Peter and the St. Paul. The latter was commanded by his lieutenant, Chirikoff, who sailed to a point near Sitka, on the North American continent. He lost two boats while trying to effect a landing, after which he returned to Avatcha.

Bering, in the St. Peter, sailed down the Alaskan coast and discovered and named that imposing sentinel of the mountain range, Mount St. Elias. This voyage, and its results, is generally accepted as the Russian discovery of Alaska. Bering touched the American continent at latitude 59 degrees, 40 minutes, at a point supposed to be near the later named Mount Fairweather, but his crew being by this time disabled by scurvy, he turned about and sailed north. Unfortunately, his ship was wrecked upon an island of the Aleutian archipelago, now bearing his name. Here he died, and after a winter spent amid unbelievable hardships, the few survivors of the expedition managed to return to Avatcha bay. They brought with them, however, a few of the beautiful pelts of the sea otter, and of the fur-bearing seal, that created particular interest upon their arrival in Siberia, and that subsequently caused a stampede to the American coast in quest of these valuable furs. It was furs, rather than scientific interest in exploration, or desire for colonizing, that made the discoveries of Bering and Chirikoff the basis of Russian settlement.

In the meantime, Chirikoff, with the St. Paul, sailed eastward. About July 11, 1741, he sighted the highland of the west coast of the archipelago Alexandria, near latitude 55 degrees, 21 minutes; and on the following morning the promontory afterward known

as Cape Addington. Next came the Hazy islands, so named later
by Dixon, 1787. July 17, 1741, the St. Paul was estimated to be in
latitude 57 degrees, 15 minutes, north, in the region of Sitka
sound. Being in need of fresh water, Chirikoff sent 10 of his best
men ashore in a small boat. They never came back. Neither did a
second party. It was thought they were all murdered by the natives.

Then followed a number of Russian fur trading voyages. It is
said that fully one-third of the frail vessels, held together in some
instances merely by thongs, were wrecked; but the fatalistic Russians persisted, in spite of all obstacles, and succeeded in building
up a rather uncertain fur trade. The furs were marketed in China,
but owing to official objections, the fur packs had to be covertly
transported overland, and not delivered by ship to Chinese ports,
in the usual way. Russian traders seem to have been in disfavor
with both the Chinese and Japanese, a circumstance that later
proved to be to the advantage of the Americans.

Contact of the Russians with Cook's expedition, 1778, seems to
have stimulated Russian interest in this fur trade. In the year
1781, a number of merchants of the coast of eastern Siberia organized a company, but it met with small success, chiefly because
of its brutal treatment of the natives. It was merged, 1799, with
the newly organized Russian-American Company. To this concern
was given by the Russian government a monopoly of the fur trade
on the American coast, from Bering strait, southerly as far as
north latitude 55 degrees. This is a fact of importance, as indicating the basis of the subsequent Russian claim to this latitude on
the American coast, and as having a bearing upon the "Fifty-four
Forty or Fight" controversy of later years. Between 1781 and
1783, Russian fur traders explored the American coast as far
south as Prince William sound, explored Kodiak island and, 1787,
founded an establishment at Cook river, on the main land.

The chief agent of the Russian-American Company in America
was Alexander Baranoff, who, later, had dealings with John Jacob
Astor in connection with his Columbia river operations. For 20
years, Baranoff ruled, sometimes with brutality, always with in-
flexible severity, his northwestern dominions. Except for the difference in the character of the two men, and their methods of
governing their domains, he is comparable to the Hudson's Bay

Company chief factor, Dr. John McLoughlin, in the extent of power and authority vested in one individual. Having made several unsuccessful attempts to locate establishments on the Alaskan coast, Baranoff, 1799, bartered with a native chief for a tract of land and built his new capital, Sitka, the "City on the Channel," which became the center from which thenceforth the Russian-American Company conducted its extensive business. The territorial ambitions of the Russians on the Pacific coast, and the resulting international complications, will be described in a later chapter.

In passing it may be mentioned that, 1786, the Frenchman, La Perouse, acting under instructions from his government, visited the north Pacific coast in the vicinity of Mount Fairweather, and there was also another voyage under the same flag by Marchand, 1791; but, excepting for this unimportant participation, the French nation had no part in the explorations in this part of the world.

2

Having introduced the Russians, we shall now return to the activities of the British. As already stated in chapter III, the government of that nation was responsible in some degree for the tardy exploration of the coast of the Pacific northwest. Something more should be said as to the monopoly of the entrenched trading companies. The exclusive privilege of British trading with the west coast of America, and within 300 leagues thereof, belonged to the South Sea Company. The East India Company was reaping a rich harvest from its trade with the East Indies, and it had the sole right of such trade east of the cape of Good Hope. These exclusive privileges hampered free trade by British fur traders by interfering with their dealings with the natives on the northwest coast, in which the South Sea Company had sole rights, but also by interfering with marketing furs in China, in which the other company had the exclusive privileges. Both companies granted some licenses, but conditions were such that the fur trade of the Pacific coast offered no inducement to extend operations of these companies themselves into that field. Rival British companies and independent British traders could not legally trade in China or on the northwest coast with the Indians, without licenses, while sailing under the British flag.

The result of this short sighted policy was that some British captains were tempted to sail under the Austrian flag, or to take out Portuguese papers at the port of Macao on the China coast. The first to try this, definitely mentioned, was James Hanna, who sailed to this coast from Macao, 1785, in the Harmon, a small brig. When he arrived at Nootka, the Indians tried to board his vessel in the open day. Many were killed in the fray that followed. Hanna, however, carried on a successful trade on the coast, and took back to Macao a cargo of sea otter skins which brought $20,000.

An attempt was made the next year to start a line of packets from Kamschatka but this was not a success. About the same time, also, small ships from Calcutta and Bombay were sent out by the East India Company. Lowrie and Guise came to Nootka in the Captain Cook, a 300-ton vessel, and the Experiment of 100 tons, fitted out at Bombay, sailed under the East India Company. The voyage, which was under the supervision of James Strange, earned $24,000.

The King George's Sound Company was organized in London, and, 1785, it sent out an expedition under Captains Dixon and Portlock, in the Queen Charlotte and the King George, carrying licenses from both the South Sea and the East India companies. Dixon's name was subsequently given to the entrance to Queen Charlotte sound, and he claimed to have discovered the region between 52 and 54 degrees north, on the ground that it had not been seen by Cook. He called the land seen, the Queen Charlotte islands. He thought it was not a portion of the mainland, and this fact was later confirmed by Capt. Charles Duncan, in command of the Princess Royal, and James Colnett, master of the Prince of Wales, of the same company, who came to the coast, 1787. Portlock cruised to Cook inlet, where he was "not a little mortified" to find other traders ahead of him, presumably Russians.

Among others resorting to the false flag subterfuge mentioned was Capt. Charles William Barkley, an Englishman, whose name is sometimes spelled Berkeley, or Barclay, operating under the flag of the Austrian East Indian Company, who, 1787, visited the northwestern coast in command of the ship, Imperial Eagle. His wife accompanied him upon this voyage and so had the distinction of being the first white woman to visit these shores. Opposite

Quadra's Isla de Dolores, Barkley discovered a river into which he sent a boatload of his men for fresh water. They were set upon by the natives and all were killed, whereupon Barkley named the stream Destruction river, which name has been since transferred to the island and the river is now called by its original Indian name, Hoh.

After anchoring at Nootka, a canoe came alongside and Mrs. Barkley was astonished when a man, appearing to be an Indian, but a very dirty one, clothed in a filthy sea otter skin, came aboard and introduced himself as Dr. John Mackay, late surgeon of the Captain Cook, who had been left there by that vessel the preceding year. So far as known Mackay was the first European to live among the northwest Indians. Captain Hanna on his second voyage, 1786, had seen Mackay and had offered to take him back to civilization, but the doctor had declined. He had begun to relish the native diet of dried fish and whale oil. During Barkley's stay at Nootka, he, with the aid of Mackay, acquired all the skins that the Indians had, and when, soon after, there arrived the Prince of Wales and the Princess Royal, respectively commanded by Colnett and Duncan, they could do no business.

From Nootka, Barkley sailed south, discovering Clayoquot sound. He anchored off a large village near what is now known as Effingham island. A successful trade was carried on, and several points and islands were named. Among them was Cape Beale, at the southern entrance to Barkley sound.

On leaving that sound, the strait of Fuca was discovered, on a July day, 1787, as the following quotation from the diary of Mrs. Barkley shows: "In the afternoon, to our great astonishment, we arrived off a large opening extending to the eastward, the entrance to which appeared to be about four leagues wide and remained about that width as far as the eye could see, with a clear easterly horizon which my husband immediately recognized as the long lost strait of Juan de Fuca, and to which he gave the name of the original discoverer, my husband placing it on his chart."

Barkley, however, did not pause to examine the opening, or to explore the strait. He proceeded down the coast, and, in latitude 47 degrees, 43 minutes, on a river supposed to be the Ohahlat, near Destruction island, the mate, Mr. Millar, the purser, Mr. Beale, and four seaman were murdered by Indians. After this loss, Barkley continued onward to Cape Fear, and thence sailed to China. The following year, when Meares visited Nootka, he saw a seal or ornament hanging from the ear of a native, recognized as having belonged to Millar.

The owners of the Imperial Eagle found they were not warranted in trading, even under the Austrian flag, with China and the northwest coast; and, through fear of loss of position with the East India Company, they felt obliged to sell the ship to avoid worse consequences. They tried to break their contract with Barkley, but he brought suit and obtained a verdict of £5000 sterling against them.

3

The second navigator actually to find the long sought strait, seen and named by Barkley, was Capt. John Meares, already mentioned in these pages. He was a retired lieutenant of the British navy and one of the spectacular characters in the early maritime annals of the Pacific northwest. He was successful as a fur trader, the first to introduce Chinese labor on the Pacific coast, and he launched the first vessel built in this region. He almost brought on a war between England and Spain, and in the controversy in which he figured, was accused of mendacity by some of his contemporaries.

Meares sailed, 1786, from Bengal, with two vessels, the Nootka and Sea Otter, names suggestive of furs and adventure. He directed his course north to Unalaska, thence to Prince William sound, where it had been arranged that he was to meet the Sea Otter, in command of William Tipping. However, that vessel which had reached the rendezvous, had left the place before Meares arrived, and was never heard of again. Meares remained there for the winter, but he, and his crew, had a miserable time. Scurvy broke out, and there was not a healthy man on the ship. The surgeon died. In Meares' journal is this entry: "We continued to see and lament a gradual diminution of our crew from this terrible disaster. Too often did I find myself called to assist in performing the dreadful office of dragging the dead bodies across the ice to a shallow sepulcher, which with our own hands we had hewn out for them on the shore. The sledge in which we fetched the wood was their hearse and the chasms in the ice their grave." Of the crew, 23 died of scurvy and exposure.

In the spring (1787), Capt. George Dixon, in the Princess Charlotte, arrived on the coast, from London. Dixon had heard, through natives, of Meares' plight, and came to his relief. He was welcomed as a "guardian angel, with tears of joy." Soon afterward Capt. Nathaniel Portlock, in the King George, arrived. The two ships were licensed by both of the monopolies, and were owned by a British company, and flew the British flag. The explorations of the two captains in this region have been mentioned. But although Meares was given some assistance, a heated controversy arose, which later found expression in pamphlets and letters published in England, full of bitter charges and counter charges, in which the veracity and good faith of Meares was assailed. Dixon charged that the scurvy was augmented by drunkenness, an assertion which was vigorously denied by Meares. Other charges, especially those showing that Meares claimed for himself much that should have been credited to others, were established. For assistance rendered by Portlock and Dixon, Meares was required to furnish bond to return to China at once, and to leave the coast clear for trade to Portlock and Dixon, on the ground that Meares was a trespasser, and so, finally, June 21, to the infinite joy of her crew, the Nootka set sail for the orient.

English merchants in India, 1787, fitted out two ships, the Felice Adventurer and the Iphigenia Nubiana, placing them under the command of the same John Meares and William Douglas. Proceeding to Macao, on the coast of China, they were provided with Portuguese flags, papers and nominal captains. This, as was afterward claimed by Meares, was to avoid port charges at Macao, or the payment of Chinese exactions, but it was really to avoid the imposition of excessive licenses by the East India and South Sea companies. A Portuguese partner was taken along, and the plan was to make it appear, in case of necessity, that the real captains were merely supercargoes and clerks.

Meares, sailing the Felice, arrived at Nootka in May, 1788, and procured from Chief Maquinna, or another local chieftain, a tract of land upon which he proceeded to build a fort. On arrival of the vessel, canoes filled with native men and women and children surrounded the ship, and, to their great surprise, Comekela, a Nootkan Indian, who had been carried to China on an earlier expedition, was restored to them. "Dressed in a scarlet regimental coat decorated with brass buttons, a military hat set off with a flaunting cockade, decent linens, and other appendages of European dress, which was far more than sufficient to excite the extreme admiration of his countrymen." A magnificent feast of whale blubber and oil followed, and the day was spent in rejoicing. Even the little children drank the oil with all the appearance of extreme gratification. A day or two later, Maquinna and Callicum, two chiefs, accompanied by a fleet of war canoes, visited Meares. The canoes moved in a procession around the Felice while the crews sang "a pleasing though sonorous melody." Each canoe had 18 men clad in robes of beautiful otter skins covering them from neck to ankle, enough to excite the cupidity of the whites. Meares presented Maquinna with copper, iron and other articles.

Meares had brought with him the framework of a schooner. He had also brought Chinese helpers, and with them and the members of his crew he straightway set about its construction and also the erection of a fort. While his men were at work at shipbuilding, he set sail upon an exploring expedition to the southward. June 29, he sighted in latitude 48 degrees, 39 minutes, north, the great inlet which had been discovered the previous year by Barkley. On the assumption that this was the passage described by Michael Lok, nearly 200 years before, he named it after its supposed discoverer, Juan de Fuca, although it had already been so named by Barkley.

Crossing to the entrance, he was hospitably entertained by Chief Tatoosh, whose name he gave to the small rock island nearby, where now is situated the United States light-house and weather station. The following is Meares' own account of what he believed was a re-discovery of the strait: "At noon, the latitude was 48 degrees, 39 minutes, north, at which time we had a complete view of an inlet, whose entrance appeared very extensive, bearing east-southeast, distant about six leagues. We endeavored to keep with the shore as much as possible, in order to have a perfect view of the land. This was an object of particular anxiety, as the part of the coast along which we were now sailing had not been seen by Captain Cook, and we knew no other navigator, said to have been this way, except Maurelle; and his chart, which we now had on board, convinced us that he had never seen this part of the coast, or that he had purposely misrepresented it. * * * * By three o'clock in the afternoon we arrived at the entrance of the great inlet already mentioned, which appeared to be 12 or 14 leagues broad. From the masthead it was observed to stretch to the east by north, and a clear unbounded horizon was seen in this direction, as far as the eye could reach * * * * The strongest curiosity impelled us to enter this strait, which we shall call by the name of its original discoverer, Juan de Fuca."

His curiosity seems, however, not to have been sufficiently compelling to induce him to explore the strait. He did send his mate in one of the ship's boats, who proceeded to sound for anchorage between the shore and Tatoosh island. But, after his return, Meares again set sail toward the south. Sighting the snow-capped mountain, formerly named Santa Rosalia by the Spaniard, Perez, he renamed it Mount Olympus, whence the modern appellation Olympics, applied to the range. Sunday, July 6, 1788, he passed the promontory, called by Heceta, Cape St. Roc or St. Roque, (Cape Disappointment) and sought the river supposed to debouch in that latitude, but he failed to find the Columbia, thus again illustrating the perversity of fate in keeping her secret hidden so long from the Spanish and English navigators.

Meares thus describes his experience off the mouth of the Columbia river: "At half past ten, being within three leagues of Cape Shoalwater, we had a perfect view of it; and with the glasses we traced the line of the coast to the southward, which presented no opening that presented anything like an harbour. An high bluffy promontory bore off us southeast, at a distance of only four leagues, for which we steered to double, with the hope that between it and Cape Shoalwater we should find some sort of a harbour. We now discovered distant land beyond this promontory and we pleased ourselves with the expectation of its being Cape St. Roc of the Spaniards, near which they are said to have found a good port. By half past eleven we doubled the cape, at the distance of three miles, having a clear and perfect view of the shore in every part, on which we did not discern a living creature, or the least trace of habitable life. A prodigious easterly swell rolled on the shore, and the soundings gradually decreased from 40 to 16 fathoms, over a hard sandy bottom. After we had rounded the promontory, a large bay, as we had imagined, opened to our view, that bore a very promising appearance, and into which we steered with every encouraging expectation. The high land that formed the boundaries of the bay was at a great distance, and a flat level country occupied the intervening space; the bay itself took a rather westerly direction. As we steered in, the water shoaled to nine, eight and seven fathoms, when breakers were seen from the deck, right ahead, and from the masthead, they were observed to extend across the bay; we therefore hauled out, and directed our course to the opposite shore, to see if there was any channel, or if we could discover any port. The name of Cape Disappointment was given to the promontory, and the bay obtained the title of Deception Bay. By an indifferent meridian observation it lies in the latitude of 46 degrees, 10 minutes, north, and in the computed longitude of 235 degrees, 34 minutes, east. We can now with safety assert that there is no such river as that of St. Roc exists, as laid down in the Spanish charts. To those of Maurelle, we made constant reference, but without deriving any information or assistance from them. We now reached the opposite side of the bay, where disappointment continued to accompany us; and being almost certain that we should obtain no place of shelter for the ship, we bore up for a distant headland, keeping our course within two miles of the shore."

Thus on account of a preconceived doubt as to the credit to be given to the Spanish suggestion of a river in these parts, and a wholesome dread of the breakers of the bar, Meares missed his opportunity to become the discoverer of the Columbia, and thereby to give to his country a strong claim to its tributary territory. It is interesting to note that, within two months after this experience, he chanced to be at King George's sound when the American sloop Washington sailed in, and its captain, Robert Gray, gave him information of his having landed at a harbor on the Washington coast that had just been vainly scrutinized by Meares.

After his return to Nootka, the schooner which had been built during the absence of Meares was launched and christened the North West America. The Russians had built vessels in Alaska before this, but here began the ship building industry that has since grown to great proportions on this part of the coast. The North West America was put in command of Robert Funter. Douglas, in the Iphigenia Nubiana, had returned from a cruise to the north, and now that vessel and Funter's command were ordered to proceed to the Sandwich islands. Meares then departed for China with the cargo of furs. An interesting entry in Meares' journal at this time is as follows: "We also took on board a considerable quantity of fine spars, fir for topmasts, for the Chinese market, where they are very much wanted and of course proportionably dear. Indeed the woods of this part of America are capable of supplying with these valuable materials all the navies of Europe." A storm arising shortly after Meares set sail, compelled him to jettison his cargo of spars, but this attempt is of interest as being the beginning of the lumbering industry on the northwestern coast of America, and an early recognition of the excellence of this timber for ship masts and spars.

It will not be necessary here to follow the particular discoveries of the English captains, Duncan and Colnett, to whom must be attributed much important exploration, and the naming of important features of the northwest coast. They were in the vicinity of Queen Charlotte island in the summer of 1788, while Meares was there, but Duncan, whose tiny vessel of 50 tons had sailed for 20 months through the Atlantic and the Pacific, and rounded South America, spent several days at anchor on the south side of the strait of Juan de Fuca. He did not penetrate further than two miles, and his ship remained at the Indian village of Claaset, although his chart indicates a knowledge of a more extensive coast line.

While rival discoverers were thus finding new islands and sounds, and were gaining additional information about these shores and the native inhabitants on the northwestern part of the American continent, and while rival fur traders were competing in bartering with the natives for the pelts of the sea otter, far more important events, changing the main current of human history, were taking place on the Atlantic shores. A confederation of free states had been formed, and the nation of the United States of America had been established on new principles of government. Its merchants of Boston, and the seafarers of the New England coast, were sailing abroad under a new flag and developing a new merchant marine. For the first time the flag of the United States was seen in foreign ports, and a new type of sailor had approached the Pacific shores, drawn hither by the attraction of undiscovered country, but more especially by the profit to be gained from whales and fur bearing animals.

CHAPTER VI

Nootka Convention

1

MEARES DID NOT, as he had planned, return to the Pacific coast in the Felice, but he organized a joint stock company which secured a license from the East India Company, allowing trade with the American coast. This license obviated the necessity of making use of double colors. Douglas and Funter, in the Sandwich islands, were ignorant of this, and this ignorance on their part led to unpleasant complications later on, as we shall see. The new company sent out two ships, the Argonaut, in command of Captain Colnett, and the Princess Royal, under Captain Hudson. Material was carried on board for the construction of another schooner at Nootka. Twenty-nine Chinamen were taken along, the intention being to procure for them Kanaka wives in the Sandwich islands, and settle them as the nucleus of a colony at Nootka. The permanent settlement to be established at that place was to be called Fort Pitt, and very elaborate plans were made for its improvement and fortification.

Meantime, the Spaniards had heard of the encroachments of the Russians from the north, and their plans to monopolize the fur trade of the Pacific northwest. Spain was still wedded to the belief that the South sea, and all the western shores of the two Americas washed by it, belonged exclusively to the Spanish people, and that any others venturing into these regions were poaching upon Spanish domain. Moreover, the coasts now being occupied and exploited by the Russians, had previously been explored to some extent by Spanish navigators and taken possession of in the name of the Spanish king. Consequently, it seemed to Florez, the Spanish viceroy of New Spain, or Mexico, that it was time to reassert the authority of his king over the disputed regions, or the opportunity might be lost. Whatever was to be done had to be done upon his own initiative, owing to the difficulty of communicating with Spain, and the dilatory habits of the home government.

The viceroy was moved to immediate action by a report brought to him, December, 1788, by a naval officer whom he had dispatched to the north to make an investigation of rumored encroachments of Russians and British. This was Ensign Don Estevan Jose' Martinez, who had sailed as second pilot with Perez to the same waters, 1774, and who had been at Nootka, 1778. He knew the basis of the Spanish claims, and knew of Cook's visit to this coast, 1778, and his instructions had directed him to ascertain and report whether any attempts had been made to establish settlements, or trading posts. On returning, he had given full details of his visit to the Russian fur trading station at Unalaska, reporting that he had been hospitably and even generously received and entertained, and had had no difficulty in drawing out from the officials that the Russian claims, by reason of the discoveries of Bering and Chirikoff, extended far down the coast. He had also reported that they were then but awaiting the arrival of four frigates from Siberia, to proceed to assert the Russian rights by ousting the English fur traders that had located at Nootka.

Florez, therefore, took immediate action, hoping in this way to get possession of Nootka before the Russian fleet could reach that port. The matter is of more than passing interest to Americans, for the first American vessels to the Pacific coast were also under surveillance. Instructions given to Martinez, who was entrusted with the command of the new expedition, ordered him to take the frigate Princessa and the packet San Carlos the Filipino, well armed and manned, and to take the convoy packet Aranzazu, with provisions and supplies. He was furnished with a copy of Cook's map of the entrance to Nootka, then but recently published in London. Four Apostolic friars were to accompany the expedition for religious work among the Indians. A building was to be erected at Nootka, with a view to demonstrating thereby the dominion of the Spanish sovereign.

Martinez was instructed, if Russian or English ships should arrive, to receive their commandants with the politeness and good manners which the existing peace and amity with those nations required, but to show them "the just reason for our establishment at Nootka, the superior right we have to continue them along the entire coast, and the arrangements which our superior government is taking to hold them." The expedition was to use prudent firmness, but if the foreigners should attempt to use force they were to be met with force and prevented from trading and bargaining with the Indians. The English were to be reminded, if they depended in any degree for priority upon Captain Cook's visit of March, 1778, that in the narrative of his voyage he had related that he had redeemed two Spanish silver spoons that had been stolen from Martinez himself at that place, 1774. As for the Americans, if any were met, they were to be dealt with according to these instructions:

"Your honor can make use of stronger argument still to the subjects of the independent American colonies, if they should appear on the northern coasts of the Californias, which up to the present time have not seen their vessels, but from an official letter of the most respected Senor, the Viceroy of Peru, I have learned that a frigate, which is said to belong to General Washington, left Boston in September of 1787, with the intention of going to the aforesaid coasts, that a storm compelled her to put in to the island of Juan Fernandez in distress, and when repaired she pursued her course.

"In case your honor should meet with this Boston frigate, or with a little packet that sailed in her convoy and which is lost in the storm they encountered, these facts will serve your honor as a guide in order to take such action as you can, and as may seem to you proper; it being well understood that our settlements are being extended in order to make it known thereby to all foreigners that we have already taken formal possession, in 1779, as far as beyond the port of Prince William, and of that port and its adjacent islands."

The American vessels were the Lady Washington and the Columbia Redivivus, from Boston. The entire correspondence, copied from the originals, is in the Library of Congress, with all the reports and accompanying documents, excepting letter No. 672, which is in the archives at Seville, Spain. In the report of Florez, Viceroy, to Valdez, Foreign Minister in Spain, the suspicion with which the voyage of the Washington and Columbia was viewed is indicated by the following passages:

"It is to be suspected that this frigate and the little packet which left Boston in her company came with the view of discovering the port and neighboring territory on our northern coasts of the Californias, in order to establish and maintain some new colony of their nation. There is no doubt that this is the enterprise, for what other object could have compelled them to such a long voyage as these two barks are making." The Viceroy proceeds to quote from Jonathan Carver's Travels and to call attention to his proposal to travel to the coast, and said: "if this man had wandered some 24 degrees of longitude further to the west he doubtless discovered Cape Gregory, or St. Gregory, on the northern coasts of New California," and he adds. "On account of all this we should not be surprised that the English colonists of America, republican and independent, are putting into practice the design of discovering a safe port on the South sea and trying to hold it by travelling across the immense territory of this continent above our possessions in Texas, New Mexico and California. Much more wandering about may be expected from an active nation, which bases all its hopes and resources on navigation and trade; and in truth it could hold the riches of Great China and of India, if it succeeds in establishing a colony on the western coasts of America."

2

In 1789, therefore, Martinez went north to build a fort at Nootka and to hold it in the name of the Spanish king. On arriving, he took possession with elaborate and impressive ceremonies, and proceeded to erect three houses, to be used as a forge, a cook house and a dwelling. A building for the troops was also constructed, with a battery of ten guns, upon a high hill commanding the entrance to the port. There were no Russians there, but he found the American vessels, Washington and Columbia, already in port, under command of Captains John Kendrick and Robert Gray. However, the "passports given by General Washington" as the report states, were found to permit a voyage of discovery around the world, and did not indicate any purpose to interfere with Spanish rights, so the vessels were not arrested. One of these was engaged in making extensive repairs, required by reason of a fire in the store room, in which the sails were kept, a misfortune that happened near Santa Barbara, and it was represented that as soon as the vessels were ready they would continue their voyage around the world. But the Spanish commander took the precaution to notify the Americans, in the name of the king, that they were "not to return by these seas and coasts without bringing a passport provided with a special license from our monarch," and that it was prohibited by ordinance for any foreign nation to "sail the coasts of America."

Martinez found also the Iphigenia Nubiana under command of

the Englishman, Captain Douglas, who, upon arrival of the Spaniards, had run up the Portuguese flag. Suspicious of the subterfuge, Martinez seized the Iphigenia, in spite of its Portuguese colors, but later, fearing international complications, released his prize, and furnished Captain Douglas with supplies for which he accepted an order upon the supposed Portuguese partner. He subsequently discovered that this partner was a bankrupt, whereupon he seized the schooner, the North West America, which had returned to Nootka early in June.

Captain Hudson arrived with the Princess Royal, June 14, 1789, took the furs from the North West America and then sailed away on another trading trip. July 3, Captain Colnett, with the Argonaut, sailed into Nootka. Regardless of the presence of the Spaniards, and in open defiance of their authority, Colnett set about aggressively with his preparations for the building and fortification of Fort Pitt. Martinez thereupon promptly seized his vessel and all of its cargo, stores and supplies, and when Captain Hudson returned to Nootka, July 14, the Princess Royal was also seized.

This was somewhat beyond the written instructions, and the seriousness of the consequences possible, the gravity of the risk of precipitating war thus assumed by subordinate local officials, became apparent, even to themselves. In August, Martinez sent his English prizes to San Blas, where Florez, the viceroy, found himself in a rather embarrassing position. He had no means at his disposal for reinforcing Martinez at Nootka, and had not received from his home government confirmation of his own acts, nor had he any assurance as to when such confirmation would come, if ever. Moreover, his successor as viceroy had been appointed, and was on his way to replace him. Eventually, he was ordered by the Spanish government to release the prizes, but, before the receipt of the order, he had already done so, refitting them and paying wages to their owners for the time of the crews' detention. Martinez abandoned the fort at Nootka, December, 1789, but early in 1790, a new Spanish garrison was sent there under the command of Lieut. Francisco Eliza.

3

The English government at this time had no desire to enter upon a war with Spain. The cabinet hoped for the continuance of

European peace, and, consequently, when they received from their minister at Madrid the first intimation of these events upon the Pacific coast, they kept the matter quiet until they should hear more details. However, the details were forthcoming upon the arrival of Captain Meares, who reached London, April, 1790. In his famous memorial to the British government he straightway set forth all the wrongs, real and imaginary, that his company had suffered at the hands of the Spaniards, and he loudly demanded redress. He set down his actual losses as amounting to 153,433 Spanish milled dollars, and the "probable" losses as 500,000 additional dollars.

The government could no longer keep this matter secret, and the furor which resulted from its publication was tremendous. The cabinet immediately took up the question of redress, and warlike preparations were begun on an extensive scale. England appealed to her allies, Holland and Prussia, and both promised to lend their aid. The fleets of these nations were put in readiness. All outlying British colonies were warned to prepare, Canada in particular, and she was advised to cultivate friendly relations with the United States. The Spanish colonies in Central and South America were approached, with the view to their taking this opportunity to throw off the Spanish yoke. A grand alliance of all these peoples was planned, to fight against Spain. The government of the United States was also approached, but this country decided to remain neutral in the case of hostilities.

The only hope that the Spaniards could reasonably look for was from France, but France at that time was in the first throes of her great revolution, which rendered any aid from that quarter out of the question. Consequently, the Spanish government felt itself forced to yield; and, October 28, 1790, all differences between Spain and Great Britain relative to their claims in the Pacific northwest were settled by the so-called "Nootka Convention." This treaty stipulated that all buildings and tracts of land on the northwest coast of America, of which Spanish officials had dispossessed any British subjects should be restored; that just reparation should be made for any acts of violence committed by their respective subjects upon the subjects of the other; that any property seized should be restored, or paid for; that subjects of Great Britain should not navigate or carry on their fishery within 10 sea leagues of any part of the coasts already occupied by Spain; that north of the coast already occupied by Spain, the subjects of both parties should have free access wherever the subjects of either of the two powers had made settlements.

This treaty met with violent opposition in both England and Spain, on the ground that it was too favorable to the other side, which probably shows that it was as fair an arrangement as could have been made under the circumstances. Several years elapsed before the terms were carried out, and, in the meantime, the Spaniards remained in possession of Nootka; but eventually, as will be seen later, the post was evacuated and left to the natives. The amount finally paid by the Spanish government by way of damages was $210,000.

It was a fortunate circumstance for the young republic, the United States, that this controversy was settled peaceably, rather than by the arbitrament of arms, for had the latter course been pursued, it is likely that Great Britain, having established her title to the Oregon Country by the right of war, would not readily have relinquished it, and that the "Fifty-four Forty or Fight" controversy might not have been so easily adjusted.

Commander Juan Francisco de la Bodega y Quadra, representing Spain, and Capt. George Vancouver, representing Great Britain, met at Nootka, 1792, in order to carry out on the spot the terms of the "Nootka Convention," which had ambiguities that were not easy to clear up; but, although the two agents became fast personal friends, witnessed by the fact that the original name given by them to Vancouver island was Quadra and Vancouver, they could not come to any satisfactory agreement. Two other representatives were subsequently sent out by their respective governments, Sir Thomas Pierce and Manuel de Alava, 1795, who finally consummated the settlement, as will be more fully shown in the next chapter.

Meanwhile, many traders and explorers were visiting the northwestern coast of America, British, Spanish, and now also American; but, before proceeding further, we must record the exploits of Vancouver, the man to whom, perhaps more than to any other, this coast is indebted for its first thorough exploration, and for the names given by him to many geographical features.

CHAPTER VII
VANCOUVER'S VISIT
1

CAPT. GEORGE VANCOUVER has left a greater impress upon the map of the Pacific northwest than has any other navigator, for not less than 75 mountains, bays, capes and sounds bear names bestowed by him, and two important cities and a large island are called by his name. Various considerations led the British government to send out this most thorough and painstaking exploring expedition. By the terms of the Nootka Convention the British were not to navigate or fish within 10 sea leagues of any part of the coast already occupied by Spain, but the limit of Spanish occupation was not fixed. Consequently, the Spanish wished to establish themselves in the northern region as speedily as possible, and a feverish period of activity on their part ensued. We find their explorers looking into every nook and cranny of the coasts of British Columbia and southern Alaska.

The French navigators, La Perouse, 1786, and Marchand, 1791, explored the coast in the northerly latitudes, and Marchand did some trading for furs, which he took to China. Their voyages circumnavigated the world, although La Perouse died before reaching home. As has already been stated, these voyages were not of particular importance to Oregon's part of the coast. Not less than seven American vessels were regularly engaged in the fur trade on the coast, in the year 1792, and the voyages and discoveries of all the active seamen aroused the anxiety of the British. It has been estimated that the growth of the fur trade on the coast was such that in 1799 there were 10 trading vessels from Boston alone, and that there were at least 15 American vessels in 1801, while in that year the British had but one. Another estimate shows that there were 108 American vessels in the trade between 1790 and 1818, and 22 British that were in the trade, mostly after 1800.

In accordance with the terms of the Nootka Convention, it was necessary, as stated in the preceding chapter, to send a commissioner to Nootka sound to meet there an emissary from Spain, and to carry out the provisions of the treaty upon the spot. The British government decided that if a commissioner was sent to the coast, he might also determine, once for all, the old question of a northwest passage, especially since Captain Meares, upon his visit to England, 1790, had published a new pamphlet, again raising the old question. The title of the pamphlet was "The Probable Existence of a Northwest Passage." The discovery of the strait of Juan de Fuca, and of fiords and inlets of southern Alaska, had led Meares to suggest that perhaps they were a part of a vast network of such waterways, through which it would be possible to sail the Atlantic. Alexander Mackenzie's overland explorations and discoveries, effectually disproving this theory, had not yet been made.

These considerations induced the British government to give Captain Vancouver other specific duties, besides meeting the Spanish commissioner, upon his memorable expedition, leaving England January, 1791. It had been originally intended to put Capt. Henry Roberts in command of the expedition, which was in readiness to sail before the close of the year 1790, but as a great European war seemed imminent, Captain Roberts was sent upon an expedition to the West Indies, for strategic reasons, and this command ultimately devolved upon Vancouver, much to his satisfaction. He had seen the coast in March, 1778, when he was a midshipman with Captain Cook.

Vancouver's instructions directed him to examine and to survey the shore of the American continent on the Pacific, from latitude 30 degrees to 60 degrees, north; and he was furthermore instructed to ascertain, particularly, the number, extent and situation of any settlement of European nations within these limits; and especially to inquire as to the nature and extent of any water communication which might tend in any considerable degree to facilitate an intercourse for the purposes of commerce between the northwest coast and the country on the opposite side of the continent, occupied by British subjects. He was also ordered to examine particularly the supposed strait of Juan de Fuca, said to be situated between the 48th and 49th parallel of north latitude, and said to lead to an opening through which the sloop Washington passed, 1789, coming out again to the northward of Nootka.

In his instructions was the following paragraph: "With respect to the first object, it would be of great importance if it should be found that, by means of any considerable inlets of the sea, or even of large rivers, communicating with the lakes of the interior of the continent, such an intercourse, as hath been already mentioned could be established; it will therefore be necessary for the pur-

Captain George Vancouver
From the painting by Lemuel F. Abbott, in the National Portrait Gallery, London.

—From Meares' "Voyages"

The Launching of the "North West America"
*At Nootka Sound, September 20, 1788, being the first vessel that was ever built
in that part of the globe.*

Spanish Fort at Nootka Sound, 1793
*Drawing by George E. Jarvis from a rough pencil sketch supplied by the Bancroft
Library. The original sketch was made at Nootka Sound in 1793.*

pose of ascertaining this point, that the survey should be so conducted as not only to ascertain the general line of the sea coast but also the direction and extent of all such considerable inlets, whether made by arms of the sea, or by the mouths of large rivers, as may be likely to lead to, or facilitate, such communication as is above described."

The expedition consisted of the sloop-of-war, Discovery, of 400 tons burden, commanded by Capt. George Vancouver himself, and the armed tender, Chatham, of 135 tons, in command of Lieut. W. R. Broughton. An ample equipment and personnel for scientific research was also carried. Vancouver, with his two vessels, sailed by way of the cape of Good Hope into the South sea, where he carried on extensive explorations, discovering several hitherto unknown islands, among them Chatham island. He spent the winter at the Sandwich islands, and the next spring proceeded toward the American coast, which he reached, April 17, 1792, in north latitude 39 degrees, off California. The Spanish captains, Valdez and Galiano, had entered the strait of Juan de Fuca during the preceding winter with their small exploring vessels, the Sutil and Mexicana, and were already exploring there, and had set up a small Spanish post at Neah bay.

Proceeding northward, he reached the Oregon coast on the 24th, near a great headland which some of his company thought might be the Cape Blanco of Martin d'Aguilar, but which Vancouver called Cape Orford, thus honoring the English earl of that name. Near this point, a number of Indians came out in their canoes to visit his ship, one of the many instances of this kind, which show that the natives of the Oregon coast were bold and skillful deep sea sailors.

For two days after this, a haze prevented Vancouver from accurate observations, but, on the evening of the 26th, he found himself off that part of the Oregon coast formerly observed by Captain Meares, with clear skies, and conditions particularly favorable for observation. Vancouver seems to have evinced a very lively interest in this section of the shore line, because of Meares' previous survey, and because he wished to take this opportunity to prove or disprove the existence of the river said by the Spaniard, Heceta, to debouch in these parts. It will be of interest to read Vancouver's description of this part of the Oregon coast, because the landmarks pictured by him will be easily recognized by any one familiar with the region as it is today. Although the description is accurate as far as it goes, nevertheless it shows that Vancouver, in general, must have kept so far off shore that he failed to see some of its more important details, and these omissions affected his judgment, and deprived him of the honor of becoming the discoverer of the Columbia river.

The following is Captain Vancouver's account: "Sunset brought us in sight of the coast which had been seen by Mr. Meares; its northern extremity in sight bore by compass N. ½ W; Cape Lookout, N. 10 E; the nearest shore N. 34 E, about a league distant. This being a remarkably steep bluff cliff, flattered us for some time with an appearance like the entrance of an harbor; but on a nearer approach the deception was found to have been occasioned by the low land to the north forming a very shallow open bay; the southernmost land in sight bore S.S.E.; in this situation we had fifty fathoms of water, black sandy bottom."

Friday, April 27: "The night which was tolerably fair, was spent as usual in preserving our station until daylight, when we pursued our examination along the coast with a favorable breeze, attended with some pleasing showers. Cape Lookout then bore by compass east, about two leagues distant. This cape forms only a small projecting point, yet it is remarkable for the four rocks that lie off from it, one of which is perforated, as described by Mr. Meares; and excepting a rock passed the preceding afternoon, these were the first we have seen north of Cape Gregory.

"From Cape Lookout,which is situated in latitude 45 degrees, 32 minutes, longitude 236 degrees, 11 minutes, the coast takes a direction about N. 8° W., and is pleasingly diversified by eminences and small hills near the seashore; in which are some shallow sandy bays, with a few detached rocks lying about a mile from the land. The more inland country is considerably elevated; the mountains stretch toward the sea, and at a distance seemed to form many inlets and projecting points; but the sandy beach that continued along the coast renders it a compact shore, now and then interrupted by perpendicular rocky cliffs, on which the surf violently breaks."

It appears from this description that Vancouver passed Tillamook and Nehalem bays without seeing them, showing that he must have sailed at a greater distance from the shore than he estimated. His narrative continues: "This mountainous inland country extends about 10 leagues to the north from Cape Lookout, where it descends suddenly to a moderate height; and, had it been destitute of its timber, which seemed of considerable magnitude, and to compose an entire forest, it might be deemed low land." The mountainous country thus described extends from the entrance of Tillamook bay to Clatsop beach, and includes the hills back of Garibaldi beach, Neahkahnie mountain, False Tillamook and Tillamook head. It seems strange that he did not notice Tillamook rock.

He is now off the Columbia river. He proceeds: "Noon brought us up with a very conspicuous point of land composed of a cluster of hummocks, moderately high, and projecting into the sea from the low land before mentioned. These hummocks are barren and steep near the sea, but their tops thinly covered with wood. On the south side of this promontory was the appearance of an inlet, or small river, the land behind it not indicating it to be of any great extent; nor did it seem accessible for vessels of our burthen, as the breakers extended from the above point two or three miles into the ocean, until they joined those on the sandy beach nearly four leagues further south. On reference to Mr. Meares' description of the coast south of this promontory I was first induced to believe it to be cape Shoalwater; but on ascertaining its latitude I presumed it to be that which he calls cape Disappointment, and the opening south of it Deception bay. This cape was found to be in latitude 46 degrees, 19 minutes, longitude 236 degrees, 6 minutes. The sea had now changed from its natural to river colored water; the probable consequence of some streams falling into the bay, or into the ocean to the north of it, through the low land. Not considering this opening worthy of more attention, I continued our pursuit to the N.W., being desirous to embrace the advantage of the breeze and pleasant weather, so favorable to our examination of the coast. * * * "

In a Journal kept by Edward Bell, one of the officers of the Chatham, the entry of April 25, 1792, is as follows: "At night with the land wind we weigh'd and stood out to the Wd. and at daylight with a fair Soly: Breeze bore away along shore. The fair and pleasant weather continued and on the 27th, at noon, we observed in the Lat: of 46.10 N. Just then, the Discovery made the Signal that we were in danger; we haul'd out; this situation is off Cape Disappointment from whence a very extensive Shoal stretches out and there was every appearance of an opening there, but to us the sea seem's to break entirely across it." The Columbia bar was therefore actually seen, but it was passed without appreciating the importance.

Vancouver's reference to the entrance of the mighty Columbia, that it was "not worthy of more attention," would be humorous had it not been fraught with such momentous consequences. It seems almost inconceivable that a navigator with the experience of Vancouver could have dismissed the evidence which he describes, of the existence of a great river. Whether he relied too much upon the judgment previously formed by Captain Meares, or was at fault in not investigating the course of the "river colored water," where he should have been alert, we cannot tell, but the fact remains that he thus lost an opportunity that was grasped shortly afterwards by Captain Gray.

Having made this cursory examination of the mouth of the Columbia, Vancouver sailed northward under a sunny sky and with a favorable breeze, gazing upon the Washington shore and being pleased with this country "furnishing so delightful a prospect of fertility." On the evening of April 28, 1792, he made the following entry in his log: "The several large rivers and capacious inlets that have been described as discharging their contents into the Pacific between the 40th and 48th degree of north latitude, were reduced to brooks insufficient for vessels to navigate, or inapplicable as harbors for refitting; excepting that one of which Mr. Dalrymple informs us that 'it is alleged that the Spanish have recently found an entrance in the latitude of 47 degrees 45 minutes North, which in 27 days' course brought them to the vicinity of Hudson's bay;' this latitude exactly corresponds to the ancient relation of John de Fuca, the Greek pilot, in 1592." With pertinacity Vancouver adhered to his preconceived opinion that there was no great river in the latitude of the Columbia, and no strait.

In passing along the Washington coast in the neighborhood of Shoalwater bay and Grays harbor, Vancouver was, as he says, very solicitous to find a port in the vicinity, and "our attention was therefore earnestly directed to this object," but every promising opening proved on closer examination to be impassable. He particularly comments on Meares' mention of two possible entrances to Shoalwater bay, where he says the breakers gave reason to consider them inaccessible and unworthy any loss of time, whilst accompanied by so favorable a breeze. He failed to find Grays harbor and ignored Shoalwater bay, now called Willapa bay.

2

It so happened, however, that upon the next day, after writing the skeptical opinions quoted above, he was to meet the very man that had been examining the entrance to the Columbia with an open mind. Early in the morning, Sunday, April 29, a sail was seen standing in toward the shore, the first strange craft observed by Vancouver in eight months. Naturally, great curiosity was evinced among the British sailors as to this lonely voyager, and its national colors. Approaching nearer, a friendly salute was fired by the stranger, which was answered in like manner by the Discovery. Both ships hove to, and it was ascertained that this was the ship Columbia, 19 months out from Boston, flying the Stars and Stripes, and under command of Capt. Robert Gray.

Vancouver sent the ship's boat, with Puget and Menzies, the former his lieutenant, and the latter the surgeon and naturalist of the expedition, to pay his respects to Captain Gray. After the proper exchange of courtesies, the British visitors ascertained from him that he had recently discovered, in latitude 46 degrees, 10 minutes, the mouth of a great river which he had not been able to enter, although he had waited nine days for weather conditions that would enable him to do so. He said that the outset, or reflux, was so strong as to prevent his entering. Commenting upon this statement of Gray, Vancouver writes in his Journal, "this was probably the opening found by me on the forenoon of the 27th, and was inaccessible, not from the current, but from the breakers which extended across it." As a matter of fact, however, Gray actually crossed the bar and sailed into the river some two weeks later.

It will be remembered that Vancouver's instructions had expressly directed him to examine the supposed strait of Juan de Fuca, leading to an opening through which the sloop Washington was reported to have passed, 1789, and to have come out again to the northward of Nootka. Concerning this report, Vancouver says: "It is not possible to conceive any one to be more astonished than was Mr. Gray on his being made acquainted that his authority had been quoted, and the track pointed out that he had been said to have made in the sloop Washington." The Bell Journal already mentioned, confirms this by the following entry: "At daylight a strange Sail was seen on the N.W. Quarter standing toward us, she hoisted American colours. About seven we spoke her, she proved to be the Ship Columbia, of Boston, commanded by Mr. Grey, on the Fur trade. She had wintered on the Coast in Port Clynquot on Berkley's Sound. This Mr. Grey being the man who Mr. Mears in his chart has published having entered the Streights of De Fuca, and after proceeding a considerable distance up, returned to sea again by another passage to the Northward of that by which he entered.—Captn Vancouver was desirous of obtaining information respecting the Streights, he therefore hoisted a boat out, and sent an officer on board the Columbia. Mr. Grey very civilly offered him any information he could possibly give him, but at the same time told him that Mr. Mears had been very much misled in his information, and had published what had never happened; for though he (Mr. Grey) did enter the Streights of De Fuca and proceeded a considerable distance, where he still saw an unbounded horizon, he return'd by the same way he entered."

It may be noted in passing that at a later date Meares defended himself and asserted that he had not ascribed the voyage around Vancouver island to Captain Gray, but to Kendrick. It is obvious that this does not improve his statement, for Captain Kendrick did not make any such voyage. An interesting suggestion has been made by a recent writer, however, that it may have been young John Kendrick whose name was intended to be used. He was a second pilot with Martinez in the Spanish expedition, 1789. This assumption is because young Kendrick was actually at the passage leading northward from Puget sound, as shown by an entry in the Martinez Diary, quoted by Lalla Rookh Boone, in Oregon Historical Quarterly, September, 1934. Still it is not shown that young Kendrick or Martinez actually circumnavigated the island.

Keeping a sharp lookout all that day for the entrance to the strait of Juan de Fuca, Vancouver's vigilance was finally rewarded with the view of its broad expanse of waters extending as far as the eye could reach, toward the east. Sailing toward its southern shore, he came to anchor in Neah bay, where the natives flocked on board in most friendly fashion, and the evening was spent amid mutual amenities and entertainment. Vancouver, however, was impatient to be under way; the new "Mediterranean Sea" beckoned him on, and we next find his ships gliding under full sail before a favoring wind, eastward, up the strait. The log of the Discovery for the days following shows the keen enjoyment, the almost boyish abandon of Vancouver and his men in their task of this important exploration and discovery. Swiftly they sailed, intent only upon the marvelous vistas opening before them of lovely archipelagoes and snow mantled mountains.

Meares had already noted and named Mount Olympus, and, as has been stated, the range is now known as the Olympics. It was Joseph Baker, the third lieutenant of the Discovery, that was the first to see the lofty summit of snow clad Mount Baker, and his captain named it after him. At seven o'clock on the evening of April 30, a fine harbor was found, which so much resembled Vancouver's home port that it was named Dungeness. In his log entry for this evening, the navigator reverts again to the negative results of his explorations along the continental coast to the southward. He enlarges upon the subject to show how minutely the coast had been examined, and deems it a very singular circumstance that on the coast of nearly 215 leagues, on which his inquiries had been made under the most favorable circumstances of wind and weather, he should not until now have seen any appearance of an opening in its shores. He asserts that the whole coast forms "one compact, solid, straight barrier against the sea." He refers again to "Mr. Gray's river" as very intricate and inaccessible to vessels of our burthen.

May Day, 1792, a short sail brought the voyagers upon the inland sea to a fine harbor, which was named Port Discovery in honor of the ship, while the island which stood guard at the entrance to the harbor was named Protection island. This proved to be such an ideal port that Vancouver decided to rest there, and to undertake a general refitting and cleaning of his ships. A week was occupied with these tasks, after which small boats were sent out in charge of Menzies, Puget, Johnstone and the captain himself.

3

It would unduly extend this narrative to attempt to follow the courses and detailed examination of Puget sound made during the summer by these men. It will suffice, for our purpose, merely to summarize their accomplishments as a whole. Vancouver's plan was to explore thoroughly every opening, beginning at the right and following the whole coast line wherever it might lead. Although in no sense the discoverer of Puget sound, Vancouver was the first to enter the sound itself. Barkley, Meares and Gray had seen the strait, and Meares had entered it, 1788. The Spaniards, Quimper and Elisa, had also entered the strait, the former, 1790, going as far as Port Discovery, and the latter, who sailed, 1791, as far as the gulf of Georgia. Gray claimed to have gone up the strait to Clallam bay, and out by the same route, although the distance may have been exaggerated in his statement. From John Boit's Journal, kept by a young officer of Captain Gray's vessel, it would appear that Gray first saw the strait November 11, 1791, but did not then enter any great distance; he passed the entrance again, April 3, 1792, and entered again with Captain Vancouver's vessels, April 29, 1792.

The origin of some of the names given by Vancouver during the stay in the Pacific northwest may be of interest. Hood Canal was explored, throughout its entire length. It was so named, as later was also the great Oregon snow-clad mountain, in honor of Viscount Samuel Hood, a commander in the British navy, who had won fame in the war of the American Revolution, fighting against de Grasse. The loftiest mountain in the northwest, rearing its summit to an altitude of 14,408 feet, was discovered and given the name of Rainier, in honor of Rear Admiral Peter Rainier, who also served with great distinction in the British navy. Port Townshend was so named after the marquis of that name, but by popular usage the spelling is now Townsend. He had served with General Wolfe, in Canada. Vashon island bears the name of Admiral James Vashon. Port Orchard was discovered by a clerk of the Discovery, bearing that name, and was named in his honor. Lieutenant Puget's memory is perpetuated in Puget sound, and, afterward this favored member of the expedition was honored again, by giving his name to an island in Columbia river. Port Gardner, Penn's Cove, Whidbey island, Port Wilson, Bellingham bay, and many other landmarks, were named by Vancouver, either in honor of his personal friends, or of others of his nation, more or less prominent at that time. The whole region on the main land, to the east of Puget sound, Vancouver called New Hanover, a name derived from the ancestral home of the British sovereign, who was also remembered in bestowing a name upon the important gulf of Georgia.

While cruising northward, after a partial circumnavigation of these inland waters, Vancouver met two Spanish vessels, the Sutil and Mexicana, bearing as commanding officers, Galiano and Valdez. They had entered by way of the strait, and had been exploring in its waters during the previous winter (1791) with their small vessels of 45 tons, before any British excepting Barkley and Meares. They presumably set up the small Spanish post at Neah bay before Vancouver had entered the strait, although Vancouver does not mention this place. Through them he learned that the Spanish commissioner, Don Juan Francisco de la Bodega y Quadra, had arrived, and now awaited him at Nootka, for the purpose of consummating the terms of the Nootka Convention. The Spaniards also told him that they had sailed past what appeared to them to be the entrance to a great river. This was in reality the Fraser river, later to be so named after its explorer; but Vancouver, with his usual dogmatism, dismissed this as not worthy of credence, and made no effort either to verify or disprove the river's existence. The British and Spanish ships sailed in company some distance northward, through the channels recently explored by the expedition's small boats. Later, however, Vancouver parted from the Spanish party, and learning from the master of the British trading vessel, the Venus, which was met in these waters, that a supply ship from England was awaiting him in Nootka, he continued northward, and thus completed the circumnavigation of Vancouver island, arriving at Nootka, August 28, 1792.

Here Quadra received his fellow commissioner with as much pomp and circumstance as the primitive conditions at Nootka permitted. There was much feasting, drinking of toasts and entertainment, in which the local Indian chieftain, Maquinna, as well as his daughter, the Princess, participated. Vancouver and Quadra were on the friendliest terms, and it was at the suggestion of the latter that the great island, upon which this meeting took place, received its name from them jointly and was called Quadra and Vancouver's island, which name has since, for convenience, been abbreviated to its present form. In spite of the good fellowship which marked the relations of the two commissioners, when it came to the transaction of the business which had called them half way around the globe to Nootka, they could reach no agreement. Vancouver contended that the provision in the treaty for restoration to the British of the buildings and tracts of land they had been dispossessed by the Spanish, April, 1789, fairly meant more than merely the identical space occupied by the house and the accessories of Meares, and he asked for the whole of Nootka; he also insisted that the Spanish settlement at Nootka was established after the treaty, at which time there was no Spanish settlement north of San Francisco bay, and that, fairly interpreted, the British were by the treaty to have free access to all Spanish settlements and establishments above San Francisco. Quadra offered to restore the exact site of the British station, but did not feel authorized to accept Vancouver's wider definition of the territory to be surrendered, and he proposed to refer to his government the question raised as to allowing free access to Spanish establishments at Nootka and north of San Francisco, one such establishment having been recently located on Neah bay, in de Fuca strait. Arriving at this diplomatic impasse, the negotiators declared the proceedings adjourned, and agreed to report to their respective governments pending further instructions.

4

During the stay of Quadra at Nootka, Captain Gray visited the place twice, the first time from July 24 to August 24, 1792, during which period he made repairs upon the Columbia. He was indebted to the Spanish governor for many favors, and the generosity of the latter is shown by the fact that he would not allow the American to pay for the supplies or assistance given, but did all in his power to aid him, entertaining Captain Gray at his own house during his stay, and turning over to him the use of a building in which to store the ship's cargo and stores while she was being overhauled. The carpenters from the Daedalus, Vancouver's supply ship, which was then awaiting the arrival of that commander, and the Spanish carpenters from Quadra's vessels, helped in the repairs.

At that time, Captain Vancouver had not yet arrived. Gray soon sailed away northward, intent on finishing his fur trading, and returned to Nootka, September 21, meeting Quadra at the entrance, just as the latter was beginning his homeward voyage. Quadra desired to purchase the American sloop Adventure, and agreed to wait for Gray at Neah bay, at the Spanish settlement, where he was going for the purpose of leaving orders. On this occasion, when Gray entered Nootka sound, he found Captain Vancouver there with his ships, the Discovery and Chatham, besides the Daedalus. Here Gray informed the British commander that he had sailed into and had named the Columbia river, in the preceding May, shortly after his first meeting with Vancouver, off the strait of Juan de Fuca. There is some question of detail as to whether Gray gave Vancouver a copy of his map of the river, or whether Vancouver had the map from Quadra, as there is conflict between the authorities on this point, but Gray soon left for Neah bay to keep his appointment with the Spanish admiral. Vancouver's demonstration that Nootka sound was not in fact on the main coast, by circumnavigating the island, was confirmation of a surmise noted in the journals of the Americans, as early as the preceding June.

Vancouver did not fail to verify Gray's discovery of the Columbia river, as will be shown in a subsequent chapter. But, before taking up the immediate events let us pause to add a word about Nootka, after the plenipotentiaries left it with its fate unsettled. During Vancouver's stay at Nootka the following named vessels were in and out of that harbor: *Spanish,* Sutil, Mexicana, Activa, Aranzazu, Princess; *English,* Discovery, Chatham, Daedalus, Venus, Three Brothers, (or 3 B's), Jenny, Butterworth, Jackal, Prince Lee Boo, Fenis (the last two named under Portuguese flag), Prince William Henry; *American,* Hope, Columbia, Adventure, Margaret. The Prince William Henry and a tender for the Margaret were built there during that summer. Vancouver sent his lieutenant, Mudge, to England with a special report on the failure of the negotiations; and a list of vessels on the coast in 1792 was enclosed. The fur trade was already overdone, and prices in China had fallen, while the natives were demanding more than formerly. The era of the fur-trader on the coast was already approaching its end.

Spain, soon after, consented to an amicable adjustment with Great Britain. The final scene occurred March 23, 1795, when in the presence of Lieut. Thomas Pierce of the royal marines, representing Great Britain, and Brigadier-General Alava, representing Spain, the Spanish flag was hauled down and the British flag was run up in its place, on the site of the buildings that had been erected by Meares. The Spanish fort was then deserted, and both nations withdrew. This place that was the center of so much activity, and the scene of so much of interest, has never since the departure been a port of commercial importance.

5

Among the voyages that might be described with interest was that of the Union, a single masted vessel, 50 or 60 feet long, sailing out of Newport, Rhode Island, August 1, 1794. It was commanded by the same John Boit who had been with Captain Gray on the discovery of the Columbia river two years before. He was now 19 years old. After calling at Cape Verde islands and Falkland islands, and rounding Cape Horn, the vessel reached Columbia cove, Vancouver island, in the month of May, 1795, and a brisk trade was begun. Soon after, it was at anchor at Houston Stewart channel, Queen Charlotte island, when it was attacked by several hundred Indians. The assault was repulsed by Captain Boit and his crew, the native chief and some forty of his warriors being slain. After trading extensively at other places of call on the northwest coast, the Columbia river was visited, but the attempt to cross the bar was unsuccessful, and trading was renewed further north. The voyage was continued around the world, with calls at Hawaii, Canton and Mauritius, and so via the cape of Good Hope, with return to Boston, July 8, 1796.

It may be appropriate to quote the language of Professor Samuel Eliot Morison, of Harvard University, from an address delivered by him at Astoria, Oregon, on the occasion of the dedication of the Astoria Column, July 22, 1926, in which he spoke of that voyage and others:

"The northwest fur trade of Boston that followed quickly on the Columbia's voyages, was one of the most remarkable lines of commerce that any people has ever pursued. Obtaining on credit consignments of cloth and blankets, strap iron and nails, sheet copper and pocket mirrors, buttons and blunderbusses, the Boston merchants loaded them on little home-made ships of 100 to 250 tons burthen, from 65 to 90 feet long, with stores for a three years' voyage. When a yacht of this size today, with all the modern inventions of auxiliary engine, radio, wire rigging and chronometer, makes a voyage across the Atlantic her exploit is written up in the newspapers as a remarkable adventure. Yet the stout New England seamen of that period thought nothing of taking their small, clumsy, heavily laden vessels around the most dangerous and difficult voyage in the world, one in which many a ship has met her end, where roaring westerlies and enormous seas put a small vessel at serious disadvantage."

In a short time the American traders, or "Bostons," as they were known to the natives, and the Russians, had control of the fur trade in the north. It is said that in one year 18,000 skins were collected on the islands and mainland of the Pacific. Later, the sea otter became so scarce that the trade grew unprofitable. There were frequent conflicts between the natives and traders. The white men did not hesitate to take by force, and the natives retaliated. The ship Boston was seized by the natives under Maquinna, 1803, by strategy, and all on board were murdered, except John R. Jewitt, armorer of the vessel, and John Thompson, a sail maker. The vessel was beached and burned, and the goods were distributed among the Indians. Jewitt and Thompson were held slaves by Maquinna until 1805, when they escaped.

In that year the Lydia, under Captain Hill, arrived at Nootka. Maquinna was anxious to resume the old relations with the traders, and bore a letter to Hill written by Jewitt, in which, without Maquinna's knowledge, Jewitt requested Hill to hold Maquinna a prisoner and as a hostage, until he and Thompson were released. The scheme was successful and they were set free.

In 1805, also, the Atahualpa, from Rhode Island, was attacked by a number of Indians who had come on board ostensibly to trade. They were repulsed after the captain, mate and six men had been killed. It may be said that while the sea otter trade enriched many, it demoralized the Indians. And Nootka, once the great port of the Pacific northwest, the scene of so many historic events, has no further part in international affairs.

In 1806, the Russians, at Sitka, were needing such food stuffs as could best be found in California, especially wheat and farm products. An expedition under Imperial Inspector Rezanof managed to overcome the obstacles in the way of trade with the Spanish authorities, who were still under strict prohibition against selling to foreigners. He obtained what was immediately needed, and gave furs in exchange. This led to the establishing of a Russian fort, sometimes called Fort Ross, on Bodega bay, California, 1812, the land having been purchased from the Indians of the locality. Agriculture, stock raising, fishing and fur hunting along the coast, were established and carried on with some success, and sporadic trade with the Spanish inhabitants grew up. The settlement comprised some 400 persons, but many were not of Russian birth, being Aleuts and Kamschatkans. The property was finally sold out, 1841, to Capt. John A. Sutter, of Sutter's Fort, and the enterprise was abandoned.

CHAPTER VIII

DISCOVERY OF THE COLUMBIA

1

YOUNG JOHN LEDYARD, who, as already mentioned, had sailed with Captain Cook as petty officer, returned home about 1782 with a story of his stirring adventures, and in the following year his book, containing an account of the famous voyage, was published at Hartford, Connecticut. His story attracted attention at Boston, and information regarding the profitable transactions of members of the Cook expedition between the northwest coast and the city of Canton reached Boston from other sources. There was much interest in the possibilities thus opened, for, although American ships were engaged in the Chinese trade, there had been no great profit. There was no salable commodity to carry to China from New England; and return cargoes of tea, and other Chinese goods, had to be paid for with actual money. This, and the long distance to China upon voyages by way of the cape of Good Hope, made Boston take keen interest in the prospect of a new trade route, with enormous profits to be made in turning in New England manufactures to the Indians in exchange for furs, and then in turning again at a good profit these furs for Chinese commodities.

One of the remote, but potent, influences that brought about the acquisition by the people of the United States of the wide domain of the Oregon Country, was the fondness of the Chinese for sea otter and other furs. Perhaps the first American trading vessel to go to the northwest coast of North America to engage in trade with the Indians and to secure furs for the China market was the ship Eleanora, Captain Metcalf, in the summer of 1788. This fur trade was the subject of conversation among a gathering of friends which met one evening, 1787, at the residence of Dr. Charles Bulfinch, Bowdoin Square, Boston, when another enterprise was there projected, that had, later, close connections with Oregon history. Besides the doctor himself there were present his son Charles, a graduate of Harvard, recently returned from a European tour; Joseph Barrell, a prosperous merchant; John Derby, a ship master of Salem; Capt. Crowell Hatch, of Cambridge; Samuel Brown, a trader of Boston; and John Marden Pintard, of the New York firm, Lewis Pintard Company.

The result of this conference was that a stock company was

formed with a capitalization of $50,000, divided into 14 shares. Two vessels were purchased, the Columbia Rediviva, a full-rigged ship of 212 tons burden, 83 feet long, and carrying 10 guns, and the Lady Washington, a small sloop of 90 tons. The development of the story told in the preceding chapter has required a mention of these vessels in connection with the events there described, but it will now be necessary to take up further particulars, and to revert to earlier dates. It is of interest to note that the great state of Washington and the mighty river of Oregon reflect the names of the two vessels of this small flotilla.

Capt. John Kendrick, of the merchant marine, a man 45 years of age, was chosen to command the Columbia, and the sloop Washington was put in charge of Robert Gray, a native of Rhode Island, who is said to have seen service in the navy in the war of the American Revolution. The last mentioned commander, as we shall see, proved the more able, and by far the more daring. Great care was exercised in preparing for this expedition. Passports were provided by the Massachusetts authorities. From the Spanish minister to the United States were procured letters recommending the voyagers to the Viceroy of New Spain, as Mexico was then called. However friendly and honest may have been the intentions of this Spanish minister, the same cannot be said of the Spanish officers in Mexico, for, upon hearing of the intended expedition, the following instructions were sent from Mexico to the commandant at San Francisco: "Whenever there may arrive at the Port of San Francisco, a ship named the Columbia, said to belong to General Washington, of the American States, under the command of John Kendrick, which sailed from Boston, September, 1787, bound on a voyage of discovery and of examination of the Russian Establishments on the northern coast of this Peninsula, you will cause the vessel to be secured, together with her officers and crew." The brief order, filled with inaccuracies as it is, again shows how the Spaniards considered the South sea their own particular preserve, and how they looked upon navigators who ventured into those waters as trespassers.

Kendrick and Gray's orders from their owners were to avoid offense to any foreign power, to treat the natives with kindness and Christianity, to obtain a cargo of furs on the American coast, to proceed with the same to China to be exchanged for a cargo of

Captain Robert Gray
Discoverer of the Columbia, famed River of the West.

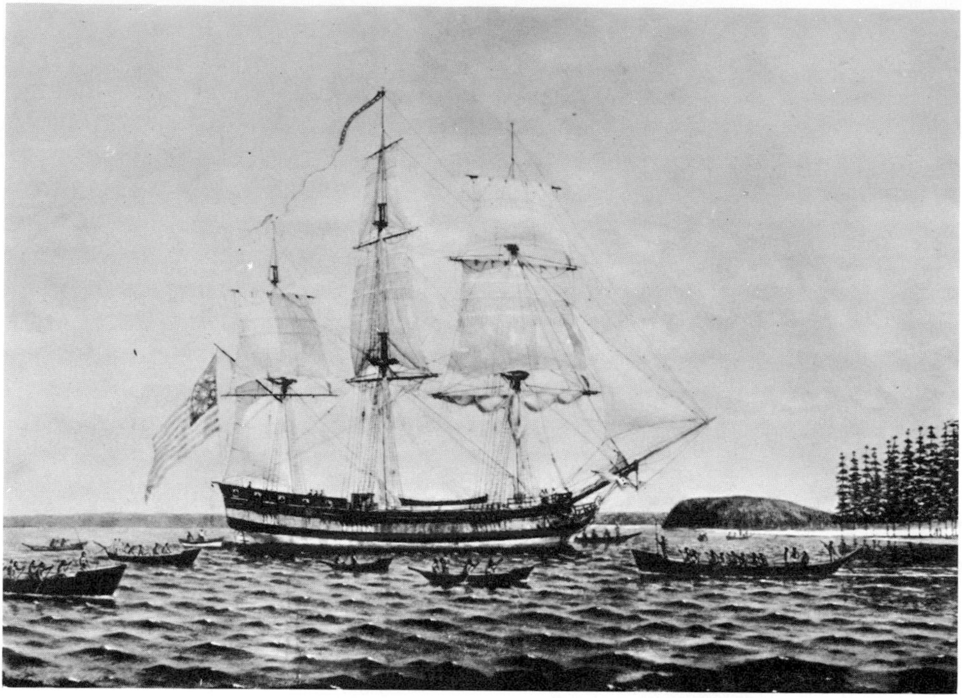

—Oregon Historical Society

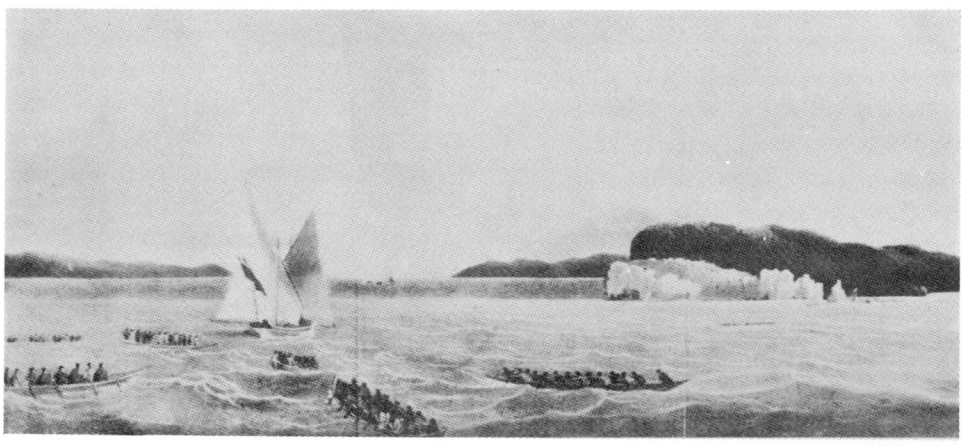

Captain Robert Gray's Ship—"Columbia"

Captain Meares at the Entrance of Strait of Juan de Fuca, June 29, 1788

The island on the right is Tatoosh Island. Meares claimed to be the discoverer of the strait but it had already been seen by Barkley. The picture is from Meares' "Voyages."

tea and to return with the tea to Boston. An outward bound cargo was taken on, consisting of such trinkets as were thought to appeal to the savage heart, beads, brass buttons, ear-rings, calico, tin mirrors, blankets, hunting knives, copper kettles, iron chisels, snuff and tobacco. The crews were carefully chosen, and, in addition to the usual complement, there was taken along a surgeon, an accountant, a trader and an astronomer. Woodruff, a member of Captain Cook's expedition, was one of the mates.

The promoters of this enterprise evidently realized the importance of the step which they were about to take, and the consequences with which it was fraught, as is shown by the fact that bronze and silver medals were struck off, to commemorate the event. These bore, on one side, the names and pictures of the vessels, together with the name of Kendrick as commander, and on the other, the names of the chief stockholders in the enterprise. The importance was realized also by the Boston people in general, for, upon the day of the departure of the little flotilla, what seemed to be the entire population of that city assembled to bid the hardy voyagers God-speed.

2

Sailing out of Boston harbor, Monday, October 1, 1787, a course was laid for the Cape Verde islands, where there was a delay of two months, the first evidence of dilatoriness and lack of enterprise on the part of Captain Kendrick. It was there that Gray took on board a young negro, Marcus Lopez, whose want of good judgment at a later period caused trouble with Indians on the Oregon coast. From the Cape Verde islands, Kendrick steered for the Falklands, where there was another delay. However, Gray and the other bolder spirits of the party finally prevailed upon him to proceed. The usual peril from stress of weather was encountered in the vicinity of Cape Horn, and there came a period of extreme cold, when the shrouds were frozen stiff. Then storms separated the two vessels, which were destined not to meet again until they reached their rendezvous at Nootka. Kendrick first landed at Mas a Tierra, one of the islands of Juan Fernandez, for water and repairs. The governor of the latter place, notwithstanding his country's objection to the intrusion of foreigners, treated Kendrick with kindness, but, for doing this, afterward received a reprimand from the Spanish government, and was dismissed from office.

Taking advantage of the prevalent southwest winds, Gray, in his little sloop, sped onward toward the coast of North America, which he first sighted near the locality of Cape Mendocino, August 2, 1788. Cruising northward along the Oregon shore, he saw "the entrance to a large river where great commercial advantages might be reaped." The latitude corresponds with that of the Siuslaw, while the Umpqua lies not far to the south. Neither stream can be properly called large, but Gray's ideas of the Oregon coast, and the bays and inlets there as he observed them, are in sharp contrast with those of previous navigators. His vessel was small and of light draft. Whether he had the courage to sail closer to the shore, and to brave the danger of entering bar bound harbors, where others were more cautious, may be a question, but certain it is that, where they had reported an impenetrable wall, with streams and inlets unworthy of serious notice, he found important bays and rivers.

Sailing along the coast of Oregon, he found what he called a "tolerably commodious harbor," near Cape Lookout, possibly the present Cape Meares. That cape is approximately 40 miles south of the mouth of the Columbia river, and one of the bays near to that cape is now known as Netarts, but surely even the optimistic Gray could not have described Netarts as tolerably commodious. For this reason geographers now believe that the bay he referred to is Tillamook. But this is not entirely clear for other reasons.

However, Gray had real excitement here. He went in, boldly, and at first the natives seemed friendly and hospitable, bringing berries and crabs, which delicacies were no doubt welcome to those on board, some of whom were suffering from scurvy, that curse that always followed the early voyagers. But a party of the men had been sent ashore to gather grass for some animals that were on board, and the colored boy, Marcus, negligently left his cutlass or knife sticking in the sand. An Indian, seeing it and coveting it, attempted to take it, when the boy ran after him and tried to wrest it from him by force. Marcus was overpowered and killed by a group of the natives, and the whole party was in danger of meeting the fate that so often came to landing parties from other ships, at other places along this coast. In making their retreat to the ship, however, which they did without worse injury to themselves than fright, several of the Indians were killed.

Conflicts of this kind can generally be traced to a lack of tact or understanding on the part of the white men. We now know, from wide experience of many explorers and travellers, that if proper representations had been made to the chief, instead of attempting forcible recovery of the boy's property, restitution probably would have been made, and bloodshed would have been avoided. Lewis and Clark had several such experiences when on the Columbia river a few years later, but, excepting on one occasion, they managed to avoid open rupture. On the other hand, many landing parties from early ships on the coast were attacked by natives. Generally speaking, the Indians were jealous of their rights, and would expect, as a white man would, to be consulted, and perhaps to be compensated, before wood, or water, or game could be taken by strangers. But, until contact with the whites made them suspicious of good intentions, most of the tribes were hospitable, generous, and trustworthy. It must be said, however, that the narrative of Gray's voyages on the coast shows that he had many conflicts with the native people; and the difficulty at this particular landing place was but one of his conflicts of the kind.

3

Gray left Tillamook after this experience and put well out to sea. He arrived at Clayoquot sound, near Nootka, August 16, 1788, just in time to witness the launching of the Northwest, built under the direction of Captain Meares, the first vessel built on the coast, excepting those built by Russians. He was welcomed by the Englishmen, Meares and Douglas, and, soon after, Captain Kendrick arrived safely at Nootka with the Columbia, much to the relief of Captain Gray.

It was during this summer that Martinez, the Spaniard, arrived here, with explicit instructions as to foreigners, but he evinced no hostility to the Americans, and they were allowed to carry on their trading without molestation. Captain Kendrick made explorations further north, during which operations one of his sons was killed by the Indians. The American captains now exchanged ships; the Columbia, with Captain Gray in command, was sent to China with the cargo of furs that had been obtained by both ships, and from China she returned to Boston. Thus Gray circumnavigated the globe, and the Columbia was the first vessel to carry the Stars and Stripes around the world.

The welcome he received at Boston was most enthusiastic, and although the venture did not prove a financial success, because he had found the Chinese market demoralized by large offerings of furs from other ships, at the time, still, the owners decided to fit out a second expedition for the same purpose. It is upon this second expedition that our interest is chiefly centered, for it was while making this voyage that Captain Gray entered the Columbia river and named it after his vessel. The elusive River of the West was at last not only found, but entered upon and named.

4

It may be well before describing the epoch making discovery of the Columbia river to bring to mind that Captain Gray's voyages were in no sense governmental in character. They were purely private enterprises. The mere discovery of, and entrance into, the mouth of a river would not be sufficient to establish rights to the country, particularly as against a nation or nations already claiming by earlier exploration and discovery the same general region, followed by actual and visible occupation. On the other hand, the actual first discovery of an important river may be the basis for priority of right to the stream and its watershed, especially when followed by occupancy and claim of sovereignty.

When Captain Gray returned to the coast, 1791, Spain was claiming the country, and England was seeking a foothold, asserting priority through Sir Francis Drake, and depending upon later exploration, besides claiming through dominion over the contiguous territory on the Atlantic seaboard. The United States, newly organized as a nation, was separated from the Pacific region by the intervening Louisiana country, extending (more or less indefinitely at this time) to the Rocky mountains from the Mississippi river. The Spanish claim reached from New Spain and California, west of the Rocky mountains, indefinitely northward. Russia by reason of exploration and a settlement at Sitka and on the Alaska peninsula, was claiming the extreme north, her southern boundaries being likewise indefinite. And England, having acquired Canada and the French claims north of the United States, claimed that her explorations and discoveries on the Oregon coast and northward gave her an outlet from the east to the Pacific. These claims, conflicting as they were, finally yielded to diplomacy. But for a half century the title to the Oregon Country was in dispute.

5

Upon Gray's return to Boston, as above mentioned, there was a reorganization of the company backing the fur trading venture. The sloop Columbia, refitted as quickly as possible, soon began the second voyage to the Oregon coast, leaving Boston harbor September 28, 1790. Clayoquot sound was reached, June 5, 1791. Gray visited the strait of Juan de Fuca and then busied himself, during the remainder of that season, in trading to the north, along the eastern shore of Queen Charlotte island. While engaged in this work, the mate and two of the crew were attacked by natives, and killed. July 23, he met the brig Hope, commanded by Captain Ingraham, of Boston, who had left Boston 10 days before him.

Returning to Clayoquot sound, he made preparations to spend the winter there. Quarters were built for officers and crew and these were securely fortified against any possible hostile demonstrations on the part of the Indians, who seemed to be in a particularly unfriendly mood that season. A small schooner, the Adventure, was built during this winter at Clayoquot, the first American vessel to be built upon the shores of the Pacific. It afterwards made a voyage to the north for furs, commanded by Capt. Robert Haswell, who had served with Gray some time before, as mate. On the return southward, the Adventure was sold to the Spaniards, as has already been said.

Gray tried to cultivate the friendship of the Indians at Clayoquot, during the winter of 1791-92, but without marked success, for a conspiracy was formed among them to seize the fort and massacre its garrison. He was warned of this by a young Hawaiian, son of a chieftain of the islands, who had made the voyage in the Columbia to Boston and again to the Pacific coast, with Captain Gray. Attoo, the Hawaiian, had been approached by the Indians, who had offered to make him their chief if he would assist them in their attack upon the whites. His part was to smuggle out to the natives as much ammunition as he could, and then wet the remaining powder in the fort. Attoo weighed this offer for some time, but finally decided upon the honorable course and informed Captain Gray, who immediately made preparations to repel the expected attack. The Columbia, which had been pulled out of the water for the winter, was again launched, and her guns were remounted. As soon as the treacherous natives saw that Gray was aware of their plans, they gave up all thought of the attack and made overtures of friendship, which, as may well be imagined, were quite futile. On leaving the vicinity, Captain Gray had an Indian village of 200 houses, at that time unoccupied, destroyed by fire, as a punishment and for a salutary example.

6

Soon after the arrival of spring, 1792, Gray took the Columbia and sailed southward in order to satisfy his curiosity regarding the great river to the south of Cape Disappointment.

He followed the coast of Washington and Oregon as closely as possible, and noted the appearance of several good harbors, but weather conditions prevented entrance. He turned back northward before he reached the California line. The weather continued unpropitious, and he was near the strait of Juan de Fuca again, April 29, 1792, when he chanced to meet Captain Vancouver, as related in a preceding chapter. His voyage along the coast and return was between April 2 and April 28, and his ship had gone as far south as latitude 42 degrees, 50 minutes. Gray told Vancouver that he saw what appeared to be the entrance of a large river, and stated that he had stood off and on for nine days, trying vainly to effect an entrance. The time was actually between April 17 and April 22, as nearly as can be figured from the records.

His statement, that he intended to return to make further investigation of the river, made little impression upon the English explorer, as is evident from the latter's Journal. Gray lingered a few days, and then, with improving weather, again turned southward, having the determination to enter where he could, and feeling certain that in new and uncharted harbors, where natives had not yet learned to measure the value of sea otter skins in trade for iron and cloth, he would secure the coveted furs at attractive prices.

7

Sailing down the Washington coast, he sighted one of the openings, which he entered without trouble. This was May 7, 1792. It proved to be a fine bay, never before discovered, which he named Bulfinch harbor, after one of his ship's owners; but, though he noted this name in his log and so marked his chart, his officers and crew preferred his own name, and called the bay Grays harbor, a name now generally used.

During the night of the eighth, while lying at anchor in this bay, the expedition had an exciting time, with little opportunity for sleep by any on board. Several canoes full of Indians were first seen passing the ship, but they were kept away by the firing of muskets over their heads. It was a bright moonlight night, and, soon after midnight, they were seen approaching again. Several cannon shot were then sent over them, but they continued to advance with war whoops, and at length one large canoe with at least 20 men, dangerously close, was blown to pieces with a direct shot, and probably all on board were killed or drowned. This put an end to the threatened assault, and the next day trading was resumed, nothing being said of the tragedy of the night. The Columbia remained at anchor here until the 10th, many Indians coming out to visit the ship and to barter.

8

On the afternoon of May 10, Gray weighed anchor and stood down the bay, emerging into the ocean at seven thirty in the evening. Proceeding slowly down the coast during the night, the dawn of the next day found his ship six leagues off the entrance of the great river, which bore east-south-east. The air was clear, the coast line being visible for a distance of 20 miles, and the breeze though light was fair. Without hesitation or faltering, Gray stood in directly for the line of breakers on the bar. The breakers had proved an impassable barrier to d'Aguilar, Heceta, Meares and Vancouver, but had no terrors for Gray, and he found exactly what he expected, a passageway through, where soundings showed from five to seven fathoms of water, deep enough to permit the entrance of vessels of more than 1000 tons burden.

The quality of Gray's courage and seamanship was often demonstrated. A few days before, when seeking an entrance to Grays harbor, the cutter in charge of the second officer, who had been sent to examine the inlet into that bay, had returned to the ship with a report that the officer could see nothing but breakers at the entrance, although beyond it had the appearance of a good harbor. Gray was determined not to give it up, and he successfully negotiated the passage with his ship. The crossing of the bar of the Columbia called for the same quality of courage. Through the channel, Gray sailed without mishap, and the ship Columbia was soon riding gently within the entrance of the great

River of the West. May 11, 1792, 300 years after the discovery of America, marks an achievement important in the history of the Pacific northwest.

In describing his first anchorage point, Captain Gray's log says: "When we were over the bar we found this to be a large river of fresh water up which we steered. Many canoes came alongside. At one p. m., came to with the small bower, in 10 fathoms, black and white sand. The entrance between the bars bore west-south-west, distant 10 miles; the north side of the river a half mile distant from the ship; the south side of the same, two and a half miles distant; a village on the north side of the river, west by north, three quarters of a mile. Vast numbers of natives came alongside; people employed in pumping the salt water out of our water-casks in order to fill with fresh, while the ship floated in. So ends." And thus ended the exciting and epoch making day.

The point then reached is now identified as off McGowan, just above Chinook point (now generally called Fort Columbia.) The Chinook village was between McGowan and the point. In October following, Lieutenant Broughton anchored at this place and found the water salty, but this was no doubt due to different stage of water in the river at that time of year, and to difference in tides.

Gray's ship went further up the stream, got aground, but was soon free again without mishap, and, after several changes of position during the days following, left the river, May 20. Native canoes crowded around the ship, and there was much trading.

The following is a quotation from the Journal of young John Boit, under-officer, then 17 years of age:

"The river extended to the NE. as far as eye cou'd reach, and water fit to drink as far down as the Bars, at the entrance. We directed our course up this noble River in search of a village. The beach was lin'd with natives, who ran along the shore following the ship. Soon after, above 20 canoes came off, and brought a good lot of furs and salmon, which last they sold, two for a board Nail. The furs we likewise bought cheap, for Copper and Cloth. They appear to view the Ship with the greatest astonishment and no doubt we was the first civilized people that they ever saw. We observ'd some of the same people we had before seen at Gray's harbour, and perhaps that was a branch of this same River. At length we arriv'd opposite to a large village, situate on the North side of the River, about 5 leagues from the entrance. Came to in 10 fm. sand, about ¼ miles from shore. The River at this place was about 4 miles over. We purchas'd 4 Otter skins for a Sheet of Copper, Beaver skins, 2 spikes each, and other land furs, 1 spike each.

"We lay in this place till the 20th May, during which time we put the ship in good order and fill'd up all the water casks along the side, it being very good. These Natives talk'd the same language as those farther South, but we cou'd not learn it. Observ'd that the canoes that came down river, brought no otter skins, and I believe the otter constantly keeps in salt water. They however always came well stocked with land furs, and capital salmon. The tide set down the whole time and was rapid. Whole trees sometimes come down with the stream. The Indians inform'd us there was 50 villages on the banks of this river.

"May 15. N. Latt. 46° 7′. Long 122° 47′. On the 15th we took up the anchor, and stood up river, but soon found the water to be shoal so that the ship took the ground, after proceeding 7 or 8 miles from our first station. However soon got off again. Sent the Cutter and found the main Channel was on the South side, and that there was a sand bank in the middle. As we did not expect to procure Otter furs at any distance from the Sea, we contented ourselves in our present situation, which was a very pleasant one. I landed abreast the ship with Capt. Gray to view the country and take possession, leaving charge with the 2d Officer. Found much clear ground, fit for cultivation, and the woods mostly clear from underbrush. None of the Natives come near us.

"May 18. Shifted the Ship's berth to her old station abreast the Village Chinoak, command's by a chief Polack. Vast many canoes, full of Indians, from different parts of the River were constantly alongside. Capt. Gray named this river Columbia's, and the North entrance Cape Hancock, and the South Point, Adams.''

7

May 20, 1792, the ship Columbia left the river that was thenceforward to bear her name, and proceeded northward, making stops on Vancouver island, both at St. Patrick harbor and Columbia cove. At each of these places there was some friction between the ship's crew and the Indians, and at the latter place a war canoe full of Indians was fired upon, "so effectually as to kill or wound every soul in the canoe."

There were similar occurrences with the Indians a few days later, when the ship reached Queen Charlotte sound, (which waters, Captain Gray called Pintard's straits after one of the owners of his ship.) The full narrative of Gray's voyage reveals many clashes with the natives, several with fatal results. Whether this was due to bad management, or not, is not entirely clear. The trading, however, was carried on vigorously, the ship returning from time to time to Columbia harbor, and several times cruising in the vicinity of Queen Charlotte sound, and even going 100 miles southerly behind Vancouver island, on a course that would, if continued, have reached the strait of Juan de Fuca, and thus would have resulted in establishing for a certainty the Americans' guess that Nootka was situated upon an island. The Adventure rejoined the Columbia in these northern waters, and delivered her cargo of 500 skins, obtained still farther to the north and west.

A Boston ship, Margaret, Captain Magee, was met with, but the captain was sick, and his trade was not good. July 28, 1792, on one of the trips to Queen Charlotte island, the Columbia had the bad fortune to strike a hidden rock, and came near being lost. She was freed successfully on the next tide, but leaked badly. The stem and other parts of her hull were badly damaged, but the ship was kept afloat by hard work at the pumps, and reached Columbia cove for repairs; ultimately, she had to be taken to Nootka sound to be beached and to have renewals that could not be completed at the former place.

8

Gray visited Nootka again in October of the same year, as already related, on which occasion he gave to Captain Vancouver the details of his discoveries of Grays harbor and Columbia river. Vancouver was at that time arranging to move his base to the Sandwich islands for the winter, and decided to revisit that part of the coast, and to make a more detailed examination, on his way southward. He began his voyage with the Discovery, accompanied by the Chatham in command of Lieutenant Broughton, and the Daedalus, in command of Lieutenant Whidbey. He left to Whidbey the duty of entering Grays harbor, or Bulfinch harbor, as Gray had named it on his map. The Discovery and the Chatham arrived off the mouth of the Columbia river October 19, 1792. The Discovery being the larger vessel, and not readily finding a feasible channel, stood off shore, while the Chatham successfully negotiated the passage of the bar. Vancouver heard a gun fired from behind a point, and saw that this salute was answered by the hoisting of the Chatham's colors, and firing a gun. The Discovery then made another effort to enter, but, a southwest gale arising, she abandoned the attempt, and put about, steering southward for the agreed rendezvous at Monterey, on the California coast, there to await the other two vessels. The vessel that was in the river when the Chatham arrived was the small fur trading schooner, the Jenny, of Bristol, England, commanded by Captain Baker, of whom more hereafter.

Broughton had observed the departure of the Discovery, but he proceeded to examine both shores of the great stream. He sailed a few miles, following the north bank, and saw a deserted Indian village. The early explorers frequently mentioned these deserted villages, which were not in fact permanently deserted, but were merely left during the summer season while the inhabitants were away in search of game and berries for winter store. He sighted and named Tongue point on the opposite shore. His ship grounded on more than one occasion, but got off without difficulty. Passing across the river to the south bank, he examined the sandy peninsula of Point Adams, and rowed in the ship's boat up a bay and small river, which he named, Young's bay, after Sir George Young, of the royal navy. While exploring this bay and river, he observed immense flocks of wild geese and ducks.

Broughton then undertook, with ship's boat and crew of oarsmen, an exploration of the river for a distance of approximately 100 miles from its mouth. His narrative of this exploration says: "The discovery of this river, we were given to understand, is claimed by the Spaniards, who call it Entrada de Ceta, [Heceta], after the commander of the vessel who is said to be its first discoverer, but who never entered it; he places it in 46 degrees, north latitude. It is the same opening that Mr. Gray stated to us in the spring, he had been nine days off the former year, but could not get in, in consequence of the outsetting current. That in the course of the late summer he had entered the river, or rather the sound, and had named it after the ship he then commanded. The extent

Mr. Gray became acquainted with [it] on that occasion is no further than what I have called Gray's bay, not more than 15 miles from Cape Disappointment, though according to Mr. Gray's sketch it measures 36 miles. By his calculation its entrance lies in latitude 46 degrees, 10 minutes, differing materially in these respects from our observations." It may be noted here that the astronomical station of the United States Coast and Geodetic Survey on the highest point of the southern extremity of Cape Disappointment is now officially gives as latitude, 46° 16′ 36.40″ north; longitude 124°, 02′, 50.37″ west.

9

Broughton's exploration up stream, was the first upon the river, and he gave names to many now familiar landmarks, some of which have already been mentioned in these pages. Puget island was named in honor of Vancouver's lieutenant on the Discovery. Baker bay was named for the captain of the Jenny, Walker island was named for the surgeon of the Chatham. Coffin mountain was so called because of the Indian burying ground which was observed there, where the dead were placed, as was the native custom, in canoes or primitive coffins, supported by stakes. A point, probably Coon island, at the mouth of the Willamette, was named Belle Vue, and it was from near this location that Broughton first saw the snow-capped summit of Mount Hood, which he named in honor of the same noble Englishman similarly honored in the naming of Hood canal. The sight of this mountain led him to think that the source of the Columbia was somewhere in the range of which it was a part, and that this could not be far away. The highest point reached on the Columbia river was at or near the mouth of Sandy river, above which he saw a projection of the north shore, that he designated as Point Vancouver. This is at the mouth of Canyon creek, several miles above the present city of Vancouver, which is near the site of the Fort Vancouver, established by Hudson's Bay Company.

The season being now far advanced and supplies being near an end, Broughton decided not to extend the reconnaissance, but to return down stream, which, after a ceremony to indicate a claim of sovereignty by the British government, was done with as much speed as possible. Returning to the Chatham, sail was spread, and the vessel proceeded to the mouth of the river, and thence in due time overtook the Discovery, Captain Vancouver, at Monterey, California, as agreed.

10

Little is known of the schooner Jenny's calls at the Columbia. Vancouver first mentions her as arriving at Nootka, October 7, 1792, shortly before his own departure. While careful to record the information he got from Gray regarding the river, he does not indicate that Captain Baker had also entered the stream. Nor, does it appear from the Journal that Captain Baker told of his plan to go there again on leaving Nootka. Yet, the fact is that on October 7, Vancouver received from the captain of the Jenny, two young girls, transported from their homes in the Sandwich islands, and undertook the duty of returning them to the islands, as the Jenny intended to go from Nootka "straight to England." As already related, the Jenny was found in the Columbia river, October 21, 1792, by Lieutenant Broughton, when he entered that river. Vancouver's statement regarding this tells of his hearing the salute fired from behind Cape Disappointment, and the answering gun of the Chatham, and seeing the hoisting of the Chatham's colors, from which he says "we concluded some vessel was there at anchor," which carries the implication that he did not know at that time that the vessel was the Jenny, which, leaving at the same time as Vancouver's ships, evidently had slipped down from Nootka in advance of the officers of the royal navy. She remained there until the departure of the Chatham.

Lieutenant Broughton's description of how the Jenny led the way out over the bar, on the 10th of November, discloses the fact that Captain Baker had an assumed familiarity, or superior knowledge, because of "having been here the earlier part of the year," which shows that Baker had been there one or more times. The earlier visit could not have been prior to Gray's discovery, in May, or priority for British entrance would have been claimed. It seems probable, therefore, that Captain Baker, like Captain Vancouver himself, had met Gray earlier in the year, and having learned of the discovery of the Columbia, had then hastened there to try the new field for fur traffic. This would have been some time between May and October. However this may be, he secured for himself and his vessel the honor of being second to enter the river, anticipating Vancouver and Broughton. Just why Vancouver did not learn of Captain Baker's first visit there, if there was an earlier visit as Broughton intimates, or was not told of the purpose to go there the second time in advance, but, on the contrary, was given to understand that Baker was going direct to England, remains unexplained.

11

In the meantime, the Daedalus had visited Grays harbor, and the report of Captain Gray concerning it was verified. Although Gray had called it Bulfinch's harbor, old English maps sometimes indicate it as Whidbey's harbor, after the lieutenant in command of the Daedalus. The name, Grays harbor, is now well established. The exploring expedition of Vancouver visited the Sandwich islands and returned to the northwest coast, where it completed the elaborate surveys.

Captain Vancouver ended his great voyage, 1795, after four years of absence from home, during which he thoroughly examined and charted the north Pacific coast of North America. For the British crown he assumed protection of the Sandwich islands, now called Hawaiian islands, where his wise course in adjusting the affairs of the native chiefs and settling the controversies that had arisen there, shows that he had the qualities of a successful administrator. He kept a full record, but his narrative was not published until 1798, after he had died. It was, however, completed and printed, under the direction of his brother, substantially as written in his own notes, a clear and readable, as well as interesting, story of the long nautical expedition.

His memory will always be respected by Americans, as well as by the British, notwithstanding the evidences throughout the narrative of prejudice against American ship masters and traders, which, in a man so fair and reasonable in his dealings with others, is to be regretted. His taking possession of the Columbia river and the country in its vicinity in his Britannic majesty's name, may be ascribed to a spirit of patriotism. He gave, as the reason, his professed belief that the subjects of no other civilized nation or state had ever entered this river before, and this was founded on the theory that Gray's entrance had led him no further than into Grays bay, as Broughton called it, meaning the lower part of the stream, thus assuming the river to end before it empties into the ocean. This was a view that was shared by Lieutenant Broughton.

Vancouver's prejudice against Gray may perhaps be ascribed in some measure to a written statement made jointly by the American captains, Ingraham and Gray, at Nootka, 1789, in response to a request of the Spanish commissioner, in which they stated what they knew or thought, of the character and location of the buildings that the English claimed to have erected before the arrival of the Spaniards, at Nootka. This statement was severely criticized by Vancouver in his Journal, and his synopsis of it is garbled and distorted, not only by suppressions, but by direct misstatements. As to Captain Ingraham, Vancouver's renaming of certain islands, discovered and named Washington islands by that American, at the same time showing by his Journal that he knew that they had previously been discovered and named, may be taken as an indication of his attitude. On the whole, his valuable work as an explorer throws into shade any criticisms that may be made of his record, and he remains one of the greatest of the early visitors to the Pacific coast.

12

After the departure of the Jenny and the Chatham from the Columbia river, November 10, 1792, the river became a resort for fur traders, and some of them wintered there instead of going to the Sandwich islands for that purpose. The records are meager, and no complete list of such vessels can now be given, but some of them may be identified. Perhaps the first trader to follow the Jenny was the brig Phoenix, of Bengal, Captain Moore, which made a call on its second voyage to the northwest coast, 1794. It spent the following winter in the Columbia, and after trading there during the summer, called at Nootka, and at the Sandwich islands, en route to China.

The Ruby was a ship owned by Sydenham Teast, of Bristol, England, who was also owner of the Jenny, already mentioned. The Ruby first reached the Columbia river, May 22, 1795. Her master was Captain Bishop, who seems to have had knowledge of the published accounts of the voyages of Cook and Meares, but not that of Vancouver, which, in fact, had not yet been published when he left England, October 16, 1794. Bishop, no doubt, had obtained from Teast all the information that had been given by

Captain Baker, of the voyage of the Jenny, for he seems to have understood the peculiarities of the channel, and to have sailed boldly over the bar, carrying full press of sail. He anchored in Baker bay, close to the bluff, a quarter of a mile from the north shore. It is a singular fact, however, if he really knew what Captain Baker could have told of the discovery and naming of the river by Gray, that in the entries in the Ruby's log he persistently alludes to the river as the Chinook.

The natives at first showed a disinclination to trade. It was evident from their methods that their experience with other vessels had not only given them knowledge of the value of their furs, but also a clear idea of just what commodities they wanted in exchange. Nevertheless, after a show of reluctance on their part, a lively trade was begun, and during the 13 days that the vessel remained in the river, Captain Bishop obtained over 100 good sea otter skins, besides a variety of others. While the trading was going on, the captain put in ballast, and secured a three months' supply of wood and water.

From what the natives said, it appeared that the Jenny had made a recent visit to the river, under command of Captain Adamson. This would have been either her second or her third call at the river. The Indians also told of a Captain Moore, or Mooen, who had spent the winter in the Columbia river, doubtless meaning Captain Moore of the Phoenix, already mentioned.

The Ruby returned to trade here again, October, 1795. Again she had a good trade. She sailed for the Sandwich islands January 23, 1796. Captain Bishop's log shows that he got on very well with the native people, finding them generous and trustworthy; but it was intimated to him by the chiefs, with whom he cultivated friendly relations, that three ship masters who were earlier visitors were in disfavor and would have a warlike reception, if they ever returned. The cause of this feeling was not clearly stated, but it appeared that they had fired upon the natives, and on one occasion they had wounded several of them. Captain Baker of the Jenny and Captain Brown of the Butterworth were accused of making a brutal attack on the Indians in October, 1792, and were also accused of piracy. Captain Magee of the American was also blamed for his transactions with the Indians.

Captain Bishop planted a small vegetable garden near Cape

Disappointment, on an island in the river, during his summer visit, and he had the satisfaction of finding, on his return in the autumn, that there was a crop of good potatoes and some beans, although the peas, mustard, cress and celery, that had been planted, were not to be found, the seed having been eaten by marauding birds. This was the first garden planted in Oregon, and, before the captain sailed away, he repeated the experiment and planted another lot of seeds, although it is probable that he never returned to get the benefit. The ship's larder was amplified and the salt rations were agreeably varied by wild fowl, fish and venison, besides wapatoes and cranberries, during the vessel's stay in the river.

After this, the names of vessels or captains coming to the Columbia river to trade are unknown, until in the winter of 1805-06, when Lewis and Clark spent some weeks at their Fort Clatsop. Memoranda found with the original note books of these explorers, list the following persons, assumed to be ship captains: Moore, Youin or Youens, Swepeton or Swipton, Mackey, Meship, Jackson, Balch or Bolch, Haley, Washilton or Washington, Lemon, Fallawan or Tallamon, Skallie or Skelley, Callallamet, and Davidson. Skelley is described as having but one eye, and Callallamet as having one leg. All these but Tallamon and Davidson, were traders, but Haley was the favorite with the natives on account of the numbers of presents given by him.

In their narrative, Lewis and Clark note, under date Friday, March 14, 1806:

"We are informed by the Clatsops that they have latterly seen an Indian from the Quin-na-chart [Quinault] nation, who reside six days march to the N. W., and that four vessels were there, and the owners, Mr. Haley, Moore, Callamon and Swipeton, were trading with that numerous nation, whale bone, oil and skins of various description." Lewis and Clark did not have the good fortune to see any of these, but were so impressed with the character of Mr. Haley, from what they heard from the Indians, that they called the bay Haley's bay, at the mouth of the Columbia, that Broughton had named Baker bay. We also learn from John Jewitt's Journal that Captain Hill, of the American brig, Lydia, got one of the Lewis and Clark written notices that they left with the natives on departing upon their return journey. The Lydia had been in the

Columbia in November, 1805, a fortnight after Lewis and Clark had passed down the river, but was not seen by them. The Lydia was on the coast until August, of the following year, and Jewitt, who was on board when the vessel was in the river soon after the departure of Lewis and Clark, mentions the fact that the natives showed medals that the explorers had given to them.

CHAPTER IX
Looking Across the Continent

1

WE NOW enter upon an entirely new and distinct period in the history of Oregon, the era of exploration carried on by land, from the east. Thus far our account has been of voyages by Spaniards, Englishmen, Americans and Russians, and others, in some cases for the sake of increasing the world's store of geographical knowledge, but more often for the sake of trade. There was always, however, the underlying nationalistic purpose or hope of acquiring dominion over these far distant regions, although at the early period with which we have been dealing the prize did not seem of sufficient value to justify engaging in war. It is true, Great Britain and Spain almost came to blows, but better sense of statesmen of these nations averted such a catastrophe, thereby indirectly aiding ultimate development of the United States.

There is a certain unity of events which must be borne constantly in mind in following the story of the Oregon Country, a certain logical sequence leading up to final establishment of American claim to this far away section of North America. The key to the possession of this fair land was the great Columbia river. The nation discovering this navigable river would have a decided advantage over rivals, provided the discovery was followed by occupation of the tributary country. We have seen how the river, again and again, as though by some providential dispensation, escaped discovery by Spanish and British navigators, to fall at last to the American captain, Robert Gray.

These early navigators had proved one thing conclusively, that to colonize this distant country would be almost impracticable by way of the sea; the long voyage around Cape Horn, or by way of the cape of Good Hope, and the perils incident, made this quite clear. The conception of an overland passage across the continent was persistent, because its advantages were seen, and it was much to be desired. Besides the early Spanish explorations in the southern part of the continent (which, however, were not particularly designed to open a way from the Atlantic to the Pacific), consideration had been given to the possibility of finding a route across the northern part of the continent, almost two centuries before Gray's discovery of the Columbia river.

In Hakluytus Posthumus, or Purchas his Pilgrimes Contayning a History of the World, first issued at London, 1625, the author gives a brief discourse upon the probability of a passage to the Westerne or South sea, illustrated with a copy of testimonials and a brief treatise and mappe by Master Brigges. This was written, 1616, and Master Brigges is therefore recommended as a thrice learned (and in this argument three times thrice industrious) Mathematician, famous for his readings in both Universities and this honorable Citie (London). From Master Brigges' argument and the accompanying map, we learn that California is an island, and this is based upon a recent Spanish map captured by the Hollanders, and which he, himself, has recently seen. (Our readers may be reminded in passing that maps showing California as an island were common during the seventeenth century.)

He thinks that it cannot be very far across America from Hudson bay to the west coast, but that a much nearer, safer, and far more wholesome and temperate route may be found through the continent by way of Virginia. "And this hope that the South sea may easily from Virginia be discovered over land is much confirmed by the constant report of the Savages, not onely of Virginia, but also of Florida and Canada; which, dwelling so remote from one another, and all agreeing in the report of a large Sea to the Westwards, where they describe great ships not unlike ours. . . ." Here we have the first suggestion of an overland route, the author arguing the probability of waterways flowing westward to the Westerne sea, which would aid in transporting the explorers and their provisions.

The author in his quaint style displays both his patriotism and his reverence by indicating that if this route is found, of which there is great probabilitie (if not full assurance) the endeavors "shall by God's blessing have a prosperous and happy success, to the encrease of his Kingdome and Glorie amongst these poore ignorant Heathen people, the publique good of all the Christian world, the never dying honor of our most gracious soveraigne, the inestimable benefit of our Nation, and the admirable and speedie increase and advancement of that most noble and hopeful Plantation of Virginia; for the good success whereof all good men with mee I doubt not, will powre out their prauers to Almighty God."

There was a similar plan outlined in a book now deemed spurious, which purported to recount the Discoveries of John Lederer, translated from the Latin by Sir William Talbot, published, London, 1672, and republished, Rochester, New York, 1902.

Then there was the story of the old Indian of the Louisiana region named Monacht Ape', who had ascended the Missouri, crossed the mountains and followed a river flowing into the ocean, where he is said to have had a hand in a conflict between local tribes and bearded strangers, who landed from a ship. The story was told to a Frenchman, residing in Louisiana, named Antoine Simon Le Page du Pratz, who published a book, 1758, in which it is given faith and credit, although it is full of inconsistencies and its inherent weakness is apparent. There were others who wrote about the possibility of crossing the continent, and for two centuries it was always about to be done. Meanwhile, numerous maps were issued from the European publishers that purported to show geographic features of the country.

As knowledge of the Pacific coast, after Cook's visit, 1778, rapidly increased by reason of the many other sea voyages already mentioned, interest in the overland exploration became more general. When Great Britain acquired the French rights in Canada, and her fur traders pushed out farther and farther west, and particularly after the publication of Carver's Travels, it became evident that it would be but a short time until the Terra Incognita of some of the old maps would be explored and definitely mapped.

Anthony Hendry, in the service of Hudson's Bay Company, visited the Blackfeet tribe, 1754, probably in the present province of Alberta. Samuel Hearne, 1769-72, made an adventurous journey as far as Coppermine river, in the Arctic regions, for the same company. Its rival, the North West Company, planned an expedition to reach the Pacific coast, 1784-85. Besides these, there were many reports of the waterways and trails of the remote parts of the Canadian great west.

2

Alexander Mackenzie was a partner in the North West Company, and one of its most enterprising and venturesome explorers. He even went around the Great Slave lake, 1789, and discovered and descended the river flowing from it into the Arctic ocean. This journey convinced him that there was no feasible passage for sea vessels from Hudson bay to the Pacific, for he found the mouth of this river closed by ice in July, and he observed, more-over, that the chain of mountains lying westward ran even farther north than the estuary of the river. The stream was named the Mackenzie river.

Mackenzie's plans for a new expedition, this time to reach the Pacific, were carried out by him, 1792 and 1793, and no more courageous feat of western exploration was ever accomplished; but instead of following down the reputed great Oregon, or River of the West, as he had originally intended, his course led him upon other streams. He spent the winter upon Peace river, and from there he crossed the continental divide and began his journey as soon as spring permitted, May 9, 1793.

After having crossed the Rocky mountain range, he came to a river that seemed to have a westerly direction. This is the stream now known as Fraser river. He had ten well seasoned men in his party, but, after continuing the perilous journey through canyons and cascades for 25 arduous days, they found the difficulties of keeping along the stream too great to be overcome. They turned northwest, therefore, crossed a divide to the Blackwater, and then to Dean river, and floated down Bella Coola, until ultimately they reached the western coast. Mackenzie's farthest point was, July 21, 1793, a place that had already been seen by Vancouver's ships, and that had already been named, Port Menzies.

Mackenzie's expedition was the first overland journey to the waters of the north Pacific, a journey full of danger and menaced by starvation and failure. The ocean was found at almost the very time that one of Vancouver's officers, Lieutenant Johnstone, in a small boat, was examining this part of the coast. The explorers missed each other, as Lewis and Clark a few years later missed the hoped-for American ships when those explorers reached the Pacific. Mackenzie, on leaving upon the return journey, left an inscription, painted in large letters on the face of a rock: "Alexander Mackenzie from Canada by land, the twenty-second of July, one thousand seven hundred and ninety three." This was on an arm of the sea where Vancouver nomenclature had given the estuary the name Cascade canal.

3

Mackenzie had not discovered the Columbia, but its lower reaches had been seen in the previous year by Gray and Broughton.

It was Vancouver's map, published in London, 1798, that gave to the world exact knowledge of the mouth of that river, with the geography of the coast line, and soon thereafter Mackenzie, publishing in London an account of his travels, made a map of his own, joining thereon his own discoveries with those of the navigator. He indicated a river, which he erroneously designated the Columbia (which of course he did not know by name until after he had returned from his journey), by a dotted line, believing that this was the same river he had followed for 25 days, and then abandoned. In reality, as was later ascertained, his was the stream called by the Indians the Tacouche Tesse, the same as Fraser river, subsequently explored by Simon Fraser and named after him.

Simon Fraser was a North West Company man of courage and enterprise, who followed Alexander Mackenzie, 1806, to a place called Nechacs, on the river that now bears Fraser's name. The next year, 1807, after establishing at that place a post called Fort George, he took a large and well equipped party down the turbulent stream. His men suffered great hardships and had thrilling adventures. After many narrow escapes from death on the way, a point near the mouth of the stream was reached, where further progress was made impossible by hostility of natives, and he returned without actually reaching the ocean, believing that he had been descending the Columbia river, although when at the mouth of Thompson river, a tributary, he was told by natives that there was another great river, further southwest, that flowed to the ocean.

Mackenzie suggested a plan, after his famous overland journey, for the consolidation of the Hudson's Bay Company with the North West Company, with the active cooperation of all the capital and organization of these two companies, to develop the fur trade on a grand scale by establishing a line of posts from the mouth of the Columbia river to the Rocky mountains, thence across to and along Saskatchewan river and Lake Winnipeg and Nelson river. His plan contemplated the use of the Columbia river, and of course the surrounding and tributary country, by British subjects.

Contiguity of territory is a great aid in carrying on national land explorations. As long as Spain, or France, owned the Louisiana country west of the Mississippi, extending westerly to the

Rocky mountains, the United States was not directly interested in the development of the Pacific coast. The wedge intervened, and the Oregon Country seemed very remote. Some there were, even at the early period now under consideration, who contemplated American development of the far west. But these, including Thomas Jefferson, who was one of the earliest to show an interest, did so with the idea that an American population under such development would have to be governed as an independent state. Even 25 years later, Senator Benton, in studying the Oregon question, at first took that view, although in time he came to realize, as Jefferson before him, that this was not necessary or desirable.

4

That Jefferson understood the menace to the welfare of the young republic of the United States of foreign settlements in the Oregon Country, may be seen from the fact that while he was residing in France, 1785, on hearing that an exploring expedition under Perouse was outfitting at the harbor of Brest for a voyage to the north Pacific, he sent John Paul Jones on a secret errand to that port with instructions to satisfy himself as to the purposes of the voyage, conducting himself, however, so as to avoid exciting suspicion. But important events after Gray's discovery came along rapidly, so rapidly as to be almost simultaneous in their happenings.

President Jefferson heard of contemplated plans in Great Britain for the exploitation of that section; owners of American sailing vessels in great number were following the lead of Bulfinch and his associates to the Pacific coast, and were building up a commercial enterprise of importance; and, finally, there was change in the ownership and the sovereignty of the Louisiana country.

5

The vast stretch, known by the name Louisiana, originally was claimed by the French, by whom it was discovered and settled. In 1762, the French government, being pressed by the English in the then pending French and Indian war, made a cession to Spain of "all the country known under the name Louisiana", including New Orleans; and when the war closed, 1763, by the treaty of peace whatever portion that may have been east of the Mississippi, was turned over to Great Britain, only to be returned to Spain again by

the treaty between Great Britain and Spain, 1783. Spain then had
the entire Louisiana from the latter date until it was secretly
ce ed to France once more, 1800. When news of this transfer
leaked out, 1802, it produced "uneasy sensations," to use Jefferson's expression, in the United States, and great effort was at
once made to acquire New Orleans by purchase. Instead of this,
a purchase of the whole of Louisiana was accomplished, 1803, as
an outcome of negotiations with Napoleon and his minister, Tal-
leyrand. Free navigation of the Mississippi, and its control from
its mouth to the source of the great river and its tributaries was
thus insured. There is, however, no ground for the claim that the
title of the United States to the Oregon Country was derived, in
whole or in part, by the acquisition of Louisiana, although that
was assumed for a time by geographers and historians, and even
by our own interior department, which once made the error of
issuing an important map of the United States, ascribing the
acquisition of Oregon to the Louisiana purchase. The Louisiana
title did not include any lands west of the Rocky mountains.

These facts will take our attention. Jefferson's interest in the
Oregon Country, though stimulated by the gradual approach toward that section from all sides, was not new born. It may be
traced through his correspondence to a much earlier period, and
to a connection with the same young John Ledyard, who had sailed
with Captain Cook, and was concerned with events already related
in this narrative. And, as will be seen, the expedition that was
sent to the Pacific ocean under the directions of this close-con-
structionist republican president, whose whole political theory and
practice should logically have made him an opponent of the plan
to acquire Louisiana, or to explore and colonize the Oregon Country, was an expedition that was really the outcome of long treas-
ured plans and deliberate purposes of his own. Such is the inconsistency of human nature. In this particular, he may be contrasted with the likewise inconsistent Gouverneur Morris, of Pennsylvania, ardent federalist, who, 1803, was equally positive that the
United States had no right to acquire new territory, or to admit
new states created therein.

But this does not go so far as to say that in sending Lewis and
Clark to the Oregon Country Jefferson had in mind, originally,
the acquisition of that territory for the United States. On the

contrary, his instructions to Lewis and Clark indicate that he was then considering the advantage of developing a fur trade that could be conducted through the Missouri river into the United States. But, as will be seen, after the expedition was formed, and Louisiana was acquired by the United States from France by purchase, he conceived the possibility of making some future claim to the Oregon Country. The expedition, however, paved the way for the subsequent settlement by the Astor party, and for the movement of Americans over the Oregon Trail, which furnished this country with the really effective arguments to prove its title to the disputed territory.

6

In treating this sequence of events chronologically it will be useful to turn to the career of the man who furnished Jefferson with the information that perhaps later on influenced his decision to send out the pathfinders, Lewis and Clark. Ledyard was born in Groton, Connecticut, 1751. His mother, who had been early left a widow, intended that her son should be educated for the ministry, and consequently we find him at the age of 21, attending Dartmouth College, noteworthy at that time as a training school for missionaries to the Indians.

Although a young man of brains, he seems to have lacked the power of application which is needful for a profession, and his own adventurous and roving proclivities, together with the unfavorable opinion formed of him by the members of the Dartmouth faculty, caused him to disappoint his mother's ambitions, and we find him embarked upon a career of adventure, which was never abandoned through his life, although it never brought him to successful personal achievement.

Urged by his overpowering wanderlust, he left college of his own volition, became a sailor before the mast for some years, and then conceived the idea of visiting relatives in London, through whom he thought his career might be advanced more rapidly. These relatives treating him with some coolness, he haughtily left them, and, after a period of want in that great city, secured a berth with the expedition of Captain Cook, then about to set out on its voyage by way of the cape of Good Hope into the South sea. This expedition brought young Ledyard to the Oregon coast, where he had an excellent opportunity to study the ways of the natives, and to appreciate the possibilities of the fur trade. In fact, so impressed was he, that it became the ruling passion of his life thereafter to promote this trade, and to be the first to reap the rich profits that he had the foresight to recognize as possible.

When the Cook expedition left Nootka, it was Ledyard who was sent by Cook to communicate with the Russian settlement, and he was with the expedition when it sailed through Bering strait. He learned the impossibility of reaching the Atlantic by way of a northwest passage.

Upon his return to England he found that country in the midst of the war of the American Revolution. He enlisted in the British navy, understanding that he would not be called upon for service against the land of his birth, but, in spite of this, he found himself, during the year 1782, on board a British ship, off the Long Island coast. The call of home was too strong to be resisted. Ledyard obtained shore leave, and, soon after landing, found his mother, with whom there was a very happy reunion. He never returned to his ship, but spent some time in New England, where he talked about the fur trade, much like a modern promoter.

7

This was the first intimation that the New Englanders had had of this commercial opportunity, and it created great interest. Ledyard tried for some time, but in vain, to organize companies and enlist capital in ventures to the Oregon coast; but at last, becoming discouraged, he sailed for England. Afterwards, he went to France, where he pursued the same objective. He was always just on the verge of success, but something always intervened to blast his hopes. It was while he was in France, that he met Thomas Jefferson, who took a genuine interest in his plans. The importance of this meeting is well set forth by one of Jefferson's biographers who writes: "To a statesman like Thomas Jefferson it was evident that a large portion of that immense territory, separated from the United States by no barrier of nature, would be eventually embraced within their boundaries. He was convinced, therefore, of the propriety of its being explored by a citizen of the United States, and regretted the failure of Ledyard's attempts in his own country to engage in a voyage before the same thing had been meditated anywhere else. These views were deeply impressed on the mind of Jefferson, and in them originated the journey of Lewis and Clark, 20 years afterwards, which was projected by him and prosecuted under his auspices."

When all of Ledyard's schemes for promoting an expedition by sea to the northwest coast had failed, he determined that he would reach his goal by proceeding overland by way of Russia and Siberia to the Pacific ocean, and thence to the American coast, as best he could. As events proved, this was about as impracticable a plan as could have been proposed, but he had the support of English friends and tried to carry it into execution. After many hardships in Russia and Siberia, the Russian authorities absolutely vetoed the project, arrested him and brought him back. This ended his attempts to exploit the fur trade of the northwest. His further adventures led him to Africa, and he died soon afterward, a failure as far as the accomplishment of his ambitions went, but, nevertheless, a man who had an important indirect influence upon the history of Oregon. Even after he had embarked on his African venture, Jefferson, as shown by a letter written to a friend, had hopes that on his return he would fulfil a promise to attempt "to penerate from Kentucke to the western side of the continent."

8

In 1795, Great Britain, involved by reason of the French Revolution, found herself again at war with Spain. The danger was instantly realized by American statesmen, that the world's greatest maritime nation might seek to take advantage of this opportunity to seize Louisiana from the Spanish, and thus not only connect Canada with the gulf, but compensate herself for the loss suffered through the independence of her American colonies. Jefferson, then secretary of state, one of the first to sense this possibility, wrote at once to the American minister at London: "We wish you, therefore, to intimate to them [the British ministry] that we cannot be indifferent to enterprises of this kind; that we should contemplate an exchange of neighbors with extreme uneasiness; that a due balance on our borders is not less desirable to us than a balance of power in Europe has always appeared to them."

Our interest in this question involved more than an anxiety as to who were to be our neighbors to the west. For many years, settlers had been going in increasing numbers to the country contiguous to the Ohio and Mississippi rivers, and these great water-ways were becoming of increasing importance for purposes of commerce. Unfortunately, the mouth of the Mississippi was not within American territory. It was within the boundaries of Louis-iana. Annoying tolls and restrictions upon through transport had sometimes been exacted by the Spanish occupants of that strategic location, and although a rather unsatisfactory temporary arrange-ment with Spain had been effected, American inhabitants of the western parts of the country were in a state of constant anxiety lest the privilege of trans-shipping by way of the river might some time be entirely suspended. Friction had also arisen respect-ing the settlement by Americans in Spanish territory, west of the Mississippi and near the Red river. This state of affairs had led the American government to carry on negotiations with Spain looking to a permanent adjustment of the differences. Progress was made, and the treaty that was signed with Spain, 1795, was an attempt to agree upon boundaries, principally east of the great river.

Jefferson had always been suspicious as to the intentions of the French in Louisiana. As early as 1790, he wrote our minister at Paris: "It is believed here that the Count de Moutier during his residence with us conceived the project of again engaging France in a colony on this continent; and that he directed his views to some of the country on the Mississippi; and attained and com-municated a good deal to his court." His suspicions were verified when, 1800, during the period of French ascendancy in Spain, the treaty of St. Ildefonso was forced upon the latter nation, which transferred the possession of the entire Louisiana territory to Napoleon. The news of this secret treaty reached America, 1801, or early in 1802. Jefferson, who was president at that time, was greatly alarmed, realizing that the possession of this contiguous territory by such a powerful nation as France was fraught with dangerous possibilities to his country.

9

He wrote at once to the American minister at Paris: "The ces-sion of Louisiana and the Floridas by Spain to France works sorely on the United States. . . . It completely reverses all the political relations of the U. S. and will form a new epoch in our political course. . . . There is on the globe one single spot, the possessor of which is our natural and habitual enemy. It is New Orleans. . . . It is impossible that France and the United States can long continue friends when they meet in so irritable a position." In spite of his lifelong admiration of the French, Jefferson openly declared that the possession of New Orleans by France would make necessary an alliance between this country and Great Britain. How deeply he was stirred may well be understood from the very fact that such an alliance could be deemed a possibility, in view of his persistent dislike of that country. But, Jefferson was essentially a man of peace. He sought some way whereby he might solve the problem of foreign ownership of the mouth of the Mississippi and at the same time retain the friendship of France.

With this end in view, he instructed Livingston, who was at that time our minister to France, to approach Napoleon with an offer to purchase New Orleans. Jefferson had already conferred with Congress on the subject and had received its consent and an appropriation for that purpose. It soon became apparent, however, that Livingston was not making progress, and apparently he was unable to get favorable results. Men of the western country were clamoring, Jefferson was impatient of delay. In that emergency, he sent his friend Monroe to Paris, as a special envoy to try to bring matters to a head.

But by this time, Napoleon had come to realize that in the acquisition of Louisiana he had assumed greater burdens than he could carry, mighty as he was. He knew he could not spare armies and fleets to protect his title, and that the time would surely come when Great Britain with her preponderant naval power would take this remote western territory from him, and thereby add to her already too extensive dominions. That Napoleon fully appreciated all this is clearly shown by his own statement on the subject: "I know the full value of Louisiana, and I have been anxious to repair the fault of the French minister who abandoned it, in 1762. A few lines of treaty have restored it to me, and I have scarcely recovered it before I must lose it. But, if it escapes from me, it shall one day cost dearer to those who obliged me to strip myself of it than those to whom I wish to deliver it. The English have successively taken from France, Canada, Cape Breton, New Foundland, Nova Scotia, and the richest portions of Asia. They shall not have the Mississippi, which they covet. . . . I have not a moment to lose in putting it out of their reach. . . . I think of ceding it to the United States. . . . They only ask of me one town in Louisiana, but I already consider the entire country as entirely lost; and it appears to me that in the hands of this growing power it will be more useful to the policy and even to the commerce of France than if I should attempt to keep it. . . . I renounce Louisiana. It is not only New Orleans that I will cede, it is the whole colony without any reservation. To attempt to retain it would be folly. I direct you to negotiate this offer with the envoys of the United States. It will be moderate, considering the necessity in which I am making the sale. . . . Irresolution and deliberation are no longer in order. Do not even await the arrival of Mr. Monroe; have an interview with Mr. Livingston this very day." This being his temper and point of view, the transaction was soon consummated.

Shortly after the conclusion of the negotiations, when the treaty had been signed, Napoleon said: "This accession of territory strengthens forever the power of the United States, and I have just given England a maritime rival that will sooner or later humble her pride."

10

Thus, at the stroke of a pen, for the comparatively paltry sum of $15,000,000 and without shedding a drop of blood, we acquired an empire almost as extensive as our original territory. We did not hesitate to purchase without consulting the wishes of the inhabitants, but nations were not particular in those days, and there was no thought of the necessity of being so. The peaceful solution of this problem of 10 years' standing was as pleasing to Jefferson as it was to Napoleon. It meant that Americans in the west could thenceforth work out their own destiny without fear of interference on the part of other nations.

It also produced another consequence of importance. It resulted in the increase of the power of the federal government. It seems like the irony of fate that Jefferson, who had always so jealously guarded the prerogatives of the individual states, should be the instrument in an act of statecraft which so greatly promoted the unity, power and sovereignty of the nation. From the very beginning of his negotiations he doubted the constitutionality of the step he was taking, and even planned, at the inception, a constitutional amendment to legalize the transfer; but, subsequently, he feared to have such a suggestion made lest ratification should fail, and he resigned himself to the exigencies of the situation. He himself said as to this: "The Constitution has made no provision for our holding foreign territory, still less for incorporating foreign nations into our union. The Executive, in seizing the fugitive occurrence, which so much advances the good of the country, has done an act beyond the constitution. The Legislatures in casting behind them metaphysical subtleties, and risking themselves like faithful servants, must ratify and pay for it, and throw themselves upon the country for doing for them what they knew they would have done for themselves, had they been in a situation to do it."

11

Jefferson's correspondence at this period shows that he had no conception of the importance of the territory as a whole. A constitutional amendment was prepared by him, which, while confirming the purchase, would prohibit grants of land therein north of the mouth of the Arkansas river, other than to Indians in exchange for lands occupied by them east of the Mississippi, until authorized by further amendment to the constitution. His object seemed then to be "to prevent emigrations, excepting to a certain portion of the ceded territory."

Looking back upon the year 1803 from our present vantage point, we can see how President Jefferson, in taking advantage of the necessities of Napoleon, paved the way for the settlement and acquisition of the Oregon Country. No sooner had Louisiana become ours than settlers and trappers began to swarm across the Mississippi and to enter the territory between the river and the Rocky mountains.

It is evident that for 20 years previous to the setting out of the expedition of Lewis and Clark, Jefferson had evolved in his mind the project of the exploration of the extreme western part of the American continent and of finding an overland route to the Pacific. The first evidence found of such a design agitating his fertile brain is in a letter which he wrote to General George Rogers Clark, December 4, 1783, wherein he says: "I find that they have subscribed a very large sum of money in England for exploring the country from the Mississippi to California. They pretend that it is only to promote knowledge. I am afraid they have thoughts of colonizing into that quarter. Some of us have been talking here in a feeble way of making an attempt to search that country; but I doubt if we have enough of that kind of spirit to raise the money. How would you like to lead such a party? Though I am afraid our prospect is not worth asking the question." Here we find the germ of the plan for the Lewis and Clark expedition.

12

This project was undoubtedly still further developed in the mind of Jefferson through his meeting with John Ledyard in Paris, 1786. Jefferson himself thus describes this meeting: "When I resided in Paris, John Ledyard of Connecticut arrived there, well known in the United States for energy of body and mind. He had accompanied Captain Cook on his voyage to the Pacific ocean, and distinguished himself on that voyage for intrepidity. Being of a roaming disposition, he was now panting for some new enterprise. His immediate object at Paris was to engage a mercantile company in the fur trade of the western coast, of America, in which, however, he failed. I then proposed to him to go by land to Kamschatka, cross in some of the Russian vessels to Nootka Sound, fall down into the latitude of the Missouri, and penetrate to and through that to the United States. He eagerly seized the idea, and only asked to be assured of the permission of the Russian government."

In 1792, Jefferson, who was a member of the American Philosophical Society of Philadelphia, proposed a western exploration and that they undertake the task, and that the necessary funds for its accomplishment be raised by private subscription. This was successfully done, and it was decided to appoint Andre Michaux, a noted French botanist, as leader, but it was soon discovered that Michaux had been associated with the French minister, Genet, in his schemes for the embarrassment of the American government, and it was considered unwise to allow him to go. This resulted in the cancellation of the plans for the expedition.

Jefferson's memorandum, dated January, 1793, of instructions to Michaux in behalf of the Philosophical Society, are in some respects similar to those later given to Lewis and Clark. It is deemed of prime importance, he said, that the Missouri shall be explored "to find the shortest and most convenient route of communication between the United States and the Pacific ocean within the temperate latitudes." "It would seem by the latest maps as if a river called Oregon interlocked with the Missouri for a considerable distance, and entered the Pacific not far southward of Nootka sound. But the society are aware that these maps are not to be trusted so far as to be the ground of any positive instructions to you." Readers need not be reminded that the foregoing is one of the early uses of the name Oregon, as shown in the first chapter hereof. It also indicates the route selected for the Lewis and Clark expedition.

13

Thus far, plans for the exploration of the far west had failed, but when Jefferson was elected president, 1800, an entirely different aspect was given to his projects. It is a fortunate circumstance for the Oregon Country, as matters transpired, that Jefferson was elected at that particular time. The federalists were not unfriendly to England, and might not have followed up the discovery of Captain Gray with an expedition, if likely to result in a dispute with that country over the ownership of the territory contiguous to the Columbia. Jefferson's communication to Congress was confidential, and its action was likewise kept from the public as far as possible, principally to avoid friction with other nations.

Solicitous, as he usually was, to act strictly in accordance with the letter of the federal constitution, Jefferson coupled with his proposal to Congress of an expedition to the Pacific, the plan of investigating the government trading posts which had been established in the west for the benefit of the Indians, the contracts for whose maintenance were about to expire. In connection with this investigation it was proposed to send an expedition up the course of the Missouri river to its source, across territory belonging at that time to France, having just been acquired by that country from Spain, and to secure a report upon the state of trade as far west as the Rocky mountains, together with recommendations of means for its further development. This communication to Congress was dated January 18, 1803.

In making the recommendation, Jefferson wrote as follows: "While other nations have encountered great expense to enlarge the boundaries of knowledge, by undertaking voyages of discovery, and for other literary purposes, in various parts and directions, our nation seems to owe to its own interests to explore this, the only line of easy communication across the continent, and so directly traversing our own part of it. The interests of commerce place the principal object within the constitutional power of Congress, and that it should incidentally advance geographical knowledge of our own continent cannot but be an additional gratification." The expedition was to have the guise of a scientific enterprise, and Jefferson wrote Lewis: "The idea that you are going to explore the Mississippi has been generally given out. It satisfies the public curiosity and masks sufficiently the real destination."

Congress promptly made an appropriation of $2500 to defray the expenses "for the purpose of extending the external commerce of the United States," and plans were immediately undertaken to start the expedition on its way. Jefferson hardly expected the expedition to keep within the modest appropriation, for it was given unlimited letters of credit. The members were also carried on the pay rolls of the army.

It will be noted that throughout all these plans up to this point, and for some time afterward, there was no thought of securing possession of the Oregon Country. The expedition was purely for commercial purposes, to promote the fur trade with the Indians in the region of the upper Mississippi, and even to attract, if possible, that of the Columbia basin and divert it across the Rockies.

At the time when these preparations were being made Jefferson may have thought that his own countrymen would be the first to undertake to reach the Pacific by an overland route. In his instructions to Lewis and Clark he said: "The northern waters of the Missouri are less to be inquired after, because they have been ascertained to a considerable degree, and are still in the course of ascertainment by English traders and travellers." Mackenzie's book, giving the account of his expedition, was first published in London, in 1801, and French and German editions were printed in 1802. Vancouver's Voyage was published in London, 1798. Albert Gallatin, secretary of the treasury, was so much interested in the success of Jefferson's plan that he suggested that General Dearborn (secretary of war) should write immediately to procure Vancouver's book, one copy of which, perhaps the only one in America, was then being offered for sale. That Lewis knew the details of Broughton's expedition up the Columbia river, before the American party began its long journey up the Missouri, is shown by the Journals of the expedition, and these leave no doubt that he had seen a copy of Mackenzie's excellent book.

CHAPTER X

LEWIS AND CLARK EXPEDITION

1

"OCEAN IN VIEW! O the joy," were the triumphant and happy words of Captain Clark, entered in his Journal, November 7, 1805, when the Pacific ocean was seen from the canoe on the Columbia river.

Here was, in fact, the consummation of a long and arduous journey. Whatever the perils and hardships of the return journey, this at least was safe, the expedition had reached its great objective, the continent had been crossed. It has been well said, that the story of the Lewis and Clark expedition is our national epic of early explorations. It is a story of adventure, and full of interesting features. And it is a story of achievement that has a profound significance to the nation.

The drama is staged in a setting of novel and picturesque scenery, among the tribes of the new west. As the story is unfolded, all the elements of a popular book of adventure are revealed, such as courage, resourcefulness, self-denial, helpfulness, manly leadership and steadfastness of purpose.

The expedition was President Jefferson's own conception. He laid the plans, selected the leaders, advised about the equipment and stores, and wrote with his own hand the careful instructions. He was solicitous about the conduct of the men and the treatment of the natives with whom they would come in contact.

President Jefferson chose as the leader of the expedition, his private secretary, Meriwether Lewis, but at the latter's request this leadership was shared with his personal friend, William Clark. More capable leaders could not have been chosen. Lewis was a Virginian of distinguished Scotch ancestry, born in 1774. His early life, which was divided between studies and outdoor sports, had fitted him for the task. As soon as he was appointed, he applied himself diligently to special studies to equip himself with some knowledge of the useful sciences. He himself had said, when upon a former occasion he had asked to be selected for a similar expedition, that he could live wherever an Indian could.

William Clark, also a native of Virginia, was a resident of Kentucky, where he had had the life of a frontiersman, and had

William Clark   *Meriwether Lewis*
Co-leaders of the Lewis and Clark expedition to the Pacific ocean.

Replica of Fort Clatsop built in 1955 for Lewis and Clark's
Sesquicentennial Celebration

Chinook Woman and Child
Showing the manner in which the heads of the children were flattened.

—From a Catlin painting, Smithsonian Institution

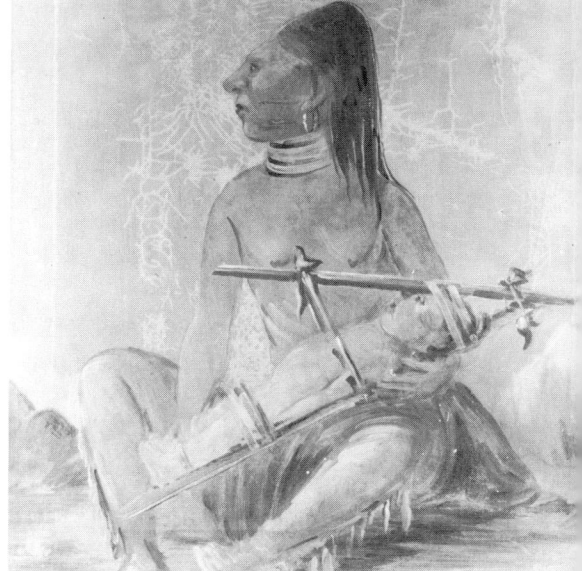

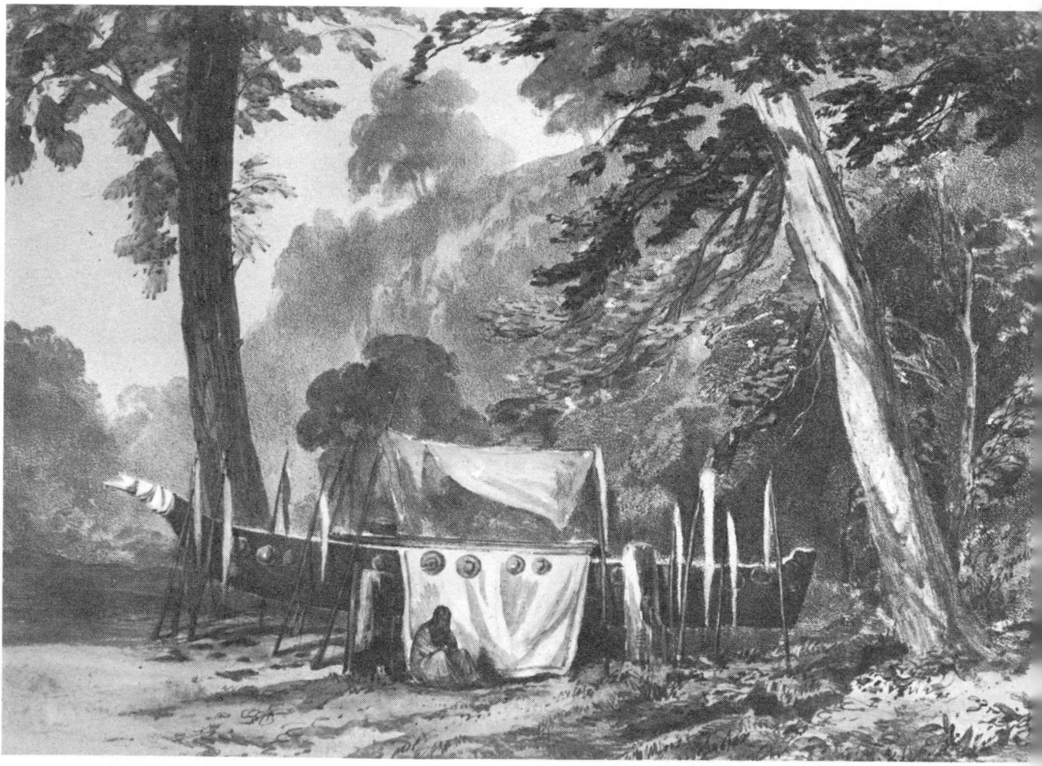

—Oregon Historical Society

Indian Canoe Burial, Lower Columbia River

gained experience in Indian warfare. Both had served in the army, and they were close friends.

In the party were four sergeants, Ordway, Pryor, Gass and Floyd; the last named died from natural causes on the way westward. There were 20 private soldiers, including Shields, Colter, two brothers named Field; also Drewyer, a half-breed, and York, who was Clark's colored servant, especially interesting to the Indians on account of his great strength, as well as for his color. There were eleven voyageurs and nine frontiersmen.

2

A wait at the rendezvous on the American side of the Mississippi river during the early months of 1804, while preparations were being made and the men were being trained for special duties, was occasioned by delay in official proceedings to transfer the sovereignty of Louisiana to the United States. It was while this training was going on, and while waiting for suitable spring weather for the start, that the neighboring outpost town, St. Louis, was the scene of interesting ceremonies indicating the successive changes in sovereignty.

Lower Louisiana had been transferred from Spain to France at New Orleans, November 30, and to the United States, December 20, 1803, at the same place. It was not until spring was opening that the Spanish authorities were ready to take similar action as to Upper Louisiana, at St. Louis, for it seems that the Spanish commandant at that station had received no official notice of transfer of Louisiana to France, much less of the acquisition from France by the United States. However, after a long wait, the Spanish colors were lowered, the French flag was then displayed, only in turn to be hauled down and that of the United States to be substituted. Captain Lewis attended the ceremonies, as the representative of the President. All this elaborate program was carried out March 9 and 10, 1804, although, as a matter of fact, Captain Lewis had learned just before he left Washington that the purchase had been consummated; furthermore, he had already received a letter from President Jefferson, dated July 15, 1803, officially informing him of the conclusion of the negotiations for the purchase. The same letter gave him his first information of Broughton's survey of the Columbia river. The treaty with France had been ratified by the Senate by a vote of twenty-five to seven, October 17, 1803.

So, it was not until May 14, 1804, that the expedition began to move up the Missouri, under the direction of Clark. Lewis joined the party at St. Charles, 21 miles above the mouth of the Missouri. The equipment consisted of a large craft, 55 feet over all, square rigged, and with 22 oars; a tow line was also provided, by which the vessel could be tracked up stream, at the rapids. There were also two small pirogues, or boats, sharp at the bow and broad and flat at the stern. Horses accompanied the expedition, being led along the bank. It had been decided to use boats as far as possible, as the plan was to follow the Missouri river to its source, but it was later learned that this was not the best method, nor was the route that was followed the best possible for crossing the Rockies to the Pacific.

The instruction of Jefferson relative to the natives was faithfully carried out. Friendship was cultivated, and a careful inquiry was everywhere made into their manners and customs. It was noted that those Indians that had been most in contact with the whites were in a worse plight than those farther in the interior, who had not had the contaminating influence of civilization.

3

The journey up the Missouri was slow and arduous, the current was swift and the obstructions many and troublesome. Buffaloes, then numerous on the vast prairies, were hunted. Indians, principally the remnants of the Missouri tribes, visited the explorers, and were hospitably entertained.

At one of the picturesque highlands bordering the river a meeting was arranged by Lewis and Clark between the chiefs of the Missouris and the Ottoes, and after much speech making, and bestowing of medals, a general agreement was reached to maintain peace and cultivate amicable relations. From this circumstance the site of the meeting has been called Council Bluffs. August 20, 1804, the site of the present Sioux City was reached, at which place the sad death of Sergeant Charles Floyd occurred.

In September, the party entered the territory of the Sioux Indians, who showed a more unfriendly disposition than any of the natives previously encountered. However, thanks to the tact of the captains, the party was able to pass through this region without mishap. The next tribe encountered was that of the Aricaras, who proved to be of a most friendly disposition, and who supplied the travellers with corn, beans, squashes and watermelons. The ethical code of these Indians was admirable, corporal punishment and the use of liquor being taboo among them.

4

Late in October, 1804, because of increasing inclemency of the weather, the leaders decided to seek a situation favorable for winter quarters. The site chosen was the village of the Mandans, who had, through the efforts of Lewis and Clark, made peace with their enemies, the Aricaras, and had become fast friends of the Americans. Here the men were set to work felling timber for the erection of winter quarters. These took the form of a triangular stockade, with barracks along two of the converging sides. At this point, near the site of the present city of Bismarck, 1600 miles from St. Louis, the members of the expedition spent a tolerably comfortable and happy winter. There was much hunting of buffalo, deer and elk, much entertainment of their Indian friends, and some slight trouble with rival traders of the North West and Hudson's Bay companies. These men were given to understand that the territory in which they were then operating on the Missouri belonged now to the United States, and that they were to obey such rules as Captains Lewis and Clark saw fit to establish.

The party had been able to employ as interpreters such Canadian French trappers as they met along their route, but from this time on they would be entering into a country where there were no trappers. Fortunately, they found at the Mandan village a former Northwester, one Charboneau, who understood the Shoshone language and who was induced to go with the expedition. Charboneau's wife was an Indian girl, Sacajawea, who had been born among the Shoshone Indians, on the western side of the Rockies, but who, at an early age had been taken captive by a hostile tribe, carried eastward, and had been bought by Charboneau.

5

April brought with it fine weather, and the party made ready to go on their way. The large boat was sent back down the river, bearing an Aricara chief and four other braves of that tribe, to pay a visit to President Jefferson. Some of the men, not needed for the remainder of the way to the coast, were released and sent back. On the seventh of April, 1805, the expedition started westward, with Charboneau, his wife and child, and a Mandan Indian who wished to visit the Shoshones and make a treaty of peace with them. The flotilla consisted of the two pirogues and six canoes.

Progress, from now on, was even slower than before, owing to the increasing swiftness of the current. From the time that the country of the Mandans was left, until that of the Shoshones was reached, no Indians were seen. Game was plentiful, however, and an ample supply of meat was secured without difficulty.

April 26, 1805, the mouth of the river called by the French the Roche Jaune, translated by the Americans into Yellowstone, was passed. After the mouths of Milk river and Dry Fork had been passed, the Journals record, May 9: "The game is now in great quantities, particularly the elk and buffalo, which last are so gentle that the men are obliged to drive them out of the way with sticks and stones." Day after day was passed through a "country beautiful in the extreme" although, as they proceeded, the river narrowed and the current was often so swift that it was necessary to "track" the boats by the use of the tow lines. Late in the month of May there was a recurrence of such cold weather that water froze on the oars, and there was an eighth inch of ice on the surface of the buckets. They named a "handsome river about fifty yards wide" Sahcajahweah (Sacajawea) or Birdwoman's river, out of compliment to Charboneau's wife.

6

Sunday, May 26, 1805, Captain Lewis, who was proceeding on foot, climbed to the summit of a cliff and saw for the first time the crests of the "Rock Mountains," which he alludes to as "the object of our hopes and the reward of all our ambition." June 8, they reached the mouth of Marias river, so named by Captain Lewis in honor of a young lady of his acquaintance. At this point the explorers were in doubt as to which of the two confluent streams was the real Missouri, and parties were sent to explore both streams. These parties were not able to decide the problem, and consequently the two leaders ascended to higher ground from which they could view a broader expanse of country. It was decided that the proper course to follow was that of the more southerly stream. A few days afterward the booming of the falls of the Missouri proved to them that their judgment had been correct. These falls impressed them greatly and they lingered here some days. Captain Lewis' description rises to more than his usual fluency, as well it might, for the Great Falls, in the heart of Montana, was an inspiring spectacle. He says he travelled toward the falls seven miles after first hearing the roar, and as he approached, a spray which seemed driven by the high southwest wind, arose above the plain like a column of smoke. He seated himself on some rocks and "enjoyed the sublime spectacle of this stupendous object which since the creation had been lavishing its magnificence upon the desert, unknown to civilization."

After this, game was not always plentiful, and at times was not to be found. The feeding of such a large party was always a serious problem, and became so serious on the return journey that the men often knew what it was to suffer with hunger and at times even to see starvation facing them. The meat of Indian dogs, and horses, became familiar food to them. A present on one occasion of about 20 pounds of fat horse meat by a generous Indian was noted in the Journals with gratitude, and roots and leaves, and unsavory looking food from the nomadic tribes, when procurable, helped to eke out the larder; but as the Indians had little that they could sell, this was not always a reliable resource.

7

Page by page throughout the Journals the narrative is distinguished for its direct style and terse but effective descriptions. July 19, 1805, they entered what they called the Gates of the Rocky Mountains, where "for five and three quarter miles these rocks rise perpendicularly from the water's edge to the height of nearly 1200 feet."

July 27, 1805, they reached what they called Three Forks, at which point they found the first comfortable camping place they had encountered for some days. The three streams meeting there caused another delay while it was being determined which one would lead them by the shortest route toward the headwaters of the Columbia. The most westerly of the streams was named the Jefferson fork, the other two being named in honor of Gallatin and Madison, respectively.

Soon after, Captain Lewis, proceeding in advance, found a plain Indian trail. He left the party somewhere below the mouth of the Big Hole or Wisdom river and followed up the main stream to the present site of Armstead, where Red creek and Horse Prairie creek join. Lewis followed the westerly or Horse Prairie creek. The Indian trail was found about five miles above Armstead on that stream.

His route thus led him by way of Trail creek to the divide. He came at last in sight of an Indian and endeavored to get an opportunity to show his friendly intentions, but the red man was suspicious and rode away.

The Journals of the expedition speak thus of the arrival at the continental divide, August 12: "The road was still plain, and as it led them directly on toward the mountains the stream gradually became smaller, till after going two miles farther, it had so greatly diminished in width that one of the men in a fit of enthusiasm, with one foot on each side of the river, thanked God that he had lived to bestride the Missouri. As they went along, their hope of soon seeing the waters of the Columbia rose almost to painful anxiety, when at the distance of four miles from the last abrupt turn of the stream, they reached a small gap, formed by the high mountains which recede on either side, leaving room for the Indian road." This is now known as the Lemhi Pass. From the foot of one of the lowest of these mountains, which rises with a gentle ascent of about half a mile, issues the most remote source water of the Missouri.

They had now reached the hidden sources of that river, never yet been seen by civilized man; and as they quenched their thirst at the chaste and icy fountain, as they sat down by the brink of that little rivulet which yielded its distant and modest tribute to the parent ocean, they felt themselves rewarded for all their labors and difficulties. They left reluctantly this interesting spot, and pursuing the Indian road through the interval of the hills, arrived at the top of a ridge, from which they saw high mountains, partially covered with snow, still to the west of them. The ridge on which they stood formed the dividing line between the waters of the Atlantic and the Pacific oceans. They followed a descent much steeper than on the eastern side, and at the distance of three-quarters of a mile reached a handsome bold creek of cold clear water, running to the westward. They stopped to taste for the first time the waters of the Columbia.

8

The chief purpose of Captain Lewis in proceeding in advance of the main party had been to come in contact as quickly as possible with the Shoshones, and to get on friendly terms with them, as he realized that it must be with their help that the expedition would find its way through the mountains and reach the basin of the Columbia in safety. Excepting the lone horseman he had seen before reaching the continental divide, whom he supposed to belong to the tribe of the Shoshones, the expedition had not seen any of the natives for several weeks, although they had seen many signs of their occupancy of the country traversed.

However, August 13, 1805, they discovered two women, a man, and some dogs on an eminence at a distance of a mile before them. The natives saw Lewis approaching and allowed him to reach a spot a half mile distant, without changing their position. Here he ordered his companions to halt while he laid down his knapsack and unfurled a small flag as signs of peace, and went forward alone. The women soon retreated; and the man remained until Lewis was within a hundred yards and then followed the women. The dogs alone remained behind and Lewis tried to attach some trinkets to their necks and thus communicate his friendly designs to the Indians, but failed. Calling upon his men to follow, he again followed the trail, and, about a mile further on, came upon three women. One of these, who was a young woman, immediately took flight, but the older woman and a child who was with her bent their heads to the ground thinking they were about to be killed. The Journals continue, "Captain Lewis instantly put down his rifle and advancing toward them took the woman by the hand, raised her up, and repeated the words *tabba bone*," which was the Shoshone for white man. The fears of the old woman were instantly relieved, and she was prevailed upon to call to the younger woman and tell her to return, which she did at once. Both the women were given presents and they readily agreed to conduct Lewis to their camp.

9

After travelling for two miles along the trail, they were met by a band of 60 warriors, well armed, and mounted on fine horses, coming at full speed. Lewis laid down his gun, halted his men and advanced to meet them. The two women began telling of their experiences with the white men, whereupon the chief of the party dismounted and embraced Lewis and his men with every show of affection, "and no small share of the grease and paint," a ceremony that was repeated with each of the 60 Indians in the party. Thus Captain Lewis had accomplished one object of his journey, and after being welcomed at the near-by village where the pipe of peace was smoked and speeches were made, he justly felt that the friendly relations so established had paved the way for the successful advance of the main party following slowly behind.

The next object of Captain Lewis was to induce the Shoshones to return with him to meet the advancing main party and assist them in transporting their supplies over the mountains. This he accomplished by telling the chief of the objects of the expedition and of how the tribe might profit by assisting them. He also told him of the Shoshone woman who was coming with the whites, and of the black man whose like the Indians had never seen. After some hesitation, due to a fear of treachery on the part of the whites, the Indians were induced to accompany Lewis and his two companions back up the trail, and the junction with the main party was finally effected.

Here, upon the meeting of the two parties, a very dramatic scene was enacted. Sacajawea recognized, at first, a young woman who had been taken captive at the same time she had been taken, but who had subsequently escaped. Next, she recognized in the chief her own brother, and her demonstrations of joy at this reunion were very much the same as would be expected of more civilized white persons. This relationship made Sacajawea invaluable to the expedition, and her knowledge of the Shoshone language proved to be a great help.

The advantage gained by cultivating the friendship of the Shoshones was immediately apparent. Captain Lewis had planned to continue his journey, beyond the Lemhi Pass, following the course of the Salmon river, but his native friends assured him that course was quite impossible, and a reconnaissance showed this to be true. The natives then volunteered to direct and accompany the expedition over the main mountain range eastward and northward, to the Bitter Root river, or Clark's fork as it is now variously called. They kept their promise faithfully, and with hardships to themselves, as well as to the whites, escorted them as far as Ross Hole, after which they departed eastward in order to replenish their well nigh exhausted food supply by a buffalo hunt. The route followed by the expedition led northward and eastward, until the Lolo Pass was reached, through which a feasible crossing of the range was found.

The journey through the Shoshone district brought the white men into frequent contact with the natives of both sexes, whom they found generous, hospitable and well clad; but there was always a dearth of nourishing food. Coming as the expedition did without previous warning, many of the Indian encampments were surprised and frightened, but they soon made the visitors welcome, and offered them gifts of ornaments and food.

10

August 25, 1805, the expedition was saved from total failure by the Shoshone wife of Charboneau. Sacajawea had learned from her tribal friends that because of the shortage of food and the approach of winter the chiefs had requested their people on the other side of the mountains to meet them for the purpose of joining in a buffalo hunt upon the Missouri river. She told this to her husband, who, not appreciating that it meant a desertion, was inclined to join in the plan. Fortunately, however, Captain Lewis was told by him, though with apparent unconcern, that he expected to meet all the Indians from the camp on the Columbia the next day. It then came out that the first chief had already sent some of his young men to make this arrangement, and the intention was for all the Shoshones to leave Lewis and Clark and their baggage. This meant that no horses would be supplied as promised. Facing now the alternative of continuing the evidently impracticable route down Salmon river the situation was desperate, but the resourcefulness of Lewis was equal to the occasion, and after conference with the chiefs in which he presented to them the necessity, and demanded that they keep faith, they agreed to stand by the promise already made.

The party now found themselves in the country of the Flatheads, who proved themselves as friendly as had been the Shoshones. After a three days' rest upon the banks of the Bitter Root, the westward journey was resumed. Although it was but September, the air was cold, due to the altitude, and the trail was difficult to follow; the horses suffered severely, game was scarce and the men were pinched with hunger.

At last level country was reached. A beautiful open plain, partially supplied with pine, now presented itself. Captain Clark, who had proceeded in advance of the slow moving caravan, continued for five miles, when he discovered three Indian boys, who on observing the party ran off and hid themselves in the grass. Clark immediately alighted, and giving his horse and gun to one of the men, went after the boys. He soon relieved their apprehensions and sent them forward to the village, about a mile off, with pres-

ents of small pieces of ribbon. Soon after the boys had reached
home, a man came out to meet the party, with great caution, but
he conducted them to a large tent in the village, and all the inhabitants gathered around to view these wonderful strangers.

The Indians now set before Captain Clark and his six men a
small piece of buffalo meat, some dried salmon berries and several
kinds of roots. After their long abstinence this was a sumptuous
feast. They returned the kindness of the people by a few small
presents, and then went on, in company with one of the chiefs,
to a second village in the same plain, at a distance of two miles.
There they were treated with great kindness, and passed the
night. These Indians were the Nez Perce's, who, in after years,
through the period of settlement by the whites, generally maintained the same friendly attitude.

At the end of September, 1805, several of the party were sick,
but cedar canoes were built, with the assistance of the natives.
Two chiefs of the Nez Perce's offered to act as guides, and accompanied the party as far as The Dalles.

The horses were branded, and together with the saddles, were
left in care of the old chief "Twisted Hair," who proved faithful
to his trust and returned them in good condition upon the eastward bound return of Lewis and Clark. At frequent intervals,
during their voyage down the Clearwater to the Snake, which they
called the Lewis river, and down that stream to the Columbia,
they mingled with the natives, who had been apprised of their
coming. The Indians were at that season engaged in catching and
drying salmon, which were then making the seasonal visitation to
the upper reaches of the streams for spawning.

At the junction of the Snake with the Columbia, the width of
both streams was measured by triangulation; that of the former
was found to be 575 yards, while that of the latter was 960 yards.
From this point Clark spent a day ascending the Columbia, and
found many Indians, all busy gathering and drying salmon, and
immense numbers of these fish were seen stranded along the
banks and deep down in the clear waters.

11

Leaving the junction with the Snake, good progress was made
down the Columbia. Many different tribes were encountered, the
one particularly noted in the Journals for friendly disposition
being the Walla Wallas, which tribe during the return journey

assisted the expedition greatly by guiding them over the hills to the Nez Perce's. October 19, 1805, Mount Adams was sighted and mistaken for Mount St. Helens, and on the same day Mount Hood, called by the Indians Tumtum, was observed.

On this day Captain Lewis, who was walking along the bank, shot a white crane on the wing. Near the spot where the bird had fallen was a group of Indian huts, but no Indians were in sight. Upon looking into the first hut Lewis found it filled with natives crouching in the most abject manner. The other huts were also filled with similar groups of terror stricken natives. It was with much difficulty that he was able to restore them to their normal frame of mind, and later learned that the Indians, hearing the explosion of the gun and seeing the crane fall from the sky, had conceived the idea that Lewis himself had descended upon them by the same route and that he was some supernatural being.

October 22, the mouth of the Deschutes was passed, called by the Indian name Towahnahiooks, and soon afterward the roar of the great falls of the Columbia, at Celilo, was heard. Throngs of Indians were found drying fish, just as a few of their descendants do today. These natives, who afterwards developed an evil reputation among the whites, were at that time peaceable and friendly, although they did make use of their opportunity to pilfer. Nez Perce's guides, who had accompanied the party thus far, were at first unwilling to go among the Indians at Celilo, alleging that they were enemies, but a satisfactory peace was arranged by the leaders of the expedition and the Nez Perce's suffered no harm; but at this point the guides left the party and returned home on horseback. The local Indians assisted in carrying some of the heavy articles, and all of the luggage was taken by land to the foot of the rapids.

12

At the lower Dalles, Lewis and Clark first came in contact with the widespread Chinook tribe, with whom they were so constantly associated afterwards, and thus it was necessary for them to acquire still another Indian tongue. As elsewhere throughout the journey, the leaders scrupulously avoided giving any cause for offense, and conducted their negotiations with the natives so skilfully that they won friendship and esteem; and it was in no small degree due to their tact and good judgment, in such dealings, that they finally brought their efforts to a successful conclusion.

The Cascades, which received from the explorers the name "Great Shoot," were reached November 2, 1805. Below this point they noticed that the river was affected by the tide, which proved to them that they would have no more rapids to encounter, and that they were at last on the bosom of the mighty Columbia, the goal for which they had braved all the dangers and hardships of their long transcontinental journey.

They no longer had rapids and whirlpools to contend with, but, were now discommoded by the rains of a more than usually wet western Oregon winter season. In the passage down stream they noted and described such well known features as Beacon Rock, Rooster Rock and the quicksands at the mouth of the Sandy river. This stream was called by them "Quicksand river." Near its mouth, and not far from Canyon creek, was Point Vancouver, the most easterly point that had been reached by Lieutenant Broughton of the Vancouver expedition, more than a decade before, in his voyage up the Columbia.

Passing down stream, they failed to notice the mouth of the Willamette river, and it was not discovered by them until on the return trip, when they named it the Multnomah. Many of the Indians, from this time on, proved to be "very assuming and disagreeable companions." They were less friendly and more sophisticated than those previously encountered, due to association with whites, whose ships already occasionally entered the Columbia for trade.

The Journals give a description of Hayden island, which the explorers named "Image Canoe Island," from the fact that it was there that they met a large canoe "ornamented with the figure of a bear in the bow, and a man in the stern, both nearly as large as life, both made of painted wood, and very neatly fixed to the boat." It was here, also, that the party was first supplied with the wapato root, which was greatly relished by them. It grew in great abundance upon Sauvie island, from which circumstance that island first gained the name "Wapato island." Game now proved quite abundant, and this, together with the roots purchased, proved the salvation of the men, who for many days had subsisted upon food which was far from palatable, or nourishing, and which had caused much sickness among them.

Frequent mention is made in the Journals, from the time the Dalles was reached, of a new annoyance, that of numerous fleas, which infested every Indian village. Another annoyance of a lesser degree is mentioned in describing the camp on the night of November 5, for on a sand island opposite were immense numbers of geese, swans, ducks, and other wild fowl, that made such noises during the night as to prevent sleep.

13

November 7, 1805, the voyagers obtained their first glimpse of the waters of the Pacific. The following is the description of this momentous event, given in the words of the Journals: "We had not gone far from this village when the fog cleared off, and we enjoyed the delightful prospect of the ocean—that ocean, the object of all our labors, the reward of all our anxieties. This cheering view exhilarated the spirits of all the party, who were still more delighted on hearing the distant roar of the breakers." They made their dreary camp at the foot of a bluff and spent the night trying to keep warm in the midst of a soaking rain. Day after day, the Journals record this same dreary downpour, and tell of clothing rotted and provisions spoiled. "It rained without intermission during last night and today." This becomes almost a stereotyped phrase in the record. Their camp on the north bank was just below present day McGowan station, and above Chinook Point, or Fort Columbia. From there Captain Clark visited Cape Disappointment and the ocean beach as far north as Long Beach.

They were held storm bound by the prevailing southwest gales and did not dare launch their canoes, until November 26, when the condition of the weather permitted them to cross to the south side. This move was hastened by the necessity of choosing a permanent winter camp as soon as possible. The Journals say: "It becomes necessary to decide on the spot for our winter quarters. The people of the country subsist chiefly on dried fish and roots, but of these there does not seem to be a sufficient quantity for our support, even were we able to purchase, and the extravagant prices as well as our small store of merchandise forbid us to depend on that resource. We must, therefore, rely for subsistence on our arms, and be guided in our choice of residence by the abundance of game which any particular spot may offer. The Indians say that the deer is most numerous at some distance above on the river, but that the country on the opposite side of the bay is better supplied with elk, an animal much larger and more easily killed than the deer, with a skin better fitted for clothing, and the meat of which is more nutritive during the winter, when they are both poor." They desired, moreover, to make their camp near the sea in order that they might renew their fast disappearing store of salt, and because of the hope of meeting some of the trading vessels, which were expected in about three months, and from which they might procure a stock of trinkets for use in trading on the way home.

They camped, at first on what the journalist calls "a very remarkable knob of land" projecting a mile and a half into the river and only 50 yards wide in its narrowest part. This will be easily recognized as what is now called Tongue Point. Here the party was storm bound again, not daring to launch their frail canoes, and they again suffered all the discomforts of lack of food and never-ceasing rain. However, December 7, they set out and entered what is now called Youngs bay. It was called by them Meriwether bay from the Christian name of Captain Lewis. On the banks of a river flowing into this bay, they established their permanent winter encampment. The stream is now known as the Lewis and Clark river. A stockade was erected, barracks were built, and there the expedition spent the winter of 1805-1806 without serious mishap.

Farther up, on Lewis and Clark river, where forage was abundant, were many herds of elk; it was seven miles across the peninsula to the ocean beach, and in that direction, on the Clatsop plains, were also deer and elk. Waterfowl were also plentiful and their Indian friends kept them supplied with the nourishing wapato. Where is now the popular town, Seaside, a site was chosen for the manufacture of salt. The location of Lewis and Clark's salt cairn at Seaside is now an object of never-failing interest to visitors at that resort, and that, and the site of the winter camp, old Fort Clatsop, are the only permanent memorials of the winter which the expedition spent at the mouth of the Columbia.

14

During the interval of sunny weather, several members of the party made an interesting diversion, southerly over Tillamook Head. It had been reported by the Indians that a large whale had been stranded upon the beach just south of the Head, and that natives were flocking there in order to obtain blubber and oil. January 5, 1806, a party led by Captain Clark made ready to set out from Fort Clatsop on this journey, when Sacajawea and her husband begged most earnestly to be allowed to accompany them.

This was granted, so that they could see the ocean and the big fish.

From the summit of Tillamook Head they saw the view which has delighted so many since that day, and of which the Journals say: "Here one of the most delightful views in nature presented itself. Immediately in front is the ocean, breaking in fury on the coast from the rocks of cape Disappointment as far as the eye can discern to the northwest, and against the highlands and irregular piles of rock which diversify the shore to the southeast. To this boisterous scene the Columbia, with its tributary waters, widening into bays as it approaches the ocean, and studded on both sides with the Chinook and Clatsop villages, forms a charming contrast; while immediately beneath our feet are stretched the rich prairies, enlivened by three beautiful streams, which conducted the eye to small lakes at the foot of the hills. We stopped to enjoy the romantic prospect from this place, which we distinguished by the name of Clark's Point of View."

Captain Clark gave the creek the name of Ecola, or Whale creek. The Journals constantly speak of the disposition of the Clatsop natives to pilfer, and also of their filthy habits, but on visiting a tribe located somewhat farther south, they found different conditions. It will be of interest to recount, by way of contrast, the comments relating to a visit of Captain Clark, as illustrating the hospitality, amiability, culture and cleanliness of some of the inhabitants. "Captain Clark was received with much attention. As soon as he entered, clean mats were spread, and fish, berries and roots were placed before him on small platters made of rushes. After he had eaten, the men of the other houses came and smoked with him. They all appeared much neater in their persons and diet than Indians generally are, and frequently washed their hands and faces, a ceremony by no means frequent elsewhere. . . . Towards evening it began to rain and blow very violently from the southwest, and Captain Clark therefore determined to remain during the night. When they thought his appetite had returned, an old woman presented him, in a bowl made of a light-colored horn, a kind of sirup, pleasant to the taste, and made from a species of berry common in the country, about the size of a cherry, and called by the Indians shelwell [salal]; of these berries a bread is also prepared, which being boiled with roots forms a soup, which was served in neat wooden trenchers; and this with cockles was his repast."

15

The Clatsop Indians, the neighbors of the white men during this winter, proved friendly. This disposition was manifested in many ways, but more especially by the fact that although the hunters of the expedition killed many elk and deer during the season, which animals were looked upon by the Indians as their tribal property, nevertheless, the Clatsops made no objection, neither did they demand payment. It is related that one of the white men was saved from intended robbery and murder planned by a Tillamook Indian, through timely revelation of a woman of the Clatsop tribe. The chief of the Clatsops in after years, maintained that, through his influence, he frustrated the design of the Klaskanies to attack the Lewis and Clark stockade.

The Clatsops were peaceful and industrious, never engaging in war with their neighbors, as far as the Americans could learn. They were mentally alert and far more cheerful than any of the interior tribes with whom the party had come in contact. These interior tribes were prone to sullenness and moroseness, a disposition that was likewise noticed in those met by Captain Clark on the lower Willamette on the return journey. The chief Kobaiway of the Clatsops, whose name the Americans incorrectly rendered as Comowool, was a particular favorite with all the party, and he showed his friendship for the white men in many ways. When the return trip was begun, the stockade and buildings were given to him.

The Journals refer to the Clatsop Indians in the following terms: "The Clatsops and other nations at the mouth of the Columbia have visited us with great freedom, and we have endeavored to cultivate their intimacy. . . . We found them inquisitive and loquacious, with understandings by no means deficient in acuteness, and with very retentive memories; and, though fond of feasts, and generally cheerful, never gay. Everything they observe excites their attention and inquiries. . . . To all our inquiries they answer with great intelligence, and the conversation rarely slackens, since there is a constant discussion of the events and trade and politics in the little but active circle of the Killamucks, Clatsops, Cathlamahs, Wahkiacums and Chinooks." As to the abstemiousness of these Indians, the Journals say: "We have not observed any liquor of an intoxicating quality used among these or any Indians west of the Rocky Mountains, the universal beverage being pure water." But they were excessively prone to the use of tobacco, and were fond of gambling.

The winter had been rainy, even for this region, the Journals mentioning only six clear days, and but 12 on which rain did not fall. The men suffered from rheumatism and influenza. By the month of March, 1806, game began to desert the usual feeding grounds for the hills, and this rendered the task of procuring a sufficient food supply more difficult. It had been the intention of Lewis and Clark to remain in their encampment until April, when it was expected that trading ships would begin to arrive, but scarcity of food supplies induced them to break camp, March 23, 1806, and to start the return journey.

16

Before leaving, several written documents were distributed among the more trustworthy of the natives, and one was posted up in the fort, with the expectation that at least one of them might fall into the hands of traders. The following is a quotation from this document, explaining its purpose: "The object of this last is that through the medium of some civilized person who may see the same, it may be known to the world that the party consisting of the persons whose names are hereunto annexed, and who were sent out by the government of the United States to explore the interior of the continent of North America, did penetrate the same by the way of the Missouri and Columbia rivers, to the discharge of the latter into the Pacific ocean, where they arrived on the 14th day of November, 1805, and departed the 23rd day of March, 1806, on their return to the United States, by the same route by which they had come out."

Of the written lists and memoranda, left with the Clatsops, one copy did eventually reach the United States. In the summer of 1806, Captain Hill, of the brig Lydia, entered the Columbia to trade. A copy of the document quoted above, with a rough draft made with a pen, outlining the outward route by which they intended to return, was given by one of the natives to Captain Hill, who took it with him on his voyage to Canton, whence it reached the United States.

The eastward journey was as replete with interest as that to the coast, but only those features of it will be described here that concern the Oregon Country. It was fraught with even more hardship than the westward journey. Upon leaving Fort Clatsop the party found the supply of merchandise suitable for use in trading with the Indians very much depleted, and they had to rely almost exclusively upon the prowess of the hunters for food, which at times was difficult to obtain. The voyage up the Columbia against the strong spring freshets seemed much longer than that down stream.

17

The most important event of the return journey, as far as Oregon history is concerned, was the discovery and partial exploration of the Willamette river. As already mentioned, this very considerable stream had not been observed on the voyage down the Columbia, because the boats had followed the north bank, and because the islands at the mouth of the Willamette concealed its entrance from view. On the return journey, the party again failed to observe it, but by mere chance, while they were encamped at a point opposite the upper entrance of the Sandy river, they were informed by Indians from the country contiguous to the Willamette of the existence of this stream. It had been thought at first that the whole region on the left bank of the Columbia, from the Cascades down, was drained by the Sandy river, but now it was learned that this stream was of minor importance and that some other river served this function. This news fired the leaders with the desire to investigate the accuracy of the report, and it was decided that Captain Clark should turn back long enough to undertake this.

The Indians who conveyed this information visited the camp of the Americans and told them that they dwelt upon the banks of a large river which flowed into the Columbia not far below where they were then camped. Their tribe, they said, lived near a waterfall of considerable proportions, undoubtedly the falls of the Willamette, at Oregon City. They made all this clear by drawing with a coal upon a skin. The Indians everywhere in the west seemed to be quite proficient at the art of map drawing. On this occasion, Captain Clark offered one of the Indians a burning glass as an inducement to accompany him as guide upon his quest of the new river.

18

Setting out with six of his men and the Indian guide, in a large canoe, Captain Clark proceeded along the south bank of the Columbia. He found a small village that he had not seen when descending or ascending the river, as it lay behind an island. He landed at another village that he had observed when going down the river, but now the grass houses, 24 in number, had disappeared and there was but one large double wooden house, which was still occupied.

In this vicinity his curiosity was attracted to a number, perhaps a hundred, of canoes of very small size that were piled up or scattered in different directions in the woods, and he ascertained that these were the property of natives living in the vicinity of the Cascades, who used them occasionally in getting the wapato at this place. The shallow lakes along the bottom land afforded an abundance of the edible roots of this plant, which constituted a staple article of diet and were even made use of by the local natives in trade for other articles procured from tribes more distant. The roots were detached from the mud of the lake beds by the women, who were adept at getting them, and who often used their feet for the purpose, when they could not get them with their hands. The small canoes, which would not sustain the weight of more than one person, were principally used to hold the wapatoes as they were gathered.

Captain Clark entered one of the rooms of the large house and offered several articles to the natives in exchange for wapatoes. He says the people were sulky, and refused to sell. His narrative, which follows, serves to show the ready resourcefulness of the man. He says in the Journals:

"I had a piece of port fire match in my pocket, off which I cut a piece one inch in length, and put it in the fire, and took out my pocket compass and set myself down on a mat on one side of the fire, and [also showed] a magnet which was on top of my inkstand. The port fire caught and burned vehemently, which changed the color of the fire. With the magnet I turned the needle of the compass about very briskly, which astonished and alarmed these natives. And they laid several parcels of wapato at my feet and begged me to take out the bad fire. To this I consented. At this moment the match being exhausted was of course extinguished, and I put up the magnet, &c. This measure alarmed them so much that the women and children took shelter in their beds, and behind the men. All this time a very old man was speaking with great vehemence, apparently imploring his god. I lit my pipe and gave the women the full amount [value] of the roots which they had put at my feet. They appeared somewhat pacified and I left them and proceeded on."

19

Clark soon passed on down the Columbia, observing that what the expedition had called Image Canoe island was in reality two islands. They are now jointly called Hayden island, and the Spokane, Portland and Seattle Railway's bridge, and the Interstate bridge for vehicle and pedestrian travel between Portland and Vancouver rest their piers partly on them in crossing the Columbia river. At 13 miles from the last Indian village he found the mouth of the great tributary stream which he was seeking and says: "I entered this river which the natives had informed us of, called Multnomah river, so called by the natives from a nation who reside on Wapato island, a little below the entrance of this river."

It was noted that it was one-fourth the size of the Columbia at this point, and was 500 yards wide and sufficiently deep for a man-of-war or a ship of any burden, and also that it had recently fallen 18 inches from its greatest annual height. He saw and named Mount Jefferson, and could plainly see three other great snow-covered mountains, Mount Hood, Mount Adams and Mount St. Helens. In the Journals the spelling of Multnomah sometimes appears as Moltnomar, but the former spelling is used on the map made at this time, not only to designate the stream, but also to indicate the location of the village of the "Multnomah Nations" on Wapato, the modern Sauvie island.

From the size of the stream it was surmised that the Multnomah might head as far south as 37 degrees north, in California, and it was believed to water the vast tract of country between the mountain ranges now known as the Cascades and the Coast range. From the opinion thus formed by Captain Clark of the length of the river, geographers' maps of the years following delineated this stream as of much greater length than subsequent investigation justified. On a map, published in 1814, for example, that accompanied the first London edition of the Lewis and Clark Journals, the stream is shown as heading near Great Salt lake, in present Utah, while other maps, some of them official maps of the United States, placed its source in California. The name Willamette, by which the stream has been known ever since permanent occupation of the Oregon Country by white men, is likewise derived from

an Indian local tribal name, but in early days it had various spell-
ings, and one of these that was preferred in pioneer times was
"Wallamet."

Captain Clark spent the night of April 2, 1806, in a camp on
that river. At 10 miles from the mouth he stopped at a large
house that was vacant at the time, on the east side of the river,
where he intended to sleep, but he found the building so infested
with fleas that it was decided to spend the night in the open.
Within this native dwelling, he found that the Indians had left
many of their valuables such as canoes, mats, bowls and trenchers,
"a proof indeed of the mutual respect for the property of each
other, though we have had very conclusive evidence that the property of white men is not deemed equally sacred."

20

Early the next day, a point was reached on the east side. Just
where this spot was is uncertain, but the best opinion seems to be
that it is where Portland University is now situated, within the
present city of Portland. The following is Captain Clark's account
of this part of his journey: "Early the next morning Captain Clark
proceeded up the river, which during the night had fallen about
five inches. At the distance of two miles he came to the center of
a bend under the highlands on the right side, from which its
course, as far as could be discerned, was to the east of southeast.
At this place the Multnomah is 500 yards wide, and for half that
distance across a cord of five fathoms would not reach the bottom.
It appears to be washing away its banks, and has more sand bars
and willow points than the Columbia. Its regular, gentle current,
the depth, smoothness and uniformity with which it rolls its vast
body of water, prove that its supplies are at once distant and regular; nor, judging from its appearance and courses, is it rash to
believe that the Multnomah and its tributary streams water the
vast extent of country between the western mountains and those
of the sea coast, as far, perhaps as the gulf of California."

On returning the same day to the camp on the Columbia at the
mouth of the Sandy river, a stop was again made at the villages,
and, at the one where his guide lived, an old Indian gave the
names of the various tribes of the Willamette valley and assisted
Captain Clark in the preparation of a sketch map on which these
tribes are marked. The map itself shows, however, that it was

"given by several different tribes of Indians," and doubtless was the result of much inquiry on his part. It is the first map on which the Multnomah or Willamette river is shown. The numerous tribes on Wapato island and along the course of the river are named, but no tribe having the name Willamette is indicated, nor do the Journals reveal knowledge on the part of Lewis and Clark of any tribe of that name.

21

The return trip of the expedition through the valley of the Columbia and over the Bitter Root mountains was greatly assisted by the Nez Perce's, who again proved themselves to be faithful friends. It was at all times the policy of Lewis and Clark to cultivate the friendship of the Indian nations through whose territory they passed, and not only the Nez Perce's were thus won over, but also the Mandans, Sioux, Shoshones, Walla Wallas, Wascos, Chinooks, Tillamooks and Clatsops. It is a noteworthy fact that in all the contacts of this expedition with the red men there was but one instance of the killing of an Indian, and that seemed to be almost unavoidable.

The circumstances were as follows: While in the Blackfeet country on the return eastward, Lewis and three of his men fell in with a party of natives who attempted to seize their weapons and make off with their horses. In order to recover the horses, which were at the time invaluable to them, and upon which, in fact, their very lives depended, it was necessary to kill two of the thieves.

When the expedition reached the Mandan villages, on the Missouri, arrangements were made to send a party of leading Indians of that locality to visit the President, at Washington. It was here also that John Colter, one of the most reliable and efficient members of the expedition, got leave to join two Illinois hunters who were on their way up the river on a fur trading and hunting enterprise. Colter was paid off, and the Journals show that the leaders parted from him with regret. His subsequent career as a hunter and trapper was colorful and his life in the far west was full of adventure.

Settlers on the Missouri were surprised to see passing down the river 30 ragged men with faces bronzed to the color of Indians. When they learned who the voyagers were, there were cheers of welcome. On September 23, 1806, the expedition landed at St. Louis, and the important exploring expedition was completed.

Captain Lewis was later appointed governor of Louisiana Territory. He died in Tennessee while en route to visit the capital city. Captain Clark settled at St. Louis and there served as territorial governor of Missouri, 1813-20, and was superintendent of Indian affairs at St. Louis from 1822 until the time of his death, 1838, at the age of 69.

Jefferson had been anxious to have the Journals printed as soon as possible. Arrangements were made with a Philadelphia firm for the publication of the work, and a prospectus was circulated asking subscriptions. Lewis was on his way on horseback from St. Louis to Washington and Philadelphia where he was to edit the Journals. He died at a settler's house where he stopped for the night some 60 miles from Nashville, Tennessee, and a report that he had committed suicide was generally accepted, but there is reason to believe he was murdered for money. Neither of these men received the recognition from their fellow countrymen that their services merited, and it is doubtful if even at the present time the importance of their achievement is sufficiently appreciated.

Upon this arduous enterprise, day by day careful and minute records were kept, as Jefferson had expressly directed. The leaders were to keep Journals, and the men were also to be encouraged to make notes. Besides the Journals and field notes kept by Lewis and Clark, four sergeants and at least one private, members of their party, kept note books. The originals of most of the Lewis and Clark records are preserved, but although Jefferson urged their early publication, and the first official edition was published, 1814, they were not printed entire until a century after they were written. Extensive and important portions, often more or less inaccurate, were, however, printed and reprinted in various editions in the meantime.

CHAPTER XI

FUR TRADE PUSHES WESTWARD

1

OREGON HISTORY is concerned with the approach of the fur hunter from Canada, as well as from the United States, and from California, as well as by more direct routes from the east. For convenience, the forward movement may be presented without strict regard to time sequence. One of the purposes in sending out the Lewis and Clark expedition was to inquire into the possibility of diverting the fur trade to the United States. With this in view, a preliminary report was made to the President, written at the Mandan villages while the expedition was wintering there, on the outward journey. This report was published. Additional information, acquired on the remaining part of the exploring trip was given out on the return to St. Louis. Manuel Lisa, a trader, of that city, seems to have been the first to make practical use of the reports, for, in the spring of 1807, he went by boat upon an adventurous and successful trading expedition up the Missouri and the Yellowstone, to the mouth of the Big Horn river.

There is meager evidence that another party of Americans (whether associated with Lisa's enterprise, or not, does not appear), were actually over the divide, and therefore in the Oregon Country, in that same summer, 1807. All that is at present known about this party comes from two sources, both connected with the visit to this region in that year of David Thompson, advance agent of the North West Company, of whom there is much to say in the following pages.

The Kootenai Indians, who lived in the vicinity of the northern tip of the modern state of Idaho, told Thompson, according to an entry in his "Narrative of the Expedition to the Kootenae," under date August 13, 1807, that about three weeks previously some 42 Americans had arrived, two of whom were men who had been with the Lewis and Clark expedition. Thompson indicated that this would seriously interfere with the plans of the North West Company to locate in that region. He said the Americans had established a military post at the confluence of the two most southern and considerable branches of the Columbia, and were preparing to locate a small advance post, lower down the river. Recent investigation has brought to light a letter in the Public Records

Office, London, purporting to be from Lieut. Jeremy Pinch, dated September 29, 1807, at "Politito palton lake." The letter, if genuine, was intended for David Thompson, and after receipt was forwarded to London by him, together with a copy of his own letter replying to the same, dated December 26, 1807. In Pinch's letter is a threat to expel British traders, in case they fail to obey American regulations; and there is a request not to supply Indians with firearms; a complaint, also, that certain Indians, whom the writer calls "Pilchenees," together with bloodthirsty allies, had attacked friendly "Polititopalton" Indians and had wounded one of Pinch's soldiers. Thompson's answer disclaimed authority to decide questions of boundary and jurisdiction, and evaded commitment as to a recognition of the claims or authority of Pinch.

2

Nothing more is known of this party. Manuel Lisa is said to have built a fort in that same year, at the confluence of the Big Horn and Yellowstone rivers, but that place is many miles east of the continental divide. It is possible that a part or all, of his men went as far as Palouse lake, or Coeur d'Alene lake, either of which may be the lake referred to in the correspondence, but heretofore there has been no general knowledge of that fact. The name Jeremy Pinch has not been identified in connection with the fur trade, and no officer of that name is found in the army lists. The narrative and the letters, being taken at face value, and, assuming Pinch to have really been an army officer with authority, as claimed, it would appear that the United States may have attempted to assume jurisdiction beyond the mountains at this early date, and moreover that the Pinch party was the first to enter the Oregon Country, overland, after Lewis and Clark, a distinction that has been accorded to David Thompson, himself.

3

We learn from a letter of the secretary of Hudson's Bay Company, dated February 23, 1846, on file in the British Foreign Office, that it was represented that Thompson wintered in the Kootenai country, on the upper waters of the Columbia, 1806 or 1807, and that James McMillan, partner of that company, wintered there, 1808. McMillan stated in a separate letter that clerks of the company visited the Kootenai some years before the establishment of a regular trading post; and that John Stuart, another

partner of the company, corroborates this statement, asserting
that the visits alluded to took place before the year 1800.

In 1807, two military escorts set out from St. Louis to go up the
Missouri river, the one under the command of Lieut. Joseph Kimball, and the other under Ensign Nathaniel Pryor, who had been a
sergeant in the Lewis and Clark expedition. These escort parties
set out together, and traders took advantage of the protection
thus afforded and went up the river at the same time. Pryor's
party was entrusted with the responsible duty of escorting to his
tribe, the Mandan chief, Shakaka, or Gros Blanc, otherwise Big
White. This chief had been induced by Lewis and Clark to accompany them to Washington to visit President Jefferson, and was
now returning to his people. The escort party under Lieutenant
Kimball had a similar duty to perform with reference to a party
of 18 men and women and six children of the Sioux tribe, a deputation that had visited St. Louis. The objects were not accomplished, owing to the hostility of the tribes through whose domains it was necessary to pass. None of these early expeditions,
except perhaps that of Pinch, crossed the continental divide and
thus reached the Oregon Country, but their operations along the
Missouri and its tributaries made the beginning that led the way.

4

The Lisa party of 1807, already mentioned, deserves further
space, although it did not go as far as the Oregon Country. It comprised some 42 men, including three that had been with Lewis and
Clark. Another remarkable member of that expedition, Colter,
was recruited on the way up the Missouri, when he was met as he
was paddling alone, down stream, on his way to civilization after a
year's stay in the upper country. At this time the Aricaras were
at war with the Mandans and were averse to letting the whites go
through, as they objected to having supplies sold in the enemy
country. After serious opposition, a compromise was effected and
Lisa was allowed to proceed, upon confiscation of a considerable
part of his outfit. The Big Horn was reached, in due course, and
Colter was sent from there to inform the Crow nation, and other
tribes, of the location of the new trading post, which Lisa erected,
and which later was known as Fort Raymond.

Colter's remarkable journey, while on this errand, is one of
the greatest feats in the annals of the west. He made an extensive
circle, on foot, alone and in the rigorous winter season, taking in

part of Yellowstone park, Jackson lake, upper Green river, and the South Pass, a distance of not less than 500 miles. Lisa returned, leaving in the late summer of 1808, and then he became active at St. Louis during the next winter, organizing a new and much larger company, called St. Louis Missouri Fur Company, which successfully escorted Big White and the Mandans to their people. This was the largest trading expedition so far assembled, and it had, in its active management and partners, many of the ablest and most experienced men of the west. At one time it had over 200 enlisted militiamen and rifle men in the organization. The force was sufficient to insure passage through the hostile districts and to establish a number of fur trading posts east of the Rocky mountain range.

It was during these operations that a group of hardy men, picked for quality and bravery, was organized to establish a western outpost close to the Rocky mountain range, in the hostile Blackfcct country. The party was under Pierre Menard, as company manager, with Maj. Andrew Henry, as field captain, and with Colter, as guide. They left Fort Mandan for Three Forks, on the Missouri, March, 1810, with what seemed an adequate force of men, well mounted and experienced in the west, and they built a stockade at Three Forks. But, the trapping for beaver in the vicinity was dangerous in the extreme, and many of the party were waylaid and killed. The place became untenable. Colter, after a thrilling escape from the Indians, successfully returned to the settlements with a companion, by making a dug-out and descending the river. Major Henry held on for a while with a small force, then retreated southward and led his men up the Madison and across the continental divide to a small branch of Snake river, afterward called Henry's fork. This was a tributary of the Columbia, and here he built a small post, where he spent the winter of 1810, regarded as the first American location west of the Rocky mountains, unless, of course, Lieutenant Pinch had already built such an establishment.

5

It will not be practicable to review in detail the history of the great fur companies, British and American, or to chronicle the stirring adventures of the men in their service who were the explorers and the pathfinders of the far west. But there is a period of

Oregon history so closely connected with the fortunes of some of them that in order to trace the beginnings of Oregon settlements and government a preliminary survey of these companies becomes essential.

The St. Lawrence river and the great lakes formed a natural route through which, and over a short portage at the western end of Lake Superior, the waterways to the westward and northward were readily reached. Montreal, therefore, from the first, was the headquarters for the Indian trade, and thus it was that the fur traders, following the numerous streams and lakes in Canada, were already far west with their operations when the dealers and trappers of the United States first became active in the Rocky mountain region and beyond. Discovery and exploration in Canadian western territory was far advanced before the district further south became known to the civilized world. The American Revolution operated to delay exploration and fur trading from the American colonies, both because of the hostility of the Mississippi valley Indians at that period, and the activity of the British military forces. During the war, moreover, Great Britain secured a firm foothold upon the northern frontier, and, even after the treaty of peace was signed, British military forces continued for a considerable time to maintain forts upon the Great lakes, contrary to the provisions of that instrument.

French Canadian trappers had long kept an intimate contact with the northwestern tribes. Having a certain sympathy for the Indian point of view, and adapting themselves rapidly to Indian methods, they not infrequently took to themselves native wives and lived according to customs of the tribes, learning the language and allowing their children to grow up as Indians. This trait, or adaptability, had given the Frenchman a familiar influence that was not easily counteracted by the Scotch and English traders, who, indeed, did not in the early period lead in extending the western frontier. The English did not venture as far as the French Canadian forts upon the Saskatchewan until the year 1771.

The fur trade, however, was already being prosecuted with great vigor by the British interests in the Canadian northwest before Lewis and Clark made their historic journey to the mouth of the Columbia; and, as already shown in these pages, the news that reached Jefferson of British activities had a direct effect in hastening that expedition. Both British and Americans were approaching the Rocky mountains. When Lewis and Clark returned from Oregon to the upper Missouri, they met hunters named Dickson and Hancock, who had been hunting on the Yellowstone, and who had spent the previous winter in company with another, named Ceautoin, in the Tetons. Two traders of the North West Company had just been killed by Indians, and another employee of that company, Charles Mackenzie, was then reported to be hunting or trapping in the district.

6

The two great British companies come directly into Oregon history. The original charter of the Hudson's Bay Company was granted by Charles II, of England, May 2, 1670. It will be noted that this was a century before the war with France that resulted in British control of Canada. Until this change of sovereignty, that British company had confined its operations to British territory, in the vicinity of Hudson bay, north of the French Canadian provinces, a district then known as Rupert's Land. Broad powers of an exclusive character were conferred by the royal charter, not only as respects trade and exploration, but also in the government of its servants and of the inhabitants of the country to which the grant applied.

The charter authorized the members of the company to hold court, "to make, ordain and constitute such and so many reasonable laws, constitutions, orders and ordinances" as should seem necessary and convenient for the good government "of the said company, and of all governors of colonies, forts and plantations, factors, masters, mariners and other officers employed or to be employed in any of the territories and lands aforesaid, and any of their voyages;" and also to revoke or alter their own enactments. It provided, furthermore, that they "shall and may lawfully impose, ordain, limit and provide such pains, penalties and punishments upon all offenders, contrary to such laws, constitutions, orders and ordinances, or any of them," and levy and impose fines and amerciaments. There was also granted the right to send ships of war, men or ammunitions, to choose commanders and officers over them, and to give them power and authority to continue or make peace or war, "with any prince or people whatsoever that are not Christians," and to make reprisals, build defences, and to man and equip them.

In fact, legislative, judicial and executive governmental powers were vested in the company in the vast district that was vaguely described in the charter, with "the whole and entire" trade and traffic to and from all havens, bays, creeks, rivers, lakes and seas into which they shall find entrance or passage by water or land out of the territories, limits, or places" described in the charter. As the monopoly of the East India Company in Asia, and that of the South Sea Company upon the Pacific, hampered independent traders along the recently rediscovered west coast of North America, and interfered with the exchange of furs for Chinese commodities, so likewise the grant to the Hudson's Bay Company interfered with inland trade by reason of its monopolistic provisions.

This grant, broad as were its provisions, did not in express words embrace the regions of the Rocky mountains or the Pacific west, that country being unknown at the time the royal charter was given, but apparently it applied to the region watered by streams flowing into Hudson bay, rather than to more remote territory, as might likewise be inferred from the title of the company. Rival traders began, therefore, to dispute the monopoly in the west, and thus, before the close of the 18th century, the profits of the fur trade having by this time become attractive, men of independence and enterprise who traded in and out of Montreal not only were pressing by canoe and paddle toward the western side of the continent, but they even turned to the north and east and dared to intrude into the particular province of the Hudson's Bay Company in Rupert's Land. Till this time, the big company had been sluggish and inert, but now competition, and trespass upon its preserves, incited it to reach out into new fields in the west.

7

The history of the North West Company was altogether different. Unlike the Hudson's Bay Company, it was purely a Canadian enterprise, growing out of earlier independent fur trading organizations. In its original form nine of the principal trading interests of Canada entered into an agreement, 1779, to divide territory and business, and this plan proved so successful after a one-year trial that the arrangement was renewed, for a further period of three years. Success was impaired, however, by failure of some of the parties to keep the agreement in good faith, and the plan was therefore abandoned at the end of two years. However, as the soundness of the principle was recognized in spite of failure, a third attempt at consolidation was made, 1783-84, largely through the influence of merchants at Montreal, who much preferred to have the fur business pass through their hands, rather than to have it controlled at Hudson bay. This time the effort was a success, and the real beginning of the North West Company resulted. It was not an incorporated company, but it gathered under the direction of responsible partners most of the enterprising and adventurous men of the trade. Nevertheless, it did not succeed in associating all of the independents, and its operations were sometimes opposed by active rivals with force and violence. For example, John Ross, one of the partners, was murdered, 1786, and this was reported to have occurred in a scuffle with the followers of Peter Pond, a dissatisfied independent who believed the North West Company had not treated him fairly. Pond is reported to have wearied of the contest and to have sold out his shares, 1790, when he retired to the United States, leaving a deep impress on the fur trade of the west. He was an adventurer of no mean attainments. His early travels and maps, and the theory he formulated as to the Athabasca drainage system, in all probability influenced Alexander Mackenzie in setting out on his overland journey to the Pacific coast.

This North West Company has a place in the Oregon history of the early years of the 19th century, not only because of its acquisition of the Astor interests on the Columbia river, but also by reason of the far-reaching effect which its competition had upon the methods and policies of the older Hudson's Bay Company, and, consequently, upon the whole fur trade and the fate of the entire region wherein that trade was plied.

8

Prior to the advent of the North West Company, the "gentlemen adventurers" of the Hudson's Bay Company had their trading posts as far west as Fort Cumberland on the Saskatchewan river, as established by Samuel Hearne, 1774. This great Hudson's Bay Company explorer already had found the Arctic ocean at the mouth of Coppermine river, 1771, and had discovered Great Slave lake. Hendry, an earlier Hudson's Bay Company explorer, had made the first authenticated visit of a white man to Lake Winnipeg from Hudson bay, 1754-55, and had gone as far as Red Deer river, in the vicinity of the present city of Calgary, where he came in contact with the Blackfeet Indians, as has been mentioned. David Thompson, then one of Hudson's Bay Company's active men, spent the winter of 1787-88 at Manchester House, and the following winter at Hudson's House, posts of the company on the Saskatchewan and its tributaries.

Hudson's Bay Company began dealing on the Missouri, about the year 1793. It suffered the disadvantage of non-resident ownership, but was stimulated to greater endeavor by the increasing competition. It had the advantage of ample capital and of chartered privilege, but this was offset by the daring and enterprise of the rival company. Hudson's Bay Company factories were located at convenient stations, generally near the mouth of streams, where it would be easy for the Indians to come with their peltries for sale. The plan of the Northwesters was rather to carry trade to the very lodges and hunting grounds of the natives.

9

The North West Company was again reorganized in 1787, with new partners and a different distribution of shares, and some of the retiring partners projected still another company, which came to be known as the X Y Company. Alexander Mackenzie's arrangement with the old Northwesters expiring, 1799, that great explorer and leader went to England, and was succeeded in his former place by Roderick Mackenzie. Soon after his arrival at London, Alexander Mackenzie published the account of his explorations, and was honored with knighthood. His book awakened widespread interest among the people of the parent country, and its success encouraged him to launch an ambitious scheme, elsewhere mentioned in these pages, for combining fur trade and fishing interests and locating trading posts, including subordinate stations on the Columbia, at Nootka, and other places on the coast. He did not succeed in organizing his company, but he did place himself at the head of the new North West Company (the X Y Company), and so succeeded in making himself a formidable rival for a time to the concern with which he had been allied.

10

War between the companies became intense. Resort was had to every questionable method. Intoxicating liquor, the disastrous effects of which on the aboriginal population had been foreseen by the early organizers, was again introduced among the Indians as a means of gaining favor. Hudson's Bay Company's legal jurisdiction was openly defied, and, attempts being made by that company to assert rights independent of the Canadian courts, it was discovered that its powers had been as yet but imperfectly determined, and were of doubtful character. Compromise between the two North West companies was effected, July, 1804, leaving unsettled, however, the war upon Hudson's Bay Company.

In the autumn of that year, development of trade with tribes on the Missouri was begun by the Northwesters, and a party sent out from the Assiniboine river station, seeking a new locality in which it might trade without contravening the inter-company arrangement as to competitive territory, quietly stole away to the southward and passed the winter in the Mandan villages, which were reached in November, 1804. The Lewis and Clark expedition was already there, and the Canadian leader, Francois Antoine Larocque, did not question the claim of the Americans that the region formed part of the territory of Louisiana, purchased in the preceding year by the United States. This Canadian party was none too successful in trade, and the field was not particularly attractive, for it was found that the tribes in this section were prosperous and independent, and were too nearly self-sustaining to hunt beaver for the advantage of the whites.

11

One of the most enterprising employees of the North West Company was the geographer and surveyor, David Thompson, already mentioned. Early in life he had been a Hudson's Bay Company man. His was the honor of being the first white man to see the entire Columbia river from source to mouth. It was in the year 1811 that he performed this feat, but he had already carried out the instructions of the North West Company in exploring the district near the headwaters of that stream, and had established trading places and organized trade with the tribes in that vicinity. A few words about the man will be of interest here.

English by birth, he was sent to a charity school in London, and at 15 years of age he began service as an apprentice with Hudson's Bay Company, at Fort Churchill and at York Factory. He showed great aptitude, and not only discharged the duties required of him in the fur trade, but studied practical methods of surveying and astronomy, and became a skilled geographer and explorer, as well as a successful trader. After 13 years with the Hudson's Bay

Company, in which he covered in his travels much of the British territory east of the Rocky mountains, he withdrew and joined the North West Company, 1797.

Thompson was in charge of the first expedition sent out by the North West Company to cross the Rocky mountains with a view to establishing trading posts; and, taking his wife and family with him, he went through the Canadian part of the range over a pass, afterwards known as the Howse Pass, named after Joseph Howse, who was an employee of the Hudson's Bay Company. Thompson established first, Kootenay House, near Lake Windemere, 1807. The following year he came to the same general district again by descending Kootenai river, dealing with the Flatheads in the vicinity of present Bonner's Ferry, Idaho, and extending his journey to Kootenai lake. The next season, 1809, found him at Rainy lake, and in the vicinity of present Winnipeg and Edmonton. In that year, also, he established Kullyspell House, at Sheepherder's Point on the north shore of Pend d'Oreille lake, near the mouth of Clark's fork, and passed through that lake; he also established Saleesh House, on a prairie on Clark's fork, now within the state of Montana.

12

In the spring, following, he tried the descent of Pend d'Oreille river to Box canyon, and stopped with Finan McDonald, one of his assistants, at Kullyspell House, where they had visits from the various tribes of Indians in that region. Thompson again went eastward, across the mountains, in that year, 1810, and this time he returned by way of the Athabasca Pass, reaching the Columbia river, January, 1811. The Athabasca Pass afterward was the one generally used by the Canadian fur traders. For his winter quarters he chose a place on the Columbia called Boat Encampment, which afterward became a place of importance on the route of the fur traders' travel across the mountains.

Later, in the same year, Thompson crossed from the source of the Columbia to Kootenai river, which he descended, until he reached the trail leading to Clark's fork. Thence he passed Saleesh House and Lake Pend d'Oreille, a new post at Spokane House, that had just been established by McDonald, about eight miles from the present city of Spokane; and later he reached Kettle Falls on Columbia river in the eastern part of present Washington state.

Here, he began his famous descent of the Columbia, July 3, 1811, after stopping long enough to build a canoe, sufficiently large to carry himself and his crew of Indians and Canadian voyageurs. As a warning to Americans and Hudson's Bay men, he posted a notice at a place near the mouth of Snake, or Shawpatin river, as follows:

"Know hereby that this country is claimed by Great Britain as a part of its territories, and that the North West Company of Merchants from Canada, finding the factory for this people inconvenient for them, do hereby intend to erect a factory in this place for the commerce of the country around.

D. Thompson.
Junction of the Shawpatin River
with the Columbia, July 9th, 1811."

He was disappointed on arriving at the mouth of the great river July 15, 1811, to find the American Fort Astor already established and occupied. After a brief stay, he began his return, as will be described in our account of the Fort Astor story. It remains to be said that Thompson completed his survey of the remaining part of the Columbia, and visited various points in the upper country, and then, after spending the winter of 1811-12 at Saleesh House, he left for Montreal in the spring.

Thompson kept elaborate journals throughout his many years in the west. In these he entered, no matter what the fatigue or excitement of the day, a full chronicle of events, geographic and topographic data, courses and distances, and latitude and longitude. Considering the difficulties of keeping such records while carrying on his rapid and arduous journey, through new country, by way of mountain streams, or difficult mountain trails, or no trails at all, his record in this respect may be considered remarkable. His fearless courage sustained him through long years of adventurous travel and through many perils. He devoted much of his time during the next two years to the preparation of his map. He did not return to the far west, and he died at Longuenil, opposite Montreal, 1857, at the age of 86 years.

It should be added that while Thompson was at Saleesh House, late in November, 1811, there arrived a large party of Northwesters, one of whom, John George McTavish, was a partner. Another of the party was James McMillan, and altogether there were 15

men and 10 horses. The party had come through from Rainy lake,
and via Kootenay House to Saleesh House, with goods and supplies.
Evidently, the North West Company meant to retain possession
and to keep out rival fur traders, for McMillan remained with
Finan McDonald at Saleesh, while McTavish located at Spokane
House.

The Thompson map, which alone would make his fame secure,
was completed in 1813 and 1814. It was for the North West Company, "from actual survey during years 1792 to 1812." It records
or locates 78 posts of that company, which shows how trade had
been stimulated by competition. The map, in after years, served
to support the British claims in the boundary dispute with the
United States. And it may be added that an offer of Thompson to
sell a copy of the map to the United States, 1845, was not accepted
by the American secretary of state.

13

To justify its right, the North West Company claimed to be the
legitimate successor of the French trappers, but recognizing the
insecurity of its position as long as the Hudson's Bay Company's
exclusive chartered privileges were asserted, it began as early as
1808 to attempt to procure for itself from the British authorities
a definite charter, which would not only warrant its making the
necessary outlays to establish a chain of posts with transportation
facilities, which it contemplated establishing from the Canadian
settlements westward to the mouth of the Columbia, but also
would grant it exclusive privileges in the western territory.

In addressing the British Board of Trade by petition for this
purpose, it represented that an irrevocable and unlimited license
from Hudson's Bay Company was, if that company had the legal
right to grant or refuse such a license, a necessity for its proposed plan. It also needed similar licenses and trading privileges
from the East India and South Sea companies, to barter goods in
China direct. The petitioners took note of the explorations of Lewis
and Clark, and the political aspect of the venture was urged in the
petition, in a statement that unless the British interests acted
promptly there was likelihood that the Americans would claim the
country from the Spanish boundary northward as far as latitude
50 degrees, by right of occupation. The "Columbia or Oregon"
river is mentioned in these documents.

14

Nothing came of this effort, but, 1811, a charter of incorporation was sought from the crown, to run for a period of 21 years, and to include the grant of exclusive privileges of trade in the vast region on the Pacific slope. The British Board of Trade, in the negotiations, agreed that the issue was important to national interests, but suggested certain modifications of the proposed charter, among others a provision that it should be revocable on three years' notice. Answering this, 1812, the company pointed out the hazards of the enterprise, which could hardly hope to establish itself in a single season, or without great outlay, and which would be unlikely to recompense its owners immediately; and, as an alternative, proposed that the charter be made terminable at the end of five, instead of three years. There are references to the opposition of the American company already on the ground, and allusion to the political value of the move. But the new war between the United States and Great Britain caused delay in these negotiations, and while they were still pending events at Astoria, recounted in another chapter, resulted in acquisition by the Northwesters of the Astor interests.

15

Now, a new force made itself felt,—the colonization scheme devised by the altruist Lord Selkirk, which, though it had its locus in the valley of the Red River of the North, illustrates the far-reaching effects of remote events on history, for from the clash of interests growing out of the attempt at permanent settlements of that section, there arose such a state of affairs that even parliament began to appreciate the necessity of a definition of the rights of the trading companies, and in the end the Hudson's Bay Company absorbed and succeeded the Northwesters in Oregon. Selkirk first fortified himself with advice of eminent counsel, to the effect that the Hudson's Bay Company had the right to sell portions of its territory for the purpose of settlement, and then proceeded to obtain control of sufficient stock of that company to insure the sale to him of the land he desired. So successful was he that the Hudson's Bay Company shareholders voted overwhelmingly, May, 1811, in favor of the sale of a tract of some 110,000 square miles lying across the present boundary line between Canada and the United States.

The Northwesters, regarding this as a blow at their fur trade, and scenting, perhaps, a plan to erect an agricultural barrier against their fur trade expansion, and, moreover, sharing in large measure the traditional contempt of the free adventurer for the plodding husbandman, were openly hostile from the beginning. But settlers began to arrive late in 1812. By January, 1814, we find the governor of the colony issuing a proclamation prohibiting exports of food from the colony, except by special license, and denying provisions to the western posts of the North West Company.

The retaliatory scheme of the Northwesters seems to have been to coax away as many as possible of the colonists, and then to make it so disagreeable for the remainder that they would be glad to escape from the country. Pitched battles were fought, in one of which, at Seven Oaks, June 18, 1816, the settlers were defeated, 20 of their number, including Governor Semple, of the Hudson's Bay Company, being killed. Selkirk reinforced himself by adding a number of discharged soldiers to his party of settlers, and then boldly assumed control. A prolonged series of charges and counter-charges followed, and the courts were appealed to by both parties; but jurisdictional questions had not yet been settled in that forma-tive period, and the trials, civil and criminal, came to little. In some instances defendants were acquitted and in others sentences were imposed, never to be executed.

Notwithstanding these, and other, disturbances which need not be recounted here, since they bear only indirectly on the history of the region with which we are dealing, the fur trade on the whole was active. However, there were far-sighted individuals among officials of both the Northwesters and the Hudson's Bay Company who realized that competition would in time become ruinous, if it had not already reached that stage. By the autumn of 1819 the Northwesters were eager for a consolidation. The prac-tice of furnishing the Indians with intoxicants, and of taking fur-bearing animals without regard to sex, and also of tolerating, if not encouraging, summer trapping, seemed likely to strip the country of its most valuable resource. The death of both Selkirk and Alexander Mackenzie came in 1820. The North West Com-pany's term was approaching an end, but the partners were re-solved to renew their agreement for another period, from 1822 until 1832. While this arrangement was pending, however, negotiations were entered into in London by Simon McGillivray, one of the North West partners, seemingly at first without official authority from the other partners, for a union with the Hudson's Bay Company. Dr. John McLoughlin, soon after to be a great figure in the Oregon Country, was present as a representative of some of the partners.

16

The outcome of the negotiations was an agreement to unite the concerns, under date March 26, 1821. The colonial office and parliament had been stirred by public reports of conditions in North America, and an act of parliament was passed, July 2, 1821, by which, after a long preamble, in which these evils were set forth and lamented, it was provided that the two companies should be united. The charter of Hudson's Bay Company should be amended, and the structure of the older company was to be retained. The license was for a period of 21 years and, while preserving all monopolistic and exclusive chartered rights, and affirming jurisdiction of the latter company, the charter conferred exclusive privilege of trading in all the region northward and westward of the territories of the United States, not incorporated in any British province or belonging to the dominion of any other country. It was stipulated that in that portion of America west of the Rocky mountains, which, according to the convention of 1818 between the governments, was to remain in joint occupancy, privileges of trade were not to be monopolized to the exclusion of American citizens. The act expressly confirmed the right of Hudson's Bay Company in the administration of justice, particularly as applied to British subjects in the regions of the fur trading enterprise. Pursuant to the act, a charter was issued, December 5, 1821, and the controversy was settled for a period of 21 years.

It remains to be said that the consolidation of the two companies proved highly successful and the business was carried on, during the license period, without serious competition in the Oregon Country. At the end of the first term, a similar license was granted, extending the privilege for a second term of 21 years. So, until 1859, the Hudson's Bay Company was a great factor in the history of the far west, and it was not until the waning of the fur trade after the latter date that that region became free for all;

and it was not until 1869 that the company finally surrendered its grant for a pecuniary consideration paid by the Canadian government. It maintains to this day, Canadian trading posts, and it still owns land in the Canadian provinces. Its part in Oregon history during the period of the first pioneer settlements and while both Great Britain and the United States were claiming title to the country was most important.

17

It will be desirable to recur again briefly to the operations of the American fur traders east of the Rocky mountains. It was found necessary to abandon the posts on the upper Missouri river, 1812, and at about this time the price of beaver declined from four dollars to two dollars and a half a pound. Reorganization of the St. Louis Missouri Fur Company was accomplished, January, 1812, almost two months before its term expired, and additional capital was invested in it. The war of 1812 interrupted progress in the Missouri river region, as it did on the Pacific coast, and gave Lisa opportunity to perform services for the United States. As sub-agent for the Missouri river tribes above Kansas, he was successful in controlling the Indians. He organized war expeditions against some of the tribes on the Mississippi, who were allies of the British, and he secured pledges of friendship from those on the Missouri. In the spring of 1815, he returned with 43 chiefs and head men, authorized to make treaties of friendship and alliance with the United States.

The fur company was again reorganized in 1819, but Lisa died in 1820, and Joshua Pilcher succeeded to the management. This man was a worthy successor to Lisa in many ways, but he was unable to make a profit, and found it necessary to take competition into account. He was a tireless traveller and made a tour of the northwest that was quite remarkable even for that time. Setting out, 1828, from the Bear river country with nine men, he went to the northwest to explore the region of the Columbia river, to ascertain its attractions and capabilities for trade. After spending the winter at Flathead lake he lost all his horses by the acts of bands of thieving Indians. With only one man of his original party, but accompanied by a British trader, he then travelled to Fort Colville on the upper Columbia. Here he accepted the hospitality of the Hudson's Bay Company and its offer of the protection of the company's express. He accompanied it on a circuitous journey by way of the Athabasca, the Saskatchewan, Cumberland House, Moose lake and the Selkirk Red River settlements to the Mandan villages; and thence made his way to St. Louis, where he arrived after nearly three years' absence from the headquarters of the company. About this time, the St. Louis Missouri Fur Company ceased to exist. Pilcher is believed to have obtained, by his long journey, a more intimate knowledge of Hudson's Bay Company posts than was then held by any other American.

18

Gen. William H. Ashley is another notable figure in the trade. He had been a partner of Maj. Andrew Henry, and was the organizer of an active company which, 1824, abandoned the Missouri river region and turned to the mountain region further to the southwest. He began the regular use of the South Pass to reach the tributaries of the great rivers whose sources were west of that pass. He made a fortune, sold out and was three times elected to Congress, where he was considered an authority on Indian affairs.

When, in his operations on the Missouri river, March, 1832, General Ashley was involved in war with hostile Aricaras, he found three young men of his company especially reliable. These were Jedediah S. Smith, David E. Jackson and William L. Sublette, who all became famous for skill and bravery in the annals of the west. Smith was a young, well educated New Yorker, and this was his first experience among the Indians. He volunteered as the bearer of an important message from Ashley to Major Henry, then on the Yellowstone, and managed to get through in safety. This was the beginning of his remarkable career. The three young men organized the firm Jackson, Smith and Sublette, 1826, and bought Ashley's interests in his company. The new organization was generally called Rocky Mountain Fur Company.

19

In that same year, Smith with a party of his men left his partners at the rendezvous, near Great Salt lake, took a southerly course by Utah lake and thence southwesterly across the desert country until he reached the neighborhood of San Diego, after about two months of severe travel through a region never before seen by white men. At San Diego, the Spanish authorities were

none too friendly, but he obtained permission to buy supplies for
a return journey. However, after penetrating some distance into
the interior, he turned his course northward, paralleling the coast.
Deep snows frustrated his attempts to cross the Sierras. He finally
located all but two of his men in a camp, where they were to
await his return, and, taking the two, set out again, May, 1827,
determined to find a crossing over the mountains and deserts to
the rendezvous of the fur traders.

This incredible feat was accomplished. The journey through the
mountains took about eight days, and the desert journey to the
southern extremity of Great Salt lake consumed 20 more. Only two
of his animals survived the latter stage, during which the sufferings of the men, as well as of the animals, was intense.

He started almost immediately afterward to rejoin his men, in
California, going by his original southwesterly course, but this
time being waylaid by the Mojave Indians. They had been peaceable enough on the first trip, but were now incited against him
by the California authorities. The Indians took him by surprise,
killed 10 of his party of 18, and captured all of his property. His
adventures for a time from this point have to do with the inhospi-
tality of local alcaldes and Mexican governors, who first cast him
into prison, and then banished him, designating the route by
which he must leave the country.

He deviated from the way he was commanded to follow, and
proceeded up the Sacramento river, spending the winter on one
of its branches, which from this circumstance derived its name,
American fork. In April, 1828, finding difficulties in the way of
returning eastward, he turned northward, but soon directed his
course through the mountains to the coast. Fortunately for history, it happened that there was with him as a member of the
party one Harrison G. Rogers. This man kept a journal, from
which, together with Smith's own records, it is possible to recon-
struct a vivid account of the journey northward to the point where
the expedition met its crowning misfortune in the Umpqua valley,
in Oregon.

Entries in Rogers' journal, June, 1828, show that the travellers
were beginning to suffer minor annoyances from the Indians.
June 25, for example, there is an entry: "The 2 men that was sent
back to hunt the mule, returned to camp a little after night and say
the Inds sallied out from their village with their bows and arrows

and made after them, yelling and screaming, and tryed to surround them; they retreated on horseback and swam a small creek, and the Inds. gave up the chase. When our horses was drove in this morning, we found 3 of them badly wounded with arrows, but could see no Inds. untill we started; we then discovered a canoe loaded with them some distance up the creek close by a thicket and did not pursue them, knowing it was in vain." On following days, there are reports of horses missing, and of smoke signals made by the tribesmen, seemingly to notify other Indians of the party's approach. July 2, they reached the mouth of Johnson creek, in what is now Coos county, Oregon, where "no accident happened to the horses today."

20

Smith seems to have been unwilling to let the Indians have things all their own way, but to have adopted a positive, though not belligerent, attitude. The Rogers diary records: July 3, 1828, "Capt. Smith, being ahead, saw the Inds, in the canoe [one which he had employed in crossing a small stream] and they tryed to get off but he pursued so closely that they run and left it. They tryed to split the canoe to pieces with their poles, but he screamed at them, and they fled, and left it, which saved us a great deal of hard labour in making rafts." July 5, two Indians who spoke Chinook, entered camp and informed the party that they were "ten days travell from Calapos [Calapooya] on the wel Hamett [Willamette]." July 7, there were about a hundred Indians in camp, according to this chronicler, and Smith bought a sea otter skin from a chief. One of the Indians had a "fusill," a number had knives and pieces of cloth, evidence of previous barter with the whites.

Indians calling themselves the Ka Koosh, undoubtedly the Coos, were encountered on the next day, but while these redskins were selling fish, berries and peltries to the whites they were also surreptitiously shooting arrows into the horses and mules. Smith, with the business of trading ever in mind, obtained valuable otter skins, as well as beaver. July 12, an Indian of authority, who was one of a number accompanying the party for a short distance, stole an ax, and the Rogers entry for the day says: "We were obliged to seize him for the purpose of tying him, before we could scare him to make him give it up. Capt. Smith and one of them caught him and put a cord around his neck, and the rest of us stood with our guns in case they made any resistance, there was about 50 Inds. present but did not pretend to resist tying the other . . ." The ax was recovered, but the Indian suffered humiliation and was resentful.

The travellers were now on the Umpqua, within a few miles of the Willamette valley, and the weather was pleasant and the Indians informed them that "after we got up the river 15 or 20 miles we will have good traveling to Wel Hammett or Multinomah, where the Callipoo Inds. live." The party had crossed to the north bank of the Umpqua, just below the mouth of Smith river, and would have followed the Umpqua and Elk creek to the low divide, where they would have come out upon the fork of the Willamette near the present town of Drain, Oregon. In another day's travel, or at most two, they would have reached the comparatively easy going of the Willamette valley region.

21

It had been Smith's practice to set out ahead in the morning to obtain an idea of the road for the coming day, and this he did as usual, July 14. He had left orders, as is confirmed by Doctor McLoughlin's account, that no Indians should be permitted to enter camp. Soon after his departure, however, it appears that they came in numbers, and soon began a general attack. The Indians had not previously manifested an unfriendly disposition, and, according to Rogers, had not taken the tying-up of the chief very much to heart. Black had just finished cleaning and loading his gun, and he fired on the Indians, obtaining a momentary advantage, which enabled him to escape.

Research by the late Maurice S. Sullivan has brought to light a transcript of Smith's own narrative of his travels, ending with the date, July 3, 1828, including his story of the journey to California and into Oregon up to that date. This is supplemented by the publication of a copy of the three months' Journal of Alexander R. McLeod, chief trader of Hudson's Bay Company, covering the day to day narrative of a special expedition sent out by Dr. John McLoughlin, chief factor at Fort Vancouver. The object of the expedition was to recover Smith's furs and horses from the marauding Indians, and to impress them with the power and authority of the Hudson's Bay Company. This Journal is in the archives of the Hudson's Bay Company in London, and it gives the cause and the particulars of the massacre as ascertained by McLeod on his expedition, upon which he was accompanied by Jedediah Smith. The Journal covers the time from September 6, to December 10, 1828.

On October 11, McLeod met the Umpqua chief and learned from him that "While Mr. Smith's people were busy fixing Canoes together by means of Sticks, to convey their Baggage over the Channel, an ax was mised and suspicion led to suspect the Indians of having embezled it consequently to recover the Property an Indian of that tribe was seized tyed and otherwise ill treated, and only liberated after the Ax was found in the Sand, this Indian happened to be of Rank, of course much irritated at the treatment he met with, declared his intentions to his tribe to retaliate on the offenders, but he was overruled, by an other Individual in higher Rank and possessing greater influence, subsequently this same man wishing to ride a horse for amusement about the Camp took the liberty of mounting one for the purpose when one of Mr. Smith's men having a Gun in his hand and an irritated aspect desired the Indian angrily to dismount, the Indian instantly obeyed, hurt at the Idea and suspecting the Man disposed to take his life he gave his concurrence to the Plan in agitation in which dicission the Indians were much influenced by the Assertions of the other Party, telling them that they were a different people from us, and would soon monopolize the trade, and turn us out of the Country these Circumstances and harsh treatment combined caused their untimely fate."

22

It appears from the narrative that on the day of the assault Smith, with John Turner, Richard Leland, and a native guide, had gone up Smith river by canoe to locate a suitable place to cross with the horses. The assault was made by some 200 natives, called Kelawatsets, all of the whites being surprised and slain, excepting Arthur Black, who succeeded in getting to the nearby forest, and who, ultimately with the help of friendly Tillamooks was delivered in safety to Fort Vancouver. Smith's canoe was returning to the camp when the assault was taking place, but the canoe was upset by the guide, and the three white men succeeded in swimming to the shore under fire from the opposite side of the stream. They made their way, northwesterly, and reached Fort Vancouver, August 10, 1828.

Doctor McLoughlin purchased Smith's furs and horses after they had been recovered. These included 700 beaver skins, besides some otter pelts of less value, and also 39 or 40 horses.

23

Smith and his men were entertained at Fort Vancouver during the winter. Governor Simpson had the satisfaction of discussing with Smith the prospects of an immigration of settlers overland to the Oregon Country and finding that traveller convinced, as he was himself, that the character of the intervening lands, as well as distance, made it unlikely that any great number of American settlers would withstand the hardships and venture so far to find homes in Oregon. In a report to the Governor and Committee of his company, Simpson wrote:

"We learn from our American visitant Smith, that the flattering reports which reached St. Louis of the Wilhamot Country, as a field for Agricultural speculation, had induced many people in the States to direct their attention to that quarter; but he has on his present journey, discovered difficulties which never occurred in their Minds, and which are likely to deter his countrymen from attempting that enterprize. In the American Charts this River, (the Wilhamot or Moltnomah) is laid down as taking its rise in the Rocky Mountains, (indeed Mr. Rush in his official correspondence with President Adams on the subject of a boundary line distinctly says so) and the opinion was, that it would merely be necessary for Settlers with their Horses, Cattle, Agricultural implements &c. &c. to get (by the Main communication from St. Louis to Sta. Fee) to the height of Land in about Lat 38, there to embark on large Rafts & Batteaux and glide down current about 800 or 1000 Miles at their ease to this 'Land of Promise.' But it now turns out, that the Sources of the Wilhamot are not 150 Miles distant from Fort Vancouver, in Mountains which even Hunters cannot attempt to pass, beyond which, is a Sandy desert of about 200 Miles, likewise impassable, and from thence a rugged barren country of great extent, without Animals, where Smith and his party were nearly starved to Death. And the other route by Louis's River, Settlers could never think of attempting. So that I am of opinion, we have little to apprehend from Settlers in this quarter, and from Indian Traders nothing; as none, except large capitalists could attempt it, and this attempt would cost a heavy Sum of Money, of which they could never recover much. This they are well aware of, therefore as regards formidable opposition, I feel perfectly at ease unless the all grasping policy of the American Government, should induce it, to embark some of its National Wealth, in furtherance of the object."

24

Turner left Smith's service here to return south, undaunted by his experience. Smith and Black remained at the fort until March 12, 1829, when they started east to rejoin Jackson and Sublette, who meanwhile, had been trading in the upper Snake river country. The partners were reunited in July of that year on Henry's fork of the Snake. As well expressed by a western writer: "We are told that there was great rejoicing over the finding of Smith; and well might this be, though it is doubtful if the importance of what this man had accomplished was thoroughly understood by his comrades. His had been the first overland party of Americans to reach California; he had been the first white man to travel the central route from Salt Lake to the Pacific, and the first to traverse the full length of California and Oregon by land. Of the 32 men who had shared in his adventures, 25 had been slain by the Mohaves and the Umpquas. During three years of wandering west of the Rockies, he had covered 14 degrees of latitude and 11 degrees of longitude. It was one of the greatest of western explorers that Sublette's men found trapping in Pierre's Hole that summer of 1829—and he was then but 31 years old!"

25

Hudson's Bay Company men, led by Peter Skene Ogden, who later became chief factor at Fort Vancouver, were hunting in the same general location in which Jackson and Sublette were operating, during Smith's prolonged absence from the partners. Ogden had made a number of long journeys for his company, including a trip through the Blackfeet country, and another through southern Oregon and into California.

During the period of Smith's absence, the Jackson-Sublette detachment had met a double misfortune. Three members of a party under the leadership of Samuel Tulloch were killed by Blackfeet Indians, who stole about $4,000 worth of furs and merchandise; and four men, who had strayed from another division that was crossing from the watershed of the Columbia to the Great Salt lake, perished in the desert country of southeastern Oregon.

Smith was a Methodist, sincerely religious, and he had been deeply touched by Doctor McLoughlin's generosity, particularly in respect of the purchase of the furs, which in accordance with the customs of that time would have been regarded by many traders as fair spoil. He is said to have decided that he would not hunt on the western slopes of the continental divide, in the region then claimed by the Hudson's Bay Company as its own territory, and to have persuaded his partners, though with some difficulty, to acquiesce in this arrangement. Thus, for a time, American fur traders did not operate in the valley of the Columbia, and the company had little real competition in that region until it finally withdrew.

Smith, the first white man to lead a party into Oregon from California, did not live long 'after. He was killed, May 27, 1831, at the age of 33, by Comanches, while quenching his thirst in the dry bed of the Cimarron river in the desert north of New Mexico.

26

The name of the American Fur Company was prominent in trading operations upon the Great lakes and upon the Missouri river for a number of years. A new organization under that name was created, 1834, with Ramsay Crooks, as president. It was a consolidation of the interests of the old company, in which Astor was the leading figure, and those of Crooks and his associates, but the operations were not as profitable as in the fur trade of earlier days. The company was for many years a keen competitor of the Hudson's Bay Company, but it did not extend its trading as far west as the Oregon Country.

CHAPTER XII

Ventures of Winship and Astor

1

A RUSSIAN PROJECT of establishing a settlement on the Columbia river, 1808, failed because the vessel sent for that purpose from Alaska was wrecked. The next essay of the kind was by Americans, and was likewise unsuccessful, but for another reason. Winship brothers, of Boston, Massachusetts, had long carried on a profitable trade with China, and incidentally with the Sandwich islands and the coast of North America. They now conceived the idea of setting up a post on the banks of the Columbia, deeming it advantageous to have a local stock of supplies and a station that would prove useful in cultivating the good will of the native tribes.

An American ship, the Albatross, was fitted out and placed under the command of Capt. Nathan Winship. This vessel sailed, July, 1809, and reached the Sandwich islands the next April. There, she took on a cargo, consisting partly of live stock, and proceeded to the mouth of the Columbia, which was reached, May, 1810. Having crossed the bar safely, the vessel at once drew up the river, not without difficulty, following the tortuous north channel. She came to a point some 45 miles from the mouth, where, upon a beautiful and apparently fertile expanse of low land, on the south bank, the expedition decided to locate the settlement. Work was immediately begun upon a fort, and seeds were planted. Disregarding high water marks of the river, the adventurers failed to observe that the site chosen by them was subject to annual inundation, and it was not long before the rise of the stream flooded their building site. A somewhat higher situation was then chosen, and the logs that had been hewn and put in place were removed to the new site.

In the meantime, Indians, who had at first seemed friendly enough, began to show signs of hostility, causing the members of the party great anxiety. Captain Winship deemed it wise to call their chief men into a conference on board the Albatross, and, on this being arranged, the natives expressed themselves quite freely. It was learned that they were decidedly averse to having the American establishment at that point, because they felt that a trading post would interfere with their own profitable trade with the Indians farther up the Columbia. It was evident that to estab-

lish the post would incur the hostility of all the Indians of the
lower river, and, furthermore, that without their friendship no
successful trade could be carried on.

Captain Winship decided, therefore, to give up his undertaking.
Other members of the party were disappointed at this outcome,
expressed themselves bitterly toward the Indians, and made
threats, but fortunately did not have an opportunity to carry these
into execution. And so, the Albatross sailed out of the Columbia
river, having accomplished nothing. Winship brothers afterward
made some plans to renew their attempt, and to send a second ship
to the river, but, on hearing of the proposed Astor expedition,
which was on a much more elaborate scale than any that they
could undertake, they finally gave up the purpose. They traded in
and out of the Sandwich islands for several years.

2

We come then, chronologically to the best known of these fur
trade expeditions, that of the great merchant prince, John Jacob
Astor. He was at this time in the noonday of his powers, conducting a great business with headquarters in New York City.

Astor was born in Germany, in the small town of Waldorf.
When but a boy in years, working in his father's butcher shop,
he ran away to London, where he set himself up in business, meeting with rather indifferent success. Shortly after the Revolution,
however, having heard that an older brother had gone to America,
he decided that the United States would offer him a more lucrative
field for his ventures, and he took a small stock of goods, which
included some musical instruments, and sailed for Baltimore. Here
a chance suggestion influenced his life, a suggestion to go to New
York and to exchange his goods for furs. This he did. He then
took his furs to the London market where he sold them at good
profit. This successful venture was the beginning of what grew to
be a great business. He soon decided that not Canada, but the
United States, was the logical center for the fur trade, and he
planned to make New York, rather than Montreal, the great continental market. His operations gradually extended, and he had
already made a great fortune when he undertook to exploit the
Pacific northwest.

A large portion of the fur-bearing regions lay within the region
explored by Lewis and Clark, and within the boundaries of the

United States, especially if the Pacific northwest were included, and at that time the Americans had, or thought they had, as good a claim to this region as the British.

Astor realized that the Hudson's Bay Company and the North West Company were working to disadvantage in sending men and supplies overland toward the Rocky mountains, and attempting control of the far west fur trade from Montreal and Hudson bay. He saw that, especially for trade beyond the mountains, a more natural plan would be to bring the traffic to the mouth of the Columbia, where a main post could be established, using the river as a route to and from the mountain region. On the coast, where the trade would be handled entirely by ship, it would be useful to have a permanent station at an accessible port.

Russians, it is true, had established themselves on the northern parts of that coast, but it would not be difficult to maintain trade relations with them, and as a matter of fact, such relations had already been established. In the spring of 1808, the Russian government had opened a correspondence with the government of the United States in relation to what Russia termed the illicit traffic of American ships with the natives inhabiting Russian territories. It appeared, in the course of the correspondence, that Russia claimed the coast at this time as far south as the Columbia river. The right to make settlements, or at least to establish trading posts, was claimed to extend beyond that southern limit.

3

Astor succeeded in arranging an understanding with the Russian-American Fur Company by which his company was given a monopoly on the business of exchanging supplies for furs, and both agreed to avoid encroachment upon each other's exclusive territory and to refrain from furnishing arms to natives, excepting to regular hunters. Astor had conceived the scheme of obtaining possession of some island in the Pacific, which would become the emporium of a great ocean traffic, and thus constitute the focal point of world-wide trade. He believed that New York had the decided advantage over any of the Canadian trade centers as a point of departure for the trading ships.

Astor would have the additional advantages of an already well established Chinese trade. The United States was in control of the route to the west by way of the Missouri, and thence over the

Rockies, and this route Astor planned to make use of as an auxiliary to that by sea. His plan was to establish a chain of posts similar to those of the Hudson's Bay Company in the north, and thus to keep open a line of communication across the continent, using this line for more rapid service, while sending heavier freight by the water route. He believed that by these means he might confine the operations of his Canadian rivals to the region tributary to Hudson bay and draw away to the United States the great bulk of the lucrative business of the far west.

The key of the whole scheme was the establishment of a Pacific coast station at the mouth of the Columbia river, which he hoped would some day occupy the same position on the Pacific coast that New York did on the Atlantic. He seems to have visualized the ultimate establishment upon the Pacific coast of a great American state, and in this general plan he had the well wishes and support of ex-President Jefferson, besides that of President Madison and Albert Gallatin, secretary of the treasury.

Jefferson wrote to Astor, 1818, after the failure of the enterprise: "I considered as a great public acquisition the commencement of a settlement on that point of the western coast of America, and looked forward with great gratification to the time when its descendants should have spread themselves through the whole length of that coast, covering it with free, independent Americans, unconnected with us, except by the ties of blood and interest, and enjoying like us the rights of self-government." Jefferson, and perhaps Astor also, seems to have had in mind a separate, although friendly state on the coast.

The far seeing carefully wrought plans of John Jacob Astor left on the Pacific coast little but the one name "Astoria;" but in spite of the apparent failure, other men followed where he had led, and Astor's expeditions had profound influence upon the history of Oregon. His company was called Pacific Fur Company. It was organized by Astor and four other partners, representing themselves and others who might become associated. The company was modelled rather closely after the great Canadian trading companies. Astor himself was the real head, holding 50 shares of the stock, and the remaining 50 shares were to be divided among the partners. He was to have the entire control at all times in his own hands. He was to furnish goods, vessels, arms and ammunition, but was not to be required to advance more than the sum of $400,000.00. He was also to bear all losses.

4

He chose his men principally from the North West Company, as that was the only available source of supply for experienced help. There seems to have been an almost feudal gradation of partners, clerks, mechanics and voyageurs, in descending scale. All beneath the grade of partner were hired at what now seems almost nothing per year, but, as if to compensate for their small remuneration, there was held out the hope of rising to a higher position in the employ of the company, as a reward for faithful service. The partners were mostly of highland Scotch extraction. The clerks were either Scotch, or French Canadian. The voyageurs were French Canadians, or half-breeds.

It was the intention of Astor, eventually to absorb the North West Company and to make it a component part of his own; in fact, overtures were opened by him, but were rejected by the Northwesters, who at that time were planning a similar consolidation with Hudson's Bay Company.

Although the personnel of the force to be sent out was largely of foreign extraction, the supervision was strictly American. The man chosen to command the ship, which would take the party to the Pacific coast was Jonathan Thorn, who had distinguished himself in the war with the Barbary pirates. He was a lieutenant in the navy, on leave of absence, and it may be, as sometimes asserted, that he was given a furlough and practically loaned by the United States government for the voyage, to give to the expedition a quasi-governmental character, in view of the possibility of controversy with Russia, or with Great Britain. Moreover, Astor required that all his employees who were of alien birth take the oath of allegiance to the United States government before setting out. This was so that United States customs laws would not apply to commodities in transit. This they did, but two of the Scotch partners went straightway to the British minister, at New York, and told him as much of Astor's plans as they knew, and they had assurance that they were not in danger of getting into difficulties with the British government by joining the enterprise.

5

As finally constituted, the company consisted of the following partners in addition to Astor himself: Duncan McDougal, Donald McKenzie, Alexander McKay, David Stuart, and his nephew, Robert Stuart, all Scotchmen, and Wilson Price Hunt, of New Jersey. Hunt was to be agent at the principal establishment on the northwest coast, for a period of five years. Later, as will be seen, he was also chosen to lead the overland party. The clerks were, Gabriel Franchere, Alexander Ross, William Matthews, James Lefevre, Russel Farnham, Thomas McKay, Donald McGillis, Ovide de Montigny, Francis B. Pillet, Donald McLennan and William Wallace. The mechanics were Stephen Weekes, armorer; William Cannon, millwright; three Lepensees and the two Bellaux, Jacques La Fontaine, Benjamin Roussel, Michel La Framboise and Giles Le Clerc. Besides these persons, the ship provided for the party that was to go by sea carried a crew of 31 men.

A more heterogeneous assortment of men, or one requiring more skill to command, it would be difficult to imagine. Washington Irving, who was a friendly critic of Astor's undertaking, calls them "a variegated band of adventurers." And yet the man chosen to command the ship was probably as unfit as any that could have been found. Jonathan Thorn had earned an excellent reputation as a naval officer, but as the commander of this polyglot assortment of Scotch Highlanders, gentlemen's sons just out of school, and rough Canadian voyageurs, he proved himself to be a complete failure. He was honest, but suspicious of the motives of others, and was a morose and bad tempered martinet. His selection proved unfortunate for himself and all others concerned.

6

The vessel destined to take the expedition around the Horn to the Pacific coast was the Tonquin, a ship of 290 tons burden, carrying 10 guns. She sailed from New York, September 8, 1810, convoyed for some distance by the old United States frigate Constitution, because it was feared that she would be searched by a British war ship for the impressment of British and Canadians on board. No sooner had the Constitution departed, and the Tonquin was left to travel alone the long and tedious voyage, than Captain Thorn began to show his domineering character. He insisted upon acting as though he was in command of a man-of-war, tried to enforce petty and irritating discipline, and even insisted on treating the partners as though they were common seamen.

An incident that occurred at the Falkland islands, where it was necessary to land to renew the supply of fresh water, well illustrates the utter unfitness of Thorn to command such an expedition. He had made repeated threats to leave some of the members of the party behind for alleged breaches of his strict orders. He now actually tried to carry his threat into execution. Two of the partners had been hunting, and failing to notice his signal for the men to return to the ship, were not at the landing on time, whereupon Thorn hoisted anchor and set out without them. Hurrying back to the appointed place, they were frantic at seeing their plight, but they seized a small boat and rowed for dear life, after the ship. Franchere says that the men on board were extremely indignant at Thorn for this unwarranted action, and that young Stuart drew a pistol and threatened Thorn with death if he did not lay the ship to, and take the partners on board. Thorn, in writing to Astor, indicated that he really intended to desert them. The wind fortunately dropping just at that time, allowed the men to overtake the Tonquin and get on board.

Upon leaving the Sandwich islands Thorn left one of his crew marooned there for some infraction of discipline. The clerk, Franchere, who was busy with the business of seeing that the water casks were properly filled, was likewise nearly left behind. It can be well imagined that the voyage from the islands to the Oregon coast was not a pleasant one. Thorn's ill temper progressively increased, and the cold and the inclemency of the weather in the more northerly clime, contrasted with what had been experienced in the tropics. Arriving off the Columbia bar, March 22, 1811, Thorn found the weather conditions very unfavorable; and it is due largely to his experiences here as subsequently related by the historian of the expedition, Washington Irving, that the Columbia river entrance gained an unfavorable reputation. Whatever bad opinion of it had been expressed by Vancouver in his narrative, was now confirmed.

A skillful pilot, seeing the unfavorable weather conditions prevailing on the bar, and being unfamiliar with the channel, would have stood off and awaited more favorable weather before attempting an entrance. Instead of pursuing this course, Captain Thorn sailed in toward the breakers, and like Vancouver on a similar occasion, ordered a whale boat to be launched and to sound a channel. It was put in charge of the first mate, Mr. Fox, with the assistance of John Martin, an old seaman, and several of the voyageurs who were not seamen, and were unaccustomed to rough weather conditions in such a place. Fox protested against the folly of this proceeding, but was answered by taunts of cowardice by the captain, and after seeking sympathy of the partners, he set out, feeling that he was going to certain death. The whale boat was soon engulfed and its occupants were never seen again.

7

The Tonquin kept her position near the bar till nightfall and then stood off shore, and in the morning it was seen that she had drifted dangerously near to the north shore. The pinnace manned by two of the partners, David Stuart and McKay, was then sent out to find, if possible, some trace of the victims of the previous day, but they met with no success and returned to the ship. A more favorable wind arose and another attempt was made to cross the bar. When the Tonquin was nearing the unbroken chain of breakers, the pinnace was again launched, this time with Mumford, the second mate, in charge. He was unable to accomplish his purpose and returned to the ship with great difficulty. Aiken, an able seaman was then put in charge of the pinnace, and still another attempt was made to sound the channel. Aiken was accompanied by John Coles, the sailmaker, Stephen Weekes, the armorer, and two kanakas who had been shipped at the Sandwich islands. The plan was for the pinnace to precede the ship and to make soundings, while the larger vessel followed slowly. Seeing that this was impracticable on the rough bar, the captain gave the signal for the boat to return, but when it was within pistol shot of the Tonquin the strong ebb tide caught it and carried it into the breakers and out of sight.

Just at that moment the ship herself was entering the breakers and it was impossible for any of her horror stricken crew to render aid. The vessel passed through in safety and the next morning two of the men, Weekes, the armorer, and one of the Hawaiians, were found alive upon the north shore. They had managed to work their way through the surf to the beach in the pinnace, having righted it when it capsized on the bar. Aiken and Coles were not seen after, and the other Hawaiian died before reaching land. As Washington Irving concluded his account of the affair, "Thus eight men were lost on the first approach to the coast, a commencement that cast a gloom over the spirits of the whole party, and was regarded by some of the superstitious as an omen that boded no good to the enterprise." The Tonquin had come to a rather unsafe anchorage within the estuary, but a little later managed to work into the shelter of Baker bay on the north shore.

The loss of eight men was but a beginning, for worse catastrophe was to follow, and a few weeks later Captain Thorn himself lost his life through his obstinacy and mismanagement. The first day in the Oregon Country closed with a pathetic burial of the body of the unfortunate Sandwich islander, by others of his people, according to the usages of the islands.

8

The story of the first settlement in the Oregon Country is full of romantic interest. Astoria will always have prestige as the first and oldest American settlement on the coast. The rights asserted by the United States to the Oregon Country, which became for many years the subject of a diplomatic struggle with Great Britain, depended in no slight degree upon the foothold gained here. If possession, when taken, had continued without interruption, and especially without voluntary surrender, the American problem of sovereignty of the country would have been greatly simplified. But Astor's plans were frustrated, and his fur trading post at the mouth of the Columbia was turned over to a rival British company, almost immediately after it was set up.

Experiences of those who built the fort were at first agreeable enough. No sooner had the Tonquin come to a safe anchorage within the shelter of Baker bay than McDougal undertook a systematic exploration of the land near the mouth of the river in search of a site for the post. He finally settled upon a place midway between Tongue Point and Point George, on the south shore of the river, as best suited to a permanent establishment. In this choice he showed excellent judgment, for the location was sheltered from the force of the southwesterly gales of winter by the hills, heavily forest clad, which rose in its rear, and, moreover, it was situated in a bight of the river, and so was less subject to boisterous waves. It seemed a convenient place for trading purposes.

The weather at the time of this reconnaissance was delightful. The banks of the river were vividly green with the verdure of spring, multicolored flowers pleased the eye, and the birds were singing gaily. Natives, who swarmed in their canoes around the ship, seemed friendly enough. Old chief Concomly, the friend of Lewis and Clark, and much depended upon, seemed well pleased to have the Bostons locate here. This friendly chief is described as "the richest and most powerful on the river; he is a short, elderly man, blind of one eye; he has three wives, and many children."

The first steps in developing the establishment at Astoria seemed slow, especially to Captain Thorn. After the site for the fort had been selected, the Tonquin was brought to anchor near by and the work of unloading the supplies was begun. Captain Thorn accomplished this task in record time, as he was in a great hurry to get rid of his unwelcome passengers and to be on his way, for it was decided that the ship should go on a trading voyage up the coast. But he was irritated at what he thought was the unnecessary delay on shore. June first, he was at last ready to sail, and on the fifth, the Tonquin passed out over the bar without accident.

The post was named Fort Astoria. The weather proved so fine that rapid progress was made in construction, and ground was cleared for the planting of a garden. But, here we must leave for the time being the members of this first American settlement on the Pacific coast, to their not uncongenial labors, while we follow the career of the Tonquin to its tragic conclusion.

9

Upon passing out of the Columbia, the Tonquin proceeded northward for the purpose of trading with the natives. An Indian had been picked up who had learned some English from contact with other ships. The commodious harbor of Clayoquot was reached, on the western shore of Vancouver island. This was a port that had often been visited by fur traders. As to the details of the disaster that happened to the ship and her crew while in this port there is much uncertainty, but of one thing we may be sure, and that is that the tragedy was due to the folly of Captain Thorn. Men who remained at Astoria set down in their diaries the story, as they heard it. The Indian interpreter who went with the ship was the only survivor, and through him, Indians along the coast heard of the tragedy soon after it happened. Rumors of it soon reached Astoria and the interpreter's story was obtained, but the exact facts will never be known.

As soon as the ship had cast anchor, natives had swarmed about in great numbers. One of the partners, Alexander McKay, who accompanied Thorn on this voyage, protested against allowing them so near, or allowing many of them at one time to come on board, this being contrary to instructions and contrary to safe practice. But, one day, when McKay was ashore with the interpreter, Thorn allowed large numbers of the Indians to come aboard to trade, and he brought out bales of goods for display. He soon got into a state of bad temper, being unable to understand or to make himself understood. Then he refused to trade at all. His anger was especially aroused by a chief, who followed him about the deck, thrusting an otter skin in his face. The Indians became more and more insolent, and the harassed and short-tempered captain could restrain himself no longer. He thought he would show them that he was master upon his own ship. The story is that he seized the chief and his pelt, striking and pushing the chief from the deck, and driving the Indians to their canoes.

Captain Thorn seems to have taken the protests and warnings of McKay and the interpreter, on their return to the ship, with all the contempt that he usually displayed toward advice and suggestions of others. He cared nothing for the savages. What could they do against an armed ship? He refused to take any precautions, and refused to depart, as he was urged to do. Although the whole tribe deeply resented the insult, the Indians were crafty enough to pretend otherwise, and to wait until they could strike an effective blow.

Early one morning, before Thorn was on deck, and while the most of the crew were still asleep, the Indians in small numbers began to come on board. They made signs of friendship and seemed to be unarmed. As the numbers increased, the officer of the deck became anxious and sent for the captain. When Thorn appeared, he affected to see no cause for alarm, and rejected McKay's urgent request that the ship leave the harbor as quickly as possible. The trade became active, the Indians appearing inoffensive, although they had left squaws in the canoes. They seemed to prefer to take knives for their peltries, and when they got blankets, or other merchandise, tossed these to the canoes, at the same time concealing the knives about their persons. As the Indians overwhelmed the decks and far outnumbered the whites, even Captain Thorn began to see that there was danger, and at last he gave orders to unfurl the sails and to hoist the anchor. The natives were so dispersed about the deck that every white man was surrounded. Suddenly, by preconcerted signal, there was a wild yell and the Indians began a murderous attack with their knives upon their unarmed victims, and the unequal fight was soon over. Captain Thorn defended himself with powerful strength, and though he had but a clasp knife, he killed more than one of his assailants before he was overpowered by superior numbers. McKay was stabbed and thrown overboard, where the women in the canoes finished him. The interpreter leaped into the sea and was taken up by one of the canoes, and was afterward treated with kindness. Lewis, the clerk, was badly hurt, but managed to get to the cabin.

In the meantime seven sailors, who were in the rigging when the assault began, now tried to get down and to get into the hold. Three were killed, but four succeeded in joining Lewis in the cabin. These barricaded themselves and from this place of vantage they poured a fusilade of shots among the murderous savages, until they drove them to their canoes and forced them to abandon the ship. When night fell the Indians had retreated, but the men on board were too few in number to navigate the ship. The four who were unhurt decided that they would take a small boat and put out to sea with the hope of reaching the Columbia river, while the fifth, who was perhaps unable to go because of his injuries, planned to sell his life as dearly as possible.

10

He is supposed to have prepared to blow up the ship. In the morning, when the Indians came, they saw but one white man on board. He appeared to be badly wounded, but made friendly signals. The Indians approached cautiously, and on venturing on board saw no one, as he had gone below. They were soon followed by others, and it was not long before the ship was surrounded by canoes and the decks were swarming with Indians. Bales of blankets and merchandise, with the furs brought on board the day before, were scattered about, and the ship itself was a rich prize.

But the white man's hour of revenge was at hand. Suddenly, at the very height of their triumph, a terrible explosion, such as they had never known before, blew up the decks and split the ship apart. The Tonquin was a mass of wreckage, and the bay was strewn with bodies of the dead. The tribe lost over a hundred warriors and chiefs, and of the squaws left in the canoes few escaped the disaster. The day of mourning was there, and it may be supposed that few families of the tribe entirely escaped the havoc.

The four sailors, who had attempted to get out of the bay with the boat, were soon caught, and they suffered the terrible fate of victims of Indian cruelty. They had found it impossible to stem the tide, and concealing themselves as best they could at the shore, were asleep when they were discovered. No word from them ever reached their friends, but natives reported that they were made a sacrifice after prolonged torture. Rumors first reached the Astorians through Indians from the strait of Juan de Fuca, but later the interpreter returned to the Columbia with more particulars, and it was said that he escaped the fate of the others by being on shore when the ship was blown up. This interpreter, who was known by the English name Ramsay, or otherwise Indian George, in after years served as a pilot on the Columbia river.

Terrible as this disaster was it benefitted the whites in one way. The Indians of the Nootka district thereafter associated the death of their fellows with the evil spirit, which they imagined existed in the interior of the Boston mens' ships, and thereafter they had a wholesome dread of entering any portion, save the deck, and this fear saved the Americans much annoyance.

The loss of the Tonquin and the massacre of its crew were due primarily to the folly of Captain Thorn, and yet he was not the only incompetent in the expedition; we see the leader of the forces at Astoria committing another folly which in its consequences was of far more serious import. When McDougal heard of the disaster to the company's ship he feared that the Indians in the neighborhood of the fort might be emboldened by the success of the natives in the north, and by the apparent weakness of the forces stationed at Astoria, to attack that post. Accordingly, in order to inspire fear in them, he summoned a conference of the chief men of the surrounding country and showed them a small vial in which he said was contained a very powerful "medicine," which if released would cause an epidemic of smallpox to break out among the natives. On account of their willing faith in the efficacy of medicine in general, the Indians readily believed, and earnestly begged McDougal not to remove the cork from the bottle. This he promised, on condition that they would always remain faithful to the whites. The threat was unnecessary, and was foolish, as the Chinooks and Clatsops were at that time, and had always been, friendly to the whites; and, as has been related, Chief Concomly had on more than one occasion given evidence of his good will. The evil result of this deception was that whenever thereafter there was an outbreak of smallpox, measles or malaria, the Indians immediately attributed it to the evil medicine of the whites. McDougal's threat was not soon forgotten.

11

While the colonists at Astoria were busy with planting their garden seeds and erecting their buildings and stockade of logs, the Northwesters were losing no time in perfecting their rival plans, as has already been shown. These plans may have been hastened to some extent by the news of the extensive designs of Astor, but for several years the North West Company had been striving to extend their operations westward and along the course of the Columbia river to the sea. Some of their men had already begun trading on the Fraser, the tributaries of the upper Columbia, and at other places west of the divide. Their first expedition for the purpose, as has been stated, was that of Simon Fraser, sent to establish trading posts on the Tacouche Tesse river, 1805. This is the river that now bears the name Fraser river after its explorer, who called the region New Caledonia, and who established posts there, 1805-07.

The North West Company's posts in the Pacific district, when the Astor expedition arrived on the Columbia river, comprised besides Fraser's forts, Kootenai House, Kullyspell House, Saleesh House, Spokane House and stations on lakes Coeur d'Alene and Pend d'Orielle, all on waters tributary to the Columbia river. In 1812, they set up a rival post on Thompson river to oppose the one established by David Stuart of the Astor party; and, 1813, in like manner they located a post in the Willamette valley close to the Astorian Fort Wallace. David Thompson's activities on the divide, and at the head waters of the Columbia, have been related in Chapter XI, but some further details of his trip down that river, 1811, may be given in connection with the story of Fort Astor.

Thompson began a descent of the river, July 3, 1811. His journal of this trip opened with the title "Voyage to the mouth of the Columbia, By the Grace of God, By D. Thompson and seven men on the part of the N. W. Company." He arrived at Astoria, July 15, 1811, and made this entry in his journal: "At 1 p. m. thank God for our safe arrival, we came to the House of Mr. Astor's company. Messrs. McDougal, Stuart and Stuart, who received me in the most polite manner, and here we hope to stay a few days to refresh ourselves."

We have it from the narrative of one of the Astor clerks, Franchere, that Thompson presented a proposal from the Northwesters to the effect that they would abandon their forts west of the continental divide, if the Astorians would agree to keep out of British territory east of the mountains, but the facts as known seem not to harmonize with this. Thompson's arrival there was two months late. Nevertheless it is a fair field for speculation as to what would have been the effect upon the sovereignty of the country had there been no such delay. As it was, the ultimate locating of the international boundary line many years later, so far north of many of the early British posts, drew forth letters recalling these events of 1811, letters to the American government and to the British government, by Thompson in his old age, telling of his services and of the importance of the Columbia valley, and protesting against establishing the boundary north of the lower Columbia river.

On the occasion of his visit, 1811, Thompson was entertained at Astoria seven days, while the Canadian voyageurs no doubt put in a happy time with those of their kind at the American depot, and the period of rest must have been welcome after the long and rapid journey by canoe, which, as his diary shows, at times flew down the stream at a speed as great as that of a modern express train. McDougal and the two Stuarts knew Thompson well, for they had been associated with him in the North West Company. Though they were now his rivals in trade, the warm friendships that had been formed in the great forests and upon the swift streams of the far north were too deep to be disturbed by new business competition. They had shared dangers and could talk the language of their craft.

McDougal, therefore, gave Thompson ample supplies for the

return trip to the upper Columbia, with the same generous hospitality that always characterized the fur traders and explorers of the west, although it must be added that the Stuarts rather doubted the wisdom of this policy, deeming it probable that if the requested outfit were not given, Thompson and his men would either have to join the Astor party, or take ship for home when an opportunity would present itself.

12

The first news at Astoria that the Northwesters had begun trading west of the Rockies came by accidental means to Astoria, before Thompson's arrival. Shortly after the Tonquin had sailed away, two Indian messengers came with a letter addressed to a Northwester named John Stuart, on the Fraser, signed by Finan McDonald, a clerk in the service of that company at Spokane House. The messengers, who were females, although one of them dressed as a man, were perhaps Iroquois. They had heard from natives up river of white men at the mouth of the Columbia, and supposed that the man for whom the letter was intended would probably be found among them. When Thompson and his canoemen came, the Astorians got at first hand more definite news of the activities of the rival company. But what they had learned from the Indians led them to consider sending an expedition at once to get suitable locations for posts in the interior, and, when Thompson arrived this plan was about ready for execution, so that it was then decided to send David Stuart on this important mission. The Astor men learned that Thompson, on his way down the river, had posted a notice at the mouth of Snake river, making claim for the North West Company and the British interests, but it had no effect upon their decision to locate trading posts in the interior.

13

The two parties for the interior started out together, July 22, 1811. Thompson had his five Canadian voyageurs and two Iroquois Indians. Stuart had with him the clerks, Ovide de Montigny, Francis Pillette, Donald McLennan and Alexander Ross, three Canadian voyageurs and two Hawaiian islanders. The newly arrived clerks, who were members of this party, after the long voyage by sea, looked forward with pleasure to this excursion. Most of them, however, were unskilled in the management of canoes, and were having their first view of real Indians at Astoria. They took pamphlets and newspapers for amusement, one carried an umbrella, and as Ross says in his narrative, being all more or less ambitious, they overlooked, in the prospect of success, both difficulty and danger.

The Stuart party reached the banks of the Okanogan, a branch of the Columbia, August 31, 1811, and there a building was put up for the Pacific Fur Company's post, about a half mile above the mouth of the Okanogan, the first American settlement in what is now the state of Washington. This afterwards became an important establishment of the North West Company, new buildings and improvements being added, but the location was slightly changed later, and the post then was protected with strong palisades, 15 feet high, flanked with two bastions, protected by brass four pounder guns, and having loop holes for the use of musketry. This post was at the gateway of the northern country, designated by Fraser as New Caledonia, and the point of delivery for the furs of that section destined for shipment through the mouth of the Columbia.

14

In passing up and down the Columbia these early expeditions had not only to reckon with the natural difficulties, such as the rapids and portages, but also the difficulty of passing the Indians located on both sides of the Columbia in the Cascade mountains. Particular reference to some of the experiences with these Indians will find place in connection with the narrative from time to time, but a few words of more general description may here be given. The river itself is over 1200 miles in length, but owing to its winding course and the obstructions to navigation it has not often been travelled from source to mouth, as was done by Thompson, and yet it has formed the great highway for most of the intercourse between the sea coast and the interior. Lewis and Clark called the Cascades "The Shutes," but the name "Cascades" seems to have been already in use in 1811, at the time now under consideration. The obstructions at the Big Eddy at the foot of the Dalles, and continuously for 10 miles, including the falls at Celilo, are even more formidable. Thompson made a portage here by way of the south bank, in going and in returning, but the usual route was along the north bank. Other rapids that are frequently mentioned in the fur traders' accounts are Rapides du Pretre, or Priest rapids, Isle de Pierre, or Rock Island rapid, Les Chaudiere or Kettle falls, and in British Columbia (originally New Caledonia), there is Les Dalles des Morts, or Death rapids.

At the dangerous portage around the swift water near Celilo was a native village on the north side, called Wishram, where from time immemorial the Indians have been accustomed to assemble in the salmon fishing season; for here the spearing of the salmon from the rocks, or dipping them up by means of long handled dip nets, was a sport requiring rare skill. Gambling was sport of another kind, much in favor at this place. But these Indians soon earned a bad reputation with the white men, which every expedition justified by its experiences. In the fishing season they numbered, perhaps 3000, comprising not only Klickitats, who lived here permanently, but numerous representatives from different tribes throughout the country. They not only exacted tribute in the form of liberal presents, but they stole whenever they could, and the white men were in constant danger of their lives, so that large expeditions carefully guarded and always on the alert for trouble, were found a necessity to make the passage.

15

It was August 2, in this year of 1811, that the Astors passed this place with Stuart in command, bearing the first shipment of supplies and traders' goods, the first freight to be carried upon the Columbia. Thompson's canoe being light, and handled by highly skilled men, had out-distanced the Stuart party, and when they reached the mouth of Snake river, they found that he had added a British flag to his posted notice. The Astorians had two canoes, which were of the dug-out pattern, and laden as they were, with all the stock intended for their proposed trading posts, put up in bales or packs of convenient size for carrying upon the back where necessary, the task of passing the natives at the Dalles, and getting all carried and set afloat again in safety, surrounded as the little party was day and night with the menacing Indians, was a severe test for some of the young clerks, just out from New York.

Ross says of this: "The length of this dry and sandy footage is nine miles; and when it is taken into consideration that we had to go and come all the distance four times in one day, without a drop of water to refresh ourselves, loaded as we were, and under a burning sun, it will be admitted that it was no ordinary task. Under any other circumstances but a struggle between life and death, it could never be performed; but it was too much; the effort was almost beyond human strength, and I may venture to say all circumstances considered, it will never be again."

CHAPTER XIII

FAILURE OF FORT ASTOR

1

THE ASTOR overlanders suffered far greater hardships than did Lewis and Clark and their men, and had a much more difficult and dangerous journey, but the story of their loyalty, their courage and their persistence will ever be told with history's thrilling tales of heroism.

This auxiliary expedition was placed under the direction of Wilson Price Hunt, the one of the partners who was a native born American. He had had no such training as would qualify him for this adventurous undertaking, for although he had traded with the Indians, at St. Louis, he knew little of wilderness life. On entering the Astor service, he first went to Montreal, July, 1810, where he hoped to recruit a crew of rivermen. He found, however, that in spite of his liberal offers, it was difficult to get the best men, as the influence of the Northwesters was against him there. However, he obtained a well constructed Canadian canoe, large enough to carry a cargo of four tons and yet so light as to be capable of transportation around the portages upon the shoulders of the men. He was successful at last in getting enough men to paddle the canoe, and he secured a cargo of supplies, put up in the usual bundles of 90 pounds each, a convenient size to be packed on a man's back when necessary. He was joined at Montreal by one of the partners, who had been detailed to go with him, Donald Mc-Kenzie, a Scot who had been with the Northwesters.

The route followed was up the Ottawa river, and through the great lakes to the head of Lake Huron, where, at the settlement at Mackinac, Michigan, then called Michilimackinac, a stop was made to secure the additional boatmen and trappers that were wanted. At this place Ramsay Crooks, one of the partners, joined the party, fortunately for them, although unfortunately for himself, as it afterward turned out. He had served with the North West Company, and knew the Indians of the upper Missouri region, where he had traded for furs after Lewis and Clark's return.

Hunt heard that the Sioux and Blackfeet tribes were hostile to the white men and might try to prevent his going through their domains. He therefore decided that he would pick up 30 additional men at St. Louis, to strengthen his party. He did not reach St.

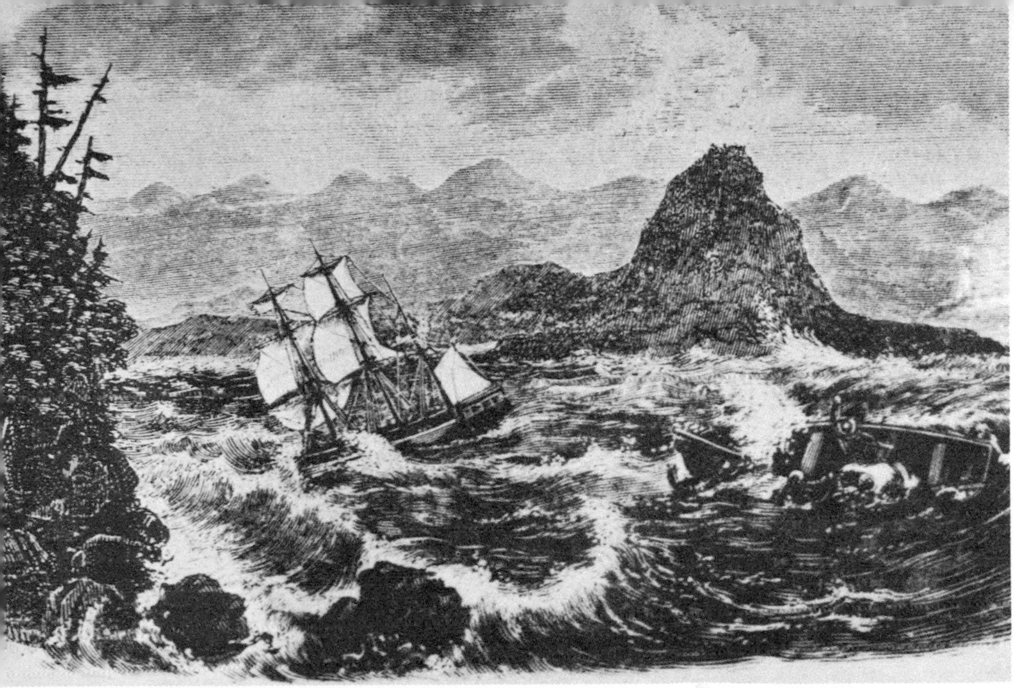

—Oregon Historical Society

Astor's "Tonquin"

The "Tonquin" ran into rough waters at entrance to the Columbia river, March 25, 1811. John Jacob Astor had dispatched the ship to set up a fur base.

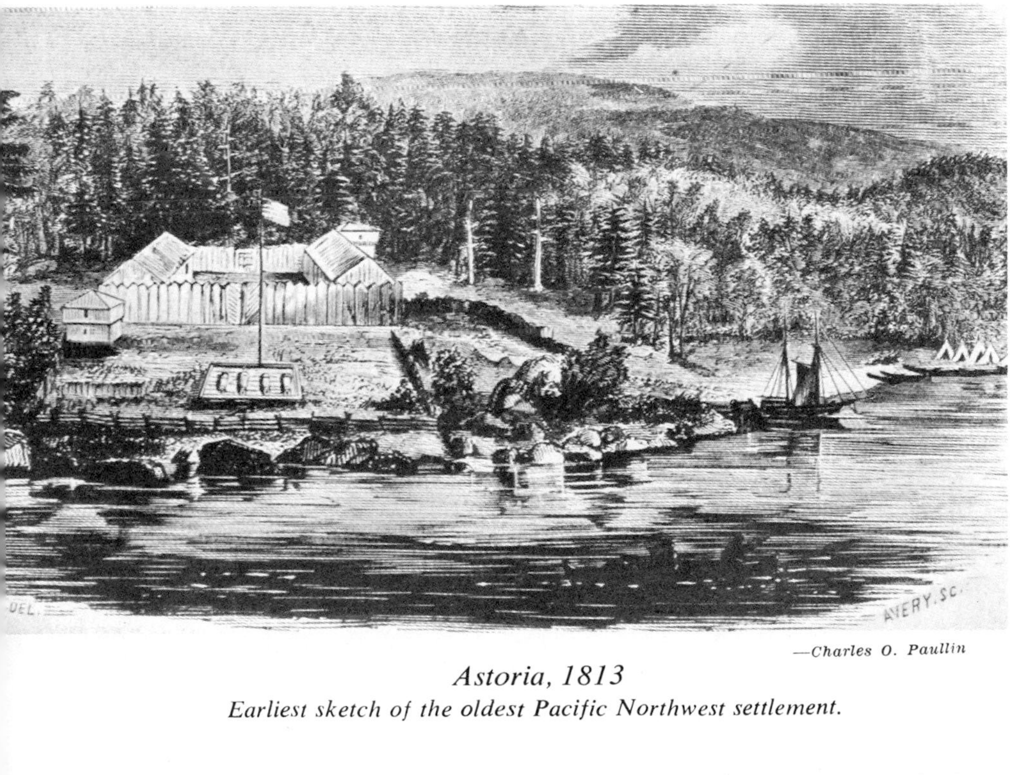

—Charles O. Paullin

Astoria, 1813

Earliest sketch of the oldest Pacific Northwest settlement.

Jonathan Thorn
Captain of the ill-fated "Tonquin."

Robert Stuart
Fur-trading partner of Astor.

Wilson Price Hunt
Leader of the Astor overland expedition.

John Jacob Astor
Founder of Pacific Fur company.

Louis until the third of September, 1810, having travelled by boats through the Fox and Wisconsin rivers and down the Mississippi. With the added delays at St. Louis the season was gone, and it was too late to proceed. While here, orders came from Astor vesting the sole command in Hunt, although prior to this it was intrusted to him jointly with McKenzie, who was experienced and reliable. This gave umbrage to the other partners and added difficulties to Hunt's position.

He was wise enough to avoid trying to winter 60 men, or more, at St. Louis, and although he knew he could not go far up the Missouri before the ice and snow would obstruct progress, he pushed forward as far as the mouth of the Nodaway, a point not far from the present city of St. Joseph. Here he went into permanent camp before November, when the river was closed by the ice. It was at this camp that Ramsay Crooks' old partner joined the expedition, Robert McLellan, an excellent shot, whose extraordinary ability in that respect, when exhibited, never failed to impress the natives. A young American also came in, John Day, whose name is perpetuated in Oregon as the name of the John Day river near the mouth of the Columbia, and the John Day river in eastern Oregon, both emptying into the Columbia. He had been in the service of Crooks and other traders. But Hunt lost some of his riflemen, for the Missouri Fur Company was getting up an expedition of its own to go up the Missouri for trade and to search for a missing partner, that same Maj. Andrew Henry, already mentioned, who had been driven by the Blackfeet from the fur trading station that had been established at Three Forks, Montana.

An interpreter was engaged, Pierre Dorion, a half-breed, the son of that Dorion that had served in similar capacity for the Lewis and Clark expedition. Dorion brought his Sioux wife, and two children, much to the surprise of Hunt, who had not bargained for this addition to his responsibilities. But Dorion was a real necessity, familiar as he was with the language of the Sioux tribe, through whose country the expedition must pass, and Hunt could not afford to let him go. The husband and wife had their differences, now and then, as the party went forward, and at times the expedition might have wished the encumbrances had been left behind, but in the end the fortitude and steadfastness of this native woman came to be recognized, and like Sacajawea of the

Lewis and Clark expedition, her heroism gained for her the good will of the party.

It was a coincidence that Sacajawea, with her husband, Toussaint Charboneau, and the little son born on the Lewis and Clark expedition, returning to the land of the Shoshones from a visit to civilization, passed up the Missouri at this time with the Missouri Fur Company's party, and thus the two brave women who first dared the overland journey came in contact with each other.

2

The ice in the river broke up earlier than usual owing to a freshet from some of its southern tributaries, and the expedition got under way in April, 1811. There were four boats, the largest of which mounted two howitzers and a swivel gun. The progress was slow and toilsome, and the route to be followed would lead them into the country of hostile savages. Dorion was half French and half Sioux, and, as already stated, his wife belonged to this tribe, which was then upon the warpath. A numerous tribe, it was considered both treacherous and fierce, and Dorion did not profess to be able to insure a safe journey through their country. To add to the anxiety from this source, the news of conditions further north and west, where the savage Blackfeet or Piegan Indians were treasuring bitter animosity against Americans, dating from the time when Captain Lewis had found it necessary to kill two of their tribe, was far from encouraging.

However, the beautiful country through which the expedition was passing in May, where the prairies were decked with flowers and where groves diversified the landscape and lent a charm to the winding river, kept those of the party who had begun to lose faith from being wholly discouraged, although two of the riflemen made an excuse and turned back. This was more than offset, however, by the addition of three experienced recruits, under circumstances quite unexpected. They were Edward Robinson, John Hoback and Jacob Rezner, all Kentucky hunters, who were perceived one morning sweeping down stream at a great pace in two canoes. They had been in the service of the Missouri Fur Company with Maj. Andrew Henry in the preceding year, in establishing his new trading post on Henry's fork, one of the branches of the Columbia river. They had actually crossed the divide therefore, and Hunt was eager to avail himself of their knowledge.

They were headed for home, when they thus met the Hunt party, but were easily persuaded to join. They were much impressed by the grand scale of the expedition, its numbers and its equipment, and caught the spirit of enthusiasm of the leaders. But it was due to their advice and the stories they brought of the Indian dangers, that Hunt decided to give up his original plan of following the Lewis and Clark route, and he determined upon a detour that would avoid the Blackfeet country. This, it was said, would take them to the sources of the Platte and Yellowstone rivers and across the mountains through an easier pass than that found by Lewis and Clark; and through a section abounding in game. The latter consideration seemed important, as the requirements of some 60 persons in the caravan, for daily meals, were far beyond the possibility of being supplied by the stores carried with the outfit. But it really proved to be a serious mistake, for while the large party could have successfully forced their way through on the Lewis and Clark route, the abandonment of the boats, and the resort to horses for transportation overland involved difficulties in procuring food, besides uncertainty as to the proper route to destination before cold weather would begin.

3

One morning two Indians were seen at a bluff opposite the camp and seemed to be haranguing the party from a distance too great to be understood. Dorion went to them and found them to be scouts of a large war party of Sioux, already numbering some 600 warriors and expecting reinforcements from other branches of their nation, who were assembling for the purpose of opposing the progress of the white men up the river. It was found that the Indians were in warlike array, painted and decorated for battle, and the outlook was serious enough. Hunt had a conference with one of the scouts, while the other made off over the hills on horseback to carry the news of the coming of the white men. The whites were so greatly outnumbered that to turn back seemed to be the only safe course, for to attempt to continue up the stream where the banks afforded every opportunity for the concealment of bands of savages, who could pick off the party without appearing in sight, seemed foolhardy.

The only alternative that offered hope of success seemed to be in a decisive battle with the whole force, in which case the superior arms of the white men might perhaps serve to secure a victory that would clear the way. The party was put in readiness for a fight, and the boats proceeded up stream. Presently the Indians in full strength were seen, and to give them some sense of respect for the white men's guns, the swivel and the howitzers were fired without shot, the tremendous reverberation echoing like thunder. Just as Hunt's men were within rifle shot of the Indians and were ready to shoot, Dorion cried out to them not to fire, and it was seen that the Indians were holding up their buffalo robes with both hands above their heads and then spreading them on the ground, a token of friendship.

After some doubt, the chief men of the Hunt party, experienced in Indian ways, landed and went forward. The Indian chiefs were seated on the bank of the river in a semi-circle, and did not rise, but remained in silence. The others of the red men lined the banks above, whence they could see the proceedings, and from which position they could take advantage of any indication of treachery upon the part of the whites, while, of the latter, those who remained on the boats were equally prepared for action.

However, the pipe of peace was produced, and the ceremonies, impressive and significant, established good will and amity, especially when Hunt produced presents of tobacco and corn and gave assurances that his purpose was to turn to the westward and not to go to the northern tribes for trade, or to interfere with plans of the Sioux by selling ammunition to their enemies. The Indians professed that they had had no unfriendly intentions, and while this statement may have been founded upon the appearance of preparedness on the part of the white men, and may have been due to the ready rifles and the big howitzers and the boom of the swivel gun, it was accepted in good part by the whites.

4

The Missouri Fur Company's boat with Manuel Lisa and 24 others, which had been hurrying forward to overtake and pass Hunt's party before they arrived at the Aricara villages, now appeared. A plan was made to proceed together for a time, although some of Hunt's best men hated Lisa, for grievances of the past, with such vindictive hatred that a union seemed out of the question, at first. The arrangement had not held for more than two days, when there was an outbreak and a violent scene, and Hunt had difficulty in preventing bloodshed.

But Hunt himself became involved with Lisa before a settlement was reached, and there was to have been a duel between these two leaders. This was avoided through the intervention of others, and the two expeditions proceeded, but without interchange of courtesies, until, as they reached the native village, a semblance of unity was arranged as a matter of policy, lest the natives should learn of their differences. The Aricaras were at the mouth of Grand river in the present state of South Dakota. At this point Hunt intended to turn from the river and follow his proposed route through the district inhabited by the Crow Indians, and leading to the Rockies by way of the Big Horn range, a route entirely unknown.

Lisa was no doubt glad to see this plan of his rival's carried out. He aided in procuring horses from the Indians, and he traded some of his own that had been held for him among the Mandans, taking Hunt's good boats in exchange and planning to use them to advantage in carrying furs down to St. Louis.

It was July 18, 1811, when the overland party set out from the Aricara villages. There were 82 horses. Some of the party were on foot, but Hunt and his partners and some others rode. The pack horses were heavily loaded, for the stores and supplies, including goods intended for use in barter, made a brave show. It was here that Edward Rose, who had lived among the Crows, was procured as an interpreter. Father and mother Dorion walked, while they led a pack horse carrying their outfit and their two small children.

In about two weeks' time the party fell in with a small group of the Cheyennes, with whom they traded and hunted, and from whom they bought 36 additional horses. The Cheyennes were friendly and showed them the crossing over the Cheyenne river, on the way leading southward toward the Big Horn range. Rose proved to be untrustworthy and was found plotting with some disaffected members of the party to steal some horses and valuable packs and to join the Crow Indians, but Hunt managed to prevent this by offering extra inducements to Rose to keep his agreement.

5

In the heat of August, the caravan proceeded through the Black hills, the hunters finding buffaloes upon the rolling plains in great herds, and in the mountains big horn sheep and black-tailed deer, which supplied ample food for the party. This range forms the dividing line between the waters of the Arkansas and those of the Missouri, and gives rise to the little Missouri, the Yellowstone and the Cheyenne, and was at that time the home of the grizzly bear. One of these treed a hunter after chasing him down a ravine, and kept him perched in this uncomfortable situation all night, and another threatened John Day and one of the younger members of the party at close quarters.

As the expedition got further into the mountains the travelling became slow and difficult, food and water became scarce. One of the hunters succeeded in killing a wolf, which was eaten and pronounced good, and the reserve supply of corn meal was used in the emergency. But, reaching the grassy plains of Powder river, they were again able to supply themselves with buffalo meat, and to dry some for future requirements. August 30, 1811, they estimated that they had travelled 400 miles from the villages of the Aricaras.

They were now in the land inhabited by the Crows, noted horse thieves. Two of these were seen and brought to camp by Rose. The next day a party of them came on horseback to invite the whites to visit their chief at the Crow camp, 16 miles distant. Friendly relations were thus established, and after presents were made and some trading was carried on, the party proceeded westward, but soon became hopelessly confused and unable to continue. They had left Rose at the Indian camp, but he now turned up with a band of Crows and with a message from the chief that they were upon the wrong road, and that they would be guided to a way across the Big Horn range, following an Indian trail.

6

The two cavalcades thus joined made a picturesque spectacle, the Indians in advance, followed by the long train of white men and their 121 horses. The Crows were excellent horsemen and delighted to show their skill. Even the women and children were expert. The white men gradually fell behind, and indeed were rather relieved when they were free from these natives, of whose good faith they were suspicious. The fears were unfounded, and no serious difficulty was experienced in the dealings with this tribe.

A small party of Shoshones was met with, who showed the way

toward Wind river, a distance of 30 miles, leading, as they said, to a pass through the mountains to the south fork of the Columbia. If Hunt had followed this direction, and had taken the advice of the men of his party who had been across the divide, his way would have been comparatively easy. But after journeying up Wind river some 80 miles, game being scarce, he abandoned the beaten trail and turned south. To the west they described snow-capped mountains, the Three Tetons, which pointed out the true route, where by crossing a single ridge the way would have been down the watershed of the Columbia.

7

The route selected carried them on a southerly detour upon the headwaters of Green river, the north fork of the Colorado. This, however, gave them another opportunity to hunt buffaloes and to lay up a supply of meat. Then they crossed the Gros Ventre range to a small stream recognized by Hoback as one on which he had trapped beaver the year previous. It still bears his name. It flows into the Snake, and so to the Columbia, and the party, on reaching the Snake after a hard struggle through the steep passes, re-joiced in the belief that their troubles were at end. The voyageurs began the construction of canoes, and every one was happy, feel-ing sure that they could now float down stream in comfort.

They were soon disillusioned, for those sent ahead by Hunt to examine the river returned with the report that it was not to be navigated. Four of the men left the party here, and began trap-ping, as it had been intended when the waters of the Columbia would be reached. They were Carson, St. Michel, Detay and De-launay. They were furnished with traps, guns and ammunition, horses and food supplies, and were to trap on the upper part of Mad river and other streams in this locality.

Robinson, Hoback and Rezner now urged upon Mr. Hunt the advisability of going direct to Henry's post. These men had been with Major Henry, and they recognized landmarks that led them to believe the fort was not far distant. At this juncture two Snake Indians appeared at the camp, and not only confirmed the state-ment that the Snake could not be navigated with canoes, but offered to act as guides to Henry's post. The whole party, there-fore, forded the river and followed a trail through Teton Pass, and on the 8th of October, 1811, succeeded in reaching this place, after some hard travelling. It was either opposite Elgin, Idaho, or a short distance below St. Anthony, Idaho, on the North, or Henry's fork, of Snake river. They found the buildings deserted, for the fact was, although they did not know it, that Henry had joined Lisa while the latter was still at the Aricara villages on the Missouri, and shortly after the departure from that place of Hunt and his party. Hoback and his two companions decided to locate for the winter to trap and hunt, and in this they were joined by Cass and Miller. Although Miller was one of the partners, and might look forward to something more than the meager pay and the hard life of the trapper, he had become discouraged and dissatisfied, and was unwilling to go farther.

It was October 19, 1811, that the overlanders took up again the toilsome journey to the ocean. The weather was already getting cold, and game was scarce. They had at this time no conception of the difficulties and hardships they were to meet in the weeks to follow. They left their horses in charge of the Shoshones, who promised to take care of them, and having built 15 canoes, anticipated a pleasant and easy voyage down stream to the sea. The Canadians were happy in forsaking the horses and again grasping their paddles, and the first day's journey met their happy expectations, for they easily made 30 miles with the swift current. But they were soon to learn that a serious mistake had been made when they abandoned their horses.

The next day was not quite so easy, for they met rapids, and portages had to be made, one around Idaho falls, and sometimes the canoes were let down with tow-lines. Twenty miles brought them to a camping place for the night, but after that difficulties rapidly multiplied. They had entered the Snake at least 600 miles above where Lewis and Clark had begun their voyage on that river, 1805, and most of the intervening distance was impassable. However, they covered 250 miles of arduous travel before they reached Shoshone falls. The canyon above and below this place, after examination, was reported unnavigable. They had already lost four canoes, with valuable contents, and it was estimated that they had no more than five days' food on hand. This was at Cauldron Linn, which may have been near the present town of Milner, Idaho, in the vicinity of Twin falls and Shoshone falls.

8

Now begins the anabasis of peril and hardship rarely surpassed in western travel. With no horses and with heavy packs that ought not to be abandoned, with no maps or reliable information of the nature of the country, with starvation near at hand, with winter coming on, and with a numerous party already much discouraged by failure to reach the objective within the estimated time, the outlook was bad enough, but the imagination fortunately could not depict the gravity of the situation in its worst aspect.

The party was now divided by Hunt into four groups, to increase the opportunities for getting game. McKenzie led one group of four men and turned northward, seeking navigable water that might be found on the Columbia, if it could be reached. His party succeeded in reaching Astoria in three months' time, after much hardship, but in advance of any of the others. Two parties, headed by Reed and McLellan, respectively, followed down the Snake on opposite sides. Crooks took six men and turned back to try to find help and food among the Shoshones, or failing in this, to try to reach Henry's post and return with the horses to overtake the main party, which would remain at the canyon with Hunt.

Hunt's men cached the goods, and caught a few beaver to help out the larder. Most of these goods were afterward taken by a band of Snake Indians, the place of concealment having been revealed by Turcotte, LaChapelle and Landry, who had left Crooks, in February, and had passed the winter with these Indians. The caches are supposed to have been on the north side of the river, opposite Milner. In three days, Crooks and his men returned to camp, having given up their attempt, realizing the impossibility of carrying it out in the face of oncoming winter.

It was decided that to follow McKenzie northward, without water, across the Snake river mountains and plains, would not be practicable, and the plan adopted was to follow down both sides of the Snake river, dividing the men into two groups of 18, led by Hunt on one side of the stream, and a like number with Crooks on the other. Dorion and his little family followed Hunt. It was now well into November. Each person, including Dorion's wife, carried a pack, and she had also during part of the time to carry her two-year-old child, while the four-year-old trudged along beside her. She was at this time nearing her birth of a third little one, but with uncomplaining courage she kept the trail with the party.

If this was an example of courage to the white men, they had another evidence of native worth on the third day out from camp when they reached a camp of Shoshones, who, although miserably poor, shared their little with the strangers, allowing them to purchase two dogs for much needed food. How Hunt and his party managed to subsist during the month that followed is a painful story. The storms of wind, and rain, and snow, added to the discomforts of hunger. Several times they met Shoshones, and procured a dog or two, or a few horses, but there was no game.

It was on December 6, 1811, that they saw Crooks and his men returning up stream on the opposite side of the river canyon, having turned back after going 60 miles below and finding it impossible to further penetrate the rugged country, where walls of rock and high ridges and deep chasms blocked their way, and where the river pushed swiftly between cliffs that rose from the turbulent water. The deep snow in the mountains made a detour away from the stream impracticable. Emaciated and hungry, these men had even eaten the soles of old moccasins.

9

Hunt returned to camp, where a horse had been slaughtered for food, and making a boat of the skin, ferried some of this food over to the starving men and brought Crooks and LeClerc across. But the boat was lost in the swift water before it could be used again, and there was no way to bring the other men over, or to share the remainder of the horse meat with them. Crooks was sick, and LeClerc was too weak to walk farther, while few of the others were fit to travel. Yet, there was nothing to do but to retrace the way. All were footsore, but the two parties proceeded slowly, leaving Hunt and five of his men behind with Crooks and LeClerc.

Dorion had somehow managed to hold possession of an old horse which he was using to carry his family. He steadfastly refused to give it up for slaughter, though starvation faced the party. But in this distress, a Shoshone camp was found, and a horse was taken and killed. The men on the other side of the river, by the insistence of Crooks, who had regained Hunt's party, were given a share by means of a boat made from the hide, but at the expense of losing a Canadian by drowning, and of losing the boat in the swift stream after a small supply had been taken over. For 10 days they had kept up their weary march without tasting food.

At this point, Hunt went forward with the main party, leaving Crooks, Day and Dubreuil. Day had given out and could not proceed, and Crooks, who was now in better condition, would not leave an old friend and employee in this plight. Fortunately some horses were procured at this place, and two were left with this small party, besides some meat.

The December weather was severe upon the underfed men, but the main body made a brave effort to go on. There were frequent snow storms, and ice was running in the Snake. The two parties retracing their course, after three weeks were united, when Hunt succeeded in crossing the Snake river in a canoe made of the skins of two horses, near the Payette or the Weiser, about where the city of Weiser, Idaho, now stands. Here three voyageurs asked permission to remain among the Shoshones, being unable to continue. The remainder now consisted of 32 men, besides Dorion and his family. They were fortunate enough to secure an Indian guide, with two of his companions who went with him part way, and who undertook to lead them by a feasible route, and, on the 24th of December, the caravan turned westward up Woodville creek, or modern Burnt river, away from the turbulent and canyon-bound Snake river, only to find other obstacles in their way.

The progress was slow and full of discomfort. They had five horses, but the men were wet with rain and snow and often had to ford streams of icy water. One meal a day was all that could be spared from the scanty store. On the third day one of the Canadians gave up in despair and lay upon the ground, unable to rise. He was put upon a horse, almost as weak as himself. The toilsome climb through the snow, taxed the strength and courage of the best of men.

10

Matters were at a serious pass when, on the 30th of December, at a place which is believed to be near the site of the present village of North Powder, Mrs. Dorion was taken with the pains of labor. Her husband had steadfastly led the miserable horse, that so far had served for her and for the little children, and for their bundle of belongings. Dorion now insisted that he would be able to do what was necessary, and that there was no cause to delay the party. Hunt left them in the snow, camped among the trees, and hastened on with his men, powerless to aid, and finding it useless to sacrifice all by lingering. Here the little family faced with courage the hour of peril for woman and child, and on that bleak day, near the close of the year 1811, a little human being came into the strange world.

Meantime another one of the Canadians with the main party collapsed and was put upon a horse, Hunt carrying the man's pack upon his own shoulders. But it was not long before they came to a place among the snow-clad hills from which they obtained sight of an open valley. This was the Grande Ronde valley, as it was afterward called, and here the famished men were delighted to find a Shoshone camp, where the Indians were friendly and hospitable.

The sun shone, there was little snow, there was food and good cheer. And here, on the 31st, came the imperturable Dorion, with his wife on the old horse, holding in her arms a new baby, while the two-year-old child wrapped in a blanket was slung at her side. The mother seemed unconcerned and none the worse for her experience. But it may be added here that a week afterward, while on the march, the infant died.

It may be as well to anticipate, and to interrupt the narrative to tell of this woman at a later period. Madam Dorion and her two children were seen among the Walla Walla Indians, April 4, 1814, when the last of the Astor expedition was passing up the Columbia en route to St. Louis. The husband and others had been killed by Indians while trapping on the Snake river during January of that year. With her children she had fled from the murderous savages, taking LeClerc, who was still alive, but wounded, and who died during the flight. She camped in a wild and secluded ravine, subsisting upon the flesh of her horses. She managed to reach the Walla Walla tribe in March, by a long tramp over the mountains, bringing her children through in spite of cold, hunger and fatigue. The Walla Wallas received her hospitably, and the helpless little ones, who had seen so many adventures in their short lives, were safe with the courageous woman, whose mother love had never failed them. On the date just mentioned, she called to the Overlanders as they were swiftly paddling up the Columbia, and it was from her that the first news of the massacre was received. Later, she married John Toupin, and was a respected resident in the French Canadian settlement in the Willamette valley. She died there September 5, 1850.

The stay at the Shoshone camp was for two days thoroughly enjoyed by the men. New Year's day, 1812, they celebrated, particularly the Canadians, with song and dance, and after their hardships the rest was welcome, while sundry horses, and dogs, and roots, furnished the sumptuous repast. Still, the end of the trail had not been reached, and the men could scarcely keep up during the journey over the Blue mountains, where the snow was waist deep. By bending every effort the head of the column came in the course of a week to a large Indian village, with well constructed and comfortable huts, made of mats. These Indians, who are designated as Sciatogas of Shahaptian family, which included the local Walla Walla tribe, were as well clad as wild hunter tribes that had buffalo and deer skin robes, and deer skin leggings and shirts. They had many utensils and implements of metal, showing that they had been in contact with tribes that knew the white men of the coast.

11

The travellers were grateful to learn that the Columbia could be reached by two days of journey. They had just one horse left, besides that one that Dorion had refused to have eaten. But now the hunger of all was satisfied and the caravan remained here in comfort, until all were refreshed and ready for the final effort. This site was upon the Umatilla river, where beaver were plenty, and the Indians agreed to collect skins ready for the white men's trade that was to be opened in the near future. These Indians had heard that a number of white men had gone down the Columbia, and Hunt decided, as was later proved true, that it was McKenzie and McLellan's party.

The route now led to the Columbia, where a crossing was made, and the trail down the north bank was followed. More tidings of the white men that had passed down stream were obtained, and also the first word of the settlement at the mouth of the river. On the last day of January, 1812, Hunt arrived at the Celilo falls and obtained canoes for the last part of his long journey to Astoria, where he arrived, February 15, 1812.

12

Thus was ended eleven months of continuous travel. As the canoes rounded the peninsula and came in sight of the fort they were greeted by the first Astorians, and also by McKenzie, Mc-

Lellan, Reed and their men, who had recently arrived. These had come together in the mountains near the Snake, and had travelled by way of the Seven Devils and the Craig mountains, on the route that Crooks and Hunt had abandoned as impossible. After extraordinary feats of endurance, they had overcome every obstacle and had reached navigable water upon the Snake, and, January 10, they had reached their destination by way of the Columbia river.

Crooks and Day, and their three Canadians, were still to be heard from. They were supposed to have perished, but Alexander Ross gives a graphic account of how Crooks and Day were found by Mr. Stuart on the banks of the Columbia, near the mouth of the Umatilla river, early in May, standing like two spectres, so changed and emaciated that they were at first not recognized as white men. Their story is a tale of starvation and sickness, and of cold and danger, incredible endurance and tenacity of life; but it is lightened by the kindness of poor and half starved Indians with whom they chanced to come in contact, and by whom their lives were saved on more than one occasion. The good Samaritan of all was found when they reached the Columbia. He was an old gray-headed Indian called Yeck-a-tap-am, who treated them like a father, and hospitably entertained them while they rested for two days. In after years, he had many dealings with the fur traders.

Their adventures did not end there, however, for proceeding down stream, they fell in with thieving Indians at the falls, who robbed them and stripped them naked, and would have put them to death, but for the intervention of three old men of the tribe. How the white men managed to get back to their friend Yeck-a-tap-am, without arms or clothing, and the desperate straits they were reduced to, in their search for food, and the kindly welcome in the humble Indian home at last, is a story in itself. This generous and kindly old man found them hungry and he fed them and found them naked and he clothed them, as best he could. He even had a horse killed, and the meat dried for them and put up in packages, and they were on the point of turning their faces eastward, with the intention of endeavoring to reach St. Louis again, when the rivermen in Mr. Stuart's canoes, sweeping down the Columbia, heard the loud and unexpected call in English, "Come on shore," and discovered these two noted and especially skillful and experienced westerners, now garbed in skins, poorer than the natives whose bounty they had been glad to accept.

Stuart presented a complete outfit of clothing to the old Indian, and the white men were soon in the canoes and on their way to Astoria. The three Canadians already mentioned had left them in the winter, preferring to take their chances with the Shoshones, whose uniform kindness to the destitute white men during this winter of misfortune was always to be relied upon.

13

On reaching Astoria after his long and arduous journey, Hunt was gratified to find the affairs of the post in a flourishing condition. The small schooner, Dolly, had been built and launched. This was the first vessel to be built on the Columbia river. The name was given in honor of Mrs. Astor. It began trading up and down the river, and was for a time put to good use, but it proved not well designed for the purpose and was soon laid up.

The tribes along the lower Columbia river with whom the Astor party came most closely in contact, such as the Chinooks, Clatsops, Wahkiacums and Cathlamets, were friendly. The outlook for profitable business was good, and, although the constant trouble experienced with the Indians, at Celilo, made the passage to the upper Columbia disagreeable and even dangerous, it was possible, by organizing large enough expeditions, to overcome this difficulty. Indians of the interior, such as the Walla Wallas, Cayuses, Nez Perce's, Shoshones, Okanogans and Kalispels, were not unfriendly, and experience showed them to be honest in the main and quite willing to have the strangers locate among them.

Early in May, 1812, the Astor sailing ship Beaver arrived at Astoria after a voyage of 212 days from New York, and this event seemed to assure the success of the whole plan, which involved not only the establishing of trading posts at the advantageous points, but also presupposed an ample stock of provisions and trading supplies always to be kept on hand at the principal station at Astoria. These were to come by sea. The Beaver had on board a cargo similar to that brought by the Tonquin, consisting of a great variety of articles attractive to the Indians, besides food, clothing and miscellaneous articles for the use and comfort of the white men. It also brought one of the partners, John Clarke, several clerks, and a number of natives of the Sandwich islands, engaged as helpers. Among the clerks was Ross Cox, a young man of intelligence, whose narrative of his experiences was published some years after. Two other clerks, Gabriel Franchere and Alexander Ross, wrote narratives, and these, supplemented by the journals of Alexander Henry, a Northwester, and the book, Astoria, of Washington Irving, afford unusually rich historical materials for the review of events of the times and place.

The commander of the Beaver, Captain Sowle, was a cautious man, who did not relish the duty of braving the bar. On his arrival at the mouth of the Columbia he stood on and off for two days firing signal guns, much in doubt whether an establishment had been located, or whether, if it had been, it was not already destroyed by the savages. He ordered out the cutter with the perilous duty of sounding the channel, in the same manner that Vancouver and Thorn before him had sought to enter the river. Fortunately, however, the weather was fair and the bar was not difficult, although the ship did strike twice in entering. The people at Astoria had already learned from the Indians of the approach of the ship, and Duncan McDougal and Donald McLellan not only answered with signal guns, but went down to Cape Disappointment, where they put up a flag and set fire to several trees, to serve in lieu of a lighthouse. The ship was met at the bar by these representatives of the company, in a barge with eight rowers, preceded by old Chief Concomly in a canoe with six Indians, whom Cox describes as "the most repulsive looking beings that ever disgraced the fair form of humanity."

McLellan took charge of the ship as pilot, and she was soon anchored in Baker bay. The recruits for the Pacific Fur Company's service went at once to Fort Astoria, where they found five proprietors, nine clerks and 90 artisans and canoe men, or voyageurs. The new party added 36 persons, including the islanders.

14

The description of the fort as it appeared to the new arrivals is of interest. It was located about three miles below Tongue Point. "The buildings consisted of apartments for the proprietors or clerks, with a capacious dining hall for both, extensive warehouses for its trading goods and furs, a provision store and trading shop, smith's forge, carpenter's workshop, etc., the whole

Figurehead of the "Beaver" — now in Beaver House, headquarters of the Hudson's Bay Company in London.

"S.S. Beaver"

The Hudson's Bay Company's "Beaver," in 1836, was the first steamer to ply the waters of the Columbia.

Crest of the Hudson's Bay Company
"*A skin for a pelt*"—*or* "*A pelt for a pelt.*"

surrounded by stockades forming a square and reaching about 15 feet from the ground. A gallery ran around the stockades, in which loopholes were placed, sufficiently large for musketry. Two strong bastions built of logs commanded the four sides of the square. Each bastion had two stories in which a number of chosen men slept every night. A six pounder was placed in the lower story, and they were well provided with small arms. Immediately in front of the fort was a gentle declivity, sloping down to the river side, which had been turned into an excellent kitchen garden, and a few hundred yards to the left a tolerable wharf had been run out, by which bateaux and boats were enabled at low water to land their cargoes without sustaining any damage. An impenetrable forest of gigantic pine rose in the rear, and the ground was covered with thick underwood of brier and huckleberry, intermingled with fern and honeysuckle. Numbers of natives crowded in and about the fort."

Soon after the arrival of the Beaver, the Astorians held a meeting of the partners to plan out the campaign for the occupation of the territory. They decided to establish a fort on Spokane river, to be under the management of Clarke, near the already located post of the North West Company. There was also to be a fort established on Flathead, or Clark's fork, and another on Kootenai river. Besides this group, the post at Okanogan, under David Stuart, assisted by Alexander Ross, was to be supported by another post, still farther north in the district called She Whaps, where the modern town of Kamloops now stands. A third region, up Snake river, was to have a post to be under the management of Donald McKenzie.

These forts and trading posts were duly established, with fair hope of success, excepting McKenzie's post on Snake river, which failed to develop a business of profit, on account of which McKenzie returned to Astoria, by January, 1813. A complete list of the stations established by the Astorians in their brief sojourn in the Oregon Country, with references to modern geographic place names is as follows: Okanogan, on the river of that name, half mile above its junction with the Columbia; She Whaps, at the junction of the branches of Thompson river, near Kamloops, British Columbia; Spokane, about 10 miles northwest of the city of Spokane, Washington; Kootenai, near Jennings, Montana; Flat-

head, between Noxon and Heron, Montana, on Bull river; Nez
Perce', at the mouth of Clearwater, at the junction of Snake and
Boise rivers, located by McKenzie, but abandoned; Wallace House,
near Salem, Oregon; and two temporary houses built by Reed,
near Fort Henry.

McKenzie failed in another duty that had been assigned to him.
He had been instructed to proceed up the Snake river to recover
the goods that had been left by the Hunt party on its overland
trip, but he ascertained that the cache had already been despoiled
by the Indians.

15

It will be seen that the Astorians made their arrangements to
spread their organization to strategic positions from the Rocky
mountain divide to the ocean, and from the Willamette valley to
Fraser river. It is apparent that, had these posts been held, it
would have been difficult for competitors to have gained a permanent footing in the Oregon Country.

The spirits of the Astorians, therefore, were cheerful enough,
after the arrival of the Beaver, in May, 1812, with the new recruits and with ample supplies. It was then thought that by securing and holding these good locations the threatened competition
of the Northwesters, who had no arrangements at the mouth of
the river, but who would have to depend upon the longer route
through Canada for supplies and shipment of furs, would not
prove serious. The Astor plans contemplated the establishing of
traffic with the Russians, who would furnish cargoes for the Astor
ships to supplement the furs obtained on the Columbia, and who
would take supplies brought from New York in exchange. It was
the intention, therefore, to have the Beaver followed by other
ships at frequent intervals. But Astor did not forsee the outbreak
of war with Great Britain, nor did he anticipate repeated loss of
vessels. Much less did he expect cowardice or treachery of his
partners and business associates.

The whole enterprise, however, seems to have been doomed beforehand to mistakes and misfortunes. One error was made that
proved serious. Hunt, who was loyal to his duty and loyal to his
flag, and who might have prevented the utter disaster that followed soon after, took advantage of the opportunity afforded by
the presence of the Beaver to get in personal touch with the Rus-

sian trade. Accordingly, he sailed with the vessel to New Archangel. He intended, of course, to return after a short absence, but upon reaching the Alaskan coast he was delayed by various causes, not the least of which was the peculiarity of the Russian potentate, Baranoff, with whom he found it necessary to deal. He survived the novel experiences at the feudal stronghold of that personage, as well as the lavish and yet primitive hospitality there dispensed, although he was not always able to drink all that was expected of him by his hard drinking host.

After many provoking delays he found that in order to get the expected cargo of furs it would be necessary to go to St. Pauls islands. He did not arrive there until the end of October, 1812, when he should have been back at Astoria. To make matters worse, the Beaver, by stress of weather, suffered injuries which seemed to require repairing at the Sandwich islands, and on this account it was decided to go there direct, after which, Hunt expected to return by some other vessel to Astoria, leaving the Beaver to go on to the Canton market. Arrived at the islands, Hunt allowed the ship to sail away, therefore, while he settled himself down to wait, employing his leisure in collecting food supplies such as he knew would be welcome at Astoria.

This might have been well enough in ordinary times, for he had every reason to expect that the annual ship from Mr. Astor would soon touch at the islands; but, after waiting until June, 1813, he found that the delay in its arrival was caused by a war between United States and Great Britain, which he now heard of for the first time, through the captain of the Albatross, a ship that came in from China, the same ship that the Winships had used on the Columbia.

Arrived at Canton, Captain Sowle, of the Beaver, held his cargo for a higher price than offered, and then found that the price fell farther, until he could not sell to advantage. Thereupon, hearing of the war, he feared capture if he returned to Astoria as directed. He therefore decided to remain in the harbor at Canton, where he borrowed money at 18 per cent, on Astor's credit, for expenses. The voyage was a complete failure.

16

It must have been provoking to find that the Albatross flying the American flag could venture on the seas and return to the islands, while the Beaver's captain still hugged safety at Canton. But Hunt's increasing anxiety to reach his post at Astoria led him, on getting the news of the war, to decide at once to charter the Albatross for his voyage to the Columbia, taking with him the food supplies that he had collected at the islands.

In March, 1812, the partners at Fort Astor agreed upon a strong expedition to go up the Columbia, which was to divide into groups to accomplish several objects. Reed was to head a party to go overland to report to Astor. Robert Stuart was to take supplies to Fort Okanogan. Russel Farnham was to recover the goods cached by the Hunt party, near Fort Henry.

The plan was but partly carried out. After having trouble with the Indians in going through the narrows of the Columbia, the party brought a considerable quantity of furs to Fort Astor, and were accompanied to that place by Crooks and Day. This large party arrived shortly after the Beaver came into the river. Mc-Kenzie made a hunting and exploring visit to the Willamette valley, and in November, 1812, Halsey and Wallace, with a large force, were sent to establish Wallace House, which was located near the present city of Salem. Early in the summer of 1812, the partners reorganized the groups that were to be sent east and up the Columbia. Robert Stuart was given the leadership of the expedition that was to carry despatches to Mr. Astor. Stuart's experiences will be described below.

17

John George McTavish, a member of the North West Company, coming to that company's post at Spokane House, direct from Montreal, January, 1813, brought news that the war had begun. According to his story, the Northwesters expected the immediate arrival in the Columbia river of a British ship, the Isaac Todd. No doubt McTavish made the most of his story, for he intimated that this vessel was to be armed and furnished with letters of marque, and that Canadians trading under the American flag would find themselves in difficulty with the British authorities on its arrival.

McKenzie, who was a Canadian before he was an Astorian, on hearing the story, at once brought the news to Astoria, where McDougal, in the absence of Hunt, was the partner in charge of the fort. Influenced by fears, or perhaps by other motives, the two partners decided at once that the Astor interests would have to be given up. McTavish descended the river not long after McKenzie's arrival at Astoria, and there he was hospitably entertained by the partners at the fort, while he gave them to understand that he was awaiting the arrival of the expected ship.

However, as the winter and spring passed without its appearance, McTavish's position at the fort became somewhat embarrassing and he withdrew up the river, but the Astoria partners, nevertheless, adhered to their view that the enterprise would have to be discontinued. It was determined that the summer should be taken advantage of for an overland return of the party to the east. By direction of McDougal, three messengers, McKenzie, Reed and Seaton, went up the river to the various forts on the Okanogan, Spokane and Pend d'Oreille, to direct the partners at these posts to bring all of their furs to Astoria. They were told to trade their remaining goods for horses, which were to be assembled at Walla Walla, and there left in charge of the tribe of that name, who were to keep them in readiness for the eastward trip with the entire stock of furs. In response to this call both Clarke and Stuart came down to Astoria from their stations, June, 1813, but both promptly objected to this abandonment of the posts. They had had good success, and this gave them assurance of profits. They could see no danger from a vessel, since, as they argued, it would be easy to remove and conceal the stores and furs that were at Astoria.

18

The North West Company had long been urging the British government to assert its exclusive sovereignty and to oust the Americans from the Columbia river country. Up to the time the war began, this had been refused, but upon the declaration of war the company renewed its appeals with more success, urging not only its own interests but the importance of the country, and the national advantage in driving out the Astor fur traders before the American enterprise developed into an actual settlement and occupation.

The North West ship, Isaac Todd, mounting 20 guns, was about to be sent by this company with a full complement of men and equipment for the establishing of a permanent base on the Columbia, and specific request was made for a convoy of armed vessels.

This was granted, and three men-of-war were furnished, under command of Commodore Hillyer. They were the frigate Phoebe, and the sloops of war Cherub and Raccoon. The Isaac Todd sailed from London, March, 1813, and was to meet the convoy at Juan Fernandez, but, being delayed, had failed to appear at the time appointed, and the war vessels proceeded to the Pacific ocean.

The Phoebe and Cherub, under the direct command of Hillyer, found and engaged the American frigate Essex, under Captain Porter, at Valparaiso, and after a fierce battle captured her. In the meantime, the Raccoon had been sent on to the Columbia to carry out the Admiralty orders "to take Fort Astoria and destroy the settlement."

On the other hand, Astor had been urging the government at Washington to furnish assistance for his enterprise. He heard of the decision of the North West Company to send its armed vessels, and suspected, if he did not actually know, that a convoy would be furnished by the British government. Being unsuccessful in his appeals for naval protection, he was full of apprehension for the fate of his establishment.

19

On Hunt's arrival at Astoria, on the Albatross, August 4, 1813, exactly a year after he had left that place, he was greeted with the disconcerting news that his partners were seriously considering selling out the posts to the Northwesters. As a matter of fact, they had decided to do so before the news of the loss of the Tonquin had been confirmed. It is to Hunt's credit that he earnestly and vigorously opposed this, but, finding that he made little or no impression upon McDougal and McKenzie, he decided to return at once to the Islands on the Albatross, which was bound for the Marquesas and could not be chartered for his cargo. His plan was to secure another ship at the Islands with which he could carry away the valuable stock of furs, which would by that time be assembled at Astoria, and at the same time he could carry out the pledge to the Islanders, in the employ of the company, to return them to their homes. These employees were some 25 in number, many of them at this time at the interior posts.

He might have succeeded in this plan but for another stroke of bad fortune. Although Hunt did not know it at the time, Astor had succeeded in spite of war perils and notwithstanding the government's refusal of naval convoy, in sending to the Pacific a third cargo vessel, the Lark. But, with the usual ill luck that followed the Astor venture, she was wrecked at the Sandwich islands and never reached the Columbia river. Hunt, therefore, did not succeed in getting the hoped for Astor ship, but after persistent effort he did succeed in chartering the American brig, Pedler.

With this vessel, taking the survivors of the crew of the Lark, he finally reached the Columbia river, February, 1814. But he was too late. The indefatigable man, had now wandered about the Pacific during 18 months of delay, disappointment and discouragement. This was time lost when his presence at Astoria was so necessary; nevertheless, he had displayed the same steadfastness and the same determination of character that had marked his conduct during the 11 months of his hard journey across the continent. Long before his arrival with the Pedler, however, the partners had sold out all of the holdings of the Pacific Fur Company, including the stock of furs he had taken such extraordinary pains to save. The Astor enterprise was at an end, and Astoria had been rechristened as Fort George. The Union Jack was flying in the place of the Stars and Stripes. The managing partner, McDougal, who had been left in charge, was now chief factor in the employ of the rival North West Company. This had been consummated October 16, 1813, and many of the partners and clerks, like McDougal himself, had accepted employment with the competitor. That company had succeeded in making a good bargain. It had become the owner of the fort at Astoria, and of the stock of furs, and the supplies at that place, and also of all of the other posts and property.

20

Hunt was soon told the unpalatable details. It seems that a few weeks after his departure on the Albatross, (the exact date was October 7, 1813,) John George McTavish had returned to Fort Astoria from the interior with a number of canoes and with a force of some 75 men, who proceeded to camp near the factory, and sat down to await the arrival of their ship. This time, as before, McTavish was compelled to wait longer than he expected, and this time he and his party were again actually dependent upon the Astorians for necessary food. The position of the Canadians became more and more awkward, as they were looked upon with suspicion by the Indians. Franchere, who was stationed at the Astoria fort at the time, says in his narrative:

"Weary at length with applying to us incessantly for food (which we furnished with a sparing hand), unable either to retrace their steps through the wilderness or to remain in their present position, they came to the conclusion of proposing to buy of us the whole establishment.

"Placed as we were in the situation of expecting day by day the arrival of an English ship of war to seize upon all we possessed, we listened to their propositions. Several meetings and discussions took place. The negotiatons were protracted by the hope of one party that the long expected armed force would arrive to render the purchase unnecessary, and were urged forward by the other in order to conclude the offer before that occurrence should intervene; at length, the price of the goods and furs in the factory was agreed upon, and the bargain was signed by both parties on the 23rd of October.

"The agent of the North West Company took possession of Astoria, agreeing to pay the servants of the Pacific Fur Company (the name which had been chosen by Mr. Astor,) the arrears of their wages, to be deducted from the price of the goods which were delivered, to supply them with provisions and to give a free passage to those who wished to return to Canada overland. The American colors were hauled down from the factory and the British run up, to the no small chagrin and mortification of those who were American citizens.

"It was thus that, after having passed the seas and suffered all sorts of fatigue and privations, I lost in a moment all my hopes of fortune. I could not help remarking that we had no right to expect such treatment on the part of the British government after the assurance we had received from Mr. Jackson, His Majesty's charge d'affaires, previous to our departure from New York, but, as I have just intimated, the agents of the North West Company had exaggerated the importance of the factory in the eyes of the British ministry, for if the latter had known what it really was —a mere trading post—and that nothing but the rivalry of the fur traders of the North West Company was interested in its destruction, they would never have taken umbrage at it, or at least would never have sent a maritime expedition to destroy it."

21

The sale of the various posts, and Astor's pelts and supplies, was for $40,000, although it is believed they were then worth over $100,000. In a letter to John Quincy Adams, Astor estimated the whole property to be worth nearer $200,000 than $40,000, the amount he received in bills on Montreal.

It was October 29, 1813, after the sale was consummated, that a large party set out for the upper river to make a transfer of the posts in the interior and to inventory and turn over the property there. Before this was concluded, Alexander Stuart and Alexander Henry, important men among the Northwesters, arrived at Fort Astoria. On the last day of that month, also, the expected British warship entered the river. It proved to be the sloop of war Raccoon, of 26 guns, under the command of Capt. William Black. The latter was greatly disappointed to learn of the sale and transfer of the post, as he had hoped to capture the goods with the fort. December 12 or 13, 1813, the American flag was hauled down and the British flag was displayed in its place. Captain Black's comment on seeing the little fort was: "What, is this the fort I have heard so much of? Great God, I could batter it down with a four-pounder in two hours!"

Captain Black's report to the British Admiralty was laconic, simply saying, regarding the sale that had forestalled him, that he "found party of North West Company here who had made arrangements with the American party before my arrival." He added that he had renamed the place Fort George, and had left the country and fort in possession and charge of the North West Company. He said "enemy's party quite broke up. They have no settlement whatever on this river or coast."

22

This indeed was true. The American settlement had come to naught and the Americans had abandoned the country by voluntary decision, a fact, which, had it remained so, would have deprived the nation of one of its most potent, if not its principal, claim in the historic controversy of future years upon the rights of sovereignty to this valuable domain. For, had Captain Black, finding the fort already in the hands of his countrymen by right of private purchase, refrained from assuming rights for his government, the restoration clause inserted a year afterward in the treaty of Ghent at the close of the war would not have applied.

That clause came to be inserted therein at the instance of President Madison, who, although he had no actual knowledge at that time of the private transfer of the fort, remembered Astor's urgent pleas for protection during the war, and therefore had issued his instructions to the American plenipotentiary with wise foresight. He had said, "Should a treaty be concluded with Great Britain and a reciprocal restoration of territory be agreed on, you will have in mind that the United States had in their possession at the commencement of the war a post at the mouth of the river Columbia, which commanded the river, which ought to be embraced in the stipulations should the possession have been wrested from us during the war." The very first article of the treaty, signed December 24, 1814, provided, therefore, as follows: "All territory, places and possessions whatsoever, taken by either party from the other during the war, or which may be taken after the signing of this treaty, * * * shall be restored without delay * * * "

By virtue of this provision the fort was later restored to American possession and the continuity of settlement and occupancy, so much relied upon by the United States in after years to establish its title to the Oregon Country, was thus re-established by international agreement. The American secretary of state, July 18, 1815, notified the British government that the President intended immediately to occupy the post at Astoria, Mr. Astor being desirous at that time to renew his plan, but as it turned out the latter did nothing further toward returning to the field of operations in Oregon, and it was three years later that the United States actually regained possession by formal delivery.

23

In September, 1817, the United States sloop of war, Ontario, under command of Capt. James Biddle, United States Navy, with whom was associated special commissioner J. B. Prevost, was ordered to the Columbia river with instructions "to assert the claim of the United States to the sovereignty of the adjacent country, and especially to reoccupy Astoria, or Fort George." On receiving information of this, the British government notified the North West Company that "due facility should be given to the reoccupation by the officers of the United States," but this was "without, however, admitting the rights of that government to the possession in question." The Ontario arrived in the river, August, 1818, although Prevost, who was detained in Chile on other governmental business, was not to arrive until later. Without waiting for him, Captain Biddle raised the American flag over the fort, August 19, 1818. Soon after, the British frigate Blossom arrived, and Mr. Prevost was on board, beside whom, James Keith, a partner of the North West Company, was a passenger. A formal writing was then drawn up, signed by Capt. F. Hickey, of the Blossom, and Mr. Keith, dated October 6, 1818, and delivered to Mr. Prevost, purporting to restore to the United States government "the settlement of Fort George on the Columbia river." The surrender was intended as a surrender of the settlement or fort, and did not purport to restore or release sovereignty of the country. But, this was not stated to the American representative at the time, or claimed by the British government in its diplomatic correspondence with the United States, until after the event. Captain Biddle, before the arrival of Prevost and the Blossom, had already posted some sort of a notice upon the river bank, making claim apparently to more than the mere property in question. The fort had been changed and enlarged. There were 23 British white men there at the time, besides 26 kanakas, 20 Canadian half-breeds and a number of women and children.

24

To recur to the situation at Astoria, or Fort George as it was now to be called. The younger Alexander Henry's journals give additional details of the sale. He tells of the altercations that arose with Hunt respecting the accounts and methods of payment. He says also that Hunt was not allowed to take more than four of the Sandwich islanders, the Northwesters insisting upon keeping the others, although they "wished much to see their own homes." The Pedler, on which Hunt had arrived, sailed away with him on board, April 2, 1814. It was not until April 22, following, that the long looked for Isaac Todd arrived in the river, with several passengers, including two more members of the McTavish name. Of the latter, one of them, Donald McTavish, arrived with authority to act as governor for the North West Company. He brought with him a handsome flaxen haired young woman, a former barmaid, Jane Burns, or Barnes by name, who is said to have been the first white woman on the Columbia river. Her superior personal charms, and also her numerous wonderful dresses, both of which she was fond of displaying at Fort George, excited the envy of the native women and the admiration of some of the males as well. The little schooner Dolly was rechristened "Jane" in her honor. Besides having a proposal of marriage from one of Chief Concomly's sons, she succeeded in making herself the subject of a jealous quarrel between Governor McTavish and young Alexander Henry. She sailed for China in 1814, and from there was returned to England at the expense of the North West Company. Young Alexander Henry and Donald McTavish and five sailors were drowned in attempting to cross the Columbia to visit the Isaac Todd, in rough weather.

25

Hunt, when he sailed away in the Pedler, early in the year 1814, carried with him some of the Astorians and some of the Islanders. Russel Farnham went with him, and he took despatches by way of Siberia and Europe to Mr. Astor, which he delivered safely in New York. On the Columbia river, it seems that the natives did not like the change of ownership, and could not understand the tame surrender to the King George men. Old Chief Concomly is reported to have offered his braves in support of the Americans, if they would fight. It is said that then and there he lost all respect for his son-in-law, McDougal, who soon found himself in bad favor with all concerned. He was taken into the North West Company, but his associates looked upon him as a cheat and the Americans thought him a traitor.

It was perhaps due to the arrival of Mr. Hunt, after the sale had been effected, as already related, that Astor's interests received any consideration. He succeeded with some effort in getting the settlement put in final form, and then he wrote a full report for Mr. Astor. Before he left he expressed to his Canadian partners his opinion of their perfidy in no uncertain terms, and in vigorous language he denounced the whole transaction, pointing out the ruinous sacrifice of values at the prices for which the furs and merchandise were sold to the competitor.

26

Before dismissing the account of the Astoria enterprise, some reference may be made to an overland party that returning to the east followed a new route which became important in the later settlement of the country. When the Beaver arrived in the river, May, 1812, at the general conference of the partners, it was agreed that, besides establishing interior posts as already described, it was advisable to send dispatches to Mr. Astor. As it was not practicable to send them by sea, the long journey overland was entrusted to young Robert Stuart.

Several parties destined to the various interior points and Stuart and his companions, altogether 62 persons, set out together from Astoria, June 29, 1812, under the command of Clarke. There was the usual trouble and delay at Celilo but while the Indians were troublesome and hostile, the entire party arrived safely at Walla Walla, by July 29, where they were to separate for their various stations. At this place, Stuart procured horses from the Indians, and he at once set off for the long journey to St. Louis. His party consisted of Benjamin Jones, Andre' Vallar, Francis LeClerc, besides two returning partners, Crooks and McLellan. John Day also began the journey with them. The party fell in with Miller and also with Hoback, Robinson and Resner, the beaver trappers, who had been furnished an outfit by Hunt. These men having been robbed by the Indians, now sought permission to rejoin the Astor party, but they soon changed their minds, and they were given a new and full equipment. They were again left to follow their trapping in the mountains. Miller, however, continued with the Stuart party.

John Day began to show new signs of his former mental malady soon after leaving Astoria, and it became necessary to turn him over to some passing Indians, who undertook to carry him back to that fort. The strain of his experiences on part of the very same general route that Stuart and his party were now to travel, apparently had resulted in a mild form of insanity, in which the sufferings upon the trail were ever present in his mind.

Stuart's party struck off southward and across the Blue mountains, but became confused and lost in the Snake river country, where they suffered every hardship imaginable. They were followed by hostile Crows, who stampeded their horses and left them to make their way as best they could on foot. Nearly starving, they reached such straits at last as to bring forth a suggestion of cannibalism from LeClerc, who urged that this was the only alternative as against the death of all. The winter was passed in temporary quarters. Stuart and his six men finally reached St. Louis, April 30, 1813, after nine months upon the arduous way, having travelled a course southerly from that of the Hunt party on their journey, thus leading to the Platte river and thence to the Missouri. This, in the after years, was substantially the Oregon Trail, although not precisely.

They had gone through the South Pass, but rather to the south of the route generally followed by settlers 30 years later. The Stuart trail, with slight exceptions, such as at South Pass, became the familiar route for ox teams and white covered wagons. Stuart's report to Astor on the posts and the prospects for trade upon the Columbia, dealt with conditions, of course, as they existed before the war, and before the serious disasters other than the loss of the Tonquin. In spite of the hardships and difficulties experienced by the expedition in entering the Oregon Country, there was enough at the time of Stuart's report to encourage Astor and to stimulate his hopes.

27

The Astorians knew the Willamette valley, and went far for furs and game. There is evidence that some of them, including Thomas McKay, Michel LaFramboise and Gabriel Franchere, explored the Santiam and Calapooia. Mention has been made of the fact that a party under McKenzie is said to have located a house near the junction of what is now called McKenzie river and the Willamette. The McKenzie river is named for this Astor partner. His journey carried him far to the south for purposes of exploration rather than for procuring furs. The valley was described as the garden of the Columbia, but it was not considered as good for beaver as some other sections, such as on the Cowlitz, and at the She Whaps, and in the blue mountains. As has been stated, Wallace and Halsey established a house near the present city of Salem in the fall of 1812. Wallace prairie, near the city, derives its name from this source. In the previous year Robert Stuart had taken a party, of which Francis Pillet and Donald McGillis were members, into the Willamette valley, returning to Fort Astor, March 30, 1812; and in 1813, another party fitted out by McDougal went still farther south. In this year also John Reed and Alfred Seton, two other clerks, took a party from Fort Astor into that valley. But the records are meager and unsatisfactory as to these expeditions, and there is doubt as to the distances covered. By 1816, their successors, the Northwesters, were in the Umpqua, as is learned from a reference to that river by Alexander Ross. How far the free men among the employees of that company, and later, of the Hudson's Bay Company, ranged in the following years cannot fully be determined, but probably they covered great distances. At the falls of the Willamette, as Ross says in his narrative, the Indians of the surrounding country were accustomed to gather in the spring to catch salmon, as also to gamble and gormandize for months together. His descriptions of the Willamette valley at this period show that it was "the frequented haunts of innumerable herds of elk and deer." It was to this fertile region that the Astorians turned for food supplies, when, by failure of the arrival of the expected ships, their supply of provisions grew scarce.

The earliest permanent residents of Oregon were members of the Astor party, who settled in the Willamette valley. Some of these, later, threw their influence in favor of the United States rather than in favor of Great Britain, when the question of a temporary government of the Oregon Country hung in the balance. These were Alexander Carson, William Cannon (both Americans), Joseph Gervais, Etienne Lucier, Louis LaBonte, DuBrueil, Thomas McKay, Michel La Framboise and Antoine Revoir (all Canadians).

After the Northwesters took possession of the business and enterprise that had cost so much in human life and human suffering they were not altogether satisfied. Alexander Henry, writing in his journal under date May 5, 1813, shortly before his untimely death, complains of the liberality shown by the Americans to the Indians in making gifts, and he criticises the price given for sea otters, thereby raising expectations too high; and he adds, "In short, the coasting trade is now of little value and will yield small profits, if any, unless something can be done with the Russians either on commission for them, or by exchanging goods for fur seals." The Northwesters were therefore beginning to see that the success of Astor's project in large measure depended upon that part of his plan which contemplated dealings with the Russians, and trading in the orient by his own vessels. Nevertheless, the transfer was a commercial triumph for the Canadian company, while it brought ruin to the Pacific Fur Company, which never recovered from the disaster.

28

So ended in failure the attempt of John Jacob Astor to establish a post and to plant the American flag at the mouth of the Columbia river. The chief reason for the failure, of the many that contributed to the result, was the unforseen war between the United

States and Great Britain. Notwithstanding the failure of the enterprise as a business, a first settlement was thus made in Oregon, and it was made by Americans. This was the logical sequel to the discovery of the Columbia river by Captain Gray, and to the first penetration of the country by the expedition of Lewis and Clark. The discovery of the transcontinental route by way of the Black hills, Wind River mountains and the Three Tetons; and finally the finding of a new road across the plains which afterward became the trail for settlers, and later the overland route for the first railroad lines,—these were important results of the Astor expedition.

The immediate effect of the failure of the Astor expedition was to add greatly to the strength of the British claims to the country, especially so, as many of the employees and some of the partners of the Astor company joined with their rivals. The restoration left the controversy as to sovereignty unsettled. The Astor enterprise made its permanent impress in several well known place names, such as Astoria, the John Day river, in Clatsop county, and that of the same name flowing to the Columbia from central Oregon, the McKenzie fork of the Willamette, and the town Gervais in Marion county.

It will not be out of place in closing this account of the ill-fated adventure to add that, some years afterward, Mr. Astor gave his own story of the expedition, with becoming dignity and restraint, in a letter that he wrote to John Quincy Adams, then secretary of state, dated January 4, 1823. He afterwards joined with partners, including Ramsay Crooks, in another western fur trading enterprise, which operated principally upon the Great Lakes, and in the Missouri river valley, but he never returned to the Oregon Country with his fur trading operations.

The purchase of Fort Astor was hardly completed before suggestions were being considered for a removal of the trading post. Alexander Henry, just before his tragic death by drowning, set out at length in his diary an argument in favor of going to the mouth of the Willamette, for a permanent site, and this was done some 10 years later. In the meantime, Fort George was maintained by the British company, although its location was changed to near Tongue Point temporarily, after which the new fort was given up and the site of the old fort was again adopted. In 1816, the

North West Company rebuilt and changed the site of Fort Okanogan, and two years later Donald McKenzie and Alexander Ross
under instructions of that company built Fort Nez Perce', afterward called Fort Walla Walla, about a half mile from the mouth
of the Walla Walla river, on the east bank of the Columbia. A
new fort at The Dalles was put under James Birnie, 1820.

CHAPTER XIV

ARCADIAN OREGON

1

IN THE EARLY YEARS of the 19th century, commercial transactions with the natives of the north Pacific coast were principally in the hands of Americans, whose ships from New England and New York would deliver furs at Chinese ports, and there get Chinese goods to be sold at home, or shipped to Europe. The British East India Company and the South Sea Company did not engage in the fur trade, but their restrictions kept British ships from the trade, and, moreover, the constant European wars during this period deterred such ships from undertaking the long voyage to the north Pacific. American vessels, on the other hand, were not hampered by British monopolies and made the most of the opportunity. Although there is no accurate record of those that visited the coast in this period, it is believed that there are unpublished records and reports of early American voyages, and that they may yet be found and published.

In the interior parts of the continent the situation was different. Bitter warfare between the North West Company and Hudson's Bay Company raged throughout British North America, from the Atlantic ocean to the Rocky mountains, for a period of 15 years, or more, but did not affect the Columbia river district, in which the Northwesters had no competitors after the surrender of the Astor interests. Hudson's Bay Company had ignored the region beyond the mountains for a century and a half. In fact, it had never sent a representative across the range until the year 1821, unless perhaps the crossing of Joseph Howse, 1810, through the pass that now bears his name, may be considered as an expedition of that company. That was little more, in fact, than an attempt to keep watch upon the movements of David Thompson, of the North West Company, who was operating for that company.

East of the Rockies, and west of the Great lakes, the contest between the two companies went to great lengths. There was fraud, theft and violence; liquor was freely used, and furs were purchased with whiskey. Indians were taught the worst and most dishonorable tricks of the white men. For 15 years, there was fierce fighting and murder, destruction of rival trading posts, corrupting of competitors' agents and employees, besides overbidding for skins and slashing of prices of trading merchandise and supplies. The attitude of the Northwesters was a general and vigorous protest against the non-resident control of the older company, and a determined opposition to its monopoly of the vast Canadian hinterland.

As has been stated (page 159), Red River colony, consisting of farmers and settlers, rather than of experienced hunters and trappers, located in Hudson's Bay Company territory, with the permission of the latter company, but was met with the violent opposition of the Northwesters. Five years afterward, 20 members of the colony, including its Governor Semple, were killed in a raid. Canadian courts were resorted to in criminal and civil cases, but warfare went on in the forests and in the open spaces, and upon the lakes and streams. Hunting and trapping in the summer season, when furs were not in the best quality, became a common practice. Young animals and females were not spared, and destructive methods seemed likely to ruin the fur trade within a few years.

2

But, by 1820, both sides were tired of the contest, and some of the wiser men began to think of a truce and a consolidation under the name of the older organization. This was effected in 1821, at London, England. The business of the North West Company in the Oregon Country had not proved profitable in the years immediately after their purchase of the Astor interests. There was friction between James Keith, in charge of the trade on the coast, with headquarters at Fort George, and Donald McKenzie, who had been with Astor's company, and who now had charge of the operations east of the Cascades. After 1816, supplies for the McKenzie trade came through Fort George, instead of overland from Canada. They came, therefore, through Keith's hands, and there was jealousy between the two Northwesters. Keith made an attempt to build up a trade in the Willamette valley, but without much success, at first, owing to conflicts with the natives. On the other hand, McKenzie, who travelled to and fro on the Columbia, established good relations with the difficult Indians at the Dalles. In fact, he lived with these natives for a long time one winter, when navigation on the Columbia was blocked by ice. He learned how to deal with these people, and he secured their confidence, but he always took precautions when he went through the narrows, and travelled with a strong body of men. He opened up a trade as far east as the continental divide.

McKenzie, at this time, had Alexander Ross for an assistant, stationed at Kamloops. Ross was a clerk, already mentioned in these pages, to whose readable account of the events of this period history is much indebted. He records the fact that orders came from the east, 1818, that required the erection of a new post on the Columbia, at the mouth of Snake river, on the site where Lewis and Clark had held a conference with the neighboring tribes. When it was ready, it was at first put in charge of Ross. The post was officially named Nez Perce′ fort, but it is now usually spoken of as Fort Walla Walla. As a matter of fact, it was not very near to the habitat of the Nez Perce′s Indians, but was close to both the Walla Wallas and the Cayuses. A great conference was held at this fort, attended by all of these tribes, and friendly relations were established with them. Snake river tribes were induced to make peace with the Nez Perce′s and to trade at the fort. McKenzie made preliminary examinations of the Snake river region, seeking to get the natives interested in trapping and hunting for the company. His first expedition was moderately successful and it was followed annually thereafter by other expeditions led by him and afterward by others, and with similar efforts to cultivate the friendship of the natives south of Snake river. McKenzie even strove to reach for trade east of the Rocky mountain range.

When he left this work, 1822, to assume a new position as governor of the Red River settlement, he had laid the foundation for a trade that almost excluded, or greatly limited, competition from American fur traders. He was, at first, succeeded by Ross, but the Hudson's Bay Company, soon after taking control, put Peter Skene Ogden in charge, and his travels reached far distances.

3

In the spring of 1825, Ogden went far south of Snake river, penetrated the country near Salt lake, and on the way his men explored and trapped the southern tributaries of the Snake for the first time. Late in the same season he went to the Klamath region. On this second journey he fell in with the Umpqua expedition under Finan McDonald, but they found the Klamath "destitute of provisions," and suffered for want of food, besides having difficulties on account of deep snow. Ogden spent some time trapping on Snake, river, and by July, 1826, returned to Fort Nez Perce'. He then proposed to lead a better equipped party of 50 men from Fort Vancouver to the unknown region west of Salt lake, as he believed that he would thus find new streams rich with beaver. He would take two years for this survey, sending a part of his men back at the end of the first season with what skins had then been secured, and keeping the other men of the expedition at work trapping during the second winter.

Always ready for new paths through unexplored country, upon arriving at Fort Nez Perce' he proceeded at once to Fort Vancouver by a new route, instead of descending the Columbia, as usual. With some of his men he crossed the country south of that river, to reach the Willamette, thence following that stream to Fort Vancouver. On this journey, he was the first to find a way over the Cascade range, perhaps by the Santiam Pass, finding snow seven feet deep on the way, and reaching his destination in the latter part of July, 1826. At Vancouver, his party of the previous winter was assembled and awaiting his arrival, not a man having been lost or injured on the long and adventurous journey into unknown territory. It was estimated that the skins secured on the expedition of 1825-26, amounted to 3800 beaver and otter pelts, yielding a profit of £2500. Ogden waited at Fort Vancouver until September 12, 1826, expecting the arrival of Governor Simpson, but the Governor did not come to the river in that year.

In the previous year, 1825, Ogden had sent a trapper, Antoine Silvaille, or Sylvaille, with five men, to the sources of the Owyhee and Malheur rivers. The Malheur river is not connected with the lake of that name, but Sylvaille had found another stream, very rich with beaver, flowing from the north and emptying in Malheur lake. This was a rediscovery of the stream, and although it was given the name Sylvaille, it is now called Silvies, or Silver river. It had previously been found by Ogden himself.

Ogden began his third Snake river expedition, September, 1826, with Thomas McKay and a party of 35, subsequently increased to 43 men, and they had over 100 horses. They crossed Deschutes river at Shearers Bridge, over a frail and rudely contrived structure, made by natives. Malheur lake and Sylvaille river were reached in due time, and the headwaters of the Deschutes were visited. The party spent the following winter on the streams east and north of Mount Shasta, including Klamath river. They may have reached as far northwest as Rogue river valley, and in the spring they travelled by way of the Malheur country to Snake river, and thence northerly to Fort Nez Perce', which was reached in July, 1827.

We may here follow the later expeditions into the Harney basin. Ogden made a fourth expedition to Snake river, 1827-28, but did not go to Harney lake. In the following year he went to the head-waters of Humboldt river, via the Owyhee, and returned by way of Sylvailles river and a tributary of John Day river. He was then succeeded in the Snake river district by John Work, who, in 1830-31, visited the Humboldt by way of Raft river, a southern tribu-tary of the Snake, and came into Oregon by Quinn river, whence he reached the southern part of Steens mountains, and then Harney lake. With the party was Payette, who had been with Ogden, 1828-29. The party trapped on Sylvailles river for several weeks, with success, and returned to Fort Nez Perce' by the John Day river and Blue mountains. In the following year, Work again had charge of the Snake river expedition, and, June 8, 1832, while en route southward he detached C. Plante to trap the Malheur river and Sylvailles river. Plante later reached Fort Vancouver, by way of the Deschutes and Columbia rivers.

4

The Snake country was not always free from American compe-tition. After the North West Company was no longer operating, 1825, some of the Hudson's Bay Company men deserted from Og-den's party, joined a party of Americans, and carried off supplies and furs, valued at £3000. Johnson Gardner was in charge of these American trappers, and, according to the report of the British company, he not only was a party to this dishonesty, but made threats that the Americans would be at the Flathead and Kootenay posts by the autumn of that year, and would drive the Hudson's Bay people from the territory. Nothing came of this, beyond stir-ring up the indignation of the Hudson's Bay Company, which re-newed its efforts, using improved methods, and with some success managed to keep out American competition, principally by gaining the confidence of the tribes, and by selling supplies and merchan-dise at prices that could not be met. Ogden found some of these

British deserters, with some Americans, in the same region, in the spring of 1826. They were 28 in number, but were having bad luck in finding beaver. Ogden got from the deserters what beaver skins they had, "in part payment of their debts," and secured, by trading, the remainder that the party had.

5

The failure of the North West Company to make profits on the Columbia river, during the years it operated there, was partly due to the loose business methods of the company in its eastern management, but was also due to the lack of convenient market for the sale of the product. The monopoly of the East India Company proved a serious obstacle in the China ports, for although a license could be obtained from that company to sell furs, and this was tried out for three voyages, from 1813 to 1816, those of the Isaac Todd, 1814, the schooner Columbia, 1815, and the brig Colonel Allen, 1816, the cost was prohibitive. No license to take on a home cargo would be allowed under any circumstances. The voyages could not be made to bring profits without getting the benefit of completing the circuit by carrying Chinese commodities to Europe. As already shown, American traders were not subject to the monopoly, and could not be so restricted. The North West Company, 1815, first tried the plan of having its supplies for the Columbia river sent from England to Boston, for trans-shipment to an American vessel, which then carried the merchandise to the Columbia, taking the stock of skins thence to China, there selling them, and putting the proceeds into teas and other Chinese commodities, and finally disposing of this cargo in Boston, for account of the North West Company, less charges for freight. This practice was followed by the North West Company from 1816 to 1820, but the profits vanished into commissions, freight and other expenses.

Transfer of interests on the Columbia to Hudson's Bay Company, 1821, put an end to such unprofitable methods, and the furs after that were taken direct to England. Still, the problem of disposing of the product to advantage continued to be serious. Various new expedients were resorted to. Without here pursuing the subject further, or going into details, it may be said that the greater efficiency of the Hudson's Bay methods, after the reorganization, improved the prospects; and, in the absence of exact figures, which the company has never published to the world, and which cannot now be accurately ascertained from available data, it may be assumed that the Columbia department was soon put upon a paying basis, and was maintained as a profit earning department.

6

When the Columbia river district, by reason of the coalition, first came under the jurisdiction of the Hudson's Bay Company there was serious consideration given, by the London office of the company, to an abandonment of operations in that district. We have this from a letter from the London authorities of the company, addressed to Governor Simpson, February, 1822, in which the subject is thus handled:

"We understand that hitherto trade of the Columbia has not been profitable, and from all that we have learnt on the subject, we are not sanguine in our expectations of being able to make it so in future. But, if by any improved arrangement the loss can be reduced to a small sum, it is worth a serious consideration, whether it may not be good policy to hold possession of that country, with a view to protecting the more valuable districts to the north of it, and we wish you to direct the attention of the council to this subject, and collect all the information which you can obtain from individuals acquainted with the country . . . Should the result of your inquiries be unfavorable to the plan of continuing the trade of the Columbia, it will be proper to consider withdrawal."

The members of Hudson's Bay Company council, according to Governor Simpson, in 1824, would have been willing to have thrown up all interest in the trade west of the Rocky mountains, and he wrote under date August 9, 1824, "If the Americans settle the mouth of the Columbia, it would in my opinion be necessary for us to abandon the Coast, and come into some arrangement respecting a division of the trade & move to the northward, as I conceive an opposition would be attended with ruinous sacrifice of money."

In the following year, Governor Pelly wrote to George Canning, secretary for foreign affairs, on the subject, and after telling him that Simpson was in London, and was ready to attend and give up to date information as to the Pacific northwest, he said:

"In compliance with a wish expressed by you at our last interview, Governor Simpson, while at the Columbia, abandoned Fort George on the South side of the River and formed a new Establishment on the North side, about 75 Miles from the mouth of the River, at a place called by Lt. Broughton Belle Vue point. Governor Simpson named the new Establishment 'Fort Vancouver' in order to identify our Claim to the Soil and Trade with Lt. Broughton's discovery and Survey. He considers the Soil and Climate of this Place to be so well adapted for agricultural pursuits, that in the course of two or three years, it may be made to produce sufficient Grain and animal Provisions, to meet not only the demands of our own Trade, but to almost any extent that may be required for other purposes, and he considers the Possession of this Place and the right to the navigation of the River Columbia, to be quite necessary for our carrying on to advantage not only the Trade of the Upper parts of the Columbia River, but also that of the Country interior from the mouth of Frasers River and the coasting Trade, all of which can be provisioned from this Place."

Governor Simpson attended and gave his testimony, and also answered a written list of questions submitted by the foreign office. Pelly's suggestion was for a boundary that would use the lower Columbia and the Snake, from the ocean to the summit of the Rockies, and thence along the divide to 49 degrees, stipulating for common use of the lower Columbia river for navigation.

Governor Simpson was of the opinion that the British government at that time was preparing to relinquish claims to the country south of the Columbia, from the mouth to Fort Nez Perce', and also to the Snake river country; but in this connection it may be of interest to note that the company soon stiffened its policy. We quote from a letter written by Governor Pelly and the London Committee to Simpson, dated January 16, 1828, following the then recent extension of the Joint Occupancy treaty of 1818, that enabled the two nations to continue for an indefinite period to occupy in peace the Oregon Country. The letter said: "The country on the West of the Mountains remaining to the Americans and us for an indefinite period, terminable by a year's notice from either Government, it becomes an important object to acquire as ample an occupancy of the Country and Trade as possible, on the South as well as on the North side of the Columbia River, looking always to the Northern side falling to our Share on a division, and to secure this, it may be as well to have something to give up on the South, when the final arrangement comes to be made."

On the whole, the policy of Hudson's Bay Company was to discourage settlement by Americans in the Oregon Country, although that policy was not strictly followed by the local management. The home office had no interest in promoting colonization by the British nation, excepting in the sense indicated by the letter quoted, and made no attempt to do so. Indeed, the region, remote from the British isles, was not easily reached either by sea or land, and was not attractive to settlers from the other side of the globe. It was to the company's interest to have it remain, just as it was, the home of wild animals, rich in furs but without permanent settlements. But Doctor McLoughlin, the chief factor at Fort Vancouver was not always in sympathy with the views of his superiors.

7

The authority for the merger of the two companies was an act of parliament, 1821, and the coalition agreement was entered into at London. This was effected under the name of Hudson's Bay Company, which retained the ancient charter rights and privileges in Rupert's Land. It also had an enlarged capital, and was granted exclusive trading rights from Rupert's Land to the Rocky mountains for a period of 21 years, and all rights in the Oregon Country, and on the northwest coast, that could be given by the British government, for a period of 21 years. In 1825, additional rights were given in the region north of the Columbia department, a province called New Caledonia.

There was a governor and a deputy governor in England, with an elected advisory committee of seven members. John H. Pelly was the first British governor. In America, there were, at first, two governors, Sir George Simpson and Governor Williams. There was also a partners' council, which was to meet annually. Governor Williams served until 1826, having charge of the southern and Montreal departments. Governor Simpson, with headquarters at York factory, on Hudson bay, had the northern department and the territory west of the Rockies; and after Williams' removal to England, Simpson became governor-in-chief, with all the American territories of the company under his authority. Field officers and wintering partners of the two old companies were organized into a partnership body, with rights defined by contract. There were 25 chief factors, and 28 chief traders, the chief factors being higher in grade, and having the principal general duties and authority, while chief traders were assigned to management of single stations, or to minor operations. Forty per cent of the annual profits were to go to the field partners, and 60 per cent to the proprietors. The 40 per cent was to be divided into 85 shares, of which two were to go to a chief factor, and one to a chief trader. Seven shares were to go into a retiring fund. There were also clerks and apprenticed clerks, the latter chiefly employed in keeping accounts and doing the necessary writing at the posts. The engages, or ordinary employees, were a still lower grade, dividing again into numerous classes.

The new organization had the energy and enterprise of the old Northwesters. Moreover, it had the unlimited capital and great prestige of the old Hudson's Bay Company, with its powerful friends in the home country, while the elimination of competition enabled it to conduct its business without indulging in practices that were reprehensible. Liquor traffic with the natives was discountenanced and suppressed, for it had become a nuisance, and an injury to the Indians, while menacing the safety of the whites. Friendship and respect of the natives was cultivated, and acts of injustice were frowned upon, even if committed by the company's agents. Ammunition was withheld from warlike tribes, in the interest of peace, but was supplied to others on liberal terms for use in hunting. Uniform prices for commodities, bought and sold, were established and maintained, experience showing that it was difficult to explain to an Indian the variation of price due to supply and demand, or the reasons for rising and falling markets. The company divided its vast domains into four departments for trade, of which the department of the Columbia comprised the waters of that stream and its tributaries, and, after 1825, New Caledonia, on the north. As already shown, early American traders were crowded out of the Oregon Country, as a result of the liberal terms offered to Indians and trappers by the big company, and by the fact that that company carried a large stock of such merchandise as the trade required, but rigorously enforced the rule that none of it would be sold to competitors to be used in competition. The goods were of excellent quality, and high standards were maintained, no inferior substitutions being forced upon the customer as just as good.

8

Governor George Simpson soon proved himself an efficient manager. He at once undertook to familiarize himself with the territory, and to inform himself as to the condition of its affairs. For this purpose he made a swift preliminary journey overland to the mouth of the Columbia river. He afterward visited Oregon in 1828 and 1841. He was on a journey around the world when he stopped in Oregon en route in 1841. He was highly regarded by his company, and his country honored him, 1839, by conferring knighthood upon him. There has, until recently, been a disposition to underestimate the extent of his influence upon the reorganization of the business in the Oregon department. But the recent publication of the journal of his first survey of the field, on his trip across the continent, 1824-25, reveals his dominating character, and supplements what little was otherwise learned from his letters and his readable, but superficial "Narrative of an Overland Journey Around the World," published, 1847.

Simpson was appointed joint governor of the vast domain of Hudson's Bay Company when he was but 33 or 34 years of age, and only two or three years after he had entered the service of that company as clerk in the London office. He continued to be governor for nearly 40 active years. He was born at Loch Broom, in Ross Shire, Scotland, 1787, or the latter part of 1786, an illegitimate son of a father of the same name. He went to London, 1809, and served as a clerk for a firm in the West Indies trade. After some commercial trading in that position, he was sent to North America, 1820, for the Hudson's Bay Company, and was first stationed in the distant Athabasca country. He remained there during the winter of 1820-21, and was given a more or less nominal appointment as governor, as already stated, without superseding the elderly Governor Williams, who was then under indictment on charges arising out of the conflict with the North West Company. He, it was, that selected Dr. John McLoughlin as chief factor of the Columbia district. Simpson was made governor-in-chief of all the territories of Hudson's Bay Company, in 1826. He died at Lachine, September 7, 1860.

9

John McLoughlin was born, October 19, 1784, at Riviere du Loup, about 120 miles below Quebec, on the east bank of St. Lawrence river. His father was a farmer, who was a son of a farmer, the latter an immigrant from Ireland. The mother, of Scotch and French extraction, was Angeligue Fraser, oldest daughter of Malcolm Fraser, a man of eminence, who had an extensive estate on the bank of the St. Lawrence, across the river from Riviere du Loup. Both parents of John McLoughlin were of the Catholic faith, and he was baptised at a nearby parish church. At the age of 16, he left home to get some training in the profession of medicine, although, like most other doctors of that period, he acquired the title without the benefit of a course at a medical school or hospital. At 19, he went to Montreal, where he is said to have practiced that profession for a time, but he soon went to Fort William, an important post of the North West Company, at the mouth of Kamanistikwa river, where he was resident physician and soon became a fur trader of marked success and ability, more and more depended upon for active work in the region east of the Rocky mountains and west of the Great lakes.

He married, about 1812, Margaret Wadin McKay, widow of the famous Northwester, Alexander McKay, who was with Mackenzie on his arduous exploring expeditions to the Pacific ocean, 1789-93, and who lost his life in the Tonquin massacre, on Vancouver island, 1811. There were four children of the McKay marriage, a boy and three girls. The boy, Tom, became in later years an active figure in the Columbia river region under the management of his stepfather, John McLoughlin. The children born to John and Margaret McLoughlin were John, Eliza, Eloisa and David. And besides these there was an older son of John McLoughlin, named Joseph, of whom the date of birth and name of mother are unknown. Physically, McLoughlin was of unusual stature, some six feet, four inches in height, well proportioned and strong, having a fine sense of dignity, but not devoid of affability. When he was chief factor of the North West Company, he was accused with others of that company of being responsible for the massacre of Governor Semple and party, of the Red River colony. He, and nine other persons, were put on trial upon this charge, at York, now Toronto, October 30, 1818, but all of the accused were acquitted.

He was present in London at the time the negotiations between the companies was going on, and took an active part at the conference. Three years afterward, when Governor Simpson was ready to take up the deferred plan of reorganizing the Columbia department, McLoughlin was his choice for the responsible duty of administration there. Simpson appointed him a chief factor, jointly with Alexander Kennedy, who was then at Fort George, and gave him the title and sole general management as soon as Kennedy retired, in the following spring. The council of the company confirmed the appointment at a meeting at Norway House, on Lake Winnipeg, June 20, 1825. McLoughlin, during the first years in this office, had an income from sixteenth seventeenths of a share of the company, which averaged about $8,000 per year, but the amount diminished, rather than increased, with the years. He had in addition an annual stipend of £500.

Governor Simpson, making a rapid first trip across the continent, 1824, had looked forward to overtaking McLoughlin somewhere on the trail. He had as yet had little opportunity to get acquainted with the man to whom such an important trust was to be confided. In his Journal he gives us a picture of Doctor McLoughlin as he appeared when he met him on the trail in the far west. It differs so much from the descriptions of him in later life, when his flowing hair was white, and when he was accustomed to dress with great regard to appearance, that the language may be here quoted. The month was September, 1824.

"On the 26th at 7 o'clock A. M. came up with the Dr. before his people had left their Encampment altho we had by that early hour come from his Breakfasting place of the preceding Day; himself and people were heartily tired of the Voyage and his Surprise and vexation at being overtaken in Riviere la Biche notwithstanding his having a 20 Days start of us from York is not to be described; he was such a figure as I should not like to meet in a dark Night in one of the bye lanes in the neighbourhood of London, dressed in Clothes that had once been fashionable, but now covered with a thousand patches of different Colors, his beard would do honor to the chin of a Grizzly Bear, his face and hands evidently Shewing that he had not lost much time at his Toilette, loaded with Arms and his own herculean dimensions forming a tout ensemble that would convey a good idea of the highway men of former Days."

10

McLoughlin had never, as yet, visited the Pacific coast, but his enterprise and ability had already been demonstrated. It was Governor Simpson's intention to expand and reorganize the business there, and if possible, to put it upon a profitable basis, operating regular ship service from England to the Columbia, opening up new trading posts, and extending the search for skins, especially beaver. Ample stocks of merchandise were to be carried, and a new central station was to be erected in the Columbia region, some place on the north side of the river. For, in compliance with a wish expressed by Hon. George Canning, His Majesty's secretary of the foreign office, the newly organized company had agreed to change the location of the old Fort George to some situation on the north bank.

It may be well to anticipate the narrative of the chapter relating to the boundary dispute, and to say that the government of Great Britain took an active interest in the reorganization of these companies, and had in mind further negotiations with the United States looking to an adjustment of the Oregon boundary. The suggestion, therefore, was no doubt prompted by the thought that in case the lower Columbia became the line between the two nations, it would be well to have the principal post of the trading company on the north bank of the stream. But, irrespective of this, the proposed change of location was desirable. It will be recalled that Alexander Henry, Jr., at Fort Astor, when the transfer to the North West Company was made, 1813, noted in his Journal the opinion that the Astor station was badly placed for trade, and that it ought to have been located at the confluence of the Willamette and the Columbia rivers.

Simpson seems to have acted promptly, after his arrival, in selecting the new site, and beginning its construction. In the early morning of the day of his departure on his return to the east, he dedicated the fort with the name Fort Vancouver. The date was March 19, 1825. The location was on the north bank of the Columbia, a short distance above the mouth of the Willamette, about one mile east of where the present United States military post stands, and a few miles down stream from the place that had been designated by Lieutenant Broughton as Point Vancouver, at the time of his examination of the river, 1792. There was a large area of fairly level, fertile land, slightly above the river and sloping gently to the stream.

11

Fort George was to have been abandoned when the new station was ready, but the company continued to own it, although it was not active as a trading post. It was put in charge of the clerk,

Donald Manson, and continued to be held for many years. Fort Vancouver could be conveniently reached by ships, as there was sufficient depth in the stream for vessels of the size used in the trade. The valleys of both the Columbia and the Willamette were easily accessible, and the Cowlitz river valley furnished a short route toward Puget sound. The post became one of the principal farming stations of the company, and from this time, under Simpson's plans, farming became a factor in selecting locations for trading posts. Four years after the dedication, the buildings were relocated and reconstructed, on low land nearer to the landing place, and, as so established, the post served as the principal trading station of the Hudson's Bay Company in the far west, until, at a date somewhat after settlement of the boundary dispute, possession was taken over by the United States and the old fort became a government military post, under the American flag. During the interval, the fur trade operations of the company radiated in all directions, and Hudson's Bay Company's influence extended from California to the Russian possessions of the north.

Among those who had charge of annual expeditions, was Alexander R. McLeod, one of the chief traders. His field was down the coast, south of the Umpqua, and into California. He was in charge of the detachment sent to recover the furs belonging to Jedediah S. Smith, taken in 1828 by the Umpqua river tribes, as elsewhere stated. About 1837, Michel LaFramboise was put in charge of the Umpqua brigade, and he, too, got out of bounds and trespassed upon the Spanish possessions in search of beaver. Another was John Work, clerk, who kept an account of his travels in the Willamette region. He had had a part in the Fraser river expedition, and in one of the Snake river expeditions, with Ogden, who was in charge. Ogden went further afield than any, visiting the Salt Lake region and central Oregon. He went also to the San Joaquin valley, in California, 1829-30, and on the way he met some Americans, about 60 in number, with Kit Carson and Ewing Young among them. In the following year Ogden was sent to the north, and founded Fort Simpson.

12

Governor Simpson's first journey to the far west was a notable feat. He took great pride in reaching Tongue Point, on the Columbia, in 84 days from York Factory, thereby "gaining 20 days on any craft that ever preceded" him. He believed he could do it in 60 days, in the next season, by taking the Saskatchewan route. He described Fort George as "a large pile of buildings covering about an acre of ground, well stockaded, and protected by bastions or blockhouses, having two Eighteen Pounders mounted in front, and altogether an air or appearance of grandeur and consequence which does not become and is not at all suitable to an Indian trading post." He added: "Everything appears to me on the Columbia on too extended a scale, except the Trade." This is characteristic of the man. He was an early example of the modern efficient business man, full of energy, thinking in terms of economy and improved organization, and intent upon eliminating waste and establishing business upon a sound basis. With a keen eye, he surveyed the district and instituted reforms, leaving orders for such changes as he deemed requisite. No detail was too small for his consideration. He was unsparing in his criticisms of the inefficient, but he had the faculty of discerning men of merit. His Journal is full of pungent expressions of opinion.

On his way to the Columbia, at the forks of Spokane river, he had his first meeting with Chief Trader Peter Skene Ogden, already mentioned. Ogden was at that time at Spokane House, but was then returning from the lower Columbia. With Ogden was John Work, clerk then stationed at Spokane House. The journalist took occasion to note that, although Ogden reported peace and quietness, and said that the company's affairs were going on as usual, this was not saying much. "If my information is correct," he wrote, "the Columbia Dep'tm't from the Day of its Origin to the present hour has been neglected, shamefully mismanaged, and a scene of the most wasteful extravagance and the most unfortunate dissension. It is high time the system should be changed and I think there is ample Field for reform and amendment."

It was in this spirit that he conducted his examination and made his report, and his Journal reveals the thoroughness of his methods, and shows that the improvement of the department that followed his visit was due primarily to Simpson, rather than to those whom he appointed to carry out his reforms.

His pleasure in the work of organizing the Columbia department, and his genuine personal interest in the plans for Fort Vancouver, may be seen from an entry in his Journal, under date Wednesday, March 16, 1825, three days before he left the new post on his return journey to the east. He said, with almost boyish enthusiasm: "I have the satisfaction to feel that the present visit has been productive of most important advantages to the Honble Coys interests; the Work of reform is not yet however thoroughly effected and to put the whole Machine in full play I find that my presence is absolutely necessary on this side the Mountain one more Winter at least. I can scarcely account for the extraordinary interest I have taken in its affairs, the subject engrosses my attention almost to the exclusion of every other, in fact the business of this side has become my hobby and however painful dangerous and harrassing the duty may be I do not know any circumstance that would give me more real satisfaction and pleasure than the Honble Committee's authority to take a complete survey of and personally superintend the extension and organization of their Trade on this Coast for 12 or 18 Months and if they do so I undertake to make its commerce more valuable to them than that of either of the Factories in Rupert's Land."

At Spokane House, at the junction of Spokane river and the Skeetshoo, or Little Spokane river, Simpson held a conference with his men. The Spokane district then comprised the posts of Spokane House and those at Kootenai and Flat Head rivers, and included also the Snake river region. There was at the time of Simpson's visit an encampment of natives of the Spokane and Nez Perce's tribes. Simpson came on horseback with Doctor McLoughlin, and Messrs. James McMillan, Peter Skene Ogden, and Thomas McKay, and found there Messrs. Finan McDonald and William Kittson, clerks, both of whom were on temporary duty at Spokane House. McDonald belonged at Flathead post, and Kittson at Kootenay House. After the conference, Ogden, and Work, his clerk, were given seven men at Spokane House; Kittson, five men at Kootenay House; McDonald, seven men at Flathead; and Ross, nine men for the Snake country expedition. All these, five officers and 28 men, were to be under superintendence of Mr. Ogden.

In this, as in many other particulars, the efficiency of Governor Simpson is clearly manifest, and his purpose to make each branch of the Columbia department justify its existence and bring net profits to the company was revealed. Incidentally, it may be noted that he had little respect for the talents of Ross, who has generally been highly regarded, chiefly on account of his excellent writings. Simpson selected the site of Fort Colville, subsequently built upon by McLoughlin, and by 1837, there were 22 trading establishments of the company in the department of the Columbia. Those established by Simpson north of 49 degrees were the most profitable to the company. They extended even to the territory of the Russians, in Alaska; two, Stikine and Tacou, were located within the Russian limits, by arrangement. At that time the company maintained six armed vessels on the north coast. Among the new posts in the north, established by him, were Langley, near the mouth of Fraser river, and McLoughlin and Simpson on the coast. Victoria trading post was not established until 1842.

13

Simpson cut down the use of European provisions and merchandise, which in the region west of the mountains had been extensively used, as they could be furnished by means of ships, and had been valued at invoice prices, not counting cost of transportation. Under his management there was an advance of 70 per cent on prime cost, which McLoughlin thought was too high. Simpson laid down the rule that the men should live on the country, and be satisfied with fish, game and such products of the farm as could be raised at the posts. He thought it unnecessary to employ great numbers of men for safe passage through the dangerous tribes along the Cascade region of the Columbia, and illustrated by citing his own experience. He insisted on discontinuing the practice of maintaining numbers of idle men through the winter months to have them available for the brigades and convoys in spring and summer. Everyone must work, and must make his services worth while. He planned to send seeds to be tried out at the various posts, and encouraged the cultivation of garden produce. He had ambitious plans for the development of agriculture, and the shipment and sale of grain.

Simpson visited the posts at Okanogan, in charge of James Birnie, clerk. He arranged to send Chief Trader James McMillan to explore the region of the Thompson and Fraser rivers. Lieut. George Vancouver, in spite of his careful survey, had missed the mouth of the Fraser, and as yet no one had attempted the ascent of the stream. An interior station, at Kamloops, on Thompson river, a tributary of the Fraser, was in charge of John McLeod, chief trader; but there was a vast region, not easily accessible, that had as yet been unexplored, and the expedition was to go from Fort George to the mouth of Fraser river, and thence inland. McMillan subsequently reported reaching the mouth of Fraser river, and exploring it for 60 miles, connecting this survey with the early survey from up stream, by Simon Fraser and John Stuart.

14

At the time Simpson took control, there was no traffic north of the Columbia river to Puget sound, or to Fraser river. Some years before, a small party of North West Company trappers had ventured as far as the southern shores of Puget sound, but they were waylaid by the natives, and one of the trappers, an Iroquois, was killed. A punitive expedition under Ogden had retaliated, and surprised and put to death a camp of natives, but there was no attempt at reconciliation, and the whites had, ever since, been careful to confine their operations to the banks of the Cowlitz. Simpson's investigation satisfied him that there was no reason for continued fear. In sending McMillan from Fort George to Fraser river in the autumn of 1824, he gave him a strong party of 42, including the experienced clerks, John Work, F. N. Annance, and Thomas McKay. They cultivated friendly relations with the tribes and opened to trade a vast country rich in furs, which later on proved profitable to the company.

At Fort Nez Perce', where chief trader, John Dease, was in charge when Simpson made his visit, which was reached by the Simpson canoes after paddling all night down the Columbia river, the post had been progressively improving for three years, but the profits were still small. The governor's shrewd eye saw opportunity for reduction of expense by discharge of some of the establishment of 11, and by "lopping off superfluities." In fact, he planned cutting down the forces throughout the whole department, from 151 officers and men, to 83 officers and men. The change would involve removing four clerks and 64 men, and would effect an annual saving of £2040 per annum, without diminishing the efficiency of the organization.

15

Simpson left specific instructions, under which the whole department of the Columbia was to be managed by McLoughlin, and there began that interesting development of western history that may be described as an American feudal state. Great rivers formed the highways. Canoes or other boats, furnished the favorite means of travel. Through forest and open prairie, mountain and valley, the area governed by McLoughlin, was, in his time, free from war. He taught peace and justice to the widely scattered native tribes, and inculcated a respect for the observance of law. With the coming of white men, gradually at first, and then in larger numbers, a new civilization crept in, and little by little the simple conditions of early years began to change. But, in all the years to come, there never was another period such as this, when the influence of one wise and good man was paramount. His word was law. And, while he had orders from his superiors in the company, he was quite the greatest man in Oregon.

At the fort, many distinguished visitors were entertained in a generous and hospitable way, and these included officials of the company, government officers sent out to explore, or to report, missionaries, travellers and settlers. Among the very early visitors was David Douglas, the botanist, called by the Indians the Grass Man, who made headquarters at Vancouver while ranging a wide extent of country in his examination of the local trees and plants. The Douglas fir was classified by him, and bears his name. He left England on board the Hudson's Bay Company brig, the William and Ann, and first arrived at Fort Vancouver, April 20, 1825. In that year he went up the Columbia, and down the Oregon valleys to the south. He was probably on the Umpqua, as well as the Santiam, and went to the coast in southern Oregon, travelling generally, all alone, and sometimes in hostile regions.

Peter Skene Ogden, one of the most important of the Hudson's Bay men, and the greatest explorer among them in this period, was in the Willamette valley, 1826, but went into central Oregon, across the Cascades, and continued on to the Humboldt river, originally called Ogden's river, and to the region north of Great Salt lake, but also went across the Rocky mountains in Idaho and Montana. The great journeys of Jedediah S. Smith through California and into the Umpqua valley, in Oregon, 1828, and the massacre of his party at that place has been told. John Work was in the Umpqua, 1834, and probably before that time the annual caravans of the Hudson's Bay Company from southern Oregon to Fort Vancouver were in regular operation.

The way to California through the Willamette valley and by trail over the Siskiyous became well established within a few years after this. Alexander R. McLeod, 1826-27, with a brigade from Fort Vancouver, having Michel La Framboise and Jean Baptiste Desportes McKay in his party of 30 or more, went by way of the Umpqua to Coos bay, and the next year went further south, perhaps to California. But, by December, 1828, McLeod returned to Fort Vancouver, and in the following year he headed another expedition, this time to the Sacramento valley, a district beyond the 42nd degree boundary, and therefore in foreign country where the expedition had no right to trade. After that, Francis Ermatinger, 1830, and La Framboise, 1831-32, and again 1834, were in California. The road from the Willamette valley settlement to the Sacramento valley and beyond became a well known trail, but the earliest explorer that had ventured into central Oregon, of whom there is positive knowledge, was Peter Skene Ogden.

16

Doctor McLoughlin became a picturesque figure. His abundant hair turned white, and he wore it long, which gave occasion for his Indian name, White Headed Eagle. He often carried a gold headed cane, and there is a story that he once used it upon a clergyman, the Rev. Herbert Beaver, although he afterward apologized for his heat. The minister had come out from England, 1836, with his English wife, Jane, he having been sent by the officers of the company, as chaplain. They stayed a year or so, and then returned home, apparently not adapting themselves very well to life in the far west. While at Vancouver, the dominie wrote some letters home, which made a point of criticising the custom of the country, whereby white men, including the Doctor himself, had taken wives of native stock, without a marriage ceremony, in times when there were neither laws, nor preachers, in the country.

A saw mill was erected on the river bank somewhat above the fort. Lumber needed in the company's operations was turned out, and some was shipped to the Sandwich islands. Carpenters and

Peter Skene Ogden
Trader, trapper, and brigade leader.

John McLoughlin
Chief factor at Fort Vancouver.

David Douglas
Early exploring botanist.

Sir George Simpson
Western governor of Hudson's Bay Company.

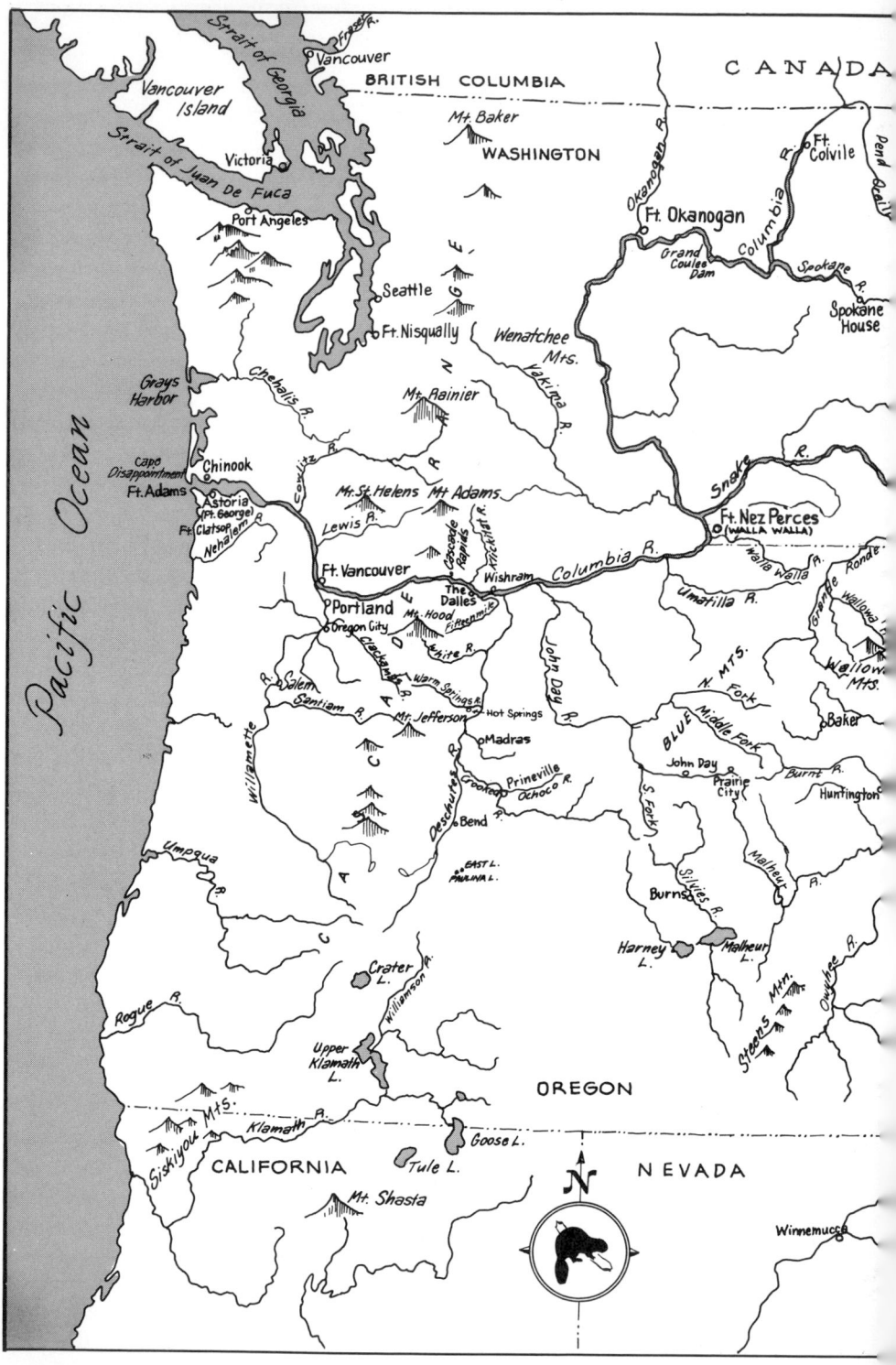

CANADA

BRITISH COLUMBIA

Strait of Georgia

Vancouver

Fraser R.

Vancouver Island

WASHINGTON

Mt. Baker

Victoria

Strait of Juan De Fuca

Port Angeles

Ft. Colvile

Pend Oreille

Okanogan R.

Ft. Okanogan

Grand Coulee Dam

Columbia R.

Spokane R.

Spokane House

Seattle

Wenatchee Mts.

Ft. Nisqually

Yakima R.

Mt. Rainier

R A N G E

Grays Harbor

Chehalis R.

Pacific Ocean

Cape Disappointment

Chinook

Mt. St. Helens

Mt. Adams

Snake R.

Ft. Adams

Astoria (Ft. George)

Ft. Clatsop

Nehalem

Lewis R.

Cowlitz R.

Cascade Rapids

Klickitat R.

Ft. Nez Perces (WALLA WALLA)

Ft. Vancouver

Wishram

Columbia R.

Walla Walla R.

Grande Ronde R.

Wallowa R.

The Dalles

Portland

Mt. Hood

Fifteenmile

Oregon City

Clackamas R.

White R.

Umatilla R.

Wallowa Mts.

Warm Springs R.

Salem

Santiam R.

Mt. Jefferson

Hot Springs

John Day R.

N. MTS.

Baker

Willamette R.

C A S C A D E

Madras

Crooked R.

Prineville

Ochoco R.

BLUE MTS.

Middle Fork

N. Fork

John Day

Prairie City

Burnt R.

Huntington

Bend

Deschutes R.

S. Fork

EAST L.

PAULINA L.

Umpqua R.

Silvies R.

Malheur R.

Burns

Rogue R.

Crater L.

Williamson R.

Harney L.

Malheur L.

Steens Mtn.

Owyhee R.

Upper Klamath L.

OREGON

N

Siskiyou Mts.

Klamath R.

Goose L.

CALIFORNIA

Tule L.

NEVADA

Mt. Shasta

Winnemucca

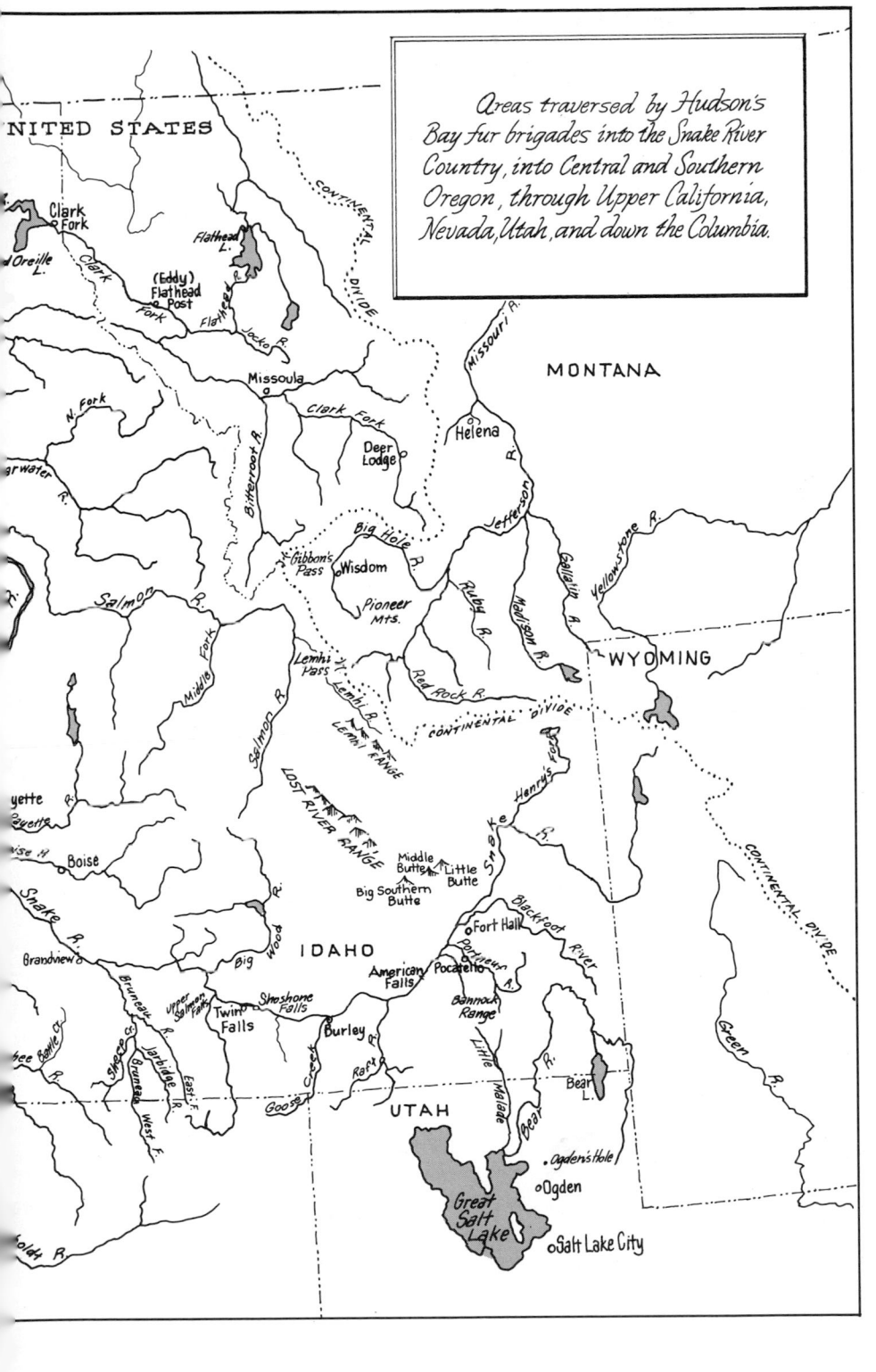

Areas traversed by Hudson's Bay fur brigades into the Snake River Country, into Central and Southern Oregon, through Upper California, Nevada, Utah, and down the Columbia.

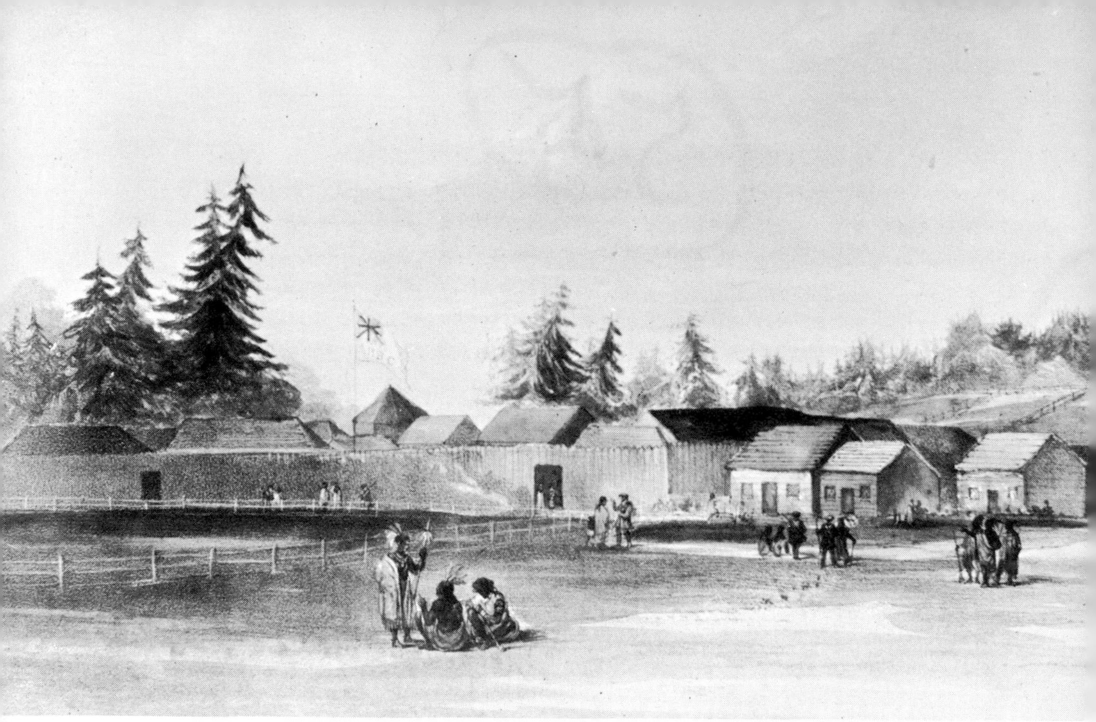

—Oregon Historical Society

Fort Vancouver, 1848
Sketched by Henry James Warre.

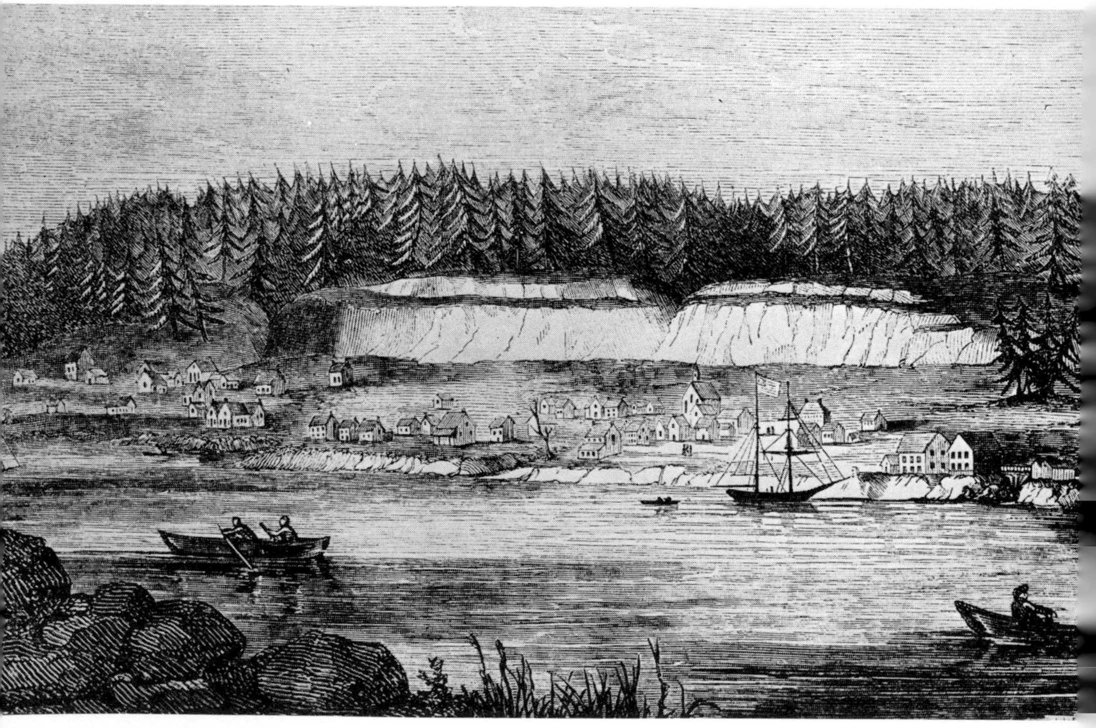

Oregon City, 1849
From a sketch originally published in Holden's "Dollar Magazine," New York, February, 1849.

other workmen were kept busy, for there was not only the building of houses and other structures to erect, but also boats and canoes, and even ocean going vessels. The various mechanical trades were represented in the variety of work undertaken, and some of the men could lend a hand as tinners, blacksmiths, machinists or millwrights. A flour mill was one of the facilities provided. It was located up stream, near a small brooklet that furnished water power, and it supplied ample quantities of flour for local use, besides some to be sold to the Russians, at Sitka. When a ship arrived, there was great bustle and activity. The place then assumed a business-like air, but, in general, Arcadian peace and tranquility prevailed.

It was not long after the stockade was built that it was surrounded by well cultivated fields, on which considerable crops of grain, vegetables and fruits were produced, for local consumption or for shipment to the Russians at Sitka. One farm where hogs were raised was on Sauvie island, and later there were extensive farms on the Cowlitz river, and at Fort Nisqually, on Puget sound. Dairy operations were carried on, and various domestic animals and poultry were produced. Even before Doctor McLoughlin's day the North West Company, in sending the ship Isaac Todd, had supplied four head of Spanish cattle, and the Astor people had had hogs and goats. With a few such animals as a beginning, others were imported from California, or elsewhere, and by wise restrictions on slaughtering brood stock, the herds and flocks were soon built up to considerable numbers.

In 1829, the buildings were torn down and removed, somewhat westward and nearer to the river, the location of the present United States army post. As rebuilt the stockade and buildings formed a parallelogram about 250 by 150 yards in dimensions, enclosed by a timber stockade, 20 feet high, secured inside by buttresses, and having bastions at the angles, each mounting two 12-pounders. Inside, there were two courts, each surrounded by buildings, built of wood, about 40 in number. These buildings were one story in height, and were used for offices, apartments for clerks and officers, fur warehouses, store houses for goods, workshops for carpenters, blacksmiths, coopers, wheelwrights and tinners. There was a school house and a chapel. A powder house was built of brick and stone. The chief factor's residence was two stories high, standing in the center. There was a public sitting room and a dining hall for clerks, officers, physicians, where meals were served with much formality, and at which Doctor McLoughlin presided, but the women were not accommodated in the general hall. Meals were substantial, and were free to those invited to partake. Wine was sometimes served, but no spirituous liquors. Here, visiting traders and distinguished guests were entertained in liberal and hospitable manner. There was, however, a gradation of rank, and Doctor McLoughlin maintained a dignity and authority that was almost that of a baron in feudal times.

The policy of the company to keep the country for fur hunting, required modification, after years. Americans began to appear, and to remain, many of them in dire distress. McLoughlin aided them, sending boats and food to meet them above The Dalles, and lending them supplies until they could get established, but for his kindness and humanity he was severely criticised by his company, and on the other hand some who were beneficiaries of his kindness failed to repay, or even joined in a movement against him. He helped the first missionaries, advising them as to favorable places for location in fertile districts, lending them boats and making them welcome at the fort, but some of them proved ungrateful. To his company he explained, at a later period, that the grain raised by the settlers, was needed to supplement that produced on the company's farms, for the cargoes sent out to Alaska and the Sandwich islands.

A native village grew up close to the stockade, for natives were not admitted, and trading was carried on through a port hole. In locating the fort, the Indians in the vicinity were assured that the company did not intend to seize their lands, and that all that would be wanted would be limited areas, and that the company wished to encourage hunting and trapping and would furnish goods in exchange for furs. They were told that war and violence would be severely punished.

17

It is a noteworthy fact, worth repeating, that, as long as Doctor McLoughlin ruled at Fort Vancouver, some 22 years, there were no wars; travel was safe, thefts were rare; and, after he resigned, although in no wise because of his resignation, there was a long period of bloody warfare, costing many lives. Prior to his arrival, white men must go in strong parties, to avoid trouble with the Indians on the way through certain districts, particularly on the Columbia river in the vicinity of The Dalles, but now the company was safe for travel while he was chief factor at Fort Vancouver, and this was in great measure due to his methods.

When Doctor McLoughlin came, the Indian population in the old Oregon Country may have been as great as 100,000, and, of these, it is estimated that there were as many as 30,000 below the mouth of Snake river. But, between the years 1829 and 1832, there was a series of fatal epidemics that had a devastating effect on the native people, especially upon the lower Columbia, so that families, whole villages, and even tribes, were totally destroyed, or so nearly obliterated as to lose their identity and become merged or absorbed with others. The effect was to greatly diminish, within a brief time, the native population. The white men's diseases, such as measles, smallpox, fevers, and various others, seemed to have a special virulence among these natives, and, of course, their filthy habits and customs, and their ignorance of proper methods of combatting these epidemics, made them an easy prey.

Doctor McLoughlin did what he could, but could do very little, to help them in these tragic years. However, he succeeded in getting them to abolish the custom of making human sacrifices. It had been usual, on the death of a chief, or other important member of a tribe, to put to death one or more of his slaves, for his use in the next world, and in some tribes the wife or wives of great men were sacrificed as a part of his funeral ceremonies.

18

The goods used for trade were brought to Fort Vancouver by ship, which required some six months for the voyage from England. The first voyage was that of the William and Ann, 1824-25. It stayed on the coast one season, and made other voyages, until it was lost at the mouth of the Columbia, 1829. Other company ships were regularly employed, including the Cadboro, Vancouver, Llama, Dryad, and steamship Beaver. The cargoes included great stores of woolen and cotton goods, tobacco, toys, tinware and household utensils.

But the company kept up its fast over-mountain express, by light canoe, for rapid communication with eastern headquarters and quick connection with Great Britain. The picturesque brigade, as it was called, having French Canadian voyageurs, skilled with the paddle, made great speed, requiring, however, approximately three months for a voyage from the Columbia river to the eastern posts of the company on Hudson bay, or Lake Superior. A messenger would reach Montreal in about 100 days from the starting time.

This passage, or voyage, as it was called, required about nine days from Fort Vancouver to Fort Walla Walla; four to Spokane House; three more to Fort Colville, the last of the company's posts in the Oregon Country on the route followed. Ten days more brought the express through the dangerous rapids and canyons of the upper Columbia to Boat Encampment, the highest point on the river to be reached with canoes. By snow shoe, thence, the men carrying heavy packs; the height-of-land, or summit, was reached in four days. Travelling down the Athabasca, horses were procured at Moose Deer Encampment, three days later. There was a ride to Jasper House, where boats were ready for quick going, down the Athabasca, to Fort Assiniboine. Horses were again used, to Fort Edmonton, and the crossing of Pembino river on the way was by rafts. From Edmonton to Fort Carlton was by boat, when horses were taken again for the Red River settlements, by way of Fort Petty and Fort Garry, (Winnipeg). Canoes were then taken for the journey of 11 or 12 days to York Factory, on Hudson bay. This was the eastern headquarters, where the American governor of the company, Sir George Simpson, resided.

The route from the United States to Oregon, which in after years became known as the Oregon Trail, gradually developed from knowledge gained by American trappers and traders in their western wanderings. It led through the South Pass, through which Thomas Fitzpatrick had passed, 1824, paralleling at that point the path that had been followed by Robert Stuart's party of returning Astorians, 1813. It developed into a regular route, used by the American fur companies, missionaries, explorers, and finally by the ox trains of the settlers.

19

In the year 1830, Edward Ermatinger, who for some time had been the accountant at Fort Vancouver, resigned and the vacancy thus occasioned was filled by the transfer of James Douglas from

Stuart lake, New Caledonia. The account books at Fort Vancouver were in his immediate charge. McLoughlin knew him and liked him from the old days at Fort William when Douglas entered the company's employment at that post as a young beginner. He was 27 years of age when he and his family arrived at Fort Vancouver. He rose in favor as the years went on. He had married, two years before, Amelia, daughter of Chief Factor William Connolly, who was located at the company's eastern headquarters. Mrs. Douglas was a favorite at the fort, where she and Mrs. McLoughlin were on most friendly terms, and under them domestic life flowed on without friction.

In 1834, Peter Skene Ogden was appointed second chief factor, with authority next to that of Doctor McLoughlin. In 1840, James Douglas was elevated to the positon of third chief factor, by order of the London office. These two, with the Doctor, were given joint power and authority, 1845, by which time there was some disposition on the part of Governor Simpson and those at London to find fault with McLoughlin's management. He retired in that year, and went to Oregon City to live, and the correspondence between McLoughlin and his superior officers, particularly his last letter written to them under date November 20, 1845, and his personal memorandum found among his papers, after his death, reveal the fact that serious friction and differences of opinion disturbed the latter part of his life. His compensation was cut down, by eliminating, without previous notice, his agreed annual salary of £500, leaving him his share of the earnings, but disgracing him, as he thought. His authority, which had been practically supreme for many years, was now diminished and was divided with others, and he could get no satisfactory or definite statement from the company as to its stand upon the important question of whether the land claim at Oregon City was to be considered as company property, or his own claim. It was intimated to him that he was subject to criticism for having engaged in business of his own, in connection with the Oregon City claim, in violation of the spirit of his contract of employment.

20

Puget Sound Agricultural Company was the outgrowth of gradual enlargement of the company's policy, which as time passed began to see that the Oregon department would become too valuable to be restricted to fur hunting. This concern was organized as a separate institution to meet objections of the conservative element among the Hudson's Bay Company directors, who feared that the company's departure from traditional fur trading policies might have an unfavorable effect on morale, by diffusing energies that should be profitably employed in that alone. However, there were advantages, too, that should be regarded, and agriculture offered profits. It was at first proposed to obtain from the government of Mexico an extensive grant of farming land in the Sacramento valley, in California; but, later, sites in the vicinity of Nisqually and the Cowlitz were preferred, as being more convenient to the headquarters post. The capital stock of the new corporation was £200,000, in shares of £100 each, and John Henry Pelly, Andrew Colville and George Simpson were named as agents. The superintendent of the company was always to be an officer of Hudson's Bay Company. Forseeing the conflict of agriculture and fur trading, the prospectus provided that no person in the employ of the agricultural company should trade in furs. In the final agreement it was provided that breeding stock should be transferred from the Hudson's Bay Company's farms to the new company, and all seeds and grains for agricultural requirements. The Nisqually post was transferred to the new company, 1842. The company established selling and buying agencies in San Francisco, and at the Sandwich islands. Thus was developed a department of Hudson's Bay Company activities not contemplated in the early plans of the founders.

Fort Nisqually, on Puget sound, had been chosen in the first instance as a branch trading post, in charge of Archibald McDonald, whose arrival at that site, May 30, 1833, is recorded in the "Journal of the Occurrences at Nisqually House." With four men, four oxen and four horses, McDonald had been 14 days on the way from the Columbia river. In the previous spring, however, while on a trading expedition to Puget sound, he had erected a small warehouse at Nisqually. The summer of 1833 was devoted to enlarging the building and constructing a stockade. Dr. William Fraser Tolmie, who had been sent from England as surgeon at Fort Vancouver, accompanied McDonald, and afterward became superintendent in charge of the agricultural company's affairs, where he remained many years.

The founding of Puget Sound Agricultural Company marked the decline of the fur trade in the Oregon Country. As the servants of Hudson's Bay Company retired from active employment in the fur trade, those of them that had wives were encouraged to remain and take up farms, although this was not in accordance with the original plan, which was to require them to leave the country when they quit the company's service. The Willamette valley attracted a number of them, and Doctor McLoughlin furnished them with seeds and livestock on favorable conditions. About 1829, a few of these former hunters, trappers and voyageurs settled in the neighborhood of the falls of the Willamette; about 1831, they removed to the vicinity of French Prairie. At first they engaged chiefly in the raising of livestock and in hunting, but as the Americans came in the farming industry spread to favorable locations.

Settlement of the boundary by treaty, 1846, at 49 degrees, north latitude, marks the end of British activities south of that line. An award of $650,000 was the amount finally decided upon as just compensation for the property taken over by the United States, consisting of 14 parcels, and was determined upon by a joint commission of the United States and Great Britain. This amount was paid by the United States, 1869, twenty-one years after Oregon territory had been created, to extinguish the private property rights that were enjoyed by the Hudson's Bay Company and Puget Sound Agricultural Company when the Oregon Country became subject to the absolute sovereignty of the United States.

21

By 1839, the annual harvest of furs obtained in the Columbia department had so far diminished from natural causes as to indicate that within a few years Fort Vancouver would no longer be the best place for the principal depot. In 1843, a new post on Vancouver island, well located for such a center of management, and well within the British domain, was erected. For several years the shift of authority to the new post was gradual, and perhaps without express intention, but in the spring of 1845, McLoughlin had written orders to remove the great bulk of the property from Fort Vancouver to Victoria. The reason given was the "jealous rancour and hostility" of the Americans, and the possibility of plunder. The foreign office was notified of this action, which no doubt had its influence on subsequent negotiations for the determination of the international boundary.

22

While it was the policy of Hudson's Bay Company to discourage settlement of the Oregon Country, it is manifest that Doctor McLoughlin was not wholly in sympathy with this. So far as the Willamette valley was concerned, he recognized that such a fertile district was essentially agricultural in character, and it appears that from an early date he had little real hope that lands south of the Columbia would become British territory. He took possession of the valuable claim at the falls of the Willamette, 1829, with knowledge and acquiescence of Governor Simpson. It is not clear whether this was originally acquired for the company, or for himself. To outsiders, it was his individual claim, but there is evidence tending to show that while as a matter of expediency it would be carried as his property, it was first taken in the interest of the company. Later he had definite views on the subject, and considered the property as his own. He began to look forward to the time when he could retire from company service, under the rules, when he would live upon his pension and make his home upon the claim. It appears from his correspondence, however, that the assumption of private ownership, was more or less due to the fact that the company did not want the claim, and that the officers of the company had made no answer to his early offer to hold the property for the company, and, indeed, were not pleased with his activities in connection with the land claim. It was certain that if the Columbia became the international division line, the claim would be in territory of the United States, and therefore subject to its land laws. So nothing was done about it.

Before retirement, 1846, when he resigned his position as chief factor, and incidentally, a comfortable income of $12,000 per annum, the relations between McLoughlin and Simpson were strained. Both of them wrote letters that show irritation, and the London office was inclined to criticise McLoughlin's conduct of affairs with the American settlers, and to indicate that the claim belonged to the company, or at least that McLoughlin had violated his duty and obligation to the company in so far as he undertook private business in relation to the land claim and mill at Oregon City. Hostile settlers, including some of the missionaries, believed that the claim belonged to the company, and complained of this to the government at Washington. McLoughlin then offered to turn it over to the company, conditioned upon reimbursement for his expenses, such as surveying and platting, erecting buildings and improvements. But, as his company did not accept, he built his home on the claim, and there he died, September 3, 1857.

It does not seem probable that the company could have acquired a title from the United States had it sought this through diplomatic channels. The last years of McLoughlin's life were embittered by a conspiracy to strip him of his land claim and to besmirch his reputation. He had decided to become a citizen of the United States, as early as 1845, and at that time consulted with Peter H. Burnett, chief justice of the provisional government, and also with Jesse Applegate, but as there was at that time no local official with authority to act in such matters, the formal application was deferred. He was, however, duly naturalized, September 5, 1851, a year after the Donation Act was adopted. Almost immediately on the organization of the territory of Oregon, under the laws of the United States, 1849, he took the required oath, and made the declaration of his intention to become a citizen. In June of that year, Samuel R. Thurston was elected delegate to Congress from the new territory, and on going to Washington was active in preparing and having passed the important Donation Land Law of September 27, 1850, which provided a grant of land to "every white settler and occupant of public lands, American half-breeds included, above the age of 18 years, being a citizen of the United States, or having made a declaration according to law of his intention to become a citizen, or who should make such declaration on or before the first day of December, 1851." The law prescribed residence and cultivation, as a condition to securing a patent for the land, and gave 320 acres to each single man, 640 acres to man and wife. The act contained, in Section 11, provisions confirming title to Abernethy island (a part of the McLoughlin claim), to claimants adverse to McLoughlin; and as to the remainder of the McLoughlin claim, expressly made it subject to the disposal of the Oregon legislative assembly, the proceeds thereof to be applied to the establishment and endowment of a university; but it confirmed title to lots that had been conveyed in the town site by McLoughlin, prior to March 4, 1849.

This unjust measure, which stripped McLoughlin of his land claim, was the result of false and malicious misrepresentations by delegate Thurston as to McLoughlin's character and conduct, and as to his rights as a settler and claimant of the land in question, accompanied by assertions that McLoughlin had refused to file his intention to become an American citizen. These statements were supported by some of the Methodist group, and by a few others, but were indignantly denied by many who knew the facts.

McLoughlin made a manly reply to the charges. He and his family continued to live in his dwelling house on the land claim, but he died before the injustice of this legislation could be rectified. In time public sentiment in the territory brought powerful influence toward remedial legislation, and five years after his death the state legislative assembly, October, 1862, passed an act authorizing the governor to convey and confirm the unsold part of the land claim, excepting Abernethy island, to the legatees under McLoughlin's will, in consideration of the almost nominal sum of $1000. Under this act, Doctor McLoughlin's son David, his daughter, Eloisa, and her husband, Daniel Harvey, got the greater part of the land claim, 12 years after the passage of the Donation Land Law, during which period the title was in the territory, or state of Oregon.

CHAPTER XV

THE AMERICAN ADVANCE

1

THE FIRST MISSIONARIES came to Oregon, 1834. This was before the settlers' movement began, and in this respect Oregon's history differs from that of some of the other parts of the United States. Before the missionaries came, there were influences at work that drew the nation's attention to the Oregon Country.

First among those who took early interest was Dr. John Floyd, of Virginia, a natural leader. He was a cousin of Sergeant Charles Floyd, of the Lewis and Clark expedition, the only member of the expedition to die on that memorable journey. He was the intimate friend of Gen. William Clark, and a warm admirer of George Rogers Clark. From a residence in Kentucky, he had gained a sympathy for frontier people and their problems. On his election to Congress to represent a Virginia district, Floyd resided at the same hotel with Ramsay Crooks and Russel Farnham, who were in Washington upon business relating to the fur trade, and who had participated in the Astoria enterprise. Senator Thomas H. Benton, of Missouri, who had been, for a time, inclined to under-estimate the value of the Oregon Country, was another resident at this hotel. Although Benton has taken credit to himself for orig-inating the Oregon agitation, it was Floyd who first presented the subject to Congress, and who first used the name Oregon for the territory on the Columbia. By persistent, vigorous and intelligent agitation, he kept this name before Congress and the people dur-ing the third decade of the 19th century. "It required not only energy but courage," wrote Benton, some years later, "to embrace a subject which, at that time, seemed more liable to bring ridicule than credit to its advocates. I had written and published some es-says on the subject the year before, which he had read." Benton here indulges in a pardonable bit of self praise, excusable in view of his later advocacy of western expansion. But the point as to Floyd is that, historically, he is the pioneer in Congress in the movement that resulted in the settlement of Oregon.

The session of Congress of 1820-21 was the first at which the question of occupation and settlement of the Columbia river terri-tory was discussed. Floyd moved, December 19, 1820, for the appointment of a committee of the House to inquire into the settlements on the Pacific ocean, and the expediency of occupying the Columbia river, and, being a member of the committee to which his resolution was referred, he made a favorable report, accompanied by a bill, January 25, 1821. The bill authorized the President to occupy "that portion of the territory of the United States on the headwaters of the Columbia river," to extinguish the Indian title thereto, to allot lands to settlers and to provide a government.

John Quincy Adams was secretary of state at that time, and his diary shows that the measure was shown to him by President Monroe, and that he not only did not approve of it, but was suspicious of the motives of Congressman Floyd in introducing it. Perhaps this was on account of its international aspects, in view of the joint occupancy agreement with Great Britain. Nothing more was done for almost a year. That bill died on the calendar, and Floyd reported another, January 18, 1822, which passed the House on second reading. It is noteworthy because it proposed to designate the region as "Oregon," this being the first official use of the name in connection with the territory, as distinguished from the river, the name having originally been applied to the stream but not to the surrounding country.

December 17, 1822, he delivered a long and able speech in support of the bill, in the course of which he intimated that transport over the route he outlined would require 24 days by steamboat to the falls of the Missouri, 14 days thence by wagon to Clark's river, and seven days additional to the mouth of the Oregon. He emphasized the advantage of obtaining control of the fur trade, the benefit to whaling and the profits of traffic with China. He reminded those of his hearers who might be inclined to regard the country as inaccessible that it had not been long since merchants first opening trade into Kentucky lost from 30 to 35 days in getting to market. From Louisville to New Orleans had formerly required a voyage of 30 to 40 days, which had been reduced to seven. The same calculations, he averred, could be applied to the journey to Oregon and, "as to distance, I have already shown that in point of time the mouth of the Oregon is not farther distant than Louisville was 30 years ago from New York, or St. Louis was 20 years ago from Philadelphia."

2

Oregon had another earnest and able champion in Francis Baylies, of Massachusetts, scholar, historian and Jacksonian federalist,
who was particularly impressed by the opportunities in the whale
fisheries of the Pacific. He was the first member of Congress to
call attention to the probable future of the Oregon timber industry.

Opponents of the Floyd bill contended that the effect of settlement of the Columbia river region would be to scatter the people
and diffuse their energies in fields in which they would be less
productive to society than they were under then existing conditions. The interests of the residents of the new territory, said one
speaker, would be in the orient rather than in the parent country.
The bill, coming to a vote in the House, January 25, 1823, was
laid on the table, 100 to 61. Much, however, had been accomplished
in the direction of stimulating interest in the Oregon question
among the people of the United States.

3

The persistent Floyd returned to the attack, January, 1824,
with a bill providing for a grant of land to each settler in Oregon,
the erection of a territorial government and authorizing the President forthwith to take military possession of the country. This
was followed by a second report, written by Floyd and submitted
to the House, April, 1824, in which was included a letter from
Quartermaster-General Thomas S. Jesup, U. S. A., who said that
he "considered the possession and military command of the Columbia necessary, not only to the protection of the fur trade, but to
the security of our western frontier." He advocated the establishment of a chain of army posts and suggested that by building
mills, cultivating the land and keeping cattle, the cost of maintenance could be greatly reduced. "As to the proposed posts on the
Columbia," he proceeded, "it is believed that they might be supplied immediately at a low rate. Wheat may be obtained at New
California, at about 25 cents per bushel, and beef cattle at three
or four dollars each. Salt, in any quantity required, may be had at
an island near the Peninsula of California." He thought that the
route from Council Bluffs to the mouth of the Columbia was practicable. "It, no doubt, presents difficulties; but difficulties are not
impossibilities. We have only to refer to the pages of our history
to learn that many operations, infinitely more arduous, have been

accomplished by Americans." He urged that the stations be designated and occupied without delay. The British companies, he said,
were wealthy and powerful, and it was not to be supposed that
they would surrender their advantages without a struggle. He
also pleaded the advantage to naval strategy of a post at the
mouth of the Columbia. "The northwest coast of America," he
said, "is an admirable nursery for seamen—many of our best
sailors are formed there. . . . The establishment might be considered a great bastion, commanding the whole line of coast to the
north and south."

The letter, and Floyd's argument in support of the bill, in the
course of which he outlined a more convenient route than had been
proposed by Jesup, nearly the route afterward travelled as the
Oregon Trail, made a favorable impression, so that December 23,
1824, the bill passed the House by a vote of 113 to 57. It empowered the President, whenever he deemed the public good might require it, to establish a port of entry on the Columbia river. This
was the first bill relating to Oregon to pass either house of Congress. It encountered opposition in the Senate, founded on belief
that it was in contravention of the treaty of joint occupancy, and
that, moreover, no territory thus occupied would ever become a
state of the United States. In the Senate, Benton supported the
bill, but it was laid on the table, March, 1825.

Another bill was introduced, December 18, 1827, but it never
came to vote, and for some years after that the subject was not
referred to again. Except for desultory references to the question
in the debates over renewal of the joint occupancy treaty, Oregon
was not discussed in Congress until late in the decade of the 30's.
Floyd had retired from Congress, 1829, to become governor of
Virginia. Baylies, of Massachusetts, retired in 1827, and the task
of keeping the Oregon issue alive was passed on to others.

4

In the meantime, however, 1824, a treaty between Russia and
the United States was concluded, that fixed 54° 51' north, as the
southern limit of Russian territory on the Pacific coast. Before
that, Russia's claim reached as far south as 51 degrees, and at an
earlier period Russia had even claimed and exercised the right of
settlement in northern California.

Where Floyd had introduced bills and resolutions, Hall Jackson

Kelley now wrote pamphlets, prospectuses and books about the Oregon Country, and urged action to save the rights of the American nation. He got up colonizing enterprises, destined never to come to fruition, and aroused the enthusiasm of various persons, whose interest he soon alienated by his vagaries. At length, though deserted by the companions who started with him, he went to Oregon, by way of Mexico overland, and through San Diego and the interior of California, the most devious route ever travelled. Arriving in the territory, October 11, 1834, already known as hostile to Hudson's Bay Company, and under auspices that made him a suspected horse thief through no fault of his, he devoted himself to making surveys and obtaining data concerning the country. Most of his visit was in a cabin at Fort Vancouver, during a long illness. He then returned home, but lost none of his enthusiasm for Oregon, and during the remainder of a long life worked industriously for the encouragement of settlement.

He taught school from 1818 until 1823. Early in life, he became involved in litigation through a venture in textile manufacturing, and one of his later obsessions was that the creditors who harassed him in the courts had been inspired by interests opposed to his plans for colonizing Oregon. He fixes the time of his own awakening interest in Oregon as 1817, or 1818, when "the word came expressly to me to go and labor in the fields of philanthropic enterprise and promote the propagation of Christianity in the dark and cruel places about the shores of the Pacific." He conceived the idea of founding a new republic of civil and religious freedom.

He presented a memorial on the subject to Congress, February 11, 1828, and he founded, 1829, the "American Society for Encouraging the Settlement of the Oregon Territory." In furtherance of his plan, he prepared a memorial setting out advantages to participants and to the government.

5

Nathaniel J. Wyeth came under the influence of the writings of Kelley. The two had an understanding that they would make the overland journey together, but Wyeth withdrew, on discovering that Kelley was unprepared to start at the appointed time. Wyeth was a man of action and his impatience with the dreamer is not hard to understand.

Kelley continued his solicitation of men of good moral character and industrious habits to join him, and also appealed to capitalists to consider the profits of such a venture. Seemingly he forgot nothing. He proposed a form of local government somewhat like that of the Michigan country. He had a scheme for allotment of lands. A pledge of $20 was exacted from each of his recruits, and at one time he claimed to have interested 3000 persons in his venture, but they never materialized. Perhaps 400 were enrolled.

6

The missionary awakening contributed to interest in Kelley's schemes, but Kelley himself seems not to have reaped much benefit from this. His obsessions, his delusions of persecution, the grandeur of his schemes for pecuniary gain, his unfortunate personality, all operated against him. The Methodist missionaries first to be enlisted for duty in Oregon owed nothing of their inspiration to this visionary. Nevertheless, he had encouragement from religious associations and individuals, and actually launched his project. He got a passport from the government for travel through Mexican territory, and was furnished by the postoffice department with free transportation down the Ohio and Mississippi rivers to New Orleans. A small party of his recruits proceeded from Boston by sea to join him at that port. Kelley loaded himself down with presents for the Indians, and with tracts and various other belongings.

His wanderings, in his effort to reach Oregon, rival those of Jedediah Smith and his trappers of 1828. Deserted and robbed by his fellow colonists, at New Orleans, and outrageously taxed by Mexican customs officials at Vera Cruz, he made his way, always with some baggage to hamper him, across Mexico, part of the way on foot, to San Blas, thence by water and land to San Diego, where he arrived, April 14, 1834. In California, he made the acquaintance of Ewing Young, who had reached the coast by travelling across from Santa Fe. Kelley's original band of colonists had been left far behind, but here, in California, he recruited a new company.

The party that was organized by them travelled north, driving a band of horses, mostly Young's, and were joined on the way by several shady adventurers, with a band of horses which afterward proved to have been stolen. As a result of this both Kelley and Young were set down as horse thieves by the Mexican governor of California, General Figueroa, who sent word by sea to Governor McLoughlin, at Fort Vancouver, that caused the gates of that post to be closed against them on their arrival, October 27, 1834.

On their way north, through the Sacramento valley, Kelley mentally outlined a branch railroad, to extend to San Francisco bay from some point on his great transcontinental line across the Rocky mountains to Oregon. Later, in the Willamette valley, the party passed the newly established mission of Jason Lee. The members of the party who arrived in Oregon with Kelley and Young were Webley J. Hauxhurst, Joseph Gale, John Howard, Lawrence Carmichael, John McCarty, W. K. Kilbourne, Elisha Ezekiel and George Winslow, the last a negro. These constituted Kelley's direct contribution to the settlement of Oregon, but they do not represent the limit of his usefulness in inducing western immigration, for doubtless many others were influenced by his pamphlets, newspaper articles and speeches, which he continued to publish and disseminate after his return to the eastern states.

7

Kelley's arrival at Vancouver on the Columbia, was an anticlimax. Doctor McLoughlin, regarding himself as governor of the region, and being disposed to treat the request of the California official in a spirit of comity between states, did not display his customary hospitality to these newcomers. He refused to receive Young. Kelley, being ill, he accommodated with a rude shelter at some distance from the post, and with food and medicine. Here Kelley in his loneliness was ignored even by his own countrymen, some of whom threatened him with bodily harm in consequence of his delay in plotting the land he had promised them for a town site. He did prepare the plan of a town to be laid out at the confluence of the Willamette and the Columbia, but it died, still born. Even Wyeth, who was then in Oregon on his second expedition, did not appear glad to see him.

Recovering somewhat from his disability, Kelley began in February, 1835, to explore the country roundabout, and to make observations, which he utilized in preparing a memoir after his return home. He was still dominated by the idea that the Hudson's Bay Company was hounding him, and so he failed to improve the bad impression he had made at the fort, on his arrival. Doctor McLoughlin, however, generously arranged for his free passage by ship to Hawaii, and presented him with a draft for seven pounds sterling. He sailed for home, March, 1835, never to return, nor ever, in the remaining 39 years that he lived, to cease to dream of the colonization of Oregon. Until 1868, he continued to publish books, pamphlets and memorials on the subject, and he died, a hermit, in Three Rivers, Massachusetts, January 20, 1874.

8

The Oregon question had been slumbering in Congress since the renewal of the joint occupancy agreement, 1827. Except for the appearance of Hall J. Kelley and his colonization schemes, and the efforts of Captain Bonneville to obtain reinstatement in the army after having been dropped from the roll for overstaying his leave, there was little to call Oregon to official attention. President Jackson, however, became interested and took steps to get reliable information. He dispatched William A. Slacum, a purser in the navy, on a mission of inquiry, 1835. Slacum received his orders from the department of state, probably on account of the dispute with Great Britain as to the title, and to give official authority, without emphasizing his military position. He had already shown his qualifications for such duty, and had made a report upon conditions in the southwest. The wisdom of choosing him is fully vindicated by the resourcefulness exhibited, and by his intelligent and comprehensive report.

His instructions required him to "proceed to and up the river Oregon, by such conveyances as may be thought to offer the greatest facilities for attaining the ends in view," and there to obtain data as to the settlements of whites on the coast and on the banks of the river, the relative number of whites and aborigines, the national character of the white residents, their sentiments toward the United States, and, in general, to possess himself of such information, "political, physical, statistical, and geographical, as may prove useful or interesting to this government." So instructed, Slacum was left to his own resources as to the manner of furthering his purposes. After several ineffectual attempts to reach the Columbia river from ports on the west coast of Mexico in small vessels that proved unseaworthy, and that nearly cost him his life, he took ship from La Paz for the Sandwich islands, where he chartered the American brig, Loriot, at his own expense. By this roundabout route he arrived in the Columbia river, December

22, 1836. He explained in his letters to the state department, that by having a vessel under his own command, he would be independent of the Hudson's Bay Company, and would also have shelter under the flag of his country, and could thus make needful inquiries unhampered by restrictions.

9

Slacum was received at Fort Vancouver with some suspicion, but not without hospitality, and he remained there for 10 days. He then travelled to the Lee missionary station. After a thorough examination of the Willamette valley and Puget sound, he went to San Francisco. On the completion of his assignments, he submitted a remarkably clear and detailed account of conditions, as he found them, at the mission and at the fur-trading posts. He told of the profits of the fur trade.

Slacum recounted a number of incidents to illustrate the monopoly held by the British fur traders, described the existence of the custom of slavery among the Indians, and the policy of the Hudson's Bay Company to encourage this as a means of saving "the company the expense of employing at least double the number of men that would otherwise be required on these [trapping] excursions."

He paid warm tribute to the work of Lee and his associates, particularly mentioning their "successful and happy efforts in establishing a temperance society among men who are generally considered as being almost without the pale of moral restraint. (I mean trappers)." At the time of his visit, he found that Ewing Young, who had been ostracized by the British company, which refused him food and other supplies, had made plans for establishing a distillery, and for that purpose had procured an old vat from Nathaniel Wyeth's abandoned establishment on Sauvie island. However, through the mediation of Slacum, Young was induced to abandon his scheme, and one of the interesting documents submitted by Slacum with his report was a copy of a petition addressed to Young and his partner, Lawrence Carmichael, by the settlers of the valley, pleading with them to consider the debasing effects of a liquor traffic on the aborigines and its peril to the infant settlement. The petitioners offered to indemnify the partners for their loss, if they would consent to abandon the scheme. This petition was signed by 30 settlers and missionaries, eight of whom were not members of Lee's Oregon Temperance Society. The missionaries obligated themselves to pay whatever amount was required, beyond what was subscribed by the others.

The partners yielded to the pressure thus brought upon them. Young explaining that he had been moved chiefly by the "innumerable difficulties and tyrannizing oppression of the Hudson Bay Company here," answered that favorable circumstances had occurred which would make it possible to "get along without making spiritous liquors," and freely promised to "stop manufacturing it for the present." He declined to receive any money payment whatever.

10

Thus, a crisis in the social life of the little community on the banks of the Willamette was averted. Slacum succeeded, at least partially, in establishing Young in the good graces of the Hudson's Bay Company authorities. Their attitude toward him arose from the mistaken accusation of the governor of California, and when this was cleared up, it was agreed that he would be permitted to get necessary supplies from Fort Vancouver on the same terms as others. Slacum offered to lend Young $150.00 and to give him and his partner free passage to California in order that Young might clear himself of the calumny resting on him.

Dr. Elijah White gives a somewhat different version of this story, and, without mentioning Slacum, attributes the efficient and diplomatic negotiations with Young to Jason Lee, and says Young acquiesced in what was represented to him to be the sense of the community upon the subject. He adds, "This was really a virtuous triumph, creditable to both parties." Mr. Lee's temperance society, he explains, was due to the custom of the Hudson's Bay Company to present a few gallons of liquor to the head of each family every holiday, especially at Christmas and New Year. This had been attended with pernicious effects, ruinous to the health and peace of the inhabitants. In some instances the brawls so produced almost resulted in murder; and at one time a woman lay insensible 30 days, brought to the point of death by the hand of her drunken husband. Mr. Lee was desirous of stopping this practice, as far as possible, and often talked with Doctor McLoughlin on the subject. As might be expected from a man of his decision of character and philosophic disposition, the governor readily and cheerfully concurred with him, and even went so far as to decide that no grains should be ground in the mills of the company for distilling liquors, and accordingly gave notice to that effect to Mr. Young.

11

Another opportunity to unite the interests of the settlers and to promote their material welfare, however, was presented. "I found," says Slacum in his report, "that nothing was wanting to insure comfort, wealth and every happiness to the people of this most beautiful country but the possession of neat cattle, all of those in the country being owned by the Hudson Bay Company, who refused to sell them under any circumstances whatever." In these circumstances, Slacum proposed the purchase of cattle in California for the settlers. Spaniards were producing cattle only for their hides and tallow, while Slacum considered the Willamette valley "as the finest grazing country in the world." He therefore offered free passage on the Loriot to as many settlers as chose to accompany him to California for the purpose of getting a herd and driving it overland to Oregon.

The proffer was accepted, and an agreement was signed, January 13, 1837. A fund amounting to several thousand dollars was subscribed by the Methodist mission, by settlers, and also by Doctor McLoughlin. McLoughlin had been won over to the plan, as it would relieve the company from the necessity of furnishing stock to newcomers. Slacum advanced Lee $500. McLoughlin subscribed for and took half of the cattle. Settlers who could not afford to invest funds were accepted as subscribers, on condition that they would go to California and assist in driving the cattle to Oregon, taking their pay in cattle. The party went south on Slacum's ship, and returned in the following spring with 700 or 800 head of cattle, a venture the significance of which was beyond the sum of money involved, since it introduced cooperation, as well as the first real feeling of independence of the Hudson's Bay Company.

12

There was another service performed by Slacum at the meeting held to organize the cattle company. "The liveliest interest appeared to be felt," he wrote, "when I told the Canadians that, although they were located within the territorial limits of the United States, their pre-emption rights would doubtless be secured when our government should take possession of the country.

I also cheered them with the hope that ere long some steps might be taken to open a trade and commerce with the country." The settlers were then receiving 50 cents a bushel for wheat at Vancouver; the Russians at Bodega bay were paying $1.50 a bushel to the company for this wheat.

In still another important respect the Slacum report is significant, for he made an earnest recommendation that the United States government hold out for possession of Puget sound. This was supported by an argument favoring the extension of the international boundary, westward to the Pacific ocean, on the 49th degree of north latitude.

Although he had been in the country only a month and a day, Slacum dropped down the Columbia river in the Loriot, January 23, 1837, and shortly thereafter put to sea, followed by the aroused hopes of the colonists, and bearing with him the members of the expedition, under the leadership of Ewing Young, to attempt a new cattle venture and lay the foundation of a self-supporting American community. Before leaving Oregon Slacum sent Lee a donation of $50.00 for the mission.

Whether due to his report, or to the missionary movement, or to the activity of promoters like Kelley, the next year, 1838, saw two bills introduced in the Senate relating to Oregon. These were the bill to authorize the occupation of Columbia, or Oregon, river, February 7, 1838, and the bill to provide for protection of citizens residing in Oregon, December 11, 1838. Neither bill passed. Charles Otho Haller and others, of Louisville, proposed to President Van Buren, 1838, a settlement of Germans in that district; and, the same year, an association was formed in New England to trade in Oregon. Neither of these projects was carried forward.

Another fact of importance occurred during Slacum's visit, which remains to be recorded. While he was in Oregon, Lee aided him in making up a complete list of all of the white settlers in the Willamette valley. The list of names included the following: Jean Baptiste McRoy, Andre Longtre, Charles Plante, Charles Rondeau, Louis Fourier, Joseph Gervais, Xavier Delarout [Laderout], Joseph Delor, E. Arquette, Jean B. Perrault, Etienne Lucier, Pierre Billique, Frederick Depau, Ewing Young, Lawrence Carmichael, William Johnson, Jas. A. O'Neal, Thomas J. Hubbard, William Cannon, Solomon H. Smith, Winslow Anderson, Charles

Roe, Elisha Ezekiel, John Hood, Webley Hauxhurst, John Turner, William Bailey, Calvin Ebbets [Tibbets], John Rowling, and George Gay. These 30 men, not including the missionaries or the Hudson's Bay Company officers, comprised the male population.

13

While farming in the Willamette valley cannot be said to have had a beginning prior to 1829, it is nevertheless true that several of the early white inhabitants, left over by the Astor enterprise, or connected with the fur companies' operations, had drifted into the valley before that date. Among those of the Astor expeditions may be mentioned Baptiste Dorion, Jean Baptiste Dubreuil, Joseph Gervais, Louis La Bonte, Michel LaFramboise, Etienne Lucier, Jean Baptiste Desportes McKay and Madame Dorion, wife of John Toupin. They with their families of native blood, managed to live by hunting, fishing and trapping, with perhaps some slight attempts at serious farming.

Etienne Lucier was perhaps the first real farmer. He left employment with the Hudson's Bay Company, 1828, and located for a short time on the Willamette, near the Stephens donation land claim, in East Portland, but about 1829 he moved up the river and located a farm three miles above Champoeg. Joseph Gervais, at about the same time began farming on French Prairie, and soon after Joseph Delor and Jean B. Perrault followed in the same district.

Father Blanchet counted 26 families in 1838, but by 1842, these had increased to 83. The population was estimated at 600 to 700 in 1845. Some scattered arrivals are enumerated in 1839, 1840 and 1841, but after 1842 the flow of settlers and ox teams began in earnest, and the population rapidly increased.

There was one party that was induced by Hudson's Bay Company to locate on Puget sound. It was from the Red River settlement in Canada, and left that colony June 15, 1841. Governor Simpson, who was making a swift journey across the continent, passed these families on the way, and gives a good description of the party in his narrative of his experiences on his round the world tour. The immigrant party was at Fort Walla Walla, October 4, the day that the fort was consumed by fire. The arrival at destination, Fort Nisqually, on Puget sound, was November 8, 1841. There were 23 families in all, including 77 men, women and children. About half of them refused to stay at that place, however, some of whom located on farms on Cowlitz river, or in the Willamette valley, although one family found its way to Edmonton, Canada, and another to California.

By 1831, Michel LaFramboise and Thomas McKay were given permission by the company to take up farms, without retiring from the service, or losing standing in the organization. McKay's location was on Scappoose creek, and in 1834, Louis La Bonte became foreman on that farm. Wyeth's expedition of 1832 brought eight or nine settlers, men who were released or discharged from the expedition. Of the latter, Calvin Tibbets and Solomon H. Smith, located on Clatsop plains, and Smith married one of the daughters of Chief Coboway. John Ball, another Wyeth man, has been mentioned in these pages, as school teacher and farmer, but he soon gave up and returned to his old home. On Wyeth's second visit, 1834, he, himself, took up an extensive farm, but he did not remain as a permanent settler. Rev. Samuel Parker, a visitor to Willamette valley, 1835, estimated that there were about 20 families in the valley.

14

Oregon settlement was influenced by immigration societies, established in many of the states to encourage and promote interest and to disseminate information regarding Oregon. One of the first was the already mentioned American Society for Encouraging the Settlement of Oregon Territory, organized in 1829, at Boston, by Hall J. Kelley. Another was the Oregon Provisional Emigrating Society that was formed at Lynn, Massachusetts, in 1838. This town was the former place of residence of Cyrus Shepard, one of the four missionaries who went to the Willamette valley in 1834. The society had for its object not only furthering actual settlement, but also to continue the work of converting the Indians. It proposed to send a colony in 1840, and it published a periodical called the Oregonian and Indian's Advocate. Then, within two or three years, there were emigrating societies in all parts of the country, and the weekly newspapers were devoting much space to their transactions. At these meetings all kinds of information concerning the route and methods of travel, the organizations forming, the character of the country and the problems of settlement, were discussed. The general promulgation of information in this way not only stimulated interest, but made it possible for those who considered the possibility of going, to join forces. The great migration of 1843, for example, was in no small degree due to such organization.

15

These last mentioned facts somewhat anticipate in point of time the sequence of our narrative. While Doctor McLoughlin was in charge at Fort Vancouver, there were two visits of historic importance by Americans. It was in no small degree through their efforts that the overland way to the Oregon Country was opened. One of these was the picturesque soldier of fortune, Captain Bonneville, whom Washington Irving has well described in his classic, "Adventures of Captain Bonneville, U.S.A., in the Rocky Mountains and the Far West." His full name was Benjamin Louis Eulalie de Bonneville; he was born in France, 1796. He had the friendship of Thomas Paine, and also of the Marquis de LaFayette. He obtained a cadetship at the United States Military Academy, West Point, from which he was graduated, 1819. While in service on the frontier, he perceived the profits to be derived from the business of trading in furs, and through his family connections, he secured financial backing for an expedition to the far west. He then obtained a leave of absence from the army for 26 months "for the purpose of . . . exploring the country to the Rocky Mountains and beyond, with a view to ascertaining the nature and character of the several tribes inhabiting those regions; the trade which might be profitably carried on with them; the quality of the soil; the productions, the minerals, the natural history, the climate, the geography and topography, as well as the geology of the various parts of the country." He was to go at his own expense, but there is some reason to believe that, outside of his written orders, there was an understanding with President Jackson, that he was to make an unofficial examination and to report upon the location and strength of the British posts in the Oregon Country. Incidentally, he planned to deal in furs on his own account. He organized a party of 110 men, provided himself with goods and equipment, and then set out from Fort Osage, 10 miles from Independence, Missouri, May 1, 1832, nearly a fortnight in advance of the departure of Nathaniel J. Wyeth, the other American visitor of this year.

16

Captain Bonneville's expedition, which was organized on military lines, was already upon the great plains. He went up the Platte and Sweetwater, and through the South Pass. On Green river, he built a post, but soon discovered that it was badly situated for winter trade, and it was never used. It was afterward known in the fur trade as Bonneville's Old Fort, or Fort Bonneville, but sometimes trappers called it Fort Nonsense, or Bonneville's Folly. He moved to the headwaters of Salmon river, and did some exploring to locate a field in which to hunt or trade for furs. He made some observations of latitude and longitude, which have since been proved erroneous, and he sent parties of hunters in different directions, who returned with stories of troubles with the Blackfeet Indians. But, after various experiences, he located for the winter on the Salmon and Snake rivers, and prepared for the spring hunt.

Wyeth, who had already been to the coast, was returning with a Hudson's Bay Company escort under the leadership of Francis Ermatinger, of the Vancouver post, and he met Bonneville here. Both had an opportunity to learn at first hand of the influence of the Hudson's Bay Company over the natives. Ermatinger, being at the time short of supplies, Captain Bonneville thought the opening was good for his own trade, but the natives were by this time so completely under the Hudson's Bay Company's influence that they refused to deal with him, and preferred to wait.

Wyeth and Bonneville planned a joint hunt, which was to have covered the country as far to the southwest as the mountains of California, but Bonneville changed his plans, and proceeded on his own account. His second season was marked by contentions with the representatives of the American Fur Company and the Rocky mountain men. He decided to explore Great Salt lake, and entrusted this part of the work to his chief lieutenant, Joseph R. Walker. He travelled on different extended journeys, sometimes hastened by a suspicion that he was being shadowed by Blackfeet, or Crows. December 4, 1833, he was ready again to go into winter quarters, this time on Portneuf river. Leaving his main party, he took three men, and started, Christmas morning, 1833, to visit the basin of the Columbia, and to ascertain the prospects for trading there. He reached the Hudson's Bay Company post, Fort Nez Perce's, or Walla Walla, March 4, 1834. But Chief Factor Pierre

C. Pambrun, while privately hospitable, made it plain that competing traders could not hope to obtain goods from his company. All that Bonneville got from him was some advice as to the safest direction to avoid hostile Indians, but from pique and suspicion the advice was not followed.

After proceeding to Bear river, Bonneville returned to within 30 miles of Fort Walla Walla, and sent another party to ask for provisions, but without success. He then travelled a short distance down the Columbia, below its confluence with the Walla Walla, but found the Hudson's Bay influence paramount everywhere, and as he could not get the natives to trade with him, he turned eastward. After spending the winter of 1834-35 in the upper Bear river valley, he returned to the settlements, which he reached, August, 1835. His leave of absence had long since expired, and he had been dropped from the rolls of the army, to which he was later restored by President Jackson, in recognition of his contributions to geographical knowledge.

17

It will be seen from this review of his activities that he covered a great territory, and penetrated the mountain country, including the upper Columbia valley. There has been some mystery about the nature of his errand, and doubt as to the extent of his official character as an investigator for the government. Research has revealed his first report to Major General Macomb, General in Chief, dated in the Crow country, at Wind river, July 29, 1833, the language of which indicates that he understood that he was to collect information as to the practicability of military occupation, but that he had found the country more extensive than he would have expected, so that he had as yet but "half a story," and would require further time to complete his report. But, he advised that the British hold on the country was weak, and could easily be taken possession of by small military contingents, which, if furnished with enough provisions to last until June, would be thereafter able to sustain themselves by farming and by living upon the local salmon. He recommended a full military company, and reported that "the information I have already obtained authorizes me to say this much, that if our government ever intends taking possession of Oregon, the sooner it shall be done the better."

The war department files show that President Jackson, before restoring Bonneville to the service, after his dismissal for over-staying his furlough, made inquiry of the department as to whether this report had been received and whether the command-ing general had approved of Captain Bonneville's continuing his exploring expedition, and had given him to understand that his furlough would be extended. Bonneville's actual contributions to the development of Oregon were small, but the publication of Irv-ing's popular book served to stimulate interest in the Oregon Country.

A station on the railroad on the south bank of the Columbia is called Bonneville. The great dam on the river at this place also bears his name. He was in command, 1853, at Fort Van-couver. There, he laid out and made a map of the military reservation of 640 acres, that had been acquired by the United States from Hudson's Bay Company. He also had a part in the war with Mexico, and in the local Indian wars in the Oregon Country. He became a general, and was twice brevetted, first for gallantry in the Mexican war, and again for meritorious services. At the time of his death, 1878, he was the oldest officer in the army.

18

In contrast to Bonneville, Wyeth was a prudent, industrious and sagacious business man, one who never lost sight of the main object of his commercial business enterprise. As a youth, at Bos-ton, he was employed by Frederick Tudor, who had the first organ-ized ice industry in the United States, and Wyeth, himself, after-ward invented many of the appliances which have been employed in the cutting and storing of natural ice. He had read much con-cerning the far west, and believed it offered a good opportunity for the use of his talents for business and organization, in fur trading and in salmon packing. He first planned to join with Hall J. Kelley, the Boston schoolmaster already mentioned in this chap-ter, who was organizing an "Oregon Colonization Society" to go out west. But he soon began to suspect that Kelley was a vision-ary, and decided not to wait for him.

Letters written by Wyeth before leaving on the first of his two expeditions show him to have been both a business man and a patriot. There is no doubt that he conceived it to be part of his mission to open the way to colonization of the Oregon Country, though the primary object of his expedition was the profit to be derived from trade. He asked for himself no monopolistic privileges. "We . . . only wish that something should be done as an inducement for Americans generally to go out to that Country," he wrote from Cambridge, Massachusetts, to Edward Everett, at Washington, January 6, 1831, "in order to form a predominating interest there to counteract that of the British already established. Government would poorly serve our interests in granting to the Oregon Society [Kelley's organization] any exclusive privileges there. Nothing on our part is desirable, excepting aid to get men out there and enacting some laws for their regulation when there, and then leave us to ourselves."

At the same time, he was making every effort to inform himself upon the methods of curing and packing of salmon for export, and as to raising tobacco for the Indian trade. Prior to setting out overland, he had arranged for shipment of a cargo of goods by sea, for which purpose he chartered a small vessel, the Sultana, subsequent loss of which contributed to the failure of his first expedition.

Wyeth left Boston harbor, March 11, 1832, with his party of 20 men. At Baltimore he was joined by John Ball and two others. On reaching Missouri, Wyeth was told by experienced up-river traders that boat wagons, with which he had provided himself, were likely to prove a hindrance rather than a help to travel, so he sold them and proceeded to Independence, Missouri. There he met Capt. W. L. Sublette, a fur trader, then on his way up-river from St. Louis on his annual expedition to the mountains. Sublette agreed to a union of forces for the trip, and the expedition left Independence, May 12, 1832. Wyeth soon lost five of his men by desertion. The two parties stayed together for mutual protection as far as Pierre's Hole. At this point, the prospect of being left without more experienced guidance, and tales that the party had heard of the perils beyond, caused fainter hearts to weaken. One of the party, a cousin of Captain Wyeth, has said that the malcontents demanded "what we had been used to at home,—a town meeting, or a parish meeting, where every freeman had a right to speak his sentiments, and to vote thereon."

Captain Wyeth, while assenting to the plan of permitting his followers to decide whether they would go on or turn back, declined to permit a vote that would be binding on the expedition. He simply ordered the roll to be called, the clerk asking each person if he would go on, or return. Seven answered that they would return, and the party was thus reduced to eleven, besides its captain. The faint hearted returned east with William L. Sublette, while Wyeth and his loyal followers proceeded westward, accompanied for a few days by Milton G. Sublette, brother of William. Milton was bound on a fur trading expedition that would take him through the Blackfeet country.

19

W. L. Sublette had trouble with the Indians, three men being killed, and several, including Sublette, wounded. Wyeth's party, on the westward journey, tried their hands at trapping on the southern tributaries of the Snake, but without much success. August 29, 1832, there is an entry in Wyeth's journal: "This day we parted from Mr. [Milton] Sublette's party with feeling of regret, for this party have treated us with great kindness, which I shall long remember." After various minor adventures, Wyeth and the remnant of his original company reached Hudson's Bay post, Fort Walla Walla, October 22, 1832, five months and 10 days from the time of departure from Independence.

P. C. Pambrun, the trader there, received them with the hospitality customary in non-official relations, and Wyeth tarried some days, at length proceeding to Fort Vancouver, where he arrived, October 29, 1832. Here disaffection was manifest again, and the party was dissolved. "I find myself," he wrote in his journal under this date, "involved in much difficulty on account of my men, some of whom wish to leave, and whom the Co. [Hudson's Bay Company] do not wish to engage, nor to have them in the country without being attached to some Co. able to protect them, alleging that if any of them are killed they will be obliged to avenge it at an expense of money and amicable relations with the Indians. And it is disagreeable for me to have men who wish to leave me."

Another entry in the journal covering the period between November 6 and 19, includes the following: "On my return from the fort [Fort George] my men came forward and unanimously desired to be released from their engagement with a view to returning home as soon as possible and for that end to remain here and work for a maintenance until an opportunity should occur. I could not refuse, they had already suffered much and our number was so small that the prospect of remuneration to them was very small. I have therefore now no men. These last were Mr. Ball, Woodman, Sinclair, Breck, Abbot and Tibbits, they were all good men and persevered as long as perseverance would do good. I am now afloat on the great sea of life without stay or support, but in good hands i.e. myself and providence and a few of the H.B.Co., who are perfect gentlemen."

Wyeth learned soon afterward that the Sultana had been lost. Being left alone, he spent the winter at Fort Vancouver, where he was entertained with hospitality. Of the party of five, including Wyeth and John Ball, that took a canoe and went to the mouth of Columbia river, Ball was the only one who had sufficient interest to try to see the ocean, after seven months of arduous journeying toward the western coast. Ball says in his journal: "I urged the men to go with me, but all declined. So I went alone to look at the broad Pacific, with nothing between me and Japan. Standing on the brink of the great Pacific with the waves washing my feet was the happiest hour of my long journey. There I watched until the sun sank beneath the water. Then, by the light of the moon, I returned to camp, feeling I had not crossed the continent in vain."

This little touch of sentiment characterizes Ball, who was to become a few days later the first school teacher in Oregon. He made this entry in his journal:

"The next day Mr. Wyeth and myself were invited by Doctor McLoughlin, the oldest partner and nominal governor, to his own table and rooms at the fort. Others were quartered out of the fort. I soon gave Doctor McLoughlin and Captain Wyeth to understand that I was on my own hook, and had no further connection with the party. We were received with the greatest kindness as guests, which was very acceptable, or else we would have had to hunt for subsistence. But not liking to live gratis, I asked the doctor, (he was a physician by professon), for some employment. He repeatedly answered me that I was a guest and not expected to work. But after much urging, he said if I was willing he would like me to teach his own son and the other boys in the fort, of whom there were a dozen. Of course, I gladly accepted the offer. So the boys were sent to my room to be instructed. All were half-breeds, as there was not a white woman in Oregon. The doctor's wife was a

'Chippewa,' from Lake Superior, and the lightest woman was Mrs. Douglas, a half-breed, from Hudson Bay. I found the boys docile and attentive and they made good progress. The doctor often came into the school, and was well satisfied and pleased. One day he said: 'Ball, anyway, you will have the reputation of teaching the first school in Oregon.' So, I passed the winter of 1832 and 1833. The gentlemen of the fort were pleasant and intelligent. A circle of a dozen or more sat at a well-provided table, which consisted of partners, the clerks, Captain Wyeth, and myself. There was much formality at the table. Men waited on the table, and we saw little of the women, they never appearing except perhaps on Sunday, or on horseback. As riders they excelled. The national boundary had not been settled beyond the mountains at this time. The traders claimed the river would be the boundary. The south side the American. The fur trade was their business, and if an American vessel came up the river, or coast, they would bid up on furs, and if necessary a price ten to one above their usual prices. So American traders soon got entirely discouraged.

"When Doctor McLoughlin found I was bent on going to farming, he loaned me farming utensils and seed for sowing, and as many horses as I chose to break in for teams. I took the seed and implements by boat, getting help up the Willamette to the falls, passing the site of Portland and beyond the now Oregon City, about 50 miles from Fort Vancouver. We carried by the falls, boat and all, and first stopped with one of the neighbors, a half-breed, J. B. Desportes, who had two wives and seven children, and plenty of cats and dogs. I caught from the prairie a span of horses with a lasso, made a harness, and set them to work. For harness I stuffed some deerskins, sewed in proper form, for collars, fitted to them for the harness, crooked oak limbs tied top and bottom with elk skin strings. Then to these, strips of hide was fastened for tugs, which I tied to the drag, made from a crotch of a tree. On this, I drew out logs for my cabin, which, when I had laid up and put up rafters to make the roof I covered with bark peeled from the cedar trees. This bark covering was secured by poles crossed, and tied at the ends with wood strings to the timbers below. Then out of some split plank I made a bedstead and a table, and so I dwelt in a house of fir and cedar."

20

Wyeth made a short excursion into the surrounding country, examined the Willamette valley, and looked into the prospects for his salmon packing industry, which seems to have been ever in his mind. He had already decided to return east, but to come again the next summer. He left for home in the following February, in company with Francis Ermatinger, of the Hudson's Bay Company, who escorted him as far as the company's post, in the Flathead country. He later fell in with Captain Bonneville, as has been related, but after failing to carry out a plan for a joint hunt, he proceeded eastward, meeting Milton G. Sublette, on the little Big Horn. He entered into a contract with Sublette to deliver to the latter, in the following spring, $3000 worth of trading goods, of which the Rocky Mountain Fur company believed itself in need, a contract which subsequently was broken by the Rocky mountain people.

One of the most picturesque incidents of his entire journey was his construction at this point of a bull boat, made of three buffalo skins, stitched together, with the seams covered with elk tallow. His voyage therein was from the head of navigation of the Big Horn to the mouth of the Yellowstone, a description of which furnishes Irving with one of his most engaging chapters. On his way down river, he observed the operations of Kenneth McKenzie, of the American Fur Company, who was running an illegal distillery for the manufacture of intoxicants, with which to corrupt the Indians, and he reported him to the government authorities at Fort Leavenworth.

He reached Cambridge, Massachusetts, November 7, 1833, and thus ended his first overland expedition to Oregon. A letter which he wrote on the following day to Hall, Tucker and Williams, in which he outlined a project for the following season, describes the extent and profits of the fur trade at that period. He mentions the contract with Sublette as one of the sources of probable profit, and also a proposed arrangement with the Hudson's Bay Company in which he had suggested that the company engage itself to buy his furs, in consideration of his restricting himself to certain territory south of the Columbia, and not to hunt or trade within 100 miles of any existing post. He also elaborates his salmon fisheries scheme, which he predicts will pay all expenses of a vessel sent around Cape Horn "and leave a large allowance for the expenses of the post at which they are caught." He describes what he conceives to be the opportunity awaiting a trader in territory occupied by neither British nor independent Americans.

He was successful in impressing his backers, and in the organization of the Columbia River Fishing and Trading Company, which outfitted the ship, May Dacre, which was then sent around Cape Horn to meet a second overland party at the Columbia. He

left Boston on his second venture, precisely three months after his
arrival home, and, at St. Louis, recruited a company of 70 men,
with whom he proceeded to Independence. This expedition is
notable for the fact that with it were the first missionaries ever
sent to the Oregon Country, led by Jason and Daniel Lee, and that
it had in the party, two distinguished scientists, Thomas Nuttall
and J. K. Townsend.

21

Wyeth was as impatient of delay on the part of the missionaries
as previously he had been of the vacillation of Hall J. Kelley.
Writing to Tucker and Williams, April 17, 1834, from Independence, Missouri, he said: "There are none of the Dignitaries with
me as yet, and if they 'preach' much longer in the States they will
lose their passage, for I will not wait a minute for them." The
missionaries having arrived, the long journey was begun, April 28,
1834, and the South Pass was reached June 14. Meeting the representatives of the Rocky Mountain Fur Company, he was surprised
and disappointed by their refusal to accept the goods they had
contracted to buy. The Rocky Mountain Company was then in the
process of dissolution, but Wyeth attributed this breach of contract to a desire to injure him, as a rival trader.

Burdened with these extra goods, which would have hampered
him in the final stages of his journey, he resorted to the building
of Fort Hall, which was begun July 16, 1834, and was so far completed by August 5, that it was left in charge of 12 of his men. The
fort was named in honor of Henry Hall, elder partner. In a letter
to Leonard Jarvis, dated October 6, 1834, Wyeth writes: "I have
built a fort on Snake, or Lewis River, which I named Fort Hall
from the oldest gentleman in the concern. We manufactured a
magnificent flag from some unbleached sheeting, a little red flannel
and a few blue patches, saluted it with damaged powder and wet
it in vilanous alcohol, and after all it makes, I do assure you, a
very respectable appearance amid the dry and desolate regions of
central America. Its bastions stand a terror to the sculking Indian
and a beacon of safety to the fugitive hunter. . . . After building
this fort I sent messengers to the neighboring nations to induce
them to come to it to trade, and am now about starting with an
equipment of goods for the winter trade. After leaving these at
the fort, I shall locate and build two more, one of which will be
situated near the Great Salt Lake."

This letter was written from the Columbia river, and the party that Wyeth dispatched to Fort Hall consisted of eight of his own men and some 13 Sandwich islanders who had arrived on the May Dacre. The bad faith shown by the Sublettes had only aroused his pugnacity. At the time of the refusal of the Rocky mountain people to accept the goods he had brought, he is said to have told Fitzpatrick and Sublette that he would yet "roll a stone into their garden which they would never be able to get out." The fort remained an important outpost for many years. The location was slightly changed afterwards, and it was twice rebuilt, but although the old structure has now entirely disappeared, the site has recently been identified.

22

Wyeth reached Fort Vancouver, September 14, 1834, one day in advance of the May Dacre, which had suffered an accident that necessitated putting in at Valparaiso for repairs; but the late arrival, after the run of salmon was over, had ended his hope of beginning salmon packing operations during the season of 1834. However, he performed other prodigious labors, during the remaining months of the year.

He established his other post, Fort William, named for another member of the firm, on Wapato island, now Sauvie island, at the mouth of the Willamette river, of which he writes in a letter dated April 3, 1835: "This Wapato island which I have selected for our establishment is about 15 miles long and about average of three wide. On one side runs the Columbia, on the other the Multnomah [Willamette]. It consists of woodlands and prairie, and on it there is considerable deer, and those who could spare time to hunt might live well, but a mortality has carried off to a man its inhabitants, and there is nothing to attest that they ever existed except their decaying houses, their graves and their unburied bones, of which there are heaps. So you see, as the righteous people of New England say, providence has made room for me, and without doing them more injury than I should if I had made room for myself, viz., killing them off."

23

Wyeth did not keep his trading post at Fort Hall, but sold it to Hudson's Bay Company. He found no buyer for Fort William, which fell into bad repair. At a later date it furnished the basis of an unsuccessful claim by Wyeth, under the land laws of the United States, to the island on which it was situated.

The whole Wyeth enterprise failed. Nothing came of the fishing venture. Although Hudson's Bay Company officials, and especially Doctor McLoughlin, were personally friendly, they treated him as a rival trader. Captain Wyeth did not attribute his defeat to unfair methods on the part of his rivals in the Columbia river country, although he was bitter toward the Rocky mountain men. His plan, broadly considered, was similar to that of Astor, though undertaken with relatively small capital, and at a time when rival fur interests had become well entrenched in the trans-Rocky mountain region.

Loss of the Sultana, delay of the May Dacre, desertion of the men of the first party, each contributed somewhat to the failure, but it now seems probable that the primary reason for failure was that the time was not ripe for success, in a business having small capital and no effective organization. Wyeth frankly admitted failure, and though showing a courageous and manly spirit throughout his correspondence, was inclined to blame the nature of the partnership, which was composed of men less venturesome than himself. His plans were well formed, and his diligence was almost superhuman. Although he failed in the west, he made a moderate success in business on his return to New England.

An important result of these unsuccessful ventures, viewed in the light of subsequent history, was development of what afterward became the Oregon Trail, and a spread of knowledge of the far west. But the road from the United States was beset with danger, and Americans had not yet awakened to the value of the Pacific coast, or begun to realize the need of measures of protection for the stream of immigration, about to begin. Bonneville and Wyeth probably did not foresee the great westward movement of population. They contributed much to geographical knowledge, and did something to establish the claim of American rights. It is a curious fact, however, that each of the American early trading expeditions into Oregon was a business failure. Henry, Winship, Astor, Smith, Bonneville, Wyeth, actually entered Oregon, but without success. The era of the fur trade was drawing to an end, Arcadia was about to be transformed, and new factors soon entered into the history of the Oregon Country.

—*Early Sketch from National Park Service*

Whitman Mission at Waiilatpu

—*John M. Stanley*

Fort Walla Walla, 1853

Pacific Ocean

CANADA

Vancouver Island

Ft. Victoria (H.B. Co., 1842-1843)

Fort Langley (H.B. Co., 1827)

Strait of Juan de Fuca

LUMMI

MAKAH

SKAGIT

DUWAMISH

QUILEUTE

SNOHOMISH

QUINAULT

SNOQUALMIE

Ft. Nisqually (H.B. Co., 1833)

Nisqually Mission (1840)

CHEHALIS

PUYALLUP

NISQUALLY

CHINOOK

COWLITZ

Clatsop (1840)

Ft. Astoria (Pac. Fur Co., 1811)

Ft. Vancouver (H.B. Co., 1825)

TILLAMOOK

St. Pauls (1839)

Willamette Falls (1840)

WASCO

KLICKITAT

St. Francis Xavier (1844)

YAQUINA

Willamette (1834)

MOLALA

ALSEA

COOS

Rogue

UMPQUA

KLAMATH

Columbia

OKANOGAN

St. Marys (1866)

St. Pauls (1845)

Ft. Colville (H.B. Co., 182..)

KUTE..

NESPELEM

Ft. Okanogan (Pac. Fur Co., 1811)

KALISPEL Kully..

Tshimakain (1839)

SANPOIL

Spokane House (N.W. Co., 1810)

Ft. Spokane (Pac. Fur Co., 1812)

WASHINGTON

WENATCHEE

White Swan (1899)

YAKIMA

St. Josephs (1846)

SPOKAN

COEUR D'ALENE

St. Michaels (1866)

Sacre..

Hear..

Ft. Walla Walla (N.W. Co., 1818)

Snake R.

WALLAWALLA

Waiilatpu (1836)

NEZ PERCE

Lapwai (1836)

K..

Clearwate..

CAYUSE Walla Walla R.

Columbia

Wascopam (1838)

UMATILLA

Salmo..

Deschutes

Umatilla R.

Oregon Trail

OREGON

IDAHO

Ft. Boise (H.B. Co., 1834)

Willamette R.

NORTHERN PAIUTE

MODOC

CALIFORNIA

BANNOCK

SASTEAN

NEVADA

Sacramento R.

Pyramid L.

	FUR-TRADING POSTS
	MISSIONS
	INDIAN TRIBES

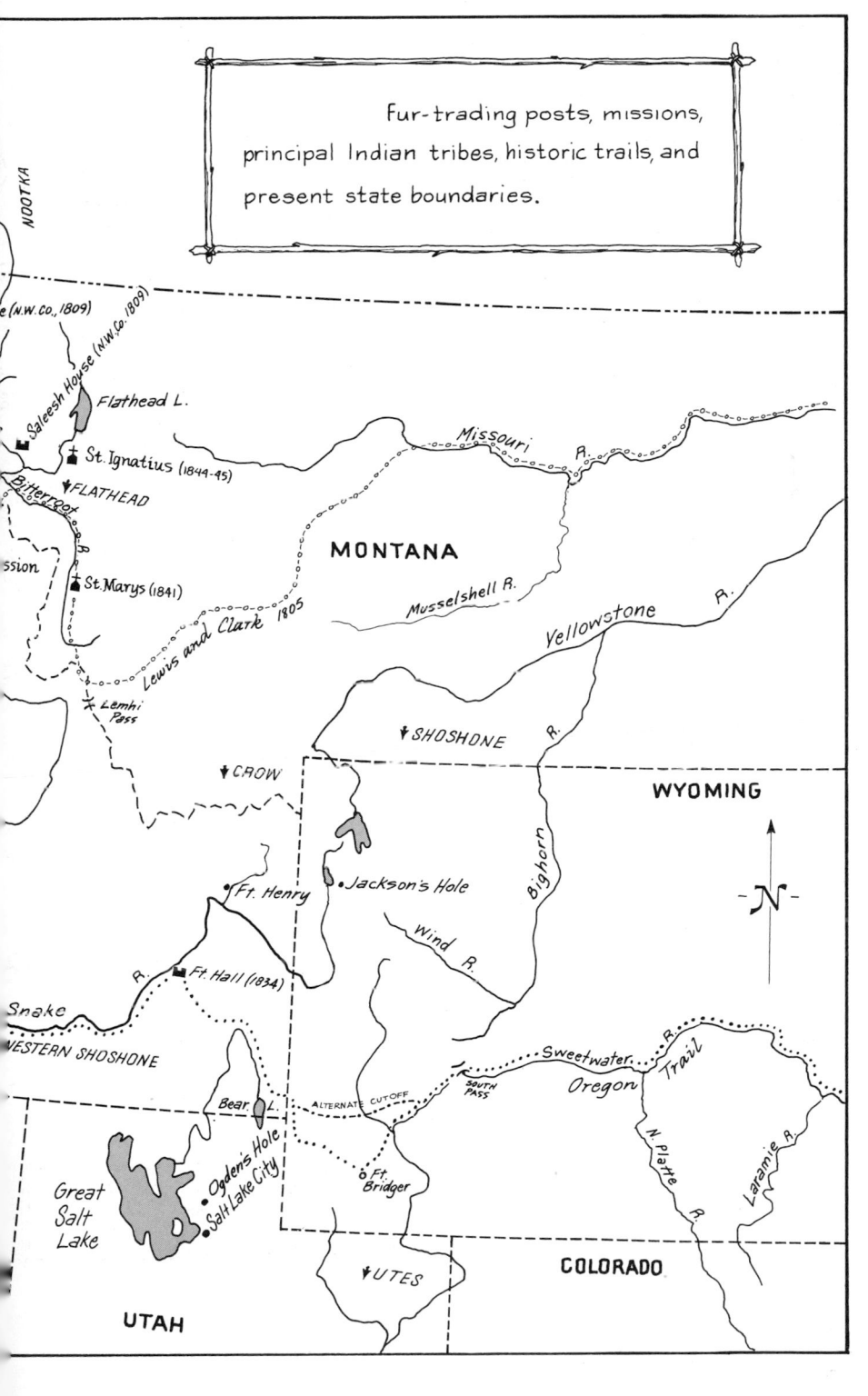

fur-trading posts, missions,
principal Indian tribes, historic trails, and
present state boundaries.

NOOTKA

e (N.W.Co., 1809)

Saleesh House (N.W.Co. 1809)

Flathead L.

St. Ignatius (1844-45)

Bitterroot R.

FLATHEAD

ssion

St. Marys (1841)

Lewis and Clark 1805

Lemhi Pass

Missouri R.

MONTANA

Musselshell R.

Yellowstone R.

SHOSHONE

CROW

WYOMING

Ft. Henry

Jackson's Hole

Bighorn

Wind R.

Snake R.

Ft. Hall (1834)

WESTERN SHOSHONE

Sweetwater R.

Oregon Trail

N
↑

ALTERNATE CUTOFF

SOUTH PASS

Bear L.

Ogden's Hole

Salt Lake City

Ft. Bridger

N. Platte R.

Laramie R.

Great Salt Lake

UTES

COLORADO

UTAH

Blue Mountains
Pioneer wagon train en route to the Columbia river valley.

Methodist Mission at The Dalles
From an oil painting by Toppin, 1849.

CHAPTER XVI
MISSIONARY SETTLEMENT

1

One of the most interesting features of Oregon's history is the part the missionary organizations had in the development, not only of the religious, but also of the social and the political life of the people of the territory. For it is a fact worth noting that preachers preceded settlers, and on the arrival of the pioneer colonists they found a welcome from little bands of missionaries that had gone out to carry the gospel to the Indians.

More than that, these missionaries became influential in a manner not originally planned, by aiding in establishing settlements of whites, in the organization of schools and colleges, and in the creation of a provisional government. The political state, as thus organized, took color from the American antecedents of the pioneers, and its form was that of a self-controlled and limited representative government. That influence of missionaries upon the civilization that ripened and expanded during the following years is traceable in many directions.

The first missionaries to arrive in the Oregon Country, 1834, comprised with a few exceptions the only Americans then in the territory. A few settlers, chiefly former servants of the fur trading companies, had established themselves in the Willamette valley, where some of them had taken Indian wives and had endeavored in a desultory way to till the soil. These were not, however, the material out of which an American commonwealth is made. There was not, as yet, a social organization in Oregon, and outside of the missions and the fur trading posts there was no responsible authority for a considerable period afterward.

These missionaries founded the pioneer schools in the new territory, at first for the instruction of the Indians in the industrial arts and handicrafts, as well as in religion. By reason of a train of events that could not have been foreseen, the missions failed to accomplish their primary object, but they laid the foundation for education of white settlers in the period of transition from the old order to the new. Moreover, they exerted a needful influence for order, and they supplied incentive for extension of the authority of the United States over the Pacific northwest country. Prior to their arrival in Oregon it cannot be said that American settlement had even been begun. Until the third decade of the century there were none who had come west for any other purpose than trade with the natives, and none who expected to remain and build up a state.

Attention of the American Board of Commissioners for Foreign Missions, at Boston, was drawn to Oregon at some time prior to 1829. The Board then had a firmly established mission in the Sandwich islands, and desiring to extend its work in the regions of the Pacific, Jonathan S. Green was sent to visit the northwest coast. The tour was undertaken by Green upon instructions from the Prudential committee of the Board. Green took passage from Oahu, February, 1829, in the bark Volunteer, Captain Taylor, which was engaged in the fur trade. The Volunteer anchored in Norfolk sound, in latitude 57 degrees north, March 11, 1829, and during the ensuing summer it sailed as far south as latitude 53 degrees, thus giving Green an opportunity to observe the northern coast Indians.

The missionary seems, from his own account, to have been exceedingly cautious, and timid. "Wherever it appeared safe," he reported to the Prudential committee, "I went ashore." He compiled a list of about 700 words of the dialects of 10 or 12 tribes, but found the natives hopelessly tainted with commercialism and debauched by white men's rum. An Alaskan chieftain, whom he pressed into service on board ship as a kind of assistant lexicographer, discovered that the missionary valued these additions to his vocabulary, and so he demanded a quid pro quo—a leaf of tobacco for a word.

The Russian governor, Chesticoff, gave Green a cordial reception and the missionary reciprocated his hospitality with a gift of "several of our Hawaiian tracts, the January and February numbers of the Missionary Herald of 1828, Mr. Dwight's address on the Greek revolution, and Mr. Stewart's Journal of a Residence in the Sandwich Islands." The feeling of the robust governor on receiving these evidences of the missionary's gratitude are not recorded.

Green made, however, a sincere effort to reach Oregon, and although he did not favor a mission among the northern Indians, for whom he saw no hope of salvation, he recommended that an establishment be set up in Oregon. Captain Dominis, of the American brig Owyhee, a doughty seafarer known up and down the length of the Pacific coast in that time, informed Green, at Norfolk sound, that the Indians of the Columbia river region, would probably be amenable to missionary teaching. "They speak of it [the Oregon Country] in terms of commendation as being a fertile country in a delightful climate," wrote Green, June 10, 1829. "The Indians are numerous and less bloody than on this part of the coast. Captain Dominis says it is unquestionably the place where a missionary station should be established. As he is soon to return to the river, he offered me a passage. I am extremely anxious to accompany him, but as there is little probability of being able to find a passage hence to the Islands, short of eighteen months, I must abandon the idea."

However, Green persuaded Captain Taylor, who had business of his own wherever there was a prospect of trade, to examine the coast further south. The Volunteer was prevented by head winds from entering Puget sound, but sailed thence to the latitude of the Columbia. "We then made for the Columbia river," Green wrote, August 31, 1829, "spent several days in the latitude of the river, and at length made land in the vicinity of the country I so much desired to visit. Cape Disappointment and Point Adams, between which land the river empties, we distinctly saw, and for several hours were within a few miles of them. Captain Taylor was no less anxious than I was to enter the river, but after arriving so near, we reluctantly abandoned the idea. So tremendous was the swell from the southwest that Captain Taylor judged that it would break in 20 fathoms of water. The danger of crossing a sandbar having four fathoms only of water, at such a time, is obvious. I am fully of the opinion that we could not have succeeded, had we attempted it. Soon after we left, we encountered a violent storm, so that we found it more pleasant as well as safe, to be at sea."

Green, while on the coast, obtained from Thomas McKay the names of 34 tribes of Indians inhabiting the vicinity of the Columbia river, and was told that they were of a race superior to the natives of the northern coast, although "Captain Simpson, an officer of the Hudson's Bay Company," as Green reported to the Prudential committee, "assured me that they had learned every vice, but not a single virtue, of their white neighbors." The officer thus alluded to was no doubt Aemilius Simpson, captain of the

Cadboro, whom Green met at Norfolk sound. Green suggested that "a regard to Christian economy would urge to the selection of the most favorable situation. . . . It seems desirable that missionary effort should commence here. This would be especially desirable, should the mission be connected with a small colony." Somewhere in the vicinity of the Columbia river, he did not doubt, such a colony "would find a salubrious climate, a fertile soil and ultimately a country of great importance. Mr. Smith [no doubt meaning Jedediah S. Smith], an American hunter, of whom you have probably heard, on his way from California to the Columbia river last winter, discovered a considerable river in the latitude of 42 degrees 30 minutes. Should this opinion prove correct the country about this river would probably be most favorable for such an object." The river alluded to may have been the Umpqua. Green continued his inquiries on his return to Oahu, where Captain Thompson, of the brig Convoy, informed him that the Columbia river Indians were friendly, and Green so reported to the American Board.

2

In 1833, an article published in a religious newspaper hastened action. A communication from Mr. G. P. Dishoway, dated at New York, appeared March 1, 1833, in the Christian Advocate and Journal and Zion's Herald, of New York, the leading publication of the Methodist Episcopal Church. It quoted a letter from an interpreter of the Wyandotte tribe, dated January 19, 1833, describing a visit of four Flathead, or Nez Perce's, Indians to St. Louis on a purported quest for religious instruction. The Wyandotte interpreter was one William Walker, a man of considerable intelligence and of good standing among his own people in Ohio.

He wrote that he had been told by Gen. William Clark, of St. Louis, that these Indians had travelled 3000 miles to learn the truth of a story told them by a white man, to the effect that the white people had "been put in possession of the true mode of worshiping the Great Spirit," that "they had a book containing directions how to conduct themselves in order to enjoy his favor and hold converse with him; and with this guide no one need go astray, but every one that would follow the direction there laid down could enjoy, in this life, the favor, and after death, would be received into the country where the Great Spirit resides and live forever with him." According to this version, the tribe at once called a council and deputed four chieftains to proceed to St. Louis and ascertain the truth of the white man's story.

3

The printed account, which has since given rise to much controversy as to its true basis, was nevertheless a spark that fired the imagination of the people. Whether or not these Indians had gone to St. Louis in quest of the "white man's Book of Life," or for some other purpose, the essential fact is that publication of the story moved the religious people of America. Indeed, it served as well as if it had been literally true in every particular, which probably it was not.

A member of the first missionary expedition to Oregon, who had first hand information, regarded the tale as an exaggeration. This was Rev. Daniel Lee, who "saw General Clark in 1834, two years after their visit, and learned from him these particulars in relation to it. . . . A high wrought account of the visit of the Indians to St. Louis, by some writer in the vicinity, was published in the Christian Advocate and Journal, New York City, March, 1833. These incorrect statements receiving the fullest confidence, many believed that the day had come and that the call was imperative to send the gospel to Oregon."

By the autumn of 1833, the story had been widely published and had evoked sympathetic response. For example, a meeting of "gentlemen desirous of bearing their part in the Christianizing and civilizing of the Indians of this country," was reported in the Illinois Patriot (of Jacksonville, Illinois), October 12, 1833, at which meeting a committee was appointed to visit St. Louis and inquire into the situation of the Indians. The committee submitted to the session of the Illinois synod a report noteworthy for its practical viewpoint. Not only was the welfare of the aborigines to be regarded, the committee suggested, but also that of the whites.

The Methodists were the first to translate thought into action. Dr. Wilbur Fisk, president of Wesleyan University at Wilbraham, Massachusetts, March 20, 1833, less than three weeks after the first publication of the story, submitted a communication to the Mission Board urging immediate establishment of a mission to the Flathead Indians. The Board communicated with the war department and learned that the department had no knowledge of any such tribe. Nevertheless it was resolved to proceed with a mission among the Indians west of the Rocky mountains.

4

Rev. Jason Lee, a former pupil of Dr. Fisk's, then laboring in the missionary field near his birthplace, Stanstead, Ontario, was chosen to lead the undertaking. Events moved rapidly. Lee was officially commissioned, July 17, 1833. In October of that year, the Mission Board appropriated $3000 for the outfitting of the mission, and a noteworthy farewell meeting was held in New York, November 20, 1833, at which there were present, among others, representatives of the American Board of Commissioners for Foreign Missions, supported chiefly by Congregationalists, but embracing also the Presbyterian and Dutch Reformed churches. This organization was subsequently to figure in an important way in Oregon history through its founding of the celebrated Whitman mission near Walla Walla, and the mission at Lapwai, in what is now Idaho, and another near the present site of Spokane, all of which represented an attempt to accomplish, east of the Cascade range, that which Jason Lee and his co-workers attempted to do farther west.

Jason Lee made a tour of the eastern states, in the course of which he presented the missionary cause to the people. An arrangement was made with Nathaniel J. Wyeth, just then preparing to set out on his second trading expedition to the Pacific coast, for transportation of the missionary party. The principal goods, garden seeds, books, farming utensils and household effects of the missionaries were to be forwarded by Wyeth's brig, the May Dacre, while the missionaries themselves were to have the advantage of Wyeth's strong organization, when they proceeded overland. Wyeth, on returning from his first expedition, 1833, had brought from the west two Indian boys, and they were present with him at a mass meeting at a Boston church one evening when Wyeth and Lee were the speakers, and money was raised for the missionary project. These Indian boys were with Wyeth until his return to the west.

Jason Lee left New England, accompanied by his nephew, Daniel Lee, and Cyrus Shepard, of Lynn, Massachusetts. The latter had been engaged as teacher, and from the time of his arrival in Oregon until his death, January 1, 1840, he carried out the mission's educational plans. As the party travelled westward, Philip L. Edwards, of Richmond, Missouri, was engaged as teacher, and Courtney M. Walker, of the same place, was retained as clerical assistant under contract for one year.

5

Wyeth had arranged to travel with the fur trading caravan of Capt. William L. Sublette, who had with him that year the naturalists, J. K. Townsend and Thomas Nuttall. The entire party when assembled on the frontier consisted of 70 persons. It left Fort Independence, April 28, 1834, and reached the rendezvous of the Rocky mountain trappers, on Hams fork, a branch of the Colorado of the West, June 20, 1834, where a stay of 12 days was made. At this point Sublette and his men left the Wyeth and Lee detachment, and turned to their fur trading and trapping.

Later, a similar stay was made necessary at the site of Fort Hall, on Snake river, at which place the missionaries received a company of Indians from the Columbia river country, led by a young chief Ish-hol-hol-hoats-hoats, known as "Lawyer," who made it known that the visitors would be welcomed by the natives as teachers of religion. This camping place on Snake river was near the mouth of the Portneuf, and here Captain Wyeth remained with those who formed his own company, and here he began the erection of the trading post which he called Fort Hall.

6

It was on Sunday, July 27, 1834, at this spot, surrounded by a congregation of mountain men and Indians in the motley and rude garb of the wild west, that Jason Lee delivered the first sermon ever preached west of the Rocky mountains. How much of it the Indians understood cannot now be known, but it must have been a picturesque sight, with the wild west background, and the varied company of white men and red, the costumes of the aborigines contrasting with those of the fur traders and preachers. It is related that after the sermon, there was a horse race, and one of the men was thrown from his horse and killed.

An incident that impressed the missionary leader deeply was the generous action of two Cayuse Indians who presented him with two white horses. "Surely," he wrote in his journal for July 30, 1834, "the hand of Providence must be in it, for they presented them because we are missionaries, and at a time when two of our horses were nearly worn out. This, if I mistake not, augurs well for our ultimate success among these generous red men." Notwithstanding this incident, opportunity for a missionary station in the immediate vicinity did not seem favorable, and, moreover, the goods of the expedition were on board the May Dacre, so the missionaries continued their journey toward Fort Vancouver. The expedition, now greatly reduced in numbers, proceeded in company with Capt. William Stewart, a Scotch sportsman and traveller who was on a hunting expedition covering a wide range in the far west, his second adventure of the kind. Thomas McKay, also, accompanied the party for a few days. He was one of the Hudson's Bay Company, and on leaving presented them with some sugar and flour, which was a welcome contribution.

7

On the way to Fort Walla Walla, they fell in with a band of Cayuse Indians who were friendly, and who urged the missionaries to stay, presenting them with four horses, for which Jason Lee made return with suitable presents. But, after a brief visit at the native encampment, the party pushed on to Fort Walla Walla with Captain Stewart, or Sir William Drummond Stewart, as he is otherwise called. They had now been nearly five months on the way. Arriving at Fort Walla Walla the party was then taken in charge by representatives of Hudson's Bay Company, and had the use of one of the company's boats for the journey down the Columbia. The voyage of 10 days was prolonged by strong head winds. At Fort Vancouver, they were hospitably entertained by the "Gentlemen of the Fort," and slept in a house this night, the first time for 152 nights. At Vancouver, the question of permanent location was prayerfully considered, and a preliminary exploration journey was then made by Jason and Daniel Lee up the Willamette river, in the company's boats.

The Flatheads, whose name had first aroused interest in the new missionary endeavor, were not destined to receive the benefits of a religious mission at this time. Doctor McLoughlin explained to the Lees, and their party, as he says in his autobiography, that "it was too dangerous for them to establish a mission [in the Flathead country]; that to do good to the Indians they must establish themselves where they could collect them around them; teach them first to cultivate the ground, and live more comfortably than they do by hunting, and, as they do this, teach them religion; that the Willamette afforded them a fine field, and that they ought to go there and they would receive the same assistance as the settlers."

8

Hudson's Bay Company officers furnished the newcomers with facilities for examining promising situations, and supplied them with men, boats and provisions for their journey. They went up the Willamette valley to a point on the east bank of the river, a few miles north of the present site of Salem, where they set up their tents in a patch of melons and cucumbers in the garden of one of the French Canadian settlers, Joseph Gervais, who had come west with the overland Astors. Here was an entrancing prospect. A broad, rich river bottom stretched along the stream for several miles, well watered, and with timber near at hand. The first house they built was located some distance above, and was of unhewn logs, into which they moved their goods while the roof was only partially completed. Cyrus Shepard, whose health was poor, had been left behind at Vancouver, where he taught a school at the post. Among Shepard's pupils were three Japanese sailors, survivors of the crew of a junk that had been wrecked on the coast, 1833, south of the strait of Juan de Fuca.

Members of the mission party became woodsmen, carpenters, rude blacksmiths and husbandmen. "Men never worked harder or performed less," wrote Daniel Lee, of this period. The first storm caught them with a roofless building; before the next storm they had a roof over part of the house and a piece of the floor was laid. Jason Lee with his jack-knife whittled sashes for the windows out of rough wood and carved a pair of wooden hinges for the door. The company got flour from Vancouver, which they made into unleavened cakes; they bought peas from the settlers; there was pork in the stores, brought from Boston in the May Dacre; the missionary cows gave a little milk, and venison was obtained occasionally from the Indians. In the spring, about 30 acres of land were broken and fenced, and planted with seed furnished by Doctor McLoughlin. Jason Lee himself salted six barrels of salmon.

In such primitive surroundings, and sustained by so plain a fare, Lee opened his school, not waiting for the building to be completed before he began to receive pupils. After a year at Vancouver, Shepard took charge of this school, and Edwards opened a school at Champoeg. Benefits of the mission were proffered to children of the white settlers as well as Indians. Indeed, as to its work among the natives, the mission was disappointing from the beginning. Three native children were received the first winter. An Umpqua lad was left there by his people, in the spring of 1835, to receive instruction in farming, and his death from consumption in that summer brought deadly vengeance on Shepard and Daniel Lee. A trapper named Shangarette died, three orphans and a number of slaves surviving him. Jason Lee added these to his family, but only on condition that the enslaved should be free, "and in the mission equal with those they once served." Thus labor multiplied, without, however, producing corresponding compensations. Two of these pupils grew tired of mission life and went away, and Daniel Lee found it in his heart to say that this was "some relief in a case in which there was so little to hope."

9

It has been estimated that out of 14 children received into the home the first year, five died, five ran away, and of the remaining four, two died in the second year. Also that of 25 children received in 1836, 16 fell ill. This is based upon the original journal of the mission. By 1842, eight years after the mission was established, the Indians had almost disappeared from the Willamette valley, and this the missionaries ascribed to the ravages of smallpox and other diseases.

There was an epidemic of a malady resembling diphtheria, and another of malaria. Both of the Lees were stricken, and Daniel Lee found it necessary to go away for his health. Worst of all, from the point of view of the devoted missionaries, deaths among the Indian pupils caused the place to be avoided by the very people for whose benefit it had been primarily founded. Little was accomplished for the Indian children, and nothing at all for adult Indians. Some interest in religion, however, was awakened among the whites, several revivals were held, and a number of converts were reported. Instruction in the mission schools combined study and recitation with work upon the farm.

March 15, 1836, Jason Lee wrote to his preceptor and friend, Dr. Wilbur Fisk, a long letter in which he expressed his discouragement. The missionaries saw no evidence that convinced them that more than one conversion had been made. Lee found the labor of building, farming, and caring for the sick took all of his time, so that he could not write letters giving information, and, on the other hand, few letters had reached the mission. He needed some lay men to help with the temporal work, so that he could give his time to other essentials.

10

Reinforcements were dispatched from the east, 1836, and again in 1837. The first party left Boston harbor in the Hamilton, July, 1836, bound for the Sandwich islands. After a stay in the islands during several months they sailed to the Columbia in the brig Diana, Captain Hinckley, reaching Fort Vancouver, May 28, 1837, where they were met by Jason Lee. In the party were Dr. Elijah White, wife and two children. Doctor White became an important figure, although soon after his arrival he became involved in difficulties with Jason Lee and returned to the east in 1840. It was his fortune in this way to take the latest information from the Oregon Country at a time of national interest. He was soon thereafter appointed by President Tyler sub-Indian agent, and became one of the leaders of the immigration to Oregon, 1842. Besides the White family, the first reinforcement included Alanson Beers, his wife and three children; J. L. Whitcomb, W. H. Willson, Miss Elvira Johnson; Miss Anna Maria Pittman, who soon afterward became Mrs. Jason Lee, and Miss Susan Downing, engaged to marry Cyrus Shepard. The women of this party were the first American white women in the Willamette valley.

11

The second party arrived, also by sea, September 7, 1837, and consisted of Rev. David Leslie, his wife and three children, Rev. H. K. W. Perkins and Miss Margaret Smith. Thus aided, Jason Lee's first thought was to extend his work. He visited Nisqually, upon Puget sound. He also chose as the site for a branch mission the point called Wascopam, now The Dalles, and placed Daniel Lee and Mr. Perkins in charge. The Wascopam mission seemed to be temporarily successful with the Indians, but presently backsliders began to out-number converts. The Indians were unable to comprehend the orthodox conception of the efficacy of prayer. Their depredations led Daniel Lee at one time to make provision for armed defense; eventually this mission was written down a failure. It was occupied by the Methodists until 1847, when it was tendered to the American Board of Commissioners for Foreign Missions, and was occupied for a short time in that year by a youthful nephew of Dr. Marcus Whitman. The American Board quit-claimed the property to the Methodist Episcopal church in 1859. The station, however, ceased, in 1847, to be used for missionary purposes.

Jason Lee had been advised that Miss Pittman would be a suitable wife, and she had been given to understand by the Missionary Society that marriage to Mr. Lee would be a possibility. Cyrus Shepard and Miss Downing were already engaged. The Journal of the mission, July 16, 1837, shows a triple wedding, including the two pairs just named and also Charles J. Roe, a Hudson's Bay Company employee, and Nancy McKay, a half-breed daughter of Capt. Thomas McKay. On this occasion there were baptisms and admissions into the church, and a sermon by Jason Lee on the sanctity of marriage. It was, however, but a few months after this, that, moved by a profound sense of duty to his trust, Lee decided to return to the east for additional help, and to ask particularly for practical farmers and mechanics. In this, he had the support of his co-workers, who joined in signing a declaration showing the necessity. He left his young wife reluctantly, and, accompanied by P. L. Edwards, began the long overland journey, March 15, 1838.

12

The decision of Jason Lee to make the journey in person was important in other respects than in its effect on the missionary enterprise. On this journey, Lee was the bearer of a memorial drawn up in Oregon, asking for the protection of the United States government.

It is interesting to note that this petition or memorial, which was afterward printed by the government at Washington, in House Document 101, of the 25th Congress, 3rd Session, bore the names of nine of the French Canadian settlers, as well as those of 27 English speaking settlers. It expressed the opinion that there were "strong inducements" for the government to take formal and speedy possession, and urged that the petitioners' interests were identified with those of the country of their adoption, and represented that they were "the germ of a great state." The loyalty of the petitioners to the United States government was manifested by the earnest language of the memorial.

In his efforts to obtain financial support for his cause, Lee delivered lectures which served to develop interest in the Oregon Country. His appearance in the various eastern states, with the stories of his experiences, and his advocacy of settlement and government by Americans, was just what was needed. He had taken two young Chinook boys with him, and also three half-breed sons of Thomas McKay; one of the former, who became ill, he left in Peoria, Illinois, for a time, from which incident sprang the organization, early in 1839, of the "Peoria party" of immigrants under the leadership of Thomas J. Farnham. It included, among those finally arriving in Oregon, Farnham, W. Blair, Robert Shortess, Sidney Smith, Francis Fletcher, Amos Cook, Joseph Holman, and Ralph L. Kilbourne. This expedition disintegrated on the way, only four of its original members reaching the Willamette settlements in that year, but Farnham, on his return, became the bearer of another memorial from the settlers to Congress, reiterating the desire for protection of the government of the United States. Farnham also wrote several popular books which further kept the Oregon question in the public mind, some of them appearing in more than one edition and having a large circulation.

The memorial conveyed by Jason Lee, and a letter that he wrote to Caleb Cushing, member of Congress from Massachusetts, in reply to the latter's request for further information, marked the merging of the missionary into the colonizer. There were, he said in the letter, two things needful for the protection and prosperity of the settlers. These were a guarantee from the government that possession of the land they had taken, and the improvements made upon it, would be granted to them; and secondly, the authority and protection of the government and laws of the United States to regulate the intercourse of the settlers with each other.

He believed that if these advantages were bestowed most of those who were then attached to the mission would remain permanent settlers in the country. To secure these objects he did not suppose that "much of a military force" would be necessary, for almost all of the settlers in the Willamette valley had signed the memorial. He closed with this prediction: "The country will be settled, and that speedily, from some quarter, and it depends very much on the speedy action of Congress what that population shall be, and what shall be the fate of the Indian tribes in that territory. It may be thought that Oregon is of little importance; but rely upon it there is the germ of a great state. We are resolved to do what we can to benefit the country; but we are constrained to throw ourselves upon you for protection."

13

Jason Lee thus succeeded in placing the political aspect of the Oregon movement before Congress at the same time that he was laboring to overcome opposition in the Board of Missions to continuance of the work—opposition based on the ground of its great cost. On his way east, he had been overtaken at Westport, Missouri, by a messenger sent by Doctor McLoughlin with news of the death of his wife and her newly born son, which had occurred, June 26, 1838, shortly after his departure for Oregon. The Mission Board paid for the services of this messenger.

Having persuaded the Mission Board to extend further aid, he subsequently married Miss Lucy Thompson, of Barre, Vermont, and returned on the ship Lausanne, in chartering which the Board is said to have received pecuniary assistance from the secret service fund of the federal government, a fact not beyond doubt. The Lausanne's company included, in addition to Lee and his wife, seven missionaries, all accompanied by their wives, as follows: Rev. Joseph H. Frost, Rev. William W. Kone, Rev. Alvan F. Waller, Rev. J. P. Richmond, Rev. Gustavus Hines, Rev. Lewis H. Judson and Rev. Josiah L. Parrish. The practical foresight of the board is shown in this personnel, for Richmond was a physician, as well as a minister; Judson, a cabinet maker; Parrish, a blacksmith. George Abernethy, who afterward was governor under the provisional regime, came as steward of the mission. There were, besides, another physician, Dr. Ira L. Babcock, four farmers, six mechanics and four teachers. The entire expedition, including children, numbered more than 50, and is known in the missionary annals of Oregon as the "Great Reinforcement." It was received with customary cordiality by the Hudson's Bay factor, at Fort Vancouver, who made provision for the entertainment of all the members. This accession to the working force enabled Lee to carry into effect at once some of his cherished plans for extension of the missionary endeavors into other parts of Oregon.

14

But, in another particular the arrival of reinforcements was important. The mission population now consisted of more than 40 adult Americans and some 50 children. Lee's assignment of Richmond to establish a Methodist mission at Nisqually, on Puget sound, gave that district its first American home. Frost was detailed to Clatsop, at which point, during Lee's absence, Solomon Smith, one of the pre-missionary arrivals, had held out hope of a successful undertaking. Hines and Kone were designated for service among the Umpquas, but this mission on further investigation was found impracticable and was not established. "The Indians," says Rev. H. K. Hines, "were few and scattered, degraded and cruel. They were evidently dying away, and as a people without hope and without remedy. Though a mission might save individuals, as a people they could not be saved. . . . They were darkly, terribly, certainly doomed."

Both the Nisqually and Clatsop stations were later abandoned. Waller, after remaining for a time to assist at the mission in the Willamette valley, was sent to Willamette Falls, now Oregon City, where he erected a substantial residence. This place later became a considerable settlement, and, 1842, the first Protestant church was built by subscription and opened for public service, 1844. A Catholic church at St. Paul was the first building erected exclusively for religious purposes in Oregon.

Meanwhile, Lee expanded his plans for the Indian manual training school, which was removed, 1841, with the original missionary headquarters, to Chemeketa, now Salem, the present capital of Oregon. With the assistance of the mechanics who had come on the Lausanne, Lee was free to plan more ambitiously. By January, 1842, he was able to lay before his co-workers a scheme for establishment of a school for the white population of the country and to obtain their approval. The projected school was to be known as Oregon Institute. The missionaries here acted in their private capacities, and not as representatives of the Methodist organization.

Among those who attended the meeting was Rev. Harvey Clark, an independent Congregationalist missionary, who had come across the mountains, 1840, without the support of the American Board, intending to labor among the Indians. Clark had been unsuccessful

in making a start, and had settled on a claim in the Willamette
valley, part of which he subsequently donated toward the founding
of Tualatin Academy, from which arose Pacific University, at
Forest Grove. Oregon Institute, initiated at Jason Lee's house at
Chemeketa, acquired the Methodist Indian industrial training
school fund of $4000, and in time became Willamette University.
These were the beginnings of higher education in Oregon.

15

Mission work in the Willamette valley, however, had now passed
its zenith. Jason Lee, on his return from the east, had observed a
striking dimunition of the native population. Disease and death
had almost destroyed the tribes. By 1842, when he conceived the
idea of an educational institution for the whites, immigration of
a different character was beginning to give a new aspect to the
Oregon situation, while the Mission Board, removed by the width
of a continent from participation in local problems, was clamorous
for a showing of religious results. How many Indians had been
converted to Christianity as the product of its vast expenditure?
Was the need of so many missionaries in Oregon as great as it
had been represented to be?

The Board, enquiring thus, July, 1843, appointed Rev. George
Gary to succeed Jason Lee as superintendent of the Oregon missions. This was without notice, and Lee, who in the meanwhile
had resolved to return east by ship, was at Honolulu, when he first
learned of the intended change. Without waiting for the arrival
of Gary, he took passage by way of Mexico to the United States,
where he devoted the few remaining months of his life to seeking a vindication, and to pressing the cause of the Americans in
Oregon upon the attention of the authorities at Washington. He
died March 2, 1845, at Lake Mephremagog, Canada. His body,
returned to Oregon, 1906, was given permanent burial at Salem,
the scene of his early labors.

The period in which Lee toiled was a time of small beginnings.
His mission, which he founded with only four assistants in 1834,
brought to Oregon upwards of 70 persons, many of whom became
permanent settlers, and constituted the nucleus of a commonwealth. It is improbable that his primary motive was to assist in
asserting the sovereignty of the United States in the new territory, but this grew upon him in his later years. It is now agreed

by impartial historians that he was unselfish, that he sought no personal emoluments, and that he was inspired throughout by missionary zeal. His political conceptions grew with his realization of failure of his Indian project. It is worthy of note that his letter to Caleb Cushing, January 17, 1839, written from Middletown, Connecticut, in elaboration of the Willamette valley settlers' memorial, dealt with the issue of emigration exclusively, and his later comprehension of Oregon's future needs is revealed by the fact that much of the time between his final return east and his death was devoted to obtaining subscriptions for Oregon Institute, to which he also bequeathed a portion of his scanty means.

16

It would be a very narrow view of the Methodist mission in Oregon to assume that because the original object of converting Indians to Christianity resulted in disappointment, and was abandoned within little more than a decade, it was therefore a failure. Lee, after his personal defeat, was still able to write to the head office of the society: "On one point I have not a shadow of doubt, namely that the growth, rise, glory and triumph of Methodism in the Willamette valley are destined to be commensurate with the growth, rise, and prosperity of our infant and rapidly increasing settlement." This was in October, 1843, and his prophecy has been abundantly fulfilled, as the subsequent history of the church will show. But, in a still different way, the importance of these early missions becomes apparent in Oregon history.

Lee had gone to Washington, 1833, before his first expedition to the Oregon Country. At that time he secured the support of President Jackson, and of the secretaries of state and war. The actual settlement of the country claimed by both the United States and Great Britain became, as time went on, a matter of importance in the eyes of a few far-seeing statesmen at Washington, although during this period there were many who failed to appreciate its advantage. Lee continued to maintain relations with the government in the years 1838, 1839 and 1840. The actual part the Methodists had in establishing a provisional political state and in urging the federal authorities to extend the laws and the protection of the United States to this region may be detailed in a more appropriate place in this narrative, but one who has given especial study to the matter has estimated that while three of the several petitions from the settlers transmitted to the government were drafted by Methodists, no less than nine of the 26 measures which the government inaugurated, including four of the nine bills introduced into Congress, were in some measure connected with Methodist initiative.

17

Charges have been made that the Methodist missions, beginning with fine altruism and deep religious fervor, soon degenerated into gross commercialism and materialism. But while this was admitted by the church itself, in withdrawing Lee from the field, he fearlessly confronted the Missionary Society, July 1, 1844, upon his arrival in New York, and was able to convince many, not only that his course was what had been agreed upon in advance, but that the spiritual and religious results were worth while. It is said that at the conclusion of Lee's address his personal vindication was complete, and that probably had not Rev. George Gary already been sent out to the field, the society would have continued Lee in charge of the mission. He announced his willingness to return and serve under Mr. Gary. His death, however, soon followed.

The one charge against this faithful minister that time has justified, in a degree, is his connivance in Rev. A. F. Waller's mean attempt to get the land claim of Doctor McLoughlin, a fact established by letters and documents. Waller was induced to drop the contest in consideration of the payment of the sum of $500.00, and the conveyance to him of eight lots and three additional blocks in the townsite. The settlement was due to the friendly offices of Dr. Elijah White, who arranged for arbitration, and the terms were recommended by the arbitrators, Messrs. James Douglas, A. L. Lovejoy and Maj. William Gilpin. But the claim of Waller and others to the island in the Willamette river, that was a part of the original McLoughlin location, was not released. Lee, who acted as agent for Waller, filed a petition in the United States supreme court after the settlement was reached, not knowing at that time of the compromise.

December, 1843, with his little daughter, Lucy Anna Maria Lee, nearly two years old, he took passage on the British bark, Columbia, from Vancouver for the Sandwich islands. His second wife, Lucy Thompson Lee, had died March 20, 1842, leaving the infant, born on the 29th of February preceding. On the ship were also

Rev. Gustavus Hines and family, who had agreed to take charge of her in Lee's absence. They later decided to return to Oregon, and she returned with them. Lee took passage for San Blas, Mexico, and continued across Mexico and to the United States. At Washington he conferred with President Tyler, Senator Thomas H. Benton, and the commissioner of the general land office, and he wrote to Hines to "please tell Bro. Waller that his claim is filed in the Office of the Commissioner General of the land office. This will probably secure his claim, though the supreme court will probably take no action till the Oregon bill passes."

18

It will be necessary to turn back a few years to review the history of some of the other churches. A call for Catholic spiritual counsellors originated with the Canadian settlers in the Willamette valley and the attaches of the Hudson's Bay Company post at Fort Vancouver. These joined, July, 1834, and again, February, 1835, in petitions to the Catholic bishop of the Red River settlements asking for religious teachers. No priests could then be spared, but a promise was given that help would be obtained from Europe as soon as possible. The priests chosen for service, however, were two Canadians, Rev. Father Francis Norbert Blanchet, who had spent his early religious life among the peaceful Acadians and the docile Micmac Indians of New Brunswick, and who was now designated as vicar-general, and Rev. Father Modeste Demers, his assistant. These two priests left Montreal, May, 1838, and reached Fort Vancouver, November 24, 1838, after a voyage of peril. They were conveyed by the Hudson's Bay Company overland express from Montreal, which also brought a number of other travellers, among whom were an English tourist, Banks, and his wife, who was the daughter of Sir George Simpson, and also the English botanist, Wallace, and his wife. One of the boats of the brigade was wrecked at the Little Dalles, of the Columbia, and 12 of the company of 26 were drowned. The dead included Banks and Wallace, and their wives.

On their way down the Columbia the Catholic missionaries made stops at Colville, Okanogan and Walla Walla. The natives professed much interest in the coming of the "black gowns," of whom they had received vague accounts from distant tribes, and from the Iroquois who had settled among them. A number of baptisms were performed, and the priests were greatly encouraged from the very beginning, although, afterward they discovered that there was reason to discount early Indian manifestation of interest in religion. At Fort Vancouver, a preliminary census accounted for 26 Catholics, including the Canadian voyageurs and the Iroquois; there were 20 Catholic families in the Willamette valley, and four on the Cowlitz. Father Blanchet lost no time in visiting the Willamette valley settlement, whither he proceeded, January, 1839. He baptised a considerable number of both whites and natives that winter. He married, according to the nuptial rites of his church, the Canadians who had taken Indian wives in the prevailing method, and precipitated considerable theological controversy by remarrying several who had been already married by Methodist ministers.

Branch missions were established on the Cowlitz and at Nisqually, on Puget sound. In connection with Father Blanchet's visit to the latter point, he met on Whidbey island "savages already acquainted with certain practices of the Catholic church, although they had never seen a missionary." Religious work was carried forward in the upper Columbia river country, although the two priests were necessarily separated and much alone.

19

Rev. Father P. J. DeSmet, sent from St. Louis, 1839, to the Flatheads, found to his great surprise that Oregon already possessed two Catholic missionaries. Hearing good reports of the western field, he went no further than to the Rocky mountains, and then he returned to St. Louis for aid. This resulted in the assignment of two additional priests and three lay brothers, who did not, however, reach the lower Columbia until the autumn of 1843. Two priests, Fathers A. Langlois and J. B. Z. Boldoc, who had been denied passage by the Hudson's Bay express in 1841, but who came from Canada by way of Cape Horn, 1842, established a school for boys at St. Paul in the Willamette valley.

DeSmet unexpectedly made his appearance at Fort Vancouver, 1842, after an exciting overland voyage. On the way down the Columbia the barge in which he was travelling was upset. Fortunately for him, he had left it to walk along the river bank. Five of his fellow travellers were swallowed up in the rapids. Afterward he made a trip to Europe and succeeded in getting a substantial reinforcement from Belgium, consisting of four priests, a lay brother and six religious sisters of Notre Dame of Namur. These arrived in a chartered vessel that entered the Columbia river, July 31, 1844. The sisters were sent to open a convent school on French Prairie, which was named St. Mary. With the arrival of the party of 1844, the school at St. Paul was strengthened, DeSmet having brought financial aid, as well as additional persons to help in the work. This school was named St. Joseph, in honor of the patron saint of Joseph Larocque of Paris, who had furnished Father Blanchet with funds for its foundation.

Father Demers, who had succeeded Archbishop Blanchet as vicar-general, was withdrawn from the Cowlitz, 1844, and placed at Willamette Falls, or Oregon City, then growing in importance as a center. Oregon was erected into an apostolic vicariate, by Pope Gregory XVI, December 1, 1843. Later, it was divided into an ecclesiastic province with three sees, namely at Oregon City, Walla Walla and Vancouver island.

Father Blanchet went to Quebec for his consecration as archbishop, and from thence made a voyage to Europe, and was so successful in arousing religious interest that, when he returned, 1847, by sea he brought with him 21 additions to the missions in Oregon, including three Jesuit priests, five secular priests, three lay brothers, and seven sisters of the same order that had previously sent recruits to Oregon. About this time, the Methodist, Rev. George Gary, successor to Jason Lee, was closing out the secular affairs of the Methodist missions, and Father Blanchet made an offer to buy the property of the Oregon Institute, which, however, was refused.

20

Rev. A. M. A. Blanchet, brother of the archbishop, was made bishop of Walla Walla, and Father Demers was created bishop of Vancouver island. The new bishop of Walla Walla arrived at that place, September 5, 1847, a little less than three months prior to the massacre at Waiilatpu, hereinafter described. With him, came Rev. Father J. B. A. Brouillet, as vicar-general, and eight other assistants.

The ecclesiastical province was by this time fully established. Its personnel then included, in addition to the archbishop, three bishops, 17 or 18 Jesuit and Oblate fathers, 13 secular priests and

13 sisters of the Order of Notre Dame of Namur. The girls' school of St. Mary and St. Joseph college for boys, had been founded. The Catholic, like the Protestant, missionaries had a large number of lay brothers in addition to the clerical.

Work among the Indians was being conducted throughout the territory, although, in common with that of the Protestant mission, it suffered reverses east of the Cascades, as the result of the Indian wars, following the Whitman massacre, wars which that tragedy precipitated. Archbishop Blanchet, who figured so largely in these events, was a man of foresight and executive ability, and continued to serve in his high office until 1881, when he resigned it to his coadjutor, and died June 18, 1883, at the age of 87 years. It was through the wise policy followed during his successful administration that the church became a strong factor of influence for peace and safety.

21

An evangelical instrument employed by the Catholic fathers, beginning in 1839, was significant as showing Father Blanchet's early understanding of the nature of the Indians' intellectual processes. It was called by the Indians the sahale stick (stick from on high) and became known as the "Catholic ladder." It was well designed for the purpose of making concrete the lessons which the fathers desired to impress upon their charges, a method analogous to the use of pictures and nature symbols in the instruction of young white children. "The great difficulty," says Blanchet in his Historical Sketches, "was to give them an idea of religion so plain and simple as to command their attention . . . and which they could carry back with them to their tribes. In looking for a plan, the vicar-general imagined that by representing on a square stick the 40 centuries before Christ by 40 marks; the 33 years of our Lord by 33 points, followed by a cross; and the 18 centuries and 39 years since by 18 marks and 39 points, his design would be pretty well answered, giving him a chance to show the beginning of the world, the creation, the fall of the angels, of Adam, the promise of a Saviour, the time of His birth, and His death upon the cross as well as the mission of the Apostles. The plan was a great success. After eight days of explanation the chief and his companions became masters of the subject . . . and started for home well satisfied with a square rule thus marked."

The "ladder" was afterward developed into the form of a chart, printed on strong paper reinforced by cloth, about five feet long by two and a half feet wide, and its use spread rapidly. The Protestant missionaries countered with a "ladder" of their own, in which the history of the Catholic church was depicted in a less favorable light. The missionary history of the period bears a good deal of evidence of sectarian bitterness.

22

A group comprising four Protestant clergymen and one lay worker, and their wives, were independents who believed that they could sustain themselves in the Indian country, or that the natives would support a mission in exchange for the benefits of spiritual leadership and education. The theory proved unsound, and all of these independent missionaries, especially the women, endured hardships, unrelieved by any evidence of success.

Rev. J. S. Griffin and his wife, and Rev. Asahel Munger and his wife were fitted out, 1839, by the North Litchfield Congregational Association of Connecticut, which appears to have been dissatisfied with the work of the American Board. They attached themselves to an American fur trading company expedition to the mountain country. Munger was already married, while Griffin found a bride in Missouri, on the way to the rendezvous, marrying her after an exceedingly brief courtship. The Griffins spent the winter of 1839 at Lapwai, the Mungers remaining at Waiilatpu, both being employed at carpenter and blacksmith work. Munger showed signs of mental derangement on the way west, and again at the Whitman mission, and an effort was made to return him to his home, without success. He later attached himself to the Methodist mission in the Willamette valley. Becoming obsessed with the idea that the Indians needed only a miracle to induce them to embrace Christianity, he impaled himself on a nail above the forge in his blacksmith shop, and was so badly burned that he died in a few days. The Griffins made an excursion into the upper Snake river country which was unproductive, were helped by the Hudson's Bay Company agent at Fort Boise, and found their way to Fort Vancouver, settling, 1841, on a claim near the present town of Hillsboro, in the Willamette valley. Griffin became pastor, in 1842, of the first Congregational church organized in Oregon, the first church of Tualatin plains. He was present at the meeting, May 2, 1843, at Champoeg, at which the provisional government was formed, and voted in favor of the organization, but he was rejected as a member of the legislative committee, on the ground that as a clergyman he ought not to participate in secular affairs.

23

The other party, which came out the next year, consisted of Rev. Harvey Clark, Rev. Alvin T. Smith, and P. B. Littlejohn, a layman, also Congregationalists, who had conceived a similar impracticable scheme of missionary endeavor without the support of a home board. Failing to find a field for usefulness among the Indians, they settled on Tualatin plains. Clark and Smith participated in the organization of the provisional government. Mr. and Mrs. Clark were self-denying and indefatigable in their educational work. Clark, who was present at the meeting held January 17, 1842, at the home of Jason Lee, at which preparations were made to establish a school for white children, at the present city of Salem, was a member of the committee which selected the site for the school. He was employed as teacher by the Methodists, and taught the children of the settlers in his own cabin, at Forest Grove. He was a prime mover in the founding of Tualatin Academy, which flourished for many years, and out of which grew Pacific University, the second institution of higher learning in point of time of its beginning, in the Oregon Country. A large part of the land on which Mr. and Mrs. Clark made their home was given by them to aid in the endowment of this school. Clark also succeeded Griffin, 1845, as pastor of the Congregational church, which in that year was removed to Forest Grove.

24

It remains to conclude the chapter with the tragic story of the Whitman martyrs. The American Board of Commissioners for Foreign Missions had taken early action by sending Rev. Jonathan S. Green to make an investigation, 1829, as has been stated, and it had his recommendation for a mission on the Columbia river. It took note of the reported desire of the Indians of the Rocky mountain country for spiritual guidance, also. May, 1834, soon after the Methodist Missionary Board had resolved to act, the American Board designated three commissioners to go overland to explore the new country, to report on its needs and to select a site suitable for a mission. Rev. Samuel Parker, of Ithaca, New York, was one of these and with companions, he left for the west, arriving at St. Louis too late, however, to join the fur trading caravan setting out that season for the Rocky mountains. Deeming it inexpedient to travel unattended, Parker's companions went to labor among the Pawnees, while Parker himself returned to the states.

He was at the frontier early in the spring of 1835, and obtained permission to travel with a brigade of the American Fur Company. The Board, meanwhile, had appointed, as his associate, Dr. Marcus Whitman, of Rushville, New York, a lay physician with strong missionary inclinations, and these two journeyed with the fur company caravan to the rendezvous of the Rocky mountain trappers on Green river. At that point, a party of Nez Perce's who had previously heard of the coming of Jason Lee, met the missionaries and requested them to establish a station in the Nez Perce's country. This convinced the travellers of the interest of the natives in religion, and Doctor Whitman turned back to report and to obtain reinforcements. W. H. Gray, who came out as lay member when Doctor Whitman returned the next year, says that this decision was hastened by incompatibility of temperaments of the two men, Parker being less adapted to the rough ways of the west than was Doctor Whitman.

Doctor Whitman, on his return east was entrusted by the Nez Perce's with two boys, while Parker, guided by the Nez Perce's, continued his westward journey. Exchanging his guides at Fort Walla Walla for canoemen of the Walla Walla tribe, and these in turn for Wascos at The Dalles, he reached Fort Vancouver, October 16, 1835. Here he passed the winter as the guest of the chief factor, who supplied him with facilities for making the exploration he desired. Parker afterward wrote and published an excellent book, in which he is revealed as one of the very first of the missionaries to comprehend the importance to the whites themselves of the new work. He visited the Lee mission and made a trip down the Columbia river to its mouth on Wyeth's brig, the May Dacre. Then he came back, up river, to explore again the region east of the Cascades. He chose a site for a mission at Waiilatpu, a name that was the Indian equivalent of Place-of-Rye-Grass, and found another suitable site at Lapwai, among the Nez Perce's, as also one in the Spokane country. Being satisfied by this time that missionary endeavors in the new country would be rewarded, he returned home by way of the Sandwich islands, arriving at Ithaca, New York, after an absence of more than two years.

Parker's belief that married missionaries were to be preferred, seems to have been also the view of the American Board; and this led Doctor Whitman, before beginning his second journey to the west, to take as his wife, Miss Narcissa Prentiss, of Prattsburg, New York. With his bride and with Rev. and Mrs. H. H. Spalding, who had just completed their studies at a theological seminary and had been planning a mission to the Osages, and with the addition of the above named W. H. Gray, Doctor Whitman made arrangements to travel in company with another company of fur traders bound for the mountain country, 1836.

The missionary expedition was outfitted with material for a blacksmith shop, and it carried a plow and various other implements, as well as seeds and clothing. On account of the ill-health of Mrs. Spalding, which made it difficult for her to ride horseback, Doctor Whitman procured a one-horse wagon, which achieved a place in history as the first wheeled vehicle to be driven as far west as Fort Boise, then a trading post of the Hudson's Bay Company, on Snake river. It arrived there as a two-wheeled cart, having been reconstructed after many mishaps on the trail.

25

The entire party reached Fort Walla Walla, September 1, 1836. The women were sent down river to Fort Vancouver, to remain until shelter at Whitman Mission, at Waiilatpu, on the site designated by Mr. Parker, could be made ready. The cabin on Walla Walla river, near the present city of that name, was constructed of sun baked mud bricks, and this had been so far completed by December 10, 1836, that Mrs. Whitman and Mrs. Spalding took up their residence there. They were the first white women to make the journey overland to the Pacific coast.

Whitman and Spalding, meanwhile, had gone to Lapwai, about 90 miles east of Waiilatpu, and about 10 miles from the location of the present city of Lewiston, Idaho. Lapwai was the site for another mission, and there Spalding began work among the Nez Perce's, while Whitman returned to the less tractable Cayuses and Walla Wallas, at Waiilatpu. Both men soon built up farms of considerable extent, aided by the labors of the Indians. Spalding in particular developed a talent for agriculture, though he is said to have been handicapped in his relations with the natives by infirmities of temperament, and to have manifested a non-cooperative spirit with other missionaries.

Ground at both establishments was broken and fenced, and the natives were taught the use of agricultural implements. Grist mills were constructed. The Indians clung to the primitive method of threshing grain by tossing the sheaves into a corral and driving wild horses over them until the grain was beaten from the heads, after which they would wait for it to be winnowed by the wind; but they soon learned that there was economy of labor in taking it to the mission mills to be ground. However, these Indians were nomadic, and it was difficult to attach them to the soil. Both Whitman and Spalding persisted, and in due time extended their farming operations, though at the expense of their primary object of spreading the gospel. They were also partly successful in persuading the Indians to breed cattle, from stock which was procured in the east. Sheep, from the Islands, were added to the herds of cattle, and the Indians received a share of them. In a material sense the natives ought to have regarded themselves as prosperous, but it was difficult to convince them of the necessity of work.

In the autumn of 1838, Gray, who had gone home the previous year, returned with a bride, and also with reinforcements for the mission, consisting of Rev. Cushing Eells and his wife, Rev. A. B. Smith and his wife, Rev. Elkanah Walker and his wife, and Cornelius Rogers. These were the only reinforcements, to reach Oregon, sent by the American Board.

26

As the magnitude of their task became apparent to Whitman and Spalding, they joined in another appeal to the Board to strengthen their forces, and Walker and Eells were sent north to establish a station at Tsimakain, near Colville, upon another site selected by the thorough-going Parker, on his scouting trip, 1835. Smith and his wife settled at Kamiah, where, among other activities, they devoted themselves to preparing a Nez Perce' lexicon and grammar. The first printing press to be set up in the territory, reached Lapwai, 1839, being the gift of the native mission at Oahu, Sandwich islands. Several books were printed in the native language. Mrs. Whitman, meanwhile, started a school for the Indian children at Waiilatpu, while her husband trained some of the more intelligent adults as assistants in his Sunday school.

The natives were troublesome from the first, and responded reluctantly to all efforts to improve their condition. Jason Lee, on his way home to the eastern states, 1838, was impressed by the success of Whitman and Spalding in controlling their wards, but Lee by that time was beginning to doubt the aboriginal capacity for absorbing civilization.

The missions, however, were far from self supporting, and their difficulties were not understood by the American Board, whose sole experience with a foreign missionary venture had been limited to experiments in Liberia and Hawaii. The Walla Wallas, in the vicinity of Waiilatpu, were "in general poor, indolent, sordid, but avaricious; and what few have property, in horses and herds, are proud, haughty and insolent." So Elijah White described them in a letter to the commissioner of Indian affairs at Washington. The Cayuses, though less numerous, were more formidable, being brave, active, tempestuous, and warlike. The Nez Perce's alone formed an honorable exception, being better disposed toward the whites and their improvements in the arts and sciences. The three tribes mentioned had become united by intermarriage and by community interest, as well as by apprehension of future encroachments of a white population.

The missionaries had endeavored to accomplish much in a short time; the Indian was not to be hurried; and the expedients adopted by the whites were oftimes unsuited to Indian character. The missionaries were repeatedly insulted. Whitman, Spalding and Smith, each was assaulted, and on one occasion a party of Indians pulled Doctor Whitman's ears and hair, and threw his hat three times in the mud at his feet. Smith and his wife, and Rogers, left the missions in 1841, and Mr. and Mrs. Gray in 1842. Instead of sending the further reinforcements that had been hoped for, the Prudential committee of the American Board dispatched a letter, which was delivered by Dr. Elijah White, who returned, 1842, with a party of settlers. The letter directed that the stations at Waiilatpu and Lapwai be closed, and only the one at Tsimakain be continued.

27

If the order of the Board had been carried out, only Doctor and

Mrs. Whitman, Reverend and Mrs. Eells and Reverend and Mrs. Walker would have remained. Doctor Whitman believed that the Board had erred gravely in its judgment in favor of the Spokane Indians. The message was received at Waiilatpu, in September, 1842. On the 26th of that month, a meeting of all the missionaries remaining in the field was held at the Whitman mission to discuss the crisis that confronted them. Doctor Whitman, notwithstanding past dissensions, resolved to start at once for the east and if possible to save the situation. He took with him a resolution signed by Walker, Eells and Spalding advising the journey. Accompanied by A. L. Lovejoy, a member of Elijah White's expedition of 1842, who had arrived only a month before, he left Waiilatpu, October 3, 1842, on a winter journey through the wilds of western North America.

28

It took them only 11 days to reach Fort Hall, a distance of 600 miles, and, as Doctor Whitman would not travel on Sunday, this was an average of 60 miles a day. At this place, they heard of Indian troubles ahead, but they pushed south over the Great Salt lake, Taos and Santa Fe route. Intense cold and blinding snow were experienced between Fort Hall and Fort Winte, but at the latter point they got a new guide and pushed on to Uncompaghre, on Grand river, then in Spanish territory. They were compelled to take refuge in a ravine for four days from another storm, after which they went into camp to wait for a change of weather. The guide said that the snow had so changed the appearance of the country that he did not know the way and they returned to Uncompaghre for a new guide.

The doctor led the way across a perilous ford of the swiftly running Grand river and by hard travelling the party reached Taos in about 30 days. Here they learned that a party of fur traders, who were ahead of them, would be leaving for St. Louis in a few days, and Doctor Whitman left Lovejoy and the pack animals behind, and pushed on with only the horse he was riding, some bedding and a small allowance of provisions. He lost his way and Lovejoy and the guide reached the rendezvous ahead of him. He finally found his bearings and arrived, much exhausted, attributing his misfortune to the circumstance that he had departed from his rule not to travel on Sunday. Undoubtedly, his choice of the southern route alone had made his trip at that season possible.

29

He proceeded without further untoward incident to St. Louis, to Cincinnati and to Ithaca, and at the last mentioned place he was welcomed by Samuel Parker. After a trip to New York and Washington, he reached Boston, where he was received without cordiality by the American Board, who were inclined to censure him for having left his station without permission. A picture of Doctor Whitman as he appeared to a fellow passenger on a steamboat is obtained from a letter by a contributor in the New York Spectator, April 5, 1843, of which the following is an excerpt: "We also had one who was the observed of all, Dr. Whitman, the missionary from Oregon. He is in the service of the American Board of Commissioners of Foreign Missions. Rarely have I seen such a spectacle as he presented. His dress should be preserved as a curiosity; it was quite in the style of the old pictures of Philip Quarles and Robinson Crusoe. When he came on board and threw down his traps, one said 'what a loafer!' I made up my mind at a glance that he was either a gentleman traveler, or a missionary; that he was every inch a man and no common one was clear. The Doctor has been eight years at the territory, has left his wife there, and started from home on the first of October. He has not been in bed since, having made his lodging on a buffalo robe and blanket, even on board the boat. He is about 36 or 37 years of age I should judge, and has stamped on his brow a great deal of what David Crockett would call 'God Almighty's common sense.' "

30

The true motive of Doctor Whitman's winter ride was long the subject of controversy, but the evidence is now regarded as complete that he undertook it to save the mission, and did not, as has been assumed by some, go for political reasons associated with extension of the authority of the United States over the Oregon Country. He was successful in his purpose. The American Board withdrew its order closing the missions among the Cayuses and the Nez Perce's, it permitted Spalding to remain in the west, and it gave its assent to a plan of inducing emigration from the east, in the view that through settlement of the country around the missions the Indians would receive an object lesson in civilization, while the missionaries would obtain the moral support of a religious community. The westward movement had been stimulated by introduction of a bill in Congress by Senator Linn, of Missouri, December, 1841, authorizing construction of a line of forts from the Missouri river to the "best pass for entering the valley of the Oregon," and immigration was already under way when Doctor Whitman reached St. Louis on his return trip. He gave valuable advice to the company of settlers who had started west in the spring of 1843. This was the first large immigration into Oregon, and it numbered among its members several who afterward became prominent in the history and development of the territory, including Peter H. Burnett, J. W. Nesmith, Jesse Applegate, Daniel S. Holman and others.

31

The immigrants held a meeting at the rendezvous, at Independence, May 18, 1843, appointed a committee to see Doctor Whitman, and adopted rules and regulations. Burnett was elected captain, and Nesmith orderly sergeant, and Capt. John Gantt, a former army officer, was engaged as guide as far as Fort Hall. Gantt fulfilled his mission, and, at Fort Hall, Doctor Whitman proffered his services, and those of several Cayuse Indians who had met the party at the fort, to act as guides for the remainder of the journey. His offer was accepted and the trip was made without accident.

At Grande Ronde he proceeded in advance of the immigrants, upon hearing that Spalding was ill. Travel by ox teams was then in the experimental stage. "Dr. Whitman," says Peter H. Burnett, "assured us that we could succeed, and encouraged and aided us with every means in his power." Thus the company, numbering more than 800 persons, reached the Whitman mission, and later, dividing into independent companies, made its way to the Willamette valley.

Doctor Whitman performed a valuable service for the immigrants of this year, and the station at Waiilatpu was a stopping place for travellers during the remaining years of its existence. In 1844, there were left at the mission the seven children of Mr. and Mrs. Henry Sager, the parents having died on the way across the plains. Doctor Whitman received them, and subsequently, by an order of court, signed by J. W. Nesmith as probate judge of Oregon, dated June 3, 1845, Whitman was appointed their guardian. By this time he had formed a clearer conception of the mission as a means of preparation for the coming of the whites, as his hospitality to travellers over the trail, and his policy toward the Indians showed.

32

While Doctor Whitman was thus engaged in administering to the temporal and spiritual needs of both races, the mission was treacherously attacked November 29, 1847, by Indians whom he had befriended. He was called to the door of his room, on the pretense of consultation about a sick Indian, and while he was talking was struck on the head from behind with a tomahawk. The Indians then overran the mission, killing on every hand and taking women and children prisoners. Fourteen persons were killed, including Doctor Whitman and Mrs. Whitman, two of the Sager boys whose guardianship the doctor had assumed, Andrew Rodgers, a young emigrant who had remained at the mission to study for the ministry, four men who were shot or stabbed on the day the massacre began, two who were discovered in hiding on the second day and slain, two men who were dragged from their beds and slaughtered the eighth day afterwards, and one man who fled to Fort Walla Walla, where admission was refused him, and who was never afterward heard from. Fifty-three women and children were held captive, the women and girls being subjected to indescribable indignities, until they were ransomed by Peter Skene Ogden, who was then chief factor of the Hudson's Bay Company, at Fort Vancouver. He had been notified of the massacre by the trader at Fort Walla Walla, and he employed the artifices of frontier diplomacy and knowledge of Indian character, supported by the traditional influence of the Hudson's Bay institution, in securing their release.

The causes of the massacre were various. It is an interesting theory that one of these was the age-old practice of the Indians to exact the penalty of death of their "medicine men" who did not succeed in effecting a cure. Measles and dysentery had been epidemic, and there were sinister whisperings among the natives that disease had been introduced by the doctor as a means of exterminating them and acquiring their lands. Then, too, the meaning of the constantly increasing stream of immigration had not escaped the Indians.

33

A mixed blood Delaware, named Joe Lewis, who had been taken in at the mission because he seemed to be perishing, had fomented trouble by giving further circulation to the story that the doctor was killing them with his medicine. The son of Peu-Peu-Mox-Mox, chief of the Walla Wallas, had been killed at Fort Sutter in California, 1844, where he had gone to buy Spanish cattle for the tribe; his death had aroused profound bitterness and had not been avenged.

But it also is probable that previous treatment of Indians in the eastern states by the United States government had aroused apprehensions of those in the west. The government had not always been prompt to keep its promises, and there was dissatisfaction, for example, among the Wyandottes and the Osages with the reservations that had been allotted them. Wandering Indians and mixed bloods had communicated this intelligence to the Indians of the mountains, who saw in the incoming tide of settlers only the doom of their race. There was a Shawnee Indian known at the mission by the name of Tom Hill, who was of this stamp, and who had complained to Doctor Whitman.

The provisional government had been set up by the settlers of the Willamette valley, 1843, but without military organization or pecuniary resources. Nevertheless it was preparing to put troops in the field to avenge the massacre, and if possible forestall a general uprising, which would have threatened the Willamette valley. Ogden, however, left Fort Vancouver, December 7, 1847, with a small party, paying toll in bullets as was the custom, to the Indians at the portages. He arrived at Fort Walla Walla on the 19th. Here he called a council of the principal men of the tribes, and warned them that if they precipitated war with the Americans every Indian would have cause to repent of his rashness. He concluded by offering to ransom the captives, but refrained from promising immunity to the offenders.

The chiefs agreed to his proposal, after long deliberation, and the survivors of the massacre were delivered to Ogden, December 29, 1847. The Spalding party at Lapwai, that had been spared through the intervention of friendly Nez Perce's, also proceeded down the river with Ogden, leaving Fort Walla Walla just as news was received that the troops of the provisional government had taken the field. The ransom was paid by Ogden in blankets, guns, ammunition, cotton shirts, and tobacco and was equivalent in value at that time to about $400.

34

The provisional troops later gave battle to the Indians, killing one who had boasted of having scalped Mrs. Whitman. They also took five prisoners, who were afterward tried, at Oregon City, convicted and hanged, June 3, 1850. The massacre resulted in the abandonment of the missions, and also of the project which Doctor Whitman had entertained of establishing an educational institution at The Dalles. Thus, the chapter of missionary endeavor by the American Board of Commissioners for Foreign Missions in the Oregon Country was closed.

Doctor Whitman's attempt to establish a mission has a larger place in the history of the region than would be ascribed to it if it had been but another of the many American failures in gaining a foothold there. The tragedy and the wide publicity given to the facts, full of pathos and of horror, stirred intense interest in the man and his work. His remarkable horseback journey of 150 days in the winter time is to be compared only with the journey of Ebberts and Meek in 1847-48, which will be described in a subsequent chapter.

It is not surprising, therefore, that in the course of time he came to be recognized as a national hero, or that the actual facts came to be expanded into a story more or less untrue. Mr. H. W. Scott has said concerning Whitman: "He was apotheosized through his fate. Hero worship, stimulated by religious or ecclesiastical devotion, has created his legend or myth, which in earlier and less critical times would doubtless have passed unchallenged. But in our age, written and printed records are preserved, and the mythopeic faculty of the human mind receives checks and corrections unknown to the composition of the Homeric poems or portions of the Biblical narrative. But the tendency to hero worship and love of the marvellous will never be wholly eliminated from the mind of man. Before the invention of writing and the use of printing, people forgot their actual history—so uninteresting was it,—and remembered only the fables they had built upon it."

The origin and purpose of Whitman's ride, the status of the Oregon question, relating to the sovereignty and occupancy of the country at that time, with Whitman's influence in changing the national policy toward holding Oregon to the present national boundary; and Whitman's real relation to the great overland move-

ment of settlers in 1843, have all been subjects of critical historical study of late years, so that an impartial decision may now be
rendered based upon the documentary evidence contemporaneous
with the events themselves.

35

Migration westward was stimulated by the printing and dis-
semination of Congressional reports and documents, including the
memorials of the first settlers that had been carried east, and was
aided by Jason Lee's campaign in 1838-9, and also by the numerous articles in the newspapers of the period. The very fact that
measures were pending in Congress to provide a free land grant
to men over 18 years of age, of a square mile in area, was in itself
enough to stir interest.

There is little doubt as to what was Doctor Whitman's purpose
in beginning his famous ride to the east, October 3, 1842. It needs
no hypothesis of a patriotic intent to save Oregon from the British, to account for his decision to leave for St. Louis at once, as
the object was stated in the conference with his associates and for
which they furnished their joint resolution of September 26, 1842,
already mentioned; and it is apparent from the resolution itself
that the urgency was to visit the United States as soon as practicable to confer with the Board in regard to the interests of the
mission.

Doctor Whitman himself made no claim of having rescued a
pending treaty from a sacrifice contemplated by the President and
cabinet, as was afterwards asserted by over-zealous advocates. No
such treaty was under consideration, and there was no such meeting as has been described. He believed his fame to rest upon other
services, and after his return he was particularly proud of the fact
that he had been able to aid the wagon train and to promote settlement by American families.

While there can be no doubt that Doctor Whitman, by his letters, (and his friends and admirers in argument in after times),
claimed too much credit for inducing the immigrants of 1843 to
take their wagons across the continent, and for his own services
in guiding them over the plains and through the mountains, he
was helpful to them in both particulars. It is not necessary to
credit him with having influenced the government to modify the
treaty with Great Britain, to recognize his services indirectly to

his country. He did not originate the great flow of settlers that started westward in 1843, and while he was not their leader or guide throughout the long journey, or the discoverer of the route followed, he did lead them and their wagons from Fort Hall to the Grande Ronde river, and they were then successfully brought to Waiilatpu. The journey to Oregon made by such a large number not only stimulated interest in Oregon, and insured a majority of Americans in the disputed territory, but doubtless strengthened the determination of the government to insist upon American rights, and it influenced the democrats to put the Oregon issue in their platform of 1844.

The services of Marcus and Narcissa Whitman need no exaggeration at the hands of any historian. They were leaders in religion and education in the eastern empire district. Their precept and example was inspiring; their ministrations to the sick and the needy, both native and white, were unselfish. They were crowned at last by death as martyrs, and their fame is imperishable in the annals of the west. If mistakes were made, they were trifling in comparison with the grandeur and the nobility of their lives of self-sacrifice, and their devotion to the cause of righteousness and of humanity.

CHAPTER XVII

BEGINNINGS OF GOVERNMENT

1

As FAR AS the British residents were concerned, there was no apparent need for a local government in Oregon, during the period of joint occupancy under the international agreement. Hudson's Bay Company had its chartered powers, including jurisdiction over its employees. And by the act of the British parliament of July, 1821, the laws of Upper Canada had been made to extend to this region.

This condition did not wholly satisfy the Americans, who, though very few in number, included some who, not satisfied with petitioning the general government at Washington for the definite extension of national laws, wanted local organization. Besides the Methodist missionaries, then in the Willamette valley, there were several independents among the Americans, such as Joseph L. Meek, Caleb Wilkins and Robert Newell, mountain men and fur hunters, who had settled in Oregon when the fur trade in the mountain region had begun to wane. Four others of the same type had recently arrived from California, having escaped with their lives from a bloody encounter with the Indians of the Rogue river district, and one of the four was the same John Turner that had escaped from Indians on Umpqua river, 1828, with Jedediah S. Smith. The others of this party from California were Dr. William J. Bailey, George Gay and John Woodward.

Hudson's Bay Company had exercised some authority, as in the case of the execution of an Indian for murder at Fort George, 1840. In 1835, a settler, T. J. Hubbard, had been exonerated of homicide, on the ground of self defense, by J. K. Townsend and Captain Lambert, of the May Dacre, after an unofficial investigation. Methodist missionaries, 1839, had designated two of their number to act as magistrates, and a number of cases had been presented to them for adjudication. In these instances there was no active participation by settlers, but these had realized the need of some species of local government, and had acquiesced. In 1835, Jason Lee had accepted appointment by McLoughlin and acted as guardian of the orphan children of the French Canadian, Louis Shangarette, deceased.

2

The settlers in the valley had addressed a petition to the United States Congress, 1840, declaring that they had "no means of protecting their own and the lives of their families, other than self-constituted tribunals, originated and sustained by the power of an ill-constructed public opinion and the resort to force of arms." This petition was signed by about 70 Willamette valley residents, and followed a similar petition of 1838. In this petition, which was committed to Thomas J. Farnham, recently from Peoria, Illinois, for transmission to Washington, the signers set forth not only the growing need of protection of law, but also the importance to the United States of the region in which they dwelt. The petitioners had put emphasis on their want of protection against crime, but it is evident from the letters and journals of this period that there was a growing feeling of apprehension that the natives in eastern and southern Oregon were in an ugly mood toward the settlers, and that a military force might be needed.

Need for law in civil cases, and to protect private rights, had not as yet been urgent. There existed, in fact, a force of public opinion not wholly inadequate to cope with violations of peace and order. A man, for example, who had stolen a number of hogs and had been betrayed by the circumstantial evidence of certain incriminating bones, found in his dooryard, had paid for the animals. In the case of Young's distillery and its abandonment, it had been shown that men valued the good opinion of their neighbors. A frontier system of extemporaneous justice might have sufficed for instances like these; it was inadequate, however, for an issue such as arose with Ewing Young's death, February 15, 1841, when the problem of administering his estate presented itself.

3

The first meeting to consider the adoption of a code of laws was held at Champoeg, then the principal settlement in the Willamette valley, February 7, 1841. The meeting appears to have been informal, and but scant record has been left. It seems to have been intended chiefly for discussion of preliminaries, such, perhaps, as those which may have preceded the preparation of the petition forwarded to Congress in the previous year. Rev. Jason Lee presided and "in a short speech in which his remarks seemed to be carefully considered, and in a manner which indicated that he felt oppressed by the grave responsibilities of the hour, he advised the selection of a committee for the purpose of drafting a constitution and code of laws for the government of the settlement south of the Columbia." Little else was done, apparently, except to recommend that the people consider the question so presented. But the death of Young, eight days later, made manifest the need for early action.

Young had taken possession of a land claim which constituted practically the entire Chehalem valley and he had thus been the first settler on the west side of the Willamette river. A man of strong initiative and boundless enterprise, he had already begun to accumulate property. He had constructed a sawmill, and the cattle he had brought from California had multiplied. He was therefore the wealthiest independent settler in the Oregon Country. His neighbors, fully understanding that there was neither a method of selling and transferring title, nor an authority for appointing an administrator to care for the cattle, began to realize the necessity of a probate court and a system of laws to govern the estates of deceased persons. There were no known heirs, and it was a question what could be done with the property. There was no state or government to which it would pass by escheat. No individual felt himself authorized to assume responsibility. Undoubtedly there were informal discussions among those who gathered at the obsequies, February 17, 1841, to pay the last formal honors to a respected fellow-resident, for, after the funeral service some remained to confer.

There was agreement that laws were needed to facilitate the settlement of estates, if for no other reasons. Rev. Jason Lee presided again at this meeting; Rev. Gustavus Hines, another of the missionaries, was named as secretary, and selection of a committee of seven to draft a constitution and a code of laws for the government of the region south of the Columbia was recommended. Although there were no white Americans, excepting missionaries, at Nisqually and east of the Cascades, it was also suggested that settlers north of the Columbia river not connected with Hudson's Bay Company be admitted to the protection of the proposed government, on making application. The meeting then adjourned until the following day to give the participants opportunity for consultation and to insure a larger attendance. The meeting also proposed a top-heavy organization, with a governor, a supreme judge with probate powers, three justices of the peace, three constables, three road commissioners, an attorney-general, a clerk of the court, a recorder, a treasurer, and two overseers of the poor.

4

Nearly all the male settlers in the valley were present at the next meeting, February 18, 1841, at the Methodist mission house. Rev. David Leslie presided on this occasion, and Sidney Smith, an immigrant with the Peoria party of 1839, and Rev. Gustavus Hines, were chosen secretaries. A committee on organization was chosen, and Rev. Father F. N. Blanchet was made chairman of the committee. His colleagues were Rev. Jason Lee, Rev. Gustavus Hines, Rev. Josiah L. Parrish, David Donpierre, M. Charlevon, Robert Moore, Etienne Lucier and William Johnson. Desire for cooperation and conciliation is shown by the composition of this committee, which represented the various elements in the young community. Blanchet was the natural leader of the Catholics and was then presumably in sympathy with the aspirations of the Hudson's Bay Company, as well as of his Canadian fellow countrymen; three were Methodist missionaries; three were French Canadians; one, Moore, was an American settler who had started from Peoria with Farnham, 1839, but had left the original party on account of a disagreement over Farnham's leadership; and Johnson, a former Englishman, was an independent settler. American citizens and British subjects, Protestants and Catholics and those of no religious predilections, were represented.

As a matter of policy the election of a governor was deferred, and Dr. Ira L. Babcock, of the missionary party, was meanwhile appointed supreme judge with probate powers; George W. LeBreton, who had come to the country on the brig Maryland, with Capt. J. H. Couch, 1840, was chosen as clerk and recorder; William Johnson, high sheriff; Zanie (or Xavier) Ladaroot, Pierre Bellique and William McCarty, constables, and Joseph Gervais, William Cannon, Robert Moore and Rev. L. H. Judson, justices of the peace. It was directed that until a code of laws should be framed, Doctor Babcock should act in accordance with the laws of the state of New York. There was not a copy of the New York code in the territory, a fact, however, that seems not to have deferred action.

The people thus had their first practical lesson in the organization of civil government in a new territory, and the settlers adjourned to meet, June 1, 1841, at the "new building near the Catholic church." This was at St. Paul, where the Catholic mission was located. Doctor Babcock, April 15, 1841, appointed Rev. David Leslie administrator of Young's estate.

5

The committee, however, failed to report at the appointed meeting in June, at which Leslie again presided. It then appeared that there was not to be that hearty unanimity that had been hoped for, that Rev. Father Blanchet had not called the members of this committee together, and, in fact, he was not in favor of organization. At any rate, he was not willing at that time to commit himself. Years afterward, he denied that he had absolutely opposed a government, explaining that he had merely counselled that the time was inopportune. He added, in further explanation, that he had told the settlers that as Commodore Charles Wilkes had been commissioned by the United States government to visit Oregon and make a report, and as his arrival was expected in the near future, it would be well to wait until his advice could be secured.

At the meeting, Blanchet's failure to cooperate had a discouraging effect. The committee was instructed in accordance with the suggestion to confer with Wilkes, and it was also decided that Doctor McLoughlin should be consulted. Thereupon, the meeting of settlers adjourned to meet at the Methodist mission house, on the first Tuesday in October, and it was recommended that the committee to draft the constitution and code of laws meet on the first Monday in August. By reconsidering the vote adopting the report of the nominating committee, this meeting annulled the election of the officers. It seems, however, that Doctor Babcock continued to be supreme judge, and in the meantime having appointed an administrator for Young's estate, caretakers were put in charge of the property, as Wilkes notes in his published narrative. The adjourned meeting, however, was not held in October, and presumably the drafting committee never acted. Except for continuance of the nominal authority of Doctor Babcock, and of the justices of the peace and constables, who found little to do, this early experiment in government may be said to have come to naught. About this time the death of one Joel Turnham occurred while resisting arrest by a posse headed by John Edmunds, the latter having been deputized as constable by Rev. L. H. Judson, justice of the peace.

6

Both Lieutenant Wilkes and Doctor McLoughlin advised against proceeding further with plans for organization. Wilkes made a journey through the Willamette valley, in the course of which he found that "these people were quite alive on the subject of laws, courts, and magistrates, including governors, judges, etc." Among those whose homes he visited was William Johnson, a member of the committee. "Johnson," wrote Wilkes in his report to his government, "trapper-like, took what I thought the soundest view, saying that they yet lived in the bush, and let all do right, there was no necessity for lawyers or magistrates."

Wilkes also conferred with Father Blanchet. "He spoke to me much about the system of laws the minority of the settlers were desirous of establishing, but which he had objected to, and advised his people to refuse to cooperate in," says Wilkes in recounting his interview, "for he was of opinion that the number of settlers in the Willamette valley would not warrant the establishment of a constitution, and as far as his people were concerned there was certainly no necessity for one nor had he any knowledge of crime having been yet committed."

Wilkes proceeded through the Willamette valley to the Methodist mission, observing on the way, as an evidence of thriftless management, that a "patent threshing machine" belonging to the mission stood uncovered and exposed to the weather, in the middle of the road. A committee of five, principally lay members of the mission, waited on him to ask his advice regarding the advisability of the pending movement. "After hearing attentively all their arguments and reason for the change," he observed, "I could see none sufficiently strong to induce the step. No crime appears yet to have been committed, and the persons and property of settlers are secure. Their principal reasons appear to me to be, that it would give them more importance in the eyes of others at a distance, and induce settlers to flock in, thereby raising the value of their farms and stock. I could not view the subject in such a light, and differed with them entirely as to the necessity or policy of adopting the change."

Wilkes held that there was "want of right" so to act, because those wishing to formulate laws were in fact "a small minority of the settlers," because necessity did not yet appear, because "the great difficulty they would have in enforcing any laws and defining the limits over which they had control" would be likely to engender discord, and "the larger part of the population being Catholics, the latter would elect officers of their party, and they would thus place themselves entirely under the control of others." He suggested further that "any laws they might adopt would be a poor substitute for the moral code they all now followed," and urged "the unfavourable impressions it would produce at home, from the belief that the missions had admitted that in a community brought together by themselves, they had not enough of moral force to control it and prevent crime, and therefore must have recourse to a criminal code."

Wilkes here overlooked the civil aspect of government, that was indeed the aspect chiefly called to critical attention, and he dwelt exclusively on restraint of crime, a matter of less importance. However, he also noted the scantiness of population and could not "avoid calling attention to the fact, that after all the various officers they proposed making were appointed, there would be no subjects for the law to deal with." Here he may have hit upon a more cogent reason for opposition to the scheme of organization. There was a not inconsiderable element, connected with neither of the principal factions, who doubted the ability of the settlers to bear the pecuniary burdens of even the simplest form of government. The people were few in number, and were widely scattered, engaged in felling trees, cultivating fields, and in other ways giving their attention to supplying immediate wants. To such as these the prospect of taxation, however slight, was far from agreeable, while the necessity for organization seemed to them remote. They had long lived without law and were willing so to continue. Conscious of their own good intentions, and relying on their own capacity for dealing with their problems, they desired only to be left in enjoyment of their Arcadia. This sentiment was at various times to find expression in the course of early efforts to establish and maintain a political state.

Wilkes also advised the people to "wait until the government of the United States should throw its mantle over them." He was afterward told that these views determined a postponement of the meeting. He made a cursory inspection of Ewing Young's farm, which he found to be much out of order, although two persons had been put in charge of it at wages of a dollar a day. The farmhouse was entirely open and everything seemed to be going fast to ruin. Young's sawmill on Chehalem creek had been partly washed away by a freshet, and there was no money to repair it, if that had been thought desirable. The cattle enterprise had prospered while Young lived, as is manifest from a report to Wilkes concerning the investment which William A. Slacum had made in the company at the time of his visit, 1836. Slacum, as has been told, furnished $500 of the capital of the concern. The administrator of the Young estate had made a division of the herds, and 86 head of cattle had been put aside as Slacum's share, after a portion for losses and accidents had been deducted. Slacum's share of the increase in four years was 63 head, although the herd had received no care, except to be driven into pens at night for protection from predatory animals. Slacum had died after leaving Oregon, and his share was now sold, at the request of his nephew, who was a midshipman on Wilkes' vessel. Doctor McLoughlin paid $10 a head for those offered at the sale.

7

Willamette valley was now well supplied with livestock, which were fast increasing in numbers. To repeat what has in effect been said in another chapter, the ship Maryland, sent by Caleb Cushing of Massachusetts, in command of Capt. John H. Couch, had arrived, 1840, with a supply of merchandise, and an American store had been established at the falls of the Willamette. The voyage was not a financial success, but Couch's owners at once outfitted the Chenamus, with which he made a second voyage to Oregon, 1842. He then settled in Oregon, later taking up a land claim and laying out a part of the city of Portland thereon.

Organization about this time of a circulating library and a debating society contributed to the general welfare. Multnomah Circulating Library was created by donation of a few books, then in possession of the residents, and a fund was collected and sent to New York for the purchase of others.

The Pioneer Lyceum and Literary Club, formed in the winter of 1842-43, met regularly at Willamette Falls, during the winter months, and discussed topics covering a wide range of popular interest. Here, organization of government was broached again. At one of the meetings Lansford W. Hastings, who, in that winter was employed by Doctor McLoughlin as his attorney, offered a resolution declaring that "it is expedient for the settlers on this coast to establish an independent government," which was warmly debated, and when it was put to a vote according to custom there resulted a decision in favor of the affirmative. The idea of forming an independent government upon the Pacific coast was not a new one. Several American statesmen, beginning with Thomas Jefferson, had advocated it, and at one time a proposal to unite with California in creating an independent Pacific coast state received some attention. Hastings did not remain in Oregon, but in the spring of 1843, went to California with a party consisting mostly of members of the immigration of 1842, and afterward was active in trying to turn immigrants from the Oregon Trail to California. He advocated an independent Pacific coast state and hoped to be the governor or president. Years afterward it was asserted by both F. X. Matthieu and George Abernethy that Doctor McLoughlin was one of those who preferred an independent government.

However, at another meeting of the Lyceum, a resolution was offered by Abernethy, who was a lay member of the mission party, and who afterward was to become provisional governor, declaring it inexpedient to form an independent government "if the United States extends its jurisdiction over this country within the next four years." A decision for the affirmative here resulted, nullifying the moral effect of the vote on the first resolution.

Meanwhile, Dr. Elijah White, who had been sent to the country with the first reinforcements furnished to Jason Lee, but had returned east, reappeared in the territory, in the fall of 1842, bearing a commission from the United States government as subagent for the Indians west of the Rocky mountains. In the course of one of the Lyceum debates he stated that he would cordially support any measure looking toward the establishment of an independent government, provided the people would elect him governor. White had been involved in an acrimonious controversy with his former fellow missionaries, and now aroused a good deal of bitterness by his exceedingly liberal construction of the authority conferred upon him by his commission, so that this declaration, even if made in a spirit of pleasantry, conveyed a suggestion by no means agreeable to his enemies.

8

The settlers' meeting of June 1, 1841, already referred to, at which Leslie was presiding officer, seems to have resulted in nothing more than to substitute W. J. Bailey, for Blanchet, on the standing committee. It is said that the meeting then adjourned until the first Tuesday in October, but there is no record of any meeting on that date, and it is evident that there was a cooling off in the ardor for creating a real government. Judge Babcock's action regarding the property of the Young estate was sufficient to meet the immediate requirement, and it seems probable that the reluctance of Doctor McLoughlin and the Catholics to join in making an effective organization had its counterpart at the Methodist mission, where Lee himself had become doubtful of the wisdom of going far with any plan of local self-government, especially as there was some hope that the United States would soon take steps to organize the territory under the American flag.

The interest at Washington at this time was not keen, being manifested principally in the introduction of legislative measures regarding the occupancy of the Oregon Country, that never passed. But, for a time the settlers were inclined to await the determination of the constantly debated question of sovereignty.

The first attempt at political organization, therefore, came to nothing of permanent character. There had been four meetings, but none of the officers took up duties, excepting the judge, who was a physician by profession, and who had appointed an administrator, but who was not even in possession of a volume of the New York statutes he was supposed to apply. The plan was allowed to die, and it seemed impossible to unite the various elements of the young community, which it is estimated then comprised 137 persons, including 34 white women and 32 white children.

9

But the idea was not to be given up without further consideration. The problem was to find some common ground upon which all could stand. Meantime, W. H. Gray, a carpenter and teacher sent out by the American Board, 1836, came down from Walla

Walla, having resigned as secular aid there, and he was employed in a similar capacity at Oregon Institute, 1842. The Institute, as already stated, was formed in that year by the Methodist missionaries, as a school for the children of white parents, and was located near the site of the present city of Salem. Here, Gray brought together an informal meeting, February 2, 1843, and for a time he seems to have been the active spirit in the organization of the settlers. The ostensible purpose of this meeting was to adopt measures for the extermination of predatory animals, a suggestion of practical character, on which all might unite, for there was perhaps not a settler possessing livestock in the whole country who had not suffered loss from this cause.

10

If the estate of Ewing Young had furnished an object lesson in what might happen in case of death of a property owner, the killing of cattle by wolves and wildcats was likewise a matter of immediate concern. Even those who regarded the extension of government as inadvisable, agreed that protection against wild animals was desirable. When, therefore, the meeting of February 2, 1843, was held, a committee of six was appointed to call a general meeting of the settlers on the first Monday in March following. This committee, again chosen with discrimination in view of the various elements in the community, included three influential settlers; a Rocky mountain hunter and two Canadian-French residents who had come to the country with the overland Astorians, under Wilson Price Hunt. They acted in accordance with the instructions, and having made a thorough canvass of the still sparsely settled neighborhood, announced a general meeting at the house of Joseph Gervais, for March 6, 1843. This constituted the first positive step in the organization of a local government.

The two assemblages of February and March, 1843, have come to be known in the history of Oregon as the first and second Wolf Meetings. The American population of the territory at this time was a little less than 250, and these were widely scattered, though all resided south of the Columbia, excepting the missionaries east of the Cascades. The missionaries at Nisqually had abandoned the station at that place. The government that was now formed by the settlers has generally been designated as the Provisional Government.

11

Doctor Babcock, who had been acting as probate judge, and who subsequently had discovered the idea of organizing a more formal government, presided at the first Wolf Meeting, but at the second, the presiding officer was James O'Neal, a member of Nathaniel Wyeth's second expedition, who owned a copy of the statutes of Iowa, and some other law books. The committee appointed at the first of these meetings made a report favoring immediate measures for the destruction of all wolves, bears, panthers and such other animals as are known to be destructive to cattle, horses, sheep and hogs, and recommended a scale of bounties. Fifty cents was to be paid for a small wolf, $3.00 for a large wolf, $1.50 for a lynx, $2.00 for a bear and $5.00 for a panther. Indians were to receive half as much as whites. An assessment of $5.00 was levied on each member, with provision for a commission of five per cent for collection. There being practically no money in the country, it was resolved that drafts on Fort Vancouver, the Methodist mission, and the milling company at Oregon City be received in payment of subscriptions.

But, when this business had been transacted, the real purpose of the movers was revealed in a resolution, which was adopted unanimously, for the appointment of a committee of 12 to "take into consideration the propriety of taking measures for civil and military protection of this colony." This organization committee consisted of Dr. Ira L. Babcock, Dr. Elijah White, James O'Neal, Robert Shortess, Dr. Robert Newell, Etienne Lucier, Joseph Gervais, Thomas J. Hubbard, Charles McKay, William H. Gray, Sidney Smith and George Gay. Growth of interest, and increase of population were reflected in the appearance of new names in these official proceedings.

The committee met at Willamette Falls, then recently platted and now called Oregon City, a few days later, most of the principal men of the neighborhood attending its deliberations. The American community, even then, was not of one mind. Jason Lee and George Abernethy now opposed organization of a government, as "both unnecessary in itself and unwise in the manner proposed." However, the organization committee resolved to call a formal meeting to be held at Champoeg, May 2, 1843, "to consider the propriety of taking measures for the civil and military protection of the colony."

12

May 2, 1843, is a red letter day in Oregon's calendar. The assembly was attended by both Americans and British. Lansford W. Hastings, an immigrant of 1842, as already mentioned herein, who was present at Champoeg when the meetings were held, departed from the Willamette valley for California, May 30, 1843. He afterward wrote a book about Oregon and California, and asserted therein that "Neither the officers of the Hudson's Bay Company, nor any persons in the service of that company, took any part in this governmental organization, nor did many of the Canadians or half-breeds, who had formerly been in the service of that company."

Champoeg, then known as "Cham-poo-ick," also by its French name, "Campment du Sable," or "place of sand," was the only region along the Willamette river and down the Columbia to the Pacific ocean where any considerable expanse of open prairie bordered on navigable water. It was one of the few places where a wagon could be driven to the stream without going through a forest. This had influenced Doctor McLoughlin in recommending the prairie country near it as a place of residence for servants of his company whose terms had expired and who did not desire to return to Canada, and these earliest settlers had formed here the nucleus of a farming community. For convenience in its agricultural and merchandising operations, Hudson's Bay Company had established a station at Champoeg. Later arrivals in the country, drawn by conveniences of trade and transportation, had located in that vicinity.

The memorable session on the second day of May was held in a small house on the open prairie. Doctor Babcock presided, and Gray, LeBreton and Willson were chosen as secretaries. The full list of those present, and indeed, the true story of what happened at the meeting are matters of doubt and confusion, owing to lack of complete contemporaneous records, and variance among the accounts given in after years by those who were present and took part in the proceedings.

The committee made its report, outlining a plan, but a motion to adopt was lost. "Considerable confusion existing in consequence," say the official minutes, "it was moved by Mr. LeBreton, and seconded by Mr. Gray, that the meeting divide, preparatory to being counted; those in favor of the objects of this meeting taking the right, and those of a contrary mind taking the left, which being carried by acclamation, and a great majority being found in favor of organization, the greater part of the dissenters withdrew."

Thus runs the formal record of the proceedings of that historic day. It elsewhere appears, however, it was not quite so simple as that; indeed, for a brief time the issue hung in the balance. Some of the Canadian settlers, who were opposed to the movement, had intended to vote no on all motions proposed by Americans. As the story is told, a test motion indicated a probable majority for the affirmative, and LeBreton, who was popular with both factions, and who seemed to be well informed as to the tactics of the opposition party, proposed a decisive stroke. W. H. Gray, who was present at the meeting, but whose account has been criticized by others, says that "by this time we had counted votes," and LeBreton proposed that the meeting divide and count. Joseph L. Meek, one of the trappers who had come to live in the Willamette valley, cried: "Who's for a divide? All for the report of the committee and an organization, follow me!" There was no mistaking Meek's meaning. The company fell into two groups: Fifty-two were shown to be in favor of organization, while only 50 were opposed to it. "Three cheers for our side," cried Meek, and the Americans cheered lustily. Thus, the popular story, as told. It may not be true in all of its details, but it has the support of not only Gray, but others. If the "great majority," mentioned in the official minutes, were actually favoring the objects of the meeting, the method taken to divide for a vote would have been unnecessary. After all, it is not now important, and indeed it is now impossible, to reconsider the accounts and to attempt to ascertain the exact number voting in the affirmative, or in the negative. The fact remains, and its official minutes so record the fact.

13

There was, among the Canadians, a young man named F. X. Matthieu, who had imbibed republican ideas before leaving Canada, and in whom the spirit of rebellion against British rule burned fiercely. According to his own story, he had been counted on by the Canadian party. When LeBreton offered his motion, and when Meek added his stentorian call for a "divide," 50 settlers immediately went over to the right side, leaving 52 Canadians; but Matthieu had determined to join the Americans, and he carried with him Etienne Lucier, whom he had previously influenced to the same course. The defection of these two from the Canadians settled the matter. Without Matthieu and Lucier, the day would have been lost. With Matthieu alone, the vote would have been a tie. The fortunate circumstance, therefore, that Matthieu had passed his first winter in the Willamette valley at the home of Lucier on the bank of the Willamette river, became a determining factor in the outcome.

Lucier's attitude in the beginning had been typical of that of a good many of the Canadian settlers, and so the manner of his alleged conversion is worth recounting here. "Among the subjects of conversation with Lucier," it is recounted in Matthieu's Reminiscences, "were the laws and customs of the United States. The old Hudson's Bay trapper was quite suspicious, and had been told that our government imposed very heavy duties, such as placing a tax on windows. Matthieu was able to tell him that the laws of the United States were just and liberal, and under them all men were equal; there was no tyranny."

The defeated faction having withdrawn, the report was considered and adopted item after item, and then the meeting proceeded to elect A. E. Wilson, supreme judge with probate powers; G. W. LeBreton, clerk and recorder; Joseph L. Meek, sheriff, and W. H. Willson, treasurer. Four magistrates, Hugh Burns, Lewis H. Judson, A. T. Smith and Charles Campo, were chosen. After this, four constables, a major and three captains were elected. The most important action taken, however, was the selection of a legislative committee of nine members, which constituted the first law-making body elected in the Oregon territory, and which was instructed to report at a public meeting at Champoeg July 5, 1843. Their compensation was fixed at $1.25 per diem, money for their payment being raised by subscription. They were limited to six days. The major and captains were instructed to enlist men to form companies of mounted riflemen.

There were settlers who would have preferred to have no government, others who favored government that would be independent of the United States, and some who felt that as Congress had before it a petition of settlers for creation of a form of government by Congressional legislation, any action by the settlers in setting up a provisional government was not desirable at this time. The persons voting in the affirmative at the public meeting, in favor of organizing, were a minority of the adult inhabitants. The majority of the members of the meeting in favor of vigorous measures to create a local government was small, but it had its way, and put through its program. There had been, in addition to the meetings of 1841, the first Wolf Meeting at Oregon Institute, February 2, 1843; the general meeting, or second Wolf Meeting, at the house of Joseph Gervais, on French Prairie, March 6, 1843; the organizing committee meeting, an open meeting at Oregon City, a few days later; the general meeting of settlers at Champoeg, May 2, 1843. The legislative committee met at Willamette Falls, May 16, and continued in session four days. It held adjourned meetings, June 27 and June 28. The general mass meeting met at Champoeg, July 5, 1843.

14

The composition of the pioneer legislative committee here chosen is worthy of especial consideration. Its members were David Hill, Robert Shortess, William H. Gray, Dr. Robert Newell, Alanson Beers, Thomas J. Hubbard, James O'Neal, Robert Moore and William Doughty. The first mentioned was a native of Connecticut, who had arrived in the territory in 1842, and represented the new settler class. Shortess, a member of Farnham's Peoria party, who had come in 1840, was a man of considerable attainments, widely read, and then generally regarded as an American extremist. During the year 1843, he became active in circulating a petition to Congress, probably drafted by Abernethy, praying for extension of the authority of the United States over the new territory, in which petition the Hudson's Bay Company and Dr. John McLoughlin were denounced, and the condition of the colony was depicted as desperate, on account of peril from encroachments of the British interests. Gray, as already stated, had come as a lay member of the Whitman mission, accompanying Doctor Whitman and Rev. H. H. Spalding, 1836, and had resigned from that mission to become a settler in western Oregon and an

[—Oregon Highway Commission]

Champoeg Meeting, 1843
Large mural in the Oregon state capitol depicting this historic meeting.

George Abernethy
First provisional governor of Oregon.

employee of Oregon Institute. Dr. Robert Newell was a Rocky mountain trapper, who had seen service with Smith, Jackson and Sublette, and had brought the first wagons from Fort Hall to Walla Walla. Beers was a blacksmith, a lay member of the first reinforcement of Methodists sent to Jason Lee, 1837. Hubbard, a member of Nathaniel Wyeth's second expedition, 1834, had been a leader in the community and had organized a cattle company, the second in the Willamette valley, the agents of which had narrowly escaped massacre by the Rogue river Indians in an attempt to reach California overland, 1840. O'Neal, also of Wyeth's party of 1834, was one of those who aided in driving to Oregon the cattle bought in California by Ewing Young. He had been chairman of the citizens' meeting of March 6, 1843. Robert Moore, a Pennsylvanian, had served in the war of 1812. He became the founder of Linn City, on the west bank of the Willamette river, nearly opposite Oregon City. William Doughty, formerly a free trapper, had arrived in the Willamette valley, 1841.

O'Neal's copy of the statutes of Iowa, which was bound with the text of the Ordinance of 1787 for government of the Northwest Territory, supplied the committee with a convenient model for shaping its deliberations. The organic act adopted verbatim many phrases from the Ordinance of 1787, and from the organic laws of Iowa. Oregon's first legislative hall, also the first on the Pacific coast, was a room in the granary of the Methodist mission at Willamette Falls, supplied without charge by the missionary authorities. This granary was a one story and a half frame structure, about 16 feet by 30, in which one end had served as church and school, the remaining space on the lower floor being used as a warehouse for grain. There were sleeping and storage quarters on the upper floor. The building was unpainted and was of the "box house" construction, with its boards upright, a type of building often used by the later pioneers. In this structure the committee met, beginning May 16, and continuing for four days. It then adjourned until June 27, and concluded its work the next day. It elected Robert Moore, chairman, and George W. LeBreton, secretary. Early in its deliberations it resolved to sit with open doors. The result of the several sessions was the preparation of an organic act for submission to a public meeting of all the citizens, July 5, following.

15

The attitude of the missionary leaders was hesitant. Lee and Abernethy at a previous meeting, as had been said, had expressed doubt of the wisdom of now organizing a government. Some of the missionaries did not support the proposal, although others had a part in the meeting. One of the devices resorted to by the government party to persuade this group to cooperate, is found in the calling of a patriotic meeting, July 4, 1843, the day before the scheduled public meeting for the consideration of the legislative committee's report, and in an invitation extended to the missionary, Rev. Gustavus Hines, to deliver the principal address. Mr. Hines, however, "dwelt principally upon the subjects of temperance, the glorious deeds of our forefathers on the other side of the Rocky mountains, and the influence and blessings of the day," but said nothing definite to show that he and his associates were ready to help form a civil government.

Nevertheless, Hines was elected chairman of the public meeting, July 5, 1843, by acclamation, when Doctor Babcock failed to attend at the opening. Unfortunately, no list of persons attending the meeting was kept. Joseph McLoughlin, eldest son of Doctor McLoughlin, was present and participated, "against the wishes and influence of his family." Jason Lee looked after the interests of his mission, Joseph Holman, Charles McKay, Robert Moore, Robert Shortess and James O'Neal made motions or took part in the debates. Doctor Babcock seems to have arrived at the meeting while it was still in session, for he is reported by Gray as having a part in the proceedings. There was a relatively large attendance of Americans, and a few of the independent French-Canadian settlers participated in the proceedings, but a greater number of the latter stood aloof, and some let it be known that they would not submit to authority so constituted. Perhaps the opposition was due to suspicion that one of the objects of the mass meeting was to vote land laws in partisan spirit, and there was, as afterward demonstrated, a fear of expense of government and of taxes to defray the expense.

If such were the grounds of the opposition, it was justified. For the enactment regarding land claims included a clause that "nothing in these laws shall be so construed as to affect any claim of any mission of a religious character made prior to this time, of extent not more than six miles square;" and another, aimed at Doctor McLoughlin, was that "no person shall be entitled to hold such a claim upon city or town lots, extensive water privileges, or other situations necessary for the transaction of mercantile or manufacturing operations."

The first was designed to enlist the support of missionaries, both Protestant and Catholic, since it was feared that without their support the government would fail. The second was directed against the claim of Doctor McLoughlin at Willamette Falls, and was championed by the most radical of the opponents of the Hudson's Bay Company. Both of these features show the control of the missionary group at this date, but the land law was changed in the next year, after the great influx of new settlers.

The provision as to the executive, was contained in Section II, Article 5, which provided that "the executive power shall be vested in a committee of three persons, elected by the qualified voters at the annual election." Hines took the floor, and denounced the body as a hydra-headed monster in the shape of an executive committee, and feared a "repetition of the Roman triumvirate— the Caesars upon the throne." This section was adopted, however, Jason Lee and most of the missionary party approving it. Of course, this plan proved crude and unworkable, and it was not long before a single executive was provided for by amendment.

Incidentally, the assemblage voted to reduce the marriage license fee of $3.00, as fixed by the legislative committee, to $1.00. The Iowa statutes were in general decided on as the basis for government of the young colony. O'Neal had just been elected a justice of the peace for the Yamhill district. There is no means of knowing what other law books were included in the purchase from him, but it has been supposed that among them was the only volume of the Iowa code then in the colony.

16

It is peculiarly true of this first public assemblage of the Oregon colonies that the citizens were strongly inclined to self assertion and to join freely in debate upon every public issue. The spirit which led to the town meeting of New England, had descended upon them. There were few lawyers in the territory at the time, but every man assumed to be a judge of right and wrong. The proceedings of the legislative committee had been openly conducted and generally discussed by the colonists. It has been intimated indeed that one reason why the formal records of those meetings were so far from complete is that those who were charged with writing the minutes were so engrossed with the discussions of the day that they had small time for their clerical duties. However, the settlers were fully informed at every stage of the proceedings, and, in the culminating meeting for the adoption of the code and for election of officials, debate was unrestrained.

It is noteworthy, therefore, that the first organic law of the territory, designed to have force "until such time as the United States of America extend their jurisdiction over us," guaranteed "freedom of worship, trial by jury, habeas corpus and the sanctity of private contracts." Adopting verbatim the language of the Ordinance of 1787, it declared that "religion, morality and knowledge, being necessary to good government and the happiness of mankind, schools and the means of education shall be forever encouraged." "The utmost good faith," said the law, "shall always be observed toward the Indians, their lands and property shall never be taken away from them without their consent, and in their property, rights and liberty they shall never be disturbed, unless it be in just and lawful laws, authorized by the representatives of the people."

Slavery or involuntary servitude, except for punishment of crime, was prohibited. Every "free male descendent of a white man," inhabitant of the territory at the time of its organization, was declared eligible to vote, and as to subsequent immigrants, a residence of six months was made precedent to citizenship. No provision was made for levying a tax, in deference to the prevailing poverty of the residents, but a voluntary subscription was made to defray immediate and necessary expenses, and fees were prescribed for recording legal instruments and for certain other public services. The subscription paper then put in circulation read: "We, the subscribers, hereby pledge ourselves to pay annually to the treasurer of Oregon Territory the sum affixed to our respective names for defraying the expenses of the government: Provided, that in all cases each individual subscriber may at any time withdraw his name from said subscription, upon paying up all arrearages and notifying the treasurer of the colony of such desire to withdraw." This informal method of meeting the costs of government was employed for some time afterward, but the legislative committee, 1844, found it desirable to provide for taxation, without, however, assuming the right to confiscate the property of those who refused payment. The expedient adopted in 1844 took the form of a section of the revenue law which read: "That any person refusing to pay tax, as in this act required, shall have no benefit of the laws of Oregon, and shall be disqualified from voting at any election in this country."

Lastly, the vast region known as Oregon was divided into legislative districts. The first of these comprised all the country "south of the northern boundary line of the United States, west of the Wallamet or Multnomah river, north of the Yamhill river and east of the Pacific ocean." The colonists, by fixing the Willamette river as the eastern boundary of the first district, making no express provision for extension of the line northward from the mouth of the river, avoided precipitating the issue as to the international boundary on the north.

The Champoeg district was bounded by a "supposed line drawn from the mouth of the Haunchauke [Pudding] river, running due east to the Rocky mountains," on the west by the Willamette river, on the south by the boundary line between Oregon and California, and on the east by the summit of the Rocky mountains. This district alone, then populated by some 200 Americans, comprised the area of an empire, and included large parts of what are now the states of Oregon and Idaho, and parts of Montana and Wyoming.

The assemblage elected David Hill, Alanson Beers and Joseph Gale as members of the executive committee provided for by the organic law. Gale was a former free trapper who had come to Oregon, 1834, by way of California, another of those intrepid adventurers of whom the earliest community was so largely composed. Hill and Beers had served as members of the committee that framed the organic law.

The Provisional Government was now established. Thus, there was created a government, republican in substance, grounded upon the broadest principles of democracy. The paternalism of the government of the Hudson's Bay Company, which had served for more primitive times, was to give way to the plan insisted upon by the American settlers, a plan of government by majority rule. Under the old system progress was hampered, for however beneficient the intentions of the baronial factor of the company, it was to the interest of the fur trade to hold a close monopoly, and to discourage competition. There was a fundamental difference between maintaining this vast domain for trade in the pelts of fur bearing animals and in devoting it to the needs of civilization.

CHAPTER XVIII

UNDER PROVISIONAL GOVERNMENT

1

THE GOVERNMENT established in the spring of 1843 was little more than a name. Until the large immigration of that year arrived, and brought some 875 additional Americans to swell the scattered population, there was no great need for the enactment of laws, and no particular object in attempting to enforce them. The obligation to obey sat lightly upon the inhabitants, and it may be said that the state rested upon good natured acquiescence in a more or less useless contrivance that nobody took too seriously. In the autumn, the newcomers began to trickle in, and a different situation presented itself. The arrivals were tired and hungry, their rosy anticipations were not realized, and they were inclined to complain. They found fault with the country, and they were critical of the provisional government. It was indeed but a loose organization, that could last only as long as there was no serious attempt to govern. It was strengthened by changes made in 1844, and was thoroughly revised in 1845.

A letter from Doctor McLoughlin to Governor Simpson, dated March 20, 1844, makes a report covering some 56 numbered paragraphs, including the various occurrences of the past year needing comment. One of these paragraphs is as follows:

"51. On the 4th inst. [March 4, 1844] a meeting of the settlers was called in the Wallamatte to petition the U. States Congress to extend their jurisdiction over this country. The Canadians were invited to attend, and did so, and being the majority (as a great part of the Americans are hostile to Dr. White who summoned the meeting, would not attend,) voted down every measure proposed, saying they were British subjects and could have nothing to do with a petition to the Congress of the U. States to extend her jurisdiction over this country and when the boundary was run they would obey the laws of the country they happened to be placed under."

There is no official record of this meeting of March 4, 1844, but an "address" purporting to be from Canadian citizens, directed to "the American citizens, and particularly to the gentlemen who called said meeting," may have been presented to the meeting of that date, mentioned by McLoughlin. It may be found printed in the Oregon Archives as if the date of the meeting was March 4, 1843. The signers were S. Smith, president; Francis Revay and Joseph Gervais, vice-presidents; and Charles E. Pickett and S. M. Holderness, secretaries.

This protest, or address, was perhaps the product of Americans as well as of Canadians. It expressed sentiments of cordiality and "desire of union and inexhaustible peace between all the people." The signers said that they did not intend to rebel against the measures previously adopted, but that they believed it would be sufficient for the magistrates already appointed to finish their time." They objected, however, to a provisional mode of government, and to overloading the colony instead of improving it. "Besides," they continued, "men of laws and science are too scarce, and have too much to do in a new country." They wished to be governed, if at all, either by a senate or a council, elected from all parts of the country; they hoped that the members would be influenced by love of doing good, rather than by hope of gain; they desired that unnecessary taxes, of whatever kind, might be avoided; they suggested that a militia would rather awaken the suspicion of the Indians than increase the security of the settlers, and also that the country should be considered, for the time being, as free to all settlers, of whatever nationality. "The more laws there are," said the petitioners, "the more opportunities for roguery for those who make a practice of it," and "in a new country, the more men employed and paid by the public, the fewer remain for industry."

The address may have been presented to the government, but the only copy received by the official clerk was unsigned and it does not appear that any official action was taken on it. The original draft was in the French language, and according to Dr. McLoughlin, it was written by one of the Catholic priests, Father Langlois, who had arrived at Willamette Falls, September 16, 1842. It was no doubt due to this petition, in great part, that an earnest attempt was thereupon made to meet the views of the Canadians, and to prevail upon them and upon British residents, to participate in the temporary government.

2

A considerable number of those who came in 1842, including Lansford W. Hastings, who had served as trail captain on the way across the plains, had found themselves disappointed with Oregon, and had decided to try California. They had held a meeting at Champoeg, May, 1843, and had again elected Hastings as captain. They started southward, but some of the party again changed their minds, and returned to the Willamette settlements after having met another party at the Rogue river, who were on their way to Oregon because they had not found California to their liking. The Hastings remnant, however, continued on the trail, and reached Fort Sutter, California, in the early summer, after having had some trouble with Indians in the Sacramento valley.

Due to the large immigration of 1843, a new element predominated in the territory when the general election was held, May, 1844, and this resulted in a turnover in the official government. The executive committee then chosen was composed of Osborne Russell, Peter G. Stewart and Dr. W. J. Bailey. Russell, an old mountain man, who had come to the territory in 1842, received 244 votes; Stewart, an immigrant of 1843, received 140, and Bailey, who represented the old-timers, 70. Alanson Beers, of the mission party, received only 49, and the rest of the votes were scattering. Joseph L. Meek was again elected sheriff, receiving 143 votes, of a total of 146 cast for that office. Philip Foster was elected treasurer, and Dr. John E. Long, recorder. Dr. Ira L. Babcock was reelected supreme judge, with 88 votes, to 39 for J. W. Nesmith. November 11, 1844, Babcock resigned, as he was about to return to the east, and in the following month Nesmith, who was one of the leaders of the train of 1843, was appointed to succeed him. The legislative committee, the first law-making body ever named by regular election in Oregon, was chosen by districts. Tualatin sent Peter H. Burnett, M. M. McCarver, David Hill and Matthew C. Gilmore; Clackamas, A. L. Lovejoy and Daniel Waldo; Champoeg, T. D. Keysur and Dr. Robert Newell. This was almost a clean sweep of the old administration, as only David Hill and Dr. Newell remained. No election was held in Yamhill in that year.

3

Considerations that influenced settlers in shaping the government in 1843, had less force now. Canadian or American numerical preponderance had been settled by the trend of events. The missionary party was less influential, and there was, on the other hand, a strong opposition to the new land law, and particularly to the provision that permitted a mission to hold a township, or 23,-040 acres.

A sharp division between the old settlers and the new, became manifest. The scheme of government by executive committee was objected to. The slavery issue was alive, and the provision of the organic act of 1843, that incorporated the clause of the Ordinance of 1787, prohibiting slave holding, was unsatisfactory to many. The legislative committee, which met June 25, 1844, supplemented the organic act upon this point with an enactment requiring all persons who had brought slaves into the country to remove them within three years, and providing that free negroes should leave within two years, under penalty of being flogged by the constable, with repetition of the flogging every six months so long as they remained in the territory in violation of law. This act was never enforced, and the legislative committee amended it at the following December session, by substituting for the flogging clause a provision that colored persons who failed to leave the country should, upon conviction, be offered publicly for hire to the "person who will obligate himself to remove such negro or mulatto from the country for the shortest term of service." The law was repealed in toto, however, 1845.

The legislative committee of 1844 also passed a prohibitory liquor law, being moved thereto by conflict between the authority of officers of the provisional government and that of Dr. Elijah White, who had construed his commission as sub-Indian agent as conferring general powers of law enforcement. White had been acting under a provision of the statutes of Iowa, prohibiting sale of liquor in Indian territory, and under its provisions he confiscated the first still set up openly in the territory since Lieutenant Slacum and Jason Lee had persuaded Ewing Young to abandon his enterprise, 1836. There was friction as a result of this dual assertion of authority, but sentiment was largely in favor of enactment and enforcement of a prohibition law by the local government.

4

The executive committee, 1844, issued a formal message, expressive of the general feeling of the community, that the government at Washington had been unduly dilatory in extending its authority over the region. This committee proposed to the legislative committee a light tax, the vesting of the executive power in a single person, instead of in an executive committee. It also proposed various amendments of the laws of Iowa to suit the particular circumstances of the colony. It called attention to the impropriety of vesting the powers of supreme, district and probate judge in one person, and recommended that the fourth article of the organic law be repealed as detrimental to the interests of the public. This was the article which declared against "either slavery or involuntary servitude."

The response of the legislative committee to this last mentioned proposal, took the form of an amendment of the existing law, so as to require the expulsion of all slaves and free negroes, thus neither recognizing the principle of freedom for the black man, nor the right of ownership of human chattels. The legislative committee, also, responded to the demand of the newly arrived immigrants that the land laws be amended. Free land having furnished the main-spring for a substantial part of the immigration of 1843, it was natural that this should now prove of paramount interest. The large grants allowed to missions was not the only feature that was causing dissatisfaction. There was objection to the requirement, in a territory in which means of travel were uncertain, that new claims should be recorded within 20 days after their location, while old settlers were allowed a year in which to make their filings. The amended land act passed by the legislative committee of 1844, at its June session, omitted the requirement for recording claims, eliminated special grants to missions, and required the making of improvements, and a bona fide intention of occupying and cultivating the land. The measure was thus aimed at land speculators.

Under the former law, as Peter H. Burnett, one of the members of this legislative body, has explained, "a man, having a number of children, could record one claim in the name of each child one month before the annual arrival of new immigrants, and that record would hold the land for six months; thus forcing the late comers either to go farther for their locations, or purchase the claims of his children." The amended land act was supplemented at the December session by an act defining the word "occupancy," as requiring the claimant to reside on the land himself, or to occupy it by the personal residence of his tenant. As a further measure of relief for those who had come late, it was provided that the settler might claim 600 acres on the prairie and 40 acres in the timber, the parts not necessarily adjoining.

5

This legislative committee was also confronted with the problem of raising revenue to support the government. Voluntary contributions had not proved dependable as a source of funds, and many of the new settlers, especially, did not feel bound to pay. To meet this situation, without antagonizing those whose support was desired, and also perhaps being still in some doubt as to the full extent of its physical power to enforce its decrees, the committee by an enactment, June 25, 1844, hit upon the plan of levying a small tax (one eighth of one per cent on certain kinds of personalty, and a poll tax of 50 cents on all male citizens over the age of 21 years, being the descendant of a white man), the law containing a proviso that "any person refusing to pay tax, as in this act required, shall have no benefit of the laws of Oregon, and shall be disqualified from voting at any election in this country." Thus, the lawmakers reached two vulnerable spots in the armor of the average American. By depriving him of his franchise, and by denying him the protection of law against any trespasser who might file an adverse claim upon his home, it supplied a strong incentive for sharing in the burdens, as well as the benefits, of government.

The first taxes were collected by Sheriff Joseph L. Meek. Four hundred names were on the tax roll of 1844, as liable to poll tax of 50 cents each, and 345 were listed for property tax. Farms were not taxed, but cattle, horses, town lots and mills produced the greater part of the revenue, the other items of taxable property being hogs, mules, watches, clocks and pleasure carriages. The largest owner of town lots was Doctor McLoughlin, but John H. Couch, Felix Hathaway, F. W. Pettygrove, Philip Foster, S. W. Moss, J. L. Morrison, Walter Pomeroy and P. H. Hatch were also listed as owners of considerable property of that classification. Doctor McLoughlin's mill property was valued at $7000, and the sawmill of Oregon Milling Company at $5950. John Force had a grist mill listed at $3000, F. N. Blanchet, another, at $2000. The principal cattle owners were Hamilton Campbell, Jesse Applegate and Daniel Waldo.

Meek had a hard time collecting the small sum due from the taxpayers, and a comical note is sounded in his report, in which he records that Joseph Gale refused to pay, and says that Gale's answer to the steward was "Darn my sole if I pay." The report showed that Louis Lumburg was "poor, very;" Tusah Peria, "blind, invalid;" Owen Sumner, "very old;" Joel Turnam, "dead." Some of those who refused to pay were Michel LaFramboise, William T. Perry, Elbridge Trask, Robert Shortess, Lewis Taylor, Thomas Owens, George Summers, Daniel McKesick and William Hobson. The sheriff reported that his failure to collect from some of those listed on the tax roll was "owing to our population being so much scattered, and to the unsettled state of the publick mind relative to the subject of taxation."

6

The estate of Ewing Young had been administered under successive judicial officers. No heir had claimed it. The subject was brought to attention by passage of a bill directing the executive committee to appoint an administrator to close the business of the estate, and to pay the moneys on hand to the treasurer of Oregon. Out of these funds, the sum of $1500 was thereupon appropriated to build a jail. The government, however, pledged its good faith for return to Young's heirs, if any should appear, of any money so converted, and some years afterward full settlement was made and the money was paid to a claimant. Doctor McLoughlin donated the site for the jail, and it was built at a cost of $1175. An interesting sidelight on the financial situation of the colony at the time, is shown in a petition presented to the legislative committee, June, 1845, by 38 citizens, praying the funds be not employed as planned, lest the government "become too much involved." "We are unaware," said the petitioners, "at what moment a demand may be made upon this Govt. for said estate. If at an early date (as is very likely) we are certain that in our present condition we shall be entirely unable to meet such demand. We have no doubt but that these demands, when paid, must be discharged in specie, a sufficient quantity of which is not in the country. A sacrifice of our property must ensue." It seems that in 1845 citizens actually believed that public debts had to be paid!

Public officials in 1844 and 1845 were not accustomed to dealing with large sums. The report of the territorial treasurer, December 18, 1844, for illustration, showed receipts from the collector of taxes of $313.31, from licenses of two ferries $40, and from one fine $5, a total of $358.31. The largest single item of the total of $115.38 expended was $60, the salary of Dr. Ira L. Babcock, as judge.

The legislature, 1844, in seeking to improve, took the liberty of destroying the charter from which it derived its own powers; for at the session which convened December 16, it received and acted on a message from the executive committee advising that provision be made for a more permanent constitution, "constructed in such a manner as would best suit the local situation of the country and promote the interests of her citizens, without interfering with the real or pretended rights of the United States or Great Britain, except where the protection of life and property actually require it." The legislative committee, therefore, prepared an amended organic law, and submitted to the people the question whether there should be a constitutional convention.

7

By a vote of 283 to 190 the voters at the general election, June 3, 1845, rejected the proposal for a constitutional convention; but at another election, held July 25, 1845, the issue, "Old organic law" or "Amended organic law," was voted on by viva voce vote, and the amended organic law was then adopted, 255 to 22. At the election of June 3, 1845, officers, as provided for by the amended act previously passed by the legislature, had been chosen.

This election was preceded by a convention held at Champoeg, at which A. L. Lovejoy was nominated for governor, but he was defeated at the polls. George Abernethy, steward of the Methodist mission, who had acquired the store and stock of goods of the Methodists, at Oregon City, but who was then absent in the Sandwich islands, received 228 votes and was elected. Osborne Russell received 130 votes, Dr. W. J. Bailey 75, and Lovejoy, nominee of the convention, 71. John E. Long was elected secretary, Francis Ermatinger, treasurer, S. W. Moss, assessor, Joseph L. Meek, sheriff, J. W. Nesmith, judge, and Marcus Ford, district attorney. Members of the legislature chosen at this election were: Clackamas district H. A. G. Lee, W. H. Gray and Hiram Straight; Champoeg district, Robert Newell, J. M. Garrison, M. G. Foisy and Barton Lee; Tuality district, M. M. McCarver, J. W. Smith and David Hill; Yamhill district, Jesse Applegate and Abijah Hendricks; Clatsop district, John McClure.

It will be noted here that the old timers are already disappearing, and that there is an infusion of new settlers. The election of June 3, 1845, is noteworthy for several reasons. For example, the election of Francis Ermatinger, as treasurer, had considerable significance, as Ermatinger was chief trader of the Hudson's Bay Company at Oregon City.

Influences were then at work, under the leadership of Jesse Applegate, to obtain support of Hudson's Bay Company for the new government. Undoubtedly there were advantages to both sides in the proposed arrangement. To the Hudson's Bay Company, it held out a prospect of protection against encroachment by Americans on its lands, it offered a method through the courts of collecting debts due the company, and gave the company a means of bringing back defaulting and deserting employees. One Henry Williamson, an American, had posted a notice bearing date February 15, 1845, on a tree near the river, about three quarters of a mile below Fort Vancouver, and erected a hut 12 feet square. By this notice he asserted a claim to some part of the company's lands, a fact that, in view of the growing prejudices against the company, led McLoughlin and Douglas to fear that force and illegal methods might be used. McLoughlin promptly reported the occurrence to Governor Simpson, and under date April 2, 1845, he wrote to Governor Pelly that he had been informed by one of the principal American immigrants of the intention to form a constitution, to have force until the boundary would be settled. The officers of the company were urged to unite in forming the new government, for its own protection. It seems clear that prior to the agreement it was arranged that Francis Ermatinger would be elected treasurer, and that on the creation of a new district north of the Columbia river, some of its officers should be Hudson's Bay Company men. James Douglas was selected as one of the judges. Other conditions were agreed upon, satisfactory to McLoughlin and Douglas.

On the other hand, from the American point of view, the compact meant an additional source of needed revenue, and avoidance of conflict. Extension of the limits of the provisional government over the region north of the Columbia river gave the Hudson's Bay Company and also any Americans who might locate north of the river, opportunity to participate in the local government.

The legislative committee that met June 24, 1845, drafted a

memorial to Congress giving information as to the establishment of the provisional government, directing attention to the colony's want of protection against hostile Indians, and to the inadequacy of its revenues to meet an emergency, praying, also, that the United States establish a territorial government. "And we pray," the memorial further said, "that in the event you deem it inexpedient as a measure, or contrary to the spirit of existing treaties, to establish a territorial government in Oregon, that you extend to us adequate military and naval protection, so as to place us, at least, upon a par with other occupants of our country." The legislature proceeded to prepare a new organic law for submission to the people at an election, to be held July 25, 1845, and then adjourned to August 5. The amended act was adopted at the polls, as has been stated.

8

The legislative committee, having adjourned pending action of the voters on the organic act, met again, pursuant to adjournment, as a house of representatives, at Oregon City, August 5, 1845, and early adopted a resolution, proposed by Applegate, setting forth that the inhabitants of the territory were not bound by acts not expressly authorized by the organic act, and consequently that no debt should be incurred without a vote of the people. This was protested by a minority as being an unwarranted imputation on the former government, but was adopted by a vote of eight to four.

At this session the negotiations conducted by Jesse Applegate with the Hudson's Bay Company officials at Fort Vancouver were carried out in full. The latter, on their part, exacted a number of conditions. The company was to be taxed on sales made to settlers only; thus preserving its established privileges of free trade with its own people and with the Indians. The district thus created north of the Columbia was to be given the name of Vancouver, after the company's principal post. All former rights of trade enjoyed by the company were to be maintained. The oath of office was to be changed as to make it acceptable to British subjects, as well as to American citizens.

Doctor McLoughlin, before this time, had come to realize the necessity for local government, and a formal letter addressed to him, August 14, 1845, by the legislature, was answered jointly by him and James Douglas, in behalf of the company, in a friendly spirit. Doctor McLoughlin, himself, regarded the compact as one merely between the people of two nations, living together in a country free to both, to enable them to maintain peace and order, which could not be kept in any other way; and he declared that it would not interfere with national allegiance. This view, too, was accepted by Lieutenants Warre and Vavasour, agents of the British government to examine into conditions in Oregon, who, in their report to the British secretary of state for the colonies transmitted a copy of the amended oath of allegiance, with the comment: "The gentlemen of the H. B. Company appear to us anxious that their motives should not be misunderstood, in uniting with the Americans for the mutual protection of their property, or that their allegiance to the mother country should not be impugned." They also reported, as to the arrangement by which the company acquiesced in the local government, that "a more judicious course could not have been pursued by all parties for the peace and prosperity of the community at large." The oath was: "I do solemnly swear that I will support the organic laws of the provisional government of Oregon, so far as said organic laws are consistent with my duties as a citizen of the United States, or a subject of Great Britain, and faithfully demean myself in office, so help me God." Many years after this settlement, in a letter written October 13, 1867, Applegate explained that one of the purposes of the agreement, which guaranteed the Hudson's Bay Company the peaceable possession of its posts and farms, was to leave the land not so occupied by the company open to settlement.

9

At this time there seems to have been some confusion in the minds of the Hudson's Bay Company officials as to the real ownership of the land claim at Oregon City. Doctor McLoughlin had ostensibly taken it up and occupied it as an individual, but he had offered to surrender all personal interest therein to his company, and had urged the company to decide whether it wanted to take it over or not; but the company had not acted, and evidently it rather expected that when the boundary dispute would be settled, the dividing line would follow the Columbia, so that the land claim would be in the United States. Correspondence has recently come to light that tends to show that while some of the American settlers were becoming violently hostile to the company and to Doctor

McLoughlin, charging that the land was kept under cover for the foreign company, the doctor was offering to surrender it to the company, if it was ready and willing to take it and pay the amount of his personal outlay for improvements.

10

The organic act of 1845 resembled a constitution, and was better suited to the needs of a growing community than its predecessor. "We, the people of Oregon Territory," the preamble ran, "for the purposes of mutual protection, and to secure peace and prosperity among ourselves, agree to adopt the following laws and regulations until such time as the United States of America extend their jurisdiction over us." Another significant phrase of the preamble was: "For the purposes of temporary government." Religious freedom, the right of habeas corpus, trial by jury and proportionate representation were preserved.

The language of the Ordinance of 1787 with respect to education was repeated. Slavery was forever prohibited. The legislative committee gave place to a house of representatives, the first in Oregon. This was to be composed of not fewer than 13 nor more than 61 members, and no more than five members were to be added in any year. The house was empowered to impeach officers of the territory for malfeasance, to create new districts, and to pass laws to raise revenue, either by levying and collecting taxes or by imposing licenses on mercantile establishments, ferries and other objects, to open roads and canals, and to regulate the intercourse of the people with the Indian tribes. The supreme powers to declare war, suppress insurrection and repel invasion, and to create a militia, were expressly bestowed on the house. It was empowered to "regulate" the introduction, manufacture and sale of ardent spirits, and to create a currency.

The executive power was vested in a single individual; the judicial power in a supreme court, and such inferior courts of law, equity and arbitration as might be established by statute. Article three, pertaining to land claims, reflected the changing circumstances of the community and the growing need of more uniform regulation of metes and bounds. Formerly, when land was plenty and settlers few, there had been lack of method; claimants were now required to conform boundaries as nearly as possible to the cardinal points and to make permanent improvements within six months of the time of entry, and no individual was permitted to hold more than 640 acres at one time, in square, or oblong, form. Officers chosen at the general election, June, 1845, were confirmed as the officers of the territory under the organic law. Amendments might be proposed by a two-thirds vote of the members of the house of representatives and made public, then to be voted on at the polls, whereupon concurrence of two-thirds of all the house members chosen at the general election was required for their enactment.

11

Another of the interesting acts of this session was a law against duelling, which arose out of a spectacular occurrence. On the sixth day of the session, Applegate rushed into the house, under considerable excitement, and moved that the rules be suspended to allow him to introduce a bill to prohibit duelling. The bill was read once for information, and twice by title, and, being duly enacted, was ordered forwarded to the executive committee forthwith for approval. Within less than an hour after its introduction it had been signed and returned and had become a law. It seems that Dr. Elijah White had engaged in a personal controversy with Samuel M. Holderness, a citizen of peppery temperament, and the latter had declared his intention of calling Doctor White to account on the field of honor. Passage of Applegate's bill forestalled the encounter and augmented Applegate's reputation as peacemaker and compromiser.

The legislative committee also adopted a resolution by Applegate, emphasizing the desire of the people that the protection of the laws of the United States be extended over them. "Adoption of the organic act by the people of Oregon," said the resolution, "was an act of necessity rather than choice, and was intended to give to the people the protection which, of right, should be extended to them by their government; and not as an act of defiance or disregard of the authority or laws of the United States." A copy of the organic law was sent with the resolution. Congress was urged, in establishing a territorial government, to legalize the previous acts of the people so far as these might be in accord with the federal constitution.

12

A brush between the legislative committee and Dr. Elijah White enlivened the annals of the August session of the legislature of 1845. He was about to return east, and was requested to convey to Congress the above mentioned memorial, signed by the members of the committee, but the motion was afterward amended to omit the requirement for signature. Dr. Robert Newell also introduced a memorial asking Congress to reimburse Doctor White for expenses he had incurred in prosecuting his work as Indian agent. It occurring later to some of the members that they had been too generous in indorsing Doctor White, a resolution by Applegate was adopted in which it was set forth that "it was not the intention of this house, in passing resolutions in favor of Dr. E. White, to recommend him to the government of the United States as a suitable person to fill any office in the territory." Speaker McCarver had signed the resolutions, notwithstanding the committee's resolution to omit signatures, and was ordered to take a leave of absence for the purpose of following Doctor White to Vancouver and "erasing his name from the said documents, to-wit: the organic law and the two resolutions in favor of Doctor White." Doctor White refused to surrender the documents for the purpose, and replied in a sardonic vein. "Being on my way," he wrote, "and having but a moment to reflect, I have been at a loss which of your two resolutions most to respect, or which to obey, but at length I have become satisfied that the first was taken more soberly and, as it answers my purpose best, I pledge myself to adhere strictly to that. Sincerely wishing you good luck in legislating, I am, dear sirs, very respectfully yours."

Doctor White then proceeded overland to Washington. But the legislative committee, not to be outwitted, ordered the secretary to prepare copies of the correspondence, together with affidavits charging Doctor White with having destroyed certain private documents. These papers were committed to Captain J. H. Couch, who was about to sail for Honolulu, and he in due time gave them to the American consul there for transmission to Washington. They were in the possession of President Polk before Doctor White arrived at the capital.

At this session of August, 1845, an act to incorporate the Multnomah Circulating Library at Oregon City was adopted, "a very good circulating library," as J. W. Nesmith called it in one of his letters. The Wahoni Milling Company and the Columbia Transporting Company were also created, and these three were the first Oregon corporations. A census taken in that year showed a total white population, 2109, of which 1261 were males, and 848 were females.

The legislature, at the August, 1845 session, attempted to meet the need of the territory for a medium of exchange by passing an act including in the list of legal tender orders, wheat, hides, tallow, beef, pork, butter, lard, peas, lumber, or other articles of export of the territory. It also adopted a resolution declaring that "one of the principal objects contemplated in the formation of this government, was the promotion and prosperity of peace and happiness among ourselves, and friendly relations which have, and ever ought to exist between the United States and Great Britain; and any measure of this house calculated to defeat the same is in direct violation of the true intention for which it was formed."

13

The legislative committee adjourned, August 20, 1845. Summarizing its accomplishments, it will be seen that the government, was now functioning under a fundamental act, adopted by the people themselves, that amendments of the act were also the work of the people, that the executive committee had been supplanted by a governor, and that governor elected by the people, while an oath of allegiance adapted to the situation of the colonists had been provided. Opposing interests had been reconciled. Property was secure and official machinery was running with little friction. Contracts were being enforced, and debts being collected, with moderation. Education was given especial consideration.

The immigration of the year 1845 was the largest that had crossed the plains. Bringing almost 3000 new settlers to the territory, it doubled its population, and added to its perplexities, because, they arrived late in the year, and few brought with them the means of subsistence while they were establishing themselves. In these circumstances the provisional legislature, no longer a legislative committee, when it met, December 2, 1845, found it expedient to modify the law for the collection of debts, allowing numerous exemptions from sale under execution, and providing that no property should be sold for less than two-thirds of its actual value.

There was a notable lack of money in the country. Primitive

methods of barter and exchange prevailed. The distinction between old and new settlers, has been well described by Peter H.
Burnett, one of the comparatively old-timers, since he had arrived
two years before. "At any public gathering it was easy to distinguished the new from the old settlers. . . . They were dressed in
broadcloth, and wore linen bosomed shirts and black cravats,
while we wore very coarse, patched clothes; for the art of patch-
ing was understood to perfection in Oregon. But while they
dressed better than we did, we fed better than they. Of the two,
we were rather the more independent. They wanted our provisions, while we wanted their materials for clothing. They, seeing
our ragged condition, concluded that if they parted with their
jeans, satinets, cottons and calicoes, they would soon be as destitute as we were; and therefore they desired to purchase our provisions on credit and keep their materials for future use. This did
not suit us precisely. We reasoned in this way: that if they wished
to place themselves in our ruddy condition, they should incur the
risk of passing into our ragged state—they should take the good
and the bad together. We, therefore, insisted upon an exchange."
The legislature, in consequence, passed an act regulating the currency, by which it made gold, silver, treasury drafts, approved
orders on solvent merchants, and good merchantable wheat, delivered at places where people were accustomed to receive wheat,
a lawful tender for taxes and judgments rendered in the courts
of the territory. This was soon changed, however, as the use of
wheat as a medium of exchange presented difficulties, and a new
enactment, December, 1847, recognized as legal tender nothing
but gold and silver and treasury drafts.

Governor Abernethy recommended in this message to the legislature, December, 1845, that a militia be organized, that a standard of weights and measures be adopted, and that surveys be made
for a new road into the Willamette valley. The valley was practically the only settled district. At this time, but one settler lived
on the Columbia, between the Willamette and Astoria. The legislature had received several applications for authority to build and
operate toll roads, among them one from Samuel K. Barlow, who
had successfully led a company of immigrants, 1845, to the Willamette valley on a route south of Mount Hood. He began constructing a toll road, and the work was so far along by August,
1846, that it was available for immigrants of that year.

14

The governor recommended that steps be taken to establish a seat of government, but for a while longer, the legislature continued to move from house to house, as occasion made necessary, and the governor, was authorized to receive sealed proposals for the erection of public buildings. The legislature also passed another prohibitory liquor law, which was vetoed by the governor. The revenue bill, passed under authority of the new organic act, December 11, 1845, levied a tax of one-fourth of one per cent advalorem, for territorial needs; local taxes were left to be fixed by the county courts, with the restriction that they should not exceed the territorial tax, and with a poll tax of 50 cents on every qualified voter under the age of 60 years. This tax law was expanded and thoroughly revised in the following year. Licenses for merchants, auctioneers and ferries, and fees for recording certain legal instruments were fixed.

A post office department was created by legislative act and William G. T'Vault, editor of the Oregon Spectator, the first newspaper published west of the Rocky mountains, became postmaster-general. The Spectator was an outgrowth of the Oregon Lyceum, the debating society which had played an important role in early efforts to organize a government. February 5, 1846, in the first issue of the Spectator, T'Vault advertised for bids for carrying of mails once in two weeks on two routes. The first, from Oregon City to Fort Vancouver, was all by water. The second, all travelled by a carrier on horseback, lay from Oregon City to Hill's, in Tuality county, thence to A. J. Hembree's, in Yamhill county, thence to Nathaniel Ford's, in Polk county, to Oregon Institute, in Champoeg county, and to the Catholic mission and Champoeg, the carrier completing his circuit by returning to Oregon City. T'Vault entered into a contract with Hugh Burns to carry mail from Oregon City to Weston, Missouri, the postage rate being 50 cents per letter, of which Burns was to receive one-fourth. The postal system was a failure, however, owing to lack of revenue.

In the election of members of the legislature, 1846, the districts north of the Columbia river were represented for the first time. The members chosen were: Champoeg, Angus McDonald, A. Chamberlain, Dr. Robert Newell and Jesse Looney; Clackamas, Hiram Straight, A. L. Lovejoy and W. G. T'Vault; Clatsop, George

Summers; Lewis, Dr. W. F. Tolmie; Polk, J. E. Williams and John
D. Boone; Tuality, Joseph L. Meek, D. H. Lownsdale and Lawrence Hall; Vancouver, Henry N. Peers; Yamhill, Thomas Jeffreys
and Absalom J. Hembree. Tolmie and Peers represented the Hudson's Bay interests, Tolmie being in charge of the Puget Sound
Agricultural Company's operations at Nisqually.

15

The legislature, which met, December 1, 1846, was not aware
that the treaty between the United States and Great Britain, fixing the 49th parallel as the northern boundary of the United
States, had been signed on June 15, preceding; but Governor
Abernethy in his message mentioned the fact that a year's formal
notice had already been given by the government, of its intention
to withdraw from the treaty of joint occupancy. Believing, he said,
that the boundary question had been settled, he left to the legislature the question whether it should adjourn, after transacting
only such business as was of most pressing importance. He recommended revision of the liquor law, however, objecting that the
power to regulate granted by the amended organic law did not
include power to prohibit, and also that the provision that fines
should be divided between the informer, the witnesses and the
officials, made the judges and witnesses interested partners in each
case. He recommended that "but one person, and that person a
physician, be authorized to import or manufacture a sufficient
quantity to supply the wants of the community for medicinal
purposes." The legislature responded by enacting a license law,
which the governor returned unsigned, with a message in which
he urged submission of the question to the voters. "If the people
say 'No liquor'," wrote Governor Abernethy, "continue to prohibit; if they say, through the ballot box 'We wish liquor', then let
it come free, the same as dry goods, or any article imported or
manufactured; but until the people say they want it, I hope you
will use your influence to keep it out of the territory." The legislature passed the bill over the veto, by a vote of 11 to five.

16

Early in 1847, it became known that the boundary controversy
had been adjusted, and that Oregon to the 49th parallel of north
latitude was part of the United States. News of the signing of the
treaty had travelled to Vera Cruz, then across Mexico to Maza-

tlan, by approximately the route taken by Hall J. Kelley, 1833-4, and by W. A. Slacum, 1836. Thence it had been conveyed by the bark Fawn to the Sandwich islands, and from there had reached Oregon by the bark, Toulon. Nevertheless, there was uncertainty concerning organization as a territory of the United States. Lively opposition to Governor Abernethy had developed from growing political hostility to the missionary influence. A. L. Lovejoy was the non-sectarian candidate for the office of provisional governor in the campaign this year. Acrimony developed in the canvass, one result of which was that Lovejoy failed to receive all of the non-mission votes, so that Abernethy was re-elected, receiving 536 votes to 520 for Lovejoy.

There was unusual political activity this year. The region was now generally prosperous, and, having had a taste of self-government, the population was unwilling to surrender its prerogatives. Rumors that President Polk would appoint an entire list of non-resident territorial officials had gained currency. The propriety of sending a delegate at once to Washington was therefore, widely discussed. It was desired that the federal government, having taken the colony under its protective wing, should proceed at once to foster the building of a railroad across the Rocky mountains. The land question was much alive. Settlers who had located claims were concerned with having them recognized in accordance with established boundaries, rather than by new section lines and subdivisions. The first wagon train to reach The Dalles from the east, arrived, August, 1847, and a large influx of settlers was expected. The exact legal status of land claims already taken was in doubt.

Besides Governor Abernethy, the officers elected, 1847, by the people were: Secretary, Frederick Prigg; recorder, Theophilus Magruder; postmaster-general, William G. T'Vault. The legislature, still a single body, but grown to a membership of 18, consisted of the following: Champoeg county, W. H. Rector, W. H. Reese, A. Chamberlain, Anderson Cox and Dr. Robert Newell; Polk, J. W. Nesmith and M. A. Ford; Clackamas, Medorem Crawford, J. M. Wair and S. S. White; Yamhill, A. J. Hembree and L. Rogers; Tuality, R. Wilcox, David Hill and J. L. Meek; Clatsop, J. Robinson; Lewis, S. Plomondon; Vancouver, H. N. Peers.

17

The great event of this year and the one following was the

Cayuse war. News of the Whitman massacre was received, December 8, the day that the legislature convened, and absorbed the interest of the colony. A company of riflemen was authorized by the legislature immediately, but the government was without funds to equip it. In this emergency a loan commission, consisting of Jesse Applegate, A. L. Lovejoy and G. L. Curry, was appointed and addressed a letter to James Douglas, the chief factor at Fort Vancouver, asking an immediate loan and inquiring what advances of funds they might expect, in view of the temporary nature of the provisional government. Douglas replied that his orders positively forbade him to grant loans for any purpose, but called attention to the force which had been equipped at the company's expense and sent, under the leadership of Peter Skene Ogden, to Walla Walla, to effect, if possible, the rescue of the survivors of the massacre. The committee solved its part of the problem by giving personal notes for a total of $999.41, signed by Applegate, Lovejoy and Governor Abernethy, in payment for supplies. Other equipment for the troops was obtained on notes aggregating $1800 given by Daniel Waldo and Joel Palmer, and all the notes were paid at maturity with money furnished by Waldo. Other donations were made by settlers, and by the Methodist mission.

Thus, the provisional government, a year and a half after the signing of the boundary treaty, was compelled to rely on the generosity of a few private citizens to finance a military campaign. A rumor that the settlers contemplated making a forced levy on the Hudson's Bay establishment at Fort Vancouver caused James Douglas to dispatch a letter of inquiry to Governor Abernethy, who replied denying that this was intended, but noting that Ogden in his passage up the Columbia to rescue the Whitman survivors had paid the Indians at the portages in powder and ball, in violation of an act of the previous legislature making it unlawful to supply Indians with munitions. Douglas replied, defending Ogden, and contending that the law was ill-advised, since friendly Indians, having emerged from the bow and arrow era, required ammunition for hunting, to prevent starvation. Douglas' counsel so far prevailed that the law was afterward repealed.

18

The legislature sent a commission to treat with the Yakima chiefs, in an effort to obtain their promise not to unite with the

Cayuses, and also to confer with the Deschutes Indians for the same purpose. A local movement was started to send a delegation to the Mormon colony in Utah with an appeal for aid, but this was frowned on by Governor Abernethy. Meanwhile, Joseph Meek was sent as a messenger to Washington with a memorial to Congress, and a party of ten men was dispatched to California under the leadership of Jesse Applegate on a similar errand. Meek made his way overland by way of Fort Hall and reached his destination, but Applegate's party failed on account of the deep snows of the Siskiyous. The memorial carried by Meek explained the situation of the territory with respect to the Indians, and its weakness as being "deficient in the grand essentials of war, such as men, arms and treasure." "For them," said the memorialists, "our sole reliance is the United States; we have the right to expect your aid and you are in justice bound to extend it." The memorialists also declared their position with reference to appointments to territorial offices. Governor Abernethy had privately dispatched J. Quinn Thornton as a delegate to Washington, in the preceding autumn, and Thornton, travelling by way of the Sandwich islands, in due time reached the national capital, where, although without official standing, he was influential in guiding legislation for the government of the new territory.

The year 1848 was one of Indian wars. A noteworthy political occurrence was submission to the people of the issue of "regulation" or "prohibition" of intoxicating liquors. At the same time there was also submitted to popular vote the question whether the county clerk of each county, instead of the secretary of the territory, should act as recorder of land claims. At the election, June 12, 1848, prohibition was carried, by a vote of 700 to 683, a majority of 17, and the county clerks were made recorders of land claims, by a large majority.

An election of general officers was also held in 1848, but an exodus to the newly discovered California gold mines had set in and the territory was being rapidly depopulated, several members of the legislature joining in the rush. On this account the December, 1848, session failed, and vacancies were filled by special election, and a special session was convened February 5, 1849, at Oregon City. The officers were: Governor, George Abernethy; secretary, Samuel M. Holderness; treasurer, John H. Couch; auditor of public accounts, G. W. Bell; attorney-general, A. L. Lovejoy; territorial auditor, Theophilus Magruder; judge of the supreme court, J. Quinn Thornton; marshal, H. M. Knighton. The members of the last provisional legislature were: Benton county, J. C. Avery; Champoeg, W. J. Bailey, Samuel Parker, William Portius; Clackamas, George L. Curry, Medorem Crawford, A. F. Hedges; Clatsop, John Hobson; Linn, H. J. Peterson, Anderson Cox; Polk, Jesse Applegate; Tuality, Ralph Wilcox, David Hill, S. R. Thurston; Yamhill, A. J. Hembree, L. A. Rice, W. J. Martin; Vancouver, A. L. Lewis.

Adjustment of the expenses of the Cayuse war, through an act to authorize the amounts due and to issue script as evidence of an obligation, which it was confidently expected the federal government would assume, was one of the chief subjects before this session of the legislature. Another was to provide for coinage. A few years before, the inhabitants had been embarrassed by total absence of a circulating medium, but they now discovered themselves handicapped by want of a standard for the gold that was pouring in from California. Holders of this uncoined metal suffered loss by abrasion; precision of division was practically impossible. In less than two years, according to some estimates, gold of the value of at least $2,000,000 had reached Oregon. The coinage act, passed February 16, 1849, allowed $16.50 an ounce for gold of virgin purity and fineness, without alloy, and provided for the establishment of a mint, for the coinage of five and ten-pennyweight pieces. The mint so authorized was never operated by the provisional government, although coins were issued as a private enterprise. Two weeks after passage of the bill, Gen. Joseph Lane, who had been appointed territorial governor by President Polk, arrived and the period of provisional government came to an end.

CHAPTER XIX

EARLY OREGON

1

AMERICAN HISTORIANS have pointed out the fact that the western frontier has had a profound influence in moulding the character of our citizenship, and upon the development of our social and political trend as a people. In truth, the United States has had many frontiers, as successive new areas have been reached for colonization and settlement. Aside from the influence of great waves of foreign immigration into the United States, perhaps no feature of American life has been more potent in making the people of our country an independent composite and unique nation than the fact that there has always been a great west, and large areas of free land. Oregon during the 1840's was a frontier, on which a sparse population of characteristic American type worked out the American plan of representative government.

The period following the establishment of the missions was one of exploration and settlement. It witnessed a change from the original plans and hopes of those who had come to Oregon to labor among the natives and to improve their condition. The total population, aside from the employees of the Hudson's Bay Company, was estimated by Rev. Jason Lee, at the beginning of 1839, at slightly more than 100. A few more or less, it did not matter, since although isolated, they were able to sustain themselves. Their principal connection with the world, outside of that coming through Hudson's Bay Company and its ships, was through trading vessels occasionally entering the Columbia river. The first of these trafficked with the Indians, perhaps took on a miscellaneous cargo of the products of the country, and went their way. However, by degrees such ventures in commerce began to exercise a new influence, by creating, as well as filling, wants among the white population, and also by giving promise of an outlet for commodities. Fully 40 vessels visited the northwest during the decade following 1830, and these afforded a means of contact, tenuous though it was, with the outside world.

As early as 1836, when Lieut. William A. Slacum visited the country, agriculture held out a promise of prosperity to the few independent settlers then living in the Willamette valley. Slacum

estimated that a large cargo of wheat, 5500 bushels, could have
been procured from these settlers, and that it would have found a
good market in the Sandwich islands, the Russian settlements, or
in Peru. He regarded the Willamette valley as the finest grazing
country in the world.

2

February, 1829, in the brig Owyhee, Captain Dominis, entered
the river a second time. His name has been mentioned in these
pages in connection with the investigation made by Rev. Jonathan
S. Green, as to the possibilities for the establishment of a mission
among the tribes on Columbia river, and the offer of Captain
Dominis to give the minister passage. The Owyhee was New Eng-
land-built and Boston-owned, and her master, being a prudent
sailor, declined to risk his vessel at the entrance of the river until
he had first carefully taken soundings and planted buoys to mark
the channel. The survey occupied two weeks, the buoys being
made of cordwood, anchored with twisted cordage made by un-
raveling condemned cables and twisting them into spun yarn. The
Owyhee had stopped, on the way to Oregon, at Juan Fernandez
island, where peach trees were taken on board, and these were
afterward planted at Fort Vancouver.

Entering the Columbia, she remained in the vicinity of Deer
island, all summer, passed the winter in Scappoose bay, and then
returned to Deer island, again trading with the natives there. Thus
she finally obtained a cargo valued at $96,000. Captain Dominis,
during his stay, put up some 50 hogsheads of salmon, the first
shipped from the Pacific coast, which later were sold in Boston
at 10 cents a pound, then regarded as excellent price for prime fish.
It may be that Nathaniel J. Wyeth's venture into salmon packing,
1834, had its inception in this Boston enterprise. Customs officials
at Boston assessed a duty on this first shipment of Oregon salmon,
and this ruling was sustained by the comptroller of the treasury,
who ruled that since the fish had been caught by Indians in a place
that "was not claimed as a part of the territory of the United
States, they must be regarded as foreign-caught fish."

3

Doctor McLoughlin had occasion to make use of his knowledge
and experience as a physician, not only among the whites, but with
the natives at Fort Vancouver. However, he trained one of the

young clerks, George T. Allan, in the rudiments, and he became an efficient assistant, whose services were especially required during the great epidemic period of the late twenties and early thirties, when various diseases proved so fatal to the native population.

Captain Dominis was blamed by the Indians for the epidemic which, during the winter of his stay, seized the natives and exterminated whole villages. Beginning as an intermittent fever, it became intensely malignant, and is said to have spread to the tribes as far south as San Francisco. The mortality rate was heightened by the ignorance of the natives of even the most rudimentary laws of hygiene, and probably by unusual susceptibility of primitive races to imported epidemics, which scientists now recognize, but are still at a loss to explain. It has been estimated that 30,000 deaths were caused by the disease, which became worse, instead of abating, in 1831 and 1832. The Indians, remembering how McDougal, Astor's factor, some 20 years before, had threatened to uncork a bottle that he told them contained a smallpox plague, were now convinced that Dominis had made good this threat by emptying a phial of "bad medicine" into the river with the purpose of destroying them. The Boston men were charged with bringing the disease, and the Owyhee's crew were saved from rough handling by the Indians only through the influence of Doctor McLoughlin. All efforts to check the spread of the blight were futile. It continued, apparently, until it had run its course, after the manner of epidemics, and it raged long after Dominis had left the Columbia river, never to return.

4

In 1833, a Japanese junk was wrecked at a point about 15 miles south of Cape Flattery, and but three out of the crew of 17 were saved. These were brought to Fort Vancouver during the following year on the Llama, Captain McNeill, and were kindly treated there. They were sent home by way of England, but after remaining in England for some time before departing thence for Japan, finally got no further than Macao, China.

There was an addition, soon after this, to the Hudson's Bay Company trading fleet. The steamer Beaver was the first steam vessel on the waters of the Pacific ocean. It was destined to play a romantic part in the marine annals of the coast. Steam engineering was then a relatively new thing, so that the Beaver's achievements were noteworthy in more ways than one. She was built in 1835, on the Thames, in England, and her launching was regarded as so important, that it was attended by King William IV, in person, and by a vast throng of spectators. She was so stoutly built that she saw 52 years of service before she was wrecked, at last, at the entrance of Vancouver harbor, July, 1888; and so well was she designed for her task that, although sent to the Pacific under canvas, rigged as a brig, she outsailed her consort on the voyage from England to Oregon, making the passage in 183 days around Cape Horn. She sailed from London, August 29, 1835, and arrived at Fort George, April 4, 1836. She proceeded to Fort Vancouver, and there, May 16, 1836, fitted with paddle wheels, which she had brought along.

June 14, she made her first trial trip,—an excursion from Fort Vancouver to the Willamette river and return. Among her passengers on this occasion was Rev. Samuel Parker, advance agent of the American Board of Commissioners for Foreign Missions, who also travelled on the vessel to Fort George, June 18 following, where he transferred to another ship for the Sandwich islands, the Beaver going north for trade with the Hudson's Bay stations and the natives on the upper northwest coast. It was while on board the Beaver, and as she was about to undertake the first venture ever made upon the Pacific ocean under the power of steam, that Rev. Mr. Parker was moved to "a train of prospective reflections upon the probable changes which would take place in these remote regions in a very few years," and it was while contemplating the Beaver's exit from the Columbia river that he observed: "Perhaps there have been more lives lost here, in proportion to the number of those who have entered this river, than in entering almost any other harbor in the world. But the calamities have been less frequent for some years past than formerly, and should a steamboat be stationed at the cape, to tow vessels over, when business shall be sufficiently multiplied to warrant the expense, the delays and dangers would be greatly diminished."

5

A tragedy of the Columbia bar before this time was the wreck of the bark William and Ann, March 10, 1829, when that vessel went ashore inside the bar, and her crew of 26 were lost. She was accompanied by the American schooner, Convoy, which made the passage in safety, but which was unable to render effectual aid.

The crew of the William and Ann were never afterward seen. There was a story, probably not true, but nevertheless believed at Fort Vancouver, that they gained the shore, wet and defenseless, but were all massacred by the Clatsop Indians. There is no doubt, however, that the Indians got possession of parts of the cargo. Hudson's Bay Company sent a punitive expedition after making demands, bombarded the village with a cannon, killed a chief and two men, and compelled surrender of some of the stolen property. Nothing more was done in the way of reprisal, but the lesson proved salutary, as was evidenced by the fact that when, a year later, the British ship, Isabella, was similarly wrecked in the same locality, her crew was not injured or assaulted, and no other demonstration of force was ever required to insure the supremacy of the authority of Fort Vancouver.

6

Lieut. William A. Slacum, 1837, made a survey of the entrance of the river, and wrote a set of sailing directions which he assured his superior officers could be relied on, and at the same time pointed out "the great facility and the advantages that would result from a cut of not more than three quarters of a mile through the lowest point of the Cape Disappointment, from Baker's Bay to the ocean." He said it would result in the creation of a deep and safe channel by tidal action. This seems to have been the first practical proposal for the improvement of conditions of navigation at the mouth of the Columbia, a subject much debated, until successful jetties were constructed by the federal government.

Under date August 8, 1826, McLoughlin wrote to Governor Simpson, reporting the launching at Fort Vancouver of a vessel, named the Broughton, "in honor of Lieutenant Broughton, who was the first European ascended the Columbia as far as this." This seems to have been the first vessel after the Dolly to be built in Oregon.

In 1829, a small sailing vessel, named the Vancouver, had been built and outfitted under Doctor McLoughlin's directions, and was sent up the coast on a trading voyage, in company with the Cadboro, commanded by Capt. Aemilius Simpson. The Vancouver remained for some time in trade on Puget Sound.

7

American competition in the river itself again threatened, in the year 1832, when the Boston brig, Llama, Capt. William Mc-

Neill came in and the Yankee skipper called on Doctor McLoughlin at the fort. He had on board a miscellaneous cargo of odds and ends, particularly attractive to the natives, and soon began an active trade. His wares were so much admired that many valuable skins appeared from hidden sources. They were eagerly bought up. The forces at Vancouver watched these operations with great concern, for the effect on the company's trade, by reason of the high prices so established, was likely to be disastrous. The result was that the doctor made a liberal offer to Captain McNeill for ship, cargo and all, and engaged him to join the Hudson's Bay Company forces. He proved to be a resourceful and enterprising agent, and for many years he and the ship were kept in the company's service.

The schooner Star of Oregon was built, 1840, on the Willamette river by a company of eight young men, led by Joseph Gale, who had come from California with Hall J. Kelley and Ewing Young. They included Felix Hathaway, a ship carpenter, Henry Wood, and R. L. Kilbourne, an immigrant from Illinois, 1839. The Star of Oregon was launched May 19, 1841, and obtained cordage and other indispensables from Lieut. Charles Wilkes, of the United States navy, then in the country on an exploring expedition. Wilkes also issued to Gale an informal license as a navigator, Doctor McLoughlin having withheld aid on the ground that the builders were inexperienced men, and that it would be suicide for them to venture to sea in such a rudely built craft. Gale, who afterward became a member of the first executive committee of the provisional government, proved his ability as a navigator. The vessel made a safe passage, 1842, to Yerba Buena, as San Francisco was then called. It was there sold, and the proceeds were invested in cattle, which were driven overland from California, and there, together with the increase from the 1837 cattle venture of Ewing Young and associates, afforded cattle for all immediate needs in Oregon.

8

The brig Maryland, commanded by Capt. John H. Couch, who was afterward a prominent figure in the marine affairs of the territory, brought a cargo of miscellaneous merchandise, and was among the arrivals of 1840. His vessel was owned by Caleb Cushing, who was not discouraged by the failure of this first venture to earn profits, but sent Captain Couch on a second voyage in the Chenamus, 1842, as already stated.

The settlers in the Willamette valley were now glad of an opportunity to find an outside market for their produce. Hudson's Bay Company, which had heretofore bought grain and other provisions from the people as a means of filling its contracts with the trading stations of the Russian-American Company, was now beginning to produce quantities sufficient for its requirements on its own farms. A typical outbound cargo consisted of "lumber, flour, salmon, beef, potatoes, butter, cheese, cranberries, turnips, cabbage and onions and also a small invoice of almanacs adapted to the meridian of Monterey."

Casualties at the mouth of the river became less frequent as sea captains became more familiar with its shoals, and an important circumstance in the development of commerce was the passage, by the provisional legislature, 1846, of a pilotage law, under which S. C. Reeves was licensed as the first authorized pilot for the Columbia river bar. Farmers on the Clatsop plain, by 1848, were so imbued with the idea that they must find a market for their own goods by their own initiative that they cooperated in building the schooner Skipanon, at a creek of that name below Astoria. The Skipanon took a cargo of butter, bacon, eggs and potatoes to Sacramento, where she arrived in time to participate in the profits of the gold rush, and the vessel itself was sold. Yet, it cannot be said that navigation of the Columbia was free from difficulties, as the experience of the brig Sequin, 1849, showed. The Sequin consumed 65 days on the voyage from Astoria to Portland. The latter city had recently been established on the densely wooded shores of the Willamette.

9

On two occasions, a cursory, although official, examination of the Oregon Country was made as an incident in a world-wide voyage. The South Sea expedition of Lieut. Charles Wilkes, U. S. N., has been mentioned. He spent some time in the region of Puget sound and the Columbia river, 1841, in an interval between other important surveys. About two years before the arrival of Wilkes, the country was visited by Capt. Sir Edward Belcher, in the British naval ship Sulphur, attended by the sloop Starling, the latter equipped with scientific instruments for making geodetic and hydrographic surveys. The Sulphur's memorable voyage consumed six years, during five of which Belcher was her commanding officer, and she rounded out her achievement by taking part in the Opium war, in China, 1840-2. It will be surmised that British official interest in the country was not keen during this period, from the circumstances that Sir Edward's instructions from the British admiralty contained nothing of a political nature. His errand was almost exclusively one of scientific research.

Belcher planned to enter the Columbia in October, 1837, but encountered a storm on the way south from Nootka sound, and preferred a safe offing to the perils of the Columbia bar, so that it was not until July 28, 1839, that he at length reached the mouth of the river, having been meanwhile occupied in California and elsewhere with matters of geographic concern. He then discovered, as other navigators were to learn after him, that sailing directions for the mouth of the Columbia were subject to change without notice; for the Sulphur grounded on a sandbar, and her consort lost her rudder, in entering the river, which inauspicious beginning naturally created an unfavorable impression of Oregon in his mind. He anchored at Fort George, however, July 31, 1839, and observed that not a vestige of the original trading post, which had been taken over from the Astors, remained. "A small house for Mr. Birnie [the Hudson's Bay Company representative in charge], two or three sheds for the Canadians, about six or eight in number, and a pine stick with a red ensign," now represented all that remained of the Fort Astoria of Washington Irving. "One would rather take it for the commencement of a village, than any fort," observes Belcher. He proceeded up-river, having difficulty in threading the intricacies of Tongue Point channel, and, after grounding occasionally, which he took to be "according to practice," the Sulphur found a soft berth for the night on an uncharted bank. The scene of this early mishap was near Pillar Rock. Relying as he did on sails for his motive power, he noted that navigation beyond Oak Point became a simple matter, since there generally was an up-river breeze from 10 a. m. to 4 p. m. August 9, 1839, after having been nearly devoured by mosquitoes, he reached Vancouver, where he devoted some time to a cursory examination of the material resources of the trading post.

James Douglas, then in charge of the Hudson's Bay Company's affairs at the post, furnished him and his staff with supplies of fresh vegetables, but sent none to the crews of the visiting vessels, and Sir Edward, although he refrained from making a formal demand, confessed surprise that, on inquiring what facilities her majesty's ships might expect in the event of touching at the Columbia for provisions, he should be told that the company was "not in a condition to supply." Having seen a profusion of cattle and potatoes, and having been told of the quantities of grain and flour procured by the trading establishment, he was inclined to believe that the factor was not much concerned over the welfare of a mere British naval expedition. He proceeded to criticize, what he took to be the policy of the Hudson's Bay Company, of encouraging settlement by American missionaries, "instead of selecting a British subject to afford them spiritual assistance," a course which he held to be "pregnant with evil consequences, and particularly in the squabble pending, as will be seen by the result. . . . They are now loud in their claim of right to the soil, and a colony of American settlers was en route in the plains when we quitted."

Sir Edward here correctly forecasts the beginning of American settlement of Oregon.

10

The old Astor fort had been burned, 1821, and, according to other records, the only vestige of the buildings, was a "bald spot," and the town then consisted of a "cabin and a shed." J. M. Shively took up a claim, 1843, and laid out Shively's Astoria. Other claims were soon after taken by Col. John McClure and A. E. Wilson, on which Astoria has since been laid out. These men, and James Birnie, Hudson's Bay Company agent, constituted the population in 1844. Birnie lived in the company's buildings near the site of St. Mary's hospital, as at present located. Other settlers were Solomon Smith, who located at Smith's point, and Robert Shortess, whose claim was at the present Alderbrook addition. James Welch located on Shively's claim during the absence of the latter, in the east, 1846, and again platted the tract. But on Shively's return, 1847, a compromise was effected by making an equal division between them. Settlers on Clatsop plains were D. Summers, Mr. Hobson and family, Rev. J. L. Parrish, Calvin Tibbets, Trask and Perry. The white settlement in the Willamette valley, according to Captain Belcher, consisted of 54 souls, when he visited Oregon, in the summer of 1839, 24 of whom were former employees of the fur company, 20 "American stragglers," and 10 clergymen, teachers and others associated with the mission of Jason Lee.

On the way down the Columbia, Belcher's smaller vessel, the Starling, lost her rudder on a snag, and in crossing the bar the Sulphur and the Starling each lost an anchor. "Heartily sick of this nest of dangers," he records, September 14, "we took our final look at Cape Disappointment and shaped our course for Bodega." The tenor of Captain Belcher's report on Oregon was pessimistic, and was not such as would revive British popular interest in the territory. Negative influence of its publication in England was favorable, on the whole, toward a settlement of the boundary, on terms generally satisfactory to the United States.

11

The French government sent a scout to Oregon, 1841, whose mission seems to have been commercial rather than political. He was Eugen Duflot de Mofras, a former attache' of the French embassy at Madrid, who was assigned by order of the Duc de Dalmatis, then minister of foreign affairs of France, to the Mexican legation, with instructions to visit the Russian stations, also the American and British settlements on the Pacific coast, "to ascertain," as he himself described his errand, "independently of political considerations, what advantages might accrue from the commercial point of view to France in a region then little known." The observations of this visitor are interesting chiefly for the light they throw upon the mode of living of the French Canadian settlers in the Willamette valley in that period. He was received by Sir George Simpson, who was then at Fort Vancouver, not very cordially, since he appears to have mislaid his official credentials, and he accompanied Simpson on a trip to the French Canadian settlements.

The friendliness of the French element impressed him deeply. "Having explored this valley with the greatest care," he wrote, "have remarked the eagerness with which the French from Canada come, sometimes several leagues, to see a Frenchman from France, as they call us. While staying at their farms we were sure of finding the most open hospitality; they lent us their horses and served us as guides in our explorations." He records having met in the valley two European Frenchmen, MM. Haiguet and Jacquet, who had come to Oregon by sea and seemed to be happily situated among their Canadian compatriots. He found the French settlers thrifty, contented and deeply imbued with a spirit of nationalism.

He estimated their cattle holdings at 3000 head; in addition to
which they had 3000 swine and 500 sheep. They harvested in a
single season 10,000 hectolitres of wheat and 3000 hectolitres of
legumes, such as field peas and kidney beans (haricots). Under
their husbandry their yield of grain was 12-fold, but de Mofras'
estimate of grain production per acre is exceedingly moderate.
"The soil," he says, "produces at least eight hectolitres per hec-
tare, [a trifle in excess of nine bushels to the acre]. Some have set
up sawmills on the numerous streams which water the valley.
Others, and particularly Stanislas Jacquet, go to California nearly
every year to buy cattle and horses. In the more favorable seasons
they trap the small numbers of beaver that yet remain, and prepare the furs and peltries, but their principal occupation consists
in agriculture."

12

Our annalist found it particularly worthy of remark in this connection that although the majority of the French colonists had
married Indian wives, they spoke only French. He noted the impression produced upon the little community by the visit of Sir
George Simpson, that had the effect of reminding them that they
were governed by one of a race and religion alien to their own. To
Simpson's greeting, "Good day, my friends; how do you do?" they
replied, "We do not speak English; we are all French here."

Local geographical names betrayed a peculiar nationalistic
sense of humor, such as "La Porte de l'enfer," "la course de
Satan," "la passage de Diable." We obtain a further impression
of this reverence of the French settlers for the institutions of the
motherland in their tendency to bestow French names upon all
things which they particularly esteemed. The finest domestic ducks
then to be found in the Willamette valley were "canards de
France"; the best shoes, though made from English leather, "des
souliers francais"; the pound sterling was a "louis"; and all
whites were "French." De Mofras relates that the Indians had so
imbibed this sense of French superiority, in all matters, that an
old Iroquois guide, on being asked where the rifle that he carried
on his shoulders had been made, replied that it had come "from the
old France of London" (de la vieille France de Londres).

French names of locality are used throughout M. de Mofras'
book. His "Jamil" river is easily seen to be the "Yamhill," but

"Camayou" is not quite so plain; the context indicates that he may mean Lackiamute. His "riviere Boudin" is, of course, the Pudding river, which was among the very first to receive a name from the French inhabitants. There are numerous interesting versions of the origin of this name, varying as to details but agreeing that it was derived from the experience of a party of French hunters, who made a blood pudding while in camp on the bank of the stream. It is certain that the river was so named in a very early time. Alexander Henry, the younger, wrote in his journal, of date January 23, 1814: "At 11 a. m. we passed a small stream on the left called by our people 'Pudding River.' " J. Quinn Thornton was responsible for the impression which long prevailed that "Pudding" was a late derivation from some other name. "The Willamette receives the Clackamus and Putin rivers," says Thornton, "which name has been corrupted to Pudding." The early Indian name was Haun-cha-uke. It is incidentally interesting to recall that the steamer Moose, owned by the Pudding River Transportation Company, made a trip up this river as far as Irving's bridge, about 10 miles from the mouth, February 18, 1860. Navigation of the stream proved impracticable, however. The name Pudding River was also used by Rev. Samuel Parker, 1835. De Mofras' "Souris" river is the French rendition of Joel Palmer's Mouse river, but the name has long been abandoned and is not found on any maps. De Mofras' efforts to render Indian names in French are sometimes confusing to English ears. Lieut. Charles Wilkes experienced similar difficulty, 1842, with reversed effect. He was misled by the French pronunciation of Campment du Sable, which he made "Camp Maude du Sable" in his official narrative. William A. Slacum fell into a similar error regarding this name.

13

The French free settlers, living apart, as M. de Mofras describes them, yet preserving a definite sense of order, and a strong desire to enjoy the peaceful social intercourse in a region far remote from the centers of civilization, were accustomed to look to the Catholic mission as a center of authority. "We were witness during our sojourn at St. Paul," writes de Mofras, "of a rather touching example of paternal justice. A French Canadian was accused of having stolen a horse from an American, and confessed his fault. The council of the fathers of families, presided over by

Abbe Blanchet, condemned him to restore the horse to its rightful owner and, besides, to remain three months at the door of the church during the offices, without being permitted to enter. He submitted to the ordeal, but upon the second Sunday Abbe Blanchet, after a short lecture, went to him, conducted him into the church, embraced him with tears in his eyes, and caused him to sit with the other settlers. Whether legal punishment by a civil judge would have produced so profound an effect may well be doubted; besides, this correction, being entirely paternal, had the great advantage of leaving no scar on the individual."

De Mofras was not so favorably impressed by an incident which occurred "when on Sunday in the church, where 600 Canadians were assembled, we heard a French priest say, in French, to a population all French: "Prions Dieu pour notre Saint Pere le Pape et pour notre bien-aime' Reine Victoria!" (Let us pray God for our Holy Father the Pope and for our well-beloved Queen Victoria.) De Mofras asked the reason for this, to him, strange invocation and was informed that it had been enjoined upon the priest as an obligation to be performed every month, under pain of forfeiting the protection of the Hudson's Bay Company.

The annalist represents Hudson's Bay Company officers at this time as somewhat apprehensive lest the establishment of new families of "free French" on the Willamette should threaten its influence, and alludes to the memorial to Congress. "The company," he says, "fears that the free population established on the Willamette may escape it some day, above all since in the month of March, 1838, when at the instigation of M. Lee, head of the American Methodists, a petition signed by 27 American and nine of the principal French Canadian colonists was addressed to Congress at Washington to claim the protection of the United States and to invite it to take possession of the territory." The names of the nine French Canadian signers of this petition as given by him were: J. B. Desportes, Joseph Gervais, J. B. Perrault, Jh. Delort, Etienne Lucier, P. Belique, Jh. Deloze, Xavier Dudevant and Andre Picord. De Mofras describes them as among the oldest and richest of the colonists.

14

Although complimentary to the French element, he was skeptical as to the Methodist missionaries, whom he suspected of secular designs, in particular, "M. Lee, the most important personage of all the Americans residing in the territory of Oregon." The domination of the Hudson's Bay Company was confirmed by his report. On his departure, he was given a free passage aboard a Company ship, but he suspected that this was prompted, not by pure generosity, but rather by a consistent policy of discouraging the establishment of American lines of communication. The tide of settlement had not set in toward Oregon, in the period of which M. de Mofras writes, and the American population not attached to the missions is thus described by him: "Almost all belong to the hardy class of 'back woodsmen,' from the western United States; they have arrived at the Columbia river overland, having for the most part for their sole possession only a rifle, and have married Indian wives. They are courageous and patient; more adept at hunting, at cutting wood and at carpentry than at agriculture. . . . One expects before many years to see the wave of the emigrants carried beyond the Rocky mountains; but up to the present it is rather toward the old Spanish provinces of Texas, New Mexico and Upper California that this movement is operating."

The American population was increased by a small immigration, 1839, stimulated by a series of lectures delivered at Peoria, Illinois, in the winter of 1838-39 by Rev. Jason Lee, then in the east in quest of reinforcements for the Methodist mission. Fourteen persons, all men, started from Peoria, May, 1839, led by Thomas J. Farnham, and most of them arrived in that year, or in 1840. Those who reached the territory in 1840 were Amos Cooke, Robert Moore, Francis Fletcher and Joseph Holman, who became permanent settlers in Oregon. Among the arrivals in 1840, came Joel Walker, Virginia-born, but an emigrant from Missouri, and his wife and five children, who are distinguished as having been the first family to cross the plains with the definite purpose of making a home in Oregon, but who somewhat later moved to California.

15

It was in 1840, that the Great Reinforcement of the Methodist mission arrived by the Lausanne, adding over 50 persons to the population, as has been related. The breaking up of the American Fur Company, also increased the population in the Willamette valley, by depriving several employees of a means of livelihood at

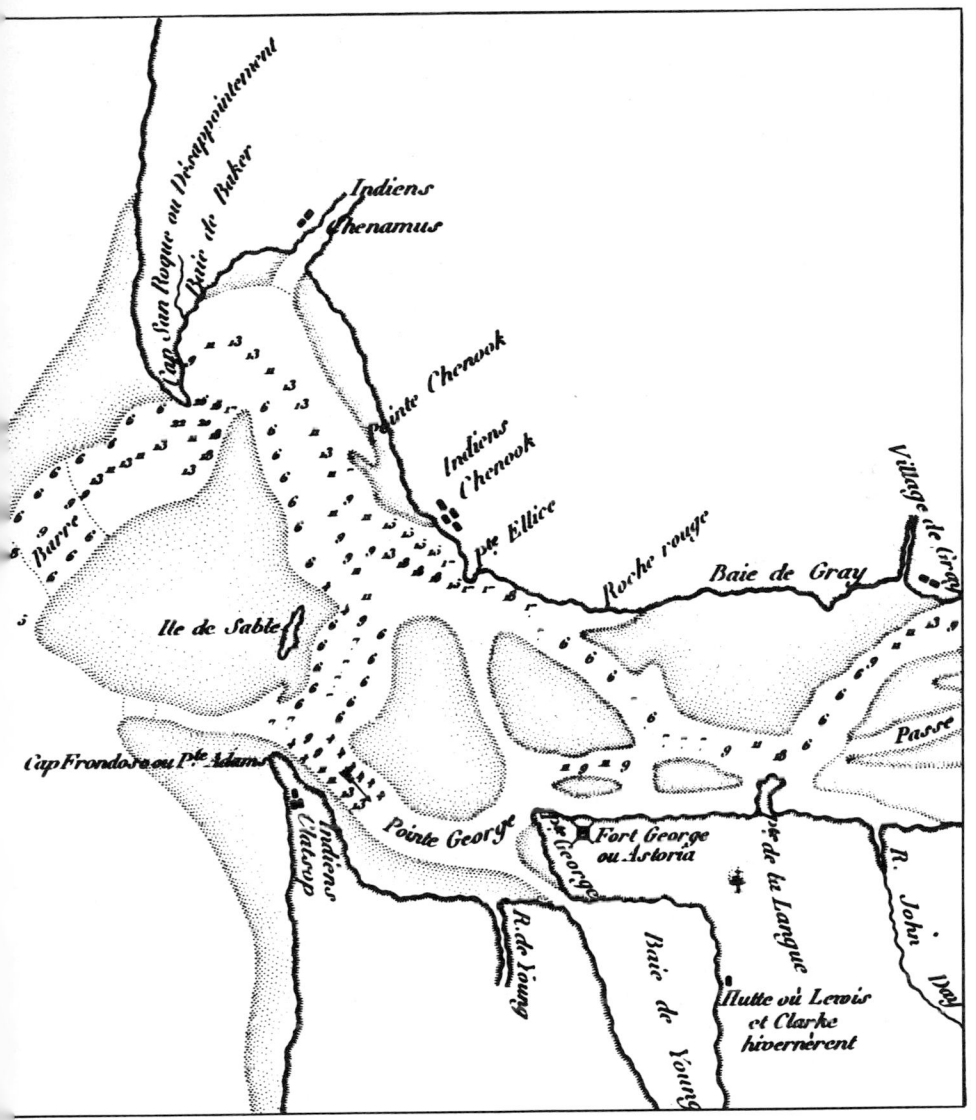

Chart of Columbia River Entrance, 1840
Part of Duflot de Mofras' "Carte du Rio Colombia," from the atlas to his "Exploration du territoire de l'Orégon, des Californies et de la mer Vermeille, exécutée pendant les années 1840, 1841 et 1842." (Paris, 1844)

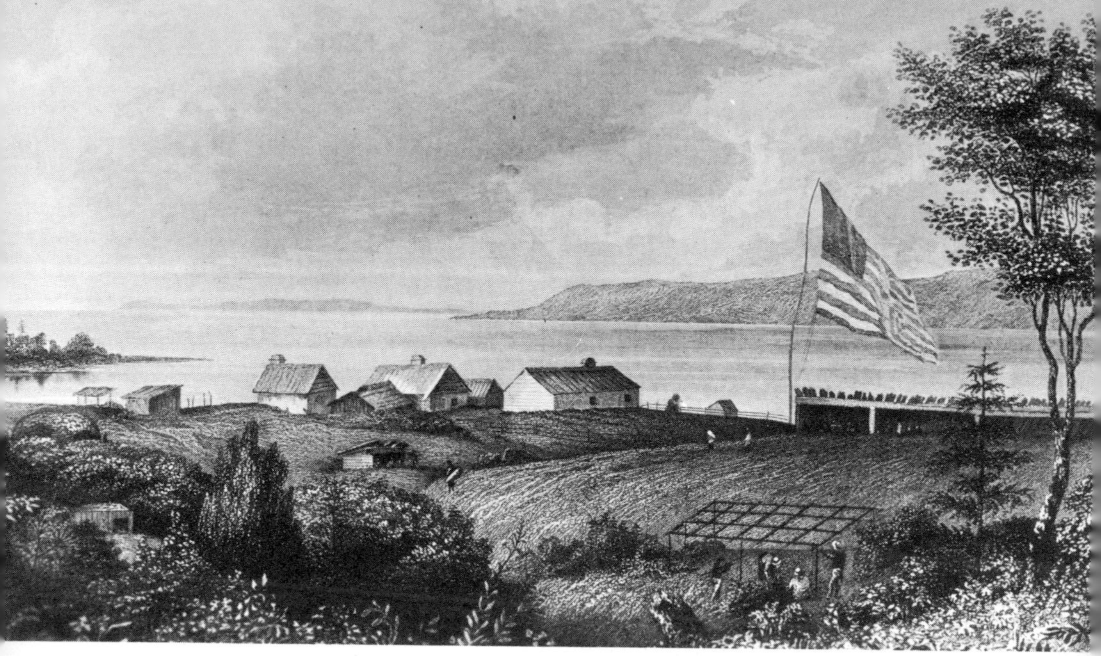

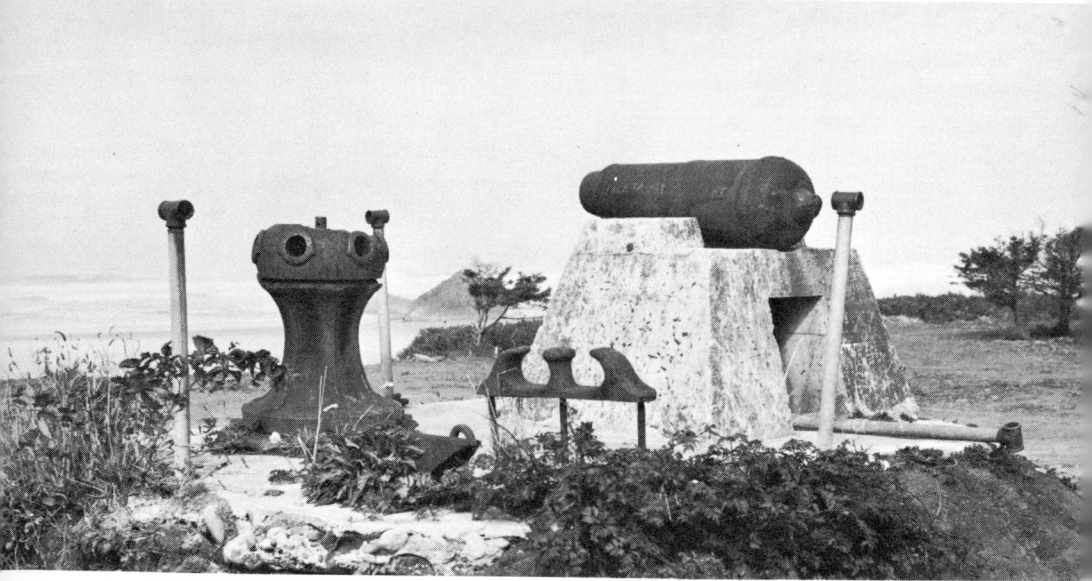

Astoria at the Time of the Wilkes Expedition, 1842

—*Oregon State Highway Commission*

Schooner "Shark's" Cannon

The "Shark" was wrecked while attempting to leave the Columbia river, September 10, 1846. Lt. Neil M. Howison attributed the loss to alteration of the channel after Lt. Wilkes' survey and to the unexpected action of the tide. No lives were lost. Howison presented the colors of the "Shark" to the citizens of the territory, through Governor Abernethy.

fur hunting, and thus compelling them to take up agriculture. Among these coming to Oregon, 1840, were Joseph L. Meek, Caleb Wilkins, Dr. Robert Newell, William Craig and John Larrison, all of whom attained prominence in the social and political life of the colony.

Arrivals of 1841 included the already mentioned colony from the Hudson's Bay Company's Red River settlements, whom the company desired to place on lands of the Puget Sound Agricultural Company, in the vicinity of Nisqually, in order to strengthen the diplomatic claim to the northern part of the territory. But they drifted to the Willamette valley, which was represented to them as having superior soil and a more agreeable climate, where land was still to be had for the asking. Dr. Robert Carlton Clark, in his History of the Willamette Valley, 1927, has endeavored to list and enumerate the Oregon arrivals in the years 1839, 1840 and 1841, a task of some difficulty on account of the somewhat sporadic and scattered sources of information. He believes that there were about 30 adults and nine children, in 1841, who came from the United States to settle in the Oregon Country, and that 25 adults and nine children settled in the Willamette valley. These figures are at least approximately correct. He adds that "the British move to settle and thus hold part of the Oregon territory brought 21 families of 116 souls, in 1841, but most of these moved later to the American section south of the Columbia."

16

The economic aspect of the country, as well as its political outlook, underwent a striking change in 1842, when the first immigrant train from the Mississippi valley to bring families, as well as single men, crossed the plains. Dr. Elijah White, whose second visit to Oregon has been mentioned herein, delivered several lectures, describing the country to audiences, chiefly assembled in churches, so that the nucleus of the expedition which was now organized, partly as the result of his efforts, had a religious character. White's activities were widely advertised in the newspapers. In May, 1842, when he arrived at Elm Grove, Missouri, more than 100 prospective settlers were waiting for a leader to make the start. In order to guard against the admission to the expedition of individuals who were likely to become a charge upon their associates, it was required that every male over 18 years of age should possess at least one mule, or horse, or wagon conveyance; should have one gun, three pounds of powder, 17 pounds of lead, 1000 caps, 50 pounds of flour or meal, 30 pounds of bacon and provisions for women and children. In this manner, those who had no property whatever, and were mere rovers, were excluded automatically; yet, even the food and supplies so required proved insufficient in some cases, notwithstanding the hunters did much to supplement the prescribed rations.

17

The ox-train, under the leadership of White, left Elm Grove, May 16, 1842, with 18 wagons, and a long line of horses, mules and cattle. He was chosen as captain, but served only 10 days, when he was superseded. No member of the party had ever made the trip across the plains. The overland party now had valuable advice from Milton Sublette, the veteran Rocky mountain fur trader, who warned White that he was taking great risks in attempting the long journey with an unorganized company, and without convoy.

A guide was engaged, who knew the country as far west as Fort Laramie, where Thomas Fitzpatrick, an old fur trader and hunter, was met, and at that place he was employed by White to go as guide as far as Fort Hall, on Snake river. Stephen H. L. Meek, brother of Joseph L. Meek, joined the caravan in the vicinity of the South Fork. There was a spirit of personal independence, disinclination to tolerate interference, manifest from the outset. The members were hardly amenable to ordinary discipline, and soon open rebellion became manifest in innumerable petty difficulties. Among other annoyances, there was a controversy over the numerous dogs owned by the travellers. White decided that all dogs be shot on the ground as they were likely to go mad on the arid plains. Twenty-two were so disposed of, but sentence was suspended as to the others. Storms were encountered on the Platte, which made everyone cold and miserable. There were other hardships and grievances; some had made bargains which they were unable to carry out; some had omitted to bring teams, or had made inadequate provision for mishaps on the road. Finally, a reorganization was voted, and Lansford W. Hastings was elected captain. The majority followed him, but White pulled out with a group that supported him, and went ahead.

The immigrants, notwithstanding these obstacles, reached Fort Laramie, June 23. Here the two parties united, on the urgent advice of Bisonette, the trader stationed there. Some traded their wagons for provisions, and at Green river other wagons were cut up and a part of the materials were made into pack saddles. The few remaining wagons were finally dispensed with at Fort Hall, at which stopping place the caravan arrived in mid-July. Here there was a division. One faction, led by White, pushed ahead, crossed the Snake river a short distance below Salmon Falls, and travelled through the Burnt river canyon and the Grande Ronde valley, and over the Blue mountains, traversing the old Hudson's Bay Company trail to Fort Nes Perce's, now called Fort Walla Walla. The other party, led by Hastings, did not cross the Snake river, but remained on the south side; travelling more slowly, it visited the Whitman mission at Waiilatpu, and were cordially received by Doctor Whitman, who supplied the weary travellers with fresh provisions. From this point the members travelled in smaller groups. A few passed down the Columbia river in Hudson's Bay Company's boats, some travelled overland to The Dalles, whence they took canoes down the river, others travelled by trail from The Dalles to the Cascades, on the south side of the Columbia, and the remainder found an Indian trail on the north side of the river, crossing again to the south bank in the vicinity of the Sandy.

18

The members of this immigration, over the age of 18, are given as follows: C. T. Arendell, Thomas Boggs, J. C. Bridges, James Brown, William Brown, Gabriel Brown, —— Barnum, Hugh Burns, C. W. Bellamy, Winsted Bennett, Vandom Bennett, —— Bailey (killed enroute), Nathaniel Crocker, Nathan Coombs, Patrick Clark, Alexander Copeland, Medorem Crawford, A. N. Coates, Allen Davy, John Dearum, John Doubenbiss, Samuel David, John Force, James Force, —— Foster, Joseph Gibbs, —— Girtman, Lansford W. Hastings, John Hoffstetter, J. M. Hudspeth, Hardin Jones, Reuben Lewis, A. L. Lovejoy, S. W. Moss, J. L. Morrison, John McKay, Alexander McKay, Stephen H. L. Meek, F. X. Matthieu, Walter Pomeroy, Dwight Pomeroy, J. H. Perry, Dutch Paul, J. R. Robb, Adam Storer, Darling Smith, A. D. Smith, Andrew Smith, Owen Summers, T. J. Sheldon, Aaron Towner, Joel Turn-

ham, Elijah White, David Weston. Ten of these had families.
Medorem Crawford gives the number of wagons as 16, the total
number of persons as 105, and the number of men over 18 years
of age as 51. Hastings gives the total number as 160, and the
number who bore arms as 80. Fremont estimated it at 64, and
Lovejoy said 70 stood guard. Lovejoy did not at this time go to
the Willamette valley. He remained behind at Waiilatpu, and he
accompanied Doctor Whitman to the eastern states as guide in
the winter of 1842-43. He later came to Oregon City, and afterward became one of the founders of Portland.

19

Three noteworthy official visitors, 1841, were Lieut. Charles
Wilkes, of the United States navy, commanding the South Sea
expedition, concerning whom something has already been said in
the foregoing pages; the Frenchman, de Mofras, whose visit has
been described; and Sir George Simpson, resident governor in
North America of the Hudson's Bay Company territories. Three
nations were thus represented. On his first approach to the Columbia river, April 26, 1841, Wilkes did not enter, on account of the
rough sea that was running on the bar. He marveled, however,
that any doubt should ever have existed that here was the mouth
of a mighty river. Mistrusting the skill of the pilot he had shipped
at the Islands, he sailed on to Puget sound, and from here he travelled overland to the Columbia and subsequently to the Willamette
valley. Further details of his visit may be deemed interesting.

His guide from Nisqually to Fort George was Simon Plomondon, an old servant of the Hudson's Bay Company, who had been
advised by Doctor McLoughlin, 1837, to take up a farm at the
lower end of Cowlitz prairie, and who thus was the first free
farmer in that locality. "A more useful person I have seldom met,"
said Wilkes, "or one that could be so well depended on. He had
been for several years in the territory, having married an Indian
wife, and was now living on a farm of about 30 acres at the Cowlitz, independent and contented."

At Astoria, Wilkes observed with regret the general run-down
condition of the famous old post, but vouched for the excellent
quality of the potatoes grown in the garden which it supported.
"In point of beauty of situation," said he, "few places will vie with
Astoria." He visited Rev. J. H. Frost and his wife, of the Metho-

dist missionary station, at Clatsop, being welcomed in a dwelling which Frost had built with his own hands. There were but two American residents then in the vicinity of Clatsop plains, Calvin Tibbetts and Solomon H. Smith, both Wyeth men, and these were the first home-making farmers to settle west of the coast range.

Agriculture, as practiced on Hudson's Bay Company plantation in the vicinity of Vancouver had attained the dignity of an art. Here Wilkes saw dairies, rich meadow land dotted with herds of fine cattle, and flocks of sheep of the finest English and Spanish breeds. The sylvan beauty of the landscape carried an irresistible appeal. Landing below Fort Vancouver, he entered a grove of large pines (firs), which had an undergrowth of various flowering shrubs. The old stumps in the road were overgrown with honeysuckle in full bloom, and other flowers were growing, even in the roadway. Fort Vancouver was a veritable hive of industry, a large manufacturing, agricultural and commercial depot, and there were few, if any, idlers, except the sick. Everybody seemed to be in a hurry, while to the naval officer there seemed to be no obvious reason for haste. In passing through the Willamette valley, as he did soon afterward, he had a good opportunity to contrast the settlers of various national origins; and, while those of French descent appeared the most contented, happy and comfortable, those of the Anglo-Saxon race "showed more of the appearance of business, and the 'go-ahead' principle so much in vogue at home."

"For some time previous to our arrival," wrote Wilkes, "they [the Hudson's Bay Company] had not been able to meet their own wants, and at the same time fulfill their contracts with the Russians. They were, therefore, obliged to purchase from the settlers in the territory, as well as send to California, to procure the requisite quantity of agricultural products. A demand was consequently created for wheat and all that could be raised in the Willamette settlements was bought for six shillings (75 cents) a bushel and paid for in drafts on their stores, in goods, at 50 per cent on the first London cost. This gave an encouragement to the small farmers that was fated to meet with grievous disappointment the next season; for the company was able not only to meet their engagements, and their own wants, but had, besides, a surplus. The prices consequently would be merely nominal, unless raised by an influx of new settlers. Whether the latter cause had any effect in creating a market, I know not, but I understand that, in 1842, the settlers fed their horses upon the finest wheat."

20

One party from Wilkes' fleet, during the summer of 1841, crossed from Puget sound, over the Cascade range by way of Naches Pass to the Yakima valley, visited the fur trading post at Okanogan, the American Board mission of Tsimakain, and stopped at Fort Colville, then travelled by a circuitous route to missions at Lapwai and Waiilatpu, returning to the starting place by the Yakima route. Another expedition was dispatched overland from Oregon to California, leaving the Columbia river late in August, with 39 men and 76 horses, and arriving at Fort Sutter, October 19, 1841. They journeyed the full length of the Willamette valley, visiting Fort Umpqua and crossing the Rogue and Klamath valleys. Besides seamen and guides, there were the votaries of science, Peale, Rich, Dana, Agate and Brackenridge. Several families, by name Walker, Burrows, Nichols, and Warfields, "joined for escort." Lieutenant Emmons was in command, and Joe Meek was guide during the first part of the journey.

Titian Ramsey Peale was a naturalist with the Wilkes expedition. He was in the wreck of the Peacock at the mouth of the Columbia. His manuscript journal is now in the Library of Congress. His entry under date Sunday, September 25, 1841, contains a reference to the massacre of the Ewing Young party, on Rogue river a few years earlier. He says: "Our camp was fixed on the banks of the river, where Mr. Young with a party of nine men were defeated, a few years since, by the Indians. Many of their bones now lay bleaching around our fires. The white people, on that occasion, suffered the Indians to come into camp in great numbers, more than 100 who professed friendship, but who waited for an unguarded moment to attack the few whites, and would have succeeded in killing all of them to obtain their property, had not a gigantic iron framed fellow [Turner] laid about him with a tremendous firebrand, keeping back the naked assailants, until his red wife brought out his rifle, when the Indians retreated with considerable loss. Two whites were killed on the spot, and two died of their wounds after returning amongst the Umpqua. Some of our volunteers were of the above party." The Turner named is the same man who had an experience with the Jedediah S. Smith party on the Umpqua in 1828, elsewhere related. Dr. Elijah White in telling of this, in other language, mentions Doctor Bailey as a leader of the Rogue river party.

A third Wilkes party began an ambitious survey of the waters of Puget sound and the Canal de Haro, but this was interrupted by news that the sloop-of-war Peacock, one of the vessels of Wilkes' squadron that had been left behind in the South Sea islands, and had followed to the coast, had been wrecked in an effort to cross the Columbia river bar, July 18, 1841. The commanding officer of the Peacock had relied on sailing directions obtained at Oahu from Captain Spalding of the Lausanne, but found himself in difficulties where he expected to find an open passage through the breakers, and the vessel was driven hard aground. The shoal on which she struck has ever since been known as Peacock spit.

The Peacock was a total loss, but all on board were saved. Wilkes then determined to complete his survey of the lower Columbia, but was unwilling to risk his flag-ship, the Vincennes, in the undertaking, so he sent the Vincennes to San Francisco bay, transferred his pennant to the brig Porpoise, another of his squadron, and completed a chart of the river to the point where, some two years later, the survey was joined by that of Lieut. John C. Fremont, dispatched overland from the east. Wilkes bought, for $9000, the American brig Thomas H. Perkins, which had entered the river with a cargo of liquor. With this vessel he replaced the lost Peacock, changing her name to the Oregon. The liquor cargo of the Perkins was bought by Doctor McLoughlin and stored to prevent its sale to the inhabitants of the country. The report of Wilkes' observations constituted the first important official description published in the United States, of the rivers and harbors of the Pacific coast.

21

The overland expedition of John C. Fremont, who was a second lieutenant of engineers, added information of the topography and natural resources of the far west. It was in the year 1843, two years after the Wilkes visit, but it may be described here.

This was his second western expedition, the one in the previous year having taken him as far as the South Pass and Wind River mountains, on the route of the Oregon Trail. His second expedition began on the same general route, but reached as far west as the Columbia river, where he was to connect his overland survey with the naval survey that had been made on the lower river by Lieutenant Wilkes. Fremont did not confine his operations to the already well established trail, but made wide detours, in the Rocky mountains and to Salt lake, as well as elsewhere on his westward progress, while keeping in mind the need of finding the best routes for pioneer travel.

He reached the Whitman mission at Waiilatpu, October 24, 1843, and was pleased to see there a "fine looking large family of immigrants, men, women and children, in robust health, all indemnifying themselves for previous scanty fare in a hearty consumption of potatoes, which are produced here in remarkably good quality." On the Columbia river, near the confluence with the Snake, he observed that a considerable body of immigrants under the direction of Jesse Applegate, whom he describes as "a man of considerable resolution and energy," had nearly completed a number of mackinaw boats in which they proposed to voyage down the river. This was the main body of the noteworthy immigration of 1843, the arrival of which in the Willamette valley was soon afterward to give a new and important turn to the political aspect of the colony.

Fremont proceeded overland to The Dalles, with only a backward glance of momentary envy at the relative comfort of the immigrant company. "As we toiled slowly through the deep loose sands, and over fragments of rock," he wrote, "our laborious traveling was strongly contrasted with the rapid progress of Mr. Applegate's fleet of boats, which suddenly came gliding swiftly down the broad river, which here chanced to be tranquil and smooth." At the Methodist mission, at The Dalles, then in charge of Rev. H. K. W. Perkins, he left most of his men, while he embarked with a few of his retinue in a canoe, bound to Fort Vancouver. He was now in a region explored by the expedition of Wilkes, as already described, and he had accomplished the object of uniting his survey with that formerly extended from the Pacific coast by the naval officer. This completed the first official survey of a transcontinental route, and the connection was made November 4, 1843.

Fremont was cordially received by Doctor McLoughlin, from

whom he bought supplies, and who readily accepted payment in bills on the government of the United States, and who also expressed a "warm and gratifying sympathy in the suffering which his great experience led him to anticipate," for the explorers on their homeward journey. The explorer tarried only two days, however, "for the rainy season had now set in, and the air was filled with fogs and rain, which left no beauty in any scenery, and obstructed observations." He departed on his return journey up the river, November 10, being accompanied by Peter H. Burnett, who was returning up stream, as he had previously left his family and property at The Dalles. Fremont's comment on the character of the immigration of that season is singularly in accord with the verdict of history. "This gentleman," he says, in allusion to Burnett, "as well as the Messrs. Applegate, and others of the emigrants whom I saw, possessed intelligence and character, with the moral and intellectual stamina, as well as the enterprise, which gave solidity and respectability to the foundation of the colonies."

22

Fremont's journey from The Dalles southward to California, associated his name most intimately with the history of Oregon, and lifts his exploit above the level of the commonplace. We obtain a clear idea of how little was then known of the country west of the Rocky mountains from the circumstance that when he left The Dalles, he was under the impression, apparently shared by Doctor McLoughlin, that there existed a large river flowing from the Rocky mountains to San Francisco bay, called the Buenaventura river. The official United States map, 1839, known as the Burr map, showed a river of that name, but in the approximate position of the Sacramento. He planned a great circuit to the southeast, and the exploration of the basin between the Rocky mountain chain and that of the Sierra Nevadas, and finally, a return to the east by a new route.

He intended to map the valley of the Deschutes river, in Oregon, and to ascertain the location of "Tlamath lake," concerning which his information was accurate, since he was able in advance to describe it as being situated "on the table land between the head of Fall river [the Deschutes], which comes into the Columbia, and the Sacramento, which goes into the bay of San Francisco, and from which a river of the same name makes its way westwardly direct to the ocean."

How much, if any, information Fremont may have had as to Peter Skene Ogden's expeditions into central and southern Oregon, or as to Alexander R. McLeod's expeditions into California, accounts of which had not been published, it is not possible now to say. There was a dearth of information as to the very early explorations and journeys of the fur traders and others in southern Oregon and California.

Reverend Mr. Perkins, at The Dalles, obtained for Fremont two Indians to act as guides as far as Klamath lake, and the expedition also enlisted, at Perkins' request, a Chinook youth of 19, formerly attached to the Perkins household, who was extremely desirous of seeing the white men and learning their ways. The cavalcade left The Dalles, November 25, 1843, at the very onset of the winter season. Fremont judged it necessary to abandon the little wagon, that had conveyed his scientific instruments across plains and mountains, and which, on all that long journey, had suffered no damage except that its glass lamps had been broken and that one of its front panels had been kicked out by a fractious horse. The thermometer registered 26 degrees at daylight; by noon, when the party left the Wascopam mission, the weather had grown colder, with flurries of snow. Quickly ascending to the uplands, the travellers found themselves in a country covered with patches of snow, although the pasture appeared good, and the new short grass was fresh and green. They camped, on the night of November 26, in the Tygh valley, being guided thither after dark by fires which had been lighted by some naked Indians, as beacons.

23

Fremont emerged from a narrow pass, November 25, by a trail which led him to a cluster of warm springs situated on either bank of the stream down which he travelled. This was Warm Springs river. Much difficulty was experienced in crossing the chasm-like valley of the Deschutes, which confirmed the explorer's judgment in abandoning his wagon, and compelled him to unlimber his howitzer, dismantle its carriage and let the parts down the declivities separately, by hand. He paused occasionally to observe the geologic formation and was particularly impressed by deposits of clay, nearly as white as chalk, and exceedingly fine grained, now known as diatomaceous earth. Fording in succession the swift, deep western tributaries of the Deschutes river, and observing that never in all his journeying had he travelled in a country in which the rivers so abounded in falls, he came, December 5, to the Metolius.

His route took him within two or three miles west of the present site of Bend. He crossed the Deschutes to the east side of the meadows, near Benham, proceeded thence to the east fork, which he forded near Vandervert's, and, close to the present site of the town of Crescent, he passed again to the east side of the stream. Some distance south of present Crescent, after making his last crossing of a branch of the Deschutes, he entered what is now known locally as the pumice desert, where the soil was generally bare, producing varieties of black pines, but not a blade of grass, so that his animals were obliged to do without food.

On the way, as he progressed through the region now embraced in the Deschutes forest reserve, he was attracted by the appearance of a species of pine tree which he saw in Oregon for the first time, the *pinus Lambertiana,* or sugar pine, which had been observed and named by David Douglas in 1825. The splendid pine forests of this part of central Oregon caused him to marvel. "The great beauty of the country in summer constantly suggested itself to our imaginations," the explorer found time to set down in his journal. "Even now we found it beautiful as we rode along these meadows, from half a mile to two miles wide. The rich soil and excellent water, surrounded by noble forests, make a picture that would delight the eye of a farmer, and I regret that the very small scale of the map would not allow me to give some representation of these features of the country."

December 10, 1843, he reached a savannah and soon afterward caught a view of an expanse of grass and a body of clear water, which he identified as the Klamath lake he had set out to find, but which was in reality an open portion of the Klamath marsh.

He was now in a region in which the Indians had earned the reputation of being hostile to all newcomers, and he took more than his usual precautions against surprise. Seeing smoke rising from the middle of the lake, or savannah, he ordered the howitzer to be fired. "It was the first time our guides had seen it discharged," he observes, "and the bursting of the shell at a distance, which was something like the second fire of the gun, amazed and bewildered them with delight. It inspired them with triumphant feelings; but on the camps at a distance the effect was different, for the smokes in the lake and on the shores immediately disappeared." He found the natives dwelling in a group of huts on the bank of a shallow marsh. The huts were large and round, about 20 feet in diameter, with rounded tops, on which were the doors by which the occupants descended into the interior. Here the explorer noted the curious facility, which certain primitive peoples acquire in making use of local materials which nature supplies. For illustration, residence in the midst of grass and rushes had given them a peculiar skill in converting these into articles of utility. They had made shoes of straw which seemed well adapted for a snowy country; and the women wore on their heads a closely woven basket which made an excellent cap. The men wore shells in their noses.

24

The explorer's impressions of the quarrelsome character of these people were confirmed when the Indians made him understand that they were at war with the tribes on the east and also on the south. Communication between the visitors and the natives was restricted by the circumstance that the language of the latter was so different from that of the Shoshone and Columbia river tribes that the Indian guides were of no value as interpreters. The guides, indeed, having fulfilled their agreement were about to return to their homes, and Fremont sought others to lead him.

The journey now assumed more the character of discovery. Fremont's entry in his journal of December 11, 1843, contains his first intimation of want of confidence in the inaccurate maps on which, until then, he seems to have depended. To this point he had relied on the fabled Mary's lake and Buenaventura river, in the vicinity of which he hoped to recruit his animals and rest his followers. "Forming, agreeable to the best maps in my possession, a connected water line from the Rocky mountains to the Pacific Ocean," he says, "I felt no other anxiety than to pass safely across the intervening desert to the banks of the Buenaventura, where, in the softer climate of a more southern latitude, our horses might find grass to sustain them, and ourselves be sheltered from the rigors of winter and from the inhospitable desert."

He then turned eastward, crossing the upper Klamath marsh in shallow water made difficult by ice, and from the headwaters of Williamson river proceeded almost due east, and south of Yamsay peak to the Sycan marsh. December 15, he crossed a stream which he then mistakenly supposed to be the principal tributary of the Sacramento river, and, December 16, ascended a gradual slope, in snow three feet deep, travelling through a deep pine forest. "The air," he records, "was dark with falling snow, which everywhere weighted down the trees. The depths of the forest were profoundly still; and below we scarcely felt a breath of the wind which whirled the snow through their branches. I found that it required some exertion of constancy to adhere steadily to one course through the woods, when we were uncertain how far the forest extended, or what lay beyond. Towards noon the forest looked clear ahead, appearing suddenly to terminate; and beyond a certain point we could see no trees. Riding rapidly ahead to this spot, we found ourselves on the verge of a vertical and rocky wall of mountain. At our feet more than a thousand feet below—we looked into a green prairie country, in which a beautiful lake some 20 miles in length was spread along the foot of the mountain, its shores bordered with green grass. Just then the sun broke out among the clouds, and illuminated the country below, while around us the storm raged fiercely. Not a particle of ice was to be seen on the lake, or snow on its borders, and all was like summer or spring . . . shivering on snow three feet deep, and stiffening in a cold north wind, we exclaimed at once that the names of Summer lake and Winter ridge should be applied to these two proximate places of sudden and violent contrast."

25

December 20, he came to another and larger lake, which he named Abert, in honor of Col. J. J. Abert, chief of the corps of topographical engineers, to which Fremont belonged. He crossed the river, now known as the Chewaucan, the same day and proceeded along the eastern shore of the lake for some distance. Here he began to experience the real hardships of the journey, finding the water hardly potable, and feed for his horses extremely scarce. Ascending the precipitous rim of the lake to the east, he travelled through the region of Flagstaff, Mugwump, Swamp and Anderson lakes, and along the ridge between the latter and a body of water near which he camped on the night of December 24, 1843. "We were roused, on Christmas morning," he says, "by a discharge from the small arms and howitzer, with which our people saluted the day, and the name of which we bestowed on the lake. It was the first time, perhaps, in this remote and desolate region, in which it had been so celebrated. Always, on days of religious or national commemoration, our voyageurs expect some unusual allowance; and having nothing else I gave them each a little brandy, (which was most carefully guarded, as one of the most useful articles a traveller can carry), with some coffee and sugar, which here, where every eatable was a luxury, was enough to make them a feast."

The body of water, which Fremont thus named Christmas lake, was not, however, the Christmas lake of present-day maps, but Hart lake. Fremont's own chart places his encampment at about longitude 119° 45′ west, while the actual situation of the eastern shore of Hart lake is 119° 50′, and the latitude of the Christmas camp, as recorded by Fremont is 42° 30′ north, which corresponds with present charts. The situation of the camp on this day was five or six miles east of the present settlement of Plush.

26

No further exploration of this region was made until 1849, when Brevet-Capt. W. H. Warner and Lieut. R. S. Williamson were directed to explore the upper reaches of Pit river, California. Warner with a party of nine men passed along the east shore of Abert lake, over Fremont's route, and entered the Warner valley at a point near Mugwump lake. The party were ambushed by Indians, September 26, 1849, and Warner was killed. Warner's name was given to the valley which reaches from about 10 miles north of the present southern boundary of Harney county, Oregon, almost to the California-Nevada line, being about 60 miles long, and from four to eight miles wide. Lieutenant Williamson's name is perpetuated by Williamson river, which was the large stream Fremont crossed on his way from Klamath marsh to Summer lake. These surveys were extended and completed by Lieutenant Abbot.

Fremont's course was then almost due south, and he camped on the night of December 26, 1843, near the 42nd parallel, then the boundary between Oregon and the Mexican province of Alta California. He passed therefore at this point out of the history of Oregon for a time, but since he is to reappear at a date somewhat later to continue his exploration of southern Oregon, it is appropriate to now record that he proceeded southward, his entire party enduring with commendable fortitude the grave hardships of a midwinter journey across desert and mountain range, and arrived at length, March 6, 1844, at Sutter's fort, on Sacramento river, in California. Part of the time the members of the party subsisted on the flesh of horses and mules; two dogs were eaten. The carto-grapher of the expedition, Charles Preuss, losing his way, was once reduced to the extremity of devouring a hill of ants, which he found to have "an agreeable, acid taste." All the plants which Fremont had collected since leaving Fort Hall, representing the typical flora of a route of 2000 miles, were lost when the mule which bore them fell over a precipice.

His quest of the Buenaventura river flowing from the eastward failed, because no river answering to its description existed, but one important result of his journey through the country was that he was enabled to make generalizations concerning the Pacific slope which had been impossible upon the basis of the unconfirmed local data then in the possession of geographers. But from his nar-rative it constantly appears that if he could have had Peter Skene Ogden in his party, he would have had the advantage of the earlier observations of that indefatigable explorer.

27

On his return to Washington, Fremont received the double brevet of captain. Afterward, 1845, he crossed the plains on his third expedition and spent some time investigating the country west of Salt lake, crossing the Salt desert and the Sierra Nevada mountains, in an effort to find a short and feasible route to Cali-fornia. He marched north from California, with the intention of discovering, if possible, a pass from the vicinity of Klamath lake into the Willamette valley. In the first week of May, 1846, he was at the northern end of Klamath lake and again in Oregon. May 9, 1846, he encountered Lieut. A. H. Gillespie, who had been sent to intercept him, and to deliver a verbal communication from Sec-retary of State Buchanan, directing him to return to California, there to "watch and counteract any foreign scheme in California, and conciliate the good will of the inhabitants toward the United States." The international issues of the northern Oregon boundary, and the Texas-Mexico question, were now at an acute stage, and Fremont's services were diverted from the field of exploration.

This marked the close of Fremont's travels in Oregon, but he was not permitted to depart without a dramatic and tragic reminder of the treachery of the Klamath Indians, against whom he had been careful to maintain a guard, in 1843. Here, on the eve of the return journey, while the camp slept, unguarded by a sentry for only the second time in 20,000 miles of wilderness exploration, the explorers were attacked in the night by a war party of 15 or 20 Klamaths. The Indians were repulsed with the loss of their chief, but not until three of Fremont's men had been killed. The dead were Basil Lajeunesse, a French hunter who had accompanied him on all three of his western expeditions, a Delaware Indian named Crane, and a half-breed Iroquois, named Dennie. The travellers then speedily withdrew southward, taking time by the way to plant a counter-ambuscade, into which the pursuing hostiles fell; and, thereafter, Fremont's name passes from the more local annals of Oregon to the history of the struggle for possession of California and, somewhat later, to the broader arena of national political affairs.

28

Theodore Talbot, one of Fremont's companions on his expedition of 1843, and with him again upon the third expedition, 1845, came to Oregon later as a lieutenant in the army service. When the rights of the United States had been established, 1849, he was assigned to duty at Fort Vancouver, with the First United States artillery. While stationed there, he was detailed to explore the Alsea river district. He left Oregon City with eight men, August 20, of that year, crossed the Willamette river at Champoeg, thence travelled by easy stages up the valley, fording the Yamhill, Rickreall and Luckiamute, and reaching the summit of the coast range by way of a branch of Mary's river, the men cutting a trail for themselves with axes as they went along. He descended the western slope of the north fork of the Siletz river, where he examined several deposits of coal, which had been found by white settlers the preceding year.

Leaving Siletz river, he went to Yaquina bay, the outlet of which he explored, and he also ascended the Yaquina river, five miles. He turned south, to Alsea bay, the entrance to which he surveyed, September 1, 1849. September 2, he made further soundings on the Yaquina bar, finding the channel of sufficient depth for navigation if further investigation should prove it not too narrow, or too much exposed. He then returned by way of Otter Rock, became mired in the delta of the Siletz, and retraced his steps from there, going by way of the Siletz sandspit to the harbor entrance, the party swimming the channel and losing a horse which was swept out to sea.

From the site of the present settlement of Taft, he ascended to the pass above the headwaters of Salmon river and descended the Yamhill, passing near where Willamina and Sheridan now stand, and arrived at Oregon City, September 15, 1849. His prediction that veins of coal of considerable size would be found in the western coast range formation, and his surveys of Yaquina and Siletz bays, particularly the former, constituted his most important work.

29

Coincident with Fremont's journey to Oregon, although conducted under vastly different circumstances, was the overland immigration of 1843, already mentioned in this chapter, which not only brought a great number of new settlers, but wholly changed the character of the population, and decided the political destiny of the region, so that it deserved the designation of "great immigration" commonly bestowed on it. It began to assemble, as if spontaneously, at the frontier rendezvous near Independence, Missouri, early in May. These immigrants were of hardy stock, many of them were inured to the privations and hardships of frontier life in the valley of the Mississippi, and its tributaries. They had a common desire to improve their economic situation, and, in addition, many were inspired by a patriotic zeal to save Oregon for the United States.

The "Oregon fever," which then prevailed, however, can be traced to no single source. One of the leaders of the significant movement of this year has candidly summarized his motives as both patriotic and pecuniary. This was Peter H. Burnett, who confessed that he was attracted by the bill proposed to donate to each immigrant 640 acres of land for himself, and 160 acres for each child. Under the provisions of this proposed law, since he had a wife and six children, he would have been entitled to 1600 acres. "I saw that a great American community would grow up in the space of a few years upon the shores of the distant Pacific," he adds, "and I felt an ardent desire to aid in this most important enterprise. At that same time, the country was claimed by both

Great Britain and the United States, so that the most ready and peaceable way to settle the conflicting and doubtful claims of the two governments was to fill the country with American citizens. If we could only show by practical test that American emigrants could safely make their way across the continent to Oregon with their wagons, teams, cattle and families, then the solution of the question of title to the country was discovered."

Burnett was in debt and saw no reasonable probability of discharging his obligations if he remained in the Missouri town in which he then resided. His own estimate of his motives in emigrating to Oregon derives additional value from the fact that it was typical. Many had similar ideas, and decided to move to Oregon. Members of the caravan, although accustomed to outdoor life, knew little or nothing about the outfitting of an expedition to cross the plains. However, by May 20, about 800 men, women and children had assembled in various camps in the vicinity of Elm Grove, Kansas, where a meeting was held and rules were adopted.

30

Start from Elm Grove was made May 22, and by the time Kansas river was reached, June 1, necessity of leadership had become apparent to most of the party, so Burnett was elected captain, and J. W. Nesmith, orderly sergeant, and a council of nine were chosen. Captain John Gantt, a former officer of the regular army, was employed as guide as far as Fort Hall, Dr. Marcus Whitman, returning to the mission after a visit to the states, overtook the main wagon train, and was welcomed as an additional adviser.

The journey was marred by no disasters of consequence, but the heterogeneous character of the company, as was the case with the train of 1842, made discipline difficult. Burnett was not entirely successful in enforcing the rules. It soon became doubtful whether so large a body could be kept together on such a journey. He resigned his leadership after eight days, and William Martin was elected captain. The expedition soon afterward divided into two parts, however, those who had no herds constituting the "light column," and the other, necessarily slower, was known as the "cow column." Jesse Applegate, who owned more livestock than any other immigrant, was made captain of the cow column. These two sections travelled for a time within supporting distance of each other, but otherwise maintained separate organizations. Still later, four separate columns were created.

The company had the advantage of fresh pastures which later immigrant trains did not have, and of good hunting, buffalo and antelope being plentiful. The monotonous passage of the Platte valley was made in the warm sunshine of June. The train arrived on the south bank of the south fork on the 29th of that month, having travelled a distance of 173 miles in the Platte valley in 11 days, and there boats were improvised, by covering their wagon boxes with green buffalo hides. In these clumsy vessels they crossed the river. This process was repeated with variations whenever the wagons reached a stream too deep to ford. At Fort Laramie, July 14, the immigrants could rest and replenish diminishing food stocks, but complained of price of supplies. They paid $1.50 a pint for coffee and brown sugar, 25 cents a pound for unbolted flour, $1.50 a pound for powder, and $1.00 a yard for an inferior grade of calico.

31

No trouble with Indians was experienced after leaving this place, as the mountain men had led the immigrants to expect, but an incident occurred which illustrates the attitude of certain of the whites toward the Indians, which may have contributed to the difficulties between the races in subsequent years. While following a band of buffaloes, August 2, a detachment of the immigrants came upon a young Sioux, alone, whom they questioned concerning the whereabouts of his tribe. He replied that they numbered 300 and were encamped on a lake three miles distant. "He was very much frightened," writes a member of the company, "when he saw that we knew he was a Sioux, expecting to be killed on the spot. We turned to go away, when the Trader observed that we ought to kill him; but the rest of us objected, and he was overruled."

Several deaths occurred on the way, and a number of new lives were ushered into the world, Doctor Whitman performing the duties of physician on some of these occasions. The travellers were in the now famous South Pass, August 5, 6 and 7, 1843, and crossed the Green river, August 11. At Fort Bridger, August 14, they overtook the Catholic missionaries, Fathers De Smet and De Vos, whom they previously had met at the crossing of the Kansas, May 31. Monotony of the fare was relieved at Bear river, where, an abundance of excellent fish, wild ducks and geese was obtained.

They arrived at Fort Hall, having travelled 213 miles from Fort Bridger in 13 days. This was regarded as good progress for a caravan of ox-teams. The virgin character of the road, however, made travel comparatively easy. Up to this point, it was the judgment of Burnett, the road over which the train had passed was perhaps the finest natural road of the same length to be found in the world.

With the encouragement of Doctor Whitman, the immigrants persisted in their determination to take their wagons to the Columbia, although they had been advised by others not to attempt to do so, and they were justified by their success. After leaving Fort Hall, the party began to break up, as Nesmith had predicted it would do, and a number of the younger men preceded the larger caravans with pack trains, which they hastily improvised. On the way to Fort Boise, they journeyed through a desolate region thickly covered with artemisia, or sagebrush. The immigrants were now travelling without respect to organization. At a point near the American falls of the Snake river, several of the party turned south and west to California, having left their wagons behind; and at Fort Boise there were other divisions, one particularly impatient company of five pushing forward on horseback.

32

Approaching the Grande Ronde, the trains were compelled to hew a way with axes through the timber, Nesmith was with the advance party, on which fell the burden of road-building, under peculiarly trying circumstances. They camped near the Whitman mission, October 10, arrived at Fort Walla Walla, October 16, and here the last semblance of organization was lost. Applegate and others built the fleet of boats which aroused the admiration of Lieutenant Fremont, who overtook the party at this point. The greater number continued by an overland route to The Dalles, where they embarked on rafts to the Cascades, and thence voyaged to Fort Vancouver in boats and canoes. A small number ventured through the Cascade mountains by Daniel Lee's cattle trail. The part of the journey after leaving Fort Walla Walla was the most difficult of all.

A son of Jesse Applegate was drowned by the capsizing of a boat in the Columbia. Travellers suffered much from the depredations of Indians, the natives in the vicinity of The Dalles fully warranting the reputation of being the worst thieves between the Missouri river and the Pacific ocean.

The journey from Independence, Missouri, to Oregon City consumed a little more than five months and a half. Many were destitute when they reached the Willamette valley, and those who could find work that winter regarded themselves as especially fortunate. Some received assistance in the form of goods on credit from Doctor McLoughlin, and others were helped by the more prosperous members of the immigration. The cattle had been left behind, either at Fort Walla Walla, or The Dalles, and only a few horses reached the Willamette valley in condition for service. The arrival of the party more than doubled the population of the territory, and imposed a heavy tax on its resources. Pork was 10 cents, and flour 4 cents a pound, not high prices by more recent standards, but prohibitive considering the scanty means of the newcomers at that time. They were nevertheless fortunate in being generally in good health, and with the hardships of the long journey behind them their good humor soon returned.

The arrivals soon scattered out over the country, acquired land claims, built cabins and even laid the foundations for new towns; Burnett and M. M. McCarver, for example, laid out a townsite, below the present location of the City of Portland, on the west bank of the Willamette river, which they called Linnton, after Senator Linn, author of the land bill which was responsible, to a great extent, for the early Oregon immigration. Many of the men who reached Oregon in this year attained some degree of eminence in the colony and were active in the work of building a new commonwealth.

33

The migration of 1844 travelled as several separate trains. The peak of privation was not attained in this year until the travellers arrived in Oregon, where, late in the autumn, they found the colony scarcely ready to receive them. Excellent crops had been harvested, it is true, but the chief need of the newcomers was clothing. They were almost barefoot and there was not a tanyard in the territory. In this emergency the pioneers were compelled to resort to makeshift and substitutes. For the first two years, after 1843, leading citizens in the community knew what it was to be without meat on their tables for weeks at a time. Nor was bread always plentiful.

In 1844, there was a movement, noteworthy because of its ultimate results, led by Michael T. Simmons, to open the country north of the Columbia to American settlement. The following year his party, all members of the immigration of 1844, opened the first wagon trail from the Columbia river to Puget sound, and Simmons settled at the falls of the Deschutes river (a different Deschutes from the famous stream in eastern Oregon), at the head of Budd's inlet, near the present town of Tumwater, Thurston county, Washington.

34

The outstanding feature of the immigration of 1845, which consisted of perhaps 3000 persons, and which differed from its predecessors chiefly in the fact that it drew more largely from the eastern and middle states, and less exclusively from the western frontier, was the tragic misadventure of a party of some 200 families who were persuaded at Fort Hall to attempt to reach the Willamette valley by way of the Malheur river. These immigrants engaged Stephen H. L. Meek as guide, but Meek lost the way and led them into the Harney basin and they passed Harney lake. They crossed an eastern branch of Sylvies river, before reaching this lake. They strayed to a region so desolate that even the Indians had avoided it. The cattle were footsore from travel over the lava formation of the Malheur mountains, there was no water that was not strongly impregnated with alkali, and a malignant fever became epidemic. Several children became ill and died, and when, at length, the party gave up trying to find a pass through the Cascades and determined to turn north, crossing the ridge between the John Day and Deschutes rivers, bitterness against Meek had become so intense that the guide was compelled to secrete himself, and afterward to flee. From The Dalles, however, he sent a rescue party to their relief.

The Deschutes was reached in due time and the travellers were again delayed by the necessity of transporting themselves, and such of their goods as were not abandoned, by means of an aerial tramway, made from a wagon box suspended from a cable across the stream. They arrived at The Dalles about the middle of October. Twenty had died along the way, and others were so weakened by the privations of the fateful journey that they succumbed after reaching their destination.

Other divisions of the immigration of this fateful year, 1845, travelling over the usual route, including the company of Joel Palmer, reached The Dalles two weeks ahead of the Meek party. Palmer, Samuel K. Barlow, and William H. Rector then proceeded in advance, by an unexplored route, in an effort to find a way to the Willamette valley around the base of Mount Hood. Those who made a trial of this approach to Willamette valley, suffered untold hardships and delays, so that the rear guard of the season's migration straggled into Oregon City, weary and destitute, in December. Barlow's exploratory work was fruitful, however, inasmuch as he applied for and received from the provisional government authorities a charter for a toll road, afterward known as the Barlow trail, which was put in order in time to be serviceable to the immigrants of 1846, and to avoid dangers and hardships that attended a voyage down the river from The Dalles. In fact, a decided stimulus was given to the desire for better roads and trails throughout the territory.

35

In the spring of 1846, some disappointed California settlers reached the Willamette valley by trail, coming from the south, and bringing information that Lansford W. Hastings, whose name has been mentioned in connection with the immigration of 1842, and in describing his activities in Doctor McLoughlin's affairs at Oregon City, in the winter of 1842-3, was planning to divert settlers from the Oregon Trail, and to induce them to turn off and go to California. The California party that brought this story and preferred Oregon, included Robert C. Keyes, John Chamberlain, Abner Frazer, Jairus Bonney and Truman Bonney. This plan of Hastings seemed to Willamette valley citizens an effort to lead astray, by misrepresentation, persons who were on their way to Oregon, and a mass meeting was at once held at the City Hotel, Oregon City, where, after organization, steps were taken to get affidavits and procure further information. Depositions were taken, and were published in the Oregon Spectator. A fund was raised to send Colonel Finley, J. S. Rinearson and W. G. T'Vault "to meet the immigration from the United States to this country," in order to prevent settlers from being deceived and led astray. Hastings and others actually went from California to points east of Fort Bridger during the summer of 1846, and diverted some settlers from Oregon.

36

A British fleet of 16 vessels, mounting 350 guns, was now in the Pacific ocean, having been assembled there, perhaps in view of the uncertain status of the northern boundary question. The Columbia river valley was officially visited, August, 1845, by Captain Park of the British royal marines, and Lieut. William Peel, of the British navy, who brought assurances to the local officials of the Hudson's Bay Company that the British government would extend protection to its nationals and to the company, in the event of an open rupture with the United States. Lieutenant Peel, moreover, was charged to ascertain whether troops might, in an emergency, be transported overland from Canada to the lower Columbia valley.

The America, flagship of the squadron, was stationed at Puget sound for a time, to be succeeded by the frigate Fisgard, 42 guns, and the gunboat Cormorant, six guns. November 2, 1845, the sloop-of-war Modeste, 18 guns, entered the Columbia river, anchoring before Vancouver, November 29.

37

These obviously warlike preparations suggested to some of the local American citizens the military need of a more practicable overland route. This idea, together with desire of settlers in the southern valleys to promote local development, induced Levi Scott, Jesse and Lindsay Applegate, and others, to organize a prospecting party, in the spring of 1846, to search for new and more direct route from the Oregon Trail to southern Oregon. These men ascended the Umpqua canyon, which, though exceedingly rough, was believed to afford a feasible way for wagons, then followed a southeastern branch of the Rogue river to the foot of the Siskiyou mountains, and, near the parallel of 42 degrees, approached an easy slope which led them to the stream now called Keene creek, near the summit of the Siskiyou ridge. Here they camped, June 30, in a little valley now known as Mound prairie, and, July 4, they crossed the summit of the Cascade range, near the place where Fremont, only a few days previously, had met Lieutenant Gillespie and had turned back to California. The prospectors now continued along the shore of lower Klamath lake, turned eastward and forded Lost river on the since famous stone bridge, a submerged causeway. Passing to the south of Goose lake they ascended a beautiful sloping meadow, which led by way of

Lassen creek, through a gap in the mountain wall to the eastward, and entered Surprise valley in northern California. The party found their way across the great desert of northern Nevada to the Humboldt meadows, ascended the Humboldt river and in due time reached Fort Hall.

The prospectors met a considerable train of immigrants at Fort Hall and persuaded a number of them to travel by this new route into southern Oregon, including J. Quinn Thornton, a fluent diarist who set down his experiences in a journal, which he afterward extended into a book. Most of the members of this division, which Thornton himself has estimated at 98 men and 50 women, followed Lindsay Applegate, who pressed ahead to improve the trail, with the assistance of a few young volunteers from among the immigrants.

The caravan was disappointed, however, for various causes, and consumed three months and five days in making the journey from Thousand springs to the Rogue river valley, which the prospectors had covered in the opposite direction in 37 days, the cattle and other impedimenta of the settlers accounting only in part for the delay. They had several skirmishes with Modoc Indians, in one of which a member of the party was killed; the desert furnished insufficient sustenance for their animals, and in a panic which overtook them when they found themselves in the Cascade mountains with winter almost on them, some of the travellers cast away their portable belongings.

They had left the old Oregon trail, August 9. They were in the canyon of the Umpqua, November 9, when Thornton wrote: "Having at various times upon the journey from Ogden's river [the Humboldt] thrown away my property, I had little remaining save our buffalo robes, blankets, arms, ammunition, watch, and the most valuable part of our wardrobe. We were very weak in consequence of want of sufficient and healthful food. The road was very muddy, and the rain was descending in the gorge of the mountains, where we were, while the snow was falling far above us upon the sides. There was a close canyon, some three miles ahead of us, down which we would have to wade three miles in cold mountain snow-water, frequently above the middle."

Thornton's party, which had now fallen to the rear, was able to judge the privations of those who had gone before by physical evidence left along the trail. "We passed many wagons," says Thornton, "that had been abandoned by their owners, in consequence of their proprietors finding it impossible to take them over. We passed household and kitchen furniture, beds and bedding, books, carpets, cooking utensils, dead cattle, broken wagons and wagons not broken, but, nevertheless, abandoned. In short, the whole road presented the appearance of a defeated and retreating army having passed over it, instead of one over which had passed a body of cheerful and happy immigrants, with high hopes and brilliant expectations." An immigrant died, leaving a widow and seven small children, and there were a number of other deaths along the way. Many were scantily clad and were not only without money, which for the moment was of no consequence, but were utterly without food.

38

Applegate received tidings of the plight of the stragglers in the rear, and made all possible haste, with the cooperation of other citizens, to send relief, which reached them in the Umpqua valley, November 14. The venture, nevertheless, provoked deep ill-feeling and was the cause of feuds which marred the neighborhood life of the settlements for some years. A weighty and prolonged controversy was waged in the columns of the Spectator. Thornton no sooner arrived at the settlements than he wrote a letter imploring the people of the Willamette valley to go to the aid of the immigrants with at least 100 head of pack horses, declaring that unless this were done all must perish. The Spectator, February 4, 1847, printed a statement on the authority of "some of the immigrants who have reached here," to the effect that the southern party had arrived safely, to which Thornton retorted with a harrowing account of the suffering he had observed. David Goff, one of Applegate's associates in locating the new route, replied denying that conditions had been misrepresented, stating that the immigrants had been plainly told that the road through the Umpqua mountains would require the labor of at least 20 men for 10 days to make it passable, and intimating that, since they had failed to furnish sufficient help, their misfortunes were chiefly due to their own fault. Goff averred that notwithstanding their unquestioned hardships, the southern party then had more cattle alive than settlers who had come by the northern route.

A number of immigrants came by the Applegate route in 1847, however, each party contributing something to the improvement of the road and profiting by the experiences of predecessors, and thus suffered fewer delays, arriving in the Willamette valley late in September. These immigrants, according to Jesse Applegate, did much for the future prosperity of the country. "By their energy and perseverance," said he, "they have redeemed the character of a road which, in the indispensable articles of grass and water, can accommodate an immense number of animals, and from the easy access which it opens to the southern valleys of the territory, the day is not far distant when they will rival the Columbia in population and wealth.

39

An experience in the Harney basin, similar to that of the Meek party of 1845, must be recorded for the year 1853, when a party of between 1000 and 2000 persons was induced by Elijah Elliott to leave the regular Oregon trail and to follow him along a proposed cut-off from Malheur river to the Middle fork of the Willamette. They reached the Deschutes and Crooked rivers after great hardships, and ultimately found their way to the Willamette valley.

40

The inflow of American settlers during this period of several years had been noted by the British, not without realization of its political significance. The presence of British warships in Puget sound and in the Columbia river, which has been noted, was supplemented by the visit to the territory of two British army officers, who travelled, under instructions, in the guise of "private travellers for the pleasure of field sports and scientific pursuits." These men were Lieut. Henry Warre and Lieut. M. Vavasour, of the British Royal Marines, who arrived at Vancouver, October 25, 1845.

The military and political character of their mission has been fully attested by recent disclosures of official records, although at one time it was assumed that they came in the character of spies upon the local officials of the Hudson's Bay Company. What they did was to scrutinize closely the possibilities of the defense of the territory in the event of war, and to report on Oregon's accessibility by the northern or Canadian routes, and also by those further south, commonly travelled by Americans. The report, dated

October 26, 1845, indicated the advantage afforded by the Oregon Trail, and recognized the preponderance of American influence in the colony.

The officers found the route usually travelled by Hudson's Bay traders, from the Red River settlements to Oregon, to be "quite impracticable for the transport of troops, with their provisions, stores, etc.," reminding their government that the Red River immigration, which Sir George Simpson had fostered, 1841, was composed of persons accustomed to the voyageur's life, and consequently it was not to be deemed a criterion by which to determine the feasibility of the route for troops; and that, on the other hand, the passage of the Rocky mountains within American territory presented little or no difficulty. "That troops might be sent from the United States to Oregon," they reported, "is evident from the fact that 300 dragoons of the United States regular army having accompanied the last emigration to the above mentioned valley through the mountains, ostensibly for the protection of said emigrants from the hostile Indians of the plains." They discovered that, even in 1844, citizens of the United States formed a large majority over the British subjects in the Oregon Country, and they estimated the total population of the Willamette valley at about 6000, of whom about 1000 might be considered as subjects of Great Britain.

41

This report reached London too late to exercise any influence whatever on the government's policy in dealing with the boundary issue, but it has value as a picture of conditions in the territory. In a second report, dated June 16, 1846, only a day after the boundary treaty had been signed, they noted the fact that "since the summer, (1845), a village called Portland has been commenced between the falls and Linnton, to which an American merchant ship ascended and discharged her cargo in September." With the voice of prophecy they observed that the situation of Portland was superior to that of Linnton, and the back country of easier access. Settlements were springing up here and there along the banks of the Willamette below the falls. A wagon road from Tualatin plains to the old settlement at Scappoose had been begun. Everywhere, the open prairies had been claimed by settlers, who were loath to begin clearing land for homes in the heavy timber.

The outstanding features of legislation thus far enacted by the provisional government, in the minds of these visitors, were the laws looking toward the opening of two lines of communication across the Cascade mountains, south of the Columbia river. One of these routes, by way of the Santiam river, the Lebanon-Warm Spring road of today, they viewed as impracticable, notwithstanding the optimism of the contractor at work on this grade.

Portland had only then received a name, and its inhabitants were felling the trees from which their first homes were constructed and from which their primitive furniture was made. With such tools only as saw, augur, pole-ax and adze, these men labored with zeal that served for want of better implements. Fireplaces and chimneys were built of sticks, protected inside and out with clay. Puncheon floors were the rule, windows were but sliding doors in the walls, without glass, and wooden pegs were almost universally used in place of nails. This description of life in Portland, in 1845 and 1846, is more or less applicable to that of the whole territory.

42

The foundation of Portland had been laid in November, 1843, when Asa L. Lovejoy, Doctor Whitman's companion on his eastward journey in the preceding winter, and William Overton, came ashore from a canoe enroute from Vancouver to Oregon City, and after examining the topography of the locality concluded that it was suitable for a townsite. Overton afterward sold his interest to F. W. Pettygrove; and it is well authenticated that the name of Portland was chosen, in 1845, by the tossing of a coin. Pettygrove, a native of Maine, favored Portland against Boston, proposed by Lovejoy, who had come from Massachusetts. Pettygrove, as events attest, won the contest. At the date of the second Warre and Vavasour report, Pettygrove was a merchant with his principal place of business in Oregon City, and conducted a branch store in Portland. Lovejoy still maintained his law offices at Oregon City.

Unexpected numbers of the immigration, 1845, made it necessary for new arrivals to labor diligently and to practice strict economy. By the spring of 1846, newly-occupied farms had begun to produce, but the wild fruits and nuts which were then abundant were gathered and stored with painstaking labor. Thrift was a virtue growing out of universal necessity.

43

The visit of Lieutenants Park and Peel, who were also commissioned by the British government to make a report, and the arrival of the Modeste in the Columbia river, stirred the patriotism of the American residents, who were now very largely in the majority, but it did not blind them to their social duties. Peel made himself agreeable while he endeavored to ascertain the sentiment of the inhabitants. He was received with cordiality by leading American settlers, and became convinced that the British cause was lost. The Modeste became a center of social gaiety during nearly a year and a half of her stay. Capt. Thomas Baillie, her commander, acted as host to the residents, without discrimination as to nationality of his guests, and at sundry amateur theatrical performances, held on board the vessel, American as well as British patriotic songs were sung.

On behalf of the United States, Lieut. Neil M. Howison was detailed, 1846, to visit Oregon with the schooner Shark; and, although he did not arrive in the Columbia river until July 1, 1846, some time after the boundary treaty negotiations had reached the last stages, he made a report concerning the trade, shipping and general development of the territory, which by reason of its official character was influential in sustaining public interest in the Oregon Country. He was received with honors by Provisional Governor Abernethy, the official salute on that occasion being fired from a hole in a blacksmith's anvil, and he was escorted on a week's ride through the Willamette valley. His journey elicited from him the observation that "a more lovely country nature has never provided for her virtuous sons and daughters than I here travelled through."

Although a sailor, Howison had a particularly keen eye for matters agricultural, and he knew how to make himself popular with the settlers. He lamented that so fruitful a region had not received more foreign plants and flowers than had yet arrived. The honey-bee had not yet been naturalized, though sweet-briar and honeysuckle, clover and wild-grape blossom wasted their sweetness on the desert air, and in various ways the newcomers had neglected obvious opportunities; yet, on the whole, he found in the settlers a great deal to admire. "Many allowances," he said, "should be made in favor of these people. They come generally from the poorer classes of the western states, with the praiseworthy design of improving their fortunes. They brave dangers and accomplish Herculean labors on the journey across the mountains, and during this time are reminded of no law but expediency. That they should, so soon after their union into new societies at their new homes, voluntarily place themselves under any restraints of law or penalties whatever, is an evidence of a good disposition which time will be sure to improve and refine." Of the population of the territory as a whole, he said that it deserved "to be characterized as honest, brave and hardy, rapidly improving in those properties and qualities which mark them for future distinction among the civilized portion of the world."

Howison's schooner, the Shark, was wrecked in attempting to leave the Columbia river, September 10, 1846. It became a total loss, a misfortunc that Howison attributed to alteration of the channel since Wilkes' survey, and to the unexpected action of the tide. No lives were lost, although there were some narrow escapes. Citizens of the territory, Hudson's Bay Company officials and officers of the Modeste, were zealous in extending aid and expressing sympathy. Howison chartered thc Hudson's Bay Company schooner Cadboro, in which he transported his crew to San Francisco, and almost his last act before his departure, January 18, 1847, was to present the colors of the Shark to the citizens of the territory, through Governor Abernethy. "With the fullest confidence that it will be received and duly appreciated as such by our countrymen here," he wrote from Bakers bay, "I do myself the honor of transmitting thc flags to your address; nor, can I omit the occasion to express my gratification and pride that this relic of my late command should be emphatically the first United States flag to wave over the undisputed and purely American territory of Oregon."

CHAPTER NOTES AND REFERENCES

PART I

CHAPTER I

Wagner, Henry R.—Spanish Voyages to the Northwest Coast, 1929, includes voyages to 1602. The same author's Spanish Explorations in the Strait of Juan de Fuca, 1933, includes voyages between 1769 and 1793.

Burpee, L. J., editor.—Journal and Letters of Pierre Gaultier de Varennes de la Verendrye and his Sons, The Champlain Society, 1927.

LaHontan, L. A.—New Voyages to North America, edited by R. G. Thwaites, 1905, vol. I, p. 167.

Coronado's expedition in search of the kingdom of Quivira is described in Hakluyt's Voyages, vol. IX, p. 164.

Nunn, G. E.—Origin of the Strait of Anian Concept, 1929.

Jefferys, Thomas.—Great Probability of a Northwest Passage, 1786, contains DeFonte's letter.

Lok's Note is published in Greenhow's History of Oregon and California, 1845, p. 407.

Elliott, T. C.—"Origin of the Name Oregon," in Oregon Historical Quarterly, vol. XXII, p. 91, contains the Proposals of Robert Rogers and the Petitions of Carver. See also "Strange Case of Jonathan Carver and the Name Oregon," by the same author, in Oregon Historical Quarterly, vol. XXI, p. 341.

CHAPTER II

Regarding the papal line of demarcation established first by Pope Nicholas V, and modified by Pope Alexander VI, consult John Fiske, Discovery of America, Appendix B. The Bull of Alexander VI, as translated in English, is in Purchas His Pilgrimes, vol. II, p. 32, and the modification is on page 65.

Nunn, G. E.—"Magellan's Route in the Pacific," in Geographical Review, October, 1934, p. 615.

As for the Spanish voyages, consult Wagner as cited in notes of Chapter I, and Greenhow, History of Oregon and California.

Relative to the features of the coast line, particularly as to modern nomenclature, see George Davidson, United States Coast Survey, Coast Pilot of California, Oregon and Washington Territory (1869 and other editions).

CHAPTER III

The principal sources of the Drake narrative are the following:

Corbett, Sir Julian S.—Sir Francis Drake, London and New York, 1890. Drake and the Tudor Navy, London, 1898, 1899.

Davidson, George.—Examination of Some of the Early Voyages, Washington, 1886. Francis Drake on the Northwest Coast of America, 1579, in Transactions of the Geographical Society of the Pacific, vol. V, series II, 1908. Identification of Sir Francis Drake's Anchorage, San Francisco, 1890.

Hakluyt, Richard.—Principal Navigators, Voiages and Discoveries of the English Nation, 1589, 1598-1600; new edition, London, 1903-05.

Nuttall, Zelia.—New Light on Drake, Hakluyt Society, London, 1914.

Purchas, Samuel.—His Pilgrimes, London, 1625-26; reprinted, Glasgow, 1905-07.

Robertson, John W.—Francis Drake and other Early Explorers along the Pacific Coast, San Francisco, 1927.

The World Encompassed, London, 1628; reprinted by Hakluyt Society, 1854.

Wagner, Henry R.—Sir Francis Drake's Voyage Around the World, its Aims and Achievements, San Francisco, 1926.

The original account of Drake's voyage is in the World Encompassed, chiefly by Francis Fletcher, chaplain, in Purchas, His Pilgrimes, vol. II. It was published as a separate narrative in 1854. For copies see Appendix to Robertson's Francis Drake, which book also discusses at length Drake in the South sea, (p. 87) and reproduces a number of beautiful early maps. A less important biography is Sir Francis Drake, by E. P. Benson, New York and London, 1927. But by far the most scholarly book on the subject (also containing maps and illustrations) is Wagner's Sir Francis Drake's Voyage Around the World. There is a conflict of opinion as to the bay on the California coast in which Drake made his protracted stay. Wagner's opinion is that Drake did not anchor in what is now known as Drakes bay, and he inclines to the view that Drake's sojourn was at Bodega bay, and also that he called at other bays on the coast. For other discussion of Drake's anchorage see George Davidson, as above cited.

CHAPTER IV

Besides the several editions of Cook's Voyages, there are two translations of a book by Henry Zimmermann that are useful to the student of the survey of the Pacific coast. These are F. W. Howay's Zimmermann's Captain Cook, Toronto, 1930; and J. C. Anderson's Zimmermann's Account of the Third Voyage of Captain Cook, Wellington, 1926. The former is well annotated.

Nootka Sound Controversy Papers, Mss. in the Library of Congress.

The story of the Yazoo Indian, Monacht Ape, is found in Le Page du Pratz, Histoire de la Louisiane. vol. III, p. 136 .

CHAPTER V

An article by F. W. Howay, "Early Days of the Maritime Fur Trade on the Northwest Coast," in the Canadian Historical Review, vol. IV, p. 26, deals with the shipping and explorations, in general.

For Bering's voyages and Russian activities see F. A. Golder, Russian Expansion on the Pacific, 1914, and Bering's Voyages, 2v. 1922; also Leonhard Stejneger's "An Early Account of Bering's Voyages," in Geographical Review, October, 1934, concerning the first authentic account of Bering's second expedition, by Peder Van Haven.

Strange, James.—Records of Fort St. George: . . . Journal and Narrative of the Commercial Expedition to the North-West Coast of America, edited by A. V. Venkatarama Ayyar, Madras, 1928.

Barkley, on arriving at Canton, had told Meares of the discovery of the strait of Juan de Fuca, although afterward (1790) Meares claimed it for himself.

Howay, F. W.—Dixon-Meares Controversy, 1920.

As to the strait and river see John Meares, Voyages to the Northwest Coast of America, 1790, ch. XIV, pp. 152-68.

In negotiations for settlement of the international boundary line, 1826-27, the British laid some stress upon what they called the discovery of the Columbia river by Meares; see Greenhow, Oregon and California, 1845, pp. 171, 178, 449.

Gray and Haswell are authorities for the statement that the Northwest America was under Portuguese colors; F. W. Howay, "Captains Gray and Kendrick: The Barrell Letters," in Washington Historical Quarterly, vol. XII, p. 257.

CHAPTER VI

One of the letters in the Nootka Sound Controversy Mss. in the Library of Congress complains that the Americans were still in Spanish waters after nearly a year had elapsed. It has always been a question why Martinez did not follow orders and treat the Americans as he did the British. This is partly explained by the so-called Barrell letters of Captains Gray and Kendrick, written to the owners of the ships at Boston, and also by the Martinez diary and Haswell's log. The American captains established friendly personal relations with Martinez, gave him presents, flattered his vanity and aided him in his plans, at the same time maintaining the pretense of being on an exploring expedition; see F. W. Howay, Washington Historical Quarterly, vol. XII, p. 243.

Nootka Sound Controversy Papers. Mss. in Library of Congress.

Manning, W. R.—Nootka Sound Controversy (In American Historical Association, Annual Report, 1904).

The Nootka treaty is set out in Greenhow, History of Oregon and California, 1845, p. 476.

Meares, John.—Authentic copy of the Memorial to the Right Honourable William Wyndham Grenville, London, 1790.

CHAPTER VII

In the Introduction to Vancouver's Voyage (p. vi) he states that recent visits of merchantmen had revived the slumbering hypothesis of a communication between the waters of the Pacific and Atlantic oceans, the archipelago of St. Lazarus was once more called into being, and its existence assumed on the authority of De Fonte, De Fonta, or De Fuentes, and of a Mr. Nicholas Shapely, from Boston in America. He was evidently unimpressed by these ancient theories, and speaks with sarcasm of those who had dared to drag the name of Captain Cook forward in support of the visionary conjectures.

The pamphlet war between Meares and Captain Arthur Dobbs in London at this time revealed Meares in a rather unenviable light.

Meany, E. S.—Vancouver's Discovery of Puget Sound, 1907.

For the negotiations and cause of the failure of the conference at Nootka, reference may be made to Bell's "Anonymous Journal," Washington Historical Quarterly, vol. VI, p. 51, and Greenhow's Oregon and California, p. 242.

According to Greenhow (p. 246) Quadra presented Vancouver with copies of charts given to him by Gray. Bell's Journal says Gray gave Vancouver a plan or map. (Washington Historical Quarterly, vol. VI, pp. 56, 59).

For names of vessels on the northwest coast, 1785-1804, consult F. W. Howay, List of Trading Vessels in the Maritime Trade, (Reprinted from the Transactions of the Royal Society of Canada, series 3, vol. 24, sec. 2, 1930, and series 3, vol. 25, sec. 2, 1931).

Boit's voyage on the Union is described by S. E. Morison in his Maritime History of Massachusetts, 1921, p. 74-76, and is referred to in Morison's "Nova Albion and New England," in Oregon Historical Quarterly, vol. XXVIII, p. 8.

Jewitt, John R.—Narrative of the Adventures and Suffering of John R. Jewitt, 1815.

CHAPTER VIII

Howay, F. W.—"Captain Simon Metcalfe and the Brig Eleanora, in Annual Report of the Hawaiian Historical Society, 1925.

As to action of Spanish officials, see Bancroft, History of California, vol. I, p. 445; Idem, Northwest Coast, vol. I, p. 186; Greenhow, p. 184.

Gray's original log of the ship Columbia is lost, but the part that relates to the visit to Grays harbor and to the Columbia river is printed in Greenhow, Appendix p. 434. This copy was made by Charles Bulfinch, 1806. See his affidavit, April 21, 1838, in Senate Document, 470, pp. 14-23, of the 25th Congress, 2nd Session; also note by E. S. Meany in Washington Historical Quarterly, vol. XII, p. 1. Haswell's Log of the voyage of the Columbia is in Bancroft, Northwest Coast, vol. I, pp. 703-35 (second edition). Haswell started on the Columbia, but was transferred to the Washington before entering the Pacific. The Journal of the young John Boit, which gives a detailed account of the visit to the Columbia river, (with one day's error in dates) is reprinted in Oregon Historical Quarterly, vol. XXII, pp. 257-351; Washington Historical Quarterly, vol. XII, pp. 1-50; Massachusetts Historical Society, Proceedings, vol. 53, pp. 217-75.

Howay, F. W.—"Ship Margaret," in Annual Report of the Hawaiian Historical Society, 1929.

Besides Vancouver's Voyage (1798), the original log of the Chatham, in the Public Record Office, at London, may be consulted. So much of the latter as applies particularly to the Columbia river is published in Oregon Historical Quarterly, vol. XVIII, pp. 231-43. Broughton's survey of the Columbia river is recorded in Bell's Journal, printed in "Columbia River Exploration," by J. N. Barry, in Oregon Historical Quarterly, vol. XXXIII, pp. 31-42, 143-55; see also Mr. Barry's article, "Broughton, Up the Columbia River, 1792," idem, vol. XXXII, pp. 301-12. Broughton called Sandy river Baring river. Lewis and Clark named it Quick Sand river, a name that did not survive. Lady island in that vicinity was called by Broughton Johnstone island, and Brant island by Lewis and Clark.

"Voyages of the Brig Jenny," by F. W. Howay and T. C. Elliott, in Oregon Historical Quarterly, XXX, pp. 197-206.

The Daedalus came out from England with instructions and supplies, and reached the rendezvous at Nootka, July 4, 1792; Vancouver, vol. II, p. 98.

Two journals of the ship Ruby have been printed in Oregon Historical Quarterly, both edited by T. C. Elliott: in vol. XXVIII, pp. 258-80, "Journal of the Ship Ruby," and vol. XXIX, pp. 337-46, "Journal of Captain Charles Bishop of the Ruby in 1795."

CHAPTER IX

Alexander Mackenzie's Voyages (1801) p. 349, narrates the story of the great expedition and describes the dramatic arrival at the ocean and the painting of the inscription. See also Lawrence J. Burpee, The Search for the Western Sea, 1908.

The Tacouche Tesse river, (the Fraser) was mentioned by Lewis and Clark before it was explored by Fraser, in 1807, and it is probable that they got the name from a map in Mackenzie's Voyages, showing "Tacoutche Tesse or Columbia river"; Original Journals of Lewis and Clark, edited by R. G. Thwaites, vol. IV, p. 60. At the time Fraser was instructed to explore that stream it was believed that it was part of the Columbia; Oregon Historical Quarterly, June 1909, p. 9.

That Jefferson's plans for acquiring Louisiana did not include lands west of the Rocky mountains, see quotations from his letters in The Louisiana Purchase, by Binger Hermann, 1908; also F. G. Young, in Oregon Historical Quarterly, vol. VI, p. 1. Constitutional questions involved in the acquisition of Louisiana: The Constitutional History of the Louisiana Purchase, by Everett Somerville Brown, 1920; Western boundary questions: A History of the Western Boundary of the Louisiana Purchase, (1819-1841), by Thomas Maitland Marshall, 1914; Diplomatic and political history: McMaster's History of the People of the United States, (1897), vols. II and III.

The letter of Thomas Jefferson to John Jay, August 14, 1785, in which he tells of sending John Paul Jones to Brest to report on the purpose of the voyage of Perouse to the coast of North America, (Writings, vol. V, p. 64) is to be read in connection with his second letter to the same correspondent, October 6, 1785, (id., p. 165), in which he indicates that the report showed "An intention to settle factories, at least for the present. However, nothing shows for what place they are destined. The conjectures are divided between New Holland and the Northwest coast of America."

The Life of John Ledyard, by Jared Sparks, Cambridge, 1828, is still the standard biography. See also, Appleton's Cyclopedia of American Biography, vol. III, p. 655. The quotations from Jefferson are from the Federal editions of his Works, vol. VI, VII, IX and X. The quotations from Napoleon are from Marbois, History of Louisiana, (1839) pp. 264 and 312. For details of the negotiations for the sale, see Henry Adams, History of the United States, First Administration of Jefferson, vol. II, ch. 1-3; D. C. Gilman, James Monroe, ch. 4; B. Marbois, History of Louisiana, part 2; American State Papers, Foreign Relations, vol. II, pp. 506-83.

CHAPTER X

On reaching the divide at Lemhi pass, Clark followed Salmon river to a point 52 miles below the mouth of Lemhi river; but as the course seemed impracticable, a change was made by the expedition and thence the course was north and east on the east side of the divide, and then through Lolo Pass. From Ross Hole, at the head of Bitter Root river, the party went to present day Weippe Prairie, near the Clearwater, Idaho, and then through Lolo Pass.

The Lewis and Clark camp on the north side of the Columbia river, November 7, was just below McGowans, and above Chinook Point, or Port Columbia. From there Clark visited Cape Disappointment and the ocean beach, as far north as Long Beach.

The latest work on Sacajawea is Grace Raymond Hebard's Sacajawea, A Guide and Interpreter of the Lewis and Clark Expedition (1933). It shows that Sacajawea died on Shoshone reservation, Wyoming, April 9, 1884, and that she is there buried. These facts and others as to her life history were subject of controversy prior to Miss Hebard's definite biography, one theory being that Sacajawea was the person referred to in Luttig's Journal of a Fur Trading Expedition on the Upper Missouri, 1812-1813, by John C. Luttig, Clerk of the Missouri Fur Company, edited by Stella M. Drumm, 1920, where it is indicated that she died December 20, 1812, on the upper Missouri (pp. 106 and Appendix, 132). The Hebard book has a full bibliography.

CHAPTER XI

The letter of Jeremy Pinch to David Thompson, September 29, 1807, and the answer of December 26, 1807, are in the Foreign Office at London, and copies are in Dr. R. C. Clark's History of the Willamette Valley, Oregon, 1927, Appendix, pp. 838-41, with letter of A. Barclay, Secretary, Hudson's Bay Company, to Foreign Office, February 23, 1846.

Thompson noted in his Narrative of the Expedition to the Kootenae and Flat Bow Indian Countries, on the Sources of the Columbia River, under the dating August 13, 1807, that the Kootenaes had informed him that about three weeks previous Americans to the number of 42 had arrived "to settle a military post" at the confluence of southern branches of the Columbia, and that two of the Americans were men who had been with Captain Lewis; T. C. Elliott, "The Discovery of the Source of the Columbia River," Oregon Historical Quarterly, vol. XXVI, p. 23.

The establishing of Henry's Fort on Henry's Fork, a tributary of the Columbia, is mentioned by Bancroft, History of Oregon, vol. II, p. 328; Northwest Coast, vol. I, p. 511; Chittenden, American Fur Trade, vol. III, p. 974.

A good statement, in brief, of the causes of the conflict between Hudson's Bay Company and North West Company, and the terms of the coalition and reorganization, is in the Introduction to Fur Trade and Empire: George Simpson's Journal, by Frederick Merk, (1931).

The history of the North West Company, and its operations prior to the union with the rival company is best set forth in the North West Company, by Gordon Charles Davidson, (1918). Recent publication of Documents Relating to the North West Company, edited by W. S. Wallace and published by the Champlain Society, 1934, throws much light on the working of the company.

The biography of David Thompson and his explorations in the northwest: The Introduction to David Thompson's Narrative of his Explorations in Western America, edited by J. B. Tyrrell, Champlain Society, 1916; see also George W. Fuller, History of the Pacific Northwest, 1931, p. 78, and his Inland Empire of the Pacific Northwest, 1928, vol. I, pp. 147-57. T. C. Elliott has published a number of articles about Thompson and his works, one of which, "David Thompson, Pathfinder and the Columbia River," in Oregon Historical Quarterly, vol. XXVI, pp. 191-202, is especially useful as a general survey. Others of these articles are the following: "Fur Trade in the Columbia River Basin Prior to 1811," Oregon Historical Quarterly, vol. XV, pp. 241-51, and "Discovery of the Source of the Columbia River," idem, vol. XXVI, pp. 23-28.

H. M. Chittenden's American Fur Trade of the Far West, 3 vols., 1902, with maps and illustrations, is still the best general history of the fur trade in western United States, and is indispensable in the study of the approach to Oregon up the Missouri and Platte rivers.

The Travels of Jedediah Smith, 1934, by Maurice S. Sullivan, is a printing of the original Journal of the explorer, with the diary of Alexander Roderick McLeod, and some quotations from the Journal of Harrison G. Rogers. The author presented a brief sketch of Smith, but reserved for another book a more complete biography. Unfortunately the death of the author, January 31, 1935, leaves his important life work unfinished. The Journal of Rogers appeared in full in The Ashley-Smith Explorations and the Discovery of a Central Route to the Pacific, 1822-1829, by Harrison Clifford Dale, 1918; and also in part in The Splendid Wayfaring, by John G. Neihardt, 1920.

CHAPTER XII

The Winship enterprise is covered in Bancroft, Northwest Coast, vol. II, pp. 130-35. The journal of William A. Gale, Winship's assistant, therein printed is a day by day account of the efforts to found a trading post on the Columbia.

The standard work on the Astor expedition is Washington Irving's Astoria, supposed to be founded on Mr. Astor's own statements. It was first published in two volumes, 1836. Most of the information regarding the venture that comes from other sources is based on narratives of three members of the expedition, Gabriel Franchere, Narrative, published in French in 1820, and translated into English and published, New York, 1854; Ross Cox, Adventures on the Columbia, 2 vols., 1831; and Alexander Ross, Adventures of the First Settlers on the Columbia River, 1849. Ross' Fur Hunters, 2 vols., 1855, deals with the operations of the North West Company after the purchase of Astoria. The authoritative biography of Astor is John Jacob Astor, Business Man, by Kenneth W. Porter, published in two volumes by the Harvard University Press, 1931. The author had access to Astor manuscripts and business accounts that have never before been used.

In the Washington Historical Quarterly, vol. XIII, pp. 83-92, F. W. Howay has set out the various accounts of the loss of the Tonquin, and after careful analysis concludes the correct version is to be found in Franchere and Cox.

The Journal of David Thompson's trip down the Columbia river, 1811, is printed in the Oregon Historical Quarterly XV, pp. 39-63; 104-125.

CHAPTER XIII

The heroic story of Madam Dorion will be found in Franchere and Cox. Her later years were spent at French Prairie, in the Willamette valley. Her marriage to John Toupin, July 19, 1841, is recorded in the parish register of St. Paul (Oregon) Catholic church. Recently her burial place was found to be in the church at St. Louis, Oregon, and on April 7, 1935, the Oregon Chapter, Daughters of 1812, placed a bronze memorial tablet in the church.

From account books of the Pacific Fur Company, Kenneth W. Porter compiled a list of all employees of the Overland Astorians, which is printed in the Oregon Historical Quarterly, vol. XXXIV, pp. 103-112.

Documents relating to the sale of Astoria are printed in Astor and the

Oregon Country, by Grace Flandrau, published in 1926, by the Great Northern Railway, and in Oregon Historical Quarterly, vol. XXIII, pp. 43-50. A complete inventory of goods transferred to the North West Company is listed in House Document, No. 45, 17th Congress, 2nd Session. See also the Henry-Thompson Journals for activities after the sale.

CHAPTER XIV

Traits of American Indian Life and Character, by a Fur Trader, London, 1853, is attributed to Ogden, depicting scenes and adventures drawn from his own life and experiences.

"Peter Skene Ogden, Fur Trader," is the title of a biographical article by T. C. Elliott in Oregon Historical Quarterly, vol. XI, pp. 229-78. Ogden's explorations and fur trading on the Snake river, and elsewhere west of the Rocky mountains, 1824-25, are covered by an article by Frederick Merk, in Oregon Historical Quarterly, vol. XXXV, pp. 93-122. Ogden's journal of his expedition of 1825-26 is in Oregon Historical Quarterly, June, 1909; for the years 1826-29, idem, vol. XI, pp. 201-22, 355-97.

George Simpson's journal of his trip to the Columbia with Dr. McLoughlin in 1824 is printed in Fur Trade and Empire, by Frederick Merk, together with correspondence of officers of the Hudson's Bay Company relating to affairs of the company in the Columbia department. His second visit to the Pacific coast and around the world is described in Narrative of a Journey Round the World in the Years 1841 and 1842, London, 1847, (2 vols.).

It seems that Dr. John McLoughlin, a partner of North West Company, went to London, 1820, with Angus Bethune to represent that company in negotiating the union, but did not succeed in doing so. The union was later concluded with the McGillivrays and Edward Ellice, and McLoughlin was very much disconcerted with the terms of the union, but accepted a commission in Hudson's Bay Company as chief factor; see Documents Relating to the North West Company, pp. 29-30, and 482; (cited supra, in these Notes, Chapter XI).

The latest and best book on Dr. McLoughlin is Richard G. Montgomery's White Headed Eagle, (Macmillan, 1934). An earlier biography is that of F. V. Holman, Dr. John McLoughlin (1907). The former volume brings out in a readable style many newly discovered facts relating to the life and career of Doctor McLoughlin, while the Holman book is chiefly valuable for reprint of documents.

The route from Fort Vancouver to York Factory may be followed in Edward Ermatinger's York Factory Express Journal, 1827-28, published in 1912 by the Royal Society of Canada.

"Journal of the Occurrences at Nisqually House," in Washington Historical Quarterly, vol. VI, p. 180.

"Dr. McLoughlin's Last Letter" to the Hudson's Bay Company, 1845, edited by Katharine B. Judson, for American Historical Review, October, 1915, reflects his grievances and explains his policy toward Americans and his position regarding the land claim at Oregon City.

After his retirement from the Hudson's Bay Company, Dr. McLoughlin took an active part in the affairs of Oregon City and was mayor, in 1851.

CHAPTER XV

Benton had advocated settlement on the Columbia in editorials written by him and published in the St. Louis Enquirer, 1819. See also Benton's Thirty Years' View, vol. I, pp. 13-14; review of Benton's work by Fred W. Powell, Oregon Historical Quarterly, vol. XVIII, p. 14.

Floyd's career is outlined in Bourne's "Aspects of Oregon before 1840," in Oregon Historical Quarterly, vol. VI, pp. 255-75; see also Scott, Oregon Country, vol. I, p. 306. Floyd's Report of 1821 is in Annals of Congress, 16th Congress, 2nd Session, p. 946.

The latest and most complete work on Kelley is Fred Wilbur Powell's Hall J. Kelley on Oregon, which contains a collection of Kelley's published works and a number of his unpublished letters, Princeton University Press, 1932. Kelley's numerous books and pamphlets leave little to be said in favor of American settlement.

CHAPTER XVI

Green's Journal of a Tour was first published in the Missionary Herald, 1830-31; it was reprinted as a book, in 1915. See also "Green's Missionary Report on Oregon, 1829," by George V. Blue, Oregon Historical Quarterly, vol. XXX, pp. 259-71.

This excursion of Green, several years before Samuel Parker was sent overland to Oregon, derives especial interest from the light it throws on the very beginning of the missionary movement in Oregon. Although nothing resulted immediately from Green's trip it was counted in an early day as a factor in missionary effort.

There is much literature on the subject of the Indians' visit to St. Louis. See E. V. O'Hara, Pioneer Catholic History of Oregon, pp. 59-72; L. B. Palladino, Indians and Whites in the North West, 1922, pp. 8-19; C. T. Johnson (pseud. of T. C. Elliott) Evolution of a Lament; R. Rothensteiner, Flathead and Nez Perce' Delegation to St. Louis, 1921; Chittenden, American Fur Trade, vol. II, pp. 640-47, 912-25.

For sketches of the members of the Lee party see Leslie M. Scott, History of the Oregon Country, vol. I, pp. 207-28.

The principal historical sources for Lee's trip overland and the establishment of missions in Oregon are his diary, printed in Oregon Historical Quarterly, vol. XVII, and Ten Years in Oregon, 1844, by Daniel Lee and J. H. Frost, and the Mission Record Book, Oregon Historical Quarterly, vol. XXIII, pp. 233-60.

McLoughlin sent a letter March 1, 1836, to the mission, containing a donation of £26, contributed by seven members of the Hudson's Bay Company; Mission Record Book, p. 243.

The Mission Record Book, Oregon Historical Quarterly, vol. XXIII, pp. 230-66, The Methodist Annual Reports, idem, vol. XXIII, pp. 303-64, and Diary of George Gary, idem, vol. XXIV, all edited by C. H. Carey, are contemporary sources. Jason Lee, Prophet of the New Oregon, by C. J. Brosnan, 1932, is the most complete biography of Jason Lee. It is especially valuable for its presentation of original documents.

W. H. Gray says that when he was at Fort Hall he received the news of the death of Mrs. Lee. He employed Paul Richardson to carry the message on to Lee, for which he was to receive $150. A Document of the Mission Board, under date January 16, 1839, says that Lee was allowed the expense of the express; "A Document of Mission History," edited by R. M. Gatke, in Oregon Historical Quarterly, vol. XXXVI, p. 77.

At this period the United States government not infrequently subsidized Indian Mission schools, and the manuscript records of the board show that it was receiving such help for a number of its Indian missions. This fact may be the source of the statement that the mission received aid from a secret fund of the government; see Document of Mission History, above cited, p. 80.

Lee's defense of his policy is printed in Brosnan, cited above. The charges against him as drawn up by the Mission Board are printed in Document of Mission History, above cited.

For Lee's part in the Waller-McLoughlin controversy, see C. H. Carey, "Lee, Waller and McLoughlin," Oregon Historical Quarterly, vol. XXXIII, pp. 187-213.

Full accounts of the Catholic missions in the Oregon Country are printed in the annual Rapports sur les Missions du Diocese de Quebec. The Catholic ladder is described in Blanchet' Historical Sketches of the Catholic Church in Oregon, 1878, p. 85; a facsimile is reproduced in the Rapport, June, 1843, and also described in C. B. Bagley's Early Catholic Missions in Old Oregon, 1932, pp. 119-22.

Dr. Whitman kept a journal of his tour with Parker in 1835, which is printed in Oregon Historical Quarterly, vol. XXVIII, pp. 239-57.

Mrs. Whitman's journal and numerous letters to her family can be found in the Oregon Pioneer Transactions, 1891 and 1893.

No circumstance in Oregon history has given rise to so much controversy as the motive of Whitman's winter ride. In W. I. Marshall's Acquisition of Oregon the whole subject is minutely examined and the arguments of advocates of the theory that Whitman saved Oregon to the United States are refuted. E. G. Bourne in Essays in Historical Criticism analyses the "Legend of Marcus Whitman." A judicial review of authorities is in Bishop Bashford's Oregon Missions. A series of articles in the Oregonian, by H. W. Scott, are reprinted with comprehensive annotations by Leslie M. Scott in History of the Oregon Country, vol. I, pp. 223-38, 302-06.

CHAPTER XVII

Copies of all petitions and memorials presented to Congress from Oregon, 1838-48, were compiled by C. J. Pike, and are in Oregon Historical Society. Mr. Pike's study of the petitions is printed in Oregon Historical Quarterly, vol. XXXIV, 216-35.

J. Quinn Thornton, in his "History of the Provisional Government," Oregon Pioneer Transactions, 1875, gives the only details of the meeting of February 7, 1841.

The various accounts of the May 2 meeting are set out in an article by Russell B. Thomas, "Truth and Fiction of Champoeg Meeting," in Oregon Historical Quarterly, vol. XXX, pp. 218-37. See also Leslie M. Scott, "Modern Fallacies of Champoeg," Oregon Historical Quarterly, vol. XXXII, p. 213.

For biographies of the voters at Champoeg, May 2, 1843, see Caroline C. Dobbs, Men of Champoeg, 1932.

Shortess said that Abernethy wrote the Shortess petition, but refused to sign it, or to allow it to be circulated in his handwriting, for fear it would injure the mission; Evans, History of the Pacific Northwest, vol. I, p. 243.

CHAPTER XVIII

McLoughlin's letter, with an introduction by Katharine B. Judson, is printed in full in Oregon Historical Quarterly, vol. XVII, pp. 215-39.

The settlers' petition therein mentioned was presented in Congress, December 2, 1845, and was printed as House Document No. 3, 29th Congress, 1st Session. It bore the same signatures as the Canadian Address; C. J. Pike, in Oregon Historical Quarterly, vol. XXXIV, pp. 227-29.

The original French manuscript of the Canadians' address is in the Oregon Historical Society; a facsimile reproduction with copies in English and French are to be found in Oregon Historical Quarterly, vol. XIII, p. 338. For discussion of the date of the address, see R. C. Clark, "How British and American Subjects unite in a Common Government for Oregon Territory in 1844," in Oregon Historical Quarterly, vol. XIII, pp. 140-59. The authorship of the address is given by McLoughlin in a letter dated July 4, 1844; see R. C. Clark, History of the Willamette Valley, Appendix p. 798.

The original tax roll is in the Oregon Historical Society. It was printed in Oregon Historical Quarterly, vol. XXXI, pp. 11-24; see also Leslie M. Scott, "First Taxes in Oregon," in the same Quarterly, pp. 1-10.

In 1855, the sum of $4994.64 was ordered paid to Joachin Young, who professed to be the heir of Ewing Young. The documentary record of the claim is set out in Oregon Historical Quarterly, vol. XXI, pp. 197-207, and the Petition of settlers protesting against the building of the jail, p. 314.

The act under which the people were permitted to make their choice of organic laws shows the simplicity of their government. At the polling places the judges of election were required to read and explain the organic laws, with and without amendments, and the voters so instructed proceeded to vote viva voce for the instrument preferred; Organic Laws and Acts, 1845.

In the Williamson case, McLoughlin complained to the executive committee, who promptly investigated and replied that Williamson had desisted from his "insolent and rash measure," and had expressed regret for the incident. The original correspondence is in the Oregon Historical Society. McLoughlin's letter to Pelly may be found in Clark, History of the Willamette Valley, p. 813, as well as letter to Simpson relating to same incident, p. 812.

Dr. John McLoughlin's Last Letter, cited above, explains his reasons for joining the compact.

The report of Warre and Vavasour is in Oregon Historical Quarterly, March, 1909. In their final report of June 1846, they criticise the policy of McLoughlin in relation to American settlers. McLoughlin's answer to their charges is printed in Oregon Historical Quarterly, vol. XXXIII, pp. 214-29.

CHAPTER XIX

The Owyhee was in the Columbia the first time June 4-14, 1827. During most of the time on that visit, the crew was cutting spars. F. W. Howay gives an account of the two voyages of the vessel in Oregon Historical Quarterly, vol. XXXIV, pp. 324-29 and vol. XXXV, pp. 10-21.

McLoughlin's policy in returning the Japanese by way of England is shown in a letter he wrote to the Hudson's Bay Company, November 18, 1834. He says, "I might have sent them to Woahoo [Honolulu] and left them to find a passage to their own country the best way they could, but as I believe they are the first Japanese who have been in the power of the British nation, I thought the British Government would gladly avail itself of the opportunity to endeavour to open communications with the Japanese Government, and that by these men going to Great Britain they would have an opportunity of being instructed and be able to convey to their countrymen a respectable idea of the grandeur and power of the British nation."

The Owyhee and the Convoy assisted in saving some of the cargo of the William and Ann. The log of the Owyhee contains the only contemporary account extant of the loss of this ship, excepting the Hudson's Bay correspondence. Jonathan Green says he heard from Captain Thompson of the Convoy that the Indians "had not the slightest agency" in the death of the crew, but a letter from George Simpson to John McLeod, May 12, 1829, says that all on board, 26 souls, were destroyed by the Clatsops, and William Todd, writing to Edward Ermatinger, July 15, 1829, makes the same statement.

Joseph Gale's account of the building of the Star of Oregon is to be found in Oregon Pioneer Transactions, 1891, pp. 181-92.

The results of the cruise of the Sulphur and Starling were published in two volumes in 1843, which were of considerable interest in England.

For literature on the 1843 immigration, see Peter H. Burnett, Recollections of an Old Pioneer; "Diary of the Emigration of 1843," by J. W. Nesmith, in Oregon Historical Quarterly, vol. VII, pp. 329-59; Day with the Cow Column, by Jesse Applegate. The latest edition of Applegate's Day with the Cow Column, with which is printed Jesse A. Applegate's Recollections of My Boyhood, was issued by the Caxton Club, Chicago, 1934, with introduction by Joseph Schafer.

Mr. Lawrence A. McNary, with the aid of diaries and personal exploration, has been able to identify the trail of the Meek Cut-off; see his "Route of Meek Cut-off," in Oregon Historical Quarterly, vol. XXXV, pp. 1-9.

The report of Lieutenant Peel, edited by Leslie M. Scott, is in Oregon Historical Quarterly, vol. XXIX, pp. 51-76.

Some details of the wreck of the Shark, and the appearance of the settlement at Astoria at that time, are given in letters of Burr Osborn, a member of the crew, in Oregon Historical Quarterly, vol. XIV, p. 355.

PART TWO—

THROUGH THE CIVIL WAR

CHAPTER XX

INTERNATIONAL BOUNDARY SETTLEMENTS

1

BY A TREATY between the United States and Spain (the Florida treaty), in 1819, and a convention with Russia in 1824, and by a treaty between Russia and Great Britain in 1825, the northwestern boundary question was reduced to an issue between Great Britain and the United States. By the Florida treaty the northern boundary of the Spanish possessions in the United States was definitely fixed as the parallel of 42° north latitude. Our convention with Russia, which nation formerly had laid claim to the entire Pacific coast north of the Columbia river, and even as far south as 38°, determined the line of 54° 40′ north latitude, which was coincident with the most southern point of Prince of Wales island, as the southern limit of the Russian territory on this continent. The treaty between Russia and Great Britain also mentioned 54° 40′ as the starting point in delimiting the boundary between the Russian and the British possessions, significant because of the bearing at a subsequent time on the contention between Great Britain and the United States.

2

The extent of the territory originally ceded by Napoleon to the United States, known as the Louisiana purchase, was never precisely determined in any official instrument. The earliest exposition of the limits of that region, as Robert Greenhow has pointed out, is found in a royal grant made September 17, 1712, by King Louis XIV, of France, to one Antoine Crozat, bestowing the exclusive trade of these countries. This grant alluded to the "territories by us possessed, and bounded by New Mexico and by those of the English in Carolina" . . . "from the seashore to the Illinois, together with the rivers St. Philip, formerly called the Missouries river, and the St. Jerome, formerly called the Wabash [the Ohio], with all the countries, territories, lakes in the land, and the rivers emptying directly or indirectly into that part of the River St. Louis." In a concession purely for the purposes of trade, and in which the right of sovereignty was retained by the French crown, the boundaries thus indefinitely described were deemed sufficient. Later, the agreement with Crozat was suffered to lapse, and after various vicissitudes the whole indefinite region reverted to the king of France.

In 1763, by a treaty of peace at Paris, ending the Seven Years' war, between France and Spain on the one hand and Great Britain and Portugal on the other, the territory known as Louisiana was ceded to "his Catholic majesty (the king of Spain) and his successors in perpetuity," and Great Britain at the same time obtained possession of Canada, Florida and the portion of Louisiana east of a line drawn along the middle of the Mississippi, from its source to the river Iberville and thence along the middle of the Iberville, and the lakes Maurepas and Pontchartrain, to the sea. Thus the eastern line of Louisiana territory was defined, while the western and northern boundaries remained vague, as before. By the treaty of October 1, 1800, which was not made public until 17 years after the purchase of Louisiana by the United States, France and Spain made an exchange of territories, France receiving Louisiana and ceding to the Duke of Parma, a prince of Spain, certain dominions in Italy. The language of this treaty of exchange did nothing to make more definite the northern and western boundaries of Louisiana. It merely ceded "the colony or province of Louisiana, with the same extent which it now has in the hands of Spain, and which it had when France possessed it, and such as it should be, according to the treaties subsequently made between Spain and other states." The language of the Louisiana purchase treaty, 1803, is no more precise. It is: "The First Consul of the French Republic desiring to give to the United States a strong proof of his friendship doth hereby cede to the United States in the name of the French Republic forever and in full sovereignty the said territory with all its rights and appurtenances as fully and in the same manner as they have been acquired by the French Republic in virtue of the above mentioned treaty concluded with his Catholic Majesty."

3

From the time of Sir Francis Drake, 1578, Great Britain claimed the northwest coast; Spain's claim was older, and was based upon its various voyages of exploration upon the coast; Russia's began with the Bering discoveries in the north, including first discoveries of bays and harbors on the North American continent, 1728; and the United States could trace the inception of its rights to 1792, when Gray discovered the Columbia river. But, for nearly two centuries after Drake's voyage there was no clash of interests, and international rivalry may be said to have been dormant until late in the eighteenth century, when, by reason of the approach of the Russians from the north, and the activities of the British after Cook's voyage, Spain was awakened to the importance of securing her rights.

After the United States had acquired Louisiana by purchase from the French, 1803, it became necessary for us to find out just what we had obtained. For as the vendors were rather uncertain as to what went with the sale, and made no deed of conveyance with a description that indicated definite boundaries, our rights were resting largely upon ability and willingness to fight, and the possibility of war was not remote. It was particularly important to us to settle the southern part of the purchase, and we soon began negotiations with Spain to establish our rights both east and west of the Mississippi.

However, negotiations between the United States and Great Britain to determine the northern boundary of the Louisiana purchase were begun almost at the time of exchanges between this government and that of Spain concerning the extent of that territory on the south. Those with the British were interrupted by the war of 1812. A strange assumption of history, for which later investigators have found no historical warrant, had led the American commissioners, in the negotiations with Great Britain, to claim for the north boundary of the Louisiana purchase a line running along the 49th parallel of north latitude, as far west as the summit of the Rocky mountains. However, the treaty of Ghent, terminating the war of 1812 between the United States and Great Britain, left that question still open and unsettled.

The north boundary of Old Oregon was likewise uncertain. Evidence that the Madison administration had kept the question of the boundary in mind during the parleys at Ghent, is found in the confidential instructions forwarded by Secretary Monroe to the American commissioners. In his letter, dated March 22, 1814, Mr. Monroe said, after calling attention to the existence of the Astor trading post on the Columbia: "On no pretext can the British government set up a claim to territory south of the northern boundary of the United States (that is, south of 49 degrees north latitude). It is not believed that they have any claim whatever to territory on the Pacific ocean. You will, however, be careful, should a definition of boundary be attempted, not to countenance, in any manner, or in any quarter, a pretension of the British government to the territory south of that line."

As a result of this, the British commissioners were informed of the attitude of the United States toward Oregon, but, as has been stated on page 218, the treaty provided only for restoration of the Astor trading post, without saying anything about the boundary. This resulted, in due course, in delivery of the post to the United States commissioner, J. B. Prevost, October 6, 1818. The provision of the treaty, signed December 24, 1814, was in Article I, that "all territory, places and possessions, whatsoever, taken by either party from the other during the war . . . shall be restored without delay."

In the course of these negotiations, the British and American commissioners had each submitted a tentative draft of an article as to the northern boundary of the Louisiana purchase. The British commissioner insisted, also, upon rights of navigation of the Mississippi river, to which the Americans were unwilling to assent. Both had proposed the line of 49° from the Lake of the Woods westward as far as the respective territories extended. But the British proposed that the line should end at the Rocky mountains, and not run to the northwest coast of America, on the theory that the United States had no title west of the Louisiana purchase. On this rock the commissioners split. The boundary therefore was not determined when the peace was concluded.

4

Restoration of what remained of old Fort Astoria was almost coincident, however, with agreement on the treaty providing for joint occupancy of the Oregon territory to cover a period of 10 years. This treaty, under date October 20, 1818, fixed also the northern boundary of the Louisiana purchase as the 49th degree of north latitude, from the Lake of the Woods to the Stony [Rocky] mountains, just as the commissioners at Ghent had unsuccessfully attempted to do. The American commissioners made a proposal that the 49th parallel be used for the boundary as far west as the Pacific ocean, and this demand became an offset to the British efforts to obtain free navigation of the Mississippi.

Resulting compromise established the boundary, as far west as the Stony mountains only. The British demands for rights of navigation on the Mississippi were dropped during the negotiations.

In the course of the discussion, the American representatives, Richard Rush and Albert Gallatin, made no claim that the United States had a perfect right to the region west of the Rocky mountains, but contented themselves with insisting that our claim was at least as good as that of Great Britain. The British here developed for the first time the theory that the Columbia river was the most convenient boundary that could be adopted, and urged that no line would be satisfactory that did not give the British government the right to a harbor at the mouth of the Columbia, in common with the United States. Thus, the issue of free river navigation was transferred from the Mississippi to the Columbia, and, no agreement as to this being possible, joint occupancy was resorted to as a temporary expedient.

5

Meanwhile, 1818, the United States requested the government of Spain to fix the northern boundary of her possessions from the Rocky mountains to the Pacific ocean, the treaty of joint occupancy with Great Britain having expressly disclaimed intent to prejudice the rights or claims of other nations. Negotiations with Spain, carried on at Washington, embraced important issues relating to Florida, and resulted in the so-called Florida, or Washington, treaty of February 22, 1819, which fixed the northern boundary of the Spanish possessions in western North America at the 42nd parallel of north latitude, the parallel which, where applicable, now constitutes the southern boundary of the state of Oregon and the northern boundary of California. Under this treaty, furthermore, as the United States contended in subsequent negotiations with Great Britain, any rights which Spain might have possessed, as the result of its early voyages and discoveries, to the northwestern region, passed to the United States. Spain's willingness to concede the Oregon boundary at 42 degrees was due to her desire to clear up her title in the region of Texas, American claims having previously embraced all the territory as far south as the Rio del Norte [Rio Grande]. Cession of the Spanish claims to Oregon was obtained, therefore, at the expense of relinquishment of American claims on Texas, more or less intangible.

Title of the United States to the Oregon Country was greatly strengthened by the treaty with Spain. While its essential provisions, as viewed by the statesmen of both countries at that time, were those that covered the cession of the Floridas, and the release of Spanish claims upon the southeast corner of what is now the United States, it turned out that the remaining part of the treaty that dealt with the Oregon south boundary was quite as important to the welfare of the United States. It was due to the farsightedness and firmness of John Quincy Adams, secretary of state, that the Spanish title and color of right to the vast domain in the far northwest, comprising the present states of Oregon, Idaho and Washington, with parts of Montana and Wyoming, was included in the treaty.

6

After the sale of Louisiana to the French, and then the resale of that section to the United States, 1803, the acquisition of the Floridas had become the cherished purpose of the authorities at Washington. But, the far away region on the Pacific, west of the Louisiana purchase, claimed by the United States by virtue of the discovery of the Columbia river and the settlement at Astoria, was with almost equal show of right claimed by Great Britain through discovery, exploration and settlement, as well as by relinquishment of Russia under treaty. The acquisition of the Spanish claim of title to Oregon, therefore, based upon early exploration of the coast, was a matter of great importance to the United States, although that fact was not generally recognized at the time, by our statesmen.

7

It is of interest to note that, at the early stage of the discussion that resulted in the Florida treaty, the Spanish foreign minister proposed that Spain cede the Floridas in return for a general release of all rights that the United States owned or claimed west of the Mississippi, from source to the Gulf, which if agreed upon, would have restored to Spain the Louisiana purchase, would have forever shut the United States from the Oregon Country, and would have prevented her expansion to the Pacific ocean. This proposal, of course, was promptly rejected. The negotiations assumed a stormy aspect by reason of encouragement given by the United States, at about this period, to the aspirations of rebellious Spanish colonies in South America, particularly Buenos Aires, which wanted independence and sought recognition by the United States. Privateers outfitted to prey upon Spanish commerce had been using ports of the United States. Complications arose, also, by reason of General Jackson's operations within the Floridas in prosecuting the Seminole Indian war. The friction between the two nations had reached a point that would, perhaps, have meant actual war, had it not been for Spain's impoverished condition at the time. John Quincy Adams, secretary of state, handled the diplomatic negotiations with signal skill and ability, and his persistence led him finally to obtaining terms more favorable than would have been required by President Monroe and others of his cabinet.

8

October, 1818, the Spanish offered the Missouri river to its source as the western boundary of the northern part of Louisiana, and Adams countered with an offer following the Sabine, the Red river, and then 41° north latitude to the Pacific ocean, but this not being accepted, was withdrawn. February 1, 1819, the Spanish minister, Louis De Onis, wrote: "I propose to you, that, drawing the boundary line from the gulf of Mexico by the river Sabine, as laid down by you, it shall follow the course of that river to its source; thence, by a line due west, till it strikes the source of the river San Clemente, or Multnomah, in latitude 41°, and along that river to the Pacific ocean; the whole agreeably to Melish's map." In the project of a treaty which De Onis offered to Adams February 9, 1819, a further concession was made. This had already been communicated by the French minister to Adams, who records in his Memoirs (vol. IV, page 244) that "the President was much inclined to accept this line; but I think it would not be acceptable to the nation, and if Onis intends to conclude at all, we can obtain better." February 11, Monroe declared decidedly for agreeing to 100° of longitude and 43° of latitude and taking the middle of the rivers, Arkansas, Red and Multnomah. The other members of the administration all inclined the same way, but Adams was convinced that more might be obtained by adhering steadily to our demands. Both proposals were rejected by Adams and the line of 42° north to the ocean was subsequently adopted as a compromise. The assumption that a line drawn due west from the source of the Arkansas river would encounter the Multnomah [Willamette], indicates the unreliability of maps upon which the negotiators were then forced to depend.

9

The Spanish minister, De Onis, was finally brought to terms. He and Adams signed and sealed the counterparts of the famous treaty. It carried the date of Washington's birthday, in the year 1819, thus closing negotiations between Spain and the United States that had more or less covered a period of twenty years. The boundary line between the two countries west of the Mississippi was made to "begin on the Gulf of Mexico, at the mouth of the river Sabine, in the sea, continuing along the western bank of that river, to the 32° latitude where it strikes the Rio Roxo, westward to the degree of longitude 100 west from London and 23 from Washington; thence crossing the Red River, and running thence, by a line due north, to the river Arkansas to its source, in latitude 42° north; and thence by that parallel of latitude, to the South Sea [Pacific ocean]." The line between California and Oregon still remains on the line of 42° north latitude, as defined in this treaty. The United States received the Floridas in consideration of a settlement of disputed claims of her citizens to an amount of not more than $5,000,000 while the Spanish claims of similar character were expunged. Spain's necessities forced her to accept terms most unpalatable.

With pardonable pride Adams entered in his diary, under date February 22, 1819, a triumphant summary of these facts, in the course of which occurs this passage: "The acknowledgment of a definite line of boundary to the South Sea forms a great epoch in our history. The first proposal of it in this negotiation was my own and I trust it is now secured beyond the reach of revocation. It was not even among our claims by the treaty of independence with Great Britain. It was not among our pretensions under the purchase of Louisiana—for that gave us only the range of the Mississippi and its waters. I first introduced it in the written proposal of 31st October last, after having discussed it verbally with De Onis and De Neuville. It is the only peculiar and approp-

riate right acquired by this treaty, in the event of its ratification."
Adams was elated with his success, and realized its importance
to the nation in the years to come. The treaty, however, was not
promptly ratified. In fact, it met opposition in both countries. In
the American senate, Benton expressed regret that the boundary
had not been extended much further westward into Texas; and
Jefferson, in his retirement at Monticello, was unalterably opposed to it on similar grounds. Clay opposed it as fixing a new
and arbitrary line in the southwest, with a large cession of territory to Spain. Adams alone seems to have grasped the importance of the provision that had the effect of surrendering to the
United States Spain's claims to the Oregon Country, an empire in
itself. The treaty was ratified at Madrid, October 24, 1820, from
which date it became effective.

To most statesmen of that day a vision of the future upon the
Pacific coast was not possible. The great consideration with them
seemed to be the settlement of the irritating questions with Spain
arising upon the lower Mississippi, and on the southern border.
To some, the acquisition of new southern territories out of which
slave-holding states might, in the course of time, be developed,
appeared to be the vital question, while others would have been
interested in seeing our pretensions in the direction of Texas and
Mexico strengthened.   But, to John Quincy Adams alone is the
credit due for securing to posterity the valuable rights that Spain
claimed by reason of centuries of exploration and discovery, west
of the Rocky mountains and north of the California line. It was
due to him that the rights of the United States, whatever they
were, by discovery and settlement upon the Columbia river, and
by the restoration by Great Britain of Astoria at the close of the
war of 1812, gained new strength, through the treaty of Florida
of 1819.

10

The rival pretensions of another nation, Russia, remained to be
disposed of before the Oregon boundary between the United
States and Great Britain was capable of final adjustment. Diplomatic relations between the United States and Russia had been
first established, 1808, and, almost immediately afterward, John
Quincy Adams, who was then American minister to St. Petersburg, had called attention to the desirability of fixing a limit to

Russian claims on the coast. He suggested that the limit should be as little advanced southward as may be. "It appears," said he, "from what passed between Spain and Great Britain, in the affair of Nootka sound, in the year 1790, that the claims of the former extended to the 60th degree of north latitude." Russia did not then commit herself definitely on the boundary, however, and at her request the subject was dropped for the time being.

Count Romanzoff told Mr. Adams that the Russian maps "included the whole of Nootka sound and down to the mouth of the Columbia river as a part of their Russian possessions." But Romanzoff realized that the time was not propitious for negotiations of a nature capable of stirring controversy. He would defer the issue "for the sake of avoiding all possible collision, and even every pretext of uneasiness or jealousy." The Napoleonic wars were at full tide, and owing to world-wide unrest then prevailing, the count professed that the first and strongest wish of his heart was "to bring all the civilized nations to pacific dispositions, and most carefully to avoid everything which could strike out a single new spark of discord among them." Count Romanzoff apparently was seriously impressed with the desirability of postponing all negotiations that might by any possibility rekindle a conflagration, for in another conversation with Adams he alluded to the minister's proposal that a treaty of commerce be arranged, and said that he presumed that this "would meet no difficulty whatsoever, unless indeed, there shall be one which he did foresee. It was, that in the violent and convulsed state of the world at this time he hardly conceived it possible to agree upon anything that, if he might be allowed the expression, had common sense in it."

11

Thus was Oregon involved in world affairs. Preoccupation of Russia with the European cataclysm at this time, the confusion in all the governments of the old world, to which Romanzoff alluded, was reason enough for a discontinuance of all negotiations for the time being. There were other and more momentous questions for solution, and Oregon was far away. The issue was precipitated anew when, September 4, 1821, the czar published a ukase by which all of the western coast of America, north of the 51st parallel, was claimed as the exclusive possession of Russia, and when regulations were issued by the Russian-American Company, with the sanction of the czar, relative to foreign commerce on the waters bordering on the establishments of that company. One of these regulations provided: "It is therefore prohibited to all foreign vessels not only to land on the coasts and islands belonging to Russia, as stated above, but also to approach them within less than a hundred Italian miles." "The transgressor's vessel," it continued, "is subject to confiscation, along with the whole cargo." Trade with the natives was also interdicted.

To this, John Quincy Adams, who had now become American secretary of state, and whose familiarity with the questions relating to the Pacific coast made him wide awake to the importance of the issue, replied, February 16, 1822, that the president "has seen with surprise, in this edict, the assertion of a territorial claim on the part of Russia extending to the 51st degree of north latitude on this continent." In the negotiations that ensued, Russia made formal claim to title by discovery, the voyages of Bering, 1728 and 1742, particularly being mentioned. To the contention of the czar's government that Captain Cook had admitted the existence of Russian establishments at Ounalaska, however, the American reply was that, according to Captain Cook's own account, the principal person at this settlement, Ismaeloff, and other Russians whom he met there, "affirmed that they knew nothing of the continent of America to the northward." The United States claimed that it had all of Spain's rights, and contended that discovery, or settlement, of an island conveyed no title to an adjacent mainland, and that Russia, having been long previously informed of the claims of Spain beyond 60° north latitude, had not protested them, but, on the contrary, had given assurance that "it was extremely sorry that the repeated orders issued to prevent the subjects of Russia from violating, in the smallest degree, the territory belonging to another power, should have been disobeyed." Thus it will be seen that within two years after the treaty of Florida the United States was asserting rights in the Pacific as successor to Spain and as the owner of what Spain's discoveries justified.

12

At the time of the attempted settlement of the Nootka sound controversy, June, 1794, it had been ascertained that the extremest eastern or southern Russian settlement on the northwest coast was in latitude 60° north. But now in dealing with the United

States the assertion was made by Russia that the treaty of 1819 between the United States and Spain conveyed only the "rights and pretensions of Spain to the territories to east and to the north of the boundary line." At one stage the Russian negotiators had asserted that "in assigning for limits . . . the 51st degree of latitude," they "had only made a moderate use of an incontestable right." Russia, insisting that it had held possession as far as 59°, said that the line of 51° was therefore no more than a mean point between New Archangel (57°) and the American colony on the Columbia.

But by gradual stages the Russian pretensions were modified and agreement was approached. Secretary Adams, March 30, 1822, firmly declined to recognize the Russian territorial claims, and noted that the parallel of 51 degrees had been fixed as equidistant between New Archangel and the mouth of the Columbia river, but, in answer to this, he called attention to the old grant made to the Russian-American Company by the czar, fixing the limit of 55 degrees. "The right of citizens of the United States," said Mr. Adams, "to hold commerce with the aboriginal natives of the northwest coast of America, even in arms and munitions of war, is as clear and indisputable as that of navigating the seas." However, he gave assurance of willingness to listen to any specific complaint of transactions which, by the ordinary laws and usages of nations, the United States was bound either to restrain or punish.

13

December 2, 1823, President Monroe, in his message to congress, in which he enunciated the now famous Monroe doctrine, said that Russia had made proposals to the United States and Great Britain for an amicable adjustment of the "respective rights and interests of the United States on the northwest coast of this continent." He added, thus extending the Monroe doctrine to the northwest coast: "In the discussions to which this interest has given rise and in the arrangements by which they may terminate, the occasion has been deemed proper for asserting, as a principle in which the rights and interests of the United States are involved, that the American continents, by the free and independent condition which they have assumed and maintain, are henceforth not to be considered as subjects for colonization by any European powers."

Preliminary inquiries were now made by the United States with a view to joint action by this nation and Great Britain in carrying on the further negotiations with Russia, concerning various issues then in controversy. But Great Britain, while frankly regarding the Russian claims as extravagant, and as appearing "to have been adopted more in deference to the recommendations of Russian trading companies on the Pacific than from a studied policy, avoided recognition of the new American state policy announced in Monroe's message, and preferred to conduct negotiations with Russia separately. George Canning, the British secretary for foreign affairs, declined to instruct the British minister at St. Petersburg to treat jointly with the representative of the United States. Informing the state department at Washington of this decision, Richard Rush, our minister at London, wrote: "The resumption of its original course by this government [of Great Britain] has arisen chiefly from the principle which our government has adopted, of not considering the American continents as subjects for future colonization by any of the European powers—a principle to which Great Britain does not accede."

14

Joint occupancy of the northwest country by the three nations —the United States, Great Britain and Russia—was then proposed by Adams in the course of the negotiations. The arrangement would have established zones. The exceptional situation of the United States by reason of location was pointed out in a letter from Adams to our Minister Middleton at St. Petersburg, July 22, 1823, in which Adams stated that the American government considered its rights from the 42nd to the 49th parallels of north latitude "as unquestionable, being founded, first on acquisition . . . of all the rights of Spain; second, by the discovery of the Columbia river, first by sea, at its mouth, and then by land, by Lewis and Clark; and third, by the settlement at its mouth, in 1811." "The territory," he wrote, "is to the United States of an importance, which no possession in North America can be of to any European nation, not only as it is but the continuity of these possessions from the Atlantic to the Pacific ocean, but as it offers their inhabitants the means of establishing hereafter water communications from the one to the other." Mr. Middleton was advised that the United States would be willing to agree to 55° as the line of demarcation of Russian rights, apart from the issue of trade with the natives.

Adams transmitted a copy of this letter of instruction to Rush, at London, as a guide to him, and Rush then proposed to Canning a treaty, stipulating that Great Britain should permit "no settlement by any of her subjects on the northwest coast of America, either south of the 51st degree of latitude, or north of the 55th degree; the United States stipulating that none should be made by their citizens north of the 51st degree. Rush supplemented this proposal with a statement that "these limits were supposed to be sufficient to secure to Great Britain all the benefits to be derived from the settlements of her North West and Hudson's Bay companies on the northwest coast, and were indicated with that view." But the answer of the British negotiators was that they "consider the whole of the unoccupied parts of America as being open to her future settlements in like manner as heretofore. They included within these parts, as well that portion of the northwest coast lying between the 42nd and 51st degrees as any other parts.

15

The tripartite occupancy proposal proved unacceptable to the British government, and subsequent negotiations with Russia were carried on by the United States and Great Britain separately. A convention, finally perfected between the United States and Russia, was formally concluded April 17, 1824, and was proclaimed January 12, 1825. The gist of it is contained in Article III, as follows: "It is moreover agreed that, hereafter, there shall not be formed by the citizens of the United States, or under the authority of the said states, any establishment upon the northwest coast of America, nor in any of the islands adjacent, to the north of 54° 40′ of north latitude; and that, in the same manner, there shall be none formed by Russian subjects, or under the authority of Russia, south of the same parallel."

Great Britain and Russia, continuing their separate negotiations, completed a treaty, which was signed at St. Petersburg, February 16, 1825, by which they established a joint boundary line, which began with 54° 40′ of north latitude on the south, the southernmost point of Prince of Wales island, and extended north along the ridge of the watershed of the coast mountains, with a provision that the distance from the coast should be no greater at any point than 10 marine leagues. It was agreed that no establishments should be set up by either party to the negotiations within the territorial limits of the other.

16

After this, for some time, nothing was done to call attention to Oregon. The region was not only remote, but almost uncharted. The intervening country had not been settled, and there was no public demand for further territorial expansion. However, the activity of John Floyd and others at Washington, in the decade of the 20's, as we have seen, led to some revival of interest, as the time approached for renewal of the joint occupancy convention with Great Britain, due to expire in 1828.

Negotiations which led to such extension, were important principally because they stiffened claims of both nations. The general provisions of the convention of 1818, were continued, but, instead of fixing a definite period, the new agreement provided that the arrangement would continue until terminated by either government on twelve months' notice. This agreement was concluded, at London, August 6, 1827, and here the issue was permitted to rest, so far as official action was concerned, until the fourth decade of the century, when natural forces, which had meanwhile been operating steadily, created a new crisis.

It is interesting to note the play of minor influences that, aside from the formal proceedings shown in the records, were shaping the course of events. Stratford Canning, British minister to the United States, conceived a violent dislike for, or at least an unsympathetic misunderstanding of, the open methods by which representatives of a democracy made known their views on delicate diplomatic questions, in debate upon the floor of congress. There are entries in the Memoirs of John Quincy Adams which indicate that there were stormy conversations between Stratford Canning and the American secretary of state on the subject of the northwest coast, conversations conducted in a temper not calculated to smooth the way for future diplomatic parleys. The tone of these conversations, rather than the substance of them, seems to have been provocative. Adams had a sharp tongue, and Canning was disturbed by the discussions in congress, kept alive by Floyd, upon the question of occupying the coast and territory adjacent to the Columbia river. For illustration, Canning called on Adams, January 26, 1821, to say that, as Adams recounts the interview, "having been some days since present at a debate in the house of representatives, he had heard some observations made by Mr. Nelson, of Virginia, importing a design in the government of this country to form some new settlement on the South sea; that he should not particularly have noticed this but that in the National Intelligencer of this morning, a paper generally considered as partaking in some sort of an official character, there was a publication signed by Mr. Eaton, a member of the senate, which was a part of the executive government, and which disclosed an avowed project for such a settlement on the Pacific ocean." Canning had called, he said, "to inquire as to the intentions of the government in that respect." Adams replied that "it was very probable that our settlement at the mouth of the Columbia would at no remote period be increased." Canning then protested that such a settlement would be a direct violation of the convention of joint occupancy of 1818, which, however, Adams did not concede.

We have the version of the other party to this conversation in a long letter written by Canning himself to Lord Castlereagh, the British foreign minister. He says he called upon the secretary of state about the bill then pending in congress introduced by Dr. John Floyd of Virginia, requiring and authorizing the president of the United States to occupy that portion of the territory of the United States on the waters of the Columbia river. Mr. Canning asked Mr. Adams as to the intentions of the United States. He says in his letter: "Mr. Adams replied in the most determined and acrimonious tones that the United States did probably mean to make a settlement on the Columbia and that they had a perfect right to do so, the territory being their own." Being asked if this answer could be said to come from the government, Mr. Adams replied with increased asperity in the affirmative. Canning adds that "he seemed determined to consider my interference respecting the Columbia as offensive and unwarranted."

Regarding Great Britain's position in 1818, which was mentioned by the British minister, Adams said that he considered the claim then put forward as "a mere chicaine of the moment." "What more," he exclaimed, "would England grasp at? Could it be worth while to make a serious question of an object so trifling as the possession of the Columbia? What would be the thought in England if Mr. Rush were to address the secretary of state on the occasion of a regiment being destined for New South Wales, or the Shetland islands? The United States had an undoubted right to settle wherever they pleased on the shore of the Pacific without being molested by the English government and he really thought they were at least to be left unmolested on their own continent of North America."

In a letter to Charles Bagot, March 30, 1823, Canning noted that the pending bill, "though ultimately set aside, made progress chiefly through the support which was given to it by members connected with the interests of commerce and the Pacific whale fishing." "Nor should I be surprised," he added with considerable perspicacity, as subsequent events were to prove, "if it were to meet with better success another year. Colonel Benton . . . made an abortive attempt to set the question on its legs in the senate." The attitude of the British representatives in this country was in general one of patronizing tolerance of the new republic. The conduct of Charles Bagot, who was in Washington during the negotiations for the restoration of Astoria, while officially correct, was tempered by his private views. In letters home he caricatured President Madison, expressed irritation over the climate ("a pint of American summer," he once wrote, "would thaw all Europe in ten minutes"), and predicted that "this will not be a great nation," on the ground that a "government founded on Jacobinical principles is an absurdity." He described Monroe as a "man altogether of a foxy appearance," who "has been made king of these parts." A man holding these views, it may reasonably be supposed, did not contribute to an early friendly understanding between the nations.

17

In 1824, while the Russian negotiations were pending at St. Petersburg, Rush, who was at London, acting on specific instructions from Washington, was endeavoring to secure a settlement with Great Britain of the northwest boundary. In this, he was somewhat embarrassed by publication of the report of the select committee of the house of representatives which embodied the letter from Brig.-Gen. Thomas S. Jesup, in which that officer had given it as his opinion that "the possession and military command of the Columbia" was "necessary not only to the protection of the fur trade, but to the security of our frontier." General Jesup had mentioned the presence in this western region of "numerous powerful and warlike Indian nations," most of whom communicated, "either with the British to the north and west, or the Spaniards to the south," and had intimated that in the event of war if measures were adopted to secure the cooperation of those Indians, "they, with the aid of a few small garrisons, would not only afford ample protection for that entire line, but would become the scourge of our enemies." A sentence in the letter of this doughty warrior, however, which was particularly disturbing to the peace of mind of British statesmen, was: "They [the proposed military posts] would afford present protection to our traders, and, at the expiration of the privilege granted to British subjects to trade on the waters of the Columbia, would enable us to remove them from our territory and secure the whole trade to our own citizens."

London negotiations of this period were conducted by Rush, for the United States, and by William Huskisson and Stratford Canning, for Great Britain, and covered a number of issues, including the northeastern boundary, admission of United States consuls to British colonial ports, and the Newfoundland fisheries. At the 12th conference of the series, Rush presented, April 2, 1824, the proposal of the United States for continuance of the treaty occupancy, with the proviso that the nations refrain from making settlements north and south, respectively, of the parallel of 51 degrees. The British plenipotentiaries made a counter proposal, July 13, 1824, that the boundary be extended westward from the Rocky mountains along the parallel of 49° to the point where that parallel crosses the northeastermost branch of the Columbia, thence down the Columbia to the sea, navigation of the river being perpetually free to both nations. This proposal was made in deference to what was thought to be the wishes of Hudson's Bay Company. As a matter of fact, Canning had later from Sir John H. Pelly, the London governor of the company (December 9, 1825), the suggestion that the boundary should start from the point where the 49th parallel crosses the Rocky mountains and follow the summit of the mountains southward to the place where Lewis and Clark crossed the mountains, in latitude 46° 42', thence westerly along the Lewis river to the Columbia, thence to the sea.

This was the first offer of the Columbia as the boundary, but there can be little doubt that British claims for some time previous would have been satisfied with the Columbia as the boundary, and certain it is that from this time forward British aspirations really went no further. But a deadlock had now been reached, and the plenipotentiaries dropped for the present any further negotiations.

18

The 1824 attempt to adjust differences failed, as in 1818, but produced, at least, a somewhat better understanding of the issues. The claims of the United States were asserted to include all the region between the parallels of 42 and 51 degrees, on the ground of discovery of the Columbia river, by Gray, at its mouth, and by Lewis and Clark at one of its sources; of effective settlement at its mouth by Astor; and by acquisition of the Spanish title through the Florida treaty of 1819. In rejecting a subsequent British counter proposal, Rush expressed a willingness on the part of his government to recede to the 49th parallel from the mountains to the sea. He then "desired it to be understood that this was the extreme limit" to which he was authorized to go and "that, in being willing to make this change" he, too, "considered the United States as abating their rights, in the hope of being able to put an end to all conflict of claims between the two nations to the coast and country in dispute."

19

George Canning, British foreign secretary from 1822 until 1827, felt keenly the mistake of restoring Astoria, which he had strongly condemned, and which he was determined to retrieve if possible. He foresaw, more clearly than many of his contemporaries, the possible future relation of the western coast of America to the oriental trade. When he formulated the policy of his government, therefore, he supported it with great pertinacity. A letter of instruction which he wrote to the British commissioners, May 21, 1824, laid out the pathway not only during his term of office, but for more than a decade afterward. He insisted that the terms offered by the American government were little calculated to satisfy the claims of Great Britain, even when those claims were reduced within the narrowest compass prescribed by the honor and just interests of the country. In thus introducing the suggestion that national honor hung upon the outcome of the negotiations, Canning erected another obstacle to approach of the issue. His able review of the British arguments, and his analysis of the historical aspects of the controversy, served as a text book for his successors, and made it difficult for any of them to abate the claims put forward by him. He characterized the American claims as "not less extravagant in regard to territorial sovereignty than those which were previously advanced by Russia with respect to maritime jurisdiction." Conceding that "an early settlement of conflicting claims might well be purchased by a reasonable concession on either side," he contended that in exchange for abandonment by Great Britain of her title to the whole coast between the parallels of 42 and 51 degrees the United States offered no quid pro quo. He expressly denied the right of the United States to rely on a series of claims. Either, he said, the American title rested on its succession to France in the possession of Louisiana, or as the representative of Spain by virtue of its last treaty with that power, or in the American "underived character, as discoverers or occupants of that territory." "It could not be tolerated," he said, "that the defect of any one of these titles should be supplied by arguments deduced from the other two."

Canning, on behalf of Great Britain, contested the claim of priority through Spain's discovery, advancing the contention that Sir Francis Drake had "received from the native authorities" in the region north of the Spanish settlements, "a voluntary submission of that country to the reigning sovereign of England." However, he gave even more weight to the proposition that "all question of title derived from Spanish discoveries north of San Francisco was set at rest by the treaty concluded with Spain in October, 1790, [the Nootka sound convention]." From this, which Canning viewed as a victory for British policy, won at the risk of war, he was unwilling to recede.

He also disputed the claim to prior discovery by Gray, which he characterized as "the casual arrival of a trading vessel at an intermediate point of the coast, other parts of which on both sides, if not the particular spot so visited, had been long before known, examined and frequented." This, he said, might not be "put in competition with the expensive operations and laborious surveys executed at the charge of the British nation, in the years 1777 and 1778 under the direction of Cook and Clerke, and in 1792, under that of Vancouver." "It was not," he added, alluding to the Lewis and Clark expedition, "until 10 years, at least, after the mouth of the Columbia had been surveyed by Lieutenant Broughton, by order of the last-mentioned navigator, that an exploring party, commissioned by the American government, penetrated to the shores of that river." Next, Canning held the title of Great Britain by right of occupancy to be superior to that of the United States, asserting that the only establishment formed west of the Rocky mountains was that of the Astorians, which had been made over by voluntary agreement to a British company, and which had been "nominally given back to the Americans by order of His Majesty's government, on a liberal construction of the first article of the treaty of Ghent, but under an express reservation of the territorial claim."

In renouncing all claim to the region between the middle of the entrance of the Columbia river and the Spanish territories on the south, said Canning, Great Britain would also surrender a portion of the interior territory already occupied by British traders, but he conceived "that we shall obtain a satisfactory return for these concessions, by securing the only point of substantial interest . . . the undisputed possession of the whole country on the right bank of the upper Columbia and a free issue for the produce by the channel of that river." He would consent, however, to a continuance of temporary occupancy for 10 years. He added that "an agreement founded on mutual convenience will naturally supersede the necessity of recurring to first principles."

20

Declarations, pro and con, from which neither side would recede, having put an end to the possibility of adjustment, the issue remained unsettled for another two years. Meanwhile, President Monroe, in his last message to congress, December 7, 1824, recommended the establishment of a military post at the mouth of the Columbia river, or at some point in that quarter within our acknowledged limits. "This," he said, "would afford protection to every interest, and have a tendency to conciliate the tribes of the northwest with whom our trade is extensive." An appropriation sufficient to authorize the employment of a frigate to survey the mouth of the Columbia was recommended. President John Quincy Adams, in his first annual message, December 6, 1825, said that "the River of the West, first fully discovered and navigated by a countryman of our own, still bears the name of the ship in which he ascended its waters, and claims the protection of our armed national flag at its mouth."

Presidential messages evoked two reports from a select committee of the house of representatives, of which committee Baylies, of Massachusetts, was chairman, which described the Oregon Country in great detail. The second report was accompanied by a bill for carrying the recommendations into effect. This bill was laid on the table by the house, but it was an indication of a development of national interest in Oregon. This second report, dated May 15, 1826, reviewed the history of exploration and settlement, and reached the conclusion that the United States "have an incontestable claim to this coast, from the 42nd parallel of latitude, north, nearly to the mouth of the strait called on the map the strait of Juan de Fuca . . . and including a part of the region called New Caledonia, extending on the north beyond the 49th parallel of latitude; and that they have a better title than any other nation to the countries watered by the strait of de Fuca and the waters themselves." The Baylies report asserted that the offer of Mr. Rush, to continue the boundary along the 49th parallel of latitude, from the Rocky mountains to the ocean, was as great a concession as would be compatible with our interests, our honor, or our rights. And so, national honor was now invoked by both countries.

The committee was not content, however, with a mere exposition of the issue, but indulged in the incidental pastime of "twisting the British lion's tail," popular in some circles even in that early day. British domination of the commerce of the world was held up as the aim of British statesmen, adopting "no policy from caprice or vanity," but as the product of a "system of wise and sagacious projects, to check, to influence, and to control all nations, by means of her navy and her commerce; in prosperity and in adversity she has pursued this grand design, and with an energy and perseverance which does infinite credit to her political sagacity and foresight." Great Britain's achievements were reviewed. "What then," asked the committee, "remains to enable her to encompass the globe? Columbia river and DeFuca's strait! Possessed of these, she will soon plant her standards on every island in the Pacifick ocean." The report called to action. "The indifference of America," it concluded by saying, "stimulates the cupidity of Great Britain. Our daily neglect weakens our claim, and strengthens hers; and the day will soon arrive when her title to this territory will be better than ours, unless it is earnestly and speedily enforced."

The report moved George Canning to write to the Earl of Liverpool, July 14, 1826: "After such language as that of the committee of the H. of Representatives, it is impossible to suppose that we can tide over the Columbia, or can make ourselves the illusion that there is any other alternative than either to maintain our claims, or to yield them with our eyes wide open." Albert Gallatin, as special commissioner from the United States to London, was made aware both of the stiffening of opposition at home, to concessions of any kind, and of the increase of determination in the attitude of the British government. Hudson's Bay Company's standing and influence, meanwhile, had been fortified by the consolidation with the North West Company. This merger had been accompanied by extension of the jurisdiction of the courts of upper Canada over the region west of the Rocky mountains. Sir George Simpson had made his journey to the west, which had resulted in the founding of Fort Vancouver, 1825. Americans, on their part, had done nothing toward effecting settlement, or recovering possession. The agitation that had been begun by Floyd, Baylies, Benton and a few others, in the second decade of the century, would not bear fruit until 10 years later. Jason Lee, it will be remembered, did not reach Oregon, as its first missionary, until 1834. Slender as was the British claim to prior settlement, based on establishment of factories exclusively for trade with the Indians, on the American side there was not even so much to hold possession, or to fortify the arguments of our diplomats.

21

Negotiations were again begun, 1826. A further declaration of the line of 49 degrees, which was to rise later to embarrass President Polk in fulfillment of the "Fifty-four Forty or Fight" slogan of the campaign of 1844, was made by Gallatin in his reply to the first proposal of new British commissioners. These commissioners repeated the offer made to Rush, 1824, of the line of 49 degrees from the Rocky mountains to the Columbia river, and down the center of that stream to the sea, with joint navigation of the river by both nations. Gallatin was acting under instructions from Henry Clay, then secretary of state, in the course of which Clay wrote, June 19, 1826: "You are then authorized to propose the annulment of the third article of the convention of 1818, and the extension of the line of the parallel of 49 from the eastern side of the Stony mountains where it now terminates, to the Pacific ocean, as the permanent boundary between the territories of the two powers in that quarter." To this Clay added: "This is our ultimatum and you may announce it. We can consent to no other line more favorable to Great Britain." It may be mentioned, in passing, that on an official map issued by the United States government, 1838, the language of the ultimatum is engraved as an inscription. The map is entitled: "Map of the United States, Territory of Oregon, West of the Rocky mountains, exhibiting various trading depots or forts occupied by the British Hudson Bay Company connected with the Western and Northwestern Fur Trade."

But Gallatin was, nevertheless, authorized by Clay to offer a concession, that, should the line of 49° cross the Columbia river or any of its tributaries at points from which they were navigable to the main stream, navigation of those rivers, should be perpetually free to the citizens of both nations. Clay proposed that the two nations engage to ascertain by experiment within 15 years whether the branches of the Columbia were navigable by boats from where the line passes them to the Columbia river, and that if it were found that they were not, the British right to navigate them should cease. Five years were to be allowed the citizens of each nation to withdraw from the other's territory.

The point was made, in support of the American offer, that if the British retained all of the region west and north of the Columbia, they would obtain all of the harbors within the strait of Juan de Fuca, while the United States, with right of access to the Columbia river only, would fare badly in the allotment of harbors. The British commissioners replied to this by conceding a detached portion of what is now known as the Olympic peninsula. They offered "the possession of Port Discovery, a most valuable harbor on the southern coast of De Fuca's inlet; and to annex thereto all that tract of country comprised within a line to be drawn from Cape Flattery, along the southern shore of De Fuca's inlet to Point Wilson, at the northwestern extremity of Admiralty inlet, from thence along the western shore of that inlet, across the entrance of Hood's inlet, to the point of land forming the northeastern extremity of said inlet; from thence along the eastern shore of that inlet to the southern extremity of the same; from thence direct to the southern point of Gray's harbor; from thence along the shore of the Pacific to Cape Flattery."

The British commissioners said that this "offer of a most excellent harbor, and an extensive tract of territory on the straits of DeFuca" constituted a "sacrifice tendered in the spirit of accommodation, and for the sake of a final adjustment of all differences, but which, having been made in this spirit, is not to be considered as in any degree recognizing the claim on the part of the United States, or as at all impairing the existing right of Great Britain over the post and territory in question."

Gallatin had also offered, tentatively, to deviate from the 49th parallel, "if on account of the geographical features of the country a deviation founded on mutual convenience was found expedient," while suggesting that "any deviation in one place to the south . . . should be compensated by an equivalent in another place to the north of that parallel." Gallatin had in view "the exchange of the southern extremity of Nootka's island [Quadra and Vancouver's], which the 49th parallel cuts in an inconvenient manner, for the whole or part of the upper branches of the Columbia river north of that parallel."

The negotiators, however, were unable to reach a settlement. What Gallatin accomplished was to obtain an extension of joint and peaceable occupation, indefinite as to term, from which either nation might withdraw on giving 12 months' notice. Viewed as a completed act, this joint occupancy now appears as an advantage gained by the United States, for if the issue were practically left to be determined by settlement, as later it was, the United States was the country from which immigration would be most likely to flow. Gallatin thus transferred the final determination of the question from the hands of statesmen to those of plainsmen and pioneers. The extension agreement was completed, August 6, 1827. George Canning, then head of the British cabinet, died August 8, two days later. The influence of his policy, however, was felt long afterward.

22

Perhaps the most striking feature of the protocols of these negotiations is the frank statement by the British plenipotentiaries, Huskisson and Addington, that "Great Britain claims no exclusive sovereignty over any portion of that territory." But here was an open challenge to the Monroe doctrine. "Her present claim," the statement continued, "not in respect to any part, but to the whole, is limited to joint occupancy, in common with other states, leaving the right of exclusive dominion in abeyance. In other words, the pretensions of the United States tend to the ejection of all other nations, and, among the rest, of Great Britain, from all right of settlement in the district claimed by the United States. The pretensions of Great Britain, on the contrary, tend to the mere maintenance of her own rights, in resistance to the exclusive character of the United States." The British commissioners made a full statement and argument, which was answered in detail by Gallatin, the respective reports being in the nature of briefs of able counsel.

The British plenipotentiaries examined the grounds upon which the claims of the United States were founded, again denying to the United States the right to supplement one right with pretensions founded upon another. "If, for example," said the British plenipotentiaries, "the title of Spain by first discovery, or the title of France as the original possessor of Louisiana, be valid, then must one or the other of those kingdoms have been the lawful possessor of that territory, at the moment when the United States claim to have discovered it. If, on the other hand, the Americans were the first discoverers, there is necessarily an end of the Spanish claim; and if priority of discovery constitutes the title, that of France falls equally to the ground." But the point upon which the British commissioners placed greatest emphasis was that Spain by the Nootka sound convention of 1790 had agreed with Great Britain that all parts of the northwest coast of America not occupied at that time by either of the contracting parties, should thenceforward be equally open to the subjects of both, for all purposes of commerce and settlement, the sovereignty remaining in abeyance. In succeeding to the rights of Spain, it was held the United States "necessarily succeeded to the limitations by which they were defined and the obligations under which they were to be exercised."

To this Gallatin replied in his counter statement that "the compact between Spain and Great Britain could only bind the parties to it, and can effect the claim of the United States so far only as it is derived from Spain. If, therefore, they have a claim in right of their own discoveries, explorations and settlements, as this cannot be impaired by the Nootka convention, it becomes indispensably necessary, in order to defeat such a claim, to show a better prior title on the part of Great Britain, derived from some other consideration than the stipulation of that convention." But, Gallatin held, the Nootka convention was, in fact, "merely of a commercial nature, and in no shape to effect the question of distinct jurisdiction and exclusive sovereignty." The contention that the treaty must have been purely of a commercial nature was important to the issue, since commercial treaties alone between Great Britain and Spain had been renewed by those nations subsequently to the war which intervened. Gallatin found it "difficult to believe, on reading those provisions and recollecting in what cause the convention originated, that any other settlements could have been contemplated than such as were connected with the commerce to be carried on with the natives." And since the right of exclusive dominion had been left in abeyance, it was contended by Gallatin, that the issue "must revive to its full extent whenever that joint occupancy may cease."

Replying to the British contention that the United States might not found its claim upon three distinct pretentions, Gallatin declared: "In different hands, the several claims would conflict one with the other. Now, united in the same power, they support each other. The possessors of Louisiana might have contended, on the ground of contiguity, for the adjacent territory on the Pacific ocean, with the discoveries of the coast and main rivers. The several discoveries of the Spanish and American navigators might separately have been considered as so many steps in the progress of discovery, and giving only imperfect claims to each party. All those various claims, from whatever considerations derived, are now brought united against the pretensions of any other nations."

Gallatin contended that the principle of contiguity, deriving force from the settlement of the northern boundary of the Louisiana purchase as the parallel of 49° north latitude, also established the American claim to the territory south of that parallel as far west as the Pacific ocean, a claim "not weakened by the fact that the British settlements west of the Stony mountains are solely due to the extension of those previously formed on the waters emptying into Hudson Bay." But he did not neglect to reassert the American claim as resulting from that which the British plenipotentiaries had designated as "proper right." "The discovery, which belongs exclusively to the United States," said Gallatin, "and in their own right, is that of the river Columbia." The continuity of the coast from the 42nd to the 48th degree of latitude having been ascertained by Quadra in 1775 and confirmed by Cook in 1778, "the object of discovery thenceforth, was that of a large river, which should open a communication into the interior of the country." The failure of Meares, and the misconception of Vancouver until informed by Gray of the existence of the bay, were recounted by Gallatin, who added: "It must again be repeated, that the sole object of discovery was 'the river,' and, coming from the sea, the mouth of the river."

Finally, Gallatin recited the exploration by Lewis and Clark, 1805, of the sources of the Columbia river, and the settlement at Astoria, 1811. With respect to the British counter claims, he denied that the trading posts of the North West Company gave title to the territory, both "because the title of the United States is considered as having been complete before any of those traders had appeared on the waters of the Columbia," and because it was "also believed, that mere factories, established solely for the purposes of trafficing with the natives . . . cannot of themselves . . . give any better title to dominion and absolute sovereignty, than similar establishments made in a civilized country."

Gallatin also looked into the future, and suggested that "the probability of the manner in which the territory west of the Rocky mountains must be settled, belongs essentially to the subject." Here he pointed out that "under whatever nominal sovereignty that country must be placed," and whatever its ultimate destinies may be, it is nearly reduced to a certainty that it will be almost exclusively peopled by the surplus population of the United States." The tone of the Gallatin counter statement was pacific. It stressed the desire of the United States to obtain a definite boundary as a means of avoiding all possibility of collision, and reminded the British negotiators that the line offered by the United States gave to Great Britain "by far the best portion of the fur trade . . . and a much greater than her proportionate share of the country, with a view to permanent settlement, if the relative geographical situation, and means of colonizing, of both parties, be taken into consideration."

23

Events in the next decade, that of the 30's, during which the Oregon Country received little attention from congress, justified the earlier contention of Gallatin that the region west of the Rocky mountains was destined to be populated most largely by citizens of the United States. First, in 1832 and 1834, the Wyeth expeditions began, and second, in 1834 and 1836, the missionary movement followed, with all that this implied as a stimulation of the imagination of the American people. Wide-spread curiosity was aroused by the missionary venture, and this was fed by publication of descriptions of the new country.

Publication of Rev. Samuel Parker's Journal, which was widely circulated, petitions to congress and numerous publications in the newspapers relating to the Oregon Country, kept alive the popular interest. Jason Lee's first memorial to congress was signed by 36 residents of the Willamette valley, including 15 French Canadian settlers, and was presented by him personally at Washington. A vivid impression of the remoteness of the missionary station from the center of government will be gained from the fact that this petition, dated March 16, 1838, was not presented to congress until January 28, 1839, when it was placed before the senate by Senator Linn. It stimulated the effort of Linn, of Representative Caleb Cushing, and a few others of a small but active minority, to obtain legislation. The people of the eastern states now had notice that their fellow countrymen in the middle west were interested, and that the few Americans then in Oregon earnestly desired the protection of the flag.

24

Linn introduced in the senate, February 7, 1838, a bill "authorizing the occupation of the Columbia or Oregon river, establishing a territory north of latitude 42 degrees, and west of the Rocky mountains, to be called Oregon Territory; authorizing the establishment of a fort on that river, and the occupation of the country by the military forces of the United States; establishing a port of entry, and requiring that the country should then be held subject to the revenue laws of the United States; with an appropriation of $50,000." In seeking to have his bill referred to the committee on military affairs, Linn suggested that there was reason to apprehend that "if this territory would be neglected, in the course of five years it would pass from our possession." Henry Clay interposed a cautious inquiry whether occupation of the country might not violate the stipulations of the existing treaty with Great Britain and give that nation cause of offense. But Linn replied that he was aware of the provisions of the treaty of joint occupancy; he desired to obtain all possible information on the subject, that the bill might be modified if found advisable, for he wished it to be as perfect as it could be. James Buchanan said that the time had come when we ought to assert our right to the Oregon Country, or abandon it forever. "We know," he said, "by information received from an agent of the government [allusion here is undoubtedly made to William A. Slacum] that the Hudson's Bay Company were establishing forts in that quarter, cutting down the timber and conveying it to market, and acquiring the allegiance of the Indian tribes, and while they had been thus proceeding, we had patiently looked on during a long period of years." Our right, said Buchanan, ought to be now asserted, but in a prudent manner. The time had come to settle this question, and there were too many such questions unsettled with the British government, already. He favored prompt assertion of the American right to the country.

The report of William A. Slacum, to which Buchanan had referred, had called attention to the topography of "Pugitt's Sound," and had urged that the point should never be abandoned. "If the United States claim, as I hope they never will," said Slacum, "at least as far as 49 degrees of north latitude . . . on the above parallel, we shall take in 'Pugitt's Sound.' In a military point of view it is of the highest importance to the United States." The Slacum report had been read in the senate, December 18, 1837, and referred to the committee on foreign relations, of which Buchanan was chairman. Consequently, Buchanan was aware of its import. Here we find still another allusion to the parallel of 49 degrees, contributing again to the circumstances that finally determined the boundary on that basis.

The years 1838 and 1839 were marked, in congress, by occasional discussions of the issue raised by Linn. This senator was as industrious as Floyd had been a decade previously. He also introduced a bill to provide for protection of the settlers on the Columbia river, and February 22, 1839, made a speech, belligerent in its tone, in which he reiterated a former prophecy that "our difficulties with Great Britain would only be adjusted by war, as the causes for hostilities were rapidly accumulating, and old sores were in a state of irritation."

25

Linn followed his bills, resolutions and requests for official information concerning Oregon, with a new bill, introduced January 8, 1841, "to authorize the adoption of measures for the occupation and settlement of the Territory of Oregon, and for extending certain portions of the laws of the United States over the same." This new bill made claim for a boundary on the line of 54° 40'. It also provided that "as soon as the boundaries of the Oregon territory are indisputably determined, one thousand acres of land shall be granted to every white male inhabitant . . . of the age of 18 and upward who shall cultivate and use the same for five consecutive years." He said in a brief speech introducing the bill: "If we have a just title to the country in dispute, it should not be abandoned to any power upon earth, nor ought we to sleep any longer upon our claims." Section 2 of this bill provided:

"That if any citizen of the United States shall within the territory or district of country lying west of the Rocky mountains, south of 54° 40' of north latitude, commit any crime, offence or misdemeanor, which, if committed elsewhere, would be punished by the laws of the United States, or if any person shall, within such part of the territory or district of country as belongs to the United States, west of the Rocky mountains, commit any such crime, offence or misdemeanor upon the property or person of any citizen of the United States, every offender on being thereof convicted, shall suffer the like punishment as is provided by the laws of the United States for the like offences, if committed within any place or district of country under the sole and exclusive jurisdiction of the United States. The trial of all offences against this act shall be in the district where the offender is apprehended, or into which he may be brought; and the supreme courts in each of the territorial districts, and the circuit courts, and other courts of the United States, of similar jurisdiction in criminal causes in each district of the United States . . . shall have, and are hereby invested with full power and authority . . . in the same manner as if such crimes, offences and misdemeanors had been committed within the bounds of their respective districts."

This Linn bill offered the first promise to the colonists of a system of American law, such as the British government had provided for its subjects when it had extended the jurisdiction of the courts of upper Canada over them and their affairs, but it will be noted that it provided a criminal code only, and still ignored the needs of settlers for a civil code.

26

Linn's view that the Oregon Country should extend as far north as 54° 40′, was shared in a report made by Lieut. Charles Wilkes to the secretary of the navy, June, 1842. Returning from the voyage of exploration, in the course of which he had advised the settlers in Oregon that the time had not yet arrived for organization of a local government, Wilkes was an ardent advocate of the rights of the United States to the whole region, on topographical grounds. He alluded to a map accompanying his report, which delineated the territory of Oregon as extending from latitude 42° north to that of 54° 40′ north, and west of the Rocky mountains. Its natural boundaries, said he, would confine it within the above geographical limits. "On the east it has the Rocky mountains running along its entire extent; on the south those of the Klamet range on the parallel of 42° and dividing it from upper California; on the west the Pacific ocean; and on the north the western trend of the Rocky mountains and the chain of lakes near and along the parallels of 54° and 55° north, dividing it from British territory, and it is remarkable that within these limits all the rivers that flow through the territory take their rise."

Wilkes then described the geography of the country in more detail. "There is no point on the coast," he said further, "where a settlement could be formed between Fraser's river, or 49° north, and the northern boundary of 54° 40′, that would be able to supply its wants." He emphasized particularly the fine harbors within the strait of Juan de Fuca, control of which, in his opinion, was requisite to peaceful possession of the interior. Wilkes also advocated prompt congressional action in the interest of future settlement by Americans. The preliminary volumes of his report were published in 1845, and had a wide circulation, greatly stimulating interest in the Oregon Country.

27

The northeastern boundary between Maine and Canada, certain fishing rights, and the issue of search and seizure on the high seas, claimed the attention of both nations, 1842, particularly because of local conflicts between residents of the disputed northeast territory. Great Britain sent Lord Ashburton to Washington as special commissioner to adjust these difficulties. He had, moreover, secret instructions to take up the Oregon question, but this was regarded as incidental to the main purpose of his mission. Tyler was then president of the United States, and Daniel Webster was secretary of state.

Little discretion was given to Ashburton by Lord Aberdeen, British secretary for foreign affairs. As to the Oregon question, he was directed to offer: (1) The line of the Columbia river from its mouth to the Lewis or Snake river, thence to the summit of the Rocky mountains. (2) The same line as laid down in the negotiations of 1824 and 1827, while Canning was directing the British foreign policy, namely, the parallel of 49° from the summit of the Rocky mountains to the northernmost branch of the Columbia river and thence to the sea, with joint free navigation of the river. He was instructed not to accept under any conditions the line of 49° from the Rocky mountains to the Pacific ocean.

28

While Webster and Ashburton were negotiating a settlement of the northeastern boundary, American statesmen were also discussing the annexation of Texas and the acquisition of that part of California lying north of the parallel of 36°, which would have given the United States the harbor of San Francisco and have mollified those who were clamoring for a port on the north Pacific coast. It was clear that Ashburton's instructions to adhere to the Canning policy permitted small hope that the Oregon boundary question would be settled through the pending negotiations, at least without involving concessions as to the northeastern boundary and the fishing rights. Neither Tyler, nor Webster, was willing to make any trade of that kind, and so Oregon was not considered in the negotiations.

The Webster - Ashburton treaty was signed in Washington, August 9, 1842, having been arrived at, as Webster afterward said, "on principles of compromise." "It would have furnished an additional cause for congratulation," wrote President Tyler in his message to congress, December 6, 1842, "if the treaty could have embraced all subjects in future to lead to a misunderstanding between the two governments. The Territory of the United States, commonly called the Oregon Territory . . . to a portion of which Great Britain lays claim, begins to attract the attention of our fellow citizens, and the tide of population which has reclaimed what was so lately unbroken wilderness, in more contiguous regions, is preparing to flow over those vast districts which stretch from the Rocky mountains to the Pacific ocean. It became manifest, at an early hour in the late negotiations that any attempt for the time being satisfactorily to determine those rights, would lead to a protracted discussion, which might embrace in its failure other more pressing matters."

This allusion to "more pressing matters" is characteristic of the official attitude toward Oregon at that time. Lord Aberdeen, writing to the British minister Fox, at Washington, October 18, 1842, began by saying, "the more important question of the disputed boundary between Her Majesty's North American provinces and the United States being thus settled," and also alluded to Ashburton's withholding discussion of the Oregon issue, because of apprehension, lest, by so doing, "the settlement of the far more important matter of the northeastern boundary should be impeded, or exposed to the hazard of failure."

29

After the Webster-Ashburton treaty had been concluded, and while Ashburton was still in the United States, Tyler and Webster conceived the idea of uniting the Oregon, Texas and California questions, with a view of obtaining for the United States the port of San Francisco, possibly in exchange for territory in the northwest. This was, perhaps, the most critical period in all the Oregon boundary negotiations for the fate of that part of the

Oregon Country lying north of the Columbia river. Webster forwarded a general outline of his plan to Edward Everett, United States minister at London. This came to be known as the "tripartite agreement." It contemplated acquisition of all of California north of the 36th parallel, in exchange for recognition of a northern boundary, beginning on the west at the strait of Juan de Fuca, running up the strait apparently to the south end of Admiralty inlet, and thence south, striking the Columbia river below Vancouver and following it to its intersection with the 49th parallel.

The advantage of acquiring the southwest and California for the United States had long been recognized. President John Quincy Adams had offered Mexico $1,000,000 for Texas, 1827; President Jackson had raised the offer to $5,000,000 in 1829, and had proposed to buy San Francisco, 1835. As negotiations now advanced the desire of American statesmen to acquire Texas and California became an important factor. Southerners wanted southern development as an offset to acquiring Oregon, and the slavery question influenced men's judgment.

American and British citizens in 1842, held large claims for indemnities against the Mexican government, which seemed unlikely to be paid, and Webster's proposal was that Mexico sell upper California to the United States, for a sum to be determined, out of which these claims should be discharged, and that Great Britain should employ its good offices to obtain Mexico's assent. This tripartite plan came to nothing. Webster's ambition to go to London as special envoy to complete it was balked by refusal of a house committee, by a vote of six to three, to agree to an appropriation to defray the cost of the mission. Great Britain was unwilling anyway to use its influence with Mexico for this purpose, and Mexico would not consider a sale of any part of its territory.

30

Linn's bill for the occupation of Oregon was passed by the senate, 1843, but was defeated in the house. Meanwhile the great westward immigration movement had begun, the large numbers, 1842 and 1843, serving to emphasize the interest of the people in a settlement of the boundary question. Meetings were held, advocating holding Oregon, as apparently there was a rumor of some purpose to give up part of the territory, or to make some trade or concessions. An "Oregon convention" was held at Cincinnati, July 4, 1843, attended by 96 delegates. This convention adopted resolutions asserting the American right to all the territory between California line and that of 54° 40′. Henry Clay's views regarding the meeting, and the objects, are fully set out in an unpublished letter, the original of which is in the possession of the New York Historical Society. It was dated June 24, 1843, and was addressed to Gen. T. Worthington, of Logan, Ohio, declining an invitation to attend the convention, and denying the expediency of immediate occupation of the Oregon Country by the authority of the government, or especially without its sanction. In this letter, he gave many reasons, and among others suggested that the nation had vast regions east of the Rocky mountains that should be developed before we thought of colonizing Oregon. While these views of Clay were shared by others, the general sentiment throughout the north favored immediate occupation.

The policy of Secretary of State Calhoun, during 1843, and early 1844, was aptly characterized by himself, later, as "masterly inactivity," but while he believed that the whole country drained by the Columbia river was destined to be populated by Americans, and therefore he was disinclined to close the negotiations by accepting 49°, there was nothing gained by the delay, as final result afterward demonstrated.

However, there was now an active demand for the vigorous assertion of American rights. The national democrat convention at Baltimore, which nominated James K. Polk for president, May 27, 1844, adopted a platform containing the following declaration: "Resolved: That our title to the whole of the territory is clear and unquestionable; that no portion of the same ought to be ceded to England, or any other power; and that the reoccupation of Oregon, and the reannexation of Texas, at the earliest practicable period, are the great American measures, which this convention recommends to the cordial support of the Democracy of the Union." A slogan of the ensuing Polk campaign was "Fifty-four Forty or Fight," an interpretation of the platform which was founded on the declaration of the Oregon convention, held in Cincinnati. Thus, the Oregon question was no longer a local question, it became a matter of interest throughout the country. Furthermore, the Polk administration was definitely charged with responsibility for Texas as well as for Oregon, and the country was facing the possibility of two foreign wars.

31

The British government saw the trend of sentiment in the United States, and again took the initiative in proposing renewal of negotiations. The first move, 1844, was made by Richard Pakenham, the new British minister, at Washington, under instructions. He wrote to our secretary of state, Upshur, February 24, that he was ready to take up the question at earliest convenience. Death of Upshur, however, interrupted the discussion for a brief period. In July, Pakenham took the subject up with the newly appointed secretary, John C. Calhoun, following it up, in August, by stating the British offer, which, in addition to previous proposals, included an offer to make free to the United States any port or ports which the United States might desire, either on Vancouver island or the mainland, south of 49°.

Calhoun rejected this offer in a statement in which he reiterated the arguments set up in previous negotiations, adding a paragraph to the effect that the claims of the United States, based on continuity, had been greatly strengthened by the rapid advance of American population.

Several resolutions directing the president to give formal notice of abrogation of the existing joint occupancy treaty were offered in congress, in that year, and the chairman of the committee on territories introduced a bill to extend the jurisdiction of the courts of Iowa over the region between the parallels of 49° and 54° 40', providing for an additional judge of Iowa, who should reside in Oregon, and granting 640 acres of land to each inhabitant. In December, 1844, after Polk had been elected, but before his inauguration, a bill for organization of a government in Oregon was introduced, but it was permitted to rest in committee, because of pending diplomatic negotiations. These measures and the increasing migration of Americans to Oregon were viewed with much concern by the British diplomats.

32

Correspondence between Lord Aberdeen, British foreign minister, and the prime minister, Sir Rober Peel, 1844, shows that these statesmen had little hope of an amicable adjustment, without submitting the controversy to arbitration. Aberdeen said that the most that could be hoped for would be to adopt the line of 49° "to the water's edge," leaving the British in possession of Vancouver island, with the northern side of the entrance to Puget sound, "and if all the harbors within the sound, and to the Columbia, inclusive, were made free to both countries, and further, if the river Columbia from the point at which it becomes navigable, to its mouth, were also made free to both," this would be a most advantageous settlement.

Peel suggested, in answer, that it might be desirable to have the Collingwood, flagship of the British naval squadron, to make a friendly visit, when she had leisure, to the Columbia. It will be recalled that the sloop Modeste, Thomas Baillie, commander, was assigned to that duty, July, 1844, and the America, J. Gordon, captain, was stationed in Puget sound, 1845.

Peel also suggested getting information from "settlers or persons connected with the Columbia, as to the practical effect on British interest, present or future which any particular arrangement with the United States might have. This idea seems to have been adopted and special agents were sent for the purpose.

In one of his letters to Peel, Lord Aberdeen, reiterating his preference for arbitration, said: "The Oregon question is principally or best suited for arbitration. Its real importance is insignificant; but the press of both countries, and public clamor, have given it a fictitious interest which renders it difficult for either government to act with moderation, or with common sense."

33

Polk was elected, November, 1844, on a platform which asserted the claim of the United States to the "whole of the territory" of Oregon, and in his inaugural message, March 4, 1845, he repeated the language of the platform, that our "title to the country of Oregon is clear and unquestionable." He declared it to be his duty to assert and maintain by all constitutional means the right of the United States to the portion of our territory which lies beyond the Rocky mountains, omitting, however, the claim to the "whole" of the territory, asserted in the platform. This aroused deep interest and some resentment, in Great Britain, and at the same time constituted notice to the statesmen of that country of the strength of American determination not to yield any material portion of the disputed region. With the accession of Polk to the presidency, James Buchanan succeeded Calhoun as secretary of state, and he renewed the negotiations in a spirit more moderate than the "Fifty-four Forty or Fight" campaign slogan would have indicated. In a letter to Pakenham, July 12, 1845, he signified President Polk's willingness to recede from the 54° 40′ line, on the ground that he had "found himself embarrassed if not committed by the acts of his predecessors." "In view of these facts," said Buchanan, "the President has determined to pursue the present negotiation to its conclusion upon the principle of compromise in which it commenced, and to make one more effort to adjust this long pending controversy." He then proposed to divide the territory on the 49th parallel, at the same time offering to make free to Great Britain any ports that it might choose on Vancouver island south of that parallel. This offer would have opened the way for a compromise, but Pakenham rejected it on the ground that it offered less than had been tendered in the negotiations of 1826. This was a bad strategic move, as Buchanan at once saw, and he was quick to withdraw the proposal, leaving the next move to be made by the British minister.

34

Lord Aberdeen disapproved Pakenham's summary action, and proposed that "unless Mr. Buchanan should be disposed to renew his late proposal, which is greatly to be desired," the "whole question of an equitable division of the territory" be submitted to arbitration. He wrote to Edward Everett, our minister to Great Britain, who was earnestly in favor of amicable settlement, January 3, 1846: "I have no resource but strongly to renew the offer of arbitration. Whether accepted or not, this places us favourably before the world. . . . But I have no particular predilection for arbitration; on the contrary, I am only driven by necessity to press it. If it should be declined . . . it may open the way for a renewed discussion of terms and conditions, and the negotiation may revive." This proposal for arbitration, when formally made by Pakenham to Buchanan, December 27, 1845, was rejected by the latter, who characterized it as a mere proposal to divide the region, and "as precluding the United States from claiming the whole territory;" and in response to subsequent advances on the part of the British minister, Buchanan declared, that the president "does not believe the territorial rights of this nation to be a proper subject for arbitration."

35

As early as 1844, Lord Aberdeen would have been willing to

concede the demand for a 49° boundary, if it was to except Vancouver island, so that the island would remain British territory. But the British cabinet feared that such a concession, after years of demanding better terms, would be deemed a cowardly retreat, and would bring much criticism from all sources in the British isles. The belligerent language of President Polk in his inaugural message had stirred up resentment, and any new concessions would be met with general opposition, as it was believed. The necessity of smoothing the way for a compromise was realized by Lord Aberdeen, it being plain to his astute mind that he could not himself do much to mold public opinion, and he would have to rely upon others.

Between October, 1845, and the actual signing of the treaty, a concerted campaign of education was carried on to convince the cabinet and people that negotiations ought to be reopened on the basis of 49°. Aberdeen kept behind the scenes in this, but that he had much to do with the plan is well understood. Edward Everett had a part in this campaign, in its early stages, and he reported to the American secretary of state that he was furnishing requisite facts and data to a well known magazine writer for the purpose. This was but a beginning, and soon reasons and arguments, too numerous to be here repeated, were set forth in great detail by editors and contributors, and appeared in many British newspapers and magazines. Even the London Times was enlisted and did valiant service, although "far from being an organ of the ministry," as Everett wrote George Bancroft, a member of the Polk cabinet. Publication of opposition literature was discouraged at the same time, and a sentiment against war was built up.

36

During the campaign of education, the Corn Laws were repealed under sensational circumstances. Owing to famine in Ireland, the British ports were to be opened for free importation of grain, a fact that was published first in the Times, although it was the leading opposition newspaper. This brought the downfall of the Peel government, as protection of farm products was almost generally accepted as necessary. An attempt was then made to form a whig government by Lord John Russell, with Lord Palmerston as foreign minister. The failure of this, and the incoming of a new government under the lead of Peel, in which

Lord Aberdeen was again minister of foreign affairs, followed. In the reorganized cabinet, there was entire harmony upon the plan to compromise the Oregon question in accord with the Aberdeen views of proper settlement. The way was open, and the new treaty was drawn by him and sent to Washington. The admission of American grain free of duty was counted upon as improving good feeling in the United States.

37

The democrat victory in the national election in the United States was a declaration against high protective tariffs, and the Polk administration was committed to tariff reform, as well as to support of the national claim for the Oregon Country. British factories were suffering for lack of profitable business. The factory owners and their employees were not much interested in distant Oregon; and a war to maintain territorial rights under existing circumstances would not have their support. The two countries had a common interest, the United States to have the British duties on cotton and agricultural products abolished, and Great Britain to have American protective tariffs on railroad iron, and other British manufactures, reduced to enable the industries of Briton to flourish. President Polk's message to congress, December 2, 1845, therefore, was reassuring to Aberdeen and Peel of his intention to carry through a reduction of tariff rates, while Peel's tariff policy was gratifying to the United States. The negotiations for mutual concessions continued until the treaty was agreed upon, and no doubt had a profound influence in bringing about a favorable conclusion.

38

As has been stated, two British military agents, Lieutenants Warre and Vavasour, were dispatched overland from Canada to examine into conditions in Oregon and particularly with reference to its possible defense; and Lieut. William Peel, son of Sir Robert Peel, the British prime minister, was sent ashore from a British frigate in Puget sound to obtain information concerning the progress of American settlement in the Willamette valley. Young Mr. Peel's confidential report, which he hurriedly carried to England, was delivered by him February 9 or 10, 1846, and he also delivered a written report of Capt. John Gordon, already mentioned herein, who was a brother of Lord Aberdeen, and in command of the ship America, which visited Puget sound in the autumn of 1845. The report of Warre and Vavasour probably did not reach London in time to have influenced the foreign office, although it is believed that the substance thereof was conveyed in advance of filing, through the medium of other agents of the government. The news that the officials of Hudson's Bay Company had taken steps to remove its principal headquarters to Victoria, and had found it expedient to unite with the Oregon provisional government, furnished additional influence upon British leaders.

39

In Washington, there had been much talk of war, which, however, responsible leaders desired to avoid. Affairs were nearing a climax, late in 1845, as is shown by an entry in Polk's diary of December 23, four days before the British proposal for arbitration was submitted. The official atmosphere was surcharged with apprehension, in the president's cabinet, lest the British arbitration proposal should be accompanied by an ultimatum. "A grave discussion took place," wrote Polk, "in view of the contingency of war with Great Britain, growing out of the present critical state of the Oregon question. Mr. Buchanan expressed himself decidedly in favor of making vigorous preparation for defense, and said it was his conviction that the next two weeks would decide the issue of peace or war. I expressed my concurrence with Mr. Buchanan, that the country should be put in a state of defense without delay. . . . A private letter of Mr. McLane [American minister to Great Britain] of the 1st instant, was also read. The opinion was then expressed by Mr. Buchanan that the British minister would soon propose arbitration, as an ultimatum. All agreed that we could not agree to arbitration, first because the question of a compromise of territorial limits was not a fit subject for such reference, and second, because in the existing state of the principal powers of the world an impartial umpire could not be found. . . . Mr. Buchanan repeated the anxiety he had often expressed to permit the negotiations to be reopened, with the hope that the dispute might be settled by compromise."

The British cabinet was not less anxious to avoid war. The government had its hands full with military operations in distant Afghanistan and China, and had recently had a stubborn fight with the Sikhs in India. There was friction with the Dutch in South Africa, and there was a famine in Ireland.

At the meeting of the American cabinet, just mentioned, Buchanan inquired whether, if the British minister should offer the parallel of 49° from the mountains to the strait of Juan de Fuca, leaving the southern end of Vancouver island to Great Britain, Polk would "submit such a proposition to the senate for their previous advice." Polk replied that "if an equivalent, by granting to the United States free ports north of 49° on the sea and to the straits of Juan de Fuca should also be offered," he would "consult confidentially three or four senators from different parts of the union, and might submit it to the senate for previous advice."

Polk did call in several senators, who agreed with him in objecting to arbitration. Turney, of Tennessee, told him that Benton would not support the administration on the question, and that Benton and Calhoun, in his opinion, would be found acting together in opposition. "He said many members from the south were opposed to war, and would follow Mr. Calhoun, while some members from the west were almost mad on the subject of Oregon, and that I was between these two fires, and whatever I might do I must dissatisfy one or the other of these sections of the party."

40

In a message to congress, March 24, 1846, the president had recommended an increase of the navy and the raising of an "adequate military force to guard and protect such of our citizens as might think it proper to emigrate to Oregon," and had called attention to warlike preparations which were even then being advocated in Great Britain. Bills were introduced in congress in furtherance of the president's recommendation, but by this time, diplomatic exchanges between the governments already had assumed a more amicable tone. The British government, however, was convinced by this time that the United States would, on account of public opinion, elect war rather than make material concessions, Sir Robert Peel increased his efforts to avoid a final rupture, and in this he was favored by a compromising spirit at Washington, so that in April, 1846, the resolution pending in congress to instruct the president to give notice of abrogation of the joint occupancy treaty was amended in the interest of peace, by inclusion of the words: "And that the attention of the governments of both countries may be more earnestly directed to the

adopting of all proper measures for a speedy and amicable adjustment of the differences and disputes in regard to the said territory."

41

Pakenham was directed to present the draft of treaty that
Aberdeen had sent to him, and to outline the project, fixing the
boundary on the line of 49° to the strait of Juan de Fuca, giving
to Great Britain Vancouver island, and granting to Hudson's Bay
Company free navigation of the Columbia river for the term of
its existing charter, guaranteeing, also, the possessory rights of
the Hudson's Bay Company and the Puget Sound Agricultural
Company south of the 49th parallel. This draft was laid before the
senate by Polk, June 10, 1846, with a message in which he said:
"In the early periods of the government the opinion and advice of
the senate were often taken in advance, upon important questions
of our foreign policy, General Washington repeatedly consulted
the senate and asked their previous advice upon pending negotiations with foreign powers. . . . This practice, though rarely resorted to in later times, was, in my judgment, eminently wise,
and may on occasions of great importance be properly revived."
The senate responded by voting, two days later, 37 to 12, in favor
of acceptance of the treaty, which was thereupon signed in Washington, June 15, 1846.

42

Some further facts concerning the history of the treaty may be
stated. Calhoun, whose position as secretary of state ended with
the close of President Tyler's administration, March 6, 1844, was
in the following November elected to the senate by the South Carolina legislature. He took his seat as senator December 22, 1845,
and thereafter continued his interest both in the Oregon question
and in the Texas question, desiring above all else to avoid war
with Great Britain or with Mexico. During the winter there was
much curiosity as to what attitude he would assume as to the
threatening posture of President Polk. He delivered an able address before the senate on the Oregon question, March 16, 1846, in
which he counselled against war, and opposed passage of any measure to provide for military occupation, or for immediate cancellation of joint occupancy. It was his opinion, as shown by his
published letters, that the speech was the best he ever delivered,

and he was pleased with the congratulations he received, which included what he called the most violent of the 54° 40′ men. Calhoun wrote to a correspondent: "Our triumph has been complete, in both Houses of Congress and the country, of which the majorities in the two Houses on the resolution for giving notice affords an indication. With little exception, the vote separates the war and peace parties. The former is rather weaker and the latter stronger than it indicates. In the Senate, the former does not exceed eight out of 56. In the country, I would say, the peace party is still stronger in proportion. This great change has been effected by the Senate against the entire influence of the Executive; a great majority in the House; and a strong current in their favour in the Community, and the weight of the press against us. The only difficulty in the way of reaping the fruits of this great victory is, that the notice may be used, not as a means of reopening the negotiations on our part, but of extorting an offer from Great Britain. In that case, the offer, if made by Great Britain, may be an ultimatum; and that in turn gives rise to new difficulties. I trust, a course so hazardous may be avoided, but I fear. . . ."

In another letter he indicated the gravity of the question of war or peace with Mexico, and said, "I fear that it may arrest, or even defeat the settlement of the Oregon question, and introduce the interference of both England and France, before it is concluded." He was pleased that a compromise of the boundary at 49° had been proposed by Great Britain, and approved by the senate vote of more than three to one, and believed that his efforts had borne fruit. He commented on the opening of the Mexican war as follows: "The Settlement is a great point, just at this critical moment, when we have a war on hand, which might have become formidable, if it had been left open. It is to me a great triumph. When I arrived here, it was dangerous to whisper 49, and I was thought to have taken a hazardous step in asserting that Mr. Polk had not disgraced the country in offering it. Now a treaty is made on it with nearly the unanimous voice of the Country. I would have had an equal triumph on the Mexican question, now the Oregon is settled, had an opportunity been afforded to discuss it. As it is, I have been forced to take a stand, which for the time has weakened me with mere partisans, but strengthened me with the patriotick and reflecting. I shall wait patiently for a fair opportunity of presenting my views in relation to it, and have no fear of regaining more than has been temporarily lost. The war has opened with brilliant victories on our side, and, I trust, may soon be brought to a close. I give it a quiet, but decided support, as much as I regret the occurrence."

In another letter he supplemented this by expressing the belief that if the British government had known that war with Mexico had already arrived, the proposal for settlement of the boundary at 49° would not have been made. He wrote: "The settlement of the Oregon question has given great, and, I may almost say, universal satisfaction. It was effected in the nick of time. It is now known that had the English proposition been delayed five days, until the news of our declaration of War against Mexico had arrived, the Settlement would not have been made. As it was, there was a division in the British Cabinet on the subject of the offer. How great the folly to endanger the Oregon settlement by the rash, thoughtless and unwarranted movement of our troops to Del Norte!"

43

It is interesting to follow the correspondence between the French government at Paris and its representatives at Washington, during the later years, 1839-46, of the diplomatic exchange as to the Oregon question. France was in the position of a disinterested observer, so far as these negotiations were concerned; but it had and expressed keen interest as to Texas and California. The letters thus exchanged show an intelligent understanding of the matters in controversy, and of the progress made in the diplomatic struggle; and when an apparent impasse had been reached, and war seemed imminent, the opinion was expressed that there would be no war, for neither of the opponents could afford it, and that in the end public opinion in the United States and in Great Britain would be counted upon to bring about an adjustment. The American moves in California, in 1843 and in 1846, were keenly watched, and every detail of the Texas question and the growing certainty of war with Mexico was reported upon. One feature of the French correspondence that is especially noticeable is the astonishing frankness and candor of statesmen in discussing these situations with the representatives of a foreign power at the very time when relations between governments were strained almost to a breaking point. January 29, 1846, the minister of foreign affairs, M. Guizot, wrote to his minister, M. Pageot, at Washington, a comment inspired by some of President Polk's perfervid references to France in his annual message: "On the special question of Oregon, we warmly desire that a pacific solution take place, for it would be doubly regrettable if the peace of the world would be disturbed by such a matter, and we are in any case firmly decided to keep the most complete neutrality so long as it will be possible for us to do so."

44

The last chapter of the Oregon boundary dispute was not written, however, until 1872, by which time the territory of Washington had been in existence nineteen years, and Oregon had long been established as a state of the Union. The treaty provided, in Article I, that the boundary shall be "continued westward along the said 49th parallel of north latitude to the middle of the channel which separates the continent from Vancouver's island; and thence southerly through the middle of the said channel and of Fuca's straits, to the Pacific ocean."

But there is a considerable archipelago in the waters between Vancouver island and the mainland, and there are at least two channels. The Americans claimed as the boundary the broadest and deepest of these, the canal de Haro, which gave them most of the islands; the British contended for the more frequented strait of Rosario, farther east. The American contention was that the primary, indeed the only, purpose of deviation from the 49th parallel was to give the whole of Vancouver island to the British, and that, besides, the canal de Haro was obviously the main channel, because of its superior volume and the greater directness of communication by this route between King George's sound and the strait of Juan de Fuca.

An attempt to settle the controversy was made, 1856, when congress appointed two commissioners and Great Britain two, who labored two years and made extensive surveys and soundings, but failed to agree. In 1859, a colony of Americans settled on San Juan island and came in conflict with the British authorities over an issue of trespass by livestock, and the governor of Vancouver island, Sir James Douglas, asserted British sovereignty over San Juan. In his official character, Douglas ordered

Admiral Baynes, then at Esquimalt with a British fleet, to drive the Americans from San Juan island; an order which, as governor of a British colony, he was authorized to give. Admiral Baynes, however, disobeyed it on his own responsibility, declaring that it would be ridiculous "to involve two great nations in war over a squabble about a pig."

A company of United States troops was sent to San Juan in this year, the company of Capt. George E. Pickett, afterward a distinguished Confederate general, and these troops were ordered off by the agent of Hudson's Bay Company, who claimed the entire island as the property of his company. Admiral Baynes blockaded the island with a flotilla of British warships, but Pickett prepared to resist attack. General Harney, commanding the United States forces in Washington territory, reinforced him with all the available troops then in the northwest. They eluded the British blockade and landed in a fog. The governor of British Columbia protested. At one time the United States had some 500 troops on San Juan, while five British ships of war, carrying 167 guns and 2140 men, held the island in a state of seige. Finally Gen. Winfield Scott was sent to the scene, whereupon all but one company of Americans was withdrawn, and the British squadron sailed away.

45

A nominal joint military occupation followed, lasting thirteen years. The British, 1860, proposed arbitration, suggesting as arbitrator either the king of the Netherlands, the king of Sweden and Norway, or the president of Switzerland. Negotiations were interrupted by the war between the states, and were resumed, 1869, when a treaty was entered into for submission of the issue to the president of Switzerland, but this treaty failed of ratification by the senate. The question was then involved with numerous differences arising between the United States and Great Britain, arising out of our own war. These were referred to the Joint High Commission of 1871, one of the members of which was George H. Williams, of Oregon. The commission agreed on a treaty by which the San Juan controversy was referred for arbitration to Emperor William I, of Germany, who decided in favor of the canal de Haro as the boundary, sustaining the claim of the United States.

The award was dated October 21, 1872. Ninety years had passed since Great Britain had first formally recognized the existence of the United States as an independent nation. From that time, wrote George Bancroft, then our minister to Germany, the controversy regarding the boundaries of the possessions of America had not ceased for a single day. "During this period," added Bancroft, "the two countries have repeatedly been on the verge of war, growing out of their opposing claims to jurisdiction. After an unrelenting strife of ninety years, the award of His Majesty, the Emperor of Germany, closes the long and unintermitted and often very dangerous series of disputes on the extent of their respective territories, and, so, for the first time in their history, opens to the two countries the unobstructed way to agreement, good understanding and peace."

CHAPTER XXI

IN TERRITORIAL DAYS (1848-1859)

1

THE PROVISIONAL GOVERNMENT met the immediate necessities of the Oregon people for a system of laws and a political organization, but they were impatient for a regular territorial government. The time seemed long between the settlement of the boundary and the consummation of a permanent local government. But the delay was due to the Mexican war and the growing bitterness of the slavery question. Congress adjourned in early 1847 without passing the act creating the territory, although such a bill passed the house of representatives, expressly reaffirming the validity of the organic act, based upon the Ordinance of 1787, forbidding slavery. The bill failed in the senate. By this time there were ten or twelve thousand people in Oregon, and the provisional government was working smoothly.

As has been elsewhere stated, Governor Abernethy, upon the advice of a number of citizens, asked J. Quinn Thornton, who was then supreme judge, to go to Washington to look after the interests of the Oregon people. He departed from Oregon City, October, 1847, some weeks before the Whitman massacre, and arrived at his destination in May, 1848, where he was well received by the president and some of the leading members of congress. He prepared and presented a memorial and later drafted a bill for the organization of the territory, in which measure there was an express prohibition of slavery. There was bitter opposition, lead by such able southerners as Jefferson Davis and Andrew P. Butler, and a duel was at one time almost precipitated between Senators Butler and Benton. But, in spite of the efforts to defeat it, the bill passed the senate August 13, 1848, after an all night session, and it was signed by President Polk on the next day, August 14. The tragedy at the Whitman mission, and the presence of Joseph Meek at Washington, contributed to this favorable result.

2

The first officers of the new territory were Joseph Lane, governor, and Joseph L. Meek, whose spectacular trip across the plains as the bearer of a memorial praying for federal aid, just after the Whitman massacre, had won for him the office of United States marshal; Kintzing Pritchette, of Pennsylvania, secretary of the territory, and General John Adair, of Kentucky, collector of customs at Astoria. The first judicial appointees were William P. Bryant, of Indiana, as chief justice, James Turney, of Illinois, and Peter H. Burnett, formerly of Oregon but then of California, as associate justices. Turney, however, declined the appointment, and O. C. Pratt, a native of Illinois then residing in California, was nominated in his stead. Judge Bryant resigned soon afterward and returned home, so that when Judge Pratt was summoned to California, early in 1850, to sit in a number of admiralty cases pending in the federal court at San Francisco, Oregon territory was actually without a judge. Thomas Nelson and William Strong were appointed in the stead of Bryant and Burnett, and the court then consisted of Nelson, Strong and Pratt. The resignation of Governor Lane, which took effect June 18, 1850, left Pritchette to act as governor two months, until August 18, 1850, when John P. Gaines succeeded to the office.

3

During the period of the territory, the following attorneys were admitted to the bar of the supreme court: Columbia Lancaster, Amory Holbrook, Aaron E. Wait, Edward Hamilton, John B. Preston, Alexander Campbell, William W. Chapman, William T. Matlock, Jesse Quinn Thornton, Simon B. Marye, David B. Brenan, Cyrus Olney, John B. Chapman, James K. Kelly, Joseph G. Wilson, Reuben P. Boise, David Logan, Milton Elliott, James McCabe, George McConaha, Matthew P. Deady, Addison C. Gibbs, A. B. P. Wood, A. Lawrence Lovejoy, W. Stuart Brock, Benjamin Stark, P. A. Marquam, Lafayette Grover, Eli M. Barnum, Benjamin F. Harding, Riley E. Stratton, James C. Strong, Mark P. Chinn, Lafayette Mosher, Stephen F. Chadwick, Columbus Sims, George K. Sheil, Delazon Smith, Noah Huber, Stukely Ellsworth, Thomas H. Smith, Sylvester Pennoyer, Benjamin F. Bonham, Andrew J. Thayer, John Kelsay, William W. Page, Lansing Stout, R. B. Snelling, Benjamin F. Dowell, Chester N. Terry, George B. Currey, John R. McBride.

4

Samuel R. Thurston had been elected the first delegate to congress from the new territory, 1849, and had proceeded by sea to

Washington, bearing a memorial from the Oregon legislature. He lost all his baggage and papers on the way east, and with true western enterprise drafted a memorial of his own, as a substitute for the one that the legislature had committed to his care, and the substitute served the purpose well enough. Thurston signalized his entry into public service by attacking Hudson's Bay Company and Puget Sound Agricultural Company. He was instrumental in framing and obtaining the passage of the donation land law, with provisions hostile to the interests of Doctor McLoughlin. The donation law was not Thurston's original conception, in its general features, but followed the structure of the early bills introduced in the senate by Senator Linn, of Missouri, as has been related in these pages.

5

The opening years of government as a territory of the United States were filled with political and legal controversy out of which came much bitterness of spirit. There was a sharp difference of opinion between the whigs and democrats, as would be natural, but it grew into a permanent state of personal and political antagonism that left a corroding effect upon prominent men of the young commonwealth, not to be erased for many years.

Governor Lane, who was a democrat, served from March 3, 1849, to June 18, 1850. He was succeeded by the whig governor, John Pollard Gaines, appointed by President Taylor. Gaines arrived in Oregon on the sloop Falmouth, August 14, 1850, and with him came the secretary, Edward Hamilton, and William Strong, who, as already stated, came as associate justice of the supreme court to fill the vacancy left by Burnett's declination. The journey by way of Cape Horn consumed nine months, during which time local democrats fulminated against alien officials who dallied on the way while the territory was left to shift as best it might with temporary government.

6

It may be interesting to add that Abraham Lincoln might have had one of these places, if he would have accepted. He was a member of congress, 1847-49. It seems that he had had some hopes that on the coming in of the whig administration, at Washington, at the end of his own term of office as congressman, he might receive the appointment as commissioner of the general land office. But he was disappointed in this, and later he was considered for appointment as secretary for Oregon territory. When he declined, he was suggested by friends for the governorship of Oregon, but again wrote that he could not consent to accept. He then proposed the name of his friend, Simeon Francis, of Springfield, Illinois, for the secretaryship. Francis afterward removed to Oregon. In a letter to the Oregon Argus, 1860, he proposed Lincoln for the republican nomination as president. He served as editor of the Oregonian for a short time in the place of Thomas J. Dryer, when the latter was absent from the state on a journey to Washington.

7

Experience of the people in managing their own affairs, ever since the beginning of the provisional government, had produced a sentiment in favor of home rule and in favor of selecting territorial officers from the territory itself. The Gaines appointment was coldly received. Although he had a fine record, as speaker of the house of representatives in congress, and as general in the Mexican war, he was somewhat pompous and aristocratic in bearing, and did not have the faculty of making friends. Moreover, the whigs were greatly outnumbered by the democrats in the territory.

In these circumstances, notwithstanding certain undeniable personal charm, Governor Gaines was predestined to encounter partisan opposition. In accordance with an editorial style that was called freedom of speech, and that was characterized by great outspokenness in personal matters, the governor was almost immediately assailed by the local press. Incidents associated with his career as an officer of the Mexican war were distorted, and bitter and protracted discussions of a personal character appeared in the columns of the newspapers. Gaines, for example, was dubbed in pure derision the "hero of Encarnacion," in allusion to the capture of his detachment by a numerically superior Mexican force, and notwithstanding he had an honorable career as a soldier.

8

The organic act, section 6, expressly provided that "to avoid improper influences which may result from intermixing in one act such things as have no proper relation to each other," every law of the territory should embrace but one object and that should be expressed in the title. However, this fundamental requirement had been overlooked by the legislature, in 1849, in adopting a law primarily intended to change the location of the seat of government to Salem, instead of keeping it at Oregon City, where it had existed under the provisional government and where the first session of the territorial legislature had been held.

The new act was entitled "An Act to provide for the selection of places for location and erection of the public buildings of the Territory of Oregon," and contained ten sections. It purported not only to locate and establish the seat of government, and to instruct the future legislative assemblies to meet there, but it located the penitentiary at Portland, and a university at Marysville (afterward called Corvallis). Governor Gaines, in a message, February 3, 1851, long before the time for the session, took the position that this law embraced more than one object and was therefore void; so that, in his opinion, the seat of government lawfully remained at Oregon City, and in this he had the support of an opinion of Amory Holbrook, the United States attorney, who was another of the new whig appointees. This view was quite contrary to the plans of some leaders of the other party, and the vials of wrath of the democrats, led by Matthew P. Deady and Asahel Bush, were then opened, and soon the quarrel raged fiercely.

In due season the majority of the members of the legislature, in defiance of the governor's message, proceeded to Salem. Governor Gaines and the territorial secretary, Edward Hamilton, refused to attend at that place. They maintained the executive offices at Oregon City, and the minority members of the legislature met there. But, having no quorum in either branch, the latter body adjourned from day to day, and finally gave up and dispersed, December 17, 1851. Two of the three judges of the supreme court, Chief Justice Thomas Nelson and Judge William Strong, in a suit entitled "Amos M. Short versus F. Ermatinger," at Oregon City, had an opportunity to express their views, and they upheld the territorial officers and the minority of the legislature. In separate and lengthy written opinions, these two judges argued that the seat of government was lawfully at Oregon City, and they demonstrated to their own satisfaction, and that of the whig office holders, that the statute attempting to change it to

Salem was absolutely void, because of the defect in the title and failure to conform to the plain requirements of the organic law.

On the other hand, the third judge of the supreme court, Judge O. C. Pratt, who was a democrat appointed by President Polk, rendered an elaborate opinion in response to a resolution of the majority members of the legislative assembly sitting at Salem, advising that the decision of Judges Strong and Nelson was void, because they had held court at Oregon City, instead of at Salem, and that the statute was entirely valid and binding. His opinion was dated December 25, 1851, and, as the views expressed by him accorded with the Salem legislature's desires and opinions, its members continued in session and proceeded to enact laws and to discharge the usual duties of such a body.

9

Judge Pratt was popular at Salem, especially among the democrats, and was commended by Asahel Bush, editor of the Statesman and public printer. On invitation, the judge read his opinion to the joint meeting of the two houses, January 9, 1852, whereupon that body gave him an ovation and voted to print three thousand copies. The opinion was printed in full in the Statesman and was highly praised by those whose views it confirmed. The question involved the supremacy of the old capital at Oregon City and the aspirations of Salem for state leadership, and a majority of the people favored the change. The Salem legislature adjourned, January 12, 1852, but the controversy continued to rage.

The minority, who had met at Oregon City, had not been able to muster more than four members. They were Columbia Lancaster, Aaron E. Wait, William T. Matlock, and R. C. Kinney, and of these Lancaster and Matlock memorialized congress on several subjects of interest to the territory, without, however, alluding to the burning question of the times. On the other hand, the Salem legislature, after full debate, sent a memorial of their own, claiming that prima facie, at least, the seat of government was at Salem, which was the only place at which court or legislature could sit, and that the majority judges had abused their high office in attempting to hold court at Oregon City or to decide the statute void. That memorial accused the judges of "fulminating" against the legislature and its acts, and of issuing paper decrees, characterizing the members as revolutionists and disorganizers. It expressed the opinion that public confidence in the judiciary department had been seriously impaired, and strongly intimated that the two judges were unfit for their high office.

As for Governor Gaines, it was plainly said that he had already proved a failure, and that his administration was characterized by a total want of confidence and sympathy between himself and the people. "Ever since he landed upon our shores and entered upon the duties of the office," said the memorialists, "either from mental perverseness or, what is more probable, the mischievous, advice of the district attorney, Amory Holbrook, he has sought by indirect and extra official acts to usurp the powers placed in the hands of the representatives of the people alone, and the consequence has been that confusion and discord have, like the cloud that precedes the storm, overshadowed our public affairs." Matthew P. Deady was chairman of the committee that prepared the memorial and no doubt this was in great part his own language.

10

The opinion of the attorney general of the United States, to whom the legal question was referred by the treasury department, was that the majority judges of the Oregon court were right, and that the only lawful seat of government was at Oregon City, thus upholding Governor Gaines and incidentally stamping as illegal all of the legislative acts adopted at Salem. The opinion upheld the refusal of the territorial secretary to issue warrants for the payment of salaries and expenses incurred at Salem.

But the triumph of the Oregon whigs was short-lived. Congress, at the instance of General Lane, the delegate from Oregon, adopted a joint resolution, May 4, 1852, which settled the legal question by ratifying and approving the act of the legislative assembly of Oregon establishing and locating the seat of government at Salem, and by declaring the laws adopted by the Salem session to be "in conformity with the provisions of the act" and "to have been held in conformity to the provisions of law." The Oregon Statesman, strong democrat organ that it was, did not refrain from pointing out that this was by unanimous vote of the committee on territories of the national house of representatives, composed of whigs as well as of democrats. It proceeded to take the satisfaction that was obviously to be derived from this situation, in an editorial, June 8, 1852, which used some words of Chinook jargon, and in general was characteristic of the political amenities of those days in Oregon, as follows:

Poor "Supreme Court"! Alas! Alas!

The "Supreme Court" is "done for," laid out, kilt; or as our classical "brother Dryer" would say, in the "jargon of the country," kockshut, memloosed, halo! It was a feeble, rickety concern to begin with, and the rough usage it received from the legislative assembly and the people nearly knocked the breath of life from it, and finally congress gave it the finishing kick, and it was no more forever. No one appeared to administer consolation in the agonies of death. Not a voice was raised, not a vote was given to succor and to save. Out of three hundred members of congress, more than one-third of them whigs, not one was found to do it reverence. Its condemnation was decreed, every voice answering aye! and it passed to the tomb "unknelled, unhonored and unsung . . . "

11

The democrats made the most of the opportunity and constantly insisted that the effect of the congressional resolution was to hold that the Salem legislative proceedings were legal. Wincing under this, Holbrook wrote to President Fillmore, complaining of the executive approval of the resolution, and sending a pamphlet with argument on the subject. The president promptly answered by letter, marked private, dated July 26, 1852, in which he expressed surprise at the claim that the congressional resolution was a decision in favor of the validity of the Salem legislative proceedings. "I did not scrutinize the resolution when presented to me for my approval," said he. "I supposed it was intended merely to legalize the proceedings of the legislative assembly at Salem, but not to express any opinion whether they were legal or illegal under the organic law. On that point the attorney-general had given his opinion, in which I fully concurred then and do now, and the very fact that this joint resolution was passed was an evidence, at least, that these proceedings were not considered as valid without being ratified by congress. There may have been some artful design in the wording of the resolution, intending to give it a local effect in Oregon, of which I was wholly unaware. I regret, however, that anything should have transpired that should have led anyone to suppose for a moment that I had changed my opinion in reference to the true construction of the organic law."

12

In December, 1852, political controversy broke out afresh, when the legislative assembly met. Excuse this time, was that the governor had sent a message to the legislature without having been requested to do so. The message itself was a comparatively innocent one, and in a later time it would have provoked no controversy. It called attention of the legislature to the necessity for immediate construction of a penitentiary, and urged the improvement of the western end of the immigrant route, in view of the hardships suffered by incoming settlers. These proposals undoubtedly would have been popular, if initiated by a governor chosen from among the residents. The message recommended the passage of a law to provide for commissioners to take acknowledgments of deeds; it reviewed the resources of the territory and urged that home industry be stimulated whenever possible; and it expressed the views of the governor as to places where spirituous liquors were for sale. "If," said Gaines, "these establishments may be regarded as public benefits, the amount exacted for a license seems to be exorbitantly high; if, on the contrary, they are justly considered as unmixed evils, the tax should be greatly augmented, or by adequate enactments they should be prohibited altogether."

A member of the assembly, George E. Cole, introduced a resolution declaring that "whereas, this house has listened to the message of the governor, but inasmuch as the legislative department of this territory is in nowise connected with or dependent upon the executive department, for legislative purposes, therefore be it resolved that the further consideration of the message be indefinitely postponed." The speaker made the point that the first message to the territorial legislature, delivered by Lane, had been submitted by request. "Now, sir," he vociferated, "the first message of this territory was a message by General Lane, at the request of the assembly. Did the assembly ask Governor Gaines for a message? No. In answer to the resolution of this house, simply informing him that we were in session and transacting business, he gives us a message, instead of a report." John H. Anderson advocated indefinite postponement of consideration of the message on the ground that there was no connection between the legislative and executive departments of the territory. "Congress,"

Anderson added, "placed the interests and rights of the people of this territory in their own hands and they exercise these rights through their representatives."

13

The legal principle involved in the seat of government contest, as applied by the whig judges, developed a juristic tangle in another direction, resulting in a situation that, however amusing to posterity, was serious enough among the politicians of the day. It was nothing short of a violent dispute as to what code of laws was in effect for the governing of the young commonwealth. If a law could embrace but one subject, to be expressed in the title, what about the validity of a statute that purported to adopt at wholesale the Iowa code, with its manifold and varied contents?

Successive provisional legislatures had on three separate occasions adopted bodily the statutes of Iowa to be the law of Oregon, July 5, 1843, July 27, 1844 and August 12, 1845. Each of these acts of the voluntary political organization of the settlers had alluded specifically to a certain compilation of the Iowa territorial statutes printed in 1839, being the statute laws enacted at the first session of the legislative assembly of that territory. This book was bound in blue boards and it came to be popularly known in Oregon, during the years from 1843 to 1849, by familiar designation as the Blue Book.

Now, when the territory of Oregon was created by congress, the first territorial legislative assembly, notwithstanding the provision in the organic act that kept alive all existing laws of the provisional government, deemed it necessary again to adopt the Iowa statutes, and proceeded to do so by an enactment, September 29, 1849, that referred to a later compilation of the Iowa statutes, printed in 1843, being the revised statutes of the territory of Iowa, contained in a more portly blue volume. Like the statute already mentioned, changing the seat of government to Salem, this action of the Oregon legislature was said to ignore the basic provision of the fundamental act of congress, which has been quoted, requiring that every act should embrace but one object to be expressed in the title. The code of laws as adopted was derisively nicknamed the "Steamboat Code," since it carried a miscellaneous cargo, an appellation attributed to Amory Holbrook.

Conflicting views of the judges in the seat of government controversy, when applied to the new code, resulted in the claim on the one side that the enactment was void and that the Steamboat Code or Big Blue Book, as it was variously called, had no authority, and that the old Blue Book or Little Blue Book was still the authorized version. The Big Blue Book (or simply the Blue Book, as distinguished from the Little Blue Book), was repudiated in the district in which Judge Nelson presided, composed of Clackamas, Marion and Linn counties, and also in Judge Strong's district, composed of Clatsop county and those north of the Columbia river, while, in the district presided over by Judge Pratt, the Little Blue Book was anathema. Judge Pratt's district covered nearly all the territory west of the Willamette river, and included the counties of Washington, Yamhill, Polk and Benton. In this district, the Big Blue Book or Revised Statutes of Iowa of 1843, came to be recognized as the compendium of law, and a compilation, or selection therefrom, was prepared by a legislative committee of which Col. W. W. Chapman was chairman.

There were but two copies of the Big Blue Book in Oregon, and the Chapman printing was not ready until the latter part of 1853, when a few copies were furnished by the territorial printer. This latter edition was generally known as the Chapman Code, and meantime Judge Pratt's court had to get along with little learning and less law, as one of the practitioners said. In the districts of Judges Strong and Nelson the difficulty was scarcely less, for there were but three or four copies of the Little Blue Book in the entire territory.

As Judge Pratt was popular with the legislature and his views coincided with those of the members, an act was passed detaching Marion and Linn counties from Judge Nelson's district, thus leaving Clackamas county alone to the latter. Of course, Judge Nelson refused to recognize the validity of such an act, adopted by what he deemed an illegal legislative body. James K. Kelly, in describing this situation in an address delivered before the Oregon Bar Association, many years afterward, said: "In the act it was provided that the terms of court in Marion and Linn counties should commence one week earlier than they did under the old law. So Judge Pratt held court at Salem and Albany under the new law, and a week later, in each county, Judge Nelson went to Salem and Albany to hold the district court under the old law. He found, however, that Judge Pratt had preceded him, held the courts, and adjourned for the term. Judge Nelson finding that no business was prepared for hearing before him by the lawyers, returned somewhat disgusted to Oregon City, and was soon after relieved by the appointment of Hon. George H. Williams (of Iowa), as chief justice of the territory."

14

The remedy was found in the passage of an act by the legislature, January, 1853, providing for the election of commissioners to draft a new code of laws. James K. Kelly, Reuben P. Boise and Daniel R. Bigelow were selected for this duty and the task was completed with the help of Joseph G. Wilson, clerk. About 200 copies were printed by the state printer for the use of the legislature in considering the report. Both Kelly and Boise were elected members of the legislature at the election, June, 1853, and when that body assembled in December of that year the code so prepared was adopted in separate parts, all to take effect May 1, 1854.

This effective date gave time for printing and binding of the code in New York, where it was sent by the state printer because of the lack of facilities in Oregon. But unfortunately all of the copies excepting about 200 were sent from New York to Oregon by way of Cape Horn, by sailing vessel, and these never reached Oregon. They were either shipwrecked or so damaged that they were useless. The 200 that came to Oregon by way of Panama were used, but the legislature at its session commencing, December, 1854, ordered a new edition, and this was printed, in New York, 1855, and contained in addition to the code such statutes as were adopted at that session, and those of the preceding session of the legislature.

Col. James K. Kelly has said: "Between May 1, 1854, when the code took effect, and the arrival of the first copies of the printed volume from New York, we were somewhat troubled for want of evidence of existing statutes, and the judges and lawyers used in the courts copies of the printed draft reported by the code commissioners. A few of these unbound volumes still remained, and such changes as had been made by the legislature were noted in them."

15

A profound change was wrought meanwhile in the financial condition of the people by the discovery of gold in California, news of which reached Oregon, July, 1848. It is no exaggeration to say that nothing in all the history of the colony, except the final determination of its nationality by the boundary treaty in 1846, so influenced its destiny. The view point of the people was changed, and many pioneer makeshifts were no longer necessary. From an agricultural community, content with the production of its own primary necessities, Oregon was transformed into an ambitious, enterprising and efficient source of supply for those who were too busy hunting for and mining gold to take the necessary time to produce the prosaic food stuffs they required. After the first flush of excitement, in which about two-thirds of the able-bodied men of the territory left hurriedly for the new El Dorado, thereby depleting the population to an extent which even the Indian war had not done, those who remained at home found opportunity to organize agricultural and industrial production on a new and better basis.

By the spring of 1849, a large inflow of gold had created a circulating medium which gave life to commerce; markets had been established which promised a certain and profitable outlet for all that farmers and lumbermen could produce; flour mills and sawmills flourished, whenever they could obtain hands to operate them. Whereas, there had been a distinct feeling of depression throughout the region due to the needy migrations culminating in 1847, this now gave way to a spirit of the optimism that was fostered by high wages and advancing prices. Debts were paid throughout the territory; new manufacturing enterprises were started; towns sprang up; the river was alive with vessels awaiting cargoes of supplies for the mines.

16

The steps by which new conditions of local prosperity were achieved were attended by picturesque and romantic incidents. The first tidings of the gold excitement in California, were brought by Captain Newell of the brig Honolulu, by way of Honolulu, whence they travelled to Nisqually, later finding their way to Fort Vancouver. At that place the captain, who was energetically obtaining supplies of picks, crowbars, axes and other hardware, had let it to be understood that he was purchasing these supplies for the use of coal miners engaged in digging fuel for mail steamers. Until his vessel was about to sail, no news of gold discoveries had leaked out, but the story soon travelled throughout the Oregon Country.

No wagons had yet ventured overland from Oregon to California, but in a few days a typical expedition had been organized, one of many in the following years to traverse the headwaters of the Willamette river and to penetrate the Shasta mountains (as the Siskiyous were then called). It consisted of 150 stout, energetic and robust men, with 50 wagons and ox teams. These men were off to the mines, leaving everything behind them. The Applegate trail from the Umpqua to Klamath lake was now pressed into service again, but from the point where it intersected Fremont's old route it lost interest for the argonauts, who were bent on making all haste, and who turned south along the general line followed by Fremont in retracing his steps to California, in 1846.

Entire settlements were deserted, as Lieutenant Talbot found, for example, on his exploratory trip across the Coast range in the summer of 1849. Crops were neglected; Indian wars were forgotten. The provisional government in this year was not able to muster a quorum of the legislature for the transaction of public business. There are gaps in the files of the newspapers of that time which bear eloquent testimony to the inability of employers to obtain help. From September 7 until October 12, 1848, for illustration, the Spectator failed to appear, and on the latter date its editor apologized to its readers in the following words: "The Spectator, after a temporary sickness, greets its patrons, and hopes to serve them faithfully, and as heretofore, regularly. That 'gold fever' which has swept about 3,000 of her officers, lawyers, physicians, farmers and mechanics of Oregon from the plains of Oregon into the mines of California, took away our printers also —hence the temporary non-appearance of the Spectator." The Oregon Free Press, which had been founded by George Law Curry, March, 1848, ceased publication, in October of the same year, mainly because of the rush to the mines. Departure of males was, in fact, nearly complete, and many families were deserted by their breadwinners.

Something has been said in an earlier chapter about the action taken by the Oregon people to create their own coinage. The provisional legislature that convened February 5, 1849, immediately before the territory began to function, had passed a law providing for coinage of gold; but this official action was never fulfilled. A coinage, however, known as beaver money, was provided by private enterprise, and the so-called Oregon Exchange Company issued some coins of pure gold, of five and ten dollar denominations. On the obverse side were the figure of a beaver and the letters "K. M. T. A. W. R. C. S." and below was "T. O. 1849." On the reverse side was "Oregon Exchange Company. 130 G., Native Gold, 5 D," or "10 pwts, 20 grains, 10 D." The T. O. letters were for Territory of Oregon, and the other letters are said to have been the initials of the men who composed the company, Messrs. Kilbourn, Magruder, Taylor, Abernethy, Wilson, Rector, Campbell and Smith. A cut of the beaver coins is shown on the title pages of the first and second volumes of this history. The coins contained about 8 per cent more gold than like denominations of United States money, and therefore soon disappeared from circulation, but they served their purpose for a time when government coins were scarce in distant Oregon. A specimen of the beaver coins, and the dies with which they were stamped, are in the possession of Oregon Historical Society.

Even missionaries left their labors for the mines. Rev. Ezra Fisher, who was striving to give the Baptist denomination a footing in the pioneer community, was actuated by the motive that led many men to abandon their usual vocations temporarily. He was among those who departed early and was one of the first to return. "I went to the mines," he wrote to the secretary of his home board, in July, 1849, being then on his way back to his missionary station in Oregon, "principally to raise something to give my family something of the bare comforts of life. God has mercifully blessed me with about $1,000 worth of gold, and in all probability if I had stayed three or four months longer and had been blessed with a continuance of my health I should have raised from $3,000 to $4,000 more." Clergymen on the way to Oregon, travelling by way of California, caught the infection and stopped short of their original destination, hoping to improve their temporal fortunes in the mines.

17

Concerning the effect upon the material and moral welfare of the people, men were then of two minds. On the debit side, there was a mighty upheaval in the community that until now was almost Arcadian in its simplicity; restlessness and speculation displaced contentment; the rough, uncouth and unruly element that accompanied the argonauts gave a new and undesirable character to the population as a whole. It was the judgment of one of the immigrants, who experienced the hardships and privations of the southern route in the memorable year of 1846, that the days "from the first settlement of this country until 1850, the time when gold commenced flooding the country from California, were the happiest days the country has ever seen. The unexpected acquisition of wealth, caused the people to discard, to a large degree, the essential elements of true happiness. All thought and effort was turned to the gaining of more wealth, paying little regard to the manner in which it was acquired." Yet, it can be said that a larger vision was made possible, that the sense of isolation was removed, that the people came to a new realization of their relationship to the world. The horizon of the community was broadened. There is no doubt that, in the United States, the era of more modern comforts, and of better facilities for transportation, dates from the discovery of gold on the Pacific coast, which, by coincidence, is associated with the launching of territorial government in Oregon.

18

Discovery of gold in southern Oregon, 1851, brought an influx of several thousand persons into Rogue river valley. Jacksonville was founded, as also Scottsburg, on the Umpqua. The California gold excitement itself led to a natural desire to prospect the mountains and valleys of Oregon, in the hope of discovering another El Dorado; and soon it was known that there was profit in the business of growing and manufacturing supplies to meet the necessities of miners, as has been shown in these pages. The liberal provisions of the new land law may be again referred to in this connection. The donation act of September 27, 1850, granted 320 acres to every male settler, or occupant of land, above the age of 18, being a citizen of the United States, or who should declare his intention of becoming one on or before December 1, 1850;

while, if he were then married, or should marry within one year
from December 1, 1850, the law allowed 640 acres, "one-half to
himself and one-half to his wife, to be held by her in her own
right," and the surveyor-general was directed to designate the
part inuring to the husband and that to the wife. Married women's right to hold real property, so generally recognized now,
but so rarely allowed in any civilized country then, was thus early
in Oregon's history established by law. Half as much land was
granted to all above the age of 21, who should settle in the territory between December, 1850, and December, 1853, with the
same provision as already stated as to married persons. The land
law not only encouraged settlement, but it was the cause of many
marriages throughout the territory. Brief courtships and early
weddings became the rule, and many brides were in their early
teens when the knots were tied.

19

It was due to the donation land law, to a great degree, that the
immigration trains of the early fifties were composed chiefly of
homeseekers and builders. The peak in numbers was attained in
1852, a year of peculiar hardships and dangers on the trail. The
Oregon Trail had now become a mighty highway, rutted hub-deep
by the great procession of ox-drawn vehicles. No authentic record
was ever kept of this movement, the very magnitude of which
involved it in confusion, but there has been a curious tendency to
underestimate its numbers rather than to exaggerate them. The
early and long accepted estimate of 2500 immigrants for 1852
falls far short of actuality. In the light of later information it
would seem that the number of immigrants who arrived in Oregon in that year was in all probability not far short of 13,000. In
that year Douglas and Jackson counties were organized, and at a
later period, Coos, Curry and Josephine were cut out of them.

The census ordered by Lane on his accession, 1849, had shown
a population of 9083, of whom 8785 were citizens and 298 were
foreigners, 5410 were males and 3673 females. The counties of
Vancouver and Lewis, then comprising all the region north of the
Columbia river, had 304 inhabitants, of whom 189 were citizens
and 115 foreigners, 231 were males and 73, females. But the
United States census of 1850, taken about the time that Gaines
assumed the governorship, showed a total population of 13,294,

of whom 1049 resided north of the Columbia river. This increase, which is not accounted for by immigration, indicated that settlers who had early flocked to California were already beginning to return, and that land hunger was operating again, this time to induce settlement of the Cowlitz valley and the region around Puget sound, as well as of other parts of Oregon.

20

A military road was provided for by an act of the 33rd congress, to extend from Astoria to Salem, and an appropriation of $25,000 was made to be expended under the direction of the secretary of war. The road was not completed. Lieut. George H. Derby, well known as a facetious writer over the signature of "Phoenix," alias "Squibob," alias "Butterfield," and sundry other nommes de plume, was ordered to take charge of the work (1855). Twenty-two miles were constructed, extending from near the custom house at Astoria, eastward. A few years later, 1857, in the midst of newspaper attacks upon General Lane by the Oregon Statesman, it was charged by that newspaper that this proposed road was a political job and Lane was blamed for the waste of money appropriated for its construction. In 1853, congress made an appropriation for a road from Fort Steilacoom, on Puget sound, to Walla Walla. It was partly built across the Cascade mountains by citizens of the territory to accommodate the expected immigrants in the fall of that year, and the government appropriation of $25,000 was spent, under the directions of Capt. George B. McClellan, upon that part of the road. The principal road, in the period of Washington territory, was the mail route road extending from the landing at the head of navigation on the Cowlitz river to Olympia, a distance of about 50 miles. The legislature, 1852, sent several memorials to congress asking for appropriations for military roads, for the improvements of rivers and harbors, and the establishment of lighthouses and other aids to navigation. A military road from Scottsburg to the Rogue river was asked for, among others.

21

It would have been too much to expect that the federal customs laws would come into operation in the new territory without friction, and these were the cause of several clashes of authority between territorial officers and British shipmasters. The situation was particularly critical at Puget sound, on account of the location of Hudson's Bay Company, at Victoria and Nisqually, on opposite sides of the boundary and at an inconvenient distance from the only Oregon port of entry, which was then Astoria.

A case which almost resulted in serious international complications arose from the seizure of the British ship Albion, which entered Puget sound, 1849, evidently ignorant of the new revenue laws. Her crew cut a quantity of spar timber, for which offense Collector Adair's deputy, George Gibbs, libeled the ship and put vessel, cargo and stores in charge of a caretaker, who either looted the vessel, or allowed others to do so. It was sold at auction, November, 1850, at Steilacoom, but the money did not reach the federal treasury. Subsequently, so flagrant were the circumstances of this seizure and sale, the British minister made formal complaint to the American secretary of state, and congress averted further trouble by authorizing the secretary of the treasury to indemnify the owners of the ship.

In that connection, a good story is told of Joseph L. Meek, by his biographer, Mrs. Frances Victor. "Nobody suspected the integrity of the marshal, but most persons suspected that he had placed too much confidence in the district attorney, who had charge of his accounts. On some one asking him, a short time after, what had become of the money from the sale of the smuggler, he seemed struck with sudden surprise. 'Why,' he said, looking astonished at the question, 'there was bar'ly enough for the officers of the court'."

Somewhat similarly, Hudson's Bay Company schooner, Cadboro, was seized in the same year, 1850, for carrying goods direct from Victoria to Nisqually, without first entering them at Astoria. The same company's steamer Beaver was seized for landing a passenger at Nisqually without first reporting at Olympia. Creation of a Puget sound collection district, 1851, removed part of the cause of trouble. Operation of customs laws, nevertheless, hastened the withdrawal of Hudson's Bay Company, and its subsidiary Puget Sound Agricultural Company, from south of the 49th parallel, for although it had the right of free navigation of the Columbia river, expressly reserved by the treaty of 1846, the customs regulations hampered the enjoyment of the privilege.

22

In territorial days, before courthouses were constructed, the judges and juries had to resort to makeshifts in some of the counties. At Eugene, the first term of court was held under a convenient oak tree. Lawyers and judges, riding the circuit together, learned to know each other intimately. Accommodations for board and lodgings were often primitive in character, and jurors attending court, officers, litigants, witnesses and accused persons were sometimes thrown together in familiar contact. Conditions under which the United States district court at Chinook, in Pacific county, in the new territory of Washington, were opened are thus described by James G. Swan, in his Three Years Residence in Washington Territory:

"The building selected as a courthouse was a small one-story affair, measuring about 12 feet by 15, or somewhere near that; at all events, it was so circumscribed in its limits that, when the jury were seated, there was barely room left for the judge, clerk of the court, and counsel, while the sheriff had to keep himself standing in the doorway. The outsiders could neither see nor hear till some one suggested that a few boards be knocked off the other end of the house, which was soon done, and served the purpose admirably. The grand jury were then called in and sworn, and the usual forms gone through. There was nothing of importance on hand except a case of homicide, and the judge charged particularly on that point. . . . The grand jury, having been duly instructed, were marched into old M'Carty's zinc house near by, as that was the only unoccupied place in town. There were but two rooms in this house, one of which contained several hogsheads of salt salmon, and all of M'Carty's nets and fishing-gear, and had certainly an 'ancient and fish-like' perfume. Now a grand jury are presumed to do their business in a very quiet manner, and, to further the ends of justice, a culprit must not know that there is any bill against him till it is popped in his face by the sheriff; but old Mac's zinc house was just as sonorous as a drum, and, for all purposes of secrecy, we had better have held our deliberations on the logs of Chinook beach than where we were. The outsiders either crawled under the house or stood outside, where they could hear perfectly well what was going on. . . . When the jury was called and the challenges exhausted, it was found that there were no more persons to draw from. So the two counsel agreed on a compromise, which was, that nine jurors should be selected from among the grand jury who had just solemnly rendered a true bill against the prisoner."

23

Journalism, also, began to flourish at about this time, being stimulated partly by growth of population, and as well by intensity of local partisanship. But three papers had existed here prior to the territorial era. In 1845, Oregon Printing Association was organized and began publication of the Oregon Spectator, February 5, 1846, with William G. T'Vault, editor, and J. Fleming, printer. As this was the first newspaper published west of Missouri river it is interesting to note that it was non-political, but claimed a circulation among 155 subscribers in its first year. The hand press is now used for making proofs in the printing office of the University of Oregon at Eugene. The second editor of the newspaper was George L. Curry, several times governor of Oregon, who, in 1848, edited a rival paper at Oregon City, the Oregon Free Press. The third paper was the Oregon American and Evangelical Unionist, published at Tualatin plains by Rev. J. S. Griffin. This was first printed June 7, 1848, and after a bold start it died a natural death, 1849.

Now, however, other newspapers were established, the first in the field under territorial government being the Western Star, first published June, 1850, by Lot Whitcomb, at Milwaukie, a town that was a rival of Portland for leadership. The paper was moved to Portland in 1851 and the name changed to Oregon Weekly Times. Following the Western Star were the Weekly Oregonian, at Portland, a whig newspaper, founded by T. J. Dryer, a printer with political ambition, the first number appearing December 4, 1850, and the Oregon Statesman, first published March 28, 1851, at Oregon City, by Asahel Bush, and afterward removed to Salem. The Oregonian and Statesman are still published. A third paper, whig in politics, was started at Oregon City in 1855, by W. L. Adams and called the Oregon Argus. With them in the field, both whigs and democrats were vigorously represented.

24

The first printing press, as has already been mentioned, was a gift. It was the only one in Oregon for a period of six years. It was known as the Mission press, and is now in the museum of Oregon Historical Society. It was a Ramage, the first press west of the Rocky mountains. The first books printed thereon were in the native dialects of the Nez Perce's and the Spokanes. This press was given to the Whitman and Spalding missions by American Board missionaries stationed at Honolulu. With it was a supply of "types, furniture, paper and other things." The outfit arrived at Lapwai, May 13, 1839, by pack train, and a printer, Mr. E. O. Hall, of Honolulu, who came at the same time, remained until 1840, when members of the missions were able to carry on the work.

There were nine of these books, printed between 1839 and 1845, after which the press was taken to The Dalles, and later served at Tualatin plains, 1848 and 1849. Nez Perce's First Book, bore the imprint, Clear-Water, Mission Press, 1839, and was an eight page grammar and lexicon in the language of that tribe. The second book, published in August of the same year, was also in the Nez Perce's language. The third, in 1840, had 52 pages and comprised an edition of 800 copies. Mr. Hall having departed, the missionaries continued the work, publishing a Spokane dialect primer, a book of simple laws, a hymn book and a book of scripture. The eighth, in 1845, bore the imprint of M. G. Foisy printer, "printed at the Press of the Oregon Mission, under the direction of the American Board, C. F. Missions, Clear Water," and was a translation of the gospel of Matthew. The last of the series was a small dictionary of Nez Perce's and English.

25

The first novel, or work of fiction, written by an American on the Pacific coast, was by Sidney Moss, at Oregon City, 1843, but his manuscript was sent to Cincinnati, Ohio, where it was printed under the name of Emerson Bennett, a popular author, with the title "The Prairie Flower." A sequel was subsequently published entitled "Leoni Loti." Both books were romantic tales of adventurous experiences in crossing the plains, and in coming in contact with the native people of the great west.

The first magazine to be printed on the Pacific coast was the Oregon Monthly. It was edited and published by S. J. McCormick, at Portland, beginning in 1852, with several poems by the editor, including one entitled "The Editor's Address to his Patrons, Friends and Readers." McCormick's printing office, from which it was issued, was on "Front Street, Opposite the Mail Steamship Landing." In 1852, W. L. Adams, under the pseudonym Brakespear, issued a political satire in blank verse, with the title, "Melodrame, Entitled Treasons, Stratagems and Spoils," the principal characters of which were readily recognized as leaders of the democrat party. It was originally printed in the Oregonian, and subsequently reprinted as a pamphlet. Another early publication was "Grains, or Passages in the Life of Ruth Rover," published at Portland, 1854, by Carter and Austin. It was published anonymously, but the author was Margaret J. Bailey. In 1859, Abigail Scott Duniway wrote "Captain Gray's Company," which was published by S. J. McCormick.

26

Now, a movement to divide the territory by establishing a new commonwealth north of the Columbia river was set on foot, and, being favored by conditions, soon acquired momentum. The river had been a natural boundary almost from the beginning of negotiations between the United States and Great Britain over the title to Oregon. In a local political sense it was hardly less a distinct division line, in 1851.

Figures from the census reports of 1849 and 1850 have already been given, and it is fairly estimated that by 1851 the number of whites living north of the river was not less than 1200. As has already been mentioned, settlement by American families, north of the river, had first begun, 1845, when a small group led by Col. M. T. Simmons located in the vicinity of Puget sound. Among these were James McAllister, Samuel B. Crockett, Jesse Ferguson, David Kindred, Gabriel Jones and George W. Bush, nearly all of them having families. They had come across the plains with the overland caravans of 1844, and had arrived at Fort Vancouver in the autumn of that year. Dr. McLoughlin advised them, as he did in other cases, that Americans were taking up the rich lands of the Willamette valley, and that a provisional government had already been erected there. However, they learned also, that this provisional government had prohibited free negroes from residing in the territory, but that the provisional laws at that time were confined in their operation to the district south of the Columbia river. Now, one of their own party, Bush, was a free mulatto, who had a white wife, and who had been generous and helpful on the overland journey, so that many of those who were in the train were under obligations to him. They all decided to stand by him.

The party remained near Vancouver, on the north side of the river, until the spring of 1845, when, in spite of hints that the region north of the river was to be British soil, they ventured to the Puget sound country for settlement. Colonel Simmons was a Kentuckian of strong personality and he became an active figure in the territory. He began to establish a town under the name Newmarket, near the present city of Olympia, but changed the name to Tumwater. It was not long until the provisional legislature passed a resolution confirming the land claim of the mulatto, Bush, and in 1855, congress passed a special act to secure his title, as under the donation act he could not qualify. Many of the party remained but a short time at Puget sound, and removed to Willamette valley. These first settlers north of the river were soon followed by others, among whom were Ford, Sylvester, Rabbeson, Chapman, Chambers, Ebey, Lansdale, Collins and Maynard. Some of these settled on Whidbey island, others found locations near Steilacoom. Prior to 1851, several settlers had located on Cowlitz river and at Chinook, Cathlamet and opposite Oak Point on the Columbia river, but the settlements, considering the vast extent of the fertile lands free for the taking, were still sparse and far apart.

27

When the Simmons party settled at the sound, the title to the region was still undetermined, although just about to be confirmed to the United States. But it was not long before the growing population north of the Columbia looked forward to forming a separate government, as a territory under the laws of the United States. The Puget sound basin had sea communication with San Francisco, where it found a rich market for its lumber and agricultural produce in the gold mining period, while travel from the settlement at Puget sound to the Willamette valley by way of the Cowlitz river was difficult and precarious. Since the Willamette valley and Puget sound had the same kind of products, trade from each locality obeyed a simple economic law in moving directly by water to San Francisco, a common market. There was so little occasion for commercial interchange between the two Oregon districts that their people were practically unacquainted, and the seat of government in Oregon seemed far away.

John B. Chapman, the fourth of July orator at Olympia, 1851, struck a responsive chord when he alluded in a flight of patriotic fancy to the "future state of Columbia," and considerable enthusiasm was manifested at a convention, held at Cowlitz, August, 1852, to take into consideration the position of the northern counties, their particular wants, and the propriety of appealing to congress for a division of the territory. Although the Cowlitz convention recommended the creation of four new counties under the existing territorial government, thereby indicating that it was not over-confident of the success of the separation movement, the action of the Oregon legislature, in the winter of 1851-2, providing for but one new county, fanned the flame of desire, and the movement was renewed, now ably supported by the first newspaper established north of the Columbia river, the Columbian, issued at Olympia, September, 1852.

Another convention was called for November 25, 1852, at Monticello, near the mouth of the Cowlitz river, a location chosen with proper consideration for settlers near the north bank of the Columbia. This meeting was attended by delegates from the new settlement at Seattle, now appearing in historical annals for the first time, and by others from as far north as Port Townsend and Whidbey island. A memorial to congress was prepared, setting forth the isolation of the northern community, and other reasons for a separate government. It urged congress to set apart the country north and west of the Columbia river, an area of some 32,000 square miles, or less than a tenth of the entire territory of Oregon. The name Columbia was proposed.

28

Success of the plan was hastened by the assent of the Oregon legislature, which, November 4, 1852, had already adopted a memorial of similar purport. Congress acted with unprecedented promptness. Pressed by Lane, the bill for the creation of the new territory was passed by the house of representatives almost immediately. It encountered little opposition in the senate, and was signed by President Fillmore, March 2, 1853. However, the name was changed to Washington, at the suggestion of Representative Stanton of Kentucky. In the senate, Stephen A. Douglas reported an amendment substituting the name Washingtonia, for the purpose of avoiding, as he said, confusion in the mails, but the amendment was not urged, since the session was then drawing to a close.

Boundaries were changed to include all that portion of Oregon territory lying and being south of the 49th degree of north latitude, and north of the middle channel of the Columbia river, from its mouth to where the 46th degree of latitude crosses said river, near Fort Walla Walla, thence with the 46th degree of latitude to the summit of the Rocky mountains. This placed in the new territory the greater portion of the present "panhandle" of Idaho and most of the part of Montana lying west of the Rocky mountains. The boundary underwent numerous readjustments before it was settled as at present.

When Oregon was made a state, 1859, its eastern boundary began on the north at the intersection of the Snake river and the 46th parallel, extending south up the middle channel of the Snake river to its junction with the Owyhee river, near the present town of Nyssa, and thence south to the present northern boundary of Nevada. The remainder of old Oregon was included in Washington territory, and in consequence, Washington had an area of about 244,000 square miles for a time, while that of the state of Oregon was 96,690 square miles. By the creation of the territory of Idaho, the area of Washington was reduced to 69,180 square miles, as at present.

29

An effort, unproductive of results, was made in 1853 and 1854 to start a movement for the creation of a separate territory in southern Oregon, where the people felt a sense of remoteness from the seat of government, and where recent mining activity was creating a population whose interests differed somewhat from those of the inhabitants of the Willamette valley. General Lane received a letter from H. L. Preston, of Crescent City, California, dated December 3, 1853, indicating that steps were being taken to carve new territories out of that state also, the ultimate aim being to create a Republican Empire on the Pacific coast.

Pursuant to a call published in the Yreka (California) Mountain Herald of January 30, 1854, a mass meeting of citizens of Jackson county was held at Jacksonville "for the purpose of taking into consideration the propriety of organizing a new territory and to devise means to effect the same." Samuel F. Culver was

elected chairman and T. McF. Patton, secretary. According to
the meager records of the meeting, L. F. Mosher, a son-in-law of
Joseph Lane, was called on to explain the purposes of the movement, and a committee of five was appointed to draft a memorial
to the Oregon legislature. Delegates were elected to attend a general convention, the date of which was set for February 25, and
the secretary was instructed to enter into correspondence with
citizens of other southern Oregon counties. The movers appear
to have been unsuccessful in their efforts to persuade their neighbors that a new territory was practicable, and the plan died a
natural death. The projected convention was never held.

30

Organization meetings of the democrat party, early in 1852,
were of considerable moment because they marked the beginning
of local political thinking in terms of national issues. Although,
as has been made plain, Americans had forced the creation of
provisional government, and had shaped its course, abating nothing of their nationalism, except on the occasion when, 1845, Applegate's expedient was used to effect a compromise with the
Hudson's Bay interests, it may be said that party lines were not
defined in the early days of territorial government. Thurston,
the first delegate, who was pro-missionary in his leanings, was a
democrat, but there was no party organization in Oregon at the
time of his election. He was decidedly against the Hudson's Bay
Company. Lane was a democrat, who had strong southern sympathies. When he ran for the place left vacant on Thurston's
death, 1851, his opponent was W. H. Willson, a former ship carpenter, who had come out with the first reinforcement of Jason
Lee's mission, 1837, and who shared the missionary hostility to
the Hudson's Bay Company. But he was also a democrat, so that
no party issue was joined and the nominations just mentioned
were not nominations made by party caucus or conventions.

It was evident that, if Oregon should aspire to statehood, the
burning question of slavery would enter into the debates. President Taylor, February 13, 1850, submitted to congress the petition of California to be accorded statehood. The constitution that
had been adopted in California prohibited slavery. By the terms
of the Missouri Compromise, which excluded slavery from all territory north of 36° 30', congress had no right to exclude slavery,

and the question was one to be decided by the people of the new territory. But a fierce debate began, that was not to end until civil war settled the question by abolishing slavery from the Union. President Taylor died July 9, 1850, and was succeeded by Millard Fillmore. Three great American statesmen who had evinced great interest in Oregon affairs died about this time, John C. Calhoun, of South Carolina, March, 1850; Henry Clay, of Kentucky, June, 1852; and Daniel Webster, of New Hampshire, October, 1852.

By 1852, opposition to Governor Gaines, as a non-resident appointee and a whig, crystallized the organization of Oregon democrats as a party, of which Lane became the logical candidate, as he had avoided making political enemies, had a record in public affairs which most of the people approved, and had talent for effective campaigning in the frontier settlements. The democrats first made themselves known as an organization by holding a convention July 4, 1851, and thereafter by holding caucusses of democrat members of the legislature of 1851, at which a central committee was chosen and J. W. Nesmith was made chairman. The population was preponderantly democratic, and the party organization had no difficulty in electing a large majority of the legislature in June, 1852.

On the accession of President Pierce, Lane was appointed by him as governor of the territory, to succeed Gaines, and he accepted the appointment as a personal tribute. He resigned, however, May 19, 1853, three days after displacing Gaines, and announced his purpose of becoming a candidate for delegate in congress to succeed himself. He preferred life at the capital of the nation. George Law Curry, who had been appointed secretary of state by Pierce, and who had taken office, May 14, 1853, by Lane's resignation became ex-officio governor, holding until December 2, of the same year, when Pierce appointed John W. Davis, of Indiana, to the vacant governorship.

Lane, who was a shrewd politician, counted his chances accurately, for he was reelected delegate by a majority of 1570, in a total vote of 7588, at the election of June, 1853. His chief opponent was Alonzo A. Skinner, formerly a judge under the provisional government, a commissioner with Gaines to treat with the Indians, 1851, and later Indian agent for the Rogue river tribes.

Skinner was nominally a whig. He knew that this was a fact unfavorable to his prospects in the then-existing political atmosphere, for the whigs were not yet organized as a party in Oregon, nor were they politically popular, but he attempted to disarm partisanship by announcing that he had become a candidate at the behest of certain of his fellow-citizens, without distinction of party. He deprecated partisan strife among neighbors in a new territory.

"I hold," said Skinner, in a statement, "that parties are unnecessary and pernicious unless when organized to effect some practical measure of a public and beneficial nature. Whilst we are in a territorial condition we have no power by our own votes, or by the votes of our representatives, to affect in the slightest degree the national politics. The introduction of them into our midst I should hold therefore fraught with no good consequences, but only of ill blood, strife, evil. I hold that a delegate from Oregon should not be the representative of a whig party, nor a democrat party, but the representative of Oregon. He ought not to endeavor to secure the adoption of either whig measures, or democratic measures, but the adoption of Oregon measures. Whatever will develop the resources, advance the interests, and promote the prosperity of the country deserves his cordial support, irrespective of its party effects."

Skinner outlined an ambitious program of internal improvement at federal expense. He favored connecting the Atlantic and Pacific oceans with an "iron track;" he advocated liberal appropriations by the general government for roads into and through the territory, "not for military purposes only, but for the benefit of the people of Oregon;" he urged appropriations for surveying and improving rivers and harbors, grants of land for schools of agriculture, revision of the land laws, to permit the heirs of a deceased settler to take such land as the settler would have been entitled to claim if he had lived, and extension of the commutation privilege to Oregon, so as to permit citizens to take land and pay for it at a price to be fixed by the government, without the requirement of residence on their claims. But his platform was 80 years in advance of the times, and he was not elected.

31

Other changes in the local government came as a result of

Pierce's election as president, among which was a clean sweep in the federal judiciary. Strong, Nelson and Pratt were superseded. The new appointments brought forward two democrats, who were destined to prominence in the affairs of territory and state. One of these was Matthew P. Deady, who had come to Oregon with the mounted ride regiment in 1849, and soon was to be regarded as a leader. He had won some distinction as chairman of the committee on judiciary in both houses of the territorial legislature. He served as territorial judge, and after the creation of the state of Oregon, he was appointed United States district judge, and continued through his life to be a prominent figure on the federal bench. The other was George H. Williams, of Keokuk, Iowa, who also became a man of mark and a potent influence in directing the thought of the people of the commonwealth.

Pratt's name was at first submitted to the United States senate, as successor to Chief Justice Nelson, but it encountered the personal opposition of Stephen A. Douglas, so that Judge Williams was named as chief justice instead. The third appointee was Cyrus Olney, a resident of the territory since 1851. Williams, Deady and Olney qualified and entered upon the discharge of the judicial duties.

32

A complete list of the judges of the supreme court of the territory of Oregon follows: William P. Bryant, chief justice, appointed 1848, resigned 1850; Peter H. Burnett, associate justice (declined) 1848; James Turney, associate justice (declined) 1848; Orville C. Pratt, associate justice, appointed (vice Turney) 1848, term expired 1853; Thomas Nelson, chief justice, appointed 1850 (vice Bryant), term expired 1853; William Strong, associate justice, appointed 1850 (vice Burnett), term expired 1853; George H. Williams, chief justice, appointed 1853, re-appointed, resigned 1858; Cyrus Olney, associate justice, appointed 1853, re-appointed, resigned 1858; Matthew P. Deady, associate justice, appointed 1853 (commission vacated as informal); Obadiah B. McFadden, associate justice, appointed 1853 (removed 1854); Matthew P. Deady, re-appointed 1854 (vice McFadden), term expired by admission of Oregon, 1859; Reuben P. Boise, associate justice, appointed 1858 (vice Olney), term expired by admission of Oregon, 1859.

33

Deady was assigned to the first district, comprising the counties of southern Oregon; Olney to the third district, originally composing the northern counties, but which had been reduced in size by the creation of Washington territory; and Williams to the remaining counties. The new judges held one term of court, when Deady was removed and Obadiah B. McFadden arrived with a commission to serve in his stead; but McFadden was appointed a judge of the territory of Washington, soon after, and Judge Deady was reinstated. In order to equalize the judicial burdens, the legislature soon redistricted the territory, placing Marion, Linn, Polk and Benton counties in the district presided over by Williams, Clatsop, Clackamas, Washington and Yamhill in Judge Olney's district and the remaining counties in Deady's district, as before. Other federal offices filled by appointment of President Pierce, 1853, were: Superintendent of Indian affairs, Joel Palmer; United States district attorney, Benjamin F. Harding; United States marshal, James W. Nesmith; collector of customs for the port of Astoria, John Adair; collector for the port of Umpqua, Addison C. Gibbs; postal agent, A. L. Lovejoy.

34

An uproar that arose in connection with the appointment of Deady was heard from one end of the territory to the other. Deady had not much more than taken his place on the bench in pursuance of his first appointment when McFadden's arrival with a commission appointing him to the same position suddenly deprived Deady of the honor and the emoluments he had scarce begun to enjoy. The regularity of the credentials which McFadden produced seemed unquestionable, so he qualified and held one term of court in the district. It was found that, in the commission issued to Deady, the latter's given name was written "Mordecai," whereas, in fact it was "Matthew." In some quarters the error was attributed to the machinations of the whig, Amory Holbrook, who was in the east at the time Deady was appointed; but this only intensified the feeling that the national administration was out of touch with Oregon affairs. Nesmith wrote to Deady, October 21, 1853: "I know that the late fed'l officers and especially Holbrook would do anything in their power to damn you, but what appears strangest to me is that a Democratic administration should take so important a step upon the recommendation of its enemies. I suppose that the thing has been brought about by that renowned Brigadier Gen'l Cushing, aided and assisted by Amory Holbrook." Lane, in Washington, disclaimed knowledge, and wrote to Nesmith: "It is not necessary for me to say that I am and have been from the first greatly pained at the removal of Deady, and if it had been possible would have had him put right before now. It must be done. But, my dear friend, you and others must have patience." And in a postscript, he added: "Deady shall be put right or I shall have a row."

At this time Deady and his group were in control of the democratic political organization. McFadden was received with extreme coolness, and the suggestion was openly conveyed to him that he ought to resign. He protested that he had had no knowledge that he was to supercede a democrat, and that he had believed he was displacing one of the whig appointees. The party was deeply stirred, but the matter was finally adjusted by President Pierce appointing McFadden judge for Washington territory, as stated above, whereupon Deady was reappointed in February, 1854, and again took the oath of office and resumed his seat upon the bench. His temperament was that of an advocate rather than a judge, and he was not of a forgiving disposition. He was unable, therefore, to withdraw entirely from partisan politics and he continued for a long time to bear a part of the responsibilities of political management.

35

The currents of politics now became turbulent, as the result of several circumstances, one of which was the early and capable organization of the democrats, who were dominated by forceful characters, like Asahel Bush, editor of the Oregon Statesman, L. F. Grover, B. F. Harding, J. W. Nesmith and R. P. Boise, usually denominated the "Salem clique." Judge O. C. Pratt, although a federal appointee, was by some regarded as also a member of the inner council. The word was humorously pronounced "kli-kew" by their political foes, and many stories of the intolerance of these leaders enliven the intimate history of the period. The attack on Joel Palmer, for appointing "know-nothing whigs" to positions under his Indian agency was laid at their door, and they opposed the naming of any others than democrats even as officers of volunteers in the early Indian wars. Deady was always consulted.

36

Governor Davis, for all that he was a democrat, was unable to propitiate them, although he profited by the experience of Gaines and sent no messages to the legislature when not asked to do so. Not even the fact that he brought with him $40,000, which congress had appropriated for the construction of a capitol building and a penitentiary, sufficed to establish him in the good graces of the dominant powers, and he resigned after nine unhappy months in office, in which the whigs made the most of the fact that a democrat president had refused to recognize the local demand for home rule, as the whig, Taylor, had likewise done in appointing Gaines. The governor enjoyed a reprisal when he declined the proffered honor of a farewell banquet, in a public letter in which he tendered the democrats of Oregon some sound, although unsolicited, advice.

Davis' letter, published in the Oregonian, August 5, 1854, was addressed to George H. Williams, and others. It assigned domestic reasons for resignation, expressed regret that the people of Oregon had voted against holding a constitutional convention, and continued:

"I will be pardoned, I know, if I say a parting word, by way of admonition, to my political friends. More than thirty years of continued advocacy of democratic principles entitles me to assume this privilege, and to you I say, you can only maintain your supremacy by being united in your efforts; all sectional and personal considerations should be abandoned, at once and forever, and principles only made the foundation of your efforts. We believe we have the right and truth with us, and want no other aids to insure success; a firm, decided, but respectful exercise of these weapons will ever keep the party in the ascendant, while division must inevitably result in defeat. Our opponents are entitled to their opinions equally with ourselves, and this difference of opinion does not necessarily bring with it an interruption of our social relations, for the old maxim is not more trite than true, that 'it is manly to differ but childish to quarrel because we differ;' and when among our political opponents there are found those who, acting upon the principles that 'the end justifies the means,' resort to slander and detraction, as adjuncts to their cause, they have more claim to pity than to anger."

With this parting shot Davis left for Indiana, with the expressed intention of returning later to make his home in the territory as a private citizen, but he died soon afterward, in the east.

37

Oregon was very far from the eastern states, but its isolation did not serve to keep it from having an interest in national, social and political issues that enlivened this period. Two of these were the great nation-wide temperance movement and the know-nothing political agitation. The Maine law, adopted in the state of Maine, 1851, prohibited manufacture and sale, directly or indirectly, of any spirituous or intoxicating liquor. But, provision was made for the appointment, in towns, of suitable agents to sell liquor for medicinal and mechanical uses. Warrants of search might be issued, and the sheriff, or constable, must search the store, shop, warehouse, or building, and if liquor were found, must seize it, but no dwelling could be searched unless liquor had been sold therein. The passage of this bold law stimulated the already active temperance movement in the states, and everywhere there were meetings advocating or denouncing proposed stringent liquor laws. Attempts to enforce such laws incited riots, much litigation was engendered and carried into the courts, and political parties were profoundly affected. By 1854, numerous cases in the courts had held that such laws were constitutional, or unconstitutional.

Oregon was deeply stirred. A temperance convention at Salem, May, 1852, was for adopting the Maine law verbatim in this territory. Delegates representing several counties attended these conventions. The Maine law was accepted as a model, and a legislative committee was appointed to confer with candidates for the legislature. Oregon newspapers reprinted numerous articles on the subject, taken from the eastern press. In April, 1854, another convention was held at Salem, at which the Maine law, with modifications, was supported, and an energetic campaign was launched with the purpose of having local conventions called and held in each of the several counties to nominate candidates for the legislature.

The effect was to present an important issue to the voters, but to divide the state on new lines of cleavage, that split both the democrat and opposition parties. For, while officially the democrats now presented a solid front against their enemies, whether whigs or know-nothings, the democrats actually were far from unanimous against the liquor control bill; and, while the opposition were charged by the Statesman with advocacy of the measure, it was by no means a certainty that all the anti-democrats were for temperance legislation. In Marion county, there was no whig ticket, but there was a support for a Maine law; the reverse was true in Washington county; and, in Polk and Yamhill counties, there were whigs and independents both for and against the Maine law. The convention of Marion county democrats, May 6, 1854, declared that democrats did not recognize the Maine law as a legitimate political issue, and the Statesman fought against it, not only because the newspaper opposed any prohibition law, on principle, but also on the ground that the temperance issue was but a trick of the whigs to aid in the defeat of the democrats.

38

The result favored the democrats, who elected the legislative candidates, with but a loss of eight seats obtained by whigs. The intensity of the fight had tended to solidify the democrat party and to eliminate factions therein. But for several years, the growing opposition in the eastern states to resident foreigners, and to the Roman Catholics, had developed a new social and political issue that had its counterpart in Oregon. By 1853, when feeling ran high, there were street riots in the larger cities of the east and various anti-foreign organizations were formed. A non-political society in New York, called the Order of United Americans, had an off-shoot, under the name Know-nothings, whose members were given opportunity to display their political and social prejudices, and did so as a secret organization, opposed to Catholics and pledged to vote for no political candidate not an American of three generations. The name of the new party was the American party, but it continued to be popularly designated as know-nothing, presumably from the fact that members, when questioned by outsiders, answered that they knew nothing of such an organization.

Immigration from Europe was reaching great figures. The United States seemed to be the refuge open to all Europe. Labor began to organize and to make demands for shorter days, better wages, and for improved and sanitary places of work. There was a ferment of socialism, generally called by the name liberalism. In Oregon, this new political movement began suddenly, and at once menaced both parties, but especially was resisted by the democrats. Most of the members of the know-nothing secret party were from the ranks of the whigs. Bush began to attack them as early as 1852, and thereafter any person suspected as an adherent was violently attacked in the Statesman, whenever occasion offered. He charged the whig party with exhibiting the unjust attitude of the old alien and sedition laws, and, by 1854, he was representing the know-nothings as a secret society with principal strength in the eastern states, advocating native Americanism, and he imputed to it all the evils of abolitionism and whiggery.

Dryer, in the Oregonian, thought the apprehension of the democrats unjustified, and sneered at the violence of his competitor, saying that for his own part he knew nothing of such an organization in Oregon; but, by October and November, 1854, Dryer found know-nothingism useful in his attacks upon the democrats and he practically supported, if he did not adopt, the principles of the secret party. His claim was that a native born American, made free by the best blood of the revolutionary sires, and educated under laws and institutions truly American, should be able to vote in accordance with dictates of his own conscience, in spite of the objections of the democrats, whom he constantly referred to as the Durhamites.

39

It is not possible to give reliable figures as to the number of voters that were members of the new organization, but there is no doubt that they increased rapidly, and that they were confident and enthusiastic. But, November 1, 1854, the Statesman came out with a complete and sensational exposure. Bush claimed that he had the statement of a reliable friend, who said that he had joined through curiosity the "Supreme Order of the Star Spangled Banner," or know-nothings, and who had now revealed all the details, including form of initiation, signs, grips, tokens and pass words, the list of Salem members, and a statement of what had transpired at meetings of the order. He condemned the whole organization for bigotry, intolerance and stupidity, and asserted that the whole was ridiculous humbug. He claimed that nearly all the members were whigs, but admitted that there were a few democrats.

A letter from Nesmith to Lane, dated January 1, 1855, gives some details: "Nothing has occurred here worthy of note since I last wrote you, with the exception of some astounding developments in relation to the 'Know Nothings.' Holbrook introduced the order into this Territory about August last. It was then supposed that its influence would be confined to the Towns, and that it could not obtain a footing in the country, but in this however, we find ourselves mistaken. The Whig leaders have made every exertion to spread it throughout the country; and I regret to say that their efforts are being crowned with success. They number now 300 in Portland, about 150 in Oregon City, about 100 at Lafayette and about 90 here, besides various lodges scattered about in different parts of the country. One of their members at this place who can be relied upon has divulged everything to Bush and he is making use of it to defeat their plans. They intend to complete a thorough Organization through the Territory so as to enable them to carry the next election, and I assure you that from present indication there is reason to fear that they may be successful in the accomplishment of their object. They avow in their Lodges that their real object is to break down and disorganize the democratic party. As a matter of course they sweep all the Whigs, Softs, tenderfooted and disaffected. Such men for instance as Wiley Chapman, of this place . . . readily fall into their ranks. These things can readily be accounted for with such Democrats who are 'out,' but why the treason should extend to the 'Ins' is more than I can account for, but such is the melancholy fact. . . ."

The next weekly number of the Statesman was mostly devoted to the know-nothing issue. The editor says that demands have been made for the name of his informant, but he refuses to reveal the source of his information. He continues his sensational exposures and defies those who threaten to hold him personally responsible. The local know-nothing organization changed its place of meeting, but there was no escape. The newspaper had inside information and continued the printing of its exposure and denunciations. It acted very much as a modern sensational newspaper would act under similar circumstances.

The result was that the American movement in Oregon had a serious set back. Few had the courage to defy the blasts and to admit membership; and Bush's assertion that no one known as a member could ever hope for political preferment, had its effect upon democrats as well as whigs, and the know-nothing party as an organization dwindled to nothing.

40

A viva voce bill, promoted by Bush and the Salem clique, was adopted by the legislature, December, 1854, to establish a censorship over voters. It was conceived in the partisan spirit of the period, and originally was aimed at the American, or know-nothing party. It provided that all votes "shall be given viva voce, or by ticket handed to the judges, and shall in both cases be cried out in an audible voice by the officer attending, and noted by the clerk in the presence and hearing of the voters." The bill was strongly supported by democrats, who made it a party issue. It passed the house, December 15, 1854, by a vote of 14 yeas to 12 nays, and the council, December 21, by five yeas to three nays. It is said to have operated well in the election of 1857, as a check on the designs of those who secretly harbored a desire to see slavery imposed on the new state.

The general provisions of this law were subsequently carried forward in the state constitution, which provided: "In all elections by the legislative assembly, or by either branch thereof, votes shall be given openly, or viva voce, and not by ballot, forever; and in all elections by the people, votes shall be given openly, or viva voce, until the legislative assembly shall otherwise direct." Difference in the use of the word "openly," in the constitution, for the phrase "by ticket handed to the judges," in the statute, may be noted, although the legal effect was the same.

41

In 1851, while Gaines was governor, a public meeting was held in Portland, at which a resolution was adopted setting forth that "there are many respectable individuals in Oregon capable of discharging the duties devolving upon the judges, as well as filling any other office under the territorial government, who would either discharge the duties or resign the office." This was published in the Statesman, April 11, 1851. The territorial legislature, December, 1851, adopted a memorial asking congress so to amend the organic act as to permit the people of the territory to elect their own officers. This was not a demand for statehood, but it was very close to that. At the following session an act was adopted, however, by the two houses and signed by their respective presiding officers, January 19 and January 20, 1852, which provided that in the event that congress should adjourn without acting upon this memorial, the president of the council and the speaker of the house of representatives should issue a proclamation authorizing a poll to be opened, within 60 days thereafter, for the purpose of taking a vote of the people upon the question of calling a convention to form a state constitution. Almost at once, therefore, after organization as a territory, the young commonwealth began to aspire to statehood and home rule.

42

The arrival of Davis, an appointee from outside of the territory, bearing a commission as governor, which made it appear that the democrat national party was no more likely than its whig predecessor had been to recognize local claims, was the signal for the passage of this act. The move for statehood met with opposition, founded, in part, on belief that the statehood movement was primarily a democratic scheme to obtain more offices, but also on the real, or pretended, ground of economy. The issue was voted on by the people, June, 1854, when the measure was defeated by a majority of 869. Commenting upon this vote, the Oregonian, August 5, 1854, foresaw a renewal of the contest and urged organization to consolidate the strength of the opposition. "Let them understand that your votes cannot be obtained for a measure, which must inevitably be destructive to the masses of the people, merely to pacify the morbid appetites for office and power on the part of a few party hucksters. . . . Tell these office hunters to go to work and earn their bread by the sweat of their brows."

But the agitation was continued, and proponents of statehood made a better showing in 1855, when 4420 votes were cast in favor of framing a state constitution, and 4835 against; a negative majority this time of only 415. Meanwhile, Curry had acted as governor ex-officio in succession to Davis, and November 1, 1854, he was formally appointed governor by President Pierce. This ought logically to have satisfied the aspirations of the home rule party, but, notwithstanding the appointment of an Oregon man, the constitution movement continued. Its adoption by the democrats as a party measure gave it the benefit of party organization, when the "democratic dogma of statehood" became the predominant issue in the territory. It also received the support of one of the whig leaders, David Logan.

43

Another bill submitting the question to the people, therefore, was passed at the legislative session of 1856, and a special election was held in April, 1856, at which the majority against a constitution was reduced to 249. Lane, in congress, introduced a bill for admission to statehood by congressional action. His bill failed to pass, for the reason that the members of congress thought the population of the territory insufficient, but also because of whig apprehensions in the east lest the new state, which had persistently sent a democrat as delegate to congress, should array itself on the side of slavery in both house and senate. Soon after this, however, there was a sweeping change of whig sentiment in the territory. The leaders of that party began to fear that President Buchanan was preparing a policy of forcing slavery upon free territories by federal action. "If we are to have the institution of slavery fastened upon us here," was the whig announcement, "we desire the people resident in Oregon to do it, and not the will and power of a few politicians in Washington City." The question was therefore submitted again in the 1857 election, and this time statehood was carried by a vote of 7617 to 1679, a decisive, overwhelming majority of 5938.

44

March 6, 1857, two days after the inauguration of President Buchanan, the Supreme Court of the United States rendered a decision in the famous Dred Scott case in which the Missouri Compromise act of 1820 was held unconstitutional. The opinion of Chief Justice Roger B. Taney in effect said that a negro had no rights, and that a slave might be taken by his master into free territory without losing his property right. Congress had no power to prohibit slavery in any state or territory. The decision was followed by a storm of protest in the newspapers of the north, and bitter denunciation of the court and its decision. The effect of the decision as applied to Oregon was a question everywhere debated in that territory.

45

There was more than the usual surface opposition to Lane for delegate to congress, in the election of 1857. This was the direct result of his known pro-slavery inclinations. A peculiar combination of circumstances by this time prevailed which made it seem not only possible, but even highly probable, that slavery might be imposed upon the territory. It is interesting now after the lapse of many years, and after the burning questions concerning slave holding are no longer living issues, to note that there were courageous men among the democrats in Oregon who did not disguise their opposition to the introduction of slavery.

As early as 1853, Judge George H. Williams, a democrat appointed to hold office under a democrat administration, dared to decide according to his conscience, although against what was then the prevailing popular opinion. In an address made by him many years afterward to the Oregon pioneers, he told the story in these words: "Among the first cases I was called upon to decide [as chief justice] when I first came to Oregon, in 1853, was an application by a colored family in Polk county to be liberated upon habeas corpus from their Missouri owner, who had brought and held them here as slaves. They were held upon the claim that the constitution of the United States protected slave property in the territories; but it was my judgment that the law made by the pioneers upon the subject (in 1844) was not inconsistent with the spirit of the constitution and was the law of the land, and the petitioners were set free; and, so far as I know, this was the last attempt at slave holding in Oregon. When the state government was formed, strenuous efforts were put forth to make Oregon a slave state; but inspired by the example and sentiments of the early pioneers we decided to go into the Union as a free state. . . ."

Williams became a member of the constitutional convention, 1857, and subsequently, when the question was before the people for decision, his speeches did much to turn the tide against admission of slavery. He was active in organizing the Union party movement, supported Lincoln during the war, and was elected, in 1864, United States senator as a Union republican. Although Oregon became a free state by majority vote, it elected an outspoken pro-slavery democrat (Whiteaker) as its first governor.

46

The undercurrents of opinion, the conflicting desires and emotions of the people, and in particular the sound reasons which the opponents of slavery had for apprehension as to the outcome, have been set forth by a keen observer of and participant in the events of that stirring time, T. W. Davenport, who said: "Some pro-slavery democrats, confident of the approval and patronage of the Washington administration, would not be silenced, and were advocates, by speech and press, of their opinions. And they were far more numerous than those democrats of free-state proclivities who dared speak out. And, of the latter, some would say, 'I shall vote against slavery, but if it carries I shall get me a nigger.' Add to all these the fact of the great donations of land by the general government, section and half-section claims occupying the valleys of the richest portion of the territory, and the scarcity and high price of labor, and we may not wonder at their anxiety. They had undoubtedly read in their histories of the frequent attempts of the settlers in Indiana territory to obtain from congress a temporary suspension of the anti-slavery ordinance of 1787, so they could obtain laborers to open their timbered farms, but the pioneers of Indiana were restricted in their land holdings as compared with the Oregonians." It was the mature opinion of this commentator, a full half century after the event, that the people of Oregon "were in far more danger of the introduction of slavery among them than the people of Kansas were at any time."

47

National democrats, in various counties, bolted the regular conventions of 1857, and their disaffection crystallized in support of G. W. Lawson, a free state democrat, for delegate to congress, who announced his candidacy as an independent. But Lane was re-elected, receiving 5662 votes to 3471 for Lawson. The republican party had now come into being as a national organization and had largely attracted former whigs and know-nothings. Meetings had been held with a view to organization, but the new party did not yet consider itself sufficiently strong, in Oregon, to venture with a territorial ticket. Division of the democrats weakened that party's hold on the government. There was a democrat majority of only one in the legislative council, and the combined opposition to the control of that party succeeded in electing ten members of the lower house of the legislature.

48

Organization of the free state republican party of Oregon was soon effected. The republicans in the territory had already laid the ground-work of an organization, as early as May, 1856, prior to the nomination of Fremont for president, at a meeting held at Lindley school house, in Eden precinct, Jackson county; and, thereafter, another meeting was held by friends of the republican cause, at Albany, August 20, 1856, to adopt measures for the organization of the republican party in Oregon. At the latter meeting James Hogue presided and Origen Thompson was secretary. The platform adopted contained the declaration: "Resolved, that we fling our banner to the breeze, inscribed, Free speech, free labor, a free press, and Fremont."

Local republican mass meetings were held in various localities in the fall of 1856, and the party had progressed so far by February 11, 1857, that delegates from eight counties attended a party territorial convention at Albany on that date. W. T. Matlock, of Clackamas, was chairman, and Leander Holmes, of Clackamas, secretary. The convention selected a committee to prepare an address to the people on the slavery question, and this address, which was not published until two months afterward, was an able, dispassionate and convincing document, placing the issue squarely before the voters for the first time. John R. McBride, of Yamhill county, one of the delegates to the Albany convention, was subsequently (in 1857), elected a delegate to the constitutional convention, being the only one chosen under that party designation. Organization of the new party was received with volleys of partisan abuse. The "nigger worshipping convention," at Albany, was referred to as a "slim affair" by the leading organ of the democrat machine. The stock name in the columns of the Statesman, for the new party, was black republican.

49

The election at which the people decided to frame a constitution was held in June, 1857; the constitution was to be submitted to the people in November for their approval. The constitutional convention met at Salem, August 17, so that the summer and autumn of 1857 were well filled with political agitation in which slavery overshadowed every other issue. This question, which now en-

grossed the nation, was fairly before the people of Oregon. Pro-
slavery democrats advocated, on the hustings and in the columns
of the newspapers, the introduction of cheap labor to develop the
country. John Whiteaker, afterward the first state governor,
championed the introduction of slavery on the ground that to do
otherwise would be to invite race equality.

The outstanding contribution to the anti-slavery political literature of the period was an exhaustive article written by Judge
George H. Williams and printed July 28, 1857, in the Oregon
Statesman, which had thrown open its columns to both sides in
the discussion. In this article Judge Williams avoided advocacy of
the abolition of slavery in those states where it already existed,
and confined himself to pointing out the inexpediency of extending
it to new territory. "One free white man," he said, "is worth more
than two negro slaves in the cultivation of the soil, or any other
business that can be influenced by zeal or the exercise of discretion," and he argued that Oregon farmers could employ free labor,
more cheaply than they could maintain slaves, which would inevitably degrade the free labor of the country and result in injury
to all concerned. The ethical aspect of the question was ignored
by Judge Williams, doubtless for prudential reasons, but his letter
was influential in determining the result, as no direct attack on the
institution of slavery itself could possibly have been. "After the
circulation of this address," says Davenport, "any observing person could notice that a change was taking place; any sensitive person could feel it."

50

The constitutional convention itself was not prepared to accept
responsibility for committing Oregon on this issue. Discussion of
the topic in the convention was disapproved. Nevertheless, Judge
Matthew P. Deady, who, in making his canvass for election as
delegate to the convention, had openly advocated slavery, was
chosen as chairman. Pro-slavery democrats controlled the organization of the convention, but it was deemed good policy by both
groups to leave the determination of the heated question to popular vote, and an understanding to that effect was reached, so that
the arguments for and against slavery were not voiced in the convention. A proposal to include the anti-slavery provision of the
Ordinance of 1787 in the new constitution was introduced by John
R. McBride, but was decisively defeated, 41 to 9. The slavery issue,

and that of admission of free negroes to the territory, were made into segregated schedules, or separate proposals, to be submitted to the people apart from the constitution itself.

51

The constitution, as at length agreed upon, fixed the salaries of the governor and secretary of state at $1500 a year, that of the state treasurer at $800, and of the supreme court judges at $2000. Establishment of banks under state charter was prohibited, the state was forbidden to subscribe to the stock of any corporation, and the limit of state debt was fixed at $50,000, except in the event of war or invasion. Counties were forbidden to incur indebtedness beyond $5000. Chinese arriving in the state after the adoption of the constitution were not permitted to hold or operate any mining claim; negroes, mulattoes and Chinese were disqualified from voting; the seat of government question was again put up to the people with a provision that it should be submitted at the first election following the meeting of the first state legislature, and when so located, the capital should not be removed for 20 years. Another clause provided that the property and pecuniary rights of a married woman should not be subject to the debts or contracts of her husband, a progressive provision that had recently been adopted in Indiana, Pennsylvania, New York, California and Wisconsin.

The final vote of the convention on the completed constitution was divided upon party lines, 34 for adoption and 11 against, with 15 absent or not voting, the affirmative vote showing the strength of the democratic ruling faction.

52

The members of the constitutional convention were: Levi Anderson, Jesse Applegate, A. D. Babcock, Reuben P. Boise, J. H. Brattain, Paul Brattain, W. W. Bristow, B. F. Burch, A. J. Campbell, Hector Campbell, Stephen F. Chadwick, Jesse Cox, Joseph Cox, R. F. Coyle, John T. Crooks, Matthew P. Deady, Thomas J. Dryer, L. J. C. Duncan, Luther Elkins, Solomon Fitzhugh, William H. Farrar, L. F. Grover, S. B. Hendershott, Enoch Hoult, James K. Kelly, John Kelsay, Robert C. Kinney, Haman C. Lewis, David Logan, A. L. Lovejoy, P. B. Marple, William Matzger, John R. McBride, S. J. McCormick, Charles R. Meigs, Richard Miller, Isaac R. Moores, Daniel Newcomb, H. B. Nichols, Martin Olds, Cyrus Olney, William H. Packwood, J. C. Peebles, P. P. Prim, J. H. Reed, Nathaniel Robbins, Davis Shannon, Erasmus D. Shattuck,

Levi Scott, James Shields, Robert V. Short, Nicholas Schrum, Delazon Smith, W. A. Starkweather, William H. Watkins, John W. Watts, John S. White, Thomas Whitted, Fred Waymire, George H. Williams.

There were 30 farmers, 19 lawyers, three mechanics, three miners, two physicians, one editor, one printer and one surveyor. At least 12 afterward became distinguished in public affairs. Boise was on the supreme court bench for many years. Chadwick served as secretary of state from 1870 to 1877 and was acting governor in 1877-8. Deady was territorial judge from 1853 to 1859 and United States district judge from 1859 until his death in 1893. Farrar was mayor of Portland, 1862. Grover was governor of Oregon from 1870 to 1877 and United States senator, 1879 to 1885. Kelly was United States senator 1871 to 1877, and chief justice 1878 to 1880. Logan was mayor of Portland in 1863. McCormick was mayor of Portland in 1859. Prim was chief justice in 1879-80. Shattuck was circuit judge and associate justice for many years and chief justice 1866-8. Delazon Smith was United States senator for the short term February 14 to March 3, 1859. Williams was chief justice of the territory 1853-9, United States senator 1865-71, one of the joint high commissioners in settling the Alabama claims in 1871, attorney-general of the United States 1872-75, and mayor of Portland 1903-4. Thirty-two of the delegates were born in northern states, 26 in southern states (including Missouri), one in Germany and one in Ireland.

53

The people adopted the constitution at a special election, November 9, 1857, by an affirmative vote of 7195 to 3195, a majority of 4000. Slavery was rejected by a vote of 2645 to 7727, a majority of 5082 against. Free negroes and mulattoes were excluded from the territory by a vote of 8640 to 1081, showing considerably more opposition to the presence of free negroes than to slaves, although the vote is partly accounted for in the desire to improve the chances of success, in view of the free state clause of the constitution, in the expected contest before congress.

The vote by counties was as follows:

Counties	Constitution		Slavery		Free Negroes	
	Yes	No	Yes	No	Yes	No
Benton	440	215	283	368	132	459
Clackamas	530	216	98	655	113	594
Clatsop	62	37	25	71	25	65
Columbia	30	66	11	84	24	66
Coos	68	26	19	72	10	79
Curry	117	14	35	95	8	121
Douglas	419	203	248	377	23	560
Jackson	465	372	405	426	46	756
Josephine	445	139	155	435	41	534
Lane	591	362	356	602	97	783
Linn	1111	176	198	1092	113	1095
Marion	1024	252	214	1055	76	1115
Multnomah	496	255	96	653	112	587
Polk	528	188	231	484	53	584
Tillamook	23	1	6	22	1	25
Umpqua	155	84	32	201	24	181
Wasco	55	89	58	85	18	122
Washington	265	226	68	428	80	393
Yamhill	371	274	107	522	85	521
Total	7195	3195	2645	7727	1081	8640
Majorities	4000			5082		7559

54

Ratification by congress was not completed until more than a year had elapsed. Whether the new state would increase the voting strength of the slave power in senate and house, was the prime consideration. Other questions, publicly debated, were the sufficiency of its population and exclusion of free negroes. Kansas had been refused admission, and the bitterness engendered by this contest had not cooled. The Oregon admission bill was, at length, however, passed by senate and house and approved by President Buchanan, February 14, 1859. An act to extend the federal laws and judicial system over Oregon was passed, March 3, 1859.

By the admission act, the state was required to accept six propositions; in substance, that sections 16 and 36 of the public lands should be reserved as school lands; that 72 sections be set apart for the benefit of a state university and for no other purpose; that 10 sections be reserved for the completion of public buildings;

that salt springs, not exceeding 12 in number, with six sections of land adjoining, be set apart to be disposed of as the legislature should direct; that five per cent of the net proceeds of the sale by congress of public lands within the state be devoted to roads and other improvements, under the direction of the legislature. These were attended by a proviso, "that the foregoing propositions, hereinbefore offered, are on the condition that the people of Oregon shall provide by an ordinance, irrevocable without the consent of the United States, that said state shall never interfere with the primary disposal of the soil within the same by the United States, or with any regulations congress may find necessary for securing the title in the said soil to bona fide purchasers thereof; and that in no case shall non-resident proprietors be taxed higher than residents." These conditions were accepted by the legislature, June 3, 1859, thereby completing the formal incorporation of Oregon into the Union.

55

The legislature of 1855-6 sat for a brief time at Corvallis, but promptly passed a bill relocating the capital at Salem, and then moved without delay to the latter place. There, it submitted the issue of permanent location to the people, to be voted on at the general election in June, 1856. The vote at that time was: Eugene City, 2627; Corvallis, 2327; Salem, 2101; Portland, 1154. The counties of Wasco, Tillamook, Jackson and Josephine failed to make returns to the secretary of the territory within the 40 days provided by law, and therefore were not to be counted, so that the result of the canvass as officially announced was: Eugene City, 2319; Salem, 2049; Corvallis, 1998; Portland, 1154. As the act required a majority to decide, another election became necessary, at which the competitors were Eugene and Salem. This special election was held on the first Monday in October, 1856. Little interest, however, was shown by the general public, and the polls were not even opened in Tillamook, Polk, Curry and Wasco counties. The vote was: Eugene, 2559; Salem, 444; Corvallis, 318.

But there was a strong sentiment among the politicians against recognition of the right of the legislature to delegate the duties conferred upon it by the organic act, which provided that "at said first session, or as soon thereafter as they shall deem expedient, the legislative assembly shall proceed to locate and establish the seat of government for said territory at such place as they may deem eligible, which place, however, shall thereafter be subject to be changed by the said legislative assembly." It was contended, therefore, that the election of October, 1856, had no binding effect, that it was at most an expression of desire, by which the legislature was not bound unless it chose to accept the suggestion. As a consequence, the result of the special election was ignored by people and legislature alike, with what seemed to be general consent. The territorial officers remained at Salem, while a bill to resubmit the question to another vote was lost in the house, at the session of 1856-7, and another, proposing to remove the capital to Portland, was summarily cast aside.

56

To anticipate future action, it may be added that the seat of government question, a by-product of the first decade of statehood, was disposed of in two elections, held in 1862 and 1864, by which Salem was made the capital. In the election of June, 1862, Salem received 3417 votes, to 1921 for Eugene City, 1787 for Portland and 1026 for Corvallis. In the election of 1864, Salem received 6108 votes, a clear majority of 79 over all other aspirants. The vote was: Salem, 6108; Portland, 3864; Eugene City, 1588; Corvallis, 289, all other places, 288. Salem had majorities in the counties of Baker, Clatsop, Columbia, Douglas, Josephine, Linn, Marion, Polk, Tillamook, Umatilla and Wasco. Portland carried the counties of Clackamas, Multnomah, Washington and Yamhill. Eugene carried Coos, Jackson and Lane. Only Benton gave a majority for Corvallis. Curry did not vote on the question.

Marion county, of which Salem was the county seat, was then the most populous county in Oregon, as indicated by the vote cast for representative in congress, the totals being 1435 for Marion and 1342 for Multnomah, the next most populous county. A change in relative positions was even then taking place, however. In the November following, Multnomah cast 1995 votes for presidential electors and Marion 1901. Growth of Portland, which was stimulated by the opening of river transportation to the new mining districts of eastern Oregon, Idaho and Montana and by trade with California and the growing territory of Washington, was now a factor in political and commercial life.

57

Section six of the schedule of the new constitution, in anticipation of early congressional action, provided that, if the constitution be ratified, then a special election would be held on the first

Monday in June, 1858, for the election of members of the legislative assembly, of a representative in congress and also of state and county officers, and that a special session of the state legislative assembly would be convened on the first Monday of July, 1858, which should proceed to elect two senators in congress, and make further provision, as necessary, to complete the organization of a state government.

It was soon evident that the convention had made the mistake of setting these dates too early. Congress did not act promptly to create the state. For a time, from the growing intensity of political feeling, it looked doubtful whether the state would be admitted at all. Lane, writing from Washington to the Statesman, indicated his hope that he might be elected as one of the senators, and advised that the state legislature should hold its regular session in September under the constitution, and the state should begin to function without waiting for congressional action. The fact that he gave such advice led to a breach among the democrats that he could not have foreseen. It is probable that his purpose was to be sure of being senator before losing his position as delegate in congress.

His advice was not followed, but there is no proof that he then entertained the wish (as afterward suspected by some of his political opponents), that, as a state neither in nor out of the Union, Oregon might later fall into the secession movement, to which he became more and more committed as time went on. However, as the spring of 1858 opened, the time came for the various party conventions. These, while nominating state tickets, and members of the state legislature, took the precaution of nominating territorial officers also, a forethought that proved fortunate and saved an otherwise impossible situation. These party conventions were rancorous and partisan in the extreme. By this time, in the nation and in the territory, the split in the democrat party was widening, so that for the first time in Oregon separate tickets were put up by the "state democrats," constituting the thorough-going pro-slavery element, or "hards," as they were sometimes called, and by the "national democrats," constituting the more moderate wing of the party, or "softs."

58

The platform of the state democrat party, which held its convention at Salem, March 16, 1858, inconsistently endorsed both the Kansas-Nebraska act and the principles of the Dred Scott decision, and declared it to be a fundamental principle that a people, in framing a state constitution, have the unconditional right to form and adopt the government which they may think best calculated to secure their liberty, without imposition by congress of any condition as to slavery. Lafayette Grover was nominated for congress by this group, and an advocate of slavery, John Whiteaker, was nominated as governor. On the other hand, members of the national democrat party in the legislative assembly, charging that the state group of democrats (the Salem clique) had juggled with the apportionment of delegates to the convention, "for the election of officers in view of the admission as a state into the federal Union," favored a convention of their own variety of democracy, which was held at Eugene, April 8, 1858, and which nominated James K. Kelly for congress, and E. M. Barnum for governor; and yet at the same time this convention endorsed the record of pro-slavery Lane, as delegate. Such was the inconsistency of political conventions of the times.

59

The republican state convention, held at Salem, April 2, 1858, adopted a resolution denouncing traffic in slaves, and declaring that the slavery question should be determined by each state for itself. It nominated John R. McBride, for congress, and John Denny, for governor.

The result of the June election was a complete victory for the so-called "state" or pro-slavery faction of the democrats, who elected their entire state ticket and most of the state legislature. They elected Grover as member of congress. They elected also for the territorial legislature nine members of the council and thirty members of the house. Thus, the people of Oregon that had just adopted a free-state constitution, and voted against slavery, elected violent advocates of slavery for the first state officers, and they now proceeded to select pro-slavery senators to represent them in the senate at Washington.

60

As directed in the schedule of the new constitution, the state legislature met at Salem, July 5, 1858, in a preliminary first session, notwithstanding the fact that no word had been received from congress, and although there was as yet no state of Oregon. William G. T'Vault was elected speaker and Chester N. Terry, clerk of the house, while Luther Elkins was elected president and George Carpenter chief clerk of the senate. Practically nothing was done, however, at this session excepting to elect Joseph Lane and Delazon Smith as United States senators. Lane was already at Washington, and Smith and Grover departed at once from Salem for the capital. The senators and the representative in congress were therefore chosen before the state of Oregon was created.

State Governor Whiteaker was escorted into the legislative hall at Salem, July 8, 1858, and, after the oath of office had been administered by Judge R. P. Boise, he read an inaugural address, in which the first paragraph was as follows: "You are assembled here today under the provisions of the fundamental law of the state. The people by their own act called a convention; that convention framed a constitution; the people ratified it, and today we put on the habiliments of a full grown man and emerge from territorial vassalage and into state sovereignty. It is worthy of note that while the people of Oregon were preparing for a state organization the government of the United States was menaced and greatly imperiled by the acts of a sister territory [Kansas] while framing for itself a constitution preparatory to entering the Union. It is a matter of gratification that no such lawless conduct and violation of rights characterized the people of our young and fair state while preparing to become one of the members of this great confederacy, and it is attributable to the fact that Oregon was peopled by a high order of citizens, a people possessing a due sense of their moral and political duties to themselves and a spirit of forbearance one toward another. The transition from a territorial existence to that of a state sovereignty is always attended with more or less disorder and delay; but when we consider the change that Oregon has passed through, the people when but a handful organized and successfully maintained a provisional government, which government was superseded by an organic act, and General Lane sent here as our first governor, the people readily accommodated themselves to the governor and his authority, and now they declare they are ready for another change and assume state sovereignty."

The anticipatory session lasted but four days, and although the validity of its action in electing senators was never challenged, the session is not now officially recognized as one of the numbered state assemblies.

61

The summer drifted away without bringing the hoped-for news from Washington. Rather against the advice of leading democrats, but in accordance with Lane's recommendation, a first regular session of the house of representatives of the legislative assembly of the state was then attempted at Salem, September 13, 1858, that being the second Monday in September, the day fixed by the new constitution for the first regular meeting of the legislative assembly. Like the preceding special session, this was too early, and it evidently could not act for a state that as yet had no legal existence, for it was generally understood by the members that congress had adjourned without passing the Oregon bill. After the speaker, W. G. T'Vault, took the chair and called the house to order, C. N. Terry, chief clerk, and J. Henry Brown, doorkeeper, appeared. Representatives Burch, Cochran, Cruzan, Crooks, Dryer, Hannah, Hedges, Jennings and Tichenor, nine in number, appeared and adjourned until the next day, but as only one additional member came at that time the house then adjourned sine die. Two members of the senate appeared, Messrs. Florence and Bristow, but no formal meeting of that body was held except to adjourn. This abortive effort is not counted in state records as a first regular legislative session.

62

The question in Oregon, in the autumn of 1858, was which of its two governors was in authority. As congress could not act until its December session, Governor Whiteaker and the state officers decided to give way to territorial Governor Curry, and the tenth and last Oregon territorial legislature was assembled December 6, 1858, pursuant to the old provisions of territorial law. The session was opened at Salem, and, after organization, a committee was appointed to wait upon territorial Governor Curry and to inform him that the two houses had effected organization and that they were ready to receive communications. The governor then read a lengthy message in which he said: "Notwithstanding the accumulation of doubt which has settled upon the question, we indulge the hope that at the present session of congress Oregon will be admitted as a state in the Union. If its population is numerically insufficient to entitle it to a representative in congress and if after all it is to be excluded on that account, we shall be obliged to hold the general government itself in a great measure responsible for the circumstances."

The message principally discussed states' rights and the slavery question. But Governor Curry, inconsistently enough, while officially acting as territorial governor, took the position that, in view of the Dred Scott decision, congress had no right to establish territorial governments "or to ordain organic laws for the government of any civil community anywhere within boundaries of the United States." He argued in the same breath that the organic act amounted to an inviolable guarantee by congress that Oregon would be admitted as a state when it had sufficient population, and he said, "Most assuredly we ought to insist upon the fulfillment of the terms of that compact."

63

At this session the question that had made trouble in the preceding territorial legislature, about slaves held in Oregon, arose again. Mr. Chapman presented a petition from Lane county asking the legislature to recognize the right of citizens of Oregon in the protection of slave property. Mr. T'Vault then presented three petitions on the same subject. Subsequently there was a majority report by the judiciary committee, through Mr. Chapman, favoring this legislation, with arguments in support thereof. The bill introduced by the majority made it a penal offense to harbor a slave without the master's consent, or to carry a slave out of the territory by boat; it also made slave property assessable, and provided that any person or persons bringing slaves to the territory and owning property in such slaves, according to the constitution of the United States as construed by the supreme court in the Dred Scott case, should have the rights and remedies in the courts of the territory allowed for protection and recovery of any other personal property of like value. There were two minority reports, one by Mr. Craner, supporting the theory that slave property was already protected by law under the Dred Scott decision, and the other by Mr. Shattuck, denying the right of the territory to make slaves property, and claiming that the Dred Scott decision did not alter the legality of the territorial prohibition of slavery. The bill passed the council by a vote of 13 to 9, but did not reach a vote in the house, and so failed. Little but routine work was undertaken during the session, as the members felt the uncertainty of their position, and this final session of the territory of Oregon adjourned January 22, 1859.

Thus it was that a bill for the protection of slave owners in Oregon was very nearly passed, just after the people had voted to adopt a constitution prohibiting slave holding. And the debates in congress on the Oregon bill, carried on during the same winter in which the territorial legislature was considering this pro-slavery measure, make it plain that had the measure been adopted anti-slavery congressmen would not have voted for the statehood bill, and it would have been defeated.

64

Notwithstanding the turbulent state of political affairs, the territory made some industrial progress in the closing days. Immigration, which had been interrupted by the Indian wars, was resumed, and the number of arrivals in 1859 was considerably larger than for several years. Mining had been stimulated by the construction of roads and trails, and a new stampede to the Fraser river country, north of the British Columbia boundary, had furnished a new outlet for restless spirits. Whereas, Indian troubles had caused business depression in the Willamette valley about the middle of the decade, there was now a revival, and southern Oregon, in particular, began to show new signs of enterprise. Large shipments of potatoes from Scottsburg to San Francisco, where they brought excellent prices, gave encouragement to settlers in the Umpqua region. The Coos bay district was attracting attention, and coal banks were being opened near Yaquina bay. Livestock, in this period, became an important source of income to the people. It was estimated by a statistician of the time that between February 1 and June 16, 1857, for illustration, 28,000 head of cattle were driven through the Umpqua valley to markets in the mining regions of southern Oregon and California.

1

THE DECADE of 1848 to 1858 was marked by Indian wars, growing out of a number of causes, among which was the inevitable conflict between the needs of an expanding nation to occupy and utilize the land, and those of a primitive race whose members could not hold exclusive possession of this vast region on economic grounds. These wars, in a large sense, were wars of destiny, perhaps inseparable from the process of quieting the Indian title to the soil. Until it became apparent that the white men were determined to possess the territory, conflicts between the races were restricted to minor and more or less individual encounters.

It is noteworthy that no collisions deserving the name of war occurred in the period preceding the arrival of the first settlers. So long as traders occupied the field, and while their interests and those of the natives were more or less mutual, manifestations of Indian hostility were not common, and were usually traceable to wrongs committed by the whites, or at least to some failure of the latter to comprehend the Indian's character or to sympathize with his customs and traditions. Historical candor requires the admission that the natives did not always lack provocation. A careful reviewer of more than one hundred cases of first contact of whites with Indians reached the conclusion that in practically every instance the attitude of the Indians in the beginning was that of admiration for superior beings. "More valuable still," says this reviewer, "their attitude was uniformly and almost without exception friendly, until it had reason to be inimical."

There is no doubt that early fur traders often took advantage of the untutored savages, and that the conduct of the whites was often selfish, brutal and arrogant, and even dishonest. Such friendly sentiments as the natives at first may have entertained, were not infrequently turned to hatred by the acts of those who should have set an example of virtue. Later arrivals reaped the harvest that their predecessors had sown. The massacre of Jedediah S. Smith's party on the Umpqua, 1828, for example, was due to harsh treatment, and did not occur until some years after the traders had stimulated in the Indians of the coast an avaricious desire for white men's goods. It is true that some tribes were more difficult to deal with than others. Yet, in the main, during the fur trade period, Indians in the Columbia valley felt no antipathy for whites. Hudson's Bay Company, during the greater part of two decades, was able, with a relatively small number of persons, to get along peaceably with these natives and to compel respect for property of the company and the persons employed in its business. This was partly due to far-seeing policy, but it was also the product of the company's community of interest with them in preserving the wilderness as the Indians themselves would have preserved it. The issue of land occupancy was unimportant during the fur trade era.

2

The earliest missionaries, arriving in Oregon in 1834 and thereafter increasing in numbers, and the first of the settlers who followed in their train, presented an issue to the natives in a new aspect. The coming of the settlers had been preceded by reports not flattering to Americans. Intercourse between the tribes east and west of the Mississippi river had long been established, and as a result those of the west were made aware of the dissatisfaction arising out of the seizure by the whites of the lands of the eastern tribes. By its treatment of the Choctaws, the Delawares, the Sacs and Foxes, the Wyandottes, the Chickasaws, the Kickapoos and the Osages, the federal government had prepared the way for discord between whites and Indians.

Already there were charges of bad faith in execution of treaties, of exchanges of bad lands for good, of delays in performance. Reports of these had been widely circulated, and were generally credited by the Oregon natives prior to the massacre at Waiilatpu, in November, 1847. Unfortunately, too, a number of incidents occurred during this period that increased distrust. It is doubtful whether at any time the missionaries really understood the Indians, and it is certain that some others of the superior race made no effort to do so. An encounter at Willamette falls, 1844, in which an Indian named Cockstock and others were killed, furnishes an example.

The Cockstock affair was the outgrowth of a private dispute between two negro settlers, Winslow Anderson and James D. Saules, and a Wasco Indian named Cockstock, who had been hired by Anderson to perform labor on a land claim, in payment

for which he was to have received a horse. Before the completion
of the contract Anderson sold the land claim and also the horse
to Saules, who refused to deliver the animal to Cockstock. The
latter then appropriated the horse; the negroes appealed to Dr.
Elijah White and he compelled Cockstock to surrender it. Cockstock threatened all concerned with violence, and White offered a
reward of $100 for Cockstock's arrest. March 4, 1844, Cockstock
and four Molalla Indians rode into Willamette falls, armed, and,
in an attempt to arrest them, George W. LeBreton, clerk and
recorder of the provisional government, a highly esteemed citizen, received a fatal gunshot wound and a man named Rogers
was wounded by a poisoned arrow, dying on the following day.
Winslow Anderson, going to the rescue of LeBreton, dispatched
Cockstock by breaking his skull with the barrel of his rifle.

The incident created great excitement in the Willamette valley
and resulted in the organization of the mounted rifle company
known as the Oregon Rangers, of which T. D. Keysur was captain, the officers being duly commissioned by the executive committee of the provisional government. This constituted the first
military force authorized in the Oregon Country. The company,
however, was never called into action. The Wasco Indians were
much agitated by the killing of their fellow tribesman, and they
believed that Cockstock had not gone to Willamette falls on a
hostile errand. Doctor White visited them and pacified them by
compensating Cockstock's widow. White's own account of the adjustment of this difficulty is: "I told them we had lost two valuable innocent men; and should our people learn that I had given
them presents, without their giving me two blankets for one, they
must expect nothing but the hottest displeasure from the whites.
After much deliberation among themselves, they with one voice
concluded to leave the whole matter to my discretion. I at once
decided to give the poor Indian widow two blankets, a dress and
a handkerchief, believing the moral influence to be better than to
make presents to the chief or tribe and receive nothing at their
hands. . . . It is to be hoped that the matter will here end, though
that is by no means certain, as at present there are so many
sources of uneasiness and discontent between the parties."

3

In the earliest Indian wars the pioneer settlers volunteered, and the campaigns were chiefly, although not wholly, carried on by them. These included the Cayuse war of 1847-8, the Rogue river wars ranging through the years between 1853 and 1858, and the Yakima war of 1855-6. The later wars, however, were largely in the management of government forces, on the side of the white men. They covered the eastern Oregon conflicts of 1865-6, the Modoc war of 1872-3, the war with the Nez Perce's, in 1877, and the war with the Bannocks, in 1878.

4

After Doctor White's appointment as sub-Indian agent, he had compiled a code of laws for the Nez Perce's. This was because of a rumor that an alliance had been formed, in the autumn of 1842, by the Walla Wallas, Cayuses and Nez Perce's for aggression against the missionary stations in the interior, and against the Willamette valley settlements. November, 1842, he obtained the services of Thomas McKay, Cornelius Rogers and Baptiste Dorion, the latter the son of Wilson Price Hunt's interpreter, Pierre Dorion; and with these and a small armed party, which was joined at Fort Walla Walla by Archibald McKinlay, the Hudson's Bay Company chief trader there, he travelled directly to the Nez Perce's country. Here he called a council of the principal chiefs, to whom he gave assurances of the kind intentions of the United States government, "and the sad consequences that would ensue to any white men, from this time, who should invade their rights, by stealing, murder, selling them damaged for good articles, or alcohol, of which they are not fond."

Doctor White was peculiarly fortunate on this occasion in his choice of companions. McKay, the half-breed son of one of the partners in the Astor company, lost on the ship Tonquin, and McKinlay, representing the Hudson's Bay Company among the tribes, were in themselves a guarantee of success of his mission. But, in assuring the natives of the "sad consequences which would ensue to any white man who should invade their rights," the subagent was not only promising more than he could perform, but was preparing the way for subsequent accusations on the part of the Indians that the whites wished to have one set of laws for the natives and another for themselves. When, for example, in 1845, Elijah Hedding, a young Walla Walla chieftain, son of Peu-peu-mox-mox, head chief of the Walla Wallas, was wantonly slain by miners at Fort Sutter, California, the occurrence created in the minds of the natives throughout the west an impression unfavorable to the whites. "The slayers of the son of Peu-peu-mox-mox were never hanged," was a rallying cry of the disaffected members of the tribes in the Cayuse war of 1848, and in subsequent Indian wars.

Doctor White reversed the time-honored policy of Hudson's Bay Company by bringing about the election of one Ellis as chief of the Nez Perce's and the appointment of twelve sub-chiefs. Hudson's Bay officers, on the contrary, knowing Indian character, had consistently avoided becoming involved in tribal politics. Furthermore, Doctor White conceived the idea that Indians should organize a more compact tribal government, not considering the effect on their future relations with the white men. His conference with the Nez Perce's was a picturesque and noteworthy incident in early American endeavors to bring about an understanding between aborigines and the people who were destined to succeed them in the possession of the territory.

5

Twenty-two chiefs, besides a large number of lesser tribal dignitaries, were present at the conference. The white visitors made speeches first, while the Indians maintained a profound, respectful and inquisitive silence. Five Crows, "a wealthy chief of 45, neatly attired in English costume," spoke. "I am glad," he said, "the chief has come. I have listened to what has been said; I have great hopes that brighter days are before us, because I see all the whites are united in this matter; we have much wanted something; hardly know what; been groping and feeling for it in confusion and darkness. Here it is. Do we see it and shall we accept?"

Bloody Chief, more than 90 years old, who had been high chief of the tribe at the time of the visit of Lewis and Clark, told the council how he had proudly shown the explorers the wounds he had received in battle with the neighboring Snakes, his hereditary foes, but had been told "it was not good, it was better to be at peace." Doctor White's own account represents Bloody Chief as saying: "Clark pointed to this day, to you, and to this occasion; we have long waited in expectation; sent three of our sons to Red River school to prepare for it; two of them sleep with their fathers; the other is here and can be ears, mouth and pen for us. I

can say no more." Six other Indian leaders spoke. Doctor White
then proposed to the Nez Perce's that they select a single high
chief, with 12 subordinate chiefs of equal power, each of whom
should have five men as a body guard, to execute his lawful commands. White read his code of laws to them. "They were greatly
pleased with all proposed," White relates in his journal, "but
wished a heavier penalty to some, and suggested the dog law,
which was annexed."

There were further councils, accompanied by much feasting,
Doctor White furnishing a fat ox for the barbecue, and Ellis, the
young man to whom Bloody Chief had alluded and who had been
put forward by White, was elected high chief. The selection afterward proved a mischievous one, since Ellis' natural virtues were
not improved by his Red River education. He became domineering
and arrogant, and attempted to enforce the new code with great
literalness and undue severity. It will be borne in mind in considering the effect of Doctor White's laws upon the Indians that
they made criminal offenses of acts which before that time had
meant to the native mind no breach of law or morals.

6

White's laws are noteworthy as the first attempt made by whites
west of the Rocky mountains to teach the Indians to govern
themselves according to alien standards. White sets them forth
as follows:

"Art. 1. Whoever wilfully takes life shall be hung.

"Art. 2. Whoever burns a dwelling shall be hung.

"Art. 3. Whoever burns an outbuilding shall be imprisoned
six months, receive fifty lashes, and pay all damages.

"Art. 4. Whoever carelessly burns a house, or other property, shall pay damages.

"Art. 5. If any one enter a dwelling, without permission
of the occupant, the chiefs shall punish him as they think
proper. Public rooms are excepted.

"Art. 6. If any one steal, he shall pay back two-fold; and
if it be the value of a beaver skin or less, he shall receive
twenty-five lashes; and if the value is over a beaver skin he
shall pay back two-fold, and receive fifty lashes.

"Art. 7. If any one take a horse and ride it, without permission, or take any article and use it, without liberty, he
shall pay for the use of it and receive from twenty to fifty
lashes, as the chief may direct.

"Art. 8. If any one enter a field and injure the crops, or

throw down the fence, so that cattle and horses go in and do damage, he shall pay all damages, and receive twenty-five lashes for every offense.

"Art. 9. Those only may keep dogs who travel or live among the game; if a dog kill a lamb, calf, or any domestic animal, the owner shall pay damage and kill the dog.

"Art. 10. If an Indian raise a gun or other weapon against a white man, it shall be reported to the chiefs and they shall punish it. If a white do the same to an Indian, it shall be reported to Doctor White, and he shall punish or redress it.

"Art. 11. If an Indian break these laws, he shall be punished by his chiefs; if a white man break them, he shall be reported to the agent, and punished at his instance."

7

The Cayuses in the vicinity of Doctor Whitman's mission meanwhile were becoming restive. They were on the line of the Oregon trail, in the path of immigration, of which Doctor White's own party had been the first important forerunner. But this tribe had heard that the custom of the whites was always to possess themselves of the Indians' lands, usually in ruthless disregard of Indian rights. Doctor White made an unsuccessful attempt to allay their misgivings as to this, but the Cayuses were manifestly suspicious, at a council called by him at Waiilatpu. Tau-i-tau, a Walla Walla chieftain, argued eloquently that the whites were much more to blame than the Indians; that three-fourths of them, though they taught the purest doctrines, practiced the greatest abominations. He gave a graphic account of his vain endeavor to reduce his own tribe to order, by flogging the young men and reproving the middle-aged, until his popularity had declined almost to zero.

White made small headway here. He returned to the Walla Walla valley, however, May, 1843, in response to a rumor that the tribes contemplated an attack on the expected immigrant train of that year. He was then accompanied by the Rev. Gustavus Hines, and learned that apprehension concerning the coming of large bodies of settlers was the chief cause of the Indians' disquietude. The young Cayuse chiefs were in favor of raising a large war party at once, marching on the Willamette settlements and cutting off the inhabitants at a swift, sharp blow. The older chiefs pointed out the difficulty of conducting an expedition across the snow covered Cascades, and advised caution. Nevertheless the tribe was deeply imbued with the feeling that their lands were to be taken from them. They told White's interpreter that they had received their information concerning the designs of the American from a half-breed, who had said that it would be useless for them to continue to cultivate their grounds, that the whites would come in the summer and kill them all off, and destroy their plantations.

8

The Cayuses were less tractable than the Nez Perce's had been. At another council, held May 23, 1843, they repeatedly reminded the American envoys that promises made to them by the whites had not been kept. Ellis, and a young chief named Lawyer, of the Nez Perce's, who had been called to meet with the other tribes, reminded Doctor White that they expected pay for being chiefs. Ellis said he had counted the months he had been in office, and thought that enough was due him to make him rich. They left at a late hour, without receiving satisfaction. One of the difficulties for the commissioners to settle was the matter of payment for some horses the Indians had given Rev. Jason Lee, when Lee first came to Oregon, in 1834. This old claim was adjusted by promise to give the Indians a cow for each horse. On the third day, the Cayuses elected Tau-i-tau chief, but he declined to serve because, being a Catholic, the majority of his tribe were of a different religion, and his brother, Five Crows, was elected in his place. Doctor White presented the Indians with a fat ox, and Mrs. Whitman gave them a hog, on which they feasted during the second day. On the third day the Indians demanded and received a second ox.

This great council was attended, according to the estimate of Rev. Gustavus Hines, who was present, by 600 Nez Perce's, and 300 Cayuses and Walla Wallas. Doctor White got them to agree to accept his laws, but they did not manifest much enthusiasm. The increasing influence of the Catholic missionaries, which was shown on this occasion, had no immediate bearing on the issue of peace or war, but operated as a cause of factionalism among the Indians themselves.

9

News of the Whitman massacre, November 29, 1847, was received at Willamette falls, seat of the provisional government,

December 8, 1847, in a letter from James Douglas, chief factor at Vancouver, to Governor Abernethy. The governor at once communicated it to the legislature, then in session, and issued a call for volunteers. Excitement spread rapidly through the valley, and a company was organized on the same day with a view to proceeding to The Dalles and guarding against passage of the hostiles down river to attack the settlements. Henry A. G. Lee, one of the conspicuous members of the immigration of 1843, was elected captain, and Joseph Magone and John E. Ross, lieutenants. This company, known as the Oregon Rifles, and consisting of 48 men, lost no time in obtaining such equipment as could be procured on the individual credit of citizens of the territory, and departed immediately for The Dalles, reaching there, December 21.

The provisional legislature, meanwhile, December 9, 1847, authorized the raising of a regiment of volunteers, and named its field officers. Cornelius Gilliam, an immigrant of 1844, was colonel; James Waters was lieutenant-colonel; H. A. G. Lee, major, and Joel Palmer, commissary-general. All of these were men of ability and well qualified for duty. The men of the territory responded promptly, many furnishing their entire equipment. An interesting phase of the recruiting was the raising of a company by the French Canadians, who, as a group, had held aloof from the organization of the provisional government. These held a meeting at French Prairie as soon as the governor's proclamation became known, and they adopted resolutions declaring that "the Canadian citizens of Champoeg county feel it their duty to assist their adopted country in the prosecution of the war against the Cayuse Indians for the horrible massacre committed by them upon American citizens at Waiilatpu." All the commissioned officers of this company were named McKay. Capt. Thomas McKay was the son of Alexander McKay, the Astor partner lost on the Tonquin, 1811. Charles McKay was first lieutenant, and Alex McKay, second lieutenant. An American flag was presented to the company. In accepting it, Captain McKay said: "This is the flag you are expected to defend, and defend it you must." The company performed conspicuous service in the brief war that followed.

10

As the result of this prompt response to the governor's call for volunteers, Colonel Gilliam was able to reach The Dalles late in January, 1848, with 50 men, the remainder of his regiment arriving a few days afterward. It was not then known how widespread the disaffection of the Indians had become, and so the legislature, taking a second thought, designated a peace commission consisting of Joel Palmer, Maj. H. A. G. Lee and Robert Newell, to treat with the eastern tribes, and if possible to forestall a general uprising.

11

As was stated, at page 359, the legislature dispatched Joseph L. Meek to Washington, with a memorial asking the national government for help, and it also sent Jesse Applegate with a party of volunteers to obtain aid from the military governor of California. Applegate was unable to cross through the deep snows of the Siskiyous and returned north, his dispatches being forwarded by sea. Meek's long trip across the continent was fruitless. The settlers in the Willamette valley, therefore, were compelled to carry on the war without help from any outside sources.

Meek was accompanied on his arduous overland expedition by George W. Ebbert, a former trapper and Hudson's Bay man, who had settled on a farm at Champoeg. They left the Willamette valley, January 4, 1848. After waiting at The Dalles until the close of the month, they went in company with Colonel Gilliam's regiment to Waiilatpu. Here the bodies of the victims of the massacre were reburied, and Meek performed this duty with the body of his own daughter, who had been in Mrs. Whitman's school. Meek and Ebbert were accompanied by troops to the Blue mountains, from which locality they departed accompanied by five other Americans who desired to return to the states, although two of these went no further than Fort Boise.

12

Colonel Gilliam began by vigorously carrying the war into the enemy's country. He established a supply station at the Cascades, which was named Fort Gilliam. A stockade erected at The Dalles was named Fort Lee, and here a nine-pounder cannon, the only piece of artillery possessed by the provisional government, was mounted. Lee's company had several skirmishes with the Indians before Gilliam reached him with reinforcements. The first provisional soldier wounded was Sergeant William Berry; those first killed were Privates Pugh and Jackson. These casualties were incurred in repelling raids by the Indians on the cattle of immigrants and the horses of the rangers. One other soldier, Private Alexander McDonald, was killed by a sentry who mistook him for an Indian. Four or five of the natives were killed and several were wounded.

13

Colonel Gilliam, the last week in January, 1848, a few days after the arrival of his first detachment, set out with 130 men in hot pursuit of the hostiles, who proved to be members of the Des Chutes, John Day and Cayuse tribes. Dispersing several war parties on the way to Meek's crossing, at the mouth of a canyon into which he sent Major Lee with a detachment, on a reconnoissance, Lee's men found the Indians, and killed one. Gilliam with the main body pressed forward, engaged the enemy, captured a number of their horses and some cattle, which resulted later in a treaty of peace with these tribes. The engagement in the canyon was a severe test of the mettle of the raw troops, but being frontiersmen and familiar with the Indian method of warfare, they stood the test well. Lee's little detachment of skirmishers, in particular, was forced to dismount and seek cover among boulders, while a superior force of pursuing Indians rolled stones down on them from the cliffs above. The main body of Gilliam's troops in the second day's fighting destroyed an Indian village, but spared the old people they found there.

14

Word came from the Yakimas that they would not join the hostiles, since the whites did not pass through their country and they had no quarrel with them, but the peace commissioners were unable to obtain assurances of pacific intentions from other tribes, and Colonel Gilliam took up the march to Waiilatpu. On the way, a battle was fought at Sand Hollow, on the immigrant trail, which was of considerable importance because it resulted in the killing of Gray Eagle, one of the Cayuse chiefs, and the wounding of Five Crows, head chief elected on the occasion of Dr. Elijah White's visit, 1843. These chiefs, both of whom laid claim to supernatural powers, had attempted a demonstration of their invulnerability by riding close to the troops and shooting a dog. Capt. Thomas McKay, of the company raised in the French Canadian settlement, shot Gray Eagle through the head, and Lieut.

Charles McKay of the same company wounded Five Crows with a shotgun so severely that the chief was forced to give up his command.

This proof that their leaders were but mortal and that the volunteers were in deadly earnest, measurably chilled the ardor of the Cayuses. The battle declined to a skirmish and the soldiers were not seriously hampered in continuing their march to Waiilatpu. They crossed the Umatilla river, despite the boast made by the Cayuse chiefs to their followers that this would be prevented, and reached the Whitman mission, March 2. The spectacle at the mission grounds, where some of the bodies of the victims had been exhumed by wolves, and the scene of general desolation, steeled the hearts of the soldiers and almost led to an open breach between the military forces and the peace commissioners.

The latter had been dispatched on their errand of diplomacy in the hope that a general war might be averted by a policy of leniency toward the friendly Indians. Their design was to inform the tribes that if the murderers of the Whitman party were surrendered for punishment no further demands would be made. Newell had been chosen as a member of the commission because of his experience as a mountain man, and his sympathy with the Indian point of view. Palmer also had been known to entertain sentiments of moderation in treating with the tribes. Colonel Gilliam chafed under restraint of his implied obligation to the peace commissioners, and because of scarcity of supplies, which were obviously insufficient for a protracted campaign.

He began at once the construction of a rude fort out of the debris of the ruined mission houses. He received overtures from Peu-peu-mox-mox, of the Walla Wallas, and from a few friendly Nez Perce's, but was unable to obtain guarantees from them that the principal conspirators of the murder would be surrendered. Gilliam proposed to grant immunity to five of the murderers in exchange for Joe Lewis, the renegade who was believed to have incited the massacre, but the peace commissioners would not assent to this. A large party of friendly Nez Perce's and Cayuses, however, approached the camp, March 6, 1848, and were acclaimed by the soldiers. A council was held, March 7, in another effort to preserve the peace, but without important results.

15

Colonel Gilliam, therefore, was restrained from forcing the fighting, at least until the commission had further opportunity to test the value of pacific measures. Although he mistrusted the motives of the Indians, and suspected them of design to gain time to prepare for further hostilities, he waited for the council. The peace commissioners were acting under specific instructions from Governor Abernethy to avoid war if possible, while exercising the utmost firmness "consistent with the honor of American citizens." Abernethy wrote that there were "some requisitions that must be complied with on the part of the Indians." All the murderers must be delivered up for punishment; "the property taken delivered up or an equivalent given, and restitution made of the property stolen last year." The governor continued: "I am aware the greatest difficulty will be in obtaining the persons of the murderers, but the Indians must be given to understand in the commencement of negotiations that this must be done; and that no compromise can be made. There may be some among those that are implicated in this affair around whom some palliating circumstances may be thrown; these you will take into consideration; but the principal actors should be executed in the presence of the tribes. . . . You will hold a council with the field officers of the army, and decide in council what steps shall be taken to accomplish the much-desired object, restoration of peace. You will use every exertion to have the property and lives of our fellow citizens that may be hereafter travelling through the Indian territory preserved; the chiefs are able to govern their own people."

The Cayuses were represented by the war chief Camaspello, whose sick child had been visited by Doctor Whitman only a short time before the massacre, and who had not warned the doctor of the conspiracy. Among the leaders of the Nez Perce's present were Joseph, their head chief in the absence of Ellis on a buffalo hunt; Jacob, half-brother of the Cayuse, Five Crows; James, a Catholic; Richard, who had accompanied Doctor Whitman on the latter's return to the United States, 1835; and Kentuck, who had been Rev. Samuel Parker's guide in Idaho, 1835. Peu-peu-mox-mox, head chief of the Walla Wallas, represented his tribe. Palmer found Peu-peu-mox-mox "decidedly friendly and withal prudent and sensible."

16

A letter from Governor Abernethy, addressed to "the Great Chiefs of the Nez Perce's and other Tribes," was brought forth and the seal broken with solemn ceremony, "after the pipe of friendship had been passed around till our hearts were all good and our eyes watery," as Palmer afterward wrote. Abernethy reminded the Indians that the early American missionaries had gone to dwell among them and instruct them at their own request, that Doctor and Mrs. Whitman had been actuated only by good motives, and that the stories the Indians had heard, that Doctor Whitman had poisoned them, were not true. "Brothers," Abernethy's letter continued, "our warriors are on the warpath; what shall be done that we may all again be friends, and not enemies? I will tell you what we want; listen to me; we want the men that murdered our brother, Doctor Whitman, and the rest of our brothers—Tiloquoit, Tamsukie and all that were engaged . . . and further that restitution of the property stolen and destroyed be made, either by returning the property, or giving an equivalent. If this is done the hatchet will be buried and the Indians and Americans will be friends and brothers. Our great chief has always been told that the Indians in this country were all friendly; he has not sent any of his war chiefs here. We have now sent word to him that our people have been killed; his war chiefs will come, and should you prefer war to peace, let me tell you, and listen to what I say, they will punish you until you shall be fully satisfied with war and be glad to make peace. . . . My advice to you as a friend is that you deliver up the murderers, or let the Americans go and take them without your interfering with them; in this case do not let the murderers shelter among you, lest your people should get killed through mistake, for which I would be very sorry."

Commissioner Palmer diplomatically informed the Nez Perce's that the Cayuses had by their conduct forfeited their lands. "We do not want these lands," he added, "but we wish to open the road for Americans to travel, as they have done before. We shall build a fort and station a number of men at Waiilatpu. Our war chief will hunt these murderers as you hunt the deer, until he drives them from the face of the earth. Suppose you were all to unite with the Cayuses and kill us off; we are but a handful; others would come with both hands full and wipe you out. We are slow to get angry, but when we begin war we never quit until we conquer." Palmer promised that a blacksmith would be sent them, and a teacher to instruct them in mechanical and agricultural pursuits, and that no whites would be permitted to intrude upon them or settle on their lands without first obtaining their consent.

Newell reminded the Nez Perce's that he had fought with them, and that some of the Indians present had been his comrades in battle. "I am not here to fight," he said, "but to separate the good from the bad and to tell you that it is your duty to help make this ground clean. Thank God, you have not helped to make it bloody. What have the Cayuses made; what have they lost? Everything; nothing but a name. All the property they took in a short time will be gone; only one thing left, that is a name, 'the bloody Cayuses.' They will never lose that, only in this way, obey the great God and keep his laws. What is our duty to the great God? This is his law: He who kills man, by man shall his blood be spilt. This is what God says, and he must be obeyed, or we have no peace in the land."

Colonel Gilliam, Major Lee and Captain McKay confirmed the promises of the other commissioners that no whites would be permitted to settle in the Indian country without the tribes' consent.

17

Camaspello, the Cayuse, declared that though his people seemed to have two hearts, he had but one. He denied that he had given his consent to the murders at the mission, though he admitted that Tamsukie had told him of the plan of the younger men. "I pointed to my sick child," said Camaspello, "and told him my heart was there, and not on murder. He went back and told his friends he had obtained my consent. It was false." Joseph spoke for all the Cayuses present and also for his own people. He did not wish war. "You speak of murderers," he said, "I shall not meddle with them. I bow my head."

Said Jacob: "It is the law of this country that the murderers shall die. This law I keep in my heart, because I believe it is the law of God,—the first law. I have heard your speech and am thankful. When I left home I believed the Americans were coming for the murderers only. I thank the governor for this good talk."

Red Wolf said that when he had heard of the murder of Doctor Whitman he had inquired whether the chiefs were responsible, and had learned that they were not all in the conspiracy, but that the young men were to blame. Richard said that the last words of his old chief, Cut Nose, were: "My children, I leave you. Love that which is good. Be always at the side of right and you will prosper." The Nez Perce's had been taught not to take bad words from their enemies and throw good words away. Ellis, who was absent, he said, would be glad to hear that his people were for peace. Kentuck said that he and his father fought with the Americans against the Blackfeet, and denied that his people's hearts were with the Cayuses. "We are glad to hear you want none but the murderers," he concluded.

Newell presented the Nez Perce's with a large American flag, which he counseled them to keep as a gift from the great white father, to be hoisted on all national occasions. The flag was accompanied by gifts of tobacco. "In the evening," wrote Palmer in his official report to Governor Abernethy, "the Nez Perce's gave us a war dance, which amused and delighted us much, and we do them but bare justice when we say the performance was well timed, the parts well acted, characters represented to the very life, and the whole first rate."

18

The main body of the Cayuses was still encamped at some distance, and evidence was lacking that Camaspello spoke for the really influential members of his tribe. The Nez Perce's chiefs, however, agreed to act as emissaries to the Cayuses, in an endeavor to persuade them to surrender the murderers. When the command moved forward, March 8, it was met by Chief Sticcas, of the Cayuses, bringing in a band of cattle and personal property and money which had been stolen from the Whitman mission and from passing immigrants. Sticcas obtained consent to the holding of a council, at which it was announced that the Cayuses refused to surrender Teloukikt or Tamsukie. Newell concluded at this point that further peace parleys would be useless and the peace commissioners returned to the Willamette valley. On the way home, Palmer conferred with Indians in the vicinity of The Dalles and persuaded them that it was to their interest to remain friendly. They were at least neutral during the remainder of the campaign.

An important point had also been gained in obtaining the neutrality of the Nez Perce's. Peu-peu-mox-mox, also known as Yellow Serpent, chief of the Walla Wallas, manifested friendship for the whites and wished an end to the whole affair, but one of the murderers had fled to the country of the Palouses, and Peu-peu-mox-mox, though he may have desired to see the guilty one in custody, could not arrest him without precipitating war between the Palouses and the Walla Wallas. The Cayuses had lost heart for war, on finding themselves abandoned to their own resources, but continued hostilities some time longer in the evident hope of forcing further concessions. They were willing to let bygones be bygones, but the peace party was unable to comply with the primary conditions laid down by the Americans. The hostile faction and the friends and relatives of the murderers retained sufficient power to defeat the aims of those who would have bought security at any price.

19

Colonel Gilliam hastened in pursuit of the Cayuses, who divided their forces. His command, numbering 158, made a night march and surprised the enemy in camp near the mouth of the Tucannon. But the Indians were prepared with subterfuge, where open fighting would not serve their end, and represented themselves as friendly Walla Wallas. While the troops were investigating the truth of their statements, the main body of the enemy escaped across Snake river. While returning from the scene, Gilliam's men were attacked in the rear by a body of about 400 Palouses and Cayuses. Skirmish fighting ensued, as the troops retreated down the Tucannon to a point within a few miles of the Touchet river. Here the men camped without food or fire, and on the morning of March 15, 1848, fought a spirited battle for possession of the ford across the Touchet.

"The history of savage warfare," says the report of Capt. H. J. G. Maxon, "contains few instances of greater Indian prowess and daring than the scene which followed. The struggle for the ford was obstinate for some time. . . . And here I may say that had it not been for the bold and decided stand of a few young men at the most vulnerable point, the army must have sustained a heavy loss in crossing the stream, perhaps been thrown into confusion and cut to pieces. In an hour, the sound of our rifles had hushed.

The long battle was ended. We were all over the river alive, and but nine or ten wounded, none mortally. It was not so with the enemy. The deafening roar of their musketry which had been sounding in our ears for thirty hours had died away,—their shrill warwhoop was changed to the melancholy death song . . . They called off their warriors, more anxious to leave the ford of the Toosha [Touchet] than they had been to gain it. We moved to the fort, at which place we arrived on the evening of the 16th, worn down with fatigue and hunger, having eaten nothing but a small colt for three days."

Victory was with the troops, the Indians being glad enough to escape into the mountains with the livestock which the army had been forced to abandon on its retirement, but the soldiers were in no condition to pursue them. A council of the officers was held on March 18, at Fort Waters (Waiilatpu), at which it was concluded that nothing effective could be done without more men and more ammunition. Pursuant to this decision, Colonel Gilliam, with two companies, about 160 men in all, moved toward The Dalles. On the way Colonel Gilliam was accidentally killed, March 24, at Well Springs, near the Umatilla river, while drawing a riata from a camp wagon, which caused a rifle to be discharged into his body.

20

Command of the division devolved on Captain Maxon, whose report to Governor Abernethy, dated March 28, 1848, and published in the Oregon Spectator of April 6, 1848, aroused the Willamette valley to a high pitch of patriotism. The death of Colonel Gilliam brought home to the people the gravity of the war. But Maxon also described the hardships of the troops and graphically depicted their forlorn condition and, further, represented that the entire colony faced the peril of annihilation unless the Indians were checked promptly and decisively.

"Something must be done," wrote Maxon, "and done at once, or abandon the war and have the Indians in the valley in a month, stealing our property and murdering our frontier settlers. . . . A force of less than 600 men cannot carry on offensive operations, as the enemy have that force or more in fifty miles of Fort Waters. What men we have are in a destitute situation. Some almost without clothing, many without horses, as the principal

portion of the horses we have taken have been claimed by friendly Indians and given up to them. . . . There are 150 of our boys
in the heart of the enemy's country, almost without ammunition,
—wholly without bread. . . . If there is a continuance of operations, I hope there will be more patriotism shown in the valley
of the Willamette. Indeed, there must be, or we are lost."

21

It was easier to stimulate patriotism than to supply the materials of war. Captain Maxon's report contained an appeal to fathers to send bread to their sons, to mothers to send warm garments, and to daughters to "evince your angelic influence for your
country's good by withholding your fair hand and fairer smile
from any young man who refuses to turn out to defend your
honor and your country's rights." Fifteen young women of the
valley responded at once by signing a compact framed in the
spirit of Captain Maxon's suggestion.

This agreement, published in the Oregon Spectator, April 20,
1848, read: "We hereby, one and all, of our own free good will,
solemnly pledge ourselves to comply with that request; and to
evince, on all suitable occasions, our detestation and contempt for
any and all young men who can, but will not, take up arms and
march to the seat of war, to punish the Indians who have not only
murdered our friends, but have grossly insulted our sex. We
never can, and never will, bestow our confidence upon a man who
had neither patriotism nor courage enough to defend his country
and the girls,—such a one would never have a sufficient sense of
obligation to defend and protect his wife. Do not be uneasy about
your claims, and your rights in the valley; while you are defending the rights of your country she is watching yours. You must
not be discouraged—fight on—be brave—obey your officers—and
never quit your post 'till the enemy is conquered; and when you
return in triumph to the valley, you shall find us ready to rejoice
with you as we now are to sympathize with you in your sufferings and dangers."

At a meeting of the "ladies of Oregon City and vicinity" held
at the Methodist church, April 12, at which Mrs. N. M. Thornton
presided, committees were appointed to obtain subscriptions of
food and clothing. Two hundred and fifty volunteers enlisted, including a company in Polk and Clackamas counties, of which

J. W. Nesmith was elected captain, a company in Linn county, of which W. P. Pugh was captain, and a company in Tualatin county, with William J. Martin as captain.

22

Money was extremely scarce in the territory and wheat was the common medium of exchange. But wheat in the raw state was not wanted by the army in the field and the process of converting grain subscriptions into goods required by the commissary was tedious and cumbersome. Supplies were collected in driblets. Lead and powder were almost non-existent. The commissary agent at Salem reported that he had been able to buy only six saddles. Provisions were obtained here and there, a few hundred pounds at one place and a few hundred at another. A forced loan of wheat from certain farmers and from Hudson's Bay Company granary at Champoeg was seriously considered at one time. The difficulties of the officers of commissary and supply were intensified by their anxiety to relieve the destitute condition of the troops in the field and to reinforce them in anticipation of a vigorous summer campaign.

There was no more fighting, however. Governor Abernethy appointed Maj. H. A. G. Lee, colonel, to succeed Colonel Gilliam, ignoring Lieutenant-Colonel Waters, who had temporarily succeeded Gilliam in command of the regiment, but Lee magnanimously resigned his commission and served as lieutenant-colonel under Waters. Two months were given to minor excursions in search of the murderers, who, with their companions among the hostile Cayuses, were supposed to have fled to the mountains in the direction of the Nez Perce's country. Suspicion of the good faith of the Nez Perce's was bred in the minds of the soldiers by the fact that the Cayuses had been permitted to escape, but friendly members of the tribe atoned for this, so far as might be, by helping to drive captured Cayuse cattle into camp at Waiilatpu. Word was received from the Rev. Cushing Eells, at Tsimikain, containing information that the Spokane Indians were divided in opinion, although none condoned the murderers. A delegation of 45 Spokanes accompanied the courier bringing Eells' message, and gave information of the whereabouts of a band of cattle belonging to one of the Cayuse culprits.

23

If money was scarce in the Willamette valley, it was even less plentiful among the soldiers, and the primitive necessity for barter to which the whole territory was then reduced is shown by a subscription paper signed at Clearwater Camp, Lapwai, by the men of Lieutenant-Colonel Lee's detachment, for the purpose of providing a reward to be offered to the Nez Perce's for the arrest of the criminals. Subscriptions were pledged in the form of wheat, blankets, shirts and miscellaneous merchandise, estimated to represent the equivalent of $125 in goods and wheat, besides 67 blankets and 104 shirts. The reward was never claimed.

The text of the subscription compact was: "We, the undersigned, promise to pay to the Nez Perce's or other Indians, or their agent, the articles, sums, and amounts annexed to our names, respectively, for the capture and delivery to the authorities of Oregon Territory, any two of the following named Indians, viz: Teloukikt, Tamsucy, Tamahas, Joe Lewis or Edward Teloukikt, or half the amount for any one of them. We also promise to pay one-fourth of the amount as specified above for the capture and the delivery of any one of the following: Llou-Llou, Pips, Frank Escaloom, Quiamashoukin, Estools, Showshow, Pahosh, Cupup-cupup, or any other engaged in the massacre. The same to be paid whenever the service is rendered and the fact that it is rendered established."

24

The futility of further efforts to arrest the murderers was apparent now that spring had come and the Indians were able to scatter out and subsist on the country. The volunteers, though willing enough to fight, were weary of the monotony of mere police duty, and their private interests in the Willamette valley called them. It was resolved by a council of officers to withdraw the main force from the Walla Walla region. A detail was sent to Lapwai to give a safe conduct out of the country to William Craig, who had been appointed resident Indian agent under the compact made with the friendly Nez Perce's, but whose situation was precarious while the murderers were free. A detachment commanded by Major Magone proceeded to Tsimikain, as an escort for Rev. Cushing Eells and Rev. Elkanah Walker, their wives and children, and a Miss Bewley, sister of the captive of that name, who had remained among the Spokanes. It was now June, and the volunteers more than ever desired to return to their homes, so that when a vote was taken by the officers on the question of leaving a garrison to occupy Fort Waters until the immigrant season closed, the proposal was rejected by a vote of six to five.

In order to induce volunteers to remain, Lieutenant-Colonel Lee, who had assumed the duties of superintendent of Indian affairs, on the resignation of Joel Palmer, offered to give written authority for the colonization of the Cayuse country and this had the desired effect. More than the requisite number offered their services. Lee wrote a letter, which was published in the Oregon Spectator, July 13, 1848, in which he informed the people of the Willamette valley that "there are now in the Cayuse country, grist and saw mills, blacksmith's anvil and bellows, with some tools, a quantity of iron, plows, harrows, a crop of wheat, peas, potatoes and corn, with almost every convenience and facility in forming a settlement." He wrote of the superior and peculiar adaptability of that section to the growth of wool and the raising of horses and cattle, while the climate, he added, "for health, and the scenery for beauty, cannot be excelled by any spot of earth."

Lee obtained the approval of Governor Abernethy for this new policy of introducing settlers into the very midst of the Indian country, and proclaimed the forfeiture of all the lands of the Cayuses, making no exception in favor of friendly members of the tribe. The insatiable land-hunger which supplied a motive for the whole immigration movement, and which subsequently constituted an important obstacle to peaceful settlement of the Indian troubles, made the settlers peculiarly receptive to this new opportunity to enlarge their domain. "In middle and eastern Oregon," wrote the editor of the Spectator in his enthusiasm, "there is more prairie land covered with a dense growth of rich grass, upon which horses, cattle and sheep will subsist throughout the year, than all the meadow pasture and plow lands in all New England. Who can estimate the wealth of such lands? The volunteers who spent the last winter in the middle country assure us that it was remarkably mild and pleasant. Some tell us that they never saw fat cattle until they saw them at Waiilatpu in February last. . . . Two lead mines were discovered in that portion of the country last winter. . . . The far-famed mountain of marble mentioned by Professor Hitchcock, in his Treatise on Geology, is in the neighborhood of the Cayuse country."

25

Notwithstanding this proposal to induce settlement, Major Lee was not yet quite sure that the country was safe for missionaries. Eells and Walker, and their families, were escorted out of the eastern region early in June, and Lee then addressed a letter to the Catholic priests at The Dalles, in which he declared it to be desirable that all missionary labors among the tribes should cease. "At present," he wrote, "the relations between the whites and Indians are too precarious to allow missionary labors with the Indians to be either prudent or effective of good. So soon as circumstances will allow I shall take much pleasure in throwing wide open the door of missionary labor amongst the Indians to all Christian missionaries; at present, prudence demands that it shall be closed against all."

26

In addition to the volunteers who had been left at Waiilatpu, a lieutenant, an orderly sergeant and thirteen privates were detailed to guard The Dalles, and the remainder of the regiment proceeded to the Willamette valley and were mustered out, July, 1848. The company on the Walla Walla passed the summer patrolling the immigrant trail. The Cayuse murderers kept well out of sight and no effort was made to apprehend them, in view of the general expectation that a regiment of United States cavalry would soon be assigned to duty in the territory. The expected regulars were, however, diverted for service in the Mexican war. The rifle regiment arrived in the autumn of 1849, by which time the Cayuses, as a nation, were thoroughly cowed and heartily weary of being fugitives. Without ammunition for the hunt, compelled to be constantly on the move, so that they could not raise crops, they were threatened with starvation. Five of the tribe, Teloukikt, Tamahas, Klokamas, Isaiachalakis and Kiamasumpkin, surrendered themselves at The Dalles. Governor Lane went to that place with an escort of a lieutenant and ten men, of the rifle regiment, and brought them to Oregon City, where they were held as prisoners on an island in the Willamette river. The trial was conducted by Judge O. C. Pratt. Amory Holbrook, United States district attorney, prosecuted. The defense was directed by the territorial secretary, Kintzing Pritchette, and was presented by R. B. Reynolds, paymaster, and Thomas Claiborne, captain of the rifle regiment. The verdict of guilty was returned and the prisoners were executed June 3, 1850.

27

While the troops were pursuing the Cayuses, some of the more restless Indians in western Oregon began a series of raids on the isolated foothill farms in the Willamette valley, apparently for the purpose of testing the temper and the resources of the settlers. A war party of Klamaths and Molallas surrounded the home of Richard Miller, a prominent citizen of Champoeg county, March, 1848, and their boldness so alarmed the people of the valley that a military organization was effected, some sixty men, young and old, volunteering for instant service. Daniel Waldo was elected colonel and R. C. Geer, Allen Davy, Richard Miller and Samuel Parker were chosen as captains. The company pursued the Indians to Abiqua creek, engaged them and killed two. Continuing the pursuit on the following morning, the younger men of the command overtook what they supposed to be the rear guard of the fleeing warriors, and again gave battle, killing seven, one of whom proved to be a woman armed with a bow and arrow. Two women were wounded. The main party of the Indians escaped, but were so effectually intimidated that they did not repeat the foray.

The "battle of Abiqua creek," so called, was kept secret for nearly 20 years after it occurred, and was seldom referred to by those who participated in it. This silence expressed better than words the regret of old settlers for the killing or wounding of non-combatants. It is probable, from the fact that the fighting was carried on at long range in the mist and haze of a March morning, that the volunteers were not to blame for their mistake.

28

Rogue river and Klamath Indians were troublesome in the south, May, 1848. A party of eight men, led by John Saxton, on the way from the Sacramento valley to the Willamette, was attacked on the California trail by members of these tribes, who stole 65 horses in broad daylight. It is said that the natives kept up the firing, throughout the day, at the narrow passes along the trail. No one was injured, excepting a Mr. Girtman, who was shot in the thigh by the accidental discharge of his own gun.

29

Notwithstanding this and other menaces in southern Oregon, there was delay and difficulty in organizing defenses. The man-power of the colony was already severely taxed for the regiment in eastern Oregon. Therefore, when Felix Scott was commissioned sub-Indian agent for southern Oregon and urged to raise a company for defense of the settlements, he was frankly told that there were no funds for payment of expenses. He accepted, neverthe-less, and raised a small company, which performed important services by protecting members of the immigration of 1848, who came in over the southern route.

30

Remoteness of the Oregon colony from the seat of national gov-ernment, and the failure at Washington to realize and take action for the needs of the settlers, prolonged the Indian wars. This is illustrated by the tardy arrival, in 1849, of the rifle regiment that had been promised in 1847. The treaty with Great Britain, by which Oregon was confirmed to the United States, became effec-tive June 15, 1846. But the act of congress creating the territory was not approved until August 14, 1848; and Joseph Lane, first territorial governor, did not take office until March 3, 1849. The result was that, although the boundary question had been ad-justed and the people looked to the national government for help, they were still compelled to rely wholly on their own resources for defense. The mounted rifle regiment, first federal troop to reach the territory, came too late to be of any practical service.

31

Governor Lane employed himself energetically in his duties as superintendent of Indian affairs, this office having been added to that of governor, but he was embarrassed by delay of the federal government to grant him authority to act. Having set the young territory on its feet, congress apparently forgot it again. The In-dians of numerous tribes bordering on the settlement, hearing that the governor had arrived, came flocking in, "chiefs, head men, warriors and in many instances entire bands, expecting presents, making known that the whites had promised, from time to time, that when the laws of the whites were extended over

Oregon, the governor would bring them blankets, shirts, and such other articles as would be useful to them." Every promise made by an Indian agent on any occasion now came home to vex the new governor. He was without funds, and was unable to give them anything, but they swallowed their disappointment, professed friendship and "generally expressed a desire to sell their possessory rights to any portion of their country that our government should wish to purchase." This was the beginning of systematic effort to obtain title peaceably to the Indian country, an enterprise which, could it have been carried to fruition with reasonable celerity and in entire good faith, and well in advance of the oncoming immigration, might have averted the conflicts that followed.

Natives with whom Lane came in contact were well-disposed, according to his various reports, and he pointed out that in the absence of a large proportion of the male population of Oregon, who had stampeded to the California mines, it was more than ever desirable that the Indian titles should be acquired by the government. "The necessity for locating them entirely out of the settlements is obviously very great," he wrote to the United States secretary of state, April 9, 1849. He outlined his policy in dealing with the Cayuses in his first message to the territorial legislature, July 17, 1849, in which he promised that on the arrival of the expected rifle regiment, the Cayuse murderers would be pursued and punished. Lane also pleaded for justice to the Indians. "Surrounded, as many of the tribes and bands now are, by the whites, whose arts of civilization, by destroying the resources of the Indians, doom them to poverty, want and crime," he wrote in his message, "the extinguishment of their title by purchase, and the locating them in a district removed from settlement is a measure of the most vital importance to them. Indeed, the cause of humanity calls loudly for their removal from causes and influences so fatal to their existence."

32

The rifle regiment that set out from Fort Leavenworth, May 10, 1849, under command of Brevet-Colonel W. W. Loring, established posts at Laramie, Fort Hall and The Dalles, but suffered incredible losses of life by accident and disease, arriving at The Dalles ragged and nearly destitute of food and supplies. More

Joseph Lane
First territorial governor of Oregon.

Benjamin L. E. Bonneville
Western explorer and adventurer.

Fort Vancouver in Transition
To the left are the American troops barracks; to the right, the Hudson's Bay Company Fort, with the Columbia beyond (Drawing by Gustavus Sohon, U. S. Pacific Railroad Report, 1855).

losses of life and property were suffered in Oregon, one party of six being drowned in the rapids at the cascades, where a raft loaded with several tons of goods was wrecked, and another party that took the wagon road over the mountains at the base of Mt. Hood losing two-thirds of the horses in their charge. The total number that deserted or died from Fort Leavenworth to the Willamette valley was 70, while the property loss included 45 freight wagons, an ambulance, and over 300 horses and mules.

No sufficient provision had been made for housing the troops, and provisions, that were sent by the ship Walpole to the Columbia river, were landed at Astoria, instead of at Fort Vancouver and at Oregon City, where the men were stationed. There were delays and expenses in getting these supplies to the places where needed. There were many desertions. One group of 70, bound for the gold mines of California, were overtaken by Colonel Loring and Governor Lane, in Umpqua valley, and returned to Oregon City with Lane, while others were followed by Loring into the snows of the Siskiyou mountains. Seven of these were found and brought back by their colonel, but a number of others were believed to have perished from hardships. Two companies of artillery, under command of Brevet-Major J. S. Hathaway, came to Oregon on board the Massachusetts, a combined sailing and steam vessel that arrived at Astoria, May 9, 1849. These companies were stationed at Fort Vancouver, but a portion of the command was afterward located at Astoria.

33

On account of the need for immediate payment of the provisional government militia, many of the men being in want, and the merchants and others who were creditors pressing for settlement, the governor recommended the issuance of scrip, with the expectation that it would ultimately be redeemed by the United States government. Accordingly this was authorized by the territorial legislature, but many persons entitled to be paid found it necessary to part with their scrip for less than face value. Efforts made to have the general government assume and pay the cost of the Cayuse war, resulted in a preliminary payment of $73,000, and a later appropriation of $75,000, with which to pay the remaining expenses. Bounties were voted for volunteers, and some private claims were paid from time to time.

34

The Klickitats, a bold and enterprising tribe north of the Columbia, made visits to the Willamette valley, where they committed a few minor breaches of the peace, as a forerunner of the more widespread alliance of all the principal northwestern tribes that was to come. A band of Snoqualmies, May 1, 1849, surrounded Fort Nisqually, the Hudson's Bay Company's station on Puget sound, in an attempt to capture ammunition kept there, and, although the attempt failed, they murdered Leander C. Wallace, an American settler. J. Quinn Thornton and Robert Newell had been appointed sub-Indian agents meanwhile, and Thornton was assigned to the region north of the Columbia river. He offered the Snoqualmies a reward of 80 blankets for the surrender of the murderers, an act that gave Lane another opportunity to assert himself upon dealing with Indians. He disapproved of Thornton's offer, although the promise, having been made, was subsequently kept. He declared that it would not be his policy under any consideration to hire Indians to make reparation. They were to be taught, said Lane, that they would be punished, not bribed, whenever they did wrong. The murder of Wallace and the violation of the security of the Hudson's Bay Company, now dependent on the American government for protection, were avenged by the arrest and execution of two Snoqualmie Indians, named Kassass and Quallawort. Four others were acquitted by the jury, which sat in judgment on all six. The whole tribe, seemingly, attended the trial and the hanging of the murderers. The proceedings had the effect of temporarily restraining that tribe, then regarded as the most fierce and warlike of the tribes on Puget sound.

35

Lane lacked authority to conclude the treaties with the Indians by which title to the land might be obtained for settlers. Congress expressly reserved, although it delayed in asserting, the right to make regulations respecting the Indians, and provided only for expenditure of a nominal sum for gifts to them.

June 3, 1850, an act was passed by congress authorizing the appointment of commissioners to treat with the tribes west of the Cascade mountains. The president appointed Anson Dart, of Wisconsin, superintendent of Indian affairs for the territory, and also named three commissioners—John P. Gaines, who succeeded Lane as governor on the change in national administration, Beverly S. Allen and Alonzo A. Skinner. The commissioners received general instructions only, from the acting commissioner of Indian affairs, at Washington, who wrote that "the information in the possession of this office is so limited that nearly everything must be left to your discretion beyond what is here communicated, and even that may be found by you to be somewhat defective."

However, the treaty commissioners were informed that the object of the government was to extinguish the title of the Indians to all the lands lying west of the Cascade mountains, "and, if possible, to provide for removal of the whole from the west to the east of the mountains." They were told to spare no effort to procure the removal of all in a body; failing in this, they were authorized to treat with tribes separately. Expenditure of $20,000 was authorized, of which $5000 was to be invested in goods suitable for presents for the Indians, which would be sent around Cape Horn. Notwithstanding their instructions to persuade the western Indians to remove to the region east of the Cascades, a policy that would have involved a revolution of their habits of living, the Gaines commissioners made treaties at Champoeg with various tribes in the Willamette valley, and Dart obtained treaties at Tansy Point, Port Orford and Oregon City with others.

36

As has been stated, the donation land law granted 320 acres to each single person and 640 acres to each married couple, who could establish a residence in Oregon prior to December 1, 1851, but made no exception predicated on extinguishment of Indian titles, and the effect of this omission was to foster settlement in advance of treaty making. Further to complicate this phase of the question, the treaties of Gaines and Dart were never ratified. The reservations which they proposed to create were chosen unfortunately, from the settlers' point of view, and the senate was bombarded with protests. To the Indians, however, who had entered into them in good faith, and who could not be brought to understand the reasons for delay in fulfillment of their provisions, this could be only an additional cause of disappointment and irritation.

The Twality band of the Calapooya tribe ceded the country between the Willamette river and the summit of the Coast range and between the Yamhill and Tualatin rivers, embracing the sites of the present towns of Lafayette, Dayton, Newberg, Amity, McMinnville and Yamhill. A reservation within this region and about six by eight miles in area was set apart for them, but certain exceptions were made within the reservation, for the benefit of all claimants under the donation land law of 1850, with the provision that "the said land claims are hereby ceded to the United States for that purpose, whenever the same shall be surveyed and marked out as required by said act." The net effect of this provision, if the treaty had been ratified, would have been to isolate perpetually those settlers whose claims were thus reserved. Since the pioneers looked forward to development of neighborhood life, the prospect, though their titles were protected, was far from pleasing to them.

The treaty provided for payment to the Twality band of $40,-000, in 20 annual installments, of which only $500 annually was to be paid in cash, the remainder being expended for merchandise for the use of the Indians. Each of the Indian treaties was similar in this regard, so that the list of articles specified is typical. The Twalities were promised annually 130 blankets, 38 coats, 26 pairs of pants, 152 shirts, 76 vests, 130 pair of shoes, 200 yards of calico, 200 yards of linsey plaid, 27 blanket shawls, 200 yards of domestic shirting, 38 hats or caps, 132 pocket handkerchiefs, 24 axes, five plows, ten plow harnesses, 24 hoes, six scythes and cradles, "all of which are to be good and substantial articles." It became the custom also to provide by treaty for certain gifts to tribal dignitaries. Thus, it was stipulated that on the occasion of payment of the first two annual installments the United States should deliver to each chief "a good Indian horse and a good bridle, for the use of the said chiefs, to encourage agriculture among the said tribe." This treaty was signed at Champoeg, April 19, 1851.

The Luck-a-mi-ute band of the Calapooyas, May 2, 1851, ceded their lands on the west side of the Willamette, south of the foregoing and embracing the present site of Corvallis, for $20,000, with similar indefinite and trouble-breeding exceptions in behalf of white land claimants. Also, the same day, the Yamhill band ceded the region on the west side between the Yamhill and Luck-a-mi-ute rivers, for $28,000, but the treaty commissioners omitted the exception in favor of white settlers, agreeing instead "to remove all persons who may be residing within the bounds of the reservation."

On the east side of the river, the principal band of the Molallas, on May 6, 1851, ceded their lands surrounding the site of Oregon City, for $22,000, obtaining a reservation from which the claims of settlers were excepted. The Santiam band, May 7, 1851, exchanged their lands, south of the foregoing, for a reservation on the upper Santiam, and $20,000.

Dart and his two sub-agents, H. H. Spalding and Josiah L. Parrish, made treaties, in August and September, with various bands of the Clatsop, Tillamook and Chinook tribes, west of the Coast range, north and south of the Columbia river, and with two bands of the Rogue river tribe, and returning to the Willamette valley in November, 1851, concluded a final compact with the Clackamas tribe, now reduced to fewer than a dozen adult males, the government granting the privilege of residing on the grounds then occupied by them at the Clackamas ferry, and protecting them in their right to fish "at all their former fishing grounds on the Clackamas river, together with the privilege of passing freely from one to the other along the river." The vagueness of this provision, which was contained also in other and later Indian treaties, was a frequent cause of friction between the races.

37

The treaty commissioners, however, contributed further to misunderstandings between the whites and the natives, and laid the foundation for that future alliance of the tribes north and south of the Columbia river, which was a few years later to inflame the entire region with war, by ignoring the claims in the Willamette and Rogue river valleys of the powerful and warlike Klickitats. In the early fur trade era, the Klickitats had confined themselves to the region near the headwaters of the Cowlitz, White Salmon, Lewis and Klickitat rivers, and they were unknown south of the Columbia when the Methodist missionaries arrived in Oregon. They were more nomadic than the Willamette valley tribes, probably because of earlier wars with the Cayuses, who had driven them westward from the foothills of the Rocky mountains. Becoming acquainted with other parts of the country, as well as with the advantages of trade, they extended the field of their operations, overflowing their natural boundaries and reaching the Columbia river, at some time between 1835 and 1840. Here, they began war on the Chinooks and other inferior tribes. Game in the Willamette valley next attracted them and they made numerous forays against the indolent Calapooyas. The Calapooyas, in this period, suffered greatly from diseases, introduced among them by the whites, and were much diminished in numbers and in powers of physical resistance.

38

The date of the irruption of the Klickitats has not been determined with exactness. J. Ross Browne says that "in 1841 they began to turn their attention to the south side of the Columbia." George Gibbs, an ethnologist and Indian linguist with George B. McClellan's division of the Northern Pacific Railroad exploration expedition of 1853, says that "it was not until 1839 that they crossed the Columbia, when they overran the Willamette valley, attracted by the game with which it abounded, and which they destroyed in defiance of the weak and indolent Calapooyas."

These Klickitats boasted that they had taught the Calapooyas to ride and hunt. They were the most skilled of all the Oregon tribes in the use of firearms, and they quickly assumed possessory rights over the entire Willamette valley, dictated terms to the conquered, established camps, exacted tribute, opened an extensive trade in furs, and made the Willamette valley their public highway to the north and their depot during the greater part of the year, where they left their property and families. After the immigration of 1843, they sought work as farm laborers, becoming skilled in husbandry, and also became acquainted with the nature and extent of the immigration movement. Their services were regarded by the settlers as superior to those of other Indians. In their systematic efforts to obtain supremacy over the southern tribes, they aided the whites in every outbreak in that region. They furnished a small but effective contingent of warriors to General Lane, on the occasion of a hostile demonstration in the Rogue river country, 1853.

39

The Klickitats, therefore, believed themselves to have acquired, by conquest, the right to be considered in the negotiations to quiet the Indian title to the Willamette valley. Moreover, they constituted a communicating bond between all the tribes. When they were removed, 1855, by the superintendent of Indian affairs for Oregon to their original country north of the Columbia, they accused the government of cheating them, contended that every right obtained in accordance with Indian usage had been violated, and they were, from that moment, in a state of war.

Judicial records bear testimony to the Klickitats' repeated assertion of their rights in the Willamette valley. At a term of court held in Washington county in 1851, Donald McLeod brought an action for trespass against a band of Klickitats who had destroyed timber he had prepared for his house. Indian Agent Parrish represented them. The Indians contended that the timber was as much theirs as McLeod's, that they had acquired the land by conquest and had warned McLeod against settling there, and that the land had never been purchased from them. The judge held that they had a possessory title which had never been extinguished by the government and refused judgment for trespass. Another farmer built a fence across a trail which was their public highway. They tore down the fence and the court gave a similar decision. Recognition of the claims of the Klickitats by the treaty commissioners would seem, therefore, to have been suggested by diplomatic considerations, if no others. Omission in this instance may have furnished a motive for the compact between the northern and southern tribes which led to widespread war, and without which it is improbable that the Indians would have deemed themselves sufficiently powerful to undertake a campaign of extermination against the settlers.

The exodus of the settlers to the gold mines in California tempted the Indians of the Klamath and Rogue river countries to commit a number of petty thefts and minor depredations. The treasure hunters, a considerable proportion of whom were of a less responsible class than the home-seeking immigrants, retaliated without discrimination, and a state of practical warfare was created which took Governor Lane south, May, 1850, to endeavor to conclude a treaty of peace. Lane's successor as governor, John P. Gaines, had been appointed meanwhile, but had not arrived in the territory, and Lane forwarded his resignation, to take effect on June 18, by which time he expected to have concluded his task.

Lane was accompanied by 15 Klickitats led by Chief Quatley, and by a small party of white men. Coming upon a camp of Rogue river warriors on Grave creek, he held a council with them, enlivened by one of the most dramatic episodes in the early history of the dealings of whites with the Indians. At a critical point in the conference, the Rogue river chief cried out to his followers, who sprang to arms, as if by pre-arrangement. Quatley, the Klickitat, seized the treacherous chief and held him fast, while Lane menaced him with a pistol, and, by threatening to kill the chief on the first sign of violence by his followers, contrived to get him out of camp as a hostage. Employing this advantage, he induced the leading men of the tribe to sign a peace compact. Lane's boldness on this occasion so impressed the Rogue river chieftain that he took the name of Jo, after the formality of obtaining Lane's consent. The governor then proceeded to the California mines and the Indians remained quiet for a short time.

40

There were repeated encounters, however, between the travellers and the Indians, particularly at the ferries, where the Indians were wont to steal canoes left by the white men, with the purpose of exacting toll for crossing the river. The treaty obtained by Lane failed of its purpose, for reasons not discreditable to the better classes of either race. The earliest settlers, who had come to the country with kindly feelings for the Indians, had been followed by some who entertained contrary sentiments. The gold mines, as has been said, attracted a more reckless class of whites. There were transient renegades also, among the Indians, who committed excesses which were charged to the tribes permanently resident in the region. It is not possible to fix with exactness the blame for the hostilities in 1851, and thereafter, that some annalists have attributed wholly to disregard of treaty obligations by the Indians, and others, with equal inaccuracy, have charged solely to the whites.

S. H. Culver, Indian agent in the Rogue river valley, wrote in a report to Joel Palmer, superintendent of Indian affairs, July 20, 1854: "With the first emigration, hostilities commenced, which were continued by both parties from year to year, owing to mutual misunderstanding, until 1850, when Governor Lane undertook the very difficult task of making peace with these bands, in which he succeeded. But it had become so much a habit with each to shoot the other at sight, that many were not able or did not wish to resist what seemed to have grown into a temptation. Early next summer hostilities again began. . . . Up to the present time much the largest portion of the outrages committed upon the whites has been the work of migratory bands of ungovernable Indians. From the want of correct information, our citizens prosecuted a vigorous warfare against the Indians of this valley for depredations in the commission of which they bore no part. The Indians were compelled . . . to take up arms in self-defense, . . . while our own people supposed themselves also to be prosecuting a defensive war."

41

A succession of encounters occurred in the spring of 1851, on the road from the Willamette valley to California, between parties of travellers and roving bands of Indians. June, 1851, Maj. Philip Kearney, with a detachment of the mounted regulars who had been ordered to leave Oregon, arrived on Rogue river. He responded promptly to an appeal by whites in the vicinity for protection, by pursuing and engaging the Indians near Table Rock, June 17. Capt. James Stuart was killed in a hand-to-hand encounter with an Indian warrior, and the loss of the hostiles was eleven dead and several wounded. Kearney then waited for reinforcements and attacked the Indians again, June 23, on which day there was skirmishing in the forenoon and a four hours' battle in the afternoon, wherein the Indians suffered severely but were not humbled. Their answer to a proposal now made by Kearney for a peace treaty was a howl of defiance. Kearney took up the pursuit again, June 30, to discover that the warriors had fled, leaving their women and children behind them. The latter, to the number of 30, were made prisoners. Lane, who had just been elected delegate to congress from the territory, and was on his way to California to look after his mining interests there, arrived in time to take part in the hunt. He was recognized by some of the Indians, who pleaded with him from a distance to use his good offices for peace.

The Indian captives were delivered by Kearney to Lane, who

committed them to the care of Governor Gaines, now approaching the valley on another peace mission. Partly, perhaps, in order to ransom their families, a party of Rogue river Indians, a few days afterward, signed an agreement to keep the peace and to restore the property they had stolen. This arrangement was ignored, however, by the war faction of the tribe. In a letter from Lane to the Statesman, June 22, 1851, he reported: "The Indians have been completely whipped in every fight. Some 50 of them were killed, many wounded and 30 taken prisoners. . . . Never has an Indian country been invaded with better success or at a better time." In a postscript he wrote: "I omitted to mention that on my way down Rogue river with the prisoners I had a conversation with a considerable number of Indians, across the river, who gave me a terrible account of the invasion of their country by our people, that they had come on horses, in great numbers, invading every portion of it—that they now were afraid to lay down to sleep, for fear the white people would be upon them before they would awake,—that they were tired of war and wanted peace."

42

Southwestern Oregon had received its first influx of settlers in 1851, when land claims were taken under the donation land act in the Umpqua valley and its tributaries. Settlement began prior to the visit of Anson Dart on his treaty-making errand. In June, 1851, the harbor of Port Orford was re-discovered, and a party of nine men was put ashore from the steamer Seagull, with a supply of provisions and a small cannon. The newcomers were ordered away by a band of Coquilles residing in the vicinity, who surrounded the camp and made an assault on it. The cannon was discharged by the defenders and several Indians were killed, or wounded, by a single shot. Notwithstanding this, natives continued the attack at close quarters, but were repulsed by the superior arms of the white men. The latter, nevertheless, took counsel of discretion and, being insufficiently supplied with ammunition for a siege, withdrew one night and set out for the settlements on the Umpqua, which they reached after a painful journey. They found salmon berries to eat the first four days, and subsisted on mussels after that, until they met some comparatively friendly Indians, with whom they exchanged the shirts they wore, for food.

Other settlers were later brought to Port Orford by the same vessel that had set the nine ashore, and by August, 1851, Port Orford had a population of about 60. In this month W. G. T'Vault, who had become prominent at Willamette falls, in 1846, as the pioneer newspaper editor of the territory, led a party of explorers in quest of an overland route to the settlements of the interior. Ten of these men, including T'Vault, after getting lost and wandering for some days in the mountains, engaged some Indians to guide them, and the latter treacherously led them into an ambush at Coquille village. Only five escaped, and the bodies of the five who were murdered were so mutilated that it was impossible later to identify them. This massacre occurred on September 14, 1851. When the news of it reached California a punitive expedition consisting of 90 United States dragoons was ordered into the field. The soldiers devoted a little more than three weeks, from October 31 until November 21, to locating and cornering the Coquilles, and then about twenty minutes to a decisive battle in which 15 Indians were killed and many wounded, and their village and stores destroyed.

The victims of the massacre just described were Patrick Murphy, of New York, A. S. Dougherty, of Texas, John P. Holland, of New Hampshire, Jeremiah Ryland, of Maryland, and J. P. Pepper, of New York. The survivors were W. G. T'Vault, Gilbert Brush, T. J. Davenport, of Massachusetts, L. L. Williams, of Vermont, and Cyrus Hedden, of New Jersey. Williams was terribly wounded by an arrow, and Brush by a paddle in the hands of an Indian. Here was a notable instance of kindness and bravery on the part of a young Indian of the village. T'Vault and Brush were in the river, into which they had leaped with a hope of getting away, but a native in a canoe overtook Brush and was beating him unmercifully with a paddle upon the swimmer's head. An Indian youth, seeing the desperate straits of the white men, pushed out from the shore in a canoe, beat off Brush's assailant, helped Brush into the canoe, gave T'Vault his paddle, and then leaping into the water, swam to the shore, and left the white men. They subsequently made their way to Port Orford, being aided near Cape Blanco by friendly Indians, to whom they owed their rescue from starvation and hardship.

43

Events of 1852, commanding attention by reason of their relation to the Indian troubles in Oregon, were the discovery of gold in Rogue river valley, near the present site of Jacksonville, marked increase of immigration to southern Oregon, and failure of the United States senate to ratify any of the treaties previously entered into with the Indians. The federal government had not yet formulated its policy, and Indian Agent A. A. Skinner, who was assigned to duty in the Rogue river valley, could only counsel patience and continue to make promises, which the government did not perform. On the other hand, the intractables among the Indians grew more menacing, acts of the peace faction were repudiated, and the increasing numbers of travellers added new opportunities to pillage. The large immigration to Oregon, 1852, over the usual trail, escaped serious encounters because of its numbers. But the smaller number of immigrants who travelled over the southern route were not so fortunate. Murderous attacks were made on immigrant trains and small parties of miners were waylaid and killed. About one hundred whites were slain in this manner.

A company of 75 volunteers, commanded by John K. Lamerick, was raised in the vicinity of Jacksonville, in July, in response to an appeal from settlers whose homes and property were believed to be in danger. One occurrence that had aroused their apprehension is thus described by Agent Skinner in his report to Superintendent Dart: "About the time of the murder of a white man at Scott's valley, Sam, the principal war chief of the Indians of this valley, went to the house of Dr. Ambrose, who resides about two miles from the Big Bar, on Rogue river (the usual winter residence of Sam), and demanded of him three beef cattle, or that he should immediately leave the place; stating that he, Sam, had previously sold the land to William G. T'Vault, Esq. Sam, at the same time, proposed to trade two Indian children, and a horse, and some money for a little girl of Dr. Ambrose, about two years of age. Sam's manner at the time was such as to cause the doctor to apprehend that he intended to take the child by force if he could not otherwise obtain it." Ambrose, himself, was impartial, and believed that much of the trouble with the Indians was caused by the whites, who on more than one occasion mistreated the natives, and in some cases killed women and children.

The volunteers, uniting with a posse from the Shasta valley, on the California side of the boundary, commanded by Elijah Steele, succeeded in surrounding a considerable band of warriors under Chief Sam, and so frightened them with a show of overwhelming force that they sued for peace. Captain Lamerick favored rejection of these overtures, declaring that the Indians would not keep their pledges and should be severely punished. The settlers urged the pacific course, fearing retaliation after the military organization had been disbanded. A vote was taken. The settlers' party won and a treaty was made by which the Rogue river warriors agreed to respect the property of the settlers and to hold no communication with the Shastas, then in particular disfavor with the whites because of their leadership in outlawry. The treaty was completed, July 21, 1852. Agent Skinner resigned soon afterward, leaving the region without even the nominal protection of a representative of the federal government.

The terms of this treaty are set forth in a letter from J. R. Hardin in the Statesman, August 7, 1852: "An agreement was made and signed which runs something after this manner: That the Rogue river Indians should have no communication with the Shasta Indians, who are in the habit of committing depredations upon the whites by stealing horses and other property and running them over into the Rogue river valley and securing succor and protection from the Rogue Rivers; that they should expect no more presents from the *hias Boston tyee* (the president of the United States) unless he wanted to do so; that the Bostons have the rights to settle where they pleased and be secure and protected by the chiefs and their counselors in their persons and property; that all cattle in the valley belonging to the whites are to be safe from molestation from the Indians; that if any property, of any kind or description, belonging to the Bostons, is stolen or destroyed by the Indians, and Sam, the chief, does not produce it in a given time, that he is to be surrendered up into the hands of the Bostons, to do with him as they think proper, even to the taking off of his head." Hardin, writer of the foregoing letter, was mortally wounded when a party of which he was a member was attacked from ambush by Indians, August, 1853.

44

Hostilities, in 1853, were restricted to southern Oregon and northern California, but this was a year of historical significance in the great struggle between the races. Here enters another dominating character, Kamiakin, chief of the Yakimas, who in this year conceived the idea of uniting all the Indians of the northwest in a mighty struggle for possession of their lands. At this time, also, Lieut. George B. McClellan arrived in the Yakima valley, with the advance guard of an expedition under command of Isaac I. Stevens, to explore the route of a railroad from the Mississippi river to the Pacific coast. Kamiakin, who had not resented the coming of the fur traders, or the missionaries, and who had shown himself amenable to progress, so that he was said to have introduced the first cattle into the Yakima region and to have built the first irrigation ditch ever constructed by Indians in the Oregon Country, was of a different mind when the soldiers of the United States appeared. Here he saw confirmation of the stories that had been told him by Indians farther east, that the white men were coming to take the Indians' hunting grounds from them.

<h2 style="text-align:center">45</h2>

Meanwhile, August, 1853, savages in the Rogue river valley, who repudiated the treaty of the previous year, among them a Rogue river sub-chief named Taylor, suddenly attacked the isolated settlements. The settlers arrested two Indians in war paint, and took them to Jacksonville and hanged them after a trial. Reprisals and counter reprisals resulted. A coalition between the disaffected Rogue rivers, Shastas, Klamaths and Siskiyous gave encouragement to the hostiles, who by this time were better armed than were the whites. Several citizens were ambushed and murdered. Lieutenant-Colonel Bonneville, the same officer who had led a fur-trading expedition across the Rocky mountains in 1833, was then stationed at Fort Vancouver, and he responded to a requisition from the governor of the territory for arms, by sending a howitzer and rifles and ammunition, with an escort consisting of Lieut. A. V. Kautz and six artillerymen. Forty volunteers from the Willamette valley, in command of J. W. Nesmith, accompanied the train. Three companies of volunteers, about two hundred men, were recruited in the Rogue river valley. Eighty residents of the Shasta valley organized into two companies. Maj. B. R. Alden, then at Fort Jones, California, joined the hast-

ily improvised army and took command, which he relinquished a
few days afterward, August 21, 1853, to Lane, who had meanwhile been commissioned by Governor Curry as brigadier-general
of volunteers. Lane had heard of the hostilities in the Rogue river
valley while at his home on the Umpqua river, and had hastened
to the scene with a company of about a dozen settlers. The Indians were driven to bay and decisively defeated, August 24,
1853, in a battle in which the whites lost three killed and five
wounded and the Indians eight killed and 20 wounded. Lane received a bullet wound in his right arm, and Major Alden a gunshot wound from which, two years afterward, he died.

The Indians by this time had discovered that Lane, for whom
they had conceived a certain admiration, was in command of the
expedition against them, and cried out to him for a parley, which
was granted with some misgivings, and this resulted in setting a
date early in September for a treaty council, Lane taking as hostage a son of his Indian namesake, Chief Jo.

46

The military position of the whites was strengthened during
the period of the armistice by the arrival of Kautz, with the
howitzer and a store of ammunition, accompanied by Nesmith
and his Willamette valley volunteers, and also by a small detachment of regulars from Port Orford in command of Capt. A. J.
Smith; so that, when the day of the historic council of Table
Rock, September 10, 1853, arrived, the troops made a formidable
showing, even against the aggregation of Rogue river warriors,
estimated by Nesmith at about 700 men. Joel Palmer had been
appointed superintendent of Indian affairs for the territory, and
he arrived on the scene, meanwhile, with authority to represent
the government in the treaty-making. Lane, whose policy it was
to show no fear in the presence of the Indians, had consented,
even before the arrival of reinforcements, to preliminary terms,
to which Nesmith, hardened pioneer and experienced Indian fight-
er that he was, demurred. These terms were, that Lane would
proceed to the Indian encampment, which lay at the base of the
perpendicular walls of Table Rock, at a distance of some two and
a half miles from the military front, attended only by a body
guard of ten unarmed men.

47

Lane kept his agreement to the letter, and Nesmith, although he afterward admitted that he had no liking for the adventure, consented to accompany the party, as interpreter. "Against those terms," said Nesmith afterward, "I protested, and told the general that I had traversed that same country five years before, and fought those same Indians; that they were notoriously treacherous, and had earned the designation of 'Rogues' by never permitting a white man to escape with his scalp, when once within their power; that I knew them better than he did, and that it was folly for eleven unarmed men to place themselves voluntarily in the power of 700 well-armed hostile Indians, in their own secure encampment." Lane replied that he had fixed on the terms of the meeting and was determined to keep his word. If Nesmith was afraid to go, said Lane, he could remain behind. Nesmith retorted that he was as little acquainted with fear as Lane was, though still insisting that he believed the white councillors were going to their own slaughter.

48

An incident of the conference almost justified Nesmith's forebodings. In the party of councillors, in addition to Lane and Nesmith, were Indian Superintendent Palmer, Indian Agent Samuel P. Culver, Capt. A. J. Smith, Capt. L. F. Mosher, Col. A. J. Ross, Lieut. A. V. Kautz, R. B. Metcalf, J. D. Mason and T. T. Tierney. Arriving at the meeting ground, they found the Indians in full panoply of war; on the plain below and within full view of the Indians, the dragoons were formed in line, the sunlight of a perfect autumn morning glinting from their white belts and burnished scabbards. Behind the Indian camp frowned the perpendicular cliff of Table Rock.

Lane and Palmer made long speeches, which were translated twice, first into the Chinook jargon, by Nesmith, and then into the Rogue river tongue by an Indian interpreter. The replies of the chiefs were also twice translated, in reversed order. Shortly before the final understanding was reached a naked Indian courier rode wildly into camp with tidings that a company of whites, at Applegate creek, had captured an Indian sub-chief known as Jim Taylor, tied him to a tree and shot him to death.

The courier's harangue threw the Indians into a turmoil, in

the midst of which the Indian interpreter informed Nesmith that the braves were threatening to tie the councillors to trees and serve them as the whites had served Chief Taylor. Nesmith "noticed nothing but coolness," however, among his companions. Lane sat immovable on a log, his arm bandaged because of his wound of a few days before. At Nesmith's suggestion, the others of the party scattered among the Indians, to avoid becoming targets for the hot-headed warriors. After a few tense moments, Lane addressed the tribe again. "Owens, who violated the armistice and killed Jim Taylor," he said, "is a bad man. He is not one of my soldiers. When I catch him he shall be punished. I promised in good faith to come into your camp with ten other unarmed men to secure peace; I do not believe that you are such cowardly dogs as to take advantage of our unarmed condition. I know that you have the power to murder us, and you can do so as quickly as you please, but what good will our blood do you? Our murder will exasperate our friends and your tribe will be hunted from the face of the earth. Let us proceed with the treaty, and in place of war have everlasting peace." Lane's bold defiance, and a promise to compensate in shirts and blankets for Taylor's death, quieted the excitement.

49

The treaty signed that afternoon was measureably effective in preserving the peace in southern Oregon for about two years. Major Alden promptly began the construction of a military post on the south bank of Rogue river, opposite the reservation, which was a military headquarters during subsequent Indian wars in the region, but was abandoned when the treaty Indians were removed to another reservation, 1856.

The Table Rock treaty was ratified by the United States senate, April 12, 1854, and proclaimed February 5, 1855. The Indians ceded about 2500 square miles of the upper Rogue river valley above Applegate creek, except approximately one hundred square miles east of Evans creek and north of Rogue river. For this they were to receive $60,000 from the United States, of which $15,000 was retained to pay for property of the whites destroyed by the Indians during the war, and about $5000 was to be expended for goods for the benefit of the tribe, under the direction of the Indian agent. The balance of $40,000 was payable in 16 equal annual instalments, in merchandise. Each of the three principal chiefs received in addition a dwelling house to cost not to exceed $500. The Indian reservation was specifically made a temporary one, the United States government agreeing to pay the Indians an additional $15,000, whenever they should be removed to another reservation.

Before leaving the country Lane made a less formal peace agreement with Chief Tip-su, whose band laid claim to the region of the headwaters of Rogue river, and September 19, 1853, Superintendent Palmer completed a treaty with the small Cow creek band of Umpquas, who relinquished their claim on the Umpqua valley in exchange for a reservation and $12,000.

50

The remaining months of 1853 and all of 1854 were nominally peaceful, though marred by several conflicts between nomadic, non-reservation Indians and whites, who were not settlers. A quarrel between two squaw-men and a band of Shastas resulted in the spreading of a false report by the squaw-men that the Indians were on the warpath. Citizens raised a company of volunteers and also obtained the help of a detachment of regular troops from Fort Jones. The captain of the volunteers, R. C. Geiger, was killed before the story of the squaw-men had been discredited and the regulars were withdrawn. But this started another series of reprisals and counter-reprisals in which a number of friendly Indians and peacefully inclined whites were killed. The murder of James Kyle, a merchant, at Jacksonville, October 7, 1853, by two Indians, who were afterward traced to the reservation, once seemed to threaten a serious breach, because one of the murderers was a relative of Chief Jo; but the guilty men were surrendered by the tribe, and were tried and hanged at Jacksonville, a proceeding which did a good deal to restore the confidence of the white settlers in the good faith of the treaty Indians.

51

A volunteer military expedition commanded by Capt. Jesse Walker deserves a place among the remembered events of 1854, because of the signal service it performed in guarding the southern immigrant trail in that season. There were rumors of disaffection among the Indians of the interior, concerning whose land no treaties had been made, and Walker's company of 71 men was recruited, August, 1854, in response to an order of Governor Davis. It proceeded at once to its task, under instructions from the governor to cultivate the friendship of the Indians, if possible, but if necessary to the safety of lives and property of the immigration to whip the hostiles and drive them from the road, an order similar to that issued by Abernethy, in 1848. The Walker expedition engaged bands of Modoc and Shasta Indians in several skirmishes and kept the immigrant trail clear during the season.

52

The cost of the Rogue river war of 1853 was assumed by the United States, and the accounts were paid with more than customary promptness, owing in all probability to the fortunate circumstance that Lane, who commanded in the campaign, was also a delegate in congress and in a position to press consideration. Lane declined compensation for himself. The volunteers were paid off in coin, at Jacksonville and Yreka, June and July, 1855. The subsistence accounts were paid by draft on Governor Curry, who made disbursements to individual creditors. The total thus expended was about $285,000. The expenses of the Walker expeditionary force, however, suffered greater delay, and were not liquidated until the close of the Civil war. Walker's volunteers were recruited with full understanding of the sacrifice expected of them. The territorial treasury was now depleted, and Governor Davis wrote to Col. John Ross, in command of the Ninth regiment of Oregon militia: "I am aware of the many embarrassments under which you will labor if it should be considered necessary to raise such a command without a single dollar to defray expenses; you will be compelled to rely upon the liberality and patriotism of our fellow citizens, who in turn will be compelled to rely upon the justness of the general government for their compensation."

53

Restiveness of interior tribes was increasing year by year. Immigrants travelling in large companies, well armed, escaped open assault, although subject to thefts of stock, and other small annoyances. But two treacherous attacks on isolated parties of whites, 1854, west of Fort Hall, at which point it was now customary for wagon trains to break up into individual units, awakened the inhabitants of the territory to a new sense of danger. United States military forces in Oregon had a nominal strength of nine companies of infantry, but these had been so depleted by desertion that they mustered no more than 350 men. About this time there arose an unfortunate controversy between responsible officers of the army, the officials of the Indian department and the territorial authorities, as to where blame should be placed for Indian hostilities. The excesses of irresponsible whites, and the acts, not always prudent, of settlers goaded to desperation by deeds of outlaw Indians, gave just enough color to the theories of those who opposed a policy of stern repression of the savages, to embarrass seriously the advocates of a moderate, but intelligent, policy of controlling the natives by force, in their own interests as well as those of the white inhabitants. The military establishment, such as it was, was kept in comparative retirement, and it did nothing to forestall the serious encounters that followed. Roving Indians, east of the Cascades, who might have been impressed by a glimpse of the power of the federal government, hardly saw the federal soldiers, and had no reason to fear them. "From what I can learn, there is a determination on the part of the Snakes to kill and rob all who may fall into their power," wrote Indian Agent R. R. Thompson to Superintendent Palmer, September 3, 1854. "They say the Americans have been continually telling them that unless they ceased their depredations, an army would come and destroy them; but no such thing has been done, and that the Americans are afraid of them, and that if we wish to fight them, to come on."

54

About 30 warriors of the Winass band of Shoshone, or Snake Indians, August 30, 1854, surrounded a train of five wagons and 21 persons, led by Alexander Ward, of Kentucky, 25 miles east of Fort Boise, and murdered all but two, under circumstances of peculiar atrocity, even for Indian warfare. The savages first attempted to steal the immigrants' horses. One of the immigrants tried to restrain them and shot one warrior dead, with a revolver. In the fighting that ensued all the white men were killed. The savages then brutally tortured and afterward murdered the women and children. Seven members of another train came upon the Indians plundering the wagons, gave battle in a fruitless effort to succor the captives, and one of the rescue party was killed. The survivors of the first train were two young sons of Mr. and Mrs. Ward. One of these, though deeply wounded with an arrow, escaped to Fort Boise, which he reached in a journey of four days, and the other was found in hiding in a thicket by the rescue party. Immigrants then in the region were too poorly armed, however, to undertake a pursuit, and were forced to abandon the captives to their fate.

Another attack, which occurred on the day before the Ward massacre, was made on a train of five wagons commanded by Moses Kirkland, of Louisiana, 95 miles east of Fort Boise, also by Snake Indians. The savages greeted the immigrants with manifestations of friendship, and then fired a volley, killing three. The whites resisted and forced their assailants to retire, but lost their horses.

A company of 37 volunteers led by Captain Nathan Olney was speedily raised in the Willamette valley and pursued and captured four Indians, who were afterward reported to have been shot while attempting to escape. Maj. Granville O. Haller, of the Fourth infantry, with 23 regulars, took the field, but was too late to render service, except in guarding the immigrant trail. In the following year, however, Haller captured three of the murderers and hanged them, one at a time, on a gallows erected near the grave of Mrs. Ward and seven of her children.

55

Want of coordination of the forces, which might have defended the territory successfully, was conspicuous in the events that immediately followed. There was, first, the failure to station a sufficient force within easy reach of the Indian country. But the inhabitants were of two minds concerning the management of an Indian campaign. Western Oregon, deeply stirred by news of the Ward massacre, cried insistently for immediate and adequate punishment of the murderers. The territorial militia had already been reorganized, with J. W. Nesmith, veteran of many frontier skirmishes, as brigadier-general, E. M. Barnum as adjutant-general, M. M. McCarver, commissary-general, and C. S. Drew, quartermaster-general; and in response to popular outcry, Governor Curry, who had succeeded Governor Davis, issued a proclamation, September 18, 1854, calling for two companies of volunteers, of 60 men each, every volunteer to furnish his own arms and equipment, for the purpose of chastising the perpetrators "by a punishment commensurate with the magnitude of their crime." But, on reflection, Governor Curry wrote to General Nesmith, September 22, 1854, inquiring whether a winter campaign in the Indian country would be practicable, and on receipt of Nesmith's reply in the negative, he rescinded the call for volunteers, an act that was received with lamentations by some of the newspapers and people of the territory. Nathan Olney's volunteers and Major Haller's regulars withdrew from the Snake river country, on receiving assurance that no more immigrants were on the way.

56

Indian Superintendent Palmer made still another effort, early in 1854, to compose the differences between the settlers and the Indians of the Willamette valley, by negotiating a new treaty with the Tualatin band of the Calapooyas, to supersede the ineffective compact of 1851, which, for want of ratification at Washington, had been wholly disregarded by the whites. Palmer outlined the controlling reasons for this treaty in a letter to the commissioner, dated March 27, 1854, in which he said that "settlers have taken and now occupy within this reserve all the lands susceptible of cultivation, without regard to the occupancy of the Indians, who in several instances have been driven from their huts, their fences thrown down and property destroyed." The feelings of the settlers and of the citizens generally toward the Indians, he continued, were such as to render the interposition of the Indian agents in their behalf ineffectual. "The Wappatoo, Kammas and other nutritious roots once produced abundantly in the marshes and lowlands around their principal residences, and constituting their principal means of subsistence, have, since the increase of swine, gradually diminished in quantity and must soon entirely fail. The wild game, formerly abundant, is also becoming scarce, and an act of the territorial legislature prohibiting all persons other than an Indian from supplying the Indians with arms and ammunition renders them unable to avail themselves of the supply the forests might still afford. . . . Their needy circumstances demanded immediate relief and I deemed it wise, expedient and humane to connect the temporary relief afforded them with provisions of permanent character for their comfort and well-being."

Palmer's sympathy for the natives may be seen from a letter written by him to General Lane, then in Washington, as delegate in congress, March 20, 1854: "I regard this treaty as but an entering wedge to the greater work before us, and if we can get action by the senate . . . we may hope to accomplish something within the coming year beyond the mere expenditure of appropriations for the payment of agents, etc. . . . You are acquainted with the conditions of affairs in Oregon and with the desire of our settlers to have these Indians removed from our midst. The provisions of this treaty may be thought by some to be too liberal toward these poor, degraded beings, and that they are not entitled to the consideration given them. Their very weakness and ignorance is one of the reasons why we should liberally provide for them. No one will for a moment pretend that the amount proposed to be paid them is any consideration, comparatively speaking, for their country."

By this treaty, which also failed of ratification, the Calapooyas agreed to cede some 1470 square miles of land, which had already been largely settled by the immigrants, in exchange for an undetermined reservation of about 40 acres for each family and an annual allotment of goods covering a period of twenty years. January 22, 1855, however, Palmer obtained a new treaty, which the senate promptly approved, March 3 of that year, with the confederated tribes of Calapooyas in the Willamette valley, by which the Indians formally relinquished all remaining title to the entire Willamette valley north of the Calapooya mountains, for about $155,000, payable in goods, the government also agreeing to furnish them with a reservation, with an industrial school, and, for a period of five years, with a physician, school teacher, blacksmith and superintendent of farming operations. It was also provided that if any of the bands who signed the treaty should subsequently establish a legitimate claim to any portion of the country north of the Columbia river, their interests therein should be preserved by future treaties. The government reserved the right to allot land in severalty at a subsequent time, on condition that these allotments should be, during the entire period of territorial government, exempt from levy, sale or forfeiture.

An attempt to restrain use of liquor by Indians was made in Article 7, which read: "In order to prevent the evils of intemperance among said Indians, it is hereby provided that any one of them who shall drink liquor, or procure it for other Indians to drink, may have his or her proportion of the annuities withheld from him or her for such time as the President may determine."

57

Of even greater importance, however, because of bearing on the later relations of the people of the entire Oregon Country with the Indians, were a number of treaties obtained late in 1854, and during 1855, by Gov. Isaac I. Stevens with tribes north of the Columbia river and west of the Cascade mountains. It will be remembered that Washington territory had been created out of the region north of the Columbia, 1853, and Stevens had been named as both governor and superintendent of Indian affairs of the new district. Notwithstanding political separation, however, community of interest in the Indian problems was so manifest that territorial boundaries were ignored. Volunteers from each territory were frequently engaged within the limits of the other. Some of the treaties made by Stevens and certain factors of dissatisfaction arising from governmental delay in acting on them, were influential in bringing about a union of tribes, north and south of the Columbia river, that prolonged the wars in both territories.

58

Stevens and Palmer, representing their respective superintendencies, also acted together in obtaining a treaty with tribes east of the Cascade mountains, whose hunting grounds embraced both Oregon and Washington. Palmer concluded a treaty with bands of the Des Chutes, Wascoes and Walla Wallas, in central Oregon, June 25, 1855, resulting, some time later, in the creation of what is now known as the Warm Springs Indian reservation, and removal of Indians to that location. With the exception of one of Stevens' treaties, however, which subsequently also became a cause of strife, ratification of this series of treaties was delayed by the United States senate, until 1859.

The exception alluded to was the treaty of Medicine creek, so called because the council at which it was agreed on was held on She-nah-nam, or Medicine creek, later known as McAllister's creek, in what is now Thurston county, Washington.

59

The Indians on Puget sound then numbered some 8500, subsisting chiefly on food from the waters, and on camas roots from the low meadows, and berries from the foothills. Captives were held in hereditary slavery. These tribes were at peace with the whites, but were in perpetual dread of the more powerful Yakimas and Klickitats on the east. There was increasing apprehension of the encroachments of white settlers on their fields and fisheries.

These Indians were chosen by Stevens for a development of the treaty policy of the government, although following to some extent previous treaties made by Palmer and Lane with the Rogue river tribes, at Table Rock, and with the Umpquas, at Cow creek. Stevens had before him a formal letter of instruction from the federal bureau of Indian affairs, approving Palmer's course. The treaties "negotiated by Superintendent Palmer," wrote Acting Indian Commissioner Mix to Stevens, August 30, 1854, "are regarded as exhibiting provisions proper on the part of the government and advantages to the Indians, and will afford you valuable suggestions."

Briefly, the plan was to concentrate the natives on a few reservations, to pay them for their lands, not in money but in useful goods, to instruct them in farming and the manual arts, to prohibit inter-tribal wars, to abolish slavery, to prevent the use of intoxicants so far as possible, to preserve for them, during a period of transition from barbarism to civilization, certain rights to fish and gather roots at accustomed places, and at an indefinite future time to allot lands to them in severalty. Tribal jealousies made it necessary to increase the number of reservations somewhat beyond the original plan, but the right was retained to remove them later to larger reservations, where they might be consolidated. Stevens' policy was determined upon after consultation with expert advisers, who examined a number of treaties already entered into by the government with eastern tribes.

60

Col. M. T. Simmons, one of the first settlers to establish a home north of the Columbia river, B. F. Shaw, whose mastery of the Chinook jargon made his services almost indispensable, James Doty, the governor's secretary, who had passed a winter among the Blackfeet and had studied Indian customs there, George Gibbs, scientist attached to the expedition to explore a route for a transcontinental railroad, Lieut. William A. Slaughter of the regular army, and several other white men prominent in the territory, were present at the council. About 700 Puget sound Indians attended, including a few Snoqualmies, who dwelt on the upper streams having their headwaters in the Cascades, and who had established relations with the Yakimas. One of the representatives of the Snoqualmies present was Chief Leschi, whose name appears attached to the official treaty.

The official record of Leschi's name in this connection was afterward the subject of controversy. Colonel Shaw, the interpreter, vouched for Leschi's presence at the council, and numerous witnesses attested that he had affixed his mark to the instrument. Ezra Meeker, a well-known Washington pioneer and a volunteer of the war of 1855-6, however, after making an investigation in a spirit of friendship for the Indians, concluded that Leschi did not sign. Meeker wrote a book on the subject, in which he says: "I have recently interviewed John Hilton, an Indian, one of the five survivors of the signers, who steadfastly refused to go into the war. He says Leschi did not sign; that he stood up before the governor and said that 'if he could not get his home, he would fight, and that the governor told him it was fight, for the treaty paper would not be changed.' Continuing, Hilton said: 'Leschi then took the paper out of his pocket that the governor had given him to be sub-chief, and tore it up before the governor's eyes, stamped on the pieces and left the treaty ground, and never came back to it again'." While the controversy was at its height, Meeker wrote, December 29, 1903: "When Col. B. F. Shaw says he saw Leschi sign the Medicine creek treaty I simply do not believe him. I believe he is mistaken. The preponderance of testimony against this one witness is so overwhelming and the probability is so much to the contrary that I think it is a moral certainty that Leschi did not sign the Medicine creek treaty, although his name is signed with a cross opposite."

61

The council lasted three days. The treaty was signed, December 26, 1854, by Stevens for the United States government and by 62 chiefs and headmen, all who were present, representing the

Nisqually, Puyallup, Steilacoom, Squawskin, S'Homamish, Steh-Chass, T'Peek-sin, Squiath and Sa-ha-wamish tribes. The Indians thus ceded the region comprising the present counties of Thurston and Pierce and parts of Mason and King, reserving an island of about 1280 acres, and two tracts on the mainland of 1280 acres each, one near the mouth of Medicine creek, and the other included within the present site of the city of Tacoma.

The seeming inadequacy of a reservation of about 3840 acres to the needs of an Indian population which was able to assemble 700 persons at the council, was sought to be atoned for by guaranteeing to the Indians the right to fish at their accustomed grounds, (except for taking shell-fish from beds cultivated by citizens,) and to hunt, gather berries and roots, and to pasture cattle on unclaimed land. They were to receive $32,500 in annuities of goods, in addition to $3250, to be expended in removing them to their reservations. They were prohibited from trading outside of the dominions of the United States, and foreign Indians were forbidden to reside on their reservations. This provision was intended to strengthen the hand of the government in dealing with the liquor problem, by checking liquor traffic across the international boundary, and also to curb the influence of the Hudson's Bay Company among the Indians.

62

Stevens concluded three other treaties with Canoe Indians of Puget sound, January, 1855, so that by early spring he was free to cross the Cascades and negotiate with the less tractable tribes of the interior. Of these, the Yakimas had been passive, if not friendly to the whites, being outwardly content with the isolation they enjoyed prior to the beginning of settlement north of the Columbia; but they now began to fear the encroachments of the settlers. To the Yakimas, as well as to the Walla Wallas, Cayuses, Nez Perce's and others, Stevens sent couriers into Oregon territory, as well as in Washington territory, advising them of his desire to meet them in a great council at which all matters at issue between the whites and Indians might be adjusted. The Walla Walla valley was chosen for the council ground, at the instance of the Yakima head chief, Kamiakin, who said: "This is the place where in ancient times we held our councils with the neighboring tribes, and we will hold it there now."

There is an interesting story, however, that Kamiakin had foreseen the issue, and had called a great preliminary council of the eastern tribes, who had met during the summer of 1854 in the valley of the Grande Ronde, at a meeting in many respects the most remarkable gathering of Indians ever held in that vast territory. Only Lawyer of the Nez Perce's, Sticcas of the Cayuses, and Garry of the Spokanes, according to the story, were in favor of making any treaty with the whites. Lawyer and Sticcas, the former because of his long-standing friendship for the whites, and the latter perhaps by reason of recent memories of the experiences of his tribe, held out strongly for a treaty council. All the chiefs except Lawyer and Sticcas thereupon agreed among themselves to mark the boundaries of their tribes, so that the chief of each could rise in council and claim his boundaries as a reservation for his people. There being no lands for sale to the whites, so reasoned the wily chieftains, the council would fail. This plan was communicated to the officials by Lawyer, who, in anticipation of the coming conference, now set about the creation of a counter coalition.

63

There was opposition, also, in official quarters, to the holding of this council, Joel Palmer, among others, deeming the time inopportune. Many who knew the Indians well had sensed an approaching storm. Stevens, however, procured an escort of 40 federal troopers from Major Rains, at The Dalles, and reached the council ground, on Mill creek, near its confluence with the Walla Walla river, May 21, 1855. A large quantity of goods to be used as gifts was transported up the Columbia to Fort Walla Walla by boat, and a company of 25 packers, organized at The Dalles, conveyed tentage and provisions to the camp. A herd of beef cattle, a huge pile of potatoes, and large stores of bacon, flour, coffee and sugar were provided for the Indians. Palmer, with two Indian agents representing Oregon, arrived on the same day and went into camp. The officials now awaited the arrival of the Indians with feelings not unmixed with apprehension.

64

The Nez Perce's, 2500 strong, commanded by Lawyer, and flying the American flag which had been given them by Newell, 1848, in appreciation of their friendship for the whites in the

Cayuse affair, arrived first, May 24, 1855, and their chiefs and sub-chiefs were banqueted by Stevens and Palmer. An ominous development of the day was the receipt of a message from Peu-peu-mox-mox that the Walla Wallas, Yakimas and Cayuses, would accept no provisions from the commissioners, but would bring their own, and the messenger refused to accept gifts of tobacco for his chief. Two priests, from the Walla Walla and Yakima country, arrived to attend the council and brought reports that Kamiakin was inclined to hostility. Three hundred Cayuses and Walla Wallas rode into camp, May 26, but their chiefs were surly and refused to smoke pipes with the commissioners. Chief Garry, of the Spokanes, came as a spectator; and a courier, who had been sent to the Palouses, returned accompanied by only one chief, whose people refused to take part as a tribe.

On May 27, which was Sunday, the Nez Perce's held religious services, a chief named Timothy preaching in the Nez Perce's language and taking the Ten Commandments as his text. Peu-peu-mox-mox, although he found opportunity to profess confidence in the whites, asked that more than one interpreter be employed, so that the Indians might know that the translations were correct. The Yakimas, encamped some distance away, were coldly formal. Peu-peu-mox-mox and a delegation of Yakima chiefs, including Kamiakin, Owhi and Skloom, rode into camp, May 28, shaking hands with the commissioners with reserved cordiality; but, during the talk with Stevens which followed, they declined tobacco proffered them and smoked their own, exclusively. Soon after this, Spotted Eagle, of the Nez Perce's, informed Stevens that the Cayuses had been long trying to create disaffection among the Nez Perce's and had invited three Nez Perce's sub-chiefs to confer with them and the Yakimas, without consulting the Nez Perce's head chiefs. The atmosphere of Indian plot and counterplot pervaded the preliminaries. On the eve of the formal opening of the council there were some five thousand Indians in the valley, including squaws and children.

65

The council opened, May 29, 1855, with the customary ceremony of smoking, and continued from day to day, until June 11, but the treaty that was finally arrived at was dated June 9. It was officially proclaimed as of date June 12, 1855. The prevailing distrust of the white people was voiced by Peu-peu-mox-mox, at one of the conferences, in a speech in which he said: "In one day the Americans became as numerous as the grass. This I learned in California. I know it is not right; you have spoken in a round-about way. Speak straight. I have ears to hear you and here is my heart. Suppose you show me goods; shall I run up and take them? Goods and the earth are not equal. Goods are for using on the earth. I do not know where they have given lands for goods. We require time to think quietly, slowly. You have spoken in a manner partly tending to evil. . . . Show me charity. I should be very much ashamed if the Americans did anything wrong. . . . Think over what I have said."

The task of the commissioners was now to convince the Indians of the advantages to them of civilization, and of the inevitable coming of the whites. But even Sticcas, friendly chief of the Cayuses, was dissatisfied with a treaty that left his tribe none of their own lands. Young Chief, also of the Cayuses, who was believed to have been secretly plotting with Kamiakin for the destruction of the whites, declared that the Indians had no right to sell the ground which God had given them for their support, unless for a good reason. Peu-peu-mox-mox asked for delay and another council. He opposed the coming of the settlers. "The whites," he said, "may travel in all directions through our country. We will have nothing to say to them, provided they do not build houses on our lands."

66

Palmer proposed a compromise to meet the desires of tribes unwilling to be placed on a reservation with the Nez Perce's, offering them another reservation which would embrace part of the region in which they were then living. This won the assent of all present, except the Yakimas, but a disturbing factor now entered the negotiations when an Indian runner arrived with news that Looking Glass, war chief of the Nez Perce's, who had been absent on an expedition into the Blackfoot country, was now on his way to the council ground. This chieftain, who was 70 years old, had ridden 300 miles in seven days, and his party presently rode into camp bearing aloft a fresh Blackfoot scalp. A great hubbub arose in all the Indian lodges, and even the Nez Perce's withdrew their promises to sign the treaty.

The Nez Perce's held a council among themselves at which it was proposed to depose Lawyer and place Looking Glass in his stead. The issue was determined by tribal politics. Lawyer's party prevailed and the majority voted that the faith of the tribe had been pledged to sign the treaty, as Lawyer had agreed to do. Peu-peu-mox-mox and Kamiakin then yielded, although Kamiakin refused to accept a present for himself when the customary gifts were bestowed. "When the government sends the pay for these lands," he said, "I will take my share."

67

A reported incident, accepted by some writers as the turning point of the negotiations, is thus described by Hazard Stevens: "Late that evening (June 2, 1855), Lawyer came unattended to see Governor Stevens. He disclosed a conspiracy on the part of the Cayuses to suddenly rise upon and massacre all the whites on the council ground,—that this measure, deliberated in nightly conference for some time, had at length been determined upon in full council of the tribe the day before, which the Young Chief had requested for a holiday; they were now only awaiting the assent of the Yakimas and Walla Wallas to strike the blow; and these latter had actually joined, or were on the point of joining, the Cayuses in a war of extermination against the whites, for which the massacre of the governor and his party was to be the signal. They had conducted these plottings with the greatest secrecy, not trusting the Nez Perce's; and the Lawyer, suspecting that all was not right, had discovered the plot by means of a spy. ... The Lawyer concluded by saying: 'I will come with my family and pitch my lodge in the midst of your camp, that those Cayuses may see that you and your party are under the protection of the head chief of the Nez Perce's.' He did so immediately, although it was now after midnight."

That Lawyer did so act is unquestioned. Only the fact of the conspiracy itself is in dispute. A. G. Splawn says he talked with many old men who were present at the council, some of them prominent in their tribes. All claimed that there was no foundation of truth to Lawyer's story, and that the Yakimas and Walla Wallas heard of it only after Lawyer had moved his lodge to Governor Stevens' camp, whereupon Kamiakin, Peu-peu-mox-mox and Looking Glass went to the Nez Perce's chief and accused him of having a forked tongue.

68

That a conspiracy of some kind existed, is indicated by the war that followed, and something is needed to explain the acquiescence of Kamiakin in the treaty, after his persistent and consistent opposition to concessions of any nature. It is Hazard Stevens' view that except for Sticcas, the friendly Cayuse, all of the hostiles—Young Chief, Five Crows, Peu-peu-mox-mox, Kamiakin and their sub-Chiefs—signed the treaties as a deliberate act of treachery. Kamiakin's lifelong policy was consistent with this supposition. As to Peu-peu-mox-mox, he was long an enigma to the whites, and his alternative name, "Yellow Serpent," a mistranslation of the Indian name, which means "yellow bird," is an indication of the appraisal of his character made by some other Indians. "Pio-pio-mux-mux," wrote Dr. W. C. McKay, "was entirely a different person at the head of a war party than when he was before the U. S. commissioners in council, urging to be let alone." Dr. McKay was a son of Thomas McKay. He also wrote: "The Walla Walla chief was emphatically chief amongst all tribes. His word was law amongst his people. He was much respected by the traders, as he was powerful and a friend to them, and in case of trouble with other Indians he could be relied on."

Palmer, colleague of Stevens in the treaty council, discredited both the story of the widespread Indian plot and the report of the conspiracy as alleged by Lawyer. Palmer wrote to Maj. Gen. John E. Wool, November 21, 1855: "The reported combination of all these tribes with intent to wage a war of extermination of the whites, is, I apprehend, but a phantom conjured up in the brains of alarmists . . . and the plot said to have been nearly consummated of cutting off those engaged in the negotiations last June, I regard as of the same character."

69

The treaties concluded by Stevens and Palmer, at Walla Walla, were three in number, and ceded more than 60,000 square miles to the whites. The Nez Perce's obtained a reservation of about 5000 square miles and $200,000.00 to be expended for industrial improvements. The Yakimas received two reservations, a large one on the Simcoe and a smaller one on the Wenatchee, with payments similar to those made to the Nez Perce's. The Umatilla reservation of 800 square miles was set aside for the Walla

Wallas, Cayuses and Umatillas, with $100,000.00 in annuities, $50,000.00 in improvements and $10,000.00 for moving the immigrant road, which then passed through the reservation. In addition, the head chief of each tribe was granted a salary of $500.00 a year for 20 years, a comfortable house, well furnished, and 10 acres of land, plowed and fenced. Peu-peu-mox-mox also demanded and received especial consideration. "The first payment to the Walla-Walla chief, to commence upon the signing of the treaty. To give to the Walla-Walla chief three yokes of oxen, three yokes and four chains, one wagon, two ploughs, twelve hoes, twelve axes, two shovels, and one saddle and bridle, one set of wagon harness and one set of plough harness, within three months after the signing of this treaty. To build for the son of Pio-pio-mox-mox one dwelling house and plow and fence five acres of land, and to give him a salary for twenty years, one hundred dollars in cash per annum, commencing September first, 1856." The salaries of all the other chiefs were to begin on ratification of the treaties, which did not occur until March 8, 1859. The Walla Walla chief was also secured for five years in his right to build and occupy a trading post at the mouth of the Yakima river, for the sale of wild cattle ranging in that district. He proved to be the best negotiator in his own interest of all the chiefs present at the council.

70

On the theory that the treaties were signed with mental reservations on the part of certain of the chiefs, it would not be difficult to explain a series of acts which, only a few months afterward, precipitated a general Indian war. There was another contributing cause, however, which deserves mention here, as showing that the whites, as a race, were not wholly without blame. This was the premature, and apparently authoritative, announcement that the region ceded by the tribes was open to settlement; whereas, as a matter of fact, the treaties were not confirmed by the United States senate for some four years afterward. Advertisements in the Oregon Weekly Times, and other newspapers, stated that the country, not included in the reservations, was open to settlement. Nothing could be done by federal administrative officials in fulfillment of the treaties in advance of their ratification. Meanwhile, settlers, acting on what to them seemed good authority, began to occupy the Indian lands; and, gold having been discovered on the Pend d' Oreille river, in the summer of 1854, prospectors and miners flocked thither in 1855.

Whether or not these Indians, when they made the compact, intended to break it, they now believed they had confirmation of their suspicions that the treaty commissioners spoke with "forked tongues." Stevens made a trip, north, after the Walla Walla council and negotiated a treaty with the Kootenais, Flatheads and upper Pend d' Oreilles, but he failed to induce the tribes in the vicinity of the Spokane and Colville rivers to treat with him. The latter, including the Coeur d'Alenes and Spokanes, were determined that settlers should not occupy their lands on any terms, and they were among the last of the tribes to yield to the final argument of force.

CHAPTER XXIII

MORE INDIAN WARS AND TREATIES (1855-1858)

1

A PARTY of prospectors crossing the country of the Yakimas on the way to the mines, in August, 1855, was reported to have disappeared, and soon afterward another party was attacked, but not annihilated, two persons being killed and three escaping to carry the news of their misadventure to the settlement. A. J. Bolon, special agent to the Yakimas, went alone to hold a conference with Kamiakin. Bolon never returned, and a Des Chutes spy, sent by Indian Agent Nathan Olney from The Dalles, ascertained that he had been treacherously shot, September 23, 1855, in the Simcoe mountains, about fifteen miles from the present site of Goldendale, Washington, by a sub-chief named Qual-chan, son of Owhi, and his body and that of his horse had been burned to conceal the crime. Kamiakin, in a talk with the spy, was said to have expressed regret only that the killing of Bolon had anticipated his plans for a later well organized and widespread uprising. But, the Yakimas and Klickitats had been preparing for war, so that when Major Haller, of the regulars, who left The Dalles, October 3, with eighty-six regulars, under orders to arrest the murderers of Bolon, reached the Simcoe, October 6, he was surrounded by a body of several hundred well armed warriors and was compelled to retreat, suffering a loss of five men killed and seventeen wounded. Haller spiked and buried a howitzer and abandoned it on the way. A company of fifty regulars, commanded by Lieut. William A. Slaughter, meanwhile had been dispatched from Fort Steilacoom to the Yakima country, by way of the Naches pass, but withdrew on learning that Haller had been repulsed and that the Yakimas and Klickitats were on the warpath in overwhelming numbers.

News of Haller's retreat, which was exaggerated in the first reports, caused excitement throughout Oregon and Washington. Maj. Gabriel J. Rains, in command of the United States military district, ordered out all the available troops at Vancouver, The Dalles and Steilacoom, and called on the governor of Oregon for four companies, and the governor of Washington for two companies of volunteers, to be mustered into service of the United

States. Acting-Governor Mason, of Washington, responded with the desired quota and at the same time summoned other volunteers to protect the settlers around Puget sound. Governor Curry, of Oregon, issued a call, October 11, 1855, for eight companies instead of the four requested, the men to furnish their own arms and equipment where possible. There was a general shortage of arms in the territory, so that some difficulty was experienced in obtaining rifles, and this was intensified by the commencement of hostilities by the Indians in southern Oregon and northern California; so that, October 15, Governor Curry called for nine additional companies for service in the Rogue river valley. J. W. Nesmith was named colonel of the regiment first called for service against the Indians in the north.

2

The Oregon volunteers were never mustered into the federal service. "It is wholly impracticable," wrote Governor Curry to Major Rains, "to induce the citizens of Oregon to enroll for service in the suppression of any Indian hostilities under the organization prescribed by the rules and regulations of the United States army. I am, therefore, constrained, in order to secure the enrollment of a sufficient force for the present critical emergency, to preserve a distinct military organization." Nesmith and four companies reached The Dalles within a few days after issuance of the governor's proclamation, but here still another difficulty confronted them. Rains declared that he had no authority to furnish supplies unless the territorial troops were first mustered in as regulars. Curry and Nesmith persisted in their determination, however, and the volunteers continued to act as an independent unit, contriving as best they could, which was not very well, to obtain subsistence.

Rains then took up the march for the Yakima country, October 30, 1855, without waiting for the volunteers, and Nesmith with five companies followed, November 1. The forces cooperated in a spirit of individual loyalty, and Rains, finding himself in straits in a skirmish with a band of hostiles at a ford of the Yakima river, December 8, sent back to Nesmith for two companies, who, with Rains' dragoons, dashed into the rapid current of the river and put the enemy to flight. Two men of Rains' command were drowned while crossing the river and Nesmith's horse was struck by a bullet. The combined forces now swept the Indians from the plains, killing a few, but unable to overtake and punish the remainder. Nesmith, at Rains' request, undertook an expedition toward Naches pass, in the course of which he destroyed several caches of provisions, but found no other trace of the enemy. The troops burned the mission on the Yakima, and a house owned by Kamiakin. It was then decided to return to The Dalles for recruits and reinforcements.

3

Two companies of volunteers commanded by Maj. Mark A. Chinn meanwhile made a foray into the Deschutes region, where they were told that Peu-peu-mox-mox had gone on the warpath, robbed Fort Walla Walla of its store of ammunition, and destroyed the buildings there. Chinn then threw up a fortification near Wells Springs, which he named Fort Henrietta, in compliment to General Haller's wife, and awaited reinforcements. These, amounting to 170 men, in three companies, were sent by Nesmith, accompanied by Lieut.-Col. James K. Kelly, who now took command. It was the fortune of this detachment to conduct the only subsequent military operations in this part of the territory during the winter. Rains, after his march into the Yakima country, retired to winter quarters at The Dalles, and Nesmith, late in November, 1855, discharged 125 men, whom he was unable to mount on horses suitable for a hard campaign, "deeming it worse than useless to retain a large unmounted force at this place to consume our scanty supplies." The volunteers were now suffering from intense cold, and from scarcity of tents and other ordinary requisites. The commissary, Nesmith informed the governor by letter, November 25, was almost destitute of every indispensable article and particularly flour and beef. The winter of 1855-6 set in early in eastern Oregon.

4

Lieutenant-Colonel Kelly's command at Fort Henrietta now numbered about 350 men; and Kelly formed a plan to march on the Indians, at Walla Walla, and take them by surprise. Failing to find the enemy there, however, Kelly proceeded without baggage or rations to a point on the Touchet, about twelve miles above its mouth, with 200 men, ordering Chinn to march to the mouth of the Touchet with the baggage train.

Peu-peu-mox-mox and six warriors rode out to meet Kelly's troop, as the latter approached an Indian encampment on the Touchet, and sought an interview. The Walla Walla chieftain began by asking why the soldiers were in his country. Kelly replied that they had come to chastise the Indians for wrongs they had committed. Peu-peu-mox-mox asked for an armistice until the next day, when he promised that he would sign a treaty of peace. Kelly feared a ruse and refused to delay attacking the village unless the chief and five others would surrender themselves as hostages until all difficulties were settled. Peu-peu-mox-mox chose to remain, promising, according to Kelly's official report, to assemble his people on the following day, to require them to surrender all property stolen from the whites, and to furnish fresh horses to remount the entire command.

Kelly now refrained from pushing the attack, thinking he had Peu-peu-mox-mox in his power, but he permitted the chief to send a messenger to his people to apprise them of the terms of the expected treaty. But Kelly was informed, on the next day, that the messenger of Peu-peu-mox-mox had in reality carried a command to the warriors to remove their women and children and to prepare for battle. In any event, the village was immediately abandoned and no more Indians appeared to treat for peace; so Kelly, holding fast to his hostages, retired to the mouth of the Touchet with the intention of establishing camp for the winter.

5

Shots were exchanged between the troops on the march, and Indians who were harrying their flanks, and a running engagement developed on the morning of December 7, 1855, the forces of the Indians increasing with every mile. At a farm, twelve miles from the mouth of the Touchet, the Walla Wallas made a stand. The position chosen by them was a rolling plain covered by clumps of sage brush and small sand knolls. Their left rested on the river bank, covered with trees and underbrush; their right was protected by a high range of hills. About fifty volunteers who were mounted on the fleetest horses, arriving first, charged the Indian front, losing a lieutenant killed and a captain and three enlisted men wounded. The attackers were now reinforced and drove the Indians back two miles. In an attempt to force them from their position, a captain and one private were killed. A howitzer was now brought to bear on the Indians, who gave way. The volunteers removed the bodies of their dead and retired in good order to camp.

While the advance troops engaged the hostiles, those in the rear halted at a small cabin, where the surgeons attended the wounded, and some of the dead were brought in. An effort was made here to bind the Indian hostages, as a precaution against treachery, which the proud chiefs resented as an indignity on no account to be suffered. There was a struggle, one of the hostages drew a knife, and in the ensuing melee Peu-peu-mox-mox and his companions were killed. In the bitterness following receipt of news of the killing of others of the volunteers on the front line, the bodies of the hostages were subjected to indignities. This involved the volunteer organization in a controversy with officers of the regular army, and hampered cooperation between federal and local authorities in the subsequent conduct of the Indian war.

The chief and four of his men were put to death, all scalped, and the head of the chief was entirely peeled, wrote Palmer to Commissioner Manypenny, enclosing a copy of the Portland Oregonian for January 5, 1856, in which the following appeared: "Dr. Shaw, assistant surgeon O. M. V., and Mr. Story, of Company A, arrived here on Tuesday evening last direct from the Walla Walla country. . . . Dr. Shaw had in his possession the ears of the celebrated Indian chief, Pee-pee-mox-mox, who was killed at the battle on the 9th Dec. Mr. Story also brought down the scalp of the noted chief." Sober minded citizens of the territory did not condone this gross barbarity, but it was strongly maintained that the proud and haughty chieftain was not slain in violation of an armistice. "Peu-peu-mox-mox," wrote Governor Stevens, on March 20, 1856, "was slain fairly. I have investigated the matter on the ground and found—having not only the witnesses of his death, but the testimony of the friendly Indians, both Cayuses and Nez Perce's, he was not entrapped by a flag of truce. I, of course, reprobate the indignities subsequently committed upon his person."

The Indians were reinforced on the night of December 7, 1855, but on the following day the volunteers took the initiative, charging bands of the enemy wherever sighted, though the latter fought with skill and bravery. The battle continued four days, the Indians withdrawing each night and the troops being too exhausted to pursue them farther. Two fresh companies arrived from Fort Henrietta, December 10, when Colonel Kelly charged with his entire command and forced an engagement which terminated the campaign. The Indians fled across the Snake river and were seen no more. Losses of the volunteers in the four days of fighting were a captain, a lieutenant and a private soldier killed, four private soldiers mortally wounded, and three captains and ten men less seriously wounded. Colonel Kelly reported having found the bodies of thirty-nine Indians on the field, and he estimated the Indians' loss at seventy-five.

6

The volunteers now built another camp, two miles above Waiilatpu, which they named Fort Bennett in memory of Capt. Charles Bennett, who had been killed, December 7. They devoted most of the winter to scouring the country in search of provision caches made by the Indians. Colonel Nesmith resigned in December, to take a seat in the territorial legislature, and Col. Thomas R. Cornelius was elected in his place. Governor Stevens returned about this time, from an expedition to treat with the Blackfeet Indians. His march was through the hostile country, on which he was escorted part of the way by a guard of sixty-nine friendly Nez Perce's. The region in which the Oregon troops were now encamped was in Washington territory, but Stevens agreed with the Oregon officers that they should hold their ground until the regulars were ready to take the field for a systematic campaign. An additional company was recruited in the vicinity of Walla Walla, with Indian Agent B. F. Shaw as captain. The members of the Nez Perce's escort were formally incorporated with the Washington volunteers, as a stroke of policy, and then formally mustered out of service. They reciprocated by furnishing the volunteers with remounts from their own bands.

7

The winter of 1855-6, passed by the volunteers in the Walla Walla valley, was memorable in the history of Indian warfare by reason of its deprivations rather than because of any fighting that occurred. There was heavy snow and the temperature frequently fell to ten or twenty degrees below zero. The men were poorly clad, the commissary and transport service from the Willamette valley having been interrupted by ice in the Columbia river, and they subsisted on a few cattle that had been spared by the Indians, on potatoes grown in the Walla Walla valley, and on meager rations of flour and sugar, and sometimes were reduced to eating young ponies, as the volunteers in the Cayuse campaign eight years previously had done. They were relieved, March, 1856, by five companies recruited in western Oregon, who opened the campaign, in April, by scouring the plains between the Walla Walla and the Columbia, in which they were resisted by Kamiakin and some 300 Yakimas and Klickitats. The Indians were repulsed, but not pursued. The volunteers by this time were reduced to the last extremity for want of equipment and forage, the territory having been stripped of its resources, and the ice in the Columbia precluding transportation of such supplies as were available, so that the regiment was mustered out and returned home. Two companies, recruited chiefly from among the veterans, were raised, however, for the defense of the Walla Walla and Tygh valleys.

8

The campaign in the Walla Walla valley added fuel to the flame of controversy between the territorial and the federal military authorities. Maj.-Gen. John E. Wool, commanding the department of the Pacific, who arrived at Fort Vancouver, November 17, 1855, and was there when tidings of the battle of Walla Walla were received, persisted in his determination not to enter on a winter campaign, and made no effort to go to the support of the territorials. He severely criticised Major Rains for having called on Governor Curry for four companies of volunteers, which he declared unnecessary, and questioned the wisdom of the volunteer expedition, the only result of which, he said, "will be to unite all the friendly tribes in that region against us, except the Nez Perce's, who still remain friendly and will continue to do so." He also impugned the motives of the officials of the territory, and intimated that the volunteer service was grossly wasteful and absurdly expensive, that it was undertaking an unnecessary campaign in the east, when the deep snows of the mountains would have afforded sufficient protection to the settlements against invasion, and that more harm than good would result from the volunteer policy. In the course of a long correspondence which ensued, Stevens retorted that but for the operations of the Oregon volunteers he and his followers would have been cut off on their return from the expedition to treat with the northeastern tribes, and that their massacre would have been followed by a "hurricane of war between the Cascades and the Bitterroot." Wool nevertheless declined to equip volunteers or receive them into the service of the United States.

The controversy between Wool on the one hand and Stevens and the local authorities on the other hand sometimes threatened to rival in bitterness the feeling engendered by the Indian wars themselves. Volumes of official reports and correspondence relate to this incidental aspect of the wars. Wool consistently championed the cause of the Indians and maintained that their hostility was largely due to excesses by the whites, and accused the settlers of advocating extermination of the natives.

9

It will have been noted that the operations of the Oregon volunteers were conducted largely within the boundaries of the neighboring territory of Washington, that had recently been created by act of congress, a circumstance inseparable from the extensive character of the Indian uprising, which now had spread to the Puget sound region and to southern Oregon and northern California, and which made the interest of each locality the concern of all. The campaigns of Nesmith and Kelly with their volunteers, and of Rains' regulars east of the Cascades, possessed a certain strategic significance, since the larger and more warlike tribes dwelt in this region. Two more destructive wars, in point of lives and property sacrificed, were being waged by the Indians of other localities.

10

Near Puget sound, for example, there was an unheralded and unprovoked massacre of settlers in the White river valley, October 28, 1855. The Indians waited until most of the regulars stationed at Fort Steilacoom had started to join Rains and Nesmith in the Yakima country, when they raided the settlers' farms, being prevented from killing the entire population by a warning sent by a friendly chieftain, Kitsap, the elder. Lieutenant Slaughter and a small detachment immediately took the field and engaged the hostiles, and Slaughter was killed, December 4, 1855,

by a lurking savage while the former was standing before an open
fire in a cabin, in conference with his brother officers. The incident illustrated the unfamiliarity of many of the regular officers,
notwithstanding their unquestioned gallantry, with the methods
of their crafty antagonists.

Eight settlers were killed in the White river valley raid, and
an infant child was either kidnapped or killed by the attackers.
Slaughter's command lost one man in the engagement with hostiles of the Klickitat, Nisqually and Green river tribes. Presence
of the Klickitats here was significant of the part played by their
tribe in the general conspiracy.

The Nisquallies had become restless by reason of discontent
with the area of the reservation allotted to them, and also as the
result of fantastic rumors to which currency had been given by
leaders of the conspiracy. One of these stories was that the government proposed to transport all the Indians to an island far
out in the Pacific ocean, where the sun never shone, a region of
perpetual night.

11

Causes similar to those which generally prevailed elsewhere
contributed to the unrest of the Indians in the south, which culminated in the most sanguinary war in all the history of the
Oregon Country. After having made a treaty with the Rogue
river Indians, the representatives of the government had virtually left them to their own resources. Those on the reservation
were not controlled. To remove friction between the races, Indian
Superintendent Palmer undertook to remove them to another
reservation, as technically the treaty permitted him to do, but
they demurred. Already there had been numerous acts of hostility, both by Indians and white men. The trail from Oregon to
the newly opened mines of California lay through this region,
and there were hopeful mining prospects in southern Oregon.
The mines attracted a class of men more venturesome and less
restrained by ties of kindred than were the present settlers.
Miners habitually travelled in small parties, or alone, and left
property for long periods unguarded. Every misdemeanor committed by an irresponsible Indian, and not punished, brought
contempt for the authority of the whites, and every reprisal made
without due examination into individual guilt became at once a

reflection on white men's justice, and a provocation for retaliation in kind.

Raiding renegades killed three miners, stole a band of horses and committed other depredations, early in June, 1855. A posse of citizens pursued them and killed three. Chief Sam, one of the signers of Lane's Table Rock treaty of 1853, repudiated the guilty men. A few weeks later, July, 1855, a series of difficulties, subsequently designated as the "Humbug war," occurred. The trouble originated in a dispute between a white man and three Indians, all of whom had been drinking, and it resulted in the death of the white man. A civilian posse in quest of the slayer met a band of Indians, who refused to answer questions, and several were arrested. Two escaped, returned to their camp and spread an alarming story that started a massacre of white miners along the Klamath river, between Humbug and Horse creeks. Eleven were thus slain. The whites, many of whom were newcomers to the district, and unacquainted with the Indians, included all natives in the reprisals that followed. Most of the twenty-five Indians, now indiscriminately shot, hanged or thrown into abandoned prospect holes, had been friendly to the whites; on the other hand, the outlaws had promptly put a long distance between themselves and their pursuers.

Other incidents at about this time further tended to destroy the possibility of effective cooperation between the white inhabitants and the few regular troops stationed in the district. For example, some of the Indians concerned in the Humbug affair surrendered to the military commander at Fort Lane, who refused to turn them over to a company of civilians, on the ground that the latter were not authorized officers of the law. The angry citizens laid siege to the fort, but after a few days' consideration thought better of the plan. In August, 1855, an Indian in the Port Orford district shot and wounded a white man, and was arrested by Indian Agent Ben Wright, who put him into the custody of the sheriff. The officer, having no place to keep him, turned him over to the military to be taken to Port Orford. On the way to the latter place, the soldiers and their prisoner were fired on by the man who had been wounded and by two companions, who had decided to take the law into their own hands. The accused Indian, and another, were killed by the first volley, whereupon the soldiers

returned the fire, killing two of the attackers and mortally wounding the third.

12

In the belief that a band of reservation Indians, encamped in a
grove near the mouth of Butte creek, were bent on mischief, a
volunteer company commanded by Maj. J. A. Lupton, a member-
elect of the territorial legislature from Jackson county, surrounded the Indian camp before daybreak, October 8, 1855, and in-
flicted summary chastisement, killing twenty-three, or more, and
wounding nearly all the others. Most of the dead proved to be old
men, squaws and children, but they made a spirited resistance,
resulting in the death of Major Lupton from a poisoned arrow
wound. The war was now under way in earnest. When the hostiles
sprang to arms, as they did on the day of the Lupton affair, they
were already well provided with rifles and ammunition, as if in
anticipation of the event. By the morning of October 9, 1855,
roving bands were attacking and murdering miners and settlers
wherever found, sparing neither men, women nor children, and
desisting only after all the survivors in the outlying sections of
the Rogue river valley had found safety in the forts and settlements. Sixteen persons of all ages and both sexes were murdered.
A deed of heroism conspicuous in the annals of the war was that
of Mrs. George W. Harris, wife of a settler, who with her young
daughter, held the Indians at bay after her husband had been
killed, firing her rifle at them through the chinks of the rude
cabin in which she hastily fortified herself. Mrs. Harris was rescued on the following day by regulars from Fort Lane, although
it has been stated that the rescue was effected by miners from
Jacksonville.

Governor Curry's call for two southern battalions of volunteers
was followed promptly, October 15, 1855, by issuance of a general
order by Adj.-Gen. E. M. Barnum, which recognized the general
belief that Indians throughout the northwest were acting in concert. "In view of the probable concert of action among the tribes
upon both our northern and southern borders," the order read,
"it is indispensably necessary that a free communication should
be kept open between the Rogue river and Willamette valleys. . . .
For the purpose of effectually chastising these savages who have
perpetrated the merciless outrages in their midst, they will treat

all Indians as enemies who do not show unmistakable signs of friendship, and they will also bear in mind, that so far as practicable, a concert of action will be maintained with the United States forces."

13

The alarm felt in the Rogue and Umpqua valleys was communicated to the Willamette valley, and spread throughout Oregon, transcending in immediate importance the campaigns of Nesmith and Kelly in the east. Southern Oregon was prepared with men anxious to volunteer for the emergency, but arms were lacking. Notwithstanding this handicap, some fifteen companies were recruited by October 20, 1855, and were detailed by Col. John E. Ross, to guard the settlements, as fast as they could be armed with such weapons as were then procurable.

The rapidity with which events now moved is shown by the circumstance that on October 17, only nine days after the date of the Rogue river massacre, volunteers met and engaged a greatly superior force of Indians, who surrounded and besieged them at Gallice creek, a camp occupied by miners, including some Chinese. Here the Indians varied their usual mode of attack by shooting lighted arrows into the cabins, to which the soldiers had retired, and the entire camp, except the buildings held by the troops, was burned. Three of the defenders were killed and another received a wound from which he died a few weeks later. The volunteers succeeded in strengthening their defenses in the night, so that the enemy retired on the following day, concealing their losses by carrying their dead with them. The battle was stubbornly contested and the soldiers were confronted by great odds. The Indians possessed superior long range rifles, making it possible for them to inflict damage from a distance, so that the fire of the troops was ineffective.

14

Regular military forces in this district now consisted of ninety dragoons from Fort Lane, and these were reinforced, late in October, by about 300 volunteers, who had answered the first call in the Rogue river valley. These combined forces were augmented, on the night of October 30, 1855, by two companies recruited under the call issued by Governor Curry. Marauding Indians having retired to the vicinity of Grave creek, the soldiers pursued and divided with a view to catching the enemy on front and rear simultaneously; but here the officers of the regulars showed a lack of caution, similar to the carelessness that cost Lieutenant Slaughter his life in the Puget sound country at nearly the same time. Captain Smith gained a position in the rear of the Indian stronghold, at which he arrived at daylight on October 31, before the division sent to occupy the front had reached its station, and, it being the dawn of an exceedingly inclement morning, he built fires to warm and refresh his men. The camp fires gave a warning to the Indians and destroyed every prospect of surprise. In the engagement that followed, known variously as the battle of Hungry Hill, of Bloody Spring and of Grave Creek Hills, the volunteers lost six men killed, and the regulars three; the volunteers fifteen wounded, and the regulars seven. Another volunteer perished from exposure.

15

This was the last battle of the winter. Both regulars and volunteers retired after the affair, which was a victory for the Indians. The volunteers proceeded to reorganize by superseding the local regiment, which had been hastily recruited in the first emergency, with battalions called for under Governor Curry's formal proclamation, and by obtaining new supplies. There were a few skirmishes between patrols and detached bands of Indians, in December. The regulars went into winter quarters, and the volunteers who remained in the service passed the season in arduous and uninspiring guard duty, in the vicinity of settlements, varied by occasional and usually futile pursuit of hostiles who had now dispersed in small parties, intent on employing their superior arms and better knowledge of the country by inflicting damage over a wide area.

Indians of the whole country, from British Columbia to the Shasta mountains, and from the Rocky mountains to the Pacific ocean, were now organized and armed. The settlers were thoroughly aroused, but not well armed. While the region east of the Cascades was practically abandoned to the natives, whites in the Puget sound country, and in the Rogue river valley, built rude forts and strengthened their blockhouses. Notwithstanding these precautions settlers lived in a state of constant apprehension. The Willamette valley shared the general feeling of insecurity. Palmer, absent from the Indian superintendency at Dayton, on another of his journeys of conciliation, was informed by his secretary that "there is much fear and quaking among our citizens . . . in consequence of the signal fires seen looming up on the heights of the Coast range, and which appear to be answered by similar lights upon the Cascade summits." Business was everywhere interrupted. A lurking savage seemed to be concealed in every roadside bush.

16

Palmer now sought to persuade his superiors in the Indian bureau of the expediency of assembling the discontented natives of western and southern Oregon on a few reservations, where their material wants could be supplied at government expense, and their hostility could be curbed by satisfaction of their physical appetites. He wrote to Commissioner Manypenny, October 9, 1855, notwithstanding only a few months previously his name had been subscribed to an advertisement proclaiming these lands open to immigrants, that much of the present difficulty "is traceable to the mistaken policy of permitting the settlement of the Indian lands prior to the extinguishment of the Indian title and the designation of proper reservations. This mistake might now be partially remedied by the immediate gathering of the Indian population on their several reservations, to do which, and make proper provision for their comfort, would involve an expense less than that of a six months' or two years' war, which must inevitably follow, as I believe, their present situation and a failure to provide for their wants."

Palmer estimated that an expenditure of $35,000 for buildings and roads, and for clothing the tribes south of Umpqua and for providing them with food during the winter, would secure peace in that quarter; $25,000 for the Table Rock reserve, $25,000 at Umatilla, and $20,000 on the Wasco reservation, he believed, would insure tranquility in the Rogue river region and in middle Oregon. "The crisis of the destiny of the Indian race in the Oregon and Washington territories," wrote Palmer also, "is now upon us; and the result of the causes now operating, unless speedily arrested, will be disastrous to the whites, destructive to the Indians, and a heavy reproach upon our national character."

17

The Indian bureau was not, however, prepared to act in accordance with Palmer's advice. Nor was it needful to go as far as the national capital for an example of the policy of delay that was now defeating all attempts to prevent war. Voluminous official correspondence of the period contains much to illuminate this topic. For illustration, Capt. H. M. Judah, Fourth infantry, acting in the capacity of Indian agent at Fort Jones, wrote to Thomas J. Henley, superintendent of Indian affairs at San Francisco, November 2, 1855, urging that provisions be made for the subsistence of those peaceful Indians who had had no opportunity to lay in food for the winter, but he received a reply in which Henley stated that he conceived it to be his duty "to provide for the reception of suffering Indians on the reservations," but expressed doubt that Indians who declined to proceed at once to the reservations designated for them were entitled to relief in any measure. Captain Judah, January 21, 1856, retorted that he "had supposed that the necessary preliminaries to removal of the Indians upon a reserve, including their preparation for the so serious a change to them, was one of the more delicate if not difficult portions of the duties appertaining to the Indian department. How the Indians are to be reconciled to the relinquishment of their homes, what inducements are to be legally offered them, how the expenses of their removal are to be provided for, Colonel Henley does not pretend to say, or advise upon."

Palmer, nevertheless, proceeded to obtain by purchase a reservation of about 6000 acres at the headwaters of the Yamhill river, to which, as expeditiously as possible, he removed certain bands of Calapooyas, Umpquas and Molallas, most of whom had been deprived of their customary supplies of roots, berries and fish, and were nearly destitute of clothing and moccasins. This was not accomplished without some opposition among the Indians themselves. The young men desired to go, but the old men were reluctant, saying that they had but a few years to live and wished to pass them in their familiar hunting grounds. These objections, at length, were overcome, so that by February, 1856, some 300 Indians were domiciled at Grand Ronde, including a small band of the Rogue river tribe, under Chief Sam, who had held to the terms of the Table Rock treaty, and had taken no part in the hostilities.

18

Now, however, still other obstacles were interposed. Political partisanship was intense, and Palmer's foes in the territorial legislature seized the occasion for their advantage. The democrat members of the legislature, thirty-five in number, January 8, 1856, addressed a protesting memorial to President Pierce, asking Palmer's removal on various grounds, among them that he was "at this moment engaged in efforts to purchase the land claims of citizens residing on the west side of the Willamette valley, with the avowed intention of bringing thousands of Indians from remote parts of the country and colonizing them in the heart of this, the Willamette valley; and this despite the remonstrances of the legislative assembly, and of our constituents, the men, women and children of the territory."

In consequence of failure to coordinate the labors of those who strove for constructive peace, the causes of irritation were not removed, nor were they much abated. In the Puget sound district the natives were still dissatisfied with their reservations, and of all their treaties, but one still remained unconfirmed. In the country of the Yakimas and the Klickitats there was increasing evidence that Kamiakin, Owhi and Skloom had discovered that the treaty signed at Walla Walla was unpopular with their people. As to the Klickitats, who had declined to attend the Walla Walla council, they were enraged when they learned that their country had been sold without their consent, and openly declared that they would not abide by an agreement in which they had had no voice. Palmer now ordered all the Klickitats resident in the Willamette and Umpqua valleys to return to their former homes. "Some left the country quietly," wrote Palmer, "and appeared satisfied; while others evinced a bad feeling, and, I am told, sought to produce a similar spirit among the Indians throughout the country."

19

Warlike factions in the Rogue river and Umpqua valleys seemed to have reached an understanding, though not a perfect coalition. Governor Curry's two southern regiments had been organized as independent commands, neither recognizing the authority of the officers of the other. These units were now consolidated, the Second regiment of Oregon mounted volunteers being created, with Robert L. Williams, colonel; W. J. Martin, lieutenant-colonel, and

James Bruce, major. Charges of intentional inactivity, preferred against Colonel Williams by a number of his subordinates, in February, 1856, resulted in the election by the legislature of John K. Lamerick, as brigadier-general in supreme command. About two-thirds of the volunteers received their discharges, some of them reenlisting in two new companies that were then recruited, and the regiment was further reorganized, in March, by election of John Kelsay, colonel, W. W. Chapman, lieutenant-colonel, and W. L. Latshaw and James Bruce, majors. Even before regimental politics had been thus adjusted, the Indians had taken the war-path again.

20

The last vestige of local sympathy for the Indians was alienated by the murder, February 22, 1856, of Ben Wright, Indian agent at Gold Beach, at the mouth of the Rogue river. Wright had been a persistent champion of the Indians and was recognized as a prudent and a just administrator, and an advocate of Palmer's plan of ending the war by conciliation. His slayer was a renegade named Enos, of an eastern tribe, who had been with Fremont as a guide, and had so far won the confidence of Wright that he had unquestioned access to the agent's office. Enos, himself, killed Wright with an ax; following which he and his followers mas-sacred twenty-five other settlers at Gold Beach. The survivors fled to a fort, where they were besieged for thirty-five days, until relieved by a detachment of regulars from Fort Humboldt, California. The military forces in the upper Rogue river valley were informed of the plight of the beleaguered people, but feared to go to their rescue lest they should expose the settlements to great-er danger. The entire coast region was over-run by Enos' Indians. Several other residents were killed. Enos then joined the up-river hostiles, and the coast Indians were pursued and subdued by reg-ulars and volunteers, in a campaign that continued into April, 1856, at the conclusion of which they begged to be taken under the protection of the government.

21

The volunteers of the Second regiment engaged in several minor skirmishes, and fought two battles, in March and April, 1856, operating throughout these months with the formal assist-ance of the regulars. Brigadier-General Lamerick wrote to the

governor, April 15, 1856: "I have reason to believe that General
Wool [of the regular army] has issued orders to the United
States troops not to cooperate with the volunteers. But the officers of Fort Lane told me they would, whenever they met me,
most cordially cooperate with any volunteers under my command." The regulars, however, in the beginning confined their
activities chiefly to the coast, while the volunteers sent scouting
parties through the mountains, with the design of driving the
Indians down the rivers toward the regulars. In the execution of
the plan the volunteers gave the hostiles no rest. They engaged a
superior force of mixed Rogue rivers, Shastas and Umpquas, late
in March, at the base of Eight Dollar mountain, where there was
sharp fighting, terminating in the escape of the Indians in the
heavy timber that covered the hills.

Again, pursuant to the plan of campaign developed by Lamerick, the northern and southern battalions, about the middle of
April, marched by two routes along the north and south sides of
the valley, scouring the foothills until they discovered the hostiles
concentrated in camp on a bar below the Little Meadows of the
Rogue river; but difficulty in crossing the river in the two canvas
boats which constituted the soldiers' only means of water transport, almost frustrated their victory. The Indians were driven
from the bar with loss, and again evaded capture by taking to the
woods. They abandoned the locality, and the volunteers established a permanent camp, named Fort Lamerick, at Big Meadows,
near the scene of their late fighting. The result of the campaign
was to clear the upper valley of Indians, and to incline many of
them to accept the protection of the regulars, whose vengeance
they feared less than they did that of the settlers and volunteers.
Citizen companies from Coos bay, Port Orford and Gold Beach,
during this period, kept up an incessant campaign of scouting in
the mountains, descending on the Indians wherever they found an
encampment, and usually giving no quarter.

22

The strategy of the regulars was similar to that of the volunteers. The dragoons from Fort Lane made a difficult march, in
rain, snow and fog, across the Coast range, in May, 1856, clearing
the country of the enemy as they proceeded, and at the mouth of
the Illinois river joined with the command of Lieutenant-Colonel

Buchanan. The base of supplies of the regulars was Crescent City, and the task of escorting the commissary trains was attended by incessant guerilla fighting. The Coquilles were particularly treacherous, repeatedly breaking promises to return to the reservation and remain there, so that if report can be credited, it came to be the practice to shoot a Coquille Indian on sight.

Palmer now redoubled his efforts to obtain peace by treaty. He sent messengers, chosen from among prisoners, to the chiefs, to tell them that unless they surrendered it would be impossible to prevent a war of extermination, and also to warn them that the conflict could terminate only to their disadvantage; and thus he gained consent to a council, but only on condition that they should be free to accept or reject the terms offered them, and that they should not be molested if the conference came to naught. Several of the chieftains of the warring tribes assembled with this understanding, May 21, 1856, at Colonel Buchanan's camp on Oak Flat, on the right bank of Illinois river, a short distance above its mouth.

The council was effective only in extracting from some of the Indians a promise to lay down their arms and permit themselves to be escorted to a new reservation, a promise subsequently broken. But Chief John refused even to give this pledge. He defied the councillors. "You are a great chief," he said, addressing Colonel Buchanan. "So am I. This is my country. I was in it when those large trees were very small, not higher than my head. My heart is sick with fighting, but I want to live in my own country. If the white people are willing, I will go back to Deer Creek and live among them as I used to do. They can visit my camp, and I will visit theirs; but I will not lay down my arms and go with you on the reserve. I will fight. Goodby." The other chiefs, less candid, agreed to assemble with their bands, May 26, to be conveyed under military guard to the reservations set apart for them, but the promise was made without intention of keeping the agreement, as subsequent events were to prove.

23

The day came, but not the Indians. Indeed, Captain Smith, who was waiting to receive them with infantry and dragoons, got word that Chief John was plotting an attack. Smith hastily moved camp and built rifle pits and breastworks, which were completed

none too soon, for on the morning of May 27, 1856, the warriors
surrounded him. Failing to gain admission by representing them
selves as having come to surrender, they assaulted from all sides,
charging on front and rear in force, under the cover of the fire
of their sharpshooters, while smaller bodies clambered up the
steep declivities that flanked the camp. The soldiers had one howitzer, but their small arms were inferior to those of the natives
and the garrison suffered heavily from long range fire which they
were unable to return effectively, so that by the afternoon of the
second day they had lost nine killed and twelve wounded, or almost one-third of their number, while the Indians had received
fresh accessions. To the sufferings of the wounded were added
the pangs of intense thirst. There was much fighting at close
range, so close that the Indians shouted epithets at their antagonists. During the previous negotiations Captain Smith had threatened them with hanging, if they were caught committing depredations after having refused peace. Chief John now threw Smith's
own words back at him. The savages derisively dangled ropes
before the troopers, accompanying the action with appropriate
taunts.

The battle, which had begun at eleven o'clock on the morning
of May 27, continued without interruption until four o'clock on
the afternoon of May 28, when a company of the Fourth infantry
sent by Buchanan arrived just as the Indians were preparing a
final assault en masse. The Indians fled, though they still largely
outnumbered the combined forces of the whites; and thereafter
they surrendered in small bands, receiving the immunities of civilized warfare and the protection of the regulars on their journey
to the reservations. Chief John persisted in his determination to
return to Table Rock. A few roving Indians remained in the
Coast range for a time, to be treated as outlaws, hunted down a
few at a time, and shot; but the war in southern Oregon was
finished.

24

The later history of these Indians was written on the reservations, to which the tribes were removed. Chief John and his Rogue
river band, with Chiefs George and Sam, were first taken to Palmer's Grand Ronde reservation, where in November, 1856, a
census showed the total number congregated there to be 1925, of

whom 909 were members of the Rogue river and Shasta tribes. In May, 1857, however, almost all of the latter were removed to the Siletz reservation of about 1000 square miles, lying along the Pacific coast between the Siletz and the Alsea rivers. Of the Rogue rivers, only Chief Sam, who had remained neutral throughout the wars, with fifty-eight men and their families, stayed on the Grand Ronde. The confederated bands of Umpquas and Calapooyas on this reservation now numbered 262, and the Willamette valley Indians, including a few scattered bands of Calapooyas, 660, constituting the pathetic remnant of the numerous people among whom Jason Lee and his missionary associates had labored some twenty years before.

25

Something more may be said of the independent and defiant Chief John. He continued his obstinate resistance to authority on the reservation. He and his son, Adam, refused to become recociled to the restrictions imposed, and were constantly making trouble, until the Indian agent, Metcalf, believed them to be planning an outbreak. At Metcalf's request, they were put under arrest in May, 1858, by the military officers of the Fourth infantry, and were first removed to headquarters at Fort Vancouver, where they were kept in close confinement. This seemed to have a salutary effect upon the others upon the reservation. It was then decided to send them to California, by steamship, for detention at Alcatraz, but while being so transported they broke out into a mutiny, in which the son was wounded, resulting in the amputation of one of his legs. They were detained in California for some time, but were ultimately returned to the Siletz reservation in Oregon.

The Indian population of the Siletz reservation, 1857, comprised 554 Rogue rivers and Shastas, with whom treaties had been made and ratified, and other coast Indians to the number of 1495. The latter included the Ioshutz, Chec-coos, Too-too-ta-ays, Mac-ca-noo-tangs, Coquille, Port Orford, Sixes, Flores Creek, Shasta-Costas and Yukers, with whom treaties had been made, though not yet ratified. A total of not many more than 3000 remained, as compared with the numerous inhabitants of western Oregon at the beginning of the nineteenth century. It cannot be said truthfully that the lot of the Indians on the reservations was happy.

Administrative difficulties disturbed their contentment, and there were inequalities of treatment. For example, the Rogue rivers and Shastas, whose treaties had been ratified, were entitled to receive certain benefits not bestowed upon other Indians, who had been driven from their homes under similar circumstances. The latter were not provided with annuities, or other advantages. Delivery of treaty goods to one tribe, and non-delivery to another, would have occasioned an outbreak. "The whites," wrote J. Ross Browne, in a report on the condition of the reservations, 1857, "are unable to justify any favoritism, and the Indians are fully aware of the fact, for they are sufficiently sagacious to understand the general principles of justice." Consequently, the agent found it necessary to resort to the unsatisfactory expedient of making presents to all the Indians at the same time, in an effort to mollify them, a subterfuge which did not increase the reverence of the Indians for the institutions of the whites. Almost innumerable other instances of inefficient administration arose, among which was delay in receipt of annuity funds. "The present year's annuities have not yet been received," wrote the special agent of the department, although it was then November. "Winter is approaching, and it is necessary the Indians should be provided with blankets and clothing. The money that should have been paid last year for goods has to be paid this year; from which it will be seen that the ruinous system of credit is kept up, even under the treaties, and that the Indians receive but a fraction of what congress provides for them."

Browne recounts several instances in which contractors extracted high prices for inferior food. A contract was made for flour at ten cents a pound, when flour was selling in Portland at $8 a barrel. Mill sweepings were delivered, the quality of which was so low that it made many of the Indians sick. "They got the idea that the whites had poisoned it, and it was only with the utmost difficulty that the agent pacified them." He did this by eating a large quantity in their presence and by telling them that the white employees used the same article. Flour costing $5 a barrel at the mills was delivered at the reservations at a contract price of $17 a barrel. Yet one of the contractors told Browne that with the apparently enormous profit "he made nothing, as he had not yet received his pay and had to borrow money at three per

cent per month to meet his liabilities for the original purchase."
The result, from the point of view of the Indians, who had no
voice in the adjustment of their accounts, was "tantamount to a
breach of faith."

26

The southern Indians were averse to labor and made no progress in civilization. An exception was Chief Sam, who built himself a house, cultivated a patch of ground and sold apples and
onions to his subjects, at twenty-five cents for an apple and twelve
and a half cents for an onion. It was the especial grievance of the
Rogue rivers that they had been removed from a congenial reservation in their own country, against their will, and only as a
temporary expedient to preserve the general peace. Believing
themselves unjustly treated, they made no effort to abandon their
old ways. When the main body of the Rogue rivers left the Grand
Ronde, they burned all the houses in which they had lived, as had
always been their custom when leaving a place. The government,
they said, which forced them to live in an unhealthful country,
must be content to abide by their customs.

Grievances to which allusion has been made were communicated
to the special agent of the government at a "wa-wa," or talk,
with the head chiefs at the Grand Ronde agency. Sam voiced the
general feeling of the Indians when he charged that the government's promises had not been kept. He was puzzled by the removal of Indian Superintendent Palmer, who had now been superseded by J. W. Nesmith. "With us," said Sam, "we are born
chiefs; once a chief we are a chief for life. But you are only common men and we never know how long you will hold your authority, or how soon the great chief may degrade you, or how soon
he may be turned out himself. We want to know the true head,
that we may state our condition to him. So many lies have been
told him that we think he never hears the truth, or he would not
compel us to suffer as we do." The Indians were told in reply
that they must work. "All white people had to work. The shirts
and blankets they wore were made by white men's labor. Were
they better than white men, that they should live without working?" Yet, it is doubtful if they were as much impressed by this
as by the agent's further warning: "If they undertook to go back
to their homes they would be shot down, and then the president's

heart would be sad, because he could no longer protect them." These grievances were adjusted slowly, and for some years two badly located military posts were maintained, nominally for the preservation of the peace and protection of the people.

27

The campaign in the north, in 1856, was involved more deeply in considerations of policy than of military strategy. The federal troops in the district were reinforced, in January, by eight companies of the Ninth infantry, commanded by Col. George Wright, who was ordered by General Wool to proceed up the Columbia and to establish headquarters at The Dalles, and branch posts in the Walla Walla and Yakima valleys, and also midway between Yakima and The Dalles. Wool, however, although he was thus determined on a policy of occupying the country, with a view to preventing the Indians from hunting or fishing at their accustomed places, and so reducing them to subjection by degrees, was not favorably disposed toward white settlements in the eastern district, in advance of ratification of treaties. His campaign did not contemplate permanent protection of the white inhabitants. Kamiakin and his fellow hostiles were first to be persuaded to enter into treaties.

Wright's mission was not entirely that of a soldier bent upon war; he was an emissary, sent to open negotiations with the disaffected tribes. Kamiakin was now the recognized leader of all the northern disaffected Indians, and an error of judgment committed by Colonel Wright, in carrying out General Wool's orders, was responsible almost at the outset for a tragic occurrence—the siege of the stations at Cascades—by Yakima, Klickitat and Cascade Indians, under Kamiakin's leadership. There is reason to believe that Kamiakin had long realized the tactical value of this point, in his scheme to advance across the Columbia river and to invade the Willamette valley; so that, when Wright sent his soldiers east to Walla Walla, and north toward Yakima, and left only a sergeant and eight men to garrison the blockhouse at the middle Cascades, Kamiakin saw that his opportunity had come. The portages were guarded by this meager military force. There were, also, a number of civilian employees, who were building a portage railroad to be used in transporting stores from the lower to the upper Columbia, a few men were at work unloading river steamers, and the other inhabitants were engaged in their usual vocations. Two steamers, the Mary and the Wasco, lay in the river. Most of the workmen were at the upper Cascades, where they made headquarters in the Bradford store, about a mile from the blockhouse.

28

The Indians attacked without warning, from ambush in the timber above the settlements, simultaneously all along the line, on the morning of March 26, 1856. At a saw mill on Mill creek, at the upper end of the portage, a workman, his wife and her young brother fell at the first fire, and were scalped, their bodies being thrown into the river. The crew of the steamer, Mary, were fired on, but they defended themselves stoutly and succeeded in building fires under the boilers and getting away. On the opposite side of the Columbia river, the steamer Wasco started up stream. She had been lying in a position from which the attack on the Mary was clearly seen. This frustration of the Indians' plans for a sudden and complete destruction of communications was disastrous to them, for the steamers took to The Dalles tidings of the attack. Colonel Wright had only recently begun his march toward Walla Walla. A courier speedily overtook his detachment and advised him of the situation at the Cascades. He returned with as little delay as possible. A friendly Indian, meanwhile, carried the news to Fort Vancouver, and while Colonel Wright was descending the Columbia, Lieut. Philip Sheridan, who subsequently distinguished himself in the war between the states, was on the way up river, on the small steamer called the Belle, with 40 regulars from the small number that had been left at Vancouver when Wool projected the eastern campaign. About seventy volunteers, who furnished their own arms and accoutrements, followed in two detachments on the next day.

The Indians meanwhile laid siege to the Bradford store, at the upper Cascades, in which forty persons, comprising eighteen men and four women who could fight, and eighteen wounded men and children, had congregated. They also surrounded the blockhouse, where the soldiers and a smaller company of civilians had fortified themselves. One soldier failed to reach the blockhouse, and was captured by the attackers and cruelly slain. At the upper Cascades, a teamster who was wounded while trying to reach the

store took refuge behind a rock, where he was protected by a hot
gunfire from the store, but it was impossible to succor him. During the two nights that the siege continued the Indians burned
buildings to light the scene and prevent his rescue. The store was
a two-story log structure, strongly built. It well served the purposes of a fort and, fortunately, contained a quantity of military
stores. The Indians kept up an incessant fire at this point, giving
variety to the attack by shooting lighted arrows and throwing
burning faggots on the roof of the store from the overhanging
bluffs. Here the civilian garrison by constant vigilance for two
days and two nights maintained its position until relief arrived.
The survivors of the first attack on the lower Cascades escaped
down the river in open boats. Fourteen persons in all, including
one woman, were killed and twelve wounded. The survivors met
Sheridan, and the men volunteered to return with him to fight.

29

Colonel Wright arrived at the upper Cascades early on the
morning of March 28, 1856. Sheridan reached the lower Cascades
only a few hours later, and landed on the Oregon side. After re-
connoitering on foot, he ascertained from friendly Cascade Indians the state of the siege, both at the blockhouse and the upper
town. Wright's men, numbering 250, speedily dispersed the enemy
at the latter place, and Sheridan's smaller force, which soon
reached the Washington side, met sharp resistance and was compelled to drop down the river and entrench. With the help, however, of Willamette valley volunteers, who arrived in the steamer
Fashion, and who divided the attention of the enemy, Sheridan
had just reached a point near the blockhouse and located a howitzer in a favorable position, and was engaging the full attention
of the Yakimas, when a cavalry bugle call signalled the approach of a troop from Wright's camp. The Indians were between the two detachments, but they were thus warned, and possible surprise and victory by Sheridan's forces faded away. The
sound of the bugle ended any hope and the Indians fled, as always
had been their practice when battle turned against them.

30

No Yakima Indians were punished for the raid, but Chenoweth,
a renegade chief of the Cascade tribe, and eight others, were
caught, tried by summary court-martial and hanged. Wright then

ordered that all members of the Cascade tribe found away from an island reservation which he set apart for them should be shot. He ordered a blockhouse to be erected on the bluff back of Bradford's store, and another at the lower Cascades. Both of these were garrisoned with troops.

A generally regretted incident growing out of the excitement engendered by the Cascade massacre was the murder of the family of Chief Spencer, a friendly Chinook, consisting of his wife, two youths, three girls and a baby. Spencer, who was an influential chief, had been sent for by Colonel Wright to act as interpreter in negotiations with the hostile tribes, and had taken his family with him to remain with relatives in eastern Oregon. When Wright went to the relief of the Cascades, Spencer sent his family down river to Vancouver, and they disappeared. Lieutenant Sheridan, at the request of Joseph L. Meek, deployed a detachment as skirmishers, across the valley, and found the bodies of the entire family. All had been strangled with strands of rope tied around their necks. "The offenders," said Sheridan in his Memoirs, "were citizens living near the middle blockhouse, whose wives and children had been killed a few days before by the hostiles, but who well knew that these unoffending creatures had nothing to do with those murders."

31

The Oregon territorial assembly, January 30, 1856, had adopted a memorial asking that General Wool be removed from command of the department of the Pacific. "He has remained inactive and refused to send troops to the relief of the volunteers," said the memorialists, "or to supply them with arms and ammunition in time of need. He has gone into winter quarters and left our settlements exposed to the ravages of our enemies. . . . Not content with the inactive and inefficient course which he has thought proper to pursue in this war . . . he has departed from this inactive policy only to censure the governor and people of this territory for their commendable zeal in defending their country." Governor Stevens reposed no greater confidence in Wool than did the Oregon legislature, and February 25, 1856, he ordered the organization of three battalions of volunteers, one of which under command of Lieutenant-Colonel Shaw, was directed to march to the Walla Walla valley, it being Stevens' plan to drive the hostile

Indians from the vicinity of Puget sound toward the interior plains.

No attention was paid in high official quarters to the protest against Wool, and Wright was left free to pursue his original course, as soon as he had recovered from the setback caused by the occurrence at the Cascades. So, while Shaw was preparing to cross the mountains by way of Naches pass, which he did in June, Colonel Wright resumed his march north, in May, in quest of Indians with whom to negotiate, engaging in a few skirmishes with irreconcilables, who set fire to his grass and otherwise committed petty annoyances. Finally, obtaining interviews with Kamiakin, Skloom, Owhi, Leschi and a young son of Peu-peu-mox-mox, who had succeeded his father in command of the Walla Walla war party, he was completely deceived by a policy which the chiefs now craftily developed, of obtaining delay by representing that they themselves were in favor of peace, but required time to bring their associates to their way of thinking. They told Wright that the whole trouble arose from the fact that the treaties of Walla Walla had been forced upon them. Wright answered with threats, tempered with expressions of sympathy, but this did not much impress the hostiles.

Nothing definite was accomplished at Wright's conferences, and the United States forces devoted the remainder of the summer to destroying Indian food caches, to driving the natives from their fishing places, and to collecting non-combatants, who were sent to Oregon to be cared for on reservations. These, however, were not closely guarded, so that they were free to come and go as they wished, and to act as spies.

The last of the Oregon volunteers were disbanded, August, 1856, largely for lack of equipment and because of the refusal of the regular army authorities to supply them with arms; but their service in keeping Indians on the move had not been without considerable value. So, too, Colonel Shaw's Washington volunteers contributed to the final suppression of the hostiles by fighting two battles on Burnt river and in the Grande Ronde valley in Oregon, which battles, although inconclusive, gave notice to the Indians that they were dealing with a persevering foe. Notwithstanding the general absence of cooperation that characterized these operations, the cumulative effect of incessant harrying

Isaac I. Stevens
First territorial governor of Washington.

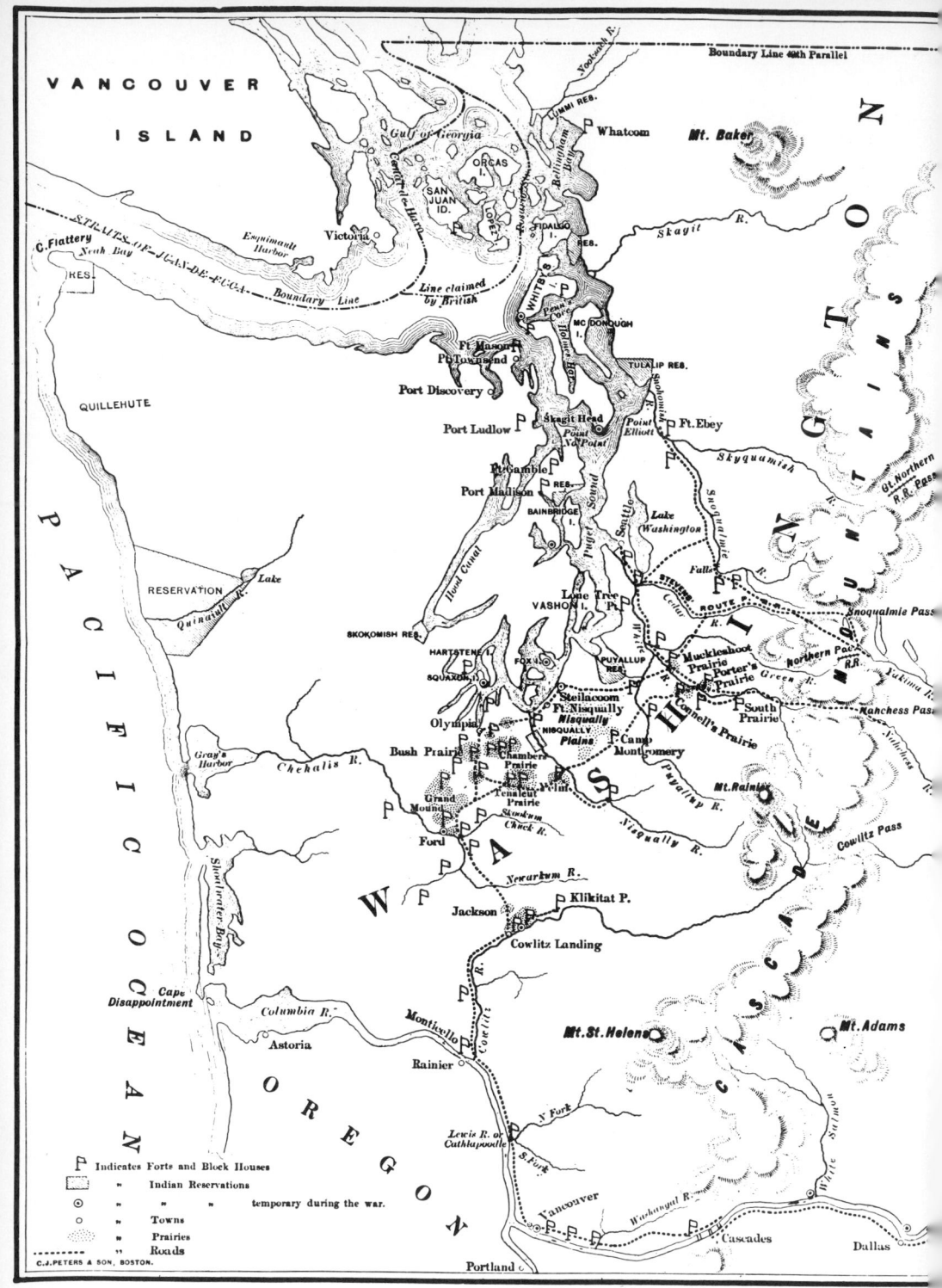

Theater of Indian War, 1855-56, on Puget Sound and
West of Cascade Mountains

of the savages, by regulars and by Oregon and Washington volunteers, began to be observed late in the summer, when eight or nine hundred wavering Wascos, John Days, Tyghs, and Des Chutes surrendered in small groups and were sent to the Warm Springs reservation.

32

Efforts were made independently by Stevens, acting as superintendent of Indian affairs in Washington territory, and by Col. E. J. Steptoe, of the regular army, in the autumn of 1856, to make peace by treaty. Steptoe was sent, in August, to establish a military post in the Walla Walla valley, and he anticipated his departure from The Dalles for that locality by issuing a proclamation, August 20, ordering all settlers out of the region the Indian title to which had not been settled by confirmation of treaties with them. "No emigrant or other person, except the Hudson's Bay Company, or persons having ceded rights from the Indians," said Steptoe in the proclamation, "will be permitted to settle or remain in the Indian country, or on land not settled, or not confirmed by the senate and approved by the president of the United States."

33

About this time Governor Stevens, in view of Wright's plans for the occupation of the Walla Walla country, went to Shaw's camp, on the present site of the city of Walla Walla, for the purpose of mustering out the volunteers, and also to attempt to hold a council with the tribes. The war faction of the Nez Perce's was now thought to be dominating, the attitude of the Cayuses was dubious, and the Walla Wallas and the Yakimas were openly hostile, so these considerations moved Stevens to request Steptoe to furnish him the protection of two companies of regulars with mountain howitzers. Steptoe refused, giving as reasons that it was unnecessary, that it would have an unfavorable effect on the Indians, and that it would be a violation of the instructions of General Wool.

The council opened September 11, and lasted a week. The Indians were surly and uncompromising from the beginning. On September 13, Stevens addressed to Steptoe another appeal for a guard, "as essential to the security of my camp." Steptoe replied by suggesting that Stevens move, instead. The governor reluctantly took the hint, and on the way to Steptoe's camp encountered a band of warriors commanded by Kamiakin, whose design to attack the volunteers, Stevens was informed, had been prevented by this unexpected move.

The council accomplished nothing. Stevens submitted his terms, which were unconditional submission to the justice and mercy of the government, and the surrender of all Indian murderers for trial. Steptoe informed the Indians that he had come to the country to establish a post, not to fight them; and that he "trusted they should get along as friends," and he appointed the following day for another council, which the Indians ignored. Instead, they set fire to the prairie around Steptoe's camp, as a further act of defiance, and started in pursuit of Stevens and the volunteers now returning to The Dalles. Fighting between Stevens' party and the hostiles of all tribes continued through the afternoon of September 19, and was renewed, September 20. Colonel Steptoe, meanwhile, sent detachments of dragoons and artillery to Stevens' aid, and the enemy were repulsed. Colonel Shaw, of the volunteers, distinguished himself in the first day's fighting by leading a charge with twenty-four men, in the course of which he was cut off by a band of 150 warriors, through whom the volunteers cut their way back to the main column. The principal casualties of the battle occurred here. Stevens' loss was one killed, and one gravely, and one slightly wounded. The Indians losses were officially reported as thirteen killed and wounded. Attended by the escort from Steptoe's camp, Stevens and the volunteers proceeded out of the region and the governor returned to Olympia.

34

General Wool did not lose hope of concluding peace by convincing the Indians that the regulars were their friends, and that settlers would be excluded from their country. Under orders from Wool, Colonel Wright called another council of Cayuse, Walla Wallas and Nez Perce's, at which about forty of the chiefs attended. The Indians reiterated their dissatisfaction with the Walla Walla treaties, declared that Lawyer had sold them out and that they wanted peace. Wright in return promised them immunity for their past conduct and assured them that no white man would be permitted to settle among them without their permission, until the treaties had been acted on or new ones made. Wright was so impressed by the results of this council that he reported officially that, in his opinion, the treaties should not be ratified and that peace and quiet could easily be maintained. Stevens took issue with Wright, who, he said in a letter of protest to the secretary of war, Jefferson Davis, had made unauthorized concessions calculated to embarrass the Indian service in its dealings with the tribes.

General Wool nevertheless accepted the view of his subordinate, which coincided with his own predilections, and, December 18, 1856, officially declared that peace had been restored. "Under present arrangements," he wrote, "I don't believe that the war can be renewed by the whites. The posts are well arranged to preserve peace and to protect the inhabitants from any hostility on the part of the Indians residing in the territories."

35

While these events were occurring east of the Cascade mountains, the people around Puget sound had at least two noteworthy conflicts with the western tribes. These are germane to a history of Oregon, although Washington had meanwhile become a separate territory, because they show the widespread character of the uprising, in the nature of which a considerable victory for the natives in any locality would have greatly improved the morale of the tribes in the entire region.

January 25, 1856, a considerable force of hostiles, led by Leschi of the Nisquallies and Owhi of the upper Yakimas, attacked Seattle and poured a hot fire into the town all day, but were repulsed by home guards, aided by men from the sloop-of-war Decatur, then in harbor. The Indians had planned to destroy Seattle and march on Fort Steilacoom, capture the ammunition there and open a war of extermination. Early in March, 1856, a band of fifty warriors committed several murders south of Steilacoom, and March 8, a battle was fought by local volunteers and Indians at Connells prairie, which resulted in a victory for the numerically inferior force of whites. Two companies of United States infantry and four companies of volunteers were busily employed in patrolling the region, with occasional skirmishes, throughout the summer.

Indians from British Columbia in this year invaded Washington territory in war canoes, and when they interpreted as a sign of weakness a missive sent to them under a flag of truce, with a friendly warning to leave the country, they were engaged in battle at Port Gamble by the crew of the United States steamer Massachusetts, who killed twenty-seven and wounded twenty-one, of a total force of 117. This put an end to apprehension of invasion by the northern tribes.

For a short time during this period, Pierce county was placed under martial law by proclamation of Governor Stevens, in consequence of Stevens' disagreement with the civil courts over the treatment of prisoners, squawmen and others, suspected of being spies for the Indians. Stevens' militia arrested Judge Edward Lander, as the latter was attempting to open court to hear applications for writs of habeas corpus in defiance of the military proclamation, and the judge retaliated by ordering the governor's arrest for contempt of court. The judge was held in nominal custody for a time, and when the war on the sound had ended, he fined Governor Stevens $50 for contempt of court. The incident not only provoked an acrimonious political controversy, but illustrated again the want of unity in dealing with the Indian question, which was a feature of the history of this period.

36

A semblance of peace existed under the policy now dictated by the regular army, a policy that conceded the Indian title to the country east of the Cascade mountains, ignored the Stevens-Palmer treaties, and closed the region to settlement. But pacification was incomplete for various reasons. First, the Indians were not able to comprehend the sentiment of benevolence, and saw in every concession an indication of weakness and nothing else. Second, they were still uneasy in view of their experience with a vacillating government, lest at some time in the future the struggle be renewed. Third, they objected that the chiefs, who had signed the treaties of 1855, lacked authority to do so, and that their acts were not approved by the tribes. Also, the partisans of the murderers of Bolon were constantly apprehensive lest their punishment should be insisted on. Still further, there dwelt in the northeastern section of the territory a pugnacious tribe that had obstinately refused to permit settlers to obtain a foothold within their boundaries. These were the Coeur d'Alenes, who had said, even to the early Hudson's Bay traders: "We are willing to barter our furs and peltries for your powder and ball, and such things as you bring for traffic, but we can make the exchange only at certain points [named by themselves]. Within the limits of our land you cannot enter; but on the banks of yonder river, which marks our border, we will meet you at stated times; and there, and there only, can we trade and traffic."

A few Jesuit missionaries had succeeded in penetrating the barrier of their distrust. They had declined to treat with Stevens, 1855, and had then made it known again that they would resist every effort to build roads through the country they called their own. Closely allied with the Coeur d'Alenes, although somewhat more corrigible, were the Spokanes, who also had rejected Stevens' advances, and who demanded only that they be let alone. Their chieftain, Garry, had gone to school in the Red River settlement, where he had acquired a certain knowledge of civilization, and he had protected the missionaries, Walker and Eells, in the troubled months immediately following the massacre at Whitman mission. Between the Spokanes and the Coeur d'Alenes, in the north, and the Walla Wallas and the Cayuses farther south, roamed the Palouses. Of all tribes between the Rocky mountains and the Cascades the Palouses were rated as the most treacherous. They were a thieving lot, and were held in low esteem, even by those of their own race. The way to the recently opened mines of the Colville district lay through the country of the Palouses and the Spokanes, and a misguided traveller strayed occasionally across the boundaries of the Coeur d'Alenes.

37

By June, 1857, when Brig.-Gen. Newman S. Clarke, who had succeeded Major-General Wool in command of the military department of the Pacific, visited Oregon, the nominal peace which Wright had made and Wool had proclaimed was at the point of breaking. The Palouses, misinterpreting the self restraint of the military, grew bolder, and on one occasion even drove off a band of horses from the military post in the Walla Walla valley, at Wright's very door. Two prospectors on the way to the Colville mines were robbed and murdered, and other miners disappeared. People living near Colville reported the nearby Indians hostile, and petitioned the military forces for protection.

General Clarke arrived in Oregon holding some of the views

of his predecessor, Wool, and began by attempting to carry out Wool's policies. Stevens was elected delegate to congress from Washington territory, July, 1857, and Joel Palmer was succeeded as superintendent of Indian affairs for Oregon by J. W. Nesmith, whose authority was now extended over the Indians of both territories. Clarke held a conference with Nesmith, at The Dalles, at which the causes of the now apparent revival of unrest among the eastern Indians were discussed. Nesmith agreed with Clarke that uneasiness for the future disposition of Bolon's murderers and fear that the Walla Walla treaties would be enforced, were two prime sources of irritation. He expressed the view that it would be impolitic to confirm the treaties, and said that he would use his influence to prevent their ratification. Colonel Steptoe, in command of Fort Walla Walla, reported, October, 1857, that in his opinion any attempt to enforce the treaties would be followed by immediate hostilities with most of the tribes. Steptoe, in a spirit of friendship for the Indians, recommended that another treaty commission be appointed and a new treaty made, "thoroughly digested and accepted by both sides."

Clarke determined, inasmuch as the Indians had been led to believe, however mistakenly, that the past would be forgiven, that he would not destroy the future influence of the government by an appearance of bad faith, and he instructed his officers so to inform them. Clarke also directed a continuance of the policy of Wool, and issued a formal order forbidding settlement east of the Salmon river, in Washington, and the Deschutes river, in Oregon. In compliance with the order, military force was used to expel settlers who persisted in coming to the Walla Walla valley. Reports of disaffection among the tribes, together with rumors, which now reached Clarke through official channels, to the effect that Mormons, in Utah, were supplying Indians with ammunition and fomenting disorder among them, caused Clarke, early in January, 1858, to direct Steptoe to place his command in a state of full efficiency, at the earliest possible date, for the purpose of going on an expedition to obtain full information in relation to the eastern tribes.

38

Steptoe reported, January 29, 1858, that he doubted that the Indians in the immediate vicinity of Walla Walla were disposed to involve themselves in war, but that he believed that the Palouse, Yakima and Spokane tribes awaited only slight encouragement to revive hostilities. Only a day later Maj. R. S. Garnett, commanding the military post at Fort Simcoe, sent word that he had received word for the second time from Skloom, brother of Kamiakin, that Mormon emissaries had been among the Yakimas, seeking to incite them to hostility toward the United States.

As a result of this condition, and in obedience to the order of General Clarke, Colonel Steptoe left Fort Walla Walla, May 6, 1858, with three companies of dragoons and a detachment of mounted infantry, 158 men in all. Two of the dragoon companies were armed with the musketoon, a short gun of musket pattern, but incapable of efficient execution at any great range. At the last moment of loading the pack train, it was found that the baggage exceeded the carrying capacity of the train, and a large portion of the ammunition was left behind. Steptoe's mission being peaceful, rather than punitive, this omission did not then attract attention.

The route of Steptoe's march also was fateful. Leaving Walla Walla, he travelled northeast to the Snake river, which he reached at the mouth of Alpowa creek, where the friendly Nez Perce's chief, Timothy, had a fleet of large canoes likely to be useful in making the crossing, and also where, he had been informed, a large party of Palouses were gathering. He then followed a succession of Indian trails which led him close to the present Washington-Idaho boundary line, and so doing, he approached very near to the country of the Cocur d'Alenes; whereas, a direct route from Walla Walla to Colville by the then travelled trails would have led him thirty miles or more to the westward. On reaching the Palouse river and being about to attempt a crossing, he was informed that the Spokanes and Coeur d'Alenes would oppose his entrance to their country. He continued his march, however, meeting occasional parties of Indians, probably spies, who professed friendship and had ample opportunity to obtain information concerning the strength of his command.

On Sunday, May 15, 1858, while the column was encamped on Pine creek, a tributary of the Palouse, a band of mounted warriors variously estimated at from 1000 to 1500, Spokanes, Yakimas, Palouses and Coeur d'Alenes, appeared suddenly from the hills. Spokanes and Coeur d'Alenes, acting as spokesmen, told Steptoe they had been informed that he had come to annihilate them, and said that if this were so they were ready to fight. In reply to Steptoe's explanation that he was merely on his way to Colville on a friendly mission, the Indians retorted that he had not come by the most direct route to Colville, and pointed to his howitzers as confirmation of their belief in his warlike purpose. Appreciating the fact that he was outnumbered seven to one, and that the Indians carried rifles of longer range than the musketoons of his own dragoons, Steptoe resolved to retrace his steps.

The Indians, who had not forgotten their early religious training, told Steptoe that they would not fight on Sunday; but they opened the attack as soon as the retrograde movement was begun, on the morning of May 18, and surrounded the troops, who took refuge on a hill near the present site of Rosalia, Washington, where the battle continued into the night. Reduced to three rounds of ammunition for each man, Steptoe then abandoned his howitzers and pack train, and retreated under cover of darkness by a forced march of eighty miles to Snake river crossing. He had suffered the loss of a captain and a lieutenant and six enlisted men, killed, and eleven wounded, and left his dead hastily buried in shallow graves on the battlefield. The prestige of the army was impaired and the confidence of the native tribes was strengthened by this military failure.

39

Steptoe's defeat, however, hastened the conclusion of hostilities in that region by putting the whole army on its mettle, and by convincing General Clarke that hostiles could be brought to terms only by punishing them. The expedition which Clarke now organized omitted no detail of equipment that would make fulfillment of its purpose certain. He obtained, as reinforcements, three companies of artillery from San Francisco, one company of the Fourth infantry from Fort Jones, and another from the Umpqua district, and he concentrated nearly 2000 men of all arms at Fort Walla Walla, where they were diligently drilled in the tactics of Indian warfare. Command of the expedition was committed to Colonel Wright, who sent three companies under Major Garnett to the Yakima country, to drive the Indians east toward the main column, which meanwhile proceeded north.

Wright took the precaution before starting out, however, to make a formal treaty of friendship with the Nez Perce's, with a view to protecting his rear, and this curious compact was signed August 6, 1858, by Wright for the government of the United States and by 38 chiefs and sub-chiefs of the Nez Perce's. It was subsequently countersigned by General Clarke, at Fort Vancouver, but it never received the consideration of the senate. However, it was faithfully kept by the tribe, until 1877, when its first article was violated by Chief Joseph, who was pursued by Gen. O. O. Howard across the present states of Idaho and western Montana, and who finally surrendered to Gen. Nelson A. Miles.

The Nez Perce's treaty was the cause of much agitation in Oregon, on the ground that Wright had promised more than he could perform, that the Indians did not understand that Wright had no authority to make treaties, and that failure to supply the Nez Perce's with arms, as the treaty provided, would result in dissatisfaction and in alienation of the friendship of the tribe. Wright maintained, however, that the treaty was justified, as an act of military necessity, and that by placing hors de combat some 1700 Hudson's Bay muskets alone, it accomplished the purpose for which it was intended.

40

Wright's division consisted of four companies of dragoons, five companies of artillery, two companies of infantry and a company of Nez Perce's allies, in United States army uniforms. There were long range rifles for the entire force and ammunition for a protracted campaign. But, even this formidable army found the Indians insolent and willing to take the initiative. The two culminating battles of the campaign were fought at Four Lakes, September 1, where the brother and brother-in-law of Chief Garry were killed, and on the Spokane plains, where Kamiakin was wounded by a tree top, blown off by a cannon and striking him on the head. Wright had no losses, either in killed or wounded, and on the entire campaign reported as casualties only two, who died from nonmilitary causes. The losses of the Indians were concealed by them.

In addition to their dead and wounded, however, they suffered heavily in loss of property. The troops captured several hundred head of cattle and a larger number of horses, the surplus of which, after remounting the command, were shot. The entire Spokane nation was practically unhorsed in two days.

The Indians were taken wholly by surprise by Wright's well trained forces, and particularly by the new long range rifles, now used for the first time, while the artillery overwhelmed them and gave them no opportunity to employ their usual tactics of sniping the troops from every convenient cover. But a natural phenomenon at this time gave a peculiar and picturesque turn to the event. Donati's comet became visible for the first time as the army under Wright drew near. "Night after night," wrote Lieut. Lawrence Kip, who accompanied the expedition as artillery adjutant, "it had been streaming above us in all its glory. Strange as it may seem, it has exerted a powerful influence with the Indians in our behalf. Appearing just as we entered the country, it seemed to them like some huge besom to sweep them from the earth. The effect was probably much increased by the fact that it disappeared about the time our campaign ended, and the treaties were formed. They must have imagined that it had been sent home to the Great Father in Washington, to be put away until required the next time."

41

Indians now approached Wright as suppliants. Garry pleaded that he had been opposed to fighting, but that his young men and many of the other chiefs had overruled him. Wright's attitude was that of conqueror. His reply to Garry embodied his policy in dealing with most of the other tribes. Wright said: "I have met you in two battles; you have been badly whipped; you have had several chiefs and many warriors killed or wounded; I have not lost a man or animal. I have a large force, and you, Spokanes, Coeur d'Alenes, Palouses and Pend d'Oreilles may unite, and I can defeat you as badly as before. I did not come to the country to make peace; I came here to fight. Now, when you are tired of war and ask for peace you must come to me with your arms, with your women and children, and everything you have, and lay them at my feet. You must trust to my mercy. If you do this, I shall then give you the terms upon which I will give you peace. If you do not do this, war will be made on you this year and the next, and until your nations shall be exterminated." Of the now terrified Coeur d'Alenes, Wright demanded that they surrender for execution the man who struck the first blow at Colonel Steptoe, give one chief and four warriors and their families to be held as hostages, and restore all property taken from Steptoe's command.

Owhi, brother-in-law of Kamiakin, entered camp seeking peace and was detained as hostage for the appearance of his son, Qual-chan, the murderer of Indian Agent Bolon. Qual-chan came unsuspectingly into camp without having met the messenger sent after him. He was recognized, seized and bound. Colonel Wright's official report reads: "Qual-chan came to me at nine o'clock this morning, and at 9 1/4 a. m. he was hung." Owhi was shot a few days later while trying to escape. Seven Palouse Indians, who sued for peace, were tried by summary court, convicted of various atrocities and six were hanged. Other Palouses followed, and were told by Wright that he would make no treaty with them until their good faith had been tested by probation. Four other notorious marauders were surrendered by their fellows, and were summarily executed. Returning to the country of the Walla Wallas, Wright called a council, at which he commanded all who had taken part in the recent battles to stand up. Thirty-five stood up, of whom Wright selected four at random, who were hanged on the spot. Sixteen Indians were thus executed by Wright's orders. Major Garnett in the same period captured and executed eight Indians, all of whom were shot.

42

The war in the north was now over. The hostile chieftains were either dead or in flight. In Puget sound region, Leschi, of the Nisquallies, had been betrayed for a reward, arrested and hanged by the civil authorities of Washington territory, February 19, 1858, after a memorable legal struggle to save his life, in which he was befriended by influential citizens who believed that he had been made a scapegoat, and that he had not signed the Medicine creek treaty, or, if he had done so had but imperfectly understood its terms. Kamiakin, instigator of the effort to unite all the tribes in a war of extermination of the whites, and Skloom, of the Yakimas, found safety in prudent flight.

The treaties made by Wright were treaties of friendship only, and left the land issue precisely as it was before. General Clarke, however, now withdrew his opposition to the Walla Walla treaties, and they, and also Palmer's treaty with the Indians of central Oregon, were ratified by the senate, March 8, 1859. The eastern country was formally thrown open to settlement, October 31, 1858, by order of Gen. William S. Harney, who became commander of the military department of Oregon upon the creation of the department, September 13, 1858.

Throughout the war period the inhabitants of Oregon territory bore a heavy burden, the great weight of which it is not easy to appraise by present standards. Isolation of the pioneer colony was never more keenly felt, perhaps, than in that time when the very existence of the people was threatened, and when no aid, or aid that was inadequate, was forthcoming from the national government. In the crisis that confronted these settlers in a remote section, when it became apparent that the government could not well furnish a sufficient military force for their protection, the people showed self-reliance. When the government could not see the pressing need, as in the period of clashing policies, of the obstinacy of Wool, and the self-assertiveness of Curry and Stevens, the people shouldered responsibilities thus imposed upon them. Patriotism and self-interest, need of protection of homes and preservation of the state, operated as incentives. While volunteers were in the field, women and children were left to manage affairs at home as best they could. The financial load was heavy, and there was constant sense of insecurity and danger. Anxiety was peculiarly distressing in southern Oregon. Throughout distant settlements, where no life was safe, the highest sacrifice made by volunteers was not to face the danger to which they themselves were exposed, but rather in being compelled to leave the women and younger children, while husbands and fathers, and in many instances half-grown sons, were away from home fighting the war.

43

The cost in human life was heavy, while loss in property as the result of depredations was enormous in proportion to the means of the settlers. Casualties were relatively higher among civilians than among soldiers, so that it was literally true that it was safer to be in the service than out of it. Many murders were committed by Indians, of which no record was ever made, but the number of those known is large. Frances Fuller Victor, who, in the course of her research into the history of the northwest, formed the habit of setting down names and numbers of white people killed by Indians in the Oregon Country, estimated the total killed and wounded between the years 1828 and 1878, as 1896, an average of more than thirty-seven annually. Unprovoked murders constituted more than half, the remainder being those occurring in warfare. But as a matter of fact, as these records also show, the greater proportion of the victims fell between the years 1850 and 1862, a loss during the period of more than 160 annually. Men thus slain were in the prime of life. Many families were destroyed, and the Indians added to the horrors of war every form of torture and outrage that it was possible for them to devise.

After congress had reimbursed the territory for its claims growing out of the Cayuse war of 1847-8, and the first Rogue river war of 1853, and had assumed the cost of the Walker expedition of 1854, which was not paid, however, until after the close of the war between the states, it engaged in debating the merits and demerits of claims growing out of the later Rogue river and Yakima wars. These ultimately became inextricably tangled in official reports and correspondence. Congress, August 18, 1856, passed an act authorizing an inquiry into these claims. A commission composed of Capt. Andrew J. Smith, Capt. Rufus Ingalls and Lafayette Grover was appointed, and it ascertained that Oregon's share of the cost of the war amounted to a total of $4,449,-949.33, of which $1,409,644.53 was represented by the muster rolls of the volunteers and $3,040,304.80 by scrip issued in payment for supplies, and the total expended by both Oregon and Washington territories was $6,011,457.36. February 8, 1859, congress directed the third auditor of the treasury to examine all vouchers, which that official, R. J. Atkinson, did by appraising the value of supplies on the basis of their cost in the eastern states. He cut the total for both states to $2,714,808.55, a reduction of 55 per cent, and this was ultimately paid. The heavy loss which was thus entailed upon the people of the sparsely settled territory was responsible for a number of business failures, and the impossibility of realizing expectations assumed the proportions of a financial tragedy. Who was responsible for the delay in getting appropriations to reimburse those who had claims became a heated political issue in Oregon, as editor Bush, of the Oregon Statesman, at Salem, denounced Senators Delazon Smith and Joseph Lane, and praised Lafayette Grover. Oregon, like other parts of the country, was experiencing hard times in the latter part of the decade of 1850, and would have welcomed a prompt payment.

44

Veterans of these wars were even less successful in getting pecuniary recognition for their services. Long after laws had been enacted for the relief of the soldiers of the Civil war, men who had fought the Indians on the frontier continued to be disregarded. The act of the territorial legislature of 1855-6, required volunteers, so far as practicable, to furnish their own arms, clothing, horses and equipment, each non-commissioned officer and private to receive $2.00 per diem and rations, besides $2.00 per diem for the use and risk of each privately owned horse. But no appropriation was made in fulfillment of this implied obligation until 1903, almost half a century later, when the state legislature authorized an appropriation of $100,000 to pay each surviving veteran $2.00 for each day of actual service. Ten years later, in 1913, an appropriation of $50,000 was made to compensate each veteran at the rate of $2.00 for each day he had furnished a horse. A further measure was enacted requiring county courts to levy a tax of not less than one-thirtieth of one mill nor more than one-tenth of one mill for the relief of indigent soldiers and sailors and their widows generally, including those who had served not less than ten days in the Indian wars.

The government made no provision for pensions for any of the veterans of our many frontier Indian wars until July 27, 1892, when congress granted pensions of $8.00 a month to the survivors and widows of survivors of the Black Hawk, Creek, Cherokee and Seminole wars of 1832 to 1842, but made no provision for any others. On April 22, 1896, Sen. John H. Mitchell, of Oregon, presented a bill proposing to include in the benefits of the already existing law the survivors of the Cayuse, Yakima and Rogue river wars, but nothing was done until June 27, 1902, when by an act of congress the provisions of the law of July 27, 1892, were extended to Oregon veterans of 1847 to 1856. A determined effort to obtain an increase of pensions for the soldiers of the various Indian campaigns resulted in the passage by the lower house of congress on August 5, 1912, of a bill increasing the rate of pension for surviving veterans from $8.00 to $30.00 a month, and the senate on January 21, 1913, passed the bill after reducing the pension to $12.00 a month.

In support of his bill Mitchell presented figures prepared by the war department, showing that in the Indian wars of Oregon, from 1847 to 1856, there had been engaged 850 regulars, of whom seventy-five per cent had served in the Mexican war, and consequently would receive their benefits under the Mexican war pension act, and 6379 militia, of whom 20 per cent, or 1276, had rendered more than one service, leaving, net 5103; a total for both militia and volunteers of 5316, from which six per cent was deducted for desertions and casualties, leaving 4997 survivors at the close of the latter war. The number of survivors of the Cayuse war was estimated by the war department, February 7, 1895, at 144, and their surviving widows at 82, a total of 226. Survivors of the wars of 1851-6 were estimated as 2399 and widows 1340, a total of 3739. Senator Mitchell said he regarded these estimates as excessive, and as probably representing more than treble the total number of survivors at that time. The average age of the survivors of the Cayuse war was then (in 1895) 68 years, and of survivors of the wars of 1851 6 was 65 years, with an average expectancy of 11.10 years. The further interesting fact was developed that the average age of all the volunteers in each war was 22 years at the dates of enlistment.

While the measure was pending in conference, the Oregon legislature adopted a memorial, which was telegraphed to the committee of the two legislative bodies, urging passage of the bill in the form in which the house had passed it. A compromise on $20.00 a month was effected, and the bill as amended became a law on February 19, 1913, fifty-seven years after the close of the volunteers' service in the Yakima and Rogue river wars and 65 years after the conclusion of the Cayuse war. As a final act of grace, congress, March 4, 1917, extended the provisions of the amended act to veterans of the Shoshone war of 1865-8, in Oregon and Idaho, and of the Modoc war of 1872-3, in Oregon, Nevada and California.

CHAPTER XXIV
THE FRONTIER IN THE CIVIL WAR

1

OREGON'S principal share in the Civil war consisted in protecting the frontier against marauding Indians and the interior from rebel sympathizers, while the troops of other states were engaged in more conspicuous and apparently more glorious, but no more essential or arduous, service on the actual fields of combat. Whiteaker, who was governor when the war began, opposed suppression of the rebellion by force, contrasting in this respect with patriotic war governors in other northern states, and his attitude caused delay in obtaining volunteers for service of any sort. Col. George Wright, who had brought the Indian wars to a close, 1858, was commander of the federal military district of Oregon and Washington, when, on the outbreak of the Civil war, the whole region was practically stripped of regulars, leaving less than a full regiment in the entire northwest. Not even a gunboat remained for patrol duty on the coast, at a time when it was locally believed that a movement for separate secession of the Pacific states was under way. In the interval between Wright's pacification of the tribes of the intermountain region and the beginning of the Civil war, those dissatisfied Indians who refused to be bound by the terms of the peace, became infected with a spirit of unrest.

The military department of the Pacific was divided into two districts, September 13, 1858, the department of California and the department of Oregon, and Maj.-Gen. William S. Harney was then assigned to the command of the latter department. One of his first orders was to revoke General Wool's prohibition of white settlement in the Walla Walla country. But the Oregon legislature adopted a joint resolution urging adequate protection of immigrants upon the overland routes, and the establishing of a military post at Fort Boise. General Harney gave orders, early in the spring of 1859, to Capt. Henry D. Wallen, of the Fourth infantry, designed to accomplish the purpose of affording a sufficient escort for the wagon trains during the immigration season, and also to search out a new route for a wagon road "up the John Day river and thence over the headwaters of the Malheur, following down that route to the Snake river."

Captain Wallen was given an ample force of dragoons, infantry and engineers, and succeeded in making the roving Indian bands understand that his force was to be feared, for they kept out of the way, and during the summer of 1859, no overland travellers were attacked. He reported to General Harney, however, that the Bannock Snakes, or southern Shoshones, were growing bolder and that they were constantly annoying small parties of whites passing through their country. He was confirmed by the experiences of those who succeeded to the command the following year. Wallen explored the Blue, Owyhee and Goose Creek mountains, and the country on both sides of these mountain ranges. He reported that some of the families among the immigrants were in destitute condition, and, that without the help he was able to give them from the military stores, they would inevitably have starved on the way. His assignment was completed, October 17, 1859, when he returned finally to Fort Dalles.

2

In the next year, 1860, General Harney sent two expeditions into the same region. Maj. Enoch Steen had the command and was to march east from Crooked river, but Capt. A. J. Smith, a veteran of the Indian wars, was to take a different route with a smaller detachment. Smith was openly attacked near the Owyhee river; Steen had several brushes with the natives, which, however, came to nothing; the Warm Springs reservation was twice raided by hostiles, and in September, 1860, there occurred a massacre of immigrants about thirty miles east of Fort Boise, more atrocious than any that had preceded it. This was subsequently known as the Salmon Falls massacre, or the Myers massacre, after the name of a family consisting of husband, wife and five children, who were among the survivors. The party, numbering forty-four, were convoyed by United States cavalry to a point a short distance west of Fort Hall, where the troops left them in supposed security. They were surrounded, September 13, 1860, by a band of a hundred Bannocks, who first exacted presents of food, then drove off the immigrants' cattle and finally attacked them, killing eleven, including one woman and two children. Abandoning their train, the surviving immigrants fled and were pursued, six being killed near Burnt river and one near the Owyhee. Four children, two boys and two girls, whose fate has never been determined, are presumed to have been taken captive by the Indians and held in slavery. Five starved to death. Four discharged soldiers from Fort Hall deserted the company, taking arms with them on the pretense of going ahead on scout duty, and two of these were reported by their companions as having been killed on the road mapped by Captain Wallen in the preceding year. The survivors were succored by troops of the Ninth infantry in command of Capt. Frederick T. Dent, brother-in-law of Ulysses S. Grant, October 25, after forty-two days of almost incredible hardship and deprivation. Of the entire party of forty-four immigrants, only fifteen were accounted for as living. In their extremity, the survivors were reduced to devouring the bodies of their dead, four children being thus disposed of.

3

These circumstances indicated that the Indians were again to be seriously reckoned with by the people of the west. The tragedy, coming on the heels of almost weekly reports of isolated outrages, moved the legislature, then in session at Salem, to address a memorial to congress asking for additional military posts at Grande Ronde, Burnt river, Boise, Warm Springs and Klamath lake, and for the removal of all Indians by treaty to reservations, where they might be held in check by a sufficient military force. Meantime Colonel Wright returned to Oregon to take command, as above stated, succeeding General Harney, who went to active duty in the south.

But, the exigencies of the Civil war interfered with any plans the federal government may have had for policing the hostile Indian country. Instead, troops were rapidly withdrawn for more pressing service elsewhere, and, in the spring of 1861, not more than 700 remained in the northwest. The opening gun of the Civil war was fired at Fort Sumter, April 12, 1861; the proclamation of President Lincoln calling for 75,000 volunteers to put down the rebellion was published in Oregon, May 11, but Governor Whiteaker did not respond to the appeal of the proclamation. In a long address to the people of Oregon, issued at Pleasant Hill, Lane county, May 28, 1861, Governor Whiteaker argued that the south could never be conquered, that Oregon's geographical situation would exempt it from demand for troops to put down the rebellion, and that since the people of the state had come from every section of the Union, "it would certainly be impolitic in us, however keenly we may sympathize with other sections, to subject ourselves to the calamities which afflict them." He favored a military policy of defense only, and urged the government to "Beware of making a war for the ultimate or immediate extinction of slavery." "Have a care," he added, "that in freeing the negro you do not enslave the white man."

4

Colonel Wright, after waiting until September 12, 1861, for the state to take action, then made a requisition on the governor for one company of volunteer cavalry for three years' service, for the purpose of checking the depredations of the Indians, east of the Cascades. Under this plan each recruit was required to furnish his own horse. To this, Governor Whiteaker responded, September 16, by issuing a call for eighty-eight men, rank and file, and by appointing A. P. Dennison, former Indian agent, recruiting officer. But nothing came of this. It was suspected that Dennison was no more enthusiastic than the governor was. He appointed five assistant recruiting officers, at a cost of $273 in all, and rendered a bill of $365 for his own services. His total bill for compensation and expenses was $1985.25. He and his assistants enrolled only twelve men.

Wright revoked his requisition, October 23, 1861, on the authority of the war department, which had seen the futility of waiting on Whiteaker, and had appointed Thomas R. Cornelius, colonel; Reuben F. Maury, lieutenant-colonel; Benjamin F. Harding, quartermaster; C. S. Drew, major, and J. S. Rinearson junior major, with directions to recruit a regiment of cavalry. These were the first appointees for volunteer service in an Oregon regiment in the Civil war and were men of whose loyalty to the Union cause there was no question. The terms of the call, however, were not of a nature to stimulate enlistment. The young men of Oregon could see no attraction in serving in the home district, with the prospect of frontier patrol duty and border Indian fighting; nor were pecuniary inducements ($31 a month for each man and his horse, a bounty of $100 at the expiration of his term of service and a land warrant for 160 acres), enticing in a period of plenty of work at good wages, with the new mines of Idaho attracting every fortune hunter.

So the ranks filled slowly. It was well toward the spring of 1862 before six companies were ready for duty, and these completed their quotas in some instances with details from other companies, recruiting for which had progressed even less favorably. Only a few more than forty enlisted east of the Cascade mountains, but this company, mustered in at The Dalles, in command of Captain George B. Currey, was first to be called on for service. The murder of a party of prospectors on the John Day river, and rumors that a considerable body of Simcoe Indians had been seen north of the Columbia with property known to have belonged to the victims, caused the commanding officer at The Dalles to order Currey, with all the men he had, to proceed against the suspects. The expedition consisted of only twelve enlisted men, although it was then March, 1862, nearly four months after recruiting had been begun. It distinguished itself for the promptness and excellent strategy with which it executed its mission, but the effort was otherwise bootless.

5

A number of Indian villages were raided by Currey's troopers, several old Indians were taken as hostages for the future good behavior of their tribes, and a good deal of ground was covered by forced marches, but the murderers of the prospectors were not found, and the soldiers treated the Indians, on the whole, with leniency and moderation.

6

Other incidents of the service which the volunteers were called on to perform, even before the organization of the regiment was completed, indicate the practical necessity for maintaining a military force as a check on disloyalty within the state. While the recruits who were mustered in at Oregon City were stationed at Camp Barlow, early in April, 1862, two men stole horses and deserted. They were pursued up the Willamette valley by Lieut. John T. Apperson, with E company and a detachment. The chase led through Salem, Albany and Corvallis to the crossing of the Long Tom at Richards' ferry, and it is significant that the pursuers found it expedient to conceal the fact that they were Union soldiers, but represented themselves as civilians in quest of horse thieves, lest the sympathy of the countryside be aroused in behalf of the deserters. "The people living in this part of the country," says Lieutenant Apperson in a letter in the Oregon Historical Society, "would not be disposed to aid us in capturing a deserter from the Union army, as they were known to be sympathizers with the south. . . . In some way it leaked out that we and the men we were after were in the Union army, and then it was all off, so far as getting assistance from the citizens who lived in that part of the country."

7

As an especial inducement to recruiting, the war department, in the order by which the general officers of the First Oregon Volunteers were appointed, had invoked the name of Senator Baker, on whose strong recommendation, said the official communication, the department "relies upon the prudence, patriotism and economy with which you will execute this trust." Baker's death, occurring before the order was received in Oregon, discouraged enlistments, but the members of the six companies that were at length assembled at Vancouver, May, 1862, believed that after they had been seasoned by a suitable period of frontier service they would have a part in the war itself, and would receive the assignment they coveted.

The feeling of the men of the First Oregon was expressed by Lieut. J. A. Waymire, in his report to Adj.-Gen. Cyrus A. Reed, April, 1866. Lieutenant Waymire wrote: "I will here say that from my personal knowledge I know that a great majority of the men who composed the First Oregon company were young men acting solely from a conviction of patriotic duty. They left pleasant homes and profitable occupations to take up arms, not only in defense of our frontiers against the Indians, but also to assist in preventing or counteracting any movement on the Pacific coast in favor of the attempt to dissolve the Union; they also hoped that, should the war prove a long one, and there should be no serious difficulty here, they would, after becoming drilled and disciplined, be ordered east to engage in active battles there. That they have fought no great battles, or won no important victories, is the misfortune and not the fault of the Oregon volunteers."

8

The six companies, in the organization of which it became necessary to consolidate some companies and to accept the resignations of certain surplus officers, were dispatched from Fort Vancouver to Fort Walla Walla, June, 1862, but were not fully equipped until July or August. Colonel Cornelius resigned, July 15, for reasons which showed his impatience at the tardy response with which his efforts to raise a full regiment had been met, and at the same time attested his unselfishness and his patriotism. No colonel was formally appointed in his place, however, until April 4, 1865, when Lieutenant-Colonel Maury, who meanwhile held command, received a commission as colonel in recognition of faithful service. A correspondent in the Oregon Argus, speaking of the resignation of Colonel Cornelius, said: "I suppose the truth in regard to his resignation is that he had the full number of field officers for a regiment, that his regiment, having been reduced to six companies, he considered that he had an unnecessary number of field officers, and that rather than require any of his subalterns to resign, he resigned himself. His whole course in the raising of the regiment, organizing it, and putting it into service has done him distinguished credit. He will return to his ample estate in Washington county with the good wishes of all the officers and men composing the regiment."

The military district of Oregon was for a time in command of Col. Justus Steinberger, who had represented Oregon as a proxy delegate in the national convention that nominated Breckenridge and Lane, 1860, a circumstance that provoked much local political controversy in the closing months of the war. Steinberger, as colonel of the First Washington infantry, raised his regiment to full strength by going to California and recruiting four companies there, so that, when Brig.-Gen. Benjamin Alvord, of the regular army, arrived and Steinberger was sent to Walla Walla, the latter outranked Lieutenant-Colonel Maury, and the Oregon cavalry during most of its term of service was under command of an infantry officer from a neighboring territory. This was another fact that had a tendency to discourage recruiting in Oregon. The Oregon men, nevertheless, were kept busy with scouting and escort duty all summer.

9

The aggregate distance covered by the various detachments of E company alone, during 1862, amounted to more than 3000 miles. Companies A, B and D patrolled the overland trail, in the summer and autumn of the same year, to protect the immigrants of that season, who arrived in considerable numbers but were largely of a different class from the homeseekers of the two preceding decades. Of about 10,000 who took the road toward Oregon, a very large proportion sought the newly prospected mining regions of Idaho and eastern Oregon, a few settled as farmers in the Walla Walla valley, and a still smaller number reached western Oregon. The immigrants received further protection from a volunteer company raised in the eastern states and commanded by Capt. Medorem Crawford. In several instances the inhabitants of the mining camps hired and equipped detachments of frontiersmen at their own expense to pursue and punish murderous bands of Indians, and these expeditions served as outlets for the combative spirits of numerous venturesome young men.

The election of Governor Gibbs, and a pro-Union legislature, 1862, gave encouragement to the friends of the Union and promise of a full participation in the war. With the support of loyal citizens, a number of newspapers were suppressed at various times for treasonable proclivities, among them being the Albany Democrat, Jacksonville Gazette, Albany Inquirer, Portland Advertiser and Corvallis Union, and one at Eugene, edited by Cincinnatus H. Miller (Joaquin Miller) that was first called the Democratic Herald, but was changed to the Democratic Register, and again to the Review. The changes of name were to evade suppression orders based upon charges of unpatriotic conduct. Miller removed from Eugene, and became a county judge at Canyon City before leaving Oregon to reside in California.

Leading supporters of the rebellion also left the state to enter the service of the Confederacy. John Lane, son of the ex-governor and ex-senator, became a colonel of Confederate cavalry. Adolphus B. Hanna, who had been United States marshal in Buchanan's administration, and John K. Lamerick, formerly brigadier-general of Oregon militia and a conspicuous figure in the early Indian wars in southern Oregon, offered their services to the Confederacy. John Adair, son of the first collector of customs at Astoria and a graduate of West Point, 1861, being ordered to join a regiment of the United States dragoons, declined duty and was dropped from the army rolls.

At the same time, a number of Oregonians went east to seek

service in the Union cause. Colonel Joseph ("Fighting Joe") Hooker, a resident of Marion county when the war began, distinguished himself as a major-general. John L. Boon, son of J. D. Boon, for several terms territorial treasurer, participated in the battles of Shiloh and Corinth. Maj. George Williams, of Salem; Volney Smith, son of Delazon Smith; Frank W. Thompson, of Linn county; Henry Butler, of Oakland, and John W. Lingenfelter, of Jacksonville, a veteran of the Cayuse war, served with credit in various eastern regiments. Lingenfelter was killed at Fortress Monroe, in 1861. Capt. Roswell H. Lamson, of Yamhill county, who was the first cadet appointed to the United States naval academy from Oregon, became famous as the "hero of Fort Fisher," from a daring exploit conducted under his leadership. He afterward served as clerk of United States circuit court, at Portland. Capt. W. L. Dall became a lieutenant in the navy, in the war. He had commanded the steamship Columbia, which began running in the Columbia river, 1851, and after the war, he again served as a steamship captain.

10

The legislature, 1862, passed a comprehensive act to organize the militia, and, with the purpose of making disloyalty hateful in every possible way, also passed a bill to require every person having a financial claim against the state to subscribe to an oath of fealty to the Union. The secretary of state, at discretion, was empowered to require of the claimant such further proof of his loyalty as he might deem requisite, and to withhold payment if not satisfied with the sufficiency of proof. The bill was vetoed by Governor Gibbs, but came very near to being passed over his veto.

The militia act, however, was accepted throughout the state as a military necessity. It required the assessor of each county to enroll all citizens liable for military duty and granted exemption only to ministers of the gospel, judges of the supreme court, county judges, county clerks, sheriffs, members of the legislature, the secretary of state, state treasurer, and clerks in telegraph offices while so employed. The military population was divided into three brigades, the whole in command of a major-general. The legislature put teeth in the law by providing for a draft, if, in response to a call for volunteers, an insufficient number should present themselves. The draft was not resorted to, however. To complete the story, some additional facts may be stated, even though the events did not occur within the period prescribed for this book.

Subsequent legislatures adopted persuasive, rather than coercive, measures. For example, there was passed, October 24, 1864, an act granting a bounty of $150 to each recruit enlisting for three years, or for the war, to meet the requirements of which an appropriation of $200,000 and a bond issue of $100,000 were authorized. At the same time, another law was passed granting additional compensation of five dollars per month to those who had previously enlisted, payment to be made to the soldier in interest-bearing bonds of the state. By still another law, the legislature in special session, December, 1865, extended the bounty provision to volunteers who enlisted for one year only, granting $50 to each of these.

11

The active existence in Oregon of the Knights of the Golden Circle, a secret organization formed to oppose the suppression of the rebellion, became known as early as the winter of 1861-2; and, by 1863, it had created widespread uneasiness, although this was due to the mystery in which all its movements were shrouded, rather than to particular acts of violence. Other names by which the order was known were "Golden Circle," "Old Guard," and "Friends of the Union," the last being the one generally adopted in Oregon, where, according to information obtained through spies, in the service of the adjutant-general of the Oregon militia, there were about 2500 members in 1863 and 1864. There were at least ten circles in the state, two in Portland, two at Salem, and one each in Scio, Albany, Jacksonville and Yamhill county. The Knights planned to resist the draft, if an attempt should be made to enforce it, and they planned to improve the first favorable opportunity of erecting a Pacific republic in the western states. Arms were imported, all the money in the treasuries of the local circles being expended for this purpose, and the members were drilled in the manual of arms in their lodges, stealthily, by night. A plot to assassinate Adjutant-General Reed was discovered and frustrated. Campaigns for membership were conducted more or less openly, representatives of the order even carrying on the propaganda at the state fair at Salem, where a number of members were initiated. These activities behind the lines kept the people, particularly those of the Willamette valley, in a constant state of apprehension. In an effort to offset the machinations of the Knights, an organization, also secret, calling itself the Union League of America for the State of Oregon, but later known as the Loyal League, was formed, its first president being Governor Gibbs, and its membership including many of the prominent and loyal citizens, but it lacked purposeful direction, and it had no appeal for those who abhorred secret political methods in general, so that it accomplished little. Gibbs and his adjutant-general, Reed, received the support of the Unionists in other and more effective ways, and the work of holding Oregon in line for the Union was carried on behind the scenes.

12

There was open complaint from official quarters, 1863, that Oregon had not raised its share of troops. General Alvord, in command of the military district, called for six additional companies to increase the First Oregon cavalry to full strength; but he was not able to give assurance of any kind of service other than such as the regiment was then experiencing. Governor Gibbs, January 10, 1863, issued a proclamation in accordance with General Alvord's requisition, and supported his appeal for men. "They will be needed," said the governor, "on the frontiers of this state and Washington territory, and for expeditions against the Snake Indians, who have so long been mercilessly engaged in robbing our fellow citizens. I cannot doubt that the citizens of Oregon, who have always responded to any demand for their military services, will in like manner respond to this call, thereby showing their loyalty to the government and aid in chastising marauding bands of Indians which infest our frontiers." Not even a rumor that the troops so raised would eventually be assigned to duty in Texas, which obtained currency about this time, had a favorable effect on recruiting, the young patriots being surfeited with promises that had come to naught. Not until March was it announced that a single company, that raised by Lieut. John F. Noble, was nearly full, and then it was said that there was a possibility that one more company might be recruited; but this, said the Argus, "will be the most that can be obtained, unless the legislature should be convened and grant an additional bounty."

In the same month, General Alvord declared in a letter to Rowland Chambers and other residents of Kings valley: "Oregon has
not raised her share of troops, California has sent nearly nine
regiments, and Oregon but seven companies into the field. California has her volunteers in Arizona, New Mexico, Utah and
Washington territory, as well as in Oregon, guarding your Willamette valley." Alvord's letter was written in reply to a petition
of inquiry to the governor, concerning the rumored intention of
the war department to abandon Fort Hoskins, in Kings valley,
and it further contained a promise that if the people of the valley
would fill the company then being recruited by Lieutenant Henry
C. Small, at Eugene, that company would be stationed at Hoskins. Both Small and Noble received commissions, and the single
additional company formed by the consolidation of the recruits
they had obtained was accepted as G company, the state's final
contribution to its cavalry regiment during the war.

<h2 style="text-align:center">13</h2>

A picturesque incident occurred in the spring of 1863 to relieve
the tedium of patrol duty and Indian skirmishing in the region
between the Rocky mountains and the Cascades. A campaign
against the unruly Snakes was projected, early in the year, by
Colonel Steinberger and four companies of Oregon cavalry. Two
companies of Washington infantry were drilled, ostensibly for
this service, but in reality for the purpose of making an impression on the Nez Perce's, who were now divided into factions, and
who had been summoned to a treaty-making council at the Lapwai
agency. The discovery of gold at Oro Fino and Florence, in what
is now the state of Idaho, had brought many trespassers to the
lands of the tribe and it was thought that a new treaty would be
necessary to satisfy them. The Nez Perce's chief, Lawyer, and his
followers were still friendly to the whites and were willing to
make further grants of land; a second group of the members of
the tribe led by Big Thunder, while not openly hostile, opposed
making concessions; a third, of which Eagle-of-the-Light and
Joseph were the spokesmen, constituted the war party and obviously awaited only a favorable opportunity to precipitate hostilities. Lawyer and Big Thunder, with about 2000 followers, attended the council, bringing some 12,000 horses to the treaty
grounds.

The spot chosen for conference was the mission established by Rev. H. H. Spalding, 1836. "The old, moss-grown apple trees planted by him at that early date," wrote W. V. Rinehart, one of the participants, "still stood as silent sentinels to mark the spot." Just before the parley began it was discovered that a large band of renegade Indians from the north, Coeur d'Alenes, Okanogans, Palouses—none of them Nez Perce's—were there mingling freely and trying to foment trouble and disorder. Companies D and E were, therefore, sent to escort them off the reservation, which was done in a way that made these Indians know they were unwelcome visitors, and they kept away, at least until the treaty was concluded.

14

In the course of the council the commissioners became anxious as to their personal safety. Ammunition was issued to the troops, and full arrangements were made for defending the position in the event of an outbreak, which was momentarily expected. A detail of twenty men, commanded by Capt. George B. Currey, proceeded to the Indian camp at the hour of midnight one night, and found fifty-three chiefs and sub-chiefs deliberating on the propositions which had been submitted to them by the commissioners. "The debate ran with dignified firmness," wrote Currey in a noteworthy account of this memorable event, "until near morning, when the Big Thunder party made formal announcement of their determination to take no further part in the treaty, and then, with a warm and emotional manner, declared the Nez Perce' nation dissolved; whereupon Big Thunder men shook hands with the Lawyer men, telling them with a kind but firm demeanor that they would be friends, but a distinct people. It did not appear from the tone of their short, sententious speeches, that either party was meditating present outbreak. I then withdrew my detachment, having accomplished nothing but that of witnessing the extinguishment of the last council fires of the most powerful Indian nation on the sunset side of the Rocky mountains."

The treaty completed soon afterward by the commissioners, therefore, bore the assent of only the Lawyer faction, about one-third of all the Nez Perce's. The more numerous element of that tribe, as well as the renegades from other tribes, the unconquered Modocs on the south, and the Bannocks of the middle country, continued to annoy and harass the whites and to keep the troops employed in the vast intermountain region until after the close of the Civil war.

15

From this time onward, duties of the troopers often took them into lands never before traversed by white men, unless by an occasional trapper of the fur trade era. In the task of convoying the immigrant trains of 1864, consisting in all of less than 400 wagons, they were assisted again by eastern volunteers recruited for that purpose, and commanded, as in 1862, by Capt. Medorem Crawford. Open war was made on disaffected Indian bands, who were pursued and shot when overtaken, if it could be shown that they had been guilty of murder or other crimes. A characteristic extract from the official account runs: "Leaving camp with thirty men late in the evening of the 2d of June, the next day we came upon the Indians. Seeing us, they attempted to escape, killed them and moved up the creek in search for more, but found only one, killed him and then returned to Camp Henderson, on the evening of the 5th of June."

This camp, named for Oregon's representative in congress at that time, was established early in 1864, near the mouth of Jordan creek, 330 miles from Walla Walla, and was the center of operations in southeastern Oregon for some time afterward. Alvord valley was discovered and named for the commanding officer of the military district. Some of the military camps during the Civil war were located as follows: Camp Polk and Camp Maury, on the Deschutes, near the mouth of Crooked river; Camp Dahlgren, slightly east thereof; old Camp Watson and Camp Lincoln on the headwaters of John Day river; Camp Logan, east of Canyon City, on the road to Colfax; Camp Colfax, at the Willow creek crossing of the Canyon City-Boise road, south of Baker City; Camp Currey, on Silver creek; Camp Wright, north of Harney lake; old Camp Alvord, on Horse creek in Alvord valley, east of Steens mountain range; Camp Lyon in the Jordan valley, east of Owyhee river; old Camp Warner, east of Warner lakes, and Camp Warner, west of the same lakes. Besides those in Oregon, Camp Lander and Camp Reed were established on Snake river in southern Idaho.

Travelling over sage brush plains one day and across the sands of the region of Harney lake on another, acting as scouts and convoys for scattered travellers to and from the mines, not infrequently in the saddle continuously for day after day with only field rations and with the lightest of equipment, the troopers suffered the usual discomforts entailed by constant marching, by drinking alkali water and by subsisting on a monotonous diet, but they won the distinction of being the first command that had ever traversed southeastern Oregon without meeting defeat. An expedition under Lieut. J. A. Waymire, acting in cooperation with a company of fifty-four citizens of the Harney valley, the latter commanded by C. H. Miller (Joaquin Miller) engaged a largely superior force of Utah and Nevada Indians, in Harney lake valley, in April, 1864, in a battle which Adjutant-General Reed has declared to be undoubtedly the hardest fought battle in which our troops participated.

16

In October, when the men, who had endured hard service in the Steens mountain region, had begun to look forward to a period of rest at Camp Alvord, orders reached Currey from district headquarters stating that it was believed that secessionist sympathizers meditated an outbreak on election day, and directing him to report at Fort Dalles at once. The prospect of fighting a white enemy, particularly one presumed to be attacking them in the rear while they were pursuing skulking redskins, so revived the energies of the troopers that they made the march from the Malheur river, at the point where it was crossed by the old emigrant road, to The Dalles, in nine days. Men from the regiment were then detailed for duty at various points where there had been rumors of sedition, but nothing unusual occurred, to the intense disappointment of most of the men.

There was said to be a plot to cast votes by large numbers of disloyal residents. General Alvord's order to the various officers commanding detachments read, in part: "It is alleged that if votes are challenged on that day, certain evil-disposed persons threaten to refuse to submit to the challenge and to resist it by arms. The legal right to challenge is indisputable and suppression of that right by armed men cannot be tolerated. You will not, however, use the military force except in subordination to the civil authority, and, if any firing on a mob occurs, let it be from the express requisition of the civil authority."

17

In addition to the exceptional hardships peculiar to the nature of their service, which were borne on the whole with fortitude, the cavalrymen suffered from the result of a congressional error which was even harder to endure, because it indicated complete lack of understanding, at Washington, of the nature of the sacrifices they were making. The order under which the regiment had been raised, based on an act of congress of 1861, required the men to furnish their own horses and horse equipment, for which the government allowed them forty cents a day. Congress, June 20, 1864, repealed the act of 1861, and the army paymaster received orders not to pay the per diem allowance. The horses that had cost the soldiers from $125 to $250 each, had now been reduced by hard marching and by poor forage to mere skeletons of the animals originally bought, and the prospect of obtaining supplies necessary to put them in passable condition for marketing, if this could be done at all, was slight. News of the repeal of the original law did not reach the troops in some instances until three months afterward. There were other causes of dissatisfaction, which included the failure of the war department to authorize the enlistment of friendly Indians, these having proved their value as scouts while serving without pay in the desert country of southeastern Oregon and northern Nevada.

The term of enlistment of the first six companies of the volunteer cavalry expired in the autumn of 1864, and the men who had been the first to respond to the call were gradually retired from the service. In the summer of this year, defense works at Point Adams, at the south side of the entrance of the Columbia river, were completed and christened Fort Stevens, for Gen. Isaac I. Stevens, of Washington territory, and were garrisoned by regulars, sent from California. The remaining Oregon cavalrymen were still held for service against the Indians, but in diminishing numbers, mere squads being compelled to patrol long stretches of infested trails.

18

A call from the federal government for a regiment of infantry was received by the governor, October, 1864, about the time that the legislature passed the bill for a bounty to encourage enlistments. Governor Gibbs issued a proclamation in which he pleaded earnestly for volunteers in order that resort to the extremity of a draft might be avoided. Private citizens subscribed funds for the payment of bounties in various localities. Polk, Josephine and Clackamas counties were among those that sought in this manner to make recruiting popular.

The dark hours for the Union had come, bringing encouragement to the friends of the Confederacy on the Pacific coast. Knights of the Golden Circle grew bolder and more militant. Between the dates of the Wilderness campaign and Sherman's march to the sea, secessionist sympathizers were supposed to be well organized and armed, particularly in the Long Tom and Siuslaw valleys. At Forest Grove, for example, the outlook was so ominous that a company of home guards was hastily formed. It was composed mainly of students of Pacific University and Tualatin Academy. This organization and others like it received Springfield rifles from the state arsenal at Salem. An effort was made to enroll all the able bodied men of the state under the militia law of 1862, in anticipation of a draft, which it was now believed would precipitate local outbreaks, and which on that account the people strongly desired to avoid.

Recruiting was stimulated by such devices as competition between counties for the honor of muster as Company A. It began almost simultaneously in Polk and Yamhill counties in November, 1864; in Polk under the direction of Lieut. Charles LaFollette, and in Yamhill and Washington under Lieut. Ephraim Palmer, a veteran of the Mexican war. Polk won, and LaFollette was rewarded with the captaincy of Company A, Palmer becoming captain of Company B. Recruiting in Washington county was stimulated at a mass meeting of citizens held at Tualatin Academy, December 1, 1864, the student element in the Tualatin valley being predominantly Unionist. Six companies were mustered in as the First Oregon Volunteer infantry, June 23, 1865, when George B. Currey, formerly captain of E company of the First Oregon cavalry, was commissioned as colonel. The higher regimental officers were drawn from the cavalry regiment, the veterans thus recruited receiving advancement in rank which they had despaired of ever winning by conspicuous deeds on the battlefield. The officers, who had served in the Oregon cavalry, besides Currey, were Lieut.-Col. John M. Drake, Maj. William V. Rinehart and Surgeon Horace Carpenter.

19

Lee's surrender at Appomattox occurred more than two months before the formal muster as a regiment of the Oregon infantry, but as had been the case with the cavalry in 1862, the companies were utilized for garrison duty while being drilled for further service. The first two companies mustered in, for example, were stationed at Fort Hoskins, where, on receipt of news of the assassination of President Lincoln, they were held under marching orders in anticipation of disturbances at Eugene, although the nearby presence of military force proved sufficient and no disturbance occurred.

20

The story of the First Oregon Volunteer infantry parallels that of the cavalry, the companies being scattered among the posts and camps of the military district of Oregon, then comprising Oregon, Washington territory, and also Idaho territory, which was set apart in 1863. Brigadier-General Wright was drowned, July 30, 1865, while on the way from San Francisco to Portland on board the steamship Brother Jonathan, having been transferred to the command of the Oregon district. The vessel was wrecked on the California coast, off Crescent City. This left Colonel Currey as ranking officer in command of the department of the Columbia, and Currey proceeded as soon as he could to organize a campaign against the Indians, in accordance with the views of western frontiersmen, which differed from those of the regular army establishment chiefly with respect to the policy of garrisoning the country in winter, which was favored by the volunteers and deprecated by the regulars. Currey's determination to test the volunteer theory was followed by characteristically prompt action; his plan contemplated sending every available man in the district against the Snake Indians and keeping them engaged, summer or winter, until the enemy were reduced to submission.

To avoid the encumbrance of unwieldy transportation trains, winter stations were selected in the midst of the Indian country and supplies were ordered sent to them during the autumn months. Of the numerous camps already mentioned as having been made use of at some stage of the military operations, the following were put into service for the particular purpose in hand; Camp Polk, near the mouth of Crooked river; Camp Logan, on the road between Colfax and Canyon City; Camp Lyon, in Jordan valley; Camp Alvord, on Horse creek in Alvord valley; a camp on Silvies river north of Malheur; Camp Colfax, at the Willow creek crossing of the Canyon City-Boise road; Camp Lander, at the site of Wyeth's old Fort Hall; and Camp Reed, near Salmon Falls. Troops were ordered to all these points with instructions to erect winter shelters for themselves.

21

It was Currey's idea that as soon as the first storms of winter were over, and the snow had hardened a little on the mountains, the troops at all the camps, except Reed and Lander, should be set in motion, concentrating in a moving column near Harney lake, travelling thence toward the region where it had been ascertained that the Indians were accustomed to congregate in winter. Currey believed that the hostiles could be forced to make a stand, either on the west side of Steens mountain range, or at the headwaters of the Owyhee, or that they would gather near the lakes west of Steens mountain, from where they would be driven, either south into Nevada or across the Goose Creek mountains to the Snake river plains, where they would be intercepted by the reserves. As incidents to the moving of the troops into position, the soldiers destroyed twenty-three Indian camps and their provision caches and killed about sixty Indians. "The only objections that can be urged against a winter campaign," wrote Currey in a subsequent official communication, "are those founded on the personal comfort of officers and men, and are totally unworthy the consideration of the soldier who is ambitious of performing soldierly duty."

Currey arranged to take the field in person, November 1, 1865. He was interrupted, however, by telegraphic orders from the war department, which had got wind meanwhile of the details of his plan, directing the mustering out of the volunteers. But the snow in the Blue mountains and the Cascades by this time had cut off communication, preventing the immediate recall of the men in the isolated camps. Currey, himself, was mustered out on October 14, 1865, together with such of the volunteers as were accessible at the time, and the remainder were gradually discharged until, in June, 1866, only two companies of Oregon men remained. The intervening winter was extremely cold, the troops stationed at the points chosen had no shelter until they provided it for themselves, and in point of hardships and privations their service probably exceeded even the miseries which fell to the lot of the cavalry.

22

The history of Oregon military participation in the Civil war, as has been seen, consists of a series of events peculiar to the still isolated nature of the northwest country. It moreover extends for a considerable period beyond the limit prescribed for this general history, beyond the formal surrender of General Lee, and into the summer of 1866, in which season Oregon volunteers were still pursuing Indians, escorting immigrant trains, guarding settlers against the depredations of small bands of thieving renegades, and occasionally laying down rifles and bayonets to perform prodigious labor with shovels and axes in clearing the way for wagon trains of settlers. At the close of the Civil war the immigrants took up the march across the plains in increasing numbers. The soldiers were not always rewarded by the gratitude of those whom they served. "I was often very much discouraged," wrote Lieut. Cyrus H. Walker, who commanded a detail assigned to duty on the Oregon trail, "in trying to help the immigrants in the way of advice. A majority of them were 'secesh,' and did not like Uncle Sam's boys much, and would not take good advice. It was quite refreshing to meet a train of Union men, a number of which passed, generally travelling by themselves."

Desultory warfare did not end, however, with the final discharge of the last Oregon companies and their replacement by regular troops, in 1866. The Indian menace was such, in the autumn of that year, that the Oregon legislature by joint resolution called on the military commander of the Pacific division for sufficient troops to furnish adequate protection to the citizens. A new turn was given to the course of events by the recruiting, under an act of congress, of two companies of friendly Indians on the Warm Springs reservation, led by William C. McKay and John Darragh, whom Gov. George L. Woods appointed first lieutenant. This precipitated a controversy between the governor and the war department over the propriety of conducting a war of extermination of the hostiles without regard to sex. The governor contended that the Ward massacre had demonstrated that Indian women were even more fiendish than the men, that they had taken the lead in devising tortures for the women and children among the captives, and that no peace could be obtained without unrelenting reprisals. Woods' instructions prevailed.

23

Brevt. Maj.-Gen. George Crook, now acting as lieutenant-colonel of the Twenty-third infantry, took the field in the Boise district in December, 1866, and by following the general policy of a winter campaign, outlined in 1865, made further progress toward restoring peace to the frontier of Oregon. He kept the hostiles constantly on the move, and this forced the larger bodies to sue for peace. This was concluded with the Warner lake and Malheur bands of the Shoshones in the closing days of 1865, leaving only a few irreconcilable Modocs and Shastas on the southern border of the state to be dealt with in the so-called Modoc war, which consisted about equally of a series of massacres by outlaw Indians, and of conflicts of authority between civil and military officials, and was not terminated until 1873.

Oregon's isolation at the time of the Civil war, and the cost of moving troops across the continent made impossible the hope that any Oregon regiment would be called to the front. The population was small and was well scattered.

The enrolled militia of Oregon, comprising all of the citizens of military age who had been listed by the county assessors under the law of 1862, consisted in 1865 of 12,793 men. Linn county led with 1300, Marion county was second with 1265, and Multnomah third with 1243. Tillamook enrolled twenty-eight. The militia organization, moreover, was complete in skeleton, with Governor Gibbs as commander-in-chief, Joel Palmer, major-general of the division, and Cyrus A. Reed, adjutant-general. Generals of the three brigades were James C. Tolman, John McCracken and Orlando Humason. These were in addition to the troops furnished for active service. The governor's staff consisted of the following: Col. Richard Williams, judge advocate; Col. Ralph Wilcox, surgeon-general; Col. Leonard J. Powell and Lieut.-Col. A. G. Hovey, John H. Mitchell, David M. Thompson, Chester N. Terry, Philip Schuyler and William P. Abrams, aides.

24

The Modoc war, to which allusion has been made, was, however, the most disastrous to the military forces of all the campaigns in the northwest, in this respect far outstripping the rout of Haller, or the defeat of Steptoe in the fifties. It cost the lives of forty-one soldiers, and more than that number were wounded. Seven commissioned officers were killed, among them Maj.-Gen. Edward

Richard Sprigg Canby, who was treacherously murdered, April 11, 1873, while a member of an unarmed peace commission that had gone to treat with Captain Jack, chief of the faction of the Modocs which had refused to go on the reservation provided for them. One other member of the peace commission, Rev. E. Thomas, a Methodist minister of California, was killed; a third, A. B. Meacham, was gravely wounded, left for dead and subsequently rescued, and two escaped. The principal part of the war was in California territory.

The Modocs were a degraded tribe, by common standards, whose men forfeited all claim to local esteem by profiting by the immoralities of their women, while affecting to be affronted by the proposal that they themselves be put to work. Nevertheless, they enlisted the sympathy of numerous sentimentalists at a distance from the scene, and civil and military authorities clashed so frequently over matters of policy in disposing of them that they were emboldened to acts of defiance which continued for about five years, from 1868 until 1873.

Officers of the regular army felt that that organization itself was open to criticism as to this tragedy, as it had been in 1858, by Steptoe's retreat, and a large force was promptly put in the field against Captain Jack's warriors. The latter, however, defeated or held off the troops in several engagements, killing twenty-two and wounding sixteen at one time, before they were at length overcome. A number of these Indians were indicted by a grand jury in Jackson county, Oregon, 1873. Governor Grover, who was then in office, issued an official protest against any action by the federal government that would give them immunity for their crime. Captain Jack and three other Modoc leaders were condemned by military court and hanged on October 3, 1873, which date may be taken as the termination of the Modoc war and of Indian warfare in Oregon.

The part that Oregon had in the Civil war was not as spectacular as it might have been had it been nearer the stage of the great national conflict. But though remote the state remained loyal and indirectly it did its full part for the Union. It would take a long honor roll to enumerate the names of those who went to the front, or those who were in the regiments locally used, and this is not the place to attempt to describe the many instances of individual heroism and courage. Most of those who survived the war became members of the Grand Army of the Republic, and the Oregon posts, though thinned in ranks, still loyally follow the flag and march at the head of every patriotic demonstration of loyal Oregon citizens. If this review has covered years beyond the opening years of the Civil war, and has therefore included details not originally embraced in the plan, excuse may be found in the natural desire to complete the entire story.

CHAPTER XXV

COUNTIES, CITIES AND TOWNS

1

"IT WOULD seem from this sorry catalogue," wrote Lieut. Neil M. Howison, U. S. N., on the occasion of his official visit to Oregon about the time that the boundary issue was decided, "that Oregon cannot yet boast of her towns and cities. Even in these, however, her improvement has been great and rapid, and population comes into the capital faster than the gigantic fir trees, which have lately been its sole occupants, can be made to disappear." A faithful picture is given by him of the territory, 1846, at the very beginning of the period of development of towns and cities.

The "capital" to which Howison alludes, is Oregon City, the pioneer urban community in all the Oregon Country, since the trading post at Fort Vancouver had remained a trading post, and Astoria was at this time, as Howison tells us, "in a state of transition, exhibiting the wretched remains of a bygone settlement, and the uncouth germ of a new one." Although a sailor, Howison had a particularly keen eye for matters agricultural, and lamented that so fruitful a region had not received more exotic plants and flowers than had yet arrived. The honey bee had not yet been naturalized, though sweet briar and honeysuckle, clover and wild grape blossom wasted their sweetness on the desert air, and in various ways the newcomers had neglected obvious opportunities; yet on the whole he found in the settlers a great deal to admire. "Many allowances," he said, "should be made in favor of these people. They come generally from the poorer classes of the western states, with the praiseworthy design of improving their fortunes. They brave dangers and accomplish Herculean labors on the journey across the mountains, and during this time are reminded of no law but expediency. That they should, so soon after their union into new societies at their new homes, voluntarily place themselves under any restraints of law or penalties whatever, is an evidence of a good disposition, which time will be sure to improve and refine." Of the population of the territory as a whole, he said that it deserved "to be characterized as honest, brave and hardy, rapidly improving in those properties and qualities which mark them for future distinction among the civilized portion of the world."

2

Oregon City, at the time of Howison's arrival, comprised some seventy buildings and a population of nearly 500 souls. Astoria had ten houses, including a warehouse, Indian lodges, a cooper's and a blacksmith shop. It had a white population of about thirty.

Linnton, which was then a town plat a short distance north of the present district bearing that name, occupied a promising situation, as the founders, Peter H. Burnett and M. M. McCarver, were men of initiative and resource, and had opened a road from their townsite to the Tualatin valley beyond the intervening ridge of hills. But its few inhabitants were "very poor and severely persecuted by mosquitoes, day and night."

Eight or nine miles above Linnton, Howison says, he came "to a more promising appearance of a town," which had been named Portland, whose proprietor had devoted his capital after the fashion of the period to "opening wagon roads, (assisted by neighboring farmers) into the Tualatin Plains." Twelve or fifteen new houses were then occupied and more were building; and "with a population of more than sixty souls, the heads of families generally industrious merchants," its prospects of increase were favorable. Opposite Oregon City was Multnomah City, claimed by Robert Moore, and a "sixth spot dignified with the name of town is Salem, of which," says Howison, "too little exists to be worthy of any attempt at description." The picture thus given by the visitor shows the very beginning of Oregon's towns.

3

But upon the determination of the northern boundary and the prospect of definite political status for the whole region, a movement of population on a great scale began, and within five years the number of ambitious and striving, or rather struggling, towns had greatly increased. Many of them had no more than a nominal pretension, for ambitious towns were laid out that never had more than a paper existence. Milwaukie, laid off on a donation of Lot Whitcomb, had 500 inhabitants, and was a rival of both Oregon City and Portland. St. Helens, already big with plans for the construction of a railroad, was scheming for control of water transportation. Milton, on Scappoose bay, not far from St. Helens, had been founded by Captains Nathaniel Crosby and Thomas H. Smith, and a number of doughty seafaring men, catching the enthusiasm of the hour, had invested considerable sums from their hard-earned savings in town lots, which, however, were soon inundated by a spring freshet that put an end to the city's hopes. No one believed that so many cities as had then been platted were needed for a population of a few thousand, but each group of town builders had faith and courage, and even confidence that its particular venture would outstrip all the rest.

The Oregon Spectator of December 13, 1849, contains a review of urban development to that time. Portland had already become a "place of general and active trade. Vessels usually discharge their cargoes at this point." "In addition," said the writer, "we have been informed that a steam sawmill will soon be in operation there." Lexington, now called Warrenton, on Clatsop plain, near the mouth of the Columbia, was then the county seat of Clatsop county. It was laid out in 1848. In contrast with the social philosophy of the present, which regards agriculture as the foundation of a sound economic structure, the Spectator observed that "the prosperity of the villages and towns of a country is the surest indication of the general prosperity of the country." Of Milwaukie it was noted: "It may be said to be the head of ship navigation on the Willamette. We are assured that any vessel that can come into the river at all can come up to Milwaukie. . . . But this is not the only thing which recommends this place to public notice. In the rapid improvement it is making, we have evidence that its citizens possess the right kind of go-ahead American energy to guarantee its prosperity. The erection of a new building is a matter of very frequent occurrence, and gives assurance of an active, busy population. Four sawmills and one grist mill are or soon will be in active operation."

Falls City, a new town then just laid out by Job Hedges, on the east side of the Willamette river, immediately above the falls and adjoining Oregon City, was the terminus of river transportation from above, and the promise was held out that "a lot will be cheerfully donated to any Christian denomination that may wish to erect a house of worship." Linn City was a town plat opposite Oregon City. Towns in Willamette valley were also spoken of. Syracuse, on the south side of the Santiam, in Linn county, Milton Hale, proprietor, was advertised as the head of navigation on the Santiam. Lafayette City was the "shire town" of Yamhill county. Between the falls of the Willamette and the mouth of the Clackamas, along a shore line of four or five miles, were not only Oregon City, but Green Point and Clackamas City, with a combined population of some twelve hundred, nearly all of whom were at the falls. "There are doubtless other paper towns in this valley," said the Spectator.

4

We get a good picture of the little town of Oregon City in the following year from the enthusiastic letter published in the Milwaukie Western Star, of December 25, 1850, evidently written by a resident of Oregon City: "Oregon City is blessed by a vast amount of water power," he said. "It has also two flouring mills, and five sawmills. There are three large hotels, one, the best in the territory, is called the Main Street House, and is kept by Col. S. Richmond. There are three dozen stores . . . there are two jewelry and watch establishments, eight or ten clothing stores, one drug store is an apothecary shop, a boot and shoe manufactory, a confectionery, hardware, crockery, and liquor stores; two bakeries, two barber shops, a tailor, saddler, the most extensive tinware manufactory in the territory, two cabinet shops, blacksmiths, a plow manufactory, a foundry, brick kiln and yard, &c. There is a Daguerrean artist, dentist, half a dozen physicians, and a score or more of lawyers. There are Methodist, Baptist, Congregational and Catholic meeting houses." A courthouse was under construction, as also a female seminary and a Baptist college.

The Main Street House, so referred to, had been operated by Sidney W. Moss, a picturesque character, assisted by a Mrs. Richardson, as housekeeper. Under that management it had been popular and successful.

In spite of the hopefulness of the Oregon City correspondent, however, there was a cloud upon the land titles of that town that would hamper its progress. Thurston, the delegate in congress, sent out numerous printed copies of an address that he had delivered in the house of representatives, December 20, 1850, "in defense of his constituents and his course as to the Oregon land bill." One of these copies reached John Orvis Waterman, editor of the Western Star, at the rival town of Milwaukie, who was glad of the opportunity to disclose the fact that Thurston had ruined Dr. McLoughlin's prospects of getting confirmation of his land title. The consequence would be that he would be unable to give deeds to lots in the town site.

In his March 13, 1851, issue the editor said: "It appears that Mr. Thurston caused a circular to be distributed among the members of congress, during the pendency of the land bill, in which he attacks Dr. McLoughlin and Hudson's Bay Company, saying many hard things of both . . . Mr. Thurston appears to seek popularity by crying British aggression and British influence, and more than insinuating that Dr. McLoughlin and his friends were aiders and abettors of the horrid massacre of Dr. Whitman and family, alleging that it was instigated by those of Catholic faith; and that he is laboring to defend 'my people' from such monsters. . . . We have made hundreds of inquiries of the first settlers, and they uniformly tell us that had it not been for Dr. McLoughlin, they must all have starved. We have yet to see the first man to corroborate Mr. Thurston's statements in that respect. . . ." In the April 10, 1851, number of the Star is printed in full the letter of Thurston to Nathaniel J. Wyeth inquiring as to the manner of McLoughlin's treatment of his enterprise and party. Wyeth writes defending and praising McLoughlin. Wyeth then writes to Hon. R. C. Winthrop, member of congress at Washington, as to what occasions the inquiry, and Winthrop says he asked Thurston whether there was anything pending in congress or before the executive in which McLoughlin's character or interest were concerned, and received answer in the negative. Then Wyeth writes to McLoughlin about Thurston's inquiry, and McLoughlin writes a defense. The fact was that Thurston had already, in drawing the donation land bill that had passed September 27, 1850, taken McLoughlin's rights from him, by making an express exception to the general provisions of the bill. The act referred to provided for the appointment by the president of a surveyor-general for Oregon, to survey the state, to set out section lines and mark the boundaries of donation claims.

5

The first number of the Western Star as a democrat weekly had appeared at Milwaukie, Thursday, November 21, 1850, with an address to the citizens of Oregon territory, and a prospectus, both of them over the name of the town proprietor, Lot Whitcomb. An editorial recited that "Milwaukie, as a town is little more than one year old, and numbers more than 500 inhabitants, with fair prospects of a rapid increase. There is in this place a good school, post office, tin shop, cabinet manufactory, shoe shop, blacksmith shop, three stores, printing office, warehouse, three taverns, two sawmills, a sawmill and grist mill being built, also a steamboat for the river navigation between Oregon City and Pacific City, touching at every point where there is business." The same newspaper stated that a free ferry had been in operation at Milwaukie for several months past, and that citizens of Portland who had suffered the evils of high prices, were resolved to establish a free ferry at that place. The information was furnished that press, type and paper, intended for the Oregonian, was on board the bark Keoka, in the river near Portland, and that T. J. Dryer, Esq., formerly city editor of the California Courier, would conduct a good readable newspaper.

There was considerable rivalry between Milwaukie and Portland in the early fifties. The Western Star was taken over by the editor John Orvis Waterman and William Davis Carter, February 27, 1851, and it and the Weekly Oregonian, under the intense and nervous management of editor T. J. Dryer, were always clashing. The first number of the Weekly Oregonian was issued December 4, 1850. When Whitcomb completed the steamboat, Lot Whitcomb, it began regular trips between Oregon City and Astoria. The boat was launched and christened on Christmas day, 1850, in the presence of Governor Gaines and other guests, but the festivity of the occasion was destroyed by the tragic death of Capt. Frederick Morse, of the schooner Merchantman, who was instantly killed by the bursting of a cannon.

In November, 1850, a new line of packet ships was advertised to operate between Milwaukie and San Francisco. The ships were the Ocean Bird, T. A. Hall, master; Keoka, D. W. Hall, master; and Louisiana, G. W. Roberts, master. They were advertised for fast sailing service, and assurance against detention in the rivers was given, "as they will be moved by a steamer from and to the mouth of the Columbia to Milwaukie." It was this kind of competition that spurred Portland to energetic effort, and caused citizens of that village to send a committee to San Francisco, where they bought and put in service the side wheel steamer Goldhunter, as elsewhere related.

6

January 9, 1851, a petition was filed in the Oregon legislature, by G. Heron and thirteen others, for a charter empowering them to build and operate a plank road from Olympia to some point on the Columbia river, and another project of the same kind was begun on a route from opposite Portland to Oregon City. The newspapers carried an advertisement for bids for carrying mails on various routes through the territory.

7

It is difficult to determine with precision the point from which Portland began to forge ahead of other cities in fulfillment of its destiny to become the metropolis of Oregon. Nevertheless, it seems to have been recognized in a very early day that the site located by Overton and Lovejoy and first improved by Lovejoy and Pettygrove, possessed natural advantages in being situated very near the head of river navigation for deep sea vessels, and also in having comparatively easy communication with the interior. "The situation of Portland," said the British officers Warre and Vavasour, in 1845, "is superior to that of Linnton, and the back country of easier access." One of the real reasons for Portland's early leadership was stated by Capt. John H. Couch, in the winter of 1846, to be that "the best water on the lower Willamette was opposite the Overton claim for shipping." Water transportation, and the means of reaching tributary farming regions, were matters of primary concern, and the opinion of so practical a man of affairs as this New England mariner and merchant carried more than ordinary weight.

The Portland townsite having been chosen and formally surveyed, as was done in 1844 and 1845, and a beginning having been made by the clearing of some land and the erection of a building or two, the personal factor in city building was a matter of importance. Lovejoy, for illustration, was a man of initiative and enterprise, as also was Pettygrove. Lovejoy was a native of Groton and a graduate of Amherst College, the first lawyer to begin the practice of law in the territory, and, with the exception of John Ball, the first to come to Oregon. Pettygrove was a Maine Yankee, a shrewd and successful merchant who had come to Oregon, 1843, by way of the Hawaiian islands with a stock of goods. Lovejoy and Pettygrove laid off four streets in 1845 and platted sixteen blocks. A few of the immigrants of 1845 saw the location of the new town and approved it, among them James Terwilliger, who acquired a claim some distance south of the first location, and also bought a lot within the townsite limits.

Couch, who had sailed into the Willamette as the representative of the Cushings, of Newburyport, Massachusetts, knew the disadvantages of Oregon City for merchandising. He had become acquainted with both the Clackamas rapids and the Ross island shoals, so that after a search for a better landing place, and in order to save expensive lighterage, he chose Portland as the future city. He selected the land claim adjoining that of Lovejoy and Pettygrove, on the north. Daniel H. Lownsdale, arriving with the immigration of 1845, found a claim to his liking, being attracted thereto by a creek afterward known as Tanner's creek, and by a small hemlock forest which served him well in a tannery enterprise that he soon established. William Johnson had located on the south of the Overton-Lovejoy townsite in 1842-3, thus being in all probability the first settler within the present limits of the city, on the west side of the river. The Johnson claim became the property of Elizabeth and Finice Caruthers, mother and son. Still beyond the Johnson-Caruthers location was the claim of Daniel Lunt, who sold later to Terwilliger, and south of Lunt's was the claim of Thomas Stephens, while the neighborhood of Portland Heights was claimed, in 1850, by Thomas Carter, an immigrant of 1848. On the east of the Willamette, James B. Stephens and Jacob Wheeler were early claimants of land along the waterfront.

Lownsdale bought Pettygrove's interest in the townsite for $5000worth of leather, and Lovejoy, whose health required a change of climate about that time, sold his interest to Benjamin Stark, who had come to the territory as purser of the Toulon.

The original founders of the city were now superseded, therefore, by Lownsdale and Stark. To these were added Stephen Coffin and W. W. Chapman, and a townsite promotion company, formed with Coffin, as president, and Chapman, as secretary, proceeded to offer lots for sale at low prices as inducements for the erection of buildings. This plan met with some success. W. S. Ladd arrived from Vermont, 1850, with plans already matured for supplying merchandise to miners, as the gold excitement was then at its height. For a brief time Portland sustained a loss of population in consequence of the stampede to the gold diggings, but soon regained its lost ground; and, in general, those who remained behind, or returned in time, fared better than those who lingered and sought fortune in the placers of California.

8

A vast change took place in something less than three years. Extracts from a contemporary diary give this picture of Portland in January and February, 1848: "Portland has two white houses and one brick and three wood colored frame houses and a few cabins. . . . We traveled four or five miles through the thickest woods I ever saw, all from two to six feet through, with now and then a scattered cedar; and intolerably bad road. . . . These woods are infested with wild cats, panthers, bears and wolves." By contrast, another observer wrote in November, 1850: "You will perhaps be astonished when I tell you that Portland has become the principal town of Oregon. . . . There are now under way not less than 150 new houses, and there have been built over 100 dwellings during the last summer and fall, eighteen stores, six publick boarding houses, two large churches, fifteen smaller stores. We have cut a road through to Tuality Plains." It was this road that connected Portland's water front with the interior valley, and made Portland the natural port for shipment of the products of the farms.

The city continued to grow rapidly. Rev. Ezra Fisher, writing January 3, 1852, thus described the settlement: "Portland is the principal port in Oregon. The present population is estimated at 700 souls. It contains thirty-five wholesale and retail stores, two tin shops, four public taverns, two steam sawmills, one steam flouring mill, with two run of stones, six or eight drinking shops and billiard tables, one wine and spirit manufactory, a variety of mechanic shops and from eight to fifteen merchant vessels are always seen lying at anchor in the river or at the wharves. . . . This is the place where nearly all the immigrants by water land and from which they will go to their various points of destination."

The first frame house, as distinguished from a cabin hewed entirely from logs, had been erected near the present corner of Front and Washington streets by Capt. Nathaniel Crosby, who brought the lumber ready-cut from Maine. The traditional carrying of coals to Newcastle was outdone by this Yankee skipper. John Waymire had set up the first whipsaw operated by hand, and William H. Bennett and associates had built the first shingle mill. The first steam sawmill was begun in 1849 and completed in 1850 by W. P. Abrams and Cyrus A. Reed. Three religious denominations, Methodist, Congregational and Catholic, had built their first churches in the settlement.

9

The city was incorporated in 1851, and at the first municipal election, held April 7 of that year, H. D. O'Bryant was chosen mayor; W. S. Caldwell, recorder, and Robert Thompson, Shubrick Norris, George H. Barnes, L. B. Hastings and Thomas G. Robinson, councilmen. The young city plumed itself, not without good reason, on the erection of three brick buildings in 1853, the builders being W. S. Ladd, on a location on Front street between Stark and Washington; Lucien Snow, on Front street between Pine and Oak; and D. C. Coleman, at the southeast corner of Front and Oak.

H. W. Corbett built what was then regarded as a highly pretentious residence on the block now bounded by Fifth, Sixth, Yamhill and Taylor streets, 1854. That year was also memorable for the creation of Multnomah county, with Portland as the county seat, the citizens having been compelled before that date to travel to the county seat of Washington county, which was Hillsboro, to transact official business. The assessed valuation of city property in 1855 had reached $1,195,034 and there was a population of 1209, which gave color to its boast that it was not only the most populous, but the richest city per capita north of the California boundary. By various and rapid stages it continued to expand. The city limits were extended, 1864, to include the Caruthers claim on the south.

The city advanced rapidly in commercial importance during the Indian wars, of the decade of the fifties, during which it was headquarters for military supplies, and it again leaped forward with the opening of a new era of mining development in Idaho, British Columbia and eastern Oregon in the sixties. Macadam road, begun in 1858, extending from the city limits southward, was the first of its kind in Oregon.

10

Litigation over titles to the lands on which the city is situated was the logical outcome of the peculiar conditions under which early settlement was made. Title to the Oregon Country was as yet unsettled when the original townsite was located and staked out, 1845, and there was no law by which land could be held, except such as had been provided by the provisional government, which had not foreseen urban growth. When Lownsdale bought the townsite and made Coffin his partner, it was agreed that lots that had already been sold should be confirmed to purchasers, as soon as the vendors would be able to obtain title for themselves. But the donation land act of 1850 required that locations when made should be for the use and benefit of the purchaser only, and there was a vexatious provision that "all future contracts, by any person or persons entitled to the benefit of this act, for the sale of the land to which he or they may be entitled under this act, before he or they have received a patent therefor, shall be void."

Multifarious issues, technical and ethical, that arose out of this situation were adjudicated in a series of suits which occupied the attention of the courts for a decade, beginning with 1863, and the essential equities were preserved in a decision by Judge Lorenzo Sawyer, of the United States circuit court, who viewed the entire litigation in the light of the history of the period in which the issues arose, and held that, in the state of society at the time Oregon was settled, a town could have been built in no other way than by means of contracts made with proprietors who would agree to perfect and convey title when opportunity should offer, as had been done. This decision, upholding the validity of such contracts, and in which Judge Matthew P. Deady concurred, cut a veritable Gordian knot of technicalities and restored a normal equilibrium by confirming the titles of a large number who had erected improvements on their holdings.

11

Another series of contests arose from the nebulous condition of the title to the water front. Lovejoy and Pettygrove had platted several blocks but had left the land immediately adjacent to the river bank for a landing place, and were regarded as having set apart this frontage for general public use. In 1850, Lownsdale had a survey made and a map was drafted by John Brady, according to which the river bank was laid off in town lots varying in depth with the meanderings of the river. The city council in 1852 adopted the Brady plat, which was the only map in existence at the time, thereby indirectly confirming the river bank lots and forfeiting its claim to what was then known as the levee. The council, 1860, attempted to rescind this action, and a crusade was begun against the holders of the property along the river, but the courts decided in favor of the lot owners.

Covered wharves, necessary to the handling of goods in winter, had been built on the water front as private enterprises. Captain

Couch had built one on his own claim north of the first townsite. The municipality held out no prospect of making wharves as public improvements, so that opposition to private ownership on the water front gathered little force, and the crusade was permitted to lapse. The courts held that there was no proof that the levee had been dedicated to public use. Coffin, however, dedicated a small tract on the river between Jefferson and Clay streets, which he designated as a public levee, and this was held to have been duly dedicated to public use.

12

From an address of Judge William Strong, delivered, 1878, before the Oregon Pioneer Association, we have a picture of Astoria as it appeared to him August 14, 1850, when he first reached the Columbia river with his family after a long voyage around the Horn. He said:

"When Astoria was pointed out as we rounded the point below, I confess to a feeling of disappointment. Astoria, the oldest and most famous town in Oregon. We had expected to find a larger place. We saw before us a straggling hamlet consisting of a dozen or so small houses, irregularly planted along the river bank, shut in by the dense forest. We became reconciled and, indeed, somewhat elevated in our feelings when we visited the shore, and by its enterprising proprietors were shown the beauties of the place. There were avenues and streets, squares and public parks, wharves and warehouses, churches, schools and theaters, and an immense population, all upon the map. Those proprietors were men of large ideas, large hopes. They assured us that in no short time Astoria was to become the commercial metropolis of the Pacific coast. Some of those proprietors have passed away and gone where they are beyond the reach of hope or fear. Some remain, and though their eyes sparkle and brighten when they talk of the future grandeur of Astoria, they manifest a slight feeling of sadness and drop the subject with the remark: 'This may not be in our day, but it will surely come. You and I may not see it, but our children will.' Astoria at that time was a small place, or rather, two places—the upper and lower town, between which there was great rivalry. They were about a mile apart, with no road connecting them except by water and along the beach. The upper town was known to the people of lower Astoria as 'Adairville.' The lower town was designated by its rival as 'old Fort George,' or 'McClure's Astoria.' A road between the two places would have weakened the differences of both, isolation being the protection of either. In the upper town was the custom house, in the lower two companies of the First U. S. Engineers [First Artillery] under command of Maj. J. S. Hathaway. There were not, excepting the military and those attached to them and the custom house officials, to the best of my recollection, to exceed 25 men in both towns."

After many disappointments and discouragements, with more than a fair share of the hope deferred that maketh the heart sick, the self-reliance of the residents of the city of Astoria asserted itself. The feeling that the facilities for commerce, if once provided, would stimulate trade has been the mainspring of civic enterprise that has led to the creation in recent years of ample docks, elevators, terminals, a sea-wall, and well paved streets, and excellent public buildings. The contrast between Judge Strong's picture and the present is remarkable.

13

The manual labor school for the benefit of the native children was originally established, 1834, by Jason Lee, ten miles below the city of Salem. But in 1841, when the mission was moved to Chemeketa, a larger school building was constructed at that place at a cost of some $10,000.

In the autumn of 1842, the Indian mission school was housed in the new building. In 1844, the manual training of native children was abandoned, and Rev. George Gary, who had come to Oregon to supersede Lee, sold the building, with possessory rights to the land on which it stood, consisting of 640 acres, to the Trustees of the Oregon Institute for $4000, to be paid at a future time. The school was converted into one for white children, and ultimately became Willamette University. The building was destroyed by fire, 1872.

Oregon Institute, however, was not so incorporated under the provisional government as to be authorized to hold lands. At a meeting of the trustees, May 25, 1845, it was decided to continue the school and to raise money for the purpose by sale of town lots, and also to survey and lay out a city. Arrangements were then made with Rev. David Leslie, Rev. L. H. Judson, Henry B. Brewer and W. H. Willson, who held adjoining tracts of land near the Institute, to extend the lines of their respective land claims. Judson provided 320 acres, Leslie 200 acres, Brewer 80 acres, Willson 40 acres, to be located by Willson in one tract, for "endowing and sustaining a literary and religious institution of learning . . . the same being situated upon the tract of land upon which the town of Salem, in the county of Champooick, in Oregon Territory, is situated." This was before the land law of 1850 was adopted.

J. Quinn Thornton was consulted as legal adviser of the parties named, and he prepared a bond in the sum of $100,000 signed by Willson, under date July 11, 1847, in favor of Brewer, Judson, Parrish, Beers, Abernethy, Roberts, Wilbur and Thornton, obligating Willson to perfect the title to the 640 acres. If this, 60 acres with the Institute building, were to be devoted to and used for an institution of learning and religion; certain proceeds from the sale of lots to be accounted for as in the bond stated, a part to be applied to payment of the $4000 of the Gary purchase, and finally, unsold portions of the tract were to be conveyed as stipulated.

But, as Mrs. Willson was not a party to the bond, and under the donation land law, became the owner of 320 acres of the tract, and as she could not be compelled to account for any part of her half of the claim, there were unforeseen complications, affecting the validity of titles in the city of Salem that were not cleared up for a long time.

The act for organizing the territory of Oregon, August 14, 1848, had an express provision, in its section 17, as follows: "All bonds, recognizances, and obligations of every kind whatsoever, valid under existing laws within the limits of said Territory, shall be valid under this Act, . . . and all penalties, forfeitures, actions and causes of action, may be recovered under this Act in like manner as they would have been under the laws in force within the limits composing said Territory at the time this Act shall go into operation."

14

In 1852, there were perhaps half a dozen families living in Salem. The store was owned by John D. Boon, who was then justice of the peace, and afterward treasurer for territory and state. The mission building and mill were standing, besides a few other buildings. When the legislature assembled at this town, 1855, there were few accommodations for the members. It met in the residence of J. W. Nesmith, located near where Salem flouring mill was afterward constructed. The supreme court, for its December, 1852, session, met in a building on High street, then recently put up by Charles Bennett. Between Commercial street and the river was a thicket, and there was a schoolhouse south of Marion square. Mill creek bottoms afforded a favorite camping place for visiting Indians, and a small chair factory was in that neighborhood. There was one barber, but several physicians could be counted.

Salem, from an early day, had an able bar, which included L. F. Grover, Joseph G. Wilson, E. M. Barnum, Elijah Williams, B. F. Harding, Cyrus Olney and Reuben P. Boise. The first courthouse was erected, 1854, but the present structure was built, 1873, upon a block donated by the original proprietor.

One of the great engineering projects of these times was the construction of a canal to supply water power and clear water for the Salem woolen mills, elsewhere described in these pages. The buildings were erected in 1856. The canal drew its water from the Santiam near Stayton. It used the bed of Mill creek for part of the distance into Salem.

15

The territorial capitol building was first at Oregon City. It was a two story frame structure, with basement. In 1854-5, however, the legislative session was convened at Salem, in a partly finished building then under construction. The legislature voted to move to Corvallis for the next session, but no sooner took up quarters at that place than it voted to go back to Salem, which it did before the session was finished. The new quarters at Salem were in the same building that had been occupied before, but now the structure was completed. A fire broke out, December 30, 1855, and this new capitol was totally destroyed. Thereafter the legislature continued its sessions in rented quarters until a new and substantial capitol was erected on the site of the one that had been burned.

In December, 1872, the state legislature appropriated $100,000, and appointed a commission, consisting of Gen. John F. Miller, Henry Klippel and Samuel Allen, who selected the site, in block 84, facing Willson Park. Several eminent architects submitted plans, but Krumbein and Gilbert's plan was accepted. The excavation was done by labor of inmates of the state penitentiary, and the corner-stone was laid with appropriate ceremonies, October 8, 1873, at which Gov. L. F. Grover presided. The building was 264 feet in length and 75 feet in width, with projection of wings, 100 feet. The dome was planned to reach a height of 180 feet, but this was not finished until 1893. This entire structure was destroyed by

fire on the evening of April 25, 1935, and when the ruins were being removed the corner-stone was opened July 31, 1935, and documents that had been deposited therein in 1873 were found in good
state of preservation. November 9, 1935, the legislature, at a special session, decided to rebuild the capitol, on the same site, at a
cost of $2,500,000.00.

16

Some further particulars as to the early history of Salem may
be of interest.

After the survey of 1846, a few lots were sold, which were paid
for in wheat, and in due time the question of selecting a name
arose. The Indian name "Chemeketa," freely translated, was
"place of rest," and this was proposed by Rev. Josiah L. Parrish
as a name for the new settlement. But Willson pointed out that by
a happy coincidence, there was also a biblical word meaning nearly the same thing, "Salem," or "Sholum," a "city of peace," which
was then decided upon. But the missionary influence diminished
somewhat with continued accessions of new and sometimes irreverent and ungodly elements to the population, so that in the summer of 1853 the subject of changing the name was seriously agitated. "Chemeketa," "Woronoco," and "Multnomah," among
others were proposed. Petitions asking that the change be made
were circulated for presentation to the legislature, and received a
considerable number of signatures.

In the proceedings of the fifth territorial legislature, which
met, December, 1853, it appears that Mr. Colby presented the
petition of R. C. Geer and others, praying that the name of
Salem be changed to "Thurston," or "Valena." On the same day
Mr. Humason presented the petition of Chester N. Terry, and
others, to change the name to "Corvallis," and a resolution was
also introduced in the council to change the name of Marysville to
Corvallis. The rather spirited contest resulted in giving the name
Corvallis to the city which now bears it. The act was passed December 20, 1853.

The various Salem petitions had been referred to a select committee of the council, which submitted a report, December 21,
1853, recommending that the name be changed to "Chemawa."
Action on the report was delayed until January 13, 1854, when
two other amendments were offered, "Willamette" and "Bronson"

being suggested, the latter without much seriousness, but apparently in honor of a respected pioneer resident. The name "Chemawa" was adopted by the council and the bill went to the house for concurrence, where it was called up, January 17, 1854. The debate seems to have been the occasion of a good deal of merriment and persiflage. Mr. Simpson moved to substitute "Valena" for "Chemawa." Mr. Scott raised a laugh by moving to amend the amendment by striking out "Valena" and inserting "Pike," and insisted on a vote. On motion of Mr. Kelly, "Chemawa" was changed to "Chemawah," whereupon on motion of Mr. Simpson "Chemawah" was stricken out and "Victoria" inserted. The prankish mood of the house having by this time exhausted itself, the bill was considered with due gravity and was indefinitely postponed, and the name Salem has been retained.

17

Motives that actuated the founders of Salem are noticeable in the beginnings of other towns in the Willamette valley. Forest Grove grew up on the site of a land claim originally located by Solomon Emerick, later a resident of the village of Cornelius, who sold his holdings to one Cary for a consideration said to have been a merchandise order on the Hudson's Bay Company for $6.00, and the land passed from the possession of Cary to that of Rev. Harvey Clark, who gave liberally of his lands and other substance to the founding of the school which has since developed into Pacific University.

18

Something of the same spirit was caught by William T. Newby, who settled, 1844, on a land claim in the present site of McMinnville, where he built a mill in 1853, laid out a town in 1855, named for his former home, McMinnville, Tennessee. He made a large donation of land for the endowment of McMinnville College (now called Linfield College) with the announced purpose of furnishing liberal culture without the necessity of travelling far from home.

Monmouth, named for Monmouth, Illinois, and largely settled by members of the Christian Church, was laid off in 1855, also with the primary motive of founding a denominational college with the proceeds of the sale of lots. The normal school of Monmouth is the outgrowth of this early planning. Bethel, in Polk county, similarly begun, gives testimony by its name to the religious spirit of the time; Amity bears witness to the resolution of another group of peace-loving citizens to foster neighborly good feeling. In the town names of such places as Sublimity, named by its United Brethren founders in tribute to the scenic grandeur of its surroundings, and Philomath, to which place they subsequently removed, are still other evidences of the aspirations of the earliest settlers for the higher things in life. A number of these settlements, however, never attained the stature of cities, and can hardly be called towns. Carlton was named for John Carl, Sr., an old settler, about the year 1875. Rainier was named for the great snow peak, that is in the state of Washington. Charles E. Fox settled there, 1851, and was the first postmaster, when the place was called Eminence. The mountain was named by Vancouver for Admiral Peter Rainier of the royal navy. Oswego was named for Oswego, New York, by A. A. Durham, pioneer of 1847. Seaside got its name from Seaside House, the name of Ben Holladay's famous hotel near the ocean shore. In fact, the first postoffice was called Seaside House. Tillamook, from the Indian tribe of that name, had the names Lincoln and Hoquarton in early times.

19

The single communist experiment associated with the early growth of neighborhood settlements, in Oregon, is suggested by the name of Aurora, which was established, 1856, on French Prairie, near Pudding river, as the result of a noteworthy movement which brought to Oregon upwards of 500 of its most industrious and thrifty settlers. This colony, which crossed the plains from an earlier settlement of the kind, Bethel, Missouri, settled at first on the shores of Willapa harbor, in Washington territory, but soon abandoned that location, partly because of its lack of communication with the outside world, and settled in Marion county instead. It prospered under the management of a strong leader, Dr. William Keil, but gradually disintegrated, as idealistic enterprises are wont to do in such circumstances, upon the death of the founder.

The Aurora colony was remarkable in many ways, and its leader a man of unusual individuality and character. Having become imbued with communistic ideas through his early associations in Prussia, where he was born, he saw in America a field of opportunity. He initiated his experiment in Bethel, whence he sent scouts, 1853, to the Pacific coast. As a result, four parties came west in 1855, two travelling by ox-teams across the plains, with the property of the community, and two coming by way of the isthmus of Panama. Dr. Keil himself chose the site of Aurora, 1856, and named it for his third daughter. The prosperity of the colony under his management is indicated by the circumstances that, although the original Aurora site was purchased by Dr. Keil for $1000, the communal property had so increased in value by 1870, when the colony had a population of 320, that the portion lying in Marion county was assessed at $80,000, and further holdings in Clackamas county were assessed at $40,000. After the death of Keil the property was divided among the members of the colony under the direction of the United States district court.

20

The names of these early towns were apt to be changed whenever they proved on trial to be unsatisfactory, efforts in that direction usually not encountering such opposition as was met at Salem. Dallas, originally Cynthia Ann, not only changed its name, but moved its townsite also. First situated on the highlands on La Creole, opposite its present location, where it was settled in 1852, it found the water supply insufficient for an ambitious town, and moved bodily a distance of a mile or so, in 1856. The county in which it was the principal settlement having been named for President Polk, it seemed only fair that the town should bear the name of Vice-president Dallas.

Marysville, first located, in 1846, by Joseph C. Avery, of Pennsylvania, and laid out as a town by him in 1848, was called after Mary's river, which had been previously named in honor of Mary Lloyd, believed to have been the first white woman to step across that stream. But Marysville, California, rapidly outstripped Marysville, Oregon, after California gold was discovered. Confusion resulted, and mail intended for Marysville, Oregon, often went astray, so that the name Corvallis, a Latin compound, intended to mean "heart of the valley," was bestowed upon it by the legislature in December, 1853, as has been noted. The name is said to have been made up by Avery, who was a pioneer of 1845. Becoming, in 1864, the site of a school conducted under the auspices of the Methodist Church, South, which subsequently surrendered its denominational claims in order that the college might be developed into a seat of agricultural and industrial instruction, under the patronage of the United States government as well as of the state, Corvallis entered the list of Oregon communities noted for their influence in education. The college is now a unit in the system of higher education adopted by the state.

Albany was named Takenah by its founders, who adopted the pleasant sounding word employed by Indians to describe the large pool or depression created by the Calapooya river, as it enters the Willamette; but the habit that certain irreverent old-timers had of freely translating this as "hole in the ground" clouded it, and on petition of the citizens the legislature, January, 1855, changed the name to Albany, chosen by Thomas Montieth, an early settler, who previously had lived in Albany, New York.

21

The history of southern Oregon towns furnishes examples of similar changes, more especially since the mining era, which induced the first settlement of that region, brought a shifting population that evinced little veneration for the traditions of the past. Waldo, for illustration, which was the original county seat of Josephine county, and bears a familiar pioneer name, was first called Sailor Diggings, from the circumstance of a party of seafaring men having found rich placers there. Phoenix, a one-time rival of Jacksonville, was previously Gasburg.

The practice of naming Oregon towns after cities in the eastern states, as illustrated by Albany, McMinnville and Portland, prevailed to a considerable extent. It was exhibited in Lafayette, named by Joel Perkins, owner of the original land claim and a former resident of Lafayette, Indiana; by Dayton, which was settled in the winter of 1848-9 by Joel Palmer and Andrew Smith; by Independence, where E. A. Thorp, a public spirited citizen, chose the name in honor of Independence, Missouri; and in double measure by Ashland, which took the name of two other Ashlands—one in Ohio, the former home of the builder of Ashland Mills, and the other, Ashland, Kentucky, which was the home of Henry Clay, many of the early settlers in that neighborhood being whigs.

The history of Lafayette recalls one of the minor tragedies in town development. This pioneer settlement was laid off in town lots, 1847, and was surveyed in 1848; it had a dozen houses early in 1849. It grew in physical proportions, and for a considerable time was important as the home of culture, the seat of the pioneer Lafayette Academy, and the occasional gathering place of important citizens. It was the county seat of Yamhill county when the county possessed relatively large political power; it obtained, 1859, a $15,000 courthouse, which was worth mentioning in that period of economy in public expenditures. It acquired a $7000 jail in 1877, an important occurrence in its time; but fortune ceased to smile when railroad building began, and the town was not included in the builders' plans. The crowning civic calamity for Lafayette was the removal of the county seat to McMinnville, 1887.

The town of Silverton, in Marion county, got its present name about 1855, although there had been sawmills and a grist mill at Milford and other near locations as early as 1852. The name Silverton was recognized by the postal department, 1855, when the postoffice with that name was established, and Charles Miller was appointed as postmaster. The name Silver creek for the stream itself was used for some years before that date. John Lewis and Joseph Jones had a blacksmith shop there in 1854, and Charles Lorraine Worthington kept a drug store, 1857. Solomon and Edward Hirsch, both of whom became distinguished, the one as United States minister to Turkey and the other as state treasurer, were partners, 1860, in a general merchandise business. They were succeeded by Henry J. Herman and Edward Hirsch, who in turn sold out to John C. Davenport and John Wolfard. The sawmills of John Smith and John Barger were located above the present location of the town, 1852. In the next year they erected a flour mill. White and Holland are said to have built the first building in the town, 1853.

22

Eugene, first called Eugene City, and Hillsboro were named for their pioneer settlers—Eugene for Eugene F. Skinner, who located a land claim in 1846 on a site which included Skinner's Butte, overlooking the present city, and Hillsboro for David Hill, a pioneer of 1842, who settled on the site in 1847, but who, however, called his place Columbus, which was converted into Hillsborough by common agreement of the neighborhood when Hill became postmaster. The name was shortened to Hillsboro in due course of time.

A letter from Eugene F. Skinner to Gen. Joseph Lane, dated February 24, 1854, gives a statement of the progress of the new town, with names of some of its first citizens. He says: "Eugene City is fast improving. There are now three stores, two blacksmith shops, and numerous small buildings going up." Among the citizens enumerated by Skinner are J. Huddleson, J. L. Bromby, P. Blair, Benjamin Davis, William Smith, F. McMurry, H. Shaw, F. Scott, H. G. Hadley, D. M. Risdon, Z. Vivert, Thomas Holland, I. M. Lakon, I. Davis, A. W. Patterson, R. Robe, S. Goff and I. Gillespie.

23

Settlement of southern Oregon was delayed, as has appeared, by the warlike character of the Indians who inhabited the region, and was alternately interrupted by Indian outbreaks and accelerated by the discovery of gold, the latter event attracting large numbers of daring and adventurous individuals who were willing to brave danger for the sake of wealth.

During the Gaines administration an extension of surveys in the southern region was undertaken, including further exploration of the Umpqua valley by Jesse Applegate. Umpqua City, Scottsburg, Elkton and Winchester were established upon Umpqua river. Scottsburg, settled by Levi Scott, who was conspicuous in the early annals of the country as trail builder for other immigrants, was founded in 1850, and became the seat of government of Umpqua county prior to the absorption of that county by Douglas. The first newspaper in southern Oregon, the Umpqua Weekly Gazette, was issued at Scottsburg April 28, 1854, Danied Jackson Lyons, editor, and William J. Beggs, publisher. Scottsburg succumbed in due course to the superior advantages of Crescent City, California, as a seaport, and to changes in the common route of travel by road, which took place when the country became better known. Winchester was laid out by Addison C. Flint, 1850. Each of these towns had an important place in pioneer history. Roseburg, another pioneer town of southern Oregon, better favored by subsequent events and especially by its location on the main line of the railroad from the Columbia river to California, was settled in September, 1851, by Aaron Rose, whose name it still bears. Roseburg soon outranked Winchester in importance, but Winchester in its time was a busy settlement. The legislature of 1851-2

authorized a road to be built from Marysville, later Corvallis, to
Winchester, and it was the first county seat of Douglas county.
When in 1852 voters decided in favor of Roseburg as the permanent county seat, the people of Winchester, not to harbor a grudge
perpetually, moved their town bodily to this new settlement and
cast their fortunes with their victorious neighbors.

24

Events of particular historical interest in southern Oregon,
however, were the discovery of gold on Jackson creek, December,
1851, or January, 1852, by two prospectors, James Cluggage and
John R. Pool, and the ensuing stampede to the region. This resulted in the founding of the town of Jacksonville, and in the establishment of a rough and ready system of government based on
the experience of the first miners in California, well calculated to
meet the immediate necessities of a mining population. Here for
a time law was administered by judges elected by popular vote
and known by the Spanish term as alcaldes. One of them was
called upon to try a case in which a miner, who had been unable
because of illness to comply with the conditions necessary for
holding title to his mining claim, charged that his partner had
taken advantage of his distress and had selfishly seized the property. The alcalde rendered a decision adverse to the plaintiff,
which was so unpopular in the community that a public meeting
was held. A supreme alcalde was elected, before whom, as a kind
of court of appeals, the case was retried and the complaining partner was reinstated by a decision in which in all probability the essential equities were preserved. At any rate, popular opinion was
sometimes given expression in judicial pronouncements then as
now. The case was conducted for the respective litigants by P. P.
Prim and Orange Jacobs, both of whom attained eminence in
their profession. Prim was later circuit judge and chief justice of
the Oregon supreme court. Jacobs later removed to Washington
territory, where he became chief justice of the supreme court.

Jacksonville became the home of the second newspaper in southern Oregon, the Table Rock Sentinel, established November 24,
1855, by W. G. T'Vault, a former editor of the Oregon Spectator,
and a pioneer journalist of the Willamette valley. Jacksonville
prospered, since it was situated near a rich mining region, and
with its advantages as a trading station on the way to California,

the city acquired a position in the political and commercial affairs of the territory and state.

Canyonville, on Canyon creek, in south Umpqua valley, was in the so-called Umpqua canyon, where pioneers coming over the new southern road to Oregon, 1846, had great hardships. The first postoffice, called North Canyonville, was established, 1852. The present name of the postoffice dates from June 1, 1892.

25

In the vast region east of the Cascades, need for local government preceded the creation of towns. Wasco county, when it was organized by act of the territorial legislature, January 11, 1854, comprised all of the territory east of the Cascades and south of the Columbia river. It had as its county seat Dalles City, afterward called The Dalles, the only town in that spacious region, a place that had grown up around the mission established by Daniel Lee, nephew of Jason Lee. In 1847, the mission was abandoned, and the property was transferred to Dr. Marcus Whitman in consideration of $600. His nephew, Perrin B. Whitman, was placed in charge. After the Whitman massacre the American Board retransferred the property to the Missionary Society of the Methodist Church. The latter subsequently asserted title, made surveys and, after much litigation, obtained a patent. In the meantime a military reservation had occupied a part of the site, and for this and for mission property destroyed the government paid to the society $24,000 damages. Walter D. Bigelow took up a donation claim of 320 acres and cultivated it until 1860. In 1852 a town was in existence on part of the land formerly claimed by the Methodist mission, and this town, under direction of Wasco county, was surveyed and laid out in lots, blocks and streets; the town was incorporated as Dalles City in 1857, and record thereof was subsequently entered in the United States land office at Oregon City. Suits brought by various plaintiffs resulted ultimately in holding that the Missionary Society had no title, and the title of various claimants was settled, whereupon the Missionary Society refunded some $23,000 to persons who had made payments in settlement of titles to lots. The name Dalles, from the French word dalle, meaning flag-stone, was applied in early Oregon to places on Columbia river where there were rapid waters flowing swiftly through or over flat surfaces of stone.

26

Baker county was cut out of Wasco, for in 1862, inhabitants of the mining camp then called Union Flat organized an election board and voted for state officers, sending the returns to the state capital as from "Baker county," although it had no legal existence at that time; but, while the ballots were not canvassed at Salem, it was partly as the result of this expedient to advertise that Baker county was created by act of the legislature, September 22, 1862, when the then thriving camp of Auburn, some nine miles from the present city of Baker, became the county seat. Here, however, prior to the organization of the new county, two miners had been poisoned, and suspicion had fallen on a third, who was detained by his neighbors in camp. Being tried before a quondam judge and jury, the accused was found guilty and was executed on the spot, in order to save the citizens the trouble and expense of conveying him to Dalles City, 250 miles away, for trial. In this general locality, also flourished in the decade of the sixties the town of Pocahontas, now almost forgotten, which received ten votes in the contest for the state capital, 1864. Baker county derived its name from Sen. Edward D. Baker.

Weston, originally intended to have been called Westen, for no particular reason except the orthographical eccentricity of its founders, was inadvertently spelled Weston in a petition for the establishment of a postoffice there. It was formally christened at a public meeting at which the names "Prineville," "Sparta," and "McMinnville," were also proposed, "Weston" receiving more votes than all the others combined.

27

Early attempts to force the growth of towns east of the Cascades were less successful than those in the Willamette valley. When Umatilla county was organized by the legislature, September 27, 1862, there was not a town within its limits. The first county seat was temporarily located "at or near the Umatilla river, opposite the mouth of Houtamia or McKay creek," at what was known as Marshall's Station, afterward called Middleton. Later, a town was laid out just above the mouth of the Umatilla river, and was first called Columbia, but the name was soon changed to Umatilla Landing, or Umatilla City. By vote of the citizens in 1865 this became the county seat. As the result of general dissatisfaction with the location, the legislature enacted a law, 1868, peculiar in the respect that it directed the people to declare, at the next general election, their choice between "the present location . . . and Upper Umatilla, somewhere between the mouths of Wild Horse and Birch creeks." The vagueness of the latter designation was natural enough, since, in the prospective county seat town there were but two buildings, a farm residence and a shed, occupied respectively by Judge G. W. Bailey as a residence, and by M. E. Goodwin, owner of the land claim on which the shed stood, as a place of casual entertainment for wayfarers. The voters, as was expected of them, chose the new location, and a committee was appointed in accordance with the law to make a more particular designation and to select a name, the choice falling on "Pendleton," as a tribute to George H. Pendleton, nominee for vice-president as the running mate of George B. McClellan in 1864, Pendleton's anti-war views being shared without limitation by the predominant faction in the locality. Judge Bailey ordered the county officers to remove the records to Pendleton, and rented his residence to the county for a courthouse, reserving the cellar for a jail. Umatilla City sued to compel the officials to return the records, and won a preliminary round in court. The final decision, however, was in Pendleton's favor. Umatilla City practically vanished on the removal of the county seat to Pendleton.

In 1866, Umatilla and Wallula were the places at the head of navigation on the Columbia river, where on alternate days stages met steamboats from Portland. The stages operated as far as La Grande and Uniontown, at which latter place another stage line connected, and operated thence to Boise City, Placerville and Idaho City, and there again connected with stages for Holladay's overland line.

28

The frontier made its last struggle for survival in central Oregon. Here city building was delayed until the last of all. The town of Burns in that region was named for a poet, and is perhaps the only city so distinguished in all the Oregon Country.

Arlington, previously called Alkali, got its new name by act of the legislature, approved November 20, 1885. Athena has the classic name of a Greek goddess. D. W. Jarvis, school principal, suggested the name. Canyon City was designated as a postoffice April 23,

1864. The location is in a canyon, south of John Day river. It had much active life during the rush to the district, 1861, when gold was first discovered in the vicinity. Condon was named as a post-office, July 10, 1884, and was named for one of the townsite proprietors, Harvey C. Condon. Heppner was named for Henry Heppner, and was founded, 1873. The town was inundated by flood waters, June 14, 1903. Lakeview, Lake county, had its name suggested by John A. Moon, at a settlers' meeting, 1876. Goose lake was larger in those times and came up to the platted townsite. Lebanon, Linn county, was called Kees Precinct, after settlers of that name; but on being surveyed and platted, 1851, Jeremiah Ralston named it after Mount Lebanon, Syria. Marshfield, Coos county, is said to have been named by Wilkins Warwick, 1854, for Marshfield, Massachusetts, but another story is that it was so named by a land owner who preceded Warwick. There were but two buildings in the town, 1867, when John Pershbaker built his sawmill, and began shipbuilding and lumber business, after which it grew rapidly.

To view in detail the history of urban development in Oregon would require far more space than can here be given. Each of these centers of activity and social interest has a story well worth the telling. It is men that make the state, as the poet has well said, and in the same sense it is also true that it is the men that make the towns and cities. The names of those to whose enterprise and industry, progress and success are due, are well worth preserving. But the parts played by industrious men and women in building and making better their own localities, however interesting and important, should be described in narratives devoted to the special subject, and all that has been attempted here is to indicate in a general way the relationship of place history to the forward march of events of state-wide significance.

29

County organization began at the historic meetings of the legislative committee of the settlers, at Wallamet, between May 16, 1843, and July 5, 1843. In forming the provisional government, at a time when the northern boundary was still a matter of international controversy, no one could say with certitude how to describe the area to be comprised within its jurisdiction. And in such a vast region, it was almost equally hard to find practical and easily recognized bounds for the counties or districts into which it was to be divided for governmental convenience. The resolution adopted solved these difficulties very skilfully. The northern boundary was not defined, and the districts were outlined in very general terms. The resolution as shown by the official record was "The legislative committee recommended that the territory be divided into four districts, as follows:

"First district to be called the Twality district, comprising all the country south of the northern boundary line of the United States, west of the Willamette, or Multnomah river, north of the Yamhill river, and east of the Pacific ocean.

"Second district to be called the Yamhill district, embracing all the country west of the Willamette, or Multnomah river, and a supposed line running north and south from said river, south of the Yamhill river to the parallel of 42 degrees, north latitude, or the boundary line of the United States and California, and east of the Pacific ocean.

"Third district to be called the Clackamas district, comprehending all the territory not included in the other three districts.

"Fourth district to be called the Champooick district, and bounded on the north by a supposed line drawn from the mouth of the Anchiyoke [Pudding] river, running due east of the Rocky mountains, west by the Willamette, or Multnomah river, and a supposed line running due south from said river to the parallel of 42 degrees north latitude; south by the boundary line of the United States and California, and east by the summit of the Rocky mountains.

"The legislative committee also recommended that the above districts be designated as Oregon territory. Approved by the people, July 5, 1843."

But after adopting this resolution, in order to make a definite claim for a north boundary sufficiently distant to include all territory that could be claimed, another act was passed, December 24, 1844, as follows:

"Be it enacted by the legislative committee of Oregon, as follows: That Oregon shall consist of the following territory: commencing at the point on the Pacific ocean where the parallel of 42 degrees of north latitude strikes the same, as agreed upon by the United States and New Mexico; thence north along the coast of said ocean, so as to include all islands, bays and harbors contiguous thereto, to a point on said ocean where the parallel of 54 degrees and 40 minutes of north latitude strikes the same; thence east along the last parallel as agreed to between the United States and Russia, to the summit of the main dividing ridge of the Rocky mountains, dividing the waters of the Atlantic and Pacific oceans; thence southerly, following said main dividing ridge, to the said parallel of 42 degrees, north latitude, and thence west to the place of beginning."

In the original territory so claimed, the districts were afterward designated as counties; and at different dates the legislature carved from them 36 smaller counties, giving them names. Sometimes after the creation of a county it was divided. The result is as follows:

Baker county, created September 22, 1862, from Wasco county, was named for Col. E. D. Baker, United States senator.

Benton county, created December 23, 1847, from Polk county, was named for Sen. Thomas H. Benton, of Missouri.

Clackamas county, created July 5, 1843, was part of the original district, named for the Clackamas Indian tribe.

Clatsop county, created June 22, 1844, from the original Tuality district, named for the Clatsop Indian tribe.

Columbia county, created January 16, 1854, from Washington county, was named for the Columbia river.

Coos county, created December 22, 1853, from Umpqua and Jackson counties, probably named for Coos-Coos Indians. Umpqua county had been created in 1851, but had a temporary existence.

Crook county, created October 24, 1882, from Wasco county, named for Maj.-Gen. George Crook.

Curry county, created December 18, 1855, from Coos county, named for Gov. George L. Curry.

Deschutes county, created December 13, 1916, named for Deschutes river.

Douglas county, created January 7, 1852, from Umpqua county, named for Sen. Stephen A. Douglas, of Illinois.

Gilliam county, created February 25, 1885, from Wasco and Umatilla counties, named for Col. Cornelius Gilliam, who was killed in the Cayuse war, 1848.

Grant county, created October 14, 1864, from Wasco and Umatilla counties, named for Gen. Ulysses S. Grant.

Harney county, created February 25, 1889, from Grant county, named for Harney lake, which was named, 1859, for Gen. William S. Harney.

Hood river county, created June 23, 1908, from Wasco county, named for Hood river, which got its name from Mt. Hood.

Jackson county, created January 12, 1852, created from original Yamhill and Champoeg districts, named for Gen. Andrew Jackson.

Jefferson county, created December 12, 1914, from Crook county, named for Mt. Jefferson, which was named for President Thomas Jefferson.

Josephine county, created January 22, 1856, from Jackson county, named for Josephine Rollins, daughter of a pioneer.

Klamath county, created October 17, 1882, from Lake county, named for Klamath lakes, which were named for Klamath tribe of Indians.

Lake county, created October 24, 1874, from Wasco county, so named on account of the many lakes therein.

Lane county, created January 28, 1851, from original Yamhill district, named for Gen. Joseph Lane, first territorial governor of Oregon.

Lincoln county, created February 20, 1893, from Benton and Polk counties, named for President Abraham Lincoln.

Linn county, created December 28, 1847, from the original Champoeg district, named for Sen. Lewis F. Linn, of Missouri.

Malheur county, created February 17, 1887, from Baker county, named for Malheur river.

Marion county, created July 5, 1843, name changed from Champoeg, September 3, 1849, in honor of Gen. Francis Marion.

Morrow county, created February 16, 1885, from Umatilla county, named for J. L. Morrow, an early settler.

Multnomah county, created December 22, 1854, from Washington and Clackamas counties, named for the Multnomah tribe of Indians.

Polk county, created December 22, 1845, from original Yamhill district, named for President James K. Polk.

Sherman county, created February 25, 1889, from Wasco county, named for Gen. W. T. Sherman.

Tillamook county, created December 15, 1853, from Yamhill and Clatsop counties, named for the Tillamook tribe of Indians.

Umatilla county, created September 27, 1862, from Wasco county, named for the Umatilla river, which was named for a tribe of Indians.

Union county, created October 14, 1864, from Baker county, named for the United States.

Wallowa county, created February 11, 1887, from Union county, took its name from Wallowa lake and river. The Nez Perce's Indians used the word to designate a tripod of poles to support fish nets.

Wasco county, created January 11, 1854, took in all of Oregon territory from the Cascade range to the Rocky mountains, named for an Indian tribe.

Washington county, created July 5, 1843, changed from Tuality, September 3, 1849, named for President George Washington.

Wheeler county, created February 17, 1899, from Crook, Grant and Gilliam counties, named for H. H. Wheeler, an early settler.

Yamhill county, created July 5, 1843, one of the original districts, named for a tribe of Indians.

CHAPTER XXVI

FARMS, GARDENS AND ORCHARDS

1

IT IS PROBABLE that farming in the Willamette valley began in 1829, although it is possible that some of the Astorians who remained in Oregon after the withdrawal of Astor's fur company had located in that valley at an earlier date, or that employees of North West Company had made their homes there. Doctor McLoughlin is authority for the date, 1829, and if there had been any actual farming before that date it must have been desultory and on an unimportant scale, or it would have been spoken of by him, or by such early observers as David Douglas or Peter Skene Ogden.

It has been mentioned in these pages that Etienne Lucier, after first locating on the Willamette river about opposite the first townsite of Portland, when he retired from active service as an employee of Hudson's Bay Company, 1828, removed in 1829 to a location in the prairie region above Champoeg. His farm was on the right bank of the river, about opposite the present town, Newberg, and in the same general district, but a few miles south, Joseph Gervais located a farm, 1829 or 1830. These were the first farmers in the valley so far as known, but other French Canadian employees of the company located in the same vicinity, about the same time or shortly afterward.

French Prairie, as the region was called from the type of its early settlers, was fertile and productive, and it was not long before farms were producing good crops, and providing a surplus of wheat, and other productions, for sale and shipment. Among the early farms was that of Thomas McKay on Scappoose creek, opposite Sauvie island, which was located prior to 1833. A favorite route for going from Vancouver to the west side of the Willamette valley and Tuality plains was by way of McKay's place, and a trail led from the farm through a pass in the hills. He furnished horses to Jason Lee and his party when they went up the valley to find a suitable location for establishing the first Methodist mission.

In enumerating farms and gardens, mention has been made of the efforts of the missionaries, both in Willamette valley and east of the mountains, to carry on farming. This was necessary for the support of the missions, but the farming operations served to give the native pupils practical schooling, in the attempt to induce them to abandon nomadic life and to adopt agriculture. The plan failed to produce practical and permanent results of value, and failure in this had much to do with the collapse of the Protestant missions. The Catholic mission did not attempt to make the Indians work, if they objected to doing so.

The Wyeth men that stayed in Oregon, John Ball, Solomon Smith and Calvin Tibbets, did some farming. Ball, the first school teacher, went from Fort Vancouver to French Prairie, where he and his comrade, John Sinclair, shared a farm together, 1833. Ball had a farming outfit and seed from Doctor McLoughlin. He was accommodated with lodgings, until he had his own house, at the cabin of Jean Baptiste Desportes McKay, not far distant. He planted 20 bushels of wheat and some potatoes and corn, but the wheat crop seems to have been all that succeeded, as the other plantings failed for lack of rain. However, he lived on meal, ground at Fort Vancouver, and the fish and venison that the country furnished. Continued illness discouraged him, so that he soon gave up the farm, and he and Sinclair returned to the east. Smith married one of Chief Coboway's daughters and settled for a time in the Chehalem valley. Later he and Calvin Tibbets settled on Clatsop plains.

Ewing Young, 1835, in the Chehalem valley, and Nathaniel Wyeth in the same year on Sauvie island, at the mouth of the Willamette, engaged in general farming. Young had a saw mill on his farm. Wyeth had a few cattle, sheep, goats and swine which had been procured for him in the Hawaiian islands. Jason Lee began farming, in connection with the Methodist mission in the Willamette valley, 1835; and Doctor Whitman broke ground for crops at Waiilatpu, 1837. By 1839, both Lee and Whitman, but particularly Whitman, were prepared to show that the territory was well adapted to agriculture, and the farms of Hudson's Bay Company were doing well.

2

We learn from the log of the Ruby, the first vessel to enter Columbia river after Gray's discovery, that on one of its early visits to the river, 1795, Captain Bishop planted a garden, with potatoes, beans and radishes, and although he did not stay to cultivate it, he reported that on calling at the river at a later date he found some of his plants were doing as well as could be expected. Both the Winship and the Astor expeditions to the river planted gardens. The Winship party found its labors vain, for the rise of the waters, shortly after, inundated the site selected for permanent location. But the Astor garden was a greater success. One of the first enterprises undertaken after locating Fort Astor was to plant garden seeds. The first harvest was not encouraging. "We had brought with us from New York," says Gabriel Franchere in his interesting narrative, "a variety of garden seeds, which were put in the ground in the month of May, 1811, on a rich piece of land laid out for the purpose on a sloping ground in front of the establishment. The garden had a fine appearance in the month of August; but although the plants were left in the ground until December, no one of them came to maturity, with the exception of the radishes, the turnips and the potatoes. The turnips grew to prodigious size; one of the largest we had the curiosity to weigh and measure; its circumference was 33 inches, its weight 15½ pounds." He tells about the first planting of potatoes and its result. "With all the care we could bestow upon them during the passage from New York," he says, "only 12 potatoes were saved, and even these were so shriveled that we despaired of raising any from the few sprouts that showed signs of life. Nevertheless, we raised 190 potatoes the first season and, after sparing a few plants for our inland traders, we planted (the next season) about 50 or 60 hills, which produced five bushels the second year. About two [bushels] of these we planted the next year, which gave us a welcome crop of 50 bushels for the year 1813."

3

Agriculture was begun in a determined way, 1825, by Dr. John McLoughlin, at Vancouver. Various seeds and grains were brought by ship from England. The crops flourished, with some ups and downs, under the thrifty management of the Hudson's Bay chief factor. Wheat, oats and other grains, and seeds of some forage grasses, were sown and prospered, although corn, or maize, failed because the nights were not sufficiently warm for its successful cultivation. The full needs of the trading establishment as to wheat and flour were met by 1828, when importation of these commodities ceased. By 1835, when Rev. Samuel Parker visited the post, such was the productivity and development in ten years' time that the farm possessed 450 neat cattle, 100 horses, 200 sheep, 40 goats and 300 hogs, and there was produced in that year 5000 bushels of wheat, "of the best quality I ever saw," and also 1300 bushels of potatoes, 1000 bushels of oats, 1000 of barley and 2000 of peas, besides a wide range of garden vegetables. Fruit growing was also begun in a very small way by the first residents at the post, the first fruit trees grown in Oregon being produced from seeds. The first peaches grown on the Columbia were from trees presented to Doctor McLoughlin, in 1829, by F. A. Lemont, who had brought them from San Juan Fernandez in the brig Owyhee. Mrs. Whitman describes the garden at Vancouver, 1836, as a "delightful place." "Here," she writes, "we find fruit of every description, apples, peaches, grapes, pears, plums and fig trees in abundance; also cucumbers, melons, beans, peas, beets, cabbage, tomatoes. Every part is very neat and tastefully arranged, with fine walks lined on each side with strawberry vines." The farms owned by the company at the post comprised 3000 acres, besides the farms operated on Cowlitz river and at Nisqually on Puget sound.

4

Requirements of the British trading posts demanded a steady and rapid increase in the growing of wheat, which was early recognized as a staple crop for this soil and climate. It had the advantage of convenience of handling, transportation and exchange. The first surplus grain from the valley farmers was sold by its producers to Hudson's Bay company. The company found a market for wheat, and also for flour, butter and other provisions at the Russian trading posts in Alaska, as well as at the Sandwich islands and in California. Russian furs were taken in exchange for the Oregon products.

Rev. Samuel Parker describes the prosperous condition of the Hudson's Bay farm at Fort Colville: "Fruit of various kinds, such as apples, peaches, grapes and strawberries, for the time they have been introduced, flourish and prove that the climate and soil are well adapted for the purpose of horticulture." Alluding also to operations at Vancouver he says: "Various tropical fruits, such as figs, oranges and lemons, have been introduced and grow with about the same care that they would require in the latitude of Philadelphia," but in this particular, later experience shows that realization did not come up to expectation.

Crops almost phenomenal in proportion to the time and care bestowed upon them were produced at these places. Willamette valley, especially in the very early period, became noted for the quality of its grain. The first immigrants were enthusiastic on the subject of the fertility of the ground. In a letter to the Iowa Gazette, November 6, 1843, M. M. McCarver wrote from the Tualatin plains: "The soil in this valley and in many other portions of the territory is equal to that of Iowa, or any other portion of the United States, in point of beauty and fertility, and its productions in many articles are far superior, particularly in regard to wheat, potatoes, beets and turnips. The grain of wheat here is more than one-third larger than any I have seen in the States. There is now growing in the fields of Mr. James Johns, less than a mile from this place where I write you, a turnip measuring in circumference four and a half feet, and he thinks that it will exceed five feet before pulling time." Curiously, the exceptional plumpness of the grain to which Mr. McCarver alludes was the cause of heavy loss to the first private exporter of the commodity, Joseph Watt, when he sent a shipload to New York. "The appearance of the wheat was unusual. It was so white and plump and round that people wouldn't believe it was a healthy product of the soil. An experienced miller gave it as his opinion that the wheat was damaged, that the cargo was wet and the wheat had swelled, so it was put up for sale under these discouraging circumstances, and the enterprising Oregonian who was trying to introduce the products of Oregon to the world pocketed a loss of about $8000." Californians knew the value of Oregon wheat even in the period of the Mexican occupancy of the region south of 42°. Sir George Simpson records that General Vallejo, governor of California in 1840, greatly prized a field of wheat planted near Monterey, "seed for which had been obtained from the Columbia river and was highly superior to his own."

A visitor at the Waiilatpu mission, 1839, was impressed by Dr. Whitman's apparently comfortable circumstances. "He has raised," said Asahel Munger, "about 100 bushels of corn, rising of a 1000 bushels of potatoes as he thinks, though they are not yet dug, some wheat, peas, beans, beets, carrots, turnips, squashes, melons, onions, broom corn, hops, summer and winter squashes, pumpkin, &c." Diversified farming, and especially the branch colloquially known as truck gardening, received a decided impetus from missionary thrift and enterprise.

The massacre at Whitman mission, 1847, and generally unsettled conditions among the Indians east of the Cascades afterward, retarded the agricultural development of the interior, but during this period the Willamette valley grew apace, furnishing settlers from its overflow to begin the settlement of the Puget sound country, 1845, the Umpqua valley, 1849, and the Rogue river valley, 1852. With all these, wheat for some time continued to be the chief product, largely because of its portability, until fear of ultimate soil exhaustion dawned, whereupon less wheat and more of other and diversified products were grown.

5

Meanwhile, new interest was created in animal husbandry by the importation of pure bred stock and this in turn invited more particular attention to forage crops, such as red and white clover. Orchards were planted. It was discovered not only that certain varieties of flax were indigenous, but that the rich soils of the valleys were capable of the production of an excellent fibre, so that linen became to no inconsiderable extent an article of home manufacture, some time prior to the introduction of modern machinery. Something more on this interesting topic will be said in later pages of this chapter.

6

The lowlands of the Willamette valley were settled first, for social reasons, but later immigrants who acquired farms in the foothills discovered that these localities vied with the lowlands in healthfulness of climate, in purity and abundance of water, and in adaptability to the culture of forage crops. The turning point for agriculture in Oregon may be said to have been reached, indeed, with the introduction of animal husbandry on a considerable scale, due to difficulty in transporting other commodities to market. The introduction of livestock, and the peculiar suitability of soil and climate for animal husbandry in particular, gave Oregon a conspicuous place in Pacific coast food production in a relatively early time. Certain species of legumes were native to the country, giving assurance that better varieties would thrive also, and red clover, now a factor of considerable consequence to Oregon agriculture, was successfully introduced in 1854 by Charles W. Bryant, of Washington county. White clover, less important in point of bulk production, yet exceedingly useful in pastures, was brought to Oregon by J. L. Parrish, one of the reinforcements to Jason Lee's mission, 1840. Vetch was brought to Oregon by William Chalmers from New York, 1870, and it has ever since had a significant double role as forage and soil restoration crop.

7

The first farm animals in the territory were the hogs and sheep brought on the Tonquin by the Astor party, 1811. To these, the Hudson's Bay Company made additions, soon after it succeeded the Northwesters in possession, 1824-5, importing some cattle from California by sea, and also three head of English Durhams of aristocratic lineage, for the production of milk, butter, and cheese. A few sheep were imported from California, also, so that both cattle and sheep were already numerous in Oregon in the early 30's. The importations from California by Ewing Young and party, 1837, were Spanish longhorns. Some of this brand roamed the hills of the Chehalem valley for years after Young's death, became wild, and troublesome to settlers on the outskirts of the Willamette valley. They were hunted with rifles and slaughtered on occasions, for their hides, and in order to make the fields safe for women and children.

There was a second herd from California, driven by Thomas J. Hubbard and others, 1840, according to Dr. Elijah White. A third importation is mentioned as having been brought, 1843, by Joseph Gale and the crew of the Star of Oregon, after they had sold the schooner at San Francisco, as stated on page 366 of volume one.

8

Better grades were introduced when American immigration began, the first in all probability being shorthorns, or Durhams, then in high favor in the middle west. David M. Guthrie, of Polk county, pioneer of 1846, was probably the earliest to introduce high bred shorthorns, and, 1847, John Wilson brought in another herd from Illinois. These cattle, which were much better than earlier livestock, were the forerunners of the dairy and domestic livestock industries, both of which have since obtained high rank. Each succeeding immigration, especially that of 1852, brought large numbers of cows as well as oxen.

9

Sheep husbandry remained exclusively in the control of the
Hudson's Bay Company, until a date probably somewhat later
than that of Ewing Young's pioneer cattle venture. A few sheep
were reported by Lieutenant Wilkes, 1841, at Waiilatpu. They had
been brought from the Hawaiian islands for use by the early missionaries, part of a far-seeing plan to introduce both flocks and
herds, as aids to civilization of the Indian. The Nez Perce's acquired
a few flocks, and doubtless would have done well with them if the
Cayuse outbreak had not put an end to missionary work in that
field. There were no sheep in western Oregon, however, aside from
the early Hudson's Bay Company importations, until 1843, when
Joseph Gale made his drive of cattle from California, as above
mentioned. By his advice, Jacob P. Leese, an American settler in
California, drove a flock of some 900 sheep in the wake of Gale's
band of 1250 head of cattle and 600 horses and mules. It is probable that all that were not owned by Leese were for the farms of
the Puget Sound Agricultural Company, at Nisqually and Cowlitz.
These sheep were low in quality, as indeed most of the previous importations of livestock had been; they were "light of body and
bone, coarse and light of fleece, of all colors of white, black, ring-
streaked and grizzled, having in an eminent degree the tenacity to
life common to all scrub stock, and giving their increase at all seasons, though principally in the spring. They responded quickly to
any cross for improvement, especially toward the merino blood,"
as has been stated by John Minto, a noteworthy pioneer figure in
the sheep business in Oregon. He says: "Bancroft mentions 2000
sheep being brought overland from California, about this date,
by the Hudson's Bay Company, indefinitely; but, as we know Dr.
W. F. Tolmie was placed at Fort Nisqually about the time of their
arrival, the supposition is reasonably probable that William Glen
Rae, the officer in charge of the Hudson's Bay Company's station
in California and son-in-law of Doctor McLoughlin, bought 2000,
or more, sheep and furnished men to drive them in company with
Mr. Leese, under Captain Gale's leadership."

10

The first sheep to reach Oregon by crossing the plains were
brought from Missouri, 1844, by Joshua Shaw and his son, Alva
C. R. Shaw, who settled in Polk county. The early success of the

Shaws induced Joseph Watt to undertake a similar venture, which he accomplished, 1848. The first pure bred merino rams came from Ohio, 1851, and consisted of three head which were driven overland by Hiram Smith. A larger flock was brought, 1853, by R. R. Thompson and David P. Thompson, both of whom achieved considerable eminence in the later history of Oregon.

Watt brought with him to Oregon, with his sheep, the cards, reeds and castings for a loom and spinning wheel, which were set up at the home of the Watt family, in Yamhill, and long served a highly useful purpose. The discovery of gold in California in the following year affected the sheep industry, as it did nearly every other industry in the territory, by giving a new stimulus to food production, and by causing a rapid advance in the prices of commodities. Yet, it checked at the same time the woolen manufacturing enterprise which Watt had had in mind when he brought his loom west with him, by discouraging investment of capital. The rush of young men from Oregon to the California mines caused at first a great depression, an unfavorable condition for projected commercial ventures.

11

A noteworthy incident in the history of sheep husbandry, occurring soon after this, relates to the shipment to Oregon of the first aristocrats of sheep, originating in Australia. Says John Minto: "In 1857, Martin Jesse, of Yamhill county, returned from the California gold mines, heard the call for a sheep sale from the deck of a ship at San Francisco. He found on inquiry that the stock were thoroughbred merinos from the Camden Park flock of the Macarthur Bros., of New South Wales, descended from the Kew flock of King George III, of England, which were drawn from the Negretti flocks of the Marchioness del Campo di Alango, by royal grant of the King of Spain, who only could permit exportation, for which courtesy the English king thanked the noble lady by a present of eight splendid English coach horses. The start of Macarthur's Australian merinos were those drawn from the English king's flock and imported into New South Wales in 1804 by Capt. John Macarthur, founder of the Camden Park flock and father of the firm of brothers who sold the sheep, herein mentioned, to J. H. Williams, United States consul at Sydney, New South Wales, for shipment to California in March, 1857. The ship had been driven out of her course and both food and water for the sheep were scarce. The latter had been given at last out of bottles and the sheep saved by that means. Mr. Jesse purchased 20 head of them and transferred them to the ship he had engaged his passage to Portland on. Thus were brought the means of reproduction of the golden fleece to Oregon. They [the sheep] could not be watered on the ship, but by drinking out of a bottle until they were landed on the farm of Coffin & Thompson, of Dayton, Oregon."

The author mentions, among other pioneers of the sheep business at this time: R. C. Geer, of Marion county, who imported Southdowns direct from England, 1858; John Cogswell, of Lane county, who imported New Oxfordshires and Hampshire Downs, 1860; Jones & Rockwell, who sold in western Oregon, 1860, forty-five head of thoroughbred merinos, mostly of the Spanish type, but which were so improved by Vermont breeders as to justify naming them American merinos, as was done. Benjamin Stark, while United States senator, sent a fine Cotswold to Oregon. Archibald McKinlay, when he retired from the Hudson's Bay Company, settled in Marion county, taking with him a number of high grade sheep from the late English importations of the Puget Sound Agricultural Company, and these became the nucleus of a number of excellent flocks.

12

Another, and unexpected, effect of the growth of the industry was felt, when, as the result of overproduction and of lack of facilities for manufacture on the Pacific coast, prices declined to unprofitable levels in the middle fifties, and wool became an article of local barter. From 1853 until 1857, there was but one wool buyer in Portland, then the commercial metropolis, and his uniform price was ten cents a pound for all grades. Home manufacture of cloth now became part of the routine of pioneer life, and homespun garments were the mode from the beginning of the depression until some time after the establishment of the first woolen factory, which was the outcome of Watt's persistence, and the story of which bears intimately upon the social and commercial life of the time.

13

Watt succeeded, 1856, in organizing a joint stock company, which obtained a charter from the territorial legislature and began operations by constructing a canal by which the waters of the Santiam river were diverted into Mill creek, at a point about 15 miles from its confluence with the Willamette river, at Salem. This was in itself an ambitious engineering feat, and the concern, known as the Willamette Woolen Manufacturing Company, bought machinery on credit in New England, borrowed funds from Daniel Waldo and from Mr. Watt, and finished its first product, a lot of fine white blankets, January, 1858. The Fraser river mining stampede in the spring of that year stopped operations, and, when the workmen returned later in the year, the stock of raw wool became exhausted, while there were no funds to buy more. In the ensuing financial readjustment, an arrangement was made by which the finished products of the factory were sold to the merchants of the territory in exchange for wool. Wages of employees were now paid in part in due bills of the company, instead of cash, and "factory scrip," as it came to be known, was for a time an important circulating medium in the Willamette valley.

The cloth made by the factory bore the brand "Hardtimes," in token of the peculiar circumstances of its production, and found a ready market along the line of the Holladay stage route, in Oregon and California, and also in Washington territory. The company earned large profits during the Civil war and rival mills were built at Oregon City, Brownsville and Ellendale as the result of the prosperity of the pioneer concern.

14

The first officers of the Willamette Woolen Manufacturing Company were: George H. Williams, president; Alfred Stanton, vicepresident; Joseph Watt, W. H. Rector, Joseph Holman, E. M. Barnum and Lafayette Grover, directors; Joseph G. Wilson, secretary; John D. Boon, treasurer. L. E. Pratt, who was manager of the mill from its establishment, 1857, until 1863, says that the business was at first financed by loans from Daniel Waldo and Joseph Watt, on which interest at the rate of two per cent a month was paid, compounded semi-annually. The early financial difficulties of the company were attributed to a flood of cheap eastern goods sent to the territory by sea during the panic of 1856-7, but the issue of factory scrip overcame this handicap, and by furnishing a new circulating medium was instrumental in alleviating distress in Oregon.

The selection of a site for a factory was attended by the usual competition between "east side" and "west side," then ever-recurrent in Oregon commercial as well as political life. When the project was first broached, 1855, subscriptions of stock were sought and offers of bonuses solicited. The articles provided for a capital stock of $25,000, and that when $9000 had been subscribed a meeting should be held to decide on the location. One party wished the mill placed on the Luckiamute, west of the Polk county hills, and the other desired it to be located at Salem, on the east side of the hills. The party favorable to the Salem site obtained a bonus of about $7000 and got control of the voting stock. At the time the factory was first talked of, according to Watt, wool was almost worthless in Oregon, and woolen cloth was exceedingly high priced. "I thought this expense would more than compensate the difference in labor between this country and the Atlantic states," was Watt's statement. He says that Polk and Yamhill counties were the first liberal subscribers to the capital stock, and that he then persuaded Salem people to subscribe, "after several weeks and a good deal of labor."

Watt's operations led also to the entry of Oregon wool for the first time into eastern markets, when the company, 1862, sold its surplus of 100,000 pounds to New England buyers. A noteworthy incident of Watt's operations, deserving mention in this connection, was his later shipment of the first cargo of wheat from the Willamette valley to Liverpool, which constituted the first Oregon agricultural venture in the great markets of the world.

15

Pure bred cattle were not brought to the Willamette valley, with the insignificant exceptions noted, until October, 1871, when two important consignments arrived under the personal supervision of their owners, Simeon G. Reed, one of the moving spirits in the Oregon Steam Navigation Company, and an enterprising citizen possessing a variety of interests, and B. E. Stewart and sons, of North Yamhill. While the importations were at dates later than the limit of time set for this volume, a few words may be allowed. These importations consisted of prize winners at state fairs in the east, and a considerable number of them had previously been imported from England and Scotland. The Reed stock, which subsequently became the foundation of an important purebred livestock industry owned by Reed and W. S. Ladd, of Portland, was selected by William Watson, son of the founder of the Aberdeen-Angus line of cattle. Stewart made his own selections and both consignments reached San Francisco at about the same time. Reed chartered the steamships Oriflamme and Ajax for his herds, and also gave passage on board one of them to Stewart and his family, and to the sheep and poultry of the Stewart importation. The remainder of the Stewart herds reached Portland on board the side-wheel steamer J. L. Stephens, after an uncomfortable passage. The Reed and Ladd herds comprised shorthorn and Ayreshire cattle, Clydesdale and trotting horses, Cotswold and Leicester sheep and Berkshire swine, while the Stewarts brought Ayreshire, Holstein and Devon cattle and Cotswold sheep. It is not exaggeration to say that these created a revolution in animal husbandry in Oregon, for they not only constituted an important object lesson in the superiority of well bred stock over the varieties then generally prevailing, but they also led to other shipments and to competition in the ownership of high bred animals, which had a lasting effect on the entire industry. Ladd afterward brought other fine animals to Oregon of various kinds, and, among other enterprises, established Jersey dairy cattle in the state. Among others to whom credit should be given for stimulating interest in well bred stock and in good husbandry was James Withycombe, afterward governor of the state.

16

An attempt to introduce pure bred stock on a considerable scale had previously been made, 1855, when the Oregon Stock Importing Company was incorporated. Wayman St. Clair, of Benton county, was president; Ralph C. Geer, of Marion, vice-president; A. G. Hovey, of Benton, treasurer; John P. Welch, of Lane, importing agent, and T. W. Davenport, of Marion, secretary. A published "abstract of intentions" stated that "the agent will proceed to Kentucky, Ohio and New York and select a few pure bred French merino sheep each year." The plan failed for want of support, but several of the individuals named were active in efforts to improve livestock breeds in the state prior to the Stewart, Reed and Ladd ventures.

Durham, or shorthorn, cattle were favorites of the pioneers, the breed having become well established in the Mississippi and

Ohio valleys about the time that immigration to Oregon began. Governor Gaines imported a number of pedigreed Durhams, 1852. A faction of the Democrat party in the territorial period were known as "Durhamites," from a circumstance arising from a cattle deal. The story then current was that Judge O. C. Pratt, who figured prominently in the politics of the day, had sold a band of Spanish cattle which he had bought from a man named Durham, the purchaser being led to believe that he was buying blooded Durham stock. Pratt's followers were consequently called "Durhamites" by their detractors.

17

It was destined from the beginning that horticulture should prosper, for numerous wild progenitors of the common domestic fruits of the eastern states were indigenous to the region, and throve in peculiar abundance and amazing fruitfulness in the hospitable soil and climate of Oregon. The earliest visitors, for example, found a species of wild crab apple, Pyrus rivularis, growing everywhere in the western part of the state, an excellent indication of the suitability of the country for the production of pome fruits in general, while a species of wild plum, prunus subcordata, which grew in profusion in both western and eastern Oregon, similarly guaranteed the success of drupes. Native grapes and a large variety of berries abounded, particularly in the more humid localities. To these were added, prior to the beginning of immigration, a number of domestic fruits grown from seeds, concerning which there is a pleasing and romantic story.

The legend says that a number of employees of the Hudson's Bay Company, faring forth from England, to aid in establishing the company's post on the lower Columbia river, 1824, were guests at a farewell dinner, at which some of the young women at the reception party presented them with seeds from the fruits of the banquet table, to be planted in Oregon in memory of their parting. The injunction was literally complied with, so runs the tale, and the fruits of these trees, planted in the spring of 1825, at Fort Vancouver, were for many years enjoyed by those who were fortunate enough to partake of the hospitality of the fur trading post.

18

Grafted fruit trees, true to the stock from which they originated, were practically unknown, however, until 1847, when Henderson Luelling, of Iowa, brought to the territory by ox team a consignment of some 800 one-year-old nursery trees. These were set out in the spring of 1848 on newly cleared land near Milwaukie, on the present grounds of the Waverly Club.

Nathaniel J. Wyeth claimed to have set out grafted fruit trees on his claim on Wappato (Sauvie) island at the time that he established the trading post he called Fort William. In his "Statement of Facts," dated at Cambridge, Massachusetts, December 13, 1847, prepared in an effort to persuade congress to recognize his title to the land in question, he says: "At this post . . . we grafted and planted apples and other fruits." No record exists, other than this, as to Wyeth's orchard, and it probably perished from neglect. Dr. J. D. Cardwell, former president of the Oregon Horticultural Society, expressed the opinion that the grafts and stock must have come from the Sandwich islands.

William Barlow, an immigrant of 1845, tells how he started from Illinois with a complete assortment of the best grafted trees that Illinois could produce and transported them as far as Independence Rock, where he met several men returning from Oregon who informed him that there was "as good fruit in Oregon as anywhere in the world," in allusion to the seedling orchards at Vancouver and on French Prairie, and also advised him that he would be unable to reach the Willamette valley with his wagons. Thereupon he abandoned the undertaking, only to learn, somewhat later, that the journey with the wagons might have been made successfully. He brought with him, however, a quantity of apple seeds, from which, in the autumn of 1846, he sold a large number of seedling trees at 15 cents each.

Barlow estimated that his own error of judgment cost him $50,000. "There were no grafted trees in all the territory," he wrote, "and I could have made a full monopoly of all the apples and pears on the coast. Mr. Henderson Luelling, who crossed the plains in 1847, two years later than I did, with substantially the same kind of fruit trees that I had, supplied the country as fast as he could grow the trees at $1.00 apiece for one-year-old trees. I paid him, in 1853, $100 for 100 grafted trees. I was talking to his son a few days ago about the profits to themselves and the benefits of their importation to the country, estimating it at a million dollars. I think their own profits ran up to the hundreds of thousands. . . . Meek, his brother-in-law, built the Standard flour mill at Milwaukie out of the profits of the nursery."

19

It is worthy of record that among the varieties brought to the territory by Luelling were several in the production of which Oregon has since attained a reputation for especial excellence. This first consignment consisted of Newtown, Baldwin, Bellflower, Rambo, Rhode Island Greening, Seek-no-further, Northern Spy, Red Cheek Pippin, White Winter Pearmain, Spitzenberg, Winesap, Golden Russet, Blue Pearmain, Gloria Mundi, Early Harvest, Gravenstein, King and Red Astrachan apples; Bartlett, Seckel, Clapp's Favorite, Early Butter, Fall Butter, Pound, Winter Nelis, and Vicar of Wakefield pears; May Duke, Black Biggereau, Kentish, Royal Anne, Black Tartarian and Early Purple Guigne cherries; and Early Crawford, Late Crawford and Golden Cling peaches.

20

The fruit industry thereafter developed into one of the most profitable branches of farming in Oregon. The natural conditions favoring it are illustrated by the circumstance that one of Luelling's nursery trees bore a great red apple while still in the nursery row, a phenomenon which attracted the attention of settlers from all parts of the country. Orchards sprang up in nearly every door yard and began to exert a definite influence on the life of the people. The discovery of gold in California again was felt, when Oregon fruit found a ready sale in California at high prices, apples yielding their growers as much as a dollar a pound, by the box, and selling at retail for a dollar and a half apiece. Six thousand bushels shipped from the state, 1855, returned the shippers $20.00 to $30.00 a bushel. The export of 1856, by which year many young orchards, set out in the autumn of 1848 and the spring of 1849, were in full bearing, was estimated at 20,000 boxes. There ensued a reaction such as quite commonly follows overproduction, the requirements of accessible markets were largely exceeded, resulting in decline of prices and, as a consequence, in neglect of orchards and the admission of insect and fungus enemies.

It may be added that horticulture suffered a period of depression in the decade of the sixties, which was not, however, without its practical lessons. In the quest of a product that would bear the high costs of transportation of the time, the Italian prune, now an important and profitable staple of Oregon, was introduced, the fruit-growing industry was organized, the spirit of research and experiment was stimulated, and agriculture as well as horticulture entered a more auspicious era. It was moreover now realized, as had been predicted early in the fifties, that settlement in a new country by a people previously accustomed to husbandry under widely different conditions was beset with problems which required individual solution. "The experience and experiments of 'the States'," Asahel Bush warned his readers in 1853, "are of little or no service now. Our climate, seasons and soil differ from those of all of them, and agriculture and horticulture here must be conducted upon different systems. New experiments must be tried, and new modes adopted. In a great measure everything is to be learned anew. Hence the importance of societies where interchange of opinions and experience may be had." This was apropos of a projected meeting of the farmers of Yamhill county at which, October 4, 1853, the first county agricultural society was organized, to be followed in the natural course of events by similar organizations in other counties, leading to formation, 1858, of the Fruitgrowers' Association of Oregon, which was the first state organization of the kind, and in 1860, of the Oregon State Agricultural Society, with which the Fruitgrowers' Association was then merged.

The state society was sponsor for the first state fair, held near Oregon City, in the autumn of 1861. The permanent location of the fair was established at Salem, however, in the following year. These early societies were social and cultural as well as utilitarian in their aims and contributed not inconsiderably to the spread of general education and to fostering neighborly amenities during the entire period in Oregon in which the rural influence predominated.

21

Immigration to southern Oregon, following the pacification of the Indians there, revealed new regions where the foothills were especially suited to the production of fruit, and after railroad communication with the eastern states was established, the industry was again extended. Commercial culture of deciduous fruits as distinguished from production as the by-product of general farming, can be said to have originated, and to have reached its highest development, in Oregon. An example of this may be taken from the experiences of a later period. It having occurred to certain apple growers in what is now Hood River county, in the decade of the nineties, that grading and packing were important to retention of permanent markets, the Oregon method was now introduced to the world. This consisted in fixing definite standards of excellence, to the maintenance of which the corporate faith of unions of fruitgrowers was pledged, and it marked the beginning of a new day in marketing methods, not only for Oregon but for a large number of communities which have followed its example.

The versatility of Oregon farmers and fruitgrowers, which has been perceptibly influenced by independent investigation, has been exhibited almost from the beginning in an exceptional capacity for discovering the products particularly adapted to various localities, as reflected in the variety of the natural products of the state. The Evergreen variety of the blackberry, which is said to have come originally from the South Sea islands, found a congenial habitat at the James Stephens place, in the early fifties, on the Willamette, where East Portland was afterward laid out; and three or four miles farther up that stream, at Milwaukie, Seth Luelling originated the Black Republican and Bing varieties of cherries in the sixties, the latter being named for a trusted Chinese helper who bore that name. It was in this neighborhood, too, that J. H. Lambert first produced the equally good Lambert variety, which he presented to the Oregon State Horticultural Society in 1876.

22

At least four varieties of native cranberry having pointed to the possibilities of domestic culture, cranberry growing has recently been engaged in with favorable results. The abundance of nectar-producing blossoms, particularly the wild clover and wild pea, which was noticed by the earliest comers, led to a number of efforts to introduce honey bees. The loss of a hive of bees by a member of the immigration of 1846, via the Applegate trail, was then with reason regarded by its owner as a calamity, because he had had a promise of $500 for a hive delivered in good condition in the territory. Further attempts to bring bees over the trail were thereby discouraged, until 1854, when John Davenport, of Marion county, succeeded. His achievement was hailed with great joy throughout the territory, since it meant a new and welcome addition to the diet of the pioneers. The Oregon Statesman recognized the importance, and made the following announcement:

"SOMETHING NEW.—John Davenport, Esq., of this county, has just returned from a visit to the States, and has brought with him a hive of honey bees, an enterprise hitherto supposed impracticable. The bees are apparently in good health and not less in numbers than when hived for the journey. The hive in which they were confined is of the ordinary size, three sides being made of wire gauze, the fourth of boards."

23

Somewhat similarly, the production of flax was pre-indicated by the appearance of plants of this species among the indigenous flora east of the Cascades. Lewis and Clark found the Clatsop Indians using fish lines from the fiber of wild flax and were told that they had obtained it by barter with their neighbors, east of the Cascades. A letter in the Portland Oregonian, by Mrs. Harriet McArthur, a daughter of Senator Nesmith, says: "That they understood, in a crude way, the retting and curing of flax, is very clearly proven by examining bags made by the Wascos, Klickitats, Warm Springs, Cayuse, Umatillas and other tribes." Lewis and Clark's entry of July 18, 1805, is as follows: "For several days past we have discovered a species of wild flax (Linum perenne) in the low grounds. . . . Today we met with a second species of flax (Campanula rotundifolia) smaller than the first, as it seldom obtains a greater height than nine or twelve inches."

Flax seed brought across the plains to Oregon from Indiana, 1844, by James Johnson, was planted near Lafayette, Yamhill county, and grew well. The fiber was woven on a home made loom, in 1845, and domestic linen manufacture was practiced quite generally by the pioneer mothers. Flax has more recently proved a profitable crop in the Willamette valley, and much is due to several who have given especial effort to establishing it on a stable basis, with a view to its industrial possibilities in the manufacture of linen products in the future.

24

Nut culture, the success of which was forecast by a high quality of wild filbert, which grew everywhere in the valleys of the state, has also become an industry of considerable commercial importance in connection with the utilization of large areas of logged-off forest lands. Several other varieties of nuts are now extensively produced, including English walnuts.

Agricultural progress of the territory has also been promoted by the introduction of products which at first were assumed to be unsuitable for the region. Indian corn, or maize, a conspicuous example of this, is now grown successfully in consequence of persistent scientific experimentation and research.

The elevated and mostly unwatered plains of eastern and central Oregon, as distinguished from the grain growing alluvial valleys, were last to be settled and for many years were chiefly given over to the production of livestock, by methods which would now be regarded as economically wasteful, but which were well enough suited to their own time. These great plateaus were exclusively a range for cattle and sheep until land became relatively scarce in the western valleys. Dry farming, a method by which the soil moisture of two seasons was approximately conserved for the production of a crop each alternate year, was rewarded with moderate results and introduced into the population a new element, who made homes on the land, built fences and set up an active opposition to the monopoly of the "cattle barons," as the owners of large herds on the ranges were sometimes colloquially called. As a supplement to dry farming, irrigation was begun in a small way, a private enterprise of this kind being initiated in Umatilla county at an early date, to be followed by others which utilized the most convenient sites for reservoirs and ditches. Of late years the United States government has invested much money and effort to reclaim lands by irrigation, but this work has been carried on after the period limited by this volume.

CHAPTER XXVII

EARLY SCHOOLS AND COLLEGES

1

VOLUMES MIGHT be written upon the history of the educational institutions of the state. An account of the life work of the men and women of note who have carried on the campaign for better schools, and of those who have unselfishly devoted themselves to giving instruction, imparting knowledge and inspiring a desire for study in the young, would well repay the labor of preparation. All that can be attempted here is an indication of the early steps. Looking back over the stretch of years since the pioneer schools were established in primitive buildings and with little or no equipment, either of books or other necessary articles for successful pedagogy, when pupils, young and old, had often to travel miles through bad roads or no roads at all, braving inclement weather and the danger of hostile savages, all for a few brief weeks of rude schooling, the contrast with present conditions is the measure of the progress of the commonwealth itself. For, as the communities have gained in numbers and in material wealth, as their comforts have increased and their opportunities have broadened, their schools and colleges have prospered and grown in strength and usefulness. It was James Russell Lowell who said in effect that in making education not only common to all, but in some sense compulsory on all, the destiny of the free republics of America was practically settled. So in Oregon. Education was made the very cornerstone of the state, and the entire structure, with all of its majestic and upstanding importance, rests upon the principle established in the beginning, that every possible facility would be furnished for a liberal and useful education. And who can doubt that, if Oregon has gained in character and dignity of citizenship with the passing years, this result is in great measure due to the schools and colleges.

We have seen that the earliest settlers fully understood and well appreciated the desirability of education, and that they manifested a practical interest in this important subject when, in forming the provisional government, they adopted verbatim the declaration of Nathan Dane's Ordinance of 1787, which ought to be put upon a tablet at the entrance of every school building in Oregon, that "religion, morality, and knowledge, being necessary to the happiness of mankind, schools and the means of education shall be forever encouraged."

2

When the uncertainty as to sovereignty was decided, and Oregon emerged from its voluntary organization and became a full-fledged territory of the United States, education was cared for in the act of congress, even more liberally than the historic ordinance dealt with the subject for the Northwest territories, 1787. To state this more specifically, the federal act for the organization of Oregon territory granted not only the 16th section in every township of the public lands for the purpose of education, as the Ordinance of 1787 provided for the states erected out of the original Northwest territory, but it doubled the gift by granting both sections 16 and 36 of every township. Oregon was thus the first American commonwealth to receive this double grant. The provision was inserted at the suggestion of J. Quinn Thornton, as he has said, when in Washington as the agent of the Oregon provisional government.

This provision was perpetuated by the act of congress admitting the territory to statehood, and the gift was formally accepted by the first state legislature. An additional congressional grant, by section 10 of the donation act of 1850, of two townships, or 72 sections of the public lands for the use and support of a university, encouraged the founding of schools for higher education.

It is to be noted, however, notwithstanding there was seeming agreement concerning the desirability of education in the abstract, and despite professed willingness, whenever the subject was presented, to make the schools a subject of public concern, the private school was preferred to the public school for a considerable time. The first schools were private schools. Those that were public in the sense that they received some support from the common treasury, were often sustained in part by tuition fees. Some of the early settlers came from states in which the public school system had not been developed, in which there was at least a remnant of social prejudice against them. There was for a time a prevalent belief, held by some of the most enterprising and patriotic Oregon citizens, that every man should educate his own children, and not tax others to do it. The early missionaries founded schools for the instruction of Indians which were later developed into schools for white children. As settlers began to come in increasing numbers, it was plainly evident that the first efforts to establish free schools would encounter opposition.

3

At page 275, supra, it was shown how the first school in Oregon began at Fort Vancouver, with John Ball as teacher. That was in 1832. Ball, it will be remembered, was a member of Nathaniel Wyeth's first expedition. Another, of the same party, was Solomon Howard Smith, who taught at the same place until, after ending his engagement with Doctor McLoughlin, in the summer of 1834, he removed to the Willamette valley and opened a school at the farm of Joseph Gervais. This was the first school within the present limits of Oregon. His pupils were natives and half-native children; and according to the statement of his son, Silas B. Smith, this second school was already in operation when Jason Lee and his party of missionaries reached the valley in that year. The Methodist mission school was soon afterward located on the river, several miles farther south. Solomon Smith and his family moved to Clatsop plains in August, 1840, where they were first settlers.

It has been mentioned that Cyrus Shepard, missionary teacher, who arrived at Fort Vancouver with the Jason Lee party, began teaching there before the mission buildings on the Willamette were ready for the missionary school, and that among his pupils were the three Japanese shipwrecked sailors, rescued from captivity among the coast Indians by order of Doctor McLoughlin. Shepard's school consisted of about 30 half-breeds in the day classes, while he also had two young men and eight boys in evening classes. In the great dining hall, at the fort, there was a Sunday evening class in singing, a feature of the school work that greatly pleased the Doctor. No doubt, the young teacher had his difficulties with the Indian dialects, plus the Japanese language, recast into evening hymns.

Shepard taught at the mission school when it was made ready, but his health was soon impaired, and he died January 1, 1840, after much suffering. His ailment affected one of his legs, and it was amputated by Doctors Elijah White and William J. Bailey. He never recovered, but while confined to his bed of pain he maintained his cheerfulness, and wrote helpful letters to his friends.

One such letter, to Daniel Lee, at The Dalles, was subscribed by him "A part of Cyrus." Philip L. Edwards and Courtney M. Walker, of Lee's original missionary party, were teachers, and other teachers came with the reinforcements.

4

Governor Lane's inaugural message addressed to the territorial legislature, July 17, 1849, had a noteworthy bearing on education. It contained a strong plea for the principle of the public school, and it served to introduce a personality of note in the annals of education in Oregon. This was Rev. George H. Atkinson, who arrived in the territory, 1848, as the representative of the American Home Missionary Society, a Congregationalist body, which had charged him especially to aid in the work of education whenever opportunity presented. Atkinson wrote, at Governor Lane's request, the portion of the inaugural message touching education.

"The law of congress," said the message, "provides that when the lands of the territory shall be surveyed . . . sections numbered 16 and 36 shall be reserved for the purpose of being applied to the schools. The magnificent spirit displayed by congress, in making so liberal a donation for this purpose, is a ground for grateful acknowledgment, and indicates an enlightened policy, which looks to the diffusion of knowledge as the surest guarantee for the continuance of good government and the substantial happiness of our people. In this grant we shall have the means of providing a system of common schools for the education of all the children of the territory. Your attention is invited to the importance of adopting a system of common schools and providing the means of putting them into operation; and when the lands become available, the system may, under wise legislation, be maintained and continued, without bearing onerously upon the people, and ultimately be productive of the end in view when the gift was made. With a system of education, sustained by such resources, there is no reason to doubt that in the course of a few years the rising generation of Oregon will proudly vie, in respect to useful knowledge and moral culture, with that of the older settled portions of our common country."

The legislature responded by adopting, September 5, 1849, the territory's first school law, a law particularly creditable as an expression of the taxpayers' willingness to tax themselves for the school system. It declared that the principal of all funds accruing, "whether by donation or bequest, or from the sale of any land heretofore given or which may be hereinafter given by the congress of the United States to this territory for school purposes, or accruing from licenses, fines, forfeitures or penalties appropriated by law to the common schools, or in any manner whatever, shall constitute an irreducible fund, the proceeds or interest from which shall be annually divided among the school districts in the territory . . . for the support of the common schools . . . and for no other use or purpose whatever."

A school tax of two mills on every dollar was levied, provision was made for the biennial election by the legislature of a school superintendent, county courts were empowered to appoint examiners to determine the qualifications of prospective teachers, a school commissioner for each county was created and directed to divide the county into school districts, and a species of local home rule in school affairs was established by a provision that there should be a public meeting in each school district on the first Friday of every November, when a majority of the taxpaying inhabitants of the district lawfully convened should have power to levy an ad valorem tax on all property of the district, for school purposes. This plan of government in local school matters by direct vote of the people was similar to the New England town meeting, and it has been retained under statehood, to some extent.

Religious freedom was guarded, as had been done by the founders of the earliest government, in a section which provided that "no preference shall be given or discrimination shown on account of religious opinion, whether with the pupils or the teacher, nor shall any laws be enacted by any district that will or may in any way interfere with the rights of conscience in the free exercise of religious worship."

5

A hopeful beginning was made in the effort to place the public school system on a solid and enduring basis. This beginning, for want of vision on the part of the early lawmakers, or, perhaps for reasons less creditable to some of them, was nullified in important essentials by subsequent failure to protect the school fund and to adopt a policy in disposing of the state's patrimony of public lands, that would prevent fraudulent land grabbing. Part of the school land was covered with heavy timber, itself a rich possession; but it was remote from market, so that it was unattractive to bona fide home builders. In later years it passed into the possession of land and timber speculators, who could hold it for private exploitation, and did so, through a series of frauds and doubtful transactions that stained the history of state government.

It may be well to anticipate the later years, and to explain that sales of school lands during the territorial regime, and for many years afterward during statehood, were made at the nearly uniform price of $1.25 an acre, although $2.00 an acre was sometimes realized. No attempt was made to set up a system under which the lands and timber would be appraised, and sold for actual value, or for reforesting denuded forest lands. The minimum price was increased to $2.00 an acre in 1878, when solemn pledges were exacted of intending locators that their purchases were not made for speculative purposes, and that no agreement, expressed or implied, had been entered into for the sale of these lands. Notwithstanding these nominal safeguards, a vast area of school lands passed into the possession of speculators, the practice reaching its height during and immediately following the period of railroad expansion, that rapidly changed economic conditions throughout Oregon, and gave to Oregon timbered lands a new value that they did not possess when the prospect of finding a market for timber products was limited by lack of means of transportation.

6

In the winter of 1843-4, while sovereignty of the region was yet in dispute and the provisional government was still cautiously feeling its way, a primary school was opened at Oregon City under the patronage of Sidney W. Moss, with John P. Brooks as teacher. No charge was made for tuition, the entire expense being assumed by Moss. In Clatsop county, where a number of scattered settlements were growing up, a subscription school was conducted in the winter of 1845-6 by Miss Lucy Jane Fisher, in a log house furnished for the purpose by Capt. R. W. Morrison, and supported by Morrison and Solomon H. Smith. Conditions during the winter of 1848-9 complicated the problem of keeping up schools, because of the absence of a great part of the male population at the California mines.

In the general neighborhood of the present settlement of Amity, citizens decided to build a school, but disagreed over the selection of the site. Two factions cut logs and hauled them to the respective locations of their choice. Ahio S. Watt, engaged to act as teacher, composed the differences of the warring elements by choosing a new site midway between the two, to which the name Amity was given as evidence of harmonious settlement and a token of brotherly cooperation. Here in 1849, Watt taught a group of youngsters of all ages, assisted by his 13-year-old sister, Roxanna. Classes were held under the spreading branches of a noble oak, when the weather was propitious, and the single McGuffey's reader that the district owned was passed from hand to hand. "There were few text books of any kind," says a pioneer teacher, "and as late as 1855, when Levi Ankeny and Harvey W. Scott were in attendance at Amity, the instruction was largely oral. A number of men noted in Oregon affairs began their careers in this little log school house. Following Watt as teacher, were Matthew P. Deady, John E. Lyle, Rev. E. R. Geary and Wyatt Harris."

In 1848, W. L. Adams, a college-bred man, arrived in Oregon, and settled on Burton Prairie, north of the town of Yamhill, where he was engaged by the few inhabitants to open a school in a lean-to addition to James Fulton's log cabin, over the door of which a sign, written with charcoal, announced the existence of "Yamhill University." In one corner of the room was a mud chimney that smoked much of the time, and here boy pupils in buckskin and moccasins, and girls in gowns of shirting colored with tea grounds, conned their lessons during the bitter winter of 1848-9, a season remarkable for low temperature, during which the thermometer fell below the zero mark. The successor to this school was another conducted by Adams in one of the three rooms of the log cabin of Dr. James McBride. Among his pupils were J. R. McBride, who was afterward a member of congress from Oregon, Judge Thomas A. McBride, who became a justice of the supreme court, George L. Woods, afterward governor of Oregon, and L. L. Rowland, later state superintendent of public instruction.

7

John E. Lyle, elsewhere mentioned herein, came to Oregon overland in 1845. He at once opened a school at the home of Nathaniel Ford, in the settlement known in early times as Dixie, but later

called Rickreall, in what is now Polk county. The school was called
Jefferson Institute. Among the children attending were those of
the families of Jesse, Lindsay and Charles Applegate, from Salt
Creek, Thomas and Mary Embree, Sarah and Caroline Ford,
Amanda Thorp, Caroline and Pauline Goff, Ann and John Howard. Later, Martha Howard, Miller Ford, and three Beagle children attended. The Oregon Spectator of March 19, 1846, contained an announcement of this Institute, indicating that "scholars
from a distance can be accommodated with boarding in the neighborhood." The tuition was $8.00 "per scholar." N. Ford, James
Howard and William Beagle were the trustees. The following description of the school is given by Julia Veazie Glenn, a descendant
of John Lyle, in Oregon Historical Quarterly, volume XXVI, at
page 137:

"Jefferson Institute was a log cabin erected for the purpose on
the land claim of Carey Embree . . . Benches made of long planks
were placed along the walls and the children sat facing the wall,
using for a desk a puncheon, a wide board, set on props against
the wall. Pens were made of sharpened goose quills, many kept in
readiness by Mr. Lyle. The first pencils were lead bullets ham-
mered flat and long. Ink was made by squeezing the juice from
oak balls and letting it stand on iron filings. The writing paper
was blue and probably purchased of the Hudson's Bay Company.
The pioneers had brought school books. Carey Embree brought
enough to keep his children advancing for three years. The Bible
was read in the morning, each child reading a verse. There was a
lunch period, also recess, during which the boys played ball with
knitted balls on one side of the house while on the other side the
girls jumped the rope with ropes made of braided rawhide.

"A pulpit was placed in Jefferson Institute. The cabin was used
for church and for all general gatherings. Lyle was a Presbyterian. Denominational differences were ignored and missionaries
of all churches were welcomed. People came from miles away and
through the Sabbath morning could be heard the men's voices
urging their ox-teams as they approached the Institute. Hospitable
cabins welcomed the arrivals and happy hours of visiting followed
the religious service before the slow moving oxen were turned
homeward."

The Jefferson Institute served its purpose for a time, but in

1855, when Dallas superseded Cynthian townsite, a new educational establishment was created, with donations of land and money and the Dallas townsite was agreed upon. The new school had the ambitious name of La Creole Academic Institute, of which Rev. Horace Lyman was principal teacher, as will be more fully stated on page 716.

There was another Jefferson Institute, on the Santiam, that was chartered in 1857. E. E. Parrish was president, J. M. Harrison, vice-president, H. A. Johnson, secretary, and W. F. West, assistant to the secretary, N. R. Doty, treasurer and J. L. Miller, J. Terhune and Jacob Conser, directors. An advertisement inserted in the Oregon Statesman, March 22, 1859, showed that Professor O. G. Carr and wife were then the teachers, and there were 89 pupils. M. C. George, afterward member of congress, was at one time at the head of this school, and in 1876, J. C. Campbell was principal.

Another school, Sublimity College, dates from 1858. It had for its first trustees, John Denny, Thomas J. Connor, Eli Hubbard, Drury S. Stayton, Jesse Harritt, William Bishop, Jeremiah Kenoyer, David R. McMillan, James Campbell, Allen J. Davie, Harley Hobson, Solomon Albrison, George W. Hunt, James Chandler, and Morgan Rudolph. The school was connected with the church of the United Brethren in Christ. The first teacher was Milton Wright, father of Orville and Wilbur Wright, inventors of the airplane.

In the winter of 1849-50, the first school in Lane county was opened at Pleasant Hill, 13 miles south of Eugene, where Elijah Bristow had made a donation of five acres for "church, school and cemetery purposes." The school, like others in the territory in this period, was built by community cooperation, the heads of families joining in furnishing materials and labor for its construction.

8

The first school law, though wisely conceived, found few communities ready to avail themselves of its provisions, but while public education waited, schooling did not. Even prior to the date of Governor Lane's inaugural message, or at about the time that it was written, the governor had been in communication with Gov. William Slade, of Vermont, a national leader in education, with a view to obtaining the assignment of young women as teachers in Oregon, who were to be reimbursed, in part, out of funds of the

American Home Missionary Society, as appears from Slade's reply, dated October 21, 1849, in which he points out the difficulty of obtaining recruits for a point so far beyond the Mississippi valley. He adds: "I shall in the meantime make efforts to find ladies of the proper qualifications who will go, and take measures to have them gathered at Hartford, or some other place, and carried through the short course, with especial reference to their very important mission."

Rev. Mr. Atkinson also had called a meeting at Oregon City at which the question, "Shall we organize a system of public education?" was decided in the affirmative by a vote of 37 to 6. It was thought on more mature deliberation, however, that the plan was too costly for the means of the community, and so, a private school, the Clackamas County Female Seminary, was incorporated instead, ex-Governor Abernethy subscribing $1500, Doctor McLoughlin donating a block of land, and others making lesser subscriptions, to a total of about $4000. To this seminary, the first non-sectarian school organized in the territory for the education of young women, exclusively, came five teachers as the result of Lane's correspondence with Governor Slade. These teachers were Elizabeth Lincoln, from Maine, who later married Alonzo A. Skinner; Margaret Wands, New York, who became the second wife of John P. Gaines; Sarah Smith, New York, who married Alanson Beers, and afterward became Mrs. Kline, of Albany; Miss Mary Gray, Vermont, later married to B. F. McLench, and Elizabeth Millar, New York, who became the wife of Joseph G. Wilson.

The seminary subsequently attained a high standing and enjoyed great prosperity, particularly in the period from about 1852 until 1858. The influence of Doctor Atkinson was exerted in this and other particulars, which makes him a commanding figure in the chapter on education in the history of Oregon. He brought to the territory, for example, the first school books which were placed on sale, and these he disposed of, without profit, at the general store of L. D. C. Latourette, at Oregon City, the first store in the territory to have a school book department. It was recalled by Doctor Atkinson, in a review of the advance of education in Oregon, that these first text books consisted of Sander's series of Readers and Spellers, Thompson's Arithmetic, Davies' Algebra, Smith's Geography, Wilson's History, Wells' Grammar and the Spencerian system of penmanship.

9

The public school encroached but slowly on the field thus dominated by the early private school, a condition that is even now reflected in the exceptional number of small, privately conducted colleges in the state. Transformation was retarded from the beginning by pecuniary considerations and sparse settlement. It was some years before the territory began to realize upon its irreducible school fund, and the first contributions to the local districts from this source were too small to be of much importance. The history of education in Portland, the richest city in the territory, and the one whose citizens might have been expected to bear with least grumbling the burden of a school tax, is illustrative.

The first school in that city was a private school, opened in the autumn of 1847, by Dr. Ralph Wilcox, who was also the first practicing physician in Portland. It was in a residence building near the foot of Taylor street. In February, 1848, Thomas Carter came to Portland and his daughter, Julia, (afterward Mrs. Joseph Shoewalter Smith) opened a private school in a log cabin at Second and Stark streets, with about 35 pupils. In the winter of 1848-9, Aaron J. Hyde opened another school in a building called the "cooper shop," which served the inhabitants as a kind of town hall, on the west side of First street, between Morrison and Yamhill. Late in December, 1849, another noteworthy event in the annals of education occurred, when Rev. Horace Lyman, who had come to Oregon as a Congregational minister, began teaching in a frame building on the west side of First street, near Oak.

Lyman, together with Josiah Failing, Col. William King, and others who were concerned with the future of the city, made an effort, in 1850, to organize a school district under the territorial law, but encountered strong opposition. Meanwhile private schools of one kind and another began with hope, but soon were given up. Cyrus A. Reed, who succeeded to Lyman's school in the spring of 1850, charged $10 a quarter for tuition and obtained 60 pupils. Delos Jefferson took up the work, August 1, 1850, where Reed had left it, and taught three months at the same charge for tuition, the year being thus made memorable by the circumstance that Portland children received six months of schooling. Rev. Nehemiah Doane, who taught for nine months, beginning December 1, 1850, received pecuniary aid from the Methodist Episcopal Home

Missionary Society fund, by reason of which he was able to reduce his tuition charge to $2.50 a quarter in the primary grades, and to $6 a quarter for advanced classes, including one in which "Burnett's Geography of the Heavens" was taught.

10

The first free public school in Portland was not realized, however, until December 15, 1851, when John T. Outhouse was employed by the district organized as the result of the earlier efforts of Lyman and others. Outhouse taught continuously, until March, 1853, at a salary of $100 a month, paid from district funds, the community agreeing with some reluctance to tax itself for the purpose. The school nevertheless proved popular, and it attracted pupils from points as far distant as Astoria. Its teacher eked out his living, when not busy with his official duties, by laying sidewalks, helping to unload ships in the harbor, and in other ways proving himself to be an industrious and useful citizen. Another triumph of the champions of public school education came November 20, 1852, when the electors of the Portland district voted a tax of $1600, thus making possible the establishing of a graded school.

The public school system in Portland was not, however, suffered to continue without challenge. There was lack of enthusiasm in 1853, largely due to the popularity of Miss Abigail M. Clarke, who had opened a private school. The usual district meeting of the first Friday in November was not held in 1853, and no funds were voted. Late in the autumn of 1854, agitation was renewed, and W. S. Ladd, Thomas Frazar and Shubrick Norris were elected directors, and A. D. Fitch, clerk. There were now two school districts in Portland, and L. Limerick, the first Portland teacher under the new organization, acted also as county school superintendent. July 7, 1855, in response to an advertisement for "a competent person to take charge of the public school in District No. 1," a young man named Sylvester Pennoyer was engaged. Pennoyer, afterward became governor of Oregon. He taught six months in 1855, after which the schools were discontinued as a charge on the district, perhaps with a view to letting funds accumulate for the construction of a building. No public school was maintained from that time until 1858, when classes were opened in the newly constructed schoolhouse, at about which time the

Portland public schools seem to have become firmly established, so that they have been maintained without interruption ever since.

11

The continued and active opposition that the advocates of the free schools were compelled to combat, has a picturesque illustration in an occurrence in May, 1856, when a meeting of the taxpayers of the Portland district was called to discuss a proposal to levy a special tax for the construction of a schoolhouse. Benjamin Stark opposed the measure, suggesting that, as the county would soon be called on to erect a jail, the school tax would be likely to prove too burdensome. Col. J. M. Keeler replied that the erection of a schoolhouse should have first consideration, and he urged that if the school interests were more carefully fostered a jail "would indeed prove a burden because of its uselessness to the community." Keeler's ready answer seems to have saved the day, for it is recorded that, in 1858, the public schools resumed their sessions in a building devoted to school purposes exclusively.

A curious objection to the free schools now found voice, that would deserve little consideration if it had not been then regarded with much gravity. It was argued that under the formerly prevailing custom of holding school only three, or at most, six months, many of the young pupils had been gainfully employed during the remainder of the year, whereby they had formed habits of industry, so that their minds and bodies grew in perfect harmony, whereas, free schools and longer terms tended to produce young men and young women less well fitted to cope with the grave problems of life. This was a condition which the private schools, and particularly the denominational academies, set themselves to remedy.

12

Tualatin Academy, at Forest Grove, based on the gift of 200 acres from the land claim of Rev. Harvey Clark, supplemented by other gifts from patriotic and self-denying citizens, became Pacific University, 1854, as has already been mentioned in these pages. Willamette University, at Salem, also mentioned, was incorporated by the legislature in January, 1853. Wilbur Academy in Umpqua county, Sheridan Academy, Dallas Academy, Santiam Academy, at Lebanon, and Portland Academy and Female Seminary, are others that were organized. The Cumberland Presbyterians, 1853, obtained a fund of $20,000, of which $4000 was expended at once for the construction of a building at Eugene. This is the school hereinafter mentioned, that was dedicated as Columbia College, November, 1856, with E. P. Henderson as principal teacher.

The Baptists, 1856, incorporated a school known as Corvallis Institute. The Disciples of Christ, better known locally as the "Campbellites," or Christian church, established a school at Mc-Minnville, which they surrendered to the Baptists on condition that the latter should organize and maintain a college; and somewhat later they founded Bethel Academy in the Eola hills in Polk county, chartered, 1856, as Bethel Institute and opened in that year with 60 pupils. Thaddeus R. Harrison was its first teacher. The Baptists had gone no further with Corvallis Institute than to incorporate it, but they obtained a charter, 1858, for West Union Institute, situated at the north end of the Tualatin plain, in Washington county, 14 miles from Portland, and they built a schoolhouse and a church, the latter being widely known as the "Lenox" church. In pursuance of their compact with the Disciples they obtained a charter for McMinnville Academy. The Disciples meanwhile encountered local opposition to Bethel Institute, and compromised this difference by organizing Monmouth University, in furtherance of a plan entered into by a number of members of the denomination in Illinois. The town of Monmouth was platted and lots were sold, as was beginning to be a custom, to realize funds for the support of the school. Monmouth University flourished under the auspices of Rev. Thomas F. Campbell, of the Christian church, who was for many years an eminent figure in education.

Albany Academy was incorporated in 1858. It became Albany Institute, 1866, and Albany College, 1867. It was first begun pursuant to the decision of the board of education of the Presbyterian church to enter the Oregon field, and then gained strength from the endeavors of Rev. E. R. Geary, a noteworthy pioneer in this field. A number of names of citizens distinguished for enterprise and public spirit appear among the trustees of the academy at the time of its incorporation. Residents of the Albany neighborhood furnished the site and subscribed several thousand dollars for a building. The entire property was conveyed to the general assembly of the Presbyterian church, 1867.

Somewhat later, although still within the period when denominational schools were prominent in Oregon educatonal affairs, Corvallis College was founded, 1864, by the Methodist Episcopal church, South, largely as the result of the efforts of Rev. B. F. Burch. This college has a peculiar interest from its subsequent designation by the state legislature, 1868, as the recipient of the congressional land grant of July 2, 1862, for the maintenance of agricultural colleges, out of which arose the present large and successful Oregon State College, now a part of the state school system of higher education.

13

The history of the various denominational schools deserves to be set forth with more particularity, as it introduces a number of persons who greatly aided cultural development in the territory and the state. Rev. Harvey Clark, for example, already repeatedly mentioned in these pages, who came to Oregon as an independent Congregational missionary, was an indefatigable laborer in the field of education and a man singularly free from denominational bias, as was illustrated by his service in various early schools without regard to denomination. The arrival of Doctor Atkinson in Oregon resulted in bringing needed aid to Clark's cherished schemes of education, by means of which a collegiate department was added to Tualatin Academy, and Pacific University was created. The first president of the new college was Rev. Sidney Harper Marsh, who continued in that office a quarter of a century, until his death in 1879, and he was also prominent in educational endeavor throughout the state.

Baptist effort began at Oregon City. No sooner had a meeting house been completed, 1848, than a school was started therein. Almost immediately afterward a movement to found a college was begun, since every denomination now deemed it of the highest importance that the young should be reared amid Christian influence. Oregon City College was organized under the direction of the Oregon Baptist Education Society, that favored the ministry as a career for young men. The college became a kind of theological seminary in embryo, struggled for a time, and finally gave up. The zeal and determination which characterized these efforts are plainly illustrated by the fact that there were reported at this time to be only 160 Baptists in all the region west of the Rocky mountains and north of California. They, however, subscribed more than $4000 to the enterprise. Notwithstanding first discouragements, the Baptists persisted and presently, 1857, McMinnville College, already mentioned, was established with the aid of several donations of land by citizens of the neighborhood. It opened under the direction of Prof. John W. Johnson, afterward the first president of the University of Oregon. It is now called Linfield College.

14

Methodist schools flourished with the impetus given by the early missionary organization, and the establishment of Oregon Institute at Chemeketa, or Salem.

January 12, 1853, the territorial legislative assembly passed an "Act to Establish the Willamette University," at Salem, and Oregon Institute was included in the university, as a preparatory department open to persons of both sexes. The first trustees were David Leslie, William Roberts, George Abernethy, W. H. Willson, Alanson Beers, Thomas H. Pearne, Francis S. Hoyt, James H. Wilbur, Calvin S. Kingsley, John Flinn, E. M. Barnum, L. F. Grover, B. F. Harding, Samuel Burch, Francis Fletcher, Jeremiah Ralston, John D. Boon, Joseph Holman, Webley Hauxhurst, Jacob Conser, Alvin F. Waller, John Stewart, James R. Robb, Cyrus Olney, Asahel Bush, and Samuel Parker.

Growth was greatly accelerated by the arrival of Rev. James H. Wilbur, who by his subsequent labors won a high place in the regard of Oregonians without regard to denomination. He arrived in Oregon on the Whiton, 1846, and went at once by small boat to the Methodist mission. Rev. John Parsons has described his first experiences in Oregon as follows:

"The story of the journey is quite heroic. The first day he got as far as Butteville, where he stayed over night with a settler, whose name was Hall. The second day brought him to the mouth of the Yamhill river. He lay on the ground that night with a bear skin for a cover, and a couple of blankets; but his rest was broken by howling wolves, and screaming beasts. Besides, it rained and the water fell on his unsheltered head. One of his helpers, a Kannacker, kneaded a bit of dough, which he baked on a board, and broiled a piece of beef, for their breakfast. After breakfast prayer was said, and they started up stream. But the stream was swift, and the water was shallow, and they were forced to wade the river and pull the boat. Wilbur was up to his waist in water, and rain fell from the clouds. The third night he slept on the ground again, and the next day the boat moved upwards about ten miles. Wilbur was in the water most of the day. They went into camp again, and remained over Sunday. . . . Wilbur added to the record, as a sort of postscript, 'I should have said that I took supper with Sister Willson, and never do I remember to have eaten a meal that I relished so well'."

"Father" Wilbur, as he was long called, taught school for a time at the Institute, but, 1849, proceeded to Portland, where he prevailed on the proprietors of the town to donate land as the site for a school. Here, with his own hands, he cleared a space on which, 1851, the first building of Portland Academy and Female Seminary was completed. The institution was incorporated, June, 1854, prospered greatly as Portland increased in population, and was one of the most important of the educational institutions in Oregon, until it was discontinued in 1879, by which time the public schools were well established. The academy and female seminary was founded in pursuance of Father Wilbur's plan to create a series of schools of academic rank to serve as preparatory schools for Willamette University.

Father Wilbur was appointed, 1853, to organize a Methodist mission in southern Oregon. He carried this idea with him, opening Umpqua Academy only a few months after his arrival in the Umpqua valley, where he chose a pleasant situation at a point then known as Bunton's Gap, and repeated his Portland feat by clearing ground himself and erecting a rude log house. The articles of incorporation specified that the school would be open to youths of both sexes. An early catalogue announced that "the object of instruction will be to form correct mental and moral habits, and to cultivate a taste for intellectual pursuits," and this policy was pursued, with such fidelity as the human shortcomings of its young pupils permitted, until it, too, was merged into the public school system, 1900, by being sold to the local school district. A peculiar and interesting phase of the useful life of Umpqua Academy was that it was for years the only institution of higher learning between Sacramento and Salem. It drew students from the larger part of two states.

Santiam Academy, a primary and grammar school at Lebanon, had as its first trustees Delazon Smith, Aaron Hyde, Alvan F. Waller, Rev. Thomas H. Pearne, John McKinney, William C. Gallager, Luther R. Woodward, Luther Elkins, Morgan Kees, Andrew Kees, Jeremiah Ralston, John Settle and David W. Ballard, all prominent citizens of the territory, and fulfilled its destiny until, 1910, it succumbed to the growing influence of the public schools. A number of other Methodist schools contributed their full part to the educational facilities of the decade immediately preceding the Civil war.

Cumberland Presbyterians were less fortunate although not much less energetic, in their attempts to influence education. Their Eugene school, already mentioned above, opened in 1856 as Columbia College, had some 50 students, but the building was destroyed on the fourth day of the opening term by an incendiary fire, and on being rebuilt was again burned, 1858, also by an incendiary. Plans were now made to rebuild once more, this time of brick and stone, which doubtless would have been done if the brethren had not fallen out among themselves over the issue of reading the Bible and holding prayers in the class room. The opponents of prayer were defeated and then withdrew their support, which ended denominational educational effort at Eugene. But, curiously, this experience ripened somewhat later in locating the state university there.

The story of the founding and development of Catholic denominational schools begins with the founding of St. Joseph's College at St. Paul in 1842. This was made possible by the liberal donation for the purpose by Joseph Laroque to Father Blanchet, the pioneer missionary. It was soon followed by girls' schools established by Sisters of Notre Dame de Namur. These missionary schools, however, were abandoned a few years after their foundation, but another girls' school was begun at Portland, 1859, called St. Mary's Academy. St. Joseph's College for boys was re-established, and again in 1861 a girls' school was reopened at St. Paul, and another at Portland. In the following year another was reopened at Oregon City. Other early schools were established at Salem, Jacksonville, The Dalles, Vancouver, Walla Walla and Steilacoom, all before Oregon was admitted into the Union.

15

A spirit of competition in the establishment of private schools prevailed in every community, in the late 1850's and early 1860's. Butteville Institute and Yoncalla Institute, both incorporated by the legislature, January, 1859, were examples. Another, already mentioned in this chapter, was LaCreole Academy, founded February 5, 1855, at a meeting of the residents of the vicinity of Dallas. Gifts of land were made by J. H. Lewis, J. E. Lyle and Solomon Sheldon, and part of the land was sold in town lots, now constituting a large part of the town of Dallas. John H. Robb gave half of all his property, a gift amounting to about $6000, as an endowment. The first teacher was Rev. Horace Lyman, later member of the faculty of Pacific University. Elizabeth Boise was his assistant. For some years the academy furnished education in accordance with the needs of individual pupils. It had no prescribed course of study, and consequently no formal graduates, no diplomas being granted until 1881. It passed at length to the control of the United Evangelical church. The first trustees of La Creole Academy were Reuben P. Boise, N. Lee, William Lewis, J. F. Roberts, J. E. Lyle, F. Waymire, A. H. Sweeney, J. H. Frederick, and Horace Lyman.

16

Indeed a community which could not boast a college, an institute, or at least an academy, at this time was apt to be held in low esteem by its cultured neighbors, and citizens vied with one another for the honor of a trusteeship in some educational institution, as the highest social distinction that the territory was able to bestow. The rosters of trustees and incorporators of these various schools constitute a directory of prominent citizens of Oregon.

The first trustees of Albany Academy were Thomas Kendall, Delazon Smith, Demas Beach, Edward R. Geary, Walter Monteith, J. P. Tate, John Swett, James H. Foster and R. H. Crawford. Of these, John Swett sometime afterward achieved prominence as superintendent of schools at San Francisco. The incorporators of Yoncalla Institute were Lindsay Applegate, E. L. Applegate, John Long, W. H. Wilson, and James Miller. The trustees of Butteville Institute were George L. Curry, G. A. Cone, George Hibler, Ely Cooley, J. W. Grim, F. W. Geer, J. C. Geer, F. X. Matthieu, and George Laroque. Monmouth University was chartered by Ira F. M. Butler, John E. Murphy, Reuben P. Boise, J. B. Smith, Sylvester C. Simpson, William Mason, T. H. Hutchinson. Thomas H. Lucas, Squire S. Whitman, and D. R. Lewis.

The trustees of Umpqua Academy, incorporated in January, 1857, were James H. Wilbur, James O. Raynes, Matthew P. Deady, Addison R. Flint, Benjamin R. Grubbe, Willis Jenkins, Flemming R. Hill, John Kuykendall, and William Royal. The trustees of Bethel Institute, in 1856, were Glen O. Burnett, Amos Harvey, Sanford Watson, W. L. Adams, A. V. McCarty, A. H. Frier, J. H. Robb, Joseph W. Downer, and S. M. Gilmore.

17

Popular education in Oregon may be said to have entered upon a new era about 1862, when the benign effect of the popular assemblage clause of the first school law was recognized. Annual district meetings, at which people were wont to gather and to determine the rate of school taxation, and to discuss other matters of intimate detail, had slowly but surely operated as a transforming force. The self-education power of the school system, its influence upon citizen, as well as pupil, its capacity for uniting the divergent elements of communities, were no longer disputed. Said Governor Gibbs in his inaugural message, 1862: "Upon the proper education of a free people depends the stability of their institutions. I doubt whether a republican form of government can long exist without general education among the masses. The subject of popular education has attracted my attention, and it will be my pleasure as well as duty, as superintendent of public instruction, to elevate the standard of education in Oregon as much as my limited influence and acquirements will permit." From 1859 to 1873, the governor of the state was ex-officio superintendent of public instruction. This was a provision of the state constitution, which also provided that the legislative assembly could after four years from the adoption of the constitution provide by law for the election of a superintendent.

18

By 1872, the legislature was ready to increase the state tax levy for schools from two mills to three, and did so. Accruals from the irreducible school fund were appreciable in amount. Local school taxes yielded larger returns with increasing wealth and population. In the fiscal year 1875-6, to illustrate, total receipts of school funds in all the districts of the state amounted to $269,821, the public school property in the state was valued at $442,540, and 48 districts reported holding school terms of six months or more. The total number of pupils enrolled in the 745 public schools was 27,426, while the number of pupils attending the 132 private schools in the state was but 3441. "The habit of sending their children from the country to the city schools adopted by the richer farmers," Doctor Atkinson reported to the state superintendent of public instruction in 1876, "on the principle that every man must look out for his own, is perhaps slowly yielding to the purpose to spend the money in providing better country schools." It is sufficient to say, in summarizing more recent developments in education in Oregon, that the trend has been uniformly toward expansion of the public common school system, without, however, ignoring wholly the historical and sentimental claims of private and denominational schools which were the pioneers in Oregon education, but which now occupy a more subsidiary relative position in the scheme of education.

19

An additional grant to the state of 90,000 acres of government lands by an act of congress approved by President Lincoln, July 2, 1862, was a step forward in education, by introducing a further motive for a state institution of higher learning. The proceeds derived by the state were to be devoted to the creation of another irreducible fund, the revenue from which should be applied inviolably to the support by the state of a college whose leading objects, without the exclusion of other scientific and classical studies, should be to teach those branches of learning particularly related to agriculture and mechanic arts. There was then no public college in Oregon, nor for that matter was there an appreciable demand for one. The public common schools were still struggling against tradition, and public higher education was still a novel idea. It will not be practicable to follow the history of higher education beyond the limit of this book, but the years that have passed since the adoption of the statute just mentioned have a tale of their own to tell.

20

Although the Agricultural College was the first publicly supported school of more than secondary rank in Oregon, a state university had been conceived in an even earlier time. As has been stated, Section 10 of the donation land law of September 27, 1850, granted two townships to the state for the support of a university, and this provision was noted in the state constitution, which provided (Article VIII, Section 5) that "no part of the university funds, or of the interest therefrom, shall be expended until the period of ten years from the adoption of this constitution." Even prior to this, however, an attempt was made to locate such an institution as was contemplated by the donation land act. The territorial legislature, January 20, 1853, designated James H. Bennett, John Trapp and Lucius W. Phelps, as commissioners to construct a territorial university at Marysville, as Corvallis was then called, on land offered by Joseph P. Friendly as a gift, or elsewhere in or near Marysville. But when, at the session of 1854-5, the state capital was located at Corvallis, a political sop was thrown to southern Oregon, in an act designating Jacksonville as the seat of the university, that town, according to a more or less malicious suggestion of the time, counting not so much on obtaining permanently a great temple of learning as on securing the expenditure of a few thousand dollars for a building which might be conveniently converted into a courthouse when the university had failed, as was prophesied. This act of location was, however, repealed January 15, 1856, without having benefitted either Jacksonville or the rest of the state.

The subsequent history of the State University, after the period intended to be covered by this volume, will not be given in detail here; but its location and development at Eugene, its gradual expansion and the widening of its field, is a story of interest. It is firmly established as a part of Oregon's system of higher education.

21

The modern normal school, or institution for the especial training of teachers, had its inception in Oregon in a relatively early time, a period corresponding quite closely with the dawning of realization of the importance of the public school system. There was an interesting meeting of the teachers of the schools of Oregon, both public and denominational, at Portland, December 28, 1858, at which the Oregon State Educational Association was organized. A noteworthy occurrence at this meeting was the presentation by the Right Rev. Thomas Fielding Scott, then Episcopal missionary bishop of Oregon and Washington, with a resolution, setting forth among other things that "the efforts for establishing local and denominational colleges, instead of uniting our means and patronage for the organizing and supporting of one institution of ample university character, are deserving of grave consideration; and whether or not it were not judicious to consider the propriety of organizing all denominational colleges in connection with the state university." The resolution also declared that the "establishment of a normal school for the training of teachers is very sensible, and that such an institution might properly be established by the legislature as the first step toward the state university and from funds belonging to that object." The organization then perfected was the first state association of teachers in Oregon, and it gave impetus to the creation of the existing normal school at Monmouth, originally Christian College, which became a state institution for the training of teachers in 1862. Other normal schools have been organized, but the two at Ashland and La Grande, with the one at Monmouth, together constitute a branch of the higher education plan of the state.

The officers of the first state association of teachers were representative of various denominations, as well as of existing public schools. Bishop Scott was president; Bernard Cornelius, W. E. Barnard, J. D. Post, James H. Rogers and W. W. Parker, vice-presidents; A. R. Shipley, treasurer; L. L. Terwilliger, recording secretary; C. S. Kingsley, corresponding secretary; C. H. Mattoon, G. H. Stebbins, G. C. Chandler, W. Carey Johnson and F. S. Scott, executive committee. The names of Bishop Scott and Bernard Cornelius, in particular, recall an early important enterprise in Oregon education. Bishop Scott appointed a committee in 1854 to obtain property for a school to be conducted by the Episcopal church at Portland, and a tract near Oswego was selected, where, in 1856, Trinity School was opened and Bernard Cornelius was its principal. Trinity School was closed in 1865, but not until it had left a marked impression on the school life of the state.

22

A further phase of education has been the growth of libraries. The present Oregon State Library, which, like the schools, has developed far beyond the conception of its originators, is an example. The second corporation authorized in Oregon was by act of the legislature of the provisional government, August 19, 1845, to incorporate Multnomah Circulating Library at Willamette Falls. Congress, by the first law for the government of the territory, (the enabling act of August 14, 1848), appropriated $5000 for a library to be maintained at the seat of government. J. Quinn Thornton in his memorial to congress had asked for an appropriation of double that amount to be expended in the purchase of a library to be kept at the seat of government for the use of the governor, legislature and officers. In making the appropriation, no restrictions were made as to the character of the books to be purchased. Those acquired had a miscellaneous character, as is evidenced by the annual report and inventory published as an appendix to the legislative journals of 1852. The list includes "The Philosophy of Living," "Terrible Tractoration," "Goth's (sic) Faust," "Works of Hannah More," "Hethergill's Sermons," "Edgeworth's Novels," "Locke's Essays," and "Dewes on Children." This library was destroyed by fire, December 29, 1855, when the unfinished capitol building was burned, whereupon the territorial legislature addressed a memorial to congress, praying for an appropriation of $20,000 for a new library, but congress granted only $500. The state government became more generous, as the value of the library as an instrument of popular education came to be better understood, and the state library has not only kept pace with the growth of public libraries elsewhere, but has under wise and progressive management greatly enlarged the field of usefulness.

CHAPTER XXVIII

FOUNDING A COMMONWEALTH

1

ARRIVAL OF the overland immigration of 1842, the first to come in large numbers and with definite intention of settling and holding the country for homes, may be said to have opened a new era. For 20 years thereafter, the annual arrivals of settlers were largely Americans from the middle west, of pioneer antecedents, well knowing the usual conditions of western life, not fearing to encounter the rigors and hardships they were sure to face while following the long trail, and while making a home in a new country. Whatever future years may have in store for the American nation, students of its history may always look back with interest upon those two decades of pioneer settlement in Oregon. Here was a people living a simple life, without pretense or ostentation, in a broad domain wherein poverty, misery and crime were scarce known. Here, generous hospitality and neighborly cooperation was the universal practice, and self-reliance, thrift and industry were commonly exercised. The pioneers supported schools and churches. They were frugal, but none of them was supported by doles from public funds.

It is true that arrivals in the first years of this period came in destitute circumstances, and that the country was at first ill prepared for their advent in such large numbers. They needed food, clothing, and almost everything necessary for existence and for comfort. But the shortage of food and clothing in the colony was temporary, and soon there was a surplus, and after that the necessity of new-comers could be taken care of, and was taken care of, and they were met with a welcome and friendly helpfulness.

As for clothing, there was at first little that could be purchased from stores, outside of supplies of cloth and calicoes carried by the Hudson's Bay Company. But, soon there were cargoes of miscellaneous merchandise brought in by vessels from New England, and cotton or woolen goods could be obtained at reasonable prices, besides a variety of articles for domestic use. As the population grew, and towns were located, general merchandise stocks to meet the demand were carried by enterprising dealers.

This does not mean that every one had money, or its equivalent, with which to buy. On the contrary, many of the settlers had to get on at first with makeshifts. Clothing that came over the Oregon Trail was about worn out by the time its owner reached destination, and, in the early years, rags and patches were fashionable and more or less inevitable. But this situation was accepted with little complaint, and was rectified in due course of time when the first years of ingenious substitutes and make-overs were no longer necessary. Worn out shoes and boots were replaced with moccasins for a time, and there were those that were known to go barefoot, if they so desired. Deer skin garments were common. There were substitutes for tea, coffee and sugar. Flour, when procurable in early years, was generally coarse ground, brown flour or grits. Early pioneers liked to tell, in after times, of the laughable features of their daily life in the new country, but most of them knew what pioneering meant, and did not complain of what they knew to be the somewhat inconvenient restrictions of life in a new country.

Before the days of gas, electric lights or even kerosene, reliance for artificial light was upon tallow candles, and almost every pioneer family had a candle mold and made its own candles. The houses were generally built of logs and covered with shakes, but window glass was common. There was, generally, a large fireplace and the cooking was done there.

Some frame or box houses were built, and the Gay house in Willamette valley was built of brick. Sometimes doors and windows were brought by ship. Water was not piped into the houses, but was carried in from a stream, a well, or a spring. Most of the furniture was home made, but after the first years it was possible to purchase ready made articles, and a few of the homes, including the McLoughlin house, built in 1846, at Oregon City, had beautiful furniture, silver, dishes and ornaments. Many of the pioneer women were skilful in spinning and weaving, and nearly all families had home made garments and household textiles.

2

The earliest settlers in Oregon had no roads, but roads were not needed. The principal streams afforded ready means of travel and transportation, where available. They were, indeed, highways in constant use by natives and by the few white people in the country. There were Indian trails, of course, and some of them were well travelled. These occupied the obvious and the convenient routes through the country, and had been located by countless footsteps passing back and forth through uncounted spans of time. When roads came with the development of white men's government and civilized occupation of the country, it was quite often found that the early trails were located just where the surveyors found it desirable to set the stakes and to locate the wider wagon trails.

In the eastern part of the state, and in the open prairies of the Willamette valley, problems of road building were simple in comparison with those encountered in the forests and mountains.

The first roads were not surfaced with stone or other durable materials, but those in western Oregon, where the rainfall in winter made mud roads impassable, were sometimes laid with planks, or the less expensive and less satisfactory corduroy. The need of a good road between Oregon City and Lee's mission was recognized by the provisional government, 1844, and a commission was appointed to mark it out. At about the same time, there were several projects for the opening of toll roads, at the expense of the promoters, who would get their profit out of tolls collected. Ferry licenses were also applied for.

3

Samuel Barlow and his party, which included among others Joel Palmer, who crossed the Cascade mountains from eastern Oregon, 1845, and suffered great hardships on the way, realized the urgent need of a graded road for immigrant trains. Theirs was a company of pioneers, with their cattle and wagons, travelling from The Dalles to Oregon City, by a route leading south of Mt. Hood. A franchise was granted to Barlow allowing him to take tolls, on condition that he would build and keep up the road. Much work was done by him in making the road passable, but it ran through rugged country, over steep grades and through heavy timber, and the difficulties of construction were such that he was not able to make an ideal wagon road of it, or to keep it fit for use.

The first party over the Barlow road included 19 men and women. They had 16 yoke of cattle, besides horses, and 13 wagons. After blazing the way, men and boys followed after, slashing about four or five miles a day. Swamps on the east side of the mountains proved especially difficult to get over, the horses becoming mired and the wagons getting stalled. When the Big Sandy was reached things went better, as there was an Indian trail, and the main trouble encountered was in getting over the stream. Several attempts to cross the Cascade range with wagons were made on other routes by early settlers, and traces may be found even to this day of the deep ruts worn in the soil, or deep cuts upon trees made by snubbing ropes when the heavy wagons were eased down steep places. These visible signs indicate the difficulties encountered by the hardy and courageous pioneers.

When Barlow got his franchise he put through his construction work in one season, using 40 men to grade, build bridges, and lay corduroy of logs. This was in 1845-6. The road, later called the Barlow road, was about 85 miles in length. It began at Tygh valley, followed the Indian trail through Warm Springs Indian Agency, as afterward defined, then over the Barlow pass at Mt. Hood, and ended at Foster road, with which it connected at Sandy river. After 1847, many immigrants used this road, and cattle were generally brought to Willamette valley by that route. The toll was $1.00 per head for stock and $5.00 per wagon.

The road was so bad, however, that a new franchise was granted by the territorial legislature, 1852, to Hall and Hall, a firm that undertook to regrade and to put it in passable condition. They are reported to have expended about $10,000 for improving grades, removing stumps and rocks, and bridging marshes and gullies. The same year brought a patronage that indicates the importance of such a road at the time. There were 1073 persons, with 673 wagons, 1396 horses and mules and 5680 cattle, although the road was still far from perfect, and there was much complaint.

Some idea of the difficulties experienced by travellers in using the road may be gained from a statement of one of them, who crossed in 1852, and who describes a particularly steep incline called Laurel hill, where his party rough-locked the wheels of their 12 wagons, and cut a tree and used it as a drag brake. One yoke of oxen went ahead to drag and guide the train of vehicles, while the remainder of the animals were led down the grade. The women and children walked. "Two days before we made the descent of Laurel hill," he said, "an emigrant who was rather set refused to unyoke his oxen. He said his oxen could hold back the wagon on any hill. The wagon bed pitched forward and killed the man and one of his wheelers."

4

In the missionary period there was a trail from The Dalles down the south bank of the Columbia river to the Sandy, and this was used by Daniel Lee in taking cattle from The Dalles mission to the Willamette valley, and was afterward used by some of the early settlers. Prior to the advent of the railroads, a feasible wagon trail from The Dalles on this same route was used and some work on the Portland end of the road was done; but the road was never very good, and later, was totally obliterated and destroyed by the grading for railroad right of way, the tracks being laid on the line of the road where there was not room for both road and railroad.

In our chapter XIX some account was given of the difficulty that the party guided by Stephen H. L. Meek, 1845, had in trying to reach the Willamette valley by way of Malheur river over a route highly recommended by him, and of the woeful experience, 1846, of the Thornton immigration, similarly induced by Levi Scott, Jesse and Lindsay Applegate, to try a new way from the Oregon Trail to southern Oregon by way of Lower Klamath lake and Umpqua canyon. These efforts to find a new and feasible road were disastrous, although the last mentioned enterprise resulted in establishing a road used by subsequent travellers with success in later years. The trails so followed can hardly be described as roads, but the need of a shorter and more direct route than that usually followed by way of the Snake and Columbia rivers was universally recognized. Exploration of various passes through the Cascades was carried on from time to time, but the difficulties were great and no easy grade could be found. In 1853, a commission was appointed to find and to open a new road that would begin in Willamette valley and reach the Oregon Trail somewhere near Fort Boise. A party of seven spent 60 days going over the proposed route, and subscriptions were taken for a road to cost $3000 and to go through what was recommended as a feasible low pass. The new road as partly constructed followed Middle fork of the Willamette river, and in the first season immigrants to the total of 610 men and 415 women and children arrived by that route, bringing 215 wagons, 3970 cattle, 1700 sheep, 222 horses and 64 mules. The road was reported by some of the new arrivals to be practicable, but it was poorly constructed and was never put into general use.

5

While, prior to 1848, travel in the Willamette valley was generally by horseback, when not on foot or by water, there was a very early road that served the eastern part of the valley, but it had no bridges over streams crossed, until 1850. This road is described as running from Oregon City, through Silverton, Lebanon, Brownsville, to Jacob Spore's on the upper Willamette. It crossed Butte creek, east of Monitor, following the line of the present Brownsville road. In 1858, there was a plan for a plank road between Silverton and Oregon City, as the existing road was almost impassable between October and June.

A post office department had been created under legislative act by the provisional government, 1846, as stated in our first volume. The mail routes mentioned in the advertisement for bids for carrying the mails included, besides a water route between Oregon City and Fort Vancouver, a land route by horseback from Oregon City to Hill's, in Tuality, to Hembree's, in Yamhill, to Ford's, in Polk, to Oregon Institute, in Champoeg county, and thence back to Oregon City by way of Oregon Institute, the Catholic mission, and Champoeg itself. This route shows the important places to be reached at that time, and foretells the need for roads to be established.

From other sources, we learn that, in 1847, a road led from Oregon City to the Oregon Institute, substantially on the line of the present road via Silverton and Marquam. The gold rush, beginning about August, 1848, when wagons were first driven to the Sacramento valley, substantially over the route of the already well defined Indian trail, definitely located an important thoroughfare. There were ambitious plans, also, for roads from the incipient towns on the lower Willamette to the Tualatin plains, in the early 1840's. For example, Linnton, planned by Peter H. Burnett and M. M. McCarver, 1844, was below the Linnton of the present day, but was near the Willamette slough. Some lots in the townsite were sold, and a road was projected and partly laid out by commissioners appointed by the provisional government, with the design of drawing to the new town the business of what was then called Tuality, a district that principally produced wheat. The road was to be 30 feet wide, and the river terminus was designated as Sauvie island.

Springville, another such paper town, was laid out one mile up stream from Linnton, and a road from its warehouse, on the river, to Tuality was opened; but it is probable that the road was a branch of the Linnton road. The town itself failed; the warehouse burned in 1872, and although the road from Tualatin plains to Springville was opened in 1867, it was never an important highway. The road now called the Germantown road was one of the early entrances from Willamette river to the Tuality plains. It enters the pass that is opposite the modern Linnton, which is above the original townsite of that name. There was also a route much travelled by horses from McKay's farm on Willamette slough to the Tuality district. Cornelius pass was not so named until a later period.

6

When Portland was founded, 1845, one of the things done was to open from the river to Tuality plains, by way of what is now known as the Canyon road. This road was on easy grade and began at deep water, where ocean going ships could dock, on which account the road soon became the principal highway leading to the fertile lands in the prairie region beyond the hills, west of the Willamette river. This factor had much to do with Portland's growth. The city was well located for trade along the Columbia and Willamette valleys. Most of the many towns on the lower Willamette river, platted with high hopes and ambitions, dwindled and died, and because Portland had deep water and a good road to the interior, it gained supremacy.

The Canyon road was planked after a few years. In 1851, a company was chartered by the territorial legislature under the name Portland and Valley Plank Road Company. The stockholders organized at Lafayette, with J. W. Nesmith for chairman. Under Major Tucker, of Fort Vancouver, as road engineer, ten miles of planking were laid by November first, and $14,593 had been expended by the following April. The first plank, on present Jefferson street, near where Portland Art Association museum building now stands, was laid with ceremonies appropriate to the important undertaking, but for lack of funds the road work came to an end before it was finished, and the road suffered heavy damage by the rains of 1851-2.

A new company, called the Portland and Tualatin Plains Plank

Road Company was created by the legislature of 1855-6. The Barnes road, from Portland, paralleled the Canyon road, but was steeper and almost impassable in winter. And a new road, from Hillsboro and Centerville to Portland was planned in 1872, with a new corporation, capitalized at $60,000, called Washington County Plank Road Company.

As to all of these enterprises for roads west of Portland, it may be said that because of the heavy forest growth, the steep hills, and the heavy rainfall in the winter months, the pioneers were confronted with a gigantic task when they undertook to lay out a road on practicable grades, with proper curvature. The immense stumps were solidly rooted, and, when removed by laborious effort, the roots and rocks in the roadbed had to be cleared away. The work was costly and the cost was always greater than estimated. Under these conditions the first roads were narrow and steep. The mud during the greater part of the year made wagon travel almost, if not quite, impossible. In the valley, there was little winter travel, and this was almost always by horseback. Where there were streams to cross, there were no bridges, or none that would withstand winter freshets. Ferries were few. A wagon journey, with a load, made progress at the rate of eight or ten miles a day.

Among the ferries in the early days was John Switzler's ferry across the Columbia river at Fort Vancouver, afterward for many years operated by his son Joseph Switzler. The first ferry across the Willamette river at Portland was established in 1848 by Israel Mitchell, the landing on the west side being at Ferry street, afterward named Taylor street. This was followed by Robert C. Fulkerson's ferry in 1851, and by James B. Stephens' ferry in 1852. Other ferries were George Griswold's on Sandy river, at Barlow road, and another across the Columbia at the Cascades; Sulger's, Taylor's and Boone's on Tualatin river. Hugh Burns had a ferry below Oregon City on the Willamette, competing with Robert Moore's ferry between Oregon City and Linn City.

In 1851, $5000 was raised by subscription to aid in building a bridge estimated to cost $8000, across the Yamhill river at Lafayette. The bridge, 50 feet above low water, was double tracked, each ten feet wide, and it was provided with a self-supporting span. The contractors were Webber and Wrenn, of Portland.

7

The general government aided in building some early roads in Oregon, such as that out of Astoria, already described. The first appropriation for that road was $10,000, provided in 1854, but $70,000 additional was furnished soon after. However, the work was never finished. Another appropriation of $20,000 was provided, 1854, for a road in southern Oregon, to cross the Siskiyou mountains and to connect with one in California; the Applegates were contractors, and Jesse Applegate aided in the survey. Still another appropriation was expended on a road to Scottsburg under Lieut. Joseph Hooker. Lieutenant Sheridan built a road between King's valley and Siletz, in the 1850's.

Due to the Indian wars in Oregon, congress provided for the construction of military roads from the Willamette valley across eastern Oregon, but these extensive enterprises, supported by grants of public land, were at a period beyond the range of these volumes. For similar reason no description of the important development of the road system of later years would be appropriate here.

8

Within a period of 20 years after the first railroad was built in the United States, men of imagination began to talk of a transcontinental railroad to Oregon. In 1832, Judge S. W. Dexter of Ann Arbor, Michigan, and in 1834, Dr. Samuel B. Barlow, a resident of Granville, Massachusetts, began to advocate the construction of a railroad from New York to the Columbia river, with government aid. The decade of the 1830's witnessed an extravagant expenditure for railroad building in the eastern states, followed by the great panic of 1837. Some of the lines built were doomed to failure beforehand, being laid out and constructed without regard to the possibility of earning anything. Some had state aid, and many that were built upon borrowed money were almost a total loss to investors. These railroads were usually short in mileage, as well as in earnings. Rails were brought from England. There was no standard of construction, and they were of varying widths, some of six feet gauge and some less than four feet in width between rails, so that there were as many as eight gauges in use upon different lines. Passengers and freight had to be transferred from one line to another in making a journey of

any considerable length. Such being the discouragements, it is the
more remarkable that the gigantic project of building to the Pacific could be seriously considered, or that it could be supposed
that there would be money enough in the country for an enterprise so great. No lines had been built west of the Mississippi,
and little was known of the country beyond.

Dexter's proposal was published in the Emigrant, at Ann Arbor, Michigan, February 6, 1832, and its essential feature was
that the project might be financed or aided by a land grant of
3,000,000 acres. Doctor Barlow seems to have made a similar suggestion without reference to Dexter's plan, but his proposal was
to have the project financed with annual appropriations of the
surplus from duties and taxes, after the public debt was paid.
These men were visionaries, but they anticipated by a generation
what became a reality. In fact, there were several other enthusi-
asts of the same type; promoters, who, not being engineers or
railroad builders, nevertheless made suggestions that are now
recalled and noted, such as John Plumbe, of Dubuque, Iowa, and
Dr. Hartwell Carver, each of whom applied to congress by memorial. Plumbe suggested what was substantially adopted by the
government in later years, when it voted such railroad aid land
grants, namely, a gift or subsidy of alternate sections on each
side of the line, the reserved sections to be so enhanced in value
by the building of the railroad that the government would lose
nothing.

An anonymous contributor to American Farmer of Baltimore,
July 9, 1819, proposed a camel route; Robert Mills, 1820, (A
Treatise on Inland Navigation), a portage railway or turnpike;
Hall J. Kelley, (Geographical Sketch of Oregon), advocated a
transcontinental railway line, after visiting Oregon, 1834, although he did not cross the plains, either in going or returning.
Rev. Samuel Parker, advance agent of the American Board of
Commissioners for Foreign Missions, whose visit to Oregon has
already been described, was impressed as early as August 10,
1835, by the apparent feasibility of a railroad to the Pacific coast
by way of the South Pass. "There would be no difficulty," he
wrote, "in the way of constructing a railroad from the Atlantic
to the Pacific ocean; and probably the time may not be far distant when trips will be made across the continent, as they have

been made to Niagara Falls, to see Nature's Wonders." Sen. Thomas H. Benton predicted, 1844, that adult men then living would see the western plains subjugated by steam transportation; he wrote many editorials and letters, and made speeches advocating transportation lines to Oregon.

Asa Whitney, of New York, a pioneer railroad promoter and locomotive builder, returning from China, was impressed with the possibilities of a trade with the orient by way of Oregon. He petitioned congress, 1844, for a grant of public lands 60 miles in width to aid in the construction of a railroad from Lake Michigan to the mouth of the Columbia. Whitney represented that by means of such a railroad, the cost of which he estimated at about $65,-000,000, the continent might be comfortably crossed in eight days, and the journey to Amoy, in China, would take 30 days. "The drills and sheetings of Connecticut, Rhode Island and Massachusetts, and other manufactures of the United States may be transported to China in 30 days, and the teas and rich silks of China, in exchange, come back . . . in 30 days more." He represented that if the railroad were built, the United States could have a naval station at the mouth of the Columbia river, and thus command the Pacific, the south Atlantic and the Indian oceans; the whole line would soon be settled by an industrious and frugal people; and Oregon would then become a state of magnitude and importance; but, otherwise she would become a separate state, which, with cities, harbors, ports all free, would monopolize the fisheries of the Pacific, control the coast trade of Mexico and South America, and draw to her ports all the rich commerce of the Sandwich islands, China, Japan, Manila, Australia, Java, Singapore, Calcutta and Bombay. If the road were built, Oregon would be held in the Union, and the United States would enjoy the commerce of the far east.

9

March 3, 1845, the house committee on roads and canals, of which Robert Dale Owen was chairman, submitted a report, which is memorable because it contains the first congressional endorsement of a transcontinental railroad project. "Your committee," wrote Owen, "are deeply impressed with the immense and far-reaching influence which the construction of such a road to a distant territory . . . is likely to exert upon her progress and destiny."

The committee urged that "the plan, if practicable and expedient, should not be too long delayed." While congress did nothing at this time, the Whitney proposal gained in popularity. It was endorsed by meetings at Benton, Missouri, and at Jeffersonville, Indiana, and Whitney addressed legislatures and mass meetings in different states. Members of congress were urged to support the project. A meeting held in Indiana petitioned for a railroad from the Mississippi to Oregon, and a bill and reports were soon presented in both houses. The senate committee on public lands considered the constitutionality of the land grant, and the practicability and advantages of such a railroad, and finally approved the plan.

In this very early period of discussion, detractors were numerous. Representative Dayton of New Jersey voiced the opinion of the conservatives when he said:

"The power of steam has been suggested. Talk of steam communication, a railroad to the mouth of the Columbia! A railroad across 2500 miles of prairie, of desert, of mountains! The smoke of an engine through these terrible fissures of that great rocky ledge, where the smoke of a volcano only has rolled before! Who is to make this great internal, or rather external, improvement? The state of Oregon, or the United States? Whence is to come the power? Who supply the means? The mines of Mexico and Peru disemboweled would scarcely pay a penny in the pound of the cost. Nothing short of the lamp of Aladdin will suffice for such an expenditure."

10

Soon afterward, 1845, George Wilkes, of New York, projected a scheme for a Pacific railroad to be built by the federal government, and he embodied in his memorial to congress a history of Oregon and also a vigorous attack on the fundamental principle of a government subsidy as proposed by Asa Whitney. He calculated $58,250,000 to be an "extravagant estimate" of the cost of the railroad, and contended at length in support of his suggestion that the government should undertake the task, reimbursing itself from the sale of lands instead of granting an immense tract to private investors, who, he said, would soon become mere land speculators, rather than railroad builders. Wilkes entitled his memorial a "Proposal for a National Railroad from the Atlantic to the Pacific." Like Whitney, he was impressed by the oriental phase of the transcontinental railroad enterprise, rather than by the idea of fostering the settlement of the Oregon Country.

Wilkes also addressed a memorial to the Oregon provisional legislature and the people of Oregon, praying for endorsement of his plan, and that body in the following December adopted a memorial to congress in the course of which it said: "We cannot but express with mixed astonishment and admiration our high estimation of a grand project (the news of which has found its way to Oregon by the memorial of George Wilkes, Esq.,) for a railroad from the Atlantic to the Pacific ocean. That such a thing should exist cannot but be obvious to every person, particularly to those who have travelled from the United States to Oregon." Meanwhile, however, a public meeting had been held at Oregon City, September 24, 1846, at which resolutions were adopted setting forth the "great importance of a national railroad across the Rocky mountains to this country," and a committee was appointed to devise further measures for calling national attention to the scheme. This committee is distinguished as the first in the annals of Oregon to take definite action favoring the building of a railroad from the eastern states to the Pacific coast.

The house committee in congress reported unfavorably upon the Wilkes project, and thought it entirely impracticable to build or operate a railroad in a cold section, where in winter it would be covered with snow and ice, and where it would extend over 3000 miles of uninhabited country, and over mountain passes 7500 feet above the sea level. But the committee recommended a survey, including the route of the Columbia and Missouri rivers, and an examination of feasible mountain passes in the Rocky mountain range.

Whitney travelled extensively through the eastern states, lecturing and educating the public to the necessity and feasibility of his project, and he put before congress, 1848, a modification of his proposal, under which he was to build at his own expense 10 miles, which when completed would entitle him to 10 miles of the land grant, and this was to be used in turn to raise money for the next section, and so on. The Mexican war, however, diverted the attention of the nation from the project, and nothing came of it.

11

Following this, H. M. Knighton, owner of the original townsite at St. Helens, Oregon, proposed, 1850, to build a railroad from that town, then a serious competitor of Portland for supremacy as the metropolis at the head of river navigation. The route of the railroad was to follow through the Cornelius pass, and across Washington county, to Lafayette. Knighton calculated that the enterprise would involve an outlay of $500,000 for construction and equipment, and he proposed to divide that sum into 1000 shares of $500 each. The scheme was advertised in the Oregon Spectator as a "brilliant chance for investment." The advertisement contained this paragraph: "N. B. It is almost useless to add that the terminus of this road should be at a point that can be reached with safety by large class vessels at any season and at any stage of the river, as the people of Oregon have already expressed their wishes upon this subject."

There were no adequate laws in Oregon for the creation of limited liability corporations in this period, however, and, for this and other reasons, the sum demanded being very large in proportion to the wealth of the territory, the plan fell through. It had the support of the owners of the townsite of Milton, and it aroused some interest in Lafayette, then the most influential town in the Willamette valley; but naturally it received no support in Portland or from other settlements on the rivers, each of which places was then hopeful of obtaining recognition as the water terminus of any line that might be built.

12

To form some conception of the conditions in Oregon at this time, as far as relates to transportation and means of communication, will aid in understanding the steps by which the Pacific railroads were brought into existence and Oregon was given railroad communication with the outside world. The members of the legislative council of the provisional government in their memorial to congress adopted June 28, 1845, had described their defenseless situation and told of the scattered condition of the people, and among other requests had asked for "a public mail, to be established, to arrive and depart monthly from Oregon City and Independence, Mo., and that such other mail routes be established as are essential to the Willamette country and other settlements."

The settlers did not await the action of congress, which at best would be slow, but actually elected a postmaster general of their

own, and outlined certain mail routes, as between Oregon City
and Vancouver, once in two weeks by water, and a circuit up the
valley and return once a week on horseback. When the Oregon
American and Evangelical Unionist was issued, June 7, 1848, at
Tualatin Plains, it said: "Probably the greatest embarrassment
to the successful operation of the presses in Oregon is the want
of mails," and it made arrangements for two carriers to make the
rounds through the settlements. It was to receive the mails from
Portland, 12 miles away, once a week, and by special express
whenever foreign intelligence reached the river.

As has already been stated in volume one, page 355, the postmaster general appointed by the provisional government was W.
G. T'Vault, editor of the Oregon Spectator. He awarded a contract to Hugh Burns to carry letters to Weston, Missouri, for the
eastern states, but Burns could not make it pay, and gave up
the contract. However, there was a general demand for mail
service, and each settlement wanted a post office. Dayton represented that it was the center of a thriving community and as
steamers were making regular trips and would carry mails at
moderate rates, it was entitled to better service. Oregon settlers
were disappointed at not receiving the regular mail rates established for all other parts of the nation.

It was in response to the settlers' memorials and other appeals
that congress inserted in the act of 1850, to establish post roads
in the United States, the following in Oregon: (1) From Astoria,
via the mouth of the Cowlitz river, Plymouth, Portland, Milwaukie, Oregon City, Linn City, Lafayette, Nathaniel Ford's,
Nesmith's Mills, Marysville, John Lloyd's, Eugene F. Skinner's,
Pleasant Hill to mouth of the Umpqua river. (2) From Umpqua
valley to Sacramento City, in California. (3) From Oregon City,
via Champoy (Champoeg), Salem, Hamilton Campbell's, Albany,
Kirk's Ferry, W. B. Malay's, to Jacob Spore's in Linn County.
(4) From Nesqually via Cowlitz settlement to the mouth of the
Cowlitz river. (5) From Portland via The Dalles of the Columbia
river. (6) From Portland to Hillsborough. (7) From Oregon City
to Harrison Wright's on Mollala. (8) From Hamilton Campbell's
to Jacob Conser's on Santiam Forks. (9) From Linn City to Hillsborough.

13

When immigration to Oregon began, Great Britain had already

introduced the use of postage stamps in the British isles, but some time elapsed before they were adopted in the United States. Congress, 1845, failed to muster a majority vote to pass a bill to authorize their use. Immediately, however, the sale of stamps without statutory authority began in a sporadic way in several cities of the eastern states, purely as private enterprises. Such stamps when bought from a postmaster were honored at his office, the letter was stamped prepaid, and he set aside for the government the amount of the value of the stamp, and the letter went out in the mails.

Stamps were so convenient that there was a public demand, and congress acceded by authorizing five and ten cent stamps to be provided by the postmaster general, to be sold to such postmasters as would pay cash for them. When used upon letters or packets they were evidence of prepayment of postage. This put an end to private issues and began the general use of postage stamps in the United States. Congress had reduced postage rates, 1845, and this not only increased the use of the mails, but created a general demand for further reductions, and in 1851, it was voted that, for a letter prepaid, the rate would be three cents postage for an ounce or fraction, provided it would be going not over 3000 miles. The rate would be five cents if not prepaid, and for distances beyond 3000 miles the rates would be doubled.

14

Mail had been sent under government arrangement from the eastern states to Oregon as early as 1845. The service was improved after the gold rush of 1849. About the close of the Mexican war, as early as 1847, a postal agent for Oregon had been appointed with power to name postmasters. He had appointed John M. Shively, at Astoria, and W. G. T'Vault, at Oregon City, and soon after, postmasters were appointed both at Salem and at Corvallis. But the fact remains that in 1850, when the first railroad project was proposed by Oregon capital, there was not even a regular mail steamer to the Oregon Country, and not a stage line yet established. Private persons carried letters and light packages at that time, overland, from Oregon to California at 50 cents an ounce. Until 1855, it required at least five months to get a letter overland across the continent.

The Pacific Mail steamship, Caroline, had made one trip to the

Columbia river, in May or June, 1850, and the steamships, Oregon and Panama, of the same company, visited the river during the summer of that year. Regular monthly mail service to the mouth of the river from San Francisco began with the visit of the steamship Columbia, of that line, in the winter or spring of 1850-51. At this period, the usual time for receipt of letters from the states was from six weeks to two months, and the postage on a single letter was 40 cents. Mail then came by way of the Nicaragua route, but, 1852, the railroad across the isthmus of Panama was completed and this became the regular route for such mail. The service was the subject of criticism by the legislature, 1852, which also requested the appointment of a postmaster in each county seat; and in 1853, it complained that, although six weeks had elapsed since its meeting began, but one mail was delivered at the capital, at Salem, during that period.

By 1852, weekly mail began between Portland and Hillsboro and Lafayette. By 1853, the following 39 post offices had been created in the valley: Portland, Linn City (opposite Oregon City), Tualatin (one mile south of Forest Grove), Hillsboro, Mountsylvania (near the present town of Metzger), Lafayette, Amity, Dayton, Cincinnati (Eola), Rickreall, Luckiamute, Spring Valley (six miles northwest of Salem), Independence, Bloomington (on Luckiamute river), Salt Creek, South Yamhill (near Sheridan), Dallas, Jennyopolis (eight miles south of Corvallis), Marysville (Corvallis), Starr's Point (one mile northwest of Monroe), Milwaukie, Oregon City, Clackamas, Butteville, Champoeg, Lebanon, Fairfield, Sublimity, Parkersville (four miles southeast of Gervais), Salem, Santiam City (five miles above mouth of Santiam river), Calapooya, Albany, Central (eight miles east of Albany), Washington Butte (near Lebanon), Willamette Forks (near Coburg), Skinner's (Eugene), Pleasant Hill, Siuslaw (12 miles southwest of Eugene).

15

Owing to increase of mail, due to gold mining and the commerce resulting therefrom, a semi-weekly mail was begun, but not kept up, between Salem and Oregon City, prior to 1850. The postmaster general said the experimental route from Oregon City to Marysville cost the government $8000 per annum, while the offices supplied by it furnished a revenue of only $688. Weekly mail service was, however, soon after permanently established between Oregon City and Salem, and also between Salem and Lafayette, via Doak's Ferry. In fact, mail service between local points in Oregon now seemed to be on a permanent basis, and bids were asked by the United States postal authorities for carrying mails weekly, for three years, beginning July, 1851. Post offices were to be operated for the net proceeds. There was at this time one semi-monthly foreign route to Astoria, but the distributing office was changed to San Francisco, about 1853, and this caused delay to valley mails, so that the legislature protested again in 1856, whereupon better service was furnished. In 1854, the steamship, Columbia, on regular schedule was arriving in Portland the fourth day out from San Francisco, and mail service between these cities was considered excellent. The growth in mail service in the territory is shown by the fact that, in 1856, the routes covered 968 miles, at a cost of $102,871 per annum. The service included two steamboat routes: From Portland to Astoria, semi-weekly, for which the contractor received $7000; and from Portland to Oregon City, semi-weekly, at $1100. The routes by coach then covered 95 miles, costing $3650.

16

There were some stage lines in the Willamette valley as early as 1851, when a line was established by Todd and Company to run from Portland to southern Oregon points. This route was later controlled by L. W. Newell, who afterward operated as Newell and Company, and this firm was succeeded, first, by Adams and Company, and then, about 1855, by Wells, Fargo and Company. The latter organization operated successfully between the ends of the railway lines until the completion of the through track, and for the greater part of this time carried express mail in competition with the postal service of the government. At Portland, the Oregonian received the eastern newspapers from the mail steamers before the steamers tied up at the wharf. Steamboats that ran from down river points to a terminus at Champoeg, in the early 1850's, were met at the latter place by stages for Salem run by E. Dupuis.

The stages from Portland to Salem, by 1857, were operated on a schedule that covered the 50-mile run in one day. Charles Ray, mail carrier out of Portland, operated the first Concord coach. It was used between that city and Ray's Landing, up the valley. Dugan and Company were the owners of a line from the mines in southern Oregon to Portland, and a pack train between Jacksonville and Oregon City did a good business after the discovery of gold in the vicinity of Jacksonville, 1852. There was a weekly stage service in 1859 between Portland and Jacksonville.

In 1853, California Stage Company was formed in that state by consolidation of existing stage lines. Weekly and semi-weekly mail service in connection with that organization and connecting stages was maintained for some time prior to 1860, thus giving mail service between San Francisco and Portland; but the post office department required this to be cut to a monthly service. About this time, however, daily stages between the two cities were put in operation, and incidentally the mail service was improved. There were 90 post offices in Oregon that were indirectly benefitted, the mail being carried by contractors. The California company connected with Chase's line at Oakland, which in turn connected with Oregon Stage Company at Corvallis, operating between Corvallis and Portland.

In 1857, the Overland Stage Company was organized and began carrying the letter mail between St. Joseph, Missouri, and Placerville, California, by contract with the postmaster general, under an act of congress of March 3, 1857, which required the mail to be carried in good four-horse coaches, or spring wagons, suitable for passengers, through in 25 days. This arrangement was continued until the completion of the Union Pacific and Central Pacific railroads, 1869.

17

Considering how dependent Oregon was from the beginning upon ships and shipping, and how much of interest in its early history comes from its ocean and river activities, it is to be regretted that so little is shown by early records. No port register of the first vessels, or history of their affairs, was kept. Visits of this ship, and that, are mentioned, and an occasional fact of interest is revealed by correspondence, or other documentary sources, but the story is far from complete. The same is in a measure true about river commerce, which in the pioneer period was an exceedingly important factor in life.

The Astors built the Dolly, 1811; the Broughton and the Vancouver were built at the Vancouver post by Hudson's Bay Company, 1826 and 1829; the steamship Beaver, that came under sail, 1835, from England, was converted into a steamship at Fort Vancouver, 1836; Captain Gale with his little company of American adventurers built and sailed the Star of Oregon to San Francisco, 1842; and at Skipanon creek, 1848, the schooner Skipanon was constructed. All of these have been mentioned in passing. But that there were many other facts of interest of similar character, worth relating, may well be believed. Vessels were coming and going, bringing cargoes and occasional passengers, or taking shipments from remote and isolated Oregon.

18

At Astoria, the steamboat Columbia, 90 feet long, was built by John Adair and associates, 1850, and her maiden trip under Captain Frost was made on July 4, of that year, reaching Oregon City, at 8 p. m., where there was a great celebration in honor of the event. She began a regular twice-a-week service between the two cities, carrying mail as well as passengers and freight. She charged $25 per ton for freight, and a like amount for a passenger, between the terminals. Oregon City had a boat building establishment at that time. It was located at Canemah, where boats, including steamers, were constructed for use above the falls. Oregon City at that time still claimed to be the head of ocean transportation, but the shoals and rapids above Portland made navigation difficult and at times impracticable.

Milwaukie was ambitious, and, in 1850, there were five deep water vessels in that port at one time. In that year, the founder of the town, Lot Whitcomb, built a steamboat, the first on the Willamette river. It was launched on Christmas day and christened with the name, Lot Whitcomb, by special request of citizens who joined in a petition. It was put on the run between Milwaukie and Astoria. It was 160 feet long, and had side wheels 18 feet in diameter. Its machinery was installed by Jacob Kamm, who became its engineer, and thus began an active career as a steamboat man on the Willamette and Columbia rivers, lasting many years. The captain was J. C. Ainsworth, who likewise became a figure of great importance in river navigation.

The civic pride of Portland's citizens was stirred, and a fund was subscribed at that place. A committee was sent to San Francisco, and a side-wheel, ocean-going vessel was bought for $48,600, named the Goldhunter, and this was the second ocean vessel to land at Portland, following the steamship, Caroline, which in June, 1850, had brought United States mail that it had received at the isthmus of Panama. Later, the Goldhunter was acquired by the federal government and was used in coast survey work, the name being changed to Active.

The Lot Whitcomb was soon purchased by Oregon City citizens, and was operated from that place. A notable event in its career was a popular excursion, May 30, 1851, to Cascades on the Columbia, returning the following day. Passengers were taken on at Oregon City, Milwaukie and Portland, fares being $25, for a gentleman and lady, the round trip. The boat was sold to California Steam Navigation Company, 1853, for use on the Sacramento, at a price of $50,000, which was $8000 more than cost.

Among the steamboats on the rivers of Oregon, 1851, were the Wallamet, Multnomah, James P. Flint, Eagle and Washington. The Wallamet, in 1854, was sold and went to the Sacramento river. Her initial run had been to Astoria, returning with mail from the eastern states. The Multnomah operated on the upper Willamette, as far as Corvallis, bringing down wheat, but later was put on the service between Portland and Oregon City. The Eagle was a small ten-ton boat, having an iron hull and copper bottom; she was brought from New York, and did a profitable business for a time between Portland and Oregon City when rates were $5.00 per passenger, and $15.00 per ton for freight.

The Allan was another boat doing business between Portland and Oregon City. She was owned by Hudson's Bay Company, when that company had a place of business at Oregon City. The Hoosier was built at Oregon City by A. L. Murray, and others. It was used on the river above the falls, as was also the Washington, which was a larger iron boat that was used on Yamhill river. Both of the last named boats proved profitable, but the Washington was soon sold, and was taken to the Umpqua river.

There is a story to the effect that when Capt. A. F. Hedges, in 1849, bought machinery in the east for a steamer, he paid for it with beaver money. He built a boat called the Canemah, at the town of that name, where boat building was active in the early period of boat navigation. It was 120 feet long, and cost approximately $32,000. It was in use on the river for many years, the first service being on the upper Willamette. It carried the mails between Oregon City and Corvallis for a time, and carried much freight from the farms of the valley, but was ruined by explosion, near Champoeg, the first steamboat explosion in Oregon.

19

A second ship to carry the name Columbia, was on the route between the river and San Francisco, 1851. She was larger than John Adair's vessel of that name, being 193½ feet in length. She made connection at San Francisco with the Panama vessels of United States Mail Steamship Company, and furnished excellent service to Portland, charging $75 for cabin and $45 for steerage passage.

Some improvement of importance in aid of navigation was effected between 1850 and 1853. The government spent $30,000 on the Clackamas rapids, below Oregon City, and some work was done in clearing the upper Willamette, as far as Salem. By 1852, it was possible for the Multnomah and Eagle to go through to Oregon City from Portland, even at low water stages. The Tualatin river had some work done upon it, and the little Rickreall (or LaCreole), had a connection with the Willamette by canal. A specially built boat, the Shoalwater, was used when low water prevented the larger boats from running. That boat subsequently was known as the Fenix, and still later as the Minnie Holmes. It is reported that river commerce in the early 50's was so active that Portland had 14 daily steamboats calling on regular schedules, besides sail boats and monthly calls of San Francisco steamships.

20

In 1854, the stern wheel steamboat was tried out by Ainsworth and Kamm, who had acquired ownership of the Belle and the Multnomah. They built a new sternwheeler, the Jennie Clark, and found that this form was well adapted for use on the Oregon streams, and the improvement was generally used thereafter in constructing boats for such use. The Jennie Clark was transferred to Oregon Steam Navigation Company, 1862.

A vessel called the Gazelle, the first of several of that name, was built, 1854, opposite Oregon City, on the Willamette, but, while lying at Canemah wharf, its boiler exploded and the boat was a total loss, besides killing 20 people and injuring others.

There was much complaint about high rates on the upper Willamette, and Salem shippers encouraged the Jamieson line to put on vessels at more moderate charges. It added the Enterprise, and afterward the Onward, built at Canemah, 1858. The Enterprise was sold and sent to Fraser river during the period of gold rush in that region. Kamm and associates acquired the Onward, 1860, but sold it three years afterward to Peoples Transportation Company.

Obstructions above Salem having been somewhat cleared, steamers began to run to Eugene, 1856-7. The James Clinton was the first, but Eugene citizens put up $5000 for stock in Peoples Transportation Company, organized by McCully, and the Surprise, a boat built at Canemah, was also put in service to Eugene. These two boats operated until 1864, and in the meantime the Elk was put on the run up Yamhill river by a group of farmers.

An important enterprise was the building and launching of the Carrie Ladd, 1858, at Oregon City. She was owned by Ainsworth and Kamm, and was built by John T. Thomas, an Englishman, who came to Oregon, 1850, and who had built many of the Willamette river vessels, including the Hoosier, Canemah, Wallamet, Shoalwater, Fannie Patton and Success. The Carrie Ladd was the finest vessel on the river, when she was built. She was equipped with a stern wheel, and made the run from Oregon City to Fort Vancouver in one hour and 45 minutes. Later she was sold to Oregon Steam Navigation Company and put in service on Columbia river, where she was sunk by running on a rock, near Cape Horn, 1862.

Yamhill people began to take an interest in transportation and rates, about 1859, when they organized a local company under the name Yamhill Steamboat Company, capitalized at $12,000. The company operated the James Clinton, Yamhill and Union, and the St. Claire. The last mentioned steamboat was piloted over the falls at Oregon City, by its Captain Taylor, 1861. That was the only vessel to try that hazard. He took his boat to the Columbia, on the Cascade route. The Yamhill was operated on Tualatin river.

21

The most important capitalization was that of the Oregon Steam Navigation Company, incorporated 1860, and in which most of the successful steamboat men were associated. The company got control of the river commerce. The leaders were Messrs. Ainsworth and Kamm; they and Gilman had the Carrie Ladd, Jennie Clark and Express; they chartered the Senorita, and Mountain Buck. Kamm had the mail contract on the Oregon City route. The interests of these men controlled the important part of the Willamette and Columbia river transportation, and they pooled their holdings, having thus a control of the new company. Altogether, there were 15 stockholders and the assets were valued at $175,000. The company got control of the portages on Columbia river, and the Florence, Idaho, gold excitement stimulated business, so that there was an enormous profit on the investment. The subsequent history of the company shows how fortunes were made for all of the stockholders that retained their shares.

Such Willamette owners as did not join the new company found it profitable to continue. These comprised the various owners of the Elk, Relief, Onward and Surprise, for whom Theodore Wygant, of Portland, acted as joint agent. The Express had connecting arrangements with the James Clinton and the Union, operating on Yamhill river.

Peoples Transportation Company acquired control of the Rival and other Willamette river boats. The Rival's maiden trip, July 4, 1860, when she was under her first owners, was a very successful excursion, carrying 700 passengers to Vancouver.

22

The most formidable and active competitor of the Oregon Steam Navigation Company was the Peoples Transportation Company, already mentioned. The company was projected by Stephen Coffin, of Portland, one of the townsite owners. The nominal capital was $2,000,000. The company persisted in cutting the rates fixed by the Navigation Company, and this brought on a relentless rate war. Fares from Portland to Salem were cut to 50 cents, including berth and meals; to Albany or Corvallis $1.00 to $1.50. There was a time when passengers were carried free from Portland to Oregon City, and freight was at the rate of 50 cents a ton. Ultimately there was a compromise and territory was divided.

In time, the Peoples Transportation Company confined its work to the Willamette river, south of Portland. It acquired other good vessels on the upper river, absorbed the Willamette Steam Navigation Company, the competition of which was proving annoying, and enjoyed a monopoly in the growing farming region of the valley. It made improvements for handling freight. At last, when the locks at the falls at Oregon City invited competition on the river and competition of the new railroad lines was threatened, it sold out to Ben Holladay interests for $200,000, 1871. He had already acquired Pacific Mail Steamship interests in the north, including six ships, and he created Willamette Transportation Company and made a treaty with Oregon Steam Navigation Company. The day of the railroad transcended that of the steamboat.

The Panama railroad, across the isthmus, a private enterprise, was completed 1855, and, after this, some mails for the coast were sent by that route; but even with this improvement in service, it required 20 to 25 days to carry a letter from New York to San Francisco, and an indefinite additional period for delivery in Oregon.

The pony express, between St. Joseph, Missouri, and Sacramento, California, was not inaugurated until April, 1860, and it continued in operation about two years. It was not maintained after the through telegraph to California was put in operation, 1864.

23

President Pierce's inauguration, March 4, 1853, revived the hopes of expansionists and brought forward the project for a Pacific railroad. The President appointed Jefferson Davis, as secretary of war, and, after much debate, congress adopted an act, 1853, authorizing surveys for a transcontinental railway. The routes to be examined were four, the most northern of which would reach Oregon. An appropriation of $150,000 was provided, to be expended under the direction of the secretary of war, who would have supervision of the work, and would report to congress. A separate bill, introduced by Senator Gwin, of California, for a railroad from Arkansas to California, with a branch from some point west of the Rocky mountains to Oregon, and also with branches to the Gulf of Mexico, was not adopted, or given serious consideration.

Pursuant to the act, the secretary of war organized surveying parties on the four proposed routes, appointing Isaac I. Stevens to take charge of the northern survey. Stevens had just been appointed governor of the new territory of Washington, and in going to take up the duties of that office, he traversed the general route that Lewis and Clark had followed nearly 50 years before. He had, among his assistants, Capt. George B. McClellan, and assigned to that young officer the especial work of exploring the Cascade range for a feasible pass for a railroad route north of Columbia river. McClellan subsequently reported to Governor Stevens that the Columbia river pass afforded the only feasible route, and that great physical difficulties stood in the way of following any other route across the Cascades. Another of the several capable army officers under Stevens was Capt. John Mullan, who was assigned to the Rocky mountain region. Several mountain passes were examined by him and other engineers. Subsequently, after resigning from the army, he surveyed and laid out a wagon road from Walla Walla, Washington, to Fort Benton, Montana, a useful thoroughfare to the mines of Idaho and Montana, much used in the early 60's, a period in which there was a great rush of prospectors, and in which Columbia river steamboat transportation reached a zenith of activity.

24

Governor Stevens made his report to the secretary of war, warmly recommending the northern route. He showed that the probable cost of such a line would approximate $117,121,000; but Davis revised and elevated this estimate to $150,000,000, and then selected for his recommendation to congress the southern route. Stevens attributed this decision to Davis' well known bias in favor of the south. The biographer of Governor Stevens says that Secretary Davis was in fact astonished and deeply disappointed at the results of the surveys, and the very favorable picture of the northern route and country given in Governor Stevens' report. "A leader among the southern public men, who were so soon to bring on the great rebellion, of which he was to be the official head, he had set his heart upon the southern route, and was anxious to establish its superiority to all others and secure its adoption as the national route, in order to aggrandize his own section."

The effect of the report of the secretary of war was to show that it was by no means impossible or impracticable to construct a Pacific railway line, and thereafter public discussion upon the subject was confined to questions of cost and preference of routes. It may be added that when congress, during the war, took action, it adopted for military reasons, the central route, now occupied by the Central and the Union Pacific railroad lines, while the Northern Pacific, afterward constructed, has substantially the course surveyed and recommended by Stevens.

25

Another of the same series of government explorations was conducted under the direction of Lieut. R. S. Williamson and Henry L. Abbot, 1853, and was productive of consequences of more immediate interest to Oregon. These engineers, whose work was greatly hampered by the Rogue river war of the winter of 1853-4, one effect of which was to deprive them of military escorts, made one survey of a line from Reading, California, to the Columbia river at The Dalles, by way of Pit river pass, east of Mount Shasta, through the Klamath lake region and down the valley of the Deschutes, finding the lower Deschutes too rugged for practical railway building. Seeking a pass through the Cascades, they reported the only acceptable one to be that known as the Middle Fork of the Willamette, leaving the valley near Eugene, crossing the Cascades south of Diamond peak, and reaching the Deschutes south of the deep canyons that had been crossed with difficulty by Fremont, December, 1843. From Eugene, also, Williamson followed a northerly course east of the Willamette valley, crossing the Santiam above its forks and leaving Salem on the west.

Lieutenant Abbot also projected a route from Vancouver along the west side of the Willamette river to Salem, where he crossed the river and continued to Eugene, and proceeded thence over the general course of the regularly travelled wagon route to Yreka, California. Military duty requiring him to pass Fort Jones, in Scott's valley, he was diverted from the more practicable route which he might otherwise have discovered, but these surveys furnished the foundation for others, which, during the period of construction of the railway projects in California, soon undertaken, stimulated effort in Oregon to establish communication with the east by building a railroad from the Columbia river south.

26

The first railroads in Oregon and Washington to use iron rails and steam locomotives were the portage railroads, built in 1861 and 1862 by the Oregon Steam Navigation Company in aid of navigation on the Columbia river. One of them, six miles long, was on the Washington side at the Cascades, and the other was on the Oregon side extending 14 miles east from The Dalles to Celilo. The latter was authorized by an act of congress giving that company a grant of a right of way over public lands in Wasco county. Prior to their construction, there was a short wooden tram road on the north side, from the middle landing to the upper Cascades, originally built by F. A. Chenowith, but afterward operated by P. F. Bradford; and a short tram road with wooden rails operated with mule power, built by Col. J. S. Ruckel and H. Olmstead, on the Oregon side of the river at the Cascades. The latter was partly supplied with strap iron rails and an engine, to operate on a part of the line. These lines were all superseded when the government many years afterward built canals and locks at both of these localities on the river. The locks at the Cascades have in turn been superseded and the improvements have been submerged by the construction of the Bonneville Dam and ship canal, 1935.

27

The outlook for a railroad across the continent was so bright, in 1863, that citizens of Jacksonville, then a booming mining town and the agricultural center of southern Oregon, subscribed to a fund, payable in money and merchandise, to defray the cost of a survey for a railroad in Oregon, to connect with a line from Marysville, California, north to the Oregon-California boundary. But these events, and the subsequent interesting history of railroad development affecting Oregon, are outside of the time limits of this volume, so that full exposition must await some other occasion.

Suffice it to say, therefore, that four railroads were chartered by the Oregon legislature of 1853-4, but they were purely local in their aims. They were the Willamette Valley Railroad Company, which proposed to build from Portland to the head of the Willamette valley; the Oregon and California, which promised to build from Eugene City to the lower Willamette river; the Cincinnati Railroad Company, to build from Cincinnati (now Eola), in Polk county, to some prospective nearby coal mines; and the Clackamas Railroad Company, to build a road around Willamette Falls. These companies never passed the preliminary stage, although the names of many citizens prominent in the territory attested the popular interest in the subject. No stock was ever issued. Similarly, in 1859, the Astoria & Willamette Valley Railroad Company was incorporated to build a railroad from Astoria to Salem, and this also failed to obtain support, so that it ultimately expired from neglect.

The history of actual railroad building in the Oregon Country is comprised within a period of only a little more than half a century. The contrast of the present with railroad conditions three-quarters of a century ago is perhaps more marked than that for any other similar period in the expansion of a state. It was not until 1861 that completion of the transcontinental telegraph to California, with an express system north to the Columbia, reduced the time required to transmit messages to about four days; and not until 1864 that Oregon was united by telegraph with California.

28

Thereafter, as has been seen, it was almost two decades before passenger travel by rail between the Atlantic seaboard and Oregon was made possible. Those who lived in the era during which the great transformation was taking place sometimes viewed the changes herein noted with sincere misgivings. "This is a fast age," wrote Senator Nesmith, in 1864, as the first through telegraph line to Oregon approached completion. "People travel by steam and talk by lightning, and it does seem to me sometimes that they have some sort of intuitive way of acquiring information. People like myself must get out of the way for the 'car of progress'. In fact, I often look upon the halcyon days when I was an honest miller as the happiest in my life."

"An Act to facilitate Communication between the Atlantic and Pacific States by Electric Telegraph," adopted by congress, was approved June 16, 1860. It provided for a line from the western boundary of Missouri to San Francisco, and section two gave the contractors the "right to construct and maintain through any of the territories of the United States a branch line so as to connect their said line or lines with Oregon." A telegraph line was in operation as early as 1858 between Yreka and Sacramento, and after that date news was carried from the end of the telegraph line to Portland, at first by horseback and then by stage. Stage from Yreka to Portland took four and a half days.

The first proposal to operate a through telegraph line from Portland and valley points to California points was by Charles F. Johnson, agent of Alta California Telegraph Company, and F. D. Towsley, 1854, but this was not built at that time. Part of this line, however, was put in operation, 1855-6, between Corvallis, Lafayette, Oregon City and Portland. A company called the Oregon Telegraph Company, promoted by J. E. Strong, of California, was organized by W. S. Ladd, H. W. Corbett, S. G. Reed and others, 1862, with John McCracken as superintendent. They undertook to build a through line to California from Portland, and were so successful that the first through message was sent out over the wires March 5, 1864, and the Oregonian issued an extra edition containing news 24 hours old from New York. The celebration at Portland was on March 8, when there was an exchange of messages between the mayors of Portland, Oregon, and Portland, Maine. The operator at Portland for many years was O. P. S. Plummer. The first line from Portland to Seattle was completed in 1864. In 1868 a line was built from Portland to The Dalles, which was extended to Boise City in 1869.

29

These facts again take the story of Oregon into recent times. Looking backward over the years since the first railroad land grant in aid of western development was proposed to congress, it is evident that besides the elements of optimism and imagination, there was much of the ingredients of ignorance and inexperience that induced our pioneers to advocate and investors to finance the first railroad construction in the far west. It is plain now, after experience has made the record, that to build a costly railroad in an undeveloped country where there were few inhabitants and no industries would be to face a lack of dividends out of earnings for many years. It would not be possible to operate such a railroad without a steady supply of money from some source to pay the monthly deficit in operating income. The hope of converting a land grant into ready money as needed, would be certain of disappointment. And where, as in the case of the Oregon and California land grant, it was weighted with a condition that prohibited sale of lands except to actual settlers, and at $2.50 per acre, the lands being far away and mostly undesirable for purposes of actual settlement, the availability of the grant as an asset to furnish the stream of ready money that would be required during the pioneer period was visionary and impracticable.

It is not surprising, therefore, that none of the early enterprises that were so vital to the Oregon people proved a success to the original investor. Looking forward from the time of Oregon's admission as a state, it may now be seen that several of the lines went through receiverships and reorganizations. Some portions of the land grants were forfeited for failure to construct within the time limit, and others were forfeited for failure to comply with the conditions. There was consequently during the years much litigation, and the activities of legislatures and public officials in connection with this phase of Oregon's railroad history would require a special treatise to present the story in detail. But no chapter of events is more important to a review of the development of the Oregon Country than that which shows the part that the prospects for the coming of the railroads had in this story.

30

In the eastern states, in 1854, owing to reckless speculation, there was a panic and a sudden stoppage of business. Banks and business houses failed, there was a cessation of railroad building and a crash in stocks and bonds. Many persons were thrown out of employment, and destitution was widespread. In five years between January 1, 1851, and January 1, 1856, railroad mileage had increased from 8600 miles to 27,760 miles, principally built upon borrowed money. According to a report of the secretary of the treasury, March 2, 1854, nearly $203,000,000 worth of American securities were held abroad. The rising prices of commodities, in 1856, were followed by increased hard times in 1857, and business failures were numerous. Specie payments were suspended. Among the causes assigned were bank expansion of credit followed by rapid contraction, building unprofitable railroads, excessive importations from Europe, loss of $2,000,000 by the wreck of a treasure ship, and speculation and extravagance.

In Oregon, the panic in the east brought no serious disaster, but it was discussed by the newspapers, and excerpts from the press of the Atlantic seaboard were liberally reprinted. The hard times in the east had the effect of stimulating migration to the Pacific coast, but the major part of the movement was toward California. It is estimated that in 1857, the shortage of labor in Oregon, due to expanding activities, was a great drawback to the various branches of business, and that a thousand laborers, in addition to those already employed, could find constant employment at good wages. It was also pointed out, that the Willamette valley, in consequence of thin settlement, due to the operation of the donation land law, could hardly keep up its schools, and that what was wanted were numerous families with plenty of children, and scores of competent male and female teachers. Another factor that interfered with growth of Oregon population, prior to 1860, was the fear of Indian raids, and the fact that the trail was not sufficiently guarded by national or local military forces.

31

About 2000 immigrants came in 1850. The total population was then estimated at 13,294. By 1860, the population was 52,465, of which 16,564 were Oregon born, and 30,474 had come from outside the state. These figures may be compared with those of 1870, when the population was 90,923, an increase of 38,458 from 1860, or a growth of 73.3 per cent in the decade.

During the period under consideration there were few industries established on a business basis. Besides salmon fishing, lumbering and merchandising there was gold mining, but little else. Merchants and express companies issued drafts on San Francisco or New York, and this practice began as early as 1850. They also acted as agencies for receiving and forwarding gold dust, money and other valuables. Couch and Company, merchants at Portland, advertised as bankers, wholesale and retail merchants. They were a mercantile firm, but sold drafts. Norris and Company, another such firm, began to advertise for such banking business, in 1851, and stated that they had connections in California and at the various cities, on most favorable terms.

The express companies that engaged in similar business were Wells, Fargo & Company and Adams & Company. Both of them received moneys on deposit. In 1851, Todd and Company acted as agents for the Adams company and were authorized to draw bills of exchange on all houses on the Atlantic, and on London, at the usual rates. But in 1852, the firm authorized to represent Adams & Company, in Oregon, was Newell & Company. Wells, Fargo & Company had a branch office at Portland, opened October, 1852, and advertised as bankers and exchange brokers, with W. H. Barnhart and Company as agents.

An important bank was established at Portland in 1859, doing business under the name Ladd & Tilton, the members being W. S. Ladd and C. E. Tilton, the capital at the beginning being $50,000, but soon this capital was increased to $250,000. It was the sole bank in Oregon for a period of seven years. At that time the usual rates of interest were from three to five per cent per month, on short commercial loans, but favored customers at Ladd & Tilton's were charged two and one-half per cent. That was a time of scarcity of capital for loaning, and mortgage loans as well as bank loans took a high rate, especially in transactions in the mining regions of southern Oregon, and later in Idaho and Montana. At the opening of the Civil war, 1861, there was an unusual scarcity of money and discounts were not obtainable at any rate per cent. This was due to delay in payment of claims against the government, and belief that agents and officials of the United States had contracted liabilities for which the government was not responsible, as well as to the grave political questions agitating the country.

CHAPTER XXIX

OPENING YEARS OF STATEHOOD

1

THE OPENING years of the young commonwealth, now an equal among equals in the Union, cover a noteworthy chapter in the history, not only of Oregon, but of the nation. New political alignments, springing from broad issues that divided the country as a whole, were now formed in Oregon. Politically, the territory of Oregon had up to this time been so overwhelmingly democratic that pre-election canvass by the party nominees was always more or less perfunctory. A nomination upon the democrat ticket was in itself an assurance of election. As for the whigs, they had made little headway during the short life of that party in Oregon; and as yet the policy of the republican party had hardly crystallized. The democrats had everything in their favor, for many of the Willamette valley settlers came from Missouri and Tennessee, bringing with them their party preferences.

Yet Oregon would not follow the national democracy into the slavery camp, whither the efforts of Lane, who now aspired to the presidency, would have led it. Inclining a receptive ear to the doctrine of popular sovereignty, as enunciated by Stephen A. Douglas, Oregon democrats did so with such reservations as might have been expected from a people determined not to have slavery introduced on their own soil. The dominant note of Oregon's new political life was loyalty to the Union. This was manifest in the promptitude with which it rejected overtures looking toward the formation of a new republic on the Pacific coast, and with which it repudiated Lane's pro-slavery ideas. On the issues of slavery, and of the integrity of the Union, the Oregon democracy divided almost as soon as statehood was gained, and on this division the newly formed republican party built its hopes of success in the state.

2

In order to visualize Oregon's place in national politics, as a state admitted into the Union, a brief examination of the background may be proper. President Fillmore, a whig, was followed by Franklin Pierce, a democrat of New Hampshire, March 4, 1853. In January of that year, Sen. Stephen A. Douglas, of Illinois,

chairman of the committee on territories of the senate, offered a
bill to organize into two territories the undeveloped regions between the Missouri river and the Rocky mountains. The northern part was to be designated Nebraska, while lands south of the
40th parallel were to be known as Kansas. On account of these
names the bill was generally alluded to as the Kansas-Nebraska
bill. In effect, it would repeal the Missouri compromise of 1820,
by allowing slavery in both territories, if locally favored, although
most of the so-called Nebraska territory was north of the parallel named in the compromise measure. It will be remembered that
the so-called Missouri compromise act of 1820, had admitted Missouri as a slave state, but excluded slavery forever from every
other area of the Union, north and west of the northern limits of
Arkansas, thus shutting it out from every state north of 36° 30',
save Missouri. Public meetings were held through the north, at
which inflammatory resolutions were adopted, and bitter denunciation of the Kansas-Nebraska bill was voiced. In Oregon, citizens took sides, speeches were made, and the newspapers debated
the question. But, in spite of opposition in and out of congress,
the act passed both houses and was signed by President Pierce,
May 31, 1853.

This meant that the Missouri compromise was no longer in
force, and that the inhabitants of the two territories were to determine for themselves whether they would admit slavery. The
people in Nebraska territory were strongly against allowing slavery to gain a foothold; but Kansas, situated below the line, became the field of a real contest. A great rush of settlers from the
northern states began at once to fill Kansas with militant opponents of slavery, while from Missouri, and elsewhere, was echoed
the determination to form organizations to hold the territory open
for the southern institution.

A conflict that was a civil war in everything but name, was
soon raging, and after much violence, the debate on the subject
of slavery in every respect engaged the attention of congress.
Sen. Charles Sumner delivered a strong speech on the Crime
against Kansas; and there were quite as bitter replies by Senators Butler, Mason, Cass, Douglas and others. Excitement
through north and south was intense. A few days after the debate, Sumner was assaulted by Preston S. Brooks, a representa-

tive from South Carolina. The assailant used a heavy cane while his victim was seated in the senate chamber, and Sumner was so badly injured that he did not return to active duty in the senate for a period of four years.

The effect of those stirring times in the east was to accentuate party differences in Oregon. Prospects for admission of the state were to be considered in the light of the vital issues before the country at large. Repeal of Missouri compromise, 1854, disrupted the whig party. The native Americans, or know-nothing party, in the autumn of that year, and also in 1855 elections, carried several states but, after the organization of the republican party, 1856, in opposition to slavery, the alignment of voters throughout the Union was based upon that vital issue. The democrat convention, at Cincinnati, 1857, nominated James Buchanan president, and John C. Breckenridge for vice-president, while the republicans met at Philadelphia and nominated John C. Fremont and William L. Dayton. Buchanan carried 19 states, Fremont 11 states, while Fillmore, the presidential nominee of the native Americans, carried one. It was at this juncture of seething politics at Washington that Oregon became a state, when President Buchanan signed the statehood bill, February 14, 1859.

3

Opposition to having negroes in this state, whether as slaves or freedmen, had been clearly voiced in the formative period of the Oregon provisional government, and this had been shown again by popular vote on the separate issues of slavery and free negroes when the constitution was adopted. The decision by Judge George H. Williams, 1853, previously mentioned herein, had established the principle of free soil in Oregon, by judicially construing the language of the fundamental instrument adopted on creating the provisional government. This decision had gone unchallenged, although undoubtedly distasteful to violently pro-slavery citizens, who constituted the minority. Williams' popularity after this decision, and while making his active canvass against slavery in the pre-convention campaign, showed the temper of the majority when the secession movement in the south began to gain headway.

These free-soil indications were offset by Lane's personal ambitions, and by a falling out between Lane and the leaders of the

Salem clique. There was a sharp division within the democrat party when its first state convention was held at Salem, April 20, 1859, to nominate a candidate for congress to succeed Lafayette Grover. The latter, although supported by the clique, was defeated by Lansing Stout, by a vote of 43 to 33 in the convention. Stout was a recent arrival from California, and was accused by his opponents of having been a member of the know-nothing party when in that state, but he had the backing of the Lane faction. The result was received with jubilation by General Lane's followers, and Lane himself was emboldened to greater activity for the pro-slavery cause, which further widened the breach in his party.

4

However, organization of the national republican party, in Oregon, received encouragement from the obvious disturbance in the democrat ranks, so that a representative and enthusiastic convention of the new party was possible by April 21, 1859, although the party, as such, had had no existence even as recently as the preceding February. This convention was held at Salem, the next day after the democrats met there, and it proceeded in all seriousness not only to choose a candidate to oppose Stout for congress, but, what was more important to its future, to adopt free soil and patriotic resolutions calculated to interpret the spirit of the progressive people of the period, however cautious such resolutions may now seem. In temper they were conciliatory, in purpose conservative. They opposed the extension of slavery, but disclaimed intent to interfere with the institution where it already existed. Intervention by congress to protect slavery in the territories was denounced. A welcome was extended to white aliens who should come into the United States to enjoy the benefit of free institutions; and it was asserted that the enforcement of existing naturalization laws was sufficient regulation of foreign immigration. The resolutions declared in favor of a homestead bill, which Lane had opposed in the preceding session of congress, and also demanded the construction of a Pacific railroad.

The convention nominated for congress David Logan, a Portland lawyer of considerable attainments, recently from California and reputed there to have been allied with the know-nothing party, and who was a former resident of Springfield, Illinois. He was the son of Samuel Trigg Logan, an eminent lawyer and judge, a friend of Lincoln. Samuel Logan, later, was a delegate to the republican national convention at Chicago that nominated Lincoln for president.

5

During the local campaign, the division of the democrats in Oregon, and the lukewarm support given Stout by the Oregon Statesman, favored the republican candidate. The sequel, surprising to republicans and democrats alike, was that, in the election, June 27, 1859, David Logan came within 16 votes of winning. The political upset was complete. Marion, stronghold of democracy, went for Logan by 782, and Clatsop, Multnomah, Tillamook, Washington and Yamhill also gave republican majorities. Only the southern counties saved Stout, and these had been held in line by strong personal devotion to Lane, founded on his record in the Indian wars.

6

In another respect the opening year of statehood was momentous for the republican party, as well as for the state, in national affairs. The republican state convention that nominated Logan also chose delegates to the national republican convention to be held in 1860, acting far in advance of the event because of the difficulties and uncertainties of transcontinental travel; and thus it set in motion a series of circumstances which were influential in bringig about the nomination of Abraham Lincoln for president.

Lincoln was first suggested to the voters of Oregon as a candidate for president by Simeon Francis, a new man in Oregon. Previously, Francis had been the founder and editor of the Illinois State Journal, of Springfield. His plea for consideration of Lincoln was in the form of a lengthy contributed article in the Oregon Argus, February, 1860. Subsequently, he served for a time as editor of the Oregonian, during absence of Thomas J. Dryer, who carried the electoral vote for Lincoln to Washington.

The delegates nominated to go to the republican national convention were A. G. Hovey, Dr. W. Warren and Leander Holmes, and they were instructed to use their influence to procure the nomination of William H. Seward, of New York, then an idol of the opponents of slavery in the nation. He had not yet alienated his supporters by the temporizing attitude assumed by him some time later. It was asserted afterward that the Seward resolution in the Oregon convention was passed surreptitiously, after the main business of the convention had been transacted, and after many of the delegates had left. However, there were sound reasons for Oregon's support of Seward, who had stoutly championed her promotion to statehood, and had been one of the 11 republican senators to vote for the statehood bill, when it passed the senate, May 1858. Seward's speech on this occasion had been well calculated to endear him to the people of the new state. "For one, sir," he had said, "I think that the sooner a territory emerges from its provincial condition, the better; the sooner the people are left to manage their own affairs, and admitted to participation in the responsibilities of the government, the more vigorous the states which these people form will be." This accorded fully with local opinion on the subject. A saving clause in the resolution of instructions empowered the Oregon delegates to act upon their own discretion, if they could not secure Seward's nomination. This convention also created a state central committee, consisting of Henry W. Corbett, W. Carey Johnson and E. D. Shattuck.

7

The state legislature was convened in special session by Governor Whiteaker, in May, 1859, a call made necessary by the premature legislative session held before congress had passed the admission bill. Growing opposition to Lane, due to his pro-slavery proclivities, and the factional bitterness consequent on the defeat of the Salem organization in the nomination of Stout, caused a deadlock and resulted in failure to elect a senator to succeed Delazon Smith, who had drawn the short term, expiring in March, 1859. His term had ended a little over two weeks after taking his seat. Smith became a candidate for re-election, but neither faction of the democrats could muster a working majority, so nothing was done about it and the seat in the senate was left vacant.

The legislature accepted the conditions imposed by congress on admission to statehood, passed an act providing for a state seal, and another calling a special election for representative in congress, and enacted some general legislation of minor importance. Political affairs now engaged the attention of lawmakers and people to the exclusion of almost every other subject and no one was in a mood for the minor details of legislation.

8

At the special election, Stout was successful over Logan, as stated, but the strength shown by the new republican organization gave the leaders of that party strong hopes for future success, and many former democrats followed such men as Williams and Shattuck into the republican party. Backed by the fervid Oregon Argus and the vigorous Oregonian, therefore, the republicans were enabled to complete their party machinery in the various counties. With Stout elected to the lower house of congress, while Lane's colleague and supporter, Delazon Smith, was retired from the senate, the situation was more than ever complicated; nor was it simplified in any degree when it was reported that the ambition of Lane was to become the pro-slavery nominee of the democrats for president. The democrat state convention at which Stout had been nominated, in April, had named a state central committee favorable to Lane's plans, but this committee, meeting at Eugene, September 24, 1859, increased the breach between the factions by determining that the basis of representation in the state convention, called for November 16, following, at Eugene, should be the vote cast for Stout in the June election. This was strictly according to precedent, but it was clearly favorable to Lane, since it increased the proportion of delegates from the southern Oregon counties in which his personal following was large, and it correspondingly curtailed the influence of the large counties in the north.

The anti-Lane forces thereupon declared that by this course the democracy of the Willamette valley was virtually disfranchised, and claimed that a one-man rule was established as the result of the objectionable acts of Lane. They vociferously demanded that in the interests of party union the vote for Whiteaker, in 1857, before the split, be made the basis of representation in the convention. Their protest going unheeded, they withdrew from the committee's sessions, and issued a separate call to the democracy of the state to send delegates to Eugene according to the Whiteaker basis of appointment.

The consequences that might have been expected then followed. The anti-Lane delegations went to the convention, but were excluded. The Lane faction, controlling the credential committee and the convention, restricted the number of delegates to those auth-

orized under the original call. Ill-feeling was intensified. Marion
county, cut down from 10 delegates to four, led a bolt. The delegates from Clatsop, Coos, Curry, Polk, Wasco, Washington and
Umpqua counties also withdrew. These objectors organized another state convention, but foolishly refrained from nominating
delegates to the national democrat convention, on the ground that
they did not constitute a majority of the counties.

The remaining delegates in the original convention proceeded
to organize without the insurgents, and elected Joseph Lane,
Judge Matthew P. Deady and Lansing Stout as delegates to the
national convention, and J. F. Miller, John Adair and John K.
Lamerick, as alternates. They also adopted a resolution recommending Lane to the consideration of the party for the office of
president or vice-president, while pledging the party in the state
to support the nominee of the national convention, "whoever he
may be." Of the 11 counties remaining after the bolt, Josephine
and Clackamas had instructed for Douglas for president, Yamhill
for Daniel S. Dickinson, and Benton had voted down a Lane resolution. Only Lane, Douglas and Jackson counties had instructed
for Lane, who thus succeeded in getting his own selections as delegates and obtained the fruits of the plan laid in the spring convention. This resulted ultimately in his nomination at Charleston, South Carolina, in the year following, for vice-president of
the United States, as the running mate of John C. Breckenridge,
for president.

9

Among republicans, several changes of particular interest were
meanwhile taking place in the development of the national program. The popularity of Seward had been dimmed since the Oregon delegates had been chosen, more than a year in advance of
the Chicago convention, and two new figures were looming on the
political horizon. One was Edward Bates, of Missouri, who attracted a considerable following among Oregon republicans because of the large number of former residents of Missouri then
living in the state. He had won the admiration of others by his
leadership in the anti-slavery movement.

Bates was proposed for president for the first time in Oregon
by W. L. Adams, in the Oregon Argus, October, 1859. Adams had
come to Oregon from Illinois. Bates was a warm friend of Jesse

Applegate, and he and Applegate were in constant correspondence. In the early stages of the "Oregon movement," when Hall J. Kelley was bombarding congress with petitions and Dr. John Floyd had reported a bill for the military occupation of the country, with grants of land to settlers, Bates had been one of the ablest opponents of the bill. He was careful to explain, however, that he believed in the justice of the claims of the early Oregonians, but opposed the measure on the ground that it violated the spirit of the treaty of joint occupancy and consequently was inexpedient at that time. There was no disposition in Oregon to discredit Bates on this account, and his following in the state was loyal and sincere.

Another name was that of Abraham Lincoln, whose debates with Douglas, in 1858, had marked him as a national character. In chapter 21, we have mentioned that Lincoln, at the end of his term as congressman, 1849, had under consideration the governorship of Oregon territory and that he, instead of Gaines, would have been appointed to succeed Lane if he had not declined the place. At the expense of some repetition further particulars may be given.

"According to the custom of the time," says Arthur Brooks Lapsley, "all the democrats were to be turned out of office and their places given to whigs who had done service in the campaign. Lincoln, with plenty of ideas concerning public improvements and with some experience as a surveyor of lands, thought he would like to be commissioner of the general land office, a place in which he would have charge of the sale and distribution of lands belonging to the United States. To the surprise of his friends and his own great disappointment, which he did not attempt to conceal, Lincoln was refused the office he sought, but was offered that of governor of the territory of Oregon. This place, however, he declined. It was not to his taste, and most likely, he was beginning to see that he had a great work on this side of the Rocky mountains. Moreover, Mrs. Lincoln was decidedly opposed to his going to the Pacific coast. She had had enough of frontier life. Years afterward, when her husband had become president, she did not fail to remind him that her advice, when he was wavering, had restrained him from throwing himself away on a distant territorial governorship. The bait held out to Lincoln at that time was that Oregon would soon come in to the Union as a state and that he could probably return as a United States senator. This glittering prospect made him pause, until his wife's opposition determined him. It is a curious coincidence that when Lincoln was president, Edward D. Baker, who was Lincoln's friend, and his successor in congress, went to Oregon from California and was elected United States senator from that state."

Lincoln had a staunch supporter in David Logan, in whose political success he expressed personal interest. In a letter to Amory Holbrook, written at Springfield, Illinois, August 20, 1860, after Logan had been defeated a second time for congress, Lincoln wrote: "It is a matter of much regret here that Logan failed to his election. He grew up and studied law in this place, and his parents and sisters still reside here. We are also anxious for the result of your U. S. Senatorial election."

10

Oregon's part in deciding the nomination of Lincoln, in the famous Chicago convention of 1860, gives an especial interest to this period of the political history of the state. The republican national convention was first planned to meet in Chicago, June 13, 1860, but afterward the proposed date was changed to May 16, in the official call. The second notification was not received in Oregon until late in March, and thus caught unprepared the Oregon delegates, although they had been chosen almost a year previously. The journey to Chicago was no slight undertaking, and the time was short. Moreover, Oregon's allotment of delegates was designated in the call as six instead of three, and, inasmuch as there would be no state convention in time to elect the additional delegates authorized, or to allow such new selections to reach Chicago for the convention, the state central committee was hastily summoned and it appointed, as additional delegates, Henry W. Corbett, Joel Burlingame and Frank Johnson, the last named a young Oregonian then attending theological seminary at Hamilton, New York. As a further measure of precaution, the delegates were empowered to appoint proxies in the event that they were unable to be present in person.

Few of the citizens of the young commonwealth could afford the expense of going so far, involving continuous travelling for five or six weeks in each direction. Of the delegation originally appointed, therefore, only one travelled from Oregon in time for the convention, Joel Burlingame. Frank Johnson, chosen partly because he was already in the east and could reach Chicago at relatively small expense, was the only other one of the regularly appointed delegates to attend and serve. Leander Holmes sent his proxy to Horace Greeley, the veteran editor of the New York Tribune, who had broken with Seward, the candidate in whose favor the Oregon state convention had instructed the party representatives. Corbett sent his proxy to Eli Thayer, of Massachusetts, who had endeared himself to Oregonians by leading a bolt of 11 republicans in the national house of representatives against the action of the republican caucus in opposing the statehood bill. Corbett and Holmes afterward left Oregon for the eastern states, but they did not arrive in time to take part in the convention proceedings, and their proxies, Eli Thayer and Horace Greeley, acted for them through the convention. The proxy of either Hovey, or Warren, was given to Henry Buckingham, of Oregon, who attended the convention, and the sixth place on the delegation remained vacant. Thus, Oregon was represented at the great convention by Burlingame, Johnson, Greeley, Thayer and Buckingham. Although originally instructed for Seward, but one vote by a member of the delegation was given in his support, while his active and untiring opponent, Greeley, found place in the delegation, from which position he made his opposition effective. Such is the uncertainty of politics.

11

The convention was held in a building known as the Wigwam, holding not less than 10,000 persons. Greeley first favored the nomination of Bates, but subsequently he exercised his great influence in directing the tide toward Lincoln on the memorable third ballot, when the choice of Lincoln was indicated and was made practically certain by the casting of four of Oregon's five votes for him. It is unnecessary to assume that Greeley would have had no place in the convention if he had not held an Oregon proxy, but it is known that he had previously resolved not to attend. It is plain that the outcome of the convention was largely determined by Oregon, whose votes on the preliminary ballot mentioned gave Lincoln within one and a half votes of the number required for a choice. It is also clear that Greeley voted with the other Oregon delegates for Bates, and against Seward, for whom the delegation had been instructed. On each of the first two ballots, Oregon cast five votes for Bates; on the third preliminary ballot four were for Lincoln and one for Seward (the latter the only vote for Seward ever cast by an Oregon delegate) ; and on the third formal ballot the five votes were for Lincoln, who was then nominated. Hannibal Hamlin, of Maine, was nominated for vice-president. Greeley, with his Oregon proxy, served in this convention as a member of the committee on resolutions, which drafted the historic republican national platform of 1860.

12

Greeley's motive in opposing Seward has been the subject of wide differences in opinion. Seward's reputed perfidy in his political dealings with his former associate and supporter would ordinarily furnish a sufficient explanation, considering the temper of the time, but Greeley's own version is entitled to examination. He said, afterward, that he had at first resolved to avoid the convention after having concluded that the nomination of Seward was both undesirable and unsafe, but that on receiving a request from Leander Holmes to act in the latter's stead he did not feel at liberty to refuse the duty imposed on him. Concerning the attitude of the people of Oregon toward the rival candidates, he wrote: "Of the four letters that simultaneously reached me, one from Mr. Holmes, another from Mr. Corbett, chairman of the republican state committee, a third from the editor of a leading republican journal [Dryer of the Oregonian, or Adams of the Argus] and a fourth from an eminent ex-editor [Simeon Francis], at least three indicated Bates as the decided choice of Oregon for president, and the man who would be most likely to carry it, a very natural preference, since a large proportion of the people of Oregon emigrated from Missouri. One of them suggested Mr. Lincoln as also a favorite, many Illinoisans being now settled in Oregon." "If ever in my life I discharged a public duty in utter disregard of my personal consideration," wrote Greeley a month after the convention, "I did so at Chicago last month . . . I did not and do not believe it advisable that he [Seward] should be the republican candidate for president."

13

The national democrat convention, which met at Charleston, South Carolina, April 23, 1860, was attended by a delegation from Oregon in complete accord with Lane's ambition, although Lane himself was committed to the cause of the slave states and was drifting rapidly toward secession. Even now it was beginning to be rumored that a movement for the establishment of a new republic on the Pacific coast was under way, and the atmosphere of plot and counterplot pervaded the politics of the entire Pacific coast, of California as well as Oregon. Six delegates were allotted to Oregon, in the Charleston national democrat convention, just as at Chicago; but of those regularly chosen by the state convention in the preceding November, only Stout and Lamerick appeared in person. Lane remained in Washington, D. C., from which place he kept in touch with the delegation by telegraph, during the convention, and when appealed to for advice, he counselled the members to withdraw with the pro-slavery wing. Oregon was represented also by ex-Governor Isaac I. Stevens, of Washington territory, then delegate in congress from that territory; A. P. Dennison, an Indian agent in Oregon; Justus Steinberger, agent of the Pacific Mail Steamship Company; and R. B. Metcalf, of Texas, formerly an Indian agent in the territorial days. The last mentioned was supplanted later in the proceedings by H. R. Crosbie, an Oregonian who had come to Oregon territory with Governor Davis. It may be recalled that the northern democrats in the Charleston convention succeeded in having a Douglas platform adopted, and that thereupon the southerners withdrew; and that afterward the two factions called separate conventions of their delegates to meet at Baltimore, in June.

The Oregon delegates acted in harmony with the Breckenridge, or southern faction, but did not at first withdraw from the party, remaining with the tacit understanding that they would join the bolt only in the event that the nomination of Douglas became probable. Stevens did, in fact, put in an appearance at the adjourned convention of the northern or Douglas, democrats, at Baltimore, June 18, 1860, where a little later he announced the withdrawal of the Oregon members, who then joined the seceders at their convention held a few days afterward, at Richmond, Virginia. They participated in the nomination of Breckenridge and Lane for president and vice-president, as the candidates of the pro-slavery democrats, while the Douglas democrats at Baltimore chose Stephen A. Douglas, for president and Herschel V. Johnson for vice-president.

Stevens subsequently directed the Breckenridge-Lane national campaign, as chairman of the national central committee, but, on the secession of the southern states, he had a change of heart and allied himself with the federal cause, became a major-general of United States volunteers, and fell in gallant combat at Chantilly, September 1, 1862, fighting for the preservation of the Union. Steinberger also joined the federal army. Lamerick and Metcalf cast their fortunes with the Confederacy, Lamerick becoming commissary of a Louisiana regiment, and Metcalf a lieutenant in the Confederate army.

The divided sympathies of the delegates thus indicated the breadth of the schism in the democrat party in Oregon. While it contained a numerous and influential element of secessionist sympathizers, it became impotent as an instrument of disunion by reason of the division of its voting strength, and by the loyalty of the minority, who adhered to Douglas and the Union. In the campaign that followed, there was a political alliance of all Union sympathizers of all shades of political opinion and of all kinds of previous affiliations.

14

The nomination of Abraham Lincoln was wholly satisfactory to Oregon republicans, whom it inspired with a new fervor. Examination of the vote in the Chicago convention, moreover, revealed that Bates had never had a real chance of nomination there. Much of the popular esteem in which Seward had been held in Oregon, due to his famous speech at Rochester, New York, October 25, 1858, in which the "irrepressible conflict" phrase was coined, had been forfeited by his change of front when the Kansas bill was under consideration in the United States senate, February 29, 1860. On the other hand, it was now remembered that Lincoln's position upon the all-absorbing question was quite as clear as Seward's had ever been. "A house divided against itself cannot stand" translated the spirit of Oregon republicanism. The enthusiasm with which Lincoln had been put forward at Chicago communicated itself to the party in Oregon and hope ran high.

15

Preceding the national conventions of 1860, the citizens pursued their usual custom of holding the general election, in June. The political parties held their conventions, in April, for the selection of state candidates. The democrats met first, at Eugene, April 17, where they nominated George K. Sheil, of Marion county, for representative in congress to succeed Lansing Stout, and adopted resolutions which declared the Cincinnati platform of 1856 to be a satisfactory statement of the principles of the democrat party, refusing, by a vote of 60 to 4, to consider an amendment which would have added the words, "as advocated and enunciated by Stephen A. Douglas." Other candidates for congress before the convention were James K. Kelly, Stephen F. Chadwick, John Adair and J. H. Reed, but the incumbent, Stout, was not even considered, he having broken with Lane and Smith. Six counties, owing to the disaffection of the preceding November, were not represented. They were Clatsop, Curry, Marion, Polk, Tillamook and Washington.

The republicans, April 19, 1860, again nominated David Logan for representative in congress, T. J. Dryer, B. J. Pengra and W. H. Watkins for presidential electors, and adopted in substance the old platform of 1859, except that the Seward instructions were omitted and a strong protest against the Dred Scott decision was added. A noteworthy occurrence, which served to introduce a new and striking personality to the political life of the state, was the appearance before this convention of Col. Edward Dickinson Baker, then recently from California, whose name had been closely associated with Lincoln's and whose fame as an orator had preceded him to Oregon. Colonel Baker had defeated Lincoln for the nomination for congress, 1844, yet had remained on terms of cordial intimacy with him. That nomination had resulted in his election to the national house of representatives as a whig. Resigning his seat, 1846, to serve with distinction in the Mexican war, he had canvassed the middle west, with Lincoln, for Zachary Taylor, 1848, and had then emigrated to California, 1852, in furtherance of his political ambitions, which were, however, temporarily thwarted when he failed of election as the whig nominee for representative in congress from that state, 1859. Although thus disappointed, his speeches in the California campaign were remarkable for their stirring eloquence.

16

It having occurred to certain Oregon republicans, that the party needed a spokesman of Baker's type, he was informally invited to assist in the canvass of the state for the Lincoln ticket. It was thought that the young republican party was wanting in leaders possessing the gift of eloquence, a deficiency that Baker was peculiarly able to supply. His eloquent eulogy, delivered before a multitude assembled in the Plaza, at San Francisco, in September, 1859, in the presence of the mortal remains of Sen. David C. Broderick, killed in a political duel by Judge Terry, was considered as a masterpiece of oratory. His brilliant campaign speeches in the California campaign established his already well earned reputation as a public speaker and an anti-secessionist.

Baker promptly accepted the invitation to stump the state of Oregon, and did most effective campaign work, bringing a needed antidote for the new scheme of disruption which now threatened the nation. This was the scheme to set up a new republic consisting of the states and territories of the Pacific coast, to which allusion has been made, said to have already gained some headway in California. General Lane was reputed to be in sympathy, if not in active cooperation, with those who originated the proposal.

17

Sheil, as the representative of the Lane-Smith faction of the state democracy, was openly opposed in the ensuing campaign by Nesmith, and other Union democrats, but on the other hand was supported by Kelly and many others, who had returned to the fold rather than risk further disorganization of the party. In the June election, therefore, Sheil defeated Logan by a small margin, notwithstanding the fact that Asahel Bush, in that organ of the democrat party, the Statesman, loudly contended that the constitution made no provision for any election of a member of congress at this time, and that therefore the election was a mere trick of the friends of Lane and Smith to "debauch and distract the democratic party, and defy the popular will."

The legislature chosen in this June election, 1860, was again overwhelmingly democratic, but upon analysis it appeared that the two factions of the democrats in the joint assembly were divided nearly evenly, there being 18 supporters of Douglas and 17 adherents of Breckenridge, or Lane. The republicans, numbering 13, thus had the balance of power in the event the warring factions should be unable to unite, which was precisely what did come to pass. Indeed, the result presaged the fusion of republicans and loyal or Union democrats, which was to follow. While there was no formal alliance between republicans and Douglas democrats, there was at least agreement as to method. In Marion county, for example, the Douglas and Lane forces each nominated candidates for the legislature; and the republicans, on the advice of Baker, supported the Douglas ticket, with the understanding that the nominees, if elected, would support Baker for senator. This was in the face of the fact that the republicans were probably strong enough in Marion county to have elected their ticket. On the other hand, in Washington and Yamhill counties, the anti-Lane democrats did not nominate candidates, but supported for the most part those of the republicans. A similar understanding, denied, or at least unconfessed, seemed to exist over the state. Judge Williams broke with the Lane-Smith faction, and travelling to Linn county, Smith's home, challenged Smith to a joint canvass. Smith accepted and the two covered the county on horseback, speaking every day, and generally, as accommodations were limited, occupying the same bed at night.

The logic of this informal political compact was unassailable, for notwithstanding existing differences of opinion between the abolitionists and the champions of squatter sovereignty, both groups, constituting a majority of the whole people of the state, realized the perils of secession. Baker, indeed, refrained from committing himself to the extreme abolition view, making it easy for Douglas democrats to support him, and throughout the campaign he pursued a policy of persuasion rather than of invective.

18

When the legislature met, September 10, 1860, at Salem, the prospect that the republican and Douglas democrats would carry out their pre-election understanding was so imminent that six of the senators representing the Breckenridge faction absented themselves in a futile attempt to prevent organization of the senate, leaving that body without a quorum. The recalcitrants were A. B. Florence and James Monroe, of Lane county; A. M. Berry, of Jackson; H. L. Brown, of Linn; Solomon Fitzhugh, of Douglas; G. S. McIteeney, of Benton, all supporters of Lane. They went into concealment, while the sergeant-at-arms sought for them in vain. Two rival conventions of the factions of the democrat party were then in session in Eugene, and these adopted resolutions respectively denouncing and upholding the conduct of the absconders. Governor Whiteaker, although allied with the Breckenridge faction, published an appeal to them to return for patriotic reasons, and they did so, September 24, 1860.

The Douglas democrats meanwhile organized the assembly, electing Benjamin F. Harding, of Marion, speaker. Luther Elkins, of Linn, was made president of the senate on its organization without a quorum. The joint assembly while waiting for the absentee members to return made several unsuccessful attempts to elect a senator, the Douglas men voting for Nesmith and Williams and the republicans for Baker and Holbrook. Being unable to proceed without the absconders, however, the two houses adjourned sine die. Governor Whiteaker then called an extra session, at which both houses had a quorum, and balloting was resumed ineffectively, October first. On the 18th ballot, October 2, 1860, Nesmith and Baker were duly elected, carrying the fusion of republicans and Douglas democrats into effect. Twenty-six votes were necessary for a choice; Nesmith received 27 votes for the long term and Baker 26 votes for the short term. Pro-slavery democrats, the opponents of Nesmith, concentrated on Judge Deady, who received 22 votes. In opposition to Baker, Judge George H. Williams received 20 votes and Ex-Governor Curry, two.

19

The result had not been attained, however, without a bitter struggle in which the Douglas democrats made several efforts to find a basis of reunion with the Breckenridge faction, which should include Nesmith and exclude Smith. So closely did the factions approach agreement that, on the ballot preceding the final one, Nesmith had 24 votes and Curry 25, within two and one, respectively, of enough to elect.

The Statesman afterward reported: "Harding turned to the Breckenridge side of the house and said if any two of their number would change to Nesmith he would vote for Curry and elect Nesmith and Curry; they refused to do it. Norton, of Coos, made the same proposition to an especial friend of Governor Curry, on the floor. It was also rejected. Every Douglas man on the floor would have done the same thing, had it been possible. . . . The Douglas members would not vote for Delusion [a derisive political nickname for Delazon Smith], and the Breckenridgers refused to support Nesmith with anybody else. Not only would they not take Williams or Curry, with Nesmith, but they refused to take Stout, Reed or any Breckenridge man with Nesmith, except Delusion. If Delusion was dropped they required that Nesmith should be. . . . Baker has been politically committed to the doctrine of non-intervention in the affairs of the territory, and squatter sovereignty, before and since his residence in Oregon. As the case was presented by the Lane and Delusion member, there were but three alternatives, the election of Delusion, no election at all, or the dernier resort adopted."

20

The 15 democrats who voted for Baker joined in issuing a statement in justification of their act. They declared the "proscriptive and intolerant course pursued by General Lane and his office holding minions toward non-intervention democrats . . . and the corruption and treachery of Delazon Smith" to have been the direct causes of the party division, and contended that the election of a majority of non-intervention democrats to the legislature had finally disposed of Lane and Smith. The Breckenridge forces, and Lane by implication, were branded as party wreckers, and those who persisted in voting for Smith were charged with seeking to create a deadlock with a view to preserving a vacancy to be filled in 1862 by "a rejected aspirant for vice-presidential honors."

In specific defense of their votes for Baker, the 15 explained that they were influenced "by his well known position upon the question of slavery in the territories, a position differing but little from that of our party." On the final ballot Holbrook declined to vote, although he subsequently expressed hope that "the people may never have cause to regret the action which has secured senators who will never submit to southern dictation." In a letter from John R. McBride to Craig, October 2, 1860, McBride accused Holbrook of perfidy in failing to do his part in carrying out the agreement. "The faltering," he wrote, "was in our ranks entirely." Nevertheless, dissension among republicans was slight, in comparison with the wide breach of the democrats, the bitterness of which was shown in the hanging in effigy of the president of the state senate, Luther Elkins, and the burning of his image, at Albany, by Lane supporters.

The facts of national significance were this election of two non-secessionist senators, and the disruption of the democrat voters. Only by such disruption could the casting of the electoral vote of the state for Abraham Lincoln have been made possible, and this consequence soon followed.

With the senatorial contest disposed of, the way was cleared for the intense autumn political campaign of 1860. Presidential elections, then as now, were held in November, while the state elections were in June. The democrat conventions which met while the legislature was jockeying over the senatorship, put two tickets for presidential electors in the field. The Breckenridge-Lane nominees were Delazon Smith, James O'Meara and D. W. Douthitt. The Douglas electors were W. H. Farrar, Benjamin Hayden and William Hoffman. The republican electors, T. J. Dryer, B. J. Pengra and W. H. Watkins, had been chosen April 19. In addition to these, the constitutional union party, with John Bell as its candidate for president, had an electoral ticket in Oregon, the nominees for electors being Stuckely Ellsworth, G. W. Grier and John Ross.

An added complication arose in the nomination of A. J. Thayer, for representative in congress, by the Douglas democrat state central committee, October, 1860, pursuant to the contention of this faction that Sheil had been illegally nominated and elected in the spring. The real issue, however, was the extension or non-extension of slavery.

Thus, it came about that, with the democrats divided, the electoral vote of the state was given Lincoln by a plurality of 270, on the crucial election day, November 6, 1860. The vote was: Lincoln, 5344; Breckenridge, 5075; Douglas, 4131; Bell, 212. For congress, Thayer received 4099 votes, to 131 for Sheil. There was practically no opposition, as both republicans and Breckenridge democrats abstained from voting for that office. The incident obtains some significance from the circumstance that, although Thayer was at first seated when he and Sheil presented their credentials to the house, that body afterward reversed its action and recognized as superior the claims of Sheil. The house committee on elections of the thirty-seventh congress, although overwhelmingly republican, reported unanimously in favor of restoring the seat to Sheil, who was well known to be a sympathizer with secession, and the house itself rejected an amendment offered by Thaddeus

Stevens declaring that neither was entitled to the place, and that the seat should be declared vacant. Stevens argued that the constitution of a state might fix the time for the congressional election first held therein, but that all subsequent elections should be regulated by congressional enactment, a point upon which he thought the provision of the United States constitution to be clear and mandatory.

22

The election of 1860 ended the memorable, and many respects spectacular, career of Lane, and at the same time put an end to the Pacific republic movement, which had spread to Oregon, and in connection with which it was freely charged during the summer and autumn of 1860 that Lane, with Senator Gwin of California, had conspired with southern secessionists to complete the destruction of the Union. Three governments, declared the Statesman, July 17, 1860, were planned, two in the east, one free and one slaveholding, the third to consist of the states and territories on the Pacific coast, which were to decide the issue of slavery for themselves. Later, it was charged that senators and representatives from Oregon and California had held a caucus, in Washington, at which the feasibility of the creation of three separate republics had been considered. A form of government was said to have been agreed on. The particulars were transmitted from California and widely circulated in Oregon, although this was after the election of November, 1860, had rendered the success of the enterprise improbable. The details are nevertheless interesting. The Statesman, quoting from the San Francisco Times, made this explanation: "On certain essentials they (the conspirators) are unanimous, said a newspaper authority on the subject. In the first place they discard universal suffrage and repudiate the people as a basis of power. Secondly, labor must be performed by a servile class, and, therefore, the immigration of coolies, South Sea islanders and negroes, is to be encouraged, who are to be reduced to slavery immediately upon their arrival. If, in the expected secession of the south from the American Union, a line of slave territory from Texas to the Pacific can be kept open, a majority of the conspirators favor an immediate combination with the southern Confederacy. But another faction, in view of the probable wars in which the aggressive portion of these states will involve all their allies and confederates, favor the establishment of an empire at once, or an autocratic system on the Venetian plan, while providing for an elective executive, deposits all power in the hands of the hereditary nobles." Nesmith, visiting San Francisco in the winter of 1860, ascertained that "the programme is for Texas to withdraw and unite with Arizona, capture some of the Mexican states and force the Pacific states into the confederacy as a matter of course, though little is said of the scheme."

Lane gave color to charges that he was a particpant in these councils by his open opposition to coercive measures for the preservation of the Union, not only in his association with the Breckenridge faction, but in speeches in congress and in his private writings. He wrote to Judge Deady, on the eve of the reassembling of the thirty-seventh congress for its final session: "Congress will assemble for the last time that a national congress will assemble under the constitution as it is now." "Consequently," he added, "look upon the Union as broken up." Almost the last day of his senatorship, he predicted that the slave states would "go out of the Union into one of their own; forming a great, homogeneous and glorious southern confederacy," and he urged peace, if not in union, then by cultivating friendly relations with the states which had established a separate government. "I know long, well and intimately, the gallant men of Oregon," he said also, "that they will not be found ready or inclined to imbrue their hands, for a godless cause, in fraternal gore." Lane was quoted in a letter to a southern friend, dated January 6, 1860, printed in the Georgia Constitutionalist, and reprinted in the Oregon Statesman, February 25, 1861, as saying: "I am glad the majority of the people of Oregon have determined to leave a Union that refuses you equality and protection."

Judge George H. Williams' estimate of Lane, many years after these events, was as follows. "I have never known a man in Oregon to whom the Latin maxim, suaviter in modo, fortiter in re, could with more propriety be applied. He had all the essential qualifications of a successful politician, and if he had not been so imbued with a desire to extend slavery, might in all human probability have represented Oregon in the senate as long as he lived. He was intensely southern in all his feelings and sympathies, a devoted friend of Jefferson Davis, and opposed to coercive measures to preserve the Union. It is due to his memory to say that he had what many shifty politicians have not, the courage of his convictions, and he stood by them to the bitter end."

23

News of the firing on Fort Sumter was received in Oregon late in April, 1861. The homecoming of Lane at this time furnished opportunity for certain Unionists to manifest a noisy patriotism by hanging the now discredited senator in effigy, as was done at Dallas, and by various other spectacular acts; but the ominous fact of war brought the serious minded opponents of secession once more into accord in an endeavor to formulate a constructive program. Enthusiastic Union meetings were held all over the state, which Governor Whiteaker, a pro-slavery democrat who had been elected before secession had become the issue, proceeded to deprecate as unnecessary and as provocative of the disunion which they professed to oppose. Whiteaker did not approve the war. Democrats denied that they were disloyal. Republican leadership in most of the Union meetings gave a partisan flavor to the union movement in the beginning, and created opposition which can be interpreted sympathetically by considering the political conditions of the period. Oregon was divided less between union and disunion than over questions of expediency. Not all were persuaded that it was yet too late for settlement by compromise.

24

Senator Baker served for a brief but eloquent period in congress. He volunteered for service at the outbreak of the rebellion, recruited a regiment in Pennsylvania which was credited to the quota of California. He served as colonel, but declined a commission as brigadier-general offered by President Lincoln. He was killed in battle while leading a charge at Ball's Bluff, Virginia, October 21, 1861. During his time in the senate he delivered several remarkable speeches. He was for the Union. His first speech, delivered January 2 and January 3, 1861, in reply to Sen. Judah P. Benjamin, of Louisiana, began with these striking words: "Mr. President: The adventurous traveller, who wanders on the slopes of the Pacific and on the very verge of civilization, stands awe-struck and astonished in that great chasm formed by the torrent of the Columbia, as, rushing between Mt. Hood and Mt. St.

Helens, it breaks through the ridges of the Cascade mountains to find the sea. Nor, is this wonder lessened when he hears his slightest tones repeated and re-echoed with a larger utterance in the reverberations which lose themselves at last amid the surrounding and distant hills. So I, standing on this spot, and speaking for the first time in this chamber, reflect with astonishment that my feeblest word is re-echoed, even while I speak, to the confines of the republic. I trust, sir, that in so speaking in the midst of such an auditory, in the presence of great events, I may remember all the responsibility these impose upon me, to perform my duty to the constitution of the United States, and to be in nowise forgetful of my obligations to the whole country, of which I am a devoted and affectionate son."

In the speech he took a strong stand against the right of secession, but in a later speech, March 1, 1861, on resolutions proposing amendments to the constitution, known as the Peace Conference Propositions, he offended some of his republican associates by temporizing, or, as they thought, encouraging the threatening states in the hope that some compromise might be effected. However, immediately after the fall of Fort Sumter he delivered one of the greatest of all of his impassioned and thrilling speeches, pledging himself to the support of the flag. This was at Union Park, New York City, before an audience described as "one of the largest assemblages ever enchained by the eloquence of a single man." After raising his regiment at Philadelphia, he attended the special session of congress, beginning July 4, 1861, and there he delivered his impromptu speech, a reply to Sen. John C. Breckenridge, of Kentucky. In this speech he pledged the loyalty of Oregon and California, although he admitted that there were "a few men there who have left the south for the good of the south, who are perverse, violent, destructive, revolutionary and who are opposed to social order."

25

Governor Whiteaker appointed to the vacancy, caused by the death of Senator Baker, Benjamin Stark, one of the townsite owners of Portland, thereby precipitating an acrimonious controversy, since Whiteaker still sympathized with the secessionist cause and Stark was widely believed to hold similar opinions. It was charged that Stark was "opposed to the vigorous prosecution of the war against the insurgent and revolted states, and in favor of the recognition of the so-called confederate states, and also in favor of establishing on this coast a separate government, and therefore an enemy of the United States, to whose councils he is appointed."

The draft of a letter in the handwriting of Henry Failing, of Portland, now in the possession of Oregon Historical Society, and which presumably was signed by citizens of Oregon and sent to the secretary of state at Washington, is in part as follows:

"Sir, the undersigned beg leave to make the following representations to you concerning Mr. Benj. Stark, recently appointed U. S. Senator from Oregon by Governor Whiteaker to fill the seat vacated by the decease of Col. E. D. Baker. . . .

"Mr. Stark who is a resident here and personally known to us all, has been for the past twelve months an ardent advocate of the cause of the rebellious states. He has openly avowed his sympathies with the South, declaring the government disrupted and openly expressing his admiration for the Confederate Constitution and advocating the absorption of the loyal states of the Union in the Southern Confederacy under that constitution, as the only means of restoring peace, thus advocating the surrender of our government to the so called Confederated States.

"Mr. Stark has thus expressed himself publicly and has in consequence been recognized as the most prominent and bold of the advocates of secession here in this state. He has been selected by Gov. Whiteaker doubtless in consequence of his secession proclivities, thus outraging sentiment of the people of Oregon, a large majority of whom are loyal to the Union. . . ."

The seating of Stark in the senate was delayed, but not prevented, by these protests, and with the assent of Nesmith, the other senator from Oregon, he was sworn in three months after his appointment. The charges against him were subsequently sustained by the senate judiciary committee, to which they had been referred, but congress was too busy with the larger concern of war to consider them more fully, and Stark's case was not reopened. While it is not the purpose to outline the events of the Civil war period, a brief mention of some facts will be appropriate in closing this volume.

26

Oregon was profoundly stirred by the victories of the Confederate arms which signalized the first months of hostilities. By January, 1862, party feeling had abated. A union party was brought into being to meet local necessity. The call, addressed to all who favored vigorous suppression of the rebellion, was signed by H. W. Corbett, E. D. Shattuck and W. C. Johnson, who then constituted the republican state central committee, and by other members of both parties. It resulted in the holding of a state convention, in Eugene, April 9, 1862. The county conventions, which chose delegates to the state convention, were organized in harmony with the general plan, according to calls issued by representatives of both parties. The state ticket chosen at Eugene also gave representation to both parties. Addison C. Gibbs, a northern democrat, law partner of George H. Williams, and a pioneer supremely devoted to the interests of Oregon, was nominated for governor, and John R. McBride, who had figured from the first in the councils of the republican party, for representative in congress. Other nominess were: For secretary of state, Samuel May; state printer, Harvey Gordon; state treasurer, Edwin N. Cooke; judge, fourth district, E. D. Shattuck; prosecuting attorney, first district, James F. Gazley; second district, A. J. Thayer; third district, J. G. Williams; fourth district, W. C. Johnson. The platform demanded the vigorous prosecution of the war.

27

A convention of democrats, held at Eugene, April 15, 1862, in answer to a call addressed to all "who are opposed to the political policy of the present administration and are in favor of the preservation of the Union as it was," nominated John F. Miller (who had been named as an alternate to the Charleston convention, 1860), for governor, and Judge Aaron E. Wait, for representative in congress. Other nominees were: For secretary of state, George T. Vining; state treasurer, J. B. Green; state printer, A. Noltner; judge, fourth district, W. W. Page.

Wait had been classified as a Douglas democrat. The platform declared for suppression of the rebellion by "constitutional" means, accused the republicans of conducting the war for the chief purpose of emancipating and enfranchising the negroes, and denounced the coalition of abolitionists with so-called democrats. Thus, the negro bogey, which had so often been utilized in Oregon politics, was made to do service again. The democrat ticket received the support of all the Breckenridge or secession democrats, and of a considerable number of former partisans of Douglas.

28

The union ticket, however, won by majorities ranging from 3177 for McBride, to 3590 for Gordon; and Gibbs received a majority of 3589. The total vote polled was about 10,400. Only one county, Josephine, gave a majority for a democratic candidate, Miller receiving ten more votes than Gibbs.

The legislature was almost solidly union, and, September 12, chose Benjamin F. Harding, of Marion (who was rated as a Douglas democrat and regarded as a supporter of Lincoln), for United States senator for the seat to which Colonel Baker had originally been elected and which Stark was temporarily occupying by interim appointment. The other leading candidates were Judge George H. Williams, who had received 20 votes for senator in 1860; Rev. Thomas H. Pearne, editor of the Pacific Christian Advocate; Elisha L. Applegate, Orange Jacobs, H. W. Corbett and John Whiteaker. Three votes cast for the last named candidate represented the full strength of the secessionist sympathizers in the joint convention. Thirty ballots were taken. Orange Jacobs, of Jacksonville, who was a republican of pronounced type, was within three votes of election on the 16th ballot, after which the republican vote veered to Corbett, who was elected.

The legislature, without audible dissent, adopted a set of resolutions, introduced by McBride (who is reported to have voted for Harding), which declared the rebellion an "unjustifiable, inexcusable and wicked attempt" to overthrow the Union, and demanded that the president be supported to the utmost in his endeavors to "subdue the present revolt against the best and wisest government ever devised by man." Loyalty and Union were the watchwords of the hour.

Governor Gibbs' inaugural message rang with patriotism. "The absorbing question of the day," he said, "is how to put down the rebellion and pay the expenses of the war." "Those who are not for us are against us," he said also. "It has been often and truthfully said," added the governor, "that eternal vigilance is the price of liberty. Mark its frequent truths at this time, and watch those who carp at every real or imaginary error of the administration, and are complaining of the 'tax bill' because a small portion of their fortunes is required to preserve civil and religious liberty in America."

29

The legislature passed as a war measure an act making United States notes legal tender for the payment of debts and taxes, a proceeding calculated to put patriotism to the test, in view of the difficult condition of state and national finances. New purchases could be made only at prices specified by the seller, and based on the value of the medium in which they were paid for, while creditors were compelled to accept payment of old debts in fluctuating currency. A partial remedy was found in 1864, when the legislature enacted a law which permitted specification by contract of the kind of money in which the obligation should be payable, and required that judgments be discharged in the specified medium.

30

A few paragraphs may be added in anticipation and as a summary to complete what has been said in this chapter. Lincoln's emancipation proclamation did not meet with universal favor in Oregon, only the radical republicans defending it, for as has heretofore appeared, the temper of the community was about as hostile to the negro as it was to the extension of slavery. There was division of opinion, therefore, in 1864, when the union party held its convention, at Albany, March 30, and the anomaly was presented of a party convention electing delegates to the national convention of a party bearing a different designation from its own. The union party of Oregon chose Rev. Thomas H. Pearne, J. W. Souther, Frederick Charman, Meyer Hirsch, Josiah Failing and Hiram Smith to represent it in the councils of the national republican party, but technically it evaded the issue by referring to the "national convention" only, and omitting the qualifying "republican." The delegates to Baltimore were instructed to support Lincoln for renomination, which they did, and the platform warmly indorsed the national administration. Oregon was at this time asking for a branch United States mint, and John R. McBride's disposition toward having it located at The Dalles raised a strong feeling against him in the western and more populous part of the state. McBride was defeated for renomination, and Rev. J. H. D. Henderson was nominated for congress. Harvey Gordon, state printer, having died, H. L. Pittock, publisher of the

Oregonian, was named to succeed him, removing this office from the control of the Oregon Statesman for the first time since its creation. The nominees for presidential electors were H. N. George, George L. Woods and J. F. Gazley.

31

Secessionist sentiment was strong in the democrat convention that met at Albany, April 13, 1864, and over which ex-Governor Whiteaker presided. Col. James K. Kelly was nominated for representative in congress; no candidate for state printer was presented; the nominees for presidential electors were Aaron E. Wait, Benjamin Hayden and Stephen F. Chadwick. Delegates to the national democrat convention were Benjamin Stark, L. P. Higbee, William McMillan, Jefferson Howell, John Whiteaker and N. T. Caton. The platform both reasserted the Virginia and Kentucky resolutions of 1798-9 and condemned the rebellion; and it directed a particular attack at the abolition of slavery.

The succeeding campaign was spirited, and at times violent. The democrats held hope, which, however, proved groundless, of controlling the legislature and electing a United States senator to succeed Harding. The result of the election, in June, was a sweeping victory for the Union ticket, Henderson winning by a majority of 2763 over Kelly, and the democrats obtaining only two members of the senate and five members of the house. One of the latter was Lafayette Lane, son of Joseph Lane. The elder Lane had emerged from political seclusion and with a little of his old-time fire had led the democrat canvass of the state.

32

The legislature chosen at this time met in September and elected as senator, George H. Williams, who was now regarded as a republican, although he had not formally announced his conversion. His leading opponent was Rev. Thomas H. Pearne. The secessionist vote was given to John F. Miller. The same session at which Judge Williams realized his twice-frustrated ambition, and made another step forward in the illustrious political career that culminated in his selection as attorney-general in the cabinet of President Grant, also brought into prominence John H. Mitchell, who was president of the state senate. He thus began what became a noteworthy political career, in the course of which he represented Oregon in the United States senate for 22 years out of the 32 years from 1873 to 1905.

The spirit of the legislature of 1864 was revealed in the names chosen for two counties, created east of the Cascade mountains, Union and Grant. Nevertheless, a change in the political character of the population was taking place, as exhibited in the vote for president, in November. Lincoln carried Oregon by 1431 over McClellan, which was satisfactory enough to the supporters of the Union cause; but Henderson's majority over Kelly in June had been almost double that number. Analysis of the returns indicates that the difference was due largely to the season's new immigration, which consisted principally of settlers from the border states who were weary of the war and who were referred to by the newspapers of the period as the "left wing of Price's army," there being a flavor of sardonic humor in the designation, referring to the defeat and retreat of the Confederate forces under General Price, who were said to have kept on running until they reached Oregon, where they could always be counted on to support the democrat party. It was a population largely secessionist in sympathy, or at least opposed to continuance of the war; and this sentiment was reflected in the vote in eastern Oregon.

The total number of ballots cast, east of the Cascades, June, 1864, was 3291; in November the total was 4560, an increase of 1269, of which increase precisely 900 were accounted for in the increased vote for the democratic nominee for president. In the state at large, Lincoln received 9888 votes, or 1129 more than had been cast for Henderson; McClellan, however, received 8457, or 2461 more than had been received by Kelly in June. The new arrivals, many of whom settled in the eastern part of the state, and had democratic sympathies, were already contributing to the restoration of the political status of ante-bellum times.

33

The legislature convened in special session December 5, 1865, by the call of Governor Gibbs, and voted for ratification of the 13th amendment to the federal constitution, abolishing slavery, 43 ayes, seven noes, the negative votes being wholly those of democrats. A year later, in September, 1866, the succeeding legislature ratified the 14th amendment, also by a large majority, although the political complexion of that body had changed somewhat.

The spring campaign of 1866, in fact, marked the beginning

of the end of the union party and the return of the democrats. The unionists nominated Rufus Mallory, of Marion county, for congress, it having by this time become a tradition that the congressional plum should be passed around; and, for governor, they chose George L. Woods, of The Dalles. S. E. May was nominated for secretary of state, E. N. Cooke for treasurer and W. A. McPherson, of the Albany Journal, for state printer. The platform, which attempted to teach both round and flat, was evidence of the increasing difficulty of meeting the views of both republicans and democrats upon issues as complex as those now arising out of reconstruction. The democrats named James K. Kelly for governor this time, and James D. Fay, of Jackson county, for congress; and in the platform warmly indorsed President Johnson in his controversy with congress over reconstruction policies. The union party leaders were largely on the side of congress as against the president, but there was confusion of opinion among the voters.

34

The union ticket won in the June election, but by conspicuously reduced majorities, that for Mallory being 553 and Woods, 277. Woods had been among the organizers of the republican party in the territory, 1857, and had served as a Lincoln elector, 1864. Mallory was a republican. He was an able young lawyer of Salem, although then practically unknown outside of Marion, Douglas and Umpqua counties. The geographical distribution of the republican nominees was shrewdly calculated to give strength to the ticket. Mallory's nomination was a bid for the strongly republican vote of Marion; McPherson was named as a sop to Linn; May was popular in Jackson county and the rest of southern Oregon; and Woods' selection was obviously in recognition of the increasing influence of eastern Oregon in the political councils of the state. The democratic leaders, however, misjudged their public and missed a possible chance for success by the inclusion of Fay and O'Meara on their ticket; both were avowed secessionists, and their selection so affronted such republicans as might otherwise have been counted upon, that these again voted the ticket straight, as they had been wont to do during the war. The democrats made gains notwithstanding their mistakes, and elected seven senators and 21 representatives to the legislature, the total membership of that body being 69.

35

Senator Nesmith was shelved in the realignment now taking place. Having voted with the war party in congress, he was viewed by democrats as a republican; but he had also supported President Johnson and offended the republicans. His situation as a candidate was thus described by him in a letter to Deady: "Some republicans commended my course during the war, but denounced me fully because I was not in favor of its prosecution after the rebels had ceased to resist. Besides I was not up to their standard with respect to the superiority of the negro over the white man. On the other hand, a portion of the democracy could not forgive me for having supported the war and because I did not support the rebellion."

A union party caucus agreed on Governor Gibbs for senator, and he would have been elected if three members had not refused to be bound by its decision. John H. Mitchell received 15 votes on the first ballot, to Gibbs' 21, after which Henry W. Corbett, a pioneer in the organization of the republican and union parties and Harding's leading opponent of 1862, gained steadily and was elected on the 16th ballot, when he received 38 votes, to 14 for Joseph Shoewalter Smith, his nearest opponent. Nesmith's highest vote had been nine, and he received but four votes on the last ballot.

The negro question, which would never subside in Oregon, the hostility between President Johnson and congress and the continued arrival of new settlers with democratic predilections restored the local democrat party to favor, in 1868. In the impeachment proceedings against Johnson in that year the entire delegation in congress was against the president. Mallory, in the house, voted for the resolution presenting the articles of impeachment; both Williams and Corbett voted "guilty" in the senate.

36

The union party convention at Salem this year adopted the name "union-republican," and nominated for congress David Logan. He was defeated, however, in the June election by Joseph Shoewalter Smith, who had a majority of more than 1200, a clear reversal of political form, while the democrats elected 43 of the 69 members of the legislature. The union-republican nominees for electors were Orange Jacobs, A. B. Meacham and Josiah Bowlby, and the convention sent delegates to the national convention of the republican party which nominated Ulysses S. Grant. The democratic electors, Stephen F. Chadwick, John Burnett and J. H. Slater, however, received the majority of the votes in November, when Oregon rejected Grant and Colfax and gave Seymour and Blair a plurality of 165.

Another incident reflecting the change in political opinion in the state occurred in 1868. A resolution originating in the house was adopted by the legislature calling on both of Oregon's senators, Williams and Corbett, to resign, on the ground that they had misrepresented their constituents by voting for measures "which were in plain and palpable violation of the constitution of the United States, among which measures are those known as the reconstruction acts of congress, which acts in their enforcement have overthrown and subverted civil liberty in 11 states of this Union, and consigned the citizens thereof to odious and despotic military dictatorship."

The legislature at about the same time adopted a resolution which had been introduced in the senate, withdrawing the assent of the state to the 14th amendment to the federal constitution, which had been given by the legislature of 1866. The rescinding resolutions, which were introduced in the senate by Victor Trevitt, of Wasco county, set forth that the three-fourths majority of the state by which the amendment had been declared adopted had included Alabama, Arkansas, Florida, Louisiana, Georgia and South Carolina, the legislatures of which "were created by a military despotism against the will of the legal voters of said states, under the reconstruction acts (so-called) of congress, which are usurpations, unconstitutional, revolutionary and void." The resolutions demanding the resignations of the senators were forwarded to the United States senate, which returned them. The curious effort to repeal the state's ratification of the 14th amendment was based on the ground that a state might withdraw its assent at any time prior to final ratification by three-fourths of all the states, and that, excluding those in which so-called "carpet bag" legislatures had voted, consent of the necessary three-fourth had not been obtained. The senate resolutions seem never to have reached their destination, but they are interesting and significant exhibits of the political temper of the day.

37

Oregon Pioneer Association, at its 1894 annual meeting, amended its constitution to extend the privileges of membership beyond the prescribed limit of 1854, to make eligible those who had come to Oregon on or before February 14, 1859, when the state was admitted into the Union. The members were justly proud of the distinction of being creators of a great state, and to have participated in the heroic adventure of crossing the plains before the Oregon Trail was a well beaten pathway. This feeling is evidenced by the fact that at the annual meeting of 1896 an explanatory resolution was adopted, to the effect that the time limit, February 14, 1859, was thereafter not to be changed, excepting by unanimous vote of the members of the Association at a regular annual meeting. It has never been changed.

But, for general purposes, the pioneer period may be somewhat enlarged. It will not be forgotten that after Oregon attained statehood there were many courageous settlers who braved the dangers of the trail and suffered the hardships of the long and arduous journey, so that until after the completion of transcontinental railroads, at least, wagons still toiled their painful way across plains and mountains, and enterprising men and women trekked to Oregon, as to the promised land.

Discovery, exploration, fur trading, missionary evangelism, settlement by home seekers, the pageant of history flashes its scenes and then pauses to show how pioneers created a simple but effective local government, without instruction or command from recognized political authority. Thereafter, boundary dispute is compromised, a territory is created, the Old Oregon domain is subdivided and new territories are organized. Indian wars are courageously faced and homes are defended with comparatively little help from the distant federal government. A state is then created, and the responsibilities of statehood are assumed on the eve of the war that divides the nation.

Oregon's early history is picturesque, and is unique in many of its features, but, if it had no pages excepting those of the pioneers, it would still have a brilliant story to tell. The early pioneer period, before the discovery of gold in California, by an Oregonian, has been called idyllic. Settlers had come as homeseekers, hoping to aid in building an American government and to strengthen the claim of the United States. Conditions of home life were simple, even primitive, but there was a total lack of pretense and artificiality. Wealth there was none, and there were no grades or social classes. Agriculture was the leading, and almost the sole industry. The production of sufficient food for the necessities of a growing population was generally recognized as the prime need of the hour. The weaving of materials for clothing, and the tanning of leather for shoes, were enterprises already engaging attention. And meantime, with wisdom and deliberation, the settlers planned and put in motion their provisional government, that operated successfully between the years 1843 and 1848.

In the summer of 1848, when congress at Washington was passing the bill to create the Territory of Oregon, the first news of the gold discovery in the Sacramento valley, and the amazing stories of the golden harvest drew away the male population of Oregon. In the months that followed the pastoral age underwent change, and money or its equivalent found its way into the channels of trade. Clothing and shoes could be bought, merchandise came by shipload. And soon the necessity for extreme economy and self denial was relaxed. Pioneer life continued, but under new and easier conditions. An era reached an imperceptible limit and another era had its beginning.

CHAPTER NOTES AND REFERENCES
Part II

CHAPTER XX

Robert Greenhow, History of Oregon and California, 1844, and later editions, is essential in a study of Oregon's international boundaries.

Western limits of the Louisiana purchase: The extent of territory granted to Crozat by Louis XIV, 1712, is set out in Greenhow, 1845, p. 277. The treaty ceding the Louisiana purchase, and the other treaties mentioned herein, are printed in Malloy, Treaties and Conventions, 1910. For discussion of the origin of the 49th parallel as the northern boundary of the Louisiana purchase, see Greenhow, pp. 281 et seq., also id., Appendix, p. 437. It was long taken for granted that by the peace of Utrecht (1713) the parallel of 49° was agreed on as the dividing line, and that this line had been confirmed in the treaty of 1763. It was accepted by the plenipotentiaries of the United States and Great Britain, in the convention of 1818, with the proviso that this shall not be construed "to extend to the northwest coast of America . . . or to the territories . . . westward of the Stony Mountains." (Greenhow, p. 282.) Hudson's Bay Company, 1714, had advised its government to propose a line so described, (R. C. Clark, History of the Willamette Valley, 414, citing C. O. Paulin, Canadian Historical Review, vol. IV. p. 127). The original suggestion is said to have come from that company.

For negotiations at Ghent, 1814, see American State Papers, Foreign Relations, vol. III; J. Q. Adams, Duplicate Letters, the Fisheries and the Mississippi, 1822; and The Great Peace Maker, the Diary of James Gallatin, 1914.

Spain's proposals regarding Florida will be found in Letters from Ministers Abroad, vol. XIV, (Pizarro to Erving), and Fuller, The Purchase of the Floridas, p. 275.

American State Papers, Foreign Relations, vol. V, contains the diplomatic negotiations with Russia; see also Writings of John Quincy Adams, edited by W. C. Ford, vols. III and IV. Brown's Political History of Oregon prints the correspondence between Poletica and Adams.

Monroe doctrine: Messages and Papers of the Presidents, compiled by J. D. Richardson, vol. II, p. 778; Dexter Perkins, Monroe Doctrine, 1933. For comments of the British foreign secretary, see Bagot, George Canning and His Friends, and Rush, Residence at the Court of London, second series, vol. II.

Adams records in his Memoirs, his conversations with Stratford Canning, vol. V, p. 243.

Floyd's so-called bill was House Resolution, No. 22, January 25, 1821; his report was published as House Report 45, 16th Congress, 2nd Session. Adams' reply to the British minister, about a United States settlement on the Columbia, is quoted by Katherine B. Judson in "Restoration of Astoria," Oregon Historical Quarterly, vol. XX, p. 329.

Jesup's letter is printed in Oregon Historical Quarterly, vol. VIII, pp. 290-94. It is referred to in Rush's Residence, vol. II, p. 267.

Boundary negotiations between United States and Great Britain, 1824, in American State Papers, Foreign Relations, vol. V, Protocol of 26th conference, p. 565.

Canning's letter of May 21, 1824, is printed in E. J. Stapleton, Some Official Correspondence of George Canning, vol. II. Other quoted letters of Canning are from this work.

The "express reservation of the territorial claim" rested on two documents not addressed to the United States. It was suggested by the British ministers to their own agents. It was never published, or communicated to the United States.

Baylies' report was printed as House Report 213, 19th Congress, 1st Session.

Negotiations of 1826: Clay's instructions to Gallatin are in American State Papers, Foreign Relations, vol. VI, p. 645; see also correspondence between the United States and Great Britain, in House Executive Document 199, 20th Congress, 1st Session. The map of 1838 is in House Document 101, 25th Congress, 3rd Session, as part of Caleb Cushing's Report.

For Gallatin's tentative offer to deviate from 49°, see American State Papers, vol. VI, p. 666.

Huskisson and Addington's statement annexed to protocol of the seventh conference, with Gallatin's counter statement, American State Papers, Foreign Relations, vol. VI. See Writings of Albert Gallatin, vol. III, p. 511-12.

George Vern Blue, Oregon Question, 1818-28, Oregon Historical Quarterly, vol. XXIII, pp. 193-219.

Linn's speeches on his bill are in the Congressional Globe, 25th Congress, 2nd and 3rd Sessions, and 26th Congress, 2nd Session, Appendix.

A portion of Wilkes' report of June, 1842, was suppressed for diplomatic reasons, and it was not until July 15, 1911, that it was printed in the Congressional Record, at the request of Representative Humphrey, of Washington. It was reprinted in Oregon Historical Quarterly, vol. XII, pp. 271-99.

The northeastern boundary question was considered more important, 1842; see Correspondence Relative to the Negotiations of the Oregon Question, Subsequent to the Treaty of Washington, printed by T. R. Harrison, London, and President Tyler's Message to Congress, December 6, 1842, in Messages and Papers, vol. IV, p. 196.

Tripartite plan: Schafer, History of the Pacific Northwest, p. 174, and his British Attitude toward the Oregon Question, in American Historical Review, vol. XVI, p. 273; Scott, Oregon, Texas and Mexico, Oregon Historical Quarterly, vol. XXXVI, p. 154; L. G. Tyler, Letters and Times of the Tylers, vol. II, p. 261; Adams, Memoirs, vol. II, p. 327. As to the various attempts of the United States to purchase California prior to the war with Mexico, and the interest that Great Britain had in acquiring that province, see History of California: The American Period, by Robert Glass Cleland, (1922). An excellent article by Gertrude Cunningham, Washington Historical Quarterly, vol. XXI, pp. 31-54, entitled The Significance of 1846 to the Pacific Coast, examines the Oregon question with its relation to Texas, Mexico and California.

See McMaster, History of the People of the United States, vol. VI, pp. 294-96, as to Cincinnati and other popular conventions.

Correspondence of Aberdeen and Peel is printed in R. C. Clark's History of the Willamette Valley, Appendix; Aberdeen's letter to Everett, January 3, 1846, is in Clark, p. 849; see also Aberdeen and Peel on Oregon, 1844, by R. C. Clark, Oregon Historical Quarterly, vol. XXXIV, pp. 32-40.

Buchanan-Pakenham correspondence is in Correspondence Relative to the Negotiations of the Oregon Question.

British government propaganda is revealed in Merk, British Government Propaganda and the Oregon Treaty, in American Historical Review, October, 1934; British Side of Oregon Question, Oregon Historical Quarterly, vol. XXXVI, pp. 263-94.

For tariff policy, see R. C. Clark, History of the Willamette Valley, pp. 336-48, and the same author's British and American Tariff Policies and their Influence on the Oregon Treaty, reprinted from Proceedings of the Pacific Coast Branch of the American Historical Association, 1926.

Report of Lieutenant Peel on Oregon, edited by L. M. Scott, Oregon Historical Quarterly, vol. XXIX, pp. 51-76.

James K. Polk, Diary, vol. I.

Calhoun letters in American Historical Association, Annual Report, 1899, vol. II.

French comment on Oregon Question is shown in Blue's France and the Oregon Question, Oregon Historical Quarterly, vol. XXXIV, pp. 39-59, 144-63.

San Juan controversy: Bancroft to German minister for foreign affairs, in Berlin Arbitration, vol. II, p. 267. Bancroft's manuscripts, books and pamphlets, relating to this arbitration are in New York Public Library. See also Andrew Fish, Last Phase of the Boundary Dispute, Oregon Historical Quarterly, vol. XXII, pp. 161-224.

Other articles on the boundary question: Henry Commager, England and the Oregon Treaty, 1846, Oregon Historical Quarterly, vol. XXVIII, pp. 49-61, 147-62; Frederick Merk, Oregon Pioneers and the Boundary, American Historical Review, vol. XXIX, pp. 681-99, reprinted in Oregon Historical Quarterly, vol. XXVIII, pp. 366-88; L. M. Scott, Influence of American Settlement on the Oregon Boundary Treaty, Oregan Historical Quarterly, vol. XXIX, pp. 1-19.

Hudson's Bay Company Claims in the Northwest, Washington Historical Quarterly, vol. XIX, pp. 214-227, letters furnished by Maj. O. W. Hoop, derived from Post Headquarters at Fort Vancouver, showing correspondence, 1857, relating to the Company's lands and improvements for which claims for compensation were being made in behalf of the Company and its subsidiary, Puget Sound Agricultural Company.

Boston officers of Oregon Emigration Society, in 1845, opened a correspondence with Lord Aberdeen, in which a proposal was made by them to colonize Oregon with armed settlers and to erect an independent government, "resembling that of England as nearly as practicable," such government to be proclaimed and all rights of, and interests of, Great Britain to be fully secured. The proposal was declined by Richard Pakenham, British minister at Washington, as incompatible with his government's engagements under the existing convention for joint occupancy. (Reprinted in Clark's History of the Willamette Valley, Appendix p. 814, from British Foreign Office, 5-429 and 430).

CHAPTER XXI

Bancroft's History of Oregon may be relied upon for general reference. Thornton's Historical Letter and the Memorial praying for the Establishment of a Territorial Government in Oregon, and for Appropriations for Various Purposes, in Oregon Pioneer Transactions, 1882; the Memorial was printed as Senate Miscellaneous Document 143, of the 30th Congress, 1st Session, dated May 25, 1848. Thornton enumerates in chapter III, volume II of his Oregon and California (1855), the subjects affecting the interests of the people of Oregon that were brought to the attention of the government at Washington.

Thurston's diary, covering the period, is in Oregon Historical Quarterly, vol. XV, pp. 153-205. Joseph L. Meek is the subject of a biographical article by Rosetta W. Hewitt, Washington Historical Quarterly, vol. XX, pp. 196-200. See also, F. F. Victor, River of the West.

Lincoln and the governorship of Oregon, see chapter 29 of this volume, and Scott's History of the Oregon Country, vol. V, pp. 47-50.

For history of capital controversy, based chiefly on Oregonian files, see Scott, History of the Oregon Country, vol. II, p. 311. House Executive Document 104, 32nd Congress, 1st Session, contains correspondence between the United States treasury department and Hamilton, territorial secretary, and also the opinions of Judges Nelson and Strong. The opinion of the attorney general is printed in full in Oregon Weekly Times, December 27, 1851, and February 7, 1852. Among manuscripts in the Oregon Historical Society are several letters from Pratt to Lane urging him to procure congressional action confirming the Salem legislative proceedings.

President Fillmore's letter to Holbrook is in the manuscript collection of the Oregon Historical Society.

For controversy between Gaines and the legislative assembly, see Oregon Weekly Times, January 1, 1853; Oregonian, December 18, 1852, January 8, 1853.

For a list of early compilations of Oregon laws, see Carey, History of Oregon (1922), p. 504; also James K. Kelly, History of the First Code, Oregon Historical Quarterly, vol. IV, pp. 185-94; A. S. Beardsley, Code Making in Early Oregon, Pacific Northwest Review, vol. XXVII, pp. 3-33.

Effect of gold discovery: P. H. Burnett, Recollections of an Old Pioneer; Ezra Fisher, Correspondence, Oregon Historical Quarterly, vol. XVII; Tolbert Carter, Pioneer Days, in Oregon Pioneer Transactions, 1906; Theodore Talbot, Journals, edited by C. H. Carey.

Astoria-Salem road: Swan, Three Years Residence in Washington Territory, p. 238; Fort Steilacoom road, id., p. 399.

For report on the Albion and Cadboro, see Senate Executive Document 30, 30th Congress, 2nd Session. The Albion and its cargo were sold for $3590.12, with a deduction of $1321 for legal charges and expenses; see letter from J. R. Browne to John Adair, October 17, 1854, custom house papers in Oregon Historical Society.

H. M. Ballou, History of the Mission Press, Oregon Historical Quarterly, vol. XXIII, pp. 39-52, 95-110. Discussion of authorship of Prairie Flower, Alfred Powers, History of Oregon Literature, 195-204; and see Washington Historical Quarterly, vol. IX, p. 155.

T. W. Prosch, Political Beginnings of Washington Territory, Oregon Historical Quarterly, vol. VI. Scott's Oregon Country, vol. II, gives a full account of pioneer beginnings on Puget Sound. E. S. Meany, Cowlitz Convention, Inception of Washington Territory, Washington Historical Quarterly, vol. XIII, pp. 3-19. For changes in the boundaries of Oregon, see J. N. Barry, Oregon Boundaries, Oregon Historical Quarterly, vol. XXXIII, pp. 259-67.

The Jacksonville meeting to organize a new county is reported in Oregon Weekly Times, February 11, 1854. A dependable authority on the political history of this time is W. C. Woodward, Political Parties in Oregon. It relies much upon newspaper sources, which have been diligently examined and freely used. The Deady correspondence with the San Francisco Bulletin, now collected in the Deady Scrapbook, in Oregon Historical Society, is especially useful.

George H. Williams, Occasional Addresses, pp. 61-62, for first negro case in the courts, and see his Address, in Carey, Oregon Constitution, Appendix, p. 498. Williams' free state letter is reprinted in the Oregon Historical Quarterly, vol. IX, pp. 263-73.

T. W. Davenport, Slavery Question in Oregon, Oregon Historical Quarterly, vol. IX, pp. 227-28.

C. H. Carey, History of the Oregon Constitution, gives an outline of the political developments, a copy of the convention journal and also copies of the current newspaper reports of the convention.

The official returns of the vote on the constitution contained an error in the total negative vote, which has been copied in all subsequent records. As reported the vote was 7195, yes, and 3215, no; majority, 3890. The correct figures are herein printed, p. 512, are given in the governor's proclamation, Oregon Statesman, December 22, 1857.

CHAPTER XXII

Reports of the commissioner of Indian affairs, Bancroft's History of Oregon and Frances Fuller Victor's Early Indian Wars are the principal sources for the history of Oregon Indian wars. Scott's History of the Oregon Country, vol. II, contains much information collected from the files of the Oregonian, and also a full bibliography of Indian wars of the northwest. The Edmond S. Meany collection of documents, donated by him to the Library of the University of Washington, January, 1930, contains papers relating to the Indian wars, 1853-7. See also George W. Fuller, Inland Empire of the Pacific Northwest, and his History of the Pacific Northwest. For distribution of linguistic families and tribes, J. N. Barry, Oregon Historical Quarterly, vol. XXVIII, pp. 49-61, 147-62; L. Spier, Tribal Distribution, Southwestern Oregon, id., vol. XXVIII. pp. 358-66.

O. B. Sperlin, Indians of the Northwest, Oregon Historical Quarterly, vol. XVII, pp. 1-38, for opinion upon original friendly character of native population. Compare A Plea for the Indians, with Facts and Features of the Late War in Oregon, by John Beeson, (1858).

White's activities as Indian agent are recounted in A. J. Allen, Ten Years in Oregon, and in W. H. Gray, History of Oregon.

Cayuse war: Oregon Spectator, 1848, prints full accounts of the operations of the Cayuse war. See also Elwood Evans, History of the Pacific Northwest, vol. I. There are a number of manuscripts in the Oregon Historical Society respecting the conduct of the Cayuse war.

F. G. Young, Finances of Cayuse War, Oregon Historical Quarterly, vol. VII, pp. 418-32.

R. H. Down, History of the Silverton Country, pp. 47-58, has an account of the Battle of the Abiqua.

Lane's report to the secretary of war, October 22, 1849, is in Senate Executive Document 1, 31st Congress, 2nd Session, vol. I.

See Theodore Talbot, Journals, edited by C. H. Carey, for the artillery companies and Journal of Osborne Cross, Senate Document 1, 31st Congress, 2nd Session, for report as to the mounted rifles.

The Indian treaties of 1851 are printed in Senate Executive Documents 41-58, 32nd Congress, 1st Session.

J. R. Browne, Report on the Subject of the Indian War in Oregon and Washington, Senate Executive Document 40, 35th Congress, 1st Session.

For the battle at Port Orford, 1851, see Orvil Dodge, Heroes of Battle Rock and Pioneer History of Coos and Curry Counties, by the same author.

Table Rock treaty: Nesmith's version is in Oregon Pioneer Transactions, 1879, also, with Lane's comment, in Oregon Historical Quarterly, vol. VII, pp. 211-221.

Ward massacre: Correspondence relating to the Massacre of Immigrants by the Snake Indians, Salem, 1854; Correspondence of George L. Curry, mss., in Oregon Historical Society; A. L. Bird, Boise, (1934) pp. 81-93.

Indian Treaties: Palmer correspondence, mss., Oregon Historical Society; Indian Affairs, Laws and Treaties, vol. II; C. F. Coan, First Stage of the Federal Indian Policy in the Pacific Northwest, 1849-52, Oregon Historical Quarterly, vol. XXII, pp. 46-89, and Adoption of the Reservation Policy in Pacific Northwest, Oregon Historical Quarterly, vol. XXIII, pp. 1-38; A. W. Hoopes, Indian Affairs and their Administration, 1849-60, with especial reference to the Far West, 1932.

Walla Walla council: Lawrence Kip, Council of Walla Walla; James Doty, Official Proceedings, photostat in Oregon Historical Society, from original in the Indian office, Washington; Journal of operations of Governor Isaac Ingalls Stevens, prepared from the original journal of James Doty, by W. S. Lewis, 1919; Hazard Stevens, Life of Isaac I. Stevens; A. J. Splawn, Kamiakin.

Medicine Creek treaty: B. F. Shaw, in Oregon Historical Society, Proceedings, 1903; Ezra Meeker, Tragedy of Leschi.

CHAPTER XXIII

Reports of the commissioners of Indian affairs; Frances Fuller Victor, Early Indian Wars.

Message of the Governor of Washington Territory and Accompanying Documents, 1857, contains correspondence with the secretary of war, Major General Wool and the officers of the regular army and the volunteer service. Letters and Report by Lt. Col. T. Morris to Gov. Stevens and to Maj. W. W. Mackall, Asst. Adjt. Gen'l, relating to military operations and state of warfare, 1856-57, Washington Historical Quarterly, vol. XIX, pp. 135-41.

Indian wars paper, mss., Oregon Historical Society.

Correspondence and Official Proceedings relating to the Expeditions against the Indians, Salem, 1855.

R. C. Clark, Military History of Oregon, 1849-59, Oregon Historical Quarterly, vol. XXXVI, pp. 14-59.

L. Kip, Army Life on the Pacific.

Indian Hostilities in Oregon and Washington, 1856, House Executive Document 93, 34th Congress, 1st Session.

Denys Nelson, Yakima Days, Washington Historical Quarterly, vol. XIX, relates to the abandonment of the Oblate missions, among the Yakimas, and the subsequent opening for settlement of the Okanogan valley in British Columbia, 1859.

Haller afterward served in the Civil war. He was dismissed from the army without a court martial. He wrote a monograph in his defense, in which he reviewed his service in the Indian wars, and gave an explanation of his retreat from the Yakimas, see Dismissal of Maj. Granville O. Haller, 1869.

T. C. Elliott, Murder of Peu-Peu-Mox-Mox, Oregon Historical Quarterly, vol. XXXV, pp. 123-30.

Wool controversy: Scott, History of the Oregon Country, vol. II; Indian Hostilities, House Executive Document 93, 34th Congress, 1st Session; R. C. Clark, Military History of Oregon, Oregon Historical Quarterly, vol. XXXVI, pp. 14-59.

Wars in Southern Oregon: A. G. Walling, History of Southern Oregon; Indian war papers, mss., Oregon Historical Society.

J. G. Lewis, History of the Grand Ronde Block House.

Chief John: Fort Hoskins letters, October 17, 1857, April 17, May 7, 23, 1858, Oregon Historical Society; Letter from Mrs. M. C. Lockwood, mss., Oregon Historical Society.

J. Ross Browne, Indian Affairs in Oregon and Washington, House Executive Document 39, 35th Congress, 1st Session.

Oregon Mounted Volunteers, under command of Maj. Mark A. Chinn, moved toward Fort Walla Walla, in November, 1855, but finding the fort had been seized by hostile Indians, he made camp at Umatilla Agency, to await support by Colonel Nesmith's separate command. (Statesman, November 24 and December 8, 1855. Also letters of James Sinclair, in the archives of British Columbia, dated February 10, 1856). The fort was destroyed by the Indians, who, however, were driven away after four days of battle. Sinclair sent warning to Fort Colville, the message being carried by a band of 150 friendly Nez Perce's, who had escorted Governor Stevens from Fort Colville to the military camp near Fort Walla Walla.

Battle of the Cascades: Robert Williams, Cascade Massacre, Oregon Pioneer Transactions, 1896. This article includes a letter of L. W. Coe, who participated in the fight. F. M. Sebring, Indian Raid on the Cascades, Washington Historical Quarterly, vol. XIX, pp. 99-107.

Expedition against the northern Indians: B. F. Manring, Conquest of the Coeur d'Alenes, covers the expeditions of Colonels Steptoe and Wright; Indian Affairs in Oregon and Washington Territories, House Executive Document 112, 35th Congress, 1st Session, contains General Clarke's official report; John Mullan, Topographical Memoir of Colonel Wright's campaign, Senate Executive Document 32, 35th Congress, 2nd Session; T. C. Elliott, Steptoe Butte and Steptoe Battlefield, Washington Historical Quarterly, vol. XVIII, pp. 243-53; S. J. Chadwick, Colonel Steptoe's Battle, Washington Historical Quarterly, vol. II, pp. 332-43.

Congressional Record, vol. XXVIII, part 5, pp. 4252-54, for figures relating to cost of wars and delayed settlements.

CHAPTER XXIV

Correspondence with Gen. Harney, relative to Affairs in the Department of Oregon, House Executive Document 65, 36th Congress, 1st Session; Copies of Correspondence with General Harney, not heretofore published in reference to his Administration in Oregon, House Executive Document 98, 36th Congress, 1st Session.

Report of Captain H. D. Wallen of his Expedition in 1859, from Dalles City to Great Salt Lake, Senate Executive Document 34, 36th Congress, 1st Session.

Expense account of A. P. Dennison, Oregon House Journal, 1862, Appendix p. 25.

Report and Journal of Captain Medorem Crawford, Commanding the Emigrant Escort to Oregon and Washington, 1862, Senate Executive Document 17, 37th Congress, 3rd Session.

Knights of the Golden Circle: W. C. Woodward, Political Parties in Oregon, p. 221; Knights of the Golden Circle and Union League mss., in Oregon Historical Society.

Nez Perce's council, W. V. Rinehart, With the Oregon Volunteers, 1862-66, mss., Oregon Historical Society.

The report of Adjutant General Cyrus A. Reed, 1866, covers the campaigns 1864-66. Other accounts are John M. Drake, Private Journal, 1864, and Reminiscences of Cyrus H. Walker, mss., Oregon Historical Society.

In the wreck of the Brother Jonathan all but 19, out of a total of 174, were lost. Among them was William Logan, superintendent of Indian affairs for Oregon, with a fund for payment of Indian treaty obligations. The loss and resulting delay in paying the Indians caused further uneasiness in the country.

Modoc war: Bancroft, History of Oregon, vol. II; C. T. Brady, Northwest Fights and Fighters; Report of Governor Grover to General Scholfield on the Modoc War, in Messages and Documents, 1874; J. C. Riddle, Indian History of the Modoc War; A. B. Meacham, Wigwam and War-path; J. F. Santee, Edward R. S. Canby, Modoc War, Oregon Historical Quarterly, vol. XXXIII, pp. 70-78.

Letter relative to the Present Difficulties with the Modoc Indians, 1872, House Executive Document 201, 42nd Congress, 3rd Session; Correspondence and Papers relative to the War with the Modoc Indians in Southern Oregon, 1874, House Executive Document 122, 42nd Congress, 1st Session; Reports of the Quartermaster-general and Commissary-general giving in detail the Costs to those Departments of the Modoc War, 1875, House Executive Document 131, 43rd Congress, 2nd Session.

CHAPTER XXV

For general reference, R. C. Clark, History of the Willamette Valley and L. A. McArthur, Oregon Geographic Names.

Howison's Report, House Miscellaneous Document 29, 30th Congress, 1st Session; also reprinted in Oregon Historical Quarterly, vol. XIV, pp. 1-60.

Jesse Douglas, Syracuse and Santiam City, Oregon Historical Quarterly, vol. XXXII, pp. 195-212; Beginnings of Jefferson, id., pp. 316-31.

The Wyeth letters and McLoughlin's defence letters in reply to Thurston's charges are reproduced in Oregon Historical Quarterly, vol. I, pp. 105-109.

Portland: H. W. Scott, History of Portland; Joseph Gaston, History of Portland; Warre and Vavasour, Report, 1845, Oregon Historical Quarterly, vol. X, (March, 1909), Historical Sketch of Portland, Portland Directory, 1863; the diary quoted on page 655, is that of Elizabeth Dixon Smith Geer, Oregon Pioneer Transactions, 1907; Ezra Fisher, Correspondence, Oregon Historical Quarterly, vol. XVII; Charlotte M. Cartwright, Glimpses of Early Days in Oregon, Oregon Historical Quarterly, vol. IV, pp. 55-69.

Portland land titles: Marlin vs. T'Vault, 1 Or. 77; Lownsdale vs. Portland, 1 Or. 381; Facts for the People of Portland relating to the Levee, 1860, gives decision of the United States supreme court. A full review of the controversies and suits affecting the land titles is given in Scott's History of Portland, Chapter IX.

J. Q. Thornton, Salem Land Titles; also printed in Salem Directory, 1874; F. H. Saylor, The Capitol of Oregon, Oregon Native Son, vol. II, pp. 429-460.

Aurora settlement: R. J. Hendricks, Bethel and Aurora; John E. Simon, Dr. William Keil, Oregon Historical Quarterly, vol. XXXVI, pp. 119-53; H. S. Lyman, Aurora Community, Oregon Historical Quarterly, vol. II, pp. 78-93; F. W. Skiff, Adventures in Americana, pp. 200-23, prints letters of Dr. Keil and other documents relating to Aurora.

R. H. Down, History of the Silverton Country.

A. G. Walling, History of Lane County.

A. G. Walling, History of Southern Oregon; Binger Hermann, Early History of Southern Oregon, Oregon Historical Quarterly, vol. XIX, pp. 53-68; W. P. Tucker, Social History of Jackson County, Oregon Historical Quarterly, vol. XXXIII, pp. 313-17.

The Dalles: Mrs. R. S. Shackleford, Review of the Methodist Mission Case, Oregon Historical Quarterly, vol. XVI, pp. 24-32; Elizabeth Lord, Reminiscences of Eastern Oregon; Fred Lockley, Reminiscences of Colonel Henry E. Dosch, Oregon Historical Quarterly, vol. XXV, pp. 61-65.

Isaac Hiatt, Thirty-one Years in Baker County.

Frank T. Gilbert, Historic Sketches of . . . Umatilla County.

Western Historical Publishing Company, Illustrated History of Central Oregon.

David D. Fagan, History of Benton County.

Orvil Dodge, Pioneer History of Coos and Curry Counties.

Polk County Pioneer Sketches, compiled by the Daughters of the American Revolution.

CHAPTER XXVI

John Ball, Autobiography. Across the Continent Seventy Years Ago, compiled from Ball's Journal, by Kate Ball Powers, Oregon Historical Quarterly, vol. III, pp. 82-106.

Journal of the Ship Ruby, edited by T. C. Elliott, Oregon Historical Quarterly, vol. XXVIII, pp. 258-80; Bancroft, History of the Northwest Coast, vol. II, pp. 131-35; Franchere, Narrative; Parker, Journal of an Exploring Tour; Whitman letters, Oregon Pioneer Transaction, 1891, 1893; Diary of Asahel Munger, Oregon Historical Quarterly, vol. VIII, p. 404; J. N. Barry, Agriculture in the Oregon Country, 1795-1844, Oregon Historical Quarterly, vol. XXV, pp. 161-68, contains an excellent bibliography.

L. M. Scott, Soil Repair in the Willamette Valley, Oregon Historical Quarterly, vol. XVIII, p. 62; John Minto, Sheep Husbandry in Oregon, id., vol. III, pp. 219-47; A. L. Lomax, History of Pioneer Sheep Husbandry in Oregon, id., vol. XXIX, pp. 99-143; C. S. Kingston, Introduction of Cattle into the Pacific Northwest, Washington Historical Quarterly, vol. XIV, pp. 163-85.

J. R. Robertson, A Pioneer Captain of Industry (Joseph Watt), Oregon Historical Quarterly, vol. IV, pp. 150-67; A. L. Lomax, Pioneer Woolen Mills in Oregon, id., vol. XXX, pp. 147-60, 238-58, 339-43; L. E. Pratt, Origin and History of the Willamette Woolen Factory, id., vol. III, pp. 245-59.

J. R. Cardwell, First Fruits of the Land, Oregon Historical Quarterly, vol. VII, pp. 28-51, 151-61; William Barlow, Reminiscences of Seventy Years, id., vol. XIII, pp. 240-86.

G. H. Himes, History of Organization of State Agricultural Society, Oregon Historical Quarterly, vol. VIII, pp. 316-52.

The production of flax, and the manufacture of linseed oil, as well as the development of the linen industry, see L. M. Scott, Oregon Country, vol. III, p. 181; W. B. Bartram, Flax Fibre in Oregon, Oregon Magazine, vol. XXVI, pp. 10-31.

CHAPTER XXVII

R. C. Clark, History of the Willamette Valley, gives much valuable information regarding early schools and colleges in that region, and has been drawn upon for facts given in this chapter.

Z. A. Mudge, Missionary teacher: A Memoir of Cyrus Shepard.

G. H. Atkinson, Early History of the Public School System, Messages and Documents, 1876.

F. G. Young, State's Land Policy, Oregon Historical Quarterly, vol. XI, pp. 121-61.

F. H. Grubbs, Early Oregon Schools, Oregon Pioneer Transactions, 1913.

Jesse Douglas, Jefferson Institute, Oregon Historical Quarterly, vol. XXXIII, pp. 60-69.

Reminiscences of Mrs. B. F. McLench, one of the Slade teachers, MS. in the Oregon Historical Society.

T. H. Crawford, Historical Sketch of Public Schools of Portland, 15th Annual Report of Public Schools, 1888; C. N. Reynolds, Portland Public Schools, Oregon Historical Quarterly, vol. XXXII, pp. 334-47.

H. E. Pemberton, Early Colleges in Oregon, Oregon Historical Quarterly, vol. XXXIII, pp. 230-42, and Commonwealth Review, vol. XIII, pp. 266-84.

C. H. Mattoon, Baptist Annals of Oregon, vol. I.

Umpqua Academy, see articles in Oregon Historical Quarterly, vol. XIX.

History of Willamette University, see Gustavus Hines, Oregon and its Institutions.

Catholic Schools: E. V. O'Hara, Pioneer Catholic History of Oregon; Gleanings of Fifty Years, by the Sisters of the Holy Names; C. B. Bagley, Letters of the Sisters of Notre Dame, in his Early Catholic Missions, vol. II, a translation of Quelques Lettres des Soeurs de Notre-Dame, first printed in Notice sur le Territoire et sur la Mission de l'Oregon, 1847.

Mirpah G. Blair, Some Early Libraries of Oregon, Washington Historical Quarterly, vol. XVII, pp. 259-70.

CHAPTER XXVIII

R. C. Clark, History of the Willamette Valley.

Barlow road: Joel Palmer, Journal; W. H. Rector, Autobiography, in Lockley, History of the Columbia River Valley, vol. I, pp. 1074-77; Walter Bailey, History of the Barlow Road, Oregon Historical Quarterly, vol. XIII, pp. 287-96.

L. M. Scott, History of the Oregon Country, vol. II, pp. 278-79, for history of plank road companies.

F. G. Young, History of Railway Transportation in the Pacific Northwest, Oregon Historical Quarterly, vol. XII, pp. 170-89. This article contains a bibliography of early proposals for railroads. George Wilkes, History of Oregon, 1845, reprinted in Washington Historical Quarterly, vols. I-V; Wilkes' memorial to the Oregon provisional legislature is in the Oregon Spectator, September 17, 1846. For a list of congressional documents bearing on railroad building, see Katherine B. Judson, Subject Index to the History of the Pacific Northwest.

T. W. Prosch, Notes from a Government Document on Oregon Conditions in the Fifties, Oregon Historical Quarterly, vol. VIII, pp. 191-200.

O. O. Winther, California Stage Company in Oregon, Oregon Historical Quarterly, vol. XXXV, pp. 131-38.

C. B. Bagley, Transmission of Intelligence in Early Days of Oregon, Oregon Historical Quarterly, vol. XIII, pp. 347-62.

E. W. Wright, Lewis and Dryden's Marine History of the Pacific Northwest.

J. D. Miller, Early Oregon Scenes, Oregon Historical Quarterly, vol. XXXI, contains an account of early navigation on the Willamette river.

Irene Poppleton, Oregon's First Monopoly, History of the Oregon Steam Navigation Company, Oregon Historical Quarterly, vol. IX, pp. 274-304.

U. S. War department, Reports of Explorations and Surveys . . . for a Railroad . . . to the Pacific Ocean, (Pacific Railroad Reports).

George L. Albright, Official Explorations for Pacific Railroads; R. W. Sawyer, Abbot Railroad Surveys, Oregon Historical Quarterly, vol. XXXIII, pp. 1-24, 115-35.

CHAPTER XXIX

W. C. Woodward, Political Parties in Oregon.

A. B. Lapsley, Abraham Lincoln, vol. VIII.

Lincoln's letter to Holbrook is in the mss. collection of the Oregon Historical Society.

L. M. Scott, Oregon's Nomination of Lincoln, Oregon Historical Quarterly, vol. XVII, pp. 201-14.

T. W. Davenport, Slavery Question in Oregon, Oregon Historical Quarterly, vol. IX, p. 347.

G. H. Williams, Political History of Oregon, Oregon Historical Quarterly, vol. II, pp. 1-35.

L. B. Shippee, Echo of the Campaign of Sixty, Oregon Historical Quarterly, vol. XII, pp. 351-60, relates to the Thayer-Sheil controversy.

Joseph Ellison, Designs for a Pacific Republic, Oregon Historical Quarterly, vol. XXXI, pp. 319-42.

Joseph Wallace, Sketch of E. D. Baker; E. R. Kennedy, Contest for California, 1861, How Baker Saved the Pacific States to the Union; D. W. Craig correspondence in Oregon Historical Society. Eloquence of the Far West, Masterpieces of E. D. Baker, edited by Oscar T. Shuck.

The Lane correspondence and the Nesmith correspondence in the Oregon Historical Society, and files of the Oregonian, Oregon Statesman, and Oregon Argus furnish interesting details for the history of this period.

APPENDIX

CHRONOLOGICAL TABLE OF OREGON HISTORY

1578—Sir Francis Drake sails along the Oregon coast.

1602—Spanish pilot, D'Aguilar, notes an opening in vicinity of Columbia river.

1765—First use of the Indian name Oregon (or "Ouragon") by Major Robert Rogers, in a petition to King George III to explore territory in search of Northwest passage.

1774—July 18, Spanish navigator, Perez, reaches 54° 40′ north, passing along the Pacific coast.

1775—August 17, Heceta, Spaniard, sees the mouth of Columbia.

1778—Captain James Cook, explorer, first Englishman to visit Oregon coast, after Drake.

1787—July—Captain Charles W. Barkley and wife discover the Strait and name it Juan de Fuca.

1792—May 11, Capt. Robert Gray, American, discovers and enters Columbia, giving it his ship's name.

1792-4—Captain George Vancouver, British, maps the Pacific northwest; gives names to many mountains, bays, capes and sounds.

1793—July—Alexander Mackenzie first to reach the Pacific overland, from Canada.

1803—Louisiana purchase brings United States territory to summit of Rocky mountains.

1805—November 7, Lewis and Clark expedition reaches the Pacific ocean, overland.

1811—April 12, erection of Astoria begun near mouth Columbia.

1813—December 12, Astoria becomes Fort George under British flag.

1818—October 6, Astoria again under United States flag.
  —First Oregon joint occupancy treaty with Great Britain. Period, ten years.

1819—Treaty with Spain fixes California's northern boundary at 42°, north, releasing to United States all claims north thereof.

1824—American treaty with Russia limits latter's southern boundary to 54° 40′, north.

1825—March 19, Fort Vancouver dedicated by Hudson's Bay Company.

1827—Second joint occupancy treaty with Great Britain, for an indefinite term.

1828—Jedediah S. Smith enters Oregon from California. July 14, Smith and two others survive Indian massacre on Umpqua river.

1829—Location at Willamette Falls (Oregon City) occupied by McLoughlin for Hudson's Bay Company.

1834—Methodist mission established under Jason Lee.

1836—Whitman and Spalding missions established.

1842—Oregon Institute (Willamette University), first west of Rocky mountains, organized at present Salem.

1843—Great immigration started; first wagons westward from Fort Hall.

—May 2, beginning of provisional government, at meeting at Champoeg; first American government on the Pacific coast.

1845—June 3, George Abernethy, first provisional governor, takes office. Revision of provisional government.

1846—Treaty with Great Britain establishes Oregon title and sets northern boundary at 49° north. (Concluded June 15; proclaimed by president August 5).

1847—November 29, the Whitman massacre, at Waiilatpu.

1848—August 14, Oregon territory established by congress.

1849—March 3, Joseph Lane, first territorial governor, takes office.

1851—Portland incorporated by territorial legislature.
April 7, H. D. O'Bryant elected mayor at municipal election.
—December 15, first free public school in Portland.

1853-9—Indian wars.

1857—August and September, constitutional convention at Salem. Constitution ratified by popular vote, 2nd Monday of Nov.

1859—February 14, Oregon admitted as a state.
—March 3, John Whiteaker becomes first state governor.

1869—May 10, United and Central Pacific railroads connected.

1873—August, great fire at Portland.

1902—June 2, constitutional amendment providing initiative and referendum adopted.

1905—Lewis and Clark centennial exposition in Portland.

OFFICERS OF THE TERRITORY AND STATE OF OREGON

Names and terms of office of governors, secretaries of state, state treasurers, supreme judges, United States senators and representatives in congress. (Partly derived from Oregon Blue Book, 1935-6).

GOVERNORS OF OREGON

Name—Politics	Term of Office	By What Authority
	Under Provisional Government	
First executive committee ... Hill, David; Beers, Alanson; Gale, Joseph	1843-1844	By vote of the people
Second executive committee.. Stewart, P. G.; Russell, O.; Bailey, W. J.	1844-1845	By vote of the people
Abernethy, George	June 3, 1845-Mar. 3, 1849	By vote of the people
	Under Territory of Oregon	
Lane, Joseph	Mar. 3, 1849-June 18, 1850	Appointed by President Polk
Pritchette, Kintzing	June 18, 1850-Aug. 18, 1850	Was secretary and became ex-officio governor on resignation of Governor Lane
Gaines, John P.	Aug. 18, 1850-May 16, 1853	Appointed by Pres. Taylor
Lane, Joseph	May 16, 1853-May 19, 1853	Appointed by Pres. Pierce
Curry, George L.	May 19, 1853-Dec. 2, 1853	Was secretary and became ex-officio governor on resignation of Governor Lane
Davis, John W.	Dec. 2, 1853-Aug. 1, 1854	Appointed by President Pierce
Curry, George L. ....,..	Aug. 1, 1854-Nov. 1, 1854	Was secretary and became ex-officio governor on resignation of Governor Davis
Curry, George L.	Nov. 1, 1854-Mar. 3, 1859	Appointed by President Pierce
	Under State of Oregon	
Whiteaker, John (Dem.)	Mar. 3, 1859-Sept. 10, 1862	Elected 1858
Gibbs, A. C. (Rep.)	Sept. 10, 1862-Sept. 12, 1866	Elected 1862
Woods, George L. (Rep.)	Sept. 12, 1866-Sept. 14, 1870	Elected 1866
Grover, LaFayette (Dem.) ...	Sept. 14, 1870-Feb. 1, 1877	Elected 1870; reelected 1874
Chadwick, Stephen F. (Dem.)	Feb. 1, 1877-Sept. 11, 1878	Was secretary of state and became governor on resignation of Governor Grover, elected to U. S. senate
Thayer, W. W. (Dem.)	Sept. 11, 1878-Sept. 13, 1882	Elected 1878
Moody, Z. F., (Rep.)	Sept. 13, 1882-Jan. 12, 1887	Elected 1882
Pennoyer, Sylv. (Dem.-Peo.).	Jan. 12, 1887-Jan. 14, 1895	Elected 1886; reelected 1890
Lord, William Paine (Rep.)..	Jan. 14, 1895-Jan. 9, 1899	Elected 1894
Geer, T. T. (Rep.)	Jan. 9, 1899-Jan. 14, 1903	Elected 1898
Chamberlain, Geo. E. (Dem.)	Jan. 15, 1903-Feb. 28, 1909	Elected 1902; reelected 1906
Benson, Frank W. (Rep.)....	Mar. 1, 1909-June 17, 1910	Was secretary of state and became governor on resignation of Governor Chamberlain, elected to U. S. senate
Bowerman, Jay (Rep.) ...... (Acting governor)	June 17, 1910-Jan. 8, 1911	Was president of the senate and became acting governor owing to inability of Governor Benson to act
West, Oswald (Dem.)	Jan. 11, 1911-Jan. 12, 1915	Elected 1910
Withycombe, James (Rep.)..	Jan. 12, 1915-Mar. 3, 1919	Elected 1914; reelected 1918
Olcott, Ben W. (Rep.)	Mar. 4, 1919-Jan. 8, 1923	Was secretary of state; became governor upon death of Governor Withycombe
Pierce, Walter M. (Dem.) ...	Jan. 8, 1923-Jan. 10, 1927	Elected 1922
Patterson, I. L. (Rep.) ---.....	Jan. 10, 1927-Dec. 21, 1929	Elected 1926
Norblad, A. W. (Rep.)	Dec. 22, 1929-Jan. 12, 1931	Was president of the senate; became governor upon death of Governor Patterson
Meier, Julius L. (Ind.)	Jan. 12, 1931-Jan. 14, 1935	Elected 1930
Martin, Charles H. (Dem.)...	Jan. 14, 1935-Jan. 9, 1939	Elected 1934

SECRETARIES OF STATE

Name—Politics	Term of Office	By What Authority
	Under Provisional Government	
*LeBreton, George W.	Feb. 18, 1841-Mar. 4, 1844	Elected by mass meeting of citizens to office of clerk of courts and public recorder in 1841, thus serving as the first secretary of provisional government
†Long, Dr. J. E.	Mar. 4, 1844-June 1, 1846	First appointed, then elected by people under provisional government
‡Prigg, Frederic	June 21, 1846-Sept. 1848	Appointed to succeed Long
Holderness, Samuel M.	Sept. 26, 1848-Mar. 3, 1849	Appointed to succeed Prigg
	Under Territory of Oregon	
Pritchette, Kintzing (Dem.)..	Mar. 3, 1849-Aug. 18, 1850	Appointed by President Polk
Hamilton, Gen. Edw. (Dem.)	Aug. 18, 1850-May 14, 1853	Appointed by Pres. Taylor
Curry, George L. (Dem.)	May 14, 1853-Jan. 27, 1855	Appointed by Pres. Pierce
Harding, Benjamin F. (Dem.)	Jan. 27, 1855-Mar. 3, 1859	Appointed by Pres. Pierce
	Under State of Oregon	
Heath, Lucien (Dem.)	Mar. 3, 1859-Sept. 8, 1862	Elected 1858
May, Samuel E. (Rep.)	Sept. 8, 1862-Sept. 10, 1870	Elected 1862; reelected 1866
Chadwick, Stephen F. (Dem.)	Sept. 10, 1870-Sept. 2, 1878	Elected 1870; reelected 1874
Earhart, R. P. (Rep.)	Sept. 2, 1878-Jan. 10, 1887	Elected 1878; reelected 1882
McBride, George W. (Rep.)..	Jan. 10, 1887-Jan. 14, 1895	Elected 1886; reelected 1890
Kincaid, H. R. (Rep.)	Jan. 14, 1895-Jan. 9, 1899	Elected 1894
Dunbar, Frank I. (Rep.)	Jan. 9, 1899-Jan. 14, 1907	Elected 1898; reelected 1902
Benson, Frank W. (Rep.) ...	Jan. 15, 1907-April 14, 1911	Elected 1906; reelected 1910
Olcott, Ben W. (Rep.)	April 17, 1911-May 28, 1920	Appointed by Governor West to fill vacancy caused by death of Frank W. Benson; elected 1912; reelected 1916
Kozer, Sam A. (Rep.)	May 28, 1920-Sept. 23, 1928	Appointed by Governor Olcott to fill vacancy caused by resignation of Ben W. Olcott; elected 1920; reelected 1924
Hoss, Hal E. (Rep.)	Sept. 24, 1928-Feb. 6, 1934	Appointed by Governor Patterson to fill vacancy caused by resignation of Sam A. Kozer; elected 1928; reelected 1932
Stadelman, P. J. (Rep.)	Feb. 9, 1934-Jan. 7, 1935	Appointed by Governor Meier to fill vacancy caused by death of Hal E. Hoss
Snell, Earl (Rep.)	Jan. 7, 1935-Jan. 2, 1939	Elected 1934

  * Killed by Indians at Oregon City, March 4, 1844.
  † Drowned in Clackamas river, June 21, 1846.
  ‡ Drowned in Willamette river, October, 1849.

TREASURERS OF OREGON

Name—Politics	Term of Office	By What Authority
	Under Provisional Government	
Willson, W. H.	1843-1844	Elected by the people in mass meeting
Foster, Philip	1844-1845	Elected by the people at a general election
Ermatinger, F.	1845-1846	Elected by the people
Couch, J. H.	Mar. 4, 1846-Oct. 15, 1847	Appointed to fill vacancy caused by the resignation of F. Ermatinger. Was also elected by legislature in December, 1846
Kilbourne, William K.	Oct. 15, 1847-Sept. 27, 1849	Appointed; elected by legislature 1849
	During Territorial Government	
Taylor, James	Sept. 27, 1849-Jan. 21, 1851	Elected by legislature of territory
Rice, L. A.	Jan. 21, 1851-Dec. 16, 1851	Elected by legislature of territory
Boon, John D. (Dem.)	Dec. 16, 1851-Jan. 24, 1855	Elected by legislature of territory
Lane, Nat H. (Dem.)	Jan. 24, 1855-Jan. 10, 1856	Elected by legislature of territory
Boon, John D. (Dem.)	Jan. 10, 1856-Mar. 3, 1859	Elected by legislature of territory
	During State Government	
Boon, John D. (Dem.)	Mar. 3, 1859-Sept. 8, 1862	Elected 1858
Cooke, E. N. (Rep.)	Sept. 8, 1862-Sept. 12, 1870	Elected 1862; reelected 1866
Fleischner, L. (Dem.)	Sept. 12, 1870-Sept. 14, 1874	Elected 1870
Brown, A. H. (Dem.)	Sept. 14, 1874-Sept. 9, 1878	Elected 1874
Hirsch, E. (Rep.)	Sept. 9, 1878-Jan. 10, 1887	Elected 1878; reelected 1882
Webb, G. W. (Dem.)	Jan. 10, 1887-Jan. 12, 1891	Elected 1886
Metschan, Phil (Rep.)	Jan. 12, 1891-Jan. 9, 1899	Elected 1890; reelected 1894
Moore, Charles S. (Rep.)	Jan. 9, 1800-Jan. 14, 1907	Elected 1898; reelected 1902
Steel, George A. (Rep.)	Jan. 15, 1907-Jan. 3, 1911	Elected 1906
Kay, Thomas B. (Rep.)	Jan. 4, 1911-Jan. 6, 1919	Elected 1910; reelected 1914
Hoff, O. P. (Rep.)	Jan. 6, 1919-Mar. 18, 1924	Elected 1918; reelected 1922
Myers, Jefferson (Dem.)	Mar. 18, 1924-Jan. 4, 1925	Appointed by Governor Pierce to fill vacancy caused by death of O. P. Hoff
Kay, Thomas B. Rep.)	Jan. 4, 1925-April 29, 1931	Elected 1924; reelected 1928
Holman, Rufus C. (Rep.)	May 1, 1931-Jan. 4, 1937	Appointed by Governor Meier to fill vacancy caused by death of Thomas B. Kay; elected 1932

SUPREME COURT OF OREGON

Name of Chief Justice	Date	Name of Associate Justices
Bryant, William P...	1848 to 1850	Peter H. Burnett, Orville C. Pratt (1)
Nelson, Thomas......	1850 to 1853	Orville C. Pratt, William Strong (2)
Williams, George H..	1853 to 1859	Cyrus Olney, Obadiah B. McFadden, Matthew Paul Deady (3)
Wait, Aaron E.......	1859 to 1862	Reuben P. Boise, Riley Evans Stratton, Paine Page Prim
Boise, Reuben P.....	1862 to 1864 ,..............	Paine Page Prim, William W. Page, Riley E. Stratton, Erasmus D. Shattuck, Joseph G. Wilson
Prim, Paine Page....	1864 to 1866	Erasmus D. Shattuck, Reuben P. Boise, Riley Evans Stratton, Joseph G. Wilson
Shattuck, Erasmus D.	1866 to 1868	Paine Page Prim, Reuben P. Boise, Riley Evans Stratton, Joseph G. Wilson, Alonzo A. Skinner
Boise, Reuben P.....	1868 to 1870 ....—..	Paine Page Prim, Joseph G. Wilson, William W. Upton, John Kelsay
Prim, Paine Page....	1870 to 1872	Reuben P. Boise, Andrew J. Thayer, William W. Upton, B. Whitten, L. L. McArthur
Upton, William W...	1872 to 1874	Paine Page Prim, Andrew J. Thayer, B. F. Bonham, L. F. Mosher, L. L. McArthur
Bonham, B. F........	1874 to 1876	Paine Page Prim, L. L. McArthur, E. D. Shattuck, John Burnett
Prim, Paine Page....	1876 to 1878	Reuben P. Boise, E. D. Shattuck, L. L. McArthur, J. F. Watson
Kelly, James K......	1878 to 1880	Paine Page Prim, Reuben P. Boise
Lord, William P.....	1880 to 1882	E. B. Watson, John B. Waldo
Watson, Edward B...	1882 to 1884	John B. Waldo, William P. Lord
Waldo, John B.......	1884 to 1886	William P. Lord, W. W. Thayer
Lord, William P.....	1886 to 1888	W. W. Thayer, Reuben S. Strahan
Thayer, W. W.......	1888 to 1890	Reuben S. Strahan, William P. Lord
Strahan, Reuben S...	1890 to 1892	William P. Lord, Robert S. Bean
Lord, William P.....	July 1, 1892, to July 1, 1894	F. A. Moore, Robert S. Bean
Bean, Robert S......	July 1, 1894, to Dec. 31, 1896	F. A. Moore, Charles E. Wolverton
Moore, F. A.........	Jan. 1, 1897 to Dec. 31, 1898	Charles E. Wolverton, Robert S. Bean
Wolverton, Charles E.	Jan. 1, 1899, to Dec. 31, 1900	Robert S. Bean, F. A. Moore
Bean, Robert S......	Jan. 1, 1901, to Dec. 31, 1902	F. A. Moore, Charles E. Wolverton
Moore, F. A.........	Jan. 1, 1903, to Dec. 31, 1904	Charles E. Wolverton, Robert S. Bean
Wolverton, Charles E.	Jan. 1, 1905, to Dec. 4, 1905	Robert S. Bean, F. A. Moore, (Wolverton resigned Dec. 4, 1905)
Bean, Robert S......	Dec. 4, 1905, to Dec. 31, 1906	F. A. Moore, Thomas G. Hailey (appointed to succeed Wolverton)
Bean, Robert S......	Jan. 1, 1907, to Dec. 31, 1908	F. A. Moore, Robert Eakin, (4) Will R. King, (4) Woodson T. Slater
Moore, F. A.........	Jan. 1, 1909, to Dec. 31, 1910	Robert Eakin, Robert S. Bean (resigned May 1, 1909; succeeded by Thomas A. McBride), (4) Will R. King, (4) Woodson T. Slater
Eakin, Robert.......	Jan. 1, 1911, to Dec. 31, 1912	F. A. Moore, Thomas A. McBride, George H. Burnett, Henry J. Bean
McBride, Thomas A..	Jan. 1, 1913, to Dec. 31, 1914	F. A. Moore, Robert Eakin, George H. Burnett, Henry J. Bean, (5) William M. Ramsey, (5) Charles L. McNary

(1) Burnett, Bryant and Pratt were commissioned at Washington, D. C., August 14, 1848, but Burnett went to California, and Bryant served but a few months.

(2) Charles R. Train, of Massachusetts, was commissioned August 31, 1852, but did not serve.

(3) Deady's first commission, April 4, 1853, was erroneously made out in the name Mordecai P. Deady. His second commission was dated February 2, 1854.

(4) Commissioners from February 26, 1907, to February 11, 1909; judges from February 12, 1909, to December 31, 1910.

(5) Appointed June 3, 1913.

SUPREME COURT OF OREGON—Continued

Name of Chief Justices	Date	Names of Associate Justices
Moore, F. A..........	Jan. 1, 1915, to Dec. 31, 1916	Robert Eakin, George H. Burnett, Henry J. Bean, Thomas A. Mc-Bride, Henry L. Benson, Lawrence T. Harris.
McBride, Thomas A..	Jan. 1, 1917, to Dec. 31, 1918	(6) Robert Eakin, George H. Burnett, Henry J. Bean, (8) F. A. Moore, Henry L. Benson, Lawrence T. Harris, (7) Wallace Mc-Camant, Charles A. Johns, Conrad P. Olson
McBride, Thomas A..	Jan. 1, 1919, to Dec. 31, 1920	Henry J. Bean, Alfred S. Bennett, George H. Burnett, Henry L. Benson, Lawrence T. Harris, Charles A. Johns
Burnett, George H...	Jan. 1, 1921, to Dec. 31, 1922	(9) Charles A. Johns, Thomas A. Mc-Bride, Henry J. Bean, (10) Henry L. Benson, George M. Brown, Lawrence T. Harris, John McCourt, John L. Rand
McBride, Thomas A..	Jan. 1, 1923, to Dec. 31, 1924	Henry J. Bean, George M. Brown, (11) Lawrence T. Harris, O. P. Coshow, George H. Burnett, John L. Rand, (12) John McCourt, Martin L. Pipes
McBride, Thomas A..	Jan. 1, 1925, to Dec. 31, 1926	Henry J. Bean, George M. Brown, George H. Burnett, John L. Rand, O. P. Coshow, Harry H. Belt
Burnett, Geo. H. (13)	Jan. 1, 1927, to Sept. 10, 1927	John L. Rand, Harry H. Belt, O. P. Coshow, Henry J. Bean, George M. Brown, Thomas A. McBride
Rand, John L........	Sept. 10, 1927, to Jan. 7, 1929	Harry H. Belt, O. P. Coshow, George Rossman, Henry J. Bean, George M. Brown, Thomas A. McBride
Coshow, O. P.........	Jan. 7, 1929, to Jan. 5, 1931	Henry J. Bean, Harry H. Belt, George M. Brown, (14) Thomas A. McBride, John L. Rand, George Rossman
Bean, Henry J.......	Jan. 5, 1931, to Jan. 2, 1933	George M. Brown, John L. Rand, George Rossman, James U. Campbell, Percy R. Kelly, Harry H. Belt
Rand, John L........	Jan. 2, 1933, to Jan. 7, 1935	Harry H. Belt, George Rossman, Percy R. Kelly, James U. Campbell, Henry J. Bean, J. O. Bailey
Campbell, James U...	Jan. 7, 1935, to Jan. 3, 1937	Percy R. Kelly, Harry H. Belt, Henry J. Bean, J. O. Bailey, John L. Rand, George Rossman

(6) Resigned January 8, 1917, and succeeded by Wallace McCamant.
(7) Resigned June 4, 1918, and succeeded by Charles A. Johns.
(8) Died September 25, 1918, and succeeded by Conrad P. Olson.
(9) Resigned October 7, 1921, and succeeded by John McCourt.
(10) Died October 16, 1921, and succeeded by John L. Rand.
(11) Resigned January 15, 1924, and succeeded by O. P. Coshow.
(12) Died September 12, 1924, and succeeded by Martin L. Pipes.
(13) Died September 10, 1927, and succeeded by George Rossman.
(14) Died September 9, 1930, and succeeded by Percy R. Kelly.

SENATORS IN CONGRESS FROM OREGON

Name—Politics	Term of Office	By What Authority
Smith, Delazon (Dem.)	Feb. 14, 1859-Mar. 3, 1859	Elected by legislature
Lane, Joseph (Dem.)	Feb. 14, 1859-Mar. 3, 1861	Elected by legislature
Baker, Edward D. (Rep.)	Mar. 4, 1861-Oct. 21, 1861	Elected by legislature
Stark, Benjamin (Dem.)	Oct. 21, 1861-Sept. 11, 1862	Appointed by governor
Harding, Benjamin F. (Dem.)	Sept. 11, 1862-Mar. 3, 1865	Elected by legislature
Nesmith, James W. (Dem.)	Mar. 4, 1861-Mar. 3, 1867	Elected by legislature
Williams, George H. (Rep.)	Mar. 4, 1865-Mar. 3, 1871	Elected by legislature
Corbett, Henry W. (Rep.)	Mar. 4, 1867-Mar. 3, 1873	Elected by legislature
Kelly, James K. (Dem.)	Mar. 4, 1871-Mar. 3, 1877	Elected by legislature
Mitchell, John H. (Rep.)	Mar. 4, 1873-Mar. 3, 1879	Elected by legislature
Grover, LaFayette (Dem.)	Mar. 4, 1877-Mar. 3, 1883	Elected by legislature
Slater, James H. (Dem.)	Mar. 4, 1879-Mar. 3, 1885	Elected by legislature
Dolph, Joseph N. (Rep.)	Mar. 4, 1883-Mar. 3, 1889	Elected by legislature
Mitchell, John H. (Rep.)	Mar. 4, 1885-Mar. 3, 1891	Elected by legislature
Dolph, Joseph N. (Rep.)	Mar. 4, 1889-Mar. 3, 1895	Elected by legislature
Mitchell, John H. (Rep.)	Mar. 4, 1891-Mar. 3, 1897	Elected by legislature
McBride, George W. (Rep.)	Mar. 4, 1895-Mar. 3, 1901	Elected by legislature
*Corbett, Henry W. (Rep.)	Mar. 4, 1897, ...	Appointed by governor
Simon, Joseph (Rep.)	Oct. 6, 1898-Mar. 3, 1903	Elected by legislature
Mitchell, John H. (Rep.)	Mar. 4, 1901-Dec. 8, 1905	Elected by legislature
Fulton, Charles W. (Rep.)	Mar. 4, 1903-Mar. 3, 1909	Elected by legislature
†Gearin, John M. (Dem.)	Dec. 12, 1905-Jan. 23, 1907	Appointed by governor
Mulkey, Fred W. (Rep.)	Jan. 23, 1907-Mar. 3, 1907	Elected by legislature
Bourne Jr., Jonathan (Rep.)	Mar. 4, 1907-Mar. 3, 1913	Elected by legislature
Chamberlain, Geo. E. (Dem.)	Mar. 4, 1909-Mar. 3, 1915	Elected by legislature
Lane, Harry (Dem.)	Mar. 4, 1913-May 23, 1917	Elected by legislature
Chamberlain, Geo. E. (Dem.)	Mar. 4, 1915-Mar. 3, 1921	Elected by the people, 1914
‡McNary, Charles L. (Rep.)	May 29, 1917-Jan. 3, 1937	Appointed by Gov. Withycombe, 1917; elected by the people, 1918; reelected 1924; reelected 1930
Stanfield, Robert N. (Rep.)	Mar. 4, 1921-Mar. 3, 1927	Elected 1920
Steiwer, Frederick (Rep.)	Mar. 4, 1927-Jan. 3, 1939	Elected 1926; reelected 1932

* The United States senate refused to seat Mr. Corbett and the state of Oregon was represented by only one senator from March 4, 1897, to October 6, 1898.

† Appointed to succeed John H. Mitchell, who died December 8, 1905.

‡ Appointed to succeed Harry Lane, who died May 23, 1917.

REPRESENTATIVES IN CONGRESS FROM OREGON

Name—Politics	Term of Office	District
Thurston, Samuel R. (Dem.).	Jan. 6, 1849-April 9, 1851	Territorial delegate
Lane, Joseph (Dem.).........	June 2, 1851-Feb. 14, 1859	Territorial delegate
Grover, LaFayette (Dem.)...	Feb. 15, 1859-Mar. 3, 1859	Representative at large
Stout, Lansing (Dem.).......	Mar. 4, 1859-Mar. 3, 1861	Representative at large
Shiel, George K. (Dem.).....	Mar. 4, 1861-Mar. 3, 1863	Representative at large
McBride, John R. (Rep.).....	Mar. 4, 1863-Mar. 3, 1865	Representative at large
Henderson, J. H. D. (Rep.)..	Mar. 4, 1865-Mar. 3, 1867	Representative at large
Mallory, Rufus (Rep.).......	Mar. 4, 1867-Mar. 3, 1869	Representative at large
Smith, Joseph S. (Dem.).....	Mar. 4, 1869-Mar. 3, 1871	Representative at large
Slater, James H. (Dem.).....	Mar. 4, 1871-Mar. 3, 1873	Representative at large
Wilson, Joseph G. (Rep.)....	Mar. 4, 1873 —— — ——	Died before qualifying
Nesmith, James W. (Dem.)..	Mar. 4, 1873-Mar. 3, 1875	Representative at large
La Dow, George A. (Dem.)..	Mar. 4, 1875 —— — ——	Died before qualifying
Lane, Lafayette (Dem.)......	Oct. 25, 1875-Mar. 3, 1877	Representative at large
Williams, Richard (Rep.)....	Mar. 4, 1877-Mar. 3, 1879	Representative at large
Whiteaker, John (Dem.)	Mar. 4, 1879-Mar. 3, 1881	Representative at large
George, M. C. (Rep.).........	Mar. 4, 1881-Mar. 3, 1885	Representative at large
Hermann, Binger (Rep.).....	Mar. 4, 1885-Mar. 3, 1893	Representative at large
Hermann, Binger (Rep.).....	Mar. 4, 1893-Mar. 3, 1897	Representative, First Dist.
Ellis, W. R. (Rep.)..........	Mar. 4, 1893-Mar. 3, 1899	Representative, Second Dist.
Tongue, Thomas H. (Rep.)...	Mar. 4, 1897-Mar. 3, 1901	Representative, First Dist.
Moody, Malcolm A. (Rep.)...	Mar. 4, 1899-Mar. 3, 1903	Representative, Second Dist.
Tongue, Thomas H. (Rep.)...	Mar. 4, 1901-Mar. 3, 1905	Representative, First Dist.
Hermann, Binger (Rep.).....	Mar. 4, 1903-Mar. 3, 1907	Representative, First Dist.
Williamson, J. N. (Rep.)....	Mar. 4, 1903-Mar. 3, 1907	Representative, Second Dist.
Hawley, W. C. (Rep.).......	Mar. 4, 1907-Mar. 3, 1933	Representative, First Dist.
Ellis, W. R. (Rep.)..........	Mar. 4, 1907-Mar. 3, 1911	Representative, Second Dist.
Lafferty, A. W. (Rep.).......	Mar. 4, 1911-Mar. 3, 1913	Representative, Second Dist.
Sinnott, N. J. (Rep.)........	Mar. 4, 1913-Mar. 3, 1929	Representative, Second Dist.
Lafferty, A. W. (Rep.)......	Mar. 4, 1913-Mar. 3, 1915	Representative, Third Dist.
McArthur, C. N. (Rep.)......	Mar. 4, 1915-Mar. 3, 1923	Representative, Third Dist.
Watkins, Elton (Dem.)......	Mar. 4, 1923-Mar. 3, 1925	Representative, Third Dist.
Crumpacker, Maur. E. (Rep.)	Mar. 4, 1925-July 25, 1927	Representative, Third Dist.
*Korell, Franklin F. (Rep.)..	Oct. 18, 1927-Mar. 3, 1931	Representative, Third Dist.
†Butler, Robert R. (Rep.) ...	May, 1928-Mar. 3, 1933..	Representative, Second Dist.
Martin, Chas. H. (Dem.).....	Mar. 4, 1931-Jan. 3, 1935	Representative, Third Dist.
Mott, James W.	Mar. 4, 1933-Jan. 3, 1937	Representative, First Dist.
Pierce, Walter M.	Mar. 4, 1933-Jan. 3, 1937	Representative, Second Dist.
Ekwall, William A.	Jan. 3, 1935-Jan. 3, 1937	Representative, Third Dist.

* Elected October 18, 1927, to succeed M. E. Crumpacker, who died July 25, 1927.

‡ Elected November 6, 1928, to succeed N. J. Sinnott, resigned; reelected 1930.

INDEX

Beers, Alanson—Continued
fails of election to executive committee, I :341
joins Lee's mission, I :291
land transfer to Oregon Institute, II :660
married Sarah Smith, II :707
member first reinforcement of Methodists, I :333
member pioneer legislative committee, I :332
trustee Willamette University, II :713
Bees
efforts to introduce, II :695-696
not naturalized in 1846, II :647
Beeswax ship legend, 1:47
Beggs, William J., II :668
Belcher, Sir Edward, I :367-369, 370
Belique, P., see Bellique or Billique, Pierre
Bell, Edward
Journal, I :73-74, 76
officer on Chatham, I :73
Bell, G. W., I :359-360
Bell, John, II :774
Bella Coola, I :108
Bellamy, C. W., I :377
Bellaux
Astor expedition, I :176
Belle (steamboat)
acquired by Ainsworth and Kamm, II :743
Cascades relief expedition, II :605
Belle Vue Point
origin of name, I :98
near site of Fort Vancouver, I :231
Bellingham bay, I :78
Bellique, or Billique, Pierre
constable, I :320
settler in Willamette valley, I :266
signs petition to congress, I :373
Bend, Oregon, I :385
Benham Falls, I :385
Bennett, Charles
erects building in Salem, 1852, II :660
killed in Walla Walla battle, II :586
Bennett, Emerson
publisher of Prairie Flower by Sidney Moss, II :487
Bennett, James H., II :719
Bennett, Vandon, I :377
Bennett, William H., II :655
Bennett, Winstead, I :377
Bennett, Fort, II :586
Benton, Thomas H.
advocates settlement on Columbia, I :413
county named for, II :675
credit for Oregon agitation, I :255
duel with Butler threatened, II :466
opposes boundary provisions of Florida treaty, II :425
prediction re western railroads, 1844, II :732
supports 1824 bill, I :258
views on Oregon question, I :110, 255; II :433, 459
Benton county
creation and derivation of name, II :675
in Judge Pratt's district, II :476
in Judge Williams' district, II :496
Lincoln county cut from, II :676
member of legislature from, 1848, I :360; II :771
votes down Lane resolution, II :762
Bering, Vitus
commissioned by Russia to explore Pacific, I :50
discoveries basis of Russian claims, I :51; II :418, 427
named Mount Saint Elias, I :33
retirement, last voyage and death, I :51
sources of information about him, I :408
Bering island, I :51

Bering strait
Cook sailed through, I :48
discovery in 1728, I :4, 7, 8, 50-51
Ledyard on Cook expedition here, I :113
Berkeley, see Barkley
Berries
native, II :691
varieties introduced, II :695
Berry, A. M., II :771, 772
Berry, William, II :530
Bethel, Missouri, II :664-665
Bethel, Oregon, II :663-664
Bethel Academy
See Bethel Institute
Bethel Institute
founded, II :711
trustees, II :717
Bewley, Esther Lorinda, II :541-542
Biddle, James, I :216
Big Blue book
See Blue book controversy
Big Eddy, I :187
Big Hole
See Wisdom river
Big Meadows, II :598
Big Sandy, I :725
Big Thunder (Indian), II :635, 636
Big White
See Shahaka
Bigelow, Daniel R., II :477
Bigelow, Walter D., II :670
Bighorn range, I :195
Bighorn river
trading post, I :147, 148
Wyeth's trip down, I :277
Billique—See Bellique
Birdwoman's river—See Sacajawea river
Birnie, James
Hudson's Bay Co. agent at Astoria, I :368, 369
in charge of fort at The Dalles, I :223
in charge of posts at Okanogan, I :241
lived near St. Mary's hospital, I :369
Bishop, Captain
anchored in Baker's bay, I :102
calls Columbia river Chinook, I :102
master of Ruby (ship), I :101
plants vegetable garden near Cape Disappointment, I :102-103; II :679
Bishop, William, II :706
Bisonette, trader, I :377
Bitter Root Indians, II :588
Bitter Root mountains, I :144
Bitter Root river, I :130
Black, Arthur
rejoins Jackson-Sublette expedition, I :169
survivor of Indian massacre, I :166, 167
Black, William
commander of Raccoon, I :215
report on transfer of Astoria, I :215
Black Hills
overland route important, I :222
Astor expedition passes through, I :195
Blackberries introduced, II :695
Blackfeet country
Missouri Fur Co. plans trading post here, I :149
Blackfeet Indians
attacked Lewis and Clark, I :144
Doty lives with, II :571-572
drive Henry from post, I :149, 191
Henry meets, I :154
hostile to Bonneville party, I :270
hostility feared by Hunt, I :190, 192, 193
kill Jackson-Sublette men, I :169
killed by Lewis and Clark, I :144, 192
Stevens' expedition to treat with, II :586
warlike attitude, I :270
Blackwater river, I :108
Blair, Prior, II :668
Blair, W. I :293

Brakespear
  nom de plume of W. L. Adams, II:487-488
Blanchet, A. M. A., Bishop, I:301
Blanchet, Rev Father Francis Norbet
  Archbishop, I.301
  "Catholic ladder," I:302-303
  census of Catholics, I:300
  chairman of committee of organization, I:320
  consecrated archbishop, brings recruits from Europe, I:301
  death, I:302
  failure to cooperate in organizing government, I:321
  finds Whidbey island savages familiar with Catholic practices, I:300
  founds St. Joseph's college, I:301; II:715
  gristmill taxed, I:344
  punishment of horse thief, I:372-373
  Willamette valley and Cowlitz settlements visited, I:300
Blanco cape—See Cape Blanco
Bloody Chief (Indian), II:525
Bloody Spring battle, II:593
Bloomington (on Luckiamute river), II:738
Blossom (frigate), I:216
Blue Book controversy, II:475-476
  See also Laws and codes
Blue mountains
  beaver plentiful, I:220
  explored by Wallen, II:625
  Hunt party crossed, I:203
  Stuart's party crossed, I:219
  White faction travels over, I:377
Boat Encampment
  highest point by canoe on Columbia, I:248
  Thompson winters here, I:156
Boats—See Canoes; Ships; Steamboats
Bodega y Quadra, Juan Francisco de la
  accompanies Arteaga's expedition, I:33
  arrives San Blas, Mexico, 1775, I:33
  continuity of coast from 42° to 48° ascertained, II:444
  crew massacred by Indians, I:29
  discovered Bucareli sound, I:32
  expedition, I:29
  fails to consummate terms of Nootka treaty, I:68, 80
  friendly relations with Vancouver, I:68, 79
  generosity to Gray at Nootka, I:80
  name given to Vancouver island, I:68, 79-80
  plans to purchase Adventure from Gray, I:81
  sighted San Jacinto, I:32
Bodega bay
  Belcher shapes course for, I:370
  Drake may have stayed here, I:408
Boggs, Thomas, I:377
Boise, Elizabeth, II:706
Boise, Reuben P.
  administers oath of office to Governor Whiteaker, II:517
  admitted to bar of supreme court, II:467
  associate justice, II:495
  commissioner to draft new code, II:477
  incorporator Monmouth University, II:716
  lawyer in Salem, II:661
  member constitutional convention and subsequent career, II:510, 511
  member legislature, 1853, II:477
  Salem clique, II:497
  trustee La Creole Academy, II:717
Boise, Fort
  division of the "great immigration" reaches, I:394
  establishment, II:624
  first wheeled vehicle reaches, I:306
  road from Willamette valley to, II:726

Boise, Fort—Continued
  Salmon Falls or Myers massacre, II:625
Boise city
  stages operated to, 1866, II:672
  telegraph line from Portland, 1869, II:751
Boit, John
  commanded Union (ship), I:82
  circumnavigated the globe, I:82
  journel re Gray's discovery of Columbia river, I:94-95
  journal re Gray's discovery of Juan de Fuca strait, I:78
Boldoc, Father J. B. Z., I:300
Bolon, A. J.
  killed by Yakimas, II:581
  murder avenged, II:619
  murderers apprehensive of punishment, II:612, 614
Bonham, Benjamin F., II:467
Bonner's Ferry, Idaho, I:156
Bonneville, Benjamin Louis Eulalie de, I:269-272
  at Vancouver barracks, 1853, I:272
  birth and training, I:269
  contributions to Oregon development, I:272
  Irving's account, I:272
  places named for him, I:272
  report to Gen. Macomb, I:271
  return to settlements and reinstatement in army, I:271-272
  sends arms and ammunition to volunteers in Rogue river war, II:560
Bonneville, Fort, I:270
Bonneville, Oregon, I:272
Bonneville expedition
  Fort Osage starting point, I:269
  Great Salt Lake exploration, I:270
  Green river post built and abandoned, I:270
  influence on Oregon through Irving's book, I:272
  joint hunt with Wyeth abandoned, I:270, 277
  Oregon trail passed over, I:280
  organization; 110 men, I:269
  route, I:270
  scientific feature a failure, I:270
  supplies refused by Hudson's Bay Co. I:270, 271
  winter quarters, I:270-271
Bonneville dam and ship canal, II:749
Bonney, Jairus and Truman, I:397
Books
  first printed, II:486-487
  nine printed, 1839-1845, II:487
Boon, John D
  justice of the peace, II:660
  member of legislature, I:356
  treasurer for territory and state, II:660
  treasurer Willamette Woolen Mfg. Co., II:688
  trustee Willamette University, II:713
Boone, John L., II:632
Boone, Lalla Rookh
  quotes Martinez diary, I:76
Boone's ferry on Tualatin, II:729
Boston (ship), I:83
Boston trading expedition, I:85-87
  Columbia and Washington separated by storms, I:87
  equipment and cargo, I:82-83
  Gray's explorations, I:87-96
  medals in honor of, I:87
  Morison quoted, I:82-83
  negro, Marcus Lopez causes trouble with Indians, I:88
  organized, 1787, I:85-86
  reorganization, 1790, I:91
  Spanish ordered to capture vessels at California port, I:86

Effingham island, I:55
Eight Dollar mountain battle, II:598
Eleanora (ship), I:85
Elections
  Alvord's order re challenge of votes,
    1864, II:638
  American party controls several states,
    II:757
  Bush charges Lane and Smith with un-
    constitutional methods, II:770
  capital controversy, II:513, 514
  congressional, 1860, against secession,
    II:773-774, 775
  constitutional convention proposal re-
    jected, 1845, I:346
  democratic control, II:755
  democratic losses, 1859, II:759, 760, 761
  failure of 1848 election, I:359
  first general election, 1844, I:341
  first law-making body elected in terri-
    tory, I:341
  importance of 1845 election, I:347
  legislature, 1846, I:355; 1847, I:357; 1848,
    I:359, 360; 1860, II:770-771; 1862, II:781;
    1864, II:783-784; 1866, II:785; 1868, II:-
    786
  methods, I:415-416, II:768; votes cast
    used as basis of representation at
    democratic state convention, 1859, II:-
    761
  state, preceding ratification of statehood
    by congress, II:516
  statehood adopted, II:757; votes, II:505
  statehood convention votes, 1852-1857,
    II:504-505
  territorial emergency ticket, 1858, II:515,
    516-517
  Union majorities, 1862, II:781; 1864, II:-
    784; 1866, reduced, II:785
  viva voce voting bill, II:503
    See also—Congressional delegates; Ex-
      ecutive committee; Governor; Legis-
      lative committee; Political parties;
      Presidential campaign; Presidential
      electors; Senators, U. S.
Elgin, Idaho, I:198
Eliza, or Elisa, Lieut. Francisco
  reached Gulf of Georgia, I:78
  succeeds Martinez at Nootka, I:66
Elk (steamboat)
  on Yamhill river, II:744; on Willamette
    river, II:745
Elkins, Luther
  hanged in effigy, II:773
  member constitutional convention, II:510
  president of senate, II:516, 772
  trustee Santiam Academy, II:715
Elkton, II:668
Ellendale, II:688
Elliott, Elijah, I:401
Elliott, Milton, II:467
Ellis, Chief
  absent from great council, II:536
  chosen chief of Nez Perce's, II:525, 526
  demands pay from White, II:528
  severity in enforcing Dr. White's laws,
    II:526
Ellsworth, Stuckely
  admitted to bar of supreme court, II:467
  presidential elector nominee, II:774
Elm Grove, Mo.
  immigrants leave for Oregon, I:376, 392
Embree, Carey, II:705
Embree, Thomas and Mary, II:705
Emerick, Solomon, II:663
Emigration
    See—Immigration
Eminence
  early name for Rainier, II:664
Emmons, Lieut. George F., I:380

English possessions
  Broughton takes possession of Oregon
    country at Vancouver point, I:98
  Canadian colonies gained, I:43, 44
  Canning-Adams controversy, II:431-433
  claims based on Thompson's map, I:157
  in 1790, I:67, 90
  joint occupancy treaty, II:763
  investigated by Russia, I:63
  strengthened by Astor failure, I:222
  weakened by Meares' failure to dis-
    cover Columbia, I:60, II:444
  Drake formally takes possession for
    England, I:41, II:436
  Drake's visit basis of claims on Pacific,
    I:41-42, 90, II:418
  forts on Great Lakes, I:150
  Jefferson fears design to exploit west,
    I:114, 118
  Louisiana seizure feared by U. S., I:114
  war with Spain re northwest claims
    threatened, I:67
    See also—Boundary dispute; Fur trade;
      Hudson's bay co.; Nootka conven-
      tion; North West co., Treaties.
Enos (Indian), II:597
Enterprise (steamboat), II:744
Entrada de Ceta
    See—Esenada de Heceta
Entrada de Perez, I:32
Eola
  Bethel Academy founded, II:711
  post office created, II:738
Epidemics
  1829-1832 McLoughlin combats, I:247
  1831-1832 Indians blamed Dominis and
    crew of Owyhee, I:363
  influence on Whitman's massacre, I:312
  Lees' mission, I:290, 296
  malignant fever attacks Meek party, I:396
  threatened by McDougal has evil conse-
    quences, I:183
Episcopal church
  schools founded, II:720
Ermatinger, Francis
  accompanies Wyeth to Flathead post,
    I:270, 276-277
  accountant of Hudson's Bay Co., I:248
  chief trader of Hudson's Bay Co. at Ore-
    gon City, I:347
  elected treasurer, I:346
  in California, I:244
  suit: "Amos M. Short vs. F. Ermatinger,"
    II:470
Escaloom, Frank (Indian), II:541
Escheats
  first exercise of government in escheat
    of estate, I:345
    See also—Young, Ewing
Esenada de Heceta (Entrada de Ceta)
  Columbia river called, I:16, 97.
Esquimalt, II:464
Essex (frigate), I:212
Estools (Indian), II:541
Eugene
  citizens listed by Skinner, 1854, II:668
  Columbia College built, II:711, 715
  democratic state convention at, 1859, II:-
    761, 771; 1860, II:768; 1862, II:780-781
  first called Eugene City, II:513
  first court under oak tree, II:485
  national democrats hold opposition meet-
    ing, 1858, II:516
  origin of name, II:667
  post office created, II:738
  Small's company recruited at, II:635
  steamers run to, 1856-7, II:744
  Union and democrat conventions, 1862,
    II:780
  university location fixed, II:719

Fitzhugh, Solomon
  absentee senator, 1860, II:771, 772
  member constitutional convention, II:510
Fitzpatrick, Thomas
  guide of White party, I:376
  through South Pass, 1824, I:248
Five Crows, Chief of Cayuses
  at Nez Perce's conference with White,
    II:525
  elected chief, II:528
  wounded at Sand Hollow, II:531-532
Flagstaff lake, I:387
Flathead fork
  See—Clark's fork
Flathead (Flat Head) Indians
  Catholic missionaries, I:300
  Dobbs mentions, I:12
  friendly to Lewis and Clark, I:131
  McLoughlin advises Lee not to locate
    among, I:288
  Methodist mission authorized, I:285-286
  religious quest, I:284-285
  Stevens negotiates treaty with, II:580
  Thompson trades with, I:156
  story of old man and handkerchiefs,
    I:47
  unknown to war department, I:285-286
Flathead lake, I:162
Flathead (Flat Head) post
  McDonald given staff of seven men here,
    I:240
  on Bull river, Mont., I:207-208
Flax
  Clatsop and other Indians used, 1805,
    II:696
  indigenous to Willamette valley, II:683
    east of Cascades, II:696
  seed brought from Indiana, II:696
Fleming, J., printer, II:486
Fletcher, Francis
  arrival in Oregon, I:293, 374
  member Peoria party, I:374
  trustee Willamette University, II:713
Flinn, John, II:713
Flint, Addison R.
  lays out Winchester, 1850, II:668
  trustee Umpqua Academy, II:717
Flora
  Howison's observations, 1846, II:647
  loss of Fremont collection, I:389
Florence, A. B.
  absentee senator, 1860, II:771, 772
  state senator, 1858, II:518
Flores, Antonio, I:25
Flores Creek Indians, II:601
Florez, Spanish viceroy of New Spain
  reasserts Spanish authority over disput-
    ed region, I:62, 64
  releases prize ship seized by Martinez,
    I:66
Florida
  cession to U. S. by Spain, II:422
  terms of settlement, II:424
Flour industry
  flour exported to Sitka, I:245
  flourishes after gold discovery, II:478
  mill at Vancouver, I:245; at Salem, II:-
    660; at Silverton, II:667; Milwaukie,
    II:693
Floyd, Charles
  cousin of John Floyd, I:255
  death, I:123, 124, 255
  Lewis and Clark expedition, I:123
Floyd, John
  Adams' antagonism explained, I:256
  bill for military occupation with land
    grants to settlers, II:763
  career, I:413
  first to use name Oregon for territory,
    I:16, 255, 256

Floyd, John—Continued
  Oregon agitation in congress, I:255, 431,
    432
  Oregon bill, 1824, passed by house, I:258
  Oregon bill, 1827, not voted on, I:258
  Oregon bills, I:15-16, 256-258; II:432
  Oregon route advocated, I:258
  Oregon route: distance and time calcu-
    lated, I:256
  report to congress re Oregon, I:15-16,
    257, 413
  retires from congress, I:258
Foisy, M. G.
  member of legislature from Champoeg,
    I:346
  printer, II:487
Fonte, Pedro Bartolome de, Admiral
  abstract of letter pub. by Arthur Dobbs,
    I:8
  account of northwest passage, I:5
  account of pretended visit to Puget
    sound, 1640, I:3
  fancied story of Archipelago of St. Laza-
    rus, I:3, 409
  Jeffrey's book based on his letter, I:6
  claims to meet ship Maltechusetts, I:6
  tales gain credence, I:8
Fonte lake, I:7
Food
  dog and horse meat, I:127, 389
  Preuss eats ants, I:389
  prices, 1843, I:393, 395
  scarcity in the 40's, I:395; II:723
  wild fruit and nuts, I:403-404
Forage plants, II:680, 684
Force, James and John, I:377
Ford, Sidney S.
  locates in Puget sound region, II:489
Ford, Caroline and Sarah, II:705
Ford, M. A.
  elected district attorney, I:346
  member of legislature from Polk, 1847,
    I:357
Ford, Miller, II:705
Ford, Nathaniel
  Jefferson Institute started in home of,
    II:704-705
  second mail route reaches, I:355; II:727
  trustee Jefferson Institute, II:705
Forest Grove
  Congregational church removed to, I:304
  home guards formed, II:640
  Pacific University located at, I:296, II:-
    663, 710
  Rev. Harvey Clark teacher here, I:304
  secessionist controversy, II:640
  site of Emerick land claim, II:663
Forts
  bill authorizes line from Missouri to
    Oregon, I:311
  See also—Names of forts
Foster, James H., II:716
Foster, Philip
  elected treasurer, I:341
  owner of town lots, I:344
Foster road, II:725
Foulweather Cape
  See Cape Foulweather
Four Lakes battle, II:617
Fourier, Louis, I:266
Fourteenth amendment
  See—Constitution—U. S.
Fox, Charles E., II:664
Fox, Charles James, British minister
  Aberdeen letter, II:450
Fox, Ebenezer D., I:178
Franchere, Gabriel
  account of sale of Astoria, I:214
  account of Thompson's proposal to As-
    torians, I:185

Franchere, Gabriel—Continued
accounts of Astoria supplement Irving's, I:206
almost left on Hawaiian island, I:177
Astor expedition, I:176
explore Santiam and Calapooia, I:220
Narrative, 1820, I:214
narrative of Astoria garden, II:680
story of Madame Dorion, I:412
Franchise
first organic law, provisions, I:336
forfeited, I:337
See also, Negroes
Francis, Simeon
Lincoln proposes as secretary of territory, II:469
serves as editor of Oregonian, II:469, 759, 766
Franciscans
Jesuit missions taken over, I:27
missions founded in California, I:26
Fraser, Abner, I:397
Fraser, Angelique
mother of Dr. McLoughlin, I:234
Fraser, Malcolm
grandfather of Dr. McLoughlin, I:235
Fraser, Simon
explored Fraser river, 1807, I:15, 109, 184
trading posts established by, I:109, 184
Fraser river
believed to be part of the Columbia, I:410
discovered by Simon Fraser, 1807, I:15, 109, 242
immigration to, II:520
Indians called Tacouche Tesse, I:109
John Stuart's survey mentioned, I:220, 242
Mackenzie follows, I:108
Mackenzie mistakes for Columbia, I:109
McMillan reaches mouth, I:242
region opened to trade, I:242
sighted by Spanish navigators, I:79
trading posts established, I:184, 208
Frazar, Thomas, II:709
Frederick, J. M., II:717
Freight
first carried on Columbia, I:188
Fremont, John C., I:381-390
abandons wagon with scientific instruments, I:384
Columbia river surveyed. I:381-382
description of Central and Southern Oregon, I:385
Enos his guide, II:597
estimate of White party numbers, I:378
expedition to California, I:383-389
expedition to Oregon country, 1842, I:381; 1843, I:381-383
finds maps inaccurate, I:386
importance in Oregon history, I:383
Klamath Indians attack party, I:389-390
knowledge of Ogden's and McLeod's expedition uncertain, I:384
loss of collection of flora, I:389
McLoughlin receives, I:382-383
nominated for president, II:757
obtains Indian guides, I:384
overtakes great immigration party and Applegate's fleet of boats, I:394
part in bringing California under U. S., I:389, 390
presidential campaign slogan, II:508
quest of Buenaventura river, I:383, 389
reaches Sutter's Fort, I:389
receives double brevet of captain, I:389
returns to Washington, I:389
route followed by gold rush expedition, II:479
routes followed, I:381-382, 383-390; II:479
third expedition, I:389

Fremont, John C.—Continued
weather encountered, I:383
French Canadians
as settlers, I:370-371
attitude toward provisional government, I:330, 334
forts on Saskatchewan, I:150
Indian wives, I:371
Lee's petition to congress signed by, I:373; II:445
pre-emption rights promised under U. S. occupation, I:265
provisional government opposed, I:330-331, 339; petition, I:340
provisional government saved by two voters, I:331
raise company for Indian war, II:529
settlements and industries described by Mofras, I:370-371, 372-373
trappers' influence with Indians, I:150
French explorations
Alaskan visits unimportant, I:53
authorized by government in Paris, 1728, I:2
directed by colonial government in Montreal, 1728, I:2
La Perouse, 1786, in northwest, I:53, 69
Marchand in the northwest, 1791, I:53, 69
Mofras' visit commercial rather than political, I:370
Pierre Gaultier de Varennes (Sieur de la Verendrye), I:2
French government
interest in California and Texas, II:462-463
French names, I:371
French possessions
Louisiana ceded to U. S., I:117, 123; II:418, 419
Louisiana grant to Crozat, II:417
secured Louisiana from Spain, I:115
French Prairie
community settlement at Aurora, II:664
early settlers, I:267; II:678, 679
Madame Dorion lived here, I:412
meeting of French Canadians re Cayuse Indian war, II:529
pioneer agricultural community established, 1829, II:678
St. Mary convent school established, I:301
second Wolf meeting, I:332
settled by Hudson's Bay Co. employes, I:251
Fretum Anian
See—Anian straits
Friendly, Joseph P., II:719
Friends of the Union
See—Knights of the Golden Circle
Frier, A. H., II:717
Frobisher, Martin, I:4, 5
Frontier
influence on character, and social and political life, I:361
military protection, II:637-639
Frost, Daniel, II:741
Frost, Joseph H.
established mission at Clatsop, I:295, 379
joins Lee's mission, I:294
visited by Wilkes at Clatsop, I:378-379
Fruit industry
effect of gold discovery on prices, II:693
exports, 1856, II:693
first fruit trees produced from seed, II:681
grafted fruit trees introduced, II:691-692
legend of fruits grown from seeds, II:691
Mrs. Whitman's description, II:681
native fruits found by early visitors, II:691

Hillyer, Commodore
  captures the Essex, I:212
  commander of convoy for Isaac Todd,
    I:212
Hilton, John, II:572
Hinckley, Capt. William S., I:291
Hines, Gustavus
  accompanies White to Walla Walla val-
    ley, II:527
  address at patriotic meeting, I:334
  assigned to Umpqua mission, I:295
  attends council called by White, II:528
  chairman public meeting, I:334
  joins Lee's mission, I:294
  member committee on organization, I:320
  on bark Columbia with Lee, I:298
  returns to Oregon and brings Lee's
    daughter, I:298
  secretary of meetings to organize a gov-
    ernment, I:319, 320
  speech at public meeting, I:335
Hirsch, Edward, II:667
Hirsch, Meyer, II:782
Hirsch, Solomon
  business in Silverton, II:667
  U. S. minister to Turkey, II:667
Hoback, John
  joins Astor expedition, I:192
  locates at Henry's post, I:198
  meets Astor's return party, I:219
  stream in Gros Ventre range named for
    him, I:197
  urges Astors to go to Henry's post,
    I:197
Hoback river, I:197
Hobson, Harley, II:706
Hobson, John
  member of legislature from Clatsop, 1848,
    I:360
  settler with family at Clatsop plains,
    I:369
Hobson, William, I:345
Hoffman, William, II:774
Hoffstetter, John, I:377
Hogs
  Astorians raise, I:684
  imported from Hawaiian islands, II:679
  McLoughlin farm, II:680-681
Hogue, James, II:508
Hoh river
  called Destruction river by Barkley,
    I:55
Holbrook, Amory
  admitted to bar of supreme court, II:467
  correspondence with President Fillmore,
    II:473
  Deady-McFadden controversy attributed
    to, II:496, 497
  declines to vote for senator, 1860, II:773
  introduces Know-nothing party in terri-
    tory, II:502
  Lincoln's letter to, quoted, II:764
  prosecutor in Whitman massacre trial,
    II:543
  "steamboat code" appellation attributed
    to, II:475
  supports Gaines in capital controversy,
    II:470, 472
  vote for senator, 1860, II:772
Holderness, Samuel M.
  controversy with White, I:351
  elected secretary of the territory, 1848,
    I:359
  secretary meeting, March 4, 1844, I:340
  signs Canadian protest, March 4, 1844,
    I:339-340
Holladay, Ben
  hotel called Seaside House, II:664
  People's Transportation Co. and Pacific
    Mail Steamship Co. bought, II:746

Holladay, Ben—Continued
  treaty with Oregon Steam Navigation
    Co., II:746
  Willamette Transportation Co., II:746
Holland, M.
  erects first building, with White, in
    Silverton, II:667
Holland, John P.
  victim of Coquille Indian massacre, II:-
    557
Holland, Thomas
  citizen in Eugene, 1854, II:668
Holman, Daniel S., I:311
Holman, Joseph
  arrival in Oregon, I:293, 374
  director Willamette Woolen Mfg. Co.,
    II:688
  member Peoria party, I:374
  meeting of July 5, 1843, I:334
  trustee Willamette University, II:713
Holmes, Leander
  chooses Greeley as proxy, II:765, 766
  delegate to republican national conven-
    tion, 1860, II:759
  secretary republican territorial conven-
    tion, II:508
Home guards
  formed at Forest Grove, II:640
Homestead bill, favored by republicans,
    1859, II:758
Honolulu
  missionaries present printing press to
    Whitman and Spalding missions, II:-
    487
Honolulu (brig), II:478
Hood, John, I:266
Hood, Viscount Samuel
  Hood canal and Mount Hood named for,
    I:78
Hood canal, I:78, 98
Hood, Mount
  Barlow road passes, II:725
  origin of name, I:78, 98
  sighted by Lewis and Clark, I:133, 142
  Tumtum, Indian name, I:133
Hood river county
  creation and derivation of name, II:676
  Oregon method of fruit packing origin-
    ated, II:695
Hope (ship)
  at Nootka, I:81
  commanded by Ingraham, I:91
Hoquarton
  early name for Tillamook, II:664
Hooker, Joseph
  builds Scottsburg road, II:730
  major-general Union army, II:632
Hoosier (steamboat), II:742, 744
Horse creek, II:590
Horse Prairie creek, I:127
Horses
  eaten for food, I:200; II:587
  Gale importation, II:685
  McLoughlin farm, II:680
Hoskins, Fort
  company G of cavalry regiment stationed
    at, II:635
  First Oregon infantry stationed at, II:-
    641
Hoult, Enoch, II:510
House of representatives
  first in Oregon, 1845, I:348-355
Houses
  See—Buildings
Hovey, A. G.
  aide, governor's staff, II:644
  delegate to republican national conven-
    tion, 1860, II:759
  proxy given to Buckingham, II:765

Indians—Continued

epidemics
  exterminate tribes, 1829-1832, I:247, 363
  in school, I:290
  McLoughlin combats, 1829-32, I:247
  one cause of Whitman massacre, I:312
  threatened by McDougal, has evil con-
    sequences, I:184
ethical code of Arikaras, I:125
ethical code understood by Capt. Cook,
  I:47-48
fear of white encroachment, I:167, 308,
  313, II:522, 527
first European to live as one of them,
  Mackay, I:55
flax used by, II:696
food, I:127, II:568, 571, 595
Fort Walla Walla conference, I:226
friendliness to whites, II:521-522
friendly to explorers
  Astorians, I:180
  Bishop, I:102
  Gray, I:88
  Hunt, I:196
  Lewis and Clark, I:124, 130, 137, 140
  Vancouver, I:77
fur trade begun by Capt. Cook, I:46
fur trade, Capt. Bishop, I:102
fur trader's exploit, II:521
government by alien standards first attempted, II:526
guides for Rogers expedition, I:9
hostile to explorers and settlers
  Astorians, I:194, 219
  Boit, I:82
  Fremont, I:389-390
  Gray, I:88, 91
  Hanna, I:54
  Heceta, I:29
  Winship trading post, I:171
hostility to Americans punished by Mc-
  Loughlin, I:317
human sacrifices abolished, I:247
immigrants' attitude toward, I:393
industrial training school, I:296
killed at Gray's harbor, I:93
land titles
  articles in payment specified by treaty,
    II:551
  conceded to, country east of Cascade
    mts., II:612
  first effort to obtain peaceably, II:456
  organic act protects, I:336
  Palmer favors extinguishing, II:594
  prices paid, II:550, 551
  purchase by government attempted,
    II:549
  settlers ordered out of region not set-
    tled by confirmation of treaties,
    II:609
  to be extinguished by Floyd bill, I:256
languages
  lexicon prepared by Smith, I:307
  list of words prepared by Green, I:282
laws of the Nez Perce's given by White,
  II:524-528
legislation re ammunition, I:358
legislation re lands and property, I:336
Lewis and Clark, desertion prevented,
  I:131
Lewis and Clark expedition, two Indians
  killed, I:144
Lewis thought to be supernatural, crane
  incident, I:133
liquor
  Calapooya treaty, II:569-570
  introduced by rival fur companies,
    I:154-155, 160
  Lewis and Clark found no use of, I:-
    138-139

Indians—liquor—Continued
  traffic abolished in Oregon country by
    McLoughlin, I:264-265
  traffic suppressed by Hudson's Bay
    Co.,I:233
locating outside of settlements advocat-
  ed, II:546
McKenzie's relations, I:225
McLoughlin's policy, I:246
map drawing facility, I:140
massacres
  along the Klamath, II:590
  Atahualpa crew, I:83
  Barkley's crew, I:30, 55
  Boston's crew at Nootka, I:83
  Butte Creek, II:591
  Cascade massacre, II:607
  Coquille Indian massacre, II:557
  Gold Beach massacre, II:597
  Gray's men, I:91
  Jedediah Smith's men, California, I:-
    164; Oregon, I:167; II:521
  miners, II:590
  prospectors, II:613
  Quadra's men, I:29
  Rogue river, I:313, 317, 380; II:591
  Russian crew near Sitka sound, I:52
  Sublette men, I:274
  Tonquin crew, I:181-183
  T'Vault party, II:557
  Ward and Kirkland, II:566
  White river valley, II:588-589
  Whitman mission, I:312-314, 358; II:-
    522, 528, 530, 532, 613; trial of mur-
    derers, II:543-544
  See also—Indians—Wars
match, compass and magnet story of
  Capt. Clark, I:141
medals given by Lewis and Clark, I:104
medicine man, I:312
military escorts hindered by, I:148
missionaries, Catholic, influence of, II:-
  528
missionaries, Catholic, welcomed by, I:299
missionaries under Lee welcomed, I:287,
  288
missionary settlers present new aspect,
  II:522
name Oregon listed in Courrier du Canada, I:13
negro episode on Gray's voyage, I:87, 88
Nootkan chief restored after trip to
  China, I:57
object to leaving familiar hunting
  grounds, II:595
organic law, provisions, I:336, 350
population during McLoughlin's regime,
  I:247
population early 19th century, I:247, 296
primitive farming methods, I:307
promises of Indian agents vex territorial
  governor, II:546
reforms instituted by McLoughlin, I:247
religious instruction sought by deputa-
  tions to St. Louis, I:284-285
removal east of Cascades fails, II:549
reputation for stealing, I:394-395
reservations: See Indian reservations
Rogers' plans, I:10
sailors, I:71
salmon fishing at Wishram, I:188
scalp of Peu-peu mox-mox possessed by
  Story, II:585
slavery, captives held in, II:571
said to be encouraged by Hudson's
  Bay Co., I:263
Sunday observance, II:575, 616
tools, copper and iron, I:29
trade, with Russians or English protested by Spanish, I:63

Lee, Jason—Continued
supplanted by Gary, I:296, 298
Waller-McLoughlin controversy, I:298, 414
Whitman mission described and methods recommended, I:308
Willamette University foundation due to, I:296
work praised by Slacum, I:263
See also—Methodist missions
Lee, Lucy Anna Maria
daughter of Jason Lee, I:298
Lee, N., II:717
Lee, Fort, II:530
Leese, Jacob P., II:685
Lefevre, James, I:176
Legal tender
act of 1845, I:353; 1847, I:354
war measure of 1862, II:782
See also—Mint; Money
Legislative committee
acts ratified by amended law, I:346, 348
designates boundaries of Oregon territory, II:674-675
first law-making body by regular election, I:341; personnel, compensation, I:331, 332-333
first meeting at Willamette Falls, I:332
forms legislative districts, I:337; II:673, 674
members, I:332
oath of office amended, 1845, I:348
officers elected, I:333
policy outlined, I:353
proceedings, 1843, I:333; 1844, I:342, 344; 1845, I:347-348
superseded by house of representatives, I:350
White correspondence, I:352
Legislative districts
boundaries defined, I:337; II:674
election of, 1843, I:341
established, I:337; II:674
first organic act, provisions, I:337
north of Columbia represented, 1846, I:355
Vancouver created, I:348
Legislative hall
first on Pacific coast at Willamette Falls, I:333
Legislature, Provisional
action of 1844, I:346
authorizes regiment of volunteers, II:529
election and proceedings, 1846, I:355-356; 1847, I:357; 1848, I:359-360
election of 1845, noteworthy, I:347; proceedings, I:348-353
election of 1848 fails, I:359
house of representatives, first in Oregon, powers, I:350
members elected, 1845, I:346
Multnomah Circulating Library incorporated, I:352
mulatto land claim upheld, I:489
special session, 1849, I:359
White controversy, August, 1845, I:351-352
See also—Law; Organic act
Legislature, State
absentees leave senate without quorum, 1860, II:771, 772
capitol commission, II:661
designates Corvallis College to receive congressional land grant, II:712
first special session, 1858, before congressional ratification, II:516, 760; not challenged, II:517; first regular adjourns, not counted in state records, II:518

Legislature, State—Continued
fourteenth amendment ratified, II:784; rescinded, II:787
loyalty bill vetoed by governor, II:632
McBride resolution on Union, II:781
organization, 1860, II:770-771
party alignments, 1864, II:783, 784; changes, 1865-6, II:784-785; 1868, II:786
premature elections raise doubt as to status, 1858, II:515
republican alignment with Douglas democrats, II:771
seal, act providing, II:760
senator not elected, 1859, II:760
senatorial contests, 1860, II:770-771, 774
special session, 1859, II:760
thirteenth amendment ratified, II:784
U. S. senators Williams and Corbett requested to resign by, II:787
war currency measure, II:782
Legislature, Territorial
asks removal of Wool, II:607
authorizes scrip to pay militia, II:547
capital controversy, Salem vs. Oregon City, II:470-473
capitol at Oregon City, Corvallis, and Salem, II:661
capitol burned, 1855, II:661
code of laws adopted and printed, 1854-1855, II:477
commission appointed to construct university, II:719
democrats in power, 1853, II:500; 1858, II:516
franchise granted to Hall and Hall, II:-725
Gaines message controversy, II:474
last assembly, 1858, II:518
meets in Nesmith home, II:660
memorial for division of territory, 1854, II:492
memorial on Salem as seat of government, II:471
memorial to Pierce for removal of Palmer, II:596
memorials to congress re home rule, II:-503-504
one new county created, II:490
Oregon City acts declared illegal by attorney-general, II:472
party members, II:500
postal service, complaints to congress, 1852-1853, II:738; 1856, II:739
power to locate capital conferred by organic act, II:513-514
public buildings act, II:470
railroad chartered, II:749
Salem change of name agitation, II:662-663
Salem proceedings confirmed by congress, II:472
viva voce act, 1854, II:503
Willamette University authorized, II:713
Leland, Richard, I:167
Lehmi Pass, I:128
Lemon, Captain, I:103
Lemont, F. A., II:681
"Lenox" church, II:711
"Leoni Loti"
sequel to "Prairie Flower", by Moss, II:487
Lepensees, or Lapensee, Oliver, Ignace and Basil, I:176
Les Chaudiere
See—Kettle Falls
Leslie, David
joins Lee's party, I:291
presides at meeting to organize government, I:320
trustee Willamette University, II:713

Polk, James K.—Continued
inaugural message re Oregon, II:454; resented by British, II:456
message to congress re tariffs, II:457
message re military protection of Oregon settlers, II:459
nomination, II:452
Oregon boundary policy and settlement, II:439-440, 459
papers re White in his possession, I:352
presents Washington treaty to senate, II:460
signs territorial bill, II:466

Polk county
Benton county cut from, II:675
Bethel Academy founded, II:711
bolt at democrat convention, 1859, II:762
creation and derivation of name, II:665, 676
in Judge Pratt's district, II:476
in Judge Williams' district, II:496
Jefferson Institute, II:705
Lincoln county cut from, II:676
members of legislature, 1846, I:356; 1847, I:357; 1848, I:360
not represented at democrat convention, 1860, II:769
subscriptions to capital stock of woolen mills, II:689
volunteers for Cayuse war, II:539
whigs and independents divided in support of Maine law, II:500

Pomeroy, Dwight, I:377
Pomeroy, Walter
member of White party, I:377
owner of town lots, I:344
Pond, Peter, I:153
Pontchartrain lake, II:418
Pony express, II:746
Pool, John R., II:669
Population
American, 1843, I:327
arrivals, 1040-1041, I.374, 375, II.482, 1850, II:753
Astoria, 1844, I:369; 1846, II:648
census, 1845, I:353; 1849, ordered by Lane, II:482; 1850, II:482
Champoeg district, 1843, I:337, 339
effect of boundary determination on, II:648
gold in Oregon brings new influx, II:481
gold rush in California reduces, II:479, 654
increase, 1860-1870, II:753
Milwaukie, II:651
missionary period, 1839, I:361, 374
north of Columbia, 1849, II:482, 483; 1851, II:488
Oregon City, 1846, II:648
Portland, 1846, II:648; 1855, II:656
Willamette valley, 1844, I:402; 1849, II:-649-650
See also—Indians
Porpoise (brig), I:381
Port Discovery
British offer to cede in boundary dispute, II:441
reached by Quimper, 1791, I:78
Vancouver's visit, I:77
Port Gamble battle, II:612
Port Gardner, I:78
Port Orchard, I:78
Port Orford
citizen companies continue scouting campaign, II:598
Dart Indian treaty, II:549
Indian shoots white man, II:590
population, 1851, II:557
settlers arrive, 1851, II:556
Port Orford Indians, II:601

Port Townsend, I:78
Port Wilson, I:78
Portage railroads, II:749
Porter, Capt. David, I:212
Portius, William, I:360
Portland
assessed valuation of property, 1855, II:656
brick buildings erected, 1853, II:656
Canyon road affects growth, II:728
capital project defeated, II:513, 514
Catholic schools founded, II:715
churches, first built, II:655
city limits extended, 1864, II:658
commerce, 1848, II:649
consideration for Pettygrove interest in townsite, II:654
county seat of Multnomah county, 1854, II:656
described by British officers, I:402-403; II:653
description, 1848-1852, II:655
Episcopal schools founded, II:720
factor in commerce, II:656
first enterprises, II:655
first ferry, II:729
first frame house in, II:655
first municipal election, II:655
first settler, II:654
first steam sawmill, II:655
first telegraph line, 1855-1856, II:751
flour cost, II:602
founded, 1843, I:403
gold rush reduces population, II:654
home rule meeting, II:503
incorporated, 1851, II:656
influence of mining development on, II:-656
jail vs. school tax, 1856, II:710
Know-nothings here, 1855, II:502
land title litigation, II:656-657
land values, early, II:654, 656
leadership, reasons for, II:653
levee dedicated to public by Coffin, II:-658
Lewis and Clark approached site, I:143
macadam roads built, II:656
McCormick's printing office on Front st., II:487
name, incident of choice, I:403
natural advantages, II:653
newspapers, II:486, 652
Oregon Monthly published at, II:487
penitentiary located at, II:470
pioneers, II:653-654
platted by Lovejoy and Pettygrove, II:-653
population, 1846, II:648; 1852, II:655; 1855, II:656
postoffice, created, 1853, II:738
richest city north of California boundary, 1855, II:656
rival of Milwaukie, II:652, 741-742
river transportation affects growth, II:-514
roads from, II:728-729
saw mill, first operated by steam, II:649
school, first opened, II:708
schools, private, II:708-709
schools, public, development to 1856, II:709-710
shingle mill, first erected, II:655
site passed by John Ball, I:276
stage line to southern Oregon, II:740
state educational association organized, II:719
steamship line acquired, II:652
telegraph lines to Seattle, The Dalles, and Boise City, II:751

Resources
  central and southern Oregon; Fremont
    description, I:384-386
    See also—Agriculture; Animal hus-
      bandry; Fruit industry; Fur trade;
      Lumber industry; Salmon fishing;
      Willamette valley
Revilla, Christoval, I:31
Revoir, Antoine, I:221
Reynolds, R. B., II:544
Rezanof, Russian imperial inspector, I:84
Rezner, Jacob
  joins Astor expedition, I:192
  meets Astor's return party, I:219
  urges Astors to go to Henry's post, I:197
Rice, L. A., I:360
Rich, William, I:380
Richard (Nez Perce'), II:533, 536
Richardson, Mrs.
  housekeeper, Main Street House, Oregon
    City, II:650
Richmond, J. P.
  assigned to establish mission at Nis-
    qually, I:295
  physician with Lee's mission, I:294
Richmond, Colonel S., II:650
Rickreall, Polk county
  Jefferson Institute established, II:704-705
  name originally Dixie, II:704-705
  post office created, II:738
Rickreall river
  connects with Willamette by canal, II:743
  forded by Talbot party, I:390
Rinearson, J. S.
  appointed junior major, II:627
  sent to meet immigrants, I:397
Rinehart, William V.
  served in cavalry and infantry, II:640
  writes of Nez Perce's treaty council,
    II:636
Rio del Norte
  See—Rio Grande
Rio Grande river, II:421
Risdon, D. M., II:668
Rival (steamboat), II:745
River d' Aguilar
  Columbia river called, I:16
River de los Estrechos
  Columbia river called, I:16
River of San Roc
  Columbia river called, I:16
River of the West
  Carver mentions, I:12
  Carver's map shows, I:11
  Columbia river called, I:16
  confused with Colorado river, I:2
  French maps show, I:2
  Indian map of Ochagach, I:2
  map in Jeffrey's book, I:6-7
  rumors lead to explorations, I:2
  Verendrye did not reach, I:2
  See also—Columbia river
River Thegayo
  Columbia river called, I:16
Rivers and streams
  Buenaventura a myth, I:386, 389
  sources of the four great rivers, Carver,
    I:11-12
  Wilkes' observation on Columbia first
    important report, I:381
  See also—Names of rivers
"Riviere Boudin"
  name given by Mofras to Pudding river,
    I:372
Riviere la Biche, I:236
Roads
  Astoria to Salem, II:483, 730
  Barnes, II:729
  Canyon, II:728
  Cascades explorations, II:726

Roads—Continued
  congressional requirements, 1859, II:513
  corduroy and plank, II:724
  Cornelius pass, II:728
  Cowlitz river to Olympia, II:483
  early building difficulties, II:729
  finest natural road Ft. Bridger to Ft.
    Hall, I:394
  first chartered toll road, I:354, 397; II:-
    724
  first wagon roads follow Indian trails,
    II:723-724
  first wagon trail from the Columbia to
    Puget sound, I:396
  Fort Steilacoom to Walla Walla, II:483
  Gaines urges improvement, II:474
  Germantown, II:728
  gold rush locates to Sacramento valley,
    II:727
  Hillsboro and Centerville to Portland,
    II:729
  immigrants' work, I:398, 399-401
  legislation, 1845, I:354; 1851-1852, II:483
  Mullan's, Walla Walla to Ft. Benton,
    II:747
  Linnton to Tualatin valley, II:648, 727
  macadam, first in Oregon, II:656
  mail route in Washington territory, II:-
    483
  mail routes, II:727
  Marysville or Corvallis to Winchester,
    II:669
  military, built by acts of congress, II:-
    483, 730
  mining stimulated by, II:520
  Oregon City to Jacob Spores, II:727
  Oregon City to Lee's mission, II:724
  Oregon City to Oregon Institute, II:727
  plank road, Silverton to Oregon City,
    II:727
  plank road from Olympia to Columbia
    river, II:652
  Portland and Tualatin Plains Plank
    Road Co., II:728-729
  Portland and Valley Plank Road Co.,
    II:728
  Portland to Oregon City begun, 1851,
    II:652
  Portland to Tualatin plains, II:648, 655
  Portland to The Dalles, II:726
  post roads established by congress,
    1850, II:736
  provisional government passes laws on
    lines over Cascade mountains, I:403
  Sandy river to The Dalles, II:726
  Scottsburg road, built by Hooker, II:730
  Scottsburg to Rogue river, requested
    from congress, II:483
  Siskiyou mountains, II:730
  Skinner urges liberal appropriations for,
    1853, II:494
  Springville to Tualatin plains, II:728
  toll prices, II:725
  Tuality to Sauvie island, II:727; to
    Springville, II:728
  Washington County Plank Road Co.,
    II:729
  Willamette valley survey, I:354; II:726
  Willamette valley to Fort Boise begun,
    II:726
  Willamette valley to Oregon trail, II:726
  wooden tram north side of Columbia,
    II:749
  See also—Barlow road, Canyon road,
    Foster road, Germantown road.
Robb, James R.
  member of 1842 immigration, I:377
  trustee Willamette University, II:713
Robb, John H.
  gift to LaCreole Academy, II:716

Robb, John H.—Continued
trustee Bethel Institute, II:717
Robbins, Nathaniel, II:510
Robe, R., II:668
Roberts, G. W., II:652
Roberts, Henry, I:70
Roberts, J. F.
land transfer to Oregon Institute, II:660
trustee La Creole Academy, II:717
Roberts, William, II:713
Robinson, Edward
joins Astor expedition, I:192
meets Astor's return party, I:219
urges Astors to go to Henry's post, I:197
Robinson, J., I:357
Robinson, Thomas G., II:656
Roche Jaune river (Yellowstone), I:126
Rock Island rapid, I:188
Rocky Mountain Fur Co.
in process of dissolution, I:278
Jackson, Smith and Sublette firm called, I:163
Jackson-Sublette trade in upper Snake region, I:169
Smith's expedition to Oregon, I:163-164
Wyeth's contract violated by, I:277, 278, 279
Rocky Mountain men, I:278-280
contention with Bonneville, I:270
Rocky mountains
Fremont expedition crossed, 1843, I:382
Gates of the Rockies described by Lewis and Clark, I:127
Lemhi pass reached by Lewis and Clark, I:128
Mackenzie crossed, I:108
riches described by Carver, I:12
Shining mountains described by Carver, I:12
sighted by Lewis, I:126
summit claimed as western boundary of Louisiana purchase, II:419, 420, 421
suggestion of Governor Pelly to follow summit south of 49th parallel as boundary, II:434
Verendrye sees, I:2; calls Bright Stones, I:13
Rodgers, Andrew, I:312
Roe, Charles J.
marries Nancy McKay, I:292
settler in Willamette valley, I:266
Rogers, Cornelius
accompanies White to Nez Perce's country, II:524
joins Whitman's mission, I:307
leaves mission, I:308
Rogers, Harrison G.
Jedediah Smith's expedition, I:164-165
Rogers, James H.
vice-president state educational association, II:720
Rogers, L.
member of legislature from Yamhill, 1847, I:357
Rogers, Robert
appointed governor-commandant at Fort Mackinaw, I:9
first expedition under Capt. James Tute, route and return, I:9-10, 11
first to outline true overland route, I:9
loaned petitions and plans to Carver, I:13
Oregon name first used in written form by, I:9
proposals to George III re search for northwest passage, I:8-9
Rogers, Sterling
fatally wounded by Indians, II:523
Rogue river
Gold Beach at mouth of, II:597

Rogue river—Continued
branch followed by Applegate prospecting party, I:398
Little Meadows battle, II:598
massacre of Young's party, I:380
military post started by Major Alden, II:563
military road to, requested from congress, II:483
Thornton party reaches, I:399
valley crossed by Wilkes' land expedition, I:380
wars, 1853-56, II:524; hampers railroad survey, II:748
Rogue river Indians
at reservations, II:595, 600, 601
burn houses on leaving reservation, II:-603
chief, Lane's namesake, II:554, 561
clash with miners, 1855, II:591
demur at removal of reservation, II:603
Eight Dollar mountain battle, II:598
entitled to receive benefits, II:602
repudiate treaty of 1852, II:560
Skinner, agent for, II:493
Table Rock council, II:561-564, 571
treaty with, II:589
Rogue river Indian war, 1851-54, II:553-563
Ambrose incident, II:558
claims settled by congress, II:621, 623
cost, II:565
hostilities renewed, 1853, II:559-560
Lane grants parley, II:561
minor raids, II:553
railroad surveys hampered by, II:748
settlers carry on, 1854-56, II:524
Table Rock conference, II:561-564
Table Rock encounter with Kearney, I:555
treachery at conference averted, II:554
treaty concluded, terms, 1852, II:559; 1853, II:571, 589
treaty with Dart, II:551
Rogue river valley
alarm felt in, II:592
Curry calls companies for service, in, II:582
first call for volunteers, II:592
free communication kept open, II:591
gold discovery, II:481, 558
massacre, 1855, II:591
military forces fear to leave exposed, II:597
settlers from Willamette valley spread to, II:683
volunteers recruited in, II:560
warlike factions reach understanding, II:596
whites build forts, II:593
Rollins, Josephine, II:676
Roman Catholic church
See—Catholic church
Romanzogg, Count, II:426
Rondeau, Charles, I:266
Rooster Rock, I:134
Rosalia, Washington, II:616
Rosario, Strait of, II:463
Rose, Aaron, II:668
Rose, Edward, I:195-196
Roseburg
county seat of Douglas county, II:669
settled by Aaron Rose, 1851, II:668
Ross, A. J., II:562
Ross, Alexander
account of Astoria supplements Irving's, I:206
"Adventures of the First Settlers on the Columbia", I:226
Astor expedition, I:176
at Okanogan post, I:207

894 GENERAL HISTORY OF OREGON

Santa Cristina island, I:28
Santa Margarita (cliff and islands), I:28
Santa Maria Magdalena, I:28
Santa Rosalia
  renamed Mount Olympus, I:59
Santiago (ship)
  Heceta assumes command, I:29
  Perez' ship, I:27
Santiago, port, I:33
Santiam Academy
  discontinued, 1910, II:715
  founded, II:710
  trustees, II:715
Santiam City, II:738
Santiäm Indians, II:551
Santiam Pass, I:227
Santiam river
  canal to Salem from, II:661
  explored, I:220
  road following pass, considered imprac-
    ticable, I:403
  Williamson railroad route survey
    crosses, II:748
Saskatchewan river
  French-Canadian forts, I:150
  fur trading planned by MacKenzie, I:109
  Hudson's Bay Co. post, I:153
  Pilcher's trip, I:163
  Thompson visits trading posts, I:154
Saules, James D., II:522-523
Sautee Indians
  See—Chippewa Indians
Sauvie island
  Clark's map, I:142
  described, I:279
  formerly called Wapato island, I:134, 279
  Fort William built by Wyeth on, I:279,
    II:692
  grafted fruit trees set out by Wyeth,
    II:692
  hog farm, I:245
  Indian tribes named on Clark's map,
    I:143
  Multnomah nations on, I:142
  natives, I:279
  origin of name Wapato, I:141
  terminus of Linnton road, II:727
  Wyeth's description, I:279
  Wyeth's farm, I:263; II:679
Sawmills
  at Milford and Silverton, 1852, II:667
  at Milwaukie, 1849, II:649
  at Marshfield, II:673
  at Oregon City, II:650
  first operated by steam, Portland, II:-
    649, 655
  flourish after gold discovery, II:478
  French settlers set up, 1841, I:371
  taxed, I:344
  Waymire sets up first whipsaw, II:655
  Young's, I:319, 324
Sawyer, Judge Lorenzo, II:657
Saxton, John, II:544
Scappoose
  described by British army officers, I:402
  McKay owned farm at, I:268; II:678
  Milton located on, II:648
  Owyhee (brig) winters here, I:362
School books, II:707
School lands
  congressional grant for higher education,
    1862, II:713, 718
  congressional requirements, 1859, II:512
  donation land act for university funds,
    II:699, 718, 719
  double grant to Oregon sets precedent,
    II:699, 701
  price paid per acre, II:703
  sale to speculators retarded school de-
    velopment, II:703

School lands—Continued
  200 acres donated to Tualatin Academy,
    II:710
School law and legislation
  county unit law, II:702
  first territorial law, II:701-702
  popular assemblage control, II:702, 717
  tax increase measures, II:717
School tax
  county jail vs., II:710
  discussed at district meetings, II:717
  first territorial law, II:701-702
  funds, 1875-6, II:717-718
  Portland votes, 1852, II:709
  state levy increased, 1872, II:717
Schools
  agricultural instruction to natives un-
    successful, II:678-679
  Amity log school house, II:704
  Clark's activities, I:304
  controlled by direct vote of people, II:-
    702
  denominational, II:710-715
  early equipment, II:705
  first in Willamette valley, I:289, 290;
    II:700
  first organic law provides for, I:336
  first school and teacher in Oregon, I:275,
    276; II:700
  funds, 1875-76, II:717-718
  Indian Manual Training School estab-
    lished by Lee, I:295-296; II:659
  Lee opens mission school, I:289-290;
    educational institution for whites,
    I:296, 304
  missionary influence, I:281
  non-sectarian, for women, incorporated,
    II:707
  Oregon City, 1850, II:650
  Oregon Institute established by Lee,
    I:295-296
  popular assemblage legislative act, II:-
    702; clause of constitution, II:717
  primary school opened by Moss, 1843,
    II:703
  rivalry between towns, II:716
  statistics, 1875-76, II:718
  subscription school, 1845, II:703
  term increased to six months, II:708
  trend toward expansion of public school
    system, 1876, II:718
  Whitman mission, I:308
  Yamhill University, II:704
  See also—Academies and seminaries;
    Church schools; Normal schools;
    School books; School law; School
    tax; Schools, private; Schools, pub-
    lic; Universities and colleges
Schools, private
  Clackamas County Female Seminary,
    II:707
  competition, II:716
  denominational, II:710-715
  first schools established, II:699
  influence hours in public schools, II:710
  Portland's early schools, II:708-709
  retard public schools, II:699-700
  tuition charged in early schools, II:708-9
Schools, public
  district organization opposed in Port-
    land, II:709
  first territorial law, II:701-702
  Governor Lane's plea, II:701
  graded schools started in Portland, II:-
    709
  jail tax vs. school tax, II:710
  objections based on long terms, II:710
  opposition to, II:700, 708, 710
  organization under first school law, II:-
    701-702

Skipanon (schooner)—Continued
cargo taken to Sacramento, I:367
Skipanon creek, I:367
schooner Skipanon constructed here, II:-
741
Skloom, Chief
brother of Kamiakin, II:615
deceives Wright, II:608
discovers Walla Walla treaty unpopular, II:596
escapes after end of war, II:619
refuses gifts at Walla Walla council,
II:575
Slacum, William A.
aids Young with Hudson's Bay Co.,
I:264
American brig Loriot chartered, I:262
Canadians promised preemption rights,
I:265
cattle enterprise furthered by, I:265
Columbia river reached, 1836, I:262-263
departs in Loriot, I:266
disposition of share in Young's farm,
I:324
distillery suppressed by, I:263
donation to Lee's mission, I:266
estimate of wheat crop, I:361-362
list of white settlers in Willamette, I:-
266-267
mission of inquiry to Oregon, I:16, 262;
return and report, I:263, 266; II:446;
referred to committee on foreign relations, II:447
navigation at mouth of Columbia, improvement proposed, I:365
nephew, midshipman on Wilkes' vessel,
I:324
Puget sound's importance to U. S. urged,
I:266; II:446
reception at Ft. Vancouver, I:263
report of Lee's mission and British
trading posts, I:263
uses term Camp Maude du Sable for
Campment du Sable, I:372
voyage via Sandwich islands, I:262
Slade, William, Governor of Vermont, II:-
706-707
Slater, James H., II:787
Slaughter, William A.
command lost one man, II:589
dispatched to Yakima country, II:581
killed in White river valley raid, II:588,
593
Medicine creek council, II:572
Slavery
among Indians, II:571; encouraged by
Hudson's Co., I:263
Baker against, II:771, 773
California constitution prohibits, II:492
congress without power to prohibit,
II:505
controversy delays territorial government, II:466
democratic party attacks abolition, II:783
emancipation proclamation supported by
radical republicans, II:782
issue in aspiration for statehood, II:492,
505, 506
divides democrat party, II:507, 755, 760,
761, 766, 767, 774, 775, 780
in 1856-57, II:505-507, 508, 757; 1858,
II:515-516
in Kansas and Nebraska territories,
II:756
Missouri compromise regulations, II:756
of alien labor proposed by Pacific conspiracy, II:775
organic act, provisions, I:336; supplemented, amended and repealed, I:342-
343, 350

Slavery—Continued
pro-slavery adherents idolize Seward,
II:759
pro-slavery officers elected, II:516
prohibition in memorial presented to
congress by Thornton, II:466
proposition submitted to people, 1857,
II:509
protection of slave property discussed
in legislature, 1858, II:519
question influences acquisition of Oregon, II:451
rejected, 1857, vote by counties, II:511-
512
republican address, 1857, II:508
republican platform, 1856, II:757; 1858,
II:516; 1859, adopts resolutions opposing extension of, II:758
republican presidential nominations advocated on basis of fight against, II:-
762
thirteenth amendment, ratified by Oregon, II:784
Williams' article, II:509
See also—Dred Scott decision
Small, Henry C., II:635
Smith, Rev. A. B.
assaulted by Indians, leaves mission,
I:308
joins Whitman's mission and settles at
Kamiah, I:307
prepares Nez Perce's lexicon and grammar, I:307
Smith, A. D.
member of immigration, 1842, I:377
Smith, Alvin T.
Congregational missionary, I:304
magistrate, I:331
Smith, Andrew
member 1842 immigration, I:377
names Dayton, II:666
Smith, Andrew J.
attends Table Rock council, II:562
battle with Chief John, 1856, II:599-600
commands detachment of regulars from
Port Orford, II:561
expedition against Indians, II:625
Hungry Hill battle, II:593
member war claims commission, II:621
Smith, Darling
member of 1842 immigration, I:377
Smith, Delazon
admitted to bar of supreme court, II:467
denounced by Bush, II:621, 770
elected U. S. senator, II:517
fails of re-election to senate, II:760, 761
fight for senate election, 1860, II:772-773
member constitutional convention and
subsequent career, II:510, 511
opposition to Stout, II:769
presidential elector nominee, II:774
trustee Albany Academy, II:716
trustee Santiam Academy, II:715
Williams challenges to joint canvass,
II:771
Smith, Hiram
delegate to national convention, II:782
sheep imported from Ohio, II:686
Smith, J. B.
incorporator Monmouth University, II:-
716
Smith, J. W.
member of legislature from Tuality district, I:346
Smith, Jackson and Sublette, I:163
Smith, Jedediah Strong, I:163-170
arrival at Ft. Vancouver, I:167
bearer of message from Ashley to
Henry, I:163
California to Oregon, I:164

Smith, Jedediah Strong—Continued
expedition a financial failure, I:280
first overland party to reach California, I:169; from California to Oregon, I:170
furs purchased by McLoughlin, I:169
Great Salt lake to San Diego and return, I:163-164
importance of routes to Great Sale lake, California and Oregon, I:169
imprisoned and banished by Mexican governors, I:164
Indians encountered, men massacred, I:164, 166, 167; II:521
joins Ashley's expedition, I:163
killed by Comanches, I:170
member Rocky Mountain Fur Co., I:163
reception by McLoughlin, I:168
rejoins Jackson-Sublette expedition, I:-169
returns McLoughlin's generosity, I:169-170
stolen ax incident confirmed by McLoughlin, I:165, 166-167
Sullivan's transcript of his travels, I:166
Turner with him, 1828, I:380-381
Umpqua river discovered, I:284
Umpqua river journey, I:166, 243
Smith, John
sawmills and flour mill near Silverton, II:667
Smith, Joseph Schoewalter
candidate for senate, 1866, II:786
congressional delegate, II:786
Smith, Mrs. Joseph Schoewalter (Julia Carter)
opened private school in Portland, II:708
Smith, Margaret J.
joins Lee's mission, I:291
Smith, Noyes
member Oregon Exchange Co., II:480
Smith, Sarah
married Alanson Beers, afterwards Mr. Kline, II:707
teacher at Clackamas County Female Seminary, II:707
Smith, Sidney
arrival in Oregon, I:293
member organization committee, I:328
member Peoria party, 1839, I:320
secretary of meeting to organize government, I:320
signs Canadian protest, March 4, 1844, I:340
Smith, Silas B.
son of Solomon Howard Smith, II:700
Smith, Soloman Howard
farmer in Chehalem valley, II:679
located at Smith's Point, I:369
marries Chief Coboway's daughter, II:079
opens first school in Oregon, II:700
settler in Clatsop plains, I:268, 379, II:-679, 700
settler in Willamette valley, I:266
supports subscription school, II:703
teaches school at Vancouver, II:700
urges mission at Clatsop, I:295
Smith, Thomas H.
admitted to bar of supreme court, II:467
founds Milton, jointly with Nathaniel H. Crosby, II:648
Smith, Volney
served in eastern regiment, II:632
Smith, William
citizen in Eugene, 1854, II:668
Smith river, I:167
Snake Indians
See—Shoshone Indians
Snake river
American fur trade competition, I:228-229

Snake river—Continued
Astors reach, I:197, 200
Cayuses escape across, II:537
Crooks' party meets hardships, I:200
crossed by White faction below Salmon Falls, I:377
eastern boundary of Oregon, II:491
factory site chosen by Thompson at junction with Columbia, I:157
Henry reaches, I:149
Lewis and Clark called Lewis river, I:132
McKenzie finds navigable waters, I:204
Ogden explorations, I:226-228
post established by Astor, I:207
Reed and McLellan follow, I:199
Steptoe's march reaches, II:615, 616
Thompson claims for British, I:186
visited by Griffins, I:303
Walla Walla Indians flee across, II:586
winter quarters of Bonneville, I:270
Wyeth builds Ft. Hall, I:278, 287
See also—Henry's Fork
Snelling, R. B., II:467
Snoqualmie Indians
Leschi, Chief, II:572
Medicine creek council and treaty, II:572
most warlike of Puget sound tribes, II:-548
raid Fort Nisqually, murder Wallace, II:548
Snow, Lucien, II:656
Socialism, agitation, 1853, II:501
Somers, George, I:356
Sonora (schooner), I:29
Soto (half-breed), legend, I:47
Souris river (Mouse river), I:372
South Pass
Ashley uses, I:163
Astor's route south to Oregon trail, I:-220
Bonneville expedition, I:270
Colter reaches, I:149
Fitzpatrick passed through, I:248
Fremont expedition passed through, I:-381
"great immigration" reaches, I:393
Stuart's party may have used, I:220, 248
Wyeth second expedition, I:278
See also—Oregon trail
South Platte
See—Platte river
South sea
design of U. S. for settlement, II:432
Pacific originally called, I:6, 18
South Sea Company
formed, 1711, I:43
monopoly hinders trade, I:43, 53, 152, 224
not engaged in fur trade, I:224
South sea islands
migration from, for slave labor, proposed, II:775
South Yamhill, II:738
Souther, J. W., II:782
Southern Oregon
effect of discovery of gold, II:668, 669
first newspaper published at Scottsburg, II:668
fruit industry, II:694-695
history of towns, II:666-668
movement to create territory defeated, II:491
political representation at democratic state convention, 1859, II:761
settlement delayed by Indian wars, accelerated by gold discovery, II:668
Southern Shoshones
See—Bannock Indians
Sowle, Captain Cornelius
Canton trip a failure, I:209
commander of the Beaver, I:206

State government—Continued
elections preceding congressional action cause confusion, II:518, 775
established by act of congress, 1859, II:-512, 757
governor ex-officio superintendent of public instruction, 1857-73, II:717
loyalty to Union democrat policy, 1859, II:755
officers: premature elections pending congressional action, II:516
political alignments at beginning of statehood, II:755-757
political reaction following Civil war, II:785, 786, 787
presidential campaign of 1860, II:759-775
school legislation, II:717
Seward's speech, II:760
slavery as a state institution opposed, II:506, 755, 756
state library support, II:721
title in the soil safeguarded by act of congress, 1859, II:513
Union party created, 1862, II:781
See also—Civil war; Congressional delegates; Conventions; Constitution, U. S.; Legislature, State; Presidential campaign; Presidential electors; Political parties; Railroads; Senators, U. S.
State House
See—Capitol, Salem
State library, Salem, II:720-721
State superintendent of public instruction, II:702-717
State University
See—University of Oregon
States' rights
discussed in Gov. Curry's message, II:509
Statesman
See—Oregon Statesman
Statutes, 1855, II:477
Stayton, Drury S., II:706
"Steamboat code"
See—Blue book controversy
Steamboats, II:739-746
before 1850, II:740-741
first steam vessel on Pacific ocean, I:363
Fitch's claim to invention, I:14
mail service from San Francisco established, II:739
meet stages at Champoeg in the 50's, II:739
on Oregon rivers, 1851, II:742
on Willamette river, II:651-652
Portland acquires steamship line, II:652
rates and fares, II:741, 742, 743, 745; complaints against, II:711
rival lines, II:745
service reaches zenith, 1860, II:747
stern wheelers, II:743
See also—Names of steamers, and names of steamship companies.
Stebbins, G. H., II:720
Steele, Elijah, II:559
Steen, Enoch, II:625
Steens mountains
reached by John Work, 1831, I:228
Steh-Chass Indians, II:573
Steilacoom
Albion (ship) sold here, II:484
Catholic school established at, II:715
early settlement, II:489
road built from, II:483
Steilacoom, Fort
Indians plan to march on, II:611
regulars leave and Indians attack, II:588
Slaughter dispatched from, II:581
troops ordered out by Rains, II:581

Steilacoom Indians, II:573
Steinberger, Col. Justus
campaign against Snake Indians, II:635
commander military district of Oregon, II:630
delegate to 1860 democrat national convention, II:630, 767
joins federal army, II:768
Stephens, J. L. (steamer), II:690
Stephens, James B.
blackberries raised on farm, II:695
establishes ferry, 1852, II:729
Portland land claim, I:267, II:654
Stephens, Thomas, II:654
Steptoe, Col. E. J.
avenged by Wright, II:618-619
commands Fort Walla Walla, II:614
council call ignored by Indians, II:610
defeated by Spokanes and Coeur d'Alenes, II:615-616
orders settlers from Indian treaty lands, II:609
peace treaty effort fails, II:609-610
Pine creek attack, and retreat, II:615-616
recommends new treaty commission, II:614
refuses Stevens' appeal for guard, II:609
sends Stevens aid, II:610
sent to investigate Mormon activities among Indians, II:615
Stevens, Hazard, II:577
Stevens, Gov. Isaac I.
chooses Puget sound Indians for development of treaty policy, II:571, 614
congressional delegate from Washington territory, II:767
delegate to 1860 democrat national convention, II:767
directs Breckenridge-Lane campaign, II:767
escorted by Nez Perce's through hostile country, II:586
expedition and report re railroad survey, II:560
Fort Stevens named for, II:639
governor and superintendent of Indian affairs of Washington territory, II:-570, 609, 747
Indian treaties
Blackfeet, II:586
Canoe Indians, concluded, II:573
Coeur d'Alenes and Spokanes decline to treat with, II:580, 613
follows Palmer plan, II:571
ignored by regular army, II:612
Kootenais, Flatheads and Upper Pend d'Oreilles conclude, II:580
Medicine creek, II:572-573
obtained, 1854-1855, II:570-573
peace attempted at, II:609
Walla Walla council, 1855, II:573-574; gifts refused by tribes, II:575
Walla Walla council, 1856, II:609-610
Indian wars
appeal to Steptoe for guard refused, II:609
battle with hostile tribes, 1856, II:610
controversy with Wool over winter campaign, II:587-588
Lander controversy, II:612
policy, II:610
protest against Wright's policy, II:611
joins federal army, II:768
killed at Chantilly, II:768
Lawyer protects, II:577
Lewis and Clark route followed, II:747
orders organization of three battalions of volunteers, II:607

Transcontinental railroads
　See—Railroads
Transcontinental routes
　See—Overland expeditions—routes
Transportation
　camel route proposed, II:731
　development on Willamette river, II:649
　mail routes, 1846, II:727, 736
　prior to 1869, II:764
　stage coach lines, II:739-740
　steamboats before 1850, II:740-741
　steamboats, 1850-1871, II:741-746
　　See also—Ferries; Railroads; Ships;
　　Steamboats
Trapp, John, II:719
Trask, Elbridge
　refuses to pay taxes, I:345
　settler on Clatsop plains, I:369
Treasure ships
　legend, I:47
　wreck in the 50's causes loss, II:752
Treaties and conventions
　British-American after Revolution, I:150
　British-American re northwest boundary,
　　I:251, 402; II:417, 434, 446
　Florida treaty, 1819, II:417, 421, 422-425
　Ghent, 1814, I:215-216; II:419, 437
　joint occupancy agreement, 1818, I:231,
　　256, 258, 262; II:420, 421, 432, 446, 453,
　　763; 1821, II:431, 459-460
　Nootka convention, terms, I:67-68
　Paris, 1763, re Louisiana, II:418
　Russo-American, 1824, I:258; II:417, 430
　Russo-British, 1825, II:417, 430
　St. Ildefonso, transfer of Louisiana to
　　France, I:115; ratified by senate, II:464
　San Juan settlement, II:464
　Spain and U. S., 1795, re Louisiana boun-
　　daries, I:115
　Tordescillas, I:22
　treaty of 1800, II:418
　Washington treaty, 1846, II:460, 463
　Webster-Ashburton, II:450
　　See also—Boundary dispute; Indians—
　　treaties
Trees
　Douglas fir, name, I:243
　near Portland, 1848, II:655
　pines described by Fremont, I:385
　sugar pine, named by Douglas, I:385
　　See also—Fruit industry; Lumber in-
　　dustry
Trevitt, Victor, II:787
Trials
　by jury: organic act, I:336
　early methods, I:318; II:485
　Indian murderers of Wallace, II:548
　miners' poison trial, II:671
　　See also—Lawsuits
Trinity School, II:720
Tsimikain
　communication from Eells re Spokane
　　Indians, II:540
　Eells and Walker escorted from, II:541
　mission allowed to continue, I:308
　mission established, I:307
　party from Wilkes' fleet visits, I:380
Tualatin Academy
　founded, becomes Pacific University, I:-
　　296; II:710
　mass meeting for recruiting, II:640
　Rev. Harvey Clark, organizer, I:304;
　　II:712; donates land, I:296
　students form home guards, II:640
Tualatin county
　name changed to Washington county,
　　II:677
　volunteer company for Cayuse war, II:-
　　540

Tualatin district, provisional government
　boundaries, II:674
　members of legislative committee, 1844,
　　I:341
　members of legislature, 1845, I:346; 1846,
　　I:356; 1847, I:357; 1848, I:360
　　See also—Clatsop and Washington
　　counties
Tualatin Indians
　land cessions, II:550
　treaty fails of ratification, II:568
Tualatin plains
　Clark, Smith and Littlejohn settle, I:304
　described by British army officers, I:402
　first church, I:303
　Oregon American and Evangelical Union-
　　ist published, II:486
　post office established, II:738
　road from Linnton, II:648, 727
　road from Portland, II:648, 655
　wagon road begun, I:402
　West Union Institute founded, II:711
　wheat main product, II:727
Tualatin river, II:743
Tuality
　See Tualatin
Tucker, Major, road engineer, 1851, II:728
Tucker and Williams, I:277, 278
Tudor, Frederick, I:272
Tullock, Samuel, I:169
Tumtum
　Indian name for Mount Hood, I:133
Tumwater, Wash.
　Newmarket changed to, II:489
　Simmons settled near site, I:396
Turcotte, Jean Baptiste, I:199
Turner, John
　encounter with Kelawatset Indians, I:167
　leaves Smith at Fort Vancouver, I:169
　settler in Willamette valley, I:267
　survivor of Umpqua Indian massacre,
　　I:167, 317, 380-381
　survivor of Rogue river massacre, I:317,
　　380
Turney, Senator H. L., II:459
Turney, James, II:467, 495
Turnham, Joel
　death, I:321-322, 345
　member of White 1842 immigration, I:377
Turnips, II:680, 682
Tute, Capt. James, I:9
T'Vault, W. G.
　adventure with Coquille Indians, II:557
　contract with Hugh Burns, I:355, II:736
　editor Oregon Spectator, I:355; II:486,
　　557, 736
　member of legislature from Clackamas,
　　I:355
　petitions legislature for protection of
　　slave property, II:519
　postmaster at Oregon City, II:737
　postmaster-general provisional govern-
　　ment, I:355, 357; II:736
　sent to meet immigrants, I:397
　speaker in state legislature, II:516, 518
　Table Rock Sentinel established, II:669
Twality
　See—Tualatin
Twin Falls, I:198
Twisted Hair (chief of Nez Perce's), I:132
Tygh Indians, II:609
Tygh valley
　beginning of Barlow road, II:725
　Fremont return party camps, I:384
　two companies recruited for defense of,
　　II:587
Tyler, John
　boundary dispute during administration,
　　II:449
　Lee conferred with, I:299

William, Fort (Canada)
  Douglas enters employment here, I:249
  McLoughlin, physician and chief trader, I:235
William, Fort (Sauvie island)
  located by Wyeth, I:279, 280; II:692
  Wyeth makes claim for land, I:280
William and Ann (bark)
  account of loss in Owyhee log, I:416
  tradition of massacre by Clatsop Indians, I:365
  wrecked at mouth of Columbia, I:247, 364
William I, Emperor of Germany
  arbitrates Juan de Fuca strait controversy, II:464, 465
Williams, Elijah
  lawyer in Salem, II:661
Williams, Major George
  Civil war service, II:632
Williams, George H.
  attorney-general, II:511, 783
  break with Lane-Smith faction, II:761, 771
  career, II:511
  chief justice, II:495, 511
  circuit judge, 1853, II:506
  decision in negro case, II:506, 757
  district, II:496
  estimate of Lane, II:776
  Gibbs, law partner of, II:780
  impeachment of Johnson voted for, II:-786
  letter from Davis, II:498-499
  mayor of Portland, II:511
  member constitutional convention, II:506, 510
  member Joint High Commission, II:464, 511
  organizes Union party movement, II:506
  president Willamette Woolen Mfg. Co., II:688
  senator, II:506, 511, 783; resignation requested, II:787
  senator, defeated for, II:772, 773, 781
  slavery decision, 1853, II:506, 757, 759; anti-slavery article, II:509
Williams, J. E.
  member of legislature from Polk, 1846, I:356
Williams, J. G.
  prosecuting attorney nominee, II:780
Williams, L. L.
  survivor of Coquille Indian massacre, II:557
Williams, Richard
  judge advocate, governor's staff, II:644
Williams, Robert L.
  colonel Second regiment Oregon mounted volunteers, II:596, 597
Williams, William
  governor in Hudson's Bay Co., I:232, 234
Williamson, Henry, I:347
Williamson, Lieut. R. S.
  party ambushed by Indians, I:388
  river named for, I:388
  surveys railroad routes, II:748
Williamson river, I:386, 388
Willson, W. H.
  candidate for congress, II:492
  incorporator Yoncalla Institute, II:716
  joins Lee's mission, I:291, II:492
  Lane's opponent, II:492
  member Oregon Exchange Co., II:480
  names Salem, II:662
  secretary Wolf meeting, I:329
  signs bond for Oregon Institute, II:660
  surrenders land for Oregon Institute, II:659-660
  treasurer, provisional government, I:331

Willson, W. H.—Continued
  trustee Willamette University, II:713
Wilson, A. E.
  Astoria claim taken, I:369
  supreme judge of provisional government, I:331
Wilson, John
  high-bred shorthorns introduced, II:684
Wilson, Joseph G.
  admitted to bar of supreme court, II:467
  clerk, code commission, II:477
  lawyer in Salem, II:661
  married Elizabeth Millar, II:707
  secretary Willamette Woolen Mfg. Co., II:688
Winass Indians, II:566
Winchester, Oregon, II:668, 669
Wind river, I:196-197
Wind river mountains
  Fremont expedition reaches, I:381
  overland route important, I:222
Windemere lake, I:156
Winnipeg, I:156
  See also—Garry, Fort
Winnipeg lake
  first white man to visit, I:153
  fur trading planned by Mackenzie, I:109
Winship, Nathan, I:171
Winship expedition
  trading post on Columbia unsuccessful, I:171-172, 280; II:680
Winslow, George, negro, I:261
Winthrop, R. C., II:651
Wishram, I:188
Withycombe, Gov. James, II:690
Wolf meetings, I:327-332
Wolfard, John, II:667
Wollamut
  See—Willamette
Women
  first American in Willamette valley, I:291
    English woman on Columbia, I:217
    white woman on northwest coast, I:54
    white women to make overland journey, I:306
  importance in missionary settlements, I:306
  McLoughlin's wife partly Chippewa, I:-275-276
  Mrs. Douglas, partly Indian blood, I:276
  occupations, II:723
  pledge during Cayuse war, II:539
  property rights of married women, II:-482, 510
Wood, A. B. P., II:467
Wood, Henry, I:366
Woodman, John, I:275
Woodruff, ——
  mate on Gray's vessel, I:86
Woods, George L.
  appoints lieutenants for Indian companies, II:643
  controversy with war department, II:643
  early school attended, II:704
  governor, II:704, 785
  nominated presidential elector, II:783
Woodville creek, I:201
Woodward, John, I:317
Woodward, Luther R., II:715
Wool, John E.
  commands military department of the Pacific, II:587
  controversy with Stevens over winter campaign, II:587-588
  criticism of Rains, II:587
  failure to cooperate with volunteers, II:-587-588, 598, 607
  Harney revokes prohibition of white set-

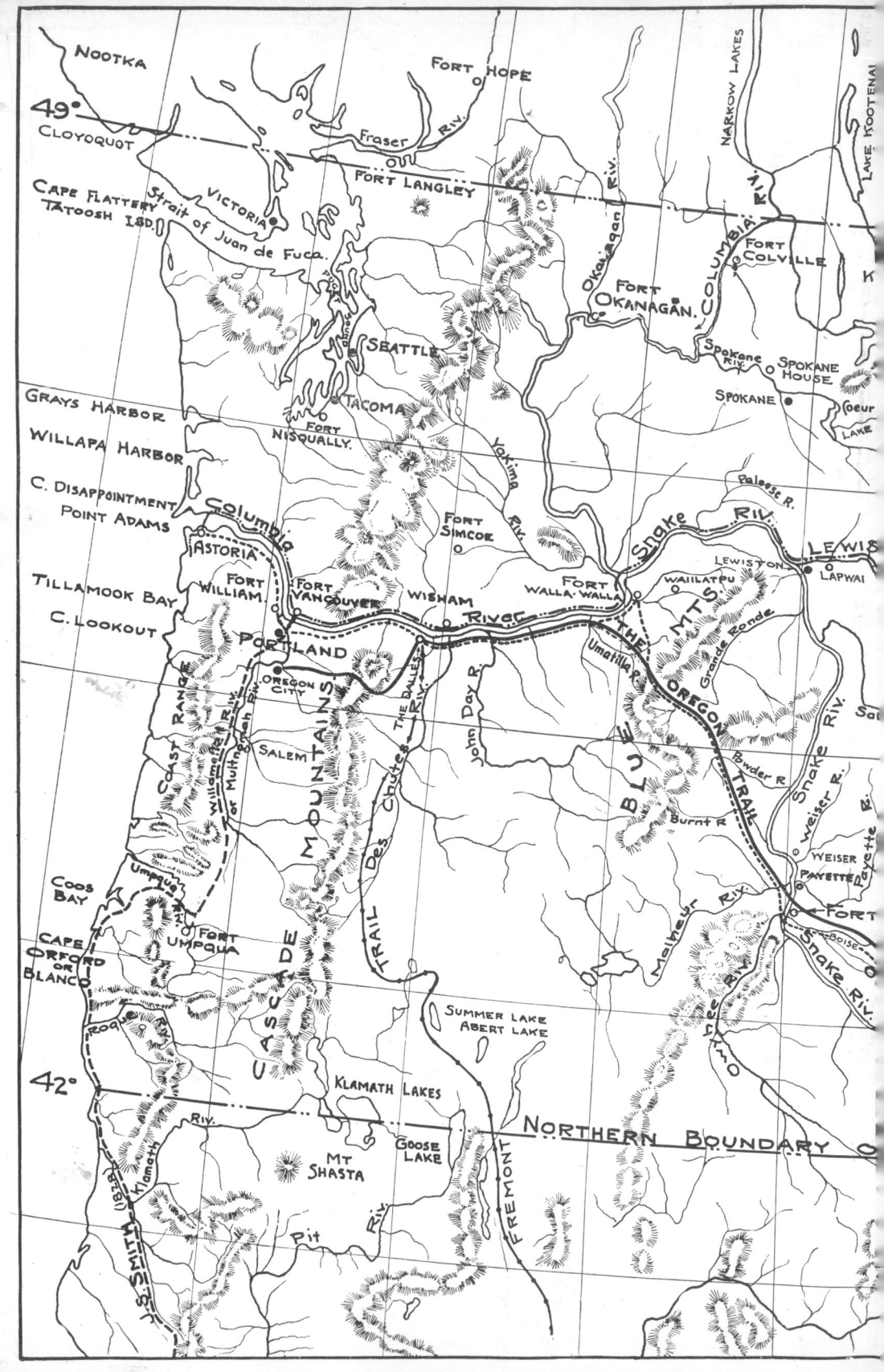